Biología centrali-americana

Aves (Volume II)

Osbert Salvin,

Frederick Ducane Godman

Alpha Editions

This edition published in 2019

ISBN : 9789353864453

Design and Setting By
Alpha Editions
email - alphaedis@gmail.com

BIOLOGIA
CENTRALI-AMERICANA.

AVES.

Vol. II.
(*TEXT.*)

BY

OSBERT SALVIN, F.R.S., &c.,

AND

FREDERICK DUCANE GODMAN, D.C.L., F.R.S., &c.

1888–1904.

CONTENTS OF VOL. II.

ERRATA ET CORRIGENDA.

BIOLOGIA CENTRALI-AMERICANA.

ZOOLOGIA.

Class AVES.

Subclass AVES CARINATÆ.

Order PASSERES.

Suborder OLIGOMYODÆ.

Fam. OXYRHAMPHIDÆ.

OXYRHAMPHUS.

Oxyrhamphus, Strickland, Ann. & Mag. N. H. vi. p. 420 (1841); Scl. Cat. Birds Brit. Mus. xiv. p. 280.

Oxyrhynchus, Temminck, Pl. Col. livr. 21, 1823 (nec Leach).

Oxyruncus, Temminck, Anal. du Syst. gén. d'Orn. in Man. d'Orn. ed. 2, i. p. lxxx (1820).

Oxyrhamphus is a genus of obscure affinities and its position cannot be satisfactorily determined until the internal structure of one of the species has been carefully studied. From an examination of its external characters it has been usually placed by recent authors with the Dendrocolaptidæ or as an independent Family. Under our present knowledge the latter position seems the most convenient.

The coloration of the plumage of *Oxyrhamphus* recalls that of *Phibalura*, a genus of Cotingidæ, but the form of the bill has no resemblance to that of *Phibalura* nor has its plumage anything in common with any recognized member of the Dendrocolaptidæ.

The bill of *O. frater* (and of both the other species) is acute, the culmen slightly curved, and the tomia nearly straight, with a small angle near the commissure; the nostrils are elongated open slits along the lower edge of the nasal fossa and have an operculum thickened along its lower edge along the upper margin. The rictal bristles are very short. The wings have ten primaries, of which the second, third, and fourth are the longest, the first being a little longer than the fifth and rather more pointed. The barbs of the central portion of the outer web of the outermost primary, in the male, have their extremities destitute of barbules, and these bare points turned rather abruptly backwards and slightly inwards, the margin of the wing thus forming a strongly serrate edge.   In the female the outer web of this feather is normal *.

The tail is of moderate length and nearly square at its tip.   The tarsi are short but stout and enclosed in scutes which cover the front and sides and nearly meet at the back ; the toes are short and nearly equal in length, the middle toe slightly exceeding the outer one, the innermost being the shortest.   The hind toe and claw are strong.

The genus is a purely Neotropical one containing three closely allied species—one, *O. flammiceps*, the oldest and best known, inhabiting South-east Brazil, another, *O. hypoglaucus*, the Guianan Highlands, and the third, *O. frater*, Costa Rica and the State of Panama.

1. Oxyrhamphus frater.

Oxyrhynchus flammiceps, Lawr. Ann. Lyc. N. Y. ix. p. 106 [1] ; v. Frantz. J. f. Orn. 1869, p. 304 [2].

Oxyrhamphus frater, Scl. & Salv. P. Z. S. 1868, p. 326 [3] ; Ex. Orn. p. 131, t. 66 [4] ; Salv. Ibis, 1869, p. 314 [5] ; P. Z. S. 1870, p. 194 [6] ; Scl. Cat. Birds Brit. Mus. xiv. p. 280 [7].

Viridis, pileo medio sericeo-coccineo utrinque nigro limbato ; capitis lateribus griseis, corpore subtus pallide flavo, ambobus nigro guttulatis ; alis et cauda nigris viridi limbatis, secundariorum et tectricum marginibus externis late et caudæ apice anguste pallide flavis, subalaribus flavis : rostro corneo, pedibus plumbeis. Long. tota 6·5, alæ 3·6, caudæ 2·2, rostri a rictu 0·8, tarsi 0·75. (Descr. maris ex Calovevora, Panama. Mus. nostr.)

♀ mari omnino similis, remige alarum primo extrorsum haud serrato.

Hab. Costa Rica (*Carmiol*), San José [1], Orosi [2] (*v. Frantzius*) ; Panama, Calovevora [3] [5] [6], Chitra [6], Castillo [7] (*Arcé*).

So far as *Oxyrhamphus frater* is concerned little information has come to hand since the account of it was published in 'Exotic Ornithology' in 1868 [4].   Even now nothing has been recorded of its habits, food, or of the kind of forests it frequents.   At the time that account was written the only other species known of the genus was *O. flammiceps* of South-eastern Brazil ; but a few years ago a third species was discovered by Mr. H. Whitely in the mountains of British Guiana, which we described under the name of *O. hypoglaucus*.   This last-named bird differs from both its allies by having the under surface of the body white (not pale yellow) spotted with black.   We thus have three very closely allied species of this genus each occupying mountainous districts situated very widely apart, and it singularly happens that no one of them occurs in any portion of the Andes or in the mountains of Venezuela.   In our country *O. frater* is restricted to a very limited area extending along the mountain-slopes from Orosi in Costa Rica to Calovevora in the State of Panama.   We have no information as to the elevations at which *O. frater* is found, but the allied *O. hypoglaucus* affects the mountains of Merume and Roraima between 2000 and 3500 feet above the sea-level.

---

* Attention was drawn to this character in the article on *O. frater* in 'Exotic Ornithology,' but it was noticed by Mikan, who, in his 'Delectus Floræ et Faunæ Brasiliensis,' figured the first primary of *O. serratus*, Mikan (=*O. flammiceps*, Temm.).

Fam. TYRANNIDÆ *.

COPURUS.

Copurus, Strickland, P. Z. S. 1841, p. 28 (type *Muscicapa colonus*, Vieill.); Scl. Cat. Birds Brit. Mus. xiv. p. 50.

Two species constitute this well-marked genus, the ranges of which are rather curiously traced : thus the Brazilian *C. colonus* extends over a large portion of Brazil and includes the eastern slopes of the Andes ; *C. leuconotus* occurs in Western Ecuador, Colombia, and Central America as far north as Nicaragua, and passes along the northern part of South America to Guiana. Both species come within the reach of the bird-collectors of Bogota, but are doubtless found on different sides of the mountain-chain.

Copurus is a rather isolated genus with no very obvious allies. Mr. Sclater places it between *Muscipipra* and *Machetornis* in the "subfamily" Fluvicolinæ, but its short tarsi and arboreal habits are at variance with his definition of that section of Tyrannidæ.

The general coloration of the plumage of *Copurus* is black with grey or white marks on the head and back. The bill is short and broad at the base, the width at the rictus being more than two thirds the length of the tomia; the bristles are well developed and reach beyond the nasal fossa; the nostrils are open, nearly circular, and situated at the end of the nasal fossa; the hook of the maxilla is rather abrupt and projects

---

* The Family Tyrannidæ forms one of the most important sections of the American bird-fauna and contains upwards of 400 described species, the greater portion of which belong exclusively to the neotropical region. The remainder are migrants spending their breeding-season in North America, some even reaching Sitka and Greenland in their northern flight. These migratory species almost without exception pass the winter months in Mexico, Central America, and the northern part of South America. The family is well represented in our region by about 104 species, the number of genera and species increasing rapidly in the more southern section of the region.

Tyrannidæ are found at almost all elevations, some occurring in the high pine-forests situated at 10,000 feet and upwards to the limits of vegetation, but it is in the damp forests of the lower lands, where insect-life abounds in endless variety, that the members of the family are to be found in greatest profusion and diversity.

As regards the classification of the Tyrannidæ we are conscious that much remains to be done. In the following pages we have conformed in a great measure to that recently published by Mr. Sclater in the 14th Volume of the Catalogue of Birds, which again is based upon the system adopted by Prof. Cabanis in the 'Museum Heineanum.' Where we have departed from the plan there laid down will be found under the notes attached to each genus. Our chief difficulty lies in the Subfamilies, as defined by Mr. Sclater, into which the system is divided. We find that their definitions are of little practical value, if not altogether misleading.

The subject, however, is an exceedingly complex one, and does not lend itself to subdivision into large groups owing to the multiplicity of forms which pass from one into the other by insensible steps. We have here not attempted to divide the family into subfamilies, but merely grouped the genera into what appear to be their natural affinities. It is only necessary to compare such genera as *Platyrhynchus* with *Serphophaga* (both placed in the Platyrhynchinæ), *Mionecetes* with *Myiodynastes* (Elaineinæ), and *Muscivora* with *Empidonax* (Tyranninæ) to show how artificial Mr. Sclater's "Key" to the subfamilies of Tyrannidæ (Catal. p. 3) is.

We see no advantage to be derived from trying to maintain divisions which seem to be incapable of accurate definition.

considerably below the closed mandible, there is a distinct notch at the end of the tomia. The tarsi are short and stout, covered with distinct scutellæ; the toes short, the outer slightly shorter than the inner. The third and fourth quills are equal and longest—2nd > 5th, 1st = 6th. The tail is nearly square at the end, with the exception of the two middle feathers, which are greatly elongated. The web on each side of these feathers is narrow in the middle but widens gradually towards the end, forming an oar-shaped spatule.

1. Copurus leuconotus.

Copurus leuconotus, Lafr. Rev. Zool. 1842, p. 335[1]; Lawr. Ann. Lyc. N. Y. vii. p. 327[2], ix.
     p. 110[3]; Scl. & Salv. P. Z. S. 1864, p. 358[4], 1867, p. 279[5], 1879, p. 511[6]; Salv. P. Z. S.
     1867, p. 146[7]; Ibis, 1872, p. 318[8]; v. Frantz. J. f. Orn. 1869, p. 306[9]; Nutt. & Ridgw.
     Pr. U. S. Nat. Mus. vi. p. 402[10]; Scl. Cat. Birds Brit. Mus. xiv. p. 51[11].
Copurus pœcilonotus, Cab. in Schomb. Guiana, iii. p. 702[12].

Niger; fronte, loris et superciliis albis; capite summo griseo-fusco; dorso medio grisescenti-albo, uropygio albo:
     rostro et pedibus nigris. Long. tota (cauda inclusa) 10·0, alæ 3·0, caudæ rectr. med. (pogoniis medialiter
     attenuatis) 7·5, reliquis 2·1, rostri a rictu 0·5, tarsi 0·5. (Descr. exempl. ex Tucurriqui, Costa Rica.
     Mus. nostr.)

Hab. NICARAGUA, Chontales (*Belt*[8]), Los Sabalos (*Nutting*[10]), Blewfields (*Wickham*[5]);
     COSTA RICA, San José, Pacuar (*Carmiol*[3]), Turrialba (*v. Frantzius*[9]), Tucurriqui
     (*Arcé*); PANAMA, Santa Fé (*Arcé*[7]), Lion Hill Station (*M'Leannan*[2][4]), Paraiso
     Station (*Hughes*).—COLOMBIA[6]; W. ECUADOR[11]; GUIANA[12]; BOLIVIA[1]?

The range of this species seems confined to Western Ecuador, Colombia west of the Andes of Bogota, and Central America as far north as Nicaragua. It has also been traced to Guiana[12], but its presence in Bolivia requires confirmation. The allied form *C. colonus* (of which we believe *C. fuscicapillus* to consist, only of darker-headed individuals) ranges throughout the Valley of the Amazons from the eastern slope of the Andes of Peru, Ecuador, and Colombia to South-eastern Brazil. The two birds may readily be recognized by the presence in *C. leuconotus* of a light grey dorsal stripe extending from the hind neck to the rump; in *C. colonus* the back is wholly black.

Salmon met with *C. leuconotus* at Remedios in the Colombian State of Antioquia[6], but he did not find its nest and made no note on its habits. Most other collectors are also silent on this subject, but Mr. Nutting, who found the species rather common at Los Sabalos on the Rio San Juan del Norte in Nicaragua, says that it builds a nest in a hole in a dry tree after the manner of a Woodpecker—perhaps the abandoned nest-holes of the latter[10]. The note he describes as weak.

PLATYRHYNCHUS.

Platyrhynchus, Desmarest, Hist. Nat. Tod. sub t. 72 (1805); Scl. Cat. Birds Brit. Mus. xiv. p. 64.

     Platyrhynchus is a well-marked genus containing nine species, which are distributed over the forests of the tropical portion of the neotropical region. Three species occur within our limits, whereof *P. cancrominus* has the most northern range, extending from the Mexican State of Vera Cruz to Nicaragua. An allied form, *P. albogularis*, takes its place in Costa Rica and thence spreads through Western Ecuador and Venezuela. Both these birds have near allies in South America in *P. saturatus* of Guiana and *P. mystaceus* of Guiana and Brazil. The third species is *P. superciliaris*, which extends from the State of Panama to Guiana and has a close ally in *P. coronatus* of Eastern Ecuador.

The general plumage of *Platyrhynchus* is brown or olive on the upper surface and ochraceous-yellowish or white on the under surface; the males, and sometimes the females, have a distinct occipital crest which can be laid open or closed by the surrounding feathers at will. The bill is a very characteristic feature, being very broad and with the lateral margins convex, the width at the base about $= \frac{3}{4}$ the tomia ; the upper surface is much flattened, the culmen slightly depressed but more abruptly so towards the tip, on either side of which there is a deep notch ; the nostrils are round and open, at the end of the nasal fossa. The tarsi and feet are very slender, the former covered with a single sheath ; the outer toe is a little longer than the inner. The wing is short and rounded, 4th quill longest, 3rd$=$5th, 2nd$=$6th, 1st$<$8th. The tail is short and nearly square, $<$twice tarsus, $=\frac{1}{2}$ wing.

a. *Stria superciliaris nulla.*

1. **Platyrhynchus cancrominus.**

Platyrhynchus cancroma, Scl. P. Z. S. 1856, p. 295 [1], 1859, p. 384 [2]; Sumichrast, Mem. Bost. Soc. N. H. i. p. 557 [3].

Platyrhynchus cancrominus, Scl. & Salv. P. Z. S. 1860, p. 299 [4]; Ibis, 1860, p. 399 [5]; Nutt. & Ridgw. Pr. U. S. Nat. Mus. vi. p. 384 [6]; Scl. Cat. Birds Brit. Mus. xiv. p. 66 [7].

Supra umbrino-brunneus ; capite summo obscuriore et crista abscondita flava ornato ; alis et cauda nigricanti-brunneis obscure cinnamomeo limbatis ; superciliis a naribus, ciliis et abdomine medio pallide ochraceis ; gula tota alba ; pectore et hypochondriis pallide umbrino-brunneis : rostri maxilla nigra, mandibula pallida, pedibus carneis. Long. tota 4·0, alæ 2·35, caudæ 1·2, rostri a rictu 0·7, tarsi 0·6. (Descr. maris ex Volcan de Agua, Guatemala. Mus. nostr.)

♀ mari similis, crista verticali nulla.

Hab. MEXICO, Hot region of the State of Vera Cruz (*Sumichrast* [3]), Cordova (*Sallé* [1]), Playa Vicente (*Boucard* [2]) ; BRITISH HONDURAS, Orange Walk (*Gaumer*) ; GUATE-MALA, Choctum [4][5], Teleman, Volcan de Agua above San Diego, El Paraiso (*O. S. & F. D. G.*) ; NICARAGUA, Sucuyá (*Nutting* [6]).

An inhabitant of the hot region of the State of Vera Cruz [3] and of the forests bordering both oceans in Guatemala, and, according to Mr. Ridgway, occurring as far south as the banks of the San Juan del Norte river in Nicaragua [6]. Sallé observed it as high as Cordova in Mexico [1], and we found it at an elevation of about 3000 feet in the Volcan de Agua, 1200 feet at Choctum [4], and at about 300 feet at Paraiso, a hacienda in the forests of the Pacific slope between the port of Champerico and Retalhuleu. Mr. Gaumer's specimen from Orange Walk was obtained close to the level of the sea. It only occurs in dense high forests, where it keeps about the growth of underwood. Mr. Nutting obtained one specimen at Sucuyá in Nicaragua in deep woods. Both *P. cancrominus* and *P. albogularis* have a close ally in *P. mystaceus* of Guiana and Brazil, but both the northern species have a whiter throat, and, moreover, *P. albogularis* has a black mandible.

2. Platyrhynchus albogularis.

Platyrhynchus albogularis, Scl. P. Z. S. 1860, pp. 68 [1], 92 [2], 295 [3]; Salv. Ibis, 1869, p. 314 [4]; P. Z. S. 1870, p. 196 [5]; Berl. & Tacz. P. Z. S. 1883, p. 553 [6]; Tacz. Orn. Pér. ii. p. 225 [7]; Scl. Cat. Birds Brit. Mus. xiv. p. 67, t. 8. f. 2 [8].

Platyrhynchus cancroma, Cass. Pr. Ac. Nat. Sc. Phil. 1860, p. 144 [9].

Platyrhynchus cancrominus, Lawr. Ann. Lyc. N. Y. ix. p. 110 [10]; v. Frantz. J. f. Orn. 1869, p. 306 [11].

P. cancromino similis, sed supra obscurior, oculorum ambitu (præter ciliam ochraceam) nigricantiore, mandibula quoque nigricante differt.

Hab. Costa Rica [4], Navarro (*J. Cooper* [10], *v. Frantzius* [11]), Irazu (*Rogers*), Naranjo (*J. Carmiol* [10]); Panama, Volcan de Chiriqui [5], Calovevora [5], Calobre [5] (*Arcé*); Panama, Truando (*Wood* [9]).—Venezuela; Ecuador [1,2,3,6]; Peru [7].

Western America, from Peru to Costa Rica, and thence eastwards to Venezuela, defines the limits of the range of this *Platyrhynchus*. Immediately to the northward in Nicaragua its place is taken by *P. cancrominus*. It is thus found throughout Panama and Costa Rica in company with *P. superciliaris*. Mr. Wood observed it on the Truando river, near its junction with the Atrato, in high trees, whence it was difficult to obtain [9]. Fraser met with it in the dark underwood of the forest at Esmeraldas [3], as well as in other places in Western Ecuador [1,2], and we have a specimen from Santa Rita in the same region, and Stolzmann also found it at Chimbo [6]. In Peru the last-named collector obtained an example at Tambillo, at an elevation of 5800 feet above the sea [7]. Jelski remarks that its note is monotonous, and that it perches on the small branches of the forest trees.

The existence of a vertical yellow crest does not seem to be always a characteristic of the male, for one of Stolzmann's Chimbo female specimens had this crest well developed.

b. Caput castaneum, stria superciliaris utrinque nigra.

3. Platyrhynchus superciliaris.

Platyrhyncha cancroma, Lawr. Ann. Lyc. N. Y. vii. p. 330 [1].

Platyrhynchus superciliaris, Lawr. Ibis, 1863, p. 184 [2]; Ann. Lyc. N. Y. viii. p. 7 [3], ix. p. 110 [4]; Salv. P. Z. S. 1867, p. 146 [5], 1870, p. 196 [6]; Ibis, 1885, p. 292 [7]; Scl. Cat. Birds Brit. Mus. xiv. p. 68 [8].

Supra olivescenti-olivaceus; alis et cauda fuscis umbrino limbatis; vertice medio castaneo utrinque nigro marginato; loris, superciliis, ciliis ipsis, tectricibus auricularibus et corpore subtus flavidis; stria postoculari et
altera infra oculos nigris; hypochondriis sordide olivaceis: rostri maxilla nigra, mandibula sordide alba,
apice albida; pedibus pallide corylinis. Long. tota 3·4, alæ 2·15, caudæ 0·8, rostri a rictu 0·5, tarsi 0·5.
(Descr. maris ex Santa Fé, Panama. Mus. nostr.)
♀ mari similis.

Hab. Costa Rica, Valza (*Carmiol* [4]); Panama, Bugaba [6], Volcan de Chiriqui, Santa
Fé [5] (*Arcé*), Lion Hill (*McLeannan* [1] [2] [3]).—Guiana [7].

This, the smallest of the three species of *Platyrhynchus* found within our region,
appears to be not uncommon in the State of Panama and in Costa Rica, as specimens
have been included in most of the large collections made in those districts. We find,
however, no accounts of its habits, though doubtless, like its congeners, it frequents
the underwood of the denser forests. Mr. H. Whitely met with the same species at
Bartica Grove in British Guiana [7]; it occurs also at Albina in Surinam. It has not
yet been noticed elsewhere in South America, though we expect it to be found in
suitable places in the country intervening between Guiana and Panama.

The only southern species at all closely resembling *P. superciliaris* is *P. coronatus*
of the Upper Amazons valley. But the latter is a larger, darker bird, with a less
clearly-defined yellow under surface.

RHYNCHOCYCLUS.

Cyclorhynchus, Sundevall, K. Vet. Ak. Handl. 1835, p. 83 (nec Kaup, 1829) (type *Platyrhynchus
olivaceus*).
Rhynchocyclus, Cab. & Heine, Mus. Hein. ii. p. 56 (1859); Scl. Cat. Birds Brit. Mus. xiv. p. 165.

Twelve species are included in *Rhynchocyclus* as a whole, all of them belonging to
the Neotropical Region, the range of the genus extending from Southern Mexico to
South Brazil. All the members are forest birds, as are the species of *Platyrhynchus*.

This genus seems to us to be quite out of place in Mr. Sclater's arrangement, where
it stands in the "Elaineinæ" next *Myiozetetes*.

The bill of *R. brevirostris* is constructed almost exactly like that of *Platyrhynchus*,
the nostrils are similarly shaped and placed in the same position, and the rictal bristles
are equally developed. The tarsi are comparatively shorter and the tail much longer.
The secondaries are longer in proportion to the primaries, and the members of the
genus generally of larger size, and of olivaceous rather than brown tints.

Rhynchocyclus is divisible into four sections, only two of which occur in our region.
In one of these sections (*R. brevirostris* and its allies) the male is distinguished by the
peculiar structure of the outer web of the outermost quill, the barbs of which are
slightly recurved and pointed so as to form a stiff pectinated edge, much as in the
genera *Stelgidopteryx*, *Oxyrhamphus*, &c.

The section containing *R. sulphurescens* and its allies has not this peculiarity.

1. Rhynchocyclus brevirostris.

Cyclorhynchus brevirostris, Cab. in Wiegm. Arch. f. Naturg. 1847, i. p. 249[1]; Scl. P. Z. S. 1856, p. 296[2]; Scl. & Salv. Ibis, 1860, p. 399[3].

Rhynchocyclus brevirostris, Cab. & Heine, Mus. Hein. ii. p. 57[4]; Salv. P. Z. S. 1867, p. 148[5], 1870, p. 197[6]; Scl. Cat. Birds Brit. Mus. xiv. p. 166[7].

Rhynchocyclus mesorhynchus, Cab. J. f. Orn. 1865, p. 414[6].

Rhynchocyclus griseimentalis, Lawr. Ann. Lyc. N. Y. ix. p. 112[9]; Salv. Ibis, 1869, p. 315[10]; v. Frantz. J. f. Orn. 1869, p. 307[11].

Supra olivaceus unicolor; alis et cauda nigricantibus extrorsum olivaceo limbatis; oculorum ambitu griseo, ciliis albis: subtus dilutior, griseo vix tinctus; ventre medio flavo; subalaribus flavo albicantibus: rostri maxilla nigra, mandibula albicante; pedibus corylinis. Long. tota 6·0, alæ 3·1, caudæ 2·75, tarsi 0·75, rostri a rictu 0·7. (Descr. maris ex Choctum, Guatemala. Mus. nostr.)

♀ mari similis, sed pogonio externo remigis primi levi nec aspero.

Hab. MEXICO, Jalapa[4] (*M. Trujillo*), Cordova (*Sallé*[2]); GUATEMALA[8], Choctum[3] (*O. S. & F. D. G.*), La Trinidad, Volcan de Fuego (*O. S.*); COSTA RICA[11] (*Carmiol*[10] & *Endres*), Dota (*Carmiol*[9]), Irazu (*Rogers*); PANAMA, Volcan de Chiriqui[6], Bugaba[6], Calovevora[6], Santa Fé[5] (*Arcé*).

Rhynchocyclus brevirostris is the Mexican and Central-American representative of a small section of the genus containing three closely allied members. The oldest known, *R. olivaceus,* is an inhabitant of the forests of South-eastern Brazil; *R. æquinoctialis* occupies the eastern forests of the Andes of Equador and enters our fauna as far north as the line of the Panama Railway; the present species then takes its place and spreads northwards as far as the forest-clad slopes of the mountains of the Mexican State of Vera Cruz. Another more remotely allied form, *R. fulvipectus,* occupies Western Ecuador and the Cauca valley of Colombia.

Several attempts have been made to divide *R. brevirostris*: thus, the Guatemalan bird was named *R. mesorhynchus* by Prof. Cabanis and the Costa Rican *R. griseimentalis* by Mr. Lawrence. The latter ornithologist correctly showed that the size of the bill, relied on for the discrimination of *R. mesorhynchus,* is a very unstable character[9], but the peculiarities of coloration set forth as distinguishing *R. griseimentalis* do not hold good when a series is examined. This is also Mr. Sclater's view[7], who confirms Salvin's note on this subject[6]. We do not, however, subscribe to Mr. Sclater's statement that *R. brevirostris* and *R. æquinoctialis* gradually merge into one another. The differences are, it is true, very slight, but we have no difficulty in assigning every specimen before us to its proper place, and their geographical boundaries appear to be quite definite.

R. brevirostris is a native of the forests of the hotter parts of the countries it inhabits. In Mexico it occurs near Jalapa at an elevation of about 4000 feet. In Guatemala we found it in the forests near Choctum, at an elevation of about 1200 feet above the sea, and on the slopes of the Volcan de Fuego as high as 3000 feet. It probably has a similar range in altitude in Costa Rica and the more western parts of the State of Panama.

The nest of *R. brevirostris* has not been discovered; but Salmon describes the eggs of *R. fulvipectus*, which he met with at Frontino, in the valley of the Atrato, as white with an indistinct zone of small, very pale-red spots.

2. Rhynchocyclus æquinoctialis.

Cyclorhynchus æquinoctialis, Scl. P. Z. S. 1858, p. 70 [1].

Rhynchocyclus æquinoctialis, Cab. & Heine, Mus. Hein. ii. p. 56 [2]; Lawr. Ann. Lyc. N. Y. vii. p. 473 [3]; Scl. & Salv. P. Z. S. 1864, p. 359 [4]; Scl. Cat. Birds Brit. Mus. xiv. p. 166 [5].

Cyclorhynchus brevirostris, Lawr. Ann. Lyc. N. Y. vii. p. 329 (nec Scl.) [6]; Cassin, Pr. Ac. Phil. 1860, p. 144 [7].

Præcedenti similis, alarum tectricibus pallido-olivaceo distincte limbatis, abdomine quoque pallidiore flavo, distinguendus. (Descr. maris ex Lion Hill, Panama. Mus. nostr.)

Hab. PANAMA, Lion Hill (*M'Leannan* [3] [4] [6]), Chepo (*Arcé*), Truando R. (*Wood* [7]).—EASTERN ECUADOR [1] [2] [5].

The bill of *R. æquinoctialis* is usually larger than that of *R. brevirostris*, but so much variation is found in this respect in the latter species that this character becomes untrustworthy. The two forms can with more certainty be distinguished by the greater definition of the edging of the wing-coverts and by the paler colour of the abdomen.

The distribution of this species is somewhat remarkable, for, as far as our present knowledge goes, there is a wide gap in its range. We have no record of its occurrence between Eastern Ecuador and the Isthmus of Darien, yet specimens from these widely separated places present no tangible points of difference.

Nothing has been recorded of the habits of this species, which inhabits the dense forests of the eastern side of the Isthmus of Panama, at a slight elevation above the sea-level, and the slopes of the Andes a few thousand feet above the sea.

3. Rhynchocyclus sulphurescens.

Platyrhynchus sulphurescens, Spix, Av. Bras. ii. p. 10, t. 12. f. 1 [1].

Rhynchocyclus sulphurescens, Cab. & Heine, Mus. Hein. ii. p. 56 [2]; Scl. Cat. Birds Brit. Mus. xiv. p. 168 [3].

Cyclorhynchus sulphurescens, Lawr. Ann. Lyc. N. Y. vii. p. 473 [4].

Rhynchocyclus flavo-olivaceus, Lawr. Ann. Lyc. N. Y. viii. p. 8 [5]; Scl. & Salv. P. Z. S. 1864, p. 359 [6]; Salv. P. Z. S. 1867, p. 148 [7], 1870, p. 198 [8]; Ibis, 1885, p. 295 [9].

Cyclorhynchus cinereiceps, Lawr. Ann. Lyc. N. Y. vii. p. 329 [10].

Rhynchocyclus marginatus, Lawr. Pr. Ac. Phil. 1868, p. 429 [11].

Supra olivaceo-viridis; capite summo cinereo lavato; loris et oculorum ambitu albidis; alis fuscis flavo-olivaceo limbatis; cauda fusca dorsi colore extrorsum limbata: subtus sulphureo-flavus; pectore et hypochondriis olivaceo tinctis; gula paulo cinerascentiore; subalaribus sulphureis: rostri maxilla nigra, mandibula pallida; pedibus corylinis. Long. tota 5·2, alæ 2·7, caudæ 2·3, tarsi 0·8, rostri a rictu 0·65. (Descr. maris ex San Pablo, Panama. Mus. nostr.)

♀ mari similis.

Hab. PANAMA, Calovevora [8], Santa Fé [7] (*Arcé*), San Pablo Station (*O. S.*), Lion Hill [4] [5] [6] [10] [11] (*M‘Leannan*).—SOUTH AMERICA from Colombia [3] to Guiana [9], Amazons valley [1] and Brazil [1] [2].

Spix described this species from specimens obtained near Rio Janeiro and in the Amazons valley, and examples from these localities agree with one another and with our series from the State of Panama. Mr. Lawrence separated the Panama bird under the name of *R. flavo-olivaceus* [5], but a specimen, in our collection, compared with his type appears to us to be inseparable from the true *R. sulphurescens*, though Mr. Sclater places *R. flavo-olivaceus* as a synonym of *R. cinereiceps* [3].

Rhynchocyclus marginatus [11] is another name, apparently applicable to this species, but the type has a slightly greyer head and darker back, the edgings of the wings are a little more distinct, and it is also a trifle greyer on the throat. Mr. Sclater places this name without question amongst the synonyms of *R. sulphurescens* [3]. We do not think the trifling differences alluded to justify its separation.

As will be seen above, *R. sulphurescens* has a very wide range over Tropical America, being probably restricted to the hot low-lying districts.

4. Rhynchocyclus cinereiceps.

Cyclorhynchus cinereiceps, Scl. Ibis, 1859, p. 443 [1]; P. Z. S. 1859, p. 384 [2]; Scl. & Salv. Ibis, 1860, p. 399 [3].

Rhynchocyclus cinereiceps, Scl. & Salv. P. Z. S. 1864, p. 359 [4], 1870, p. 837 [5]; Lawr. Ann. Lyc. N. Y. ix. pp. 146 [6], 201 [7]; Bull. U. S. Nat. Mus. no. 4, p. 26 [8]; Nutting, Pr. U. S. Nat. Mus. v. p. 395 [9]; Nutting & Ridgw. Pr. U. S. Nat. Mus. vi. pp. 374 [10], 384 [11]; Scl. Cat. Birds Brit. Mus. xiv. p. 169 [12].

Rhynchocyclus sulphurescens, Lawr. Ann. Lyc. N. Y. ix. p. 112 [13].

Precedenti similis, sed capite undique cinereo, gutture toto quoque cinereo, alarum marginibus minus distinctis et abdomine pallidiore, distinguendus. Iride (ave viva) alba.

Hab. MEXICO, Oaxaca [1] and Playa Vicente [2] (*Boucard*), Teapa (*H. H. Smith*), Tapana, Sta Efigenia (*Sumichrast* [8]), Merida in Yucatan (*Schott* [7]), Peto in Yucatan, Izalam (*G. F. Gaumer*); BRITISH HONDURAS, Orange Walk (*G. F. Gaumer*); GUATEMALA, Chisec, Choctum, Cahabon (*O. S. & F. D. G.*), Volcan de Agua above San Diego, Escuintla [3] (*O. S.*); HONDURAS, San Pedro (*G. M. Whitely* [5]); NICARAGUA, San Juan del Sur [10] and Sucuyá [11] (*Nutting*); COSTA RICA, La Palma (*Nutting* [9]), Angostura (*Carmiol* [6] [13]); PANAMA, Lion Hill (*M‘Leannan* [4]).

On comparing a series of specimens recently sent us from Teapa, in the Mexican State of Tabasco, by Mr. Herbert Smith, with our examples from Panama, we find no differences, and considering how closely allied the species is to *R. sulphurescens*, its characters are exceedingly constant.

A good deal of confusion has arisen respecting the references to this species and *R. sulphurescens* in Costa Rica and the State of Panama, but we believe we have here correctly assigned them. In the former country the southern form does not appear to be found, though they both occur on the line of the Panama Railway [4].

R. cinereiceps was first characterized by Mr. Sclater from specimens obtained by Boucard in Oaxaca and others from Playa Vicente in the State of Vera Cruz. We have received specimens from various places in the lowlands of Yucatan and Eastern Guatemala, its range in altitude reaching to about 2000 feet. It also occurs throughout the districts bordering the Pacific, up to about the same height, in the forests which clothe the volcanos of Guatemala. In Nicaragua Mr. Nutting says it is abundant at Sacuyá, where it is a rather silent bird, fond of the deep woods [11].

Mr. Nutting also secured the nest of this species at La Palma in Costa Rica. Mr. Ridgway describes it as follows [9]:—"The nest of this bird is a most remarkable structure, well worthy of description. It is a pendulous inverted pouch, suspended from a single twig, composed almost entirely of slender black filaments resembling horse-hairs (probably a vegetable fibre, related to, if not identical with, the 'Spanish Moss' or *Tillandsia* of the Southern United States), and so loosely built as to be easily seen through when held up to the light. The entrance is at the extreme lower end, the nest proper being a sort of pocket on one side, about two inches above the entrance. The total length of the entire structure is ten inches, the greatest width four inches, the lower 'neck' or wall of the entrance being about two and a half inches in diameter."

TODIROSTRUM.

Todirostrum, Lesson, Traité d'Orn. p. 384 (1831); Scl. Cat. Birds Brit. Mus. xiv. p. 69.

Sixteen species are now recognized of this varied genus, which may be distinguished by the elongated flattened bill of its members. Most of the species are well marked, and are distributed over the greater part of the Neotropical region. Two species reach the forests of Southern Mexico, the widely-distributed *T. cinereum* and *T. schistaceiceps*, which, spreading throughout Central America, pass into Colombia. The third species is *T. nigriceps*, a bird of the north-western part of South America, which enters our fauna as far as Panama and Costa Rica. The upper valleys of the Amazons basin are the headquarters of the genus, and here some beautiful and distinct species are found.

Todirostrum contains birds of very varied coloration, many of them being brightly clad in olive, black, and clear sulphur-yellow on the under surface, others have greyer tints. *T. cinereum* has an elongated flat bill, the sides of which are nearly parallel until they converge gradually towards the tip, the width at the base is a little more than a third of the length of the tomia, the terminal hook and subterminal notches are small; the nostrils are situated towards the end of the nasal fossa, and are surrounded by a slightly overhanging membrane; the rictal bristles are well developed. The tarsi are long and feeble, covered with distinct scutellæ, the toes short. The wing is rounded,

2*

the 3rd, 4th, and 5th quills nearly equal and longest, 2nd=7th, 1st=10 th. The tail is long and much rounded, the feathers narrow, $=\frac{5}{6}$ wing, >2 tarsus.

a. *Abdomen flavum, gula quoque flava.*

1. Todirostrum cinereum.

Todus cinereus, Linn. Syst. Nat. i. p. 178[1]; Bp. P. Z. S. 1837, p. 117[2].

Todirostrum cinereum, d'Orb. Voy. Am. Mér., Ois. p. 315[3]; Scl. P. Z. S. 1856, p. 141[4], 1857, p. 203[5]; Scl. & Salv. Ibis, 1859, p. 124[6]; P. Z. S. 1864, p. 358[7], 1870, p. 837[8], 1879, p. 512[9]; Lawr. Ann. Lyc. N. Y. vii. p. 295[10], viii. p. 182[11], ix. p. 110[12]; Salv. P. Z. S. 1867, p. 147[13], 1870, p. 196[14]; Cat. Strickl. Coll. p. 301[15]; Ibis, 1885, p. 292[16]; v. Frantz. J. f. Orn. 1869, p. 307[17]; Nutt. & Ridgw. Pr. U. S. Nat. Mus. v. pp. 384[18], 402[19]; Tacz. Orn. Pér. ii. p. 225[20]; Scl. Cat. Birds Brit. Mus. xiv. p. 71[21].

Triccus cinereus, Cab. J. f. Orn. 1861, p. 243[22].

Supra olivaceo-cinereum; capite nigro; alis caudaque nigris, illis olivaceo limbatis, hujus rectrice utrinque extima in pogonio externo et ad apicem late albida, rectricibus reliquis (præter duas medias) anguste albo terminatis; subtus omnino flavissimum: rostri maxilla cornea, mandibula flava; pedibus plumbeis. Long. tota 3·6, alæ 1·7, caudæ 1·9, rostri a rictu 0·7, tarsi 0·7. (Descr. exempl. ex Dueñas, Guatemala. Mus. nostr.)

Hab. MEXICO, Tlacotalpam (*Sallé*[5]), Teapa in Tabasco (*H. H. Smith*), Mugeres I., coast of Yucatan (*Gaumer*); BRITISH HONDURAS, Orange Walk (*Gaumer*), Belize (*O. S.*[6]); GUATEMALA (*Velasquez*[2], *Constancia*[15]), Choctum, Coban, Dueñas, Escuintla, Retalhuleu (*O. S. & F. D. G.*); HONDURAS, San Pedro[8] (*G. M. Whitely*); NICARAGUA, Sucuyá[18], Los Sabalos[19] (*Nutting*), Greytown (*Holland*[11]); COSTA RICA, Nicoya (*Arcé*), Turrialba[12], Pacuar[12] (*Carmiol*), Irazu (*Rogers*), San José (*v. Frantzius*[17]); PANAMA, David (*Bridges*[4]), Bugaba[14], Volcan de Chiriqui, Mina de Chorcha[14], Calovevora[14], Santa Fé[13], Calobre[14] (*Arcé*), Lion Hill (*McLeannan*[7][10]), Paraiso Station (*Hughes*).—SOUTH AMERICA, Colombia[9] to Bolivia[3], South Brazil, Amazons valley and Guiana[16].

Though apparently rare in Southern Mexico (where our only records of its presence are those of Sallé, who found it at Tlacotalpam, and of Herbert Smith at Teapa), *Todirostrum cinereum* is a common species in Guatemala and throughout the rest of Central America, being for the most part a bird of the lowland forests, but occasionally, though rarely, ascending the mountains to a height of about 5000 feet. Its usual resort is the forest, but it may at times be seen in trees situated in more open country. In South America *T. cinereum* is one of the most widely spread of Tropical birds, notwithstanding its small size. It seems to be generally distributed in the forests of South-American lowlands to the confines of Southern Brazil. In Guiana it occurs up to an elevation of at least 3500 feet, and on the slopes of the Andes doubtless to a still greater height.

Salmon, who took the eggs of this species, says they are white, but he makes no mention of its nest, nor of the situations in which it is placed. The iris in life is white [9].

b. *Abdomen flavum, gula alba.*

2. Todirostrum nigriceps.

Todirostrum nigriceps, Scl. P. Z. S. 1855, p. 66, t. 84. f. 1 [1]; Cat. Birds Brit. Mus. xiv. p. 72 [2]; Cassin, Pr. Ac. Phil. 1860, p. 144 [3]; Lawr. Ann. Lyc. N. Y. vii. p. 330 [4], ix. p. 110 [5]; Scl. & Salv. P. Z. S. 1864, p. 358 [6].

Supra flavo-olivaceum; alis et cauda nigris, rectricibus et remigibus primariis stricte, secundariis et alarum tectricibus latius flavido limbatis; pileo toto cum nucha et capitis lateribus nigerrimis; subtus flavum, gutture albo; rostro et pedibus nigris. Long. tota 3·0, alæ 1·4, caudæ 1·1, rostri a rictu 0·6, tarsi 0·6. (Descr. maris ex Lion Hill, Panama. Mus. nostr.)

Hab. COSTA RICA, Angostura (*Carmiol* [5]); PANAMA, Lion Hill (*McLeannan* [4][6]), Turbo (*Wood* [3]).—COLOMBIA, Santa Marta [1]; ECUADOR [2].

This pretty little species appears to have a limited range restricted to the northwestern parts of South America, the Isthmus of Panama, and thence to Costa Rica; but from the latter country we have only a single record of its occurrence. No specimens of it were included in the collections sent us from Chiriqui or from the neighbourhood of Santiago de Veraguas. M'Leannan, however, met with it on the line of the Panama Railway, and sent specimens both to Mr. Lawrence and ourselves, and Mr. C. J. Wood found it at Turbo, on the Isthmus of Darien, in the drier parts of the forest [3]. It had the same habits as *T. cinereum*, but was not common.

Mr. Sclater's type was obtained near Santa Marta [1].

c. *Abdomen album.*

3. Todirostrum schistaceiceps.

Todirostrum schistaceiceps, Scl. Ibis, 1859, p. 444 [1]; P. Z. S. 1859, p. 384 [2]; Cat. Am. B. p. 208, t. 18. f. 2 [3]; Cat. Birds Brit. Mus. xiv. p. 74 [4]; Scl. & Salv. Ibis, 1860, p. 399 [5]; P. Z. S. 1864, p. 358 [6]; Lawr. Ann. Lyc. N. Y. vii. p. 473 [7]; Bull. U. S. Nat. Mus. no. 4, p. 26 [8]; Nutting & Ridgw. Pr. U. S. Nat. Mus. vi. p. 402 [9]; Zeledon, Pr. U. S. Nat. Mus. viii. p. 108 [10].

Todirostrum superciliaris, Lawr. Ann. Lyc. N. Y. x. p. 9 [11].

Olivaceo-viride; pileo toto cum nucha schistaceis; loris albis; alis et cauda nigris illis viridi-olivaceo hac olivaceo extrorsum limbatis, hujus quoque rectricum externarum bitriente basali cinerascente: subtus cinerascens; abdomine albido; hypochondriis olivaceo indutis; subalaribus et campterio alari flavissimis: rostro nigricante, tomiis pallidis; pedibus corylinis. Long. tota 3·6, alæ 1·9, caudæ 1·4, rostri a rictu 0·6, tarsi 0·75. (Descr. exempl. ex Choctum, Guatemala. Mus. nostr.)

Hab. MEXICO [1], Playa Vicente (*Boucard* [2]), Guichicovi (*Sumichrast* [8]), Teapa in Tabasco (*H. H. Smith*); British Honduras, Orange Walk (*Gaumer*); GUATEMALA, Choctum (*O. S. & F. D. G.* [5]); NICARAGUA, Los Sabalos (*Nutting* [9]); COSTA RICA (*Zeledon* [10]); PANAMA, Lion Hill (*M'Leannan* [7][6]).—COLOMBIA [4]; VENEZUELA? [11].

Specimens from Playa Vicente, in the hot region of the Mexican State of Vera Cruz, were described by Mr. Sclater under this name. The species was soon after found by us in the forests of the basin of the Rio de la Pasion, in northern Vera Paz, and it has since been traced to Tehuantepec, Tabasco, and British Honduras. It occurs again on the banks of the San Juan del Norte river, in Nicaragua, and on the line of the Panama Railway. Mr. Zeledon includes its name in his list of Costa Rica birds, but has not yet stated in what part of that country it is found [10]. The bird from the mainland of South America has been separated by Mr. Lawrence as *T. superciliaris* on the ground of the under surface being rather whiter, and the white lores extending further over the eye [11]. These differences are indeed slight, and hardly of specific value in our opinion.

ONCOSTOMA.

Oncostoma, Scl. Ibis, 1862, p. 12; Cat. Am. Birds, p. 208; Cat. Birds Brit. Mus. xiv. p. 76.

Only two species are known of this curious form—one from Southern Mexico and Central America, as far south as the Volcan de Chiriqui in the State of Panama, the other peculiar to the isthmus itself along the line of railway.

The two species of this genus are olive-green above, greyish below, with the abdomen yellow, and thus resemble such members of the genus *Todirostrum* as *T. schistaceiceps*. But *Oncostoma* has several important differences. The bill is strongly arched, the culmen still more so, giving the bill a very different outline from that of *Todirostrum*, which is flat, and the culmen nearly straight; the tail is composed of narrow feathers, but is not nearly so rounded; the proportions of tail, wings, and tarsi are much as in *Todirostrum*.

1. Oncostoma cinereigulare.

Todirostrum cinereigulare, Scl. P. Z. S. 1856, p. 295 [1]; 1859, p. 384 [2].

Oncostoma cinereigulare, Scl. Cat. Am. B. p. 208, t. 18. f. 1 [3]; Cat. Birds Brit. Mus. xiv. p. 77 [4];
    Salv. Ibis, 1866, p. 194 [5]; P. Z. S. 1870, p. 196 [6]; Lawr. Ann. Lyc. N. Y. ix. p. 111 [7];
    Bull. U. S. Nat. Mus. no. 4, p. 26 [8]; Sumichrast, Mem. Bost. Soc. N. H. i. p. 557 [9]; Boucard,
    P. Z. S. 1883, p. 447 [10].

Olivaceum; capite summo vix saturatiore; alis et cauda fusco-nigricantibus, extrorsum olivaceo limbatis; capitis
    lateribus et gutture toto cinereis, hoc albicante striolato; abdomine medio flavicante: rostro corneo; pedibus
    pallide corylinis. Long. tota 4·0, alæ 2·0, caudæ 1·6, rostri a rictu 0·55, tarsi 0·6. (Descr. exempl. ex
    Coban, Guatemala. Mus. nostr.)
♀ mari similis.

Hab. MEXICO, Cordova (*Sallé* [1]), hot region of Vera Cruz (*Sumichrast* [9]), Teotalcingo
    and Playa Vicente (*Boucard* [2]), Guichicovi, Cacoprieto, Tapana, Sta Efigenia (*Sumi-
    chrast* [10]), Tizimin [8] and Peto in Yucatan (*Gaumer*); BRITISH HONDURAS, Orange
    Walk (*Gaumer*); GUATEMALA, Coban [5], Teleman, Choctum, Savana grande, Volcan
    de Agua above San Diego, Retalhuleu (*O. S. & F. D. G.*); COSTA RICA, Angostura
    (*Carmiol* [7]); PANAMA, Bugaba (*Arcé* [6]).

A species of the hotter parts of the State of Vera Cruz according to Sumichrast [9], but found near Cordova by Sallé [1]. The former naturalist also met with it in several places on the Isthmus of Tehuantepec [8], thence it spreads over the forest lands of Guatemala bordering the Pacific Ocean, ascending the mountains to an elevation of 3000 or 4000 feet. On the Atlantic side of the cordillera it occurs in the forest-region of northern Vera Paz and in the valley of the Polochic river, and is also not at all uncommon in the neighbourhood of Coban in January at an elevation of about 4500 feet above the sea-level.

The southern extension of this species is rather remarkable, as it does not terminate, like that of so many species where a second is found in the southern section of our fauna, in Honduras and Nicaragua, but it reaches Chiriqui, the allied form occurring on the line of the Panama Railway.

Its habits much resemble those of the various species of *Todirostrum*. The iris in life is greyish white.

2. Oncostoma olivaceum.

Todirostrum olivaceum, Lawr. Ibis, 1862, p. 12 [1].

Oncostoma olivaceum, Scl. Ibis, 1862, p. 12 (note) [2]; Cat. Birds Brit. Mus. xiv. p. 77 [3]; Lawr. Ann. Lyc. N. Y. vii. p. 473 [4]; Scl. & Salv. P. Z. S. 1864, p. 358 [5].

Præcedenti similis, sed capite summo olivaceo dorso concolore; gula quoque et abdomine concoloribus pallide flavo-olivaceis, tectricibus alarum magis distincte flavido limbatis, distinguendum. (Descr. maris ex Lion Hill, Panama. Mus. nostr.)

Hab. PANAMA, Lion Hill (*M'Leannan* [1] [2] [3] [4] [5]).

Oncostoma olivaceum is a close ally of *O. cinereigulare*, but at the same time easily recognized. So far as we know the only specimens that have been obtained were secured by M'Leannan during the time he was station-master at Lion Hill on the Panama Railway.

LOPHOTRICCUS.

Lophotriccus, H. v. Berlepsch, P. Z. S. 1883, p. 553 (type *Todirostrum spicifer*, Lafr.); Scl. Cat. Birds Brit. Mus. xiv. p. 86.

The two species which now constitute this genus were included in *Euscarthmus* until Count Berlepsch separated them in 1883, but without giving any characters. *L. spicifer* is a species of the upper Amazons valley up to the base of the Andes. *L. squamicristatus* has a wider and more northern and western range over Venezuela, Colombia, and Ecuador, entering our region as far as Costa Rica.

Compared with *Todirostrum* this genus has a much less elongated flattened bill, the sides of which converge from the gape to the tip, the membrane over the nostrils is more developed, the tarsi are covered with a single shield, the tail is less rounded, and the feathers of the head are wide and produced into a conspicuous crest.

1. Lophotriccus squamicristatus.

Todirostrum squamæcrista, Lafr. Rev. Zool. 1846, p. 363 [1].

Todirostrum squamicristatum, Scl. P. Z. S. 1859, p. 144 [2].

Euscarthmus squamicristatus, Lawr. Ann. Lyc. N. Y. ix. p. 111 [3]; v. Frantz. J. f. Orn. 1869, p. 307 [4]; Salv. P. Z. S. 1870, p. 196 [5].

Lophotriccus squamicristatus, Berl. P. Z. S. 1883, p. 553 [6]; Tacz. Orn. Pér. ii. p. 230 [7]; Scl. Cat. Birds Brit. Mus. xiv. p. 87 [8].

Lophotriccus squamicristatus, subsp. *luteiventris*, Berl. apud Tacz. Orn. Pér. ii. p. 230 [9].

Supra olivaceus; alis et cauda nigricantibus flavo-olivaceo limbatis; plumis cristæ elongatis nigris late ferrugineo limbatis: subtus griseo-albidus; abdomine medio flavo vix tincto; gutture toto griseo indistincte striolato; hypochondriis olivaceo indutis: rostro corneo; pedibus corylinis. Long. tota 3·8, alæ 2·0, caudæ 1·5, rostri a rictu 0·5, tarsi 0·6. (Descr. maris ex Calovevora, Panama. Mus. nostr.)
♀ mari similis.

Hab. Costa Rica, Cervantes [3], Grecia [3] (*Carmiol*), Dota [3] (*Zeledon*), Quebrada Honda [4] (v. *Frantzius*), Turrialba, Tucurriqui (*Arcé*); Panama, Chiriqui [5], Calovevora [5], Chitra [5], Boquete de Chitra [5] (*Arcé*).—Colombia [1]; Ecuador [2][6]; Peru [7]; Venezuela [8].

Some of our Central-American specimens are rather yellower beneath than others from Ecuador, but the difference is not always appreciable; moreover, a Venezulan example is yellower than any of the rest of our series.

L. squamicristatus was described from Colombian specimens, whence it has since been traced southwards to Central Peru [7]. In Ecuador it occurs in many places on both sides of the cordillera. It is also found in Venezuela, Mr. Göring having met with it on the Cumbre de Valencia. It appears to be absent in the low-lying lands of the Isthmus of Panama, but to occur in some numbers in the more mountainous parts near Calovevora and Chiriqui, and also in similar districts of Costa Rica. In the latter country v. Frantzius says that it is common in the cool forests of the mountain slopes of Quebrada Honda. Hence we infer that it must not be looked for near the sea-level.

Fraser says that the irides in life are orange, the legs and feet flesh-colour, the bill blackish [2].

ORCHILUS.

Orchilus, Cabanis in Tschudi's Fauna Per. p. 164 (1845) (type *Platyrhynchus auricularis*, Vieill.); Scl. Cat. Birds Brit. Mus. xiv. p. 88.

Three species are included in *Orchilus*, viz. *O. auricularis* of South-eastern Brazil, *O. ecaudatus* of Bolivia, Peru, and Venezuela, and *O. atricapillus* of Costa Rica. The two latter species are somewhat abnormal, having remarkably short tails, whereas the type of the genus (*O. auricularis*) is not so definitely marked in this respect.

Orchilus, as represented by the somewhat abnormal *O. ecaudatus*, is another departure from *Todirostrum*, and is mainly distinguished by its very short square tail; the bill is similar to that of *Lophotriccus*, but is longer and rather more arched. Like *Todirostrum* it has no occipital crest.

1. Orchilus atricapillus.

Todirostrum ecaudatum, Lawr. Ann. Lyc. N. Y. ix. p. 110 [1].

Orchilus atricapillus, Lawr. Ibis, 1875, p. 385 [2]; Scl. Cat. Birds Brit. Mus. xiv. p. 89 [3].

"The entire crown is black; the lores are also black, except a white mark extending from the bill to the eye on each side, separating them from the black crown; eyelids white; under the eye blackish-ash; the colour on the sides of the head behind the eye, extending to the hind neck and on the upper part of the back, is of a clear bluish-cinereous; breast also cinereous, but lighter in colour; throat greyish-white; abdomen pale yellow; flanks and thighs blackish-ash; under wing-coverts pale yellow; back, rump, and upper tail-coverts yellowish-green; wings black, the primaries narrowly edged with olive-green, the secondaries and wing-coverts conspicuously margined with yellow of a greenish tinge; tail black, the feathers with margins of the colour of the back; bill black; tarsi and toes very pale flesh-colour. First primary shorter than the fifth, third and fourth equal and longest. Length $2\frac{3}{4}$ inches, wing $1\frac{7}{16}$, tail $\frac{5}{8}$, bill $\frac{7}{16}$, tarsus $\frac{1}{2}$."—*Lawrence*, loc. cit.

Hab. COSTA RICA, Angostura (*Carmiol* [1]), Volcan de Irazu (*Zeledon* [2]).

We have copied Mr. Lawrence's description of this species, as we have no specimen of it ourselves. *O. atricapillus* resembles *O. ecaudatus*, but has a black head instead of a grey one. The first specimen was obtained by Carmiol at Angostura, but being in poor condition was referred by Mr. Lawrence to *O. ecaudatus*. A second and better one was secured during the late Prof. Gabb's expedition to the Talamanca country, this, with a suggestion of Salvin's to the effect that the bird was really distinct and undescribed, led to a fresh examination of the specimens and to their description under the name of *Orchilus atricapillus* [2]. The allied species has a wide range from Venezuela to Bolivia, but is everywhere rare.

COLOPTERUS.

Colopterus, Cabanis, Monatsber. Ak. Berlin, 1845, p. 216 (type *Motacilla galeata*, Bodd.); Scl. Cat. Birds Brit. Mus. xiv. p. 90.

This singular genus contains two species which differ from one another in that *C. galeatus*, the type, has elongated occipital feathers like *Lophotriccus*, while *C. pileatus* is not so adorned. The range of the genus extends from the State of Panama to Colombia, Venezuela, Guiana, and the lower part of the Amazons valley.

In the form of the bill, tail, and tarsi this genus is like *Lophotriccus*, but the peculiar modification of the wings makes it easy to recognize both from *Lophotriccus* and the rest of this group of genera. In the male of *C. pileatus* the outermost four primaries are attenuated and shortened to little more than half the longest of the remaining normal feathers. Of these four shortened feathers the outermost is the longest, and the rest are gradually shorter, the fourth being the shortest of the series. In the female this feature is not carried to nearly the same extent, moreover the outermost or first primary is the shortest, and the fourth nearly attains its normal place in the wing. In *C. galeatus* the male has three attenuated primaries instead of four.

1. Colopterus pilaris.

Todus pilaris, Licht. Mus. Berol. (fide Cabanis [1]).

Colopterus pilaris, Cab. Arch. f. Naturg. 1847, i. p. 253, t. 5 [2]; Cab. & Heine, Mus. Hein. ii.
    p. 52 [3]; Salv. P. Z. S. 1867, p. 147 [4]; Salv. & Godm. Ibis, 1880, p. 124 [5]; Scl. Cat. Birds Brit.
    Mus. xiv. p. 90 [6].

Todirostrum exile, Scl. P. Z. S. 1857, p. 83, t. 125. f. 3 [7]; Cassin, Pr. Ac. Nat. Sc. Phil. 1860,
    p. 144 [8].

Todirostrum megacephalum, Lawr. Ann. Lyc. N. Y. vii. p. 330 (nec Swainson) [9].

Supra olivaceus, pileo vix obscuriore; alis et cauda fusco-nigris, extrorsum pallide olivaceo limbatis; loris et
    capitis lateribus pallide fuscis: subtus margaritaceo-albus; hypochondriis flavido tinctis; gutture et pectore
    griseo obsoletissime striolatis: rostro nigro, mandibulæ basi pallida; pedibus carneis. Long. tota 3·5,
    alæ 1·7, caudæ 1·5, rostri a rictu 0·5, tarsi 0·65. (Descr. maris ex Santa Fé, Panama. Mus. nostr.)

Hab. PANAMA, Santa Fé (*Arcé* [4]), line of railway (*M'Leannan* [9]).—COLOMBIA [3 5 7 8].

The headquarters of this curious species seem to be Colombia, where it has been
noticed in several places.   Specimens occur, but not very frequently, in the trade
collections made in the neighbourhood of Bogota, but the bird is more common in the
northern parts of the country.   Within our region it has been observed by two collectors
—M'Leannan, who met with it on the line of the Panama Railway, and sent specimens
to Mr. Lawrence, in whose lists they appear as *Todirostrum megacephalum* [9]; and Arcé,
who sent us two male specimens from Santa Fé in the State of Panama [4].   Mr. C. J.
Wood says he met with this species near Carthagena, in the bushes and low trees,
constantly flying after insects, and uttering a single chirp, by which it could easily be
traced and shot [8].   He frequently saw it in the month of April.   Mr. Simons, who sent
us specimens from Minca in the Sierra Nevada of Santa Marta, says that the iris in life
is white, shading into brown or yellowish white [5].

LEPTOTRICCUS.

Leptotriccus, Cabanis & Heine, Mus. Hein. ii. p. 54 (1859) (type *Muscicapa sylviola*, Licht.);
    Scl. Cat. Birds Brit. Mus. xiv. p. 99.

Leptotriccus, which was founded on the Brazilian *L. sylviola*, contains but two
species, that just named and *L. superciliaris* of the State of Panama.

With a bill similar to that of *Lophotriccus* the rictal bristles appear to be longer,
there is no occipital crest, the 2nd, 3rd, 4th, and 5th quills are nearly equal, 1st = 8th,
the tail is long and very slightly rounded, and the feathers wider than in *Todirostrum*,
nearly = wing, the tarsus = $\frac{1}{3}$ wing.

1. Leptotriccus superciliaris.   (Tab. XXXVI. fig. 2.)

Leptotriccus superciliaris, Scl. & Salv. P. Z. S. 1868, p. 389 [1]; Salv. P. Z. S. 1870, p. 196 [2]; Scl.
    Cat. Birds Brit. Mus. xiv. p. 100 [3].

Supra viridi-olivaceus; alis caudaque nigricantibus, flavicanti-olivaceo extrorsum limbatis; pileo et collo postico nigricanti-cinereis; superciliis castaneis; linea frontali et regione parotica albis: subtus margaritaceo-albus; pectore præcipue ad latera cinereo perfuso; ventre et crisso flavicantibus; subalaribus albis: rostro nigro; pedibus obscure corylinis. Long. tota 4·0, alæ 1·95, caudæ 2·0, rostri a rictu 0·55, tarsi 0·65. (Descr. feminæ ex Calovevora, Panama. Mus. nostr.)

Hab. Panama, Calovevora [2], Chitra [1][2] (*Arcé*).

Of this pretty species we have as yet only seen the two original specimens sent us by Arcé in 1868, and described in the 'Proceedings' of the Zoological Society for that year. Both these specimens are marked as females, so that the male is not yet known, but it, in all probability, is quite similar to the female in its plumage.

In its long slender tarsi and delicate feet this species resembles *Leptotriccus sylviola* of Brazil, and it also has the pointed wings and long tail of that bird; the bill, however, is somewhat larger and wider.

The distinct chestnut superciliary streak over each eye is a strongly marked characteristic feature of *L. superciliaris.*

POGONOTRICCUS.

Pogonotriccus, Cabanis & Heine, Mus. Hein. ii. p. 54 (1859) (type *Muscicapa eximia*, Temm.); Scl. Cat. Birds Brit. Mus. xiv. p. 97.

Mr. Sclater recognizes four species as belonging to this genus, its range extending from Costa Rica to South Brazil.

The general colour of all the species is bright olive above and yellowish beneath, the head varying from grey to dark plumbeous. The bill in *P. eximius* narrows rather abruptly, the width at the rictus being considerably more than half the length of the tomia; the culmen is gradually curved from the forehead, more rapidly towards the tip; the rictal bristles are very fully developed; the tarsi are rather short and slender, the enclosing scutellæ almost obliterated into one shield; the feet are feeble, the outer and middle toes being nearly equal, the inner one shorter. The wing is rounded, the 3rd quill a little < 2nd and 4th, 5th = 2nd, 1st = 9th; tail rather long and square, the feathers narrow, a little < wing, > 3 times tarsus.

1. **Pogonotriccus zeledoni.**

Pogonotriccus ? *zeledoni*, Lawr. Ann. Lyc. N. Y. ix. p. 144 [1].

Supra olivaceus; capite summo et nucha plumbeis; alis caudaque fusco-nigris, extus pallide olivaceo limbatis; capitis lateribus et gula cinereo-albis; loris albis: abdomine toto olivaceo-flavo, medialiter cum subalaribus flavido-albidis: rostro et pedibus obscure corylinis, mandibula pallida. Long. tota 4·2, alæ 2·4, caudæ 2·0, tarsi 0·65. (Descr. feminæ exempl. typ. ex Barranca, Costa Rica. Mus. G. N. Lawrence.)

Hab. Costa Rica, Dota Mountains, Barranca (*Carmiol* [1]).

We have never obtained a specimen of this species, but have taken our description from the type of the female lent us by Mr. Lawrence. This bird has a close ally in *P. plumbeiceps*, Lawr., of Colombia, but the bill is rather wider, the mandible paler,

3*

and the spots on the wing-coverts not quite so prominent. Mr. Sclater regards this species as probably the same as *P. ophthalmicus* (Cat. Birds Brit. Mus. xiv. p. 98), over which name *P. zeledoni* has several years' priority.

SERPHOPHAGA.

Serpophaga, Gould, Zool. Voy. Beagle, iii. p. 49 (1841) (type *Sylvia subcristata*, Vieill.).
Serphophaga, Cabanis & Heine, Mus. Hein. ii. p. 53 ; Scl. Cat. Birds Brit. Mus. xiv. p. 101.

Serphophaga consists of seven species widely distributed over South America as far south as the Argentine Republic. Only one species, the wide-spread Andean *S. cinerea*, enters our fauna as far as Costa Rica.

Black, grey, and white are the prevailing colours of the various species of *Serphophaga*. They are all small birds, some of them with peculiar habits as described below. The bill of *S. cinerea* is rather wide for its length, the sides converging rather rapidly to the tip, the width at the rictus being about half the length of the tomia, the nostrils are open at the end of the nasal fossa, the rictal bristles not very well developed, considerably less than those of the foregoing genera, but more so than in *Mionectes*, which follows ; the tarsi and feet are rather stouter than in the preceding genera, the former being covered with scutellæ ; the wing is rounded, the 3rd quill slightly > the 2nd and 4th, 1st = 8th ; tail moderate and slightly rounded, considerably < wing, < 3 tarsus. Wing a little > 3 tarsus.

1. **Serphophaga cinerea.**

Euscarthmus cinereus, Strickl. Ann. & Mag. N. H. xiii. p. 414 [1].
Serpophaga cinerea, Scl. P. Z. S. 1858, p. 458 [2]; Salv. P. Z. S. 1867, p. 147 [3]; Ibis, 1869, p. 319 [4];
    Boucard, P. Z. S. 1878, p. 62 [5].
Serphophaga cinerea, Cab. & Heine Mus. Hein. ii. p. 53 [6]; Scl. & Salv. P. Z. S. 1879, pp. 512 [7],
    613 [8]; Salv. Cat. Strickl. Coll. p. 304 [9]; Tacz. Orn. Pér. ii. p. 236 [10]; Scl. Cat. Birds Brit.
    Mus. xiv. p. 103 [11].
Serpophaga grisea, Lawr. Ann. Lyc. N. Y. x. p. 139 [12].

Supra cinerea, uropygio fusco ; capite summo (aliquando albo medialiter notato) et lateribus nigricantibus ; alis
    et cauda ejusdem coloris, illarum tectricibus, hujus apice albido terminatis : subtus albida ; hypochondriis
    et crisso griseo tinctis : rostro et pedibus nigris. Long. tota 4·0, alæ 2·0, caudæ 1·7, rostri a rictu 0·45,
    tarsi 0·6. (Descr. exempl. ex Costa Rica. Mus. nostr.)

Hab. COSTA RICA (*Endres* [4], *Carmiol* [12]), Naranjo (*Boucard* [5]) ; PANAMA, Santa Fé
    (*Arcé* [3]).—COLOMBIA [7] ; ECUADOR [10] ; PERU [10] ; BOLIVIA [8].

The only difference we can see between Central-American and Southern specimens is their small size, a character we seldom like to admit to be of specific value. In the present case there is more difference between two examples from Sical in Ecuador than between any of the Central-American and the other South-American specimens before us, so that size cannot here be considered of much importance.

The other characters referred to by Mr. Lawrence when defining his *S. grisea* as distinguishing it from *S. cinerea* all break down ; for the vertical feathers of the head of some of our northern specimens have white at their bases, just as in southern ones ; the wing-coverts are tipped with dusky white, and the under surfaces of the two forms are not to be distinguished in colour.

Serphophaga cinerea was described in 1844 by Strickland from a specimen said to have come from Chili [1], probably a wrong locality ; but the species has a wide range throughout the Andes from Bolivia northwards to the valley of the Cauca. Missing the Isthmus of Panama, it reappears in the more mountainous parts of that State and in Costa Rica. It frequents the highland forests up to an elevation of 5000 and 10,000 feet, for Tschudi records it from the Sierra de Tarma (10,000 feet), Fraser from Cuenca (8200 feet), and Salmon from Envigado (5500 feet), but it is also found, according to Jelski and Stolzmann, at a low level in the environs of Lima [9].

Its habit of living near running streams has been recorded by several travellers. Fraser speaks of it as hopping from stone to stone in the Gualaquiza river, and Boucard, who observed it at Naranjo in Costa Rica, says it lives along the streams and sits on the stones lying in or near the water just in the manner of *Sayornis aquatica*. Stolzmann also speaks of its having the same habits in Peru. The last-named traveller found its nest towards the end of June attached to the extremity of a bough, to which it was suspended over the surface of the water. The nest was composed almost exclusively of moss and lined with feathers, and fixed by its lower surface to the branch. Salmon also found its nest, which he does not describe, but says the eggs are creamy white [7].

MIONECTES.

Mionectes, Cabanis in Tschudi's Fauna Per. p. 147 (1845) (type *Muscicapa straticollis*, d'Orb. & Lafr.) ; Scl. Cat. Birds Brit. Mus. xiv. p. 111.

Mionectes is the first of our genera which is placed in the "Elaineinæ" by Mr. Sclater, but the rictal bristles, though shorter than in most of the "Platyrhynchinæ," are quite obvious, and the structure of the bill is similar to that of the genera we have just discussed.

The genus itself is a neotropical one spread over the greater part of South America as far as South Brazil on the one hand and Southern Mexico on the other. Of the two sections into which the four species of *Mionectes* are now divided, *M. olivaceus* reaches Costa Rica and *M. oleagineus* Southern Mexico, both being also found in the southern continent.

The general plumage of the members of *Mionectes* is olivaceous, with the abdomen either yellowish or cinnamon. The bill of *M. olivaceus* is rather elongated and compressed, the sides converging gradually to the tip, the width at the gape being considerably less than half the length of the tomia, the culmen is nearly straight for the greater part of its length and then curves abruptly to the tip ; the nostrils are open, oval, and surrounded by membrane, the rictal bristles rather feeble; the tarsi and feet are moderately stout, the former covered with well-defined scutellæ, the outer toe is a little longer than the inner; the wing is rounded, 4th and 5th quills longest, 3rd=6th, 2nd =7th, 1st = longest secondaries; the tail is moderate, nearly square at the end, > 3 tarsus, > ¾ wing.

1. Mionectes olivaceus.

Mionectes striaticollis, Lawr. Ann. Lyc. N. Y. vii. p. 328[1]; Scl. & Salv. P. Z. S. 1864, p. 358[2]; 1868, p. 628[3] (nec d'Orb. & Lafr.).

Mionectes olivaceus, Lawr. Ann. Lyc. N. Y. ix. p. 111[4]; Salv. Ibis, 1869, p. 314[5]; P. Z. S. 1870, p. 196[6]; Boucard, P. Z. S. 1878, p. 63[7]; Scl. Cat. Birds Brit. Mus. xiv. p. 112[8].

Supra viridi-olivaceus; capite summo vix obscuriore; alis et cauda umbrino-fuscis, extrorsum olivaceo limbatis, illis introrsum cervinis; macula postoculari flavida: subtus gutture toto, cum pectore et hypochondriis olivaceis, plumis omnibus medialiter flavis; abdomine medio et subalaribus flavis: rostro nigro, mandibulæ basi pallida; pedibus corylinis. Long. tota 5·0, alæ 2·75, caudæ 2·15, rostri a rictu 0·6, tarsi 0·6. (Descr. maris ex Chiriqui, Panama. Mus. nostr.)
♀ mari similis.

Hab. COSTA RICA, Barranca[4], Dota[4], Buena Vista (*Carmiol*), San Mateo (*Boucard*[7]); PANAMA, Volcan de Chiriqui, Chitra, Boquete de Chitra, Calovevora (*Arcé*[6]), Lion Hill (*M'Leannan*[1][2]).—VENEZUELA[3]; ECUADOR[8].

This *Mionectes* is readily distinguished from its near ally *M. striaticollis* by its olive head and throat, which in the other species are slate-coloured. The distribution of the two forms is rather curious. *M. striaticollis* spreads from Bolivia and Peru to Colombia, being probably found in Western Ecuador. It occurs in the trade collections of Bogota, and Salmon found it near Medellin in the Cauca valley of Colombia; this seems to be its most northern limit. *M. olivaceus* spreads over the whole of Costa Rica and the State of Panama; it occurs again in Venezuela and in Eastern Ecuador.

We have no records of the habits of *M. olivaceus*; but *M. striaticollis* according to Stolzmann* has a considerable range in the mountains of Peru, being found as high as 9300 feet above the sea at Cutervo. He adds that it frequents thick forests, keeping amongst the low herbage, but sometimes ascending into the upper part of the higher trees. Salmon obtained the eggs of *M. striaticollis* at Santa Elena in the Cauca valley; they were pure white.

2. Mionectes oleagineus.

Muscicapa oleaginea, Licht. Verz. Doubl. p. 55[1].

Mionectes olcagineus, Cab. in Tsch. Faun. Per., Orn. p. 148[2]; Scl. P. Z. S. 1856, p. 296[3]; Cat. Birds Brit. Mus. xiv. p. 112[4]; Scl. & Salv. P. Z. S. 1864, p. 358[5], 1879, p. 512[6]; Salv. P. Z. S. 1867, p. 147[7], 1870, p. 196[8]; Nutt. & Ridgw. Pr. U. S. Nat. Mus. vi. p. 402[9]; Tacz. Orn. Pér. ii. p. 245[10].

* Tacz. Orn. Pér. ii. p. 244.

Mionectes assimilis, Scl. P. Z. S. 1859, pp. 46 [11], 366 [12]; Scl. & Salv. Ibis, 1859, p. 124 [13]; P. Z. S.
1870, p. 837 [14]; Lawr. Ann. Lyc. N. Y. vii. p. 328 [15], ix. p. 111 [16]; Sumichrast, Mem.
Bost. Soc. N. H. i. p. 556 [17].

Olivaceus; alis et cauda fusco-nigricantibus, pallide fulvescenti-viridi extrorsum limbatis; abdomine et
subalaribus fulvis: subtus gutture et pectore cinerascenti-olivaceis: rostro nigro, mandibulæ basi rufescente; pedibus corylinis. Long. tota 4·8, alæ 2·7, caudæ 2·0, rostri a rictu 0·65, tarsi 0·6. (Descr.
maris ex Volcan de Agua, Guatemala. Mus. nostr.)
♀ mari similis.

Hab. MEXICO, Cordova (*Sallé* [3]), Jalapa (*de Oca* [12], *M. Trujillo*), hot region of the
State of Vera Cruz (*Sumichrast* [17]), Hacienda de los Atlixcos (*F. D. G.*), Teapa
(*H. H. Smith*); BRITISH HONDURAS, Vicinity of Belize (*Blancaneaux*); GUATEMALA
(*Skinner* [13]), Choctum, Coban, Lanquin, Volcan de Agua above San Diego, Retal-
huleu (*O. S. & F. D. G.*); HONDURAS, San Pedro (*G. M. Whitely* [14]); NICARAGUA,
Los Sabalos (*Nutting* [9]); COSTA RICA, Angostura, Guaitil, Pacuar (*Carmiol* [16]),
Turrialba (*Arcé*); PANAMA, Chiriqui, Bugaba [8], Boquete de Chitra [8], Calovevora [8],
Santa Fé [7] (*Arcé*), Lion Hill (*M'Leannan* [5] [15]).—SOUTH AMERICA, from Colombia [6]
to Bolivia [4], Amazons valley [4], Eastern Brazil [1], and Guiana [4].

Mr. Sclater separated the Mexican and Guatemalan form of this species under the
name of *M. assimilis*, defining it as of larger size, as having a longer bill, and with the
throat and neck more tinged with ash-colour. The difference of dimensions between
the northern and southern forms is slight and not more than can be found in a series
of either of them. The difference in the colour of the throat is not very pronounced,
and though more apparent in northern examples seems to be less evident in those from
Costa Rica and the State of Panama, so that the two forms blend so gradually the one
into the other that we think they should both pass under the title *M. oleagineus*. In
South America *M. oleagineus* enjoys a wide range over nearly the whole of the tropical
portion of the continent, for it is not until we come to Southern Brazil that we find a
race that is perhaps distinct, having a dark grey head and darker fulvous abdomen;
this is the *M. rufiventris* of Cabanis.

Little has been recorded of this species. In Guatemala we found it only in the
heavily forested country of Vera Paz, where it occurs from near the sea-level to an
elevation of upwards of 4000 feet, and on the mountain-slopes stretching towards the
Pacific Ocean. In Mexico its range does not extend beyond the forests of the hotter
portions of the State of Vera Cruz, and it has not been noticed on the Isthmus of
Tehuantepec, though a little further south it occurs at Retalhuleu.

In British Guiana Mr. H Whitely obtained specimens near the sea-level at Bartica
Grove and at an altitude of 3500 feet in the mountains of Roraima.

LEPTOPOGON.

Leptopogon, Cabanis in Tschudi's Fauna Per. p. 161 (1845) (type *L. superciliaris*, Cab.); Scl. Cat. Birds Brit. Mus. xiv. p. 114.

Leptopogon contains eleven or twelve species, all belonging to the Neotropical region, only three of which enter our fauna, viz. the typical species, *L. superciliaris*, which reaches Costa Rica and has an extended range in South America; *L. pileatus*, one of the doubtful forms of the Brazilian *L. amaurocephalus*, found only in part of Central America and the Mexican State of Vera Cruz; and *L. flavovirens* of Panama.

Leptopogon has a bill shaped much as in *Mionectes*, but the nostrils are more linear and are overhung by a membrane; the rictal bristles are more strongly developed, the tarsi comparatively shorter, and the feet weaker; the 3rd, 4th, and 5th quills are nearly equal and longest, 2nd > 6th, 1st < longest secondaries; tail long, nearly = wing, = 4 tarsus.

1. Leptopogon superciliaris.

Leptopogon superciliaris, Cab. in Tsch. Fauna Per. p. 161, t. 10. f. 2 [1]; Salv. Ibis, 1870, p. 115 [2]; P. Z. S. 1870, p. 197 [3]; Scl. & Salv. P. Z. S. 1879, p. 613 [4]; Tacz. Orn. Pér. ii. p. 246 [5]; Scl. Cat. Birds Brit. Mus. xiv. p. 115 [6].

Supra viridi-olivaceis; pileo toto plumbeo; superciliis albo et cinereo variegatis; macula auriculari fusca; alis et cauda nigricantibus viridi-olivaceo limbatis, illarum tectricibus rufescenti-ochraceo terminatis: subtus gutture toto usque ad pectus griseo-olivaceo; abdomine viridi-sulphureo: rostro et pedibus plumbeis, mandibulæ basi pallida. Long. tota 5·3, alæ 2·7, caudæ 2·5, rostri a rictu 0·65, tarsi 0·65. (Descr. exempl. ex Costa Rica. Mus. nostr.)

Hab. COSTA RICA (*Carmiol* [2]); PANAMA, Volcan de Chiriqui, Bugaba, Calovevora (*Arcé* [3]). —COLOMBIA [6]; ECUADOR [6]; PERU [1][5]; BOLIVIA [6].

Leptopogon superciliaris was discovered by Tschudi in Peru, where it has since been found in many places by Jelski and Stolzmann up to an elevation of 4000 feet. It spreads southwards to Bolivia, where Buckley met with it, and it is also found in Colombia, as skins of it occur in the trade collections of Bogota. In Ecuador it is found on both sides of the Cordillera, as we have skins of it obtained by Buckley at Sarayacu and others from the Balzar Mountains near Guayaquil; but between the eastern and western birds Dr. Taczanowski and Graf von Berlepsch trace some differences and call the western one *L. s. transandinus*. The head seems to be a trifle greener, but the difference is not greater than what we find between birds of opposite sexes from the State of Panama. Our Central-American examples have the tips of the wing-coverts a little less rufescent than those from more southern localities, with the exception of Bolivia; our only skin from that country has hardly any rufescent tint on these feathers.

L. superciliaris probably lives in forests lying at a higher elevation than those frequented by *L. pileatus*, but our information concerning both species is very meagre.

2. Leptopogon flavovirens.

Tyrannula flaviventris, Lawr. Ann. Lyc. N. Y. vii. p. 328 [1].

Leptopogon flavovirens, Lawr. Ann. Lyc. N. Y. vii. p. 472 [2]; Scl. Cat. Birds Brit. Mus. xiv. p. 119 [3].

Supra olivaceus: alis et cauda nigricantibus, illis distincte olivaceo-albido marginatis et bifasciatis, hac olivaceo limbata; oculorum ambitu albo: subtus olivaceo-flavidus, mento albicante; subalaribus dilutioribus: rostro corneo, mandibula pallida; pedibus plumbeis; iride (ave viva) brunnea. Long. tota 4·2, alæ 2·1, caudæ 2·0, rostri a rictu 0·6, tarsi 0·7. (Descr. exempl. typ. ex Panama. Mus. G. N. Lawrence.)

Hab. PANAMA, line of Railway (*M‘Leannan* [1] [2]).

This species is closely allied to *L. tristis*, Scl. & Salv., which may have to be merged with it when a better series of specimens is available for comparison. Compared with our only specimen of *L. tristis* from Bolivia the type of *L. flavovirens* is rather brighter olive-colour on the back, the wing-bars are more confluent and not so much broken into spots as in *L. tristis*. The latter bird, too, has a distinct spot on several of the median secondaries on the outer web near the tip which we do not see in *L. flavovirens*.

The type specimen in Mr. Lawrence's collection, which we now have an opportunity of describing, is the only example we have seen of this species. It was contained in one of M‘Leannan's collections made on the Isthmus of Panama. It was found on high trees.

3. Leptopogon pileatus.

Leptopogon amaurocephalus, Scl. P. Z. S. 1859, p. 384 [1] (nec Cabanis); Scl. & Salv. Ibis, 1860, p. 399 [2]; P. Z. S. 1864, p. 358 [3]; Lawr. Ann. Lyc. N. Y. vii. p. 328 [4].

Leptopogon pileatus, Cab. J. f. Orn. 1865, p. 414 [5]; Salv. Ibis, 1869, p. 319 [6]; P. Z. S. 1870, p. 197 [7]; Scl. Cat. Birds Brit. Mus. xiv. p. 117 [8].

Olivaceus; capite toto summo umbrino-brunneo; alis et cauda nigricanti-brunneis, extrorsum ochraceo-olivaceo limbatis, illarum tectricibus pallide umbrino terminatis: subtus gutture toto usque ad pectus pallide olivaceo; abdomine medio flavo-olivaceo; subalaribus et alis intus pallide umbrinis: rostro corneo, mandibulæ basi albicante; pedibus corylinis. Long. tota 4·8, alæ 2·4, caudæ 2·1, rostri a rictu 0·65, tarsi 0·5. (Descr. exempl. ex Choctum, Guatemala. Mus. nostr.)

Hab. MEXICO, Playa Vicente (*Boucard* [1]), Teapa in Tabasco (*H. H. Smith*); GUATEMALA [5], Choctum (*O. S. & F. D. G.* [2]); COSTA RICA, Valza (*Carmiol* [6]); PANAMA, Calovevora (*Arcé* [7]), Lion-Hill Station (*M‘Leannan* [3] [4]), San Pablo Station (*O. S.*).

This is a northern race of the Brazilian *Leptopogon amaurocephalus*, from which it differs but slightly; the size is considerably less, the crown of the head rather darker, and the under wing-coverts, as well as the inner margin of the wing-feathers, of a darker umber tint.

For some years our bird was not considered to be separable from *L. amaurocephalus*, but in 1865 Dr. Cabanis named it *L. pileatus* from Guatemalan examples. Since then the latter title has been adopted.

The range of this species seems to be strictly confined to the denser hot tropical forests, and at present has only been found in such districts in Mexico and Guatemala which lie on the eastern side of the Cordillera. Our specimens from Costa Rica and Panama are also from the Atlantic side of the mountains.

The specimen obtained by Salvin at San Pablo Station on the Panama Railway was shot from a tree on the edge of the forest near the railway-bridge which crosses the Chagres river at Barbacoas.

MYIOPAGIS, gen. nov.

(Type *Elainea placens*, Scl.)

The form of the nostril of *Elainea placens* and its allies makes it necessary to separate this section of *Elainea* and place it under a distinct generic name; and though the outlines of the bill of *Myiopagis* are similar to those of *E. pagana*, we think that it is best placed near *Leptopogon*, which has somewhat similar nostrils, but a higher, more compressed bill.

The species we think ought to be removed from *Elainea* and placed under the new genus are:—*E. placens*, *E. subplacens*, *E. cotta*, *E. gaimardi*, *E. flavivertex*, *E. caniceps*, and perhaps *E. ruficeps*.

The general colours of the plumage of *Myiopagis* are olive above, with greyish throat and yellowish abdomen; there is also a concealed vertical crest of yellow or white: this crest is not, like that of *Elainea*, simply a few white feathers, but one constructed after that of *Tyrannus* and many other genera of this family.

The bill is moderately long, the sides nearly straight, converging gradually from the gape, the width of which is about half the length of the tomia; the nostrils are open, oval, and placed at the end of the nasal fossa, a membrane bordering them along the upper and hinder edges; the rictal bristles are moderately developed, hardly so much so as in *Elainea*; the tarsi are moderately stout and covered with distinct scutellæ; the outer toe is a little less than the inner toe; the 3rd and 4th quills are the longest in the wing; 5th > 2nd, 1st = 8th; the tail is long and scarcely emarginate, nearly = wing, wing nearly = 4 tarsus.

The distribution of *Myiopagis* includes nearly the whole of tropical America from Southern Mexico to Paraguay.

1. **Myiopagis placens.**

Elainea placens, Scl. P. Z. S. 1859, p. 46[1]; Cat. Birds Brit. Mus. xiv. p. 148[2]; Scl. & Salv. Ibis, 1859, p. 123, t. 4. f. 2[3]; P. Z. S. 1864, p. 359[4]; Salv. Ibis, 1860, p. 194[5]; P. Z. S. 1870, p. 197[6]; Lawr. Ann. Lyc. N. Y. vii. p. 328[7], ix. pp. 112[8], 201[9]; Mem. Bost. Soc. N. H. ii. p. 286[10]; Grayson, Pr. Bost. Soc. N. H. xiv. p. 279[11]; Ridgway, Pr. U. S. Nat. Mus. viii. p. 571[12].

Elainea, sp. ?, Scl. P. Z. S. 1856, p. 297, no. 113[13].

Sylvia viridicata, Vieill. N. Dict. d'Hist. N. xi. p. 171[14] ? (*cf.* Scl. Cat. Birds Brit. Mus. xiv. p. 148).

Muscicapa viridicata, d'Orb. Voy. Ois. p. 325[15].

Elaenea regulus, Licht. Nomencl. p. 17[16].

Supra olivaceo-viridis; capite summo obscure cinereo, medialiter læte flavo subcristato; loris et capitis lateribus cinereis albo intermixtis; alis et cauda nigricantibus, extrorsum olivaceo-viridi stricte limbatis: subtus gula albicante; pectore pallide cinereo; abdomine crisso et subalaribus pallide sulphureis: rostro et pedibus nigris. Long. tota 4·7, alæ 2·5, caudæ 2·3, tarsi 0·6, rostri a rictu 0·6. (Descr. maris ex Jalapa, Mexico. Mus. nostr.)

♀ mari similis.

Hab. Mexico, Tres Marias I. (*Grayson*[11], *Forrer*), Cordova (*Sallé*[13]), Jalapa (*M. Trujillo*), Alvarado (*Deppe*), Merida in Yucatan (*Schott*[9]), Mugeres I. (*Gaumer*), Cozumel I. (*Benedict*[12], *Gaumer*); Guatemala (*Skinner*[3]), Coban[5], Cahabon, Choctum, Retalhuleu (*O. S. & F. D. G.*), Volcan de Agua (*O. S.*); Costa Rica, Barranca, Guaitil, Grecia (*Carmiol*[8]); Panama, Volcan de Chiriqui, Chitra[6], Boquete de Chitra[6], Calovevora[6] (*Arcé*), Lion Hill (*M'Leannan*[4][7]).—South America, Colombia to Bolivia[15]; Brazil; Paraguay[14]?

It is quite possible that this bird should bear the name of *M. viridicata* (Vieill.), which was based upon a bird of Paraguay, the "Contramaestre pardo verdoso corona amarilla" of Azara; but until specimens are examined from that country it is safer to continue the use of Mr. Sclater's name, *Elainea placens*, bestowed upon a Mexican bird which formed part of M. Sallé's first collection made in the vicinity of Cordova[13].

The species enjoys a wide range in our country, being abundant in Guatemala in the more heavily forested parts of the temperate and hot districts. We found it especially abundant in the cocoa-plantations near Retalhuleu in the Pacific coast district of Guatemala. Here it frequented the lower branches of the forest trees, its habits being similar to those of the arboreal species of the family. The northern range of *M. placens* reaches the Tres Marias Islands, where both Grayson and Forrer met with it, but where it is not common. It occurs nowhere else in Western Mexico, but in the forests of the eastern slope of the mountains it has been found in several places.

M. placens occurs rarely in Yucatan, but appears to be very common on the island of Cozumel. Mr. Ridgway seemed doubtful whether the bird of this island was really the same as that of the mainland, but with many specimens from both places before us we do not see any grounds for their separation.

2. Myiopagis macilvaini.

Elainea macilvainii, Lawr. Ann. Lyc. N. Y. x. p. 10[1].
Elainea caniceps?, Scl. & Salv. P. Z. S. 1864, p. 359[2]; Salv. Ibis, 1874, p. 315[3].

Præcedenti similis, sed crista pallida et fasciis alarum duabus obviis, distinguenda. (Descr. feminæ ex Panama. Mus. nostr.)

Hab. Panama, Lion-Hill Station (*M'Leannan*[2]).—Venezuela?[1].

In 1864 Sclater and Salvin considered this Panama bird to belong probably to *E. caniceps* (Sw.), recognizing at the same time *E. elegans* of Pelzeln as distinct[2]. In his recent revision of the Tyrannidæ, Mr. Sclater unites the so-called *E. caniceps* with

4*

E. elegans, and places them under d'Orbigny's older title *E. gaimardi,* at the same time using Swainson's name for a very different bird.

We, however, still think the Panama bird distinct from *E. elegans* sive *E. gaimardi;* and, as it is not, as we supposed, *E. caniceps,* Sw., Mr. Lawrence's name, *E. macilvaini,* is available for it. In 1874 Salvin compared Mr. Lawrence's type with the Panama bird, and found them to agree [3].

The type of *E. macilvaini* was supposed to have been obtained in Venezuela; but as the true *E. gaimardi* occurs there it is probable that country is not included in its domicile.

E. macilvaini is closely allied to *E. gaimardi,* but may be distinguished by its yellower crest. In this respect it is intermediate between *E. gaimardi* and *E. placens.* From the latter it may be also recognized by the bands on the wings.

We have only seen three specimens of this bird, besides the type; these were all obtained by M'Leannan on the line of the Panama Railway.

CAPSIEMPIS.

Capsiempis, Cabanis & Heine, Mus. Hein. ii. p. 56 (1859) (type *Muscicapa flaveola,* Licht.); Scl. Cat. Birds Brit. Mus. xiv. p. 120.

A genus of two species, whereof the widely-ranging *C. flaveola* is only known to us.

Its affinities are not very clear, and its position here, close to *Ornithion* and *Elainea,* open to question.

The general colour is olivaceous above and yellowish beneath. The bill is wider at the base than that of *Mionectes,* and the rictal bristles much longer and stronger; the culmen is gradually decurved from the forehead, and the nostrils oval and open, without overhanging membrane as in *Leptopogon.* The wing is short and rounded, the points of the quills acute; 3rd, 4th, and 5th quills longest; 2nd=6th, 1st<10th; the tail is long and rounded, =wing, >3 tarsus.

1. **Capsiempis flaveola.**

Muscicapa flaveola, Licht. Verz. Doubl. p. 56 [1].

Capsiempis flaveola, Cab. & Hein. Mus. Hein. ii. p. 56 [2]; Pelz. Orn. Bras. p. 104 [3]; Scl. Cat. Birds Brit. Mus. xiv. p. 120 [4].

Muscipeta flaveola, Burm. Syst. Ueb. ii. p. 488 [5].

Tyrannula modesta, Sw. Orn. Draw. t. 48 [6].

Elainea semiflava, Lawr. Ann. Lyc. N. Y. viii. pp. 177 [7], 182 [8]; Salv. P. Z. S. 1867, p. 147 [9].

Supra olivacea, capite summo vix obscuriore; alis et cauda nigricanti-fuscis, extrorsum flavo limbatis, harum tectricibus mediis et majoribus sordide flavo-albido terminatis; loris, superciliis et corpore toto subtus flavis: rostro fusco-corneo, mandibula ad basin pallida; pedibus nigricantibus. Long. tota 4·0, alæ 2·0, caudæ 2·0, rostri a rictu 0·5, tarsi 0·65. (Descr. exempl. ex Chiriqui, Panama. Mus. nostr.)

Hab. Nicaragua, Greytown (*Holland*[8]); Panama, David (*Hicks*[7]), Chiriqui (*Arcé*).—Colombia?; Brazil[1 2 3 4 6].

Though this species has been traced as far north as Greytown in Nicaragua, and has also been noticed in the neighbourhood of Chiriqui, it is apparently a rare bird in our region, whence at present we have only one Chiriqui specimen. This agrees closely with an example from Bahia, and we have no doubt as to the identity of the species, though its range is so great, and, so far as we know at present, interrupted in the Amazons region, whence no examples have yet reached us.

Mr. Lawrence's *Elainea semiflava* we have no doubt belongs here. Some years ago we examined his type and came to this conclusion, which was confirmed more recently by a re-examination and comparison of the type with our own and Mr. Sclater's examples.

In Brazil *C. flaveola* appears to be more common. Natterer obtained five specimens, and speaks of having met with a small flock at Goiaz in the month of August.

ORNITHION.

Ornithion, Hartlaub, J. f. Orn. 1853, p. 35 (type *O. inerme*, Hartl.); Scl. Cat. Birds Brit. Mus. xiv. p. 125.

A genus of four species of small size and dull colour, the species of our region being of a brownish plumage hardly relieved by yellowish beneath. The rictal bristles are but feebly developed and less conspicuous than in *Elainea*, to which *Ornithion* has some affinity. The bill is much compressed, the sides concave, the width at the gape being about ½ the length of tomia, the culmen is gradually arched from the forehead; the nostrils are in the middle of a membrane, and thus differ from the foregoing genera, but resemble those which immediately follow; the tarsi are long, and the feet comparatively strong. The wing is short and rounded, offering no peculiar feature; the tail is short and square at the end, $= \frac{5}{6}$ wing, wing $= 3$ tarsus.

1. **Ornithion imberbe.**

Camptostoma imberbe, Scl. P. Z. S. 1857, p. 203[1]; Ibis, 1859, p. 444, t. 14. f. 1[2]; Scl. & Salv. Ibis, 1860, p. 400[3]; Lawr. Ann. Lyc. N. Y. ix. p. 201[4]; Mem. Bost. Soc. N. H. ii. p. 286[5].

Ornithion imberbe, Coues, Bull. U. S. Geol. Surv. v. p. 406[6]; Ridgw. Man. N. Am. B. p. 346[7]; Scl. Cat. Birds Brit. Mus. xiv. p. 126.

Ornithion incanescens, Scl. P. Z. S. 1873, p. 577[8]; Lawr. Bull. U. S. Nat. Mus. no. 4, p. 26[9] (nec Wied).

Ornithion imberbe ridgwayi, Brewster, Bull. Nutt. Orn. Club, vii. p. 208[10]; Ridgw. Man. N. Am. B. p. 346[11].

Supra fuscum; pileo vix obscuriore; uropygio sensim dilutiore; alis fusco-nigricantibus, extrorsum pallide fusco limbatis, harum tectricibus majoribus et mediis ferrugineo-fusco terminatis; stria superciliari et corpore subtus albicanti-fuscis; campterio alari et subalaribus flavido vix suffusis: rostro corneo, mandibula

pallida; pedibus saturate plumbeis. Long. tota 3·70, alæ 1·95, caudæ 1·45, rostri a rictu 0·4, tarsi 0·6.
(Descr. exempl. ex Cozumel I., Yucatan. Mus. nostr.)

Hab. NORTH AMERICA, Texas [6] [7], Arizona [10] [11].—MEXICO, Xenotencal and Aldama in
   Tamaulipas (*W. B. Richardson*), Mazatlan, San Blas (*Grayson* [5]), Presidio near
   Mazatlan (*Forrer*), San Andres Tuxtla (*Sallé* [1]), Tehuantepec (*Sumichrast* [9]), Merida
   in Yucatan (*Schott* [4]), Cozumel I. (*G. F. Gaumer*); GUATEMALA, Escuintla (*O. S.*[3]);
   NICARAGUA, Corinto (*O. S.*).—ECUADOR [8]; BRAZIL, Bahia (*Mus. nostr.*).

The specimen described above is of rather small dimensions, another larger one from
the same source has a wing 2·1 inches long, and is as large as one from the vicinity of
Mazatlan.   The birds found along the Mexican frontier in Arizona and the valley of
the Rio Grande have been separated by Mr. Brewster, and recognized by Mr. Ridgway
as *O. imberbe ridgwayi* and *O. imberbe*, the former being described as larger and greyer
with hardly any sulphur-yellow tint to the lower plumage, and with a bill larger and
thicker.   This race extends, according to Mr. Ridgway, as far south as Mazatlan.   We
have a specimen from the last-named locality, but are unable to see wherein it differs
from our series from more eastern and southern places.   Moreover, it seems to us that
an example from Sarayacu in Ecuador and two from Bahia in Brazil are not sufficiently
distinct to admit of separation.   The former is a young bird the latter adult, slightly
darker in general tint, and with somewhat darker heads and greyer chests.

Mr. Sennett first discovered this species in the valley of the Rio Grande at Lomita [6],
where others have since been found by Mr. Frazer [9].   Mr. Richardson has now sent us
specimens from the State of Tamaulipas on the southern side of the valley.

The Arizona birds were shot by Mr. F. Stephens near Tucson, where, however, they
were not common.   The males he describes as having a habit of perching on the tops
of trees and uttering a singular song at sunrise.

We only met with *O. imberbe* on one occasion in Guatemala, when a female was
secured in January near Escuintla, others being observed in the vicinity.   Our two
specimens from Nicaragua were shot, 16th March 1863, close to Corinto on the Pacific
coast; they are both young birds in their first plumage.   On both occasions the birds
were observed on the outer branches of forest-trees on the edge of clearings.

2. Ornithion pusillum.

Myiopatis pusilla, Cab. & Heine, Mus. Hein. ii. p. 58 [1]; Pelz. Orn. Bras. p. 106 [2].

Ornithion pusillum, Scl. P. Z. S. 1873, p. 577 [3]; Cat. Birds Brit. Mus. xiv. p. 126 [4].

Camptostoma imberbe, Lawr. Ann. Lyc. N. Y. vii. p. 473 [5]; Taylor, Ibis, 1864, p. 86 [6].

Camptostoma flaviventre, Scl. & Salv. P. Z. S. 1864, p. 358 [7], 1867, p. 576 [8]; Salv. P. Z. S. 1870,
   p. 197 [9]; Ibis, 1885, p. 294 [10].

Præcedenti similis, sed dorso toto olivaceo, fasciis alarum duabus sordide albis et corpore subtus flavicante
   distinguendum.

Hab. PANAMA, Bugaba (*Arcé* [9]), Lion-Hill Station (*M'Leannan* [5] [7]). — COLOMBIA [1];
   AMAZONS VALLEY [2] [8]; TRINIDAD [6]; GUIANA [10].

O. pusillum was described in 1859 from a specimen in the Berlin Museum from Cartagena in Northern Colombia, and it received another name, *Camptostoma flaviventre*, in 1864, the latter being based upon Panama examples. There can be little doubt both these names refer to the same species, which has a wide range over the northern portion of South America from the mouth of the Amazons and Guiana to Colombia and Western Ecuador, entering the Isthmus as far north as Chiriqui.

TYRANNULUS.

Tyrannulus, Vieillot, Analyse, p. 31 (1816) (type *Sylvia elata*, Latham); Scl. Cat. Birds Brit. Mus. xiv. p. 128.

All three of the species forming this genus occur within our limits, the type *T. elatus*, which is widely spread in South America, entering our border as far as Chiriqui. Both the other species are confined to Central America—*T. semiflavus* ranging from Southern Mexico to Nicaragua, and *T. brunneicapillus* from Costa Rica to Panama.

The latter species are closely allied, but differ from the type in their shorter tails and the absence of an occipital crest.

The bill of *Tyrannulus* is compressed, but hardly so much so as in *Ornithion*, the nostrils are similarly placed in the middle of a membrane, the rictal bristles are short and feebly developed, the wings offer no peculiarity, the tail (in *T. elatus*)$=\frac{4}{5}$ wing$=3$ tarsus (in *T. semiflavus*$=\frac{1}{2}$ wing$=\frac{3}{2}$ tarsus).

a. *Crista verticalis conspicua.*

1. **Tyrannulus elatus.**

Sylvia elata, Lath. Ind. Orn. p. 549[1].

Tyrannulus elatus, Vieill. N. Dict. d'Hist. N. xxxv. p. 94[2]; Gal. Ois. i. p. 93, t. 71[3]; Scl. P. Z. S. 1856, p. 141[4]; Cat. Birds Brit. Mus. xiv. p. 128[5]; Pelz. Orn. Bras. p. 106[6]; Scl. & Salv. P. Z. S. 1879, p. 512[7]; Salv. Ibis, 1885, p. 294[8].

Olivaceus; capite summo nigricante; crista verticali elongata flava ornata; alis et cauda nigricanti-fuscis, harum secundariis in pogonio externo ad apicem, tectricibus majoribus et mediis pallide viridi-flavo limbatis: subtus dilutior; gula grisea; abdomine medio flavo: rostro et pedibus nigris. Long. tota 4·0, alæ 2·0, caudæ 1·6, rostri a rictu 0·4, tarsi 0·5. (Descr. maris ex Remedios, Antioquia, Colombia. Mus. nostr.)

Hab. PANAMA, David (*Bridges*[4]), Paraiso Station (*Hughes*).—SOUTH AMERICA from Colombia[7] to Amazons valley[6], Guiana[8], and Brazil.

This well-known Tyrant enjoys a wide range over the northern part of South America, and has been recorded from South-eastern Brazil. It appears to be far from uncommon in Colombia, Guiana, and the Amazons valley. Within our limits we know but little of it; a specimen was contained in the small collection made by Bridges in Chiriqui, and described by Sclater in 1856[4], and one was sent us by Mr. Hughes from Paraiso station on the Panama Railway. We have never seen specimens in any of the other large collections made in the State of Panama, nor have any been recorded.

T. elatus is easily recognized by its yellow crest, the rest of the plumage resembling that of several species of *Tyranniscus*, none of which, however, are crested.

b. *Crista verticalis nulla, cauda abbreviata.*

2. **Tyrannulus semiflavus.** (Tab. XXXVI. fig. 1.)

Tyrannulus semiflavus, Scl. & Salv. P. Z. S. 1860, p. 300[1]; Ibis, 1860, p. 400[2]; Lawr. Ann. Lyc. N. Y. viii. p. 182[3]; Scl. Cat. Birds Brit. Mus. xiv. p. 129[4].

Olivaceus; pileo toto cinereo; fronte et superciliis elongatis albis, alis et cauda fuscis olivaceo limbatis: subtus pure flavus: rostro et pedibus nigris. Long. tota 3·0, alæ 1·8, caudæ 1·1, rostri a rictu 0·4, tarsi 0·5. (Descr. exempl. typ. ex Choctum, Guatemala. Mus. nostr.)

Hab. MEXICO, Teapa in Tabasco (*H. H. Smith*); GUATEMALA, Choctum (*O. S. & F. D. G.*[1][2]); NICARAGUA, Greytown (*Holland*[3]).

This distinct form was described from a specimen obtained by one of our collectors in the neighbourhood of the hamlet of Choctum in the forest-region of Northern Vera Paz at an elevation of 1200 feet above the sea. Subsequently others were procured from the same district. We have no record of its occurrence elsewhere in Guatemala; but Mr. Lawrence includes its name in his list of the birds of Mr. Holland's collection made in the vicinity of Greytown, Nicaragua[3], and we have recently received a female specimen from Teapa in Tabasco which was sent us by Mr. Herbert Smith.

3. **Tyrannulus brunneicapillus.**

Tyrannulus brunneicapillus, Lawr. Ibis, 1862, p. 12[1]; Ann. Lyc. N. Y. vii. p. 473[2]; ix. p. 111[3]; Scl. & Salv. P. Z. S. 1864, p. 359[4]; Scl. Cat. Birds Brit. Mus. xiv. p. 129[5].

Præcedenti similis, sed capite summo brunneo nec cinereo dintinguendus. (Descr. maris ex Lion Hill, Panama. Mus. nostr.)

Hab. COSTA RICA, Angostura (*Carmiol*[3]); PANAMA[1], Lion Hill Station (*M'Leannan*[2][4]).

A close ally of *T. semiflavus*, but readily distinguished by its brown head. The first specimens were sent to Mr. G. N. Lawrence from Lion Hill on the Panama Railway by M'Leannan, who subsequently forwarded others to us from the same place. Its range northwards extends to Costa Rica, where Carmiol met with it at Angostura. We have no record of it from the intermediate districts of Chiriqui and Veraguas.

TYRANNISCUS.

Tyranniscus, Cabanis & Heine, Mus. Hein. ii. p. 57 (1859) (type *Tyrannulus nigricapillus*); Scl. Cat. Birds Brit. Mus. xiv. p. 130.

About twelve species constitute this genus, which is closely allied to *Tyrannulus*, but, besides being devoid of an occipital crest, it has a shorter, wider bill, and more fully developed rictal bristles. The tail is normal, not short as in *Tyrannulus semiflavus*.

The range of *Tyranniscus* extends over most of Tropical America as far north as Guatemala, where *T. vilissimus* occurs, its place being taken in Costa Rica and the State of Panama by *T. parvus*, the two constituting the only representatives of the genus within our border.

1. **Tyranniscus vilissimus.**

Elainia vilissima, Scl. & Salv. Ibis, 1859, p. 122, t. 4. f. 1[1]; Salv. Ibis, 1860, p. 194[2].
Tyranniscus vilissimus, Scl. Cat. Am. B. p. 216[3]; Cat. Birds Brit. Mus. xiv. p. 132[4]; Scl. & Salv. P. Z. S. 1870, p. 843[5].

Olivaceus; pileo nigricanti-cinereo; fronte et superciliis albis; alis fusco-nigris, tectricibus majoribus, secundariis et primariis secunda, tertia, quarta et quinta ad basin viridi-flavo extrorsum anguste limbatis; cauda fusco-nigricante olivaceo marginata: subtus cinerascens; abdomine toto viridi-flavicante, medialiter pallidiore; hypochondriis olivaceo substriatis: rostro nigricante, mandibula pallidiore; pedibus nigricantibus. Long. tota 4·7, alæ 2·35, caudæ 2·0, rostri a riotu 0·4, tarsi 0·65. (Descr. maris ex Volcan de Fuego, Guatemala. Mus. nostr.)
♀ mari similis, sed (ut videtur) minor.

Hab. GUATEMALA (*Skinner*[1]), Dueñas, Calderas, Tactic, Choctum (*O. S. & F. D. G.*), Coban (*O. S.*[2]); HONDURAS, San Pedro (*G. M. Whitely*[5]).

This species, though also found in the low forest-country near Choctum, is very common in the neighbourhood of Coban at an altitude of about 4000 feet, and many specimens were brought us by the Indian boys of that town killed by their blow-guns[2]. *T. vilissimus* frequents the margins of the forest-clearings and the hedgerows dividing gardens or fields. Near Dueñas it is more rare than at Coban, but we obtained several specimens from the woods clothing the Volcan de Fuego up to an elevation of 7000 feet above the sea-level.

T. vilissimus is included both by Mr. Lawrence and Mr. Zeledon in their lists of Costa Rican birds, but, from specimens in our possession from that country, *T. parvus* is the *Tyranniscus* of this form that is found there. This view is confirmed by a specimen from Angostura sent us by Baird as *T. vilissimus*, but which is undoubtedly *T. parvus*.

2. **Tyranniscus parvus.**

Tyranniscus parvus, Lawr. Ibis, 1862, p. 12[1]; Ann. Lyc. N. Y. vii. p. 473[2]; Scl. & Salv. P. Z. S. 1864, p. 359[3], 1870, p. 843[4]; Salv. P. Z. S. 1867, p. 147[5], 1870, p. 197[6]; Scl. Cat. Birds Brit. Mus. xiv. p. 132[7].
Tyranniscus vilissimus, Lawr. Ann. Lyc. N. Y. ix. p. 111[8].

Præcedenti similis, sed multo minor; corpore subtus albicante, hypochondriis et crisso tantum olivaceo tinctis distinguendus. (Descr. exempl. ex Panama. Mus. nostr.)

Hab. COSTA RICA, Turrialba (*Arcé*[5]), Angostura, Dota, Turrialba, and Barranca (*Carmiol*[8]); PANAMA[1], Chiriqui[6], Bugaba[6], Calovevora[6], Boquete de Chitra[6], Santa Fé[5] (*Arcé*), Lion Hill (*McLeannan*[1 2 3]).

This is a southern form of *T. vilissimus* of Guatemala, differing in its smaller size and paler under surface, which is a very pale grey, with the flanks and crissum alone olive-coloured. These differences are not very trenchant, but they seem to be associated with a distinct region, the mountain-system of Costa Rica and Panama. We have received many specimens from the State of Panama, where this bird would appear to be quite common.

Mr. Sclater, in a note appended to Mr. Lawrence's original description [1], states that this bird is allied to *T. chrysops*, but its alliance is certainly with *T. vilissimus*. *T. chrysops*, besides having the head almost the same colour as the back, has, as its name implies, the forehead yellow.

ELAINEA.

Elænea, Sundevall, K. Vet.-Ak. Handl. 1835, p. 89 (type *Muscicapa pagana*, Licht.).
Elainea, Scl. Cat. Birds Brit. Mus. xiv. p. 136 (partim).

Upon close examination of the species included in *Elainea* by Mr. Sclater, we find that they belong to two different groups, easily separated by the form of the nostril as described below. Moreover, that the somewhat peculiar *Elainea arenarum* is best placed in the genus *Sublegatus*, being, in fact, identical with *E. glaber*, the type of *Sublegatus*!

Elainea, then, according to our views, contains only the first portion of Mr. Sclater's first section and part of the second; we remove from *Elainea* altogether the small bright-crested species forming sections *b* and *c* of his key.

This leaves only the *E. pagana* section to deal with, of which three species occur within our limits, none of them being peculiar, but also found in South America or the Antilles.

In the structure of the bill *Elainea* (*E. pagana*) is similar to that of the preceding genera, but is rather wider in comparison with its length and not so compressed; the nostrils are surrounded by membrane, the rictal bristles moderately developed; the wings offer no peculiarity, being comparatively short and rounded as in most non-migratory Tyrannidæ, the outermost primary $=$7th; the tail is nearly square, a little $<$ wing, $=$4 tarsus.

1. Elainea pagana.

Muscicapa pagana, Licht. Verz. Doubl. p. 54 [1].
Platyrhynchus paganus, Spix, Av. Bras. ii. p. 13, t. 16. f. 1 [2].
Elainea pagana, Scl. Cat. Birds Brit. Mus. xiv. p. 137 [3].
Elainea subpagana, Scl. & Salv. Ibis, 1860, p. 36 [4]; P. Z. S. 1864, p. 359 [5], 1870, p. 837 [6]; Cab. J. f. Orn. 1861, p. 244 [7]; Scl. P. Z. S. 1862, p. 369 [8]; Lawr. Ann. Lyc. N. Y. vii. p. 328 [9],

viii. p. 176 [10], ix. p. 112 [11]; Pr. U. S. Nat. Mus. i. p. 59 [12]; Salv. P. Z. S. 1867, p. 147 [13]; Ridgw. Pr. U. S. Nat. Mus. v. p. 500 [14].

Elainea chiriquensis, Lawr. Ann. Lyc. N. Y. viii. p. 176 [15]; Salv. P. Z. S. 1867, p. 147 [16].

Fusco-olivacea, pileo obscuriore; crista mediana celata alba; alis caudaque nigricanti-fuscis, tectricibus alarum albido terminatis, secundariis pallide olivaceo stricte limbatis: subtus pallide flava, pectore et hypochondriis cinereis; gutture albicantiore: rostro nigricante corneo, mandibula ad basin carnea; pedibus nigricantibus. Long. tota 6·3, alæ 3·3, caudæ 3·1, tarsi 0·8, rostri a rictu 0·65. (Descr. exempl. ex Sakluk, Guatemala. Mus. nostr.)

♀ mari similis.

Hab. MEXICO [3][8][12], Teapa in Tabasco (*H. H. Smith*), Peto in Yucatan (*G. F. Gaumer*); BRITISH HONDURAS (*Blancaneaux*); GUATEMALA, Sakluk near Peten (*O. S.*), Dueñas (*O. S.*[4]); HONDURAS, San Pedro (*G. M. Whitely* [6]); COSTA RICA, San José (*Hoffmann* [7], *Carmiol* [11], *Nutting* [14]), Irazu (*Rogers*); PANAMA, Volcan de Chiriqui, Chitra, Calovevora, Santa Fé [13][16] (*Arcé*), David (*Hicks* [10]), Lion Hill (*M'Leannan* [5][9]), Paraiso Station (*Hughes*), line of Railway (*Arcé*).—SOUTH AMERICA [3], from Colombia to South Brazil (Bahia [1], Rio [2]) and Guiana.

Lichtenstein's description of this species was founded on a bird from Bahia [1], and specimens from that place agree fairly with others from nearly every part of continental Tropical America. We note, however, that they are of rather a paler colour than the majority of specimens from other parts.

At one time it was thought that the Central-American birds were separable from those of the South, and they passed under the name of *E. subpagana*. With a much larger series available for comparison than formerly, it now appears that no distinction can be maintained. The Chiriqui bird has also been separated, but this too has been merged in the southern form.

In Mexico *E. pagana* is apparently a scarce bird; until recently only two specimens had reached us from that country, but Mr. Herbert Smith has now sent us an example from Teapa in Tabasco, and Mr. Gaumer one from Peto in Yucatan. Mr. Lawrence records it from the valley of Mexico [12].

In the highlands of Guatemala we only met with it on one occasion, when two birds were shot at the end of July at Dueñas, nearly 5000 feet above the level of the sea.

In the southern portion of Central America this bird would appear to be much more numerous, and we have many specimens from various points as far south as the Isthmus of Panama.

It is usually found in open situations; one killed at Sakluk near Peten was in an open savanna, those near Dueñas in a willow-tree in a hedgerow. Mr. Nutting says it is common in the hedgerows near San José, Costa Rica. Salmon found both its nest and eggs at Medellin in Colombia. The nest he describes as being built of coarse grass mixed with bark or lichen, and lined with fine grass and feathers. The eggs, two in number, are white, spotted at the larger end with brown, generally placed in a ring.

2. Elainea martinica.

Muscicapa martinica, Linn. Syst. Nat. i. p. 325 [1].

Tyrannula martinica, Cass. Pr. Ac. Phil. 1860, p. 375 [2].

Elainia martinica, Cory, Auk, 1886, p. 230 [3]; Scl. Cat. Birds Brit. Mus. xiv. p. 141 [4].

Elainea martinica?, Ridgw. Pr. U. S. Nat. Mus. viii. p. 571 [5].

Elainea subpagana, Salv. Ibis, 1864, p. 380 [6].

Elainea cinerescens, Ridgw. Pr. U. S. Nat. Mus. vii. p. 180 [7].

Præcedenti similis, sed supra unicolor, pileo dorso concolore; subtus magis grisea, abdomine medio albido vix
flavo tincto. (Descr. exempl. ex insl. Cozumel. Mus. nostr.)

Hab. MEXICO, Mugeres I., Meco I., Cozumel I. (*Benedict* [5], *G. F. Gaumer*); BRITISH
HONDURAS, Half Moon Cay (*O. S.* [6]).—ANTILLES [3], from St. Thomas [2] to Barbados [4],
Grand Cayman I. [3], Old Providence I. [7]

The Cozumel birds agree closely with specimens from the West Indies typical of
Elainea martinica; but some of those from the islands further to the north (Mugeres
&c.) have the under surface tinged with yellow, and in this respect conform to *E. pagana*,
and in fact are intermediate between these closely allied birds. With these, however,
we find examples not separable from the more typical *E. martinica*, and it seems probable, considering the short distance the islands lie from the mainland, an occasional
individual crosses over and pairs with the island form.

The distribution of *E. martinica* is singular, for though it is found in all the small
West Indian islands from St. Thomas to Barbados, it is absent from the larger islands;
but it appears again in Grand Cayman and the island of Old Providence, for, with a
specimen from the latter island before us, we do not see how *E. cinerescens* of Mr.
Ridgway can be distinguished from the true *E. martinica*.

3. Elainea frantzii.

Elainea frantzii, Lawr. Ann. Lyc. N. Y. viii. p. 172 [1], ix. p. 112 [2]; v. Frantz. J. f. Orn. 1869,
p. 307 [3]; Salv. P. Z. S. 1870, p. 197 [4]; Scl. & Salv. P. Z. S. 1879, p. 513 [5]; Ridgw. Pr. U. S.
Nat. Mus. v. p. 496 [6]; Nutt. & Ridgw. Pr. U. S. Nat. Mus. vi. p. 393 [7]; Scl. Cat. Birds Brit.
Mus. xiv. p. 145 [8].

Elainea pudica, Scl. P. Z. S. 1870, p. 833 [9].

Elainea, sp. ?, Salv. Ibis, 1866, p. 194 [10].

Supra saturate olivacea; crista verticali celata albida; alis et cauda nigricantibus, alarum tectricibus flavido
terminatis fasciis duabus formantibus, secundariis intimis extrorsum flavido late limbatis: subtus flavido-
olivacea: abdomine medio flavicanti-albido: rostro corneo, mandibula carnea; pedibus obscure corylinis.
Long. tota 6·0, alæ 3·2, caudæ 2·7, tarsi 0·7, rostri a rictu 0·55. (Descr. maris ex San Pedro Martyr,
Guatemala. Mus. nostr.)

♀ mari similis.

Hab. GUATEMALA, Dueñas (*O. S. & F. D. G.* [10]), Volcan de Agua, Barranco Hondo, Medio
Monte, S. Pedro Martyr (*O. S.*); NICARAGUA, Omotepe I. (*Nutting* [7]); COSTA RICA,
San José (*v. Frantzius* [1][2]), Barranca, Dota Mts. (*Carmiol* [2]), Irazu (*Rogers, Nut-
ting* [6]); PANAMA, Chiriqui (*Arcé* [4]).—COLOMBIA [5][9]; VENEZUELA [8].

Elainea frantzii was first described by Mr. Lawrence from specimens obtained by Dr. von Frantzius in Costa Rica [1], and soon afterwards the same species was named *E. pudica* by Mr. Sclater, whose description was based upon examples from Colombia, Venezuela, and Chiriqui [9]. In 1879 [5] it was recognized that both descriptions referred to the same species.

In Guatemala *E. frantzii* is a local bird, as our specimens were all obtained on the slope of the mountains between the volcanos of Agua and Fuego at elevations varying between 5000 and 1500 feet above the sea-level. Here it frequented the forests which so densely clothe these mountains.

On the island of Omotepe in the lake of Nicaragua Mr. Nutting found this species rather common, usually in the dense woods [6] : this would be at an elevation of a few hundred feet above the sea.

In Costa Rica this species is common, according to Mr. Nutting, who says it frequents hedgerows in the neighbourhood of San José [7]; though found on the slopes of the Volcan de Chiriqui [4] it seems absent from the rest of the State of Panama. In Colombia and Venezuela it reappears, and was found breeding near Medellin, in the Cauca valley, by Salmon [5], who describes its eggs as white with a few small spots near the larger end. The nest is placed on a low branch of a tree.

SUBLEGATUS.

Sublegatus, Sclater and Salvin, P. Z. S. 1868, p. 172 (type *S. glaber*, Scl. & Salv.) ; Scl. Cat. Birds Brit. Mus. xiv. p. 157.

Sublegatus is like *Elainea* in general appearance, but has a much wider bill, nearly round nostrils at the end of the nasal fossa, with no membrane along the anterior and lower edges ; the bill itself is wide and the edges slightly convex, the width at the gape being more than half the length of the tomia ; the rictal bristles are moderately developed, the tarsi and toes much as in *Elainea*; the 3rd, 4th, and 5th quills are nearly equal and longest ; 6th < 2nd, 1st=8th ; the tail is moderate and slightly emarginate, <wing, =4 tarsus.

This genus was founded on *S. glaber* of Venezuela, a species we now find inseparable from *Elainea arenarum* of Costa Rica, the latter being the older specific title.

Three species are included in *Sublegatus*, spread over a wide area, extending from Costa Rica to the Argentine Republic.

1. **Sublegatus arenarum.** (*Elainea arenarum*, Tab. XXXVI. fig. 3.)

Elainea arenarum, Salv. P. Z. S. 1863, p. 190 [1]; Lawr. Ann. Lyc. N. Y. ix. p. 112 [2]; v. Frantz. J. f. Orn. 1869, p. 307 [3]; Scl. Cat. Birds Brit. Mus. xiv. p. 153 [4].

Sublegatus glaber, Scl. & Salv. P. Z. S. 1868, p. 171, t. 13. f. 2 [5]; Wyatt, Ibis, 1871, p. 333 [6]; Scl. Cat. Birds Brit. Mus. xiv. p. 157 [7].

Empidonax atrirostris, Lawr. Pr. Ac. Phil. 1871, p. 234[8]; *cf.* Salv. Ibis, 1874, p. 316[9].

Muscicapa griseicollis, Licht. Mus. Ber. (*apud* Sclater)[10].

Supra fuscus; dorso olivaceo vix tincto; pileo, alis et cauda nigricantibus, tectricibus alarum (ad apices), secundariis extrorsum et caudæ apice pallide fuscis: subtus ad medium pectus cinereus; abdomine et subalaribus pallide flavis: rostro et pedibus nigricantibus. Long. tota 5·5, alæ 2·75, caudæ 2·6, tarsi 0·7, rostri a rictu 0·55. (Descr. maris ex Punta Arenas, Costa Rica. Mus. nostr.)

Hab. COSTA RICA, Punta Arenas (*O. S.*[1]).—COLOMBIA [6][7]; VENEZUELA [5].

A single male specimen shot by Salvin when in company with Captain J. M. Dow in the outskirts of the town of Punta Arenas in March 1863 is the only example that has yet been obtained of this species within our limits. On comparing the types of *E. arenarum* and *Sublegatus glaber* we find them not specifically different, so that this bird must be removed from *Elainea* and transferred to *Sublegatus*, its short stout bill and moderately developed bristles rendering it an abnormal member of *Elainea*.

The identification of these birds extends the range of *Sublegatus arenarum* to Colombia and Venezuela, Mr. Wyatt having found it in the former country [6], and Mr. Göring in the latter [5], and skins of it also occur in the trade collections of Bogota.

LEGATUS.

Legatus, Sclater, P. Z. S. 1859, p. 46; Cat. Birds Brit. Mus. xiv. p. 155 (type *Tyrannus albicollis,* Vieill.).

This genus contains but one species, which is spread over nearly the whole of tropical America from the eastern slopes of the Cordillera of Southern Mexico to Paraguay and South Brazil.

The character of the coloration of *L. albicollis* differs in many respects from that of the genera near which it is placed, and, though resembling *Myiozetetes* so far as the head is concerned, differs in having a striped breast and flanks.

The bill is wide, the width at the gape being rather more than three quarters the length of the tomia; the culmen is gradually curved from the forehead; the nostrils are at the lower anterior edge of the nasal fossa, which is large and covered with membrane, the rictal and frontal bristles are short, leaving the nostril completely exposed; the tarsi are short and covered with scutellæ; the toes rather short, the outer and inner toes being nearly equal; the 2nd and 3rd quills are the longest, 3rd > 1st, 1st = 5th; tail moderate and slightly marginate, $= \frac{3}{4}$ wing, $= 4$ tarsus.

1. **Legatus albicollis.**

Tyrannus albicollis, Vieill. N. Dict. d'Hist. Nat. xxxv. p. 89 [1].

Legatus albicollis, Lawr. Ann. Lyc. N. Y. vii. p. 472 [2], viii. p. 177 [3], ix. p. 112 [4]; Scl. & Salv. P. Z. S. 1864, p. 359 [5]; Salv. P. Z. S. 1870, p. 197 [6]; Scl. Cat. Birds Brit. Mus. xiv. p. 155 [7].

Elænia variegata, Scl. P. Z. S. 1856, p. 297 [8].

Legatus variegatus, Scl. P. Z. S. 1859, p. 366 [9], 1864, p. 175 [10]; Scl. & Salv. Ibis, 1859, p. 123 [11]; Cab. J. f. Orn. 1861, p. 245 [12]; Lawr. Ann. Lyc. N. Y. vii. p. 328 [13], ix. p. 112 [14]; v. Frantz. J. f. Orn. 1869, p. 307 [15]; Sumichrast, Mem. Bost. Soc. N. H. i. p. 557 [16].

Supra brunneus; capite summo saturatiore, crista celata flava ornato et linea alba undique circumcincto; loris et regione parotica nigricanti-brunneis; alis et cauda nigricantibus, illarum secundariis et tectricibus stricte albido limbatis: subtus pallide flavis; pectore et hypochondriis fusco maculatis; gutture albo; stria utrinque rictali fusca: rostro et pedibus nigris. Long. tota 6·2, alæ 3·7, caudæ 2·55, tarsi 0·75, rostri a rictu 0·6. (Descr. maris ex Cordova, Mexico. Mus. Brit.)

Hab. MEXICO, State of Vera Cruz (*Sumichrast* [16]), Jalapa (*de Oca* [9]), Cuesta de Misantla (*M. Trujillo*), Cordova (*Sallé* [8]), Atoyac and Teapa (*H. H. Smith*); GUATEMALA (*Skinner* [11]), Las Salinas, Cahabon (*O. S. & F. D. G.*); COSTA RICA [12][14][15], San José [4] (*v. Frantzius, Carmiol*), Tucurriqui, La Barranca (*Arcé*), Guaitil [4], Turrialba [4] (*Carmiol*); PANAMA, Bugaba [6], Chitra [6] (*Arcé*), Lion Hill (*M'Leannan* [2][5][13]), Paraiso Station (*Hughes*).—SOUTH AMERICA [7], from Colombia to Guiana and South Brazil [1].

A tropical species of very wide range. *Legatus albicollis* occurs throughout our region as far north as the mountain-slopes of the State of Vera Cruz; it thence spreads over Eastern Guatemala and crosses to the western side of Central America in Nicaragua, and in Costa Rica and the State of Panama is doubtless found on both sides of the mountain-range. We have no record of it in Western Mexico, the isthmus of Tehuantepec, or any portion of the Pacific coast-region of Guatemala.

In South America *L. albicollis* is found everywhere in the hotter districts as far south as Southern Brazil. It is the Paraguayan "Suiriri choreado siu roxo" of Azara, upon whose description Vieillot founded his name [1].

The Mexican bird was at one time separated under the name of *L. variegatus*, Sclater [8], on its supposed larger size and brighter colours. It has now been proved that some southern examples are fully as large as Mexican. The smallest of our series are from the State of Panama and Costa Rica. The Mexican birds are a little brighter yellow on the under plumage, but the difference is very slight and moreover variable.

This species is essentially an inhabitant of the hotter forest-region. Sumichrast says that it is confined to such districts in the State of Vera Cruz [16], and the specimens we have received from there confirm this statement. In Guatemala we met with it in similar places; one shot at Cahabon was in a tree in the outskirts of the village.

The nest and eggs are, we believe, unknown.

MYIOZETETES.

Myiozeta, Bonaparte, Consp. Syst. Orn. p. 30 (1854).

Myiozetetes, Sclater, P. Z. S. 1859, p. 46; Cat. Birds Brit. Mus. xiv. p. 159.

Myiozetetes is a well-marked genus, but contains several species the limits of which are not readily defined. Mr. Sclater recognizes seven species, but as we are unable to separate *M. texensis* from *M. similis* we reduce this number to six. Three of these are found within our limits, viz. the widely ranging *M. similis*, *M. cayennensis* of northern South America, which enters our fauna as far as Costa Rica, and *M. granadensis* of western South America, which ranges northwards to Nicaragua.

The last-named bird belongs to the section of the genus which has no white superciliary mark, the other two to the section where this mark is present.

Myiozetetes belongs to the group of genera which have the supranasal feathers and bristles very fully developed, so that the nostrils themselves are almost covered; the nostrils are at the lower anterior end of the nasal fossa, are open but surrounded above and behind by membrane; the bill is strong, compressed, and rather wide, the width at the gape being more than half the length of the tomia; the rictal bristles are long, extending along two thirds of the bill; the tarsi are stout and covered with scutellæ; the wing is rounded, 2nd, 3rd, 4th, and 5th quills nearly equal and longest, 6th > 1st, = 7th; tail moderate and very slightly emarginate, < $\frac{4}{5}$ wing, tarsus = $\frac{1}{5}$ wing.

1. **Myiozetetes cayennensis.**

Muscicapa cayennensis, Linn. Syst. Nat. i. p. 327 [1].

Elainea cayennensis, Cass. Pr. Ac. Phil. 1860, p. 144 [2].

Myiozetetes cayennensis, Lawr. Ann. Lyc. N. Y. vii. p. 295 [3]; Salv. Ibis, 1885, p. 295 [4]; Scl. Cat. Birds Brit. Mus. xiv. p. 160 [5].

Myiozetetes marginatus, Lawr. Ibis, 1863, p. 182 [6]; Ann. Lyc. N. Y. viii. p. 8 [7], ix. p. 112 [8]; v. Frantz. J. f. Orn. 1869, p. 307 [9].

Myiozetetes texensis, Scl. & Salv. P. Z. S. 1879, p. 513 [10].

Supra saturate olivaceus; capite summo nigro, crista aurantiaca subcelata ornato; fronte et superciliis cum gutture albis; alis et cauda nigricantibus, illarum primariis medialiter rufo limbatis, illis quoque subtus ad basin rufescentibus: subtus flavissimus; subalaribus concoloribus: rostro et pedibus nigris. Long. tota 6·0, alæ 3·3, caudæ 2·75, tarsi 0·7, rostri a rictu 0·75. (Descr. exempl. ex Paraiso, Panama. Mus. nostr.)

Hab. Costa Rica (*Carmiol* [8] [9]); Panama, Paraiso Station (*Hughes*), Lion Hill (*M'Leannan* [3] [6]), Turbo (*C. J. Wood* [2]).—South America, Colombia [10], Ecuador [5], Venezuela [5], Guiana [4].

This is the oldest known species of the genus, having been described by Linnæus. It is, moreover, the only one of this section found in Guiana, so that its determination can hardly be a matter of doubt. Its range extends along the northern portion of South America, and on the western side as far south as Ecuador. It enters our fauna and spreads northwards as far as Costa Rica. Panama specimens were described by Mr. Lawrence under the name of *M. marginatus*, but he compared it with *M. similis*, from which it can readily be distinguished.

Salmon, who found its nest at Medellin in Colombia [10], describes the eggs as white, spotted, especially at the larger end, with red; they thus, as might be expected, resemble those of *M. similis*.

2. Myiozetetes similis.

Muscicapa similis, Spix, Av. Bras. ii. p. 18, t. 25 [1].

Myiozetetes similis, Scl. Cat. Birds Brit. Mus. xiv. p. 161 [2].

Tyrannula texensis, Giraud, Birds of Texas, t. 1 [3]; Scl. P. Z. S. 1855, p. 65 [4].

Elænea texensis, Scl. P. Z. S. 1856, p. 296 [5].

Myiozetetes texensis, Moore, P. Z. S. 1859, p. 56 [6]; Scl. P. Z. S. 1859, pp. 366 [7], 1864, p. 176 [8]; Cat. Birds Brit. Mus. xiv. p. 162 [9]; Scl. & Salv. Ibis, 1859, p. 123 [10]; P. Z. S. 1870, p. 837 [11]; Owen, Ibis, 1861, p. 64 [12]; Cab. J. f. Orn. 1861, p. 245 [13]; Lawr. Ann. Lyc. N. Y. viii. p. 183 [14], ix. pp. 112 [15], 201 [10]; Mem. Bost. Soc. N. H. ii. p. 286 [17]; Bull. U. S. Nat. Mus. no. 4, p. 26 [18]; v. Frantz. J. f. Orn. 1869, p. 307 [19]; Sumichrast, Mem. Bost. Soc. N. H. i. p. 557 [20]; Salv. Cat. Strickl. Coll. p. 309 [21]; Nutt. & Ridgw. Pr. U. S. Nat. Mus. vi. pp. 374 [22], 384 [23], 402 [24]; Ridgw. Pr. U. S. Nat. Mus. v. p. 500 [25]; Perez, Pr. U. S. Nat. Mus. ix. p. 154 [26].

Myiozetetes colombianus, Cab. & Hein. Mus. Hein. ii. p. 62 [27]; Lawr. Ann. Lyc. N. Y. vii. p. 328 [28], viii. p. 178 [29]; Scl. & Salv. P. Z. S. 1864, p. 359 [30]; Salv. P. Z. S. 1870, p. 197 [31].

Tyrannula cayennensis, Sw. Phil. Mag. new ser. i. p. 367 [32].

Muscicapa cayennensis, Licht. Preis-Verz. mex. Vög. p. 2 (cf. J. f. Orn. 1863, p. 58) [33].

Tyrannus superciliosus, Bp. P. Z. S. 1837, p. 118 (nec Swains.) [34].

Supra obscure olivaceus; capite summo nigricanti-griseo, crista celata coccinea ornato; fronte griseo-albida, superciliis elongatis albis; loris et genis nigricantibus; alis et cauda fusco-nigris, illis medialiter obscure olivaceo stricte limbatis: subtus flavissimus, subalaribus concoloribus; gutture toto albo: rostro et pedibus nigris. Long. tota 7·0, alæ 3·8, caudæ 3·0, tarsi 0·8, rostri a rictu 0·7. (Descr. maris ex Vera Cruz, Mexico. Mus. nostr.)

Hab. MEXICO [33], Mazatlan (*Grayson* [17], *Xantus* [17], *Forrer*), Tepic (*Grayson* [17]), plains of Colima and Tonila (*Xantus* [17]), Acaguizotla, Dos Arroyos (*Mrs. H. H. Smith*), Acapulco (*A. H. Markham, Mrs. H. H. Smith*), Aldama and Tampico (*W. B. Richardson*), State of Vera Cruz (*Sumichrast* [20]), Jalapa (*de Oca* [7], *F. D. G.*), Chietla (*Ferrari-Perez* [26]), Cordova (*Sallé* [5]), Vera Cruz (*W. B. Richardson & F. D. G.*), Teapa (*Mrs. H. H. Smith*), Juchitan, Barrio, Chihuitan, Sta. Efigenia (*Sumichrast* [18]), Tabi in Yucatan (*F. D. G.*), Buctzotz and Peto (*G. F. Gaumer*), Merida in Yucatan (*Schott* [16]), Cozumel I. (*G. F. Gaumer*); BRITISH HONDURAS, Orange Walk (*G. F. Gaumer*), Belize (*Blancaneaux*); GUATEMALA [34] (*Constancia* [21]), Choctum, Coban, Tactic, Dueñas [10], Escuintla, Patio Bolas, Retalhuleu (*O. S. & F. D. G.*), San Gerónimo (*R. Owen* [12]); HONDURAS, Omoa (*Leyland* [6]), San Pedro (*G. M. Whitely* [11]); NICARAGUA, Greytown (*Holland* [14]), S. Juan del Sur [22], Sucuyá [23], Los Sabalos [24] (*Nutting*); COSTA RICA (*Hoffmann, v. Frantzius* [13]), San José (*Nutting* [25]), San José, Angostura (*Carmiol* [15]), Cartago (*Cooper* [15]); PANAMA, David (*Hicks* [29]), Castillo, Chitra, Bugaba, Calovevora (*Arcé* [11]), Lion Hill (*M'Leannan* [28][30]).—SOUTH AMERICA from Colombia and Amazons valley [1] to South Brazil [12].

The northern birds of this widely ranging species have hitherto been called *Myiozetetes texensis* as distinguished from the Brazilian *M. similis*, the distinction resting upon the darker upper surface and the redder margins to the wings of the southern form. Generally speaking these characters hold, but they are of very slight value, and in themselves variable, so much so that they cannot always be depended upon. Thus a specimen from Coban and one from Minas Geraes are not distinguishable specifically, and we see no reason why this species should be separated any more than *Tyrannus melancholicus*, which has even a wider range.

Regarding dimensions, to which Mr. Sclater calls attention [2], no dependence can be placed, as we have Mexican specimens fully as large as others from Brazil; the smallest of our series being from Costa Rica and the State of Panama.

The name *M. similis* was applied by Spix to the bird of the Amazons valley [1]. Mr. Sclater, who admits the distinction between the bird of South-east Brazil (*M. erythropterus*) and that of the rest of Tropical America (exclusive of Guiana) with considerable reluctance, calls a specimen from Pebas in the Amazons valley *E. texensis*; it follows that whatever the ultimate status of the South-Brazilian bird may be, all the rest should take Spix's title. We therefore apply *E. similis* to the Mexican and Central-American bird without hesitation.

The name *Tyrannula texensis* was given by Giraud to a bird supposed to have been shot in Texas, and the species has been admitted into the North-American fauna on the strength of this statement. We have not as yet been able to trace it beyond Aldama in Tamaulipas, that is the edge of the lowland tropical forest. On the Pacific side of Mexico, Mazatlan is our most northern record. In Central Mexico and the southern side of the Rio Grande valley we have not yet traced it.

M. similis is a very familiar bird throughout our region, being found everywhere in open places from the sea-level to a height of 5000 or 6000 feet in the mountains. It is noisy and conspicuous, like the equally abundant *Tyrannus melancholicus*.

At Dueñas, in Guatemala, it builds in the month of May a nest of small roots and strong grass of light construction and covered over, having a large hole in the side. The eggs, generally three in number, are of a rich creamy white, thinly spotted at the obtuse end with red; they measure, axis 10·25 lines × 8 lines [10].

3. Myiozetetes granadensis.

Myiozetetes granadensis, Lawr. Ibis, 1862, p. 11 [1]; Ann. Lyc. N. Y. vii. p. 473 [2], ix. p. 112 [3]; Scl. & Salv. P. Z. S. 1864, p. 359 [4], 1867, p. 279 [5]; v. Frantz. J. f. Orn. 1869, p. 307 [6]; Salv. Ibis, 1872, p. 318 [7]; Nutting & Ridgw. Pr. U. S. Nat. Mus. vi. pp. 384 [8], 402 [9]; Scl. Cat. Birds Brit. Mus. xiv. p. 163 [10].

Præcedenti similis, sed capite summo griseo nec nigricante, superciliis albis absentibus distinguendus. (Descr. maris ex San Pablo, Panama. Mus. nostr.)

Hab. NICARAGUA, Chontales (*Belt* [7]), Los Sabalos [9] and Sucuyá [8] (*Nutting*), Blewfields River (*Wickham* [5]); COSTA RICA (*Van Patten*), Orosi (*Carmiol* [3] [6]); PANAMA, Chiriqui (*Arcé*), Lion Hill (*M'Leannan* [1] [2] [4]).—SOUTH AMERICA, Colombia, Ecuador, and Peru.

M. granadensis can readily be distinguished from either of the preceding species by its greyer head and the absence of the white superciliary stripe so conspicuous in both the allied forms.

Its range is restricted to the western portions of the South-American continent from Peru northwards; the limit of its range in this direction being Nicaragua, where Mr. Nutting speaks of it as abundant at Sucuyá [8].

PITANGUS.

Pitangus, Swainson, Zool. Journ. iii. p. 165 (1827); Scl. Cat. Birds Brit. Mus. xiv. p. 174.

This genus contains ten species, if we include the abnormal *P. parvus*, Pelz., which is perhaps more naturally placed in *Megarhynchus*. These are distributed over the greater part of the Neotropical Region from Northern Mexico to the Argentine Republic, a section of the genus with white under surface being well represented by four species in the Bahamas and West-Indian Islands. In our region *P. derbianus* is the only one which is nearly universally spread; but in the State of Panama the southern *P. lictor* occurs, and there also *P. albovittatus* is found, a little known species not hitherto noticed elsewhere.

Pitangus belongs to the group of Tyrannidæ which has the supranasal feathers elongated, extending over the maxilla so as to completely cover the nostrils; the latter are open and nearly circular, and without any overhanging membrane; the bill itself is very strong, the culmen slightly decurved and terminating in a prominent hook, the sides of the bill are nearly straight, converging gradually from the gape to the tip, the width at the gape is considerably less than half the length of the tomia, the rictal bristles are well developed; the tarsi are short but strong, and the toes strong, the middle toe long, the lateral ones short and subequal; the 3rd and 4th quills are equal and longest, 5th > 2nd, 1st = 8th; tail moderate, square, < $\frac{4}{5}$ wing, tarsus = $\frac{1}{5}$ wing.

1. Pitangus derbianus.

Saurophagus derbianus, Kaup, P. Z. S. 1851, p. 44, t. 36 [1]; Finsch, Abh. nat. Ver. zu Bremen, 1870, p. 329 [2].

Pitangus derbianus, Scl. P. Z. S. 1856, p. 297 [3], 1859, p. 366 [4], 1864, p. 176 [5]; Cat. Birds Brit. Mus. xiv. p. 175 [6]; Moore, P. Z. S. 1859, p. 56 [7]; Scl. & Salv. Ibis, 1859, p. 120 [8]; P. Z. S. 1870, p. 837 [9]; Owen, Ibis, 1861, p. 63 [10]; Lawr. Ann. Lyc. N. Y. ix. pp. 114 [11], 201 [12]; Bull. U. S. Nat. Mus. no. 4, p. 26 [13]; Mem. Bost. Soc. N. H. ii. p. 286 [14]; Sumichrast, Mem. Bost. Soc. N. H. i. p. 557 [15]; v. Frantz. J. f. Orn. 1869, p. 307 [16]; Coues, Bull. U. S. Geol. Surv. v. p. 407 [17]; Nutting, Pr. U. S. Nat. Mus. v. p. 394 [18]; Salv. P. Z. S. 1883, p. 424 [19]; Boucard, P. Z. S. 1883, p. 448 [20]; Nutting & Ridgw. Pr. U. S. Nat. Mus. vi. pp. 374 [21], 384 [22]; Ridgw. Pr. U. S. Nat. Mus. vii. p. 500 [23]; Perez, Pr. U. S. Nat. Mus. ix. p. 154 [24].

Tyrannus sulphuratus, Sw. Phil. Mag. new ser. i. p. 368 [25].

Lanius flavus, Licht. Preis-Verz. mex. Vög. p. 2 (cf. J. f. Orn. 1863, p. 58 [26]).

Saurophagus guatemalensis, Lafr. Rev. Zool. 1852, p. 462 [27].

Supra brunneus; capite nigro; fronte, superciliis cum linea nuchali conjunctis albis; crista verticali magna flava, lateribus suis nigro intermixtis: subtus flavus, subalaribus concoloribus; gutture albo: alis fuscis, remigibus omnibus (præter primum) usque ad rhachides rufis, pogoniis internis pro majorem partem rufis; cauda fusca, extrorsum stricte rufo limbata, pogoniis internis quoque plerumque rufis: rostro et pedibus nigris. Long. tota 9·0, alæ 4·9, caudæ 3·6, tarsi 1·05, rostri a rictu 1·4. (Descr. exempl. ex Jalapa, Mexico. Mus. Brit.)

♀ mari similis.

Hab. NORTH AMERICA, Lower Rio Grande valley [17].—MEXICO, Rio Camacho in Nuevo Leon (*Armstrong*), Aldama, Xicotencal, Altamira, Tampico, all in Tamaulipas (*Richardson*), Zacatecas (*Wollweber* [1]), Mazatlan (*Grayson* [14], *Bischoff* [14] & *Forrer*), Plains of Colima (*Xantus* [14]), Acapulco (*A. H. Markham* [19], *Mrs. H. H. Smith*), Chietla, Acatlan (*Ferrari-Perez* [24]), State of Vera Cruz (*Sumichrast* [15]). Colipa (*F. D. G.*), Jalapa (*de Oca* [4]), Cordova (*Sallé* [3]), Atoyac, Teapa (*Mrs. H. H. Smith*), Alvarado (*Deppe*), Chihuitan [13], Sta. Efigenia [13], Tapana [13], Tonola (*Sumichrast*), Tabi in Yucatan (*F. D. G.*), Merida in Yucatan (*Schott* [12]), Buctzotz in Yucatan (*G. F. Gaumer*), Meco I., Mujeres I., Cozumel I. (*G. F. Gaumer*); BRITISH HONDURAS, Orange Walk (*G. F. Gaumer*), Belize (*Leyland* [7], *O. S.* [8], *Blancaneaux*); GUATEMALA, San Gerónimo [10], Dueñas [8], Escuintla, Retalhuleu (*O. S. & F. D. G.*); HONDURAS, Omoa (*Leyland* [7]), San Pedro (*G. M. Whitely* [9]); NICARAGUA, San Juan del Sur [21] and Sucuyá [22] (*Nutting*); COSTA RICA, San José [23] and La Palma [18] (*Nutting*), Sta. Anathole (*v. Frantzius* [16]), Santa Ana (*M. Lopez* [11]).—SOUTH AMERICA, Colombia, Venezuela, and Trinidad [6].

Specimens of this species from all parts of our region are very uniform in their coloration, but in the northern portion of South America the rufous colour of the outer surface of the wings is more developed, and thus a species or race has been separated under the name of *P. rufipennis*. It is somewhat remarkable that no specimens of this form have yet been found in Panama, Costa Rica being the southern recorded limit of *P. derbianus*. From this it would appear that the ranges of the latter species and of *P. rufipennis* are separated by a considerable interval. The northern limit of the range of this Tyrant extends to the lower Rio Grande valley, and we have many specimens from the frontier States of Tamaulipas and Nuevo Leon; thence it spreads all through the hot and temperate regions on both sides of the Cordillera, its limit in altitude reaching about 5000 feet. Grayson says:—"This is a common and abundant species, inhabiting the western and north-western parts of Mexico. I found it equally as common in Tehuantepec as in the region of Mazatlan, where its loud shrill notes of *hip-see-dee hip-see-dee* may be heard at all seasons of the year, but more particularly during the breeding-season, when it is excessively garrulous. It is more frequently met with in the neighbourhood of freshwater streams and lagoons, and I have often seen them dart into the water after water-insects and minnows that were swimming near the surface not unlike a Kingfisher, but they usually pursue and capture on the wing the larger kinds of Coleoptera and Neuroptera, swallowing their prey entire after first beating it against a branch. They are usually in pairs, but I have also seen as many as twenty about a stagnant pool watching its turbid water for insects and small fish, for which they seem to have a great partiality."

The nest of this species is very large, and its construction differs from that of all the Tyrannidæ of which we have any knowledge except *Myiozetetes texensis*. It is dome-shaped or covered, with the entrance on the side, whilst the other species build a nest saucer-shaped. The nest of the Bull-headed Flycatcher is usually placed in the forks of branches of very thorny trees, twenty-five or thirty feet from the ground; it is composed of very coarse material of either straw or lichen, sometimes both; the lining, however, is of firmer and more elastic fibres. Other birds sometimes make their nests in the same or nearest tree, such as *Myiozetetes texensis, Cacicus melanicterus*, and *Icterus pustulatus*.

In Guatemala *P. derbianus* builds its nest in April and May: one found at Dueñas was a large loose structure with a great deal of superfluous matter about it, its entrance being at one side: it was composed entirely of small twigs, and placed at the end of a branch about twenty feet from the ground: another, taken at San Gerónimo, had two openings, but one seems to be the rule. A favourite haunt is the banana-groves, where the nest may be found wedged in among the clusters of fruit. The eggs are slightly pear-shaped, of a pale creamy-white colour spotted and blotched with brick-red; they vary considerably in size and colour, especially as to the magnitude and density of the spots.

We never noticed *P. derbianus* feeding on fish and water-insects, as described by Grayson; but Mr. Hudson ascribes similar habits to *P. sulphuratus* in the Argentine Republic.

2. Pitangus lictor.

Lanius lictor, Licht. Verz. Doubl. p. 49[1].

Saurophagus lictor, Gray & Mitch. Gen. B. i. p. 246, t. 62[2]; Burm. Syst. Ueb. ii. p. 462[3].

Pitangus lictor, Lawr. Ann. Lyc. N. Y. vii. p. 327[4]; Scl. & Salv. P. Z. S. 1864, p. 359[5]; Salv. Ibis, 1885, p. 296[6]; Scl. Cat. Birds Brit. Mus. xiv. p. 178[7].

Muscicapa cayennensis, Wied, Beitr. iii. p. 846[8] (nec Linn.).

Supra olivaceo-fuscus; capite nigro, fronte, superciliis cum linca nuchali albis, crista magna flava, plumis nigro terminatis; uropygio ferrugineo tincto: subtus flavus, subalaribus concoloribus; alis fuscis, extrorsum stricte rufo marginatis, introrsum ad basin fulvis: rostro et pedibus nigris. Long. tota 6·3, alæ 3·4, caudæ 2·7, tarsi 0·8, rostri a rictu 1·0. (Descr. maris ex Panama. Mus. nostr.)

Hab. PANAMA, Lion Hill (*M'Leannan*[4][5]).—SOUTH AMERICA, Colombia[7], Guiana[6], Amazons valley[7], and Brazil[3].

A species of wide range in Tropical South America, which just enters our fauna, reaching the line of the Panama Railway. Here M'Leannan found it and sent specimens both to Mr. Lawrence and ourselves.

Though like *P. derbianus* in general colour it may at once be distinguished by its much smaller size and slender bill.

Though specimens occur in the trade collections sent from Bogota we have no record of the existence of this species in Ecuador, Peru, or Bolivia. It thus appears that its range hangs to the northern and eastern portions of South America rather than to the western.

3. **Pitangus albovittatus.**

Pitangus albovittatus, Lawr. Ibis, 1862, p. 11 [1]; Ann. Lyc. N. Y. vii. p. 471 [2]; Scl. Cat. Birds Brit. Mus. xiv. p. 178 [3].

Supra olivaceus; alis et cauda nigricanti-fuscis vix olivaceo limbatis; pileo et litura a rostro utrinque per oculos ducta nigricanti-brunneis, superciliis latis ad nucham conjunctis albis, stria verticali læte flava aurantio haud tincta: subtus flavus, gula alba; subalaribus flavis, remigum pogonio interno flavido-albo, haud castaneo: rostro brevi ad basin lato, robusto, nigro; pedibus nigris. Long. tota 6·3, alæ 3·15, caudæ 2·6, rostri a rictu 0·9, tarsi 0·65. (Descr. maris exempl. typ. ex Panama. Mus. G. N. Lawrence.)

Hab. PANAMA, Line of Railway (*M'Leannan & Galbraith* [1] [2]).

This bird differs in many respects from *P. lictor*, which is also found on the Isthmus of Panama. It has a shorter stouter bill, the crest is wholly yellow without any admixture of orange, the back is more olivaceous, and neither the rump nor the margins of the wings above or below have any chestnut colour.

The bird also somewhat resembles in general colour *Myiozetetes cayennensis*, but that species, besides its smaller bill with its curved culmen, has an orange crest, and the edges of the wing-feathers inside and out are, like those of *Pitangus lictor*, chestnut.

We have recently had an opportunity of examining Mr. Lawrence's type, which is the only specimen we have seen. It was contained in one of M'Leannan and Galbraith's collections made on the line of the Panama Railway.

So like is *P. albovittatus* in general colour to *M. cayennensis* and *P. lictor* that its apparent rarity may be due to its having been mistaken by collectors for one or other of those birds.

SIRYSTES.

Sirystes, Cabanis & Heine, Mus. Hein. ii. p. 75 (1859) (type *S. sibilator*); Scl. Cat. Birds Brit. Mus. xiv. p. 181.

Sirystes contains three rather closely allied though sufficiently defined species, whereof *S. albogriseus* is alone found in the State of Panama, *S. albocinereus* in the Amazons valley, and *S. sibilator* in Eastern Brazil. In coloration they somewhat resemble the Antillean species of *Pitangus*, but are destitute of the occipital crest.

In many respects *Sirystes* resembles *Pitangus*, but the bill is not nearly so strong, and is wider in proportion to its length, the width at the gape being half the length of the tomia, the sides are slightly concave, the supranasal feathers cover the nostril, and the rictal bristles are strong; the tarsi and feet are more feeble than in *Pitangus*; the 2nd, 3rd, and 4th quills are longest, 1st = 7th; the tail is rather long = $\frac{5}{6}$ wing, tarsus < $\frac{1}{5}$ wing.

1. Sirystes albogriseus. (Tab. XXXVII. fig. 1.)

Lipangus albogriseus, Lawr. Ann. Lyc. N. Y. viii. p. 9 [1].
Sirystes albogriseus, Scl. & Salv. P. Z. S. 1880, p. 156 [2]; Scl. Cat. Birds Brit. Mus. xiv. p. 182 [3].

Supra cinereus; uropygio albo; capite summo nigro; loris fuliginosis; alis nigris, secundariis et tectricibus late albo marginatis; cauda nigra, stricte albo terminata: subtus albus; gutture et hypochondriis cinereo tinctis: rostro corneo, mandibula ad basin albicante; pedibus nigricantibus. Long. tota 7·3, alæ 4·1, caudæ 3·5, tarsi 0·8, rostri a rictu 0·9. (Descr. exempl. ex Panama. Mus. nostr.)

Hab. PANAMA, Veraguas (*Arcé* [2]), Lion Hill (*M'Leannan* [1]).

Very little is known of this species, the first specimen of which was sent by M'Leannan to Mr. Lawrence, who described it under the name of *Lipangus albogriseus* [1]. We have since received two specimens from the State of Panama, but we are not informed of the exact spot where they were obtained. The species most nearly allied to the one under consideration is *S. albocinereus* of the valley of the Upper Amazons. This differs in having the wing-coverts much more narrowly edged with greyish white.

MYIODYNASTES.

Myiodynastes, Bonaparte, Compt. Rend. xxxviii. p. 657; Notes Orn. p. 87 (1856); Scl. Cat. Birds Brit. Mus. xiv. p. 182 (type *Muscicapa audax*, Gm.).
Hypermitres, Cabanis, J. f. Orn. 1861, p. 247 (type *Scaphorhynchus chrysocephalus*, Tsch.).

This genus is divisible into two well-marked sections—one characterized by the breast and flanks being conspicuously marked by black guttate spots, in the other the under surface is uniformly coloured.

In our region we find two of the former section, viz. *M. luteiventris* and *M. audax*, nearly universally distributed, and one of the second, *M. hemichrysus*, restricted to Costa Rica and the adjacent parts of the State of Panama.

Of the first section we find it impossible to recognize more than three species, though this view differs from that of several authorities on the subject. Thus Mr. Ridgway in his 'Manual of North-American Birds' (p. 332), omitting all mention of *M. solitarius*, recognizes two species, *M. luteiventris* and *M. audax*; but divides the latter into three races, *M. audax* proper, *M. a. nobilis*, and *M. a. insolens*. We, so far as the number of species are concerned, confirm Mr. Ridgway's views, but we fail to discriminate his subspecies of *M. audax*. Mr. Sclater in his recent revision of the Tyrannidæ divides this section of the genus into four species, namely *M. luteiventris*, *M. nobilis*, *M. audax*, and *M. solitarius*. We now merge *M. nobilis* and *M. audax* under the latter name, and somewhat alter the range defined of all the species, except *M. solitarius*.

The question of distribution of these *Myiodynastes* is very singular, for with few exceptions wherever *M. luteiventris* is found *M. audax* occurs with it, and moreover *M. solitarius* overlaps the range of *M. audax* in many places. In spite of this concurrent range each form keeps its characters with great precision.

The bill of *Myiodynastes*, like that of the genera just dealt with, is strong, but not so elongated as that of *Pitangus*, being wider at the gape, the proportion of which to the length of the tomia is rather more than 1 to 2, the sides are slightly convex, the supranasal feathers and nostrils are as in *Pitangus*, the tarsi and toes are moderately strong; the 2nd and 3rd quills are the longest, 1st=6th; tail moderate and nearly square, $<\frac{3}{4}$ wing, tarsus$=\frac{1}{6}$ wing.

a. *Corpus subtus, pectore et lateribus guttatis.*

1. Myiodynastes luteiventris.

Myiodynastes luteiventris, Bp. Compt. Rend. xxxviii. p. 657 [1]; Not. Orn. p. 87 [2] (descr. nulla) ; Scl. P. Z. S. 1859, pp. 42 [3], 366 [4], 383 [5], 1864, p. 176 [6]; Cat. Birds Brit. Mus. xiv. p. 183 [7]; Moore, P. Z. S. 1859, p. 56 [8]; Scl. & Salv. Ibis, 1859, p. 120 [9]; P. Z. S. 1870, p. 837 [10]; Cab. & Heine, Mus. Hein. ii. p. 75 [11]; Cab. J. f. Orn. 1861, p. 250 [12]; Sumichrast, Mem. Bost. Soc. N. H. i. p. 557 [13]; Lawr. Ann. Lyc. N. Y. ix. p. 114 [14]; Bull. U. S. Nat. Mus. no. 4, p. 26 [15]; Mem. Bost. Soc. N. H. ii. p. 287 [16]; v. Frantz. J. f. Orn. 1869, p. 308 [17]; Salv. Ibis, 1872, p. 318 [18]; Tacz. P. Z. S. 1874, p. 537 [19], 1882, p. 21 [20]; Henshaw, Wheeler's Rep. v., Zool. p. 346, t. 14 (1875) [21]; Boucard, P. Z. S. 1883, p. 448 [22]; Ridgw. Man. N. Am. B. p. 332 [23]; Tacz. Orn. Pér. ii. p. 290 [24].

Tyrannus audax ?, Scl. P. Z. S. 1856, p. 297 [25].

Supra pallide brunneus, vix olivaceo lavatus, plumis singulis medialiter nigricantibus; uropygio et cauda castaneis, illo nigro guttato hujus rectricibus medialiter nigricantibus ; alis quoque nigricantibus, secundariis et tectricibus omnibus albido distincte extrorsum limbatis; capite summo crista celata flava ornato, fronte cana, superciliis et stria malari utrinque albidis: subtus sulphureus, gutture albo, mento et stria utrinque gulæ nigricantibus, pectore et hypochondriis conspicue nigro striatis: rostro nigricante, mandibulæ basi pallida; pedibus nigris. Long. tota 7·75, alæ 4·6, caudæ 3·4, tarsi 0·75, rostri a rictu 1·15. (Descr. maris ex Jalapa, Mexico. Mus. nostr.)

♀ mari similis.

Hab. NORTH AMERICA, Arizona [21].—MEXICO, Rio Comacho in Nuevo Leon (*F. B. Armstrong*), Sierra Madre above Ciudad Victoria in Tamaulipas (*W. B. Richardson*), Yaleta in Sonora (*W. Lloyd*), Mazatlan (*Grayson* [16], *Xantus* [16]), Presidio near Mazatlan (*A. Forrer*), mountains of Colima (*Xantus* [16]), Acapulco (*Mrs. H. H. Smith*), State of Vera Cruz (*Sumichrast* [13]), Jalapa [11] (*de Oca* [4], *M. Trujillo*), Cordova (*Sallé* [4,25]), Juquila (*Boucard* [5]), Orizaba (*Botteri* [4]), Atoyac (*Mrs. H. H. Smith*), Tapana (*Sumichrast* [15]), Buctzotz in Yucatan (*G. F. Gaumer*); BRITISH HONDURAS, Belize (*Blancaneaux*); GUATEMALA (*Skinner* [3,7]), Peten (*Leyland* [8]), Savana of Santo Toribio (*O. S.*), Cahabon, Choctum (*O. S. & F. D. G.*), Escuintla (*L. Fraser*); HONDURAS, San Pedro (*G. M. Whitely* [10]); SALVADOR, La Union (*J. M. Dow*); NICARAGUA (*Delattre* [1,2]), Chontales (*Janson* [18]); COSTA RICA (*Hoffmann* [12]), Irazu (*H. Rogers*), Barranca [14], Turrialba [14], and Santa Rosa [7] (*Carmiol*), Birris (*Zeledon* [14]), San Mateo [17], Cervantes [17] (*v. Frantzius*); PANAMA (*M'Leannan*). — EASTERN ECUADOR; PERU [24].

Bonaparte's name for this species was based upon specimens brought from Nicaragua by Delattre. The bird is common in Costa Rica, but in the State of Panama *M. audax* is the prevalent species, while in South America we only know of its occurrence from a single specimen * obtained by Buckley in Eastern Ecuador; Dr. Taczanowski, however, includes it in the birds of Peru [19].

The most northern point reached by this species is probably the Chiricahua Mountains in Southern Arizona. Here Mr. W. H. Henshaw met with old and young birds in August 1874. They were discovered at the mouth of one of the deep ravines which intersect the mountains in every direction [21]. In Nuevo Leon Mr. Armstrong found it not far to the south of the Rio Grande, and it also occurs in the eastern Sierra Madre above Ciudad Victoria at an elevation of 5000 feet above the sea. Further south it appears to be equally common both on the Atlantic and Pacific slopes of the mountains. Grayson, who met with it at Mazatlan, considered it to be migratory, as he only found it in the months of May and June nesting in the tall trees of the woods. He believed that it passed southwards during the winter months.

In Guatemala it frequents the low-lying land on both sides of the cordillera, occurring in the brushwood rather than the denser forests of mixed trees. In such a situation Salvin obtained a specimen near Santo Toribio, a hamlet on the road from Cahabon to Peten.

2. Myiodynastes audax.

Muscicapa audax, Gm. Syst. Nat. i. p. 934[1].

Myiodynastes audax, Scl. P. Z. S. 1859, p. 43[2]; Cat. Birds Brit. Mus. xiv. p. 185[3]; Scl. & Salv. P. Z. S. 1879, p. 514[4]; Salv. Ibis, 1885, p. 296[5].

Myiodynastes nobilis, Scl. P. Z. S. 1859, p. 42[6]; Cat. Birds Brit. Mus. xiv. p. 183[7]; Lawr. Ann. Lyc. N. Y. vii. p. 295[8], viii. p. 178[9], ix. p. 114[10]; Scl. & Salv. P. Z. S. 1864, p. 360[11]; v. Frantzius, J. f. Orn. 1869, p. 307[12]; Salv. P. Z. S. 1867, p. 148[13], 1870, p. 198[14]; Nutting, Pr. U. S. Nat. Mus. vi. p. 394[15].

Myiodynastes audax, nobilis et *insolens*, Ridgw. Man. N. Am. B. p. 332[16].

Præcedenti similis, sed fronte, superciliis et stria utrinque malari ochraceo-albidis, mento albo; abdomine toto albo, nonnunquam vix flavo tincto: rostro plerumque majore mandibula pro majorem partem pallida. (Descr. maris ex Jalapa, Mexico. Mus. nostr.)

♀ mari similis.

Hab. MEXICO, Sierra Madre above Ciudad Victoria in Tamaulipas (*W. B. Richardson*), Jalapa (*M. Trujillo*), Mirador (*Sartorius* [16]), Buctzotz in Yucatan (*G. F. Gaumer*); COSTA RICA, Barranca (*Carmiol* [10]), San Mateo (*J. Cooper* [10]), Barranca, Cervantes, Turrialba (*v. Frantzius* [10]), Bebedero (*Arcé*); PANAMA, David (*Hicks* [9]), Chitra [14], Calobre [14], Bugaba [14], Santa Fé [13] (*Arcé*), Lion Hill (*M'Leannan* [8] [11]), Paraiso Station (*Hughes*), Chepo (*Arcé*).—SOUTH AMERICA, Colombia [4], Ecuador [3], Venezuela [3], Guiana [5].

* This appears in Mr. Sclater's catalogue under the name of *M. nobilis*, but it has all the characteristics of *M. luteiventris*, viz. yellow under surface, black chin, grey forehead, and white superciliary and malar stripes.

The range of this species coincides, to a great extent, with that of *M. luteiventris*. For though it has not yet been noticed in Southern Arizona, it occurs with the allied species in the Sierra Madre of Tamaulipas, and thence southwards along the eastern slope of the mountains of Vera Cruz into Yucatan, Costa Rica, Panama, and a large portion of Northern South America. It has not yet been traced in Western Mexico or Guatemala, but is doubtless found in the latter country.

M. nobilis is said to differ from *M. audax* in being "brighter, and the breast-spots narrower," but with the series before us we cannot fix any such difference to any particular district. Nor is it otherwise with *M. a. insolens*, the bill of which is said to be shorter, and the upper plumage devoid of rusty tinge.

Mr. Sclater speaks of his *M. nobilis* as an intermediate form passing into *M. luteiventris* and *M. audax* at the northern and southern extremities of its range. We only find this to be the case as regards *M. audax*, for we can always distinguish *M. luteiventris* by the characters upon which Mr. Ridgway lays stress.

The fact of two closely allied species being found together is no doubt difficult of explanation, and we have no solution to offer. So far as our specimens go it appears that the sexes are alike in both species.

Salmon, who found the nest and eggs of *M. audax* in the Cauca valley of Colombia [4], describes the former as made of fern-stalks and twigs, and placed in the fork of a tree or high bush; the eggs are white spotted with red.

b. *Corpus subtus immaculatum.*

3. **Myiodynastes hemichrysus.** (Tab. XXXVIII. fig. 1.)

Hypermitres chrysocephalus, Cab. J. f. Orn. 1861, p. 246 [1].
Hypermitres hemichrysus, Cab. J. f. Orn. 1861, p. 247 [2]; Salv. P. Z. S. 1870, p. 193 [3].
Myiodynastes hemichrysus, Lawr. Ann. Lyc. N. Y. ix. p. 114 [4]; Scl. Cat. Birds Brit. Mus. xiv. p. 188 [5].
Myiodynastes superciliaris, Lawr. Ann. Lyc. N. Y. viii. p. 470 [6].

Supra olivaceus, uropygio fuscescentiore; capite summo nigricanti-olivaceo, crista magna celata flava ornato; superciliis elongatis et stria utrinque malari latescenti-albis; fascia lata a naribus per oculos nigra; alis et cauda fuscis; secundariis intimis albido extrorsum limbatis; tectricibus et primariis internis rufo limbatis; rectricibus utrinque rufo marginatis: subtus flavus; gula albicantiore; hypochondriis olivaceis: rostro et pedibus nigris. Long. tota 8·0, alæ 4·0, caudæ 3·35, tarsi 0·75, rostri a rictu 1·15. (Descr. maris ex Calovevora, Panama. Mus. nostr.)
Av. juv. cristam celatam caret.

Hab. Costa Rica (*v. Frantzius* [1] [4]), Barranca (*Carmiol* [6]); Panama, Chitra, Calovevora, Calobre (*Arcé* [3]).

This species is a near ally of the Andean *M. chrysocephalus*, from which it may be distinguished by the clearer yellow of its throat and under surface. Its range is very restricted, as it is not found beyond the mountains of Costa Rica and the adjoining part of the State of Panama. No member of this section of the genus is found on the line of the Panama Railway, but at Concordia in the Cauca valley of Colombia *M. chryso-cephalus* appears, and continues its range to Peru.

M. hemichrysus was separated by Dr. Cabanis with some hesitation in 1861, and a few years after Mr. Lawrence described the same bird as *M. superciliaris*, both names being founded on Costa Rica specimens.

MEGARHYNCHUS.

Megarhynchus, Thunberg, Disq. de genere Megarhyncho (1824), cf. Heine, J. f. Orn. 1859, p. 337 (type *Lanius pitangua*, Linn.) ; Scl. Cat. Birds Brit. Mus. xiv. p. 189.

Scaphorhynchus, Wied, Beitr. iii. p. 982.

Though several geographical races have from time to time been proposed for *Megarhynchus pitangua*, it is now found that no such divisions are capable of definition, so that the genus now contains a single species of very wide distribution, extending from Southern Mexico to Southern Brazil. When the classification of the Tyrannidæ is recast it will be well to consider the propriety of adding *Pitangus parvus* and the *Hypermitres* section of *Myiodynastes* to *Megarhynchus*.

The general colour of *M. pitangua* resembles that of many other species of Tyrannidæ, such as *Pitangus derbianus*, *Myiozetetes similis*, &c., but the great development of the bill at once distinguishes the present genus. The bill is very large, the culmen curved, the terminal hook large, the sides of the maxilla are convex, and the tomia curved; the width at the base is about half the length of the tomia; the nostrils are like those of *Pitangus*, covered by the projecting supranasal feathers; the tarsi are short, and the feet moderately strong; the 3rd quill is the longest, 2nd=4th, 6th>1st; tail moderate, slightly emarginate, $<\frac{3}{4}$ wing, tarsus $<\frac{1}{6}$ wing.

1. Megarhynchus pitangua.

Lanius pitangua, Linn. Syst. Nat. i. p. 136[1]; Wagl. Isis, 1831, p. 529[2].

Muscicapa pitangua, Licht. Preis-Verz. mex. Vög. p. 2 (cf. J. f. Orn. 1863, p. 58[3]).

Megarhynchus pitangua, Nutting, Pr. U. S. Nat. Mus. v. p. 394[4]; Nutting & Ridgw. Pr. U. S. Nat. Mus. vi. pp. 374[5], 393[6]; Salv. Cat. Strickl. Coll. p. 311[7]; Scl. Cat. Birds Brit. Mus. xiv. p. 189[8].

Scaphorhynchus mexicanus, Lafr. Rev. Zool. 1851, p. 473[8]; Scl. P. Z. S. 1857, p. 204[10], 1859, p. 366[11]; Scl. & Salv. Ibis, 1859, p. 120[12]; Taylor, Ibis, 1860, p. 113[13]; Lawr. Ann. Lyc. N. Y. vii. p. 295[14]; Sumichrast, Mem. Bost. Soc. N. H. i. p. 556[15].

Megarhynchus mexicanus, Cab. J. f. Orn. 1861, p. 246[18]; Scl. & Salv. P. Z. S. 1864, p. 360[17], 1870, p. 837[18]; Lawr. Ann. Lyc. N. Y. viii. p. 183[19], ix. pp. 114[20], 201[21]; Bull. U. S. Nat. Mus. no. 4, p. 26[22]; v. Frantz. J. f. Orn. 1869, p. 308[23]; Salv. Ibis, 1872, p. 318[24].

Supra olivaceo-brunneus ; capite nigro ; fronte et superciliis elongatis, albis ; crista magna celata plerumque castanea, nonnunquam flavo intermixta ; alis et cauda nigricantibus, extrorsum stricte rufo limbatis : subtus flavissimus ; subalaribus concoloribus ; gula alba : rostro et pedibus nigris. Long. tota 9·0, alæ 4·9, caudæ 3·6, tarsi 0·75, rostri a rictu 1·45. (Descr. maris ex Volcan de Agua, Guatemala. Mus. nostr.)

♀ mari similis, sed crista celata flava distinguenda.

Hab. MEXICO, Presidio (*Forrer*), Tampico (*W. B. Richardson*), State of Vera Cruz (*Sumichrast* [15]), Misantla, Jalapa (*F. D. G.*), Jalapa (*Sallé, de Oca* [11]), Cofre de Perote (*M. Trujillo*), Orizaba (*Botteri*), Atoyac (*Mrs. H. H. Smith*), Vera Cruz (*Richardson*), Tehuantepec (*Deppe* [3]), Teapa (*Mrs. H. H. Smith*), Guichicovi, Chihuitan, Sta. Efigenia (*Sumichrast* [22]), Merida in Yucatan (*Schott* [21]), Buctzotz and Peto (*G. F. Gaumer*); GUATEMALA (*Skinner* [12], *Constancia* [7]), Yaxcamnal, Choctum, San Gerónimo, Barranco Hondo, Volcan de Agua above San Diego, Savana Grande, Volcan de Fuego (*O. S. & F. D. G.*); HONDURAS, Taulevi (*Taylor* [13]), San Pedro (*G. M. Whitely* [18]); NICARAGUA, San Juan del Sur [5], Omotepe I. [6] (*Nutting*), Chontales (*Belt*), Greytown (*Holland* [19]); COSTA RICA, Barranca, San José, Grecia, Turrialba (*Carmiol* [20]), Irazu (*H. Rogers, v. Frantzius*), La Palma (*Nutting* [4]); PANAMA, Calovevora, Chiriqui (*Arcé*), Paraiso (*Hughes*), Panama (*M'Leannan* [14] [17]).—SOUTH AMERICA, Colombia to Guiana, Ecuador, Amazons valley, and Southern Brazil.

Only one species of this genus is now admitted, the common *M. pitangua*, which ranges throughout Tropical America from Southern Mexico to South Brazil. The only specimen that at all departs from the normal type is a male from Presidio, near Mazatlan; this has the top of the head grey rather than black. It is the only record we have of the existence of the species in Western Mexico, but without a larger series for comparison we do not think it advisable to do more than note the fact of its difference. The northern range of *M. pitangua* does not extend quite so far as that of *Pitangus derbianus*, Tampico being its limit on the eastern side of the cordillera. Sumichrast speaks of it as frequenting both the hot and temperate country [15]. Our specimens from this district were obtained from the slopes of the Cofre de Perote down to the port of Vera Cruz. In Guatemala too its vertical range is very considerable, as it is to be found as high as 5000 feet in the Volcan de Fuego down to the level of the sea. It is one of the commonest birds throughout our region.

MUSCIVORA.

Muscivora, Cuvier, Leç. An. Comp. tab. 2 (1800) (type *Todus regius*, Gm. apud G. R. Gray, List Gen. Birds, ed. 2, p. 42 (1842)); Scl. Cat. Birds Brit. Mus. xiv. p. 191.

In this remarkable genus the development of the crest, characteristic of so many species of Tyrannidæ, is carried to a much greater extent than in any other form, and constitutes one of its most marked features.

Four species are now recognized as belonging to *Muscivora*, all of them strictly birds of hot tropical forests of the Neotropical Region. The single species of our country is found in such situations from Southern Mexico to the State of Panama, and in the most northern parts of Colombia. *M. occidentalis* is the bird of Western Ecuador, *M. regia* that of Guiana and the Amazons valley, and *M. swainsoni* that of the forests of Eastern Brazil.

The bill in *M. mexicana* is long but rather slightly formed, the culmen very gradually depressed, but the terminal hook large, the sides are convex, converging gradually towards the tip; the nostrils are open, and nearly round, the supranasal feathers covering the membranous base of the nasal fossa, but not extending, except as bristles, over the nostrils themselves; the rictal bristles are very strong and long; the tarsi and toes are feeble; the 3rd and 4th quills are longest, 5th > 2nd, 2nd = 6th, 1st = longest secondaries; tail moderate and nearly square, $< \frac{5}{6}$ wing, tarsus $> \frac{1}{6}$ wing.

Muscivora is allied to *Myiobius* in many respects, especially as regards the great development of the rictal bristles, and this group of genera seem to us out of place between *Megarhynchus* and the *Empidonax* group. When the Tyrannidæ are again revised their relationship to *Platyrhynchus* and *Rhynchocyclus* is worth consideration.

1. Muscivora mexicana. (Tab. XXXIX. figg. 1 ♂, 2 ♀.)

Muscivora mexicana, Scl. P. Z. S. 1856, p. 295 [1], 1858, p. 301 [2]; Cat. Birds Brit. Mus. xiv. p. 193 [3];
Moore, P. Z. S. 1859, p. 56 [4]; Scl. & Salv. Ibis, 1859, p. 124 [5]; P. Z. S. 1864, p. 360 [6];
Lawr. Ann. Lyc. N. Y. vii. pp. 295 [7], 329 [8], ix. pp. 114 [9], 201 [10]; Bull. U. S. Nat. Mus.
no. 4, p. 26 [11]; Salv. P. Z. S. 1867, p. 148 [12], 1870, p. 198 [13]; Cat. Strickl. Coll. p. 312 [14];
v. Frantz. J. f. Orn. 1869, p. 308 [15]; Boucard, P. Z. S. 1878, p. 63 [16]; 1883, p. 448 [17]; Salv.
& Godm. Ibis, 1879, p. 202 [18]; Nutting, Pr. U. S. Nat. Mus. v. p. 395 [19]; Nutting & Ridgw.
Pr. U. S. Nat. Mus. vi. p. 402 [20].

Supra brunneus; crista permagna coccinea chalybeo-purpureo terminata; uropygio pallide cinnamomeo; alis nigricantibus dorsi colore limbatis; secundariis et tectricibus alarum pallide fulvo terminatis; cauda cinnamomea, dimidio apicali brunnescentiore: subtus fulvus; pectore et hypochondriis fusco variegatis: rostro obscure brunneo, mandibula pallidiore; pedibus corylinis. Long. tota 7·0, alæ 3·5, caudæ 2·8, tarsi 0·7, rostri a rictu 1·2. (Descr. maris ex Choctum, Guatemala. Mus. nostr.)

♀ mari similis, sed crista aurantiaca nec coccinea distinguenda.

Hab. MEXICO, Cordova, Acatepec (*Sallé* [1]), Tapana, Sta. Efigenia (*Sumichrast* [11]), Merida in Yucatan (*Schott* [10]), Panabá (*Gaumer* [17]); BRITISH HONDURAS (*Blancaneaux*); GUATEMALA (*Skinner* [5]), Rancho Chahak, Rancho Tuilhá on track to Peten, Choctum, Chisec, El Paraiso (*O. S. & F. D. G.*), Coban (*L. L. Dillwyn* [14]); HONDURAS, Chilomo (*Leyland* [4]); NICARAGUA, Los Sabalos (*Nutting* [20]); COSTA RICA, Mirabayes, Bebedero (*Arcé*), Atenas (*v. Frantzius* [9]), San Ramon (*Boucard*), La Palma (*Nutting* [19]); PANAMA, Volcan de Chiriqui [13], Mina de Chorcha [13], Calovevora [13], Chitra, Calobre, Santa Fé [12] (*Arcé*), Paraiso Station (*Hughes*), Lion Hill (*M'Leannan* [6 7 8]).—NORTHERN COLOMBIA [17].

This beautiful species was first described by Mr. Sclater from specimens obtained near Cordova, in Southern Mexico, by M. Sallé [1]; but the first example sent to Europe was probably the one in Strickland's collection, obtained near Coban, in Guatemala, in 1849 [14]. Its range in Mexico is probably confined to the forests of the southern portion of that country, extending from Southern Vera Cruz to Yucatan and the Isthmus of Tehuantepec; but it appears to be nowhere abundant. In Guatemala it is much more numerous in the low-lying heavily forested country north of Coban, and thence northward in the direction of Peten. Here we obtained several specimens in the early months of 1862. It was usually found in the neighbourhood of streams, its note being familiar to the Indian hunters, to whom it is known by the name of "Pilok," and by the Spanish name of "Resplendor.." It is also found in the forests of the Pacific side of the cordillera, where our hunters obtained examples at Retalhuleu and at Paraiso, half-way to the port of Champerico.

Mr. Nutting found it both in Nicaragua and in Costa Rica, and gives the following note on its occurrence at La Palma in the latter country:—

"This exquisitely ornamental Flycatcher is abundant in the vicinity of La Palma, especially along the watercourses. Indeed, I never saw it away from the water. It builds its nest on a branch overhanging a stream, seems to be quite content to remain in the vicinity of its home, and is quiet and modest in its manner.

"Never having seen this bird before, my surprise and admiration were unbounded when I held one in my hand for the first time and saw its wonderfully beautiful fan-shaped crest. The bird was only wounded, and the crest was fully spread, while the head was slowly moved from side to side, which gave it the appearance of a bright flower nodding in the wind. While admiring this new wonder I heard a twitter of distress immediately above me, and, looking up, was delighted to see the female perched on a twig not more than ten feet above me, with her crest erected and spread, and making the same waving motion of the head. Is it not possible that this bird is provided with its remarkable crest for the purpose of attracting its insect-prey, and that the slow and regular waving motion is calculated to still further deceive by a simulation of a flower nodding in the breeze?"

Galbraith describes [8] the nest of this species as placed in very secluded spots, and surrounded with a mass of loose straggling material, so that he had no suspicion of its being a bird's nest until he observed the bird enter it; inside of the loose grass &c. is a curious hanging structure about three feet in length, large in the centre, and decreasing in size towards each end; the entrance is on the side where the diameter is largest and where the nest proper is placed, this being very perfect in form; the number of eggs was found to be invariably two. These appear small for the size of the bird; the ground-colour is dull pale reddish white, marked for half the length with dull reddish brown, lighter at the ends, which gives the appearance of a confused broad belt just beyond the middle; the smaller end is irregularly spotted and streaked with the same dark colour.

CNIPODECTES.

Cnipodectes, Scl. & Salv. P. Z. S. 1873, p. 281 (type *Cyclorhynchus subbrunneus*, Scl.); Scl. Cat. Birds Brit. Mus. xiv. p. 197.

A genus of uncertain position having the appearance of a *Rhynchocyclus* of the larger

R. brevirostris section, but with softer plumage, longer secondaries in comparison with the primaries, and the male with the web of the outermost primary normal and not serrated.

Mr. Sclater recognizes two species as belonging to this genus, but we doubt if there is more than one ranging from the State of Panama to the mountain-slopes of Eastern Ecuador.

In the form of the bill there is little to distinguish *Cnipodectes* from *Myiobius*, but the rictal bristles are not so fully developed as in the typical species of *Myiobius* (*M. barbatus* &c.), though not differing from *M. nœvius* in this respect. The wings are short and much rounded, 3rd, 4th, and 5th quills longest, 2nd=6th, 1st=8th, the longest secondaries =6th primary; the tail is rounded, a little <wing, tarsus $=\frac{1}{4}$ tail.

1. Cnipodectes subbrunneus.

Cyclorhynchus subbrunneus, Scl. P. Z. S. 1860, pp. 282[1], 295[2]; Lawr. Ann. Lyc. N. Y. vii. p. 473[3].

Cnipodectes subbrunneus, Scl. & Salv. P. Z. S. 1873, p. 281[4]; Scl. Cat. Birds Brit. Mus. xiv. p. 197, t. 16[5].

Cnipodectes minor, Scl. P. Z. S. 1883, p. 654[6]; Cat. Birds Brit. Mus. xiv. p. 197[7].

Myiochanes, sp. ?, Scl. & Salv. P. Z. S. 1864, p. 360[8].

Supra olivaceo-brunneus; alis fuscis fulvo limbatis; cauda brunnea unicolore: subtus obscure olivaceus; pectore et hypochondriis brunneo lavatis; alis intus et subalaribus pallide fulvis: rostro nigricante, mandibula pallida; pedibus corylinis. Long. tota 5·5, alæ 2·8, caudæ 2·5, tarsi 0·6, rostri a rictu 0·75. (Descr. maris ex Panama. Mus. nostr.)

Hab. PANAMA, Lion Hill (*M'Leannan* [3] [8]).—COLOMBIA [5], ECUADOR [1] [2], and PERU [5].

Mr. Sclater has recently separated this species into a larger and smaller race, the Panama bird being placed with the latter. From the specimens before us we notice that both large and small forms occur together at Chamicuros on the Upper Amazons (whence the type of *C. minor* came), and also in Western Ecuador; nor is the difference in size a sexual character, if the sexes of the specimens before us have been rightly determined. Five of them are marked males, two of them being of the small form and three of the large. Under the circumstances we think it best to recognize only one species. At the same time we notice that the Panama birds are rather more olivaceous on the belly, but they hardly differ from a Colombian specimen from Salmon's collection.

MYIOBIUS.

Myiobius, Gray, List Gen. Birds, ed. 1, p. 30 (1840) (type *Muscicapa barbata,* Gmel.); Scl. Cat. Birds Brit. Mus. xiv. p. 198.

Myiobius is a characteristic Tyrannine genus, the wide bill and elongated rictal bristles of all the species rendering them especially adapted for preying on insects. The genus is strictly a Neotropical one, and spreads from Southern Mexico to the Argentine Republic. The number of species contained in it is about twenty-three, which are divisible into several groups, most of which are represented by the five species found within our boundaries.

Of the typical form we have two species, *M. sulphureipygius*, which occurs throughout Central America, and *M. barbatus*, the prevalent southern bird, which enters our fauna as far north as Costa Rica. These have wings without cross bands, dark tails, and a sulphur rump. The males, too, are crested. The little *M. fulvigularis* has no crest, the rump is coloured like the back, and the tail cinnamon: this is a bird of wide range, represented in Guiana by *M. erythrurus*; it reaches Costa Rica in our fauna. *M. nævius* not only occurs in the State of Panama, but has a wide range in South America as far south as Buenos Ayres: the breast of this species is more or less streaked, and the head crested. Lastly, we have *M. capitalis*, a rather abnormal bird of Costa Rica and Nicaragua, about which we know very little. It has been transferred to *Mitrephanes* by Mr. Ridgway, but is certainly more out of place there than in *Myiobius*. The rictal bristles are not so fully developed as in the typical birds.

M. sulphureipygius has a wide bill, the width at the rictus being about half the length of the tomia. The nasal fossa is extended forwards, and the nostrils are large and open at the end; the rictal bristles extend beyond the end of the bill; the tarsi and feet are rather feeble; the wings are much rounded, the 4th quill longest, 3rd = 5th, 2nd = 6th, 1st much < the rest; tail slightly emarginate, = $\frac{6}{7}$ wing, >3 tarsus.

1. **Myiobius barbatus.**

Muscicapa barbata, Gm. Syst. Nat. i. p. 933 [1].

Myiobius barbatus, Lawr. Ann. Lyc. N. Y. vii. p. 328 [2]; Salv. Ibis, 1885, p. 295 [3]; Scl. Cat. Birds Brit. Mus. xiv. p. 199 [4].

Myiobius atricaudus, Lawr. Ibis, 1863, p. 183 [5]; Ann. Lyc. N. Y. viii. p. 8 [6]; Scl. & Salv. P. Z. S. 1864, p. 360 [7]; Salv. P. Z. S. 1870, p. 198 [8]; Nutting, Pr. U. S. Nat. Mus. v. p. 396 [9].

Supra obscure olivaceus; crista verticali flava celata; uropygio sulphureo; tectricibus caudæ superioribus et cauda ipsa nigris; alis nigricantibus, dorsi colore extrorsum limbatis: subtus pallide flavus; pectore et hypochondriis fulvo lavatis; subcaudalibus fuscis: rostri maxilla fusca, mandibula pallida; pedibus obscure corylinis. Long. tota 4·6, alæ 2·4, caudæ 2·3, tarsi 0·7, rostri a rictu 0·55. (Descr. exempl. ex Panama. Mus. nostr.)

♀ mari similis, sed cristam flavam caret.

Hab. Costa Rica, La Palma (*Nutting* [9]); Panama, Calovevora (*Arcé* [8]), Lion Hill (*M'Leannan* [2 5 6 7]).—Colombia [4] and Ecuador [4] to Amazons valley [4], Guiana [1 3], and Brazil [4].

The country of the typical *M. barbatus* is Guiana, and on comparing specimens from there and the State of Panama we find no material difference. On an average the tails of birds from the latter country are rather blacker than those from Guiana, but the difference is quite insignificant.

La Palma, in Western Costa Rica, seems to be the extreme limit of the range of this species within our country. Here Mr. Nutting met with it, but it is probably more abundant in the State of Panama, whence specimens have been sent us from various places.

Wherever it occurs in Central America the allied *M. sulphureipygius* occurs with it, the two species living independently in the same words. *M. barbatus*, however, has a much wider southern range, whilst *M. sulphureipygius* is found further northwards nearly to the extreme limits of the hot tropical forests of Eastern Mexico.

2. Myiobius sulphureipygius.

Tyrannula sulphureipygia, Scl. P. Z. S. 1856, p. 296 [1].

Myiobius sulphureipygius, Scl. P. Z. S. 1859, p. 384 [2]; Ibis, 1873, p. 373 [3]; Cat. Birds Brit. Mus. xiv. p. 200 [4]; Scl. & Salv. Ibis, 1860, p. 399 [5]; Cassin, Proc. Ac. Phil. 1860, p. 144 [6]; Lawr. Ann. Lyc. N. Y. viii. p. 8 [7], ix. p. 114 [8]; Salv. P. Z. S. 1867, p. 148 [9], 1870, p. 198 [10]; Sumichrast, Mem. Bost. Soc. N. H. i. p. 557 [11]; v. Frantz. J. f. Orn. 1869, p. 308 [12]; Nutting & Ridgw. Pr. U. S. Nat. Mus. vi. p. 402 [13].

Myiobius citrinopygius, Cab. & Heine, Mus. Hein. ii. p. 67 [14].

Myiobius mexicanus, Licht. Mus. Berol. (fide Cabanis [15]).

Præcedenti similis, sed pectore et hypochondriis ferrugineo lavatis. (Descr. maris ex Rio de la Pasion. Mus. nostr.)

Hab. MEXICO [15], State of Vera Cruz (*Sumichrast* [11]), Cordova (*Sallé* [1]), Playa Vicente (*Boucard* [2]), Valle Real (*Deppe*), Cozumel I. (*G. F. Gaumer*); BRITISH HONDURAS, Cayo (*Blancaneaux*); GUATEMALA, Rio de la Pasion, Choctum [5] (*O. S. & F. D. G.*); NICARAGUA, Chontales (*Belt* [3]), Los Sabalos (*Nutting* [13]); COSTA RICA, Angostura (*Carmiol* [8]), Tucurriqui (*Arcé*), La Palma (*Nutting*); PANAMA, Chiriqui [10], Bugaba [10], Calovevora, Calobre [10], Santa Fé [9] (*Arcé*), Panama Railway (*M'Leannan* [7]), Truando (*Wood* [6]).

The first specimens of this species sent to Europe were probably those obtained by Deppe at Valle Real in Mexico, which remained undescribed under Lichtenstein's MS. name, *M. mexicanus*, in the Berlin Museum. In 1856 Mr. Sclater received examples from M. Sallé which he named *M. sulphureipygius*, comparing the species with the allied *M. barbatus*. The range of this bird in Mexico appears to be extremely limited, and probably strictly confined to the hot low-lying forests of the State of Vera Cruz. It also occurs on the island of Cozumel, whence Mr. Gaumer sent us a single specimen. It is found too in British Honduras and in some abundance in Northern Vera Paz in the heavily forested country, lying at an elevation of about 1500 feet above the sea. We are not aware that it inhabits the forests bordering the Pacific Ocean on the western side of the cordillera, or indeed in any part of the west coast until we come to Costa Rica and the State of Panama. In these last-named countries it occurs together with *M. barbatus*, but not beyond the Isthmus of Darien, which appears to be the extreme limit of its range in this direction.

M. sulphureipygius inhabits the dense forest, living amongst the lower branches of the forest trees. Its nest and eggs are unknown.

3. Myiobius fulvigularis, sp. n.

Myiobius cinnamomeus, Lawr. Ann. Lyc. N. Y. vii. p. 328 [1].

Myiobius erythrurus, Lawr. Ann. Lyc. N. Y. vii. p. 472 [2], ix. p. 114 [3]; Salv. P. Z. S. 1867, p. 148 [4],
    1870, p. 198 [5]; Scl. Cat. Birds Brit. Mus. xiv. p. 203 (partim) [6].

Supra olivaceo-cinereus; alis extus, uropygio et cauda cinnamomeis: subtus omnino fulvus; gula paulo
    pallidiore: rostro corneo, mandibula pallida; pedibus corneis. Long. tota 3·5, alæ 2·0, caudæ 1·55,
    tarsi 0·55, rostri a rictu 0·5. (Descr. maris ex Santa Fé. Mus. nostr.)
♀ mari similis.

Hab. Costa Rica, Angostura and Pacuar (*Carmiol* [3]); Panama, Bugaba [5], Vibalá, Santa
    Fé [4], Chepo (*Arcé*), line of Railway (*M'Leannan* [12]).—South America, Colombia,
    Ecuador, Peru, and Amazons valley.

We have hitherto considered this bird inseparable from the Guiana *M. erythrurus*,
but having received a fair series of specimens from British Guiana we are able to make
an accurate comparison, and find that the Guiana bird can be distinguished by its
greyer throat and less olivaceous head and back; the belly, too, is paler fulvous.
M. erythrurus seems to be strictly confined to Guiana, whereas the bird we now
describe enjoys a wide range, reaching Costa Rica in its north-western extension. It
appears to be not uncommou throughout the State of Panama.

4. Myiobius nævius.

Muscicapa nævia, Bodd. Tabl. Pl. Enl. p. 34 [1].

Myiobius nævius, Salv. P. Z. S. 1867, p. 148 [2], 1870, p. 198 [3]; Scl. & Hudson, Arg. Orn. i. p. 151 [4];
    Scl. Cat. Birds Brit. Mus. ix. p. 209 [5].

Supra brunneus; uropygio paulo dilutiore; crista celata flava; alis et cauda fusco-nigricantibus; alarum
    tectricibus fulvo terminatis, fasciis duabus formantibus; secundariis internis quoque fulvo extrorsum
    limbatis: subtus sordide albidus; pectore et hypochondriis fusco guttatis. Long. tota 4·5, alæ 2·2,
    caudæ 2·0, tarsi 0·6, rostri a rictu 0·55. (Descr. exempl. ex Santa Fé, Panama. Mus. nostr.)

Hab. Panama, Castillo, Calovevora [3], Santa Fé [2] (*Arcé*), Lion Hill (*M'Leannan*),
    Paraiso Station (*Hughes*).—South America from Colombia to Buenos Ayres [4].

Some birds of this species have the crest rufous, others yellow, and we suspect that
the former will prove to be males, the latter females, but dissected specimens do not
altogether confirm this view.

Myiobius nævius has a very wide range over Tropical America, where it is one of
the commonest birds, skins being nearly always found in the trade collections of
Brazil and elsewhere. The bird of Western Ecuador has been separated under the
name of *M. crypterythrus* and that of the eastern slope of the Andes of Ecuador as
M. cryptoxanthus, both birds being hardly separable from *M. nævius*.

From Central America but few specimens have reached us, and those all from the
State of Panama. Some of these came from the low-lying forest tract crossed by the
Panama Railway, others from the more mountainous parts further to the westward.

We have no account of its habits in Central America, but in the Argentine Republic, which is the most southern part of the range of this species, Mr. Hudson says that it is a summer visitor [4]. It is shy and solitary, and flits about the upper foliage of the trees, uttering a sorrowful monotonous note.

The nest is placed in a bush or low tree and built of various soft materials compactly woven together, and the inside lined with feathers or vegetable down. The eggs are four in number, of a pale cream-colour with large well-defined spots of dark red.

5. Myiobius capitalis. (Tab. XL. fig. 1.)

Myiobius capitalis, Salv. P. Z. S. 1864, p. 583 [1]; Nutting & Ridgw. Pr. U. S. Nat. Mus. vi. p. 403 [2].
Mitrephanes capitalis, Scl. Cat. Birds Brit. Mus. xiv. p. 220 [3].

Supra olivaceus; capite cinereo; loris albidis; alis et cauda obscure fuscis, illis distincte fulvo limbatis: subtus gula albida; pectore obscure fulvo; abdomine et subalaribus flavidis: rostro obscure corneo; pedibus corylinis. Long. tota 4·5, alæ 2·5, caudæ 2·2, tarsi 0·6, rostri a rictu 0·6. (Descr. exempl. typ. ex Tucurriqui, Costa Rica. Mus. nostr.)

Hab. NICARAGUA, Los Sabalos (*Nutting* [2]); COSTA RICA, Tucurriqui (*Arcé* [1]).

Until recently the single specimen sent us from Tucurriqui in Costa Rica by Arcé was the only one known. Mr. Nutting has since obtained a second at Los Sabalos in Nicaragua, which he found in dense forest. The bird has no near allies in the genus *Myiobius*, but its resemblance in some respects to *Mitrephanes aurantiiventris* suggested to Mr. Ridgway that it should be placed in *Mitrephanes* rather than *Myiobius*.

We do not concur in this view, and believe that it would be better to leave it where it was originally placed. *Mitrephanes* as here understood contains two perfectly congeneric species, distinguishable by their distinct crests and long, deeply-forked tails. Neither *M. capitalis* nor *Empidonax atriceps* possess either of these characters.

Though both *M. capitalis* and *Mitrephanes aurantiiventris* occur at Tucurriqui in Costa Rica, it is probable that the former belongs to the lowlands and the latter to the uplands, and that they meet here at the opposite extremes of their vertical range.

PYROCEPHALUS.

Pyrocephalus, Gould, Zool. Voy. Beagle, iii. p. 44 (1841) (type *Muscicapa rubinea*, Bodd.); Scl. Cat. Birds Brit. Mus. xiv. p. 211.

In its coloration *Pyrocephalus* stands alone amongst the Tyrannidæ, no other members of the family having the brilliant red breast and head which distinguish *P. rubineus* and its allies.

Mr. Sclater includes four species in the genus, but *P. mexicanus* is hardly separable from *P. rubineus* and the status of *P. obscurus* is not very satisfactory, as it is not improbably only a dark form of the common *P. rubineus*. The fourth is the *P. nanus* of the Galapagos Islands—a dwarf form of the mainland bird.

The bill is moderately stout, the length of the tomia being rather more than twice the width at the rictus, the sides converge gradually to the tip; the nostrils are open

8*

at the end of the nasal fossa, the rictal bristles moderately developed; the tarsi and toes rather short.   The wings are rather long, 2nd, 3rd, and 4th quills longest, 1st=6th; tail moderate and nearly square, $>\frac{2}{3}$ wing, < 4 tarsus.

1. Pyrocephalus rubineus.

Muscicapa rubinus, Bodd. Tabl. Pl. Enl. p. 42 [1].

Pyrocephalus rubineus, Cass. B. Cal. and Texas, p. 127, t. 18 [2]; Cab. & Heine, Mus. Hein. ii. p. 67 [3]; Scl. P. Z. S. 1856, p. 296 [4]; Cat. Birds Brit. Mus. xiv. p. 211 [5]; Baird, Mex. Bound. Surv., Zool., Birds, p. 9 [6]; Dresser, Ibis, 1865, p. 475 [7]; Scl. & Huds. Arg. Orn. i. p. 152 [8].

Pyrocephalus mexicanus, Scl. P. Z. S. 1859, pp. 45 [9], 366 [10], 1864, p. 176 [11]; Cat. Birds Brit. Mus. xiv. p. 213 [12]; Moore, P. Z. S. 1859, p. 56 [13]; Scl. & Salv. Ibis, 1860, p. 399 [14]; Sumichrast, Mem. Bost. Soc. N. H. i. p. 557 [15]; Lawr. Ann. Lyc. N. Y. ix. p. 201 [16].

Pyrocephalus rubineus var. *mexicanus,* Baird, Brew., & Ridgw. N. Am. B. ii. p. 387 [17]; Lawr. Bull. U. S. Nat. Mus. no. 4, p. 27 [18]; Mem. Bost. Soc. N. H. ii. p. 287 [19].

Pyrocephalus rubineus mexicanus, Sennett, Bull. U. S. Geol. Surv. iv. p. 34 [20], v. p. 409; Coues, Key N. Am. B. (ed. 2), p. 444 [21]; Perez, Pr. U. S. Nat. Mus. ix. p. 154 [22]; Ridgw. Man. N. Am. B. p. 345 [23].

Muscicapa coronata, Gm. Syst. Nat. i. p. 932 [24]; Licht. Preis-Verz. mex. Vög. p. 2 (cf. J. f. Orn. 1863, p. 58 [25]).

Tyrannula coronata, Sw. Phil. Mag. new ser. i. p. 367 [26]; Bp. P. Z. S. 1837, p. 112 [27].

Pyrocephalus obscurus, Scl. P. Z. S. 1864, p. 176 [29].

Supra obscure fuscus; alis nigricantibus, extrorsum pallide fusco vix limbatis; cauda quoque nigricante: rectrica externe in pogonio externo pallide fusca; loris et regione parotica dorso concoloribus; capite summo et corpore subtus læte coccineis; subalaribus fuscis: rostro et pedibus nigris. Long. tota 5·5, alæ 3·3, caudæ 2·3, tarsi 0·7, rostri a rictu 0·65.

♀. Supra cinerea; capite summo ad frontem pallidiore; alis et cauda nigricantibus, illis sordide albo limbatis: subtus alba; pectore fusco guttato; abdomine aurantiaco. (Descr. maris et feminæ ex Monterey, Nuevo Leon, Mexico. Mus. nostr.)

Hab. NORTH AMERICA [17], Southern California, Arizona, and Southern Texas [7,23].— MEXICO [27] (*Bullock* [26]), Topochico in Nuevo Leon (*F. B. Armstrong*), Realito in Sonora (*W. Lloyd*), Mazatlan (*Forrer, Grayson* [19]), Plains of Colima (*Xantus* [19]), Amula, Chilpancingo, and Tierra Colorada in Guerrero (*Mrs. H. H. Smith*), Jerez in Zacatecas, Calvillo, Aguas Calientes, Valle del Maiz, and Tampico (*Richardson*), Mexico city (*White* [11,28]), San Martin, Texmelucan, Tlaxcala, Jalapa (*Ferrari-Perez* [22]), Cordova (*Sallé*), Jalapa (*Sallé, de Oca* [10], *M. Trujillo*), Cofre de Perote (*M. Trujillo*), Orizaba, Morelia (*F. D. G.*), Oaxaca (*Fenochio*), Sta. Efigenia and Tehuantepec city (*Sumichrast* [18]), Northern Yucatan (*G. F. Gaumer*), Merida (*Schott* [16]), Cozumel I. (*G. F. Gaumer*); BRITISH HONDURAS, Orange Walk (*G. F. Gaumer*), Belize (*Blancaneuux*); GUATEMALA (*Constancia* [14]), Pine Ridge of Poctum, Santa Ana (*O. S*), Peten (*Leyland* [13]).—SOUTH AMERICA generally from Colombia to Guiana and Argentine Republic [5,8].

On comparing freshly-moulted specimens from Northern Mexico with others from South America in similar condition we find no grounds whatever for recognizing more than one continental species of this genus, unless indeed *P. obscurus* is really separable. Under any circumstances *P. mexicanus* and *P. rubineus* must pass under the same name. With at least one hundred and fifty specimens before us from various localities no other conclusion seems possible. An occasional example from S. America is blacker than others, but this does not appear to be the rule in any one locality.

M. rubineus appears to be a very common bird on the southern side of the Rio Grande and Gila rivers, but rarer on the Texan side of the northern limit of its range. Thence it passes southwards through a large portion of Mexico, extending from ocean to ocean and living in equal abundance in the highlands of the valley of Mexico. It occurs also in Northern Yucatan and on Cozumel Island, as well as in British Honduras in the pine districts so characteristic of that country. In Guatemala it was found by Constancia, but in what locality we were never able to ascertain, for we only once met with it in our many journeys through that country and it certainly does not come within the hunting-grounds of the bird-collectors of Coban. It was only on emerging from the vast forests of Northern Vera Paz between the villages of San Luis and Poctum that Salvin found it abundant in the large open pine-tract crossed by the road to Peten. It was equally common in all similar districts of that region, but always in open country and not in the forests which line the river-banks.

The brilliant plumage of the male bird and its habit of rising in the air and descending somewhat after the manner of *Anthus pratensis* render *P. rubineus* a conspicuous bird wherever it is found, and one not easily overlooked in a country inhabited by it.

Its absence from all the country south of Guatemala until we reach Colombia is remarkable and not easily accounted for, as localities apparently suitable to it are to be found through most of the intervening countries.

Mr. Hudson [7] has published some interesting notes on this species as observed by him in the Argentine Republic. In that country *P. rubineus* is a migratory bird, arriving about the end of September and soon afterwards commencing to breed. Its nest is composed of lichens, webs, and thistle-down, which are neatly woven into a compact nest and sometimes lined with feathers. The eggs, four in number, are pointed, and spotted at the broad end with black and usually with a few large grey spots.

SAYORNIS.

Sayornis, Bonaparte, Ann. Sc. Nat. sér. 4, Zool. i. p. 133 (1854) (type *Sayornis saya*) ; Scl. Cat. Birds Brit. Mus. xiv. p. 32.

Aulanax, Cabanis, J. f. Orn. 1856, p. 2 (type *Sayornis nigricans*).

Theromyias, Cab. & Heine, Mus. Hein. ii. p. 68 (1859) (type *Sayornis saya*).

Empidias, Cab. & Heine, Mus. Hein. ii. p. 69 (1859) (type *Sayornis phœbe*) ; Scl. Cat. Birds Brit. Mus. xiv. p. 264.

The position of this genus and its limits have been and still remain uncertain. Prof. Cabanis, who divides it into three genera, places all of them near *Myiarchus* in the section Tyranninæ of the Family. Writers on North-American birds assign to it a similar position, but Mr. Sclater considers *Sayornis* to belong to the South-American Fluvicolinæ ; but he employs Cabanis's name *Empidias* for *E. fuscus* (= *E. phœbe*), and places it at the other end of the Family after *Myiarchus*. We do not see our way to following this arrangement, and prefer to place *Sayornis* near *Myiarchus* and *Empidonax* rather than with the strictly terrestrial Fluvicolinæ. At the same time we admit that *Sayornis* and *Ochthœca* have characters in common.

Sayornis in its wide sense contains three groups of species—one consisting of *S. saya*, the type of the genus, the second *S. nigricans* and two other species, *S. aquatica* and *S. cineracea*, the third *S. phœbe*. All these species frequent places near streams of water, the group of *S. nigricans* being especially partial to river-banks, where they sit on stones on or close to the margin and take their insect food from near the surface of the water. All the species have similar nesting-habits and lay white or slightly spotted eggs.

Sayornis saya has a somewhat flattened bill, rather broad at the base ; the culmen is nearly straight for most of its length and then curves suddenly to form the terminal maxillary hook ; the nostrils are covered with strong bristles and the rictal bristles are also very fully developed ; the tarsi are short and the feet feeble ; the 2nd, 3rd, and 4th primaries are nearly equal and longest in the wing, the 1st = 6th ; the tail is very slightly forked, = $\frac{6}{7}$ wing, < 4 tarsus.

1. Sayornis saya.

Muscicapa saya, Bp. Am. Orn. i. p. 20, t. 2. f. 3 (1825) [1].

Tyrannula sayii?, Sw. Orn. Draw. t. 70 [2].

Sayornis sayus, Baird, Mex. Bound. Surv., Zool., Birds, p. 9 [3] ; Dresser, Ibis, 1865, p. 473 [4] ; Sumichrast, Mem. Bost. Soc. N. H. i. p. 557 [5] ; Baird, Brew., & Ridgw. N. Am. B. ii. p. 347 [6] ; Lawr. Bull. U. S. Nat. Mus. no. 4, p. 25 [7] ; Sennett, Bull. U. S. Geol. Surv. v. p. 404 [8] ; Perez, Pr. U. S. Nat. Mus. ix. p. 154 [9].

Sayornis saya, A. O. U. Check-list N.-Am. B. p. 233 [10] ; Ridgw. Man. N. Am. B. p. 336 [11].

Theromyias sayi, Cab. & Heine, Mus. Hein. ii. p. 68 [12].

Tyrannula pallida, Sw. Phil. Mag. new ser. i. p. 367 [13].

Sayornis pallida, Scl. P. Z. S. 1857, p. 204 [14], 1859, p. 366 [15] ; Cat. Am. B. p. 200 [19] ; Cat. Birds Brit. Mus. xiv. p. 32 [17] ; Dugès, La Nat. i. p. 141 [18].

Griseo-fusca ; capite summo et tectricibus supracaudalibus obscurioribus ; cauda nigricante ; alis fuscis, tectricibus majoribus et secundariis extrorsum sordide griseo limbatis : ventre et crisso pallide cinnamomeis ; subalaribus pallide cervinis : rostro et pedibus nigris. Long. tota 6·5, alæ 4·0, caudæ 3·2, rostri a rictu 0·8, tarsi 0·8. (Descr. exempl. ex urbe Mexico. Mus. nostr.)

Hab. NORTH AMERICA, western portion from the plains to the Pacific [11], Texas [4] [8].— MEXICO, Nuevo Larido and Topochico (*F. B. Armstrong*) ; Caretas, La Mula, Chupadero in the State of Chihuahua (*W. Lloyd*), Santa Isabel, Espia (*Kennerly* [3]), Plains of San Luis Potosi (*Richardson*), Tablelands (*Bullock* [13]), Guanajuato (*Dugès* [18]), valley of Mexico (*le Strange*), Hacienda Eslava, Culhuacan, Mexicalcingo,

Ixtapalapa, S. Antonio Coapa, Chimalpa, and Coajimalpa, all in the neighbourhood of Mexico city *(Ferrari-Perez)*, State of Vera Cruz *(Sumichrast* [5]*)*, Jalapa *(Sallé, de Oca* [15]*)*, Chapulco *(Sumichrast* [7], *Ferrari-Perez* [9]*)*, Puebla and Atlixco *(F. D. G.)*.

Sayornis saya has a wide range over Central Mexico, occurring as far south as Jalapa in the State of Vera Cruz, and Chapulco in the State of Puebla. It does not, however, appear to leave the plateau, as nowhere in the south does it approach the coast. To what extent this species is migratory does not seem to be clearly stated. Sumichrast was uncertain as to its movements in the State of Vera Cruz, and other Mexican records are silent on the subject *. Within the States it would appear to be migratory so far as regards the northern and upland portions of its range. Thus Dr. Coues says it is a summer resident at Fort Whipple in Arizona, but that it winters in the Colorado valley and in the southern parts of Arizona. Dr. Cooper speaks of it as chiefly a winter visitor to the southern and western parts of California. It certainly winters in the frontier States of Mexico, Chihuahua, Nuevo Leon, and Tamaulipas, as we have specimens from several places obtained between January and March. In summer it visits the plains of the interior as far north as the 60th parallel.

Mr. Ridgway describes a nest, placed on a shelf inside a small cave on the shore of an island in Lake Pyramid, as a globular mass consisting chiefly of spiders' webs mixed with fine vegetable fibres of various kinds; the cavity was shallow and lined with the down of ducks. The eggs are uniform chalky white.

The specific name *saya* proposed by Bonaparte in 1825 and adopted by North-American writers seems to us to be the right title for this species. Mr. Sclater employs Swainson's name *pallida*, though dating from 1827.

2. Sayornis phœbe.

Muscicapa fusca, Gm. Syst. Nat. i. p. 931 (nec Müll. nec Bodd.) [1].

Sayornis fuscus, Baird, Mex. Bound. Surv., Zool., Birds, p. 8 [2]; Dresser, Ibis, 1865, p. 473 [3]; Sumichrast, Mem. Bost. Soc. N. H. i. p. 557 [4]; Baird, Brew., & Ridgw. N. Am. B. ii. p. 343 [5].

Myiarchus fuscus, Scl. P. Z. S. 1859, p. 366 [6].

Muscicapa phœbe, Lath. Ind. Orn. ii. p. 489 (ex Penn. Arctic Zool. ii. no. 275) [7].

Sayornis phœbe, Stejn. Auk, 1885, p. 51 [8]; Ridgw. Man. N. Am. B. p. 336 [9].

Empidias fuscus, Cab. & Heine, Mus. Hein. ii. p. 69 [10]; Scl. Cat. Birds Brit. Mus. xiv. p. 264 [11].

Supra olivaceo-fusca; capite summo nigricante; alis et cauda quoque nigricantibus, illarum secondariis et tectricibus majoribus, hujus rectrice extima utrinque in pogonio externo albido limbatis: subtus lactescenti-alba; mento et pectoris lateribus fusco notatis: rostro et pedibus nigris. Long. tota 6·0, alæ 3·4, caudæ 3·0, tarsi 0·7, rostri a rictu 0·75. (Descr. feminæ ex Orizaba, Mexico. Mus. nostr.)

Hab. NORTH AMERICA, Eastern States [11], Texas [3].—MEXICO, Nuevo Laredo in Tamaulipas *(Armstrong)*, Tamaulipas *(Couch* [2]*)*, Tampico *(Richardson)*, Jalapa *(de Oca* [6],

---

* In Prof. Ferrari-Perez's collection we find that specimens were obtained in and about the valley of Mexico from the end of December to the 11th April.

F. D. G.), Orizaba, Misantla (*F. D. G.*), Vera Cruz (*Richardson*), S. Antonio Coapa (*Ferrari-Perez*), Tierra templada of the Pacific slope, Morelia (*le Strange*).—CUBA?

A well-known species of the Eastern States of North America as a summer visitor, where it remains to breed. In the valley of the Rio Grande some birds of this species may be found throughout the year, for we have records of it in March from the river itself at Nuevo Laredo and opposite Brownsville, and in June Mr. Dresser found it in numbers near Houston. However, neither Mr. Sennett nor Dr. Merrill include its name in their lists. In Southern Mexico it is chiefly found on the eastern slope of the mountains of Vera Cruz from Orizaba and Jalapa to the low ground about Misantla and near the sea-coast at Vera Cruz. In the valley of Mexico it is a much rarer bird, for we only find a single specimen in Prof. Ferrari-Perez's large collection, and this was shot at S. Antonio Coapa near Tlalpam. Mr. le Strange, however, considered it a bird of the temperate districts of the Pacific slope, such as the vicinity of Morelia.

The habits of *S. phœbe* resemble those of *S. saya*, and its nest is described as similarly placed and made of similar materials. The eggs, too, are usually unspotted white, but a small proportion show reddish-brown dots at the larger end.

3. Sayornis nigricans.

Tyrannula nigricans, Sw. Phil. Mag. new ser. i. p. 367 [1].

Sayornis nigricans, Scl. P. Z. S. 1856, p. 296 [2], 1859, p. 383 [3], 1864, p. 175 [4]; Cat. Birds Brit. Mus. xiv. p. 33 [5]; Baird, U. S. Bound. Surv., Zool., Birds, p. 8 [6]; Sumichrast, Mem. Bost. Soc. N. H. i. p. 557 [7]; Baird, Brew., & Ridgw. N. Am. B. ii. p. 340 [8]; Lawr. Mem. Bost. Soc. N. H. ii. p. 285 [9]; Bull. U. S. Nat. Mus. no. 4, p. 25 [10]; Perez, Pr. U. S. Nat. Mus. ix. p. 154 [11].

Aulanax nigricans, Cab. & Heine, Mus. Hein. ii. p. 68 [12].

Myiarchus nigricans, Dugès, La Nat. i. p. 141 [13].

Muscicapa atrata, Licht. Preis-Verz. mex. Vög. p. 2 (cf. J. f. Orn. 1863, p. 58 [14]).

Muscicapa semiatra, Vig. in Beechey's Voy. p. 17 [15].

Sooty Flycatcher, Sw. Orn. Draw. t. 69 [16].

Fuliginoso-nigra; dorso medio paullo dilutiore; secundariis extrorsum, dimidio pogonii externi rectricis extimæ, subalaribus, ventre et crisso albis: rostro et pedibus nigris. Long. tota 6·0, alæ 3·5, caudæ 3·2, rostri a rictu 0·7, tarsi 0·7. (Descr. maris ex Mazatlan, Mexico. Mus. nostr.)
♀ mari similis.

Hab. NORTH AMERICA, South-western States from Texas to Arizona and California and northwards to Oregon [8].—MEXICO (*Bullock* [1]), Espia (*Kennerly* [6]), Cadereita (*Couch* [6]), Rio de Monterey and Rancho de las Triviñas (*Armstrong*), Mazatlan (*Grayson* [9]), Presidio near Mazatlan (*Forrer*), Venta de Zopilote in Guerrero (*Mrs. H. H. Smith*), Valle del Maiz, Aguas Calientes, and Sierra de Calvillo (*Richardson*), Guanajuato (*Dugès* [13]), valley of Mexico (*White* [4]), Chimalpa, Coapa, Mexicalcingo, Ixtapalapa, Culhuacan, all near Mexico city (*Ferrari-Perez*), Temperate and Alpine regions of Vera Cruz (*Sumichrast* [7]), Tanatepec (*Sumichrast* [10]), Puebla and Orizaba (*F. D. G.*), Cordova (*Sallé* [2]), Morelia (*F. D. G.*), Cinco Señores (*Boucard* [3]), Oaxaca (*Boucard* [3], *Fenochio*).

This species appears to be found throughout Mexico as far as the south-western confines of that country, but as yet we have no record of it or of the allied form in Yucatan *.

Sumichrast states that it is a very common species in the temperate and colder parts of the State of Vera Cruz, and that it builds its nest in the houses of Orizaba[7]. It is not, however, solely confined to these districts, for both Grayson[9] and Forrer met with it near the sea-level in the vicinity of Mazatlan.

It frequents the banks of streams, and most of its insect prey is taken from near the surface of the water. It builds a nest with an outer wall of mud like that of a Swallow; this is fastened to a wall or placed on a shelf, beam, or ledge of rock, with an over-hanging projection to protect it from rain. The nest is lined with fine grass or moss and horse- or cow-hair. The eggs are pure white.

S. nigricans appears to be resident in Mexico and also in Arizona and California, but in more northern districts where its insect food fails in the cold weather it is a summer visitor, migrating southwards at the approach of winter.

4. Sayornis aquatica.

Sayornis aquatica, Scl. & Salv. Ibis, 1859, p. 119[1]; Lawr. Ann. Lyc. N. Y. ix. p. 110[2]; v. Frantz. J. f. Orn. 1869, p. 306[3]; Boucard, P. Z. S. 1878, p. 62[4]; Scl. Cat. Birds Brit. Mus. xiv. p. 33[5].
Aulanax aquatica, Cab. J. f. Orn. 1861, p. 247[6].
Sayornis nigricans, Bp. Compt. Rend. xxxviii. p. 657[7]; Notes Orn. p. 87[8].

S. nigricanti similis, sed crisso fuliginoso distinguenda.

Hab. GUATEMALA, Quezaltenango, Dueñas[1], Retalhuleu, Escuintla, R. Michatoya near San Pedro Martyr, San Gerónimo (*O. S. & F. D. G.*); NICARAGUA (*Delattre*[7][8]); COSTA RICA (*v. Frantzius*[2][3], *Arcé, A. R. Endres*), San José (*Boucard*[4]).

Sayornis aquatica takes the place of *S. nigricans* in Guatemala and the rest of Central America as far south as Costa Rica, and may be recognized by its dusky under tail-coverts, those of the allied form being white. In the north-western parts of South America another form of *Sayornis* occurs with dusky under tail-coverts, *S. cineracea* (Lafr.), but may be distinguished by the broader white edgings to its wings and tail and its blacker plumage.

S. aquatica is a familiar bird in many parts of Guatemala, where, like its congener, it frequents streams, often resting on a stone on the margin or even surrounded by water; from such a point of observation it will fly suddenly and seize passing insects. In its general habits it is more active than Tyrant Flycatchers usually are, and may not unfrequently be seen about houses, some running stream being near. We never met with the nest of this species.

* Brewer states that *S. nigricans* is resident in Guatemala, and he quotes Salvin as his authority, adding that the note may refer to *S. aquatica*; a curious inaccuracy, as the passage quoted is appended to the original description of *S. aquatica*, no mention whatever being made of *S. nigricans*!

MITREPHANES.

Mitrephanes, Coues, Bull. Nutt. Orn. Club, vii. p. 55 (1882); Scl. Cat. Birds Brit. Mus. xiv.
    p. 218, vice
Mitrephorus, Scl. P. Z. S. 1859, p. 45 (nec Schönherr).

The genus *Mitrephorus* was founded in 1859 by Mr. Sclater upon *M. phæocercus* of
the Mexican and Guatemalan highlands, but the name being preoccupied, *Mitrephanes*
was substituted for it by Dr. Coues in 1882.

According to Mr. Sclater the genus includes five species, as he, following Mr. Ridgway, includes *Myiobius capitalis* and *Empidonax atriceps* in it, as well as *M. ochracei-
ventris* of Peru, a bird we have not yet examined. *M. capitalis* and *E. atriceps* we
leave in the genera in which they were originally placed, so that we have only two
species to deal with, viz. *M. phæocercus,* already mentioned, and *M. aurantiiventris* of
Costa Rica and the State of Panama.

In many respects *M. phæocercus* resembles *Empidonax,* but the bill is narrower, the
margins not so convex, and with a well-defined concave curve towards the tip; the
rictal bristles are more fully developed, the nostrils more distinctly exposed; there is,
moreover, a conspicuous crest formed of the prolonged occipital feathers, and the tail
is longer in proportion to the wings, thus, tail $> \frac{9}{10}$ wing, and in *Empidonax trailli*
$< \frac{5}{6}$ wing.

1. Mitrephanes phæocercus.

Tyrannula, sp.?, Scl. P. Z. S. 1856, p. 296, no. 104 [1].
Empidonax, sp.?, Scl. P. Z. S. 1858, p. 302, no. 82 [2].
Mitrephorus phæocercus, Scl. P. Z. S. 1859, pp. 44 [3], 366 [4], 384 [5]; Scl. & Salv. Ibis, 1859, p. 122 [6];
    Sumichrast, Mem. Bost. Soc. N. H. i. p. 557 [7]; Lawr. Mem. Bost. Soc. N. H. ii. p. 287 [8];
    Salv. Cat. Strickl. Coll. p. 313 [9].
Mitrephanes phæocercus, Scl. Cat. Birds Brit. Mus. xiv. p. 210 [10].
Mitrephanes phæocercus tenuirostris, Brewst. Auk, 1888, p. 137 [11].

Supra obscure olivaceus, capite obscuriore; loris rufo-albidis; alis et cauda fusco-nigricantibus; alarum
    tectricibus fulvo terminatis: subtus ferrugineis; mento, abdomine imo, pallidioribus: rostri maxilla
    nigricante, mandibula pallida; pedibus obscure corylinis. Long. tota 5·0, alæ 2·7, caudæ rect. med. 2·25,
    rect. ext. 2·45, tarsi 0·55, rostri a rictu 0·55. (Descr. exempl. ex Jalapa. Mus. nostr.)
Juv. supra saturate brunneis, capite nigricante, plumis omnibus fulvo limbatis.

Hab. MEXICO, Oposura in Sonora, Presidio near Mazatlan (*J. C. Cahoon* [11]), Mazatlan
    (*Bischoff* [8], *Grayson* [8]), Ciudad in Durango (*Forrer*), Sierra de Valparaiso in Zaca-
    tecas (*W. B. Richardson*), Amula and Omilteme in Guerrero (*Mrs. H. H. Smith*),
    Tetelco and Ixtapalapa (*Ferrari-Perez*), State of Vera Cruz (*Sumichrast* [7]), Jalapa
    (*de Oca* [4], *Höge, M. Trujillo*), Cofre de Perote (*M. Trujillo*), Talea (*Boucard*),
    Cordova (*Sallé* [1]), Orizaba (*F. D. G.*), Oaxaca (*Fenochio*); GUATEMALA (*Constancia* [9],
    Skinner [6]), Coban, Volcan de Fuego, Dueñas, Ridge above Totonicapam, Quezalte-
    nango (*O. S. & F. D. G.*).

Originally described from a Cordova specimen, with which others from Jalapa, Orizaba, Cofre de Perote, &c. agree. They are all rather darker than examples from the valley of Mexico, Oaxaca, and the Sierra Madre of North-western Mexico, the latter having been described by Mr. Brewster as *M. p. tenuirostris*.

The difference of colour is extremely slight, but follows the usual rule where the birds of Eastern Mexico, with its greater rainfall, are rather darker than those from the drier plateau and the western sierras. The difference in the size of the bill is hardly appreciable in the series before us. In the series obtained by Mrs. Smith in the months of July and August in the Sierra Madre del Sur are light and dark coloured birds as well as young in their first plumage.

In Guatemala *M. phœocercus* is common in the oak-forests lying at an elevation of 4500 feet and upwards, and is one of the most characteristic species of these woods. We never met with its nest or eggs.

2. Mitrephanes aurantiiventris.

Mitrephorus aurantiiventris, Lawr. Ann. Lyc. N. Y. viii. p. 174[1], ix. p. 114[2]; Salv. Ibis, 1869, p. 315[3]; P. Z. S. 1870, p. 198[4]; v. Frantz. J. f. Orn. 1869, p. 308[5].
Mitrephanes aurantiiventris, Scl. Cat. Birds Brit. Mus. xiv. p. 219[6].
Mitrephorus phœocercus, Lawr. Ann. Lyc. N. Y. ix. p. 114[7].

Præcedenti similis, sed supra magis olivaceus, abdomine medio aurantiaco distinguendus. (Descr. exempl. ex Irazu, Costa Rica. Mus. nostr.)

Hab. Costa Rica, Tabacales[1], La Palma[2], Candelaria (*v. Frantzius*[2][5]), Tucurriqui (*Arcé*), Irazu (*Rogers*), Dota[2], Barranca (*Carmiol*); Panama, Volcan de Chiriqui, Chitra, Calovevora[4], Calobre (*Arcé*).

The specimens of this species differ considerably from each other in the colouring of the top of the head, some being much darker than others; but this variation seems to be due to individual, seasonal, or perhaps sexual characters.

M. aurantiiventris is closely allied to the bird of the Mexican and Guatemalan highlands, *M. phœocercus*, but appears to frequent places lying at a lower level, descending in some cases as low as 2000 feet above the sea. It is a common bird both in Costa Rica and the State of Panama, but its nest and eggs still remain unknown.

EMPIDONAX.

Empidonax, Cabanis, J. f. Orn. 1855, p. 480 (type *E. pusillus* (Sw.)); Scl. Cat. Birds Brit. Mus. xiv. p. 221.

Empidonax is one of the most complex genera of the Tyrannidæ as regards the differential characters of some of its species, comparable in this respect to the Old-World genus *Phylloscopus*. Several distinguished American ornithologists have paid great attention to *Empidonax*, and descriptions, "keys," and all such aids to determining the various species abound in their writings. The most recent of these is Mr. Ridgway's, who, in his ' Manual of North-American Birds,' gives a key whereby to determine the North-American and Mexican species. This key was adopted almost in its entirety by Mr. Sclater in the fourteenth volume of the Catalogue of Birds in the British Museum, and we have studied it closely for our present work. If we except the use of subspecific names the result we come to is not very different from Mr. Ridgway's, though we arrive at our conclusions by rather different means. We have not taken much account of comparative measurements, for experience shows how greatly these vary in the members of the same species.

In endeavouring to determine Mexican and Central-American individuals of the migratory *Empidonaces*, we are met with the difficulty arising from having to compare birds of different seasons together. By far the greater part of the birds collected in the south are obtained in the winter and early spring months, *i. e.* in the dry season. In the States, collecting commences on the arrival of the spring migrants and extends through the summer. Thus the only birds that are properly available for comparison, so far as their plumage is concerned, are those shot in the latter part of the spring in the south just as they are preparing to leave, and those just arrived in the north from the south. Our materials do not always include birds prepared under these conditions.

Our task, however, has been vastly lightened by having before us the collection of Messrs. Henshaw and Merriam with its extensive series of carefully named specimens of North-American species.

Empidonax is almost exclusively a genus of America north of the Isthmus of Panama. There are a few species located in the north-western parts of South America, and a small section occurs as far south as the Argentine republic; but it is doubtful if the latter do not belong rather to *Empidochanes*.

Of eighteen species recognized by us, no less than fourteen occur within our limits, of which perhaps eight may be wholly or partially migrants, leaving six residents. The birds that perform the longest migrations are *E. acadicus, E. trailli, E. minimus, E. flaviventris,* and *E. hammondi.* The partial migrants are *E. fulvifrons, E. bairdi,* and *E. obscurus.* Mexico retains as residents *E. affinis* and *E. canescens,* Guatemala *E. salvini,* Mexico and Central America generally *E. albigularis,* Costa Rica and Panama *E. flavescens* and *E. atriceps.*

Like *Tyrannus, Empidonax* has short stiff setose feathers, which almost hide the open nostrils, and the rictal bristles are well developed but not so long as in *Mitrephanes*; the bill is wide, the width at the rictus being rather more than half the length of the tomia, the sides of the bill are convex from the base to the tip; the tarsi are slender; the 3rd quill is the longest in the wing, the 2nd=4th, 1st=6th; tail moderate, $> \frac{4}{5}$ wing, wing > 4 tarsus.

A. *Pileus aut olivaceus aut umbrino-brunneus, haud niger.*

a. *Rostrum latiusculum.*

a'. *Subtus cinnamomeus.*

1. **Empidonax fulvifrons.**

Muscicapa fulvifrons, Giraud, Sixteen B. Texas, t. 2. f. 2[1].

Empidonax fulvifrons, Scl. P. Z. S. 1858, p. 301[2]; Cat. Birds Brit. Mus. xiv. p. 222[3]; Ridgw. Ibis, 1886, p. 462[4]; Man. N. Am. B. p. 344[5].

Mitrephorus fulvifrons, Scl. P. Z. S. 1859, p. 45[6]; Scl. & Salv. Ibis, 1860, p. 275[7].

Empidonax rubicundus, Cab. & Heine, Mus. Hein. ii. p. 70[8].

Empidonax fulvifrons rubicundus, Perez, Pr. U. S. Nat. Mus. ix. p. 154[9]; Ridgw. Ibis, 1886, p. 463[10]; Man. N. Am. B. p. 345[11].

Empidonax pygmæus, Coues, Ibis, 1865, p. 537.[12].

Empidonax fulvifrons pygmæus, Ridgw. Ibis, 1886, p. 463[13]; Man. N. Am. B. p. 345[14].

Empidonax pallescens, Coues, Pr. Ac. Phil. 1866, p. 63[15].

Mitrephorus fulvifrons, var. *pallescens*, Baird, Brew., & Ridgw. N. Am. B. ii. p. 386[16]; Coues, B. N. W. p. 259[17]; Henshaw, U. S. Geogr. Surv. West 100th Mer. v. p. 364[18].

Mitrephanes fulvifrons pallescens, Coues, Key N. Am. B. ed. 2, p. 443[19].

Supra omnino brunneus; capite summo paulo saturatiore; alis nigricantibus, tectricibus fulvo terminatis, secundariis quoque albo limbatis; cauda nigricante, rectrice extima utrinque in pogonio externo alba: subtus rufescenti-fulvus; gutture et abdomine paulo dilutioribus: rostri maxilla nigricante, mandibula flava; pedibus nigricantibus. Long. tota 4·6, alæ 2·5, caudæ 2·0, tarsi 0·6, rostri a rictu 0·5. (Descr. maris ex Coapa prope urbem Mexico. Mus. nostr.)

♀ mari similis.

Hab. NORTH AMERICA, Southern Arizona[18] and New Mexico[18].—MEXICO[8], Tutuaca and Rio Verde in Chihuahua (*W. Lloyd*), Amula and Omilteme in Guerrero (*Mrs. H. H. Smith*), Ixtapalapa, Hacienda Eslava, Huipulco, Coapa, Mexicalcingo, Culhuacan, Axotla, Chimalpa, Coajimalpa, all near Mexico city (*Ferrari-Perez*), valley of Mexico (*H. le Strange*), Huehuetlan (*Ferrari-Perez*[9]); GUATEMALA, Quezaltenango, Dueñas[7] (*O. S. & F. D. G.*).

Mr. Ridgway recognizes three forms of this species, namely, *E. fulvifrons* from Eastern Mexico and Southern Texas, *E. fulvifrons rubicundus* from Southern Mexico, and *E. fulvifrons pygmæus* from New Mexico southwards into Western Mexico. We have now specimens from all these districts except of course from Texas, where its presence is doubtful. Our largest series comes from the vicinity of the city of Mexico, and amongst these the three forms appear to be fully represented, and, moreover, they are united by every intermediate gradation. Our ruddiest birds come from the highlands of Guatemala, where the species is doubtless resident, as it is elsewhere, except, perhaps, at the northern extremity of its range.

Mr. Henshaw found this bird breeding at Inscription Rock in New Mexico, and he also met with it in Arizona, where, according to Dr. Coues, it is a rare summer visitor.

b'. *Subtus aut albidus aut vix flavicans.*

a''. *Supra umbrino-brunneus.*

2. Empidonax albigularis. (Tab. XL. fig. 2.)

Empidonax albigularis, Scl. & Salv. Ibis, 1859, p. 122[1]; P. Z. S. 1864, p. 360[2]; Salv. Ibis, 1874, p. 309[3]; Ridgw. Ibis, 1886, p. 463[4]; Man. N. Am. B. p. 340[5]; Scl. Cat. Birds Brit. Mus. xiv. p. 223[6].

Empidonax axillaris, Ridgw. in Baird, Brew., & Ridgw. N. Am. B. ii. p. 363[7].

Supra sordide olivaceo-brunneus; uropygio rufescente tincto; gutture albo; pectore et cervicis lateribus grisescenti-brunneis; ventre et crisso pallide flavis; alis et cauda fusco-nigricantibus, illis pallide brunneo bifasciatis, secundariis extus albido anguste limbatis; subalaribus ochraceis: rostri maxilla fusca, mandibula pallida; pedibus nigricantibus. Long. tota 4·75, alæ 2·3, caudæ 2·1, tarsi 0·6, rostri a rictu 0·6. (Descr. maris ex Dueñas, Guatemala. Mus. nostr.)

Hab. MEXICO, Acapulco and Dos Arroyos in Guerrero (*Mrs. H. H. Smith*), Huipulco (*Ferrari-Perez*), Orizaba (*Botteri*[6]), Jalapa (*M. Trujillo*); GUATEMALA, Dueñas (*O. S.*[1], *L. Fraser*), Coban (*O. S. & F. D. G.*); PANAMA (*M'Leannan*[2]).

This species was discovered by Salvin during his first expedition to Guatemala in 1858, when he obtained a single example near Dueñas at an elevation of about 5000 feet above the sea. Other specimens were subsequently secured at the same place, and also at Coban, but the bird is nowhere abundant.

Its northern range reaches to the Mexican State of Vera Cruz, whence specimens have been sent from several places, and also from the neighbourhood of the city of Mexico.

Southward we have no trace of it until we come to the Isthmus of Panama, where its presence is attested by a single specimen procured by the late James M'Leannan near Lion Hill Station.

b''. *Supra olivascens aut cinerascens.*

3. Empidonax acadicus.

Muscicapa acadica, Gm. Syst. Nat. i. p. 947[1].

Empidonax acadicus, Dresser, Ibis, 1865, p. 475[2]; Baird, Brew., & Ridgw. N. Am. B. ii. p. 374[3]; Sennett, Bull. U. S. Geol. Surv. v. p. 405[4]; Coues, Birds N. W. p. 249[5]; Key N. Am. B. ed. 2, p. 441[6]; Ridgw. Ibis, 1886, p. 465[7]; Man. N. Am. B. p. 342[8]; Scl. Cat. Birds Brit. Mus. xiv. p. 228[9].

Empidonax bairdi, Lawr. Ann. Lyc. N. Y. vii. p. 327 (nec Scl.)[10].

Empidonax griseigularis, Lawr. Ann. Lyc. N. Y. vii. p. 471[11].

Supra olivaceus; alis nigricantibus, tectricibus fulvo-albido late terminatis, fasciis duabus formantibus; secundariis extrorsum pallide olivaceo limbatis; cauda nigricanti-olivaceo vix limbata: subtus albus; pectore griseo; hypochondriis olivaceo lavatis; subalaribus pallide fulvis: rostri maxilla nigricante, mandibula pallida; pedibus obscure corylinis. Long. tota 5·0, alæ 2·7, caudæ 2·2, tarsi 0·5, rostri a rictu 0·6. (Descr. exempl. ex Insula Ruatan, Honduras. Mus. nostr.)

Hab. NORTH AMERICA, Middle and Eastern States.—MEXICO, Yucatan; HONDURAS,

Ruatan I. (*Gaumer*); Costa Rica (*Endres*); Panama (*M'Leannan* [10] [11]).—Ecuador; Cuba.

A species of the Eastern States of North America, whose southern migration in winter extends to Ecuador, and it is also found sparingly in the southern portion of Central America; it has been recorded from Yucatan, and we have received several specimens from the island of Ruatan, but its southern range does not appear to spread westwards into Mexico or Guatemala.

Its breeding-ground is certainly in the middle districts of the United States, but Mr. Dresser states that it is not uncommon in Texas in summer [2]. Its nest is described as made of strips of bark or stalks of weeds woven loosely together so as to make a very slight structure, so thin that the eggs may be seen from below. It is placed in the fork of a small branch from six to ten feet from the ground. The eggs are rich cream-colour with a reddish-brown shade, and marked irregularly at the larger end with vivid blotches of red and reddish brown.

4. Empidonax trailli.

Muscicapa trailli, Aud. Orn. Biogr. i. p. 236 [1]; B. Am. i. p. 234, t. 65 [2].

Empidonax trailli, Baird, B. N. Am. p. 193 [3]; Lawr. Ann. Lyc. N. Y. viii. p. 8 [4], ix. pp. 114 [5], 201 [6]; Coues, Birds N. W. p. 252 [7]; Scl. Cat. Birds Brit. Mus. xiv. p. 226 [8].

Empidonax trailli, var. *pusillus*, Henshaw, U. S. Geogr. Surv. West 100th Mer. v. p. 356 [9]; Lawr. Bull. U. S. Nat. Mus. no. 4, p. 27 [10]; Mem. Bost. Soc. N. H. ii. p. 287 [11].

Empidonax pusillus, var. *trailli*, Baird, Brew., & Ridgw. N. Am. B. ii. p. 369 [12].

Empidonax pusillus trailli, Ridgw. Ibis, 1886, p. 464 [13]; Man. N. Am. B. p. 343 [14].

Platyrhynchus pusillus, Sw. Phil. Mag. new ser. i. p. 366 (? ?) [15].

Empidonax pusillus, Baird, B. N. Am. p. 194 [16]; Sumichrast, Mem. Bost. Soc. N. H. i. p. 557 [17]; Baird, Brew., & Ridgw. N. Am. B. ii. p. 366 [18]; Nutting & Ridgw. Pr. U. S. Nat. Mus. vi. p. 384 [19]; Scl. Cat. Birds Brit. Mus. xiv. p. 225 [20].

E. acadico similis, sed supra magis fuscus et alarum fasciis fuscescentioribus: subtus quoque grisescentior, cauda æquali fere rotundata.

Hab. North America generally, from Sitka southwards.—Mexico, Mazatlan (*Grayson* [11]), Sierra Madre above Ciudad Victoria in Tamaulipas, Vera Cruz (*Richardson*), Orizaba (*Sumichrast* [17]), Tehuantepec citry (*Sumichrast* [10]), Merida in Yucatan (*Schott* [6]); Guatemala, San José de Guatemala (*O. S.*); Costa Rica, Dota (*Carmiol* [5]); Nicaragua, Sucuyá (*Nutting* [20]); Panama (*M'Leannan* [4]).—Ecuador.

We agree with Dr. Coues in considering Swainson's name *Tyrannula pusilla* of difficult, if not of impossible, application, and as the type is no longer extant, we see no hope of its being identified with certainty. It has usually been considered to refer to the species described and figured in the 'Fauna Boreali-Americana' under this name; but the original description was based upon a specimen from the "maritime parts of Mexico," and it is thus possible that the bird with its "even tail" we now know as *E. flaviventris* was that originally described by Swainson as *T. pusilla*, whereas the bird described and figured in the 'Fauna Boreali-Americana' with its emarginate tail was *E. minimus*! Under this uncertainty we think it much better to use Audubon's later name *E. trailli* for this species; and as we wholly fail to distinguish between the eastern and western races called *E. trailli* and *E. trailli pusillus* by recent American writers, we use the term *E. trailli* to include the whole series. As a rule it is a larger bird than *E. minimus*, and has the wing-bands of a brownish grey, the tail is even or slightly rounded, not emarginate as in *E. minimus*. *E. trailli* appears to be a very common bird during the summer months in North America; but we have not hitherto observed it in any numbers in Mexico or Central America, though specimens obtained as far south as Panama and even Ecuador seem referable to it.

Our Mexican localities for this species include places near the sea-level and up to an elevation of 4000 or 5000 feet above the sea; but Sumichrast says it is a bird of the temperate region, where it is resident, being common around Orizaba in June and July [17]. The eggs of *E. trailli* are creamy white spotted with deep rusty brown.

5. **Empidonax minimus.**

Tyrannula minima, W. M. & S. F. Baird, Pr. Ac. Phil. 1843, p. 284 [1].

Empidonax minimus, Baird, Mex. Bound. Surv., Zool., Birds, p. 9 [2]; B. N. Am. p. 193 [3]; Scl. P. Z. S. 1859, p. 384 [4]; Cat. Birds Brit. Mus. xiv. p. 227 [5]; Scl. & Salv. Ibis, 1859, p. 122 [6]; P. Z. S. 1870, p. 837 [7]; Dresser, Ibis, 1865, p. 474 [8]; Baird, Brew., & Ridgw. N. Am. B. ii. p. 372 [9]; Lawr. Bull. U. S. Nat. Mus. no. 4, p. 27 [10]; Sennett, Bull. U. S. Geol. Surv. v. p. 405 [11]; Coues, Birds N. W. p. 254 [12]; Key N. Am. B. ed. 2, p. 442 [13]; Ridgw. Ibis, 1886, p. 465 [14]; Man. N. Am. B. p. 343 [15].

Tyrannula pusilla, Sw. Faun. Bor.-Am. ii. p. 144, t. 46 [16]?

Empidonax pectoralis, Lawr. Ann. Lyc. N. Y. viii. p. 402 [17].

Empidonax gracilis, Ridgw. Pr. Biol. Soc. Wash. iii. p. 23 [18]; Pr. U. S. Nat. Mus. viii. p. 571 [19].

Præcedenti similis et vix diversus, sed paulo minor, fasciis alarum albicantioribus et cauda sensim furcata distinguendus.

Hab. EASTERN NORTH AMERICA.—MEXICO (*Boucard*), Sierra Madre above Ciudad Victoria, Xicotencal and Tampico in Tamaulipas, Aguas Calientes and Plains of San Luis Potosi (*W. B. Richardson*), Venta de Zopilote, Acaguasotla, Tepetlapa, Rincon and Tierra Colorada in Guerrero (*Mrs. H. H. Smith*), Orizaba (*Botteri, F. D. G.*), Atoyac (*Mrs. H. H. Smith*), Vera Cruz (*F. D. G., Richardson*), Playa Vicente (*Boucard* [4]), Chihuitan, Sta. Efigenia, Tapana, Guichicovi, Gineta Mts. (*Sumichrast* [10]), Peto in Yucatan (*G. F. Gaumer*), Merida, Tabi (*F. D. G.*), Holbox Mujeres and Cozumel Is. (*G. F. Gaumer*); BRITISH HONDURAS, Orange Walk (*G. F. Gaumer*), Belize (*O. S.* [6]); GUATEMALA, Coban, Dueñas [6], Escuintla, Retalhuleu (*O. S. & F. D. G.*); HONDURAS, San Pedro (*G. M. Whitely* [7]); PANAMA (*M'Leannan* [17]).

It is exceedingly difficult from skins always to distinguish this species from *E. trailli*. Though the characters are laid down with considerable precision by the most recent writers on the subject, experience shows that they cannot always be depended upon to discriminate every individual. A hundred and odd specimens before us conform fairly to the characters of this bird as given above, but we notice slight differences in coloration which we believe to be due to differences of season : thus birds shot in Central America in early spring agree fairly well with North-American examples killed during the breeding-season, but autumn birds have greyer throats and more distinctly yellow bellies. The slightly forked tail of *E. minimus* seems to be the best character by which to distinguish it from *E. trailli,* and in naming our series from Mexico and Central America we have been governed by it rather than by measurement and slight modifications of colour. The difference in the colour of the eggs of *E. minimus*, which are spotless buffy white, and those of *E. trailli,* which are spotted with deep rusty brown, at once shows that the two birds are really quite distinct.

E. minimus enjoys a wide range throughout Eastern Mexico and Central America in the winter months, but it appears to be absent from Western Mexico and the central plateau, and only crosses to the Pacific coast at the Isthmus of Tehuantepec. In Guatemala it occurs on both sides of the cordillera and in the mountains up to an elevation of 5000 or 6000 feet. At higher altitudes in the Volcan de Fuego its place is taken by *E. hammondi.*

c'. *Subtus flavus.*

6. Empidonax flaviventris.

Tyrannula flaviventris, W. M. & S. F. Baird, Pr. Ac. Phil. 1843, p. 283 [1].

Empidonax flaviventris, Baird, B. N. Am. p. 198 [2]; Scl. P. Z. S. 1859, p. 366 [3]; Cat. Birds Brit. Mus. xiv. p. 230 [4]; Scl. & Salv. Ibis, 1859, p. 122 [5]; P. Z. S. 1864, p. 360 [6], 1870, p. 837 [7]; Lawr. Ann. Lyc. N. Y. viii. p. 8 [8], ix. p. 114 [9]; Bull. U. S. Nat. Mus. no. 4, p. 27 [10]; Sumichrast, Mem. Bost. Soc. N. H. i. p. 557 [11]; Baird, Brew., & Ridgw. N. Am. B. ii. p. 378 [12]; Salv. P. Z. S. 1870, p. 199 [13]; Coues, Birds N. W. p. 255 [14]; Key N. Am. B. ed. 2, p. 442 [15]; Nutting & Ridgw. Pr. U. S. Nat. Mus. vi. p. 384 [16]; Ridgw. Ibis, 1886, p. 466 [17]; Man. N. Am. B. p. 341 [18].

Tyrannula ——?, Scl. P. Z. S. 1856, p. 296, no. 107 [19].

Supra olivaceus; capite summo vix obscuriore; alis nigricantibus, tectricibus flavo-albido late terminatis fasciis duabus formantibus, secundariis internis late reliquis anguste extrorsum flavo-albido limbatis; oculorum ambitu pallide flavido: subtus flavus; pectore et hypochondriis olivaceo limbatis; subalaribus flavidis: rostri maxilla nigricante, mandibula flava; pedibus nigricantibus. Long. tota 4·5, alæ 2·6, caudæ 2·0, tarsi 0·7, rostri a rictu 0·6. (Descr. maris ex Jalapa, Mexico. Mus. nostr.)

Hab. EASTERN NORTH AMERICA.—MEXICO, Sierra Madre above Ciudad Victoria and Xicotencal in Tamaulipas (*W. B. Richardson*), State of Vera Cruz (*Sumichrast* [11]), Colipa (*F. D. G.*), Jalapa (*de Oca* [3], *M. Trujillo*), Cordova (*Sallé* [19]), Teapa in Tabasco (*Mrs. H. H. Smith*), Guichicovi, Sta. Efigenia (*Sumichrast* [10]); GUATEMALA (*Skinner* [5]), Choctum, Coban, Dueñas, Retalhuleu (*O. S. & F. D. G.*); HONDURAS, San Pedro (*G. M. Whitely* [7]); NICARAGUA, Sucuyá (*Nutting* [16]); COSTA RICA, Angostura, Grecia[9] (*Carmiol*), Navarro (*Cooper*[9]); PANAMA, Vibalá, Chiriqui, Calove-vora[13] (*Arcé*), Lion-Hill Station (*M'Leannan*[6 8]).

E. flaviventris is the sole representative in Eastern North America of the yellow-bellied section of the genus, and it is the only one which has the wing-bands rather conspicuously of a yellowish white; those of the allied forms being more or less tinged with grey or buff. The under surface, too, is of a brighter paler yellow, and the under wing-coverts are pale yellow rather than buff.

In our country it is most probably a migratory species, breeding in the Northern United States, and still further north, occurring even in Greenland, and passing in autumn and spring along the eastern flank of the mountains of Mexico, thence through Guatemala generally, and southwards as far as the State of Panama. So far as the evidence before us goes it is absent from Central and Western Mexico, but it appears on the shores of the Pacific at Tehuantepec.

Its nest is placed in clefts of old stumps or logs or similar situations, and is bulky, being composed of mosses &c. The eggs are buffy white or pale buff, speckled, chiefly round the larger end, with rusty brown or cinnamon.

7. Empidonax bairdi.

Empidonax bairdi, Scl. P. Z. S. 1858, p. 301[1]; Cat. Birds Brit. Mus. xiv. p. 230[2]; Baird, Brew., & Ridgw. N. Am. B. ii. p. 363[3]; Ridgw. Ibis, 1886, p. 466[4]; Man. N. Am. B. p. 341[5].

Empidonax difficilis, Baird, B. N. Am. p. 198, t. 76. f. 2[6]; Ridgw. Ibis, 1886, p. 466[7]; Man. N. Am. B. p. 340[8]; Scl. Cat. Birds Brit. Mus. xiv. p. 229[9].

Empidonax flaviventris, var. *difficilis*, Baird, Brew., & Ridgw. N. Am. B. ii. p. 380[10]; Henshaw, U. S. Geogr. Surv. West of 100th Mer. v. p. 359[11]; Lawr. Mem. Bost. Soc. N. H. ii. p. 287[12].

Supra olivaceus; alis nigricantibus, tectricibus ochrescenti-flavis, secundariis eodem colore limbatis; cauda fusco-nigricante, ochraceo vix limbata; oculorum ambitu pallide flavo: subtus pallide ochraceo-flavidus; pectore ochraceo-olivaceo: rostri maxilla nigricante, mandibula flavida. Long. tota 5·0, alæ 2·7, caudæ 2·3, tarsi 0·7, rostri a rictu 0·6. (Descr. maris ex Presidio, Mexico. Mus. nostr.)

Hab. NORTH AMERICA, Western United States from Sitka southwards[8].—MEXICO, Yecara in Sonora (*Lloyd*), Mazatlan, Tres Marias Is. (*Grayson*[12], *Forrer*), Plains of Colima (*Xantus*[12]), Amula, Omilteme, Venta del Peregrino, Venta de Camaron, Tepetlapa, and Dos Arroyos in Guerrero (*Mrs. H. H. Smith*), Sierra de San Luis Potosi (*Richardson*), Coapa, Chimalpa, Cuajimalpa (*Ferrari-Perez*), Amecameca, El Pinal near Puebla, Jalapa (*F. D. G.*), Cordova (*Sallé*[1]).

According to Mr. Ridgway's key of the genus *Empidonax* the bird called *E. bairdi* falls into the section which has the under wing-coverts yellow like those of *E. flaviventris*; but from the specimens before us, from Mr. Sclater's collection, supplemented by others recently received from various parts of Mexico, we find that *E. bairdi* in this respect agrees with *E. difficilis*, and in fact is, in our opinion, undistinguishable from that species. It is true some specimens have the tips of the wing-coverts rather more ochraceous than others, but we are unable to trace anything like definite distinction between them. The range of the species, as a whole, is very extensive, and doubtless the northern birds occur only in the far north during the breeding-season; at the same time it is very probable that in the highlands of Mexico birds of this species are to be found throughout the year, their numbers receiving a large accession during the winter. It is certainly found in the tablelands of Mexico as late as the end of April.

The two names *E. bairdi* and *E. difficilis* were published apparently in the same year, 1858. Though the titlepage of Baird's 'Birds of North America' bears the date 1860, copies, we believe, were distributed in 1858, the date of the preface. Mr. Sclater's title *E. bairdi* appears in the 'Proceedings of the Zoological Society' for 1858, the paper containing the description having been read at a meeting held on 8th June. There can thus be but little doubt that the name *E. bairdi* has a slight priority over *E. difficilis*.

Grayson says this species is common on the Tres Marias Islands as well as at Tepic and Mazatlan [12]. All his specimens were obtained in the winter and spring months, so that he was not certain whether it remained throughout the summer. On the Tres Marias it frequented the thick forest beneath the foliage of the trees; it also might often be met with near some secluded and shady brook, from the surface of which it took its insect food.

The nest and eggs are described as resembling those of *E. flaviventris*.

8. Empidonax salvini.

Empidonax salvini, Ridgw. Ibis, 1886, pp. 459 [1], 467 [2]; Scl. Cat. Birds Brit. Mus. xiv. p. 231 [3].
Empidonax bairdi, Scl. & Salv. Ibis, 1860, p. 36 [4].

E. bairdi similis, sed supra paulo olivacior: subtus quoque pectore clare olivaceo distinguendus. (Descr. maris ex Calderas, Volcan de Fuego. Mus. nostr.)

♀ mari similis.

Hab. GUATEMALA, Coban (*Constantia* [4], *O S. & F. D. G.*), Choctum, Calderas, Volcan de Fuego, Volcan de Agua above San Diego (*O. S. & F. D. G.*); HONDURAS? (*Dyson*).

This is a species closely allied to *E. bairdi*, but may be distinguished by its rather brighter upper surface; the chest, too, is brighter olivaceous, and the throat and belly clearer yellow. Regarding the under wing-coverts we do not see much difference. When the axillary plumes overlie the coverts the latter appear to be yellow, but when the axillaries are raised the coverts are shown to be ochraceous.

E. salvini is by no means uncommon in the woods of the Volcanos of Agua and Fuego up to an elevation of 7000 or 8000 feet. It is also found in Alta Vera Paz, near Coban, and northwards in the direction of Choctum.

9. Empidonax flavescens.

Empidonax flavescens, Lawr. Ann. Lyc. N. Y. viii. p. 133 [1], ix. p. 115 [2]; Frantz. J. f. Orn. 1869,

10*

p. 308 [3]; Salv. P. Z. S. 1870, p. 199 [4]; Baird, Brew., & Ridgw. N. Am. B. ii. p. 363 [5]; Ridgw. Ibis, 1886, p. 467 [6]; Scl. Cat. Birds Brit. Mus. xiv. p. 231 [7].

Empidonax viridescens, Ridgw. Pr. U. S. Nat. Mus. vi. p. 413 [8].

Quam præcedentes pectore multo magis ochraceo.

Hab. Costa Rica, Barranca [1] [2], Dota Mountains, Grecia [2] (*Carmiol*), Quebrada Honda (v. *Frantzius* [2]), Irazu (*H. Rogers*); Panama, Volcan de Chiriqui [4], Calovevora [4] (*Arcé*).

This species seems fairly separable from the more northern *E. salvini* and *E. bairdi*, the most obvious character being the ochraceous tint on the chest. In some specimens the head and back are of a browner olive, but this is an evanescent character. Upon the specimens with the more olivaceous upper plumage Mr. Ridgway founded his *E. viridescens*, but with a typical specimen of *E. flavescens* before us, and others compared with the type of *E. viridescens*, we do not see how two Costa-Rican species can be established—some allowance must be made for age, season, &c.

b. *Rostrum angustulum.*

10. Empidonax hammondi.

Tyrannula hammondi, Xantus de Vesey, Pr. Ac. Phil. 1858, p. 117 [1].
Empidonax hammondi, Baird, B. N. Am. p. 199, t. 76. f. 1 [2]; Coues, Pr. Ac. Phil. 1866, p. 52 [3]; Birds N. W. p. 257 [4]; Key N. Am. B. ed. 2, p. 443 [5]; Sumichrast, Mem. Bost. Soc. N. H. i. p. 557 [6]; Baird, Brew., & Ridgw. N. Am. B. ii. p. 383 [7]; Henshaw, U. S. Geogr. Surv. West 100th Mer. v. p. 362 [8]; Lawr. Bull. U. S. Nat. Mus. no. 4, p. 27 [9]; Ridgw. Ibis, 1886, p. 467 [10]; Man. N. Am. B. p. 344 [11]; Scl. Cat. Birds Brit. Mus. xiv. p. 232 [12].

E. *obscuro* similis et forsan haud distinguendus, caudæ rectrice utrinque extima pogoniis ambobus fere unicoloribus. Long. tota 5·2, alæ 2·8, caudæ 2·3, tarsi 0·65, rostri a rictu 0·55. (Descr. exempl. ex Orizaba, Mexico. Mus. nostr.)

Hab. Western North America, from the Lesser Slave Lake southwards [11].—Mexico, Sierra de Valparaiso in Zacatecas (*Richardson*), State of Vera Cruz (*Sumichrast* [6]), Orizaba (*F. D. G*), Gineta Mountains (*Sumichrast* [9]); Guatemala, Calderas 7500 feet, Pine-forest of Volcan de Fuego, between 10,000 and 12,000 feet (*O. S. & F. D. G.*).

We are not at all sure that skins of this bird can always be distinguished from *E. obscurus*, the point chiefly relied upon lies in the colour of the outer web of the outermost tail-feather on either side, which in *E. hammondi* hardly differs from the inner web, but in *E. obscurus* is always whitish; moreover, *E. hammondi* is usually a smaller bird than *E. obscurus*. We find, however, small birds with the outer web of the tail-feather paler than the inner, so that it becomes very difficult to determine accurately every individual. *E. hammondi* has the long narrow bill of this section of *Empidonax*, so that we have little doubt that it is with *E. obscurus* that it should be compared, and this is the opinion of both Dr. Coues and Mr. Ridgway, though Mr. Henshaw considered that its affinity is with *E. minimus* [8].

We know very little of this bird in Mexico, but two specimens obtained in September in the Sierra de Valparaiso by Richardson and two by Godman at Orizaba in 1888 undoubtedly belong to it, also two examples from the upper portion of the Volcan de Fuego, in Guatemala, are inseparable from the Mexican birds *. One of these was obtained near Calderas, at au elevation of between 7000 and 8000 feet above the sea, the other in the upper pine-region which commences at a little over 10,000 feet and continues to the summit. According to Mr. Lawrence, specimens obtained by Sumichrast in the Gineta Mountains of the State of Chiapas are referable to this species [9].

The northern range of *E. hammondi* extends to the Lesser Slave Lake a little beyond the 49th parallel; thence it spreads over the intervening States to Arizona. It is, however, a summer visitor to the north, reaching Arizona in April and leaving again in October. Mr. Henshaw says it leaves the low country entirely in summer and retires to the mountains, where it may be met with in pine-woods or alders fringing some mountain-stream.

There seems to be some doubt about the nest and eggs of this species, as the latest authority on the subject, Mr. Ridgway, says they are like those of *E. minimus*, but qualifies his statement with a ?.

11. Empidonax obscurus.

Tyrannula obscura, Sw. Phil. Mag. new ser. i. p. 367 [1].

Empidonax obscurus, Baird, Mex. Bound. Surv., Zool., Birds, p. 9, t. 9. f. 3 [2]; B. N. Am. p. 200, t. 49. f. 3 [3]; Scl. P. Z. S. 1862, p. 19 [4]; Cat. Birds Brit. Mus. xiv. p. 232 [5]; Sumichrast, Mem. Bost. Soc. N. H. i. p. 557 [6]; Baird, Brew., & Ridgw. N. Am. B. ii. p. 381 [7]; Coues, B. N. W. p. 258 [8]; Key N. Am. B. ed. 2, p. 443 [9]; Henshaw, U. S. Geogr. Surv. West 100th Mer. v. p. 360 [10]; Ridgw. Ibis, 1886, p. 468 [11]; Man. N. Am. B. p. 344 [12].

Epidonax wrighti, Baird, B. N. Am. p. 200 [13].

Supra olivaceo-griseus; capite saturatiore; alis nigricantibus, tectricibus et secundariis internis sordide albo limbatis; cauda nigricante, rectrice extima utrinque in pogonio externo sordide alba: loris et gutture griseo-albidis; pectore pallide fusco; abdomine toto pallide flavicante: rostro corneo; pedibus nigricantibus. Long. tota 5·3, alæ 2·8, caudæ 2·6, tarsi 0·7, rostri a rictu 0·6. (Descr. maris ex Mexicalcingo, prope urbem Mexico. Mus. nostr.)

♀ mari similis.

Hab. NORTH AMERICA, Western United States from Rocky Mountains westward, south-wards from Nevada and Utah.—MEXICO (*Bullock* [1]), Micoba in Sonora (*Lloyd*), Amula and Omilteme in Guerrero (*Mrs. H. H. Smith*), Patzcuaro, Morelia (*F. D. G.*), Chimalpa, Coapa, Hacienda Eslava, Mexicalcingo, Tetelco, near city of Mexico (*Ferrari-Perez*), Amecameca, Alixco (*F. D. G.*), Villa de Etla, La Parada (*Boucard*), State of Vera Cruz (*Sumichrast* [6]).

Swainson's description of this species was based upon a specimen stated to have come from "Mexico." It is now known as a bird of the plateau, being common in the

---

* These birds are called *E. minimus* in Mr. Sclater's Cat. Birds Brit. Mus. xiv. p. 228.

environs of the city of Mexico and thence southwards to La Parada and the highlands of the State of Vera Cruz. Westwards of the plateau it is found near Patzcuaro and Morelia, and in the Sierra Madre of Sonora. It has also been found at El Paso, and thence northwards to Utah and Nevada, and also in most of the country lying to the westward of the Rocky Mountains. Dr. Coues speaks of *E. obscurus* as migratory in Arizona, arriving in March or April and leaving in October. Some further valuable notes on this bird will be found in his 'Birds of the North-West,' which we have no space to transcribe here. Mr. Henshaw says it is an abundant species in many localities in the middle and southern regions of the United States, though in others it appears to be absent. In summer it is a bird of the mountains, resorting to the deciduous trees and bushes on the banks of streams, or, as in Arizona, the oaks. In other places it is found in the barren pine-clad hills where there is no deciduous vegetation. In the autumn it leaves the hills and may be met with in its journey southwards wherever trees and bushes afford it suitable shelter [10].

The nest is placed in aspen bushes, and is, like that of *E. minimus*, compactly felted, cup-shaped, composed chiefly of greyish fibres, and placed in a fork of an upright branch of a bush or small tree. The eggs are plain buffy-white.

12. **Empidonax affinis.**

Tyrannula affinis, Sw. Phil. Mag. new ser. i. p. 367 [1].
Empidonax affinis, Salv. Cat. Strickl. Coll. p. 314 [2].
Empidonax fulvipectus, Lawr. Ann. Lyc. N. Y. x. p. 11 [3]; Salv. Ibis, 1874, p. 310 [4]; Baird, Brew.,
  & Ridgw. N. Am. B. ii. p. 310 [5]; Ibis, 1886, p. 468 [6]; Man. N. Am. B. p. 344 [7].

Præcedenti similis, sed omnino olivaceo, mento tantum albicante ; mandibula omnino flavida ut videtur distinguendus. Long. tota 5·2, alæ 3·0, caudæ 2·6, tarsi 0·7, rostri a rictu 0·55. (Descr. feminæ ex Ciudad in
 Durango. Mus. nostr.)
♂ feminæ similis.

Hab. MEXICO, Tutuaca in Sonora (*W. Lloyd*), Ciudad in Durango (*Forrer*), Sierra de
 Valparaiso de Zacatecas (*Richardson*), Amula, Omilteme, and Tepetlapa in Guerrero
 (*Mrs. H. H. Smith*), city of Mexico (*fide Lawrence* [3]), Chimalpa, Hacienda Eslava near
 city of Mexico (*Ferrari-Perez*), La Parada (*Boucard*), Cinco Señores (*Galeotti* [2]).

Swainson's name *Tyrannula affinis* was given to a bird in Bullock's collection, stated to have been obtained in the "maritime parts of Mexico." Various attempts to recognize this name have been made. Mr. Sclater, in 1859, thought it possible that it might refer to the bird he was then describing as *Mitrephorus phæocercus*; and, in 1866 (Proc. Ac. Phil.), Dr. Coues thought that his *M. pallescens* was perhaps meant. It was not until 1882 that Salvin examined Swainson's type and identified thereby a specimen from Cinco Señores in Mexico in the Strickland collection at Cambridge, and referred to it Mr. Lawrence's *E. fulvipectus*. We have since compared the Strickland bird with a specimen compared with Mr. Lawrence's type, so that our identification of *E. fulvipectus* is hardly open to question. Unfortunately this identification has been entirely overlooked by subsequent writers. Mr. Ridgway makes no reference to *Tyrannula affinis*, and the name does not appear in Mr. Sclater's recently published catalogue.

The latter author, though he otherwise adopts, almost in its entirety, Mr. Ridgway's classification of *Empidonax*, does not admit the distinctness of *E. fulvipectus*, Lawr., from *E. obscurus*. But with a more extensive series before us we have little difficulty in separating them by the characters pointed out above.

E. affinis occurs throughout the valley of Mexico, together with *E. obscurus* and the species next described as *E. canescens*, all of them being equally common. It also occurs with *E. obscurus* at La Parada, in the Sierra Madre del Sur, and northwards in the Sierra Madre of Durango and Sonora. Whether the three birds occupy different areas in the breeding-season remains to be proved.

13. **Empidonax canescens**, sp. n.

E. obscuro quoque affinis, sed corpore supra multo magis griseo, dorso vix olivaceo tincto: subtus usque ad pectus griseus, gutture medio albicante, abdomine albicante flavo vix lavato: rostro angusto elongato, mandibula ad basin pallida. Long. tota 5·8, alæ 3·1, caudæ 2·6, tarsi 0·7, rostri a rictu 0·7. (Descr. maris ex Mexicalcingo prope urbem Mexico. Mus. nostr.)

♀ mari similis.

Hab. Mexico, Ixtapalapa, Culhuacan, Huipulco, Coapa, Mexicalcingo, and Chimalpa, near city of Mexico (*Ferrari-Perez*).

In Prof. Ferrari-Perez's collection of birds made during the winter and spring months of 1887–88 are many specimens of this species, all taken in the valley of Mexico and the surrounding hills. Compared with *E. obscurus* and *E. affinis* it is a much greyer bird, with a longer narrower bill. Two specimens, in ragged plumage, *q* and *r* of Mr. Sclater's Catalogue, and there considered young birds of *E. obscurus*, belong to this species.

B. *Pileus niger.*

14. **Empidonax atriceps.** (Tab. XL. fig. 3.)

Empidonax atriceps, Salv. P. Z. S. 1870, p. 198 [1]; Ridgw. Pr. U. S. Nat. Mus. vi. p. 413 [2].

Mitrephanes atriceps, Ridgw. Ibis, 1886, p. 461 [3]; Scl. Cat. Birds Brit. Mus. xiv. p. 220 [4].

Supra fuscus; uropygio et collo postico paulo dilutioribus; pileo toto nigro; alis et cauda nigricanti-fuscis, secundariis et tectricibus alarum majoribus sordide albo marginatis; rectricibus utrinque extimis extrorsum albo limbatis: subtus ochraceo-fuscus; gula et ventre imo albicantibus; loris et macula postoculari albidis; campterio et subalaribus sordide albis: rostri maxilla nigra, mandibula flava; pedibus nigris. Long. tota 4·5, alæ 2·3, caudæ 2·0, tarsi 0·6. (Descr. exempl. typ. ex Volcan de Chiriqui. Mus. nostr.)

Hab. Costa Rica, Irazu (*Rogers* [4]), Pirris (*J. Cooper* [3]); Panama, Volcan de Chiriqui (*Arcé* [1]).

This very distinct species was discovered by our collector Arcé on the southern slope of the Volcan de Chiriqui, and it has since been found in Costa Rica.

Mr. Ridgway, followed by Mr. Sclater, places *E. atriceps* in the genus *Mitrephanes*, but we still think it fits much better in *Empidonax*. It has no crest, the tail is not elongated, the outer web of the external rectrices is white, and its general coloration are all points wherein it differs from *Mitrephanes phæocercus*, the type of *Mitrephanes*.

CONTOPUS.

Contopus, Cabanis, J. f. Orn. 1855, p. 479 (type *Muscicapa virens*, Linn.); Scl. Cat. Birds Brit. Mus. xiv. p. 234.

Nuttallornis, Ridgway, Man. N. Am. B. p. 337 (type *Tyrannus borealis*, Sw.).

This is also one of the obscure genera of Tyrannidæ, some of the species of the *C. virens* group being exceedingly difficult to define.   Others, again, are well-marked and easily distinguished.   Mr. Sclater recognizes nine species of *Contopus*, but there are several others the status of which he was unable to establish.

In our region we find eight species, whereof three are migratory, spending their breeding-season in North America.

The type of *Contopus* (*C. virens*) is very like several species of *Empidonax*, but larger and always to be distinguished by its proportionally shorter tarsi.   The form of the bill, the supranasal feathers, &c. are much the same in both genera, as are also the proportions of the wings and tail.

C. borealis departs from the type in being a larger, stouter bird, with a much stouter bill and shorter tail.   *C. musicus* is also different in other ways, the tail being long and somewhat forked.   Both these sections are also marked by having a large white patch on the flanks on either side, but this is also present in a less degree in *C. virens*.

a. *Species majores.*

a'. *Abdomen in medio album.*

1. **Contopus borealis.**

Tyrannus borealis, Sw. Faun. Bor.-Am. ii. p. 141, t. 35 [1]; Salv. Ibis, 1866, p. 203 [2].

Contopus borealis, Baird, B. N. Am. p. 188 [3]; Lawr. Ann. Lyc. N. Y. ix. p. 115 [4]; Bull. U. S. Nat. Mus. no. 4, p. 27 [5]; Salv. P. Z. S. 1870, p. 199 [6]; Baird, Brew., & Ridgw. N. Am. B. ii. p. 353 [7]; Coues, Birds N. W. p. 243 [8]; Key N. Am. B. ed. 2, p. 438 [9]; Perez, Bull. U. S. Nat. Mus. ix. p. 156 [10]; Tacz. Orn. Pér. ii. p. 316 [11]; Ridgw. Man. N. Am. B. p. 337 [12]; Scl. Cat. Birds Brit. Mus. xiv. p. 234 [13].

Muscicapa cooperi, Nutt. Man. i. p. 282 [14].

Tyrannus cooperi, Scl. P. Z. S. 1856, p. 297 [15].

Contopus cooperi, Cab. J. f. Orn. 1861, p. 248 [16].

Muscicapa mesoleuca, Licht. Preis-Verz. mex. Vög. p. 2 (cf. J. f. Orn. 1863, p. 58) ? [17].

Contopus mesoleucus, Scl. P. Z. S. 1859, p. 43 [18]; Scl. & Salv. Ibis, 1859, p. 122 [19]; Sumichrast, Mem. Bost. Soc. N. H. i. p. 557 [20].

Supra brunneo-ardesiacus; capite obscuriore; alis et cauda nigricantibus; alarum tectricibus pallide fusco terminatis, secundariis internis extrorsum albido limbatis: subtus medialiter albus; abdomine vix flavo tincto; hypochondriis plaga magna alba notatis: rostri maxilla nigricante, mandibula flava; pedibus nigris.

Long. tota 7·0, alæ 4·4, caudæ rect. med. 2·5, rect. lat. 2·85, tarsi 0·6, rostri a rictu 0·95. (Descr. maris ex Sierra Madre, Tamaulipas, Mexico. Mus. nostr.)

Hab. NORTH AMERICA, from Canada southwards.—MEXICO, Rio de Papagaio in Guerrero (*Mrs. H. H. Smith*), Hacienda de las Escobas (*F. B. Armstrong*), Sierra Madre above Ciudad Victoria (*W. B. Richardson*), State of Vera Cruz (*Sumichrast* [20]), Cuesta de Misantla (*M. Trujillo*), Orizaba (*Botteri* [18]), Cordova (*Sallé* [15]), La Parada (*Boucard*), Cacoprieto (*Sumichrast* [5]); GUATEMALA (*Skinner* [19]), Coban, Dueñas (*O. S. & F. D. G.*); COSTA RICA (*Hoffmann* [16]), Irazu (*Rogers*); PANAMA, Calobre [6] (*Arcé*).—COLOMBIA; PERU [11].

It is possible that Lichtenstein's *Muscicapa mesoleuca*, described as "*Graugrünlich, mit weisslicher Kehle und dergl. Bauch,*" is meant for this species; and, if so, the name has one year's priority over Swainson's *Tyrannus borealis*. But, though the specific name is suggestive, the description is very meagre, so that we are not disposed to displace the specific name *borealis* in favour of *mesoleucus* * for this *Contopus*. Mr. Sclater's use of the same name in 1859 was made without reference to Lichtenstein's prior application of it. *Contopus mesoleucus* of the later author is certainly a synonym of *C. borealis*.

Though this species is rare in the Atlantic States of North America, it enjoys a wide summer range in the northern districts from Massachusetts westwards, and throughout the South-western States to the Mexican border. We have no record of it along the western slope of the Mexican cordillera north of the State of Guerrero nor on the plateau, but it is found abundantly on the flank of the mountains facing the Atlantic, and thence southwards to the Pacific on the Isthmus of Tehuantepec. In Guatemala it occurs in the mountainous parts, and in similar districts of Costa Rica and the State of Panama, and also in South America as far as Northern Peru. The nest of *C. borealis* is usually placed near the extremity of a horizontal branch of a pine or other tree, and is composed of strips of bark, roots, mosses, &c. loosely put together to form a shallow structure. The eggs are creamy buff, spotted, usually in a more or less distinct ring around the larger end, with deep rusty brown or chestnut and purplish grey.

b'. *Abdomen in medio haud album haud ochraceum.*

2. Contopus musicus.

Tyrannula musica, Sw. Phil. Mag. new ser. i. p. 368 [1].
Contopus pertinax, Cab. & Heine, Mus. Hein. ii. p. 72 [2]; Scl. Cat. Am. B. p. 231 [3]; Cat. Birds Brit. Mus. xiv. p. 235 [4]; Salv. Ibis, 1866, p. 203 [5]; Cat. Strickl. Coll. p. 314 [6]; Sumichrast, Mem. Bost. Soc. N. H. i. p. 557 [7]; Baird, Brew., & Ridgw. N. Am. B. ii. p. 356 [8]; Henshaw, Rep. Geogr. Surv. West 100th Mer. v. p. 351 [9]; Lawr. Mem. Bost. Soc. N. H. ii. p. 287 [10]; Bull. U. S. Nat. Mus. no. 4, p. 27 [11]; Coues, Key N. Am. B. ed. 2, p. 439 [12]; F.-Perez, Pr. U. S. Nat. Mus. ix. p. 155 [13]; Ridgw. Man. N. Am. B. p. 337 [14].

---

* *Elainea mesoleuca*, Licht. Nomencl. p. 17; Cab. & Heine, Mus. Hein. ii. p. 60, from Montevideo, may also possibly refer to the same bird, wrongly attributed to Mexico. In Lichtenstein's 'Nomenclator' *Contopus borealis* is called *Myiarchus villicus*.

Contopus borealis, Scl. P. Z. S. 1858, p. 301 [15], 1859, pp. 44 [16], 366 [17], 384 [18]; Scl. & Salv. Ibis, 1859, p. 122 [19].

Supra griseo-olivaceus; pileo obscuriore; alis et cauda fusco-nigricantibus, illarum tectricibus et secundariis pallide fusco obscure limbatis; remige primo in pogonio externo albo marginato: subtus sordide olivaceo-grisescens; gula pallidiore; abdomine medio fulvescente, lateribus plaga magna alba celata ornatis: rostri maxilla fusca, mandibula flava; pedibus obscure corylinis. Long. tota 8·0, alæ 4·3, caudæ rect. med. 3·4, rect. lat. 3·7, tarsi 0·7, rostri a rictu 0·9. (Descr. exempl. ex Jalapa, Mexico. Mus. nostr.)

Av. juv. obscurior, tectricibus et secundariis alarum fulvo conspicue limbatis.

Hab. NORTH AMERICA, Southern Arizona [8] *.—MEXICO (*Bullock* [1]), Sierra Madre of Sonora and Chihuahua, Rio Verde, Yecera, Tutuaca (*W. Lloyd*), Ciudad in Durango (*Forrer*), Mazatlan and Tepic (*Grayson* [10]), Plains of Colima (*Xantus* [10]), Omilteme, Chilpancingo, Amula and Rincon in Guerrero (*Mrs. H. H. Smith*), Chimalpa, Ixtapalapa, Tetelco (*Ferrari-Perez*), Chietla and Actopam (*Ferrari-Perez* [13]), State of Vera Cruz (*Sumichrast* [7]), Jalapa [2] (*de Oca* [17], *Höge, M. Trujillo*), Cofre de Perote (*M. Trujillo*), Parada [15], Cinco Señores [18] (*Boucard*), Sta. Gertrudis (*Galeotti* [6]), Gineta Mts. (*Sumichrast* [11]); BRITISH HONDURAS, Southern Pine Ridge near Cayo (*Blancaneaux*); GUATEMALA (*Skinner* [19]), Volcan de Fuego [3], Volcan de Agua (*O. S. & F. D. G.* [4]).

The birds from the Sierra Madre of North-Western Mexico, including those from Southern Arizona belonging to the same mountain-system, are of a greyer cast of plumage than the typical form of *Contopus pertinax* from Jalapa, those of the valley of Mexico agreeing with the northern rather than with the eastern type. The bird of Guatemala appears to be of a browner colour on the upper plumage and not so grey as that of the Western Sierra Madre; but it differs little, except in being rather small, from the Jalapa bird. Moreover the differences appear to be to some extent due to season and age, the young individuals being darker and browner than the old ones. This is especially to be noticed in Mrs. Smith's specimens from the Sierra Madre del Sur in Guerrero; the older birds resemble those of the valley of Mexico, the younger ones those of the Eastern Sierras. Perhaps the most distinct of these forms is that found in Guatemala, the bird of the State of Vera Cruz being intermediate, but we see no sufficient grounds for giving any of them separate names.

It is probable that only in the northern and higher portion of its range this species is migratory. It certainly breeds in Arizona, the Sierras of Durango, Cofre de Perote, &c., and also in Guatemala, as specimens before us were shot in September, at which time birds were still in the Sierras of Arizona.

There can be little doubt that Swainson's name *Tyrannula musica* is applicable to this bird and has many years' priority over *Contopus pertinax* of Cabanis and Heine. Unfortunately the former title has been entirely overlooked since it was published, so that the latter has come into general use. We believe *C. musicus* to be strictly applicable to the bird of the tablelands and thence northwards to Arizona. If separ-

---

* Capt. P. M. Thorne (Auk, 1887, p. 264) records a single specimen from Colorado.

able the Jalapa bird should be called *C. pertinax*, and on the American system of nomenclature a basis for a trinomial can be found for the latter if required.

Though, generally speaking, a bird of the upland regions of the countries where it is found, *C. musicus* is not strictly confined to such districts, for Grayson met with it at all seasons near Mazatlan and at Tepic. In Guatemala it usually frequents the second-growth woods at an elevation of 4000 to 6000 feet above the sea, and here it is not an uncommon bird at all seasons of the year.

In Arizona Mr. H. W. Henshaw met with this species in abundance from July to September, young birds being well fledged by the middle of the former month, so that the eggs must have been laid early in June. He gives a full account of the habits of the species as observed by him in Arizona; but he appears to have reached that country too late in the season to find it in the early stages of its breeding, and neither nest nor eggs have yet been discovered. Its chief resort is amongst the pine-woods and oaks at a lower elevation.

3. **Contopus lugubris.**

Contopus lugubris, Lawr. Ann. Lyc. N. Y. viii. p. 134[1], ix. p. 115[2]; Frantz. J. f. Orn. 1869, p. 308[3]; Baird, Brew., & Ridgw. N. Am. B. ii. p. 351[4]; Salv. Ibis, 1874, p. 310[5]; Scl. Cat. Birds Brit. Mus. xiv. p. 236[6].

C. musico similis, sed valde minor et omnino obscurior.

Hab. COSTA RICA, Barranca[1], Birris, and Dota (*Carmiol*[2]); PANAMA, Chiriqui (*Arcé*[6]).

Our single specimen of this species agrees closely with Mr. Lawrence's type, being only slightly smaller; its darker plumage is due to its feathers being more freshly moulted. This is but a small dark form of *C. musicus*, probably restricted in its range to the mountain-system of Costa Rica and the State of Panama. Its isolation no doubt renders its recognition certain.

4. **Contopus ardesiacus.**

Tyrannula ardosiaca, Lafr. Rev. Zool. 1844, p. 80[1].
Sayornis ardosiacus, Cassin, Pr. Ac. Phil. 1860, p. 144[2].
Contopus ardesiacus, Scl. & Salv. P. Z. S. 1879, pp. 515[3], 615[4]; Tacz. Orn. Pér. ii. p. 317[5]; Scl. Cat. Birds Brit. Mus. xiv. p. 237[6].

Supra ardesiacus, capite nigricantiore; alis et cauda nigricantibus: subtus pallidior: rostri maxilla nigricante, mandibula cornea; pedibus nigris. Long. tota 6·5, alæ 3·5, caudæ rect. med. 2·8, rect. lat. 3·1, tarsi 0·6, rostri a rictu 0·85. (Descr. maris ex Santa Elena, Colombia. Mus. nostr.)

Hab. PANAMA, Truando (*Wood*[2]).—SOUTH AMERICA, from Colombia[1][3] to Bolivia[4], Venezuela[6] and Guiana[6].

This species just comes within our limits, as it was met with at the falls of the Truando river by Mr. C. J. Wood, who accompanied Lieut. Michler's exploring expedition. He observed a pair about some rocks at the foot of the mountains on the Truando. Its notes were very pleasing and almost formed a continued song.

11*

Stolzmann observed this bird on trees in the forests of Palto in Peru, and it was not rare at Tambillo [5]. It lives at elevations between 6000 and 9000 feet above the sea.

In British Guiana Whitely met with it at Roraima and one of the neighbouring mountains at an elevation of about 3500 feet.

c'. Abdomen omnino ochraceum.

5. Contopus ochraceus. (Tab. XXXVIII. fig. 2.)

Contopus ochraceus, Scl. & Salv. P. Z. S. 1869, p. 419 [1]; Salv. Ibis, 1870, p. 115 [2], 1874, p. 313 [3]; Ridgw. Ibis, 1883, p. 401 [4]; Scl. Cat. Birds Brit. Mus. xiv. p. 237 [5].

Supra olivaceus, pileo obscuriore; alis caudaque nigricantibus, secundariis et tectricibus ularum ochraceo late marginatis: subtus ochraceus, in ventre medio clarior, mentum versus obscurior: rostri maxilla nigra, mandibula flava; pedibus nigris. Long. tota 6·5, alæ 3·3, caudæ 2·9, tarsi 0·6, rostri a rictu 0·9, (Descr. exempl. typ. ex Costa Rica. Mus. nostr.)

Hab. COSTA RICA (Carmiol [1]).

The single specimen which we now figure was sent us from Costa Rica by Carmiol and described in 1869, and is, we believe, still the only one known.

The species is a very distinct one without near allies and may at once be recognized by the yellowish-ochre colour of its under plumage.

b. Species minores.

6. Contopus virens.

Muscicapa virens, Linn. Syst. Nat. i. p. 327 [1]; Licht. Preis-Verz. mex. Vög. p. 2 (cf. J. f. Orn. 1863, p. 58) [2].

Contopus virens, Baird, B. N. Am. p. 190 [3]; Scl. & Salv. Ibis, 1859, p. 122 (?) [4]; P. Z. S. 1870, p. 837 [5]; Cab. J. f. Orn. 1861, p. 248 [6]; Lawr. Ann. Lyc. N. Y. ix. p. 115 [7]; Bull. U. S. Nat. Mus. no. 4, p. 27 [8]; Sumichrast, Mem. Bost. Soc. N. H. i. p. 557 [8]; Baird, Brew., & Ridgw. N. Am. B. ii. p. 357 [10]; Sennett, Bull. U. S. Geol. Surv. iv. p. 33 [11], v. p. 405 [12]; Coues, Key N. Am. B. ed. 2, p. 439 [13]; Ridgw. Man. N. Am. B. p. 338 [14]; Scl. Cat. Birds Brit. Mus. xiv. p. 238 [15]; Gundl. Orn. Cab. p. 75 [16].

Contopus albicollis, Lawr. Ann. N. Y. Ac. Sc. iii. p. 156 [17]; Ridgw. Man. N. Am. B. p. 338 [18].

Supra olivaceo-brunneus, capite obscuriore; supracaudalibus fuscescentibus; alis et cauda nigricantibus, alarum tectricibus fusco limbatis, secundariorum marginibus albidis: subtus cervicis et pectoris lateribus et hypochondriis fuscis; gutture et abdomine medio albicantibus, hoc sulphureo lavato: rostri maxilla fusca, mandibula flavida; pedibus nigris. Long. tota 5·7, alæ 3·3, caudæ 2·5, tarsi 0·5, rostri a rictu 0·6. (Descr. maris ex San Augustin, Nuevo Leon. Mus. nostr.)

Hab. EASTERN NORTH AMERICA, from Canada southward, westward to the great plains [10] [14], Texas [11] [12].—MEXICO, Vaqueria, San Agustin and San Antonio in Nuevo Leon (F. B. Armstrong), State of Vera Cruz (Sumichrast [9]), Tapana (Sumichrast [8]), Cozumel I. (Gaumer); HONDURAS, Ruatan I. (Gaumer [16]), San Pedro (G. M. Whitely [5]); COSTA RICA (Hoffmann [6] [7]).—COLOMBIA and ECUADOR; CUBA [16].

This is a bird of the Eastern States of North America, where it abounds in many parts during the breeding-season. The line of its southern migration does not appear quite clear. We certainly find it in the North Mexican State of Nuevo Leon and again on the islands of Cozumel and Ruatan and on the mainland of Honduras, but we have not met with it again till we come to Santa Marta in Colombia, where Mr. Simons obtained a bird undoubtedly of this species in 1879; thence it passes into Ecuador. It will be noticed that we have not included Guatemala or Panama as within the winter range of this bird, though specimens from those countries, which we now believe to belong rather to *C. richardsoni*, have been assigned by Mr. Sclater to *C. virens*. We think on the whole they are best placed here. Other Mexican localities are inserted on the authority of Sumichrast's specimens [8][9]; and as regards Costa Rica, Hoffmann's example, as determined by Prof. Cabanis [6], is the only record we have of its occurrence there.

The habits of *Contopus virens* are fully given by American authors, with whom it is a very familiar bird. Its nest is described as a beautiful saucer-shaped structure, covered exteriorly with green and grey lichens, and usually secured to a thick horizontal branch of a tree. The eggs are pale creamy buff or creamy white, spotted, generally in a ring round the larger end, with rich madder-brown and lilac-grey.

7. Contopus richardsoni.

Tyrannula richardsoni, Sw. Faun. Bor.-Am. ii. p. 146, t. 46 [1]; Salv. Ibis, 1866, p. 203 [2].

Contopus richardsoni, Baird, Mex. Bound. Surv., Zool., Birds, p. 9 [3]; Birds N. Am. p. 189 [4]; Scl. & Salv. P. Z. S. 1864, p. 360 [5], 1879, p. 615 [6]; Lawr. Ann. Lyc. N. Y. ix. p. 115 [7]; v. Frantz. J. f. Orn. 1869, p. 308 [8]; Salv. P. Z. S. 1870, p. 199 [9]; Ridgw. Man. N. Am. B. p. 338 [10]; Scl. Cat. Birds Brit. Mus. xiv. p. 239 [11].

Contopus virens, var. *richardsoni*, Baird, Brew., & Ridgw. N. Am. B. ii. p. 360 [12]; Lawr. Mem. Bost. Soc. N. H. ii. p. 387 [13]; Bull. U. S. Nat. Mus. no. 4, p. 27 [14]; Henshaw, Rep. U. S. Geogr. Surv. West 100th Mer. v. p. 353 [15]; Coues, Key N. Am. B. ed. 2, p. 440 [16].

Contopus sordidulus, Scl. P. Z. S. 1859, p. 43 [17]; Scl. & Salv. Ibis, 1859, p. 122 [18]; Sumichrast, Mem. Bost. Soc. N. H. i. p. 557 [19].

Contopus plebeius, Cab. & Heine, Mus. Hein. ii. p. 71 [20] (?); Cab. J. f. Orn. 1861, p. 248 [21].

Præcedenti similis, sed plerumque major, supra minus olivaceus : subtus pectore latiore fusco, abdomine flavido vix tincto. (Descr. exempl. ex San José, Costa Rica. Mus. nostr.)

Hab. WESTERN NORTH AMERICA, eastward to the great plains [10][12].—MEXICO [17], Mazatlan (*Grayson* [13]), Presidio near Mazatlan (*Forrer*), Chilpancingo, Venta de Zopilote, Venta de Camaron and Acapulco in Guerrero (*Mrs. H. H. Smith*), Monterey (*Couch* [3]), Vaqueria in Nuevo Leon (*F. B. Armstrong*), Sierra Madre above Ciudad Victoria (*W. B. Richardson*), Chimalpa (*Ferrari-Perez*), State of Vera Cruz (*Sumichrast* [19]), Orizaba (*Botteri* [11]), Tapana, Tehuantepec city (*Sumichrast* [14]); BRITISH HONDURAS, Orange Walk (*Gaumer*); GUATEMALA [17] (*Skinner* [18]), Coban, Dueñas, Retalhuleu (*O. S. & F. D. G.*); COSTA RICA [20] (*Hoffmann* [21]), San José (*Frantzius* [7][8]), Frailes, Barranca (*Carmiol* [7]), Irazu (*Rogers*); PANAMA, Volcan de Chiriqui [9],

Bugaba[9], Calovevora[9] (*Arcé*), Lion Hill (*M'Leannan*[5]), Chepo (*Arcé*).—SOUTH AMERICA, Ecuador[11] and Bolivia[6].

A series of specimens of this Tyrant-Flycatcher from the northern part of its range when compared with a similar series of *C. virens* shows that these species are barely separable. The upper plumage, however, of *C. richardsoni* is slightly less olivaceous than that of *C. virens*; the chest is more continuously and distinctly cinereous and the abdomen scarcely tinged with yellow. When, however, we come to the migratory flocks which spread southward at the approach of winter and distribute themselves throughout Mexico and Central America, we find the greatest difficulty in discriminating between these two birds. In naming our specimens we have been governed a good deal by their geographical distribution, and we believe that the western form in winter spreads over the greater part of Mexico, Guatemala, Costa Rica, and Panama, and thence southwards as far as Bolivia. The only point where the two birds come into contact as shown by our specimens is in the North Mexican State of Nuevo Leon, whence Mr. Armstrong has recently sent us specimens which must certainly be referred to *C. virens*, while others are almost as certainly referable to *C. richardsoni*.

In general appearance *C. richardsoni* is also exceedingly like *C. brachytarsus*; but the latter may be distinguished by its shorter and more rounded wing, the first primary hardly exceeding the fifth in length. In *C. richardsoni* it is obviously longer.

We are in some doubt whether *C. plebeius* applies to this species or to *C. brachytarsus*, and the question cannot be settled without an examination of the types, which are said to have come from Mexico[20]. The measurement of the wing points rather to the latter bird.

The writings of North-American ornithologists give full details concerning this bird, and from them we gather that its breeding-range comprises a vast area extending from Arizona and Texas to the Great Slave Lake. The nest is described as constructed chiefly of plant-fibres, sometimes, though rarely, ornamented with lichens and secured in the fork of a branch of a tree. The eggs are like those of *C. virens*.

8. Contopus brachytarsus.

Empidonax brachytarsus, Scl. Ibis, 1859, p. 441[1]; Lawr. Ann. Lyc. N. Y. vii. p. 327[2].

Contopus brachytarsus, Salv. Ibis, 1861, p. 354[3]; P. Z. S. 1870, p. 199[4]; Scl. & Salv. P. Z. S. 1864, p. 360[5]; Ridgw. Man. N. Am. B. p. 339[6], x. p. 589[7]; Scl. Cat. Birds Brit. Mus. xiv. p. 240[8].

Contopus schotti, Lawr. Ann. Lyc. N. Y. ix. p. 202[9]; Ridgw. Pr. U. S. Nat. Mus. viii. p. 571[10].

Contopus depressirostris, Ridgw. Pr. U. S. Nat. Mus. vi. p. 403[11].

C. virenti quoque similis, sed minor, alis magis rotundatis, remige primo quinto fere æquali haud longiore ut videtur distinguendus. (Descr. feminæ exempl. typ. ex Cordova, Mexico. Mus. Brit.)

Hab. MEXICO, Cordova, Santecomapan (*Sallé*[1]), Teapa (*Mrs. H. H. Smith*), Merida in

Yucatan (*Schott* [9]), Cozumel I. (*Benedict* [10], *Gaumer*); BRITISH HONDURAS, Orange Walk (*Gaumer*); GUATEMALA, Chisec, Choctum, Cahabon, Retalhuleu (*O. S. & F. D. G.*), Escuintla (*Fraser* [3]); HONDURAS, Segovia river (*Henderson* [7]); NICARAGUA, Los Sabalos (*Nutting* [11]); PANAMA, Bugaba, Calovevora [4] (*Arcé*), Lion Hill (*M'Leannan* [2 5]), Paraiso (*Hughes*).—SOUTH AMERICA, Colombia, Venezuela, and Guiana to the Amazons valley, Brazil, and the Argentine Republic [8].

This is a small short-winged resident race of this section of *Contopus*, tolerably common from the State of Vera Cruz southwards through Yucatan and Guatemala to Panama and thence throughout the greater portion of Tropical South America. In Guatemala we found it in the forest regions on both sides of the cordillera up to an elevation of about 1500 feet.

Regarding the synonyms of this bird which have been founded on Central-American specimens, *C. schotti* is now admitted on all hands to be *C. brachytarsus*. *C. depressirostris* we believe to be also referable to it. Some time ago Mr. Ridgway kindly sent us his types for examination, and as we could not distinguish them specifically from a specimen of *C. brachytarsus* from Escuintla, Guatemala, we then considered and still consider them to belong to that species.

MYIARCHUS.

Myiarchus, Cabanis in Tsch. Fauna Per., Aves, p. 152 (1845) (type *Muscicapa ferox*, Gm.); Scl. Cat. Birds Brit. Mus. xiv. p. 246.

Myiarchus is one of the most characteristic genera of Tyrannidæ and is found throughout the Neotropical Region and beyond it as far north as Canada (where *M. crinitus* occurs in summer) and the Rocky Mountains, the summer-quarters of *M. cinerascens*. Other species, such as *M. magister* and *M. lawrencii*, reach the Rio Grande valley, but the majority of the known species are more strictly neotropical in their range.

We now know twenty-six species of *Myiarchus*, of which ten occur in our region.

The relationship of *Myiarchus* is evidently with *Tyrannus*, but it is of slighter build, with longer tail and more slender bill. There is no occipital crest and the outer wing-feathers have their inner webs entire to the tip and not marginate as in *Tyrannus* and *Milvulus*. The wing is rounded, the 3rd and 4th quills being longest, 2nd = 5th, 1st = 7th; the tail is rather long and nearly even, $> \frac{7}{8}$ wing, < 5 tarsus.

a. *Majores* (M. CRINITUS &c.).

a'. *Rostrum angustum, elongatum, pectus haud flammulatum.*

a''. *Rectrices externæ in pogonio interno plerumque rufæ.*

1. Myiarchus crinitus.

Muscicapa crinita, Linn. Syst. Nat. i. p. 325 [1].

Myiarchus crinitus, Scl. & Salv. Ibis, 1859, p. 121 [2]; Cab. J. f. Orn. 1861, p. 250 [3]; Lawr. Ann. Lyc. N. Y. vii. p. 327 [4], ix. p. 115 [5]; Bull. U. S. Nat. Mus. no. 4, p. 27 [6]; Frantz. J. f. Orn. 1869, p. 308 [7]; Coues, Pr. Ac. Phil. 1872, p. 63 [8]; Key N. Am. B. ed. 2, p. 434 [9]; Baird, Brew., & Ridgw. N. Am. B. ii. p. 334 [10]; Dugès, La Nat. i. p. 141 [11]; Salv. Cat. Strickl. Coll. p. 315 [12]; Berl. J. f. Orn. 1884, p. 303 [13]; Ridgw. Man. N. Am. B. p. 333 [14]; Scl. Cat. Birds Brit. Mus. xiv. p. 247 [15].

Myiarchus cinerascens, Scl. & Salv. Ibis, 1859, p. 121 (partim) [16].

Supra olivaceus, capite paulo obscuriore; alis nigricantibus, rectricibus et secundariis internis pallide fusco limbatis, remigibus medialiter stricte rufo marginatis; cauda nigricante, rectricibus omnibus præter duas medias in pogonio interno usque ad apicem rufis, parte rhachidi proxima stricte nigricante: subtus usque ad pectus cinereus; abdomine et subalaribus sulphureis: rostro corneo, pedibus nigris. Long. tota 8·0, alæ 3·75, caudæ 3·4, tarsi 0·85, rostri a rictu 1·0. (Descr. feminæ ex Livingston, Guatemala. Mus. nostr.)

♂ feminæ similis.

Hab. NORTH AMERICA, Canada and Eastern States to the edge of the great plains southwards [10][14].—MEXICO (*Galeotti* [12]), Soto la Marina in Tamaulipas (*W. B. Richardson*), Guanajuato (*Dugès* [11]), Tehuantepec city (*Sumichrast* [5]); BRITISH HONDURAS, Cayo (*Blancaneaux*); GUATEMALA (*Skinner* [2]), Livingston [16], Choctum (*O. S. & F. D. G.*); COSTA RICA [3] (*v. Frantzius* [6], *Carmiol* [4]); PANAMA, Lion Hill (*M'Leannan* [4]).—COLOMBIA [15]; CUBA.

The decidedly olive tint of the back, the deeper grey of the throat and breast, and the brighter yellow of the under surface render this species readily distinguishable both from *M. cinerascens* and *M. magister*, though in the distribution of the rufous colour on the inner web of the lateral tail-feathers all these birds resemble one another.

M. crinitus is a familiar species in the Eastern States, where it is a summer visitor during the breeding-season, and its habits are fully described by writers on North-American birds. Its nest is placed in a hole in a tree and the eggs " curiously marked with fine ' pen-lines ' and intricate pencillings of black and various shades of rich purplish brown over a buffy or creamy brown " [10].

2. **Myiarchus inquietus**, sp. n.

M. crinito similis, sed multo minor, abdomine pallidiore flavo distinguendus. Long. tota 7·0, alæ 3·4, caudæ 3·3, rostri a rictu 0·9, tarsi 0·8. (Descr. feminæ ex Acaguisotla, Mexico. Mus. nostr.)

Hab. MEXICO, Acaguisotla, Chilpancingo, Tierra Colorada, Rio Papagaio and Acapulco in the State of Guerrero (*Mrs. H. H. Smith*).

In the large collection of birds recently received from Mr. and Mrs. Herbert H. Smith from the State of Guerrero are several specimens of a *Myiarchus* which we are unable to associate with any known species. At first we thought they might belong to the long disputed *M. mexicanus*, but the shorter wings and brighter yellow abdomen show that this is not the case. The species is evidently a small resident form of the migratory *M. crinitus* of Eastern America, which, being isolated in the Sierra Madre del Sur, has acquired distinctive characters.

The series includes several specimens in fresh plumage and others in full moult; the former shot in October, the latter in August 1888. A young example has a great deal of rufous colouring on the tail, the shaft and a small portion of the webs on either side being fuscous. In the adults the proportion of rufous is much as in *M. crinitus*, and that colour runs out to the tip of the lateral tail-feathers. They thus differ from typical *M. cinerascens*, and also in their yellower abdomen and more olivaceous mantle.

This species appears to be not uncommon in the State of Guerrero, and ranges from the sea-level at Acapulco to an altitude of 4600 feet at Chilpancingo.

3. Myiarchus magister.

Tyrannula cooperi, Kaup, P. Z. S. 1851, p. 51 (nec Nuttall) [1].

Myiarchus cooperi, Baird, B. N. Am. p. 180 [2]; Scl. P. Z. S. 1859, p. 384 [3]; Scl. & Salv. Ibis, 1859, p. 122 [4]; P. Z. S. 1870, p. 837 [5]; Lawr. Ann. Lyc. N. Y. ix. p. 202 [6].

Myiarchus crinitus var. *cooperi*, Coues, Pr. Ac. Phil. 1872, p. 67 [7]; Baird, Brew., & Ridgw. N. Am. B. ii. p. 331 [8]; Lawr. Bull. U. S. Nat. Mus. no. 4, p. 28 [9].

Myiarchus erythrocercus var. *cooperi*, Ridgw. Pr. U. S. Nat. Mus. i. p. 138 [10].

Myiarchus crinitus erythrocercus, Coues & Sennett, Bull. U. S. Geol. Surv. iv. p. 32 [11]; Sennett, Bull. U. S. Geol. Surv. v. p. 402 [12]; Coues, Key N. Am. B. ed. 2, p. 435 [13].

Myiarchus mexicanus, Dresser, Ibis, 1865, p. 473 [14]; Sumichrast, Mem. Bost. Soc. N. H. i. p. 557 [15]; Grayson, Pr. Bost. Soc. N. H. xiv. p. 278 [16]; Lawr. Mem. Bost. Soc. N. H. ii. p. 287 [17]; Ridgw. Pr. U. S. Nat. Mus. iii. p. 13 [18]; Man. N. Am. B. p. 333 [19]; Scl. Cat. Birds Brit. Mus. xiv. p. 250 [20].

Myiarchus mexicanus magister, Ridgw. Pr. Biol. Soc. Wash. ii. p. 90 [21]; Man. N. Am. B. p. 333 [22].

Supra pallide olivaceo-brunneus, capite summo paulo brunnescentiore; uropygio rufescente tincto; alis nigricantibus interne rufo marginatis, tectricibus et secundariis internis sordide albo extrorsum limbatis, remigibus medialiter extrorsum rufo marginatis; cauda nigricante, rectricibus (præter duas medias) in pogonio interno late rufo marginatis, parte rhachidi proxima nigricante, rectrice extima utrinque in pogonio externo pro dimidio proximo albido limbata; loris, cervicis lateribus et corpore subtus usque ad pectus cinereis; abdomine et subalaribus pallide sulphureis: rostro et pedibus nigricantibus. Long. tota 8·5, alæ 4·3, caudæ 3·9, tarsi 0·9, rostri a rictu 1·1. (Descr. maris ex Vera Cruz, Mexico. Mus. nostr.)

Hab. NORTH AMERICA, Southern Arizona [22] and Texas [14].—MEXICO, Ysleta in Sonora (*W. Lloyd*), Mazatlan, Tres Marias Is. [16] (*Grayson, Forrer*), Ceralvo, Hacienda de los Treviños, Vaqueria, Hacienda de las Escobas, Villa Grande, Rio de la Silla, Topo Chico, Estancia (*F. B. Armstrong*), Sierra Madre above Ciudad Victoria, Soto la Marina, Tampico (*W. B. Richardson*), Vera Cruz (*F. D. G. & W. B. Richardson*), Teapa (*Mrs. H. H. Smith*), Peto, Buctzotz, Cozumel I. (*G. F. Gaumer*); BRITISH HONDURAS, Cayo (*Blancaneaux*), Orange Walk (*G. F. Gaumer*); GUATEMALA (*Skinner* [4]); HONDURAS, Ruatan I. (*G. F. Gaumer*), San Pedro (*G. M. Whitely* [5]).

This species is involved in considerable difficulty both as to its limits and as to its proper title. Putting the South-American species aside, Mr. Ridgway, in his recent

'Manual of North-American Birds,' recognized two forms which he called *M. mexicanus* and *M. m. magister*—the former a smaller bird, ranging from the lower Rio Grande valley through Eastern and Southern Mexico to Guatemala and Salvador; the latter a larger bird, ranging from Southern Arizona through Western Mexico to Tehuantepec. As the character of size completely fails to distinguish every individual, and it is the only one he relies upon to discriminate his races, we have no alternative but to treat them all as one species. The fifty-two specimens before us seem fully to justify this view. Mr. Sclater places these forms under the name of *M. mexicanus*, and he includes with them two birds from Southern Mexico which we hesitate to associate with the rest; their general dimensions do not differ materially from the more northern bird, but the bills are obviously very much smaller. These two birds undoubtedly belong to the true *M. mexicanus* of Kaup—not only do they agree with the description, but they have been compared with the type with which they correspond; they are again mentioned under the account of the next species. The larger-billed bird is the *Tyrannula cooperi* of Kaup (nec Nuttall), as long ago recognized by Baird; and it would have saved much perplexity if Baird's suggestion for the employment of this name had been followed by subsequent writers. The fact of *Muscicapa cooperi* of Nuttall being a synonym of *Contopus borealis* has caused its rejection in the present case. As we now unite the birds of Eastern and Western Mexico, Mr. Ridgway's name for the western bird becomes available. *M. magister* is not easily differentiated from the South-American *M. tyrannulus*; but the northern seems to be the larger bird, rather lighter on the back, and with the rump rather more rufescent. These differences, however, are very trivial, and were the range of the two birds continuous we should hardly hesitate to unite them; but there is a wide tract of country lying between Colombia and Honduras unoccupied by this form, thus rendering slight differences of more importance.

M. magister is common in the valley of the Rio Grande and also in Yucatan and the islands off the north and east coasts of that promontory. It is much rarer in Guatemala, where we never met with it ourselves, though a specimen from one of Skinner's collections must certainly be referred to it.

Merrill found it breeding abundantly in the Lower Rio Grande valley, the nests being composed of felted locks of wool and hair, and placed not far from the ground, either in old holes of Woodpeckers or in natural hollows in decayed trees or stumps.

Mr. W. E. D. Scott speaks of *M. m. magister** as common in spring and summer about Tucson and other places in Arizona, including the foot-hills of the Catalina Mountains up to an altitude of about 4500 feet. A nest found in a deserted Woodpecker's hole in a dead stump of a sycamore was quite like that of *M. crinitus*. The eggs also are similar to those of that species but a little larger.

* 'Auk,' 1887, p. 17.

4. Myiarchus cinerascens.

Tyrannula cinerascens, Lawr. Ann. Lyc. N. Y. v. p. 121 (1851) [1].

Myiarchus cinerascens, Scl. & Salv. Ibis, 1859, p. 121 (partim) [2]; Scl. P. Z. S. 1859, p. 384 [3];
    Coues, Pr. Ac. Phil. 1872, p. 69 [4]; Lawr. Mem. Bost. Soc. N. H. ii. p. 288 [5]; Bull. U. S.
    Nat. Mus. no. 4, p. 28 [6]; Ferrari-Perez, Pr. U. S. Nat. Mus. ix. p. 155 [7].

Myiarchus crinitus var. *cinerascens*, Baird, Brew., & Ridgw. N. Am. B. ii. p. 337 [8].

Tyrannula mexicana, Kaup, P. Z. S. 1851, p. 51 [9].

Myiarchus mexicanus, Baird, B. N. Am. p. 179, t. 5 [10].

Myionax mexicanus, Cab. & Heine, Mus. Hein. ii. p. 74 [11].

Myiarchus pertinax, Baird, Pr. Ac. Phil. 1859, p. 303 [12].

M. *magistro* similis, sed abdomine pallidiore, rostro minore, rectrice caudæ extima utrinque in pogonio interno fere ad rhachidem (præter apicem) fulva. (Descr. maris ex Atlixco, Mexico. Mus. nostr.)

Hab. NORTH AMERICA, Western States from the Rocky Mountains westward, and from Wyoming southwards, Lower California [8].—MEXICO [9] [11], Yecera in Sonora (*W. Lloyd*), Mazatlan (*Grayson* [5], *Forrer*), Topo Chico in Nuevo Leon (*F. B. Armstrong*), San Juan del Rio (*Rébouch*), Huehuetlan (*Ferrari-Perez*), Atlixco (*Boucard & F. D. G.*), Oaxaca (*Boucard* [3], *Fenochio*), Tapana, Sta. Efigenia, Tehuantepec city (*Sumichrast* [6]); GUATEMALA, Dueñas [2], Barranco Hondo, Chuacus (*O. S. & F. D. G.*).

This species is distinguished from its near ally *M. magister* chiefly by its smaller bill, the paler colour of the abdomen, and the distribution of the fulvous in the tail-feathers, which in most cases occupies the greater part of the inner web of the outer feather, and diverging from the shaft as it approaches the tip leaves the tip itself dark. But the variation in the amount of the dark tip in different individuals is very considerable. In the young bird in the first plumage the distribution is somewhat different, as the rufous colour runs close to the shaft to the end of the feather; this fact gives us a clue to unravel the complicated synonymy of this species. We have already stated that *Tyrannula mexicana* of Kaup is the smaller-billed of the two birds described by him in 1851, that with the larger bill being the preceding species.

We have two specimens before us which have been compared with Kaup's type in the Darmstadt Museum, one of these is from Atlixco, the other from Oaxaca; they differ from the typical *M. cinerascens* in that the tip of the inner web of the outer tail-feather is rufous, but with the young of *M. cinerascens* before us we have little doubt that in their next moult their tails would be normally coloured. It therefore comes to this, that Baird was perfectly right when he placed *Tyrannulus cinerascens* of Lawrence as a synonym of *T. mexicana* of Kaup; but the latter name has been so differently applied and in so many ways by various authors for the last thirty years, during which the title *M. cinerascens* has acquired increasing stability, that we at least have no hesitation in employing *M. cinerascens* here instead of the ill-defined *M. mexicanus*, which may or may not have a slight priority.

M. cinerascens is a bird of the south-western portions of the United States, where it is a summer visitor. Dr. Coues found it abundant in Arizona, arriving late in April and leaving again towards the end of September. It usually resorted to openings in the oak-forests, bushy ravines, and the fringes of wood along the streams. In its habits it resembles *M. crinitus* in every way, building in old Woodpeckers' holes and laying cream-coloured eggs marked and speckled with purplish-red dashes and blotches of neutral tint.

In Guatemala we found this species in several places, but chiefly on the flank of the cordillera between the volcanos of Agua and Fuego amongst the groves of oaks which abound there.

5. **Myiarchus nuttingi.**

Myiarchus nuttingi, Ridgw. Pr. U. S. Nat. Mus. v. p. 390[1]; Pr. Biol. Soc. Wash. ii. p. 92[2]; Man. N. Am. B. p. 334[3]; Nutting & Ridgw. Pr. U. S. Nat. Mus. vi. pp. 374[4], 393[5]; Scl. Cat. Birds Brit. Mus. xiv. p. 250[6].

M. cinerascenti similis, sed rostro paulo majore, caudæ rectricibus lateralibus in pogonio interno usque ad rhachidem rufis.

Hab. MEXICO, Guanajuato, Tehuantepec, Chiapas (fide *Ridgway*); NICARAGUA, Omotepe I.[5] and San Juan del Sur[4] (*Nutting*); COSTA RICA (*Carmiol*[6]), La Palma (*Nutting*).

We know very little of this bird, which was separated by Mr. Ridgway on Costa Rica specimens. It is closely allied to *M. magister*, but is of rather smaller dimensions, though the bill is a little larger; the chief difference is in the tail, the inner web of the lateral rectrices being rufous to the shaft *.

b''. Rectrices omnes nigricantes haud rufo ornatæ.

6. **Myiarchus ferox.**

Muscicapa ferox, Gm. Syst. Nat. i. p. 934[1]; Berl. Ibis, 1883, p. 139[2].

Myiarchus ferox, Cassin, Pr. Ac. Phil. 1860, p. 143[3]; Scl. Cat. Birds Brit. Mus. xiv. p. 253[4].

Myiarchus panamensis, Lawr. Ann. Lyc. N. Y. vii. pp. 284[5], 295[6], ix. p. 115[7]; Scl. & Salv. P. Z. S. 1864, p. 360[8]; v. Frantz. J. f. Orn. 1869, p. 308[9]; Salv. P. Z. S. 1870, p. 199[10].

Myiarchus tyrannulus, Coues, Pr. Ac. Phil. 1872, p. 71 (nec Müll.)[11].

Supra olivascenti-fuscus, capite obscuriore plumis medialiter fuscis; supracaudalibus brunneis; alis nigricantibus, extrorsum pallide fusco limbatis; cauda nigricante: subtus usque ad pectus cinereus; abdomine et subalaribus sulphureis. (Descr. maris ex Panama. Mus. nostr.)
♀ mari similis.

Hab. PANAMA, Calovevora (*Arcé*[10]), Lion Hill (*M'Leannan*[5][6][8]), Paraiso (*Hughes*),

---

* *Myiarchus brachyurus* (Ridgw. Man. N. Am. B. p. 334) is no doubt included in the references to *M. nuttingi* given above, as it is based on one of Mr. Nutting's Omotepe specimens. Its claims to distinction rest on its larger size, comparatively short tail, and rusty tail-coverts. With only a single Costa Rican specimen supposed to belong to *M. nuttingi* before us, we are not in a position to give any opinion concerning *M. brachyurus*.

Truando river (*C. J. Wood*[3]).—SOUTH AMERICA generally southward to the Argentine Republic[4].

This bird is subject to very considerable variation throughout its wide range, some examples being much more olivaceous and paler on the back than others which are darker brown with darker heads. In most South-American localities we find darker and lighter birds together with intermediate forms in nearly equal proportions, but in the State of Panama we have as yet only met with the paler olivaceous form. This was described by Mr. Lawrence as *Myiarchus panamensis*; but we are not convinced of its specific distinctness, for it is by no means confined to the State of Panama, and in the south becomes inextricably involved with darker forms.

Mr. Lawrence[7] (followed by von Frantzius[9]) includes *M. panamensis* in his list of Costa Rica birds on the authority of " Enrique Arcé," but we cannot find any record of specimens having been sent us from Costa Rica by that collector.

b. *Minores* (M. LAWRENCII &c.).

7. Myiarchus yucatanensis.

Myiarchus yucatanensis, Lawr. Pr. Ac. Phil. 1871, p. 235[1]; Ridgw. Pr. Biol. Soc. Wash. ii. p. 92[2];
Man. N. Am. B. p. 334[3]; Scl. Cat. Birds Brit. Mus. xiv. p. 260[4].
Myiarchus mexicanus, Lawr. Ann. Lyc. N. Y. ix. p. 202[5].

Supra obscure olivaceus, capite paulo saturatiore; supracaudalibus rufescente tinctis; alis nigricantibus, tectricibus pallide fusco limbatis, secundariis internis albido marginatis, remigibus intus et extus stricte medialiter rufo limbatis; cauda nigricante, rectrice extima utrinque anguste, reliquis (præter duas medias) in pogonio interno late rufo marginatis: subtus usque ad pectus griseus; abdomine et subalaribus pallide sulphureis: rostro et pedibus nigris. Long. tota 7·0, alæ 3·3, caudæ 3·3, tarsi 0·85, rostri a rictu 0·85. (Descr. maris ex Tabi, Yucatan. Mus. nostr.)

Hab. MEXICO, Merida in Yucatan (*Schott*[5]), Tabi (*F. D. G.*), Peto, Cozumel I. (*G. F. Gaumer*[4]).

An obscure species, the position of which is not very clear. Mr. Ridgway separates it from *M. lawrencii* by the shape of the bill, which is less flattened and deeper through the middle. This is not altogether a satisfactory character, and we see very little difference between these Yucatan birds and the form of *M. lawrencii* found in Eastern Mexico from Vera Cruz northwards. Both have a considerable margin of red on the inner web of the tail-feathers (except the outermost pair), but *M. lawrencii*, from the district named, has a more elongated wider bill and is of rather larger dimensions. Compared with *M. lawrencii* from more southern localities, including Yucatan itself, the amount of red in the tail of *M. yucatanensis* becomes a more conspicuous character, and the difference between the two is more obvious.

We have now a fair series of this species, which shows that its range is restricted to the promontory of Yucatan and the adjoining island of Cozumel.

Mr. Lawrence's description was based upon a specimen in poor condition obtained by Dr. A. Schott near Merida. Godman found it during his recent visit to Yucatan, but most of our examples are from our indefatigable correspondent, Mr. G. F. Gaumer.

8. Myiarchus lawrencii.

Muscicapa lawrencii, Giraud, Sixteen B. Texas, t. 2. f. 1 [1].

Myiarchus lawrencii, Baird, B. N. Am. p. 181, t. 47. f. 3 [2]; Mex. Bound. Surv., Zool., Birds, p. 8 [3]; Scl. P.Z.S.1859, pp. 366 [4], 384 [5]; Scl. & Salv. Ibis, 1859, p. 121 [6]; P.Z.S. 1870, p. 837 [7]; Taylor, Ibis, 1860, p. 114 [8]; Cab. J. f. Orn. 1861, p. 249 [9]; Lawr. Ann. Lyc. N. Y. viii. p. 183 [10], ix. pp. 115 [11], 204 [12]; Mem. Bost. Soc. N. H. ii. p. 288 [13]; Bull. U. S. Nat. Mus. no. 4, p. 28 [14]; Sumichrast, Mem. Bost. Soc. N. H. i. p. 557 [15]; v. Frantz. J. f. Orn. 1869, p. 308 [16]; Grayson, Pr. Bost. Soc. N. H. xiv. p. 279 [17]; Coues, Pr. Ac. Phil. 1872, p. 74 [18]; Salv. Cat. Strickl. Coll. p. 316 [19]; Ridgw. Man. N. Am. B. p. 335 [20]; Scl. Cat. Birds Brit. Mus. xiv. p. 256 [21].

Myiarchus mexicanus, Scl. P. Z. S. 1856, p. 296 (nec Kaup) [22].

Myiarchus rufomarginatus, Cab. & Heine, Mus. Hein. ii. p. 73 [23].

Myiarchus nigricapillus, Cab. J. f. Orn. 1861, p. 250 [24]; Salv. P. Z. S. 1867, p. 148 [25], 1870, p. 199 [26]; Scl. & Salv. P. Z. S. 1867, p. 279 [27]; Lawr. Ann. Lyc. N. Y. ix. p. 115 [28]; Scl. Cat. Birds Brit. Mus. xiv. p. 257 [28].

Myiarchus lawrencii nigricapillus, Nutt. & Ridgw. Pr. U. S. Nat. Mus. vi. pp. 384 [30], 393 [31].

Myiarchus lawrencii olivaceus, Ridgw. Pr. Biol. Soc. Wash. ii. p. 91 [32]; Man. N. Am. B. p. 335 [33].

Myiarchus tristis var. *lawrencii*, Baird, Brew., & Ridgw. N. Am. B. ii. p. 333 [34].

Myiarchus platyrhynchus, Ridgw. Pr. Biol. Soc. Wash. iii. p. 23 [35]; Man. N. Am. B. p. 335 [36].

Supra obscure olivaceus, capite brunnescente; uropygio rufescente tincto; alis nigricantibus, remigibus et secundariis externis rufo limbatis, secundariis internis albido marginatis; cauda nigricante, rectricibus extrorsum anguste, introrsum late rufo marginatis, hoc colore frequenter absente: subtus, usque ad medium corporis, pallide cinereus; abdomine toto pallide sulphureo. Long. tota 7·0, alæ 3·5, caudæ 3·35, tarsi 0·7, rostri a rictu 1·0. (Descr. maris ex Misantla, Mexico. Mus. nostr.)
♀ mari similis.

Hab. NORTH AMERICA, Southern Arizona, Texas [1].—MEXICO [23], Yecera, Realito, and Guadalupe in Sonora (*W. Lloyd*), Tres Marias Is., Mazatlan (*Grayson* [17], *Forrer*), Plains of Colima (*Xantus* [13]), Chilpancingo, Amula, Omilteme, Acaguisotla, Tepetlapa, Dos Arroyos, and Rincon in Guerrero (*Mrs. H. H. Smith*), San Diego in Nuevo Leon (*Couch* [3]), Ceralvo, Hacienda de las Escobas, Rio de las Escobas, Topo Chico and Monte Morelos in Nuevo Leon (*F. B. Armstrong*), Sierra Madre above Ciudad Victoria, Tampico (*Richardson*), Cordova (*Sallé* [22]), Jalapa (*de Oca* [4]), Misantla, Jalapa, Orizaba (*F. D. G.*), Talea (*Boucard* [4]), Cofre de Perote (*M. Trujillo*), Atoyac and Teapa (*Mrs. H. H. Smith*), Comaltepec (*Galeotti* [19]), Sta. Efigenia and Dondominguillo (*Sumichrast* [14]), Merida in Yucatan (*Schott* [12]), Peto in Yucatan (*G. F. Gaumer*), Cozumel I. (*Benedict, Gaumer* [36]); BRITISH HONDURAS, Orange Walk (*G. F. Gaumer*), Belize, Cayo (*Blancaneaux*); GUATEMALA, Choctum, Yaxcamnal, Coban, Tactic, Teleman, San Gerónimo, Dueñas [6], Volcan de Agua, Retalhuleu (*O. S. & F. D. G.*); SALVADOR, La Union (*O. S*); HONDURAS, San Pedro (*G. M. Whitely* [7]),

Tigre I. (*G. C. Taylor*[8]); NICARAGUA, Blewfields (*Wickham*[27]), Greytown (*Holland*[10]), Sucuyá[30], Omotepe I.[31] (*Nutting*); COSTA RICA[9], Angostura[11], Sarchi[11], Grecia[28], Barranca[28], San José[28], Pacuar[11] (*Carmiol*), Irazu (*Rogers*), Tucuriqui (*Arcé*); PANAMA, Volcan de Chiriqui, Chitra[26] and Santa Fé[25] (*Arcé*).

We have before us about 130 specimens of this species from various points ranging from Southern Arizona and Northern Mexico down to the State of Panama, and, though we can see obvious differences in selected birds from several places, other specimens undoubtedly blend the whole series together. Thus the Arizona birds separated by Mr. Ridgway as *M. l. olivascens* are, for the most part, as he describes them—pale, with the top of the head hair-brown or olive, very little darker than the back, the tail-feathers in the adult bird without rufous edgings on the inner web.

Birds from Sonora exactly resemble those from Arizona, while those from Mazatlan are a trifle darker, and have the top of the head more distinctly coloured. Specimens from Northern Yucatan included in the same race by Mr. Ridgway are, again, a trifle darker as regards the head, and we can match them with some specimens from Teapa selected from numbers of the more typical form, and from them, too, Cozumel birds cannot satisfactorily be discriminated. Returning to Mexico we find that birds from the north-eastern States of Nuevo Leon and Tamaulipas and the slopes of the mountains of Northern Vera Cruz are distinguished by their larger size and by the broad rufous edging to the tail-feathers. This latter character seems gradually to disappear in birds from further south; in those from Orizaba it is but slightly shown, and in Tabasco examples it has altogether disappeared. The Guatemala bird precisely resembles that of Tabasco, nor do we see how that of Costa Rica and the western portion of the State of Panama can be satisfactorily discriminated. Under these circumstances we think it best to unite all these forms under one specific name. The plan adopted by American ornithologists would be much as follows:—We should have *M. lawrencii* from North-eastern Mexico and a portion of the State of Vera Cruz, *M. l. olivascens* from Arizona southwards through Western Mexico and Yucatan including Cozumel, and, lastly, *M. l. nigricapillus* from Vera Cruz southward through Tabasco to Guatemala, Costa Rica, and the State of Panama; but such an arrangement would not enable us to name with certainty many intermediate birds; we therefore prefer to include them all under one comprehensive name.

Myiarchus lawrencii is a common bird wherever it is found, its chief abode being the low lands bordering both oceans up to an elevation of 4000 or 5000 feet. On the Tres Marias Islands Grayson says it is abundant in all parts of the woods. In Guatemala it is common, and though more often seen in the forests of the hotter parts of the country may not unfrequently be met with in the temperate districts, such as Coban, Tactic, and Dueñas.

The eggs of this species taken by M. Boucard at Talea[5] are described as pure white, with spots of two shades of brown, principally towards the larger end, where they form a ring.

9. **Myiarchus nigriceps.**

Myiarchus nigriceps, Scl. P. Z. S. 1860, p. 68[1]; Cat. Birds Brit. Mus. xiv. p. 258[2]; Lawr. Ann. Lyc. N. Y. vii. p. 327 (?)[3]; Scl. & Salv. P. Z. S. 1864, p. 360[4]; Tacz. Orn. Pér. ii. p. 324[5].
Myiarchus brnnneiceps, Lawr. Ann. Lyc. N. Y. vii. p. 327[6].

M. lawrencii persimilis, tectricibus alarum haud rufo limbatis distinguendus.
Av. juv. primariis plus minusve rufo marginatis.

Hab. PANAMA, Lion Hill (*M'Leannan*[3][4][6]).—SOUTH AMERICA, Colombia, Ecuador, Peru[5], Venezuela, Guiana, and Amazons valley[2].

We believe that this bird, when adult, may always be distinguished from *M. lawrencii* by the absence of the rufous edgings to the quill-feathers. The crown, too, is more intensely black, but this is a very variable feature in the allied form. The boundary between the two birds seems fairly definite: *M. nigriceps* just enters our fauna as far as the line of the Panama Railway; a little further westward *M. lawrencii* takes its place.

M. nigriceps was first described from specimens obtained by Fraser at Pallatanga in Ecuador, and it has since been discovered to exist over a wide area of northern South America from the valley of the Amazons to the Caribbean sea. In Peru Stolzmann speaks of it as common at Tambillo, frequenting the edges of the forests and in other places even at an elevation of 9500 feet at Cutervo.

b'. *Rostrum latum, breviusculum, pectus distincte flammulatum.*

10. **Myiarchus flammulatus.**   (Tab. XXXVII. fig. 2.)

Myiarchus flammulatus, Lawr. Ann. Lyc. N. Y. xi. p. 71[1]; Bull. U. S. Nat. Mus. no. 4, p. 28[2]; Ridgw. Pr. Biol. Soc. Wash. ii. p. 93[3]; Man. N. Am. B. p. 335[4]; Scl. Cat. Birds Brit. Mus. xiv. p. 263[5].

Supra olïvaceus, capite vix obscuriore; alis fuscescentibus, tectricibus pallide rufo terminatis, remigibus et secundariis externis eodem colore limbatis, secundariis internis sordide albo terminatis; cauda fuscescente stricte extrorsum limbata: subtus usque ad pectus albidi-cinereo flammulatus; abdomine pallide sulphureo, ṣubalaribus ochraceo tinctis: rostro et pedibus nigricantibus. Long. tota 6·3, alæ 3·2, caudæ 3·0, tarsi 0·7, rostri a rictu 0·8. (Descr. exempl. ex Tehuantepec, Mexico. Mus. nostr.)

Hab. MEXICO, Mazatlan (fide *Ridgway*[4]), Cacoprieto, Tehuantepec (*Sumichrast*[1][2][5]).

A very distinct species, doubtfully referable to *Myiarchus*. The bill is much shorter than in typical *Myiarchus*, and broader in comparison with its length. We only know of its occurrence on the Isthmus of Tehuantepec, where Sumichrast discovered it. Mr. Ridgway, however, extends its range to Mazatlan.

TYRANNUS.

Tyrannus, Cuvier, Leç. An. Comp. i. t. 2 (1800); Scl. Cat. Birds Brit. Mus. xiv. p. 267.
Laphyctes, Reich. Av. Syst. t. lxvi. (1850).
Melittarchus, Cab. & Heine, Mus. Hein. ii. p. 80.

Of the eleven recognized species of *Tyrannus* seven occur within our limits, of which *T. pipiri* is a winter visitor from the north, *T. griseus* and *T. magnirostris* stragglers from the Antilles, and *T. verticalis* from western North America. This leaves three resident species, of which *T. melancholicus* is by far the most abundant, being found in all but the more elevated districts; the others are *T. crassirostris* of Western Mexico and Guatemala, and *T. vociferans* of the Mexican and Guatemalan highlands, a bird which also occurs in Western North America.

Tyrannus has a stout bill, the width of which at the gape is considerably less than half the length of the tomia; the sides of the bill are nearly straight or slightly convex, the terminal hook being well developed; the supranasal feathers are short and stiff, the setæ extending over the otherwise open nearly round nostril; the rictal bristles are short but strong; the tarsi are short, and with the feet moderately strong. The wings have the outer feathers pointed by the abrupt reduction of the width of their inner webs; but this is characteristic of the male, these feathers in the female being normal. The 3rd quill is slightly shorter than the 2nd and 4th; 1st < 6th > 7th; the tail is forked in some species, slightly rounded in others, $>\frac{4}{5}$ wing, <5 tarsus.

A. *Rostrum mediocre haud incrassatum.*

a. *Subtus albus.*

1. Tyrannus pipiri.

Lanius tyrannus, Linn. Syst. Nat. i. p. 136[1].
Tyrannus tyrannus, Ridgw. Man. N. Am. B. p. 328[2].
Lanius tyrannus, γ. carolinensis, Gm. Syst. Nat. i. p. 302[3].
Tyrannus carolinensis, Baird, B. N. Am. p. 171[4]; Lawr. Ann. Lyc. N. Y. viii. p. 183[5]; Bull. U. S. Nat. Mus. no. 4, p. 28[6]; Baird, Brew., & Ridgw. N. Am. B. ii. p. 316[7]; Sennett, Bull. U. S. Geol. Surv. iv. p. 31[8]; Coues, Birds N. W. p. 235[9]; Key N. Am. B. ed. 2, p. 432[10]; Ridgw. Pr. U. S. Nat. Mus. i. p. 471[11].
Tyrannus pipiri, Vieill. Ois. Am. Sept. i. p. 73, t. 44[12]; Scl. & Salv. P. Z. S. 1870, p. 837[13]; Gundl. Orn. Cub. p. 74[14]; Boucard, P. Z. S. 1883, p. 448[15]; Scl. Cat. Birds Brit. Mus. xiv. p. 267[16].
Tyrannus intrepidus, Vieill. Gal. Ois. p. 214, t. 133[17]; Sw. Phil. Mag. new ser. i. p. 368[18]; Scl. P. Z. S. 1858, p. 302[19], 1859, p. 383[20]; Moore, P. Z. S. 1859, p. 55[21]; Scl. & Salv. Ibis, 1859, p. 120[22]; Lawr. Ann. Lyc. N. Y. vii. p. 295[23]; Salv. Ibis, 1864, pp. 378[24], 380[25]; Sumichrast, Mem. Bost. Soc. N. H. i. p. 557[26].

Supra griseo-nigricans; capite nigro, crista coccinea celata ornato; uropygio nigro albido limbato; alis nigris albo limbatis ; cauda nigra albo terminata : subtus albus, pectore cinerascente, subalaribns fumosis ; alis et cauda nigris.   Long. tota 8·3, alæ 4·9, caudæ 3·5, tarsi 0·75, rostri a rictu 0·95.   (Descr. exempl. ex Cozumel I.   Mus. nostr.)

Hab. NORTH AMERICA, temperate districts, Rocky Mountains eastward, rarer towards the Pacific [2].—MEXICO (*Bullock* [18]), Acatepec (*Boucard* [19]), Playa Vicente (*Boucard* [20]), State of Vera Cruz (*Sumichrast* [26]), Ventosa [26], Tapana [6] (*Sumichrast*), Tizimin [15], Buctzotz, Cozumel I. (*G. F. Gaumer*); BRITISH HONDURAS, Saddle Cay [24], Half Moon Cay [25] (*O. S.*); GUATEMALA (*Skinner* [22]), Yzabal, Retalhuleu (*O. S. & F. D. G.*); HONDURAS, Omoa (*Leyland* [21]), San Pedro (*G. M. Whitely* [13]); NICARAGUA, Greytown (*Holland* [5]); PANAMA, Lion Hill (*M‘Leannan* [23]), Paraiso Station (*Hughes*).—SOUTH AMERICA, Colombia, Amazons valley, and Bolivia [16]; BAHAMAS [2]; CUBA [14].

Tyrannus pipiri is a very well-known bird in North America during the spring and summer months, where it is a migratory species.   It passes southwards in autumn, and returns again in spring.   In Mexico and Central America it is probably only present during the winter months and during passage.

In Mexico its range seems strictly confined to the eastern slope of the mountain-range until we come to the Isthmus of Tehuantepec, where it crosses to the Pacific and is found on both sides of the cordillera of Guatemala and thence southwards to Panama.   In South America its range is very extensive, as it reaches across the Amazons valley to Bolivia [16].

Its habits in North America, where it is a very familiar bird, have been very fully described [7].   Its nest resembles those of *T. griseus* and *T. melancholicus.*   The eggs are white, with a roseate tinge and spotted with blotches of purple, brown, and red-brown, which are sometimes collected in a ring round the larger end, and sometimes scattered over the whole surface of the egg.

2. **Tyrannus griseus.**

Tyrannus griseus, Vieill. Ois. Am. Sept. i. p. 76, t. 46[1]; Sw. Phil. Mag. new ser. i. p. 368 (?) [2]; Lawr. Ann. Lyc. N. Y. viii. p. 183[3]; Scl. Cat. Birds Brit. Mus. xiv. p. 271[4].

Melittarchus griseus, Gundl. Orn. Cub. p. 73[5].

Lanius tyrannus, β. dominicensis, Gm. Syst. Nat. i. p. 302[6].

Tyrannus dominicensis, Baird, B. N. Am. p. 172[7]; Baird, Brew., & Ridgw. N. Am. B. ii. p. 319[8]; Ridgw. Pr. U. S. Nat. Mus. i. p. 470[9], viii. p. 570[10]; Man. N. Am. B. p. 329[11]; Coues, Key N. Am. B. ed. 2, p. 433[12]; Cory, Auk, 1886, p. 244[13].

Tyrannus rostratus, Scl. & Salv. P. Z. S. 1864, p. 361[14].

Supra griseus, capite crista celata aurantiaca ornato, loris et regione parotica nigricantibus ; alis nigricantibus, tectricibus et secundariis albido limbatis ; cauda nigricante albo stricte marginata : subtus albus, pectore et hypochondriis pallide griseo lavatis, subalaribus albis flavo vix tinctis.   Long. tota 8·5, alæ 4·6, caudæ rect. lat. 3·5, rect. med. 3·1, tarsi 0·7, rostri a rictu 1·2.   (Descr. maris ex Santa Marta, Colombia.   Mus. nostr.)

Hab. NORTH AMERICA, Florida [8].—MEXICO (*Bullock* ?? [2]), Cozumel I. (*Benedict* [10]);

Nicaragua, Greytown (*Holland* [3]); Panama, Lion Hill (*M'Leannan* [14]).—Colombia [4]. Bahamas, Greater Antilles to Virgin Islands [13].

This species is probably of only casual occurrence in our region. It is a very common and characteristic bird in the Greater Antilles and Virgin Islands, but in the Windward Islands is represented by *T. rostratus*, which is doubtfully distinguished by its larger bill.

The accounts of this species in the West Indies are numerous and full of interesting details as to its habits, nesting, &c.; and copious extracts from the writings of Gosse, Hill, Professor Newton, and others are given by Brewer in the 'History of North-American Birds' [8]. It is there also stated to appear in Florida as a migratory species, arriving in March and leaving again in September. It is also said to migrate to and from Jamaica. The rarity of the species on the mainland of Central and South America makes us doubt whether there is any very general movement from the larger islands, for were this the case we should undoubtedly find it in greater abundance on the mainland. As it is, we have a very few instances of its occurrence on record, and these only of single individuals from widely distant points.

The nest and eggs of this species are very similar to those of *T. melancholicus*.

b. *Subtus flavus.*

a'. *Cauda fere rotundata.*

3. Tyrannus vociferans.

Tyrannus vociferans, Sw. Quart. Journ. Sci. xx. p. 273 [1]; Phil. Mag. new ser. i. p. 368 [2]; Baird, B. N. Am. p. 174, t. 48 [3]; Mex. Bound. Surv., Zool., Birds, p. 8 [4]; Scl. & Salv. Ibis, 1859, p. 121 [5]; Scl. P. Z. S. 1859, p. 383 [6], 1864, p. 176 [7]; Cat. Birds Brit. Mus. xiv. p. 269 [8]; Sumichrast, Mem. Bost. Soc. N. H. i. p. 557 [9]; Baird, Brew., & Ridgw. N. Am. B. ii. p. 327 [10]; Coues, Birds N. W. p. 238 [11]; Key N. Am. Birds, ed. 2, p. 433 [12]; Henshaw, Rep. Geol. Surv. West 100th Mer. v. p. 343 [13]; Lawr. Mem. Bost. Soc. N. H. ii. p. 288 [14]; Dugès, La Nat. i. p. 141 [15]; Ridgw. Pr. U. S. Nat. Mus. i. p. 480 [16]; Man. N. Am. B. p. 330 [17]; Zeledon, Cat. Av. de Costa Rica, p. 15 [18]; Perez, Pr. U. S. Nat. Mus. ix. p. 155 [19].

Laphyctes vociferans, Cab. & Heine, Mus. Hein. ii. p. 77 [20].

Tyrannus cassini, Lawr. Ann. Lyc. N. Y. v. p. 39, t. 3. f. 2 [21].

Muscicapa satelles, Licht. Mus. Berol. [22]

T. melancholico similis, sed rostro minore, pectore saturate cinereo, cauda quadrata stricte albo terminata, facile distinguendus.

Hab. North America, Rocky Mountains from Wyoming southwards, Southern California [17].—Mexico [20] (*Bullock* [2]), Santa Rosa, Trinidad, Micoba in Sonora (*W. Lloyd*), Los Nogales (*Kennerly* [4]), Plains of Colima (*Xantus* [14]), Guanajuato (*Dugès* [15]), near Mexico city (*White* [7], *le Strange*), Culhuacan, Coapa, Ixtapalapa, Coajimalpa, and Chimalpa in the vicinity of Mexico city (*Ferrari-Perez*),

Huexotitla and Llano de San Baltazar (*Ferrari-Perez* [18]), Chilpancingo and Amula in Guerrero (*Mrs. H. H. Smith*), Morelia, Atlixco (*F. D. G.*), State of Vera Cruz (*Sumichrast* [9]), Oaxaca (*Boucard* [6]); GUATEMALA, Salamá (*Skinner* [5]), Dueñas (*L. Fraser*); COSTA RICA (*Zeledon* [18]).

Sumichrast states [9] that this species is common in the hot and temperate regions of the State of Vera Cruz, and is also found on the plateau; but, so far as our experience goes, it is the only species of the highlands, and is far more abundant on the western side of Mexico than elsewhere. Xantus found it breeding on the Volcano of Colima, but at what elevation is not stated.

Northwards it spreads throughout the Western Sierra Madre, and thence across the United States frontier to the Rocky Mountains, as far north as Wyoming. But in the north it is only a summer visitor, retiring southwards after the breeding-season, at the approach of winter. In Guatemala it is perhaps more abundant than would appear at first sight, as its resemblance to *T. melancholicus* is close enough to render it easily mistaken for that bird.

Many years ago Skinner gave us a specimen said to have been shot near Salamá in Vera Paz, and during his short stay in Guatemala Fraser obtained one near Dueñas. These are the only authentic specimens from that country we have seen.

Its occurrence in Costa Rica rests on a statement to that effect in the 'History of North-American Birds,' and its mention in Zeledon's 'Catalogue of Costa Rican Birds.' We have no record to add of its occurrence so far south.

The nest obtained by Xantus is described by Brewer as a slight structure composed of wiry grass mixed with bits of wool and lined with finer grasses. The eggs are pure white, freckled on the larger end with purplish brown and greyish lilac.

4. Tyrannus verticalis.

Tyrannus verticalis, Say in Long's Exp. ii. p. 60 [1]; Baird, B. N. Am. p. 173 [2]; Baird, Brew., & Ridgw. N. Am. B. ii. p. 324 [3]; Coues, Birds N. W. p. 236 [4]; Key N. Am. B. ed. 2, p. 433 [5]; Lawr. Mem. Bost. Soc. N. H. ii. p. 288 [6]; Henshaw, Rep. Geol. Surv. West 100th Mer. v. p. 342 [7]; Sennett, Bull. U. S. Geol. Surv. v. p. 401 [8]; Ridgw. Man. N. Am. B. p. 330 [9]; Scl. Cat. Birds Brit. Mus. xiv. p. 269 [10].

T. melancholico quoque similis, sed rostro minore alarum tectricibus vix lavatis, cauda quadrata rectrice extima utrinque in pogonio externo omnino alba ab omnibus hujus generis distinguendus. Long. tota 8·0, alæ 4·9, caudæ 3·6, tarsi 0·75, rostri a rictu 0·95. (Descr. feminæ ex Volcan de Agua. Mus. nostr.)

Hab. WESTERN NORTH AMERICA together with the great plains southwards.—MEXICO, Tepic (*Grayson* [6]), Plains of Colima (*Xantus* [6]); GUATEMALA, Volcan de Agua (*O. S. & F. D. G.*), Dueñas (*F. Oates*).

Though a well-known bird in Western North America, *T. verticalis* appears to be seldom found in Mexico, and at present the only records we have of its occurrence in that country are those of Grayson and Xantus mentioned above at Tepic and Colima [6].

In Guatemala it has only been found on the slopes of the cordillera, between the volcanos of Agua and Fuego. Here the late Mr. Frank Oates, who a few years afterwards lost his life in South Africa, discovered it near Dueñas, where we subsequently met with it. The white margin to the outer tail-feathers shows rather conspicuously when the bird is flying, rendering it distinguishable from the common *T. melancholicus*.

In California the species is stated to be migratory, arriving towards the end of March, and leaving again in October. Where these birds pass the winter months has yet to be determined.

The nest is described as built on a low branch, and constructed of lichens, twigs, coarse grass and wool, and lined with hair. The eggs are creamy white, spotted with purple of two shades near the larger end [3].

b'. *Cauda furcata.*

5. **Tyrannus melancholicus.**

Tyrannus melancholicus, Vieill. N. Dict. d'Hist. N. xxxv. p. 48 [1]; Scl. P. Z. S. 1856, pp. 141 [2], 297 [3], 1859, p. 366 [4]; Ibis, 1873, p. 373 [5]; Cat. Birds Brit. Mus. xiv. p. 273 [6]; Moore, P. Z. S. 1859, p. 55 [7]; Scl. & Salv. Ibis, 1859, p. 121, t. 5. f. 4 (egg) [8]; P. Z. S. 1870, p. 837 [9]; Taylor, Ibis, 1860, p. 113 [10]; Cassin, Pr. Ac. Phil. 1860, p. 143 [11]; Owen, Ibis, 1861, p. 63 [12]; Lawr. Ann. Lyc. N. Y. vii. p. 295 [13], ix. p. 116 [14]; Salv. P. Z. S. 1867, p. 148 [15]; Cat. Strickl. Coll. p. 317 [16]; Scl. & Hudson, Arg. Orn. i. p. 158 [17].

Muscicapa despotes, Licht. Verz. Doubl. p. 55 [18]; Preis-Verz. mex. Vög. p. 2 (cf. J. f. Orn. 1863, p. 58) [18].

Tyrannus couchi, Baird, B. N. Am. p. 175, t. 49. f. 1 [20]; Mex. Bound. Surv., Zool., Birds, p. 8 [21].

Tyrannus melancholicus, var. *couchi*, Baird, Brew., & Ridgw. N. Am. B. ii. p. 329 [22]; Lawr. Mem. Bost. Soc. N. H. ii. p. 288 [23].

Tyrannus melancholicus couchi, Sennett, Bull. U. S. Geol. Surv. iv. p. 31 [24], v. p. 401 [25]; Coues, Key N. Am. B. ed. 2, p. 434 [26]; Ridgw. Pr. U. S. Nat. Mus. viii. p. 570 [27]; Man. N. Am. B. p. 329 [28]; F.-Perez, Pr. U. S. Nat. Mus. ix. p. 155 [29].

Laphyctes satrapa, Cab. & Heine, Mus. Hein. ii. p. 77 [30]; Cab. J. f. Orn. 1861, p. 251 [31].

Tyrannus satrapa, Scl. & Salv. P. Z. S. 1864, p. 360 [32], 1867, p. 279 [33]; Lawr. Ann. Lyc. N. Y. viii. p. 183 [34], ix. p. 204 [35].

Tyrannus melancholicus, var. *satrapa*, Lawr. Mem. Bost. Soc. N. H. ii. p. 288 [36]; Bull. U. S. Nat. Mus. no. 4, p. 28 [37].

Tyrannus melancholicus satrapa, Ridgw. Pr. U. S. Nat. Mus. v. p. 394 [38], vi. p. 496 [38]; Nutting & Ridgw. Pr. U. S. Nat. Mus. vi. pp. 374 [40], 384 [41], 393 [42], x. p. 589 [43].

Supra cinereus, dorso toto plus minusve viridi-olivaceo lavato; vertice crista celata coccinea ornato; subalaribus nigricantibus olivaceo limbatis; alis et cauda nigricantibus sordide albido limbatis; loris et regione parotica griseo-nigricantibus: subtus sulphureus, gula grisescente, pectore olivaceo-griseo, subalaribus flavis: rostro et pedibus nigris. Long. tota 8·0, alæ 4·5, caudæ 3·7, tarsi 0·7, rostri a rictu 1·1. (Descr. maris ex Teapa, Tabasco, Mexico. Mus. nostr.)

♀ mari similis.

Hab. NORTH AMERICA, Arizona [29], Texas [24] [25].—MEXICO (*Deppe* [19], *Sallé* [3], *Galeotti* [16]),

San Diego in Nuevo Leon (*Couch* [21]), Ceralvo, San Antonio, Estancia, and Topo Chico near Monterey (*F. B. Armstrong*), Sierra Madre above Ciudad Victoria, Soto la Marina, Aldama, Tampico (*W. B. Richardson*), Hacienda de los Atlixcos (*F. D. G.*), Cuesta de Misantla (*M. Trujillo*), Jalapa (*de Oca* [4], *Ferrari-Perez* [28]), Vera Cruz (*Richardson*), Teapa in Tabasco (*Mrs. H. H. Smith*), Merida in Yucatan (*Schott* [35]), Peto and Buctzotz in Yucatan (*G. F. Gaumer*), Tabi (*F. D. G.*), Holbox, Meco, Mujeres Is. (*G. F. Gaumer*), Cozumel I. (*Benedict* [27], *G. F. Gaumer*), Rio Mayo in Sonora (*W. Lloyd*), Mazatlan (*Grayson* [23] [36], *Forrer*), Tierra Colorada (*Mrs. H. H. Smith*), Acapulco (*A. H. Markham, Mrs. H. H. Smith*), Plains of Colima (*Xantus* [36]), Chihuitan [37], Tapana [37], Barrio [37], Dondominguillo [37], Sta. Efigenia, Tehuantepec (*Sumichrast*); BRITISH HONDURAS, Belize (*Blancaneaux*); GUATEMALA (*Constancia* [16]), Coban, Tactic, Yzabal, San Gerónimo [12], Dueñas [8], Escuintla, Retalhuleu (*O. S. & F. D. G.*); HONDURAS (*G. C. Taylor* [10]), Omoa (*Leyland* [6]), San Pedro (*G. M. Whitely* [9]), Segovia River (*Henderson* [43]); NICARAGUA, Blewfields (*Wickham* [33]), Greytown (*Holland* [34]), Chontales (*Belt* [5]), Omotepe I. [40], San Juan del Sur [41], and Sucuyá [42] (*Nutting*); COSTA RICA (*v. Frantzius* [31]), San José [14], Grecia [14], Sarchi [14], Barranca [14] (*Carmiol*), Bebedero, Nicoya, Tucuriqui (*Arcé*), Irazu (*Rogers*), La Palma (*Nutting* [38]); PANAMA, David (*Bridges* [2]), Calovevora, Calobre, Castillo (*Arcé*), Lion Hill (*M'Leannan* [13] [32]), Paraiso (*Hughes*), Truando R. (*Wood* [11]).—SOUTH AMERICA generally to the Argentine Republic [6] [17].

Specimens from the extreme southern range of *Tyrannus melancholicus* differ from those of the extreme north in having rather greyer throats, and blacker and more deeply forked tails. In Guiana and other parts of the northern portion of South America intermediate forms occur; and though the species has been separated into three races they are admitted on all hands to be not capable of precise definition. There is considerable variation in individuals from the same district, and the upper surface varies from dark olive to nearly pure grey; the throat, too, is whiter in some specimens than in others. Some stress has been laid on the colour of the tail between northern and southern birds; but this seems to be due to a considerable extent to the age of the feathers in the individuals examined, for in freshly moulted birds we see no difference in this respect.

The various names given to this bird are strictly applicable as follows:—*Tyrannus melancholicus* to the southern bird, *T. couchi* to that of the Rio Grande valley, and *T. satrapa* to that of the northern part of the South-American continent. *T. despotes* is probably a synonym of *T. melancholicus*, and so also is *Muscicapa furcata* of Spix, and *T. crudelis* of Swainson.

Except in the higher lands of Mexico, *Tyrannus melancholicus* is a very common species almost everywhere throughout our region, and in all the more open country may be seen in constant pursuit of its insect food, and from its conspicuous yellow plumage and its noisy restless habits is a species that is more frequently noticed than almost any other. At Dueñas, in Guatemala, it builds in May an open nest of slight structure, composed chiefly of small sticks and dried roots, with a little horse-hair for a lining. It is placed at the end of a branch of a low tree, at various heights from the ground. The eggs, usually four in number, are creamy white spotted with three shades of red.

B. *Rostrum incrassatum*.

6. **Tyrannus crassirostris.**

Tyrannus crassirostris, Sw. Quart. Journ. Sc. xx. p. 278[1]; Phil. Mag. new ser. i. p. 368[2]; Scl. & Salv. Ibis, 1860, p. 399[3]; Scl. P. Z. S. 1862, p. 19[4]; Cat. Birds Brit. Mus. xiv. p. 271[5]; Lawr. Mem. Bost. Soc. N. H. ii. p. 288[6]; Bull. U. S. Nat. Mus. no. 4, p. 28[7]; F.-Perez, Pr. U. S. Nat. Mus. ix. p. 155[8].

Melittarchus crassirostris, Cab. & Heine, Mus. Hein. ii. p. 80[9].

Megarhynchus crassirostris, Finsch, Abh. nat. Bremen, 1870, p. 329[10].

Muscicapa gnatho, Licht. Mus. Berol.[11]

Supra brunneus; dorso medio olivaceo vix tincto; capite summo nigricanti-brunneo, crista celata flava ornato; alis et cauda nigricanti-fuscis; regione parotica nigra: subtus flavus; gutture albo; pectore cinerescente; subalaribus flavis: rostro et pedibus nigris. Long. tota 9·0, alæ 5·2, caudæ 4·1, tarsi 0·8, rostri a rictu 1·2. (Descr. maris ex Tehuantepec. Mus. nostr.)

♀ mari similis.

Hab. MEXICO, Sauz in Sinaloa (*W. Lloyd*), Mazatlan (*Grayson* [6], *Forrer*), Chilpancingo, Omilteme and Acaguisotla in Guerrero (*Mrs. H. H. Smith*), San Juan del Rio (*Rébouch*), Chietla (*Ferrari-Perez*), Oaxaca (*Boucard*[4]), Cacoprieto, Chihuitan[7], Los Cues[7] (*Sumichrast*); GUATEMALA, Escuintla (*O. S.*[3]).

This is a species exclusively found on the western side of the cordillera of Mexico from Western Sonora in the north to the Isthmus of Tehuantepec, and thence to Western Guatemala, where we found it on one occasion at Escuintla, in the forest region bordering the Pacific[3].

Grayson met with it on the banks of the Rio Mazatlan, where he says it frequents the tops of the loftiest trees, preferring a withered branch for its perch, whence to watch for passing insects, which it seizes in the air, and returning to its perch beats to death against the branch and swallows entire. During the breeding-season pairs consort together, and are very tyrannical, attacking with great ferocity every bird that passes too near their domicile[6].

The species is probably resident wherever it is found, and resorts chiefly to the lowlands, but ascends the mountains up to an elevation of 8000 feet above the sea.

7. **Tyrannus magnirostris.**

Tyrannus magnirostris, d'Orb. in R. de la Sagra's Hist. Fis. y Pol. de Cuba, iii. p. 69, t. 13[1]; Bryant, Pr. Bost. Soc. N. H. xi. p. 66[2]; Cory, Auk, 1886, p. 243[3]; Scl. Cat. Birds Brit. Mus. xiv. p. 273[4].

Melittarchus magnirostris, Cab. J. f. Orn. 1855, p. 477[5]; Gundl. Orn. Cub. p. 73[6].

Supra griseo-brunneus; capite nigricante, crista celata fulvo-aurantiaca ornato; alis nigricantibus, tectricibus
et secundariis internis sordide albo limbatis; cauda nigricante, rectricibus omnibus albido stricte
terminatis: subtus albus; subalaribus pallide flavo vix lavatis: rostro et pedibus nigris. Long. tota 9·5,
alæ 5·2, caudæ 3·75, tarsi 0·9, rostri a rictu 1·65. (Descr. exempl. ex insula Mugeres. Mus. nostr.)

Hab. Mexico, Mujeres I. (*G. F. Gaumer* [3]).—Cuba [1 3 4 5 6]; Bahamas [2].

Mr. Gaumer's collection from the island of Mujeres off the extreme north-eastern
point of the promontory of Yucutan contained a single specimen of this species. The
species had previously only been known from the island of Cuba, and with some doubt [3]
from the island of Inagua.

In Cuba, according to Gundlach [6], *T. magnirostris* is not an uncommon bird, being
sedentary, and living in the woods, and on the plains where large trees grow. Its food
consists of insects, young birds, and lizards, and it also preys to some extent on honey-
bees.

Its nest is composed of twigs, fibrous roots, and grasses, and is placed on a horizontal
branch of some large tree, such as the Ceiba (*Eriodendron*); its eggs are like those of
T. griseus.

MILVULUS.

Milvulus, Swainson, Zool. Journ. iii. p. 165 (1827) (type *Muscicapa tyrannus*, Linn.); Sclater, Cat.
    Birds Brit. Mus. xiv. p. 277.

The two species constituting the genus *Milvulus* have, as a common character, very
elongated deeply forked tails, the bills also and the development of the supranasal
feathers are similar, but in other respects they differ rather widely, not only in coloration
but also in the way in which the outer quill-feathers in the males are reduced at their
extremities. Thus in *M. forficatus* the outermost feather only is narrowed in this way,
whereas in *M. tyrannus* three are involved.

The range of the two species is widely different, *M. forficatus* being a bird of the
prairies of South-western North America, Eastern Mexico, Guatemala, and thence southwards as a rare visitor to Costa Rica. *M. tyrannus*, on the other hand, occurs in
suitable open localities over the greater part of South America, and in Central America
as far north as Southern Mexico.

1. **Milvulus tyrannus.**

Muscicapa tyrannus, Linn. Syst. Nat. i. p. 325 [1].
Milvulus tyrannus, Scl. P. Z. S. 1856, pp. 141 [2], 297 [3]; Cat. Birds Brit. Mus. xiv. p. 277 [4]; Moore,
    P. Z. S. 1859, p. 55 [5]; Cab. J. f. Orn. 1861, p. 251 [6]; Lawr. Ann. Lyc. N. Y. viii. p. 178 [7],
    ix. p. 116 [8]; Scl. & Salv. P. Z. S. 1864, p. 361 [9], 1879, p. 516 [10]; Salv. P. Z. S. 1867, p. 149 [11],
    1870, p. 199 [12]; Ibis, 1872, p. 318 [13]; v. Frantz. J. f. Orn. 1869, p. 309 [14]; Sumichrast,
    Mem. Bost. Soc. N. H. i. p. 556 [15]; Baird, Brew., & Ridgw. N. Am. B. ii. p. 309 [16]; Ridgw.
    Pr. U. S. Nat. Mus. v. p. 496 [17]; Nutt. & Ridgw. Pr. U. S. Nat. Mus. vi. p. 375 [18]; Scl. &
    Huds. Arg. Orn. i. p. 160 [19].
Tyrannus violentus, Vieill. N. Dict. d'Hist. N. xxxv. p. 89 [20].

Tyrannus (Milvulus) monachus, Hartl. Rev. Zool. 1844, p. 214[21].

Milvulus monachus, Scl. & Salv. Ibis, 1859, p. 121[22]; P. Z. S. 1859, p. 384[23]; Taylor, Ibis, 1860, p. 114[24]; Lawr. Ann. Lyc. N. Y. vii. p. 295[25].

Supra griseus; uropygio nigricante; capite nigerrimo, crista celata sulphurea ornato; alis fuscis, tectricibus et secundariis sordide griseo limbatis; cauda nigra, rectrice extima utrinque in pogonio externo pro dimidio basali alba: subtus pure albus. Long. tota 14·5, alæ 4·1, caudæ rect. med. 2·5, rect. lat. 10·5, tarsi 0·7, rostri a rictu 0·8.

♀ mari similis, sed cauda multo breviore. (Descr. maris et feminæ ex Poctum, Guatemala. Mus. nostr.)

Hab. NORTH AMERICA, accidental[16].—MEXICO, Playa Vicente (*Boucard*[23]), Plains of Vera Cruz (*Sallé*[3], *Sumichrast*[15]): BRITISH HONDURAS, Old River and Pine-ridges of Belize (*Leyland*[5]), Saddle Cay[24], Half-Moon Cay[25] (*O. S.*); GUATEMALA[21], Peten (*Leyland*[5]), Pine-ridge of Poctum (*O. S. & F. D. G.*), San Gerónimo, Estansuelas[22] (*O. S.*); HONDURAS, Omoa and Comayagua (*Leyland*[5]), Langui and Agua Azul (*Taylor*[24]); NICARAGUA, Chontales (*Belt*[13]), San Juan del Sur (*Nutting*[18]); COSTA RICA[6] (*v. Frantzius*[14]), Orosi and San José[8] (*Carmiol*), Irazu (*Nutting*[17], *Rogers*), Turrialba (*Arcé*); PANAMA, David (*Bridges*[2], *Hicks*[7]), Castillo[12], Calovevora[12], Calobre[12], Santiago de Veraguas[11], Santa Fé[11] (*Arcé*), Lion Hill (*M'Leannan*[9 25]).—SOUTH AMERICA generally[4], from Colombia[10] to the Argentine Republic[19].

The occurrence of this species in North America appears to be quite accidental, and most of the records rest upon Audubon's observations[16]. In Mexico it is stated by Sumichrast to be abundant in winter in the savannahs of the hot lands of Vera Cruz, up to an elevation of about 2300 feet[15]. We, however, know little of its occurrence in Mexico, as none of our recent collections from that country contained specimens. There is, however, one example from that country in the British Museum, obtained by M. Boucard, but without precise locality. That traveller, however, is stated to have found it at Playa Vicente[23]. In the pine-districts and more open country of British Honduras and the adjoining parts of Guatemala in the district of Peten, *Milvulus tyrannus* is tolerably common, and several specimens were obtained in the pine-ridge of Poctum, where small flocks were observed frequenting the patches of trees and flying about displaying conspicuously their long forked scissor-like tails. Southwards of this district of Guatemala this species appears to occur in all suitable localities to the State of Panama, and thence over the greater part of South America to the Argentine Republic[19]. Mr. Hudson has given some interesting notes on this bird as observed by him in the Argentine Republic, where he states it is migratory.

Salmon, who found it breeding in the Colombian State of Antioquia, describes its nest as made of grass-stalks, roots, and fibres, intermixed with cotton, silk, and a variety of other substances, the lining being composed of dry roots or grass. This structure is placed on the spreading branch of a tree at no great height from the ground. The eggs are creamy white, distinctly spotted with dark red, especially at the larger end[10].

2. Milvulus forficatus.

Muscicapa forficata, Gm. Syst. Nat. i. p. 931 [1].

Milvulus forficatus, Scl. P. Z. S. 1857, p. 204 [2]; Cat. Birds Brit. Mus. xiv. p. 279 [3]; Baird, Mex. Bound. Surv., Zool., Birds, i. p. 7 [4]; Scl. & Salv. Ibis, 1859, p. 121 [5]; Cab. & Heine, Mus. Hein. ii. p. 79 [6]; Taylor, Ibis, 1860, p. 114 [7]; Cab. J. f. Orn. 1861, p. 252 [8]; Dresser, Ibis, 1865, p. 472 [9]; v. Frantz. J. f. Orn. 1869, p. 309 [10]; Sumichrast, Mem. Bost. Soc. N. H. i. p. 556 [11]; Lawr. Ann. Lyc. N. Y. ix. p. 116 [12]; Bull. U. S. Nat. Mus. no. 4, p. 28 [13]; Salvin, Ibis, 1872, p. 318 [14]; Baird, Brew., & Ridgw. N. Am. B. ii. p. 311 [15]; Sennett, Bull. U. S. Geol. Surv. iv. p. 30 [16], v. p. 401 [17]; Nutt. & Ridgw. Pr. U. S. Nat. Mus. vi. pp. 374 [18], 384 [19]; Ferrari-Perez, Pr. U. S. Nat. Mus. ix. p. 155 [20].

Supra griseus, dorso medio aut ochraceo aut roseo nonnunquam lavato; capite summo crista parva coccinea ornato; alis nigricantibus, tectricibus et secundariis albido limbatis; cauda elongata, rectricibus sex mediis nigris, duabus utrinque albis roseo tinctis et nigro terminatis: subtus griseo-albus, axillaribus rosaceo-rubris, hypochondriis crisso et subalaribus eodem colore lavatis: rostro corneo, pedibus nigris. Long. tota 14·0, alæ 4·8, caudæ rect. med. 2·6, rect. lat. 8·8, tarsi 0·75, rostri a rictu 1·0.

♀ mari similis, sed cauda multo breviore. (Descr. maris et feminæ ex Tampico, Mexico. Mus. nostr.)

Hab. NORTH AMERICA, Lower Mississippi valley [15] and Texas [7][16][17].—MEXICO, San Antonio, San Augustin, and Vaqueria in Nuevo Leon (*F. Armstrong*), Tamaulipas (*Couch* [4]), Soto la Marina, Tampico (*W. B. Richardson*), Hacienda de los Atlixcos, Otrobanda (*F. D. G.*), Vera Cruz (*Richardson*), Huehuetlan (*F. Ferrari-Perez* [20]), Chihuitan and Tehuantepec city (*Sumichrast* [13]); BRITISH HONDURAS, Cayo (*Blancaneaux*); GUATEMALA (*Skinner* [5]), Coban, San Gerónimo, Dueñas and near Guatemala city, Sta. Isabel near the port of San José (*O. S. & F. D. G.*); HONDURAS, Langui (*Taylor* [7]); NICARAGUA, Sucuyá [19], San Juan del Sur [18] (*Nutting*), Chinandega (*Henshaw coll.*); COSTA RICA (*von Frantzius* [8][10][12], *Carmiol*).

Milvulus forficatus is probably more abundant in the prairies of Texas and the lower Rio Grande valley than elsewhere; but it appears to be almost equally common over the eastern districts of Mexico and thence to British Honduras and Guatemala, being generally distributed in the open parts of the latter country. Its southern extension includes Nicaragua and Costa Rica, where, however, it is rare.

At Langui in Honduras G. C. Taylor says *M. forficatus* was very plentiful [7]. Numbers of birds would here assemble in the evening on the tops of trees, where they would remain till nearly dark and then fly off to the woods.

In Mexico it is chiefly a denizen of the eastern low-lands, but occasional individuals ascend the mountains as high as 4000 feet [11]. At the Isthmus of Tehuantepec it crosses to the Pacific side of the cordillera and thence spreads along both sides of the mountains of Guatemala, and is also found in open places up to an elevation of 5000 feet near the city of Guatemala, occurring at the same time near the sea-level at Santa Isabel, a few miles from the port of San José de Guatemala.

We are not aware if it remains to breed in Central America or Southern Mexico; but in the Rio Grande valley it does so in numbers, building in the mesquite trees, and laying pure white eggs blotched with large spots of dark red.

Fam. PIPRIDÆ *.

Subfam. *PIPRINÆ*.

PIPRITES.

Piprites, Cabanis, in Wiegm. Arch. f. Naturg. xiii. pt. i. p. 234 (1847); Scl. Cat. Birds Brit. Mus. xiv. p. 283.

Hemipipo, Cab. l. s. c.

Piprites is a small genus containing five species, found in the mountainous parts of South America, one species occurring in Costa Rica, having near allies in Guiana, the Andes of Colombia and Ecuador, and in South-eastern Brazil. The genus, as now understood, comprises both *Piprites* and *Hemipipo* of Cabanis. The former contains *P. pileatus* alone; the latter the other four species including *P. griseiceps* of Costa Rica. In general structure there seem to be insufficient grounds for separating the two groups, the difference resting almost entirely on the coloration of the plumage. Unlike the general rule in the Piprinæ, the sexes are similarly clothed. The bill in *P. griseiceps* is strong, wide at the base, and with a very distinct notch near the end of the tomia of the maxilla; the nostrils are large, and open at the end of the nasal fossa, and overhung by the setose supra-nasal feathers; the rictal bristles are strong. The second, third, and fourth primaries are subequal, the first < fifth. The tail is rounded; the tarsi and toes slender, the outer toe a little longer than the inner.

1. **Piprites griseiceps.** (Tab. XLI. fig. 3.)

Piprites griseiceps, Salv. P. Z. S. 1864, p. 583 [1]; Lawr. Ann. Lyc. N. Y. ix. p. 116 [2]; Pelz. & Madar. Mon. Pipridæ, pt. i. p. 9, t. 3. fig. 2 [3]; Scl. Cat. Birds Brit. Mus. xiv. p. 285 [4].

---

* The Pipridæ is a purely neotropical family containing about seventy species, which are distributed over the hotter forest-clad parts of South America, from Paraguay northwards, and through Central America to the middle of the Mexican State of Vera Cruz. Thirteen species only occur within our limits, belonging to five of the nineteen genera into which the family has been divided. Mr. Sclater, in his recent Catalogue (Cat. Birds Brit. Mus. xiv. p. 282), divides the family into two subfamilies—Piprinæ and Ptilochlorinæ. The former, represented in our country by the genera *Piprites*, *Pipra*, *Chiroxiphia*, and *Chiromacheris*, he distinguishes by the bill being short and wide at the base, the maxilla hardly notched near the tip, the rictal bristles feebly developed, and the general contrast between the sexes as regards the coloration of their plumage, the males in most cases being brightly clad. The latter subfamily is represented by *Heteropelma* alone, in which the above characters are reversed. The Pipridæ as well as the Cotingidæ have the toes united at the base, but the tarsi are differently covered. The divisions of the Pipridæ as thus defined will have to be reconsidered at some future time, for the contrast between such birds as *Piprites* and *Metopothrix* is so great that they cannot well remain under the common definition assigned to them. In *Piprites* the bill is short, wide at the base, the subterminal notch quite distinct, and the rictal bristles well developed. In *Metopothrix* the bill is long and narrow, the tomia of the maxilla is destitute of a notch, and there are no traces of rictal bristles. We can only here indicate these discrepancies, and leave the reconstruction of the classification of these complex families to a future monographer.

Supra olivaceo-viridis, alis et cauda nigricantibus, dorsi colore limbatis, illarum secundariis intimis in pogonio interno lactescenti-albidis; capite toto griseo, oculorum ambitu albo: subtus viridi-flavus, pectore et hypochondriis olivaceis, subalaribus flavido-albidis, tectricibus elongatis, margine alarum juxta nigris remigibus interne ochraceo-albidis: rostro et pedibus plumbeis. Long. tota 4·5, alæ 2·5, caudæ 1·8, rostri a rictu 0·5, tarsi 0·5. (Descr. exemp. typ. ex Tucurriqui, Costa Rica. Mus. nostr.)

Hab. Costa Rica, Tucurriqui (*Arcé* [1-4]).

A single specimen sent us by our collector Enrique Arcé from Costa Rica in 1864 is the only one that has as yet come under our notice. It belongs to a little group of four species which are distributed over the chief mountain masses of South America; thus Eastern Brazil has *P. chloris*, the Andes of Colombia, Ecuador, and Peru *P. tschudii*, and Guiana *P. chlorion*, whilst *P. griseiceps* belongs to the mountains of Costa Rica.

P. griseiceps is perhaps most nearly allied to *P. tschudii*, but differs in having the whole of the top of the head grey, and in the absence of the yellowish-white tips to the greater wing-coverts, innermost secondaries, and the rectrices.

Our figure is taken from the type, which also served for that in Von Pelzeln's and Von Madarász's Monograph on the Pipridæ.

PIPRA.

Pipra, Linnæus, Syst. Nat. i. p. 338 (1766); Scl. Cat. Birds Brit. Mus. xiv. p. 292.

Five of the eighteen known species of *Pipra* occur within the limits of Central America, only one of which, however, *P. mentalis*, is found as far north as Guatemala, British Honduras, and the southern portion of the Mexican State of Vera Cruz. The rest occur in Nicaragua and the countries lying to the south-eastward.

Mr. Sclater divides the genus into three chief sections, based upon the coloration of the sexes. The first of these alone is represented in our region.

Pipra mentalis has a much more elongated nostril than *Piprites*, which occupies the anterior lower portion of the nasal fossa and is slightly overhung by the membrane; the subterminal notch of the tomia is not so distinct, but the rictal bristles are well developed; the wings, tail, and tarsi are much shorter. The sexes, too, are very differently coloured.

a. *Gula plerumque nigra (mento interdum flavo).*

a′. *Vertex aut coccineus aut flavus.*

1. Pipra mentalis.

Pipra mentalis, Scl. P. Z. S. 1856, p. 299, t. 121 [1]; 1859, p. 285 [2]; Cat. Birds Brit. Mus. xiv. p. 295 [3]; Scl. & Salv. Ibis, 1859, p. 125 [4]; P. Z. S. 1864, p. 362 [5]; 1870, p. 837 [6]; Sumichrast, Mem. Bost. Soc. N. H. i. p. 558 [7]; Lawr. Ann. Lyc. N. Y. ix. p. 116 [8]; v. Frantz. J. f. Orn. 1869, p. 309 [9]; Salv. P. Z. S. 1870, p. 200 [10]; Ibis, 1872, p. 318 [11]; 1889, p. 364 [12]; Boucard, P. Z. S. 1878, p. 66 [13].

Chiroxiphia mentalis, Lawr. Ann. Lyc. N. Y. vii. p. 296 [14].

Nitide nigerrima; capite toto coccineo, plumis ad basin albis, mento, femoribus et subalaribus citrinis: rostro et pedibus carneis. Long. tota 4·0, alæ 2·3, caudæ 1·1, rostri a rictu 0·5, tarsi 0·5.

♀ olivaceo-viridis: subtus pallidior, subalaribus pallide flavidis. (Descr. maris et feminæ ex Choctum, Guatemala. Mus. nostr.)

Hab. Mexico, Cordova (*Sallé* [1]), Playa Vicente (*Boucard* [2]), Teapa in Tabasco (*Mrs. H. H. Smith*), Tizimin in Yucatan, Meco and Mugeres Islands (*Gaumer*); British Honduras, Orange walk (*Gaumer*), Cayo (*Blancaneaux*); Guatemala, Choctum, Yzabal (*O. S. & F. D. G.*); Nicaragua, Chontales (*Belt* [10]); Costa Rica, Tucurriqui [8], Turrialba (*Arcé*), Angostura (*Carmiol* [8]); Panama, Bugaba, Mina de Chorcha (*Arcé* [10]), Lion Hill (*M'Leannan* [5]).

M. Sallé was the first to discover this pretty *Pipra* in the forests in the vicinity of Cordova in the Mexican State of Vera Cruz, and this is the most northern point recorded of its range; but from this place southwards it occurs nearly uninterruptedly in the forests on the eastern side of the Cordillera to the State of Panama, where it is also found in the forests bordered by the Pacific Ocean.

It has not yet been met with in any portion of Western Mexico or Guatemala; but in the hotter portions of British Honduras and Vera Paz it is abundant up to an elevation of about 2000 feet. It frequents the underwood in the mixed tropical forest of lofty trees.

Pipra mentalis is the only species having a yellow chin, thighs, and under wing-coverts. *P. chloromeros* of Peru and Bolivia also has yellow thighs, but the chin and under wing-coverts are black.

2. Pipra auricapilla.

Manacus aurocapillus, Briss. Orn. iv. p. 448, t. 34. f. 2 [1].

Pipra erythrocephala, Linn. Syst. Nat. i. p. 339 [2].

Pipra auricapilla, Licht. Verz. Doubl. p. 29 [3]; Cab. & Heine, Mus. Hein. ii. p. 92 [4]; Scl. Cat. Birds Brit. Mus. xiv. p. 296 [5].

Nitide nigerrima; capite et nucha aureis, margine postico coccineo; femoribus extrorsum coccineis, introrsum albis; subalaribus albido intermixtis: rostro et pedibus carneis. Long. tota 3·5, alæ 2·2, caudæ 0·8, rostri a rictu 0·45, tarsi 0·55. (Descr. maris ex·Chepo, Panama. Mus. nostr.)

♀ olivaceo-viridis, subtus pallidior.

Hab. Panama, Chepo (*Arcé*). — South America, Colombia, Venezuela, Guiana [1], and Amazons valley.

This common South-American species can hardly be called a member of our fauna, but we include it here since we possess a male specimen from Chepo, on the isthmus of Panama, a little to the south-eastward of the railway. As *P. mentalis* occurs on the line of railway itself, the boundary of the ranges of the two species is probably thus indicated to within a few miles. *P. auricapilla* is also found in the Cauca valley, Venezuela, Trinidad, Guiana, and the whole of the Amazons valley up to the base of the Andes.

Linnæus's name *P. erythrocephala* is chiefly applicable to this species, but as it conveys a wrong impression as to the colour of the head, it has never been generally used.

b'. *Vertex cœruleus.*

3. Pipra velutina.

Pipra velutina, Berl. Ibis, 1883, p. 492 [1]; Scl. Cat. Birds Brit. Mus. xiv. p. 299 [2].

Chiroxiphia cyaneocapilla, Lawr. Ann. Lyc. N. Y. vii. p. 296 (nec Hahn) [3].

Pipra cyaneocapilla, Scl. & Salv. P. Z. S. 1864, p. 362 [4]; 1879, p. 519 [5]; Salv. P. Z. S. 1867, p. 149 [6]; 1870, p. 200 [7].

Nitide nigerrima; capite summo læte cyaneo, fronte nigra. Long. tota 3·5, rostro et pedibus nigricantibus, alæ 2·3, caudæ 1·0, rostri a rictu 0·4, tarsi 0·5.

♀ viridis, subtus pallidior, pectore et hypochondriis dorso fere concoloribus. (Descr. maris et feminæ ex Panama. Mus. nostr.)

Hab. PANAMA (*Ribbe* [1]), Bugaba [7], V. de Chiriqui [7], Santiago de Veraguas [6] (*Arcé,*), Lion Hill (*M'Leannan* [3] [4]).—NORTHERN COLOMBIA [5].

This species, which was separated by Count Berlepsch, is very closely allied to *P. cyaneocapilla* of the Amazons valley, but the blue of the crown of the head is of rather a deeper tint, the forehead is more decidedly black, and there is no indication of the indigo tint which suffuses the lower back of *P. cyaneocapilla*.

The bird has been known to us for some time from specimens sent us by M'Leannan from Lion Hill, on the Panama Railway. In the list of the birds of his collection allusion was made to the differences presented between them and typical examples of *P. cyaneocapilla*, but it was not then thought advisable to separate the Panama bird as was subsequently done by Count Berlepsch from specimens obtained in the State of Panama by the entomological collector Ribbe.

Its range is limited to the State of Panama, as we have no record of its occurrence in Costa Rica; but southwards it spreads into the Cauca valley of Colombia. Nothing has been recorded of its habits.

c'. *Vertex albus.*

4. Pipra leucocilla.

Pipra leucocilla, Linn. Syst. Nat. i. p. 340 [1]; Cab. & Heine, Mus. Hein. ii. p. 93 [2]; Salv. P. Z. S. 1867, p. 149 [3]; 1870, p. 200 [4]; Scl. Cat. Birds Brit. Mus. xiv. p. 297 [5].

Pipra coracina, Scl. P. Z. S. 1856, p. 29 [6].

Nitide nigerrima; capite toto summo et nucha niveis, rostro et pedibus nigricantibus. Long. tota 4, alæ 3·3, caudæ 1·1, rostri a rictu 0·5, tarsi 0·5. (Descr. maris ex Chitra, Panama. Mus. nostr.)

♀ olivacea; subtus medialiter dilutior, gula et subalaribus grisescentibus.

Hab. PANAMA, Cordillera de Tolé [3], Chitra [4], Calovevora [4], Santa Fé (*Arcé*).—SOUTH AMERICA, Colombia and Guiana to Brazil [2].

Adult males from our country are hardly so glossy as specimens from the south, but the difference is insignificant. The species appears to be not uncommon in the State of Panama, the limit of its range in this direction; it thence spreads southwards over the greater part of Tropical South America to the southern confines of Brazil.

b. *Gula alba.*

5. Pipra leucorrhoa.

Pipra leucorrhoa, Scl. P. Z. S. 1863, p. 63, t. 10 [1]; Cat. Birds Brit. Mus. xiv. p. 301 [2]; Salv. P. Z. S. 1867, p. 149 [3]; 1870, p. 200 [4]; Ibis, 1872, p. 318 [5]; Lawr. Ann. Lyc. N. Y. ix. p. 116 [6].

Supra nitide purpureo-nigra, gutture et crisso albis; rostro et pedibus nigricantibus. Long. tota 3·5, alæ 2·3, caudæ 1·2, rostri a rictu 0·5, tarsi 0·6. (Descr. maris ex Chitra, Panama. Mus. nostr.)
♀ supra viridis; subtus medialiter albicans, gutture griseo-albicante.

Hab. NICARAGUA, Chontales (*Belt* [5]); COSTA RICA, Tucurriqui (*Arcé*), Angostura, Guaitil (*Carmiol* [6]); PANAMA, Chiriqui [4], Bugaba [4], Laguna de Castillo [4], Boquete de Chitra [4], Calovevora [4], Santa Fé [3] (*Arcé*).—COLOMBIA [1].

This species is a close ally of *P. gutturalis* of Guiana, but may be readily distinguished by the upper surface being of a uniform shiny purple, *P. gutturalis* having a dull ring round the back of the neck and a dull patch on the lower back; moreover the last-named species has a large white patch on each wing, which must show conspicuously when the wing is extended. The ends of the under tail-coverts of *P. leucorrhoa* are white. The females are very like that sex of *P. leucocilla*, but may be distinguished by the upper surface being of a uniform green: the best character, however, for distinction is in the nostrils; these in *P. leucorrhoa* are more open than in *P. leucocilla.*

CHIROXIPHIA.

Chiroxiphia, Cabanis, in Wiegm. Arch. f. Naturg. xiii. pt. i. p. 235 (1847); Scl. Cat. Birds Brit. Mus. xiv. p. 307.

Chiroxiphia contains six well-defined species, which are distributed over Tropical America from the Isthmus of Tehuantepec to S. Brazil and Bolivia. Two occur in Central America, of which *C. lanceolata* is a species of the northern portion of South America, which enters our fauna in the State of Panama. The other, *C. linearis,* is peculiar to Central America, and ranges from Costa Rica to Tehuantepec, but is found almost exclusively in the forests bordering the Pacific Ocean.

In general structure *Chiroxiphia* resembles *Pipra*; but the male has peculiar characters of coloration, and the nostrils open at the end of the nasal fossa, though hidden by the supra-nasal feathers. The central rectrices of *C. linearis* are much lengthened, those of *C. lanceolata* less so; but this character is not found in all the members of the genus.

1. Chiroxiphia lanceolata.

Pipra lanceolata, Wagl. Isis, 1830, p. 931 [1].

Chiroxiphia lanceolata, Cab. & Heine, Mus. Hein. ii. p. 96 [2]; Scl. & Salv. P. Z. S. 1864, p. 362 [3]; Salv. P. Z. S. 1867, p. 150 [4]; 1870, p. 200 [5]; Scl. Cat. Birds Brit. Mus. xiv. p. 309 [6].

Pipra melanocephala, Vieill. Enc. Méth. p. 389 (?) [7]; Scl. P. Z. S. 1856, p. 141 [8].

Pipra pareola, Hahn & Küst. Vög. Lief. xvi. t. 4 (nec Linn.) [9].

Chiroxiphia caudata, Lawr. Ann. Lyc. N. Y. vii. p. 296 (nec Shaw) [10].

Niger; dorso toto cæruleo, crista verticali triangulari miniata, loris et fronte stricte nigris; caudæ rectricibus duabus mediis modice elongatis: rostro nigricanti-corneo, pedibus carneis. Long. tota 4·5, alæ 2·8, caudæ rect. lat. 2·4, rect. med. 3·1, rostri a rictu 0·5, tarsi 0·7.

♀ virescens; subtus pallidior, abdomine medio albicante, subalaribus albicantibus. (Descr. maris et feminæ ex Panama. Mus. nostr.)

Hab. PANAMA, David (*Bridges*), Mina de Chorcha [5], Chitra [5], Boquete de Chitra [5], Castillo [5], Calovevora [5], Santa Fé [4] (*Arcé*), Lion Hill Station (*M‘Leannan* [3]), Paraiso Station (*Hughes*).—SOUTH AMERICA, Colombia [2], Venezuela [2], Trinidad.

This species of the northern part of South America occurs in the State of Panama as far as the confines of Costa Rica, where its place is taken by *C. linearis*. From this bird the male may at once be distinguished by its much less lengthened central rectrices. *C. pareola* of Guiana has a square tail.

2. Chiroxiphia linearis.

Pipra linearis, Bp. P. Z. S. 1837, p. 113 [1]; Gould, Zool. Voy. Sulph., Birds, p. 40. t. 20 [2].

Chiroxiphia linearis, Bp. Consp. Av. i. p. 172 [3]; Scl. & Salv. Ibis, 1859, p. 124 [4]; Salv. Ibis, 1860, p. 100 [5]; 1872, p. 318 [6]; Cab. & Heine, Mus. Hein. ii. p. 95 [7]; Lawr. Ann. Lyc. N. Y. ix. p. 116 [8]; Lawr. Bull. U. S. Nat. Mus. no. 4, p. 29 [9]; Nutting, Pr. U. S. Nat. Mus. v. p. 396 [10]; vi. p. 384 [11].

Ceropæna linearis, Bp. Consp. Vol. Anisod. p. 6 [12].

Pipra fastuosa, Less. Rev. Zool. 1842, p. 174 [13].

Præcedenti similis, sed fronte latiore nigro et caudæ rectricibus duabus mediis valde elongatis (5·5) facile distinguenda.

♀ cauda elongata quoque distinguenda.

Hab. MEXICO, Tapana, Tehuantepec (*Sumichrast* [9]); GUATEMALA, Volcan de Agua above San Diego, La Trinidad, Medio Monte and Savana Grande on the slopes of the Volcan de Fuego, Retalhuleu (*O. S. & F. D. G.*); NICARAGUA, Virgin Bay (*Bridges*), Sucuya (*Nutting*), Chontales (*Belt* [6]); COSTA RICA, Bebedero, Gulf of Nicoya (*Arcé*), Dota mountains (*Carmiol*), San Juan (*von Frantzius*), Irazu (*Rogers*).

The Pacific side of the Isthmus of Tehuantepec is the extreme limit of the range of this species in this direction; thence it spreads throughout Central America to the confines of the State of Panama, but is restricted northward of Nicaragua to the forests bordering the Pacific Ocean, being entirely absent from the more eastern forests of Mexico and Guatemala. In Guatemala it is far from uncommon in the wooded slopes of the Volcanos Agua and Fuego, up to an elevation of about 3500 feet, and though we never actually met with it ourselves, our Indian hunters frequently brought us specimens from that district.

Sumichrast, who met with this species on the Isthmus of Tehuantepec, writes concerning it as follows [9] :—"This Manakin, the only one I have found in the western part of the isthmus, dwells only in certain localities, thickly wooded, at the foot of the Cordilleras, on the banks of streams, and still it is only in the solitary ravines and most shady nooks that they need be looked for. Very difficult to discover at any other time in the midst of the thick forests that they choose for their dwelling, their retreat is easily discovered in the breeding-season by the loud continuous cries made by the males during the greater part of the day. Two males are almost always found together perched side by side on the same branch, a curious fact which I have a long time wondered at, but the following observation enlightened me. A female pluming herself is perched a few steps away from these two gallants, who, anxious to please her, begin a loving joust the most diverting, ascending and descending with their wings half closed, their feathers disheveled, and their throats inflated with pleasure and the effort of singing. This continues sometimes for more than a quarter of an hour, and recommences after a few minutes rest, during which the female shows her pleasure by the trembling of her body and the fluttering of her wings. Nothing can be more graceful than this picture when a ray of sunlight piercing the dark vault of the forest enlivens the scene and brings out the bright tints of black velvet, of azure and purple that adorn the coats of these little feathered actors. With an excessive natural confidence the *Chiroxiphiæ* allow themselves to be approached very near without showing any fear, and the sound of a gun hardly frightens them."

Mr. Nutting [10], who observed two males dancing, says that they were upon a bare twig about four feet from the ground; the two birds were about a foot and a half apart and were alternately jumping about two feet into the air, and alighting exactly upon the spot whence they jumped. They kept time as regularly as clockwork, one bird jumping up the instant the other alighted, each bird accompanying himself to the tune of " *to-lé-do, to-lé-do, to-lé-do*," sounding the syllable " *to* " as he crouched to spring, " *lé* " while in the air, and " *do* " as he alighted.

CHIROMACHÆRIS.

Chiromachæris, Cabanis, in Wiegm. Arch. f. Naturg. xiii. pt. 1, p. 235 (1847); Scl. Cat. Birds Brit. Mus. xiv. p. 312.

Chiromachæris contains seven species, which are spread over Tropical America from Southern Mexico to Southern Brazil. Three of these species occur within our limits, of which *C. vitellina* alone enters the northern part of Colombia.

The plumage of *Chiromachæris* differs in texture from that of *Pipra*, being rather looser and fuller. None of the species are so brightly coloured as some members of *Pipra*; but they are, nevertheless, peculiar birds, the males having long gular feathers, pointed remiges, the shafts of the inner primaries and the secondaries are thickened. The tail and tarsi are longer than in typical *Pipra*.

1. Chiromachæris candæi.

Pipra candei, Parz. Rev. Zool. 1841, p. 306[1].

Manacus candei, Bp. Consp. i. p. 171[2]; Scl. P. Z. S. 1856, p. 399[3]; 1859, p. 285[4]; Moore, P. Z. S. 1859, p. 56[5]; Scl. & Salv. Ibis, 1859, p. 124[6]; 1860, p. 37[7]; Sumichrast, Mem. Bost. Soc. N. H. i. p. 558[8].

Chiromachæris candæi, Cab. & Heine, Mus. Hein. ii. p. 97[9]; Lawr. Ann. Lyc. N. Y. viii. p. 184[10]; ix. p. 117[11]; Scl. & Salv. P. Z. S. 1870, p. 837[12]; Nutting, Pr. U. S. Nat. Mus. vi. p. 403[13]; Ridgw. Pr. U. S. Nat. Mus. x. p. 580[14]; Scl. Cat. Birds Brit. Mus. xiv. p. 314[15].

Supra nigra, dorso postico et tectricibus caudæ superioribus olivaceis; cervice tota, tectricibus alarum pro majore parte, genis et gutture toto albis; abdomine flava: rostro nigro, pedibus carneis. Long. tota 4·7, alæ 2·2, caudæ 1·4, rostri a rictu 0·6, tarsi 0·9.

♀ olivacea, uropygio paulo dilutiore, abdomine toto flavescentiore. (Descr. maris et feminæ ex Choctum, Guatemala. Mus. nostr.)

Hab. MEXICO, Cordova (*Sallé*[3]), Playa Vicente (*Boucard*[4]), State of Vera Cruz (*Sumichrast*); BRITISH HONDURAS, Orange Walk (*Gaumer*), Belize (*Blancaneaux*); GUATEMALA, Peten (*Leyland*), Choctum, Teleman, Yzabal (*O. S. & F. D. G.*); HONDURAS[9], Truxillo (*Townsend*[14]), San Pedro (*G. M. Whitely*); NICARAGUA, Greytown (*Holland*[10]), Los Sabalos (*Nutting*[13]); COSTA RICA, Tucurriqui (*Arcé*), Angostura (*Carmiol*[11]).

Chiromachæris candæi is a bird of the eastern forests of our country throughout its range, which extends from the vicinity of Cordova in the State of Vera Cruz to Costa Rica, and is common in that region from near the sea-level to a height of from 2000 to 3000 feet. It frequents the undergrowth of the denser forests, and its presence is easily detected by its note, which resembles the crack of a whip, followed by a rustling noise, probably produced by the quills of the wing-feathers.

We have no knowledge of the nesting-habits of this species, which probably resemble those of *C. vitellina* described below.

2. Chiromachæris vitellina.

Pipra vitellina, Gould, P. Z. S. 1843, p. 103[1]; Zool. Voy. Sulph., Birds, p. 41, t. 21[2]; Lafr. Rev. Zool. 1847, p. 69[3]; Bp. Consp. i. p. 173[4].

Chiromachæris vitellina, Cab. & Heine, Mus. Hein. ii. p. 97[5]; Scl. & Salv. P. Z. S. 1864, p. 22[6]; 1879, p. 517[7]; Scl. Cat. Birds Brit. Mus. xiv. p. 315[8].

Chiroxiphia vitellina, Lawr. Ann. Lyc. N. Y. vii. p. 296[9].

Supra nigra ; dorso postico, supracaudalibus et abdomine toto olivaceis ; cervice tota, genis et gutture toto luteis : rostro nigro, pedibus carneis.   Long. tota 4·0, alæ 2·1, caudæ 1·1, rostri a rictu 0·5, tarsi 0·85.

♀ olivacea ; subtus dilutior, abdomine medio flavescente.   (Descr. maris et feminæ ex Lion Hill, Panama. Mus. nostr.)

Hab. PANAMA[1][2], Veraguas (*Arcé*), Lion Hill (*McLeannan*[6][9]), Obispo (*O. S.*), Paraiso Station (*Hughes*).—NORTHERN COLOMBIA[7].

Specimens obtained by Salmon in the Cauca Valley in Northern Colombia have the throat a little paler yellow than in typical Panama examples, but the difference is very slight.   Mr. Sclater includes Nicaragua in the range of this species, on the strength of a specimen in the British Museum, said to have been obtained by Delattre in that country ; we believe, however, an error in the record of the locality of this specimen has been made, for we have been unable to trace the species beyond the immediate neighbourhood of the Panama railway.

C. vitellina is common in the woods about Obispo on the Panama railway, where Salvin observed males on several occasions.   He could not be certain how the sharp noise like the crack of a whip was produced, but the wings when the bird flies make a buzzing noise like the rattling of quills together.   The male also utters a double note, thrusting forward its long chin-feathers at the same time.   Salmon says[7] that the eggs are creamy white (reddish in some specimens), thickly blotched with chocolate-red ; these blotches in some specimens are almost, in others quite, confluent at the larger end.   He also found the nest of *C. manacus*, an allied species ; this he describes as a shallow slight structure of grasses, suspended from the fork of a branch of a low shrub.

3. **Chiromachæris aurantiaca.**   (Tab. XLI. figg. 1 ♂, 2 ♀.)

Chiromachæris aurantiaca, Salv. P. Z. S. 1870, p. 200[1] ; Scl. Cat. Birds Brit. Mus. xiv. p. 316[2].

Præcedenti similis, sed colore luteo multo magis aurantio abdomineque aurantio nec olivaceo distinguenda.

Hab. PANAMA, Bugaba, Mina de Chorcha (*Arcé*[1]).

A species closely allied to *C. vitellina* but obviously distinct, its range lying between those of *C. vitellina* and *C. candœi*, and confined to a very limited district at the western end of the State of Panama.

Subfam. *PTILOCHLORINÆ.*

HETEROPELMA.

Heteropelma, Bp. Consp. Vol. Anisod. p. 4 (1854) ; Scl. Cat. Birds Brit. Mus. xiv. p. 318.

This is the only genus of the subfamily Ptilochlorinæ found within our limits.   It contains nine species, which are divisible into two groups, one of which comprises six ill-defined species ; the members of the other group all have yellow occipital crests, a

feature so common in the Tyrannidæ.   In our country we find two species of the first
section and none of the second.

They are dull-coloured birds, alike as to the sexes, and without bright markings of
any sort.   Their range extends from Southern Mexico to Panama, and the allied
southern forms spread over most of Tropical America to South-eastern Brazil.   Like
other Pipridæ they are found only in dense forest.

The bill is much more compressed than in the typical Piprinæ, and the subterminal
maxillary notch is very distinct; the nostrils are elliptical and open, and are situated
at the lower end of the nasal fossa: the rictal bristles are well developed.   The wings
are rounded, the fourth primary a little longer than the third and fifth, the first equals
the tenth.   The tarsi and toes are slender, the outer toe united to the middle toe a long
way from the base.

1. **Heteropelma veræ-pacis.**

Heteropelma veræ-pacis, Scl. & Salv. P. Z. S. 1860, p. 300 [1]; 1870, p. 837 [2]; Ibis, 1860, p. 400 [3];
    Scl. P. Z. S. 1862, p. 19 [4]; Cat. Birds Brit. Mus. xiv. p. 320 [5]; Lawr. Ann. Lyc. N. Y. vii.
    p. 473 [6]; ix. p. 116 [7]; Salv. P. Z. S. 1870, p. 200 [8].

Supra olivaceo-brunneum; alis et cauda rufescentioribus; abdomine medio olivaceo: rostro et pedibus corneis,
    mandibulæ basi pallida.   Long. tota 6·5, alæ 3·5, caudæ 2·5, rostri a rictu 0·8, tarsi 0·8.   (Descr. maris
    ex Choctum, Guatemala.   Mus. nostr.)
♀ mari similis.

Hab. MEXICO, Playa Vicente (*Boucard* [4]); BRITISH HONDURAS, Orange Walk (*Gaumer*);
    GUATEMALA, Choctum [1], Yzabal (*O. S & F. D. G.*); HONDURAS, San Pedro (*G. M.*
    Whitely [2]); COSTA RICA, Balza, Angostura, Cervantes (*Carmiol*); PANAMA, Volcan
    de Chiriqui, Bugaba, Chiriqui, Castillo, Chitra, Calovévora (*Arcé* [8]).

The specimens of this species from Costa Rica and Panama are rather darker than
typical examples from Vera Paz, but the difference is hardly tangible.   The darkest of
all our specimens are from Chitra and Calovevora, these contrast strongly with examples
obtained close to the line of railway which we attribute to *H. stenorhynchum.   Heteropelma veræ-pacis* is an inhabitant of the forest-region of Eastern Guatemala, where it is
not uncommon; it spreads northward to Playa Vicente in the Mexican State of Vera
Cruz [4].   Its range in altitude extends from the sea-level to an altitude of about
1500 feet.   It frequents the undergrowth of the lofty forest, keeping near the ground.

2. **Heteropelma stenorhynchum.**

Heteropelma stenorhynchum, Scl. & Salv. P. Z. S. 1868, pp. 628, 632 [1]; Scl. Cat. Birds Brit. Mus.
    xiv. p. 320 [2].
Heteropelma veræ-pacis, Salv. P. Z. S. 1883, p. 424 [3].

Præcedenti similis, sed supra pallidior; alis minus rufescentibus, pileo rufescente tincto, abdomine toto grises-
    cente.   (Descr. exempl. ex Panama.   Mus. nostr.)

Hab. PANAMA (*A. H. Markham* [3], *Arcé*).—VENEZUELA [1].

We have two specimens of this bird from the neighbourhood of Panama which agree much better with the Venezuelan form than with specimens from countries lying more immediately to the north.

H. stenorhynchum is scarcely distinguishable from *H. amazonum* from the Amazons Valley, but the head is rather more rufescent and the belly somewhat paler. The narrowness of the bill, on which some stress was laid in the original descriptions, seems to us now to be of slight importance. Mr. Goering, who discovered this species at San Esteban in Venezuela, states that in life the iris of the eye is white [1].

Fam. COTINGIDÆ*.

Subfam. *TITYRINÆ*.

The Tityrinæ can be distinguished from the other five subfamilies of Cotingidæ by a singular well-marked feature—the adult males in all the species having the second or penultimate primary so reduced in size as to be not more than half the length of the outermost primary (see Scl. Cat. Birds Brit. Mus. xiv. p. 327). In the female this feather is of the normal shape and size.

TITYRA.

Tityra, Vieillot, Anal. p. 39 (1816); Scl. Cat. Birds Brit. Mus. xiv. p. 328.

Mr. Sclater makes two main divisions of *Tityra*—one with bare lores, the other with the lores feathered. This second section has also a more flattened bill and is probably of generic rank, and might be separated under Kaup's title *Erator*. The genus, as a whole, according to Mr. Sclater, contains five species, to which we now add two of the *Erator* section.

The bill of *T. semifasciata* is stout (wider and flatter in *T. albitorques*), with a distinct

---

* Mr. Sclater (Cat. Birds Brit. Mus. xiv. p. 326) recognizes six subfamilies of Cotingidæ, all of which, except the Rupicolinæ, are represented in our region.

The family, as a whole, strictly belongs to the Neotropical Region, a few members reaching its northern limits in Mexico, and others the confines of the Argentine Republic. It numbers about 110 species, of which twenty-six are found within our borders.

The family Cotingidæ as at present constituted is one of the most heterogeneous of all the groups of birds. One has only to compare the little brightly coloured *Calyptura cristata* with the large sombre Umbrella-birds (*Cephalopterus*) to see how obviously this is the case. Unfortunately the anatomy of a large number of the species has not yet been studied, so that the classification of the family mainly rests upon external characters. The bond of union at present is the structure of the tarsal covering, which, to use Sundevall's term, is "pycnaspidean." This structure includes the Phytotomidæ, which are again separable by their serrate bills.

subterminal maxillary notch ; the nostrils are round, placed at the end of the nasal
fossa, which is ill-defined ; the lores are almost, and the area round the eye quite,
destitute of feathers.   (In *T. albitorques* both lores and ocular region are fully
feathered.)

The tarsi and toes are strong, the outer toe united at the base to the middle toe for
fully the length of the first phalanges.   The tail is short and even.   The wings rather
pointed, the third, fourth, and fifth quills the longest.

1. **Tityra semifasciata.**

Pachyrhynchus semifasciata, Spix, Av. Braz. ii. p. 32, t. 44. f. 2[1].

Tityra semifasciata, Scl. Cat. Birds Brit. Mus. xiv. p. 330[2].

Tityra personata, Jard. & Selb. Ill. Orn. i. t. 24[3]; Moore, P. Z. S. 1859, p. 56[4]; Scl. & Salv. Ibis,
    1859, p. 124[5]; P. Z. S. 1864, p. 361[6]; 1870, p. 837[7]; 1879, p. 517[8]; Scl. P. Z. S. 1859,
    pp. 285[9], 366[10]; 1864, p. 176[11]; Cab. J. f. Orn. 1861, p. 252[12]; Lawr. Ann. Lyc. N. Y. vii.
    p. 295[13]; ix. pp. 116[14], 204[15]; Bull. U. S. Nat. Mus. no. 4. p. 28[16]; Bost. Soc. N. H. ii.
    p. 289[17]; Salv. P. Z. S. 1867, p. 149 ; 1870, p. 199[18]; Ibis, 1872, p. 318[16]; Sumichrast,
    Mem. Bost. Soc. N. H. i. p. 558[20]; Nutting, Pr. U. S. Nat. Mus. v. p. 397[21]; vi. p. 393[22];
    Boucard, P. Z. S. 1883, p. 448[23]; Ferrari-Perez, Pr. U. S. Nat. Mus. ix. p. 156[24]; Ridgw.
    Pr. U. S. Nat. Mus. x. p. 589[25].

Psaris mexicanus, Less. Rev. Zool. 1839, p. 41[26].

Tityra mexicana, Scl. P. Z. S. 1856, pp. 141[27], 297[28].

Psaris tityroides, Less. Rev. Zool. 1842, p. 210[29].

Supra pallide grisea ; vertice postico et nucha albicantibus ; alis et cauda nigris, hujus rectricum dimidio basali
    et apicibus albis ; alarum rectricibus dorso concoloribus ; fronte, capitis lateribus nigris : subtus alba ;
    pectore et hypochondriis leviter griseo tinctis : rostri dimidio basali rosaceo, dimidio apicali nigro, oculorum
    ambitu quoque rosaceo, pedibus nigris.   Long. tota 8·5, alæ 5·0, caudæ 3·0, rostri a rictu 1·2, tarsi 1·0.

♀ brunnea ; capite summo obscuriore, alarum tectricibus griseo tinctis.   (Descr. maris et feminæ ex Teapa,
    Mexico.   Mus. nostr.)

Hab. MEXICO (*Salle*[28], *White*[11]), Presidio de Mazatlan (*Forrer*), Mazatlan (*Grayson,
    Bischoff*), San Blas (*W. B. Richardson*), Sierra Madre de Colima (*Xantus*), Santiago
    near Manzanillo, Tolima, and Beltran in Jalisco (*W. Lloyd*), Dos Arroyos in Guerrero
    (*Mrs. H. H. Smith*), Real del Monte (*Jenkins*[3]), State of Vera Cruz (*Sumichrast,
    Ferrari-Perez*), Jalapa (*de Oca*[10]), Huatusco and S. Lorenzo near Cordova (*F. Ferrari-
    Perez*), Orizaba (*Sumichrast*), Playa Vicente (*Boucard*[9], *M. Trujillo*), Tapana, Sta.
    Efigenia (*Sumichrast*[16]), Yucatan (*Gaumer*), Merida (*Schott*) ; BRITISH HONDURAS,
    Pine-ridges (*Leyland*[4]), Cayo Western District and Belize (*Blancaneaux*) ; GUA-
    TEMALA, Choctum, San Gerónimo, Iguana, Barranco Hondo (*O. S. & F. D. G.*) ;
    HONDURAS, San Pedro (*G. M. Whitely*), Segovia River (*Henderson*[25]) ; NICARAGUA,
    Omotepe I. (*Nutting*[22]), Chontales (*Belt*[19]) ; COSTA RICA, San José (*v. Frantzius*),
    Guaitil, Barranca (*Carmiol*), Caché (*Rogers*), La Palma (*Nutting*) ; PANAMA, David
    (*Bridges*), Bugaba, Calovevora (*Arcé*[15]), Lion Hill (*M'Leannan*[6]).—SOUTH AMERICA
    from Colombia[8] to Bolivia and the Amazons valley[1].

It has long been the custom to keep Mexican and Central-American *Tityræ* of this form distinct under the name of *T. personata*, but with a large series before us from all parts of its range we are unable to find any tangible grounds for separation, and therefore follow Mr. Sclater in uniting them all under the name of *T. semifasciata*, which was originally applied to the Brazilian bird.

Comparing a specimen from Misantla, in Eastern Mexico, with one from Lion Hill on the Panama Railway we find scarcely any perceptible difference; the back of the latter is a little paler, and this seems to be generally the case in southern specimens.

As will be seen from the list of localities where this species occurs, its distribution is pretty general throughout our region, except in the northern and central States of Mexico, and its range in altitude extends from the sea-level to a height of about 4000 feet in the mountains. Grayson [17] says that in the neighbourhood of Mazatlan it is generally seen in very lofty trees, either in small flocks, but more usually solitary or in pairs. It feeds on various kinds of fruit and also insects, which he saw it dart after like the Flycatchers. He found it near Mazatlan in the months of November, February, April, and June. It doubtless breeds in the mountain region of that latitude. It has no song, the voice being rather harsh.

Mr. Nutting [21] gives a similar account of its food and method of catching insects, except that he does not include fruit as part of its diet. Salmon [8], on the other hand, mentions fruit as its only food. No doubt much depends upon the time of year and the food most accessible, as all these birds, including some of the Tyrannidæ, eat both insects and fruit. Though chiefly a denizen of the forest country, it also frequents pine-regions, such as are found in British Honduras; and Mr. Nutting shot one at La Palma in Costa Rica in a large tree standing in an open field.

Salmon says the nest is placed in a hole in a decayed tree almost on a level with the entrance. The egg is white.

The bare portion round the eye and the basal half of the bill in life is a reddish flesh-colour. The iris is dark red, and the feet and toes lead-colour.

2. **Tityra albitorques.**

Tityra albitorques, Du Bus, Bull. Ac. Brux. xiv. pt. 2, p. 104 [1]; Moore, P. Z. S. 1859, p. 56 [2]; Scl.
P. Z. S. 1859, p. 284 [3]; Scl. & Salv. Ibis, 1860, p. 400 [4]; Lawr. Ann. Lyc. N. Y. vii. p. 295 [5];
viii. p. 182 [6]; ix. p. 116 [7].

Exetastes albitorques, Cab. & Hein. Mus. Hein. ii. p. 84 [8].

Erator albitorques, Sumichrast, Mus. Bost. Soc. N. H. i. p. 558 [9].

Tityria fraseri, Kaup, P. Z. S. 1851, p. 47, tt. 37, 38 [10]; Salv. P. Z. S. 1870, p. 199 [11]; Scl. & Salv.
P. Z. S. 1870, p. 837 [12]; Boucard, P. Z. S. 1883, p. 449 [13]; Ridgw. Pr. U. S. Nat. Mus.
x. p. 589 [14].

Tityria albitorques fraseri, Nutting, Pr. U. S. Nat. Mus. v. p. 397 [15].

Supra pallide grisea; loris et capite summo nigris; alis nigris, remigibus interne ad basin albis; tectricibus minoribus dorso concoloribus, majoribus nigris; cauda alba, fascia subterminali et rhachidibus supra nigris:

rostro et pedibus nigris.   Long. tota 7·0, alæ 4·3, caudæ 2·5, rostri a rictu 2·35, tarsi 0·95.   (Descr. maris ex Choctum, Guatemala.   Mus. nostr.)

♀ supra pallide brunnea, fronte et capitis lateribus rufescentibus, aliter mari similis.   (Descr. feminæ ex Oaxaca, Mexico.   Mus. Brit.)

Hab. MEXICO, Sochiapa (*M. Trujillo*), Playa Vicente (*Boucard* [3]), hot region of Vera Cruz (*Sumichrast* [9]), Teapa (*Mrs. H. H. Smith*), Tizimin in Northern Yucatan (*Gaumer*); BRITISH HONDURAS (*Blancaneaux*); GUATEMALA, Peten (*Leyland* [2]), Choctum (*O. S. & F. D. G.*); HONDURAS, San Pedro (*G. M. Whitely* [12]), Segovia River (*Henderson* [14]); NICARAGUA, Greytown (*Holland* [6]); COSTA RICA, Bebedero (*Arcé*), La Palma (*Nutting* [15]), Pacuar (*Carmiol* [7]); PANAMA, Volcan de Chiriqui, Bugaba (*Arcé* [11]), Lion Hill (*M'Leannan* [5]).—SOUTH AMERICA from Colombia to Ecuador and Peru [1].

The name *T. albitorques* was applied by Du Bus to Peruvian specimens [1], and the bird from southern localities seems to be strictly conspecific with that of Central America and Mexico, to which the name *T. fraseri* has sometimes been applied [10].   Females differ a good deal in the intensity of the brown colouring of the back, which is sometimes almost replaced by grey of a darker shade than that of the male, but none of them possess the spotted mantle found in *T. inquisitor*.

A young bird from Bugaba, marked as a female, has the crown rufous like the sides of the head, the subterminal band of the tail is almost broken into spots on the central feathers.   *T. albitorques* is easily distinguished from *T. inquisitor* not only by the coloration of the tail, but also by its white instead of black ear-coverts; the female, too, has the mantle spotted with black.   Besides these two forms there are two others which cannot be satisfactorily placed with either of them.   One, which we describe below as *T. pelzelni* *, was obtained in Matto Grosso by Natterer, and more recently by Mr. Herbert H. Smith; this has the tail of *T. albitorques*, but the black ear-coverts of *T. inquisitor*.   The other, which we propose to call *T. buckleyi* †, has the tail of *T. inquisitor*, and the white ear-coverts of *T. albitorques*, moreover the lower back of this bird is much whiter than that of any of its allies.

Tityra albitorques, though a much rarer bird than *T. semifasciata*, has a very similar range, but it appears to be absent from Western Mexico and Western Guatemala, and

* Tityra pelzelni.

Tityra albitorques, Pelz. Orn. Bras. p. 120 (nec Du Bus).

T. albitorqui affinis et cauda eodem modo fasciata, auricularibus nigris sicut in *T. inquisitore* differt.

Hab. Brazil, Prov. Matto Grosso (*Natterer, H. H. Smith*).

† Tityra buckleyi.

T. inquisitori affinis et cauda nigra basi tantum alba, auricularibus albis sicut in *T. albitorque* dorso imo pure albo quoque distinguenda.

Hab. Ecuador orientalis, Yanayacu (*C. Buckley*).

also from the Amazons valley. Its range in altitude is also restricted to a lower level, which probably does not exceed 1500 feet, the approximate altitude of Choctum in Guatemala.

Very little is recorded of its habits. Mr. Nutting[10] says that it is common at La Palma in Costa Rica, and is usually found in rather open country associating in flocks of six or eight, and that it is noisy and quarrelsome.

HADROSTOMUS.

Hadrostomus, Cabanis & Heine, Mus. Hein. ii. p. 84 (1859); Scl. Cat. Birds Brit. Mus. xiv. p. 333..

Five species are included in the genus *Hadrostomus*, which range from Northern Mexico to Southern Brazil, one species, *H. aglaiæ*, even passing beyond these limits into Southern Arizona.

Two species only are found within our borders, the widely spread and variable *H. aglaiæ* and *H. homochrous*, and these appear to be not very definitely separable.

Though very similar in structure to *Pachyrhamphus*, with which it was long united, *Hadrostomus* is a fairly natural genus, being composed of birds of larger size and stouter build. The bill is larger in proportion, and the colours of the plumage more uniform and devoid of definite pattern. The males are grey or blackish, the females more or less rufous.

1. **Hadrostomus aglaiæ.**

Pachyrhynchus aglaiæ, Lafr. Rev. Zool. 1839, p. 98[1].

Psaris aglaiæ, Kaup, P. Z. S. 1851, p. 46[2].

Pachyrhamphus aglaiæ, Scl. P. Z. S. 1856, p. 297[3]; Scl. & Salv. Ibis, 1859, p. 124[4]; Owen, Ibis, 1861, p. 64[5].

Platypsaris aglaiæ, Scl. P. Z. S. 1859, p. 285[6]; Sumichrast, Mem. Bost. Soc. N. H. i. p. 558[7]; Ridgw. Man. N. Am. B. p. 240[8].

Hadrostomus aglaiæ, Cab. & Heine, Mus. Hein. ii. p. 85[9]; Cab. J. f. Orn. 1861, p. 252[10]; Scl. P. Z. S. 1864, p. 176[11]; Cat. Birds Brit. Mus. xiv. p. 335[12]; Lawr. Ann. Lyc. N. Y. ix. pp. 116[13], 204[14]; Bull. U. S. Nat. Mus. no. 4. p. 28[15]; Frantz. J. f. Orn. 1869, p. 309[16]; Scl. & Salv. P. Z. S. 1870, p. 837[17]; Grays. Pr. Bost. Soc. N. H. xiv. p. 279[18]; Ferrari-Perez, Pr. U. S. Nat. Mus. ix. p. 156[18].

Platypsaris affinis, Elliot, Ibis, 1859, p. 394[20]; Scl. P. Z. S. 1859, p. 366[21]; Sumichrast, Mem. Bost. Soc. N. H. i. p. 558[22].

Hadrostomus aglaiæ, var. *affinis*, Lawr. Mem. Bost. Soc. N. H. ii. p. 289[23].

Pachyrhamphus latirostris, Bp. Compt. Rend. xxxviii. p. 658[24]; Not. Orn. p. 87[25]; Scl. P. Z. S. 1857, p. 74[26].

Hadrostomus latirostris, Nutting, Pr. U. S. Nat. Mus. vi. p. 393[27].

Platypsaris latirostris, Ridgw. Man. N. Am. B. p. 240[28].

Hadrostomus albiventris, Lawr. Mem. Bost. Soc. N. H. ii. p. 289[29]; Scl. Cat. Birds Brit. Mus. xiv. p. 335[30].

Platypsaris albiventris, Ridgw. Man. N. Am. B. p. 325 [31]; A. O. U. Check-list N. Am. B., 2nd Suppl.,
    Auk, vii. p. 62 [32].
Platypsaris insularis, Ridgw. Man. N. Am. B. p. 325 [33].

Supra nigricanti-cinereus; capite summo pure nigro; alis et cauda nigricantibus; scapularibus ad basin albis:
    subtus fusco-cinereus, plaga magna gulari rosacea: rostro et pedibus nigricanti-plumbeis. Long. tota 7·0,
    alæ 3·7, caudæ 2·9, rostri a rictu 0·9, tarsi 0·9.
♀ rufa; capite summo nigricante, fronte sordide fusca; alis extus et cauda castaneis: subtus pallidior. (Descr.
    maris et feminæ ex Misantla, Mexico. Mus. nostr.)

Hab. MEXICO, Rio Camacho, Villa Grande, Rio de Monterey (*Armstrong*), Sierra Madre
    above Ciudad Victoria, Soto la Marina, Aldama, Tampico (*Richardson*), hot, tempe-
    rate, and alpine regions of Vera Cruz (*Sumichrast* [7]), Misantla, Colipa (*F. D. G.*),
    Jalapa [9] (*F. D. G., de Oca* [21], *M. Trujillo*), Coatepec, Huatusco (*F. Ferrari-Perez*), Cor-
    dova (*Sallé* [3]), Vera Cruz (*F. D. G., Richardson*), Playa Vicente (*Boucard* [6]), Sochiapa
    (*M. Trujillo*), Rancho de Almihinte in Puebla, Yauhuitlan in Oaxaca (*F. Ferrari-
    Perez*), Oaxaca (*Boucard* [6]), Dondomingillo (*Sumichrast* [15]), Teapa in Tabasco (*Mrs.
    H. H. Smith*), Santiago and San Blas (*W. B. Richardson*), Tres Marias Is. (*Grayson* [18] [33]),
    Ysleta in Sonora (*W. Lloyd*), Presidio de Mazatlan (*Forrer*), Mazatlan (*Grayson,
    Bischoff* [29]), Zapotlan, Beltran, and Sta. Ana in Jalisco (*Lloyd*), Plains of Colima
    (*Xantus* [29]), Amula in Guerrero (*Mrs. H. H. Smith*), Sola, Juchatengo (*M. Trujillo*),
    Merida in Yucatan (*Schott* [14]), Buctzotz, Peto, Tizimin, Holbox I. (*Gaumer*),
    Cozumel Island (*Devis*), Tonila, Cacoprieto, Tehuantepec (*Sumichrast* [15]); GUATE-
    MALA, Retahuleu, Barranco Hondo, Calderas on the Volcan de Fuego [5], Chuacus
    (*Owen* [5]), Chisec, Choctum, Cahabon (*O. S. & F. D. G.* [5]); HONDURAS, San Pedro
    (*G. M. Whitely* [17]); NICARAGUA (*Delattre* [24]), Omotepe I. (*Nutting* [27]); COSTA RICA
    (*Ellendorf* [10]).

This species, taken as a whole, is subject to a great amount of variation, not only as
regards the intensity of the colour of the back and under surface, but also as regards
the rosy spot on the throat. The females also vary in the intensity of their general
rufous coloration. The darkest males are found in the province of Tabasco, and thence
southwards through Eastern Guatemala, and northwards along the coast of the State of
Vera Cruz to Tampico. At Jalapa and in the Eastern Sierra Madre the back is
generally a little greyer; and this is the case in birds from the Tres Marias Islands, the
mountains facing the Pacific coast of Guatemala, and also in those from Nicaragua. The
palest examples are from Western Mexico, in which the back is grey and the under
surface nearly white, and with these specimens from the northern part of Yucatan agree
very closely. The assumption of the rosy spot of immature males appears usually to
commence at an early stage, and is often of full size before the wing-feathers have
assumed their adult coloration. In other specimens, which are apparently fully adult
in other respects, this rosy spot can barely be traced. We have already referred to the
variation in the rufous colouring of the female; the crown of the head also varies from

deep black to grey, and even to chestnut, as in a specimen before us from Vera Cruz the crown is but a few shades darker than the back. The bill also varies greatly in size. Our specimen with the largest bill is from the island of Cozumel, but this is almost matched by others from Yucatan.

Regarding the names applied to this bird, *H. aglaiæ*, the oldest, seems applicable to the Jalapa form, in which the back is slightly tinged with grey. The type appears from the description to have been somewhat immature, as in the adult the nape and rump cannot be said to be slightly rufescent. *Platypsaris affinis* of Elliot is probably strictly congeneric with *H. aglaiæ*. *H. latirostris* of Bonaparte was applied to a Nicaraguan individual without a rosy throat, a character which we believe to be strictly individual, as we find it represented in birds associated with numbers of the ordinary type and intermediate examples occur connecting the two. *H. albiventris* was applied to the bird of Western Mexico, and with them Mr. Ridgway has recently associated the pale birds of Northern Yucatan. The distribution thus indicated for *H. albiventris* is so completely severed by a wide tract of country occupied by darker forms, that we are convinced that the similarity of the birds of the divided districts is not due to relationship but to some local cause acting so as to produce a similar effect, and we are further inclined to attribute the existence of dark and intermediate forms to a difference of climate and greater rainfall and density of vegetation. The various forms in which this bird presents itself are not sufficiently pronounced to enable us to define them with certainty and attach to them specific names. We may add that we have before us upwards of 150 specimens from nearly all the localities mentioned above. It is right, however, to quote here Sumichrast's opinion on the varieties of this bird, which is as follows [7]:—" I am led to believe that there are two varieties of this bird in the State of Vera Cruz. The one, especially found in the hot and temperate regions, of stouter proportions, and in the adult male at least with darker plumage, &c. The other, which I have met with several times in the Alpine region, is appreciably inferior in size to the preceding, and with lighter tints in the adult male. It is possible that to the latter variety the name of *P. affinis* has been given."

In all parts of our region the range in altitude of this species is very considerable, and extends from the sea-level to an altitude of at least 8000 feet. In the Tres Marias, Grayson [18] found it only in the thick woods, where it is seen searching for insects, sometimes darting after them when on the wing, at other times looking for them amongst the leaves and branches, not unlike the Warblers. Its notes are feeble and but seldom uttered, and its habits are solitary. This island bird has been separated by Mr. Ridgway as *Platypsaris insularis*. Mr. Robert Owen [5] found a nest of this bird on 15th May, 1860, at Chuacus in Guatemala, and sent us the female, its nest, and two eggs. The nest was entirely composed of tendrils, strips of bark, and grass, so as to form a hanging nest open at the top and about two inches deep. It was built between and hung from the forked branch of a sapling at the foot of a mountain. The egg is white, beautifully

16*

marked with pencilings of pinkish red and scattered spots of the same colour; these markings are much blended and concentrated at the larger end.

H. aglaiæ is included in the birds of North America as an inhabitant of the Rio Grande Valley, but it has not yet, so far as we know, occurred north of the river. The western form, *H. albiventris*, is found in Southern Arizona [32].

2. **Hadrostomus homochrous.**

Hadrostomus homochrous, Scl. P. Z. S. 1859, p. 142 [1]; Cat. Birds Brit. Mus. xiv. p. 334 [2].
Hadrostomus homochrous?, Ridgw. Pr. U. S. Nat. Mus. v. p. 397 [3].
Pachyrhamphus homochrous, Lawr. Ann. Lyc. N. Y. vii. p. 473 [4].

Supra niger; capite summo saturatiore; scapularibus ad basin albis; subtus cinereis; rostro et pedibus nigricantibus. Long. tota 7·0, alæ 3·5, caudæ 2·5, rostri a rictu 1·0, tarsi 0·85. (Descr. maris ex Ecuador. Mus. nostr.)

♀ supra cinnamomea fere unicolor; subtus multo pallidior. (Descr. feminæ ex Lion Hill, Panama. Mus. nostr.)

Hab. Costa Rica (?), La Palma (*Nutting* [3]); Panama, Lion Hill (*M'Leannan*).—South America, from Colombia to Peru.

This species very closely resembles examples of *H. aglaiæ* in which the rosy patch on the throat is not developed, a character which is never seen in southern specimens, but it is evanescent in examples from Nicaragua.

Its southern range extends to Peru, and it is apparently common in Western Ecuador [1]. Its range northward of the Isthmus of Panama is a little doubtful, and rests, so far as Costa Rica is concerned, on a female specimen obtained by Mr. Nutting at La Palma [3]. We have no examples from Chiriqui, but a female from the Isthmus of Panama agrees best with others from Western Ecuador. Salmon described the nest and eggs of a bird referred to *H. homochrous*, but his description differs so widely from that of the nest and eggs of the allied *H. aglaiæ* sent us by Mr. Owen, about which we have not the smallest doubt, that we think Salmon wrongly identified the nest he found.

PACHYRHAMPHUS.

Pachyrhynchus, Spix, Av. Bras. ii. p. 31 (1825).
Pachyrhamphus, Gray, List Gen. B. p. 31 (1840); Scl. Cat. Birds Brit. Mus. xiv. p. 337.

Of the fourteen species included in this genus, six occur within our limits, the most northern of which, *P. major*, extends its range to the middle of the Mexican State of Tamaulipas. The genus is strictly a neotropical one, and spreads over South America as far as the Argentine Republic.

As compared with *Hadrostomus*, the species of *Pachyrhamphus* are smaller and more slender birds, usually with more mottled plumage, longer wings, and rounder tails, and a wide difference in the coloration of the sexes; but *P. cinnamomeus* and *P. rufus* are exceptions in the latter respect, the sexes being alike, and only to be distinguished by the form of the second primary in the male.

Mr. Ridgway gives us a character whereby to distinguish *Platypsaris* (=*Hadrostomus*) from *Pachyrhamphus*, by the covering inner surface of the posterior half of the tarsus, which in the former, he says, is covered with a series of large scales, but in the latter is naked; this seems to hold good when *H. aglaiæ* and *P. major* are compared, but nearly all the other species of *Pachyrhamphus* agree in this respect with *Hadrostomus*, so that this character does not seem to be trustworthy for diagnostic purposes.

A. *Sexes dissimiles, marium rectricibus stricte albo marginatis.*

1. Pachyrhamphus versicolor.

Vireo versicolor, Hartl. Rev. Zool. 1843, p. 289 [1].
Callopsaris versicolor, Cab. & Heine, Mus. Hein. ii. p. 89 [2].
Pachyrhamphus versicolor, Boucard, P. Z. S. 1878, p. 65 [3]; Scl. Cat. Birds Brit. Mus. xiv. p. 339 [4].

Supra niger; dorso imo cinereo; alis nigris; secundariis internis et tectricibus albo marginatis; cauda cinerea albido stricte terminata: subtus albus nigro indistincte fasciatus; loris, gula et cervicis lateribus viridi-flavo lavatis; subalaribus albis: rostro et pedibus nigricantibus. Long. tota 4·7, alæ 2·7, caudæ 1·9, rostri a rictu 0·55, tarsi 0·6.

♀ supra viridi-olivacea, capite summo griseo; alis castaneo marginatis: subtus mari similis, sed undique viridi-flavo lavatus. (Descr. maris et feminæ ex Intac, Ecuador. Mus. nostr.)

Hab. Costa Rica, Candelaria (*Boucard* [3]).—Colombia [1] [2]; Ecuador.

This species is included here on the authority of M. Boucard, who obtained a single specimen at Candelaria in Costa Rica during his visit to that country in 1877. It occurs in the Colombian State of Antioquia, is commonly seen in the trade collections made in the vicinity of Bogota, and is also found in the northern districts of Ecuador.

P. versicolor stands alone in the genus, no other species having the under surface barred in a similar manner.

Nothing as to its habits is on record.

2. Pachyrhamphus cinereus.

Pipra cinerea, Bodd. Tabl. Pl. Enl. p. 43 [1], ex Daub. Pl. Enl. 687, p. 1 [2].
Pachyrhamphus cinereus, Lawr. Ann. Lyc. N. Y. vii. p. 320 [3]; Scl. & Salv. P. Z. S. 1864, p. 361 [4]; Scl. Cat. Birds Brit. Mus. xiv. p. 341 [5].

Supra cinereus; dorso medio olivaceo lavato; capite summo nigro; loris et fronte stricte albis; alis nigris, tectricibus et secundariis intimis griseis albo marginatis; cauda grisea, plumis omnibus medialiter nigris albido stricte marginatis: subtus albidus, pectore et hypochondriis cinereis, illo quoque olivaceo vix tincto: rostro et pedibus nigricantibus. Long. tota 5·0, alæ 2·75, caudæ 2·0, rostri a rictu 0·65, tarsi 0·7.

♀ cinnamomea, capite paulo obscuriore; alis nigricantibus extus et intus cinnamomeo marginatis. (Descr. maris et feminæ ex Lion Hill, Panama. Mus. nostr.)

Hab. Panama, Lion Hill (*M'Leannan* [4]), Paraiso (*Hughes*), Chepo (*Arcé*).—South America from Colombia to Guiana.

The females of this species are very like those of *P. cinnamomeus*, and are only to be distinguished by their smaller size; the males of course are widely different, being cinereous above and white beneath, instead of wholly of a cinnamon colour like the female.

P. cinereus has a wide range along the northern portion of the South American continent. It just enters our fauna, occurring along the line of the Panama railway, but not, so far as we know, farther to the westward.

B. *Sexes similes, cinnamomei.*

3. **Pachyrhamphus cinnamomeus.**

Pachyrhamphus cinnamomeus, Lawr. Ann. Lyc. N. Y. vii. p. 295[1]; viii. p. 182[2]; ix. p. 116[3]; Scl. & Salv. P. Z. S. 1879, p. 518[4]; Ridgw. Man. N. Am. B. p. 326[5]; Scl. Cat. Birds Brit. Mus. xiv. p. 342[6]; Ridgw. Pr. U. S. Nat. Mus. x. p. 589[7].

Pachyrhamphus sp. ?, Scl. & Salv. Ibis, 1860, p. 36[8].

Pachyrhamphus sp. ?, Lawr. Ann. Lyc. N. Y. vii. p. 296[9].

Supra cinnamomeus; capite summo paulo saturatiore; alis nigricantibus extus et intus castaneo marginatis: subtus dilutior, loris, mento et abdomine medio albicantioribus: rostro et pedibus nigris. Long. tota 5·5, alæ 3·0, caudæ 2·3, rostri a rictu 0·7, tarsi 0·8.

♀ mari similis remige secundo integro. (Descr. maris et feminæ ex Lion Hill, Panama. Mus. nostr.)

Hab. BRITISH HONDURAS, Cayo (*Blancaneaux*); GUATEMALA, Coban, Choctum (*O. S. & F. D. G.*); HONDURAS, Segovia river (*Henderson*[7]); NICARAGUA, Greytown (*Holland*[2]); COSTA RICA, Tucurriqui (*Arcé, Zeledon*[3]), Angostura, Turrialba (*Carmiol*[3]); PANAMA, Lion Hill (*M‘Leannan*[1]), Chepo (*Arcé*).—SOUTH AMERICA, Colombia[4] and Ecuador.

It is now generally considered that the sexes of this species are alike in coloration, and differ only in the form of the second primary, which is much reduced in size in the male but normal in the female. At one time it was believed that all these cinnamon-coloured birds were either young birds or females of a species having a black or cinereous male; against this supposition is the fact that no such male has yet been found in Central America north of the Isthmus of Panama, whereas the supposed females and young birds are common in many places up to the confines of Mexico. The probability, therefore, is that *P. cinnamomeus* is a distinct species in which the sexes are similarly coloured.

Though this species is common in the forest-region of Vera Paz and the adjoining parts of British Honduras, it is absent from all the low-lying lands bordering on the Pacific Ocean, but in the State of Panama it is found all across the isthmus.

C. *Sexes dissimiles, rectricibus amborum macula magna terminatis.*

4. **Pachyrhamphus cinereiventris.** (Tab. XLIII. fig. 1.)

Pachyrhamphus cinereiventris, Scl. Cat. Am. B. p. 242 [1]; Cat. Birds Brit. Mus. xiv. p. 344 [2]; Scl. &
Salv. P. Z. S. 1864, p. 361 [3]; Salv. P. Z. S. 1867, p. 149 [4]; 1870, p. 199 [5]; Lawr. Ann. Lyc.
N. Y. ix. p. 116 [6]; Nutting, Pr. U. S. Nat. Mus. vi. p. 385 [7].

Pachyrhamphus marginatus ?, Lawr. Ann. Lyc. N. Y. vii. p. 330 [8].

Supra niger; capite summo nitido; alis nigris, plumis omnibus late albo marginatis; cauda nigra albo terminata:
subtus cinereus, subalaribus et remigibus interne albicantibus. Long. tota 5·3, alæ 2·7, caudæ rect. med.
2·2, rect. lat. 1·6, rostri a rictu 0·6, tarsi 0·65. (Descr. maris ex Lion Hill, Panama. Mus. nostr.)

♀ olivacea; capite summo obscure cinerescente; alis nigricantibus fulvo marginatis; cauda nigricante fulvo
terminata, rectricibus intermediis dorso concoloribus: subtus medialiter flavescens. (Descr. feminæ ex
Bugaba, Panama. Mus. nostr.)

Hab. GUATEMALA, Choctum (*O. S. & F. D. G.*); NICARAGUA, Sucuya (*Nutting* [7]); COSTA
RICA, Angostura, San Mateo, Barranca (*Carmiol* [6]); PANAMA, Bugaba [5], Calovevora,
Santa Fé [4] (*Arcé*), Lion Hill (*M'Leannan* [3] [8]).—COLOMBIA [1].

This species is doubtfully distinct from the Brazilian *P. polychropterus*, but seems to
be smaller and to have the white tips to the tail-feathers rather wider and extending
further along the outer web of the feather.

It was originally described from a specimen obtained near Santa Marta in Colombia,
and skins of it occur in the trade collections made in the neighbourhood of Bogota.
In our country it is much more common in the portion bordering the southern
continent. Mr. Nutting says [7] that it is not common in the deep woods near Sucuya in
Nicaragua, and we have only seen one or two specimens in native collections made in
Vera Paz, Guatemala, so that we have no personal acquaintance with the species.

5. **Pachyrhamphus major.**

Bathmidurus major, Cab. in Wiegm. Arch. 1847, i. p. 246 [1]; Cab. & Heine, Mus. Hein. ii. p. 89 [2];
Sumichrast, Mem. Bost. Soc. N. H. i. p. 558 [3].

Pachyrhamphus major, Scl. P. Z. S. 1857, p. 204 [4]; 1858, p. 97 [5]; 1859, p. 366 [6]; 1864, p. 176 [7];
Cat. Birds Brit. Mus. xiv. p. 346 [8]; Scl. & Salv. Ibis, 1860, p. 36 [9].

Pachyrhamphus marginatus ?, Scl. P. Z. S. 1856, p. 298 [10].

Pachyrhamphus polychropterus, Moore, P. Z. S. 1859, p. 56 [11]; Lawr. Ann. Lyc. N. Y. viii. p. 182 [12].

Pachyrhamphus polychropterus ?, Scl. & Salv. Ibis, 1859, p. 124 [13].

Supra cinereus; capite summo nitide nigro; interscapulio plus minusve nigro notato; alis nigris, plumis omnibus
late albo marginatis; scapularibus albis; cauda nigra late albo marginata, rectricum medianarum bitriente
basali cinereis: loris et corpore subtus cinereo-albis; subalaribus et remigibus interne albis: rostro et pedibus plumbeis. Long. tota 6·0, alæ 3·4, caudæ rect. med. 2·6, rect. lat. 1·75, rostri a rictu 0·75, tarsi 0·8.

♀ castanea; capite summo nitide nigro; alarum plumis omnibus late rufo marginatis; cauda nigra, rectricibus
duabus mediis et reliquis ad apicem castaneis: subtus flavido undique tinctus. (Descr. maris et feminæ
ex Jalapa, Mexico. Mus. nostr.)

Hab. MEXICO (*Sallé* [10], *White* [7]), Sierra Madre above Ciudad Victoria (*Richardson*), Jalapa [2]

(*Sallé*[4], *de Oca*[6], *Höge*, *M. Trujillo*, *F. D. G.*), Huatusco (*Ferrari-Perez*), Amula in Guerrero (*Mrs. H. H. Smith*), Peto, Buctzotz in Yucatan (*Gaumer*); GUATEMALA, Choctum, Coban, Dueñas, Medio Monte, Calderas on the Volcan de Fuego (*O. S. & F. D. G.*); HONDURAS, Omoa (*Leyland*[11]); NICARAGUA, Greytown (*Holland*[12]).

This species, so far as the male is concerned, is exceedingly like the South-American *P. atricapillus*; but besides being decidedly smaller, appears never to have the back quite so black as in some individuals of the southern bird. The female may at once be distinguished by its cinnamon back and black crown.

P. major has a wide range in Mexico, extending northwards as far as the high ground above Ciudad Victoria in Tamaulipas, and also occurring in the Sierra Madre del Sur, near the town of Chilpancingo. Sumichrast[3] found it in the State of Vera Cruz in the lowlands, and at various elevations up to an altitude of more than 8000 feet, and we observed that it had a similar range in altitude in Guatemala, where it occurs in the Volcan de Fuego as high as between 7000 and 8000 feet, and at Choctum which is less than 1500. It occurs also near the sea-level in Yucatan, and at Omoa in Honduras. It is nowhere common.

6. **Pachyrhamphus albogriseus.**   (Tab. XLIII. figg. 2 ♂, 3 ♀.)

Pachyrhamphus albogriseus, Scl. P. Z. S. 1857, p. 78 [1]; Scl. Cat. Birds Brit. Mus. xiv. p. 347 [2]; Salv. P. Z. S. 1870, p. 199 [3].

Præcedenti similis, sed dorso cinereo unicolore diversus.
♀ supra olivacea, capite summo rufescente.

Hab. NICARAGUA, Corinto (*O. S.*[2]); PANAMA, Bugaba, Calovevora (*Arcé*[3]).—COLOMBIA; ECUADOR; VENEZUELA.

This is a smaller species than *P. major* and may be distinguished by its cinereous back, in which there is no admixture of black; the female, too, differs in having an olive-coloured back and a red instead of a black crown, so that the two species are really very distinct. Moreover it would appear that *P. albogriseus* takes to a great extent the place of *P. major* in the more southern portion of our country, and thence passes southwards into the north-western districts of South America.

The only part of our country where it appears to be at all common is the neighbourhood of Chiriqui, whence Arcé sent us several specimens; our single Nicaraguan example was shot by Salvin in the bush at the back of the seaport town of Corinto.

Subfam. *LIPAUGINÆ.*

Lipauginæ, Scl. Cat. Birds Brit. Mus. xiv. p. 348.

The Lipauginæ form the first subfamily of Mr. Sclater's second section (B) of the Cotingidæ, in which the second primary in the male is normal and not abbreviated as in the Tityrinæ; it is further defined as one of the "smaller forms; bill turdine; rictus bristled; bill broader, slightly hooked." Looking at the various genera comprised in this second section of the Cotingidæ, we doubt if these characters are sufficiently definite for practical use. In the first place, there are species of *Lathria* considerably exceeding in size *Querula cruenta*, a species of Gymnoderinæ; the bills of all this section are very varied in form and cannot be satisfactorily classed as "turdine" in character. At the same time it is obvious that *Chirocylla, Lathria, Aulia,* and *Lipaugus* form a fairly natural group of allied genera. The structure of the feet, the form of the wings (if we except *Chirocylla*) and tail are similar in all of them; though there are minor points of difference which we mention under each genus.

LATHRIA.

Lathria, Swainson, Classif. B. ii. p. 255 (1837) ; Scl. Cat. Birds Brit. Mus. xiv. p. 350.

There are eight known species of this genus, which are distributed over Tropical America from Southern Mexico to Bolivia and South Brazil. Only one species occurs within our limits, which spreads from Southern Mexico to the northern portion of the United States of Colombia. The bill in *Lathria unirufa* is stout, wide at the base, the culmen arched, terminating in a distinct hook, with a well-defined subterminal notch on the tomia of the maxilla; the nostrils are nearly round, and placed at the end of the nasal fossa, and are only partially covered by the supra-nasal plumes; the rictal bristles are moderately strong; the tarsi are short and not rough beneath at their proximal ends; the outer toe is a little longer than the inner toe and is united to the middle toe as far as the end of the first phalange; the wings are rounded, the third and fourth primaries being the longest (second < the fifth, first = the tenth); the tail is long and nearly even.

1. **Lathria unirufa.**

Lipaugus unirufus, Scl. P. Z. S. 1859, p. 385 [1]; 1861, p. 211 [2]; Scl. & Salv. Ibis, 1860, p. 36 [3];
    P. Z. S. 1864, p. 361 [4]; 1867, p. 279 [5]; Ex. Orn. pp. 1, 6, t. 1 [6]; Cass. Pr. Ac. Phil. 1860,
    p. 143 [7]; Lawr. Ann. Lyc. N. Y. vii. p. 330 [8]; Salv. P. Z. S. 1867, p. 149 [9]; 1870, p. 199 [10];
    Ibis, 1872, p. 318 [11]; Sumichrast, Mem. Bost. Soc. N. H. i. p. 558 [12].

Lathria unirufa, Scl. & Salv. P. Z. S. 1879, p. 518 [13]; Nutting, Pr. U. S. Nat. Mus. vi. p. 404 [14];
    Scl. Cat. Birds Brit. Mus. xiv. p. 353 [15].

Cinnamomea, subtus pallidior, remigibus intus brunnescentibus; rostro corneo, pedibus corylinis. Long.
    tota 9·5, alæ 5·3, caudæ 4·5, rostri a rictu 1·0, tarsi 0·8. (Descr. exempl. ex Choctum, Guatemala.
    Mus. nostr.)

♀ mari similis.

Hab. Mexico, Playa Vicente (*Boucard* [1]) ; British Honduras (*Blancaneaux*); Guate-
    mala (*Skinner* [1]), Coban [1] [3], Choctum (*O. S. & F. D. G.*); Nicaragua, Chontales
    (*Belt* [11]), Los Sabalos (*Nutting* [14]), Blewfields (*Wickham* [5]); Panama, Bugaba [10],
    Veraguas [9] (*Arcé*), Lion Hill (*M'Leannan* [4]), Chepo (*Arcé*), Turbo, R. Truando
    (*C. J. Wood* [7]).—Colombia [13].

This *Lathria* is easily distinguished from all other members of the genus by its uniform cinnamon plumage. It was first described by Mr. Sclater from a specimen obtained in March 1859 by Boucard[1] at Playa Vicente in the State of Vera Cruz, near the foot of the eastern slope of the mountain-range which traverses the State of Oaxaca, and others from Guatemala collected by Skinner and Salvin. From Southern Mexico it spreads over the low-lying forest-region of British Honduras and Guatemala, and ascends the mountains up to an elevation of about 2000 feet. It is absent, so far as we know, from the forests bordering on the Pacific, both in Mexico and Guatemala, until we come to the State of Panama. In South America it is only known in the extreme north-west of Colombia, in the State of Antioquia, where Salmon obtained it at Nichi and Remedios in the Cauca valley[13].

L. unirufa frequents the interior of the forest, and is usually found perched among the lower branches of the larger trees; its food consists principally of fruit, and, according to Mr. C. J. Wood, of large Coleoptera which abound in the dry parts of the forests at Turbo and the cordillera of the Isthmus of Darien[7].

AULIA.

Aulia, Bonaparte, Consp. Vol. Anis. p. 4 (1854) ; Scl. Cat. Birds Brit. Mus. xiv. p. 354.

Aulia contains two species, of which one, *A. rufescens*, alone is found in our country, and has nearly the same range as *Lathria unirufa*, though its northern limit does not extend beyond Eastern Guatemala ; the other species, *A. hypopyrrha*, has a wide range in South America, extending over the Amazons valley and South-eastern Brazil.

In many points of structure *Aulia* resembles *Lathria* ; but the outer and middle toes are more united at the base, the rictal bristles not so strongly developed, and the male has peculiarities in its plumage, described below, which are not found in the other allied forms.

1. Aulia rufescens.

Lipaugus rufescens, Scl. P. Z. S. 1857, p. 276[1] ; 1861, p. 211[2] ; Scl. & Salv. Ibis, 1859, p. 124[3] ;
  P. Z. S. 1864, p. 361[4] ; Ex. Orn. pp. 5, 6, t. 3[5] ; Lawr. Ann. Lyc. N. Y. vii. p. 330[6] ; ix.
  p. 116[7] ; Salv. P. Z. S. 1867, p. 149[8].
Aulia rufescens, Scl. & Salv. P. Z. S. 1879, p. 519[9] ; Scl. Cat. Birds Brit. Mus. xiv. p. 355[10].
Laniocerca rufescens, Ridgw. Pr. U. S. Nat. Mus. x. p. 589[11].

Cinnamomea, subtus pallidior ; uropygio et corpore subtus fusco transvittatis ; pectore et abdomine maculis rotundis nigris sparsim irregulariter notatis ; hypochondriis plumarum fascicula flavarum utrinque ornatis ; alis nigricantibus, intus et extus cinnamomeo limbatis, tectricibus mediis et majoribus ad apicem cinnamomeis purpureo-nigro terminatis, subcaudalibus longissimis eodem modo ornatis : rostro corneo, pedibus orylinis. Long. tot. 8·5, alæ 4·4, caudæ 3·6, rostri a rictu 1·0, tarsi 0·7. (Descr. maris ex Santa Fé, Panama. Mus. nostr.)

♀ mari similis, maculis abdominis nigris et alarum tectricum apicibus nigris absentibus distinguenda.

Hab. GUATEMALA, Coban (*Delattre, mus. Derb.*[1][3]); HONDURAS, Segovia River (*Henderson*[11]); COSTA RICA, Barranca (*Carmiol*[7]), Tucurriqui (*Zeledon*[7]); PANAMA, Santa Fé (*Arcé*[8]), Lion Hill (*McLeannan*[4]), Chepo (*Arcé*).—COLOMBIA[9].

The type of this species, now in the Derby Museum at Liverpool, is stated to have been obtained at Coban in Guatemala[1]; but as no other examples for a long period came under our notice, we were inclined at one time to doubt the correctness of the locality[4][5]. There was, however, in 1873, a Guatemalan specimen in the Museum of the Sociedad Economica de Guatemala, and more recently a specimen from Coban was submitted to us by M. Boucard, thus confirming the original statement. It must, however, be an exceedingly rare bird in Guatemala, as we have never found another example amongst the thousands of skins from that country that we have examined. Southwards of Guatemala its presence has been recorded in several parts of Central America, and in the State of Panama Arcé and McLeannan obtained a few specimens. In Colombia, Salmon found it near Remedios, in the State of Antioquia[9], and this point seems to be the southern limit of its range. The two specimens from his collection before us are perhaps not quite adult, and have a greyish tinge on the throat, head, and lower back, not found in our Central-American examples. The dark spots on the under surface and the dark tips to the wing-coverts appear to be characteristic of the male sex; the flank-tufts are also of a reddish-orange hue in the female, those of the male being clearer yellow.

This species, like *Lathria unirufa* and *Lipaugus holerythrus*, can be distinguished from the rest of its congeners by the cinnamon colour of its plumage.

LIPAUGUS.

Lipaugus, Boie, Isis, 1828, p. 318; Scl. Cat. Birds Brit. Mus. xiv. p. 356.

There are three species in this genus which have their representatives, so far as their coloration is concerned, in the genera *Lathria* and *Aulia*; but they are of smaller size, the rictal bristles are much more fully developed, and the tarsi beneath are rough towards their proximal end; the nostrils, too, are more hidden by the supra-nasal feathers.

1. **Lipaugus holerythrus.**

Lipaugus holerythrus, Scl. & Salv. P. Z. S. 1860, p. 300[1]; 1864, p. 361[2]; 1867, p. 279[3]; 1879, p. 519[4]; Ibis, 1860, p. 400[5]; Ex. Orn. p. 6[6]; Lawr. Ann. Lyc. N. Y. vii. p. 330[7]; ix. p. 116[8]; Salv. P. Z. S. 1867, p. 149[9]; 1870, p. 199[10]; Wyatt, Ibis, 1871, p. 334[11]; Berl. J. f. Orn. 1884, p. 318[12]; Scl. Cat. Birds Brit. Mus. xiv. p. 357[13].

Cinnamomeus unicolor, subtus pallidior; alis nigricantibus utrinque cinnamomeo limbatis; rostro corneo, pedibus corylinis. Long. tot. 8·3, alæ 4·2, caudæ 3·8, rostri a rictu 0·85, tarsi 0·9. (Descr. exempl. typ. ex Choctum, Guatemala. Mus. nostr.)

♀ mari similis.

17*

Hab. Mexico ?[13]; Guatemala, Choctum (*O. S.*[1] & *F. D. G.*); Costa Rica, Angostura (*Carmiol*[8]), Tucurriqui (*Arcé*); Panama, Volcan de Chiriqui[10], Chitra[10], Boquete de Chitra[10], Calovevora[10], Santa Fé[9] (*Arcé*), Lion Hill (*M‘Leannan*[2][7]).— Colombia[4][11][12].

The occurrence of this species in Mexico is somewhat doubtful, and at present rests on the authority of a single skin formerly in Gould's collection said to have come from that country[13]. Like *Lathria unirufa* it is very likely to be found in the southern parts of the State of Vera Cruz. In Guatemala we only know of its occurrence in the forest country north of Coban, drained by the affluents of the Rio de la Pasion: here the type was obtained, and the bird is found in some abundance. Southward of Guatemala it occurs probably in all low-lying heavily-forested country as far south as the Colombian State of Antioquia[4]. According to Salmon the food of this species consists of insects.

L. holerythrus may at once be distinguished from all its South-American congeners by its cinnamon-coloured plumage.

Subfam. *ATTILINÆ.*

The position of the *Attilinæ* has long been a matter of doubt, and it has been assigned to the families Tyrannidæ, Formicariidæ, and Cotingidæ. Sundevall placed it in the last-named family, and in so doing he was followed by Mr. Sclater, though with doubt. In this, we think, the last-named writer was justified, for the form of the bill, the greater length of the tarsi, and the greater separation of the toes are all suggestive of a different position from that now assigned to it. It is to be hoped that when the internal structure is examined, more satisfactory indications of the affinities of *Attila* will be revealed.

ATTILA.

Attila, Lesson, Traité d'Orn. p. 360 (1831); Scl. Cat. Birds Brit. Mus. xiv. p. 358.

The number of species in the genus *Attila* as at present known cannot be stated exactly. In his recently published Catalogue, Mr. Sclater admitted twelve species, but half of these he only separated " geographically ; " he also mentioned six other names which applied to birds with which he was unacquainted. We now add two names, so that there may be twenty nominal species of *Attila*, possibly a larger number than actually exist. The difficulty connected with these birds lies in the apparent instability of their characters, which seem to be to some extent independent of age, sex, or locality; and it is only by apparently insignificant characters that we are enabled to define the various local forms, of which there appear to be six within the limits of our fauna. These may be characterized as follows:—

  a. Abdomine albo.
     a'. Cauda obscure rufa . . . . 1. *citreopygius.*

b′. Cauda brunneo-rufa.
    a″. Gutture cinereo.
        a‴. Uropygio pallide cinnamomeo . . 2. *gaumeri.*
        b‴. Uropygio saturate cinnamomeo . 3. *cozumelæ.*
    b″. Gutture viridescente . . . . 4. *sclateri.*
  c′. Cauda læte rufa . . . . 5. *cinnamomeus.*
b. Abdomine flavo . . . . 6. *hypoxanthus.*

The bill in *Attila* is very strong, rather wide at the gape, and gradually converging to the end, the culmen is nearly straight for most of its length, when it curves rather abruptly into a strong hook; there is a distinct subterminal notch on the tomia of the maxilla, which is slightly convex; the tomia of the mandible is slightly upturned, and there is a notch near the end; the nostrils are oval and open at the end of the nasal fossa and partly covered by the setose supra-nasal feathers; the rictal bristles are long and strong. The third and fourth primaries are the longest in the wing, the second < the fifth, first = the tenth; the tail is slightly rounded. The tarsi are long, the toes and claws rather slender; the outer toe is united to the middle toe near the base, the inner toe cleft to the base.

1. **Attila citreopygius.**

Dasycephala citreopygia, Bp. Compt. Rend. xxxviii. p. 657 [1]; Not. Orn. p. 86 [2].
Attila citreopygius, Scl. P. Z. S. 1857, p. 228 [3]; 1859, pp. 41 [4], 366 [5], 383 [6]; Ibis, 1859, p. 438 [7]; Cat. Am. B. p. 194 [8]; Cat. Birds Brit. Mus. xiv. p. 361 [9]; Scl. & Salv. Ibis, 1859, p. 120 [10]; P. Z. S. 1870, p. 837 [11]; Lawr. Ann. Lyc. N. Y. viii. p. 7 [12]; Bull. U. S. Nat. Mus. no. 4, p. 25 [13]; Nutting, Pr. U. S. Nat. Mus. vi. p. 385 [14].

Supra ferrugineo-brunneus; fronte et capitis lateribus albis, plumis omnibus medialiter nigris; capite summo quoque nigro striato; uropygio pallide cinnamomeo; alis nigricantibus, tectricibus et secundariis cinnamomeo limbatis; cauda obscure rufa ad basin magis ferruginea: subtus albus; gutture toto et pectore nigro striatis, hoc quoque pallide olivaceo lavato; hypochondriis cinnamomeis; subcaudalibus flavescentibus; subalaribus pallide cinnamomeis: rostro corneo, pedibus corylinis. Long. tota 7·5, alæ 3·7, caudæ 3·2, rostri a rictu 1·15, tarsi 0·95. (Descr. maris ex Choctum, Guatemala. Mus. nostr.)

Hab. MEXICO, Jalapa (*de Oca* [5]), Santa Efigenia, Tehuantepec (*Sumichrast* [13]); GUATEMALA (*Skinner* [10]), El Zapote, Choctum, Kamkhal (*O. S. & F. D. G.*); NICARAGUA (*Delattre* [12]), Sucuya (*Nutting* [14]); COSTA RICA (*Carmiol*); PANAMA, Chiriqui (*Arcé*).

This name has usually been applied to the bird found in Eastern Mexico and Guatemala and southward to Nicaragua; but we believe that its range extends to Chiriqui, and that it occurs in that country and in Costa Rica with the allied form *A. sclateri,* but whether the two are found in the same woods remains to be proved. The throat and chin in *A. citreopygius* are more or less greyish white, whereas in the allied species this portion of the under surface as well as the breast is greenish yellow, and the streaks not quite so well marked. Southern birds have a rather more slender bill than northern ones; but the breast, in all specimens, is more or less washed with greenish yellow.

2. **Attila gaumeri.**

Attila citreopygius, Boucard, P. Z. S. 1883, p. 149 (nec Bp.) [1].

A. cozumclæ similis et cauda ejusdem coloris; corpore subtus quoque griseo, uropygio tamen multo magis pallide cinnamomeo. (Descr. exempl. ex Tizimin, Mexico. Mus. nostr.)

Hab. MEXICO, Tizimin [1], Peto in Northern Yucatan, Meco, Holbox, and Mugeres Is. (*G. F. Gaumer*).

This form is closely allied to *A. cozumelæ*, but appears always to have a much paler rump, though the colour of the under surface is nearly the same in both forms. Its range appears to be confined to the northern portion of Yucatan and the islands off the coast north of Cozumel.

3. **Attila cozumelæ.**

Attila cozumelæ, Ridgw. Pr. Biol. Soc. Wash. iii. p. 23 [1]; Pr. U. S. Nat. Mus. viii. p. 572 [2]; Salv. Ibis, 1889, p. 364 [3].

Attila sp. ?, Salv. Ibis, 1885, p. 191 [4].

A. citreopygio similis, sed supra pallidior: subtus grisescentior; cauda brunnescente ad basin vix cinnamomea, uropygio saturate cinnamomeo. (Descr. exempl. ex Cozumel I. Mus. nostr.)

Hab. MEXICO, Cozumel I. (*Benedict* [1][2], *Deirs* [4], *G. F. Gaumer* [3]).

This form appears to be restricted to the island of Cozumel. It may be distinguished from *A. citreopygius* by its greyer throat and breast, the latter seldom showing a trace of greenish yellow; the rump is of a darker cinnamon, and the tail much browner.

4. **Attila sclateri.**

Attila spadacea, Lawr. Ann. Lyc. N. Y. vii. p. 327 (nec Gmel.) [1].

Attila sclateri, Lawr. Ann. Lyc. N. Y. vii. p. 470 [2]; ix. p. 110 [3]; Scl. & Salv. P. Z. S. 1864, p. 358 [4]; Salv. P. Z. S. 1867, p. 146 [5]; 1870, p. 196 [6]; Nutting, Pr. U. S. Nat. Mus. vi. p. 404 [7]; Scl. Cat. Birds Brit. Mus. xiv. p. 361 [8].

A. citreopygio similis, sed undique multo magis virescens; dorso medio palliore cinnamomeo-brunneo; cauda paullo obscuriore; uropygio multo flavescentiore. (Descr. maris ex San Pablo, Panama. Mus. nostr.) Femina mari similis.

Hab. NICARAGUA, Los Sabalos (*Nutting* [7]); COSTA RICA, Guaitil (*Carmiol* [3]), Irazu (*Rogers*), Tucurriqui (*Arcé*); PANAMA, Volcan de Chiriqui [6], Calovevora [5] (*Arcé*), Lion Hill (*M'Leannan* [1][2]), San Pablo (*O. S.* [4]).—SOUTH AMERICA, Eastern Ecuador.

This is another of the brown-tailed group, differing, however, from the preceding in having the under surface from the throat to the abdomen yellowish green, with dark central streaks to the feathers. Its distinctness from *A. citreopygius* is obvious when the more typical specimens are compared; but Costa Rican examples sometimes have the base of the tail more rufous, so that the line of distinction becomes obscured.

5. Attila cinnamomeus.

Attila cinnamomeus, Lawr. Ann. Lyc. N. Y. x. p. 8[1]; Mem. Bost. Soc. N. H. ii. p. 285[2].

A. citreopygio similis, sed supra multo pallidior et magis cinnamomeus; cauda pallide cinnamomea, uropygio quoque pallidiore. (Descr. maris ex Santiago Tepic, Mexico. Mus. nostr.)

Hab. Mexico, Santiago Terr. de Tepic (*W. B. Richardson*), Beltran, Hacienda de San Marcos and Tonila in Jalisco, Santiago in Colima (*Lloyd*), Omilteme, Amula, and Rincon in Guerrero (*Mrs. H. H. Smith*), Juchatengo and Sola in Oaxaca (*M. Trujillo*).

This is a western form of *Attila*, extending from the territory of Tepic to Oaxaca. Generally speaking it is of a more cinnamon tint on the upper surface, and the tail is of a brighter cinnamon than in any of the allied forms. The under surface as far as the abdomen is usually pale grey with dark streaks, and few specimens have any tinge of yellow.

6. Attila hypoxanthus.

Præcedentibus similis, sed subtus undique sulphureo suffusus; uropygio sicut in *A. cozumelæ* et *A. citreopygio*; cauda fere ut in *A. cinnamomeo*. (Descr. exempl. ex Vera Paz, Guatemala. Mus. nostr.)

Hab. Mexico, Venta de Pelegrino in Guerrero (*Mrs. H. H. Smith*); Guatemala, Vera Paz (*O. S. & F. D. G.*).

The two birds we here separate appear to differ so much from the other forms that we are strongly inclined to consider them distinct. None of the others have the yellow of the underparts spread over the whole surface, all of them having more or less white on the abdomen, and grey tints usually prevail over the throat and breast. Though we separate these birds under a distinct name, we confess that the distribution of this and the allied forms is difficult to understand: that two forms should coexist in the same area is not what we should expect. If, on the other hand, these two birds are only extreme forms of the prevalent local race of the area in which they were found, one of them would belong to *A. cinnamomeus* and the other to *A. citreopygius*, the two individuals being practically inseparable.

The whole question of the separation of the various forms of *Attila* is, as we have already said, so complicated that no certain decision can at present be arrived at. In separating *A. hypoxanthus* the problem seems to be a little clearer, but we should not be surprised if the whole group had to be entirely recast.

Subfam. COTINGINÆ.

This subfamily contains some of the most highly coloured birds of the family Cotingidæ, the members of the genus *Cotinga* being amongst the most beautiful of South-American birds.

The development of the rictal bristles has been used as a character by which to separate the Rupicolinæ and Cotinginæ from the Lipauginæ and Attilinæ, but we doubt if their supposed absence or presence will eventually prove of much use in the classification of these groups. In *Cotinga* the bristles are small, and in *Carpodectes* they appear to be wholly wanting; but in all the other genera they can be traced without much difficulty. Their development, of course, is not nearly so advanced as in *Attila* and *Lipaugus*, but still they can be seen.

The Cotinginæ had therefore better for the present be defined as Cotingidæ in which the rictal bristles are absent or small. This will bring *Chasmorhynchus* into the Cotinginæ and remove it from the Querulinæ, in which the rictal bristles are very strong.

COTINGA.

Cotinga, Brisson, Orn. ii. p. 339 (1760); Scl. Cat. Birds Brit. Mus. xiv. p. 382.

Cotinga contains eight species which are spread over the tropical portions of the Neotropical Region from the forests of the southern parts of the Mexican State of Vera Cruz to South-eastern Brazil. Two allied species are found within our region—one, *C. amabilis*, extending from Southern Mexico to Eastern Costa Rica; the other, *C. ridgwayi*, occurring in Western Costa Rica and the State of Panama.

The bill in *C. amabilis* is short, wide at the base, and converging in concave lines to the tip; the culmen is gradually curved from the base, a little more abruptly towards the tip, and there is a small subterminal notch on the tomia of the maxilla; the nostrils are open and fully exposed, the short thick-set frontal and supra-nasal feathers not extending to the proximal end of the opening. The rictal bristles are small; the tarsi are short, and the outer and middle toes are but slightly united at the base.

The differences in the comparative lengths and form of the primaries in *Cotinga* are most remarkable. In *C. amabilis* the second primary is the longest, the first longer than the third, the fourth shorter than the fifth; none of them are much reduced in width, and the ends are rounded.

In *C. ridgwayi* the fourth is the longest, the third and fifth are equal, the first=the sixth, the second a little longer than the first. Both first and second are reduced in width, the second more than the first, and it is moreover slightly curved inwards towards the tip. The two species are thus quite different as regards the form of the wing.

Of the other species of *Cotinga*, *C. cœrulea* and *C. cincta* resemble *C. amabilis* in having a shortened fourth primary, but the first three are all more pointed. *C. cayana* has a fourth primary as long as the third, and the first and second are pointed, the third being normal. *C. maynana* has the third primary a trifle shorter than the second and fourth, and both it and the first are narrower towards the tip than the second. The wing of *C. nattereri* is a slight modification of that of *C. ridgwayi*.

C. porphyrolœma has a normal wing, none of the feathers being shortened out of order or attenuated.

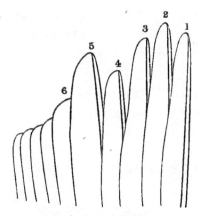

Wing of *C. amabilis*.

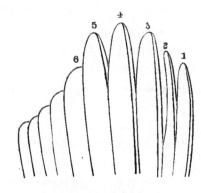

Wing of *C. ridgwayi*.

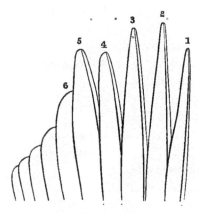

Wing of *C. cœrulea*.

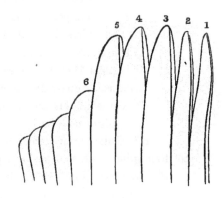

Wing of *C. cayana*.

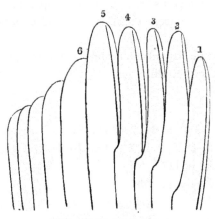

Wing of *C. maynana*.

All the variations in the wings of the various species of *Cotinga*, where they occur, appear to be found in the male alone, the wings of the females being of normal structure, except, perhaps, in the female of *C. ridgwayi*, in which (we have only one immature specimen) the first and second primaries are abnormally narrow, though much less so than in the adult male.

Using the structure of the primaries as a chief character with others whereby to define the members of the genus *Cotinga*, the following key may be useful :—

Clavis specierum Cotingarum.

a. Remigibus abnormalibus irregulariter abbreviatis aut attenuatis; coloribus nitidis cæruleis et purpureis.

  a′. Remigibus subtus omnino nigris.

    a″. Remige 4° quam 3us et 5us breviore.

      a‴. Remigibus 1° et 2° angustatis acutis, 2° et 3° longissimis.

        a⁴. Pectore et abdomine medio rubro-purpureis, fascia pectorali cærulea nulla . . . . 1. *cærulea.*

        b⁴. Fascia pectorali cærulea . . . . 2. *cincta.*

      b‴. Remigibus 1° et 2° fere normalibus, vix attenuatis aut acutis, 2° longissimo . . . . 3. *amabilis.*

    b″. Remigibus 4° et 5° fere æqualibus, 1° et 2° attenuatis sed haud acutis, 2° quam 1us angustiore.

      c‴. Gulæ plumis ad basin fuscis, fascia transversa mediana nigra notatis . . . . 4. *nattereri.*

      d‴. Gulæ plumis fascia alba nec nigra transnotatis . . . . 5. *ridgwayi.*

  b′. Remigibus subtus ad basin in pogonio interno plus minusve albis.

    c″. Corporis plumis cæruleis ad basin nigris; remigibus 1°, 2°, 3°, et 4° fere æqualibus, duobus exterioribus ad apicem attenuatis . . . . 6. *cayana.*

    d″. Corporis plumis cæruleis ad basin albis in medio rubro-purpureo transfasciatis; remigibus 2°, 3°, et 4° fere æqualibus, 1° breviore, omnibus ad apicem attenuatis, 3° multo magis quam reliquis . . . . 7. *maynana.*

b. Remigibus normalibus haud irregulariter abbreviatis aut attenuatis; coloribus plerumque nigro et albo . . . . 8. *porphyrolæma.*

1. Cotinga amabilis.

Cotinga amabilis, Gould, P. Z. S. 1857, p. 64, t. 123 [1]; Scl. & Salv. Ibis, 1859, p. 125 [2]; Salv. Ibis, 1860, p. 100 [3]; Scl. P. Z. S. 1860, p. 252 [4]; Cat. Birds Brit. Mus. xiv. p. 354 [5]; Lawr. Ann. Lyc. N. Y. vii. p. 473 [6]; ix. p. 117 [7].

Ampelis amabilis, Cab. J. f. Orn. 1861, p. 253 [8].

Nitide cærulea; capite summo cyanescentiore; alis et cauda nigris extrorsum cæruleo limbatis; gula et abdomine medio vinaceo-purpureis; pectore et hypochondriis dorso concoloribus; tectricibus caudæ supra et subtus elongatis, fere ad finem rectricum medianarum extensis. Long. tota 7·1, alæ 4·6, caudæ 2·5, rostri a rictu 0·75, tarsi 0·8. (Descr. maris ex Choctum. Mus. nostr.)

♀ supra fusca, plumis omnibus albido terminatis : subtus albida, plumis pectoris et hypochondriorum fuscis, albido limbatis ; alis et cauda nigricantibus ; secundariis et tectricibus albido limbatis. (Descr. feminæ ex Coban, Guatemala. Mus. nostr.)

♂ juv. feminæ similis, plumis maris cæruleis et purpureis huc illuc apparentibus.

Hab. MEXICO, Orizaba (*Sallé*[4]), Chimalapa, Tehuantepec (*W. B. Richardson*); GUATE-MALA, Choctum, Coban (*F. D. G. & O. S.*), Vera Paz (*Skinner*[2]); COSTA RICA (*Van Patten*), San José (*v. Frantzius*[7]); PANAMA (?) (*M'Leannan*[6]).

This well-marked *Cotinga* represents in Central America the well-known *C. cincta* of Brazil, having the same distribution of colours; but the pectoral band and the flanks, as well as the upper surface, are of a much paler shade of blue than in the southern bird, and there is some difference in the form of the primaries.

C. amabilis was first described by Gould from specimens sent him from Guatemala by Skinner[1]. During our visits to Vera Paz we found it not uncommon in the vicinity of Coban and in the forest-country lying to the northward. Near Coban the country is broken up by a series of isolated hills, on the summits of most of which a patch of forest remains, the lower country being occupied by cultivated ground and second-growth woods. In these patches of forest *C. amabilis* was to be found at seasons when certain fruits on which they fed were ripe, at other times they frequented the lower forest-country.

The northern extension of this species reaches Orizaba, where Sallé met with it and obtained one female example[4]. It must, however, be a very rare bird in this district, as Sumichrast omits all mention of it in his list of the birds of Vera Cruz, and no specimens have reached us from that part of Mexico; but Mr. Richardson has recently sent us a skin of a female bird which he shot at Chimalapa, on the eastern side of the Cordillera of Tehuantepec, in March 1890. Its southern range extends to Eastern Costa Rica, whence we have specimens certainly referable to this bird. Mr. Lawrence includes *C. amabilis* in his list of M'Leannan's collections made on the Isthmus of Panama; but this identification requires to be reconsidered, for we believe that M'Leannan's skins will prove to belong to *C. ridgwayi* or to be Guatemalan specimens wrongly attributed to Panama.

The peculiar structure of the wing of *C. amabilis* and its difference in this respect from that of *C. ridgwayi* is described under the genus.

2. Cotinga ridgwayi.

Cotinga amabilis, Lawr. Ann. Lyc. N. Y. vii. p. 473[1]; Salv. P. Z. S. 1870, p. 200[2].

Cotinga ridgwayi, Zeledon, Pr. U. S. Nat. Mus. x. p. 1[3]; Scl. Cat. Birds Brit. Mus. xiv. p. 384[4].

C. amabili similis sed minor, colore cæruleo pallidiore, ciliis oculorum et frontis lateribus ad basin nigris (nec cæruleis), tectricibus caudæ multo brevioribus et alis diversis facile distinguenda.

♀ supra cervino-punctata, subtus abdomine fusco ; plumis omnibus cervino limbatis.

Hab. COSTA RICA, Pozo Azul (*Zeledon*[3]); PANAMA, Bugaba (*Arcé*[2]).

An immature bird sent us by Arcé from Chiriqui, and described in 1870 as doubtfully

C. amabilis, belongs to this species, which was fully characterized by Mr. Ridgway in 1887 from an adult male sent him by Mr. Zeledon from Pozo Azul in Costa Rica. Mr. Sclater, in his recent Catalogue, doubted its distinctness from *C. amabilis*, but we think there can be no question on the subject; the several points of distinction referred to above and also by Mr. Ridgway are quite sufficient to determine its status as an excellent species.

Its occurrence on the line of the Panama Railway is probable, but requires confirmation; its extension further southwards rests on the authority of a skin of Bogota make in the National Museum at Washington, which also should be re-examined, as we believe it will prove to be the allied species *C. nattereri*, Boiss.*

CARPODECTES.

Carpodectes, Salv. P. Z. S. 1864, p. 583; Scl. Cat. Birds Brit. Mus. xiv. p. 389.

This peculiar genus, remarkable for the nearly pure white plumage of the males, contains only two species, both of them found in Costa Rica—one on the eastern side of the Cordillera and extending northwards into Nicaragua, the other on the western side.

The bill in *Carpodectes* is stronger and more compressed than in *Cotinga*, and the culmen more arched; the nostrils are open and fully exposed. The rictal bristles appear to be altogether absent or at least very small. The wings are normal, none of the quills being narrowed or shortened out of order; the fourth quill is the longest, the second, third, and fifth a little shorter and equal, first=seventh. The tail is short and nearly even, the upper coverts covering less than half the rectrices.

Compared with *Ampelio*, *Carpodectes* has a stouter, more compressed bill, with a more arched culmen. The rictal bristles in *Ampelio* are much more evident, the wings shorter and the tail longer. In addition to these differences the great diversity in colour is very obvious.

1. **Carpodectes nitidus.** (Tab. XLII., ♂ ♀.)

Carpodectes nitidus, Salv. P. Z. S. 1864, p. 583, t. 36[1]; Lawr. Ann. Lyc. N. Y. viii. p. 184[2]; ix. p. 117[3]; v. Frantz. J. f. Orn. 1869, p. 310[4]; Boucard, P. Z. S. 1878, p. 65[5]; Ridgw. Pr. U. S. Nat. Mus. i. p. 255[6]; Scl. Cat. Birds Brit. Mus. xiv. p. 389[7].

Albus plumbeo vix tinctus; capitis lateribus, alis et corpore subtus fere pure albis: rostro plumbeo, pedibus nigris. Long. tota 8·0, alæ 5·5, caudæ 2·7, rostri a rictu 0·95, tarsi 1·0. (Descr. exempl. typ. ex Tucurriqui, Costa Rica. Mus. nostr.)

♀ supra saturate grisea; fronte, capitis lateribus et gula albicantioribus, oculorum ambitu albo; alis nigris,

---

* Of *C. nattereri*, Boiss. (Rev. Zool. 1840, p. 2), there is a single adult male specimen in the British Museum. It is the bird marked *c* under the name of *C. ridgwayi* of Mr. Sclater's Catalogue (vol. xiv. p. 384). It differs from the true *C. ridgwayi* in having the bases of the purple feathers of the throat and abdomen dusky, with a black band dividing that colour from the blue extremity, whereas in the allied species this median band is white. The first and second primaries are rather wider and longer in *C. nattereri* than in *C. ridgwayi*, and the fifth instead of the fourth is the longest in the wing.

extus pallide griseo limbatis : subtus dilutior, abdomine imo, subcaudalibus, subalaribus et tibiis albicantibus ; cauda supra nigricante, subtus cinerea.   (Descr. feminæ ex Costa Rica.   Mus. Boucard.)

Hab. . NICARAGUA, Greytown (*Holland* [2]) ; COSTA RICA, Tucurriqui (*Arcé* [1]), Pacuare (*Zeledon* [6]), San Carlos (*Boucard* [5]).

The first specimen of this remarkable bird was sent us by our collector Arcé in 1864 [1], and formed the type of the description and figure in the ' Proceedings of the Zoological Society ' for that year.   It was shot near Tucurriqui, a hamlet in a valley on the Atlantic slope of the mountains of Costa Rica.   Another specimen, a male, was obtained by Mr. H. E. Holland in the following year near Greytown in Nicaragua [2].   Others have since been obtained by Mr. Zeledon and M. Boucard ; the last-named traveller shot an adult female at San Carlos, which is the only female we have seen, and owing to his kindness is that figured on our Plate.   A young male in the Museum of the University of Cambridge resembles the adult, but has the first (unmoulted) primary in each wing like that of the female.

All the places where this bird has hitherto been found are on the Atlantic slope of the Costa-Rican Cordillera, where a dense tropical forest prevails.

2. Carpodectes antoniæ.

Carpodectes antoniæ, Ridgw. Ibis, 1884, p. 27, t. 2 [1] ; Pr. U. S. Nat. Mus. vi. p. 410 [2] ; x. p. 20 [3] ; Scl. Cat. Birds Brit. Mus. xiv. p. 389 [4].

Præcedenti similis sed pure albus, capite summo, dorso et cauda plumbeo tantum tinctis : rostro flavo, culmine nigro.   Long. tota 8·0, alæ 5·6, caudæ 2·6, rostri a rictu 0·9, tarsi 0·9.

♀ supra plumbea, alis et cauda nigricantibus, illarum tectricibus et secundariis albo limbatis, pagina quoque inferiore (remigum apicibus exceptis) alba : subtus pallide grisea, ventre medio et crisso albis : rostro corneo ad basin albido, pedibus nigris.   (Descr. maris et feminæ ex Pirris, Costa Rica.   Mus. nostr.)

Hab. COSTA RICA, Pirris (*Zeledon* [1] [2] [3]).

The only specimens hitherto obtained of this second species of *Carpodectes* all come from the neighbourhood of Pirris, on the western slope of the mountains of Costa Rica. They were all collected by Mr. Zeledon, to whom we are indebted for a male and a female skin, which are now in the British Museum.   Mr. Zeledon says " the bird cannot be called common, and it was by mere accident that I came across a tree with ripe fruit for which it shows much partiality, and there I stationed a man to watch and shoot the birds as they arrived to feed.   I have not heard its song, nor has anyone else that I know of.   The call-note resembles very much that of *Tityra personata*."

CHASMORHYNCHUS.

Casmorhinchos, Temminck, Man. d'Orn. éd. 2, p. lxiii (1820).
Chasmorhynchus, Temminck, Pl. Col. livr. 9 (1823) ; Scl. Cat. Birds Brit. Mus. xiv. p. 403.

Four species constitute the genus *Chasmorhynchus*, all of them remarkably distinct from one another.   The ranges of these species spread over a considerable portion of tropical America. Thus, in South-eastern Brazil we find *C. nudicollis*, iu Guiana *C. niveus*, and in the western portion of that country, together with Venezuela and Trinidad, *C. variegatus* is found; in our country *C. tricarunculatus* occurs in Costa Rica and the adjoining State of Panama. It thus appears that *Chasmorhynchus* is unrepresented in Colombia, in all of the countries traversed by the Andes, and in the valley of the Amazons. The latter fact is not so surprising, as all the species appear to affect the mountain forests of some elevation.

The genus *Chasmorhynchus* has no near allies, so much so that its position in the family is by no means satisfactorily settled; there are even points in its structure, such as the absence of a bifurcation to the manubrium of the sternum, which have caused its position in the Passeres to be questioned.

Mr. Sclater places *Chasmorhynchus* in his subfamily of Gymnoderinæ, that is Cotingidæ of large form with "corvine bills." The bill conforms more strictly to the cotingine series, and the absence of rictal bristles also suggests the same position.

The forehead, the chin, and the portions of the face surrounding the bill and eyes of *C. tricarunculatus* are destitute of feathers. A long caruncle proceeds from the forehead and one from the rictus on either side; the nostrils are open and situated at the end of the nasal fossa; the culmen is moderately and regularly curved, and there is a distinct subterminal notch towards the end of the tomia of the maxilla. The wings are without special features, the third primary is slightly the longest, the second, fourth, and fifth being a little shorter, the first=seventh; the tail is nearly even; the tarsi are short, the inner and outer toes equal, the latter more united to the middle toe than the former.

1. Chasmorhynchus tricarunculatus.

Chasmorhynchus tricarunculatus, J. & E. Verr. Rev. Zool. 1853, p. 193 [1]; Cab. J. f. Orn. 1861, p. 253 [2]; Salv. Ibis, 1865, p. 92, t. 3 [3]; P. Z. S. 1867, p. 150 [4]; 1870, p. 200 [5]; Scl. Ibis, 1866, pp. 406 [6], 407 [7]; Lawr. Ann. Lyc. N. Y. ix. p. 117 [8]; Frantz. J. f. Orn. 1869, p. 310 [9]; Ridgw. Pr. U. S. Nat. Mus. v. p. 496 [10].

Castaneus; capite toto et cervice usque ad pectus niveis; loris nudis, setis nigris sparsim vestitis; carunculis tribus elongatis ornatus—una frontali, duabus rictalibus: rostro et pedibus nigris. Long. tota 11·0, alæ 6·5, caudæ 4·1, rostri a rictu 1·5, tarsi 1·1.

♀ olivacea; alis et cauda introrsum fuscis: subtus flavescens, plumis olivaceo utrinque limbatis; gutture, ventre medio et subalaribus immaculatis: rostro et pedibus nigris, carunculis rictalibus vix ullis.

♂ *juv.* feminæ similis, plumis maris undique apparentibus, carunculis obviis. (Descr. exempl. ex Tucurriqui, Costa Rica. Mus. nostr.)

Hab. Costa Rica, Tucurriqui (*Arcé* [3]), San José, Dota Mts., Cervantes (*Carmiol* [8]), Turrialba (*Cooper* [8]), La Palma (*Nutting* [10]); Panama, Boca del Toro (*Verreaux* [1]), Volcan de Chiriqui [5], Cordillera de Tolé [5], Calovevora [5], Veraguas [4] (*Arcé*).

This species has almost exactly the same range as *Cephalopterus glabricollis*, being found in the same mountains over a similar area. It was first described from specimens sent from Boca del Toro on the Atlantic side of the cordillera of Panama [1], and many specimens have since been forwarded from Costa Rica and the Colombian State of Panama. Our specimens from the former country were mostly obtained by Arcé at Tucurriqui, at an elevation of about 3000 feet above the sea, but one secured by M. Boucard was killed on the slopes of the Volcan de Irazu at a height of 6000 feet above the sea. Our series includes males in all stages of development, from which it would appear that the caruncles commence their growth on the assumption of the adult plumage, and that they acquire their full development almost before the fully adult feathers are assumed, showing that their growth must be very rapid. The upper caruncle from the base of the bill first shows itself, the rictal ones appearing later and growing unevenly. In Wolf's plate, accompanying the paper in 'The Ibis' for 1865, the caruncles are represented as flat and stiff; we doubt if they are ever so, but when relaxed are vermiform and hang loosely downwards.

Subfam. *GYMNODERINÆ*.

Gymnoderus, from which this subfamily takes its name, is a bird of a very isolated character, and its relationship to *Hæmatoderus*, *Cephalopterus*, and the other genera with which it has been generally associated is not at all obvious. After the removal of *Chasmorhynchus* from the Gymnoderinæ, *Gymnoderus* is the only genus in which the rictal bristles appear to be wholly absent. The bill cannot strictly be called "corvine," and the flanks have large white powder-down patches similar to those found in the Herons! no such character, so far as we know, being possessed by any other passerine bird. *Querula* and *Cephalopterus*, the two genera of Gymnoderinæ with which we are now concerned, belong to the section in which the rictal bristles are strongly developed. The bill is strong and conforms more to the corvine outline said to be characteristic of the subfamily, the lores are densely feathered. So different are these birds from *Gymnoderus* that we think they, with *Hæmatoderus* and *Pyroderus*, had better be separated as :—

Subfam. *QUERULINÆ*.

QUERULA.

Querula, Vieillot, Anal. p. 37 (1816); Scl. Cat. Birds Brit. Mus. xiv. p. 396.

A single species constitutes this genus, which has a wide range, extending from Costa Rica southward to Peru and eastward to Guiana.

The bill is stout, rather wide at the base, the sides converging in nearly straight lines to the tip, the culmen is curved throughout its length, more abruptly towards the end, and there is a distinct subterminal notch on the tomia of the maxilla; the nostrils are open, but partially hidden by the setose supra-nasal feathers, the rictal bristles are long and strong; the fourth and fifth primaries are the longest, the third=fifth, the second=the seventh, the first is a little shorter than the tenth; the tarsi are short, and the feet generally rather feeble, the outer toe is a little longer than the inner toe and more united to the middle toe; the tail is moderate and nearly even, and the general plumage like that of *Cephalopterus*, black, the male being adorned by a rich vinous red throat.

1. Querula cruenta.

Muscicapa cruenta, Bodd. Tabl. Pl. Enl. p. 23, ex Daub. Pl. Enl. 381 [1].

Querula cruenta, Cass. Pr. Ac. Phil. 1860, p. 143 [2]; Lawr. Ann. Lyc. N. Y. vii. p. 296 [3]; ix. p. 117 [4]; Scl. & Salv. P. Z. S. 1864, p. 361 [5]; Scl. Cat. Birds Brit. Mus. xiv. p. 396 [6].

Muscicapa rubricollis, Gm. Syst. Nat. i. p. 933 [7].

Nigra; gula tota plumis elongatis vinaceo-rubris ornata; mento nigro: rostro plumbeo, pedibus nigris. Long. tota 11·0, alæ 7·2, caudæ 4·7, rostri a rictu 1·4, tarsi 1·0.

♀ omnino nigra, gula inornata. (Descr. maris et feminæ ex Panama. Mus. nostr.)

Hab. Costa Rica, Angostura, Pacuar (*Carmiol* [4]); Panama, Montaña del Vermejo (*Arcé*), Lion Hill (*M'Leannan* [3][5]), Turbo (*C. J. Wood* [2]).—South America, from Colombia to Peru, Amazons valley, and Guiana [6].

This is a distinct species with no near allies, which has a wide range in the northern portion of South America. It occurs commonly on the Isthmus of Panama, and thence northward to Costa Rica; it frequents the higher forests, living in the branches of the loftier trees and feeding on fruit.

CEPHALOPTERUS.

Cephalopterus, Geoffroy, Ann. d. Mus. xiii. p. 235 (1809); Scl. Cat. Birds Brit. Mus. xiv. p. 398.

There are three species of this remarkable genus, one of which (*C. glabricollis*) occurs in Costa Rica and the adjoining State of Panama, another (*C. penduliger*) in Western Ecuador, and a third (*C. ornatus*) has a wide range over the Amazons valley from Colombia to Bolivia, it is also said to occur in Guiana; no species is found in the forests of South-eastern Brazil.

One of the most peculiar features of this genus is the long caruncle or appendage proceeding from the throat, densely feathered in two species, nearly naked in *C. glabricollis*, which has only a few long terminal feathers. The feathers of the crown and forehead are long and curved towards their ends, and form a kind of hood, from which these birds take their trivial name of umbrella-birds. The bill is very stout and the culmen arched; the nostrils have an overhanging membrane and are situated at the lower end of the nasal fossa; the fifth primary is the longest in the wing, the fourth and sixth are equal, the second=the seventh, the first is less than the tenth; the tail is short and rounded; the tarsi and toes are strong, the outer toe a little shorter than the middle toe, the inner toe being the shortest.

1. Cephalopterus glabricollis.

Cephalopterus glabricollis, Gould, P. Z. S. 1850, t. 20 [1]; Cab. J. f. Orn. 1861, p. 254 [2]; Salv. P. Z. S.
1867, p. 150 [3]; 1870, p. 201 [4]; Lawr. Ann. Lyc. N. Y. ix. p. 117 [5]; Frantz. J. f. Orn. 1869,
p. 310 [6]; Boucard, P. Z. S. 1878, p. 66 [7]; Scl. Cat. Birds Brit. Mus. xiv. p. 400 [8].

Niger, supra chalybeo-nitens; crista elongata ad basin nigra undique expandente: gula tota calva, rubra;
carunculo pectorali quoque calvo, plumis elongatis sparsis tantum ad ejus apicem: rostro nigro, pedibus
plumbeis. Long. tota 16·0, alæ 10·0, caudæ 4·7, rostri a rictu 2·2, tarsi 1·9.

♀ mari similis, sed obscurior; capitis plumis minus elongatis; gula tantum utrinque calva, linea mediana plumosa vestita, carunculo parvo. (Descr. maris et feminæ ex Turrialba, Costa Rica. Mus. nostr.)

Hab. COSTA RICA, Turrialba (*Arcé, Carmiol*), Tucurriqui (*Arcé*), San Carlos (*Boucard* [7]),
San José (*v. Frantzius* [5]), Angostura and Dota Mountains (*Carmiol* [5]); PANAMA,
Cordillera de Chiriqui [1] (*Warszewicz* [1]), Cordillera de Tolé, Calovevora (*Arcé*).

The first specimens of this species sent to this country were obtained by Warszewicz
in the Cordillera of Chiriqui at an elevation of about 8000 feet above the sea; these
were described by Gould in 1850 [1]. It was subsequently found in Costa Rica, where
M. Boucard tells us it occurs in the forests at all altitudes up to an elevation of 10,000
feet [7]. Its peculiar cry renders it easily detected in the forests which it frequents.
Unlike *C. ornatus* of the Amazons valley, *C. glabricollis* appears to be strictly confined
to the high mountains, and this is probably the reason it does not occur in the lowlands bordering the Panama Railway, and why its northward extension is determined by
the valley of the San Juan river.

Suborder TRACHEOPHONÆ.

Fam. DENDROCOLAPTIDÆ *.

Within our limits we are more or less acquainted with about forty-six species of
Dendrocolaptidæ, the total number contained in the family being about 300. The focus
of the family is probably the great basin of the Amazons river; but its members as a
whole are by no means confined to the forests of the more tropical countries of South
America, for the large section or subfamily of the Furnariinæ belongs chiefly to the
southern portions of the continent, to the arid districts bordering the Pacific Ocean,
or to the highlands of the Andes throughout their length. This subfamily is not
represented in Central America.

The other subfamilies of Mr. Sclater's arrangement (Cat. Birds Brit. Mus. xv. p. 3)
are :—

* The Dendrocolaptidæ forms another of the characteristic families of South-American birds, and is strictly
confined to the Neotropical Region, with the exception of the Antilles, where no representative is found.

II. Synallaxinæ;

III. Philydorinæ;

IV. Sclerurinæ;

V. Dendrocolaptinæ:

the subordinate characters being taken from the size of the bill and the length of the tarsus.

When the definitions of these subfamilies are submitted to test, we find that they do not give satisfactory results, so that we are obliged to modify them considerably by introducing the shape and structure of the nostrils as a character of importance; the relative length of the hallux is also useful as a diagnostic feature.

We cannot here go into all the modifications involved in Mr. Sclater's classification when the shape of the nostrils is taken into consideration, but in illustration we note that when the nostrils of *Pseudocolaptes* are examined it will be seen that they are linear and overhung, and not open and oval. This character places *Pseudocolaptes* in the Synallaxinæ and not with the Philydorinæ. The Philydorinæ are also affected by this character, and great changes must be made in the grouping of a large number of South-American genera, and even the species of some genera must be re-examined—as, for example, *Thripophaga*, which, as exemplified by its type *T. striolata*, has an open oval nostril and is allied to *Philydor*; but all the other birds associated with it have linear overhung nostrils, and must be placed in the Synallaxinæ, perhaps in the genus *Placelodomus*.

The Dendrocolaptidæ of Mexico and Central America may be divided as follows:—

A. Rectrices laxæ, rhachidibus ad apicem haud rigidis.
    a. Nares lineares et membrano obtectæ ad marginem inferiorem
        fossæ nasalis positæ . . . . Synallaxinæ.
    b. Nares apertæ, ovales, ad finem fossæ nasalis sitæ . . . . . Philydorinæ.
B. Rectrices rigidæ, rhachidibus prolongatis, acutis.
    c. Hallux longus fere digitum medium æquans.
        a'. Nares apertæ, ovales . . . . Sclerurinæ.
        b'. Nares lineares, membrano obtectæ . . . . Margarornithinæ.
    d. Hallux brevis, quam digitum medium multo brevior.
        c'. Nares lineares, arcuatæ, membrano obtectæ . . . . . Glyphorhynchinæ.
        d'. Nares apertæ, ovales . . . . Dendrocolaptinæ.

The Central-American Synallaxinæ as thus defined contain three genera including in all six species; the Philydorinæ four genera and fifteen species; the Sclerurinæ the genus *Sclerurus*, with three species; the Margarornithinæ the genus *Margarornis*, with two species; the Glyphorhynchinæ, *Glyphorhynchus*, with one species; and the Dendrocolaptinæ seven genera and nineteen or, perhaps, twenty species: the total number of genera being seventeen, with forty-six or forty-seven species. Of the genera not one is peculiar to Central America; but of the species twenty-nine are not found elsewhere, eighteen occurring also in South America. In Mexico and Guatemala the family is but poorly represented, but the numbers, both of genera and species, increase as the mainland of South America is approached.

Subfam. *SYNALLAXINÆ*.

SYNALLAXIS.

Synallaxis, Vieillot, N. Dict. d'Hist. N. xxxii. p. 309 (1819); Scl. Cat. Birds Brit. Mus. xv. p. 37.

Until recently this genus was made to include a ten tail-feathered and a twelve tail-feathered section. The former is now restricted to *Synallaxis* proper, and the latter is referred to *Siptornis*.

According to Mr. Sclater's recently published Catalogue, *Synallaxis* contains twenty-eight species, but the names of five others are given of which no specimens exist in the British Museum. The twenty-eight species are separated into seven sections defined chiefly by their colour. Sections II. and IV. are the only ones represented in our country: Section II. by *S. albescens* and *S. pudica*, in which the crown and the wings outwardly are rufous and the tail brown; and Section IV. by *S. erythrothorax*, in which the whole upper surface is nearly uniform rufous brown, and the breast and wings externally chestnut.

This last-named bird is the only one which reaches Southern Mexico, so that its range is that of the genus in this direction.

S. albescens and *S. pudica* are both South-American birds, the former with a wide range reaching even to the Argentine Republic. The latter occurs also in Colombia and Ecuador.

The bill in *S. erythrothorax* is moderate, the culmen slightly arched and without a notch near the end of the tomia of the maxilla, the nostrils are overhung by a membrane, the opening being a long slit on the lower edge of the nasal fossa; the wings are short and much rounded, the fourth, fifth, sixth, and seventh quills being nearly equal. The tarsi are moderately long and the toes and claws slender, the outer toe separate from the middle toe nearly to the base. The tail is moderately long and much rounded, the lateral feathers about half the length of the middle ones; all are pointed, and the barbs towards the end nearly destitute of barbules. The number of rectrices is ten.

1. **Synallaxis albescens.**

Synallaxis albescens, Temm. Pl. Col. 227. fig. 2 (27th Sept., 1823)[1]; Salv. P. Z. S. 1867, p. 143[2]; Scl. P. Z. S. 1874, p. 9[3]; Cat. Birds Brit. Mus. xv. p. 43[4]; Scl. & Salv. P. Z. S. 1879, p. 521[5].

Synallaxis albigularis, Scl. P. Z. S. 1858, p. 63[6].

19*

Supra murino-brunnea, fronte et cauda vix saturatioribus, vertice postico et nucha cum tectricibus alarum minoribus et mediis rufis; capitis et cervicis lateribus et pectore griseo-murinis; loris et abdomine medio albis; hypochondriis rufescenti-murinis, gula alba plumis singulis ad basin nigris; subalaribus albis cinnamomeo lavatis: rostro corneo, mandibulæ basi albida; pedibus corylinis. Long. tota 6·0, alæ 2·1, caudæ rect. med. 3·1, rectr. lat. 1·1, rostri a rictu 0·6, tarsi 0·75. (Descr. maris ex Medellin, Columbia. Mus. nostr.).

♀ mari similis, sed forsan rufescentior.

Av. juv. supra et subtus omnino rufescentior, vertice et fronte dorso concoloribus.

Hab. PANAMA, Santa Fé (*Arcé* [2] [5]).—SOUTH AMERICA, from Colombia [3], Ecuador [6], and Venezuela [5] to Guiana [5], Brazil [1], and the Argentine Republic.

The evidence of the occurrence of this species within our limits rests upon a single female specimen sent us by Arcé from Santa Fé in the State of Panama in 1866 [2].

This specimen is perhaps hardly adult, and is rather lighter and more rufescent on the upper surface than the male from Medellin described above, which again is in older, more abraded plumage. There can, however, be little doubt that both birds belong to the same species.

Synallaxis albescens has a wide range in Tropical America, and a long series of specimens in the British Museum, from various points of the southern continent, as far south as Buenos Ayres, confirm Mr. Sclater's view that the species, though variable, is not capable of subdivision, and that the bird described by him as *S. albigularis* [6] from an imperfect skin, from the valley of the Napo, is not really separable from the rest.

Salmon, who met with this species at Medellin in the Cauca Valley of Colombia, gives the following interesting account of its eggs and nest [3]. The former are described as of a very pale greenish-blue, almost white, colour, and measure ·88 by ·65. The nest, he says, is placed in a tree or high bush, 6 or 8 feet from the ground, and is made of sticks and twigs, the eggs being placed on a few small green leaves. In shape it resembles a pear lying horizontally, with an extended tunnel at the smaller end.

"I have seen," he says, "the nest as large as that of an English Magpie, and as firmly made, though the bird is not larger than a Sparrow. The body of the nest is composed of sticks, many of them from four to six inches in length and a quarter of an inch in diameter; the tunnel entrance, which is often of considerable length, is composed of fine twigs beautifully interlaced, the entrance only just admitting the body of the bird; it is sometimes straight, sometimes winding. The top of the nest is roofed with a mass of large leaves, a protection against the heavy rains. Altogether it is a remarkable construction, and it would be interesting to know how so small a bird can carry and fix such large sticks; but the bird at this time is exceedingly shy, always keeping at a distance from its nest when anyone is near, even if carefully hidden from view.

"The nest is difficult of approach, being placed where the underwood is very thick; and the eggs can only be obtained by making an opening on one side, which is not an easy operation."

2. Synallaxis pudica. (Tab. XLIV. fig. 2.)

Synallaxis pudica, Scl. P. Z. S. 1859, p. 191[1]; Ibis, 1873, p. 373[2]; Cat. Birds Brit. Mus. xv. p. 45[3]; Scl. & Salv. P. Z. S. 1864, p. 354[4]; 1879, p. 521[5]; Salv. Ibis, 1870, p. 110[6]; Boucard, P. Z. S. 1878, p. 59[7]; Nutting, Pr. U. S. Nat. Mus. vi. p. 404[8]; Ridgw. Pr. U. S. Nat. Mus. x. p. 590[9].

Synallaxis brunneicaudalis, Lawr. Ann. Lyc. N. Y. vii. p. 319 (nec Scl.)[10].

Synallaxis nigrifumosa, Lawr. Ann. Lyc. N. Y. viii. p. 180[11], ix. p. 105[12]; Salv. P. Z. S. 1867, p. 143[13]; Frantz. J. f. Orn. 1869, p. 304[14].

Synallaxis brachyurus, Lafr. Rev. Zool. 1843, p. 290[15]; Salv. Ibis, 1874, p. 322[16].

Supra murino-brunnea, vertice et tectricibus alarum cum remigibus in pogonio externo ad basin (duobus externis exceptis) læte rufis; fronte et corpore subtus saturate cinereis, abdomine medio pallidiore, gula sericea albido indistincte variegata; hypochondriis murinis, subalaribus cinnamomeis: rostro et pedibus plumbeo-nigricantibus, mandibula medialiter albicante. Long. tota 6·5, alæ 2·15, caudæ rectr. med. 3·0, rectr. lat. 1·0, rostri a rictu 0·7. (Descr. maris ex Costa Rica. Mus. nostr.)

♀ mari similis.

Av. juv. supra omnino murinus, vertice dorso concolore, subtus albicantior.

Hab. HONDURAS, Segovia river (*C. H. Townsend*[9]); NICARAGUA, Chontales (*Belt*[2]), Greytown (*Holland*[11]), Los Sabalos (*Nutting*[8]); COSTA RICA[14], Peje, Pacuar[11] (*Carmiol*), Naranjo (*Boucard*[7]); PANAMA, Chiriqui (*Arcé*), Lion Hill (*McLeannan*[10][4]). —COLOMBIA[15]; ECUADOR[3].

This species was described from Colombian specimens, one in the British Museum and one in Mr. Sclater's collection[1]. Others have since been sent from Western Ecuador, the Cauca Valley[5], and Central America, as far north as the Segovia River in Honduras[9] and the district of Chontales in Nicaragua[2]. The more northern birds were separated by Mr. Lawrence as *S. nigrifumosa*[11], the chestnut colour of the crown and wings being said to be a little darker than that of typical *S. pudica*, and the other colours darker and of different shades. These supposed differences seem to be hardly borne out when a large series is examined, and are not more than can be accounted for by differences of sex and age of plumage. Thus an adult example from the Balzar Mountains in Western Ecuador resembles one from Panama, being only very slightly paler on the abdomen.

There is a question as to the name this bird should bear; for it is quite possible *S. brachyura*, Lafr.[15], is applicable to it. This title was founded upon three immature birds with imperfect tails, now in the Collection of the Museum of Natural History at Boston. When Salvin examined them in 1874[16], he was inclined to believe them to be of the same species as Mr. Sclater's *S. pudica*, but the types being young and defective he thought the latter name had best be retained for the species, and this is still our impression.

Mr. Nutting, who observed *S. pudica* at Los Sabalos in Nicaragua, says[8] it is very Wren-like in its habits, and is found hopping about thick bushes or brush heaps. Regarding its notes, he says that they resemble those of a Wren, being loud, varied,

and melodious.   On the other hand, McLeannan says that it has no song [10].   The
iris is noted as reddish [8] and as brown [10].

3. Synallaxis erythrothorax.

Synallaxis cinerascens, Bp. P. Z. S. 1837, p. 118 (nec Temm.) [1].

Synallaxis erythrothorax, Scl. P. Z. S. 1855, p. 75, t. 86 [2]; 1856, p. 288 [3]; 1859, p. 382 [4]; 1874,
     p. 17 [5]; Cat. Birds Brit. Mus. xv. p. 55 [6]; Scl. & Salv. Ibis, 1859, p. 117 [7]; 1860, p. 35 [8];
     P. Z. S. 1870, p. 837 [9]; Sumichrast, Mem. Bost. Soc. N. H. i. p. 555 [10]; La Nat. v.
     p. 247 [11]; Sanchez, An. Mus. Nac. Mex. i. p. 97 [12]; Salv. Cat. Strickl. Coll. p. 335 [13];
     Boucard, P. Z. S. 1883, p. 449 [14].

Supra brunnea, capite summo obscuriore, cauda saturate rufo-brunnea: subtus gula nigra, menti plumis
     lateraliter albo marginatis, pectore et alis extus læte castaneis; hypochondriis brunneis, abdomine medio
     griseo-albo variegato: rostro et pedibus nigris.   Long. tota 6·0, alæ 2·15, caudæ rect. med. 2·6, rectr. lat.
     0·8, rostri a rictu 0·6, tarsi 0·8.   (Descr. maris ex Atoyac, Mexico.   Mus. nostr.)
♀ mari similis.

Av. juv. subtus pallide brunneus, gula cinerascentiore, abdomine albicantiore, rostri mandibula pallida.   (Descr.
maris juv. ex Retalhuleu, Guatemala.   Mus. nostr.).

Hab. MEXICO, hot region of the State of Vera Cruz [10], Uvero [11], and Omealca [11]
(*Sumichrast*), Cordova (*Sallé* [3]), Atoyac (*Mrs. H. H. Smith*), Vera Cruz (*Sanchez* [12],
F. D. G.), Playa Vicente (*Boucard* [4], *M. Trujillo*), Sochiapa (*M. Trujillo*), Teapa
in Tabasco (*Mrs. H. H. Smith*), Eastern Yucatan (*G. F. Gaumer* [14]); BRITISH
HONDURAS, Belize (*Dyson*), Orange Walk (*Gaumer*), Cayo (*F. Blancaneaux*);
GUATEMALA (*Velasquez* [1], *Constancia* [13]), Coban (*Delattre* [2][7]), Choctum, Chisec,
Kamkhal (*O. S. & F. D. G.*), Yzabal (*O. S.* [8]), Retalhuleu (*O. S.*, *W. B. Richard-
son*); HONDURAS, San Pedro (*G. M. Whitely* [10]).

The first specimens of this *Synallaxis* sent to Europe were doubtless those that
came into Prince Bonaparte's hands from Col. Velasquez, who obtained them in
Guatemala [1].   They were then supposed to belong to *S. cinerascens*, Temm., a species
of South Brazil, but quite a different bird.   Mr. Sclater's description was based upon
a specimen in the Derby Museum in Liverpool, obtained by Delattre (probably in 1846)
near Coban in Guatemala; other examples being in the British Museum and in his
own collection [2].   In 1851 Strickland received a specimen from Guatemala [11]; the bird
was afterwards traced to the State of Vera Cruz by Sallé [13] and Boucard [4], and is now
known, as Sumichrast says, to be not uncommon in the hot low-lying portions of that
State as far north as the town of Vera Cruz, where Godman found it in February 1888.
Southwards of Vera Cruz it is common, and probably spreads over the whole of
Yucatan, the State of Tabasco, British Honduras, and Guatemala, to the neighbourhood
of the town of Coban, and to Yzabal on the Golfo Dulce [8].   On the side of the moun-
tains sloping to the Pacific Ocean, *S. erythrothorax* is common about Escuintla and
Retalhuleu, but we have not traced it so far as the State of Chiapas in this direction.
Returning to the Atlantic seaboard, the most southern record we have is that of

Whitely, who found this bird at San Pedro in Honduras, a short way inland from the coast [9].

Our observations on this bird extend to January, August, and September, but we never met with the nest. This, Mr. Gaumer tells us [12], is a monstrous structure of large sticks, well laid together, with the entrance below and some 18 inches from where the eggs are placed. Mr. Gaumer thought that the bird does not build the nest itself, but occupies the deserted one of some other bird or animal. The Maya name for this species is "Tzapatan." The bird is active and restless in its movements, frequenting the lower growth of the forest. It has a harsh cry, with nothing melodious about it as that ascribed to *S. albescens*.

SIPTORNIS.

Synallaxis (partim), auctt.

Siptornis, Reichenbach, Handb. p. 171 (1853); Scl. Cat. Birds Brit. Mus. xv. p. 58.

Siptornis contains the species with twelve rectrices which were formerly included in *Synallaxis*, but which are better placed under a separate name. In general appearance the members of the genus resemble *Synallaxis*, but they may at once be distinguished by the number of their rectrices. Most of them also have the ends of these feathers more rounded, and the barbules of the barbs complete to the end. This, however, does not apply to such species as *S. anthoides*, &c., forming Section VI. of Mr. Sclater's arrangement.

Two species only are found in our country, both of them in Costa Rica, *S. rufigenis* being peculiar to that country. The other, *S. erythrops*, occurs also in the State of Panama and in Western Ecuador.

1. **Siptornis erythrops.** (*Synallaxis erythrops*, Tab. XLV. fig. 1.)

Synallaxis erythrops, Scl. P. Z. S. 1860, p. 66 [1]; 1874, p. 19 [2]; Lawr. Ann. Lyc. N. Y. ix. p. 105 [3];
    Frantz. J. f. Orn. 1869, p. 304 [4]; Salv. P. Z. S. 1870, p. 191 [5]; Boucard, P. Z. S. 1878, p. 59 [6];
    Scl. & Salv. P. Z. S. 1879, p. 521 [7]; Berl. & Tacz. P. Z. S. 1883, p. 560 [8]; 1884, p. 298 [9].
Siptornis erythrops, Scl. Cat. Birds Brit. Mus. xv. p. 60 [10].

Supra brunneus, capite summo, fronte, loris et genis, alis extus et cauda læte rufis: subtus pallidior, gula
    albicantiore: rostro corneo, mandibula infra ad basin pallida; pedibus corylinis. Long. tota 6·0, alæ 2·6,
    caudæ rect. med. 2·8, rect. lat. 1·4, tarsi 0·7. (Descr. exempl. ex Irazu, Costa Rica. Mus. nostr.)
♀ mari similis.
Av. juv. capite summo dorso concolore nec genis rufo notatis, superciliis elongatis pallide cervinis.

Hab. Costa Rica, Barranca and Dota Mountains (*Carmiol* [3][4]), Pirris (*Zeledon* [3]), Irazu
    (*Rogers, Boucard* [6]), Navarro (*Boucard* [6]); Panama, Volcan de Chiriqui (*Arcé* [5]).—
    Colombia [7]; Ecuador [1][8][9].

Siptornis erythrops was described by Mr. Sclater in 1860, from specimens obtained by Fraser at Pallatanga in Ecuador [1].

It has since been traced through the western portions of that country, and thence northwards to the Cauca Valley in Colombia, where Salmon met with it at Frontino [7]. It has not been noticed either on the Isthmus of Darien or on the line of the Panama Railway, but it reappears at Chiriqui and throughout Costa Rica. Nothing has been recorded of its habits beyond a note of Salmon's, to the effect that it lays white eggs, and that its food consists of insects.

The only species at all nearly allied to the present bird, if indeed it be distinct, is the next, *S. rufigenis*. None of the other members of this section of the genus have the rufous of the crown extending over the sides of the head, as is the case in *S. erythrops*.

2. **Siptornis rufigenis.** (*Synallaxis rufigenis*, Tab. XLV. fig. 2.)

Synallaxis rufigenis, Lawr. Ann. Lyc. N. Y. ix. p. 105 [1]; Frantz. J. f. Orn. 1869, p. 304 [2]; Salv. P. Z. S. 1870, p. 191 [3]; Scl. P. Z. S. 1874, p. 19 [4].

Siptornis rufigenis, Scl. Cat. Birds Brit. Mus. xv. p. 60 [5].

S. erythropi persimilis, corpore subtus magis rufescente et superciliis pallide rufis forsan distinguendus. (Descr. maris ex Costa Rica. Mus. nostr.)

Hab. COSTA RICA [2] (*A. C. Garcia* [1], *Carmiol* [3]).

This bird was described by Mr. Lawrence from a specimen sent him by Mr. A. C. Garcia from Costa Rica, but the precise locality where it was obtained was not recorded. We have a similar bird sent us by Carmiol, which, though marked as a male, is also without exact locality. These two specimens were compared by Mr. Sclater and found to agree [5]. The points of difference between these specimens and adult *S. erythrops* consist, as Mr. Lawrence says, in the crown being olive rather than dark cinnamon; the under surface pale cinnamon rather than greyish brown; the under wing-coverts a shade lighter, more distinct superciliaries, &c.

Our specimen of *S. rufigenis* appears to be immature, and we still are doubtful whether the supposed distinctive characters are not those of immaturity. On the other hand, a young individual of *S. erythrops* has a greyer under surface than that of *S. rufigenis* and paler though equally well-defined superciliary stripes.

Materials are still wanting to settle the status of *S. rufigenis* definitely.

PSEUDOCOLAPTES.

Pseudocolaptes, Reichenbach, Handb. p. 209 (1853); Scl. Cat. Birds Brit. Mus. xv. p. 77.

Pseudocolaptes is a peculiar genus having much the general appearance of a *Philydor* or *Automolus*, but the shape of the nostrils shows its relationship with the Synallaxinæ; they are long slits overhung by membrane, and placed along the lower edge of the nasal fossa: the bill is very straight and sharp; the toes are short and the claws strong but short; the wings long, the primaries considerably exceeding the secondaries, the third, fourth, and fifth primaries the longest in the wing.

Two species, rather doubtfully separable, are included in *Pseudocolaptes*: one of these ranges throughout the Andes from Venezuela and Colombia to Bolivia; the other occurs in Costa Rica and the State of Panama.

1. Pseudocolaptes lawrencii.

Pseudocolaptes boissoneauti, Salv. P. Z. S. 1870, p. 192 (nec Lafr.) [1]; Boucard, P. Z. S. 1878, p. 59 [2].

Pseudocolaptes lawrencii, Ridgw. Pr. U. S. Nat. Mus. i. p. 253 (10 Dec., 1878) [3]; Scl. Cat. Birds Brit. Mus. xv. p. 79 [4].

Pseudocolaptes costaricensis, Boucard, Bull. Soc. Zool. Fr. v. p. 230 (1880) [5].

Supra ferrugineus, pileo et cervice postica nigris illius plumis medialiter anguste hujus late cervino striatis; capitis lateribus nigrescentibus stria superciliari anguste cervina: subtus gula et cervicis lateribus (conspicue) pallide cervino-albidis; pectore cervino, plumis singulis nigro marginatis; abdomine medio cervino, hypochondriis rufo-brunneis, subalaribus et subcaudalibus rufis; alis nigricantibus, secundariis internis et tectricibus apicibus rufo-brunneis; cauda ferruginea dorso concolore: rostro corneo, mandibula infra pallida; pedibus corylinis. Long. tota 8·0, alæ 4·3, caudæ rectr. med. 3·7, rectr. lat. 2·6, rostri a rictu 1·0, tarsi 1·05. (Descr. maris ex Calobre, Panama. Mus. nostr.)

Hab. COSTA RICA, Navarro (*Boucard* [2], *Zeledon* [3]), La Palma (*Zeledon* [3]); PANAMA, Cordillera del Chucu [1], Calobre (*Arcé*).

This species is very closely allied to the well-known widely ranging *P. boissoneauti*, so much so that Salvin hesitated to separate it from a single specimen from the State of Panama, believed by him to be hardly adult [1]. M. Boucard, too, did not at first consider the specimen he obtained in Costa Rica sufficiently distinct [2], though he subsequently described his bird as *P. costaricensis* [4]. In the meantime Mr. Ridgway called it *P. lawrencii*, from adult and young specimens sent him by Mr. Zeledon from Costa Rica [3]. All these birds, so far as they go, confirm the characters of distinction given it by Mr. Ridgway, except perhaps the markings of the jugulum, which seem to us to be variable in intensity. There remain, however, the fawn-coloured cervical tufts and the dark primaries, which in *P. boissoneauti* are pure white and dark umber respectively. We note, nevertheless, that Bolivian examples have the cervical tufts just tinged with buff, though the primaries are umber, as in typical *P. boissoneauti*.

Of the habits of this species nothing has been recorded, but of *P. boissoneauti*, Salmon (P. Z. S. 1879, p. 521) tells us that it feeds on insects, makes its nest in a hole in a tree, and lays white eggs.

Subfam. *PHILYDORINÆ*[*].

AUTOMOLUS.

Automolus, Reichenbach, Handb. p. 173 (1853); Scl. Cat. Birds Brit. Mus. xv. p. 87.

Automolus, *Philydor*, and *Anabazenops* are three very closely allied genera; all have

[*] *Antea*, p. 146.

open oval nostrils and their definition is not very satisfactory. Mr. Sclater separates *Automolus* from *Philydor* upon their size, but a glance at the measurements of the various species of the two genera shows that they cannot be thus defined.

So far as the Mexican and Central-American species of these genera are concerned, we find that those assigned to *Automolus* have the wing as long as or longer than the tail, whereas in *Philydor panerythrus* the reverse is the case and the tail is longer than the wing. *P. fuscipennis*, however, has a tail considerably shorter than the wings, and thus spoils the definition. In fact the whole of the species of *Automolus* and *Philydor* require rearranging, when it will probably be found advisable to include all under one genus (*Philydor*), and to group the species partly by measurements, partly by characteristic coloration. In the meantime we follow the most recent arrangement of Mr. Sclater as regards these genera.

The range of *Automolus* extends northwards as far as the slopes of the mountains of the Mexican State of Vera Cruz, and on the west side to the Sierra Madre del Sur. In Guatemala, and no doubt in all the intervening country to the Isthmus of Panama, *Automolus* is found in all suitable forest districts. Nine species occur within our region, all of which, except *A. pallidigularis*, are endemic.

a. *Corpus subtus plus minusve striatum.*

1. **Automolus rufobrunneus.** (*Philydor rufobrunneus*, Tab. XLVI. fig. 2.)

Philydor rufobrunneus, Lawr. Ann. Lyc. N. Y. viii. p. 127 [1]; ix. p. 106 [2]; Frantz. J. f. Orn. 1869, p. 304 [3]; Boucard, P. Z. S. 1871, p. 59 [4].

Automolus rufobrunneus, Berl. Pr. U. S. Nat. Mus. xi. p. 565 [5]; Scl. Cat. Birds Brit. Mus. xv. p. 89 [6].

Supra rufo-brunneus, pileo paullo obscuriore, plumis singulis medialiter pallidioribus, uropygio et cauda ferrugineis; capitis lateribus et gula cinnamomeo-rufescentibus, hujus plumis anguste, illorum late nigro marginatis: corpore subtus reliquo ferrugineo, pectoris plumis obscure fusco limbatis, hypochondriis brunnescentioribus; tectricibus subalaribus et remigibus ad basin intus cinnamomeis, his clarioribus: rostro nigro, pedibus obscure corylinis. Long. tota 9·0, alæ 3·5, caudæ rectr. med. 3·5, lat. 2·1, rostri a rictu 1·1, tarsi 1·15. (Descr. exempl. ex Irazu, Costa Rica. Mus. nostr.)

Hab. COSTA RICA, San José (*v. Frantzius* [1] [2] [3]), Barranca (*Carmiol* [2]), Navarro (*Boucard* [4]), Volcan de Irazu (*Rogers* [6]).

This species, described as a *Philydor*, has of late years been placed in *Automolus* as an ally of *A. rubiginosus* [5]. Its relationship to that bird, however, is not very close, for apart from its somewhat striated under surface, the bill is relatively shorter and stouter and the culmen more curved; the tail, too, is more rounded. The wings are like those of *Automolus rubiginosus*, the third, fourth, and fifth primaries being only slightly longer than those next adjoining on the inside, instead of the fifth considerably exceeding the sixth, as in *Philydor panerythrus*.

But few specimens of *A. rufobrunneus* have reached Europe. One was obtained by Boucard at Navarro, and several were sent us by Rogers when collecting in Costa Rica in 1876. These latter were from the slopes of the Volcan de Irazu, but Rogers omitted to give any particulars concerning them. Our figure is drawn from one of these birds.

2. **Automolus virgatus.**

Philydor virgatus, Lawr. Ann. Lyc. N. Y. viii. p. 468[1]; ix. p. 106[2]; Frantz. J. f. Orn. 1869, p. 304[3].
Automolus virgatus, Berl. Pr. U. S. Nat. Mus. xi. p. 565[4].

" The feathers of the head above, hind neck and back, and also the sides of the head and of the neck, are blackish brown, with a clear ochreous stripe down the centre of each [feather], the lower part of the back is of a dull rusty olivaceous brown, the upper tail-coverts deep reddish cinnamon ; the tail deep cinnamon, not so bright as the coverts ; the wings are dull cinnamon-brown, with the inner webs of the primaries and the ends of the secondaries brownish black ; the under wing-coverts and inner margin of quills light cinnamon ; the chin and throat are pale fawn-colour with faint brownish edgings to the feathers, on the lower part of the throat the feathers are of a light brownish colour striped down their centres with pale fawn ; on the breast the feathers are of a deeper fawn-colour with dusky edges ; the abdomen, sides, and under tail-coverts are of an olivaceous brown, lighter than the lower part of the back, with rather indistinct paler centres to the feathers ; bill brownish black, with the lower part of the under mandible yellow ; irides brown ; feet brown. Total length 7½ in., wing 3¼, tail 3¼, bill ⅞, tarsi $\frac{7}{16}$." (*Lawrence, l. s. c.*)

Hab. COSTA RICA, Angostura (*Carmiol* [1][2]).

We do not know this bird, the type of which, however, has been examined by Count von Berlepsch[4], who has given the following note respecting it:—"This may be a valid species, but not of the genus *Philydor*, as I think ; in fact it seems to be a close ally of *Automolus subulatus*, Spix, ex Amazonia, from which it may be distinguished by the following points of difference. Bill longer and somewhat stronger, the upper mandible darker in colour. The ground-colour of the top of the head more blackish. The ochraceous stripes there, and still more on the hind neck and the upper back, are more pronounced. The ground-colour everywhere on the upper parts darker or more blackish. The underparts of the body are rather lighter in colour ; throat and breast of a clearer ochraceous ; wings and tail somewhat longer (al. 84½, caud. 72, culm. 23¾, tars. 20½ mm.)."

It will be noticed that the measurements taken by Mr. Lawrence and Count von Berlepsch of the same specimen do not agree. The length of the tarsus, according to the former writer $\frac{7}{16}$ in., appears to be very small ; in *Automolus rubiginosus* and its allies it usually exceeds an inch in length.

b. *Corpus subtus uniforme haud striatum.*

a'. *Stria superciliaris nulla.*

3. **Automolus rubiginosus.**

Anabates rubiginosus, Scl. P. Z. S. 1856, p. 288[1]; 1859, p. 365[2]; Sumichrast, Mem. Bost. Soc. N. H. i. p. 555[3]; Sanchez, An. Mus. Nac. Mex. i. p. 97[4].

Automolus rubiginosus, Sumichrast, La Nat. v. p. 247 [5]; Scl. Cat. Birds Brit. Mus. xv. p. 91 (partim) [6].

Supra saturate brunneus, pileo obscuriore; alis extus, uropygio, cauda et pectore saturate rubiginoso-rufis, gula pallidiore; tectricibus auricularibus grisescentioribus; abdomine brunneo, hypochondriis et tectricibus subcaudalibus obscurioribus dorso fere concoloribus, tectricibus subalaribus et remigibus ad basin intus clare rubiginosis: rostro et pedibus saturate corylinis, illius mandibula infra pallida. Long. tota 8·0, alæ 3·8, caudæ rectr. med. 3·45, rectr. lat. 3·1, rostri a rictu 1·1, tarsi 1·1.

♀ mari similis.

Hab. MEXICO, Cordova (*Sallé* [1]), Vera Cruz (*Sanchez* [4]), Jalapa (*de Oca* [2], *M. Trujillo*), Coatepec near Jalapa (*M. Trujillo*), Hot region of Vera Cruz, Uvero (*Sumichrast* [3]).

Automolus rubiginosus was one of Sallé's discoveries [1], whose specimens were procured not far from Cordova in the State of Vera Cruz, where he collected for some time. Other specimens have since been obtained in the same district, namely, at Jalapa and its neighbourhood. Sumichrast states that this bird is an inhabitant of the hot region of Vera Cruz [3]; but we must add to this the more temperate portions of that State, as its range extends to an elevation of at least 5000 feet and probably higher. It is doubtless resident in the district in which it is found; the specimens secured by our collector, Mateo Trujillo, were shot at various times from May to October.

It has hitherto been the practice to include the Guatemalan birds of this form under the name *A. rubiginosus*, but with the series now before us we think it necessary to separate several forms from the typical bird, which, according to our views, inhabits a restricted area confined to the mountains of Central Vera Cruz sloping towards the Atlantic Ocean.

4. **Automolus veræpacis.**

Anabates rubiginosus, Scl. & Salv. Ibis, 1859, pp. 5, 117 (nec Scl.) [1].

Automolus rubiginosus, Salv. Cat. Strickl. Coll. p. 337 [2]; Scl. Cat. Birds Brit. Mus. xv. p. 91 (partim) [3].

A. rubiginoso similis, sed omnino pallidior, supra magis cinnamomeus, pileo, uropygio et cauda clarioribus; pectore pallide haud saturate rubiginoso quam abdomen paullo obscuriore. (Descr. exempl. ex Coban, Guatemala. Mus. nostr.)

♀ mari similis.

Hab. GUATEMALA (*Constancia* [2], *Skinner* [1]), Coban, Tactic, Choctum (*O. S. & F. D. G.* [3]).

Hitherto this *Automolus* has been considered inseparable from the Mexican *A. rubiginosus*, and was so named in the lists of the birds of Guatemala [1], and in the catalogues of the Strickland Collection [2] and in that of the British Museum [3]. With a much larger series of specimens before us than Mr. Sclater examined when compiling the last-named work, we find that it is necessary to recognize several well-marked forms of *A. rubiginosus*, all of which have definite ranges so far as our present materials indicate.

This bird is found in the highland forests of Vera Paz in Guatemala, and at a lower elevation where these blend with the forests of the lowlands to the northward. Comparing specimens from Vera Paz with others from the Volcanoes of Agua and Fuego, we find sufficient difference to separate them; the former being rather darker than the latter justifies this subdivision, though the difference is much less than that subsisting between the Vera Paz birds and the true *A. rubiginosus* or any of the other forms.

The first example of this bird sent to Europe was probably that received by Strickland from his correspondent José Constancia[2]; that in the late Sir W. Jardine's collection[3] being most likely from the same source. Skinner subsequently sent others from the same country[1], and we found the bird not uncommon in Vera Paz.

5. **Automolus umbrinus**, sp. n.

Automolus rubiginosus, Scl. Cat. Birds Brit. Mus. xv. p. 91 (partim)[1].

Supra umbrino-brunneus, pileo multo saturatiore; alis extus paulo rufescentioribus, uropygio et cauda saturate rubiginosis: subtus cervinus, gula pallide cinnamomea, hypochondriis et tectricibus subcaudalibus brunnescentioribus, tectricibus subalaribus et remigibus intus ad basin cinnamomeis: rostro et pedibus corylinis, illius mandibula infra pallida. Long. tota 8·0, alæ 3·9, caudæ rectr. med. 3·5, rectr. lat. 2·6, rostri a rictu 1·2, tarsi 1·1. (Descr. maris ex Sta. Maria prope Quezaltenango, Guatemala. Mus. nostr.)

Hab. GUATEMALA, Vicinity of Santa Maria near Quezaltenango (*W. B. Richardson*), Volcan de Fuego, Volcan de Agua, Savana Grande, Barranco Hondo (*O. S. & F. D. G.*[1]).

Comparing our series of specimens from the forests of the volcanoes bordering the Pacific coast of Guatemala with others from Vera Paz, we find that the former are decidedly paler, more fawn-colour beneath, and with the back umber rather than rufous-brown, differences sufficiently marked to render their separation necessary.

The species is not rare in the upland forests of the great volcanoes of Guatemala from an elevation of about 2500 feet to as high as 7000 or 8000 feet above the sea.

Our specimens were all obtained on the slopes of the Volcanoes of Agua and Fuego, but Mr. Richardson has recently sent us two examples which he shot in the department of Quezaltenango, on the slopes of the Volcan de Santa Maria.

6. **Automolus guerrerensis**, sp. n.

Supra cinnamomeo-brunneus, fronte et pilei dimidio antico concoloribus, pilei dimidio postico, nucha, uropygio et cauda læte rubiginosis, oapitis lateribus (tectricibus auricularibus obscuris exceptis) ejusdem coloris sed paulo clarioribus; alis extus quam dorsum vix rufescentioribus: subtus cervinus, pectore cinnamomeo, gula albicantiore, hypochondriis et crisso brunnescentioribus; subalaribus læte cinnamomeis: rostro et pedibus corylinis, illius mandibula infra pallida. Long. tota 8·0, alæ 3·5, caudæ rectr. med. 3·5, lat. 2·6, rostri a rictu 1·0, tarsi 1·05. (Descr. maris ex Omilteme, Guerrero, Mexico. Mus. nostr.)

Hab. MEXICO, Omilteme and Xautipa, State of Guerrero (*Mrs. H. H. Smith*).

This is the palest of all these forms on the upper surface, and, moreover, has the forehead and anterior portion of the crown of the same colour as the back, instead of being of a uniform dark cinnamon or rufous-brown tint over the whole crown; the sides of the head below the eyes are also clearer cinnamon than in any of the allied forms. In other respects it most resembles the Guatemala bird from the Volcanoes of Agua and Fuego.

Mrs. Herbert Smith's large collection made in the Sierra Madre del Sur in the summer of 1888 contains two specimens of this species—the male taken at Omilteme at an elevation of 8000 feet above the sea; the other, marked female, at Xautipa, a village in the same range of mountains, both places being not far from Chilpancingo, a town on the road from the port of Acapulco to the interior.

The female differs slightly from the male in the almost total absence of the rufescent colour on the nape, the upper surface being thus almost uniform as far as the rump. We have not enough specimens to be able to judge if this difference is a normal one between the sexes, but from analogy it would not be so.

7. Automolus fumosus, sp. n.

Automolus cervinigularis ?, Scl. Cat. Birds Brit. Mus. xv. p. 92 (specimen *n*) [1].

Supra saturate fumoso-brunneus, pileo vix obscuriore, uropygio saturate rubiginoso, cauda obscuriore; alis extus fere dorso concoloribus: subtus cervino-brunneus, gula et pectore rufescentioribus, hypochondriis fumoso-brunneis, tectricibus subcaudalibus rubiginosis, tectricibus subalaribus et remigibus intus ad basin cinnamomeis: rostro et pedibus obscure corylinis, illius mandibula infra pallida. Long. tota 8·0, alæ 3·25, caudæ rectr. med. 3·1, rectr. lat. 2·25, rostri a rictu 1·15, tarsi 1·1. (Descr. maris ex Bibalaz, Chiriqui. Mus. nostr.)

Hab. PANAMA, Bibalaz in Chiriqui (*Arcé* [1]).

On the upper surface this is the darkest of all these forms of *Automolus*, darker even than *A. rubiginosus*, and has much darker wings. On the underside it is more like the Guatemalan *A. umbrinus*, but the sides of the head and flanks are much darker and the wings outwardly very differently coloured.

Of this species we have only a single male specimen, which was sent us by our collector, Enrique Arcé, in one of his last collections. He obtained it near a place called Bibalaz, on the slopes of the Volcan de Chiriqui.

b'. *Stria superciliaris plus minusve distincta.*

8. Automolus cervinigularis.

Anabates cervinigularis, Scl. P. Z. S. 1856, p. 288 [1]; 1859, p. 382 [2]; Scl. & Salv. Ibis, 1860, p. 35 [3].

Automolus cervinigularis, Scl. P. Z. S. 1864, p. 175 [4]; Cat. Birds Brit. Mus. xv. p. 91 [5]; Salv. P. Z. S. 1867, p. 143 [6]; Lawr. Ann. Lyc. N. Y. ix. p. 106 [7]; Sumichrast, Mem. Bost. Soc. N. H. i. p. 555 [8]; La Nat. v. p. 247 [9]; Frantz. J. f. Orn. 1869, p. 304 [10]; Sanchez, An. Mus. Nac. Mex. i. p. 97 [11].

Supra saturate rufo-brunneus, pileo nigricanti plumis singulis medialiter vix pallidioribus, uropygio et cauda cum tectricibus subcaudalibus saturate rubiginoso-rufis ; loris superciliis elongatis et cervicis lateribus saturate cervinis gula dilutiore : abdomine pallide cervino-brunneo, pectoris plumis leviter brunneo marginatis ; hypochondriis brunneis, subalaribus et remigibus intus ad basin cinnamomeis : rostro et pedibus corylinis, illius maudibula infra pallida. Long. tota 7·5, alæ 3·5, caudæ rectr. med. 3·0, rectr. lat. 2·5, rostri a rictu 1·15, tarsi 0·9. (Descr. maris ex Choctum, Guatemala. Mus. nostr.)

♀ mari similis.

Hab. Mexico (*G. H. White*[4]), Vera Cruz (*Sanchez*[11]), Hot region of Vera Cruz[8], Omealca[9] (*Sumichrast*), Cordova (*Sallé*[1]), Atoyac (*Mrs. H. H. Smith*), Playa Vicente (*Boucard*[2]), Chimalapa, Isthmus of Tehuantepec (*Sumichrast*[9]) ; Guatemala, Coban[3], Choctum (*O. S. & F. D. G.*[5]) ; Costa Rica (*v. Frantzius*[9]), Tucurriqui (*Arcé*), Angostura, Valza (*Carmiol*[7]) ; Panama, Boquete de Chitra, Santa Fé (*Arcé*[6]).

Discovered by Sallé near Cordova, in Mexico, this species was first described by Mr. Sclater in 1856[1], and since then its range has been traced throughout Central America to the State of Panama[4]. In Costa Rica and the adjoining portion of the State of Panama it is found associated with its near ally *A. pallidigularis*, some specimens from this region being somewhat intermediate in character between the two birds. As a rule *A. cervinigularis* may be distinguished by its darker head as contrasted with the back, the deeper fawn-colour of the under surface, and rather more definite edges to the feathers of the breast, more definite superciliaries, &c. In size there is no appreciable difference between the two.

In Guatemala, *A cervinigularis* is restricted in its range to the forest-region of Vera Paz, which spreads northwards of Coban to Mexican territory. It has not been noticed in any of the forest country bordering the Pacific Ocean. Of its nesting-habits nothing has been recorded.

9. **Automolus pallidigularis.**

Anabates ochrolæmus (?), Lawr. Ann. Lyc. N. Y. vii. p. 319 (nec Tschudi)[1].

Anabates cervinigularis, Lawr. Ann. Lyc. N. Y. vii. p. 294 (nec Scl.)[2].

Automolus pallidigularis, Lawr. Ann. Lyc. N. Y. vii. p. 465[3]; ix. p. 106[4]; Scl. & Salv. P. Z. S. 1864, p. 354[5]; 1879, p. 522[6]; Frantz. J. f. Orn. 1869, p. 304[7]; Salv. P. Z. S. 1870, p. 192[8]; Nutting, Pr. U. S. Nat. Mus. vi. p. 404[9]; Scl. Cat. Birds Brit. Mus. xv. p. 94[10].

A. cervinigulari similis sed supra pallidior, capite quoque summo fere dorso concolore nec nigricante, superciliis vix ullis, gula albicante, pectore et abdomine pallide murinis differt. (Descr. maris ex Lion Hill, Panama. Mus. nostr.)

Hab. Nicaragua, Los Sabalos (*Nutting*[9]) ; Costa Rica, Pacuar, Guaitil, Angostura (*v. Frantzius*[6], *Carmiol*[4]) ; Panama, Bugaba[7], Boquete de Chitra[7], Calobre (*Arcé*[8]), Lion Hill (*McLeannan*[1 2 3 5]).—Colombia[6] ; Ecuador[10].

Typical birds of this species from Panama are much paler than the more northern

A. cervinigularis on the throat and under surface generally, and there is hardly any difference between the colour of the head and back; but specimens of the latter from southern localities are somewhat intermediate and not always easy to recognize. They have, however, their characteristic marks in a modified degree.

A. pallidigularis was one of McLeannan's discoveries, and was described by Mr. Lawrence in one of his papers on the birds of Panama [3]. It is now known to extend as far as Nicaragua in our region, Mr. Nutting having obtained a specimen in thick forest near Los Sabalos in that country [6]. On the southern continent Salmon met with it at Remedios in the Cauca Valley of Colombia [9], and we have examples from several places in Western Ecuador [10].

PHILYDOR.

Philydor, Spix, Av. Bras. i. p. 73 (1824); Scl. Cat. Birds Brit. Mus. xv. p. 96.

Mr. Sclater includes thirteen species in *Philydor*, only two of which occur within our limits. Of these *P. panerythrus* belongs to the same section as *P. rufus*, and is distinguished by its long tail, which considerably exceeds the wings. The other, *P. fuscipennis*, comes near to *P. pyrrhodes*, and has a comparatively short tail, as is the case with many species of *Automolus*.

All the species of *Philydor* belong to the Neotropical Region, Costa Rica being the extreme northern limit of the range of the genus.

a. *Cauda quam alæ longior.*

1. **Philydor panerythrus.**

Philydor panerythrus, Scl. P. Z. S. 1862, p. 110[1]; Cat. Birds Brit. Mus. xv. p. 100[2]; Salv. Ibis, 1870, p. 110[3]; Berl. Pr. U. S. Nat. Mus. xi. p. 565[4].

Automolus rufescens, Lawr. Ann. Lyc. N. Y. viii. p. 345[5]; ix. p. 106[6]; Frantz. J. f. Orn. 1869, p. 304[7]; Ridgw. Pr. U. S. Nat. Mus. vi. p. 414[8].

Supra olivaceo-brunneus, uropygio vix pallidiore, pileo postico et nucha grisescentioribus; fronte superciliis latis elongatis, genis et corpore subtus cinnamomeis, abdomine et hypochondriis brunnescentioribus; alis extus, remigibus ad basin intus, tectricibus subalaribus et cauda quoque cinnamomeis: rostro et pedibus corylinis, illius mandibula ad apicem pallida. Long. tota 8·0, alæ 4·0, caudæ rectr. med. 3·6, rectr. lat. 3·0, rostri a rictu 0·9, tarsi 1·0. (Descr. exempl. ex Costa Rica. Mus. nostr.)

Hab. Costa Rica (*Carmiol* [3][5], *v. Frantzius* [8]), Pirris [7], Cervantes (*J. Cooper* [8]); Panama (*mus. nostr.*), Veragua (*mus. Berlepsch* [4]).—Colombia [1].

P. panerythrus may readily be distinguished from all the other allied species of the genus by its cinnamon-coloured wings. It is rather larger than its congeners, quite equalling many species of *Automolus*; the bill, however, is weaker that that of the members of that genus, and the nostrils rather more elliptical; the tail, too, is longer and not so much rounded.

The original description of *P. panerythrus* was founded by Mr. Sclater in 1862 upon a single specimen, a trade skin, from Bogota [1], but no other examples have reached us from that country. Several have been sent from Costa Rica and the State of Panama, but even there the bird would appear to be rare.

Mr. Lawrence described the Costa Rica bird in 1866 as *Automolus rufescens*[5], under which name it is mentioned by Mr. Ridgway in 1884[8]; but in 1870 Salvin referred *A. rufescens* to *Philydor panerythrus*, and we see no reason for altering this decision, which was endorsed by Mr. Sclater in the 'Catalogue of Birds in the British Museum'[2].

Nothing is on record concerning the habits of this bird.

b. *Cauda quam alæ brevior.*

2. Philydor fuscipennis. (Tab. XLVI. fig. 1.)

Philydor fuscipennis, Salv. P. Z. S. 1866, p. 72[1]; 1867, p. 143[2]; Scl. Cat. Birds Brit. Mus. xv. p. 99[3].

Cinnamomeus, pileo et capitis lateribus obscurioribus, dorso obscuriore et olivaceo tincto; stria postoculari, corpore subtus et tectricibus subalaribus cinnamomeis; gula pallidiore, hypochondriis brunnescentioribus; alis fuscis; cauda et uropygio intense cinnamomeis: rostro et pedibus corylinis, illius mandibula infra pallida. Long. tota 7·0, alæ 3·5, caudæ rectr. med. 2·75, rectr. lat. 2·5, rostri a rictu 0·8, tarsi 0·75. (Descr. maris exempl. typ. ex Veraguas, Panama. Mus. nostr.)

Hab. Panama, Santiago de Veraguas (*Arcé*[1][2][3]).

The single male specimen sent by Arcé from Santiago de Veraguas in 1866 is still the only example known to us.

The species is closely allied to *P. pyrrhodes*, a bird from Guiana and enjoying a wide range in the valley of the Upper Amazons to the foot of the Andes of Ecuador and Peru. From this bird *P. fuscipennis* differs in its darker, more rufescent rump and tail, its more cinnamon-coloured back, and browner body beneath.

ANABAZENOPS.

Anabazenops, Lafresnaye, Dict. Univ. d'Hist. N. i. p. 411 (1847); Scl. Cat. Birds Brit. Mus. xv. p. 105.

Anabazenops is very closely allied to *Automolus* and *Philydor*, and perhaps hardly to be distinguished from them. The chief, if not the only difference, is in the shape of the bill, which is slightly upturned; this character is carried much further in *Xenops*, so that *Anabazenops* occupies, as its name implies, an intermediate position between *Automolus* and *Xenops*.

The tail in some of the species is rather longer than the wing, but in others the reverse is the case.

Of the eight species included in this genus by Mr. Sclater, two only occur within our limits—one of them, *A. variegaticeps*, having a wide range, and extending from the State of Panama to Southern Mexico; the other, which is also found in Ecuador, does not pass beyond Costa Rica.

1. **Anabazenops variegaticeps.**

Anabazenops variegaticeps, Scl. P. Z. S. 1856, p. 289 [1]; 1859, p. 382 [2]; Cat. Birds Brit. Mus. xv.
p. 106 [3]; Scl. & Salv. Ibis, 1860, p. 398 [4]; Lawr. Ann. Lyc. N. Y. ix. p. 106 [5]; Frantz.
J. f. Orn. 1869, p. 304 [6]; Sumichrast, Mem. Bost. Soc. N. H. i. p. 555 [7]; La Nat. v. p. 247 [8];
Salv. P. Z. S. 1870, p. 192 [9]; Boucard, P. Z. S. 1878, p. 59 [10]; Sanchez, An. Mus. Nac.
Mex. i. p. 97 [11]; Ridgw. Pr. U. S. Nat. Mus. vi. p. 414 [12].

Supra rufo-brunneus, pileo nigricante-olivaceo, plumis singulis medialiter pallidioribus, superciliis a naribus et
macula infra oculos cervinis, tectricibus auricularibus nigris albido intermixtis; alis dorso paulo rufescentioribus, tectricibus majoribus ad apicem nigricantibus: subtus gutture sordide albo, plumis indistincte
fusco marginatis; abdomine toto pallide brunneo, hypochondriis saturatioribus; cauda læte cinnamomea,
tectricibus subalaribus et remigibus intus ad basin cervinis: rostro pallide corneo, mandibula albida,
pedibus corylinis. Long. tota 6·0, alæ 3·2, caudæ rectr. med. 2·65, rectr. lat. 2·2, rostri a rictu 0·8,
tarsi 0·7. (Descr. exempl. ex Jalapa, Mexico. Mus. nostr.)

Hab. MEXICO, Vera Cruz (*Sanchez* [11]), Hot region of Vera Cruz [7], Uvero [8] and Omealca [8]
(*Sumichrast*), Jalapa (*de Oca*), Cofre de Perote (*M. Trujillo*), Cordova (*Sallé* [1]),
Omilteme in Guerrero (*Mrs. H. H. Smith*), Villa Alta (*M. Trujillo*), Totontepec
(*Boucard* [2], *M. Trujillo*), Choapam (*Boucard* [2]), Chimalapa (*Sumichrast* [8]);
GUATEMALA, Pie de la Cuesta in San Marcos, Santa Maria near Quezaltenango
(*W. B. Richardson*), Barranco Hondo and Savana Grande between the Volcan de
Fuego and V. de Agua, Choctum [4], and Kamkhal in Vera Paz (*O. S. & F. D. G.* [3]);
COSTA RICA, Dota and Barranca (*Carmiol* [5]), Rio Sucio (*J. Cooper* [12]), Candelaria
(*Boucard* [10]); PANAMA, Volcan de Chiriqui [9] and Bibalaz (*Arcé*).

We can detect no variation in this widely-spread species, the range of which extends
from Southern Mexico to the State of Panama. In the former country it has long
been known as an inhabitant of the State of Vera Cruz, where it was discovered by
Sallé near Cordova [1], and where Sumichrast tells us it is found in the hot region [7].
This statement is no doubt correct so far as it goes, but *A. variegaticeps* has a considerable vertical, as well as a horizontal range, for de Oca found it near Jalapa, 4000
feet above the sea, Trujillo at a still higher elevation on the slopes of the Cofre
de Perote, and Mrs. Smith's collection from Guerrero contained a specimen which was
shot in July near Omilteme at an elevation of 8000 feet in the Sierra Madre del Sur.
In Guatemala, too, this species is found as low as 1200 feet, and as high as 6000 or
7000 feet above the sea.

Like most of the members of this family it is a denizen of forest districts, and is
probably resident wherever it occurs.

Its nearest ally is *A. temporalis* of Ecuador, the differences being but slight, consisting
in the paler, less rufescent back of *A. variegaticeps* and the breast also less tinged with
that colour.

2. Anabazenops subalaris.

Anabates subalaris, Scl. P. Z. S. 1859, p. 141[1].

Anabazenops subalaris, Scl. Cat. Am. B. p. 159[2]; Cat. Birds Brit. Mus. xv. p. 108[3]; Salv. Ibis, 1870, p. 110[4]; P. Z. S. 1870, p. 192[5]; Berl. & Tacz. P. Z. S. 1884, p. 300[6].

Anabazenops lineatus, Lawr. Ann. Lyc. N. Y. viii. p. 127[7], ix. p. 106[8].

Anabazenops subalaris lineatus, Berl. Pr. U. S. Nat. Mus. xi. p. 565[9].

Supra brunneus, uropygio et cauda saturate ferrugineis, pilei plumis, colli postici, dorsi antici, capitis laterum et pectoris medialiter cervino striatis, gutture quoque striis latioribus notatis; gula cervina fere immaculata; abdomine brunneo, hypochondriis obscurioribus, tectricibus subalaribus et remigibus intus ad basin cinnamomeis: rostro et pedibus saturate corylinis, illius mandibula infra albida. Long. tota 7·0, alæ 3·5, caudæ rectr. med. 3·1, rectr. lat. 2·25, rostri a rictu 0·8, tarsi 0·9. (Descr. maris ex Costa Rica. Mus. nostr.)

Av. juv. pileo et dorso antico vix striatis, striis cervicis latioribus et rufescentioribus; pectore cinnamomeo fere immaculato.

Hab. COSTA RICA, Angostura (*Carmiol*[7][8]), Pirris and Cervantes (*Zeledon*[8]), Volcan de Irazu (*Rogers*[3]); PANAMA, Calobre, Calovevora[5] (*Arcé*).—COLOMBIA[3]; ECUADOR[1][2].

There is considerable difference in plumage between the adult and young in this species, the latter being much less generally striated than the former, though the stripes on the back of the neck are more pronounced. The breast, too, is much more rufescent. Some of our young specimens show feathers of the adult, so that, different as the adult and young are, their relationship is proved.

There also appears to be a certain amount of individual variation between members of the species. Costa Rica specimens, as a rule, are not so distinctly striped on the head as some from Ecuador, but others from the latter country are not on this account to be distinguished from northern examples. The most definite stripes are possessed by our specimen from Colombia.

In 1870 Salvin[4] stated his impression as to the identity of Mr. Lawrence's *A. lineatus* with Mr. Sclater's *A. subalaris,* and on reconsidering this question with a much larger series at our disposal, we do not think that decision should be altered. Count Berlepsch, however, after examining Mr. Lawrence's type, gives *A. lineatus* subspecific value in its relationship with *A. subalaris*[9]. But the differences of size and colour to which he draws attention are hardly confirmed by our series, and we therefore place both the Central-American and Ecuadorean birds under one title.

The types of *A. subalaris* were obtained by Fraser near Pallatanga in Ecuador[1], and were described by Mr. Sclater in 1859. Mr. Lawrence's type of *A. lineatus* was sent by Carmiol from Angostura in Costa Rica, and was described in 1865[7]. Other examples have since been procured in both countries, and from several intermediate points, but no account of the habits of the bird has reached us.

XENOPS.

Xenops, Illiger, Prodr. p. 213 (1811); Scl. Cat. Birds Brit. Mus. xv. p. 110.

An easily recognized genus from the peculiar form of the bill, the culmen of which is straight, the tomia of both maxilla and mandible ascending in a gradual curve, and the lower edge of the mandible is also curved rather abruptly upwards, the whole bill being much compressed in the middle.

Only two species are now admitted of the genus *Xenops*, though others have been claimed as distinct. Their ranges are nearly coincident, and extend over the greater part of Tropical America. *X. rutilus*, however, only reaches Costa Rica, whereas *X. genibarbis* spreads northwards to Eastern Mexico.

The wings of both species are coloured in the same way as those of *Sittosomus*, *Margarornis*, and *Glyphorhynchus*—that is to say, they have a tawny transverse band extending to all but the three outer primaries. The anterior toes are all closely united at the base; the middle toe considerably exceeds the lateral toes in length and is a little longer than the hallux. The tail is soft at the end and the feathers rounded; the coloration of the tail is peculiar, being cinnamon, with the inner webs of the third and fourth feathers from the outside black.

1. **Xenops genibarbis.**

Xenops genibarbis, Ill. Prodr. p. 213 [1]; Temm. Pl. Col. 150. f. 1 [2]; Scl. & Salv. P. Z. S. 1879, p. 523 [3]; Scl. Cat. Birds Brit. Mus. xv. p. 110 [4].

Xenops mexicanus, Scl. P. Z. S. 1856, p. 289 [5]; 1859, p. 382 [6]; Lawr. Ann. Lyc. N. Y. vii. p. 320 [7]; ix. p. 106 [8]; Salv. Ibis, 1861, p. 353 [9]; P. Z. S. 1867, p. 143 [10]; 1870, p. 192 [11]; Scl. & Salv. P. Z. S. 1864, p. 354 [12]; Nomencl. Av. Neotr. p. 66 [13]; Frantz. J. f. Orn. 1869, p. 304 [14]; Sumichrast, Mem. Bost. Soc. N. H. i. p. 555 [15]; La Nat. v. p. 247 [16]; Sanchez, An. Mus. Nac. Mex. i. p. 97 [17].

Supra rufescenti-brunneus, capite obscuriore, uropygio ferrugineo-rufo, loris albicantibus, stria superciliari elongata pallide cervina, regione auriculari brunnea cervino striato infra eam plaga elongata nitide alba: subtus brunneus, gula albicante; alis nigris cinnamomeo terminatis, secundariis intimis cinnamomeis, fascia lata mediana obliqua per remiges interiores et secundarios proximos transeunte cinnamomea, remigibus externis extus cinnamomeo limbatis, subalaribus quoque cinnamomeis; cauda cinnamomea, rectricibus duabus utrinque mediis proximis nigris, duabus iis exterioribus ad basin gradatim nigris: rostro et pedibus corylinis, illius mandibula pallidiore et infra albicante. Long. tota 5·0, alæ 2·7, caudæ rectr. med. 2·1, rectr. lat. 1·6, rostri a rictu 0·63, tarsi 0·6. (Descr. maris ex Teapa, Mexico. Mus. nostr.)

♀ mari similis.

Hab. MEXICO, Vera Cruz (*Sanchez* [17]), Cordova (*Sallé* [4]), Playa Vicente (*Boucard* [6]), Uvero (*Sumichrast* [16]), Teapa (*Mrs. H. H. Smith*); BRITISH HONDURAS, Orange Walk (*Gaumer*), Cayo (*Blancaneaux*); GUATEMALA, Choctum (*O. S. & F. D. G.* [9]); COSTA RICA, Angostura, San José, Pacuar, and Grecia (*Carmiol* [8]), Tucurriqui (*Arcé*); PANAMA, Bugaba [11], Bibalaz, Calovevora [11], Santa Fé [10] (*Arcé*), Lion Hill

($M^{c}Leannan$ [7] [12]).—SOUTH AMERICA generally from Colombia to Guiana and Eastern Brazil [4].

Several names have been applied to this bird based upon supposed local differences. One of these, $X.$ $mexicanus$ [5], long passed current for the South Mexican and Central American form, which was stated to differ from the typical South American bird by being larger, more olive-coloured beneath, and in its ochraceous-white throat. The accumulation of a larger series proves that only one species can be satisfactorily recognized.

In our country, $X.$ $genibarbis$ is strictly confined to the forests of the hot country, such as are found on the eastern side of the Cordillera of Southern Mexico and Guatemala. Its northern range does not extend beyond the middle of the State of Vera Cruz; but southward of this, on the Atlantic side of the mountains, it is probably found wherever any large tract of virgin forest occurs. Its range in altitude extends from the sea-level to a height of about 1500 or 2000 feet.

On the western or Pacific side of the main mountain-chain we have not yet met with $X.$ $genibarbis$ northward of Costa Rica, but in that country, as well as in the State of Panama, it occurs on both sides of the mountains.

2. Xenops rutilus.

Xenops rutilus, Licht. Verz. Doubl. p. 17 [1]; Scl. & Salv. P. Z. S. 1879, p. 522 [2]; Scl. Cat. Birds Brit. Mus. xv. p. 111 [3].

Xenops heterurus, Cab. & Hcine, Mus. Hein. ii. p. 33 [4]; Salv. Ibis, 1869, p. 319 [5]; P. Z. S. 1870, p. 192 [6].

Supra cinnamomeo-brunneus, uropygio clariore, capite summo brunneo cervino striato, cervice postica et dorso antico quoque plus minusve striatis, superciliis et stria utrinque rictali albis, tectricibus auricularibus nigro et albo variegatis, gula alba, corpore subtus reliquo fusco albido striato; alis nigris extus cinnamomeis, remigibus omnibus (tribus externis exceptis) medialiter fascia cinnamomea notatis, apicibus quoque cinnamomeis; cauda cinnamomea, rectricibus duabus intermediis utrinque in pogonio interno nigris: rostro corneo, mandibula infra pallida; pedibus corylinis. Long. tota 4·75, alæ 2·6, caudæ 1·9, rostri a rictu 0·6, tarsi 0·55. (Descr. maris ex Chiriqui. Mus. nostr.)

Hab. COSTA RICA (*Carmiol* [5]); PANAMA, Volcan de Chiriqui (*Arcé* [6]).—SOUTH AMERICA generally [3] from Colombia [2] [4] to South Brazil [1].

Xenops rutilus may readily be distinguished from $X.$ $genibarbis$ by the colouring of the head and under surface, both of which have on each feather a definite central stripe which occupies the shaft and the portion of the web adjoining on either side. In $X.$ $genibarbis$ both the head and under surface are nearly uniformly coloured.

The range of the two species is nearly the same throughout the southern continent; but in Central America $X.$ $rutilus$ does not, so far as we know, pass beyond Costa Rica, $X.$ $genibarbis$ reaching Southern Mexico.

The name $X.$ $rutilus$ was bestowed by Lichtenstein upon a Brazilian bird which was also called *X. rutilans* by Temminck and *X. affinis* by Swainson.	The Colombian bird was separated by Cabanis and Heine as *X. heterurus* [4], but it now appears that it has no tangible points of distinction.

The present species appears to be much rarer in our country than its congener *X. genibarbis*; we have as yet only seen two specimens, one from Costa Rica and one from Chiriqui.	Mr. Zeledon did not possess a Costa Rica specimen in 1882, as shown by his Catalogue of that date.

Subfam. SCLERURINÆ [*].

SCLERURUS.

Sclerurus, Swainson, Zool. Journ. iii. p. 356 (1827); Ridgway, Pr. U. S. Nat. Mus. xii. p. 21 (5 Feb., 1890); Scl. Cat. Birds Brit. Mus. xv. p. 113.

The number of species in this genus is variously estimated, Mr. Sclater admitting six and Mr. Ridgway no less than ten; of these, three occur within our limits, the most northern of which, *S. mexicanus*, is found in Eastern Mexico.	The usual haunts of the members of *Sclerurus* are in the dense forest, where they frequent the underwood near the ground.

The bill (*S. mexicanus*) is long and slender, slightly depressed towards the tip, and with a small notch near the distal end of the tomia of the maxilla; the nostrils are open, not overhung by a membrane, but the nasal septum appears in the opening. The inner toe is freer from the middle toe than the outer one, and the hallux is long with a long comparatively straight claw; the tail is short and rounded, the shafts of each feather stiff, sharp, and slightly projecting beyond the webs.

1. **Sclerurus canigularis.**

Sclerurus canigularis, Ridgw. Pr. U. S. Nat. Mus. xi. p. 542 [1]; xii. p. 24 [2].
Sclerurus albogularis, Scl. Cat. Birds Brit. Mus. xv. p. 114 (partim) [3].

" Prevailing colour of upper parts plain dark sooty brown, overlaid on hind neck, back, scapulars, wing-coverts, and tertials with a wash of burnt-umber, this changing into dark chestnut on rump and upper tail-coverts; tail brownish black; sides of head dull greyish brown, this changing gradually into dull greyish white on chin and upper throat, and to dull ash-grey on lower throat; chest deep chestnut-brown (abruptly defined against grey of throat), this changing into dull dark sooty brown on rest of underparts: lower tail-coverts tinged with dark chestnut.	Upper mandible black, lower chiefly light-coloured; legs and feet brownish black.	Length (skin) 6·0, wing 3·45, tail 2·55, exposed culmen ·85, tarsus ·85." (*Ridgway, l. s. c.*)

Hab. COSTA RICA, Turrialba (*J. J. Cooper* [1]).

We have not seen a specimen of this bird, and opinions differ as to its distinctness from the bird from Venezuela and Tobago called *S. albogularis*, Sw.	Mr. Sclater

---

* *Antea*, p. 146.

considers *S. canigularis* to be inseparable from *S. albogularis*[3]; but Mr. Ridgway adheres to his first statement as to their distinctness[2] and summarizes their differences as follows :—

"Underparts dull greyish olive, becoming tawny olive on chest; back and scapulars bistre-brown tinged with olive; lower half of throat dull light grey; upper half, including chin, dull white . . . . *S. albogularis.*

"Underparts dark slaty, tinged on some feathers with bright mummy-brown, the chest deep burnt-umber brown; lower half of throat deep greyish; upper half, including chin, paler, but scarcely approaching white; back and scapulars deep vandyke-brown . . . . *S. canigularis.*"

The type of *S. canigularis* is, we believe, unique, and examples of *S. albogularis* are scarce, so that additional specimens of both are required to decide the status of the two birds. In the meantime we follow Mr. Ridgway in keeping them separate.

2. Sclerurus mexicanus.

Sclerurus mexicanus, Scl. P. Z. S. 1856, p. 290[1]; 1859, p. 365[2]; 1864, p. 175[3]; Cat. Birds Brit. Mus. xv. p. 115[4]; Scl. & Salv. Ibis, 1860, p. 35[5]; Salv. Ibis, 1861, p. 143[6]; P. Z. S. 1867, p. 142[7]; 1870, p. 191[8]; Lawr. Ann. Lyc. N. Y. vii. p. 465[9]; Sumichrast, Mem. Bost. Soc. N. H. i. p. 555[10]; La Nat. v. p. 247[11]; Sanchez, An. Mus. Nac. Mex. i. p. 97[12]; Ridgw. Pr. U. S. Nat. Mus. xii. p. 25[13].

Sclerurus guatemalensis, Lawr. Ann. Lyc. N. Y. viii. p. 4[14].

Supra brunneus, pileo vix obscuriore, uropygio castaneo, cauda nigricanti-fusca : subtus gula et pectore castaneis illa pallidiore; abdomine toto et tectricibus subcaudalibus dorso fere concoloribus, tectricibus subalaribus rufis : rostro et pedibus saturate corylinis, mandibula infra pallida. Long. tota 6·0, alæ 3·1, caudæ rectr. med. 2·2, rectr. lat. 1·6, rostri a rictu 1·15, tarsi 0·85. (Descr. exempl. ex Raxché, Guatemala. Mus. nostr.)

Hab. MEXICO (*White*[3]), Vera Cruz (*Sanchez*[13]), Jalapa (*de Oca*[2], *F. Ferrari-Perez*), Cordova (*Sallé*[1]), Hot region of Vera Cruz[10], Orizaba[11], and Potrero[11] (*Sumichrast*), Mirador (*Sartorius*[13]); GUATEMALA, Coban[5], Raxché[6], Savana Grande, and Volcan de Agua above San Diego (*O. S. & F. D. G.*); PANAMA, Calovevora[8], Santiago de Veraguas[7], Cordillera de Tolé[7] (*Arcé*), Lion Hill (*M'Leannan*[13]).— COLOMBIA and Amazons Valley; Bahia ?[13].

Sclerurus mexicanus was discovered by Sallé near Cordova, in the Mexican State of Vera Cruz, and was described by Mr. Sclater in 1856[1]. It has subsequently been met with in other parts of the same State, where, Sumichrast tells us[10], it chiefly inhabits the hot region, but ascends the mountains to a height of upwards of 4000 feet above the sea. It is absent from Western Mexico, but in Guatemala it occurs in sparing numbers in the heavily forested districts on both sides of the main mountain-chain. Its home is in virgin forest, where it lives amongst the undergrowth.

Though no specimens are recorded as having been obtained between Guatemala and the State of Panama, the bird most probably occurs in suitable localities. In the State of Panama it has been found in several places both along the line of railway and in districts lying nearer the Costa Rica frontier *.

The range of *S. mexicanus* in South America is generally admitted to be extensive and to reach to the Amazons Valley throughout its length, and even to extend to Bahia, though the latter point requires confirmation.

Central American examples appear to have the chestnut colour of the breast spread further over the abdomen than is the case with those from South America. Within our limits, birds from the State of Panama are a shade darker than those from Guatemala, but on the whole the variation is slight for a bird having so wide a range.

In habits *Sclerurus mexicanus* resembles some Troglodytidæ. It was not seen to climb like other Dendrocolaptidæ, but to hop about the brushwood and to scratch amongst leaves on the ground. The cry is shrill, and may be heard at some distance [6].

3. **Sclerurus guatemalensis** †. (Tab. XLIV. fig. 1.)

Tinactor guatemalensis, Hartl. Rev. Zool. 1844, p. 370 [1].

Sclerurus guatemalensis, Scl. & Salv. Ibis, 1859, p. 118 [2]; P. Z. S. 1864, p. 354 [3]; Salv. Ibis, 1861, p. 352 [4]; Ridgw. Pr. U.S. Nat. Mus. xii. p. 30 [5]; Scl. Cat. Birds Brit. Mus. xv. p. 117 [6].

Sclerurus caudacutus, Lawr. Ann. Lyc. N. Y. vii. p. 320 (nec Vieillot) [7].

Supra brunneus fere unicolor, uropygio vix rufescentiore, cauda nigricanti-fusca: subtus paullo rufescentior, gula albida, plumis singulis fusco marginatis, plumis, cervicis laterum et pectoris medialiter rufis, scapis pallidioribus: rostro et pedibus nigricanti-corylinis, mandibulæ basi albicante. Long. tota 6·5, alæ 3·5, caudæ rectr. med. 2·35, rectr. lat. 1·9, rostri a rictu 1·05, tarsi 0·9. (Descr. exempl ex Choctum, Guatemala. Mus. nostr.)

Mas et femina similes.

Hab. GUATEMALA (*Hartlaub*), Choctum (*O. S. & F. D. G.* [4]); COSTA RICA, Jimenez and San Carlos (*A. Alfaro* [5]), Sibuhuc in Talamanca (*J. C. Zeledon* [5]); PANAMA, Lion Hill (*M'Leannan* [3][7]).—ECUADOR? [6].

We have a specimen from Guatemala which agrees fairly with Dr. Hartlaub's

---

* There seems some confusion respecting M'Leannan's specimens of *Sclerurus*, obtained on the Isthmus of Panama. These have been recently re-examined by Mr. Ridgway, and we follow his determination of them.

† We are uncertain as to the proper name for the bird from the Isthmus of Darien called by Cassin

Sclerurus brunneus.

Sclerurus brunneus, Scl.; Cass. Pr. Ac. Phil. 1860, p. 193; Ridgw. Pr. U. S. Nat. Mus. xii. p. 29.

Hab. Rio Ingador, Colombia (*W. S. Wood, Jun.*).

Mr. Ridgway considered the specimen thus named to be young, and it was the only example which he attributed to *S. brunneus* when writing his monograph of the genus. It is described as having "the throat white, with brown or dusky margins to the feathers," a character better suiting *S. guatemalensis* than *S. brunneus*, the throat-feathers of which are very indistinctly edged with dusky.

description of this species, the type of which came from the same country. It is there, however, a rare bird, for we have never succeeded in securing another example. In Costa Rica it is a better known bird, for Mr. Ridgway, when compiling his monograph of the genus [5], had five specimens before him for examination, besides several from the Isthmus of Panama, whence also we have a single female bird. All these seem to agree fairly as to their characters and to possess white throats, each feather being edged with dark brown; the feathers of the breast, too, and of the sides of the neck have lighter centres contrasting with darker edges. These points and the greater size and less rufous rump of *S. guatemalensis* readily serve to distinguish it from *S. mexicanus*.

Regarding its extension southwards into Western Ecuador we are in some doubt, as the birds from that country attributed to *S. guatemalensis* by Mr. Sclater in his recently published Catalogue appear to us to belong to a distinct species [*]. They are much darker in general colour, and have longer bills (1·2 inch). The breast is less rufous and the rump darker. It is possible these birds may belong to Dr. Cabanis's *S. olivaceus*, but without examining the type of that bird it would be unsafe to pronounce a definite opinion.

S. olivaceus has been placed as a synonym of *S. brunneus* by Mr. Sclater, but is given a distinct position by Mr. Ridgway, but neither author has examined the type.

Subfam. MARGARORNITHINÆ [†].

MARGARORNIS.

Margarornis, Reichenbach, Handb. p. 179 (1853); Scl. Cat. Birds Brit. Mus. xv. p. 121.

Margarornis contains six species, of which two occur within our region in Costa Rica and the State of Panama. The others are found in the Andes from Venezuela and Colombia to Bolivia, none occurring in Guiana or any portion of Brazil.

The bill of *Margarornis* (*M. brunnescens*) is slender, the culmen slightly curved, and the tomia without a subterminal notch; the nostrils are overhung by a membrane, leaving the opening a long slit on the lower edge of the nasal fossa. The toes are rather long, the outer and middle toes united towards the base, the inner toe more free, the hallux long, its claw curved much as in those of the other toes. The tail is not nearly so stiff as in *Glyphorhynchus* and *Sittosomus*, but the shafts of the feathers project beyond the webs as in all the Dendrocolaptinæ.

---

[*] "*Sclerurus brunneus*," specimen *b* (Scl. Cat. Birds Brit. Mus. xv. p. 116), from the Balzar Mountains, is precisely like "*S. guatemalensis*," specimen *c*, from Santa Rita. It is to these two birds that the above note refers.

[†] *Antea*, p. 146.

1. **Margarornis rubiginosa.** (Tab. XLVII. fig. 1.)

Margarornis rubiginosa, Lawr. Ann. Lyc. N. Y. viii. p. 128 [1]; ix. p. 106 [2]; Frantz. J. f. Orn. 1869, p. 304 [3]; Boucard, P. Z. S. 1878, p. 60 [4]; Scl. Cat. Birds Brit. Mus. xv. p. 122 [5].

Supra rubiginoso-cinnamomea, capite summo paullo fuscescentiore, capitis et cervicis lateribus cum nucha ochraceo tinctis, superciliis latis ochraceo albidis : subtus gula alba, pectore et abdomine ochraceo-rufis, illius plumis macula discali albida extrorsum nigro limbata ornatis, hypochondriis rubiginosis ; alis extus et cauda dorso concoloribus, primariis subtus nigricantibus internis eum secundariis ad basin fascia indistincta fulva notatis : rostro et pedibus pallide corylinis, illius mandibula albicante. Long. tota 6, alæ 2·9, caudæ rectr. med. 2·8, rectr. lat. 1·7, rostri a rictu 0·65, tarsi 0·8, dig. med. 0·75, hallucis 0·72. (Descr. exempl. ex Irazu, Costa Rica. Mus. nostr.)

Hab. Costa Rica, San José [1][2], Quebrada Honda [3] (*v. Frantzius*), San Mateo (*J. Cooper* [2]), Irazu (*Rogers* [5]), Navarro (*Boucard* [4]); Panama, Calobre (*Arcé* [5]),

This species and *M. stellata* of Ecuador belong to a section of *Margarornis* distinguished by their cinnamon-coloured plumage and by the small spots which occupy the discal portion of each feather of the breast. Their wings, too, are longer than those of *M. brunnescens* and much less rounded. From *M. stellata*, *M. rubiginosa* may be distinguished by its paler colour both above and beneath, its more definite superciliary stripes, and by the fainter pectoral spots; but this difference is by no means well defined, as the spots on the breast vary considerably in size, being nearly obsolete in a specimen from Calobre and fairly distinct in our Costa Rica examples.

M. rubiginosa has a very limited range, extending from Eastern Costa Rica to Calobre in the State of Panama; but it appears to be by no means a common bird. M. Boucard obtained two specimens at Navarro in May, and Mr. Rogers others from the slopes of the Volcan de Cartago or Irazu.

2. **Margarornis brunnescens.** (Tab. XLVII. fig. 2.)

Margarornis brunnescens, Scl. P. Z. S. 1856, p. 27, t. 116 [1]; Cat. Birds Brit. Mus. xv. p. 123 [2]; Salv. P. Z. S. 1867, p. 143 [3]; 1870, p. 192 [4]; Lawr. Ann. Lyc. N. Y. ix. p. 106 [5]; Frantz. J. f. Orn. 1869, p. 304 [6]; Tacz. Orn. Pér. ii. p. 166 [7]; Ridgw. Pr. U. S. Nat. Mus. vi. p. 414 [8].

Margarornis brunneicauda, Lawr. Ann. Lyc. N. Y. viii. p. 130 [9].

Supra brunnea, dorso rufescentiore, capite cinerascentiore, plumis omnibus obsolete fusco marginatis, capitis lateribus et corpore subtus cervinis, plumis (gula excepta) fusco marginatis, alis et cauda fusco-brunneis : rostro et pedibus obscure corylinis, illius mandibula pallida. Long. tota 6·0, alæ 2·5, caudæ 2·5, rostri a rictu 0·7, tarsi 0·75, dig. med. 0·7, hallucis 0·7. (Descr. maris ex Chiriqui, Panama. Mus. nostr.)

Hab. Costa Rica, San José [5], Quebrada Honda [6] (*v. Frantzius*), Rancho Redondo, Barranca (*Carmiol* [5]), San Mateo (*J. Cooper* [5]), Pirris (*Zeledon* [5]), Rio Sucio (*J. Cooper* [8]); Panama, Chiriqui, Chitra [4], Tolé [3], Cordillera de Chucu [4], Calovevora, Calobre (*Arcé*).—Colombia [1]; Ecuador and Peru [2].

Mr. Sclater first described this species from specimens from Colombia, being part of a collection sent to him by MM. Verreaux, of Paris, in 1856 [1]. Its southern range was subsequently traced to Ecuador [2] and Peru [7]. Northwards it has been found in the

Colombian State of Antioquia, in the State of Panama, and in Costa Rica. Specimens from nearly all these places are before us, and we find that they agree in every respect.

Compared with *M. rubiginosa* this species is very distinct, for not only is the general plumage very much browner and the spots on the under surface more numerous and larger, but the wings are relatively short and much rounded.

We have no record of this bird beyond Salmon's note that the iris in life is dark and that its food consists of insects.

Subfam. *GLYPHORHYNCHINÆ**.

a. *Rostrum latum, turdiforme, haud cuneiforme; cauda brevis, quam alæ brevior.*

DENDROCINCLA.

Dendrocincla, Gray, List Gen. Birds, p. 18 (1840); Ridgway, Pr. U.S. Nat. Mus. x. p. 488 (6 Jan. 1888); Scl. Cat. Birds Brit. Mus. xv. p. 162.

This genus is a somewhat isolated one, for with a great general resemblance to the Dendrocolaptinæ in the shape of the wings, tail, and feet, and the bill not very unlike that of *Dendrocolaptes*, it has the nostrils completely covered with a membrane, so that the nasal openings are curved slits lying along the lower edge of the nasal fossa; this membrane, too, is to a great extent covered with short feathers. This peculiar nostril is almost exactly like that of *Glyphorhynchus*, so that *Dendrocincla* finds perhaps its most natural position near that genus; but the form of the bill is very different, and the tail much less elongated, the shafts of the central rectrices being not nearly so much produced.

The genus *Dendrocincla* has been examined recently both by Mr. Ridgway and Mr. Sclater. The former admits twelve species, and names three others as unknown to him; the latter gives ten species as known to him, and three unknown. This difference does not affect the numbers of the Central-American birds, both authors allowing four species as inhabitants of our region.

The extreme northern limit of the range of *Dendrocincla* reaches the hot forests of

* In framing our introductory remarks on the family Dendrocolaptidæ (*antea*, p. 146) we had intended to assign the genus *Dendrocincla* to the Dendrocolaptinæ, and to place it, as Mr. Sclater has done, with *Dendrocolaptes* as a broad-billed section of that subfamily. A further examination of the species of *Dendrocincla*, however, shows us that this arrangement is not compatible with our definitions, for *Dendrocincla* has the nostrils completely overhung by a thick membrane, and not open as in the other genera of the subfamily. This character brings *Dendrocincla* in juxtaposition to *Glyphorhynchus*, notwithstanding the great difference in the form of the bill and structure of the tail, which are described elsewhere under the respective genera. Our scheme set out on p. 146 will still stand as it is, but the distribution of the genera in the various subfamilies must be altered as follows :—The Glyphorhynchinæ to contain two genera, *Glyphorhynchus* with one species and *Dendrocincla* with four species; and the Dendrocolaptinæ six genera, instead of seven, with fifteen species.

Vera Cruz, where both *D. anabatina* and *D. homochroa* occur; and these two birds spread through Central America to the State of Panama, being joined in Costa Rica by *D. olivacea*, and at Panama by *D. ruficeps*.

1. Dendrocincla anabatina.

Dendrocincla anabatina, Scl. P. Z. S. 1859, p. 54, t. 150 [1]; Cat. Birds Brit. Mus. xv. p. 162 [2]; Scl. & Salv. P. Z. S. 1868, p. 54 [3]; Boucard, P. Z. S. 1883, p. 450 [4]; Nutting, Pr. U.S. Nat. Mus. vi. p. 404 [5]; Ridgw. Pr. U. S. Nat. Mus. x. pp. 490, 590 [6].

Dendromanes anabatinus, Scl. P. Z. S. 1859, p. 382 [7]; Scl. & Salv. Ibis, 1860, p. 35 [8]; P. Z. S. 1870, p. 837 [9]; Salv. P. Z. S. 1870, p. 192 [10].

Dendrocops anabatinus, Scl. & Salv. Ibis, 1859, p. 118 [11].

Supra olivaceo-brunnea, dorso postico pallidiore, tectricibus supracaudalibus et cauda rubiginosis, loris et gula cervino-albidis, stria postoculari cervina indistincta: subtus pallidior, pectore striis rhachidalibus cervinis indistinctis notato; alis extus rufo-cervinis, remigum apicibus nigricanti-brunneis, tectricibus omnibus dorso concoloribus, tectricibus subalaribus et alis subtus (præter apices) pallide cinnamomeis: rostro corneo, pedibus saturate corylinis. Long. tota 7·0, alæ 3·7, caudæ 2·85, rostri a rictu 1·05, tarsi 0·9. (Descr. feminæ ex Teapa, Tabasco. Mus. nostr.)

Hab. MEXICO, Mirador and Potrero in Vera Cruz (*U.S. Nat. Mus.*), Playa Vicente (*Boucard* [7]), Teapa in Tabasco (*Mrs. H. H. Smith*), Northern Yucatan (*Gaumer*); BRITISH HONDURAS, Orange Walk (*Gaumer*); GUATEMALA, Rancho Tuilhá on the Cahabon-Peten road, Choctum and Coban [8] (*O. S. & F. D. G.*); HONDURAS, Omoa (*Leyland* [1 10]), San Pedro (*G. M. Whitely* [9]), Segovia River (*Townsend* [8]); NICARAGUA, Los Sabalos (*Nutting*); PANAMA, Chiriqui, Bugaba [9] (*Arcé*).

A specimen obtained at Omoa in Honduras by Leyland formed the type of this species, and was described by Mr. Sclater in 1859 [1]. The bird has since been traced over the whole of the forest-region of the eastern side of the Cordillera, from Playa Vicente, in Mexico [7], in the north to Chiriqui [10] in the south. We have no record of its occurrence in Costa Rica, though it is doubtless found there, as it has been observed at Chiriqui and specimens sent us from there by our collector Arcé. These latter birds are rather dark in colour, but not, in our opinion, separable.

D. anabatina, like *D. homochroa*, lives in the dense forest of the lowlands, the two birds being often seen on the trunk of the same tree picking ants from the surface of the bark.

2. Dendrocincla homochroa.

Dendromanes homochrous, Scl. P. Z. S. 1859, p. 382 [1]; Salv. Ibis, 1861, p. 353; P. Z. S. 1870, p. 193 [2].

Dendrocincla homochroa, Scl. & Salv. P. Z. S. 1868, p. 54 [3]; Boucard, P. Z. S. 1883, p. 450 [4]; Nutting, Pr. U. S. Nat. Mus. vi. pp. 385 [5], 414 [6]; Ridgw. Pr. U.S. Nat. Mus. x. p. 491 [7]; Salv. Ibis, 1889, p. 365 [8]; Scl. Cat. Birds Brit. Mus. xv. p. 163 [9].

Dendrocincla homochroa ruficeps, Ridgw. P. U.S. Nat. Mus. x. p. 491 [10].

Fusco-rubiginosa fere unicolor, pileo, alis et cauda magis cinnamomeis, dorso postico pallidiore, remigibus externis nigro terminatis: rostro et pedibus corylinis. Long. tota 7·5, alæ 4·0, caudæ 2·7, rostri a rictu 1·0, tarsi 1·0. (Descr. maris ex Chimalapa, Tehuantepec. Mustr. nostr.)

Hab. MEXICO, Teotalcingo (*Boucard* [1]), Chimalapa, Tehuantepec (*W. B. Richardson*), Northern Yucatan (*Gaumer*), Mugeres I., Meco I. off the coast of Yucatan (*Gaumer* [8]); BRITISH HONDURAS, Orange Walk (*Gaumer*); GUATEMALA, Rancho Tuilhá on the Cahabon-Peten road, Choctum, Volcan de Agua above San Diego (*O. S. & F. D. G.*); NICARAGUA, Chinandega, and El Volcan near Chinandega (*W. B. Richardson*), Sucuyá (*Nutting* [10]); COSTA RICA (*Carmiol*), Navarro (*J. Cooper* [6]); PANAMA, Volcan de Chiriqui (*Arcé* [2]).

Dendrocincla homochroa was one of M. Boucard's discoveries [1], the first specimen having been obtained by that traveller at Teotalcingo, a village on the eastern slope of the mountains of the Mexican State of Oaxaca. As its name is not included by Sumichrast in his list of the birds of Vera Cruz, and as none of our collectors who have worked in that State have sent us specimens, we conclude that the bird is not found to the northward of Teotalcingo. Southward of this place and over the whole of the forest-region of Yucatan and Guatemala, on both sides of the Cordillera, it is to met with pretty frequently. It occurs also in various parts of Nicaragua, on both sides of the great lakes, and in Costa Rica and the adjoining district of Chiriqui.

Whether the bird found at Panama is really distinct must remain for the present in some doubt. No specimen of the large series of the more northern bird quite corresponds with the type of *D. ruficeps*; some equal it in size, and some have the head of the same rufous tint, but none have so large a bill, and all are rather more rufescent both above and below.

D. homochroa is not unfrequently found in company with *D. anabatina* in some numbers together picking ants from the trunks of the forest-trees. They are less active than the other members of the climbing Dendrocolaptidæ.

3. **Dendrocincla ruficeps.**

Dendrocincla, sp.?, Lawr. Ann. Lyc. N. Y. vii. p. 320 [1]?
Dendromanes homochrous, Lawr. Ann. Lyc. N. Y. viii. p. 466 [2]?
Dendrocincla ruficeps, Scl. & Salv. P. Z. S. 1858, p. 54 [3]; Scl. Cat. Birds Brit. Mus. xv. p. 164 [4].

Brunnescenti-olivacea: pileo, alis extus, et cauda tota castaneis: subtus, præcipue in gula, paulo dilutior; remigum quinque externorum apicibus nigricantibus; rostro corneo, pedibus corylinis. Long. tota 8·0, alæ 4·2, caudæ 3·2, rostri a rictu 1·2, tarsi 0·9. (Descr. exempl. typ. ex Panama. Mus. Brit.)

Hab. PANAMA (*Chambers* [3]).

Mr. Ridgway includes all the birds found between Nicaragua and the line of the Panama railway under the name *Dendrocincla homochroa ruficeps*; but our series hardly confirms this view, for amongst the specimens from Chinandega and its neighbourhood are some not to be distinguished from the Mexican type, whilst others are darker. Moreover, there is a considerable difference in size, the males being apparently a little larger than the females. None of our Nicaraguan, Costa Rican, or Chiriqui specimens quite correspond with the type of *D. ruficeps*, so that for the present we keep this bird distinct. At the same time we have doubts as to its status, and believe that it will some day have to be merged with *D. homochroa*.

The single specimen brought from Panama by the late Mr. Hoggetts-Chambers, and formerly in Mr. Sclater's collection, is the only one we have seen.

4. **Dendrocincla olivacea.**

Dendrocincla fumigata, Lawr. Ann. Lyc. N. Y. vii. p. 320 (nec Licht.) [1].

Dendrocincla olivacea, Lawr. Ann. Lyc. N. Y. vii. p. 466 [2]; Ridgw. Pr. U. S. Nat. Mus. x. pp. 492 [3],
    590 [4]; Scl. Cat. Birds Brit. Mus. xv. p. 166 [5].

Dendromanes atrirostris, Scl. & Salv. P. Z. S. 1864, p. 355 (nec Lafr.) [6]; Salv. P. Z. S. 1870, p. 193 [7].

Dendrocincla atrirostris, Scl. & Salv. P. Z. S. 1868, p. 54 [8].

Supra olivaceo-brunnea, capite summo et uropygio paulo dilutioribus; tectricibus supracaudalibus et cauda obscure rubiginosis, tectricibus alarum dorso concoloribus, remigibus extus paulo rufescentibus: subtus pallidior, gula grisescente et cum pectore striis obsoletis rhachidalibus cervinis notatis; subalaribus et remigibus (præter apices) cinnamomeis: rostro et pedibus nigricantibus, illius mandibula infra pallida. Long. tota 7·5, alæ 4·1, caudæ 3·2, rostri a rictu 1·35, tarsi 1·0. (Descr. maris ex Panama. Mus. nostr.) ♀ mari similis.

Hab. HONDURAS, Segovia River (*Townsend* [4]); COSTA RICA, Talamanca (*U.S. Nat. Mus.* [3]), Cartago and Pacuar (*C. R. Nat. Mus.* [3]), Angostura (*Carmiol* [5]); PANAMA, Chitrá (*Arcé* [7]), Lion Hill (*M'Leannan* [1]).—COLOMBIA; ECUADOR [3].

This species was at first referred by Mr. Lawrence to *D. fumigata*, Licht.[1], but subsequently described as distinct under the name of *D. olivacea* [2]. It was then considered by Sclater and Salvin to belong to the Bolivian bird described by d'Orbigny and Lafresnaye as *Dendrocolaptes atrirostris* [6]—an opinion upset by Mr. Ridgway [3], who, on examining the supposed types of that species, pronounced the Panama bird to be different, and reinstated Mr. Lawrence's name. This decision we now follow.

D. olivacea is limited in its northern range to Honduras; thence it passes along the Isthmus to Panama, and into the north-western portion of the southern continent. Being found on the line of the Panama Railway it is doubtless a bird of the hot tropical forests, and probably does not ascend the mountains to any considerable elevation. M'Leannan obtained the types transmitted to Mr. Lawrence, and many specimens were sent by him to us.

b. *Rostrum angustum, breve, cuneiforme ; cauda elongata, alæ æquans.*

GLYPHORHYNCHUS.

Glyphorhynchus, Wied, Beitr. iii. p. 1149 (1831); Scl. Cat. Birds Brit. Mus. xv. p. 124.

In many respects the single member of this genus resembles *Dendrornis* and its allies; the general coloration is similar, and the structure of the tail and feet, with their short hallux, the same. The bill, however, is very differently constructed; it is short, the culmen and gonys are gently curved downwards and upwards, and both maxilla and mandible expand laterally towards the tip and are rounded at their ends ; the nostrils are completely overhung with a membrane, leaving the opening a narrow curved slit lying along the lower edge of the nasal fossa.

The range of the genus extends over the greater part of Tropical America, *G. cuneatus* being a denizen of the low-lying virgin forests.

1. Glyphorhynchus cuneatus.

Dendrocolaptes cuneatus, Licht. Abh. Ak. Berl. 1820, p. 204, t. 2. f. 2[1]; 1821, p. 266[2]; Spix, Av. Bras. i. p. 89, t. 91. f. 3[3].

Glyphorhynchus cuneatus, Strickl. P. Z. S. 1841, p. 28[4]; Scl. P. Z. S. 1858, p. 63[5]; Cat. Birds Brit. Mus. xv. p. 124[6]; Scl. & Salv. Ibis, 1860, p. 35[7]; Lawr. Ann. Lyc. N. Y. vii. p. 320[8]; Salv. Ibis, 1866, p. 205[9]; Sumichrast, La Nat. v. p. 248[10]; Boucard, P. Z. S. 1878, p. 60[11]; Nutting, Pr. U. S. Nat. Mus. vi. p. 404[12].

Glyphorhynchus ruficaudus, Wied, Beitr. iii. p. 1150[13].

Glyphorhynchus pectoralis, Scl. & Salv. P. Z. S. 1860, p. 299[14]; 1864, p. 354[15]; Lawr. Ann. Lyc. N. Y. viii. p. 181[16]; ix. p. 106[17]; Frantz. J. f. Orn. 1869, p. 305[18]; Salv. P. Z. S. 1870, p. 192[19].

Glyphorhynchus major, Scl. Cat. Am. Birds, p. 161[20]; P. Z. S. 1862, p. 369[21]; Sumichrast, Mem. Bost. Soc. N. H. i. p. 555[22].

Xiphorhynchus mayor, Sanchez, An. Mus. Nac. Mex. i. p. 97[23].

Supra rufescenti-brunneus, uropygio et cauda saturate cinnamomeis, superciliis indistinctis et capitis lateribus cervinis fusco variegatis : subtus brunneis, plumis singulis medialiter pallide cervinis, gula paulo magis fulvescente, abdomine vix striato ; subalaribus albis, primariis (duobus externis exceptis) et secundariis omnibus fascia obliqua fulva medialiter notatis : rostro et pedibus corylinis. Long. tota 5·5, alæ 2·1, caudæ 2·7, rostri a rictu 0·6, tarsi 0·7. (Deser. maris ex Yzabal, Guatemala. Mus. nostr.)

♀ mari similis.

Hab. MEXICO, Hot region of Vera Cruz[22], Uvero[11] (*Sumichrast*), Vera Cruz (*Sanchez*[23]) ; GUATEMALA, Choctum[20], Yzabal[7] (*O. Salvin*) ; NICARAGUA, Greytown (*Holland*), Los Sabalos (*Nutting*[12]) ; COSTA RICA, Tucurriqui (*Arcé*), Naranjo (*Boucard*[11]) ; PANAMA, Bugaba[19], Mina de Chorcha[19], Volcan de Chiriqui[19], Chitra (*Arcé*), Lion Hill (*M'Leannan*[8][15]).—SOUTH AMERICA, from Colombia to Guiana and South Brazil[6].

Our first Central-American specimen (shot by Salvin at Yzabal, in Guatemala, on 19th June, 1859) was referred with doubt to *G. cuneatus*[7], but on the receipt of more examples from Choctum in Vera Paz in January 1860, the Guatemalan bird was named by Sclater and Salvin *G. pectoralis*, in a paper read before the Zoological Society on 22nd May, 1860[14]. In 1862[20] Mr. Sclater, overlooking the previous description of the same bird, re-described one of the Choctum skins as *G. major*, and in the same year referred to a Mexican skin under this name[21]. It is now pretty generally admitted that the Central-American bird cannot be distinguished from the Continental form, and there is certainly no tangible difference between the Yzabal bird and others from the neighbourhood of Bahia either in size or colour.   The Amazons bird is perhaps a little more tawny on the throat and slightly more rufescent on the back, but the difference is trivial.   This bird is the *G. castelnaudi* of Des Murs.

In its distribution *G. cuneatus* is found in Mexico and Central America almost exclusively in the low-lying forests of the eastern side of the Cordillera at least as far south as Nicaragua, where it also occurs in the forests bordering the Pacific Ocean. In South America it spreads over most of the tropical portion of that continent as far as the forests of Eastern Brazil, and occurs throughout the great valley of the Amazons.

In habits it is strictly a bird of the dense forest, and climbs trees like a Woodpecker.

Subfam. *DENDROCOLAPTINÆ* *.

We have some hesitation in placing *Sittosomus* with the Dendrocolaptinæ, as the bill is so much more feeble than in the other genera of the subfamily.   Moreover, the nostrils are not quite so distinctly open, the upper edge being slightly membranous. The hallux is short, as in *Glyphorhynchus* and the Dendrocolaptinæ generally, and the tail distinctly spinous.   Whenever the arrangement of the whole of the Dendrocolaptidæ is undertaken again, the position of *Sittosomus* will have to be reconsidered.   In the meantime we retain the genus in the subfamily Dendrocolaptinæ, but separate it from the other genera under the following characters :—

A. *Rostrum debile ; nares apertæ sed supra membrano marginatæ.*

SITTOSOMUS.

Sittasomus, Swainson, Zool. Journ. iii. p. 355 (1827); Scl. Cat. Birds Brit. Mus. xv. p. 118.

Two species constitute this genus, whereof one (*S. erithacus*) is restricted in its range to Eastern Brazil and thence southwards to the Argentine Republic.   The other (*S. olivaceus*) also occurs in Brazil, but spreads northwards to the Mexican State of Vera Cruz.   The leading characters of the genus have been already given under the subfamily.   Mr. Sclater groups *Sittosomus* with *Margarornis*, distinguishing them by the greater stiffness of the rectrices of the former.   The shortness of the hallux of *Sittosomus*, compared with that of *Margarornis*, alone seems to us to indicate the radical distinctness of the two genera.

1. **Sittosomus olivaceus.**

Sittasomus olivaceus, Wied, Beitr. iii. p. 1146 [1]; Scl. & Salv. P. Z. S. 1869, p. 353 [2]; Salv. P. Z. S. 1870, p. 192 [3]; Sumichrast, La Nat. v. p. 247 [4]; Nutt. Pr. U. S. Nat. Mus. vi. p. 385 [5]; Boucard, P. Z. S. 1883, p. 450 [6]; Ferrari-Perez, Pr. U. S. Nat. Mus. ix. p. 156 [7].
Sittosomus olivaceus, Scl. Cat. Birds Brit. Mus. xv. p. 119 [8].

----

* *Antea*, p. 146.

Sittasomus sylvioides, Lafr. Rev. Zool. 1849, p. 331 [9]; 1850, p. 590 [10]; Scl. P. Z. S. 1856, p. 290 [11]; 1859, p. 365 [12]; 1864, p. 175 [13]; Salv. Ibis, 1861, p. 353 [14]; Lawr. Ann. Lyc. N. Y. ix. p. 106 [15]; Sumichrast, Mem. Bost. Soc. N. H. i. p. 555 [16]; Frantz. J. f. Orn. 1869, p. 304 [17]; Sanchez, An. Mus. Nac. Mex. i. p. 97 [18].

Sittosomus pectinicaudus, Cab. & Heine, Mus. Hein. ii. p. 33 [19].

Supra olivaceo-rufescens, capite summo cinerascentiore, uropygio, cauda et tectricibus subcaudalibus læte cinnamomeis: subtus olivaceo-cinereus; alis nigricantibus, secundariis ad apicem et extrorsum (intimis omnino) cinnamomeis, remigibus internis quoque eodem modo ornatis, subalaribus et fascia alarum pallide cinnamomeis, primariis tribus externis omnino nigricantibus: rostro et pedibus corneis, mandibula pallida. Long. tota 6·0, alæ 3·2, caudæ 3·2, rostri a rictu 0·8, tarsi 0·7. (Descr. exempl. ex Jalapa, Mexico. Mus. nostr.)

♀ mari omnino similis.

Hab. MEXICO [10] (*Deppe* [19], *White* [13]), Hot region of Vera Cruz [16], Potrero [4] (*Sumichrast*), Jalapa (*de Oca* [12], *F. D. G.*, *M. Trujillo*, *F. Ferrari-Perez*,), Coatepec (*F. Ferrari-Perez*, *M. Trujillo*), Cofre de Perote, Cuesta de Misantla (*M. Trujillo*), Cordova (*Sallé* [11]), Vera Cruz (*Sanchez* [18]), Sochiapa (*Trujillo*), Teapa (*Mrs. H. H. Smith*), Santa Efigenia (*Sumichrast* [4]), Northern Yucatan (*G. F. Gaumer*); BRITISH HONDURAS, Orange Walk (*Gaumer* [6]); GUATEMALA, Pie de la Cuesta in San Marcos (*W. B. Richardson*), Choctum [14], Savana Grande between the Volcanoes of Agua and Fuego (*O. S. & F. D. G.*); NICARAGUA, Sucuyá (*Nutting* [5]); COSTA RICA, Tempate Nicoya (*Arcé*), Dota Mountains (*Carmiol* [15]); PANAMA, Chiriqui [3], Chitrá, Calovevora [3] (*Arcé*).—SOUTH AMERICA generally, from Colombia to Guiana and South Brazil [1].

Sittosomus olivaceus is a common characteristic species of Tropical South America, and is also found in nearly the whole of the lowland forests of Central America and Southern Mexico as far north as the middle of the State of Vera Cruz. It is absent from Western Mexico, but occurs on both sides of the mountain-range of Guatemala. Its range in altitude extends to about 4000 feet in the neighbourhood of Jalapa, in Vera Cruz, and perhaps higher on the slopes of the neighbouring mountain, the Cofre de Perote. In Guatemala it chiefly affects the forests of Vera Paz lying at an elevation of about 1500 to 2000 feet down to the sea-level, and has the habits of all the stiff-tailed members of the family, climbing trees like a *Certhia* or Woodpecker, its food being insects.

Several names have been proposed for this species to distinguish local forms, but none of these seem capable of definition in view of the very wide uninterrupted range enjoyed by the bird as a whole. To the Mexican bird Lafresnaye gave the name of *S. sylvioides*, which Cabanis and Heine supplanted by *S. pectinicaudus*. The former was long used in lists of Mexican and Central-American birds, but it gradually became evident that no real distinction could be drawn between them and birds from the southern continent, so all have latterly been united under *S. olivaceus*, the title bestowed by Prince Wied upon the Brazilian bird.

B. *Rostrum robustum; nares omnino apertæ.*

a. *Rostrum plus minusve falcatum, angustum, compressum,
ad apicem vix hamatum.*

DENDRORNIS.

Dendrornis, Eyton, Contr. Orn. 1852, p. 23; Scl. Cat. Birds Brit. Mus. xv. p. 127; Elliot, Auk vii. p. 160.

Mr. Sclater admits sixteen species of *Dendrornis* and gives the names of four others which he was unable to determine. Mr. Elliot, going over the same ground, includes twenty-two species in the genus. These are distributed over nearly the whole of Tropical America, from the Mexican States of Tamaulipas and Sinaloa to Southern Brazil. Five species are found within our limits, of which two occur in Southern Mexico and Guatemala and the other three in the more southern districts. *D. eburneirostris* is the only distinct endemic species, but the doubtful *D. nana* reaches the extreme limits of our region and probably passes beyond them into South America. Compared with that of *Picolaptes*, the bill of *Dendrornis* is stout and rather straighter, the culmen curving rather more abruptly at the end. In other respects the two genera, as well as *Xiphocolaptes*, are very similar, having plumage similarly marked, the wings, tail, and feet are similarly constructed, and the nostrils in all are quite open.

1. **Dendrornis eburneirostris.**

Xiphorhynchus flavigaster, Sw. Phil. Mag. (new ser.) i. p. 440[1]; Bp. Consp. Av. i. p. 208[2].

Dryocopus flavigaster, Des Murs, Icon. Orn. livr. 9[3].

Nasica flavigaster, Lafr. Rev. Zool. 1850, p. 383[4].

Dendrornis flavigastra, Scl. P. Z. S. 1856, p. 289[5]; 1859, p. 381[6]; Scl. & Salv. Ibis, 1860, p. 398[7]; Sumichrast, La Nat. v. p. 248[8]; Ferrari-Perez, Pr. U. S. Nat. Mus. ix. p. 156[9]; Elliot, Auk, vii. p. 178[10].

Dryocopus eburneirostris, Less. Echo du Monde Sav. 1843[11]; Des Murs, Icon. Orn. t. 52[12].

Dendrornis eburneirostris, Eyton, Contr. Orn. 1852, p. 23[13]; Cab. & Heine, Mus. Hein. ii. p. 37[14] Lawr. Ann. Lyc. N. Y. ix. p. 201[15]; Bull. U. S. Nat. Mus. no. 4, p. 25[16]; Scl. & Salv. P. Z. S. 1870, pp. 834, 840[17]; Nutting, Pr. U. S. Nat. Mus. vi. pp. 375[18], 385[19]; Boucard, P. Z. S. 1883, p. 450[20]; Ridgw. Pr. U. S. Nat. Mus. x. p. 580[21]; Scl. Cat. Birds Brit. Mus. xv. p. 130[22].

Picolaptes validirostris, Eyton, Contr. Orn. 1851, p. 75[23].

Dendrocolaptes pœcilonotus, Wagl. in Mus. Berl. (apud Cabanis & Heine)[24].

Dendrornis mentalis, Lawr. Ann. Lyc. N. Y. viii. p. 481[25]; Mem. Bost. Soc. N. H. ii. p. 285[26]; Sanchez, An. Mus. Nac. Mex. i. p. 97[27].

Dendrornis albirostris, Lafr. MS. (apud Elliot)[28].

Supra brunnea, capite summo et cervice postica nigris, plumis singulis stria mediana cervina, dorsi plumis quoque striatis, striis nigro limbatis; uropygio, alis extus et cauda cinnamomeis: subtus gula cervina, atria utrinque angusta nigra, plumis capitis lateribus cervinis nigro marginatis, pectoris et gutturis postici plumis fusco leviter terminatis, plumis abdominis pallide brunneis cervino striatis (striis singulis utrinque nigro marginatis), his marginibus ad ventrem obsoletis; subalaribus et alis subtus (præter apices fuscos) cinnamomeis: rostro albicante corneo, pedibus plumbeis. Long. tot. 10·0, alæ 4·5, caudæ 4·1, rostri a rictu 1·65, tarsi 0·95. (Descr. maris ex Cordova, Mexico. Mus. nostr.)

♀ mari similis.

Hab. MEXICO [3] [4], Altamira, Tamesi and Tampico in Tamaulipas (*W. B. Richardson*), Misantla and Colipa (*F. D. G.*), Vega del Casadero (*M. Trujillo*), Jalapa (*de Oca* [9], *F. D. G.*, *Ferrari-Perez*), Cordova (*Sallé* [5]), San Lorenzo near Cordova, Plan del Rio, Hacienda Tortugas (*F. Ferrari-Perez*), Playa Vicente (*Boucard* [6], *M. Trujillo*), Mazatlan [25] (*Grayson, Xantus, Bischoff, Forrer*), Tepic [26] (*Xantus*), Santiago de Tepic (*W. B. Richardson*), Santiago de Colima and Tecolapa (*W. Lloyd*), Chietla (*Ferrari-Perez* [9]), Temascaltepec (*Bullock* [1]), Chimalapa, Sierra de San Domingo, Tehuantepec (*W. B. Richardson*), Guichicovi, Ishuatlau, Cacoprieto [8], Tapana [8], and Sta. Efigenia [8] (*Sumichrast*), N. Yucatan [15], Peto, Buctzotz, and Tuloom (*G. F. Gaumer*), Tabi (*F. D. G.*), Meco I. (*Gaumer*); BRITISH HONDURAS, Orange Walk (*Gaumer*), Southern Pine-ridge, Cayo and Belize (*Blancaneaux*); GUATEMALA, Retalhuleu (*O. S. & F. D. G.*, *W. B. Richardson*), Savana Grande, between the Volcanoes of Agua and Fuego, Choctum [7] (*O. S. & F. D. G.*); SALVADOR, La Libertad and Volcan de San Miguel (*W. B. Richardson*); HONDURAS, San Pedro (*G. M. Whitely* [17]), Truxillo (*Townsend* [21]); NICARAGUA, Realejo (*A. Lesson* [2] [11]), Chinandega (*W. B. Richardson*), San Juan del Sur [18], Sucuyá [19] (*Nutting*); COSTA RICA (*fide D. G. Elliot* [10]).

This is the commonest and most widely spread species of *Dendrornis* found in our country, its range extending from the Mexican State of Tamaulipas in the north-east and that of Sinaloa in the north-west, southwards to Guatemala, Honduras, and Nicaragua. Mr. Elliot, in his recent monograph of the genus, also includes Costa Rica in its range, but omits to give his authority for so doing [10].

Its range in altitude reaches from the sea-level to a height of about 4000 feet in the mountains. It lives in the forests, climbing trees like a Woodpecker, and feeding on insects.

The bird of Western Mexico was separated under the name *D. mentalis* by Mr. Lawrence, and has long been considered distinguishable from the eastern and southern *D. eburneirostris*; but Mr. Elliot, after examining a large number of specimens, came to the conclusion that the distinctness of the two could not be upheld. We are now entirely of the same opinion, and, with an extensive series before us from all parts of the range of the species, no separation appears to us possible.

Birds from Western Mexico are, as a rule, paler than the average in the general tone of their plumage, but they can be exactly matched by examples from Tamaulipas and Yucatan, and these are connected with the darker birds of Vera Cruz and other places by gradual steps, the extreme forms often occurring, as on the Isthmus of Tehuantepec, in the same district at the same time of year. Great variation also occurs in size and in the dimensions of the bill, but also without reference to locality.

Swainson's name for this species was based upon a bird sent by Bullock from

Temascaltepec in the tableland of Mexico [1]. The description is very imperfect, but we think certainly refers to the bird subsequently described by Lesson as *Dryocopus eburneirostris* [11]. The latter title, however, has been more frequently employed than the former, partly from the brevity of Swainson's description, partly from the hybrid formation of his name.

2. Dendrornis nana.

Dendrornis guttatus, Cassin, Pr. Ac. Phil. 1860, p. 193 [1]; Lawr. Ann. Lyc. N. Y. vii. p. 292 (nec Licht.) [2].

Dendrornis nana, Lawr. Ibis, 1863, p. 181 [3]; Ann. Lyc. N. Y. viii. p. 4 [4]; Scl. & Salv. P. Z. S. 1864, p. 355 [5]; 1870, p. 837 [6]; Salv. P. Z. S. 1870, p. 193 [7]; Elliot, Auk, vii. p. 174 [8].

Dendrornis pardalotus, Lawr. Ann. Lyc. N. Y. viii. pp. 4 [9], 181 [10]; ix. p. 107 [11]; Frantz. J. f. Orn. 1869, p. 305 [12].

Dendrornis susurrans, Scl. & Salv. P. Z. S. 1870, p. 839 [13]; Boucard, P. Z. S. 1878, p. 60 [14].

Dendrornis lawrencii, Ridgw. Pr. U. S. Nat. Mus. x. p. 509 [15].

Dendrornis lawrencii costaricensis, Ridgw. Pr. U. S. Nat. Mus. x. pp. 510 [16], 589 [17].

D. eburneirostro affinis sed minor, rostro minore, maxilla nigricante, mandibula quoque interdum nigra, striis dorsalibus paucis et angustioribus : subtus magis rufescens, abdomine et tectricibus subcaudalibus vix striatis. Long. tota 9·0, alæ 4·1, caudæ 3·4, rostri a rictu 1·3, tarsi 0·9. (Descr. maris ex San Pablo, Panama. Mus. nostr.)

Hab. HONDURAS, Medina (*G. M. Whitely* [13]), Segovia River (*Townsend* [17]); COSTA RICA [12], Angostura, Tucurriqui [11] (*Carmiol*), San Carlos (*Boucard* [14]); PANAMA, Bugaba, Calovevora (*Arcé* [7]), Lion Hill (*M'Leannan* [1 2 3 4 5]), San Pablo Station (*O. S.*), near Panama city (*A. H. Markham*).

The differences distinguishing this bird from *D. susurrans* of the island of Tobago and the northern portion of the continent of South America are very slight, and perhaps hardly of specific value, consisting as they do in the rather deeper tint of the fawn-coloured markings of the under surface and the more elongated stripes of the abdomen of the Central-American bird. A good deal of variation exists in individuals of both forms, but on the whole they seem to conform to these points of distinction. We confess at the same time that we are straining a point in admitting *D. nana* to be different from *D. susurrans*, and we do so with much hesitation. Mr. Sclater places the two birds under *D. susurrans*, while Mr. Elliot keeps them distinct, considering *D. nana* to be easily recognizable, which may be the case in the series examined by him, but is not so in ours.

The range of *D. nana* has been traced to the north coast of Honduras [13], and thence southwards through Nicaragua, Costa Rica, and the State of Panama. All southern birds beyond this seem to be referable to *D. susurrans*.

From *D. pardalotus* this species may be distinguished by its stouter bill; the markings of the breast, too, are less definite, the margins to the central stripes being not so black.

3. Dendrornis erythropygia.

Dendrornis triangularis, Scl. P. Z. S. 1856, p. 289[1]; Scl. & Salv. P. Z. S. 1879, p. 622[2].

Dendrornis erythropygia, Scl. P. Z. S. 1859, pp. 365[3], 381[4]; Cat. Birds Brit. Mus. xv. p. 131[5];
  Scl. & Salv. Ibis, 1860, p. 35[6]; P. Z. S. 1864, p. 355[7]; Elliot, Auk, vii. p. 187[8].

Supra obscure olivacea, secundariis extus, dorso postico, uropygio et cauda rubiginosis, pilei et dorsi antici
  plumis medialiter pallide cervinis, illorum maculis latioribus guttiformibus: subtus obscure olivacea,
  plumis singulis medialiter pallide cervinis iis gulæ tantum olivaceo limbatis; alis subtus rubiginosis
  fusco terminatis: rostro corneo, mandibula pallida. Long. tota 9·0, alæ 4·7, caudæ 4·1, rostri a rictu 1·5
  tarsi 0·95. (Descr. maris ex Cofre de Perote, Mexico. Mus. nostr.)
♀ mari similis.

Hab. Mexico, Jalapa (*de Oca*[3]), Coatepec, Huatusco (*F. Ferrari-Perez*), Cofre de Perote
  (*M. Trujillo*), Cordova (*Sallé*[1]), Chilpancingo (*Mrs. H. H. Smith*), Oaxaca
  (*Boucard*[4]); Guatemala, El Rincon in San Marcos (*W. B. Richardson*), Las
  Nubes on the slope of Cerro Zunil, Coban[6], Chisec, and Choctum in Vera Paz
  (*O. S. & F. D. G.*); Panama, Lion Hill (*M'Leannan*[7]).—South America,
  Bolivia[2].

The only differences between this species and its near ally *D. triangularis* consist in
the lower back being chestnut like the wings and tail instead of olive, and in the wings
being more rufescent.

It was long considered that one form of this *Dendrornis* (*D. erythropygia*) belonged
to Central America, whilst the other (*D. triangularis*) was found in the southern
continent, and specimens in collections were generally so named according to locality.
But it now appears that the more northern bird has a wide range in South America,
examples from Bolivia being inseparable from the Mexican bird. *D. triangularis*
appears to be confined to a comparatively small tract of country lying within the
hunting-grounds of the bird-collectors of Bogota, to the valley of the Cauca, and to
Venezuela. A third form (*D. punctigula*) occurs in Costa Rica and elsewhere, whose
range is mixed with that of the present bird in a way difficult of explanation; this
bird is mentioned below.

Dendrornis erythropygia was discovered near Cordova in Mexico by M. Sallé[1], and
specimens were contained in his first collection described by Mr. Sclater in 1856; its
difference from *D. triangularis* was, however, not noticed until a few years afterwards,
when both Boucard[4] and de Oca[3] had also found it. It is now known as a fairly
common bird in the State of Vera Cruz, whence it spreads southwards through Guatemala, where it occurs on both sides of the main mountain-range. In South-western
Mexico we know of its occurrence only in the Sierra Madre del Sur, in the State of
Guerrero.

4. Dendrornis punctigula.

Dendrornis triangularis, Cassin, Pr. Ac. Phil. 1860, p. 193 (nec Lafr.) [1].

Dendrornis erythropygia, Cab. & Heine, J. f. Orn. 1861, p. 242 [2]; Salv. P. Z. S. 1867, p. 144 [3]; 1870, p. 193 [4]; Lawr. Ann. Lyc. N. Y. ix. p. 107 [5]; Ridgw. Pr. U. S. Nat. Mus. vi. p. 414 [6].

Dendrornis erythropygia æquatorialis, Berl. & Tacz. P. Z. S. 1883, p. 563 [7].

Dendrornis punctigula, Ridgw. Pr. U. S. Nat. Mus. xi. p. 544 (1888) [8]; Elliot, Auk, vii. p. 188 [9].

D. erythropygiæ persimilis, sed pileo fere immaculato et dorso striis vix ullis forsan distinguenda. (Descr. maris ex Augostura, Costa Rica. Mus. nostr.)

Hab. COSTA RICA, Augostura, Pacuar and Barranca (*Carmiol* [5]), Rio Sucio [6], Naranjo [8] (*J. Cooper*), Tucurriqui (*Zeledon* [7]); PANAMA, Chiriqui [4], Bugaba [4], Castillo, Cordillera del Chucu [4], Boquete de Chitrá [4], Calovevora [4], Santiago de Veraguas [3] (*Arcé*), Rio Truando (*W. S. Wood* [1]).—ECUADOR [6].

Mr. Ridgway's name for this bird is taken from the character of the spots on the throat, which are nearly round and situated at the end of the feather. All our Costa-Rican and Panama specimens have this character, which is also to be found in some, but not all, examples of *D. erythropygia*, the exceptions having the throat-feathers edged rather than spotted with olive. The best character by which to distinguish *D. punctigula* is its nearly uniform unspotted crown and the almost total absence of dorsal streaks. An Ecuador specimen has this coloration, and belongs, we do not doubt, to the race described by Graf v. Berlepsch and Taczanowski as *Dendrornis erythropygia æquatorialis*. This example is not separable from others from the State of Panama, referable to *D. punctigula* of Ridgway. According to Mr. Elliot [9], the specimen obtained by Mr. W. S. Wood, jun., during Lieut. Michler's Darien Expedition, and referred by Cassin to *D. triangularis* [1], belongs here, and not to the true *D. erythropygia*, which occurs on the Isthmus of Panama.

5. Dendrornis lacrymosa. (Tab. XLVIII. fig. 1.)

Dendrornis, sp. ?, Cassin, Pr. Ac. Phil. 1860, p. 194 [1]; Lawr. Ann. Lyc. N. Y. vii. p. 292, no. 48 [2].

Dendrornis lacrymosa, Lawr. Ann. Lyc. N. Y. vii. p. 467 [3]; Scl. & Salv. P. Z. S. 1864, p. 355 [4]; 1867, p. 279 [5]; 1879, p. 523 [6]; Salv. P. Z. S. 1867, p. 144 [7]; 1870, p. 193 [8]; Ibis, 1872, pp. 313, 317 [9]; Zeledon, Cat. Av. de Costa Rica, p. 11 [10]; Scl. Cat. Birds Brit. Mus. xv. p. 133 [11]; Elliot, Auk, vii. p. 181 [12].

Supra nigra usque ad dorsi medium plumis omnibus medialiter macula guttiformi cervino-albido notatis, dorso postico, uropygio, alis et cauda castaneis: subtus (præter gulam) undique guttata, plumis singulis medialiter cervino albido nigro marginatis, abdomine quoque fusco intermixto, gula immaculata albida cervino tincta: rostro corneo, pedibus plumbeis. Long. tota 9·0, alæ 4·75, caudæ 4·0, rostri a rictu 0·55, tarsi 0·9. (Descr. maris ex Bugaba, Panama. Mus. nostr.)

♀ mari similis.

Hab. NICARAGUA, Blewfields River (*Wickham* [5]), Chontales (*Belt* [9]); COSTA RICA (*Zeledon* [10]); PANAMA, Volcan de Chiriqui [8], Bugaba [8], Bibalaz, Santiago de Veraguas [7] (*Arcé*), Lion Hill (*M'Leannan* [2,3,4]), Rio Truando (*W. S. Wood* [1]).—COLOMBIA, Antioquia [6].

The first specimen obtained of this fine species was probably that brought to Washington by Lieut. Michler from the Isthmus of Darien [1]. To this bird Cassin did not give a name, nor did Mr. Lawrence to M'Leannan's first specimens from the Isthmus of Panama [2]; but the latter ornithologist subsequently [3] described M'Leannan's specimens, and the bird has since been traced through the State of Panama and Costa Rica to the Mosquito coast [5] and the Nicaraguan province of Chontales [9].

The species is a very distinct one without near allies, the definite tear-shaped spots of the anterior portion of the body forming a prominent feature in its coloration. We figure one of M'Leannan's specimens.

XIPHOCOLAPTES.

Xiphocolaptes, Lesson, Rev. Zool. 1840, p. 269; Ridgway, Pr. U.S. Nat. Mus. xii. p. 1 (5th Feb., 1890); Scl. Cat. Birds Brit. Mus. xv. p. 142.

Xiphocolaptes is a large form of *Dendrornis* with similar structural characters, but with a long strong bill, the gonys of which is slightly decurved as in *Picolaptes*. Its range extends from Southern Mexico to the Argentine Republic.

The number of species contained in it is very variously estimated. Mr. Sclater admits five, whilst Mr. Ridgway recognized twelve species and subspecies. As we are now treating, according to our views, with only one valid species, this great difference of opinion must be tested by an examination of a large series of specimens from South America—ground we must not trespass upon here.

1. Xiphocolaptes emigrans.

Xiphocolaptes albicollis, Scl. P. Z. S. 1857, p. 202 (nec Vieill.) [1].

Xiphocolaptes emigrans, Scl. & Salv. Ibis, 1859, p. 118 [2]; Ex. Orn. p. 69, t. 35 [3]; Cab. & Heine, Mus. Hein. ii. p. 36 [4]; Sumichrast, Mem. Bost. Soc. N. H. i. p. 554 [5]; La Nat. v. p. 248 [9]; Sanchez, An. Mus. Nac. Mex. i. p. 97 [7]; Ridgway, Pr. U. S. Nat. Mus. xii. p. 7 [8]; Scl. Cat. Birds Brit. Mus. xv. p. 145 [9].

Xiphocolaptes sclateri, Ridgway, Pr. U. S. Nat. Mus. xii. p. 6 [10]; Scl. Cat. Birds Brit. Mus. xv. p. 143 [11].

Xiphocolaptes emigrans costaricensis, Ridgway, Pr. U. S. Nat. Mus. xii. p. 8 [12].

Supra brunneus, capite obscuriore et cum cervice postica striis angustis rhachidalibus cervino-albidis notatis, uropygio, secundariis extus et cauda ferrugineis: subtus brunneus, gula albicante, capitis lateribus, cervice et pectore striis rhachidalibus albidis, subcaudalibus quoque indistincte striatis; alis subtus cinnamomeis fusco terminatis, subalaribus cervinis nigro maculatis: rostro corneo, pedibus plumbeis. Long. tota 12·0, alæ 5·5, caudæ 4·4, rostri a rictu 2·3, tarsi 1·3. (Descr. exemp. typ. ex Guatemala. Mus. Brit.)

♀ mari similis.

Av. juv. Striis capitis latioribus, pectore nigro maculato, abdomine et tibiis nigro transfasciatis.

Hab. MEXICO, Orizaba [10] (*Sumichrast* [5]), Vera Cruz (*Sanchez* [7]), La Parada (*Rébouch* [9]), Omilteme in Guerrero (*Mrs. H. H. Smith*), Oaxaca (*Fenechio* [9]), Tonaguia in Oaxaca (*M. Trujillo*); BRITISH HONDURAS (*Blancaneaux* [9]); GUATEMALA, Pine-ridge of Poctum, San Gerónimo (*O. S. & F. D. G.*[9]), Cahabon (*F. Sarg*[9]); Costa Rica, Naranjo (*Zeledon*[12]).

A species sparingly distributed over a wide area extending from Southern Mexico to Costa Rica, and rather variable in the markings of its plumage, which has led to the separation of the Mexican from the Guatemalan bird and the Costa-Rican from both.

The chief point relied upon is the presence or absence of dark transverse marks on the abdomen, the Mexican birds having, as a rule, these marks more clearly shown than in others from more southern localities. The type from Guatemala is destitute of these marks, but other specimens from the same country have them in varying degrees, and it seems to us impossible from the series before us to separate these birds on so slender and variable a character. Mr. Ridgway, however, strongly insists upon the distinctness of *X. sclateri* from *X. emigrans*, and we can only conclude that the specimens seen by him tell him a different story from ours. As for the Costa Rica bird, we can give no independent opinion, as we doubt the origin of a specimen in the British Museum said to be from that country, but which belongs, we think, to one of the South-American forms and not to *X. emigrans* at all.

Mr. Ridgway only makes a subspecific form of the Costa Rica bird, and gives as its difference from *X. emigrans* its slightly larger size and broader streaks on the breast &c.

X. emigrans is an inhabitant of the pine-districts where it is found. It is a shy bird and difficult of approach. A specimen shot in the Pine-ridge of Poctum flew from tree to tree, and after alighting on the trunk it rapidly ascended to the top, from whence it flew to another tree. The range in altitude of the species extends from about 800 to 1200 feet in British Honduras to at least 8000 feet in the mountains of Mexico. Sumichrast speaks of the species as inhabiting the pine-forests of the highlands of Orizaba, where it was not uncommon, taking its food from the bark of the tree-trunks. In the stomach of a bird he shot he found a tree-frog (*Hyla myotympanum*), which had probably been captured among the tufts of an *Æchmæa* (Bromeliaceæ), to which these batrachians resort during the dry season.

PICOLAPTES.

Picolaptes, Lesson, Traité d'Orn. p. 313 (1831); Scl. Cat. Birds Brit. Mus. xv. p. 146.

This genus contains the weaker forms of Dendrocolaptinæ allied to *Dendrornis* and *Xiphocolaptes*. The bill especially is more slender and feeble, as well as more curved, than in either of the above-named genera. In all other points of structure *Picolaptes* shows no essential difference. In the number of its component species it fully equals *Dendrornis*, Mr. Sclater reckoning them at seventeen, and giving the names of two others unknown to him. These are widely distributed from Central Mexico in the north to Paraguay and South Brazil. Four species, all peculiar to it, are found within our country; of these, *P. leucogaster* is peculiar to the uplands of Mexico, *P. gracilis* to Costa Rica. Of the other two, *P. affinis* and *P. compressus* range nearly over the whole area—the former in the highlands, the latter in the lowlands of the same countries.

1. Picolaptes leucogaster.

Xiphorhynchus leucogaster, Sw. Phil. Mag. new ser. i. p. 440 [1].

Picolaptes leucogaster, Lafr. Rev. Zool. 1850, p. 150 [2]; Scl. P. Z. S. 1858, p. 297 [3]; Cat. Birds Brit. Mus. xv. p. 147 [4]; Sumichrast, La Nat. v. p. 248 [5].

Thripobrotus leucogaster, Cab. & Heine, Mus. Hein. ii. p. 37 [6].

Picolaptes atripes, Eyton, Contr. Orn. 1851, p. 76 [7]; 1852, p. 22 [8].

Supra olivaceo-brunneus, capite summo nigro, plumis macula discali pallide cervina, cervice postica quoque striis cervinis nigro utrinque limbatis notata; dorso postico, alis extus et cauda rubiginosis, tectricibus alarum dorso concoloribus: subtus gula alba, plumis corporis reliquis macula magna elongata discali albida utrinque nigro limbata ornatis, tectricibus subcaudalibus medialiter striatis, subalaribus fulvis remigibus cinnamomeis fusco terminatis: rostro corneo, pedibus plumbeis. Long. tota 9·0, alæ 4·8, caudæ 3·9, rostri a rictu 1·55, tarsi 0·8. (Descr. maris ex Rio Frio Ixtaccihuatl, Mexico. Mus. nostr.) ♀ mari similis.

Hab. MEXICO, Nuri in Sonora (*W. Lloyd*), Ciudad in Durango (*A. Forrer* [4]), Sierra de San Luis Potosi, Sierra de Bolaños, Sierra de Nayarit, Sierra Nevada de Colima, Tenango del Valle, Rio Frio Ixtaccihuatl in Puebla (*W. B. Richardson*), Temascaltepec (*Bullock* [1]), San Salvador el Verde in Puebla (*F. Ferrari-Perez*), Alpine region of Orizaba (*Sumichrast* [5]), La Parada (*Boucard* [3]), Omilteme and Amula in Guerrero (*Mrs. H. H. Smith*).

P. leucogaster was described by Swainson from a specimen procured by Bullock at Temascaltepec in the highlands of Mexico [1]. Its range has now been ascertained to extend over a wide area, from the State of Sonora in the north-west to that of Guerrero and Oaxaca in the south. Specimens from different parts of this extensive tract of country do not vary to any appreciable extent; the northern birds are perhaps a shade paler, but that is all.

The species is easily recognized amongst its allies by the size and white colour of the spots of its plumage, which have no fawn-colour or buff tint as is the case in *P. affinis* and *P. compressus*.

2. Picolaptes affinis.

Dendrocolaptes affinis, Lafr. Rev. Zool. 1839, p. 100 [1].

Picolaptes affinis, Lafr. Rev. Zool. 1850, p. 275 [2]; Eyton, Contr. Orn. 1852, p. 22 [3]; Scl. P. Z. S. 1856, p. 289 [4]; 1859, pp. 365 [5], 381 [6]; 1864, p. 175 [7]; Cat. Birds Brit. Mus. xv. p. 149 [8]; Scl. & Salv. Ibis, 1860, p. 35 [9]; Lawr. Ann. Lyc. N. Y. ix. p. 107 [10]; Sumichrast, Mem. Bost. Soc. N. H. i. p. 555 (partim) [11]; La Nat. v. p. 248 [12]; Salv. P. Z. S. 1870, p. 193 [13]; Sanchez, Ann. Mus. Nac. Mex. i. p. 97 (partim?) [14]; Ridgw. Pr. U. S. Nat. Mus. v. p. 497 [15]; Ferrari-Perez, Pr. U. S. Nat. Mus. ix. p. 156 [16].

Thripobrotus affinis, Cab. & Heine, Mus. Hein. ii. p. 38 [17].

Supra brunneus; uropygio, alis extus et cauda rubiginosis, tectricibus alarum dorso concoloribus; capite summo maculis discalibus cervinis extrorsum nigro marginatis notato, dorsi plumis quoque leviter striis rhachidalibus angustis ornatis: subtus gula cervina, corpore reliquo maculis elongatis discalibus utrinque nigro marginatis notato; subalaribus pallide cinnamomeis, remigibus (præter apices fuscos) quoque cinnamomeis: rostro albicante corneo, pedibus fuscis. Long. tota 8·7, alæ 4·1, caudæ 3·7, rostri a rictu 1·3, tarsi 0·8. (Descr. exempl. ex Jalapa, Mexico. Mus. nostr.)
♀ mari similis.

Hab. MEXICO [1], Valley of Mexico (*White* [7]), Alpine region of Vera Cruz [11], Omealca [12] (*Sumichrast*), Vera Cruz (*Sanchez*), Côfre de Perote (*M. Trujillo*), Jalapa [5][17] (*de Oca, Ferrari-Perez, F. D. G., Trujillo*), Cordova (*Sallé* [4]), Hueytamalco (*Ferrari-Perez* [16]), El Patio, Villa Alta (*Trujillo*), Totontepec (*Boucard* [6], *Trujillo*), Omilteme in the Sierra Madre del Sur, State of Guerrero (*Mrs. H. H. Smith*); GUATEMALA, Santa Maria and Chuipaché in Quezaltenango, Toliman (*W. B. Richardson*), Volcan de Fuego [9], Volcan de Agua, and Santa Barbara in Vera Paz (*O. S. & F. D. G.*); COSTA RICA, Dota, Barranca, and San José (*Carmiol* [10]), San Francisco (*Rogers*); PANAMA, Volcan de Chiriqui (*Arcé* [13]).

Picolaptes affinis, originally described by Lafresnaye from a Mexican specimen in the collection of Mons. C. Brelay [1], is now known to have a wide range over the highlands of Mexico and Central America from the State of Vera Cruz to the mountains of Costa Rica and Chiriqui. It also occurs on the uplands of the intervening country wherever the mountains attain a sufficient elevation, 4000 feet being about the lower limit of its vertical range. We note no appreciable variation in specimens from many points of its wide range, notwithstanding that this range must be interrupted in several places. In the lowlands of the same countries where *P. affinis* occurs, another species (*P. compressus*) takes its place. From that species it may readily be distinguished by the spots on the head being much shorter and bounded outwardly by black, and the streaks on the neck and upper back are not nearly so well defined; the marks, too, of the under surface are much more definite. The bill, too, is darker.

P. affinis is not uncommon in the oak-forests of the volcanoes of Guatemala at an altitude of from 6000 to 8000 feet above the sea.

3. Picolaptes compressus.

Picolaptes lineaticeps, Scl. P. Z. S. 1860, p. 252 (nec Lafr.) [1]; Cat. Am. B. p. 166 [2]; Salv. Ibis, 1861, p. 353 [3]; Lawr. Ann. Lyc. N. Y. ix. p. 107 [4]; Salvad. Atti Acc. Sc. Tor. iv. p. 179.

Picolaptes affinis, Scl. & Salv. Ibis, 1859, p. 117 [5]; Sumichrast, Mem. Bost. Soc. N. H. i. p. 555 (? partim) [6].

Thripobrotus compressus, Cab. J. f. Orn. 1861, p. 243 [7].

Picolaptes compressus, Lawr. Ann. Lyc. N. Y. ix. p. 107 [8]; Salv. Ibis, 1869, p. 314 [9]; P. Z. S. 1870, p. 193 [10]; Frantz. J. f. Orn. 1869, p. 305 [11]; Scl. & Salv. P. Z. S. 1870, p. 837 [12]; Boucard,

P. Z. S. 1878, p. 60 [13]; Nutting, Pr. U. S. Nat. Mus. v. p. 397 [14]; Ridgw. Pr. U. S. Nat. Mus. x. p. 590 [15]; Scl. Cat. Birds Brit. Mus. xv. p. 153 [16].

Dendrornis tenuirostris, Lawr. Ann. Lyc. N. Y. vii. p. 292 [17].

P. affini similis, sed capitis et dorsi antici striis multo magis distinctis, illis magis elongatis et utrinque nigro marginatis: subtus striis paulo minus obviis angustioribus. (Descr. maris ex Playa Vicente, Mexico. Mus. nostr.)

Hab. Mexico, Orizaba (*Sallé* [1]), San Lorenzo near Cordova, Orizaba and Alvarado (*F. Ferrari-Perez*), Playa Vicente (*Trujillo*), Rincon in Guerrero and Teapa in Tabasco (*Mrs. H. H. Smith*); British Honduras, Belize and Cayo on the Belize river (*Blancaneaux*); Guatemala, Pine-ridge of Poctum, Chisec, Volcan de Agua, Volcan de Fuego, El Baul [8], near Santa Lucia Cosamalguapa, Retalhuleu (*O. S. & F. D. G.* [16]); Salvador, Volcan de San Miguel (*W. B. Richardson*); Honduras, Puerto Cabello (*G. M. Whitely* [12]), Segovia River (*Townsend* [15]); Nicaragua, Chinandega (*W. B. Richardson*); Costa Rica, Navarro (*Boucard* [13]), La Palma (*Nutting* [14]), Bebedero Nicoya (*Arcé* [8]); Panama, Bugaba, Mina de Chorcha (*Arcé* [10]).

This species, at one time attributed to *P. lineaticeps*, Lafr. [1], at another confused with *P. affinis* [5], was ultimately described by Prof. Cabanis under its present title from Costa Rica specimens [7].

Its range extends over the lowlands of our country from the States of Vera Cruz and Guerrero in the north to the Colombian State of Panama, specimens from the various points of this wide area showing no appreciable differences.

P. compressus is essentially a bird of the lowland forests, its range in altitude probably not passing a height of about 2000 feet. In the uplands of the countries where it is found, as we have already remarked, *P. affinis* takes its place, there being no relationship or signs of transition between the two, though they have been not unfrequently confounded. From Sumichrast's remarks as to the range of the bird of Vera Cruz he calls *P. affinis*, we have little doubt that even he failed to distinguish them [6].

4. Picolaptes gracilis.

Picolaptes gracilis, Ridgw. Pr. U.S. Nat. Mus. xi. p. 542 [1]; Scl. Cat. Birds Brit. Mus. xv. p. 154 [2].

" Pileum, hind neck, back, scapulars, and wing-coverts light sepia-brown or bistre, but this broken, except on lower back, scapulars, and wing-coverts, with broad guttate mesial streaks of pale buff, bordered with blackish, the latter almost forming the ground-colour on top of the head. Tertials, greater part of secondaries and primaries (except basally, where more olivaceous), rump, upper tail-coverts, and tail plain chestnut or hazel, the terminal portion of inner webs of primaries dusky. Sides of head and neck pale buffy, streaked with brownish black or dusky brown; chin plain pale buffy; throat similar, but feathers narrowly bordered with dusky, producing a squamate appearance. Ground-colour of other underparts hair-brown, but this relieved by broad mesial streaks of buff, each margined laterally by a narrower but very distinct blackish streak; these markings, especially the blackish streaks, becoming nearly obsolete on belly, flanks, and under tail-coverts. Bill blackish, with basal half of lower mandible whitish; legs and feet dusky; 'iris black.'

" Length (skin), 7·10; wing, 3·55; tail, 3·60; the lateral feathers 1·05 shorter; exposed culmen, ·81; tarsus, ·85."

Hab. Costa Rica, Monte Redondo (*Zeledon* [1]).

" The only Central-American species at all closely related to the present one is *P. compressus*, Cab., which comes rather close in the coloration of the upper parts, which, however, are decidedly more rufescent ; but the lower parts are very decidedly different, the lighter markings being in *P. gracilis* much paler (buffy whitish instead of deep buff), and the blackish streaks much broader ; besides, *P. compressus* has the bill much longer, and light brown instead of mainly blackish." (*Ridgway, l. s. c.*[1])

The above is Mr. Ridgway's description of this distinct species, no specimen of it having as yet reached us.

XIPHORHYNCHUS.

Xiphorhynchus, Swainson, Zool. Journ. iii. p. 354 (1827) ; Chapman, Bull. Am. Mus. Nat. Hist. ii. p. 153 (5 July, 1889) ; Scl. Cat. Birds Brit. Mus. xv. p. 158.

The long arched bill possessed by all the members of this genus renders it easily recognized. It is, in fact, an exaggeration of the bill of *Picolaptes*, being much longer and more curved ; it is also compressed much more abruptly at and beyond the nostrils. In other respects *Xiphorhynchus* is structurally like *Dendrornis, Picolaptes*, &c.

Regarding the number of species contained in the genus, authorities differ. Mr. Sclater in his recent Catalogue admits six (including *X. pucherani*) ; Mr. Chapman (excluding *X. pucherani*) recognizes nine species. We have only been partially into the question of this difference of opinion, as we are now only concerned with two species ; but though we think that *X. trochilirostris* as understood by Mr. Sclater is perhaps too comprehensive a term, we are hardly disposed to carry its subdivision so far as Mr. Chapman. Questions of this nature can only be settled by an examination of very ample and well collected materials, and no sufficient number of specimens have been yet got together to make a satisfactory decision possible.

1. **Xiphorhynchus trochilirostris.**

Dendrocolaptes trochilirostris, Licht. Abh. Ak. Berl. 1820, p. 207, t. 3 [1] ; 1821, p. 263 [2].
Xiphorhynchus trochilirostris, Wied, Beitr. iii. p. 1140 (partim) [3] ; Scl. Cat. Birds Brit. Mus. xv. p. 159 [4].
Xiphorhynchus lafresnayanus, Lawr. Ann. Lyc. N. Y. vii. p. 292 (nec d'Orb.) [5].
Xiphorhynchus venezuelensis, Chapman, Bull. Am. Mus. N. H. ii. p. 156 [6].

Supra rufo-brunneus, uropygio, alis extus et cauda rubiginosis, pilei et cervicis plumis nigris stria rhachidali cervina, ad dorsum anticum angustioribus : subtus fusco-brunneus, plumis omnibus (abdomine et crisso exceptis) cervino-albido medialiter striatis, pectoris striis angustioribus, gulæ et cervicis latioribus nigricanti-fusco utrinque marginatis, subalaribus et remigibus intus (præter apices) cinnamomeis : rostro rubido, pedibus plumbeis. Long. tota 9·5, alæ 3·6, caudæ 3, rostri a rictu (chord) 2·7, tarsi 0·8. (Descr. exempl. ex Panama. Mus. nostr.)

♂ et ♀ similes.

Hab. Panama, Lion Hill (*M‘Leannan* [5]).—Colombia [6], Venezuela [6], and Eastern Brazil [1][4].

Mr. Chapman places the birds from Panama, called by Mr. Lawrence *X. lafresnayanus*, with the Venezuelan form of this species under the name of *X. venezuelensis*. Our single specimen, though rather small, also agrees with Venezuelan examples. But we are unable to distinguish these from other examples from Colombia (Bogota trade skins), or indeed from others from Bahia and Eastern Brazil, which we take to be the true *X. trochilirostris* of Lichtenstein. Mr. Chapman separates *X. venezuelensis* from *X. trochilirostris* by the longer bill of the former and the more distinct edges to the feathers of the throat, but the differences are very slight and we cannot think them of specific value.

X. trochilirostris just enters our fauna, and the only specimens obtained were shot by M‘Leannan at Lion Hill Station on the Panama Railway. Three of these he sent to Mr. Lawrence and one to us.

Salmon, who took a nest of this or a very nearly allied species at Remedios, in the Valley of the Cauca, Colombia, says the eggs are white and nearly round, and that the nest was placed inside a decayed tree which had been cut off about three feet from the ground and become hollow to the roots, so that the nest had no protection from the rain.

2. **Xiphorhynchus pusillus.** (Tab. XLVIII. fig. 2.)

Xiphorhynchus pusillus, Scl. P. Z. S. 1860, p. 278 [1]; Cat. Birds Brit. Mus. xv. p. 160 [2]; Salv. P. Z. S. 1870, p. 193 [3]; Boucard, P. Z. S. 1878, p. 60 [4]; Scl. & Salv. P. Z. S. 1879, p. 524 [5]; Chapman, Bull. Am. Mus. N. H. ii. p. 157 [6].

Supra saturate rufo-brunneus, alis paulo brunnescentioribus, cauda saturate castanea, uropygio rufescentiore; pileo et cervice postica nigris striis rhachidalibus cervinis notatis : subtus brunneus, gutture, pectore et abdomine antico striis rhachidalibus cervinis ornatis, iis ad gulam majoribus, iis ad abdomen angustioribus; subcaudalibus et remigibus intus (præter apices fuscos) cinnamomeis : rostro corneo haud rubido, pedibus plumbeo-nigricantibus. Long. tota 10·0, alæ 3·8, caudæ 3·5, rostri a rictu 2·3, tarsi 0·8. (Descr. maris ex Boquete de Chitra, Panama. Mus. nostr.)

Hab. Costa Rica (*Endres* [2]), Naranjo (*Boucard* [4]); Panama, Chiriqui, Chitrá, Boquete de Chitrá [3] (*Arcé*).—Colombia [1][5].

This species may be readily distinguished from *X. trochilirostris* by the colour of the bill, which is horn-colour, without any of the red tint so conspicuous a feature in the allied form. The wings and tail are also much darker, but this character is more apparent in specimens from Central America than in the type and other southern examples.

X. pusillus was described by Mr. Sclater from a trade skin of Bogota make [1]. Other examples have reached us from that country, and we have received many from our collector Arcé from the neighbourhood of Chiriqui, and the bird has been found by several travellers in Costa Rica. Beyond this State it has not yet been traced.

b. *Rostrum plerumque magis rectum, latum, depressum, ad apicem hamatum.*

DENDROCOLAPTES.

Dendrocolaptes, Hermann, Obs. Zool. p. 135 (1804) ; Scl. Cat. Birds Brit. Mus. xv. p. 169.

Dendrocolaptes belongs strictly to the same subfamily, Dendrocolaptinæ, as *Dendrornis* and its allies, as it has the same structure of wings, tail, and feet, as well as the open oval nostrils of those birds. Its difference lies in the form of the bill, which is much wider at the base and not compressed ; the culmen curves slightly towards the tip, where it bends rather abruptly to form a distinct hook to the maxilla, and there is a slight notch near the end of the tomia.

Some difference of opinion prevails as to the number of species contained in *Dendrocolaptes*, Mr. Sclater admitting nine, *D. intermedius* of Count Berlepsch being unknown to him. Of these, three occur within our borders, the commonest of which, *D. sanctithomæ*, is found from British Honduras to the State of Panama and passes beyond into Colombia. Another, *D. puncticollis*, occurs on higher ground in Guatemala and Costa Rica. The third is the South-American *D. validus*, which penetrates our country as far as Costa Rica, and has an extensive range in the northern portion of the Southern continent.

1. **Dendrocolaptes puncticollis.**

Dendrocops multistrigatus, Scl. & Salv. Ibis, 1860, p. 275 [1].
Dendrocolaptes multistrigatus, Scl. Cat. Am. B. p. 162 [2].
Dendrocolaptes puncticollis, Scl. & Salv. P. Z. S. 1868, p. 54, t. 5 [3] ; Scl. Cat. Birds Brit. Mus. xv. p. 171 [4].

Supra olivaceo-brunneus, tectricibus supracaudalibus, alis extus et cauda rubiginosis, tectricibus alarum dorso concoloribus, capite summo nigro cum cervice postica et dorso antico obsolete striis rhachidalibus cervinis notatis : subtus pallidior, plumis omnibus a gula usque ad pectus medialiter albidis fusco marginatis, striis ad pectus angustioribus, abdomine et crisso transversim fusco-nigro vittatis, subalaribus et remigibus (præter apices fuscos) cinnamomeis, illis fusco variegatis ; rostro corneo, mandibula pallidiore, pedibus plumbeis. Long. tota 10·5, alæ 5·2, caudæ 4·5, rostri a rictu 1·65, tarsi 1·05. (Descr. exempl. typ. ex Tactic, Guatemala. Mus. nostr.)

Hab. GUATEMALA, Tactic, San Gerónimo (*O. S. & F. D. G.* [1][3]).

A near ally of the Brazilian *D. picumnus*, from which it may be distinguished by its more rufous wings, narrower shaft-stripes on the head, neck, and under surface, and by its larger paler bill.

We know very little of this species in Guatemala, and the two specimens, one from Tactic and one from San Gerónimo, which served as the types are the only ones we have seen from that country. They were both shot at an elevation of about 4500 feet above the sea, the San Gerónimo bird in the pine-woods covering the hills skirting the plain of Salama, and the Tactic bird in the hilly country of Alta Vera Paz, also covered at intervals with pine-forest.

2. Dendrocolaptes validus.

Dendrocolaptes validus, Tsch. Fauna Per. p. 242, t. 21. f. 2 [1]; Scl. & Salv. P. Z. S. 1866, p. 184 [2]; 1879, p. 523 [3]; Scl. Cat. Birds Brit. Mus. xv. p. 172 [4].

Dendrocolaptes multistrigatus, Eyton, Contr. Orn. 1851, p. 75 [5]; Lawr. Ann. Lyc. N. Y. ix. pp. 106, 146 [6]; Frautz. J. f. Orn. 1869, p. 305 [7].

Dendrocolaptes puncticollis, Lawr. Ann. Lyc. N. Y. ix. p. 146 (nec Scl. & Salv.) [8]; Boucard, P. Z. S. 1878, p. 60 [9]; Ridgw. Pr. U.S. Nat. Mus. xi. p. 545 [10].

D. puncticolli similis, sed abdomine toto usque ad pectus transversim nigro distincte striato; striis pectoralibus utrinque nigro irregulariter marginatis distinguendus. Long. tota 11·0, alæ 5·0, caudæ 4·5, rostri a rictu 1·4, tarsi 1·1. (Descr. feminæ ex Naranjo, Costa Rica. Mus. Boucard.)

Hab. Costa Rica, Navarro (*J. Cooper* [6 7 10]), Naranjo (*Boucard* [9]); Panama (*mus. nostr.* [4]).—Colombia [3]; Ecuador; E. Peru [1]; Venezuela [2] and Upper Amazons [2].

Through M. Boucard's kindness we have been able to examine one of the specimens of this *Dendrocolaptes* obtained by him at Naranjo in Costa Rica during his expedition to that country in 1877. We find that it agrees fairly with a specimen in our collection, said to be from Panama, which Mr. Sclater in his Catalogue decided to belong to the South-American *D. validus* of Tschudi; the latter, however, is rather more rufescent in the general tint of its plumage. The Costa Rica bird has been called *D. multistrigatus*, Eyton [6] (now proved to be a synonym of *D. validus*), and subsequently referred to the Guatemalan *D. puncticollis* [8], but we cannot find that specimens from the two countries have been compared.

Compared with the last-named bird, *D. validus* presents several points of difference, to which attention is drawn above. *D. validus*, however, varies considerably both in the clearness of its markings and the intensity of its colour, but we doubt the possibility of our being able to distinguish any definite races of the species as a whole. The Central-American birds agree very closely with a Venezuelan specimen in our collection and are hardly so strongly marked as examples from other places.

Salmon, who found a nest of this species, describes it as placed in a hole in a tree, and the eggs as white and two in number [3]. The birds shot by M. Boucard were busy with their nest in a hole in a tree [9].

3. Dendrocolaptes sancti-thomæ.

Dendrocops sancti-thomæ, Lafr. Rev. Zool. 1852, p. 466 [1].

Dendrocolaptes sancti-thomæ, Scl. P. Z. S. 1858, p. 96 [2]; 1859, p. 54 [3]; Cat. Birds Brit. Mus. xv.
p. 174 [4]; Scl. & Salv. Ibis, 1859, p. 118 [5]; P. Z. S. 1864, p. 355 [6]; 1868, p. 56 [7]; Lawr.
Ann. Lyc. N. Y. vii. p. 320 [8]; viii. p. 181 [9]; ix. p. 106 [10]; Salv. P. Z. S. 1867, p. 144 [11];
1870, p. 193 [12]; Frantz. J. f. Orn. 1869, p. 305 [13]; Wyatt, Ibis, 1871, p. 331 [14]; Boucard,
P. Z. S. 1878, p. 60 [15]; Nutting, Pr. U. S. Nat. Mus. vi. p. 385 [16]; Ridgw. Pr. U. S. Nat.
Mus. x. p. 589 [17].

Supra olivaceo-brunneus, capite fulvescente, dorso postico, alis extus et cauda rubiginosis, pileo, cervice et dorso
antico cum scapularibus frequenter nigro transfasciatis: subtus cervinus, mento grisescente, pectore
saturatiore, undique nigro frequenter transfasciatis, subalaribus cervinis nigro variegatis, remigibus intus
(præter apices fuscos) cinnamomeis: rostro nigricanti-corneo, mandibula basi pallida, pedibus obscure
corylinis. Long. tota 10·0, alæ 4·5, caudæ 4·3, rostri a rictu 1·65, tarsi 1·05. (Descr. exempl. ex
Orange Walk, British Honduras. Mus. nostr.)

Hab. MEXICO (*fide Verreaux* [2]); BRITISH HONDURAS, Orange Walk (*Gaumer*), Belize
(*Leyland, Blancaneaux*); GUATEMALA, Vera Paz (*O. S. & F. D. G.*); HONDURAS,
Omoa (*Leyland* [3]), Segovia River (*Townsend* [17]); NICARAGUA, Greytown (*Holland*),
Sucuyá (*Nutting* [16]), Momotombo (*W. B. Richardson*); COSTA RICA, San José [10],
Aguacate Mountains [13] (*v. Frantzius*), Navarro (*Boucard* [15]), Tucurriqui (*Arcé* [4]);
PANAMA, Bugaba [12], Santiago de Veraguas [11] (*Arcé*), Lion Hill (*M'Leannan* [6] [8]).—
COLOMBIA [14].

Though a rare bird in British Honduras and Guatemala, and probably very locally
distributed, this species becomes much more common in Costa Rica and the State of
Panama, whence a number of specimens have been sent us; but of its habits little has
been recorded, and we never actually met with the bird ourselves.

Compared with *D. puncticollis*, *D. sancti-thomæ* may easily be distinguished by the
transverse black bands which cover the head, upper back, and under surface, *D. puncticollis* being striped longitudinally except on the abdomen. It belongs to the larger
section of the genus, its near allies being *D. certhia* and *D. radiatus*, but from both it
may be known by the distinct character of the bars on the under surface.

Lafresnaye's name, *D. sancti-thomæ*, was suggested by his specimen being stated to
have come from the island of St. Thomas; no doubt the small sea-port town of Santo
Tomas in Honduras, situated near Omoa, was really its origin.

The occurrence of *D. sancti-thomæ* in Mexico rests on the authority of a skin said
to be from that country which was submitted to Mr. Sclater for examination by
MM. Verreaux in 1858. As neither M. Sallé nor M. Boucard nor any of the collectors
who have more recently collected in Southern Mexico have met with this bird, its
occurrence in Mexico requires confirmation.

Fam. FORMICARIIDÆ.

In Mr. Sclater's recently published catalogue of this family (Cat. Birds Brit. Mus. xv. pp. 176–328) we find the names of 254 species given in the body of the work, and, in addition to these, 37 other names are mentioned in footnotes as belonging to birds with which the author was not acquainted. The total number of species in the family, therefore, may be taken at about 300. Of these 52 occur within our limits, belonging to 19 genera. By far the larger proportion of these species belong to the southern section of our fauna, *i. e.* that lying between Nicaragua and the Isthmus of Darien. In the more northern section the number of species rapidly diminishes until we find but a single species, *Thamnophilus doliatus*, ranging beyond the State of Vera Cruz, and none on the western side of Mexico beyond the State of Guerrero. The same diminution of numbers is found towards the southern limit of the range of the family, only four species being found in the Argentine Republic. A great concentration of species takes place in the Amazons Valley, especially in the upper or western portion of that vast district; Guiana, too, is very rich.

Regarding the classification of the Formicariidæ, we are met with the same difficulties that we encountered when dealing with the Dendrocolaptidæ and some of the preceding families, and this chiefly affects the recognition of subfamilies.

Though we adhere pretty nearly to the sequence of the genera as set forth in Mr. Sclater's recently published system, and we also divide the family into two main groups, we arrange the genera under these sections differently and define them by different characters. One of these sections contains the tree and bush frequenting genera, most of which have comparatively short tarsi. The other contains the terrestrial birds, some of which (comprised in the genera *Gymnopithys*, *Gymnocichla*, *Myrmeciza*, *Hypocnemis*, &c.) follow the hordes of foraging ants (*Eciton*) and feed on the insects started from their path. The others are more solitary in their habits, and are usually found singly on the ground in the deepest parts of the forest. We have used small characters which fairly define these groups, but our knowledge of the habits of these birds and of their internal structure is so fragmentary that many modifications of their arrangement will have to be made before a settled system is established.

Of the nests and eggs of the members of this family little is yet known, and we are chiefly indebted to the late T. K. Salmon for the scanty knowledge we possess. From his notes we gather that probably all the species make their nests in trees or bushes, and this applies even to the birds that pass most of their time on the ground. The nests are often hanging structures, suspended in a forked branch near the extremity of a bough. The eggs are very varied, some being white (*Myrmotherula*), some white and thickly spotted (*Thamnophilus*), some creamy white sparsely spotted (*Dysithamnus*), some mahogany colour with darker shades of the same (*Cercomacra*), while *Grallaria* lays rich dark greenish-blue eggs, very different, apparently, from the others.

All the species feed on insects, which they capture amongst the foliage or branches of trees or pick from amongst the fallen débris on the ground. The statement that the food of many species of Formicariidæ consists largely of ants, is open to question, and the late Thomas Belt, we think, satisfactorily explains how this observation has arisen. In writing of the habits of the various species of *Eciton* found in Nicaragua ('The Naturalist in Nicaragua,' p. 20) he says:—"Several species of Ant-Thrushes (*i. e.* Formicariidæ) always accompany the army ants in the forest. They do not, however, feed on the ants, but on the insects they disturb. Besides the Ant-Thrushes, Trogons, Creepers, and a variety of other birds are often seen in the branches of trees above where an ant army is foraging below, pursuing and catching the insects as they fly up."

A. *Arboricolæ: tarsi plerumque breves.*

a. *Nares omnino apertæ, rostrum quam caput vix longior.*

a'. *Vibrissæ vix obviæ, tarsi undique scutellati.*

a''. *Rostrum robustum, valde hamatum.*

a'''. *Rostrum minime compressum.*

CYMBILANIUS.

Cymbilanius, Gray, List Gen. Birds, p. 36 (1840) ; Scl. Cat. Birds Brit. Mus. xv. p. 178.

This genus contains a single species, distinguished by its comparatively short, thick, tumid bill, which is wider at the base than that of *Thamnophilus* and not compressed ; the terminal hook of the maxilla is very pronounced, and is preceded by a very deep notch, the rest of the tomia being nearly straight ; the mandible has also a well-marked notch near the end and a wide indentation in the tomia just before it. The culmen curves slightly from the base until it descends rapidly to form the terminal hook ; the gonys ascends rather abruptly. The nostrils are quite open, slightly oval, the frontal feathers just reaching the proximal end of the opening. The tarsi are covered, both in front and behind, with well-defined scutella ; the claws are short, strongly curved, and compressed. The distribution of the genus is that of the species which follows.

1. Cymbilanius lineatus.

Lanius lineatus, Leach, Zool. Misc. i. p. 20, t. 6 (1815) [1].

Cymbilanius lineatus, Gray, List Gen. Birds, p. 36 (1840) [2] ; Lawr. Ann. Lyc. N. Y. vii. p. 293 [3];

ix. p. 107[4]; Scl. & Salv. P. Z. S. 1864, p. 355[5]; 1879, p. 524[6]; Salv. P. Z. S. 1867, p. 144[7]; 1870, p. 194[8]; Scl. Cat. Birds Brit. Mus. xv. p. 178[9].

Cymbilanius lineatus fasciatus, Ridgw. Pr. U. S. Nat. Mus. vi. pp. 404[10], 415[11]; Zeledon, An. Mus. Nac. Costa Rica, 1887, p. 114[12].

Thamnophilus nigricristatus, Bouc. P. Z. S. 1878, p. 60[13].

Supra niger, albo (præter pileum) tenuiter transfasciatus : subtus omnino frequenter et æqualiter nigro et albo transfasciatus ; subalaribus quoque fasciatis, remigibus internis in pogonio interno irregulariter albo marginatis: rostro et pedibus nigricanti-plumbeis, illius mandibula pallidiore. Long. tota 6·5, alæ 3·0, caudæ rectr. med. 2·75, rectr. lat. 1·9, rostri a rictu 1·0. (Descr. maris ex Calobre, Panama. Mus. nostr.)

♀ supra nigra cum alis et cauda ochraceo transfasciatis, pileo castaneo: subtus pallide ochracea, gula albicante undique (medialiter tenuiter, lateraliter late) nigro transfasciata. (Descr. feminæ ex Panama. Mus. nostr.)

Hab. NICARAGUA, Los Sabalos (*Nutting*[10]); COSTA RICA, Angostura (*Carmiol*[4]), Rio Sucio (*J. Cooper*[11]), Jimenez (*Zeledon*[12]), San Carlos (*Boucard*[13]); PANAMA, Mina de Chorcha[8], Calovevora[8], Calobre[8], Santiago de Veraguas[7], Santa Fé[7] (*Arcé*), Lion Hill (*McLeannan*[3][5]).—SOUTH AMERICA, from Colombia[6] to Peru, Amazons Valley, and Guiana[1][9].

A species of wide range, extending over the whole of the Amazons Valley, and thence northwards to the Caribbean Sea, and westwards to Panama, where it enters the isthmus, and spreads through Central America as far as Nicaragua. Here Mr. Nutting met with it at Los Sabalos and obtained two specimens[10]. These, with others from Costa Rica and Panama, Mr. Ridgway proposed to separate from the bird of Guiana under the name of *C. lineatus fasciatus*[10]. Our series of specimens does not show any grounds for this suggestion, for both males and females from Central America can be exactly matched by others from Guiana and other parts of the southern range of the species. Individuals vary in the width of the white bands, both of the upper and under surfaces of the body; but this variation is to be found everywhere, and we have no doubt is due to the age of the birds, those with narrower bands being the older. In some examples the crown of the head also shows transverse bands, but in general the crown is pure black.

C. lineatus was first described in 1815 by Leach[1], who placed it in the genus *Lanius*. It was transferred by Vieillot to *Thamnophilus*, and to *Cymbilanius* by Gray[2], where it remained a monotype without a synonym till Mr. Ridgway's attempt to divide it a few years ago.

Little has been recorded of the habits of this bird. Mr. Nutting says that it has a clear note, but without variation, and that its iris is red[10]. The latter character it shares with the larger *Thamnophili*, such as *T. transandeanus*. It appears to be an inhabitant of the dense tropical forest, wherever that is found within the limits of its range. Its food, according to Salmon, consists of insects[6].

b'''. Rostrum compressum.

THAMNOPHILUS.

Thamnophilus, Vieill. Anal. p. 40 (1816); Scl. Cat. Birds Brit. Mus. xv. p. 180.

Thamnophilus is by far the largest genus of the Formicariidæ, containing between sixty and seventy species, according to Mr. Sclater, of which fifty-five were more or less known to him. These are distributed over the whole area of the family, which is represented both in the extreme northern and southern limits by members of the genus. In Mexico and Central America nine species occur, of which two only reach Southern Mexico and Guatemala, the rest all belong to the southern section of our fauna.

Mr. Sclater divides *Thamnophilus* into six sections, basing their characters upon size and the colour of their plumage.

The first Section A, represented by the great *T. leachi*, is not found within our area, but the other five sections are all present.

Whether all these sections should be merged under *Thamnophilus* is a doubtful question, a revision of them would probably result in the recognition of several genera. For them many names are available, proposed at various times, chiefly by Reichenbach and by Cabanis and Heine. *T. doliatus* is usually considered the type of *Thamno-philus*. Its plumage is soft and lax, the bill smooth, the culmen slightly curved till it descends rather abruptly to a well-marked but not very prominent hook, before which, at the end of the tomia, is a moderately deep notch; the tomia of the mandible has also a small subterminal notch; the tomia of both maxilla and mandible is nearly straight, but the gonys of the latter ascends in a gradual curve; the tarsi have well-defined scutella, both in front and behind; the claws are short and curved, and have deep grooves on both inner and outer lateral surfaces. The tail is moderate and rounded, and the wings short and rounded, the fourth to the eighth primaries subequal, third = tenth, the first much the shortest, the second halfway between the first and third.

T. melanocrissus, belonging to Mr. Sclater's Section B, has much less soft plumage, the bill is more compressed, larger in proportion, and with the terminal hook and subterminal notches well developed; the wings are similarly shaped to those of *T. doliatus*, but the tail is longer in proportion. The colour of the plumage is pure white beneath, black above in the male, brown in the female. *T. bridgesi* of Section D, besides its differently coloured plumage, has a differently shaped wing, the second primary being much longer than in *T. doliatus*, falling little short of the third and fifth, and the fourth the longest in the wing; the tail, too, is longer in proportion to the wing than that of *T. doliatus*. *T. atrinucha* (Section D) has soft plumage like *T. doliatus*, but differs chiefly in its style of colour being grey and black, but without transverse bars; the male, too, has the white concealed dorsal spot so frequently present in other Formicariidæ. *T. punctatus*, a representative of Section C, has plumage like that of

T. bridgesi, so far as texture goes ; the tail, too, is long ; the wings are more rounded, resembling those of *T. doliatus* ; and the tarsi are covered like that type. *Thamnophilus immaculatus* is also referred to this section, but we think it best removed from *Thamnophilus* altogether as we explain elsewhere. Section E is represented by *T. pulchellus*, which just enters our limits.

α. *Majores: rostrum robustum profunde uncinatnm ; ptilosis bicolor, infra alba, supra in mare nigra, in femina castanea ; alæ rotundatæ.*

1. **Thamnophilus melanocrissus.**

Thamnophilus melanurus?, Scl. P. Z. S. 1857, p. 203 (nec Gould)[1] ; 1859, pp. 57[2], 383[3] ; Scl. & Salv. Ibis, 1859, p. 119[4].

Thamnophilus melanocrissus, Scl. P. Z. S. 1860, p. 252[5] ; Cat. Birds Brit. Mus. xv. p. 184[6] ; Salv. Ibis, 1866, p. 203[7] ; Sumichrast, Mem. Bost. Soc. N. H. i. p. 556[8] ; La Nat. v. p. 248[9] ; Scl. & Salv. P. Z. S. 1870, p. 837[10] ; Nutting, Pr. U. S. Nat. Mus. vi. p. 405[11] ; Ridgw. Pr. U. S. Nat. Mus. xiv. p. 471[12].

Thamnophilus hollandi, Lawr. Ann. Lyc. N. Y. viii. p. 181 (cf. Salv. Ibis, 1874, p. 310)[13].

Supra nigerrimus ; tectricum alarum apicibus macula dorsali celata et corpore subtus albis ; tibiis, subalaribus et remigibus internis in pogonio interno albis ; subcaudalibus nigris ; cauda omnino nigra : rostro et pedibus nigris. Long. tota 7·5, alæ 3·6, caudæ rectr. med. 3·0, rectr. lat. 2·4, rostri a rictu 1·2, tarsi 1·3.

♀ supra cum alis, cauda et subcaudalibus castaneis, corpore reliquo subtus albo, rostro et pedibus nigris. (Descr. maris et feminæ ex Playa Vicente, Mexico. Mus. nostr.)

Hab. MEXICO, Orizaba[5] and Santecomapam[1] (*Sallé*), Playa Vicente (*Boucard*[3], *Trujillo*), hot region of Vera Cruz[8], Omealca[9] (*Sumichrast*), Teapa (*Mrs. H. H. Smith*) ; GUATEMALA, Choctum, Chisec (*O. S. & F. D. G.*) ; HONDURAS, Omoa (*Leyland*[2][4]), San Pedro (*G. M. Whitely*[10]), San Pedro Sula (*Wittkugel*[12]) ; NICARAGUA, Los Sabalos (*Nutting*[11]), Greytown (*Holland*[12]).

This species, *T. transandeanus*, and *T. melanurus* are very close allies, and can only be distinguished with any certainty by the colour of the under tail-coverts. These feathers in *T. melanocrissus* are black ; in *T. transandeanus* they have white tips, and in *T. melanurus* the exposed portion is wholly white. This is the rule with the colour of these feathers in these birds, but it is, as might be expected, not always easy to recognize the species. Thus a specimen, apparently adult, from Teapa, has a slight white edging to the under tail-coverts, and might, for this reason, be called *T. transandeanus* were it not for the locality whence it came.

The most southern place where *T. melanocrissus* has been found is Greytown in Nicaragua, whence Mr. Holland sent specimens[12]. It is true that these were described by Mr. Lawrence as *T. hollandi* ; but Salvin, who examined the types in 1874[13], considered them to be indistinguishable from *T. melanocrissus*, notwithstanding their somewhat large size. Mr. Nutting obtained examples in the same country, which were referred, without comment, to the northern bird by Mr. Ridgway[11]. Its range northwards from Nicaragua extends along the eastern sea-board, as far as the middle of the

Mexican State of Vera Cruz. We have no record of it from any point on the western side of the Cordillera.

Mr. Nutting found this bird rather common at Los Sabalos in Nicaragua, where it frequented some freshly burnt forest and fed on the insects found there. He did not hear its note, but remarked that the iris in life is red [11].

2. Thamnophilus transandeanus.

Thamnophilus transandeanus, Scl. P. Z. S. 1855, p. 18 [1]; Cat. Birds Brit. Mus. xv. p. 185 [2];
　　　Cassin, Pr. Ac. Phil. 1860, p. 188 [3]; Lawr. Ann. Lyc. N. Y. vii. p. 293 [4]; Scl. & Salv.
　　　P. Z. S. 1864, p. 355 [5]; 1879, p. 524 [6]; Salv. P. Z. S. 1867, p. 144 [7]; Zeledon, An. Mus.
　　　Nac. Costa Rica, 1887, p. 114 [8].
Thamnophilus melanurus?, Scl. P. Z. S. 1856, p. 142 (nec Gould) [9].
Thamnophilus melanocrissus, Lawr. Ann. Lyc. N. Y. ix. p. 107 (nec Scl.) [10].

T. melanocrisso persimilis, sed tectricibus subcaudalibus distincte albo marginatis forsan distinguendus.

Hab. Costa Rica, Tucurriqui (*Arcé* [10]), Jimenez, Las Trojas, Pacuare (*Zeledon* [8]);
　　　Panama, David (*Bridges* [7] [9]), Mina de Chorcha (*Arcé*), Lion Hill (*M'Leannan* [4] [5]),
　　　Turbo (*Wood* [3]).—Colombia [2]; Ecuador [1] [2].

This race seems to be the prevailing one in Costa Rica and Panama, as all the specimens from those countries that we have seen have the white edging to the under tail-coverts. The species was first described by Mr. Sclater from a specimen from Guayaquil sent to the British Museum by Mr. G. Barclay [1]. Other examples have reached us from Ecuador, and Salmon found it in the Cauca Valley of Colombia [6]. It would thus appear that the bird has a somewhat limited range, extending along the countries bordering the Pacific, from Costa Rica to Guayaquil, and doubtless to the southern extremity of the forest region of the western side of the Andes of Ecuador. Salmon noted the iris in life as red [6], in which respect *T. transandeanus* agrees with *T. melanocrissus* and with *Cymbilanius lineatus*.

β. *Minor: rostrum debilius, ptilosis plerumque nigra; alæ rotundatæ; sexus similes.*

3. Thamnophilus punctatus. (Tab. XLIX. fig. 1.)

Thamnophilus punctatus, Cab. J. f. Orn. 1861, p. 241 [1]; Salv. Ibis, 1870, p. 110 [2]; P. Z. S. 1870,
　　　p. 194 [3]; Zeledon, An. Mus. Nac. Costa Rica, 1887, p. 114 [4]; Scl. Cat. Birds Brit. Mus.
　　　xv. p. 191 [5].

Supra niger, macula dorsali celata alba; tectricibus alarum puncto terminali albo notatis: subtus niger, abdo-
　　　mine et hypochondriis saturate cinereis, subalaribus et remigibus interioribus intus albis; cauda nigra,
　　　rectrice extima albo terminata: rostro et pedibus nigris. Long. tota 6·5, alæ 3·0, caudæ rectr. med. 2·95,
　　　rectr. lat. 2·2, rostri a rictu 0·9, tarsi 0·9. (Descr. maris ex Bugaba, Panama. Mus. nostr.)
♀ mari similis, macula dorsali celata vix ulla, abdomine cinerascentiore. (Descr. feminæ ex Mina de Chorcha,
　　　Panama. Mus. nostr.)

Hab. Costa Rica (*Hoffmann* [1], *Carmiol* [2]), Las Trojas, Pozo Azul de Pirris (*Zeledon* [4]);
　　　Panama, Volcan de Chiriqui, Bugaba, Mina de Chorcha (*Arcé* [3]).

T. punctatus was described by Dr. Cabanis from a specimen sent from Costa Rica by Dr. Hoffmann, and made the type of a group *Abalius*[1]. The species, however, appears to be rare in that country, as only a single specimen has reached us, and Mr. Zeledon had none before him when he compiled his first catalogues of the birds of Costa Rica; but the National Museum of Costa Rica now contains several examples[4]. In the portion of the State of Panama adjoining Costa Rica this bird would seem to be more numerous, as Arcé found it in some numbers in the neighbourhood of Chiriqui[3], and all but the Costa Rican example already mentioned which have come before us are from his collections.

Nothing has been recorded of the habits of this species, which is doubtless a denizen of the dense forest of the countries in which it is found.

γ. *Minor: rostrum debile; ptilosis plerumque saturate cinerea albo striata; alæ magis elongatæ, remige secundo longiore; sexus similes.*

4. **Thamnophilus bridgesi.** (Tab. XLIX. fig. 2.)

Thamnophilus bridgesi, Scl. P. Z. S. 1856, p. 141[1]; Cat. Birds Brit. Mus. xv. p. 194[2]; Salv. P. Z. S. 1867, p. 144[3]; 1870, p. 194[4]; Lawr. Ann. Lyc. N. Y. ix. p. 107[5]; Zeledon, An. Mus. Nac. Costa Rica, 1887, p. 114[6].

Supra fusco-cinereus; capite nigro striis rhachidalibus albis notato; alis fusco-nigricantibus, tectricibus puncto albo terminatis: subtus pallidior, gutture, pectore et abdomine striis rhachidalibus latis albis ornatis, subcaudalibus quoque indistincte striatis; cauda fusco-nigra, rectrice extima utrinque albo terminata; subalaribus et remigibus internis intus albis: rostro et pedibus nigris. Long. tota 6·0, alæ 2·8, caudæ rectr. med. 2·6, rectr. lat. 2·1, rostri a rictu 0·95, tarsi 0·9. (Descr. maris ex Bugaba, Panama. Mus. nostr.)

♀ mari similis, sed colore fusco-cinereo dilutiore.

Hab. COSTA RICA, San Mateo (*J. Cooper*[5]), Las Trojas, Pozo Azul de Pirris (*Zeledon*[6]); PANAMA, David (*Bridges*[1]), Mina de Chorcha[4], Bugaba[4], and Bibalaz (*Arcé*).

This *Thamnophilus* has no near allies, the white stripes covering the whole head and the under surface of the body rendering it distinct from all the other members of the genus except *T. nigriceps*, which again is reddish brown where *T. bridgesi* is dark grey and has the wings and tail chestnut.

It was first described by Mr. Sclater in 1856, in his paper on Bridges's collection made near David in the State of Panama[1]. Arcé subsequently procured us several specimens near the same place[4], and it has also been traced to Costa Rica[5][6].

Bridges stated that he found only one individual of this bird in the thick bush on the margin of the river near David[1]. This he shot, and this is the specimen described by Mr. Sclater, and is now in the gallery of the British Museum.

5. **Thamnophilus virgatus.**

Thamnophilus, sp. ?, Cassin, Pr. Ac. Phil. 1860, p. 189, no. 89[1].
Thamnophilus virgatus, Lawr. Pr. Ac. Phil. 1868, p. 361[2].

Supra saturate cinnamomeus, alis extus et cauda concoloribus ; capite toto et cervice nigris, plumis omnibus stria rhachidali alba notatis : pectore et abdomine cinereo-fuscis, plumis quoque obscuriore et latiore albido striatis ; ventre imo et tectricibus subcaudalibus rufescentibus ; subalaribus et remigibus intus cinamomeis : rostro nigricanti-plumbeo, mandibula pallidiore, pedibus plumbeis. Long. tota 6·0, alæ 3·0, caudæ 2·4, tarsi 1·0. (Descr. exempl. typ. ex Colombia. Mus. Brit.)

Hab. Panama, Turbo (*Lieut. Michler* [1] [2]).

The type of this species has been kindly sent to us from Philadelphia, it being the property of the Academy of Natural Science of that city. It is in poor condition, the bill being much injured. The species is closely allied to *Thamnophilus nigriceps*, Scl. (*cf.* Cat. Birds Brit. Mus. xv. p. 194, t. 12), and indeed before we placed the types together we were under the impression that they belonged to one species. Compared with *T. nigriceps* the wings and tail of *T. virgatus* are clearer cinnamon, the shaft-stripes of the head considerably wider, the head thus being not nearly so dark ; the stripes, too, of the under surface are wider and more numerous on the abdomen instead of being confined to the central portion ; the under surface of the wings and inner edge of the quills are cinnamon and not fawn-colour, as in *T. nigriceps*.

The two birds are peculiar in their style of plumage, and unlike any other members of the genus *Thamnophilus*. In their striated head and neck they resemble *T. bridgesi*, but that bird has no cinnamon colour in its plumage.

The only known example of this bird is the type, which was obtained during Lieut. Michler's Expedition to Darien. Cassin did not give it a name in his list of the birds, but Mr. Lawrence described it in 1868.

δ. *Minimus: rostrum debile ; ptilosis cinerea ; alæ rotundatæ, remigibus albo limbatis ; tectricibus albo maculatis ; sexus dissimiles.*

6. **Thamnophilus atrinucha,** sp. n.

Thamnophilus nævius (nec Gm.), Cassin, Pr. Ac. Phil. 1860, p. 188 [1] ; Scl. & Salv. P. Z. S. 1864, p. 355 [2] ; 1879, p. 524 [3] ; Lawr. Ann. Lyc. N. Y. ix. p. 107 [4] ; Salv. P. Z. S. 1867, p. 144 [5] ; Boucard, P. Z. S. 1878, p. 60 [6] ; Ridgw. Pr. U. S. Nat. Mus. x. p. 590 [7] ; Tacz. Orn. Pér. ii. p. 8 [8] ; Zeledon, An. Mus. Nac. Costa Rica, 1887, p. 114 [9] ; Scl. Cat. Birds Brit. Mus. xv. p. 197 (partim) [10].

Thamnophilus amazonicus, Lawr. Ann. Lyc. N. Y. vii. p. 325 (nec Scl.) [11].

Cinereus, pileo et dorso medio nigris, hoc plaga magna celata alba notato ; alis nigris extrorsum cinereo limbatis, tectricibus alarum et caudæ superioribus nigris distincte albo terminatis ; cauda nigra, rectricibus omnibus albo terminatis, rectrice extima utrinque quoque macula mediana in pogonio externo notata : subtus dilutiore cinereus, subalaribus et remigibus internis intus albis : rostro et pedibus nigris. Long. tota 5·5, alæ 2·7, caudæ rectr. med. 2·15, rectr. lat. 1·8, rostri a rictu 0·9, tarsi 0·9.

♀ brunnea, capite rufescente macula dorsali celata alba, alarum marginibus et maculis tectricum terminalibus cervinis ; rectricibus cervino-albido terminatis, externis utrinque macula mediana in pogonio externo ejusdem coloris ; subtus multo pallidior, gula grisescente. (Descr. maris et feminæ ex Panama. Mus. nostr.)

Hab. Honduras, Puerto Caballo and Medina (*G. M. Whitely* [10]), Segovia river (*Townsend* [7]) ; Costa Rica, Angostura and Pacuare (*Carmiol* [4], *Zeledon* [9]), San Carlos

(*Boucard* [6]); PANAMA, Santiago de Veraguas (*Arcé* [5]), Lion Hill (*M‘Leannan* [2] [11]), Chepo (*Arcé* [10]), R. Truando (*Wood* [1]).—SOUTH AMERICA, Colombia [3] and Western Ecuador [10].

The typical form of this bird, the true *Thamnophilus nœvius*, is from Cayenne, and compared with specimens from British Guiana the Central American bird is a little darker with rather more black on the middle of the back and nape; the female, too, is darker and not nearly so rufescent on the crown.

These differences, which were noticed by Taczanowski [8], seem to be so strictly associated with the definite range indicated above, that we think it best to separate this northern and western form from the true *T. nœvius*; with the latter bird we associate v. Pelzeln's *T. cinereinucha*, but whether the bird of South-eastern Brazil forms another distinct race we are hardly in a position to determine, the series before us being insufficient. A Brazilian bird in the British Museum we believe to be a female of this form differs considerably from specimens of that sex from Guiana and Central America, and also from the female of *T. cœrulescens*, which is another closely allied race of *T. nœvius*.

At one time Mr. Lawrence considered the Panama bird to belong to *T. amazonicus*, Scl. [11], but he subsequently referred Costa Rica examples to *T. nœvius* [4], and this has been the practice of all subsequent writers until now. The colour of the iris was noted by M‘Leannan as brown [11], whilst Salmon gives it as white [3]. As this section of the genus has little to do with that of which *T. doliatus*, a white-irised species, is typical, we are inclined to consider M‘Leannan's determination correct.

The same collector states that the bird is not common at Panama, where it is found in low trees and bushes [11]. Mr. Wood, who accompanied Lieut. Michler's expedition to Darien, frequently saw individuals of this species, generally on the ground in patches of the plant called Spanish bayonet, where they seemed to be catching insects [1].

ε. *Minores: caput plus minusve cristatum; alœ nigrœ, albo marginatœ; cauda albo terminata.*

7. Thamnophilus pulchellus.

Thamnophilus, sp.?, Cassin, Pr. Ac. Phil. 1860, p. 189. no. 88 [1].
Hypolophus pulchellus, Cab. & Heine, Mus. Hein. ii. p. 16 [2].
Thamnophilus pulchellus, Berl. Ibis, 1881, p. 245 [3]; Scl. Cat. Birds Brit. Mus. xv. p. 204 [4].

Supra rufo-brunneus, capite toto nigro, lateribus cum fronte et gula albo variegatis; alis nigricanti-fuscis albo late limbatis, tectricibus supra caudalibus longioribus nigris albo terminatis; cauda nigra albo terminata, rectrice extima in pogonio externo quoque albo: subtus albus, pectore et abdomine antico nigris, hypochondriis rufo lavatis: rostro nigricante, mandibula infra pallida, pedibus plumbeis. Long. tota 6·0, alæ 2·8, caudæ rectr. med. 2·3, rectr. lat. 1·7, rostri a rictu 0·9, tarsi 1·1. (Descr. maris ex Santa Marta, Colombia. Mus. nostr.)

♀ supra rufa, capite summo dorso concolori, capitis lateribus albidis nigro variegatis: subtus cervina, abdomine medio albicantiore; alis fuscis, tectricibus et secundariis internis albido limbatis, reliquis cum remigibus externo rufis ; cauda nigricanti-fusca albo terminata, rectrice extima utrinque quoque albo in pogonio externo. (Descr. feminæ ex Atrato, Colombia, U. S. Nat. Mus.)

Hab. PANAMA, R. Truando (*W. S. Wood*).—COLOMBIA.

We have to thank Mr. Ridgway for sending us two specimens, both females or young males, obtained by Mr. A. Schott, one at Carthagena, the other on the R. Atrato. They doubtless belong to the same species as that referred to by Cassin as occurring on the Rio Truando and allied to *T. atricapillus.* *T. pulchellus*, which was described from a Carthagena specimen, has a very limited range in Northern Colombia.

> ζ. *Minores: rostrum mediocre; alæ rotundatæ; ptilosis plerumque albo et nigro transfasciata; sexus dissimiles.*

8. **Thamnophilus doliatus.**

Lanius doliatus, Linn. Syst. Nat. i. p. 136 [1].

Thamnophilus doliatus, Bp. P. Z. S. 1837, p. 117 [2]; Scl. P. Z. S. 1856, pp. 141 [3], 295 [4]; 1859, pp. 366 [5], 383 [6]; Cat. Birds Brit. Mus. xv. p. 207 [7]; Scl. & Salv. Ibis, 1859, p. 118 [8]; Moore, P. Z. S. 1859, p. 57 [9]; Cab. J. f. Orn. 1861, p. 242 [10]; Salv. P. Z. S. 1867, p. 144 [11]; Cat. Strickl. Coll. p. 345 [12]; Sumichrast, Mem. Bost. Soc. N. H. i. p. 556 [13]; La Nat. v. p. 248 [14]; Boucard, P. Z. S. 1878, p. 60 [15]; 1883, p. 450 [16]; Nutting, Pr. U. S. Nat. Mus. vi. pp. 585 [17], 405 [18]; Ferrari-Perez, Pr. U. S. Nat. Mus. ix. p. 156 [19]; Zeledon, An. Mus. Nac. Costa Rica, 1887, p. 114 [20].

Thamnophilus rutilus, Bp. P. Z. S. 1837, p. 117 [21].

Thamnophilus affinis, Cab. & Heine, Mus. Hein. ii. p. 17 [22]; Lawr. Ann. Lyc. N. Y. viii. p. 183 [23]; ix. pp. 107 [24], 201 [25]; Scl. & Salv. P. Z. S. 1864, p. 355 [26]; 1870, p. 837 [27]; Salv. Ibis, 1869, p. 314 [28]; P. Z. S. 1870, p. 194 [29].

Thamnophilus doliatus affinis, Nutting, Pr. U. S. Nat. Mus. v. p. 397 [30].

Thamnophilus intermedius, Ridgw. Pr. U. S. Nat. Mus. x. p. 581 [31].

Thamnophilus doliatus mexicanus, Allen, Bull. Am. Mus. N. H. ii. p. 151 [32].

Supra niger, fronte et cervice postica albo punctatis, crista nigra plumis omnibus ad basin albis ; dorso, alis et uropygio albo tenuiter transfasciatis, cauda quoque fasciis sex aut septem interruptis notata : subtus gula albo et nigro striata, corpore reliquo cum tibiis et tectricibus subcaudalibus subæqualiter albo et nigro transfasciatis : rostro plumbeo tomiis albicantibus, pedibus plumbeis. Long. tota 6·5, alæ 2·9, caudæ 2·6, rostri a rictu 0·85, tarsi 1·1.

♂ *juv.* colore albo corporis et alis plus minusve cervino tincto, abdomine medio sæpe fere immaculato.

♀ castanea, capite summo, alis et cauda saturatioribus, capitis et gulæ lateribus cum nucha albicantibus nigro striatis. (Descr. maris ad. et juv. et feminæ ex Vera Cruz, Mexico. Mus. nostr.)

Hab. MEXICO [32] (*Sallé* [4]), Tampico (*W. B. Richardson*), Hot and temperate regions of Vera Cruz (*Sumichrast* [13]), Jalapa [22] (*de Oca* [5], *F. D. G., M. Trujillo*), Coatepec (*M. Trujillo*), Misantla (*F. D. G.*), Vera Cruz (*W. B. Richardson*), Orizaba (*Sumichrast* [14], *F. Ferrari-Perez, F. D. G.*), Huatusco (*F. Ferrari-Perez*), Cordova (*Sumichrast* [14], *Sallé*), Choapam (*Boucard* [6]), Playa Vicente (*Boucard* [6], *M. Trujillo*), Hueytamalco (*F. Ferrari-Perez* [19]), Tomatla, Tonaguia (*M. Trujillo*), Santa Efigenia and Tapana (*Sumichrast* [14]), Teapa (*Mrs. H. H. Smith*), Merida (*Schott* [25]),

Buctzotz and Peto in Yucatan, Meco and Cozumel Is. (*G. F. Gaumer*); BRITISH HONDURAS, Orange Walk (*G. F. Gaumer*), Belize, San Antonio and Cayo (*Blancaneaux*); GUATEMALA (*Velasquez* [1][21], *Constancia* [12]), Choctum, Chisec, Cahabon, Coban, San Gerónimo, Savana Grande, Escuintla road, Volcan de Fuego, Dueñas [8] (*O. S. & F. D. G.*), Retalhuleu (*W. B. Richardson*); HONDURAS, Omoa (*Leyland* [9]), San Pedro (*G. M. Whitely* [27]), Truxillo (*Townsend* [31]); SALVADOR, La Libertad and Volcan de San Miguel (*W. B. Richardson*); NICARAGUA, Chinandega and Volcan de Chinandega (*W. B. Richardson*), Sucuyá [17] and Los Sabalos [18] (*Nutting*), Greytown (*Holland* [23]); COSTA RICA, San José (*v. Frantzius* [24]), San Mateo (*Cooper* [24], *Boucard* [15]), Sarchi (*Cooper* [24]), Bebedero de Nicoya (*Arcé*), La Palma (*Nutting* [30]), Jimenez, Las Trojas, Cartago, Naranjo de Cartago, Pozo Azul de Pirris (*Zeledon* [20]); PANAMA, David (*Bridges* [3]), Bugaba (*Arcé* [29]), Lion Hill (*M'Leannan* [26]).—VENEZUELA [7]; TRINIDAD [7]; GUIANA [1][7]; LOWER AMAZONS [7].

The position of the Central American form of this species with respect to the typical bird from Guiana has long been a matter of doubt. When the bird was first found in Guatemala by Velasquez [2] his specimens were referred by Bonaparte the male to *T. doliatus* (L.) and the female to *T. rutilus* (Vieill.); the relationship of the sexes being then not understood. The birds obtained by Sallé and Boucard in Southern Mexico and by ourselves in Guatemala were also called *T. doliatus*. Cabanis and Heine, in 1859, separated the Mexican bird as *T. affinis* [22] on its supposed larger size and the wider separation of all the transverse bands. Mr. Allen, in 1889 [32], endorsed these differential characters, but changed the name of the Mexican bird to *T. doliatus mexicanus*, the term *affinis* having been used for a bird of the same or an allied genus. The name *T. affinis* had in the meantime been often applied to the Central American bird. A further separation was made by Mr. Ridgway when he described a male and a female from Honduras as *T. intermedius* [31]. The latter birds he compared with *T. nigricristatus*, but from the fact of the bases of the feathers of the crest being white *T. doliatus* must be its nearest ally. The type of the male, which Mr. Ridgway has kindly sent us for examination, proves this to be the case, and we are inclined to think *T. intermedius* to be an unusually dark form of *T. doliatus*, just as the Yucatan birds are unusually light.

We have now a large series of this bird before us from all parts of its range, and comparing Mexican specimens with others from Guiana we do not see any tangible grounds for separating them. Difference in size there is practically none, and as for the width of the alternate black and white bands of the plumage, so much variation occurs everywhere that we are unable to associate any particular style with any particular area. We believe that the birds which have the narrowest white bands on the upper surface are the oldest, as young birds with only a trace of immaturity are often widely banded, and even, as in the case of some Yucatan specimens before us, nearly spotless white on the abdomen.

Thamnophilus doliatus is a bird of the hot and temperate regions, where it is found ranging from the sea-level to an altitude of 5000 or 6000 feet in the mountains. It occurs as far north in Eastern Mexico as Tampico, and is abundant in the State of Vera Cruz, and thence southwards to the State of Panama. It appears not to be found in Western Mexico north of the State of Oaxaca, but occurs in the isthmus of Tehuantepec, and abundantly on the Pacific side of the cordillera of Guatemala.

It frequents the denser brush-wood, keeping near the ground, and uttering at intervals a loud cry, which may be heard at a considerable distance.

9. **Thamnophilus nigricristatus.**

Thamnophilus doliatus, Lawr. Ann. Lyc. N. Y. vii. p. 293 (nec Linn.) [1].

Thamnophilus radiatus, Scl. & Salv. P.Z.S. 1864, p. 355 (nec Vieill.) [2]; Salv. P.Z.S. 1870, p. 194 [3].

Thamnophilus nigricristatus, Lawr. Pr. Ac. Phil. 1865, p. 107 [4]; Scl. Cat. Birds Brit. Mus. xv. p. 209 [5].

T. doliato similis, sed plumis pilei omnino nigris distinguendus.

♀ quam femina *T. doliati* pallidior, gula albicantiore immaculata. (Descr. maris et feminæ ex Panama. Mus. nostr.)

Hab. PANAMA, Mina de Chorcha, Chitra [3], Calovevora [3], Calobre (*Arcé*), Paraiso Station (*Hughes*), Lion Hill Station (*M'Leannan* [1,2,4]).—SOUTH AMERICA, from Colombia and the Upper Amazons Valley to Matto Grosso in Brazil [5].

Though separated in 1865 as a distinct species by Mr. Lawrence [4], this bird has been generally considered inseparable from *T. radiatus*, until Mr. Lawrence's name was again restored to it by Mr. Sclater in his 'Catalogue' [5], though he there expressed great doubt as to its distinctness even from *T. doliatus*. Count von Berlepsch, too, has further divided this form by naming the Upper Amazonian birds *T. subradiatus*. We are unable to distinguish between the Amazonian and Colombian birds, to which the title *T. nigricristatus* is applicable; but the true *T. radiatus* seems to be distinct, the under surface of the male being much less banded and even almost white along the middle of the abdomen, and the female a much whiter bird beneath than that sex of the more northern bird.

T. nigricristatus may readily be distinguished from *T. doliatus* in the male by the feathers of the crown, which are black to their bases, and in the female by the lighter coloured and unspotted chin and throat.

The range of this bird in Central America is limited to the State of Panama, where it appears to be found alone as far as the middle of the State; in the district of Chiriqui it occurs with *T. doliatus*, which entirely supplants it to the north.

We are unacquainted with the nest and eggs of either this species or of *T. doliatus*. But Salmon says that an allied bird (*T. multistriatus*) builds a hanging nest and lays whitish eggs, which are thickly spotted and streaked at the larger end with red-brown.

THAMNISTES.

Thamnistes, Scl. & Salv. P. Z. S. 1860, p. 299; Scl. Cat. Birds Brit. Mus. xv. p. 215.

This genus contains two, perhaps three or even four, closely allied species, one of which is widely spread in our country from Eastern Guatemala to the State of Panama; another is found in Eastern Ecuador, and a third, if distinct, in Peru; the fourth is the bird described by Count Salvadori (Atti Soc. Ital. vii. p. 154) as *T. affinis,* a bird we do not know, and not referred to in Mr. Sclater's Catalogue. There is little to separate *Thamnistes* structurally from *Thamnophilus;* the bill in the type is rather wider at the base than is usual in *Thamnophilus,* but this character is hardly maintained in *T. æquatorialis,* and the fullness of the feathers of the lower back, upon which Mr. Sclater divides the two genera, is not a very tangible character and does not distinguish *Thamnistes* from all species of *Thamnophilus.* In coloration, however, the genus is very peculiar, being destitute of marks either longitudinal or transverse, except an indistinct superciliary streak. The concealed dorsal patch so frequently present in male Formicariidæ is found in *Thamnistes,* but instead of being white as is the case in nearly every other instance, it is of a pale chestnut colour. On the whole we think it best to keep *Thamnistes* distinct from *Thamnophilus,* especially in view of the probable subdivision of the latter genus at some future date. It is, however, more nearly allied to some sections of *Thamnophilus* than they are to one another.

1. **Thamnistes anabatinus.** (Tab. L. fig. 1, ♂.)

Thamnistes anabatinus, Scl. & Salv. P. Z. S. 1860, p. 299[1]; Ibis, 1860, p. 399[2]; Lawr. Ann. Lyc. N. Y. ix. p. 107[3]; Salv. P. Z. S. 1870, p. 194[4]; Zeledon, An. Mus. Nac. Costa Rica, 1887, p. 114[5]; Scl. Cat. Birds Brit. Mus. xv. p. 216[6].

Olivascenti-brunneus, subtus dilutior; superciliis gula concoloribus macula postoculari obscura; alis extus rufescentibus, cauda dilute castanea unicolore; plaga magna dorsali celata pallide castanea, hoc colore extrorsum nigro marginato: rostro corneo, maxillæ tomia et mandibula pallida, pedibus nigricantibus. Long. tota 5·5, alæ 2·6, caudæ rectr. med. 2·2, rectr. lat. 1·8, rostri a rictu 0·9, tarsi 0·8.

♀ mari similis, sed plaga dorsali nulla. (Descr. maris et feminæ exempl. typ. ex Choctum, Guatemala. Mus. nostr.)

Hab. GUATEMALA, Choctum[1], Cahabon, Teleman (*O. S. & F. D. G.*); COSTA RICA, Angostura (*Carmiol*[3], *Zeledon*[5]), Tucurriqui (*Arcé, Zeledon*[3][5]), Pacuare, Naranjo de Cartago (*Zeledon*[5]); PANAMA, Bugaba, Calovevora (*Arcé*[4]).

The original specimens of this species were obtained in January 1860, in the forest country of Vera Paz lying to the north of Coban, at an elevation of about 1200 feet above the sea-level[1]. Others were subsequently secured in the same district, and in the valley of the Polochic and Cahabon rivers, these places being the only ones in Guatemala where, so far as we know, the bird occurs. We have no record of its presence in the country situated to the southward of Guatemala until we come to Costa Rica, where it is found on the eastern side of the Cordillera up to an elevation of about

3000 feet. From the State of Panama we have received specimens both from the district of Chiriqui and from Calovevora, lying further in the direction of the isthmus, but the bird has not been noticed on the line of railway nor to the southward. The Panama birds are a little darker on the upper surface than the types, and thus approach the Ecuador form, which has been separated by Mr. Sclater as *Thamnistes æquatorialis*. The last-named bird is very closely allied to *T. anabatinus*, and the existence of an intermediate form indicates that there is probably no specific difference.

Of the habits of this species nothing has been recorded; our Guatemalan specimens were secured by Indian hunters.

b″. *Rostrum debile, leviter hamatum.*

DYSITHAMNUS.

Dysithamnus, Cabanis, in Wiegm. Arch. f. Naturg. 1847, xiii. p. 223 ; Scl. Cat. Birds Brit. Mus. xv. p. 219.

Dysithamnus is closely allied to the smaller forms of *Thamnophilus*, and there seem to be no obvious characters by which to distinguish them. The bill is certainly some-what feeble, but when the size of the birds is considered this point loses its value. The bill, as well as the wings and legs, conform to those of such species as *Thamnophilus nævius*. The tail seems less rounded.

Mr. Sclater places fourteen species in *Dysithamnus*, and mentions the names of two others unknown to him. These are distributed over a wide area, extending from Guatemala to South Brazil. Only three species occur within our region, of which *D. semicinereus* has a wide range. The other two are both peculiar to the southern section of our Fauna, both occurring in Costa Rica and one of them in the State of Panama.

α. *Pileus unicolor.*

1. Dysithamnus semicinereus.

Dysithamnus semicinereus, Scl. P. Z. S. 1855, p. 90, t. 97 [1] ; Cat. Birds Brit. Mus. xv. p. 221 [2] ; Scl. & Salv. Ibis, 1860, p. 399 [3] ; Salv. P. Z. S. 1867, p. 144 [4] ; 1870, p. 194 [5] ; Lawr. Ann. Lyc. N. Y. ix. p. 107 [6] ; Boucard, P. Z. S. 1878, p. 60 [7] ; Tacz. Orn. Pér. ii. p. 29 [8] ; Zeledon, An. Mus. Nac. Costa Rica, 1887, p. 114 [9].

Olivaceo-cinereus, capite summo unicolore pure cinereo; alis et cauda dorso concoloribus; tectricibus alarum minoribus nigris, his et reliquis anguste albo limbatis : subtus cinereo-albicans, pectore obscuriore ; hypochondriis vix olivaceo lavatis; subalaribus et remigibus intus albis flavido tinctis : rostro et pedibus plumbeis. Long. tota 4·5, alæ 2·3, caudæ 1·55, rostri a rictu 0·67, tarsi 0·75.

♀ supra fuscescens haud cinereo tincta ; alis et cauda concoloribus, hujus tectricibus apicibus pallidis ; capite summo rufescente unicolore : subtus ochraceo-alba, gula fere alba, pectore et hypochondriis fuscescentibus : rostro et pedibus plumbeis. (Descr. maris et feminæ ex Veræ Pacis septentrionali. Mus. nostr.)

Hab. GUATEMALA, Choctum [3], Chisec (*O. S. & F. D. G.*); COSTA RICA, Dota Mts., Grecia, Turrialba (*Carmiol* [6]), Guaitil (*Cooper* [6]), Naranjo (*Boucard* [7]), Cartago (*Zeledon* [9]); PANAMA, Volcan de Chiriqui [5], Chitra [5], Calovevora [5], Calobre [5], Santa Fé [4] (*Arcé*).—SOUTH AMERICA, from Colombia to Peru [9].

Mr. Sclater's description of this species was based upon specimens in the British Museum [1] from Bogota; the bird has since been traced over a large portion of Central America and southwards to Peru [8]. In South-eastern Brazil a very closely allied species, *D. mentalis*, takes its place, from which it can only be distinguished with difficulty. The Brazilian bird, however, is yellower on the abdomen, and the white of the throat spreads to the breast, the latter being thus less ashy.

In Guatemala we found this species very abundant in the great forest region which spreads over the northern portion of Vera Paz into the department of Peten. It frequents the underwood of the forest, seeking its food near but not on the ground. We know nothing of the nesting-habits of this bird, but another member of the genus (*D. unicolor*), Salmon says, lays creamy white eggs sparsely spotted with small red spots, and with a zone of large blotches of the same colour round the middle *.

Stolzmann met with *D. semicinereus* at Huambo and at Santa Rosa in Peru, at an elevation of 6000 feet above the sea-level. He says it is strictly a forest bird, moving about in small flocks either alone or with the wandering bands of birds. It flies usually near the ground, when it follows, like *Pithys*, the hordes of foraging ants [8].

β. Pileus aut guttatus aut striatus.

2. **Dysithamnus puncticeps.** (Tab. L. figg. 2 ♂, 3 ♀.)

Dysithamnus puncticeps, Salv. P. Z. S. 1866, p. 72 [1]; 1867, p. 144 [2]; Zeledon, An. Mus. Nac. Costa Rica, 1887, p. 115 [3]; Scl. Cat. Birds Brit. Mus. xv. p. 223 [4].

Supra cinereus, pilei et nuchæ plumis nigris ad basin utrinque cinereis et maculis duabus subapicalibus rotundis albis notatis; alis et cauda nigricantibus fusco-cinereo marginatis; tectricibus alarum albido terminatis; loris et capitis lateribus albis cinereo intermixtis: subtus gutture toto et pectore albis, hoc nigro lineato; abdomine medio albido; hypochondriis et tectricibus subcaudalibus ochraceo-fuscis, subalaribus albis: rostro et pedibus plumbeis, illius mandibula pallida. Long. tota 4·5, alæ 2·2, caudæ 1·5, rostri a rictu 0·75, tarsi 0·8.

♀ supra obscure olivaceo-fusca, pilei plumis fulvis, rhachide nigra et nigro terminatis: subtus gula alba nigro indistincte striata, pectore et abdomine pallide fulvis illo nigro striato, hypochondriis fuscescentibus; alis extus brunneis, tectricibus fulvo maculatis; cauda fusco-nigricante. (Descr. maris et feminæ exempl. typ. ex Santiago de Veraguas, Panama. Mus. nostr.)

Hab. COSTA RICA, Pacuare (*Zeledon* [3]); PANAMA, Santiago de Veraguas (*Arcé* [1][2]).

We only know this well-marked species from the type specimens sent us by our collector Enrique Arcé from Veraguas in 1865, and described by us in the following

---

* P. Z. S. 1879, p. 525, t. 43. f. 9.

year[1]. These we now figure. It, with *D. striaticeps*, belongs to a section of *Dysithamnus* with mottled heads, the present bird being spotted, its ally striped over the whole surface of the crown. The presence of *D. puncticeps* in Costa Rica is proved by a specimen in the national museum of that country from Pacuare[3].

3. Dysithamnus striaticeps.

Dysithamnus striaticeps, Lawr. Ann. Lyc. N. Y. viii. p. 130[1]; ix. p. 107[2]; Boucard, P. Z. S. 1878, p. 60[3]; Zeledon, An. Mus. Nac. Costa Rica, 1887, p. 115[4]; Scl. Cat. Birds Brit. Mus. xv. p. 223[5].

Supra cinereus, pileo et nucha nigro striatis, dorso postico, alis et cauda brunnescentibus, tectricibus alarum nigris albo terminatis: subtus gutture cinerea albo intermixta; pectore et ventre medio albis, illo nigro striato; hypochondriis et tectricibus subcaudalibus fulvo tinctis: rostro et pedibus plumbeis, illius mandibula pallidiore. Long. tota 4·5, alæ 2·25, caudæ 1·3, rostri a rictu 0·7, tarsi 0·75. (Descr. maris ex La Balza, Costa Rica. Mus. nostr.)

Hab. Costa Rica, Angostura (*Carmiol*[1][2], *Zeledon*[4]), La Balsa (*Carmiol*), San Carlos (*Boucard*[3]).

A rare species, restricted in its range to Costa Rica, whence but few specimens have been sent. The first of these formed part of the large collections made for the United-States National Museum by Carmiol and others, and was described by Mr. Lawrence in 1865[1]. Carmiol also sent us a male example, and M. Boucard obtained another[3].

We have never seen a female of this species, but Mr. Lawrence describes it as having a bright rufous head, each feather with a narrow black central stripe. In other respects the sexes appear to differ very much as do those of *D. puncticeps*.

MYRMOTHERULA.

Myrmotherula, Sclater, P. Z. S. 1858, p. 234; Cat. Birds Brit. Mus. xv. p. 229.

This is numerically one of the larger genera of Formicariidæ, containing some twenty-four or twenty-five species, which are divisible into several well-marked groups. The genus has a wide range over Tropical America, extending northwards to the forests of Northern Vera Paz, and southwards to the southern confines of Brazil, its focus being the valley of the Amazons throughout its length and Guiana. In Central America *Myrmotherula* is poorly represented by four species, not one of which is peculiar to the country. Two out of the four do not range beyond Costa Rica, and the fourth, the common *M. ménétriési*, occurs in all the heavily-wooded country as far as Eastern Guatemala. No member of the genus reaches Southern Mexico.

Of the sections into which Mr. Sclater divides the genus, the first, of which *M. surinamensis* is typical, is the most distinct. Besides the difference in the style of coloration, the bill is relatively longer and rather wider at the base, where the culmen is less elevated, the nostrils are situated a little further from the longest supranasal feathers, the hind tarsal scutella are more definite, and the tail shorter and squarer.

In general characters *Myrmotherula* is a diminutive *Thamnophilus*, but with a much feebler structure in every way; but we can find no features to justify these forms being placed in distinct subfamilies.

α. *Rostrum debile, cauda brevis, ptilosis plus minusve striata.*

1. Myrmotherula surinamensis.

Surinam Nuthatch, Lath. Gen. Syn. ii. p. 654, t. 28 [1].

Sitta surinamensis, Gm. Syst. Nat. i. p. 442 [2].

Myrmotherula surinamensis, Cassin, Pr. Ac. Phil. 1860, p. 190 [3]; Lawr. Ann. Lyc. N. Y. vii. p. 293 [4]; Scl. & Salv. P. Z. S. 1864, p. 356 [5]; 1879, p. 525 [6]; Salv. Ibis, 1874, p. 311 [7]; Scl. Cat. Birds Brit. Mus. xv. p. 231 [8].

Myrmotherula pygmæa, Cassin, Pr. Ac. Phil. 1860, p. 190 [9]; Lawr. Ann. Lyc. N. Y. vii. p. 325 [10]; Salv. Ibis, 1874, p. 311 [11]; Tacz. Orn. Pér. ii. p. 37 [12].

Supra nigra, plumis omnibus lateraliter stricte albo marginatis, uropygio griseo, plaga dorsali celata alba: subtus alba, plumis omnibus stria rhachidali nigra in gutture fere obsoleta; alis nigris, remigibus stricte albido marginatis, tectricibus albo terminatis; cauda nigra, medialiter albo limbata et albo terminata: rostro et pedibus plumbeis, illius mandibula pallida. Long. tota 3·5, alæ 1·9, caudæ 1·85, rostri a rictu 0·72, tarsi 0·7.

♀ supra dorso striato et alis notatis sicut in mare, capite toto et nucha rufis plumis medialiter indistincte fuscis: subtus fulva, gula et abdomine medio albicantioribus, subalaribus albis. (Descr. maris et feminæ ex Panama. Mus. nostr.)

Hab. PANAMA, Veraguas (*Arcé*), Lion Hill Station (*M'Leannan* [4] [5]), San Pablo Station (*O. S.*), R. Truando [9], Turbo [3] (*Wood*).—SOUTH AMERICA, from Colombia [6] to Peru [12], Upper Amazons Valley [8] and Guiana [8].

A bird of wide range over nearly the whole of the northern portion of the South-American continent, and occurring in the State of Panama, but not beyond its northern limits.

Males vary to some extent as regards the black central stripe of the feathers of the under surface. *M. multistriata*, Scl., was based upon specimens in which these stripes are wide and spread more strongly over the throat, but it now appears that such birds are not specifically distinct, every gradation being found between them and the normal bird. Gmelin's title for this species [2] was founded upon Latham's Surinam Nuthatch [1]. With a Nuthatch (*Sitta*) it of course has nothing to do, and it was placed in the Formicariidæ by Cabanis in 1847 under the genus *Formicivora*, and thence in 1858 transferred to *Myrmotherula* by Mr. Sclater.

Mr. W. S. Wood, who accompanied Lieut. Michler's Expedition to the Isthmus of Darien, obtained specimens of both sexes, though Cassin, who named his collection, did not recognize them as such. The bird is described as abundant on the " Cremantina " trees, especially at Camp Toucey in January 1858, and as also frequently seen on the Bananas constantly searching for insects amongst the fruit and leaves. The male was at first mistaken for the Black-and-White Creeper of the United States (*Mniotilta varia*), as its habits resemble those of that bird—running along the upper and lower sides of the branches, frequently with its head downwards [3]. Salmon describes the nest as made of very fine roots and grass, and placed in low bushes, a slight network hanging at the end of a thin bough, very deep, and suspended between a fork with the natural leaves of the shrub or bush above to protect it from the rain. The eggs are white [6]. Stolzmann found *M. surinamensis* in small numbers at Yurimaguas in Peru living in the lofty trees like the small species of Tyrannidæ, and accompanying the bands of wandering birds [12].

β. *Rostrum robustius, cauda longior, ptilosis haud striata.*

α′. *Gula albo maculata.*

2. Myrmotherula fulviventris.

Myrmotherula ornata, Cassin, Pr. Ac. Phil. 1860, p. 190, partim (cf. Salv. Ibis, 1874, p. 311)[1].
Myrmotherula, sp. no. 216, Lawr. Ann. Lyc. N. Y. vii. p. 325[2].
Myrmotherula fulviventris, Lawr. Ann. Lyc. N. Y. vii. p. 468[3]; ix. p. 108[4]; Scl. & Salv. P. Z. S. 1864, p. 356[5]; 1879, p. 525[6]; Wyatt, Ibis, 1871, p. 331[7]; Salv. Ibis, 1874, p. 311[8]; Ridgw. Pr. U. S. Nat. Mus. x. p. 590[9]; Zeledon, An. Mus. Nac. Costa Rica, 1887, p. 115[10]; Scl. Cat. Birds Brit. Mus. xv. p. 234[11].

Supra obscure brunnea fere unicolor, cauda vix fulvescentiore; tectricibus alarum nigris cervino terminatis: subtus fulva, gula alba plumis singulis basi nigra, subalaribus et remigibus interne pallide cervinis: rostro et pedibus nigricanti-plumbeis, mandibula pallida. Long. tota 4·0, alæ 2·0, caudæ 1·25, rostri a rictu 0·65, tarsi 0·65.

♀ mari similis, sed gula quam pectus vix pallidiore, haud alba, plumarum basi nigra. (Descr. maris et feminæ ex Panama. Mus. nostr.)

Hab. HONDURAS, Segovia river (*Townsend*[9]); COSTA RICA, Angostura (*Carmiol*[4]), Pacuare, Jimenez (*Zeledon*[10]); PANAMA, Veraguas (*Arcé*), Lion Hill Station (*M'Leannan*[2 3 5]), R. Truando (*Wood*[1]).—COLOMBIA[6 7]; ECUADOR[11].

The true position of this species as a distinct bird was not recognized at first. Cassin referred specimens obtained during Lieut. Michler's expedition to Darien with doubt to *M. ornata*[1]. Mr. Lawrence hesitated to describe the first specimens sent him by M'Leannan[2], but afterwards gave them the name now borne by the species[3], which proves to be quite distinct. It belongs to a section of the genus which has the throat of the male spotted with white, but is the only known form having a fulvous breast and brown back. On the Isthmus of Darien this bird is said by Mr. W. S. Wood to be found at Camp Toucey on the Truando and at Turbo, where it was observed in high trees, and also occasionally in the bushes, being very active and constantly in motion[1].

The range northwards of *M. fulviventris* from the Isthmus of Panama is extensive, for though it does not reach Guatemala, it has been traced to the northern side of the valley of the Segovia river in Honduras, where Mr. Townsend obtained two specimens[8]. It is not apparently a common bird either in Costa Rica or the State of Panama beyond the line of railway, as none of Arcé's earlier collections contained examples.

β′. Gula nigra.

3. Myrmotherula melæna.

Formicivora melæna, Scl. P. Z. S. 1857, p. 130[1]; Lawr. Ann. Lyc. N. Y. viii. p. 6[2].

Myrmotherula melæna, Cassin, Pr. Ac. Phil. 1860, p. 191[3]; Scl. & Salv. P. Z. S. 1864, p. 356[4];
    Lawr. Ann. Lyc. N. Y. ix. p. 107[5]; Salv. Ibis, 1874, p. 311[6]; Boucard, P. Z. S. 1878,
    p. 61[7]; Tacz. Orn. Pér. ii. p. 48[8]; Zeledon, An. Mus. Nac. Costa Rica, 1887, p. 115[9];
    Scl. Cat. Birds Brit. Mus. xv. p. 239[10].

Myrmotherula ornata, Cassin, Pr. Ac. Phil. 1860, p. 191[11] (partim, nec Scl.) (cf. Salv. Ibis, 1874,
    p. 311).

Myrmotherula albigula, Lawr. Ann. Lyc. N. Y. viii. p. 131[12]; ix. p. 108[13] (cf. Salv. Ibis, 1874,
    p. 317).

Nigra, supra unicolor, tectricibus alarum omnibus albo terminatis, subalaribus et hypochondriis pure albis,
    caudæ rectricibus quoque albo terminatis : rostro et pedibus nigris. Long. tota 4·0, alæ 2·1, caudæ 1·4,
    rostri a rictu 0·6, tarsi 0·65. (Descr. maris ex Angostura, Costa Rica. Mus. nostr.)

♀ olivaceo-brunnea, alis et cauda nigricanti-brunneis extrorsum paulo rufescentibus, illius tectricibus fulvo
    terminatis : subtus pallide cervina, gula albicantiore. (Descr. feminæ ex Panama. Mus. Brit.)

Hab. Costa Rica (*Boucard*[7]), Angostura[12][13], Pacuare (*Carmiol*[5], *Zeledon*[9]), Naranjo
    de Cartago, Las Trojas (*Zeledon*[8]); Panama, Lion Hill (*McLeannan*[2][4]), Chepo
    (*Arcé*), R. Truando (*Wood*[3]).—South America from Colombia to Peru[9] and the
    Upper Amazons Valley[8].

M. melæna was separated from its near ally *M. axillaris* by Mr. Sclater in 1857, his
description being founded on trade skins from Bogota[1]. Its difference from the latter
consists in the blacker, less cinereous tint of its plumage ; both birds have the pure
white flanks peculiar to this section of the genus.

From Colombia *M. melæna* ranges widely southwards to Peru and over the portion
of the valley of the Amazons appertaining to that republic. Northwards it spreads
through the Isthmus of Panama to Costa Rica, where it has been met with in the
forests of the eastern part of that country by several collectors.

The diversity of sexes of this species has been a source of confusion to several
writers. Cassin failed to recognize the specimens from Darien that came before
him, and mixing them with examples of *M. fulviventris*, called them all with doubt
M. ornata[11]. Mr. Lawrence, again, described the female as a distinct species under
the name *M. albigula*[12]. These names are now rightly, we believe, assigned to
M. melæna.

Of the habits of this species little has been recorded. Salmon merely says of the iris
that it is dark in life. Stolzmann states that it is a rather common bird at Yurimaguas in Peru, where it lives, like other species of the virgin forest, amongst the tops of
the lower trees and follows the wandering bands of birds[8].

4. Myrmotherula ménétriési.

Myrmothera menetriesi, d'Orb. Voy. Am. Mér., Ois. p. 184[1].

Myrmotherula menetriesi, Salv. P. Z. S. 1867, p. 144[2]; 1870, p. 195[3]; Ibis, 1874, p. 310[4]; Boucard,

P. Z. S. 1878, p. 61 [5] ; Tacz. Orn. Pér. ii. p. 45 [6] ; Zeledon, An. Mus. Nac. Costa Rica, 1887, p. 115 [7] ; Scl. Cat. Birds Brit. Mus. xv. p. 240 [8].

Myrmotherula, sp. ?, Salv. P. Z. S. 1867, p. 145 [9].

Myrmotherula modesta, Lawr. Ann. Lyc. N. Y. ix. p. 108 [10].

Formicivora schisticolor, Lawr. Ann. Lyc. N. Y. viii. p. 173 [11] ; ix. p. 108 [12].

Myrmotherula nigrorufa, Boucard, Ann. Soc. Linn. Lyon, 1878, p. 38 (cf. Ibis, 1879, p. 215 [13]).

Supra saturate cinerea unicolor ; alis nigricantibus extrorsum cinereo limbatis, tectricibus nigris albo terminatis : subtus gutture toto et pectore medio nigris, corpore reliquo cinereo ; subalaribus cinereis, remigibus interne albis: rostro et pedibus nigris.   Long. tota 4·0, alæ 2·3, caudæ 1·65, rostri a rictu 0·52, tarsi 0·6.

♀ supra fusco-olivacea, pileo, alis et cauda paulo rufescentioribus ; capitis lateribus et corpore tóto subtus fulvis, hypochondriis fuscescentibus, gula pallidiore, remigibus interne pallide cervinis.   (Descr. maris et feminæ ex Chiriqui, Panama.   Mus. nostr.)

Hab. GUATEMALA, Choctum, Vera Paz (*O. S. & F. D. G.*[9]) ; NICARAGUA, Matagalpa (*W. B. Richardson*) ; COSTA RICA, Grecia [10], Turrialba [12] and Barranca [12] (*Carmiol*), Naranjo (*Boucard* [5]), Pozo Azul de Pirris (*Zeledon* [7]) ; PANAMA, Chiriqui [3], Bugaba [3], Santiago [2], Calovevora [3], Santa Fé [9] (*Arcé*).—SOUTH AMERICA from Colombia and Venezuela to Ecuador, Peru, and Bolivia [8].

It has long been the practice to associate d'Orbigny's *Myrmothera ménétriési* [1] with this widely spread species, though no specimens have been included in recent collections from Bolivia, the origin of the types.   The range of the bird seems to be practically unbroken from Eastern Guatemala southwards through Central America, Colombia, Ecuador, and Peru to the confines of Bolivia, so that d'Orbigny's bird may well be the same as that so well known to us.   Should, however, it prove different we still have plenty of names for the northern bird, for Mr. Lawrence described the male as *Formicivora schisticolor* [11], and the female as *Myrmotherula modesta* [10], both Costa Rica birds. A young male from Guatemala has also been named *M. nigrorufa* by M. Boucard [13].

In Guatemala *M. ménétriési* is not a common bird, and is restricted in its range to the forest country of Vera Paz lying to the northward of the town of Coban.   We were long in doubt what this bird could be, for our collectors only sent us female examples ; on the receipt of an adult male from the same district the question of its identity was decided.   In Costa Rica and the adjoining portion of the State of Panama this *Myrmotherula* is common, but it appears to be absent from the line of the Panama Railway, as it was unrepresented in M'Leannan's collections ; Salmon, too, did not meet with it. In Western Ecuador both Fraser and Stolzmann met with it, the latter collector at Chimbo [6].   The specimens obtained by him were noticed by Count von Berlepsch to differ slightly in dimensions and colour from Panama examples.   So far as the specimens before us indicate, the grounds for separation are hardly tangible.

Little has been recorded of the habits of this species.   Fraser states that its food consists of insects ; and Stolzmann, who found it rather common at Huambo in Peru, says that it travels in small flocks near the ground, where it appears to seek the places in the forest free from bushes and small trees, and where the ground is scantily covered with grass [6].

TERENURA.

Terenura, Cabanis & Heine, Mus. Hein. ii. p. 11 (1859); Scl. Cat. Birds Brit. Mus. xv. p. 257.

Terenura is a peculiar genus of doubtful affinities, but remarkable for the bright colours of its members. These colours (black, bright yellow, chestnut, and olive), it is true, are all to be found in different species of Formicariidæ, but in *Terenura* alone are they associated in a single bird.

Cabanis and Heine, who founded the genus, placed it between *Ramphocœnus* and *Ellipura* (=*Formicivora*), and in this position it was left by Mr. Sclater. We cannot see that it has much in common with either of these forms, which, different as they are, both possess well-defined rictal bristles, not a trace of which can we see in *Terenura*. Mr. Sclater speaks of the presence in the latter genus of a slightly membranous nasal operculum such as is found in *Rhamphocœnus,* but the specimens of *Terenura callinota* before us have open nostrils without any overhanging membrane.

On the whole, and in the absence of any information as to the habits of any species of *Terenura,* we are inclined to place the genus near *Myrmotherula,* notwithstanding the difference of coloration and the much longer tail.

The bill is longer than that of *Myrmotherula surinamensis,* but is otherwise very similar. The wings are decidedly longer and less rounded. The tarsi are covered behind with large scutella, the sutures of which are, however, rather indefinite.

Four or five species constitute the genus *Terenura,* all more or less rare birds. These are distributed over a wide area of Tropical America—one or two in South-eastern Brazil, one in Guiana, one in Eastern Ecuador, and *T. callinota,* a western and north-western bird the range of which is given below.

1. Terenura callinota.

Formicivora callinota, Scl. P. Z. S. 1855, p. 89, t. 96 [1].

Terenura callinota, Tacz. Orn. Pér. ii. p. 52 [2]; Scl. Cat. Birds Brit. Mus. xv. p. 237 [3].

Supra viridi-olivacea, pileo et nucha nigris, loris et superciliis cinereo-albicantibus, dorso postico læte castaneo plumis quibusdam nigris superne marginato; alis et cauda nigricantibus olivaceo limbatis; tectricibus alarum nigris flavo-albido terminatis, campterio, humeris et subalaribus flavissimis: subtus a mento usque ad pectus cinerea, abdomine flavicante: rostro et pedibus plumbeo-nigricantibus, mandibula pallida. Long. tota 4·0, alæ 2·0, caudæ 1·63, rostri a rictu 0·5, tarsi 0·57. (Descr. maris ex Veraguas, Panama. Mus. nostr.)

♀ supra viridi-olivacea; subtus flava, pileo fusco-olivaceo, uropygio lætissime rufo, gula albida, pectore cinerascente. (*Taczanowski, l. s. c.*[2])

Hab. PANAMA, Veraguas (*Arcé*[3]).—COLOMBIA[1]; ECUADOR[3]; PERU[2].

This pretty species was described and figured in 1855 by Mr. Sclater from a specimen (a trade skin from Bogota) in the British Museum[1]. We have since seen other examples from the same country. Buckley obtained a bird of the same species near Nanegal in Ecuador, and one was sent us from the State of Panama by our collector Arcé after the second list of his birds, published in 1870, was issued. All these birds are males, and the female still remains unknown to us, though specimens of both sexes were obtained at Ropaybamba in Peru by Jelski, who shot them from a wandering band of birds as they searched the leaves at the ends of the branches of the trees [2].

T. callinota is the only species of its genus which has a plain black crown, a yellowish abdomen, and yellow edges to the wing.

b'. *Vibrissæ obviæ, acrotarsium scutellatum, planta integra.*

c''. *Rectrices decem.*

CERCOMACRA.

Cercomacra, Sclater, P. Z. S. 1858, p. 244; Cat. Birds Brit. Mus. xv. p. 263.

A genus of about ten species, of which two only occur within our limits, both of them widely spread species on the southern continent—*C. tyrannina* extending its range to Southern Mexico, *C. nigricans* to the State of Panama.

Cercomacra is a peculiar genus in several respects, the tail having the abnormal number of ten feathers. The bill is wide, and the rictal vibrissæ clearly shown. The nostrils are round and open, the dense nasal feathers reaching to the posterior margin of the nostrils. The tail is long and much rounded.

1. Cercomacra tyrannina.

Pyriglena tyrannina, Scl. P. Z. S. 1855, pp. 90 [1], 147, t. 98 [2].

Cercomacra tyrannina, Scl. P. Z. S. 1859, pp. 55 [3], 383 [4]; Cat. Birds Brit. Mus. xv. p. 265 [5]; Scl. & Salv. Ibis, 1859, p. 119 [6]; 1860, p. 36 [7]; 1864, p. 356 [8]; 1870, p. 837 [9]; Salv. P. Z. S. 1867, p. 145 [10]; 1870, p. 195 [11]; 1883, p. 424 [12]; Lawr. Ann. Lyc. N. Y. ix. p. 109 [13]; Boucard, P. Z. S. 1878, p. 61 [14]; Nutting, Pr. U.S. Nat. Mus. vi. pp. 386 [15], 405 [16]; Tacz. Orn. Pér. ii. p. 54 [17]; Zeledon, Ann. Mus. Nac. Costa Rica, 1887, p. 115 [18].

Hypocnemis schistacea, Lawr. Ann. Lyc. N. Y. vii. p. 325 (nec Scl.) [19].

Disythamnus rufiventris, Lawr. Ann. Lyc. N. Y. viii. p. 131 (cf. Salv. Ibis, 1874, p. 316) [20].

Nigricanti-cinerea, humeris et tectricibus alarum marginibus albis, plaga dorsali celata alba: subtus pallidior, abdomine imo murino-brunneo tincto, subalaribus cinereis, remigibus interne albo marginatis; cauda nigricante, rectricibus externis vix albido stricte terminatis: rostro et pedibus nigris. Long. tota 5·5, alæ 2·4, caudæ rectr. med. 2·4, rectr. lat. 1·5, rostri a rictu 0·75, tarsi 0·9. (Descr. maris ex Teapa, Tabasco, Mexico. Mus. nostr.)

♀ supra rufo-brunnea, plaga dorsali celata alba: subtus omnino rufa, gula pallidiore, subalaribus rufis, remigibus interne pallide cervino marginatis: rostro et pedibus corylinis, illius mandibula pallida. (Descr. feminæ ex Chisec, Guatemala. Mus. nostr.)

♂ *juv.* feminæ similis, sed supra obscurior et pectore plumis cinereis mixto.

Hab. MEXICO, Playa Vicente (*Boucard* [4], *M. Trujillo*), Sochiapa (*Trujillo*); BRITISH HONDURAS, Belize (*Leyland* [3]); GUATEMALA, Chisec, Choctum, Coban [6], Yzabal (*O. S. & F. D. G.*); HONDURAS, San Pedro (*G. M. Whitely* [9]); NICARAGUA, Matagalpa (*W. B. Richardson*), Sucuya [15], Los Sabalos [16] (*Nutting*); COSTA RICA, Tucurriqui

(*Arcé*), Angostura (*Carmiol* [13]), Pacuare, Pozo Azul de Pirris, Jimenez (*Zeledon* [18]), San Carlos (*Boucard* [14]) ; PANAMA, Bugaba [11], Mina de Chorca [11], Santa Fé [10] (*Arcé*); Lion Hill (*M'Leannan* [8] [19] [20]), Panama (*A. H. Markham* [12]), Chepo (*Arcé*).— COLOMBIA [1] ; ECUADOR [5] ; PERU [17] ; GUIANA [5].

Mr. Sclater first described this species in 1855 as a *Pyriglena* from Bogota trade skins in the British Museum [1], and a few years later it was discovered in Mexico [4] and Guatemala [6], and afterwards in the State of Panama [19] and in Costa Rica [13]. It is now known as a common bird in the low-lying hot forest districts of Central America on the eastern side of the mountain-range northwards of Costa Rica, and from there to the mainland of South America on both sides of the Cordillera.

A little variation is to be traced between birds selected out of the series before us, but the differences do not seem to be localized. One of the darkest birds is from Santa Fé, in the State of Panama; others from the line of Railway being paler, like the Mexican, Guatemalan, and Guianan birds.

The synonyms of this bird are not many. Mr. Lawrence first placed the Panama birds as *Hypocnemis schistacea* [19], which is a bird of the Upper Amazons and still retained in *Hypocnemis*. The same author subsequently described a young male from the same country as *Dysithamnus rufiventris* [20].

Cercomacra tyrannina is a bird of the dense tropical forest, where it lives amongst the underwood. We noticed nothing of special interest in its habits, and little has been recorded by other travellers. Stolzmann, who observed it as high as Chirimobo in Peru (5400 feet), says that it lives both in the interior of the forests and on the edges, but always in pairs. Its cry is peculiar, and unlike that of other Formicariidæ [17].

2. Cercomacra nigricans.

Cercomacra nigricans, Scl. P. Z. S. 1858, p. 245 [1] ; Cat. Birds Brit. Mus. xv. p. 267 [2] ; Scl. & Salv.
 P. Z. S. 1879, p. 526 [3].
Pyriglena maculicaudis, Scl. P. Z. S. 1858, p. 268 (?) [4] ; Lawr. Ann. Lyc. N. Y. vii. p. 325 [5] ; Scl.
 & Salv. P. Z. S. 1864, p. 356 [6].
Cercomacra maculicaudis, Scl. Cat. Birds Brit. Mus. xv. p. 268 [7].

Atra, plaga dorsali celata, campterio alari, tectricum alarum et rectricum apicibus albis : rostro et pedibus
 nigris. Long. tota 6·0, alæ 2·6, caudæ rectr. med. 2·8, rectr. lat. 1·9, rostri a rictu 0·9, tarsi 1·0. (Descr.
 maris ex Paraiso, Panama. Mus. nostr.)
♀ grisea, gutturis et pectoris plumis medialiter albis nigricanti-griseo marginatis. (Descr. feminæ ex Santa
 Rita, Ecuador. Mus. nostr.)

Hab. PANAMA, Lion Hill (*M'Leannan* [5] [6]), Paraiso Station (*Hughes*).— COLOMBIA [3] ;
 ECUADOR ; VENEZUELA ? ; TRINIDAD ?

We are unable to distinguish between adult males of *C. nigricans* and *C. maculicaudis*, and the type of the former seems to us to be a young bird. Mr. Sclater does not separate the skins in the British Museum geographically, for he places birds from Panama and Colombia under both names.

We have skins from Panama sent us by Mr. Hughes from Paraiso Station. One of these and another from M'Leannan are males in fully adult black plumage; the third is immature, slightly greyer on the flanks, and with white streaks on the throat. We refer all of them to *C. nigricans*, a bird we trace to Western Ecuador and Northern Colombia, but not beyond the line of Railway in the State of Panama.

Salmon [3] describes the nest of this species as made of dry grasses and placed between a fork at the extremity of the boughs of low bushes. The eggs are mahogany-colour, mottled with darker shades of the same colour.

d''. Rectrices duodecem.

FORMICIVORA.

Formicivora, Swainson, Zool. Journ. ii. p. 145 (1825); Scl. Cat. Birds Brit. Mus. xv. p. 248.

Formicivora contains about eighteen or nineteen described species, fifteen of which are included in Mr. Sclater's Catalogue. These are widely distributed over Tropical America from Southern Mexico to South Brazil. The well-known *F. boucardi* and the somewhat doubtful *F. virgata* are the only representatives of the genus found within our limits, and both belong to a small section of it in which the plumage of the males is mostly black and the tail comparatively short.

The bill in *F. boucardi* is feeble, but does not present any peculiar characters, the nostrils being quite open, the supranasal feathers dense and reaching nearly to the nostrils. There are well-developed rictal bristles. The tarsi are covered behind with ill-defined scutella, the claws have all deep lateral grooves. The wings and tail are much rounded.

1. **Formicivora boucardi.**

Formicivora boucardi, Scl. P. Z. S. 1858, p. 300[1]; 1859, p. 383[2]; Cat. Am. Birds, p. 183, t. 16[3]; Cat. Birds Brit. Mus. xv. p. 254[4]; Moore, P. Z. S. 1859, p. 55[5]; Scl. & Salv. Ibis, 1859, p. 119[6]; P. Z. S. 1864, p. 356[7]; 1870, p. 837[8]; Lawr. Ann. Lyc. N. Y. vii. p. 469[9]; ix. p. 108[10]; Salv. P. Z. S. 1870, p. 195[11]; Ibis, 1872, p. 318 (?)[12]; Boucard, P. Z. S. 1878, p. 61[13]; Nutting, Pr. U. S. Nat. Mus. vi. p. 405[14]; Zeledon, An. Mus. Nac. Costa Rica, 1887, p. 115[15].

Formicivora quixensis, Cassin, Pr. Ac. Phil. 1860, p. 190[16]; Lawr. Ann. Lyc. N. Y. vii. p. 325[17].

Nigra; plaga magna dorsali celata alba; tectricibus alarum omnibus et rectricibus (quatuor medianis exceptis) macula alba terminatis; subalaribus et remigibus interne albis; hypochondriis griseo tinctis: rostro et pedibus nigris. Long. tota 4·3, alæ 1·9, caudæ rectr. med. 1·85, rectr. lat. 1·15, rostri a rictu 0·65, tarsi 0·6.

♀ supra grisea, macula dorsali sicut in maris, alis et cauda quoque albo similiter maculatis; subtus omnino rufo-castanea. (Descr. maris et feminæ ex Choctum, Guatemala. Mus. nostr.)

Hab. MEXICO, Acatepec[1], Playa Vicente[2] (*Boucard*); GUATEMALA, Choctum, Yzabal, Teleman (*O. S. & F. D. G.*); HONDURAS, Omoa (*Leyland*[5][6]), San Pedro (*G. M. Whitely*[8]); NICARAGUA, Chontales (*Belt.*[12]), Los Sabalos (*Natting*[14]); COSTA RICA,

Angostura [10], Pacuare [10], Peje (*Carmiol*), San Carlos (*Boucard* [13]), Pozo Azul de Pirris, Jimenez, La Balsa (*Zeledon* [15]); PANAMA, Chiriqui, Bugaba [11] (*Arcé*), Lion Hill (*M'Leannan* [7 9 17]), R. Truando (*Wood* [16]).

M. Boucard appears to have been the first collector to notice this species, and a male from one of his collections obtained at Acatepec in the Mexican State of Oaxaca, now in the British Museum, was described by Mr. Sclater in 1858 [1]. The same traveller afterwards obtained examples of both sexes at Playa Vicente [2]. The female, in the meantime, had been found by Leyland at Omoa, and was described by Mr. Sclater in 1859 [5] *.

Shortly after this we obtained many specimens of both sexes from the hot forest country of Vera Paz, where and at Yzabal *F. boucardi* has alone been found in Guatemala.

Southwards of Guatemala this bird occurs in some abundance as far as the Isthmus of Darien. This appears to be the extreme limit of its range, for in the Colombian State of Antioquia and in Western Ecuador *F. consobrina* takes its place.

Leyland says of this bird that it is solitary in its habits and is found in thickets [5]. Mr. Nutting, on the other hand, observes that it seems to be truly gregarious, and is usually seen in flocks of ten or a dozen [14]. He adds that, in marked contrast to all the others of its family, these birds seem to keep to the trees at a considerable distance from the ground, the Formicariidæ in general being never seen much above the earth. Mr. Wood observed *F. boucardi* in abundance at the camp in the cordillera on the Rio Truando. It frequented high trees, and was never seen to descend to the bushes [16].

2. **Formicivora virgata.**

Formicivora virgata, Lawr. Ibis, 1863, p. 182 [1]; Ann. Lyc. N. Y. viii. p. 6 [2].
? *Formicivora boucardi*, Salv. Ibis, 1872, p. 318 [3].

F. boucardi similis, sed pectore striolis celatis albis forsan distinguenda. Femina ut dicitur quoque differt.

Hab. NICARAGUA, Chontales (*Belt* [3]); PANAMA, Lion Hill (*M'Leannan* [1 2]).

We do not feel very confident that this bird is really distinct from *F. boucardi*, as the chief if not the only character possessed by the male, viz. the concealed white streaks on the breast, does not seem of much importance in view of the fact that *F. virgata* is found in the country where *F. boucardi* is common. Our specimen from Chontales possesses white streaks on the sides of the breast; they are, however, not shaft-streaks, but white edges to the feathers on each side near the base.

* In his 'Catalogue of American Birds,' p. 183, and in the recently published 'Catalogue of Birds in the British Museum,' xv. p. 255, Mr. Sclater names a male and female from "Oaxaca" as the types of *F. boucardi*; but this cannot be correct, as the male was first described from the Acatepec specimen now in the British Museum, and acquired in 1858 from M. Sallé. The type of the female described from Leyland's specimen is doubtless in the Derby Museum at Liverpool.

Mr. Lawrence describes the female as resembling the male on the upper surface, but of a very deep chestnut-red on the under surface. The female of *F. boucardi* would thus appear to differ considerably, being decidedly grey above and lighter chestnut beneath. The type, which as well as the male has been kindly lent us by the authorities of the American Museum of Natural History, shows these differences; but the tint of the under surface is not pronounced, and can be nearly matched in specimens of *F. boucardi*.

We do not know enough of this bird to be able to form a decided opinion as to its status with respect to *F. boucardi*.

b. *Nares operculatæ, rostrum quam caput longior, mandibulæ tomia levis.*

RHAMPHOCÆNUS.

Ramphocænus, Vieill. N. Dict. d'Hist. Nat. xxix. p. 5 (1819).
Rhamphocænus, Scl. Ibis, 1883, p. 92; Cat. Birds Brit. Mus. xv. p. 260.

Rhamphocænus is one of the most peculiar genera of Formicariidæ, and to whatever position it is assigned in the family it must occupy an isolated position. Cabanis and Heine place it at the head of their family Eriodoridæ—*Terenura* and then *Ellipura* and *Formicivora* following. Mr. Sclater includes it in the subfamily Formicariinæ, and places it between *Terenura* and *Cercomacra*. We are not satisfied with either arrangement. The bill of *Rhamphocænus* is very long, the culmen slightly curved, with hardly any terminal hook and a very slight subterminal notch on the tomia of the maxilla and none whatever on the mandible. The nostrils are situated a considerable distance beyond the frontal feathers; they are elongated and overhung to some extent by a membrane which has a lobe near the middle. Rictal bristles are well developed. The tarsi are covered behind by a continuous entire scutellum, which bears no signs of divisional sutures; the toes are rather feeble, the hallux being rather long. The wings are rounded, but present no peculiarity; the tail in one section of the genus is long, much rounded, the rectrices being narrow: in the other section it is shorter and squarer.

On the whole, we think *Rhamphocænus* best placed near *Formicivora*, notwithstanding the very different form of the bill and the structure of the nostrils. Both genera have well-developed rictal bristles, a feature not at all usual in Formicariidæ.

Mr. Sclater divides *Rhamphocænus* into two sections—a long-tailed section and a short-tailed section *. This arrangement we follow. One member of each section

---

* Mr. Sclater places in the second section *Microbates collaris*, but we are doubtful if this is correct. Apart from its peculiar coloration, *M. collaris* has open oval nostrils, thus differing considerably from *Rhamphocænus*. That *Microbates* is allied to *Rhamphocænus* is obvious; both have similar bills, the mandible being destitute of any trace of a subterminal notch. This character might be used to separate these two genera from the rest of this section of the Formicariidæ, and the nostrils to divide them from one another.

occurs within the limits of our country. The whole genus has a wide range in Tropical America, the most southern member occurring in South-eastern Brazil.

1. Rhamphocænus semitorquatus.

Rhamphocænus semitorquatus, Lawr. Ann. Lyc. N. Y. vii. p. 469[1]; ix. p. 108[2]; Salv. P. Z. S. 1867, p. 145[3]; 1870, p. 195[4]; Boucard, P. Z. S. 1878, p. 61[5]; Zeledon, An. Mus. Nac. Costa Rica, 1887, p. 115[6]; Scl. Cat. Birds Brit. Mus. xv. p. 262[7].

Rhamphocænus cinereiventris, Scl. & Salv. P. Z. S. 1879, p. 525 (nec Scl.?)[8].

Supra rufescenti-murinus, pileo rufescentiore; capitis et cervicis lateribus rufis, hoc colore infra nigro marginato: subtus gula alba, abdomine toto cinereo, pectore nigro striato; cauda nigricanti-brunnea, rectricibus immaculatis: rostri maxilla nigricanti, mandibula albida, pedibus obscure corylinis. Long. tota 3·7, alæ 2·0, caudæ rectr. med. 1·1, rectr. lat. 0·9, rostri a rictu 0·9, tarsi 0·9. (Descr. maris ex Veraguas, Panama. Mus. nostr.)

♀ mari similis.

Hab. COSTA RICA, La Balsa (*Carmiol*[2]), Rio Sucio (*Zeledon*[6]), San Carlos (*Boucard*[5]); PANAMA, Santiago de Veraguas[3], Calovevora[4] (*Arcé*), Lion Hill (*M'Leannan*[1][6]).— COLOMBIA[8].

This species must for the present be considered doubtfully distinct from *R. cinereiventris*, a bird described and figured by Mr. Sclater in 1855 from a specimen now in the Derby Museum at Liverpool, obtained by Delattre at Pasto in Colombia. At our request the type has been kindly lent us for re-examination, and we can now affirm that a male from Veraguas in our collection exactly agrees with it in all respects except that it lacks the conspicuous brown postocular stripe that exists in the type as shown in Wolf's drawing. There is just a trace of this stripe in one of our specimens, but in the rest it is absent. Our impression is that this stripe is not constant; and if so Mr. Lawrence's name will have to be placed as a synonym of *R. cinereiventris*, a course adopted by Sclater and Salvin in 1879[8]. If, however, the receipt of more specimens confirms the differences now apparent, *R. semitorquatus* must stand, but the bird called *R. cinereiventris* in Mr. Sclater's Catalogue, from Sarayacu in Ecuador, having no postocular spot whatever must be either considered distinct from both described species or merged with *R. semitorquatus*.

The range of this species in our country is limited to Costa Rica and the State of Panama, but it appears to be everywhere rare. The first specimens procured were from the line of Railway[1]. A small number were afterwards sent us by our collector Arcé from the neighbourhood of Santiago de Veraguas[2], and it has also been found by several of the collectors of Costa Rica[2][5][6].

2. Rhamphocænus rufiventris.

Scolopacinus rufiventris, Bp. P. Z. S. 1837, p. 119[1].

Rhamphocænus rufiventris, Gray, Gen. B. i. p. 157, t. 47. f. 2[2]; Scl. P. Z. S. 1857, p. 202[3]; 1859,

p. 383 [4]; Ibis, 1883, p. 95 [5]; Cat. Birds Brit. Mus. xv. p. 261 [6]; Scl. & Salv. Ibis, 1860, p. 399 [7]; P. Z. S. 1864, p. 356 [8]; 1879, p. 525 [9]; Lawr. Ann. Lyc. N. Y. viii. pp. 6 [10], 183 [11]; Salv. P. Z. S. 1867, p. 145 [12]; 1870, p. 195 [13]; Ibis, 1869, p. 319 [14]; Nutting, Pr. U.S. Nat. Mus. vi. pp. 386 [15], 405 [16]; Ridgw. Pr. U. S. Nat. Mus. x. p. 581 [17].

Supra cinereus, capite summo et nucha cum alis extus leviter rufescente tinctis, capitis lateribus et corpore toto subtus (gula alba excepta) pallide rufis; cauda nigricante, rectricibus tribus externis (extima rhachide et pogonio externo fere tota alba) albo terminatis; subalaribus albidis rufescente lavatis: rostro corylino, mandibula pallida, pedibus plumbeis. Long. tota 4·8, alæ 2·0, caudæ rectr. med. 1·75, rectr. lat. 1·2, rostri a rictu 1·2, tarsi 0·9. (Descr. maris ex V. de San Miguel, Salvador. Mus. nostr.)

♀ mari similis.

Hab. MEXICO, Vera Cruz (*W. B. Richardson*), San Andres Tuxtla (*Sallé* [3]), Playa Vicente (*Boucard* [4]); BRITISH HONDURAS, Orange Walk (*Gaumer*); GUATEMALA (*Velasquez* [1]), Choctum [7], Chisec, Lanquin [7], Retalhuleu (*O. S. & F. D. G.*); HONDURAS, Truxillo (*Townsend* [17]); SALVADOR, La Libertad, Volcan de San Miguel (*W. B. Richardson*); NICARAGUA, Chinandega (*W. B. Richardson*), Sucuya [15], Los Sabalos [16] (*Nutting*), Greytown (*Holland* [11]); COSTA RICA, Bebedero de Nicoya (*Arcé* [14]); PANAMA, Bugaba [13], Santa Fé [12], Calobre [13] (*Arcé*), Lion Hill (*M'Leannan* [8] [10]).—COLOMBIA [9].

The first specimens of this bird that reached Europe were those obtained by Col. Velasquez in Guatemala, and described by Prince Bonaparte in 1837 [1]. The bird is now known as an inhabitant of the hot forest region of the whole of Central America, beyond which area it reaches the middle of the Mexican State of Vera Cruz in one direction and the northern part of Colombia in the other, being nearly everywhere tolerably abundant. It is absent from Western Mexico, but occurs on both sides of the mountain-range of Guatemala. It is only in Costa Rica that this bird seems to be rare, for though we have a specimen from Bebedero in that country [14], it appears from Mr. Zeledon's most recent list of the birds of Costa Rica that only a Guatemala example of *R. rufiventris* exists in the National Museum of Costa Rica.

Mr. Nutting [16] [17] obtained his specimens in dense forest, and he tells us that these birds climb about trees like Nuthatches (*Sitta*). Salmon says [9] that the iris in life is red, and that this bird feeds on insects and builds its nest in low bushes. He does not, however, tell us how the latter is constructed, nor give us any information about the eggs.

Stolzmann, writing of the closely allied *R. albiventris*, says that the only specimen he shot at Yurimaguas was in the top of a low tree in the forest, its movements recalling those of a *Polioptila*.

B. *Terrestres: tarsi plerumque elongati.*

c. *Regio ocularis plus minusve nuda.*

c'. *Nares semioperculatæ.*

GYMNOPITHYS.

Gymnopithys, Bonaparte, Ann. Sc. Nat. (iv.) i. p. 132; Scl. Cat. Birds Brit. Mus. xv. p. 296.

Mr. Sclater places *Pithys leucaspis* and its allies with *P. albifrons*, the type of the genus *Pithys*; but it belongs rather to *Gymnopithys*, of which *G. rufigula* is the type.

P. albifrons is a very peculiar species with no near allies. It has oval open nostrils which are situated high up near the culmen; the orbital space is feathered and the formation of the crest is quite *sui generis*. *G. fulvigula* has a naked orbital space and operculated nostrils, in both of which characters it is followed by *G. leucaspis* and its allies.

The range of *Gymnopithys* extends from Guiana over the Amazons Valley to Colombia, and thence northwards to Nicaragua; two closely allied species occurring within our limits.

1. **Gymnopithys bicolor.**

Pithys leucaspis, Lawr. Ann. Lyc. N. Y. vii. p. 326 (nec Scl.) [1].
Pithys bicolor, Lawr. Ann. Lyc. N. Y. viii. p. 6 [2]; Scl. & Salv. P. Z. S. 1864, p. 357 [3]; Salv. P. Z. S. 1867, p. 145 [4]; Scl. Cat. Birds Brit. Mus. xv. p. 296 (partim) [5].

Supra rufo-brunnea, fronte et capitis lateribus nigricanti-cinereis, tectricibus auricularibus nigris, regione postoculari nuda: subtus alba, cervicis lateribus, hypochondriis et tectricibus subcaudalibus brunneis; subalaribus fuliginosis, remigibus interne umbrino marginatis: rostro nigricante, mandibula pallida, pedibus corylinis. Long. tota 5·0, alæ 3·0, caudæ 1·9, rostri a rictu 0·75, tarsi 1·05. (Descr. maris ex Panama. Mus. nostr.)

♀ mari similis.

Hab. PANAMA, Santa Fé (*Arcé* [4]), Lion Hill Station (*M'Leannan* [1 2 3]), Paraiso Station (*Hughes*), Chepo (*Arcé*).

This species was at first referred to *G. leucaspis* by Mr. Lawrence [1], who soon, however, appreciated its differences from that bird and described it under its present name [2]. From *G. leucaspis* it differs in being duller on the upper surface and in having the forehead and sides of the head cinereous instead of reddish; moreover the male of *G. bicolor* has no concealed dorsal spot as in *G. leucaspis*. Both birds have a naked space behind the eye, which in the case of *G. leucaspis* is said to be light blue, the legs being of the same colour and the iris red. Concerning *G. bicolor* we have no information on these points.

The range of this species is strictly confined to the southern portion of the State of

Panama. A little way further south, in the Valley of the Cauca, *G. ruficeps* takes its place, whilst northward at Chiriqui and beyond *G. olivascens* prevails.

G. leucaspis is probably restricted to the forests of the eastern slope of the Cordillera drained by the upper waters of the Amazons and Orinoco. We have lately received a specimen from Mr. T. H. Wheeler from the Llanos of the Rio Meta.

2. Gymnopithys olivascens.

Pithys bicolor, Lawr. Ann. Lyc. N. Y. ix. p. 109 [1]; Salv. P. Z. S. 1870, p. 195 [2]; Scl. Ibis, 1873, p. 373 [3]; Cat. Birds Brit. Mus. xv. p. 296 (partim) [4]; Boucard, P. Z. S. 1878, p. 62 [5]; Zeledon, An. Mus. Nac. Costa Rica, 1887, p. 115 [6].

Pithys bicolor olivascens, Ridgway, Pr. U.S. Nat. Mus. xiv. p. 460 [7].

G. bicolori similis, sed capite toto summo et fronte rufo-brunneis, hac haud nigricanti-cinerea. (Descr. maris ex La Balza, Costa Rica. Mus. nostr.)

♀ mari similis.

Hab. HONDURAS, Santa Ana (*Wittkugel* [7]); NICARAGUA, Chontales (*Belt* [3]); COSTA RICA, Angostura [1], La Balsa (*Carmiol*), Navarro de Cartago (*Zeledon* [6]), San Carlos (*Boucard* [5]); PANAMA, Volcan de Chiriqui, Bugaba (*Arcé* [2]).

This bird has hitherto been placed with *G. bicolor*, but it evidently belongs to a distinct species, with a more northern range than its near ally. One of the characteristic features of *G. bicolor* is its dark grey forehead; in this bird the forehead is reddish brown to the base of the bill. Like *G. bicolor* the male has no concealed dorsal patch, as is the case in *G. leucaspis*; moreover that bird has a black band bordering the white under surface on either side, separating it from the dark neck and flanks. *G. olivascens* has its nearest ally in a Colombian bird which has hitherto been confounded with *G. leucaspis*, but which is clearly distinct from that bird and we therefore describe it as *G. ruficeps* *.

The range of *G. olivascens* appears to extend from Chiriqui northwards to Honduras. We are not certain whether all the Costa Rica references belong to it, but as our specimen from that country is clearly of this species, we assume that it, and not *G. bicolor*, alone is found there.

Mr. Ridgway, who has kindly lent us his types for examination, considered this bird only subspecifically distinct from *G. bicolor*, but we think its characters quite definite. The relationship of both birds to *G. leucaspis* is remote.

---

* **Gymnopithys ruficeps**, sp. n.

G. olivascenti affinis, sed fronte et pileo rufescentioribus, hypochondriis magis rufis et statura majore differt. Long. alæ 2·5.

Hab. COLOMBIA, Cauca Valley (*Salmon*).

There are four specimens of this species in the British Museum, a male and a female from Salmon's collection and two of Bogota make. They are specimens *b*, *e*, *g*, and *h* of "*Pithys leucaspis*."

d'. *Nares apertæ.*

e'. *Plumæ supranasales plus minusve criniformes.*

GYMNOCICHLA.

Gymnocichla, Sclater, P. Z. S. 1858, p. 274 ; Cat. Birds Brit. Mus. xv. p. 271.

The most obvious feature of this genus is the bare head of the male, on which the feathers are reduced to hair-like bristles, the colour of the naked skin in life being light blue. The bill is moderately strong, the nostrils open and nearly round. The tarsi are rather strong, the acrotarsium distinctly divided by scutella, the planta being smooth. The tail is moderate and rounded.

Two closely allied species constitute this genus, one of which is found in the State of Panama and the adjoining portion of the mainland of Northern Colombia. The other occurs in Costa Rica and thence northwards to Honduras.

1. Gymnocichla nudiceps.

Myiothera nudiceps, Cassin, Pr. Ac. Phil. v. p. 106, t. 6 [1].

Pyriglena nudiceps, Scl. P. Z. S. 1854, p. 113 [2].

Gymnocichla nudiceps, Scl. P. Z. S. 1858, p. 274 [3] ; Cat. Birds Brit. Mus. xv. p. 272 [4] ; Lawr. Ann. Lyc. N. Y. vii. p. 294 [5] ; Scl. & Salv. P. Z. S. 1864, p. 356 [6] ; Salv. P. Z. S. 1870, p. 195 [7].

Pithys rufigularis, Lawr. Ann. Lyc. N. Y. vii. p. 293 (nec Bodd.) [8].

Myrmeciza ferruginea, Lawr. Ann. Lyc. N. Y. vii. p. 470 [9].

Niger unicolor, pileo et capitis lateribus sparsim crinitis, quasi nudis, cute (ave vivo) cærulea ; plaga dorsali celata, tectricum alarum marginibus anguste atque remigis primi margine albis, rectricibus lateralibus vix albo terminatis : rostro et pedibus nigris. Long. tota 6·5, alæ 3·0, caudæ 2·3, rostri a rictu 0·95, tarsi 1·2.

♀ supra ferrugineo-brunnea fere unicolor, cauda saturatiore, alis extus castaneis : subtus saturate cinnamomea, gula vix pallidiore, remigibus interne pallide rufescenti-fusco marginatis. (Descr. maris et feminæ ex Lion Hill, Panama. Mus. nostr.)

Hab. PANAMA [2] (*Bell* [1]), Chiriqui, Bugaba [7], Mina de Chorcha [7], Chitra (*Arcé*), Lion Hill (*M'Leannan* [5] [6] [8] [9]).—NORTHERN COLOMBIA [2].

The bare head of the male of this species, the skin being blue in life, renders it remarkable. The feathers of the head, however, are not wholly absent, but appear as bristles thinly scattered over the otherwise bare surface.

The first specimen of this species was obtained at Panama by Mr. J. G. Bell, and is the one now in the collection of the Academy of Natural Science of Philadelphia, which was described and figured by Cassin [1]. Other examples were secured near Santa Marta [2] in Northern Colombia, and both M'Leannan [5] and Arcé [7] sent us many specimens of both sexes from various parts of the State of Panama as far north as Chiriqui and the Costa Rican frontier. Whether this species is found on the Pacific side of the mountains of that country, which seems probable, or not remains yet to be determined; on the eastern side of the range the allied form, *G. chiroleuca*, takes its place.

The female of this species was described by Mr. Lawrence as *Myrmeciza ferruginea*[9], as was pointed out by Sclater and Salvin in 1864 in their paper on M‘Leannan's collections[6].

2. **Gymnocichla chiroleuca.**

Gymnocichla nudiceps, Moore, P. Z. S. 1859, p. 55[1]; Scl. & Salv. Ibis, 1859, p. 119[2]; Lawr. Ann. Lyc. N. Y. ix. p. 109[3].

Gymnocichla chiroleuca, Scl. & Salv. P. Z. S. 1869, p. 417[4]; Salv. Ibis, 1869, p. 314[5]; Scl. Cat. Birds Brit. Mus. xv. p. 272[6]; Ridgw. Pr. U.S. Nat. Mus. xiv. p. 469[7].

Præcedenti similis, sed tectricibus alarum majoribus late albo marginatis, tectricibus minoribus externe omnino albis, plaga dorsali alba minore et nucha plumosa distinguenda. (Descr. exempl. typ. ex Tucurriqui, Costa Rica. Mus. nostr.)

♀ supra schistaceo-brunnea, capite summo et cervice postica saturate ferrugineis; alis fuscis extus obscure ferrugineis, tectricibus omnibus nigricantioribus et late rufo terminatis: subtus late ferruginea.

♂ juv. feminæ similis, sed capite supra obscuriore, tectricibus alarum majoribus haud rufo terminatis. (Descr. feminæ et maris juv. ex Santa Ana, Honduras. U.S. Nat. Mus.)

Hab. HONDURAS, Omoa (*Leyland*[1][2][4]), Santa Ana (*Wittkugel*); COSTA RICA, Tucurriqui (*Arcé*[4]).

Though only two male specimens are known to us, this bird is evidently distinct from *G. nudiceps*. Not only are the wing-coverts much whiter, but the denudation of the head is not carried nearly so far back as in the allied species. This fact is of importance, as *G. chiroleuca* thus serves as an intermediate step between *G. nudiceps* and *Myrmelastes immaculatus* and the allied forms which we now place next the genus *Gymnocichla* rather than in *Thamnophilus*, where they have latterly rested.

Leyland obtained his specimen at Omoa, where he says only two or three birds came under his notice. They frequent thickets, and make a noise like the breaking of small twigs.

Our single specimen was sent us from Tucurriqui, on the Atlantic side of the Cordillera of Costa Rica, by our collector Arcé, but without any note concerning it. The authorities of the Derby Museum at Liverpool have kindly lent us Leyland's specimen, so that its specific identity with the Costa Rica type is assured.

We are indebted to Mr. Ridgway for an inspection of a female and a young male of this bird. The former is darker on the upper surface than the female of *G. nudiceps*, and has the edges of the wing-coverts more clearly defined.

MYRMELASTES.

Myrmelastes, Sclater, P. Z. S. 1858, p. 274.

Thamnophilus, Scl. Cat. Birds Brit. Mus. xv. p. 180 (partim).

The type of this genus is *M. plumbeus*, with which *Thamnophilus immaculatus* auct.,

Myrmelastes corvinus, Lawr., and *Myrmeciza exsul* and its close ally *M. sclateri* seem strictly congeneric. *Thamnophilus leuconotus* also belongs here.

The larger black species are evidently closely allied to *Gymnocichla*, the chief difference being in the feathering of the head, *Gymnocichla* having the crown bare, thinly strewn with hair-like feathers; a tendency to this denudation is shown in *Myrmelastes*, in which the frontal and loral feathers are thin, leaving the skin visible, which in all cases appears to be light blue in life, as in *Gymnocichla*.

Myrmelastes, as we understand it, contains four or five species, of which four occur within the limits of the southern section of Central America. All are forest-loving terrestrial species, and all hang round the hordes of foraging ants (*Eciton*), feeding on the insects started from their path.

1. **Myrmelastes immaculatus.**

Thamnophilus immaculatus, Lafr. Rev. Zool. 1845, p. 340[1]; Salv. Ibis, 1870, p. 114[2]; P. Z. S. 1870, p. 194[3]; Berl. & Tacz. P. Z. S. 1883, p. 564[4]; Scl. Cat. Birds Brit. Mus. xv. p. 189[5].
Pyriglena ellisiana, Scl. P. Z. S. 1855, p. 109, t. 100[6].

Niger, margine alarum proximo et macula dorsali celata parva albis, rostro et pedibus nigris. Long. tota 6·5, alæ 3·3, caudæ rectr. med. 3·1, rectr. lat. 2·1, rostri a rictu 1·0, tarsi 1·3. (Descr. maris ex Tucurriqui, Costa Rica. Mus. nostr.)

♀ saturate brunnea, subtus dilutior; fronte, capitis lateribus et cauda nigricantioribus, mandibula infra pallida. (Descr. feminæ ex Calovevora, Panama. Mus. nostr.)

Hab. COSTA RICA, Tucurriqui (*Arcé*[2]); PANAMA, Volcan de Chiriqui[3], Boquete de Chitra, Calovevora[3], Calobre[3] (*Arcé*).—COLOMBIA[1][5]; ECUADOR[1][4][5].

Lafresnaye first described the male of this species in 1845 from Colombian specimens[1], and the female also received a name from Mr. Sclater in 1855, based upon an example in the British Museum from the same country[6]. The two birds were associated as sexes of the same species by Salvin in 1870[2], on receipt of several birds from Panama and Costa Rica, both males and females, sent us by our collector E. Arcé.

The range of *Myrmelastes immaculatus* is somewhat restricted, and extends from Western Ecuador northwards to Costa Rica. It is also found in the valley of the Magdalena, as specimens are sometimes to be found in the trade collections of skins sent from Bogota. Salmon, however, did not meet with it in the State of Antioquia, nor did M'Leannan on the Isthmus of Panama.

We are without any record of its habits, but may safely assume that it is an inhabitant of the forest. Stolzmann's specimens were obtained at Chimbo, in Western Ecuador, a heavily-forested district. That excellent collector noted the colour of the iris as burnt-sienna, the naked part of the sides of the head greyish blue, brighter on the auricular region, but nearly white in the female[4].

Though placed in *Thamnophilus* by recent writers, we now consider that this species comes much better in *Myrmelastes* near *Gymnocichla*. The tarsi are too long for *Thamnophilus*, and they are covered at the back by a single shield, and not a number of scutella, as in *Thamnophilus*. The feathers of the front portion of the head are thin and scattered, showing a tendency towards the bare head of *Gymnocichla*. The frontal feathers of *Pyriglena* are full and dense, but *Gymnocichla* is not distantly related to that genus, in which Mr. Sclater originally located the female when he described it as *Pyriglena ellisiana* [6].

2. **Myrmelastes lawrencii.**

Myrmelastes corvinus, Lawr. Ibis, 1863, p. 182 [1] (nec *Thamnophilus corvinus*, Gould) ; Ann. Lyc. N. Y. viii. p. 7 [2].

Gymnocichla nudiceps, Salv. P. Z. S. 1870, p. 195 (partim) [3] ; 1874, p. 317 [4].

Thamnophilus immaculatus, Scl. Cat. Birds Brit. Mus. xv. p. 189 (partim) [5].

Niger, unicolor, macula celata dorsali et tectricibus alarum apicibus anguste albis : rostro nigro, pedibus obscure corylinis. Long. tota 6·0, alæ 3·0, caudæ 2·45, rostri a rictu 1·0, tarsi 1·15. (Descr. maris ex Mina de Chorcha, Panama. Mus. nostr.)

♀ adhuc nobis ignota.

Hab. PANAMA, Chiriqui [3], Mina de Chorcha (*Arcé*), Lion Hill (*McLeannan* [1 2]).

Mr. Lawrence's *Myrmelastes corvinus* was placed by Mr. Sclater, following Salvin [4], as a synonym of *Gymnocichla nudiceps* [5], but a re-examination of the question makes us believe that this is not its true position. On carefully comparing all our specimens called *Thamnophilus immaculatus* and *Gymnocichla nudiceps* we find two adult males agreeing with one another, and differing in several particulars from both those birds. There is no white margin towards the base of the wing as in *T. immaculatus*, and the lesser wing-coverts are edged with white and not black as in that bird ; moreover, they are smaller, and have a shorter tarsus. From *G. nudiceps* they differ in having the crown feathered, the forehead alone showing scanty feathering ; the wing-coverts have less white, the larger ones being wholly black.

Mr. Lawrence's description [1] was based upon a young male in changing plumage, the wing-coverts being tinged with rufous ; except so far as this rufous colouring goes, our adult birds agree very closely with the type, which, through the kindness of the authorities of the American Museum of Natural History, is now before us.

The peculiarities of this bird are best recognized by placing it in *Myrmelastes*, and by removing *Thamnophilus immaculatus* to the same genus. These two birds, with some others, thus form a genus allied to *Gymnocichla* in which the feathers of the forehead and lores are so thin as to allow the skin beneath to be seen. This feature is a step in the direction of the bare head of *G. nudiceps*, *G. chiroleuca* being somewhat intermediate.

It unfortunately happens that Mr. Lawrence's name clashes with Gould's *Thamnophilus corvinus*, a synonym of *T. leuconotus*, which we now remove from *Thamnophilus* and place in *Myrmelastes*. This involves a change of name, and we propose to call Mr. Lawrence's bird *M. lawrencii*.

3. Myrmelastes intermedius. (*Myrmeciza immaculata*, Tab. LI. figg. 2 ♂, 3 ♀.)

Myrmeciza exsul, Cassin, Pr. Ac. Phil. 1860, p. 191 (?) (nec Sclater) [1]; Lawr. Ann. Lyc. N. Y. vii. p. 325 [2].

Myrmeciza immaculata, Scl. & Salv. P. Z. S. 1864, p. 357 [3]; Salv. P. Z. S. 1870, p. 195 [4]; Lawr. Ann. Lyc. N. Y. ix. p. 109 [5]; Boucard, P. Z. S. 1878, p. 61 [6]; Nutting, Pr. U. S. Nat. Mus. vi. p. 405 [7]; Zeledon, An. Mus. Nac. Costa Rica, 1887, p. 115 (partim) [8]; Scl. Cat. Birds Brit. Mus. xv. p. 279 [9].

Myrmeciza intermedia, Cherrie, Pr. U. S. Nat. Mus. xiv. p. 345 [10]?

Supra obscure badius ; capite toto et corpore subtus usque ad medium ventrem nigricanti-plumbeis, pileo et gula obscurioribus, ventre imo dorso concolore, campterio alari albo : rostro nigro, pedibus obscure corylinis. Long. tota 5·5, alæ 2·6, caudæ 1·75, rostri a rictu 0·9, tarsi 1·15.

♀ mari similis, sed pileo obscure badio tincto, gula tantum plumbea, abdomine et pectore dorso concoloribus. (Descr. maris et feminæ exempl. typ. ex Panama. Mus. nostr.)

Hab. NICARAGUA, Los Sabalos (*Nutting* [7]); COSTA RICA, Pacuare [5], Angostura [5], La Balsa (*Carmiol*), San Carlos, San Mateo (*Boucard* [6]), Jimenez (*Zeledon* [9]), Carillo (*C. F. Underwood*); PANAMA, Bugaba (*Arcé* [4]), Lion Hill Station (*M'Leannan* [2] [3]), Chepo (*Arcé*), Turbo (*Wood* [1]).

This species is closely allied to *Myrmeciza exsul* of Colombia *, from which it differs in having the wing-coverts unspotted. Panama specimens were at first referred to the southern form [1] [2], but were separated therefrom by Sclater and Salvin in 1864, under the name of *Myrmeciza immaculata* [3], which name must again give way, as there is already a species called *immaculatus* in the genus now used.

The range of this bird has now been traced through the State of Panama and Costa Rica to Eastern Nicaragua †, Mr. Nutting having met with it at Los Sabalos [7] on the Rio San Juan del Norte which drains the great lake. Here he states that *M. intermedius* is common, and lives upon the ground in the dense forest. Mr. Wood [1] noticed this bird in the thick and dry parts of the forest at Turbo on the Isthmus of Darien in some

---

* In Mr. Sclater's original description (P. Z. S. 1858, p. 540) this species is assigned to Panama (*Delattre*) and Nicaragua, but it almost certainly lives further south.

† If Mr. Cherrie's *Myrmeciza intermedia* [10] is distinct from *M. immaculata*, which seems to us very doubtful, the range of *M. immaculata* must be further curtailed, and it must have a new name. Mr. Cherrie gives it as extending from Panama to Talamanca (S.E. Costa Rica), that of *M. intermedia* from Panama and the Atlantic lowlands of Costa Rica (*i.e.* inclusive of Talamanca) to Nicaragua. Thus these two supposed forms are found together over a considerable area. We have not seen authentic specimens of *M. intermedia*, but our single adult male from Costa Rica, which ought to be of this form, seems absolutely undistinguishable from the Panama types. The first primary is not edged with white in any of our Panama birds, nor can the under wing-coverts be described as white—both characters, according to Mr. Cherrie, of *M. immaculata*.

numbers; but specimens were not easily secured, as the bird runs on the ground very swiftly, and hides amongst the leaves. It utters loud, rather musical notes, resembling those of the Golden-crowned Thrush of the United States.

4. **Myrmelastes occidentalis.**

Myrmeciza immaculata, Pr. U. S. Nat. Mus. v. p. 398 [1]; Zeledon, An. Mus. Nac. Costa Rica, 1887, p. 115 (partim) [2].

Myrmeciza immaculata occidentalis, Cherrie, Auk, viii. p. 191 [3].

M. sclateri persimilis, et mares forsan haud distinguendi; femina pallidior, et subtus gutture inferiore et pectore lætte castaneis haud castaneo-brunneis dignoscenda.

Hab. Costa Rica, La Palma (*Nutting* [1]), Las Trojas, Pozo Azul de Pirris (*Zeledon* [2]), Bebedero (*F. C. Underwood* [3]).

This bird is very closely allied to *M. intermedius*, but as it is apparently separated by the great mountain-range of Costa Rica from its relative a distinctive name for it is perhaps desirable. Mr. Ridgway has kindly lent us a typical male and three females of this form, and comparing them with a series of twelve examples of *M. intermedius*, we find no tangible difference in the males, but the females of *M. occidentalis* are decidedly of a brighter chestnut on the breast and lower part of the throat. Mr. Cherrie speaks of a decided difference of size; but his measurements only show an average difference in the length of the wing of ·02 inch, which does not strike us as of any importance whatever.

The range of this form is, according to Mr. Cherrie, restricted to the lowlands of Costa Rica bordering the Pacific Ocean. How far south-eastwards it extends we are unable to say, as we have only male specimens from Chiriqui, and these do not show to which form they belong.

Several specimens in the National Museum of Costa Rica are noted as having the bare orbital skin cobalt-blue, and the iris as chestnut [3].

f'. *Plumæ supranasales normales.*

MYRMECIZA.

Myrmeciza, Gray, List Gen. Birds, p. 34 (1841); Scl. Cat. Birds Brit. Mus. xv. p. 277.

Myrmeciza as at present constituted contains rather a heterogeneous group of species, but we do not propose to recast the genus, beyond removing from it *M. exsul* and *M. immaculata*, which come much better into the genus *Myrmelastes*. This leaves ten or eleven species in *Myrmeciza*, whereof three occur within our limits. Of these, the southern *M. swainsoni* does not penetrate beyond Panama, whilst *M. lœmosticta* and *M. stictoptera* are peculiar to Costa Rica, or its southern frontier.

M. swainsoni has a somewhat slender bill, the nostrils oval and open, the nasal feathers short, but fully developed, not reaching so far as the nostrils. The naked space round the eye is small, and chiefly behind the orbit. The tail is rather long and rounded ; the tarsi are slender, the acrotarsium scutellate, the planta entire. *M. lœmosticta* has a rather stouter bill, the nasal feathers extend to the posterior margin of the nostrils ; the tail is shorter and less rounded.

1. **Myrmeciza swainsoni.**

Myrmothera longipes, Vieill. N. Dict. d'Hist. Nat. xii. p. 113 (??) [1].
Drymophila longipes, Sw. Zool. Ill. (2) i. t. 23 [2].
Myrmeciza longipes, Scl. P. Z. S. 1858, p. 249 (partim) [3]; Cat. Birds Brit. Mus. xv. p. 278 ;
    Lawr. Ann. Lyc. N. Y. vii. p. 325 [4]; Scl. & Salv. P. Z. S. 1864, p. 357 [5].
Myrmeciza swainsoni, Berl. Ibis, 1888, p. 130 [6].
Myrmeciza boucardi, Scl. Cat. Birds Brit. Mus. xv. p. 279 (partim, nec Berlepsch) [7].

Supra rufo-castanea, plaga dorsali parva celata alba, pileo et cervice postica cinereis plumis medianis medialiter rufo-brunneis ; capitis lateribus infra oculos, gutture et pectore nigris ; abdomine medio albo utrinque cinereo ; hypochondriis et tectricibus subalaribus fulvescentibus, subalaribus griseo-albis, remigibus interne cervino marginatis : rostro nigro, pedibus carneis. Long. tota 6·0, alæ 2·7, caudæ rectr. med. 2·1, rectr. lat. 1·6, rostri a rictu 0·9, tarsi 1·2.

♀ supra mari similis, subtus, præter abdomen medium album, fulva, gula albicantiore. (Descr. maris et feminæ ex Veraguas, Panama. Mus. nostr.)

Hab. PANAMA, Veraguas (*Arcé* [7]), Lion Hill Station (*M'Leannan* [4] [5]). — VENEZUELA ; TRINIDAD ; GUIANA [7].

The bird of this form, obtained by the hunters of Bogota, was separated by Count Berlepsch as *M. boucardi,* the chief difference consisting in the whole of the top of the head and back of the neck being dark cinereous instead of the middle feathers having rufous-brown centres. But the typical bird also comes from Colombia, as Mr. T. H. Wheeler has recently sent us skins from Villavicencio in the llanos of the R. Meta which agree with the Guiana form.

Mr. Sclater places the Panama birds with *M. boucardi* [7]; but this is an error, as they differ in no way from the form found in the countries lying along the north coast of South America, which is the bird usually called *M. longipes* (Vieill.), a name misapplied according to Count Berlepsch, who substituted *M. swainsoni* for it [6].

M. swainsoni and its close ally *M. boucardi* form a distinct section of the genus, distinguished by the uniform chestnut-red of the back, wings, and tail.

The range of this species in the State of Panama is very limited, and does not appear to extend much beyond the Line of Railway. No specimens have reached us from the Chiriqui district.

2. **Myrmeciza læmosticta.** (Tab. LI. fig. 1.)

Myrmeciza læmosticta, Salv. P. Z. S. 1864, p. 582 [1]; 1867, p. 145 [2]; Lawr. Ann. Lyc. N. Y. ix. p. 109 [3]; Scl. Cat. Birds Brit. Mus. xv. p. 280 [4].

Supra badia, capite toto et corpore subtus a gula ad medium ventrem nigricanti-plumbeis, hoc dilutiore, mento et gula nigris, plumis singulis vitta transversa subapicali angusta alba; abdomine imo et hypochondriis dorso concoloribus; alarum tectricibus mediis et minoribus cum campterio nigris, apicibus albo terminatis, tectricibus majoribus badiis ferrugineo terminatis, plaga dorsali celata magna alba, hoc colore extrorsum nigro margiuato: rostro nigro, mandibula pallida, pedibus obscure corylinis. Long. tota 5·3, alæ 2·5, caudæ 1·9, rostri a rictu 0·9, tarsi 1·1. (Descr. exempl. typ. ex Tucurriqui, Costa Rica. Mus. nostr.)

Hab. Costa Rica, Tucurriqui (*Arcé* [1][3]); Panama, Sante Fé (*Arcé* [2]).

The two specimens sent us by our collector Arcé, one from Costa Rica, which we now figure, the other from Panama, are the only ones, so far as we know, in existence. None were in the United States National Museum when Mr. Lawrence wrote his list of Costa Rica birds, and it would appear from Mr. Zeledon's lists that he has not yet met with the bird. Its rarity, therefore, seems assured.

As a species *M. læmosticta* is a very distinct one, and has no near allies except *M. stictoptera* and the bird described below. With a general resemblance to *Myrmelastes intermedius* it has many points of distinction, some of which are of generic value. The bill is less stout, and the feathers of the forehead and lores more closely set; there is hardly any bare space behind the eye, and there is a large concealed white dorsal patch wholly absent in *M. intermedius* *.

3. **Myrmeciza stictoptera.**

Myrmeciza stictoptera, Lawr. Ann. Lyc. N. Y. viii. p. 132 [1]; ix. p. 109 [2]; Cherrie, Pr. U. S. Nat. Mus. xiv. p. 532 [3].

M. læmostictæ similis, sed paulo major, mento et gula nigris immaculatis, humeris quoque albis distinguenda. (Descr. maris exempl. typ. ex Angostura, Costa Rica. U. S. Nat. Mus.)

Hab. Costa Rica, Angostura (*Carmiol* [1][2]), San Carlos (*Alfaro* [3]).

There can be no question that this species is distinct from *M. læmosticta*, the types

---

* There is a specimen in the British Museum of a species closely allied to *M. læmosticta* from Ecuador, which appears to be unnamed. We propose to call it:—

Myrmeciza nigricauda, sp n.

Myrmeciza exsul, Scl. Cat. Birds Brit. Mus. xv. p. 279 (specimen *c*).

M. læmostictæ similis et gula eodem modo albo maculata, sed omnino saturatior, dorso nigricanti-cinnamomeo, cauda fere nigra, maculis tectricum alarum majoribus; plaga magna dorsali celata alba.

Hab. Ecuador, Intac (*C. Buckley*).

This bird seems clearly distinct, both from *M. læmosticta* and *M. stictoptera*, the spotted throat separating it from the latter bird. It has nothing to do with "*Myrmeciza*" *exsul.*

of which we have, through Mr. Ridgway's kindness, had an opportunity of comparing. It also differs in many respects from *M. exsul*, which also has white-tipped wing-coverts. Its throat is much darker and the abdomen deeper chestnut, besides other differences. Until recently the type of this species was the only known specimen, but now, Mr. Cherrie tells us[3], there is an example in the National Museum of Costa Rica.

HYPOCNEMIS.

Hypocnemis, Cabanis, in Wiegm. Arch. f. Naturg. 1847, xiii. p. 212; Scl. Cat. Birds Brit. Mus. xv. p. 284.

Seventeen species of this genus are recognized by Mr. Sclater in his catalogue, and the names of two others are mentioned. These belong almost exclusively to the valley of the Amazons and Guiana, only one species, *H. nævioides*, and this a bird of the southern continent, entering our fauna as far as Costa Rica.

Compared with *Myrmeciza*, *Hypocnemis* does not present much difference, but both genera contain a number of species belonging to distinct groups. *H. nævioides* has a much shorter squarer tail than *M. swainsoni*, the type of *Myrmeciza*, the bill is stouter and wider at the base, the nostrils being similarly formed; the development of the frontal and supranasal feathers and of the vibrissæ is the same in both forms, and both have a small postocular bare space. The tarsi, as in most of these terrestrial forms, have the planta entire.

1. **Hypocnemis nævioides.**

Conopophaga nævioides, Lafr. Rev. Zool. 1847, p. 69[1].

Hypocnemis nævioides, Cassin, Proc. Ac. Phil. 1860, p. 190[2]; Lawr. Ann. Lyc. N. Y. vii. p. 326[3]; ix. p. 109[4]; Scl. & Salv. P. Z. S. 1864, p. 357[5]; Tacz. & Berl. 1883, p. 566[6]; Zeledon, An. Mus. Nac. Costa Rica, 1887, p. 113[7]; Scl. Cat. Birds Brit. Mus. xv. p. 293[8].

Supra castanea, plaga dorsali celata alba, capite saturate cinereo; alis nigris, tectricibus minoribus albo terminatis, tectricibus reliquis et secundariis interioribus maculis magnis rufis notatis, his quoque in pogonio externo eodem colore irregulariter limbatis: subtus alba, mento et gula nigris plumis ad basin albis, pectore et abdominis antici lateribus maculis magnis nigris notatis, hypochondriis cinerascentibus; cauda rufescenti-brunnea, fascia subapicali nigra et rufo terminata: rostro nigro, pedibus corylinis. Long. tota 4·5, alæ 2·5, caudæ 1·4, rostri a rictu 0·85, tarsi 0·9. (Descr. maris ex Panama. Mus. nostr.)

♀ mari similis, supra brunnescens dorso castaneo tincto: subtus alba, maculis pectoralibus fuscescentibus. (Descr. feminæ ex Tucurriqui, Costa Rica. Mus. nostr.)

Hab. COSTA RICA, Angostura, Turrialba (*Carmiol*[4]), Tucurriqui (*Arcé*), Jimenez, Pacuare (*Zeledon*[7]); PANAMA, Lion Hill (*M'Leannan*[3][5]), Paraiso Station (*Hughes*), Chepo (*Arcé*), R. Truando (*Wood*[2]).—WESTERN ECUADOR[6].

The chestnut back and conspicuous large round black spots on the breast of this species render it remarkable amongst the Formicariidæ of Central America, though its size is small.

The type described by Lafresnaye[1] was said to have come from Pasto; but we have not seen specimens in recent collections from that country, though a little further south in Western Ecuador it was found by Fraser at Esmeraldas, and by Stolzmann at Chimbo[6], and from this region it would seem to range uninterruptedly through Western Colombia and the State of Panama to Costa Rica, and we have seen many examples from both the last-named countries.

Mr. Wood, who found it near the falls of the Truando river, says[2] it was abundant near the camp in the Cordilleras, running on the ground amongst bushes in damp and marshy places, much resembling in its actions the Water-Thrush of the United States.

g'. *Plumæ supranasales culminis utrinque extensæ.*

FORMICARIUS.

Formicarius, Boddaert, Tabl. Pl. Enl. p. 44; Scl. Cat. Birds Brit. Mus. xv. p. 301.

Formicarius is one of the most isolated genera of the family to which it belongs, so much so that it is difficult to say to what genus or genera it is most nearly allied. It has usually of late been compared with *Phlogopsis*, but the points of structure in common are of slight importance, consisting, in Mr. Sclater's key of the genera of Formicariinæ, of size, the similarity of the bill in each, and in the plumage being tinted with almost the same colours. The latter, however, are very differently arranged. The points of difference are very obvious, *Formicarius* being a more thick-set form, with much closer, more compact plumage, much shorter, less rounded tail, the supra-nasal feathers shorter and closer, and extending further along the bill on either side of the culmen; the tarsi are long in both forms, but in *Formicarius* the covering scutella are plainly seen, whereas the tarsus of *Phlogopsis* has a single shield both in front and behind; the claws of the former are shorter and straighter than those of the latter.

Seven species, of which one is of doubtful value, constitute this genus, and these are distributed over nearly the whole of the forest-regions of Tropical America from Southern Mexico to South Brazil. Four species occur within our limits, of which *F. moniliger* of South Mexico and Guatemala is the only one that is endemic; the other three, which all belong to the southern section of our fauna, extend their range into the southern continent, one of them reaching Bolivia.

The habits of the species of *Formicarius* are strictly terrestrial; but of their nests and eggs nothing that we know of has been recorded.

α. Macula loralis alba, tectrices auriculares parte distali rufa.

1. **Formicarius moniliger.**

Formicarius moniliger, Scl. P. Z. S. 1856, p. 294[1]; 1859, p. 383[2]; Cat. Birds Brit. Mus. xv. p. 303[3];
    Salv. Ibis, 1861, p. 353[4]; P. Z. S. 1866, p. 75[5]; Sumichrast, Mem. Bost. Soc. N. H. i.
    p. 556[6]; La Nat. v. p. 248[7].

Furnarius * *pallidus*, Lawr. Ann. N. Y. Ac. Sc. ii. p. 288[8]; Boucard, P. Z. S. 1883, p. 450[9].

Supra brunneus, pileo obscuriore, cervice postica et tectricibus supracaudalibus rufescentioribus, loris nigris
    macula subtriangulari alba notatis; capitis laterum parte postica (dimidio distali tectricum auricularium
    includente), cervicis lateribus et torque gutturali saturate rufis, area infra oculos (auricularium parte
    proxima includente) et gula nigris: corpore subtus reliquo cinerescenti-brunneo medialiter pallidiore ad
    ventrem imum albicante, tectricibus subcaudalibus rufo-brunneis; cauda rufo-brunnea nigro terminata,
    subalaribus minoribus cervinis nigro terminatis, majoribus fere omnino nigris, remigibus ad basin in
    pogonio interno cervinis: rostro nigro, pedibus corylinis. Long. tota 7·0, alæ 3·3, caudæ 2·0, rostri a
    rictu 1·05, tarsi 1·2. (Descr. exempl. ex R. de la Pasion, Guatemala. Mus. nostr.)
♀ mari similis.

Hab. MEXICO, Cordova (*Sallé*[1]), Cerro de la Defensa near Potrero (*Sumichrast*[6][7]),
    Atoyac (*Mrs. H. H. Smith*), Playa Vicente (*Boucard*[2]), Tizimin in Northern
    Yucatan (*Gaumer*[9]); BRITISH HONDURAS, Cayo (*Blancaneaux*); GUATEMALA,
    Forests of Vera Paz, Chisec[4], Kampamac, Choctum, &c. (*O. S. & F. D. G.*),
    Tactic (*Sarg*).

Formicarius moniliger was discovered by M. Sallé near Cordova, in the Mexican
State of Vera Cruz, and was described by Mr. Sclater in 1856[1]. Sumichrast says that
it inhabits the interior of the great woods of the hot region of that State, being common
at Cerro de la Defensa near Potrero, reaching an altitude of 2600 feet and upwards
above the level of the sea[6]. M. Boucard also found it at Playa Vicente in the same
State, and Mr. Herbert Smith at Atoyac, near the foot of the mountains between Vera
Cruz and the plateau.

The Yucatan bird was separated by Mr. Lawrence as *F. pallidus*[8], birds from that
country, as the name implies, being unusually pale in general colour, a very common
feature in many forms of the birds of Yucatan. This contrast of colour is quite apparent
when specimens from that country are placed side by side with the typical form; but
the difference seems to be of much less value when Guatemalan and British Honduras
examples are mingled in the series, and it is undesirable to make any separation.

Sumichrast says[6] that *F. moniliger* is a shy bird. Its cry as heard at a distance is a
series of ascending notes, not unlike, though more sonorous than, those of *Catherpes
mexicanus*. It is almost always to be seen on the ground, turning over with its beak
the dry leaves or the moss in search of insects.

* Corrected to *Formicarius* in the Index to the Volume.

2. Formicarius hoffmanni.

Myrmornis hoffmanni, Cab. J. f. Orn. 1861, p. 95 [1].

Formicarius hoffmanni, Scl. & Salv. P. Z. S. 1864, p. 357 [2]; 1879, p. 526 [3]; Lawr. Ann. Lyc. N. Y. ix. p. 110 [4]; Salv. P. Z. S. 1866, p. 75 [5]; 1870, p. 195 [6]; Boucard, P. Z. S. 1878, p. 62 [7]; Nutting, Pr. U. S. Nat. Mus. vi. p. 405 [8]; Zeledon, An. Mus. Nac. Costa Rica, 1887, p. 115 [9]; Scl. Cat. Birds Brit. Mus. xv. p. 304 [10].

Formicarius analis, Lawr. Ann. Lyc. N. Y. vii. p. 326 (cf. Lawr. l. c. ix. p. 110) [11].

F. moniligero affinis, sed torque gutturali rufo vix ullo (aut omnino absente), tectricibus subcaudalibus clare rufis distinguendus.

Hab. NICARAGUA, Los Sabalos (*Nutting* [8]); COSTA RICA (*Hoffmann* [1] [4]), San Carlos (*Boucard* [7]), Las Trojas, Jimenez, Pacuare (*Zeledon* [9]); PANAMA, Chiriqui, Bugaba [6] (*Arcé*), Lion Hill (*McLeannan* [2] [11]), Obispo (*O. S.*), Paraiso Station (*Hughes*), Chepo (*Arcé*).—COLOMBIA [3].

Dr. Cabanis [1] separated this species in 1861, basing his description upon a Costa-Rican specimen sent to the Berlin Museum by the late Dr. Hoffmann. It is readily to be distinguished from *F. moniliger* by the characters given above, but its difference from the Guiana *F. crissalis* is not so obvious, and opinions have varied on this subject. Mr. Sclater in his recent catalogue keeps the two birds separate, which is at variance with the verdict of Dr. Finsch. If *F. crissalis* is to be recognized, its range will be found to be almost restricted to Guiana, specimens from which country are pale ashy beneath, almost white on the abdomen, and the under tail-coverts bright, almost brick-red, the sides of the neck, too, are less prominently rufous. Mr. Sclater places the Antioquia bird with *F. crissalis*; but we think it goes much better with *F. hoffmanni*, to which it was first assigned [3].

F. hoffmanni was a common bird in the forest near Obispo Station on the Panama Railway in 1873, and its clear call could almost always be heard near the forest paths. The bird itself was not easy to see, except by remaining quite motionless, when it would be observed walking about on the ground with its tail erect searching for insects, every now and then uttering its cry.

Mr. Nutting says [8] this bird is rather common at Los Sabalos, but exceedingly shy. He describes its actions, when suddenly approached, as follows:—"Instead of at once resorting to flight like most birds, it spreads its wings, lowers its head, and sneaks silently and quickly along, taking advantage of every inequality of the ground and bunch of dried leaves until at a safe distance from the intruder, when it takes flight." Its note, he says, is a loud clear whistle, followed at a considerable interval by two or more lower less accentuated ones, and has a very remarkable ventriloqual quality; so pronounced is this, that when the bird is quite near the note seems to issue from the trees instead of from the ground, whence it really proceeds.

β. Macula loralis nulla, tectrices auriculares omnino nigræ.

3. **Formicarius analis.**

Myothera analis, d'Orb. & Lafr. Syn. Av. i. p. 14[1]; d'Orb. Voy. Am. Mér. i. p. 191, t. 6 bis. f. 1[2].

Formicarius analis, Scl. P. Z. S. 1858, p. 68[3]; Cat. Birds Brit. Mus. xv. p. 304[4]; Salv. P. Z. S. 1866, p. 75[5]; 1867, p. 145[6]; Lawr. Ann. Lyc. N. Y. ix. p. 110[7]; Tacz. Orn. Pér. ii. p. 78[8].

F. moniligero quoque affinis, sed multo obscurior, capite tota (auricularibus omnino inclusis), gutture et pectore nigris, macula lorali alba nulla, neque torque gutturali; cervicis lateribus vix rufo tinctis; subcaudalibus sicut in *F. hoffmanni* rufis. Long. tota 7·5, alæ 3·6, caudæ 2·0, rostri a rictu 1·25, tarsi 1·3. (Descr· exempl. ex Costa Rica. Mus. nostr.)

Hab. Costa Rica (*Carmiol*), Tucurriqui (*Arcé*[5]); Panama, Santiago de Veraguas (*Arcé*[6]).—South America from Western Ecuador to Peru[8] and Bolivia[1][2].

Adult birds of this *Formicarius* are readily distinguished from *F. moniliger* and its allies by their dark colour, the whole head, neck, and breast being black, the back of a much darker shade of brown, the absence of a white spot on the lores and of rufous colour on the under surface.

The range of *F. analis* is very extensive, as it has been found almost uninterruptedly from Costa Rica and the State of Panama to Bolivia, where it was first discovered by d'Orbigny[1]. It also occurs in the valley of the Upper Amazons, but not apparently further east.

Fraser noted that the irides are hazel, the bill black, the bare space round the eyes flesh-colour, the legs and feet brownish. His specimen was shot near a cane-patch at Esmeraldas in Western Ecuador.

D'Orbigny says[2] that this bird always lives in the virgin forest on the ground, turning the leaves in search of the insects on which it feeds. Stolzmann adds[8] that it runs quickly, and carries its tail erect like a Water-hen. Its cry is loud, resembling at a distance that of a Cock.

4. **Formicarius rufipectus.**

Formicarius rufipectus, Salv. P. Z. S. 1866, p. 73, t. 8[1]; 1867, p. 145[2]; Scl. Cat. Birds Brit. Mus. xv. p. 306[3].

Formicarius thoracicus, Tacz. & Berl. P. Z. S. 1885, p. 101[4]?

Fusco-niger, uropygio obscure rufo, capite summo et cervice postica quoque rufo tinctis, loris, auricularibus omnino et gula nigris, pectore toto et tectricibus subcaudalibus castaneo-rufis, abdomine medio dilutiore, hypochondriis fuliginosis, subalaribus et remigibus sicut in *F. moniligero*: rostro nigro, pedibus fuscis. Long. tota 7·0, alæ 3·4, caudæ 2·1, rostri a rictu 1·15, tarsi 1·6. (Descr. exempl. typ. ex Veraguas, Panama. Mus. nostr.)

Hab. Panama, Santiago de Veraguas[1] (*Arcé*).—Ecuador[3].

This well-marked species comes next to *F. analis* in many of its characters, such as the absence of the white spot on the lores and the wholly black ear-coverts. Its

30*

rufous breast, however, renders it readily distinguishable as well from *F. analis* as from all its congeners.

F. rufipectus was described from a single skin (marked ♀) obtained by our collector Arcé at Santiago de Veraguas [1]; he some years afterwards secured us a second specimen. We have also received from the late Clarence Buckley a skin, agreeing with the type, from Baisa in Ecuador, suggesting that *F. thoracicus* [4] may refer to the same species.

h'. *Plumæ supranasales elongatæ, prorectæ.*

PHLOGOPSIS.

Phlegopis, Reichenbach, Av. Syst. t. 57 (1850).
Phlogopsis, Scl. P. Z. S. 1858, p. 276; Cat. Birds Brit. Mus. xv. p. 299.

This genus contains five or six species, all more or less remarkable for their structure and colour. One species, *P. macleannani*, is characteristic of the southern section of the Central-American fauna. The rest belong to the Amazons Valley from the eastern slopes of the Andes to Para.

The bill in *P. macleannani* is rather stout, the culmen somewhat elevated and slightly curved, the nostrils are slightly oval and open, the frontal feathers are rather elongated and directed forwards, the lower portion of the lores and the whole orbital space, except a small tuft of short, curved feathers over the anterior portion of the latter, quite nude; both the acrotarsium and planta are devoid of scutella; the tail is long and much rounded.

Most of these characters are in strong contrast to those of *Formicarius*, near which *Phlogopsis* has usually found a place.

1. **Phlogopsis macleannani.**

Phlogopsis macleannani, Lawr. Ann. Lyc. N. Y. vii. pp. 285 [1], 294 [2]; ix. p. 109 [3]; Scl. & Salv.
   P. Z. S. 1864, p. 357 [4]; Ex. Orn. p. 17, t. 9 [5]; Salv. P. Z. S. 1867, p. 145 [6]; 1872, p. 318 [7];
   Ridgw. Pr. U. S. Nat. Mus. vi. p. 415 [8]; Zeledon, An. Mus. Nac. Costa Rica, 1887, p. 115 [9];
   Scl. Cat. Birds Brit. Mus. xv. p. 300 [10].

Capite summo umbrino-brunneo, fronte et superciliis magis canescentibus; cervice postica fascia transversa
   rufo-castanea; dorso, scapularibus et tectricibus alarum omnibus umbrinis, plumis singulis macula magna
   subapicali nigra, dorso postico umbrino immaculato; tectricibus supracaudalibus longissimis, ad apicem fere
   nigris: subtus gutture toto nigro, pectore et abdomine castaneis, plumis singulis sicut dorso nigro maculatis,
   maculis pectoralibus fere celatis, colore castaneo ad crinum in umbrinum transeunte; oculorum ambitu
   nudo, ave vivo cæruleo: rostro nigro, pedibus cum unguibus flavis. Long. tota 7·5, alæ 3·5, caudæ rectr.
   med. 3·3, rectr. lat. 2·45, rostri a rictu 1·0, tarsi 1·25. (Descr. maris ex Santiago de Veraguas, Panama.
   Mus. nostr.)

♀ mari similis.

Hab. NICARAGUA, Chontales (*Belt* [7]); COSTA RICA, Tucurriqui (*Arcé* [5]), Angostura
   (*Carmiol* [3]), Rio Sucio (*J. Cooper* [8], *Zeledon* [9]); PANAMA, Santiago de Veraguas
   (*Arcé* [6]), Lion Hill (*MᶜLeannan* [1] [2] [4]).

This fine *Phlogopsis* was discovered on the line of the Panama Railway by the late James M'Leannan, to whose exertions we are mainly indebted for our knowledge of the ornithology of the Isthmus. It was described by Mr. Lawrence in 1860 and named after its discoverer [1].

We have no knowledge of the range of *P. macleannani* southward of the Line of Railway, as Lieut. Michler's Darien Expedition did not meet with it, nor did Salmon in the Cauca Valley; but northwards it is found through the State of Panama, Eastern Costa Rica, and as far as the province of Chontales in Nicaragua [7]. It is thus a characteristic bird of the southern section of our fauna.

We have no record of the habits of this species beyond the fact that it lives in the high woods and feeds amongst the underwood. The bare skin round the eye in life is light blue [2].

d. *Regio ocularis vestita.*

i'. *Vibrissæ modicæ, tarsi elongati.*

e''. *Rostrum robustum, latum.*

PITTASOMA.

Pittasoma, Cassin, Pr. Ac. Phil. 1860, p. 189; Scl. Cat. Birds Brit. Mus. xv. p. 309.

This remarkable form, containing two closely allied species both peculiar to our fauna, has many points in common with *Grallaria*, such as the large stout body, short tail, and long tarsi; but the bill is much larger, wider at the base, and less compressed generally. The coloration too is peculiar, differing much from that of all *Grallariæ*.

1. **Pittasoma michleri.**

Pittasoma michleri, Cassin, Pr. Ac. Phil. 1860, p. 189 [1]; Lawr. Ann. Lyc. N. Y. vii. pp. 294 [2], 326 [3]; Scl. & Salv. P. Z. S. 1864, p. 357 [4]; Salv. P. Z. S. 1867, p. 146 [5]; 1870, p. 196 [6]; Scl. Cat. Birds Brit. Mus. xv. p. 309 [7].

Supra brunneum (?), plumis omnibus nigro marginatis; capite summo toto nigro, loris et area infra oculos cum mento albo variegatis; tectricibus auricularibus et torque nuchali castaneis: subtus gula nigra castaneo maculata, corpore reliquo albo nigro fasciato, pectoris plumis castaneo marginatis; alis et cauda fusco-nigricantibus extrorsum dorso concoloribus, illius tectricibus et secundariis internis macula cervina terminatis: rostro nigricante, mandibula pallida, pedibus corylinis. Long. tota 7·0, alæ 3·9, caudæ 1·4, rostri a rictu 1·4, tarsi 2·05. (Descr. maris ex Santa Fé, Panama. Mus. nostr.)

♀ supra mari similis, subtus multo minus fasciata, abdomine medio fere immaculato; gutture ferrugineo lavato. (Descr. feminæ ex Lion Hill, Panama. Mus. nostr.)

Hab. PANAMA, Santa Fé [5], Calovevora [6] (*Arcé*), Lion Hill (*M'Leannan* [2] [3] [4]), Rio Truando (*Wood* [1]).

This remarkable species was discovered by Messrs. W. S. Wood and C. J. Wood, jr., when with Lieut. Michler's Expedition to the Isthmus of Darien. It was found on the River Truando on 22nd Jan., 1858, above its junction with the Atrato, but before reaching the Cordillera. It was not common, but frequented woody places, running on the ground very swiftly and scratching amongst the leaves. M'Leannan soon after found this bird on the Panama Railway, and the specimens of both collectors were before Cassin when he described the species in 1860 [1].

Some of M'Leannan's birds were found on the ground in retired places in the forest, where they appeared to feed on ants [2]. Others were noticed in low shrubs in company with *Phlogopsis macleannani* [3].

Darien seems to be the southern limit of the range of *P. michleri* in this direction. Northwards we have not traced it beyond the Santa Fé district. We have no specimens from Chiriqui, and in Costa Rica the closely allied form, *P. zeledoni*, seems to take its place.

2. Pittasoma zeledoni.

Pittasoma michleri zeledoni, Ridgw. Pr. U. S. Nat. Mus. vi. p. 414 [1]; Zeledon, An. Mus. Nac. Costa Rica, 1887, p. 115 [2].

Pittasoma zeledoni, Scl. Cat. Birds Brit. Mus. xv. p. 310 [3].

P. michleri similis, sed multo major, capite toto nigro, auricularibus tantum castaneo vix notatis. Long. alæ 4·35, caudæ 1·6, tarsi 2·0. (Descr. ex Ridgway *l. s. c.*)

Hab. Costa Rica, Rio Sucio (*J. Cooper* [1]), Jimenez (*Zeledon* [2]).

Though closely allied to *P. michleri* this species appears to have definite characters. We do not possess a specimen of it, and Mr. Ridgway's description gives all the information we have concerning it.

f″. *Rostrum robustum, compressum.*

GRALLARIA.

Grallaria, Vieillot, Anal. p. 43 (1816); Scl. Ibis, 1877, p. 437; Scl. Cat. Birds Brit. Mus. xv. p. 311.

Mr. Sclater's account of the genus *Grallaria* in the 'Catalogue of Birds in the British Museum' is based upon his paper in 'The Ibis' for 1877. The same divisions are adopted, but the number of recognized species is raised from 27 to 31, to which we now add another, *G. intermedia*, not recognized by Mr. Sclater, and the recently described *G. lizanoi*. This leaves only *G. przewalskii*, Tacz., as unknown to us.

The genus is distributed over nearly the whole of Tropical America, the dense forests of the eastern slopes of the Andes possessing by far the larger number of species. In Central America and Mexico only seven species are found, three of them belonging to Mr. Sclater's second Section B, GRALLARIÆ REGES, and the other four to his fourth Section D, GRALLARIÆ FLAMMULATÆ. Sections A and C are unrepresented in our fauna.

All the species of *Grallaria* seem to be solitary in their habits. They live upon the ground in the dense forest, seeking their food amongst the decaying vegetation. The following note of Salmon's gives a good idea of their mode of life. Writing (P. Z. S. 1879, p. 527) of *Grallaria ruficapilla* he says :—" In the morning, and shortly before sunset, may be heard a melancholy cry as this Ant-Thrush creeps amongst the brush-wood. Many times have I followed to obtain a specimen, and after a tough scramble of an hour given it up for a bad job. At one time you seem to stand right upon it, and a moment after you hear it four yards off; again you reach the spot, and you hear it twenty yards behind you; you return, then it is on your right; soon after you hear it on the left. At first you imagine the bird has the power of a ventriloquist; but by dint of patience and watching you may see it creeping swiftly and silently among the grass and brushwood in places where it has to pass a rather more open spot, and the mystery is explained. The nest is also difficult to obtain : it is placed at some height from the ground, and made of a mass of roots, dead leaves, and moss, lined with roots and fibres. The eggs are two in number, rather round, and blue."

Salmon also took the eggs of *Grallaria ruficeps*, which he describes as " rich dark greenish-blue."

It would thus appear that the species of *Grallaria*, though practically terrestrial in their habits, seek the greater safety of bushes for their nests. Their blue eggs differ widely from those of other Formicariidæ known to us.

The bill in *Grallaria* (*G. guatemalensis*) is stout, the culmen arched, the tomia of both maxilla and mandible slightly decurved; the former has a distinct but not very prominent notch near the end; the latter hardly shows any notch but only a slight depression; the surface of the maxilla is nearly smooth, without longitudinal ridges. The nostril is quite open, nearly round, and exposed, and a portion of the turbinals is distinctly seen within the cavity. The frontal feathers just reach the proximal end of the nostrils. There are no simple rictal bristles strictly speaking, but the feathers bordering the rictus end in black hair-like points. The legs are long, the tibia feathered nearly to the tibio-tarsal joint; the tarsi have indistinct scutella in front, which become better defined towards the distal end, the back is covered with a single shield. The toes are short and the claws short and only moderately curved. The wings are short and rounded, the third primary slightly the longest and the first = the tenth. The tail is short and slightly rounded and considerably shorter than the tarsi.

α. Grallariæ reges, majores.

1. Grallaria guatemalensis.

Grallaria guatemalensis, Prévost, Voy. Vénus, Zool. p. 199, Atl., Ois. t. 4 [1]; Scl. & Salv. Ibis, 1859, p. 119 [2]; Salv. Ibis, 1861, p. 354 [3]; Scl. Cat. Birds Brit. Mus. xv. p. 313 [4].

Grallaria guatemalensis?, Ridgw. Pr. U. S. Nat. Mus. xiv. p. 470 [5].

Supra olivaceo-brunnea, plumis omnibus nigro limbatis, pileo postico et nucha cinereis; alis et cauda ferrugineo-brunneis, hac rufescentiore: subtus saturate fulva, gulæ et pectoris lateribus brunnescentioribus; loris, macula rictali utrinque et plaga mediana gutturali albicantibus; pectore irregulariter nigro maculato; subalaribus et remigibus intus pallide castaneis: rostro corneo, pedibus pallide corylinis. Long. tota 7·2, alæ 4·5, caudæ 1·6, rostri a rictu 1·2, tarsi 2·0. (Descr. maris ex Volcan de Fuego, Guatemala. Mus. nostr.)

♀ mari similis, sed minor, pectore toto brunnescentiore fulvo striato, maculis pectoralibus nigris magis obviis. Long. tota 6·0, alæ 4·0, caudæ 1·5, rostri a rictu 1·15, tarsi 1·85. (Descr. feminæ ex Yaxcamnal, Guatemala. Mus. nostr.)

Juv. nigra, plumis omnibus fulvo medialiter guttatis, guttis capitis angustis, corporis latioribus, abdomine imo fulvo.

Hab. GUATEMALA (*Prévost* [1]), Coban (*Delattre* [2]), Forests of Northern Vera Paz [3], Choctum, Yaxcamnal &c., Calderas, Savana Grande and Barranco Hondo between the Volcanoes of Agua and Fuego, Pajal Grande (5000 feet) and Calderas (7000 feet), Volcan de Fuego (*O. S. & F. D. G.*); HONDURAS, Santa Ana (*Wittkugel*); NICARAGUA, Matagalpa (*W. B. Richardson*).

This *Grallaria* is sparingly distributed in the heavily forested districts of Guatemala, but irrespective, within certain limits, of altitude; for it is found as high as 7000 or 8000 feet in the mountains and down as low as 1000 feet above the level of the sea. It lives on the ground amongst the underwood overhung by the forest trees, seeking its insect food amongst the leaves &c.

Guatemalan birds seem to be darker and smaller than those found in Mexico, but the difference is not great. Sumichrast thought that he found two species in Mexico, one inhabiting the hot low-lying forests, the other the woods of the Alpine region; but we doubt if any such distinction can be made. Certainly none can be traced in Guatemalan specimens from very different elevations, and it seems highly improbable that a different rule prevails in Southern Mexico.

Grallaria guatemalensis is no doubt resident in the places where it is found. We have evidence of its breeding in the upland forests, as young birds in their first spotted plumage have been shot in these districts in August. June and July would thus be the time of laying, but we have no record of its nesting-habits or of the colour of its eggs.

Mr. Ridgway refers a young bird from Honduras with doubt to this species. We have a similar one from Matagalpa in Nicaragua, which also cannot be satisfactorily determined.

2. Grallaria mexicana.

Grallaria guatemalensis, Scl. P. Z. S. 1856, p. 294[1]; 1859, pp. 366[2], 383[3]; Sumichrast, Mem. Bost. Soc. N. H. i. p. 556[4]; La Nat. v. p. 248[5].

Grallaria mexicana, Scl. P. Z. S. 1861, p. 381[6]; 1864, p. 175[7]; Cat. Birds Brit. Mus. xv. p. 313[8]; Sumichrast, La Nat. v. p. 248[8].

Grallaria ——?, Sumichrast, Mem. Bost. Soc. N. H. i. p. 556[16].

Similis præcedenti, sed plerumque major; subtus pallidior, abdomine fere albicante, maculis pectoralibus magis obviis. Long. tota 7·5, alæ 5·1, caudæ 2·1, rostri a rictu 1·4, tarsi 2·1. (Descr. exempl. typ. ex Jalapa, Mexico. Mus. Brit.)

Hab. MEXICO, Valley of Mexico (*Le Strange, White*[7]), Chimalpa (*F. Ferrari-Perez*), Ajusco (*W. B. Richardson*), Alpine[10] and hot regions[4] of Vera Cruz, Moyoapam[10], Cordova[9], Omealca[9], Uvero[5] (*Sumichrast*), San Andres Tuxtla[5], Potrero[5], Cordova (*Sallé*), Jalapa[6] (*de Oca*[2]), Playa Vicente (*Boucard*[3]), Omilteme in Guerrero (*Mrs. H. H. Smith*).

We are not very confident of the distinctness of this form from *G. guatemalensis*, as some Mexican specimens approach those of Guatemala more nearly in size than the type, which appears to be an exceptionally large example. The plumage of the underside of the former seems to be always paler in colour, especially on the middle of the abdomen, which is nearly white in the more northern bird; but our difficulty in deciding this point is increased from the limited series of specimens before us, and several of those we have are young birds and therefore of no use for comparison. For the present we keep all the Mexican birds under the title *G. mexicana*.

Sumichrast[10], as already stated, thought that two species of this form of *Grallaria* are to be found in the State of Vera Cruz; one he found at an elevation of upwards of 8000 feet above the sea, the other in the hot country at a much lower level. This difference of elevation in the range of this *Grallaria* does not, we think, imply much, as *G. guatemalensis* is found within the same range of elevation without showing any difference in size or colour.

G. mexicana is chiefly known as a resident in the forests of the State of Vera Cruz, but it also occurs in the Valley of Mexico and in the State of Guerrero. We have young birds still possessing much of their first spotted plumage which were shot at Omilteme (alt. 8000 feet) in the Sierra Madre del Sur, Guerrero, in July, and at Ajusco in the Valley of Mexico, in September.

3. Grallaria princeps. (Tab. LII.)

Grallaria guatemalensis, Salv. P. Z. S. 1867, p. 146[4].

Grallaria princeps, Scl. & Salv. P. Z. S. 1869, p. 418[2]; Salv. Ibis, 1869, p. 312[3]; P. Z. S. 1870, p. 196[4]; Zeledon, An. Mus. Nac. Costa Rica, 1887, p. 115[5]; Scl. Cat. Birds Brit. Mus. xv. p. 314[6].

G. guatemalensi quoque similis, sed omnino obscurior et, præter rostrum robustum, minor ; capite summo fere
    nigro, plumarum marginibus nigris latioribus: subtus saturate ferruginea: rostro longiore, robustiore.
    Long. tota 7·2, alæ 4·3, caudæ 1·6, rostri a rictu 1·3, tarsi 1·85.   (Descr. exempl. ex Calovevora, Panama.
    Mus. nostr.)

Hab. COSTA RICA, Irazu (*Rogers*), Turrialba (*Zeledon*[5]) ; PANAMA, Volcan de Chiriqui[4],
    Calovevora[4], Santa Fé[1] (*Arcé*).

Though the bill is somewhat stouter, this is a small dark form of *G. guatemalensis*
found in Costa Rica and the State of Panama, another still smaller allied form
(*G. regulus*) occurring in Guiana, Colombia, and Ecuador.

G. princeps was discovered by our collector Arcé, who sent us several specimens from
the State of Panama.   It was subsequently found in Costa Rica, whence we have also
an example and where Mr. Zeledon has met with it.

β. *Grallariæ flammulatæ, minores.*

4. Grallaria perspicillata.   (Tab. LIII. fig. 2.)

Grallaria perspicillata, Lawr. Ann. Lyc. N. Y. vii. pp. 303[1], 326[2] ; Scl. & Salv. P. Z. S. 1864,
    p. 357[3] ; Salv. P. Z. S. 1867, p. 146[4] ; 1870, p. 196[5] ; Scl. Cat. Birds Brit. Mus. xv.
    p. 325[6].

Supra olivaceo-brunnea ; capite summo et cervice postica saturate cinereis ; loris, oculorum ambitu, maculis
    dorsalibus elongatis et tectricum alarum apicibus cervinis : subtus alba, pectore pallide cervino, plumis
    omnibus utrinque nigro late marginatis, stria rictali nigra ; hypochondriis cervinis, nigro distincte striatis ;
    alis fusco-nigris, remigibus extrorsum et interne ad apicem et in margine interno cum subalaribus et
    campterio cinnamomeis : rostri maxilla cornea, mandibula præter apicem pallida ; pedibus carneis.   Long.
    tota 5·0, alæ 3·2, caudæ 1·1, rostri a rictu 0·9, tarsi 1·4.   (Descr. maris ex Panama.   Mus. nostr.)
♀ mari similis.

Hab. PANAMA, Volcan de Chiriqui[5], Mina de Chorcha[5], Santa Fé[4], Santiago de Vera-
    guas[4] (*Arcé*), Lion Hill (*M'Leannan*[1 2 3]).

This *Grallaria* was one of M'Leannan's discoveries during his residence on the
Isthmus of Panama.   Mr. Lawrence described his first specimens in 1861[1], and the
bird has since been traced as far as the district of Chiriqui[5].   Other records of it are
given in Costa Rica and Nicaragua, but the birds there referred to doubtless belong—
the former to *G. intermedia* and the latter to *G. dives.*

The olive-brown back, with its fawn-coloured elongated shaft-stripes, render this
species distinct from all its southern allies and from the closely affined Central-
American birds which follow.

M'Leannan says *G. perspicillata* is not common on the Isthmus of Panama, where it
it is to be observed in the dense woods and jungle, leading a solitary life on the
ground[2].

5. Grallaria lizanoi.

Grallaria intermedia, Zeledon, An. Mus. Nac. Costa Rica, 1887, p. 115 (partim ?) [1].
Grallaria lizanoi, Cherrie, Pr. U. S. Nat. Mus. xiv. p. 342 [2].

G. perspicillatæ similis, sed dorso saturate cinereo pileo concolore, striis rhachidalibus dorsi paucis et tenuis-
simis, striis corporis subtus latis : rostro nigro, mandibulæ basi pallida, pedibus pallide plumbeis.
Long. tota 5·0, alæ 3·1, caudæ 1·2, rostri a rictu 1·0, tarsi 1·4. (Descr. maris exempl. typ. ex Trojas,
Costa Rica. U. S. Nat. Mus., No. 119951.)

Hab. COSTA RICA, Trojas (*A. Alfaro* [2]), Pozo Azul de Pirris (*Zeledon* [1]).

Mr. Ridgway has kindly sent us the type of this *Grallaria*, which was recently
described by Mr. Cherrie. It is most nearly allied to *G. perspicillata* of Panama,
having striated flanks like that bird and not plain fulvous ones like *G. intermedia*,
though it has the dark grey back of the latter bird, in that respect differing from
G. perspicillata.

According to Mr. Cherrie, the range of *G. lizanoi* is probably restricted to the lowlands of the Pacific side of the mountains of Costa Rica.

Chiriqui specimens of *G. perspicillata* are somewhat intermediate between the typical
Panama birds and *G. lizanoi*. The fawn-coloured shaft-stripes of the feathers of the
back are narrow, and the whole back is slightly greyer. The ultimate status, therefore, of *G. lizanoi* with regard to *G. perspicillata* is hardly established.

6. Grallaria intermedia.

Grallaria perspicillata, Lawr. Ann. Lyc. N. Y. ix. p. 110 (?) [1]; Boucard, P. Z. S. 1878, p. 62 [2].
Grallaria intermedia, Ridgw. Pr. U. S. Nat. Mus. vi. p. 406 [3]; Zeledon, An. Mus. Nac. Costa Rica,
1887, p. 115 (partim ?) [4]; Cherrie, Pr. U. S. Nat. Mus. xiv. p. 534 [5].

Præcedenti similis, sed dorso cinereo immaculato, hypochondriis fulvis haud striatis, facile distinguenda.
(Descr. maris ex La Balsa, Costa Rica. Mus. nostr.)

Hab. COSTA RICA, Angostura [1], La Balsa (*Carmiol*), Talamanca (*Gabb* [3] ?), Jimenez
(*Zeledon* [4], *Alfaro* [5]), San Carlos (*Boucard* [2]).

In many respects this bird is intermediate between *G. perspicillata* and *G. dives*,
having the spotted wing-coverts, the rictal stripe, and the striped chest of the former,
and the unspotted grey back and rufous flanks of the latter. These characters, we
think, render it quite distinct, and we consider Mr. Ridgway was right in separating
it specifically. Its range would appear to be confined to Costa Rica, where it occurs
on the eastern side of the Cordillera.

7. Grallaria dives. (Tab. LIII. fig. 1.)

Grallaria dives, Salv. P. Z. S. 1864, p. 582 [1]; Lawr. Ann. Lyc. N. Y. viii. p. 183 [2]; ix. p. 110 [3];

31*

Nutting & Ridgw. Pr. U. S. Nat. Mus. vi. p. 406 [4]; Scl. Cat. Birds Brit. Mus. xv. p. 323 [5]; Cherrie, Pr. U. S. Nat. Mus. xiv. p. 534 [6].

Grallaricula perspicillata, Scl. Ibis, 1873, p. 373 [7].

G. perspicillatæ quoque similis, sed dorso cinereo immaculato; tectricibus alarum haud maculatis; stria rictali nigra nulla; pectore et hypochondriis fulvis, illo vix striato, his quoque unicoloribus, distinguenda. A *G. intermedia* differt tectricibus alarum immaculatis; stria rictali nulla; pectore vix striato et hypochondriis saturate fulvis. (Descr. exempl. typ. ex Tucurriqui, Costa Rica. Mus. nostr.)

Hab. NICARAGUA, Chontales (*Belt* [6]), Los Sabalos (*Nutting* [4]), Greytown (*Holland* [2]); COSTA RICA, Tucurriqui (*Arcé* [1]).

Grallaria dives was described from two specimens sent us in 1864 by our collector Arcé from Tucurriqui in Eastern Costa Rica [1]; but it has not, so far as we know, until quite recently, been since found in that country, as all subsequent notices of it were from Nicaragua, until Mr. Cherrie in writing on Costa Rica birds mentioned and described a young bird from that country [6]. Mr. Holland obtained a specimen near Greytown [2], and Belt another in the province of Chontales [6]. More recently Mr. Nutting secured an example at Los Sabalos [4], where it was apparently rare, as the only one seen was observed running along the ground in the thick woods.

The deep russet unstriped flanks, the faint streaks on the breast, the unspotted wing-coverts, and the absence of a black rictal stripe on either side of the throat render this species easily distinguishable from its two Central-American allies described above.

We have figured one of the types from Tucurriqui, Costa Rica.

j'. *Vibrissæ elongatæ; tarsi breviores.*

GRALLARICULA.

Grallaricula, Sclater, P. Z. S. 1858, p. 283; Cat. Birds Brit. Mus. xv. p. 325.

According to Mr. Sclater there are five species in this genus, one of which, *G. flavirostris*, occurs within our limits in the State of Panama and in Costa Rica. In general appearance *Grallaricula* resembles some of the small forms of *Grallaria*, but the tarsi are considerably shorter in proportion to the length of the wings, the bill wider at the base, the open nostrils are covered by the supranasal feathers, and the vibrissæ are long—indeed much longer than in any other form of Formicariidæ.

The osteology of *Grallaricula* is not known, hence the position of the genus must remain in some doubt. *Conopophaga*, which has two notches on either side of the posterior end of the sternum, is so like *Grallaricula* in many respects that it may well prove that both should belong to the same family, Conopophagidæ.

1. Grallaricula flavirostris.

Grallaria flavirostris, Scl. P. Z. S. 1858, p. 68 [1].

Grallaricula flavirostris, Scl. Cat. Birds Brit. Mus. xv. p. 326 [2].

Grallaricula costaricensis, Lawr. Ann. Lyc. N. Y. viii. p. 346 [3]; ix. p. 110 [4]; Salv. P. Z. S. 1867,
    p. 146 [5]; 1870, p. 196 [6]; Ridgw. Pr. U. S. Nat. Mus. vi. p. 415 [7].

Supra brunnescenti-olivacea, pileo obscuriore; loris et capitis lateribus rufescentibus: subtus gutture et pectore
    rufis, illius plumis ad basin albis, hujus fuscis et nigro limbatis; abdomine albo, hypochondriis rufescenti-
    olivaceis nigro indistincte striatis; subalaribus et remigibus interne cinnamomeis: rostro corneo, mandi-
    bula flavicante, pedibus corylinis. Long. tota 4·0, alæ 2·6, caudæ 0·96, rostri a rictu 0·6, tarsi 1·0.
    (Descr. maris ex Calovevora, Panama. Mus. nostr.)

♀ mari similis.

Hab. COSTA RICA, Barranca [4], Buenavista [3] (*Carmiol*), Rio Sucio (*J. Cooper* [7]); PANAMA,
    Chitra [6], Cordillera de Tolé [5], Calovevora [6], Calobre (*Arcé*).—COLOMBIA [2];
    ECUADOR [1].

This bird was first noticed on the banks of the Napo in Eastern Ecuador, and was
described by Mr. Sclater in 1858. We have other examples from the same country, as
well as from Colombia, the State of Panama, and Costa Rica, the last-named country
having furnished Mr. Lawrence with the type of his *G. costaricensis*.

Considerable variation prevails between members of this species, but we are unable
to localize them. Panama examples agree so closely with others from Ecuador that it
seems not possible to separate them. The variation chiefly affects the extent of black
streaks on the breast and flanks: in some birds these are well defined, in others they
are obsolete.

We have no account of the habits of this bird, but Salmon obtained eggs of *Grallaricula cucullata*, which he describes as pale coffee-colour spotted and blotched with
dark red-brown spots. They thus differ widely from the eggs of *Grallaria*.

Fam. CONOPOPHAGIDÆ.

This family, which is strictly South American, is not represented in the Central-
American fauna. With the Pteroptochidæ, it differs from the other families of
Tracheophonæ in having two pairs of notches to the distal margin of the sternum.

Fam. PTEROPTOCHIDÆ.

This is another peculiarly Neotropical family of Tracheophonæ, containing eight genera, several of the most characteristic of which are restricted to Chili and the southern part of South America. *Scytalopus*, however, ranges throughout the Andes, and a species of this genus has lately been discovered in Costa Rica.

SCYTALOPUS.

Scytalopus, Gould, P. Z. S. 1836, p. 89; Scl. Cat. Birds Brit. Mus. xv. p. 337.

Mr. Sclater recognizes nine species of this genus, but several others have been described which were unknown to him. The species described below is also an addition to the list.

The range of *Scytalopus* is very extended, and reaches from the Straits of Magellan to Colombia and Venezuela and also to Costa Rica. It is unrepresented in Guiana, but occurs in South-eastern Brazil.

All the species are small Wren-like birds. The wings are short and much rounded; the tail moderate, consisting of soft feathers the stems of which are slender; the bill is short and somewhat compressed towards the tip, the maxilla having a distinct notch near the end of the tomia. The nasal covers are very tumid, and the nostrils are elongated slits lying along the lower edge of the nasal fossa.

1. **Scytalopus argentifrons.**

Scytalopus argentifrons, Ridgw. Pr. U. S. Nat. Mus. xiv. p. 475 [1].

Supra saturate schistaceo-brunneus, fronte et pileo antico argenteo-cinereis, dorso postico et tectricibus supra-caudalibus saturate brunneis his rufescentioribus: subtus obscure schistaceus, ventre medio albicanti-cinereo, hypochondriis et tectricibus ad apices ferrugineo-rufis; alis et cauda dorso fere concoloribus: rostro nigro ad rictus carneo, pedibus corylinis. Long. tota 4·30, alæ 2·15, caudæ 1·55, rostri a rictu 0·55, tarsi 0·8, dig. med. 0·68. (Descr. maris exempl. typ. ex Volcan de Irazu, Costa Rica. U. S. Nat. Mus.)

Juv. supra undique nigricanti-fusco et saturate brunneo indistincte transfasciatus: subtus saturate fuscus, mento et gutture cinerascentibus cervino mixtis, abdomine ferrugineo notato. (Descr. juv. ex Volcan de Irazu, Costa Rica. U. S. Nat. Mus.)

Hab. Costa Rica, Volcan de Irazu (*A. Alfaro* [1]).

We are indebted to the authorities of the United States National Museum for the loan of two specimens (the types described by Mr. Ridgway) of this interesting species, which was discovered by Don Anastasio Alfaro on the Volcan de Irazu in April 1891, and forms an interesting and important addition to the fauna of Costa Rica.

S. argentifrons has its nearest ally in the southern *S. analis*, a bird described by

Lafresnaye from a specimen supposed to have come from Paraguay or Chili, but which is now recognized as a bird of Colombia and Ecuador. From *S. analis* the Costa Rican bird differs in being smaller, in having a less robust bill and more slender feet. In colour the two birds are very much alike, but the legs appear to be darker.

A specimen in the British Museum from Bogota has a whitish patch on the centre of the crown, but it is not so silvery grey as in *S. argentifrons*, nor does it extend so near to the base of the culmen.

Regarding this silvery patch on the crown of certain species of *Scytalopus* some difference of opinion prevails. In *S. magellanicus*, as understood by Mr. Sclater, this feature is only shown in some individuals from Chili and Patagonia, others being destitute of this mark, in which respect they agree with more northern birds, which do not appear to possess it. Chilian birds with the silvery mark were described by Landbeck as *Pteroptochus albifrons*. The specific limits of several of the species are not well defined, and as yet sufficient materials have not been collected to justify a decided opinion on several points connected with the genus.

Of the breeding-habits of *Scytalopus magellanicus* the following note of Salmon's is of interest. He says (P. Z. S. 1879, p. 528):—

" The nest is placed in a mass of moss on a bank; it is also composed entirely of moss. The female lays two eggs, large for the size of the bird, and white. I was first attracted to this bird by a harsh cry continually repeated near me, and immediately looked round to discover what animal it could be, expecting something of considerable size, but, after carefully searching, saw what appeared a small black mouse creeping along the ground. Upon killing it I found it to be a specimen of this bird."

Darwin also (Voy. ' Beagle,' iii. p. 74) speaks of the peculiar cries and skulking habits of the same species in Tierra del Fuego. He adds that it carries its tail erect, as do most other species of Pteroptochidæ.

Genus et Species insertæ sedis.

ZELEDONIA.

Zeledonia, Ridgway, Pr. U. S. Nat. Mus. xi. p. 537 (1888).

Mr. Ridgway has kindly lent us the type of this genus from the treasures of the United States National Museum. It is a very peculiar bird, and its position in the system cannot satisfactorily be decided from an examination of the skin alone.

Mr. Ridgway in his original description compares it with *Catharus* (Turdidæ), *Basileuterus* (Mniotiltidæ), *Scytalopus* (Pteroptochidæ), and *Xenicus* (Xenicidæ of New Zealand); but he justly remarks that nothing but an examination of its internal anatomy can decide to which of these very different families it belongs. In a footnote he adds that skeletons of *Catharus* and *Zeledonia* had been received at Washington, and had been submitted to Mr. Frederick A. Lucas, who was only prepared to say at the time that *Zeledonia* is not related to *Catharus*. A glance at the posterior margin of the sternum would have thrown much light on its supposed affinity to *Scytalopus*.

With the skin only before us we can merely make the following notes upon the external characters :—

The resemblance to *Basileuterus* is hardly more than a similarity in the colouring of the crown, for that genus has much longer, stronger vibrissæ, wider, more depressed bill, longer tail and wings, shorter tarsi, and other differences.

Compared with *Xenicus* the nostrils are operculated instead of open and lying next the culmen, with a membrane below, a very peculiar structure.

So far as the Pteroptochidæ are concerned, in some respects *Zeledonia* comes nearer *Liosceles* rather than *Scytalopus*, the covering of the tarsi being somewhat similar; but the bill is more feeble, and the nasal operculum much less developed. It has too fairly defined rictal bristles, softer plumage, and a much shorter tail.

For the present the position of this genus must remain in abeyance pending a full examination of its internal structure.

1. Zeledonia coronata.

Zeledonia coronata, Ridgw. Pr. U. S. Nat. Mus. xi. p. 538[1].

Supra saturate oleagineo-brunnea, pileo medio aurantio-ochraceo utrinque nigro limbato ; capite reliquo et
  corpore subtus schistaceis, hypochondriis dorso fere concoloribus, tectricibus subcaudalibus olivaceo-griseis :
  rostro et pedibus nigris. Long. tota 4·35, alæ 2·4, caudæ 1·55, rostri a rictu 0·6, tarsi 1·02, dig. med. 0·6.
  (Descr. feminæ exempl. typ. ex Laguna, Volcan de Poas, Costa Rica. U. S. Nat. Mus.)

Hab. Costa Rica, Laguna del Volcan de Poas (*A. Alfaro* [1]).

The only specimen that we have seen of this curious bird is the type, which was obtained by Don Anastasio Alfaro in November 1888 on the Volcan de Poas, in a district of Costa Rica hitherto somewhat neglected. No notes of its habits have as yet been published, and we wait with interest particulars on them as well as a further examination of the structure of this singular form.

Order MACROCHIRES.

Suborder TROCHILI.

Fam. TROCHILIDÆ.

This purely Neogean Family of birds contains, according to the most recently prepared catalogue, about 470 species, which are divided into 127 genera. Of these no less than 118 species, belonging to 50 genera, occur within the limits of Central America and Mexico. By far the larger number of these inhabit the more tropical portion of the country, the number of species becoming less as the northern frontier is approached, and, on the other hand, they are more numerous both in species and genera in the mountainous parts of Costa Rica and the State of Panama. Thus, in Northern Mexico we can only record 14 species, while in Costa Rica and Panama we know of the existence of no less than 65, Southern Mexico possessing 48, and Guatemala 38. Though the Trochilidæ are thus fully represented in our country, there are still a very considerable number of genera, mostly belonging to the Andes, not found within our limits. They include some of the most remarkable forms of the Family : thus we do not find any representative of *Diphlogœna, Helianthea,* or *Bourcieria,* nor *Cyanolesbia, Sappho,* or *Lesbia, Heliangelus* or *Urosticte,* and many other brilliant forms. Nor do any of the characteristic genera of the higher Andes occur, such as *Oreotrochilus, Oreonympha, Rhamphomicron, Oxypogon, Aglœactes,* or *Eriocnemis.* Nevertheless our region has 20 genera belonging to it, none of which are found in the southern continent : these are *Iache, Phœoptila, Microchera, Callipharus, Eupherusa, Elvira, Panterpe, Arinia, Basilinna, Sphenoproctus, Phœochroa, Eugenes, Cœligena, Oreopyra, Delattria, Lamprolœma, Abeillia, Tilmatura, Calothorax,* and *Atthis.* This is a much larger proportion of genera peculiar to our region than is found in any other group of birds, and is due in a great measure to the treatment the Trochilidæ have received as regards the subdivision of genera, which has been carried further than in any other Family of birds. At the same time it must be noted that this very remarkable group, so specialized as a whole, is very highly differentiated as regards its species, and the genera, numerous as they are, do no more than link together the most obviously allied forms. If any considerable reduction of their number were attempted, the result would hardly prove satisfactory, as the uniformity of many genera would scarcely fail to suffer thereby. In fact many more genera than the number here accepted have been proposed, so that the present system is a compromise between the extreme views held on this point.

A few words on the classification of the Family seem necessary, as the system adopted differs in many points from any hitherto promulgated. So various are the characters possessed by the Trochilidæ that hardly any serve to divide the Family into large groups of genera; the form of the bill, the modifications of the tail, all vary to such a degree that they cannot be used except in a subordinate sense. A plan has been adopted which is no doubt somewhat artificial in its application: this takes the serration of the bill as a character by which to divide the whole Family into three sections. In some genera these serrations are very plainly visible, in others no trace of them can be seen, whilst in others they are very feeble and can only be traced with difficulty. Out of these three states three sections have been formed, dividing the Family into three subequal groups of genera: we do not call them Subfamilies as they can hardly have so high a value placed upon them. The application of this character brings several genera into a not unnatural proximity, and introduces a decided improvement in the system of arrangement. Thus *Hemistephania* stands near *Androdon*, *Thalurania* not far from *Chlorostilbon*, *Avocettula* next to *Lampornis*. *Pinarolæma* proves to belong to the same neighbourhood, and not to that of *Oreotrochilus*. Even *Loddigesia* is not unnaturally associated with *Bellona* and *Cephalolepis*. All these points are in favour of the system here adopted and seem to justify its trial.

As the structure of the Trochilidæ has been very fully described in systematic works on ornithology, and their habits have also been recorded in the many special works on this favourite family, we do not propose to enter at length upon either subject here.

We are much indebted to Mr. Ridgway for a complete list of the Mexican and Central-American Trochilidæ contained in the United States National Museum. All the localities he gives us not previously published are quoted in the following pages.

TROCHILI.

Sect. A. TROCHILI SERRIROSTRES.

Tomia maxillæ ad apicem distincte serrata ; mandibula quoque eodem modo sæpe serrata.

a. *Rostrum cuneatum, ad basin latum, apicem versus gradatim compressum.*

HELIOTHRIX.

Heliothrix, Boie, Isis, 1831, p. 547 ; Salv. Cat. Birds Brit. Mus. xvi. p. 30.

A genus of three species, though others have been suggested. These are distributed over the greater part of the forest regions of Tropical America, from British Honduras and Eastern Guatemala to South Brazil. One species, *H. barroti*, occurs within our region and spreads southwards to Western Ecuador.

Heliothrix is a well-marked genus, having a peculiar bill, which is cuneate, being wide at the base and gradually compressed towards the tip. The tail is cuneate, the central rectrices being considerably longer than the lateral ones. The nasal covers are completely feathered, so that the nostrils are not at all exposed. The only genus that approaches *Heliothrix* is *Schistes*, which has a similar bill and similar glittering auricular patches; but the tail is rounded, and the nasal covers are partly exposed. *Augastes*, too, has some resemblance to these genera, but the relationship is more remote.

Mr. Lawrence inserts *Heliothrix auritus* in his list of M'Leannan's Panama birds (Ann. Lyc. N. Y. vii. p. 291), but the occurrence of this bird so far from its usual range requires confirmation.

1. Heliothrix barroti.

Trochilus barroti, Bourc. Rev. Zool. 1843, p. 72 [1].

Ornismya barroti, Bourc. & Muls. Ann. Sc. Phys. et Nat. Lyon, vi. p. 48 [2].

Heliothrix barroti, Gray, Gen. B. i. p. 115 [3]; Gould, Mon. Troch. iv. t. 217 (Oct. 1853) [4]; Salv. Ibis, 1860, pp. 272 [5], 400 [6]; 1872, p. 320 [7]; P. Z. S. 1867, p. 155 [8]; 1870, p. 209 [9]; Cat. Birds Brit. Mus. xvi. p. 32 [10]; Lawr. Ann. Lyc. N. Y. vii. p. 291 [11]; ix. p. 125 [12]; Scl. & Salv. P. Z. S. 1864, p. 365 [13]; Tacz. Orn. Pér. i. p. 258 [14].

Heliothrix purpureiceps, Gould, P. Z. S. 1855, p. 87 [15]; Mon. Troch. iv. t. 216 (May 1859) [16].

Heliothrix violifrons, Gould, Intr. Troch. p. 122 [17].

Supra nitenti-aureo-viridis, gulæ lateribus a mandibulæ basi micantibus, loris et tectricibus auricularibus nigerrimis, pileo et plaga postauriculari micanti-purpureo-cyaneis: subtus albus, rectricibus tribus utrinque lateralibus quoque albis, quatuor mediis chalybeo-nigris: rostro et pedibus nigris. Long. tota circa 4·5, alæ 2·6, caudæ rectr. med. 1·6, rectr. lat. 1·2, rostri a rictu 1·0.

♀ mari similis, colore purpureo-cyaneo, pilei et regionis postauricularis absente striam a mandibulæ basi micanti-viridem quoque caret; gutture medio indistincte fusco guttato, cauda multo longiore. Long. tota circa 5·3, alæ 2·6, caudæ rectr. med. 2·45, rectr. lat. 1·4, rostri a rictu 1·0. (Descr. maris et feminæ ex Choctum, Guatemala. Mus. nostr.)

Hab. British Honduras, Belize, San Felipe, and Cayo in the Western District (*F. Blancaneaux* [10]); Guatemala, Las Salinas [6] [10] and Choctum, track between Cahabon and San Luis [6] [10], Polochic Valley between Teleman and Panzos [6] (*O. S. & F. D. G.*); Honduras, Chamelicon (*Wittkugel, in U. S. Nat. Mus.*); Nicaragua, Chontales (*Belt* [7]), La Libertad in Chontales (*W. B. Richardson*); Costa Rica, Tucurriqui (*Arcé* [10], *Zeledon*), Angostura, Cervantes (*Carmiol* [12]); Panama, Volcan de Chiriqui [9], Bugaba [9], Boquete de Chitra [9], Castillo, Laguna del Castillo, Calovevora [10], Santa Fé [8] (*Arcé*); Veraguas (*Warszewiez* [4]), Line of Railway (*Arcé*), Lion Hill (*M'Leannan* [11] [13]), Obispo (*O. S.*).—Northern Colombia [1] [2]; Western Ecuador [10] [14] [16].

This beautiful species has been rather unfortunate in its names, two wholly unnecessary synonyms having been bestowed upon it by Gould.

It received its first appellation from Bourcier, who named a specimen sent him by the French Consul-General at Carthagena, M. Barrot, after its discoverer. Gould then described a male from Popayan as *H. purpureiceps*, supposing it to differ from *H. barroti*, which he recognized in a specimen from Veragua sent him by Warszewiez. The Popayan bird, he stated, had a shorter tail and greater extension over the nape of the blue colour of the crown than the bird from Veragua. The former character is due to the age of the bird, the latter to the make up of the skin. The Veragua bird was figured in the 'Monograph of the Trochilidæ' as *H. barroti*. Females from Ecuador were associated with *H. purpureiceps*. Gould, subsequently, in his 'Introduction to the Trochilidæ,' changed his view and placed *H. purpureiceps* as a synonym of *H. barroti*, and supposing the Veragua bird to have come from Carthagena (the original locality of *H. barroti*!), gave it a new name, *H. violifrons*. We do not see any ground whatever for supposing that more than one very constant species of this blue-headed form of *Heliothrix* exists. The way the feathers of the head are arranged when the skin is made up fully accounts for the apparent difference in the extension of that colour on the crown; and as regards the length of the tail of the male, we find considerable variation exists, due, we believe, entirely to the age of the birds compared. The sexual difference in the length of the tail is very obvious, and it seems nearly certain that this difference becomes as it were more emphasized by the gradual shortening in successive moults of the tail of the male as it advances in age.

The range of *Heliothrix barroti* is now known to extend over the whole of Central America, from the confines of Mexico southwards. It is not uncommon in the great forest-districts of Eastern Guatemala and British Honduras, and in the former country we not unfrequently met with it during visits to the low-lying hot districts. The white under surface of the body and white lateral rectrices render it a conspicuous object in some forest-path or in an opening by a running stream, and these features contrast strikingly with the dark green of the surrounding vegetation. It is, nevertheless, rather a shy bird, and never seen in any numbers together.

It seems to be wholly absent from the forests of Western Guatemala, but passes southwards on the eastern side of the cordillera to the State of Panama, where it occurs on both sides of the main mountain-chain. Its southern extension probably reaches as far as the end of the forest-region of Western Ecuador. In all cis-Andean regions, throughout the valley of the Amazons and Guiana, *Heliothrix auritus* alone is found, *H. auriculatus* finding a home in South-eastern Brazil.

Taczanowski [14] tells us that M. Siemiradski, when at the Bridge of Chimbo in Ecuador, observed a male of *H. barroti* bathing in a stream. The bird chose for that operation a small cascade of a few inches in height, into which it plunged, returning quickly and shaking itself an instant in the air a few inches above the stream. Repeating this manœuvre for about five minutes it flew away.

b. *Rostri latera subparallela, ad apicem nonnihil abrupte convergentes.*

a'. *Rostri tomia (et maxillæ et mandibulæ) plus minusve distincte serrata; corpus subtus simplex, nullo modo coloribus nitentibus ornatum.*

a". *Rostrum elongatum, rectum, debile, nonnihil sensim recurvum, haud uncinatum, tomiæ debile serratæ; cauda brevis, rotundata; frons maris micans.*

HEMISTEPHANIA.

Doryfera, Gould, P. Z. S. 1847, p. 95 (nec Illiger, Coleoptera).
Helianthea, α. *Hemistephania*, Reich. Aufz. d. Col. p. 9.
Hemistephania, Elliot, Syn. Troch. p. 81 (ex Reich.).

A well-defined genus, distinguished by its long, straight, even slightly upturned bill, the tomia of both maxilla and mandible being finely serrated; the nasal covers are fully exposed, the frontal feathers only reaching their proximal ends. The tail is short and rounded. In several respects *Hemistephania* resembles *Androdon*, especially in the form of the tail; but the latter genus shows much more strongly serrate edges to the cutting-edges of the bill, and the male has a well-defined terminal hook to the maxilla.

Four species of *Hemistephania* are now recognized, three of them being closely allied, whereof the only species in our region is one. The fourth member of the genus, *H. johannæ*, is more distinct, and enjoys a wide range, extending from the Andes of Colombia and Ecuador to Guiana.

As Gould's name *Doryfera* for this genus, though an appropriate one, has been previously used by Illiger for a genus of Phytophagous Coleoptera, Reichenbach's subgeneric title, *Hemistephania*, raised to generic rank by Mr. Elliot, must be employed.

The range of *Hemistephania* extends from Costa Rica to Bolivia, and eastwards to the mountains of British Guiana.

1. Hemistephania veraguensis. (Tab. LV. fig. 1.)

Dorifera veraguensis, Salv. P. Z. S. 1867, p. 154 [1].
Hemistephania veraguensis, Elliot, Syn. Troch. p. 82 [2]; Salv. Cat. Birds Brit. Mus. xvi. p. 40 [3].
Doryfera veraguensis, Gould, Mon. Troch. Suppl. t. 22 (Jan. 1883) [4].
Doryfera ludoviciæ?, Lawr. Ann. Lyc. N. Y. ix. p. 121 [5].

Supra nitenti-viridis, nucha et cervice postica nigricantibus certa luce læte æneo-nitentibus, tectricibus supra-caudalibus cinereo-cæruleis; fronte usque ad lineam inter oculos olivaceo-cæruleo-viridi micante: subtus fusco-nigricans, abdomine toto obscure viridi lavato, subcaudalibus concoloribus; cauda purpureo-nigra, rectricibus tribus utrinque cinereo terminatis: rostro nigro, pedibus corylinis. Long. tota circa 4·4, alæ 2·2, caudæ rectr. med. 1·3, rectr. lat. 1·1, rostri a rictu 1·5. (Descr. maris exempl. typ. ex Cordillera de Tolé, Panama. Mus. nostr.)

♀ mari similis, sed pallidior, fronte inornata, pileo concolore. (Descr. feminæ ex Chiriqui, Panama. Mus. nostr.)

Hab. Costa Rica, Cervantes (*Carmiol* [5]), Irazu (*Rogers* [3]); Panama, Chiriqui [3], Cordillera de Tolé [1] (*Arcé*).

A close ally of the well-known common species of the interior of Colombia, *H. ludoviciæ*, from which it differs in being generally darker in colour, the throat being nearly black, the glittering forehead of a bluer shade, and the wings rather shorter. These differences are more obvious in the adult male, the female being hardly separable from that sex of *H. ludoviciæ*.

The first specimen that reached us of this bird was sent us by our collector, Enrique Arcé, who shot it in the Cordillera de Tolé, in the State of Panama. He subsequently obtained several other examples in the district of Chiriqui. The bird is also found in Costa Rica, whence we have several examples agreeing with the type. There can be little doubt that *H. veraguensis* is an inhabitant of forests situated in the mountains at some elevation above the level of the sea. It is absent from the low-lying lands crossed by the railway, and in Colombia its near relative, *H. ludoviciæ*, occurs in the mountains near Bogota, at an elevation of from 8000 to 9000 feet above the sea-level. In Ecuador and Peru another allied form, *H. rectirostris*, occurs. In the former country Stolzmann found it both at Huambo and Chirimoto, at elevations ranging from 3700 to 8000 feet, and it was also not rare at Ray-Urmana, at an altitude of 7500 feet. This last-named bird only differs from *H. ludoviciæ* in its larger size and longer bill.

b″. *Rostrum elongatum, arcuatum ; cauda longior, rotundata : sexus similes.*

GLAUCIS.

Glaucis, Boie, Isis, 1831, p. 545; Salv. Cat. Birds Brit. Mus. xvi. p. 41.

Though Gould includes no less than twelve species in the genus *Glaucis*, and another has since been proposed by Mr. Lawrence, it is now pretty generally admitted that there are only two definite species in the genus, viz. *G. hirsuta* and *G. dohrni*, the others having been based upon various stages of maturing individuals of *G. hirsuta* and the sexes of *G. dohrni*, or to belong to the genus *Threnetes*.

In many respects *Glaucis* resembles *Threnetes* and the genus *Phaethornis*, a relationship suggested by the form of the bill, which is much arched in all these forms. Mr. Elliot goes so far as to merge *Threnetes* in *Glaucis*, but we believe their relationship to be quite remote. The serration of the tomia in both maxilla and mandible is very evident in *Glaucis*, but not a trace of such a character can be found in *Threnetes* or in *Phaethornis* and the allied genera. Moreover, there are peculiarities in the coloration of the members of *Threnetes* suggestive of no near alliance to *Glaucis*.

The bill of *Glaucis* is long and much arched, more so in the female than in the male, the serration of the tomia of the maxilla towards the end being very distinct, that of the mandible less so; the nasal covers are bare, and so also is the inter-ramal space;

the feet are small and feeble, the distal portion of the tarsus bare; the tail is rounded, the central rectrices not projecting beyond the curve of the rest.

The range of *Glaucis* is very extensive, including nearly the whole of tropical America from Costa Rica southwards, and it also occurs in the West-Indian island of Grenada. According to Reichenbach his *Rhamphodon chrysurus* is a Mexican species. This bird is undescribed, but Mulsant says it is the same as *Glaucis dohrni*, a Brazilian species. The Mexican habitat is altogether doubtful.

1. Glaucis hirsuta.

Trochilus hirsutus, Gm. Syst. Nat. i. p. 670 [1].

Glaucis hirsuta, Boie; Gould, Mon. Troch. i. t. 5 (May 1858) [2]; Lawr. Ann. Lyc. N. Y. vii. p. 319 [3]; Salv. & Elliot, Ibis, 1873, p. 276 [4]; Zeledon, An. Mus. Nac. Costa Rica, 1887, p. 121 [5]; Salv. Cat. Birds Brit. Mus. xvi. p. 42 [6].

Glaucis affinis, Lawr. Ann. Lyc. N. Y. vi. p. 261 [7]; Gould, Mon. Troch. i. t. 7 (Sept. 1861) [8]; Scl. & Salv. P. Z. S. 1864, p. 363 [9].

Glaucis æneus, Lawr. Pr. Ac. Phil. 1867, p. 232 [10]; Ann. Lyc. N. Y. ix. p. 121 [11].

Supra nitenti-viridis, capite summo multo obscuriore, tectricibus supracaudalibus elongatis sordide albido marginatis, auricularibus fuscis: subtus rufo-brunnea, gutture, cervicis lateribus et hypochondriis obscurioribus, mento albido, tectricibus subcaudalibus sordide albis medialiter obscuris; caudæ rectricibus mediis nitenti-viridibus albo terminatis, reliquis castaneis fascia subterminali nigra et apicibus albis: rostri maxilla nigricante, mandibula carnea apice fusca. Long. tota circa 4·5, alæ 2·3, caudæ rectr. med. 1·55, rectr. lat. 1·35, rostri a rictu 1·35.

♀ mari similis, sed paulo minor, rostro magis arcuato, subtus pallidior et magis rufescens, stria maxillari pallida magis obvia. (Descr. maris et feminæ ex Lion Hill, Panama. Mus. nostr.)

Hab. COSTA RICA (*Endres* [6] [10] [11]), Pozo azul de Pirris (*Zeledon* [5]); PANAMA, Lion Hill (*O. S.* [9], *M'Leannan* [7] [9]), Chepo (*Arcé*).—SOUTH AMERICA generally, from Colombia to South Brazil; island of Grenada [6].

In 1873 Messrs. Salvin and Elliot [4] examined the claims of the various forms of this bird to be considered distinct species, and came to the conclusion that only one could be admitted; and now reviewing this decision we are of opinion that it is correct. Comparing specimens of approximately the same age and sex from the State of Panama, from Guiana, and Southern Brazil, we find no tangible difference whatever between them.

So far as the bird found within our limits is concerned, it has been called by two names before being finally referred to *G. hirsuta.* The specimens obtained by M'Leannan on the line of the Panama Railway were first considered by Mr. Lawrence to belong to his *G. affinis* of Ecuador [7], and the Costa Rica bird was described as new by the same author as *G. æneus* [10]. Both names now rank as synonyms of *G. hirsuta.*

The range of this species covers a wide area, and it embraces the low-lying hot districts of tropical America rather than the slopes of the mountain-ranges from Costa Rica to South Brazil. In the former country it appears to be rare, but on the line of the Panama Railway it is a common bird, frequenting the edges of the forest and clearings about the stations of the railway-line.

b'. *Maxillæ tomia tantum distincte serrata ad apicem ; corpus subtus plerumque*
(Phæoptila *excepta*) *plumis nitidis ornatum.*

c''. *Spatio inter mandibulæ ramos nuda, culmen usque ad basin quoque nudum,*
tegulæ nasales nullo modo plumatæ.

a'''. *Rostrum longius, sensim decurvum.*

a[4]. *Sexus dissimiles.*

IACHE.

Circe, Gould, Mon. Troch. v. t. 338 (May 1857) (nec Mert.).
Iache, Elliot, Syn. Troch. p. 234 (vice *Circe*) ; Salv. Cat. Birds Brit. Mus. xvi. p. 59.

In this genus the bill is comparatively longer than in *Chlorostilbon* and not quite so straight, being slightly decurved ; the culmen is bare to the base, the nasal covers fully exposed, and the inter-ramal space nude. The sexes are very differently coloured, the males having the under surface more or less bright, the females greyish white.

Four species are included in the genus, some of which are not well defined ; these are separable into two groups, one of which contains larger birds, having the crown the same colour as the back ; in the other the single species is smaller and has the crown glittering blue or greenish blue. The range of *Iache* is restricted to Mexico, one species reaching the confines of Arizona and thence spreading over the whole of the Mexican uplands to the valley of the city of Mexico. This species, *I. latirostris*, also reaches the coast of the Pacific in the State of Sinaloa. The other birds all belong to Western Mexico and range from Mazatlan and the Tres Marias Islands to the Isthmus of Tehuantepec.

This genus was first separated by Gould in 1857, and called by him *Circe*. This name having been previously used in zoology, Mr. Elliot substituted *Iache* for it in 1879.

α. *Pileus dorso concolor ; tectrices subcaudales albæ.*

1. Iache latirostris.

Cynanthus latirostris, Sw. Phil. Mag. new ser. i. p. 441 [1].
Circe latirostris, Gould, Mon. Troch. v. t. 338 (May 1857) [2] ; Scl. P. Z. S. 1858, p. 297 [3] ; 1859, p. 367 [4] ; 1864, p. 177 [5] ; A. Dugès, La Nat. i. p. 141 [6] ; Villada, La Nat. ii. p. 366 [7] ; Lawr. Mem. Bost. Soc. N. H. ii. p. 292 [8] ; de Oca, La Nat. iii. p. 65 [9] ; Boucard, Ann. Soc. Linn. Lyon, xx. p. 281 [10] ; Sumichrast, La Nat. v. p. 250 [11] ; Sanchez, An. Mus. Nac. Mex. i. p. 96 [12] ; Henshaw, in Wheeler's Geogr. & Geol. Surv. v. Zool. p. 380 [13].
Iache latirostris, Elliot, Syn. Troch. p. 235 [14] ; Salv. Cat. Birds Brit. Mus. xvi. p. 60 [15] ; Herrera, La Nat. (2) i. p. 322 [16].
Ornismya lessonii, Delattre, Rev. Zool. 1839, p. 15 [17].

Supra nitenti-gramineo-viridis æneo vix tincta, capite summo obscuriore : subtus obscure cæruleo-viridis, gutture medio plus minusve micanti-cæruleo ; tectricibus subcaudalibus albis ; cauda saturate chalybeo-cærulea, rectricibus mediis saturate griseo terminatis : rostro corallino-rubro, apice nigro. Long. tota circa 3·8, alæ 2·1, caudæ rectr. med. 1·1, rectr. lat. 1·25, rostri a rictu 0·9.

♀ supra mari similis : subtus grisea, abdomine medio et tectricibus subcaudalibus pallidioribus, regione auriculari fusca, stria postoculari elongata, alba ; caudæ rectricibus lateralibus albo terminatis, rectrice extima utrinque quoque medialiter grisea, cauda minus furcata. Long. caudæ rectr. med. 1·0, rectr. lat. 1·2. (Descr. maris et feminæ ex Bolaños, Jalisco, Mexico. Mus. nostr.)

Hab. SOUTHERN ARIZONA [13].—MEXICO, District of Moctezuma in Sonora (*F. Ferrari-Perez* [15]), Nuri and Ysleta in Sonora (*W. Lloyd* [15]), Mazatlan (*Grayson* [8], *Forrer*), Guanajuato (*Dugès* [6], *Sanchez* [6] [12]), Sierra de Victoria in Tamaulipas (*W. B. Richardson* [15]), San Luis Potosi (*Jouy, in U. S. Nat. Mus.*), Jalapa (*de Oca* [4]), Alpine region of Orizaba (*Sumichrast* [11]), Aguas Calientes and Calvillo, Bolaños, San Blas, Lake Chapala (*W. B. Richardson* [15]), Santa Ana in Jalisco (*W. Lloyd* [15]), Plains of Colima (*Xantus, in U. S. Nat. Mus.*), Patzcuaro (*F. D. G.* [15]), Valley of Mexico (*de Oca* [9], *White* [5], *Boucard* [10], *Herrera* [16]), Hacienda Eslava and Tetelco in the Valley of Mexico (*F. Ferrari-Perez* [15]).

This now well-known Mexican species was described by Swainson [1] in his paper on Bullock's collection, the type being supposed to have been obtained in the "Table lands," which was most probably the case. Floresi collected many specimens during his residence in Mexico, but no record of the exact localities was preserved ; but very probably his specimens were secured near Bolaños, where the bird seems to be very common. Its range northwards extends beyond the Mexican political frontier into Southern Arizona, and it appears to be found nearly everywhere on the western side of the mountains from Sonora to Colima and to the Valley of Mexico. Its range in altitude, too, is great and extends from the sea-level to a height of 7000 or 8000 feet. *I. latirostris* is not confined to Western Mexico, for Mr. Richardson found it in the Sierra above Ciudad Victoria in Tamaulipas, and it is included in de Oca's list of Jalapa birds [4], and Delattre obtained a young male near the same place [17] ; but we suspect that these specimens were shot in the higher parts of the Cofre de Perote, on the flank of which Jalapa is situated. This would agree with Sumichrast's statement that it occurs in the Alpine region of Orizaba [11]. In the Valley of Mexico it occurs, according to de Oca [9], from November to the beginning of March, which is its time of nesting. It is not, however, a very common species.

Mr. Richardson secured us a number of specimens at Bolaños in the State of Jalisco, all shot in the month of February. These show considerable variation in the intensity of the bright blue colour of the throat, some specimens being almost green, others deep blue. This fact is of importance when the specific value of *I. magica* is considered.

Señor A. Herrera describes [16] a nest of this species which he found at Chimalcoyoc in the Valley of Mexico as composed of the seeds of *Asclepias linaria*, and placed in a plant of an *Opuntia* in such a manner that a section of the plant shaded it from sun and rain.

2. Iache magica.

Hylocharis magica, Muls. & Verr. Class. Troch. p. 38 [1]; Ann. Soc. Linn. Lyon, xviii. p. 110 [2].
Circe magica, Muls. Hist. Nat. Ois.-Mouches, ii. p. 40, t. 33 [3].
Iache magica, Elliot, Syn. Troch. p. 235 [4]; Salv. Cat. Birds Brit. Mus. xvi. p. 61 [5].

I. latirostri persimilis, sed minor, alis, rostro et cauda brevioribus, vix distinguenda.

Hab. MEXICO [1] [2] [3], Mazatlan (*Forrer* [5]).

Mr. Elliot separated this bird from *I. latirostris* chiefly on account of the throat being, as he says, " metallic bluish green " instead of " sapphire-blue " and its smaller size. One of our specimens from Mazatlan seems to belong to this form, but we much doubt if it is really distinct from *I. latirostris*. The latter bird shows so much variation in the amount of blue on the throat in specimens shot at the same time of year and at the same place, Bolaños, that, so far as the colour of the throat is concerned, *I. magica* may well be a greenish-throated *I. latirostris*, both being found at Mazatlan. The difference of size is not great:—

    I. latirostris: wing 2·1 in.; tail 0·93.
    I. magica: „ 1·9 in.; „ 0·87.

But this difference seems the sole tangible ground for the separation of *I. magica*. This name was first introduced by MM. Mulsant and Verreaux in their Classification of Trochilidæ, but without description [1]. The type passed into Mr. Elliot's hands and was characterized in his ' Synopsis ' [4].

3. Iache lawrencii.

Circe latirostris, Grayson, Pr. Bost. Soc. N. H. xiv. p. 282 [1]; Lawr. Mem. Bost. Soc. N. H. ii.
   p. 292 [2].
Iache lawrencii, Berl. Ibis, 1887, p. 292 [3]; Salv. Cat. Birds Brit. Mus. xvi. p. 61 [4].

I. latirostri quoque similis, sed gutture omnino micanti-viridi vix cæruleo tincto; tectricibus subcaudalibus
  obscure griseis disco late chalybeo-nigris nec albis quoque distinguenda.

Hab. MEXICO, Tres Marias Islands (*Grayson* [1] [2], *Forrer* [3] [4]).

This bird was separated from *I. latirostris* by Count Berlepsch in 1887 [3], his description being based upon specimens obtained in the Tres Marias Islands by Mr. Alphonse Forrer. We have a pair from the same source which fully confirm the points of distinction indicated by its describer, and which are referred to in the above diagnosis. The only question as regards this bird which demands special attention is its range, for it is said to occur with the common species, *I. latirostris*, on the mainland near Mazatlan, and that *I. latirostris* also occurs on the Tres Marias Islands. If this is, so the presence in the same localities of two so nearly related forms is remarkable,

but we think that further investigation will show that *I. lawrencii* is the sole inhabitant of the islands and does not occur on the mainland at all. Its position as a distinct species will then be fully established. Little has been noted of the habits of this species beyond the description by Grayson [1] of its nest, which is as follows:—
" This elegant structure (*i. e.* the nest of *I. lawrencii*) I found attached to a slender twig and shaded with its leaves, about five feet from the ground. The situation was facing the sea but a few paces from the water's edge..... Its form is cup-shaped, and composed of the down of the silk cotton (*Eriodendron*) intermingled with the down of other plants and spiders' webs, the whole exterior neatly studded with diminutive whitish lichens; it contained two newly hatched young but little larger than flies."

β. *Pileus nitenti-cœruleus aut viridi-cœruleus ; tectrices subcaudales fuscœ aut chalybeœ.*

4. Iache doubledayi.

Trochilus doubledayi, Bourc. P. Z. S. 1847, p. 46 [1].
Circe doubledayi, Gould, Mon. Troch. v. t. 339 (Sept. 1860) [2]; de Oca, La Nat. iii. p. 302, fig. 45 [3];
　　Lawr. Bull. U. S. Nat. Mus. no. 4, p. 33 [4]; Sumichrast, La Nat. v. p. 250 [5].
Iache doubledayi, Elliot, Syn. Troch. p. 235 [6]; Salv. Cat. Birds Brit. Mus. xvi. p. 62 [7].
Iache nitida, Salv. & Godm. Ibis, 1889, p. 240 [8]; Salv. Cat. Birds Brit. Mus. xvi. p. 62 [9].

Supra nitenti-æneo-viridis, pileo micanti-cæruleo-viridi : subtus nitenti-cærulea, abdomine viridescentiore, tectricibus subcaudalibus brunneis; cauda chalybeo-cyanea, tectricibus mediis cinereo terminatis : rostro corallino, apice nigro. Long. tota circa 2·8, alæ 1·9, caudæ rectr. med. 0·8, rectr. lat. 1·1, rostri a rictu 0·8. (Descr. maris ex Chinautla, Mexico. Mus. Brit.)

♀ supra nitenti-viridis : subtus fusca, pectoris lateribus et hypochondriis viridi lavatis : caudæ dimidio basali viridi, dimidio apicali chalybeo-cyaneo, rectricibus duabus utrinque externis griseo-albo terminatis : rostro nigricante, mandibula, præter apicem, carnea. (Descr. feminæ ex Rincon, Guerrero. Mus. nostr.)

Hab. MEXICO, Chinautla (*Dr. Saucerotte* [2]), Venta del Pelegrino, Rincon, Dos Arroyos, Acapulco (*Mrs. H. H. Smith* [8]), Chihuitan, Juchitan [5] (*Sumichrast* [4][5]), Salina Cruz and Tehuantepec (*W. B. Richardson* [9]).

Bourcier's description of this species was based upon a specimen supposed to have come from the Rio Negro [1]. This type is now in the American Museum of Natural History and was described by Mr. Elliot in his 'Synopsis'; another, according to Gould, is in the Loddiges Collection [2]; and a third, the only one we have seen closely agreeing with the description, is in the British Museum. The last named was figured by Gould in his 'Monograph of the Trochilidæ' and was obtained by him from Dr. Saucerotte, who had it from Chinautla in the Mexican State of Puebla. Compared with the types of *I. nitida* this species as represented by Gould's specimen has a greener crown, and the under tail-coverts are brown instead of steel-blue, but we do not feel certain whether these differences are not due to the age of the specimens compared.

We have a series of specimens of this species obtained by Mrs. H. H. Smith between Acapulco and the mountains of the State of Guerrero, and by Mr. W. B. Richardson on the western side of the Isthmus of Tehuantepec at Salina Cruz and Tehuantepec city, which we have hitherto considered distinct from *I. doubledayi* and have called *I. nitida*; and we should still have so treated them had not Mr. Ridgway informed us that he had compared a specimen in the United States National Museum from Dos Arroyos and found it to agree exactly with the type of *I. doubledayi*. This fact and the evident variation existing between individuals of this bird now compel us to place *I. nitida* as a synonym of *I. doubledayi*. Mrs. Smith's specimens were all collected in the months of September and October, Mr. Richardson's in February. The heads of the latter are a little greener on the crown than the others, due probably to the feathers being older; but all these birds have deep blue throats and steel-blue under tail-coverts and thus differ slightly from the Chinautla specimen of *I. doubledayi*.

We have no notes of the habits of this species, the range of which seems to be restricted to the sea-coast of South-western Mexico and the low-lying land immediately adjoining.

b⁴. *Sexus similes, mas sicut femina vestitus.*

PHÆOPTILA.

Phæoptila, Gould, Mon. Troch. v. t. 340 (July 1861); Salv. Cat. Birds Brit. Mus. xvi. p. 63.

A genus containing a single species the range of which is given below. Its position in the systematic arrangement of the Trochilidæ has been altered many times. Gould placed it near *Iache*, which we think is its right place. Mr. Elliot separated the two genera nearly as widely as possible, but gave no reasons for so doing. Mr. Ridgway locates it next *Amazilia*.

In many points of structure *Phæoptila* resembles *Iache*. The serration of the maxilla is similar in both, so also is the denudation of the nasal covers and the inter-ramal space, as well as the general colour of the female.

Phæoptila differs from *Iache* in the coloration of the sexes, the males in the latter genus being brightly tinted, whilst in the former the male is dull and hardly differs from the female except in the colour of the tail, in which the difference is one not unfrequently seen in the Trochilidæ, the bases of the outer feathers and their tips being pale grey, those feathers of the male being uniform.

1. **Phæoptila sordida.**

Cyanomyia (?) *sordida*, Gould, Ann. & Mag. N. H. 1859, iv. p. 97 [1]; Scl. P. Z. S. 1859, p. 386 [2].
Phæoptila sordida, Gould, Mon. Troch. v. t. 340 (July 1861) [3]; de Oca, La Nat. iii. p. 210 [4];
        Salv. Cat. Birds Brit. Mus. xvi. p. 63 [5].
Doleromya sordida, Boucard, Ann. Soc. Linn. Lyon, xx. p. 282 [6].
Phæoptila zonura, Gould, Intr. Troch. p. 170 [7]; de Oca, La Nat. iii. p. 304 [8].

Supra obscure nitenti-viridis, pileo sordidiore, auricularibus nigricantibus: subtus obscure cinerea, cervicis
lateribus et pectore vix viridi lavatis, tectricibus subcaudalibus cervino tinctis, cauda quam dorsum paulo
saturatiore: rostro carneo, apice nigricante. Long. tota circa 4·0, alæ 2·1, caudæ rectr. med. 1·1, rectr.
lat. 1·4, rostri a rictu 0·95. (Descr. maris ex Chilpancingo, Mexico. Mus. nostr.)

♀ mari similis, sed supra aureo suffusa: subtus pallidior; caudæ rectricibus lateralibus cinereis, fascia transversa subterminali nigra. (Descr. feminæ ex Omilteme, Guerrero, Mexico. Mus. nostr.)

Hab. MEXICO, Bolaños? (*Floresi*[8]), Chilpancingo, Omilteme, Tepetlapa, Venta de
Zopilote, in the Sierra Madre del Sur, Guerrero, Mexico (*Mrs. H. H. Smith*[5]),
Cuernavaca, Puebla (*Boucard*[6]), Oaxaca (*Boucard*[1 2 6], *Fenochio*[5], *M. Trujillo*[5]),
Atlixco (*Boucard*[6]).

This species was described by Gould from specimens obtained in the State of Oaxaca
by M. Boucard in 1856, and other examples have since been secured in the same
district by Señor Fenochio and Mateo Trujillo, and the bird appears to be not
uncommon in the vicinity of the town of Oaxaca. We have also received a series of
specimens from Mrs. H. H. Smith from various places in the Sierra Madre del Sur,
where it occurs as high as an elevation of 8000 feet.

Though described from M. Boucard's birds, there is little doubt that the first specimen sent to Europe was one obtained by M. Floresi, it is supposed at Bolaños in the
State of Jalisco, and forwarded to Loddiges. This bird was described by Gould in his
'Introduction to the Trochilidæ' as *Phæoptila zonura*[7], but it is almost certainly a
female of *P. sordida*. Similar examples have since reached us with males of *P. sordida*,
and they agree with a drawing made by Gould of the type of *P. zonura*. No specimens
of *P. sordida* have occurred in recent collections made at Bolaños and its neighbourhood,
and its presence in the Sierras north of the Rio Lerma requires confirmation.

M. Boucard[6], who found this bird in considerable abundance at Puebla in 1865,
says that it enters the gardens of the town and even builds its nest there. The female
sits about fifteen days, and in about twenty days after the young bird is hatched it
leaves the nest.

b'''. Rostrum fere rectum, breve.

CHLOROSTILBON.

Chlorostilbon, Gould, Mon. Troch. v. sub t. 355 (May 1853); Salv. Cat. Birds Brit. Mus. xvi. p. 44.

This genus was founded by Gould in 1853, his typical species being *Chlorostilbon
pucherani* of Brazil, a bird closely allied to the Mexican and Central-American species of
the genus, all of them, except *C. assimilis*, having the maxilla as well as the mandible
flesh-coloured towards the base in the dried skin, the colour in life being coral-red.

The shape of the bill in *Chlorostilbon* is similar to that of most Humming-birds so
far as regards the outline towards the tip. It is nearly straight, of moderate length,
the nasal covers partially exposed, and the inter-ramal space nude. The tomia of the
maxilla are distinctly serrate towards the tip, but the mandible is nearly smooth, except

near the tip. The plumage of the male is glittering green on the under surface, that of the female dingy white. The tail is forked in all the Central-American species, more deeply in *C. auriceps* and *C. forficatus* than in any other member of the genus. Some of the South-American species have the tail very slightly forked and even a little rounded.

The number of species in *Chlorostilbon* is variously estimated, owing to the slight characters separating many of them. In his recent Catalogue, Salvin defines thirteen species, Mr. Elliot having recognized only eight. Other ornithologists might admit a greater number, but their definition cannot fail to be very obscure.

The thirteen species are distributed over the greater part of Tropical America, from Western Mexico to South Brazil. Four species occur within our limits, one of them, *C. auriceps*, being peculiar to Western Mexico; a second, *C. forficatus*, to the islands off the coast of Yucatan; a third, *C. caniveti*, has a wide range from Eastern Mexico to Costa Rica; and the fourth, *C. assimilis*, seems to be restricted to Panama *.

α. *Rostrum carneum ad apicem nigrum; rectrices intermediæ cinereo terminatæ.*

1. Chlorostilbon auriceps.

Trochilus auriceps, Gould, Contr. Orn. 1852, p. 137[1].

Chlorostilbon auriceps, Gould, Mon. Troch. iii. t. 350 (May 1857)[2]; Villada, La Nat. ii. p. 361[3]; de Oca, La Nat. iii. p. 160[4]; Sanchez, An. Mus. Nac. Mex. i. p. 96[5]; Salv. & Godm. Ibis, 1889, p. 366[6]; Salv. Cat. Birds Brit. Mus. xvi. p. 45[7]; Herrera, La Nat. (2) i. p. 322[8].

Supra nitenti-aureo-viridis, pileo corruscante: subtus micanti-viridis, aureo suffusus; cauda elongata, profunde furcata, chalybeo-cærulea, rectricibus omnibus, extima utrinque exceptis, plus minusve griseo terminatis: rostro carneo, apice nigro. Long. tota circa 3·75, alæ 1·7, caudæ rectr. med. 0·6, rectr. lat. 1·6, rostri a rictu 0·65. (Descr. maris exempl. typ. ex Mexico. Mus. nostr.)

♀ *juv.* cauda minus furcata, rectrice externa utrinque breviore et albo terminata; corpore subtus griseo-albo, plumis viridibus intermixtis.

♀ supra nitenti-aureo-viridis: subtus sordide alba, regione auriculari fusca; caudæ rectricibus sex intermediis viridibus dorso fere concoloribus, duabus utrinque externis fascia lata subterminali chalybeo-cærulea, extima utrinque quoque albido terminata et fascia albida mediana notata. Long. caudæ rectr. med. 0·62, rectr. lat. 1·0. (Descr. maris juv. et feminæ ex Tepic, Mexico. Mus. nostr.)

Hab. MEXICO (*Floresi*[1]), Santiago de Tepic, Tepic, San Blas (*W. B. Richardson*[7]), Valley of Mexico (*de Oca*[4], *Sanchez*[5], *Herrera*[8]), Tonila (*W. Lloyd*[7]), Chilpancingo and Acaguizotla in Guerrero (*Mrs. H. H. Smith*[7]).

Gould's description of this species was based upon specimens obtained by Floresi in Mexico, but in which district was not recorded, and it is only recently that we have ascertained that it occurs chiefly in Western Mexico from Tepic and San Blas to the mountains of the State of Guerrero. Our collectors in these portions of Mexico have secured us a series of specimens exactly agreeing with the types. According to de Oca[4]

---

* *C. insularis*, Lawr. Ann. Lyc. N. Y. vii. p. 457, was founded upon a specimen of the Brazilian *C. pucherani*. See Berl. Pr. U. S. Nat. Mus. xi. p. 564.

and other authorities[5][8] it also occurs in the Valley of Mexico, where, however, it is a rare bird.

As a species, *C. auriceps* may be distinguished from *C. caniveti* by its deeply forked tail, the outer feathers of which are narrow. The crown is rich golden green.

2. Chlorostilbon forficatus.

Chlorostilbon forficatus, Ridgway, Pr. Biol. Soc. Wash. iii. p. 23[1]; Pr. U. S. Nat. Mus. viii. p. 574[2]; Salv. Ibis, 1889, p. 366[3]; Cat. Birds Brit. Mus. xvi. p. 46[4].

Chlorostilbon caniveti, Salv. Ibis, 1885, p. 191 (nec Less.)[5].

C. auricipiti persimilis, sed paulo major, rostro longiore, colore viridi corporis et capite summo minus aureo; caudæ rectricibus latioribus ut videtur differt.

♀ statura majore quoque differt. (Descr. maris et feminæ ex Cozumel I., Yucatan. Mus. nostr.)

Hab. Mexico, Mugeres and Holbox Is., off the coast of Yucatan (*Gaumer*), Cozumel I. (*Devis*[5], *Benedict*[1][2], *Gaumer*[3][4]).

A close ally of *C. auriceps* and *C. caniveti*, but more like the former than the latter, though in their geographical range the latter is interposed between the other two. As in *C. auriceps*, the tail is deeply forked, but the lateral rectrices are wider; the size, too, is somewhat larger. The range of *C. forficatus* appears to be restricted to Cozumel Island and some of the other islands situated off the north-east coast of Yucatan. We are not quite certain if it occurs on the mainland immediately adjoining, as no collections of birds have been made there; but a little further to the westward at Tizimin and Merida the true *C. caniveti* is found, and probably spreads to the north and east coasts, the only physical barrier in that direction.

C. forficatus was first described by Mr. Ridgway from specimens collected by Mr. Benedict[1][2]. Others were subsequently procured for us by Mr. Gaumer[3].

3. Chlorostilbon caniveti.

Ornismya caniveti, Less. Suppl. Ois.-Mouches, p. 174, tt. 37, 38[1]; Rev. Zool. 1839, p. 15[2].

Sporadinus caniveti, Scl. P. Z. S. 1859, p. 367[3].

Chlorostilbon caniveti, Gould, Mon. Troch. v. t. 351 (May 1860)[4]; Scl. & Salv. Ibis, 1859, p. 130[5]; de Oca, La Nat. iii. p. 59[6]; Salv. Cat. Strickl. Coll. p. 370[7]; Cat. Birds Brit. Mus. xvi. p. 47[8]; Boucard, P.Z. S. 1883, p. 451[9]; Stone, Pr. Ac. Phil. 1890, p. 206[10].

Chlorolampis caniveti, Lawr. Bull. U. S. Nat. Mus. no. 4, p. 33[11]; Sumichrast, La Nat. v. p. 250[12]; Herrera, La Nat. (2) i. p. 322[13].

Chlorostilbon osberti, Gould, P. Z. S. 1860, p. 309[14]; Mon. Troch. v. t. 354[15]; Salv. Ibis, 1860, p. 271[16]; 1866, p. 204[17]; Nutting, Pr. U. S. Nat. Mus. vi. pp. 375[18], 394[19].

Chlorolampis salvini, Cab. & Heine, Mus. Hein. iii. p. 48[20]; Cab. J. f. Orn. 1863, p. 164[21]; Lawr. Ann. Lyc. N. Y. ix. p. 128[22].

Chlorostilbon salvini, Berl. Pr. U. S. Nat. Mus. xi. pp. 375[23], 394[24]; Zeledon, An. Mus. Nac. Costa Rica, 1887, p. 122[25].

Chlorostilbon osberti salvinii, Nutting, Pr. U. S. Nat. Mus. v. p. 501[26].

Supra nitenti-aureo-viridis, pileo micante: subtus nitenti-viridis; cauda chalybeo-cærulea, rectricibus intermediis cinereo terminatis: rostro carneo ad apicem nigro. Long. tota circa 3·3, alæ 1·7, caudæ rectr. med. 0·65, rectr. lat. 1·4, rostri a rictu 0·7.

♀ supra nitenti-viridis, pileo obscuriore: subtus sordide griseo-albida, regione auriculari fusca, rectricibus mediis et duabus utrinque proximis nitenti-viridibus, tribus utrinque externis griseo terminatis et fascia subterminali chalybeo-cærulea notatis, extima utrinque quoque medialiter cinerea. Long. tota circa 3·0, alæ 1·75, cauda rectr. med. 0·9, rectr. lat. 1·1, rostri a rictu 0·7. (Descr. maris et feminæ ex Cordova, Mexico. Mus. nostr.)

Hab. MEXICO, Tampico (*W. B. Richardson*[8]), Misantla, Hacienda de los Alixcos and Vera Cruz (*F. D. G.*[8]), Jalapa (*Delattre*[2], *de Oca*[3][6], *Trujillo*[8]), Coatepec (*de Oca, Trujillo*), Mirador (*Sartorius, in U. S. Nat. Mus.*), Cordova (*de Oca, Sallé, Sumichrast*[10]), Orizaba (*le Strange*), Atoyac (*Mrs. H. H. Smith*), Playa Vicente (*Trujillo*[8]), Valley of Mexico (*Herrera*[13]), Chimalapa, Tehuantepec (*W. B. Richardson*[8]), Guichicovi (*Sumichrast*[11][12]), N. Yucatan (*G. F. Gaumer*[9]), Merida (*Schott, in U. S. Nat. Mus.*), Tabi (*F. D. G.*[8]), Aguada de Shkolak (*Stone*[10]); BRITISH HONDURAS, Orange Walk (*G. F. G.*[8]), Belize (*Blancaneaux*[8]); GUATEMALA[7] (*Delattre, Skinner*[5]), Dueñas[14], Volcan de Fuego, San Gerónimo, Coban, Lanquin (*O. S. & F. D. G.*); SALVADOR, Acajutla (*J. M. Dow, in U. S. Nat. Mus.*), Volcan de San Miguel, La Libertad (*W. B. Richardson*[8]); NICARAGUA, Chinandega and El Volcan Chinandega (*W. B. R.*[8]), Omotepe (*Nutting, in U. S. Nat. Mus.*), San Juan del Sur (*O. S.; Nutting, in U. S. Nat. Mus.*); COSTA RICA (*A. R. Endrés*), Cartago (*Cooper, in U. S. Nat. Mus.*), Tucurriqui (*Arcé*), San José (*Carmiol*[22], *Zeledon*[25]), Liberia (*Zeledon*[25]), La Palma (*Nutting*[26]).

In his original description Lesson gave Brazil as the habitat of this species[1], but afterwards mentioned Jalapa in Mexico as its domicile, on the authority of Delattre[2]. Examples from Eastern Mexico have, as a rule, more deeply forked tails than those from Guatemala and places still further south, but we are unable to distinguish any definite races of this bird. Guatemalan examples have rather less grey on the tips of the central rectrices, but this is an eminently variable character, though always present in fully adult birds. Some specimens have these feathers tipped with green, which is probably a character of immaturity or perhaps only observable in perfectly freshly-moulted feathers. One Dueñas specimen before us has the left central rectrix tipped with green, whilst the right one is plain.

Guatemalan specimens were described by Gould as *C. osberti*[14], and Costa Rican ones by Cabanis as *C. salvini*[20]. These last have the tail still less deeply forked, but in view of the apparently continuous range of the species we doubt the possibility of recognizing any really definite races. We note, however, that the specimens from the islands of Ruatan and Bonacca have the outer rectrices unusually wide.

C. caniveti was a very familiar species with us during our various visits to the Hacienda at Dueñas, and specimens could generally be seen in the garden adjoining the house searching the plants in bloom for their insect food. At San Juan del Sur, in Nicaragua, Salvin noticed it in May in some numbers feeding from the flowers of the tamarind-trees which line the shore of the bay.

In the neighbourhood of Jalapa it is found, according to de Oca, in greatest abundance in the months of June and July, at which time it builds its nest [6].

β. *Rostrum omnino nigrum ; rectrices uniformes.*

4. Chlorostilbon assimilis.

Chlorostilbon assimilis, Lawr. Ann. Lyc. N. Y. vii. p. 292 [1]; ix. p. 128 (?) [2]; Gould, Intr. Troch. p. 178 [3]; Salv. Cat. Birds Brit. Mus. xvi. p. 54 [4].

Chlorolampis assimilis, Scl. & Salv. P. Z. S. 1864, p. 365 [5]; Salv. P. Z. S. 1867, p. 156 [6]; 1870, p. 211 [7].

Similis præcedentibus, sed capite summo dorso concolore haud micanti-viridi, cauda paulo furcata et rectricibus omnibus unicoloribus nullis griseo terminatis, et rostro omnino nigro distinguendus.
♀ quoque rostro nigro dignoscenda. (Descr. maris et feminæ ex Paraiso, Panama. Mus. nostr.)

Hab. PANAMA, Volcan de Chiriqui [7], Chitra [7], Castillo [7], Cordillera del Chucu, Santiago de Veraguas [6], Santa Fé [6], Calovevora, Calobre, Line of Railway (*Arcé*), Paraiso Station (*Hughes* [4]), Lion Hill (*M'Leannan* [1] [5]).

This species is closely allied to *C. melanorhynchus* and *C. pumilus*, having like them a black bill and a forked tail, the lateral rectrices of which are rather narrow. It is, however, the only one of the three which has the crown of a comparatively dull green like the back, the crown in both the other species being of a more or less glittering hue.

C. assimilis was first described by Mr. Lawrence from specimens sent him by M'Leannan from the Isthmus of Panama [1]. It is there a common bird, and also throughout the whole State of Panama, at least as far as the frontier of Costa Rica. We have no evidence before us that it is found in the latter State, but Mr. Lawrence includes it in his list of the birds of that country [2]. Nor have we any evidence that it occurs on the mainland of South America. In the State of Antioquia the bright-headed allied form *C. pumilus* takes its place, and this, too, is the prevalent bird in Western Ecuador.

d″. *Spatio inter mandibulæ ramos plumis vestita.*

c‴. *Rostrum debile, maxillæ tomia ad apicem incurva : sexus dissimiles.*

c⁴. *Cauda furcata, pileus anticus nitide violaceus, rectrices laterales haud albo notatæ.*

THALURANIA.

Thalurania, Gould, P. Z. S. 1848, p. 13 ; Salv. Cat. Birds Brit. Mus. xvi. p. 76.

Two only of the fourteen recognized species of *Thalurania* are found within our limits, one of them, *T. colombica*, being a common bird in the northern part of South America and reaching Nicaragua in our country; the other, *T. townsendi*, has as yet only been found in Honduras.   The genus generally extends from Honduras to South Brazil.

Compared with the genera which follow, *Thalurania* has a more or less deeply forked tail, the lateral rectrices have no white at the base, and glittering blue enters more or less into the coloration of the plumage of most of the species.

1. Thalurania townsendi.

Thalurania townsendi, Ridgw. Pr. U. S. Nat. Mus. x. p. 590 [1]; Salv. Cat. Birds Brit. Mus. xvi. p. 78 [2].

Supra saturate nitenti-gramineo-viridis, fronte et pileo antico læte micanti-cyaneis, humeris et plumis inter- scapularibus cyaneo lavatis : subtus micanti-viridis, subcaudalibus cyaneis albo limbatis ; cauda chalybeo- cyaneo : rostro nigro.   Long. tota 3·8, alæ 2·1, caudæ rectr. lat. 1·4, rectr. med. 1·0, rostri a rictu 0·9.

♀ supra omnino nitenti-viridis ; subtus sordide alba, rectricibus lateralibus albido terminatis.   (Descr. maris et feminæ exempl. typ. ex Segovia R., Honduras.   U. S. Nat. Mus.)

Hab. HONDURAS, Segovia River (*C. H. Townsend* [1] [2]).

The type specimens of this bird kindly lent us by Mr. Ridgway are the only ones we have seen.   They were obtained by Mr. C. H. Townsend during an expedition to the Segovia River, which forms the boundary between Honduras and Nicaragua.

In having the under surface of the body glittering green *Thalurania townsendi* resembles the Brazilian *T. glaucopis*, but the violet-blue of the shoulders of the wings and interscapular feathers as well as the colour of the under tail-coverts (dark blue edged with white) suggest that its real relationship lies with its near neighbour *T. colombica*.

We shall look anxiously for further news of this interesting species.

2. Thalurania colombica.

Ornismya colombica, Bourc. Ann. Sc. Phys. et Nat. Lyon, vi. t. 6 [1]; Rev. Zool. 1843, p. 2 [2].

Thalurania columbica, Gould, P. Z. S. 1852, p. 8 [3]; Mon. Troch. ii. t. 106 (Sept. 1858) [4]; Boucard, P. Z. S. 1878, p. 69 [5]; Zeledon, An. Mus. Nac. Costa Rica, 1887, p. 121 [6]; Salv. Cat. Birds Brit. Mus. xvi. p. 79 [7].

Trochilus (Thalurania) venusta, Gould, P. Z. S. 1850, p. 163 [8].

Thalurania venusta, Gould, P. Z. S. 1852, p. 9 [9]; Mon. Troch. ii. t. 108 (Sept. 1858) [10]; Lawr. Ann. Lyc. N. Y. vii. p. 292 [11]; ix. p. 122 [12]; Scl. & Salv. P. Z. S. 1864, p. 365 [13]; Salv. P. Z. S. 1867, p. 153 [14]; 1870, p. 207 [15]; Ibis, 1872, p. 319 [16].

Supra nigra (a fronte adspecta) cupreo-viridis (a tergo adspecta), interscapuliis, humeris, fronte usque ad medium pilei et abdomine micanti-cyaneis, gutture toto micanti-viridi, subcaudalibus cyaneis albo marginatis ; cauda chalybeo-cyanea : rostro nigro.   Long. tota 4·0, alæ 2·05, caudæ rectr. med. 0·9, rectr. lat. 1·6, rostri a rictu 0·85.

♀ supra nitenti-viridis, pileo obscuriore et cupreo tincto, uropygio cærulescentiore, capitis lateribus et corpore subtus sordide albis, hypochondriis viridi lavatis, rectricibus mediis cærulescenti-viridibus lateralibus chalybeo-cyaneis albo terminatis.   (Descr. maris et feminæ ex Panama.   Mus. nostr.)

Hab. NICARAGUA, Chontales (*Belt* [16]), La Libertad in Chontales (*W. B. Richardson*);

Costa Rica (*Endres*), Tucurriqui (*Arcé* [7], *Zeledon* [6]), Angostura (*Carmiol* [12]), Naranjo de Cartago, Jimenez (*Zeledon* [6]); Panama, Volcan de Chiriqui (*Warszewiez* [9], *Arcé*), Boquete de Chitra [15], Chitra [15], Castillo, Laguna, Santiago de Veraguas [14], Calovevora [15], Santa Fé [14], Line of Railway (*Arcé*), Lion Hill (*M'Leannan* [11] [13]), Paraiso (*Hughes* [7]).—Colombia [1] [2] and Venezuela [7].

The original specimens of this species, as its name implies, came from Colombia [1]; and we now know it as one of the very common species of that country, large numbers of specimens being sent from time to time in the trade collections made in the vicinity of Bogota.

T. venusta was described by Gould from specimens sent him by Warszewiez [9] from Chiriqui, and it was stated to differ from *T. colombica* by the greater extent of the violet-blue colouring on the shoulders and back, that colour occupying in adult birds the whole of the interscapular region. As a rule, northern birds, *i. e.* those found at Panama and thence northwards to Nicaragua, have more blue in this portion of the plumage than southern ones, but it is certainly a variable character and at most only seen in older birds. As the bird is an inhabitant of the lowlands, and as it is very improbable that any line of demarkation divides the two forms, we think it best to keep them together under one specific name.

T. colombica is not uncommon on the line of the Panama Railway, whence M'Leannan sent us several specimens [13]. We have also received many others from various parts of the State of Panama, and also from Costa Rica.

Belt's collection, too, made at Chontales in Nicaragua, contained several specimens in very perfect plumage [16]; and we have lately received others from the same country from Mr. W. B. Richardson.

[Note.—*Thalurania luciæ*, described by Mr. Lawrence from a specimen said to have been obtained by Xantus on one of the Tres Marias Islands, now proves, according to Count Berlepsch, to be *T. glaucopis* of Brazil, an error having been made as to its origin.]

d[4]. *Cauda plus minusve rotundata.*

a[5]. *Rostrum fere rectum, rectrices laterales ad basin albæ.*

a[6]. *Pileus niveus, plumæ supra tegulas nasales extensæ.*

MICROCHERA.

Microchera, Gould, Mon. Troch. ii. t. 116 (Sept. 1858); Salv. Cat. Birds Brit. Mus. xvi. p. 66.

This genus was established by Gould in 1858 upon the wonderful little bird described by Mr. Lawrence some years previously as *Mellisuga albocoronata*. A second species was discovered in Costa Rica in 1865; and these two birds now constitute the genus, which is restricted in its range to Nicaragua, Costa Rica, and the mountainous portion of Western Panama.

The position of *Microchera* is always likely to be questioned, so peculiar is the coloration of the two birds belonging to it. Gould placed it next to *Florisuga*, with *Lophornis* following; Mr. Elliot associated it with *Mellisuga*. Neither view seems to us to be correct. A careful examination of the bill shows that the tomia of the maxilla are distinctly serrate towards the end, *Lophornis*, *Florisuga*, and *Mellisuga* having it perfectly smooth. The inter-ramal space is feathered, the bill slender, and the tomia of the maxilla are curved inwards towards the tip; the sexes are dissimilar, the tail more or less rounded, the bill nearly straight, and the lateral rectrices white at the base. These characters bring *Microchera* and *Callipharus* together, a not unnatural arrangement seeing how largely black is a prevalent colour in their plumage. They also bring these genera into the vicinity of *Eupherusa*, from which genus *Callipharus* was separated. *Microchera* can be at once distinguished from *Callipharus* by the white crown, and by the complete feathering of the nasal covers.

1. **Microchera albocoronata.**

Mellisuga albocoronata, Lawr. Ann. Lyc. N. Y. vi. p. 137, t. 4 (1855) [1].

Microchera albocoronata, Gould, Mon. Troch. ii. t. 116 (Sept. 1858) [2]; Salv. P. Z. S. 1867, p. 154 [3]; 1870, p. 207 [4]; Cat. Birds Brit. Mus. xvi. p. 66 [5].

Supra (a fronte adspecta) fere nigra læte niteuti-cupreo-rubida (a tergo adspecta), pileo toto sericeo-niveo: subtus dorso concolor, gula saturate viridi lavata, tectricibus subcaudalibus albis; caudæ rectricibus mediis saturate cupreo-brunneis, reliquis bitriente basali albis, triente terminali chalybeo-nigra, apicibus ipsis albis: rostro omnino nigro. Long. tota 2·7, alæ 1·5, caudæ 0·75, rostri a rictu 0·6.

♀ supra nitenti-viridis, uropygio et rectricibus mediis magis aureis, rectricibus reliquis albis fascia subterminali chalybeo-nigro; subtus alba, gutture toto vix griseo-lavato. (Descr. maris et feminæ ex Cordillera del Chucu, Panama. Mus. nostr.)

Hab. Panama, Santiago de Veraguas [3], Cordillera del Chucu [4] (*Arcé*), Belen (*Merritt* [1] [2]).

Concerning this species, its discoverer, Dr. J. K. Merritt, writes as follows [1]:—" It was in the autumn of 1852, while stationed in the district of Belen, Veraguas, New Granada, that I obtained several specimens of this diminutive Humming-Bird. The first one I saw was perched on a twig pluming its feathers. I was doubtful for a few moments whether so small an object could be a bird, but upon close examination I convinced myself of the fact and secured it. Another I encountered while bathing, and for a time I watched its movements before shooting it; this little creature would poise itself about three feet or so above the surface of the water, and then as quick as thought dart downwards, so as to dip its head in the placid pool, then up again to its original position, quite as quickly as it had descended.

" These movements of darting up and down, it would repeat in rapid succession, which produced not a moderate disturbance of the surface of the water, for such a diminutive creature. After a considerable number of dippings it alighted on a twig near at hand, and commenced pluming its feathers."

Dr. Merritt considered that the flight of this species was not so persistent as that of other Humming-Birds, as it appeared to rest more frequently: this he attributed to the extreme shortness of its wings.

Our collector Arcé procured us many specimens of *M. albocoronata*, most of which he obtained near Santiago de Veraguas. These include adults of both sexes, as well as young males in various states of advancing plumage. The latter at first resemble the female, the dark feathers of the under surface are then gradually developed, and last of all the white crown is assumed.

Gould's drawings were taken from the typical specimens lent him by Mr. Lawrence.

2. Microchera parvirostris.

Panychlora parvirostris, Lawr. Pr. Ac. Phil. 1865, p. 39 [1].

Microchera parvirostris, Salv. P. Z. S. 1867, p. 154 [2]; Ibis, 1872, p. 319 [3]; 1892, p. 327 [4]; Cat. Birds Brit. Mus. xvi. p. 67 [5]; Lawr. Ann. Lyc. N. Y. ix. p. 122 [6]; Boucard, P. Z. S. 1878, p. 69 [7]; Gould, Mon. Troch. Suppl. t. 30 (Aug. 1880) [8]; Zeledon, An. Mus. Nac. Costa Rica, 1887, p. 121 [9].

M. albocoronatæ similis, sed colore plerumque lætiore nitenti-cupreo-rubido; caudæ fascia terminali latiore, margine suo interno male definito.

♀ feminæ *M. albocoronatæ* quoque similis, sed cauda ad basin angustiore, alba fascia subterminali latiore, et margine suo interno male definito. (Descr. maris et feminæ ex Chontales, Nicaragua. Mus. nostr.)

Hab. NICARAGUA, Matagalpa (*W. B. Richardson* [4]), Chontales (*Belt* [3]); COSTA RICA, Tucurriqui (*Arcé* [2]), Angostura [1][6], La Balsa [5] (*Carmiol*), Rio Sucio (*Zeledon* [9]).

Mr. Lawrence's description [1] of this bird was based upon a female which he considered to belong to the genus *Panychlora*, and, having a shorter bill than usual in members of that genus, he called it *P. parvirostris*, a specific name that loses its signification now that the bird is better known, and proves to be a *Microchera* closely allied to, but quite distinct from, *M. albocoronata*.

The range of this species extends from Costa Rica, where it was first discovered, to Nicaragua. In the latter country Belt obtained a series of beautiful specimens at Chontales [3], and quite recently we have received a young male example from Mr. Richardson, who shot it near Matagalpa in the mountains near the sources of the Segovia river [4].

b[6]. *Pileus niger, tegulæ nasales haud omnino plumis obtectæ.*

CALLIPHARUS.

Eupherusa (*Clotho*), Mulsant, Ann. Soc. Linn. Lyon, xxii. p. 205 (1875).

Callipharus, Elliot, Syn. Troch. p. 211; Salv. Cat. Birds Brit. Mus. xvi. p. 67.

The single species included in this genus was described by Mr. Lawrence as a

Eupherusa. It was then separated as a subgenus under the title *Clotho*, which being used elsewhere in zoology, was supplanted by *Callipharus* by Mr. Elliot in 1879.

The position assigned to the genus has always been near *Eupherusa*; and this we think correct, for the structure of the bill is similar as well as other points of resemblance.

From *Microchera* it differs in having the crown black and the nasal covers partly exposed.

The distribution of the genus is that of the single species which follows.

1. **Callipharus nigriventris.** (*Eupherusa nigriventris*, Tab. LVII. figg. 3 ♂, 4 ♀.)

Eupherusa nigriventris, Lawr. Pr. Ac. Phil. 1867, p. 232[1]; Ann. Lyc. N. Y. ix. p. 127[2]; Salv. P. Z. S. 1870, p. 210[3]; Muls. Hist. Nat. Ois.-Mouches, i. p. 270, t. 23[4].

Callipharus nigriventris, Elliot, Syn. Troch. p. 211[5]; Sharpe, in Gould's Mon. Troch., Suppl. t. 56[6] (Mar. 1887); Zeledon, An. Mus. Nac. Costa Rica, 1887, p. 122[7]; Salv. Cat. Birds Brit. Mus. xvi. p. 67[8].

Supra nitenti-cupreo-viridis, tectricibus supracaudalibus longioribus et rectricibus quatuor intermediis magis saturate cupreis; pileo et corpore subtus omnino nigris, tectricibus subcaudalibus et rectricibus tribus utrinque albis; alis purpureo-nigris, primariis interioribus et secundariis ad basin castaneis: rostro nigro. Long. tota 3·5, alæ 1·9, caudæ 1·15, rostri a rictu 0·65.

♀ supra omino viridis, pileo vix obscuriore, capitis lateribus fuscis; subtus sordide alba, tectricibus subcaudalibus et rectricibus lateralibus sicut in mare albis. (Descr. maris et feminæ ex Cordillera del Chucu, Panama. Mus. nostr.)

Hab. COSTA RICA (*Carmiol*[8], *Endres*[1]), Cervantes (*Cooper*), Naranjo de Cartago (*Zeledon*[7]), Peorsnada (*Zeledon, in U.S. Nat. Mus.*); PANAMA, Cordillera del Chucu[3], Calobre (*Arcé*).

Mr. Lawrence's type of this species formed part of a small collection of birds made in Costa Rica by the botanical traveller A. R. Endres[1], and sent by him to the United States National Museum. Other specimens reached this country from the same source, and also from the well-known collector Julian Carmiol. In the higher parts of the State of Panama this bird is also found, as Arcé sent us a good series of specimens, including adults of both sexes and young males, from the Cordillera del Chucu and other places in the same district.

In young males the feathers of the mature plumage begin to appear in the middle of the under surface, and gradually spread to the sides, and lastly cover the crown.

b[5]. *Rostrum sensim arcuatum; rectrices laterales ad basin albæ.*

c[6]. *Rostrum longius, rectius.*

EUPHERUSA.

Eupherusa, Gould, Mon. Troch. v. t. 324 (Sept. 1857); Salv. Cat. Birds Brit. Mus. xvi. p. 72.

Three species now constitute this genus, all of them belonging exclusively to our country—*E. poliocerca* to South-western Mexico, *E. eximia* to Guatemala and Central Nicaragua, and *E. egregia* to Costa Rica and the adjoining part of the State of Panama.

As in *Microchera* and *Callipharus* the inter-ramal space is more or less feathered; the bill is slender, the tomia of the maxilla turned inwards towards the tip; the sexes dissimilar; the tail rounded. It differs from those genera in having a decurved bill, which is comparatively long, the white at the base of the lateral rectrices does not extend to the whole of the outer webs, and the size of the birds is considerably larger.

1. Eupherusa eximia.

Ornismya eximia, Delattre, Echo du Monde Savant, 1843, p. 1069 [1].

Eupherusa eximia, Gould, Mon. Troch. v. t. 324 [2]; Scl. & Salv. Ibis, 1859, p. 130 [3]; Salv. Ibis, 1860, p. 271 [4]; Cat. Birds Brit. Mus. xvi. p. 72 [5]; Boucard, Ann. Soc. Linn. Lyon, xx. p. 280 [6]; Salv. & Godm. Ibis, 1892, p. 327 [7].

Supra nitente, subtus micanti-gramineo-viridis, tectricibus subcaudalibus niveis; alis purpureo-nigris, secundariis castaneis apicibus nigris; cauda nigricante, rectricibus mediis cupreo-viridi lavatis, rectricibus duabus utrinque lateralibus in pogonio interno cum rhachidis bitriente basali albis: rostro nigro. Long. tota 3·8, alæ 2·3, caudæ 1·4, rostri a rictu 0·8.

♀ supra mari similis, subtus omnino sordide alba. (Descr. maris et feminæ ex Coban, Guatemala. Mus. nostr.)

Hab. MEXICO, Chinautla (*Boucard*), Chimalapa and Sierra de Santo Domingo in Tehuantepec (*W. B. Richardson* [7]); GUATEMALA, Coban (*Delattre* [1], *O. S. & F. D. G.* [4]), Kamkhal, Choctum and track between Cahabon and San Luis (*O. S. & F. D. G.* [5]); NICARAGUA, Matagalpa (*W. B. Richardson* [7]).

The French traveller Delattre discovered this species at Coban in Guatemala, and subsequently described it in 1843 [1]. It was at Coban that Salvin found it in 1859 to be one of the commonest Humming-Birds during the month of November, frequenting the flowering-plants, principally *Salviæ*, which abound at that season in the vicinity of the town. *E. eximia* is also found in the forest-region lying to the northward of Coban as low as about 1200 or 1500 feet above sea-level. We never met with it in any other part of Guatemala; but its range passes a little beyond the limits of that country both to the northward and southward, as M. Boucard says that it occurs at Chinautla in Puebla in the month of August, and Mr. Richardson found it on the Isthmus of Tehuantepec, both at Chimalapa and in the Sierra de Santo Domingo, in March and April, and also near Matagalpa in the highlands of Central Nicaragua in July. The eastern slopes of the mountains of Central America between these limits probably mark the limits of the range of this species.

Though observed in great numbers at Coban we never found a nest, and noticed nothing peculiar in its habits.

2. Eupherusa egregia.

Eupherusa egregia, Scl. & Salv. P. Z. S. 1868, p. 389[1]; Lawr. Ann. Lyc. N. Y. ix. p. 146[2]; Salv.
P. Z. S. 1869, p. 316[3]; 1870, p. 210[4]; Cat. Birds Brit. Mus. xvi. p. 73[5]; Boucard, P. Z. S.
1878, p. 71[6]; Sharpe, in Gould's Mon. Troch., Suppl. (text)[7]; Zeledon, An. Mus. Nac. Costa
Rica, 1887, p. 122[8].

Eupherusa eximia, Lawr. Ann. Lyc. N. Y. ix. p. 127 (nec Delattre)[9].

E. eximiæ similis, sed rectricibus mediis pallidiore cupreis, rectricibus duabus utrinque externis in pogonio
externo (margine ipso excepto) albis.

♀ caudæ rectricibus duabus utrinque lateralibus omnino albis, interdum ad apicem utrinque nigro stricte limbatis. (Descr. exempl. typ. ex Costa Rica. Mus. nostr.)

Hab. COSTA RICA (*Carmiol, Endres*), Cervantes, Barranca (*Carmiol*[9]), Cervantes de
Cartago (*Zeledon*[8]); PANAMA, Volcan de Chiriqui, Castillo[1], Calovevora[1] (*Arcé*).

An immature male from Castillo and a female from Calovevora were the first
specimens we received of this species, and formed the types of the description[1]. About
the same time Mr. Lawrence examined specimens from Costa Rica, but referred them
to the more northern ally *E. eximia*[9]. Now that the bird is better known to us from
adult specimens sent us both from the Volcan de Chiriqui and Costa Rica, it proves to
be readily distinguishable from its near ally, the greater extent of white on the outer
rectrices being sufficient to separate them.

3. Eupherusa poliocerca.

Eupherusa poliocerca, Elliot, Ann. & Mag. N. H. 1871, viii. p. 266[1]; Syn. Troch. p. 212[2]; de Oca,
La Nat. iii. p. 302, fig. 44[3]; Muls. Hist. Nat. Ois.-Mouches, i. p. 271, t. 24[4]; Gould, Mon.
Troch., Suppl. t. 55 (April, 1881)[5]; Salv. Cat. Birds Brit. Mus. xvi. p. 74[6].

E. eximiæ similis, quoad corporis et alæ colores; caudæ rectricibus mediis pallide cupreo-viridibus et rectricibus quatuor utrinque ad basin albis ad apicem et ad pogonium externum ad purpureo-griseum gradatim
mutandis.

♀ adhuc ignota.

Hab. MEXICO, Omilteme (*Mrs. H. H. Smith*[6]), Putla (*Rébouch*[1]).

Mr. Elliot described this species from specimens obtained at Putla in Western
Mexico by the French collector Rébouch, who sent them to M. Boucard[1]. The only
other specimens we have seen formed part of the collection formed for us by Mrs.
Herbert H. Smith in the Sierra Madre del Sur at Omilteme, a small place situated
in the mountains above Chilpancingo at an elevation of 8000 feet above sea-level.
Mrs. Smith secured two males in beautiful condition in the month of July, but no
females; and that sex still remains unknown to us.

d[6]. *Rostrum brevius, magis arcuatum.*

ELVIRA.

Leucochloris (*Elvira*), Mulsant & Verreaux, Class. Troch. p. 32 (1865).

Elvira, Muls. Hist. Nat. Ois.-Mouches, i. p. 266; Salv. Cat. Birds Brit. Mus. xvi. p. 74.

The birds belonging to this genus were formerly placed either in *Thaumantias* (=*Agyrtria*) or *Eupherusa*, to neither of which genera do they strictly belong. *Agyrtria* has the tomia of the maxilla very feebly serrate, moreover the lateral rectrices are not white at the base. *Eupherusa*, on the other hand, though resembling *Elvira* in many points of structure, has a comparatively longer and less curved bill. Both species of *Elvira* are found exclusively in Costa Rica and the State of Panama.

1. **Elvira chionura.**

Trochilus (Thaumatias ?) chionura, Gould, P. Z. S. 1850, p. 162 [1].

Thaumatias chionurus, Gould, Mon. Troch. v. t. 300 (May 1852) [2]; Lawr. Ann. Lyc. N. Y. viii. p. 349 [3].

Thaumantias chionura, Salv. P. Z. S. 1867, p. 156 [4]; 1870, p. 210 [5].

Eupherusa chionura, Lawr. Ann. Lyc. N. Y. ix. p. 127 [6].

Elvira chionura, Muls. Hist. Nat. Ois.-Mouches, i. p. 166 [7]; Salv. Cat. Birds Brit. Mus. xvi. p. 75 [8].

Eupherusa niveicauda, Lawr. Ann. Lyc. N. Y. viii. p. 134 [9].

Supra saturate nitenti-gramineo-viridis, tectricibus supracaudalibus longioribus et rectricibus mediis cupreo-viridibus : subtus micanti-gramineo-viridis, fronte stricte et genis concoloribus, abdomine imo et tectricibus subcaudalibus albis ; caudæ rectricibus tribus utrinque lateralibus albis, chalybeo-nigro terminatis : rostri maxilla nigra, mandibula albicante apice nigra. Long. tota 3·3, alæ 2·0, caudæ 1·15, rostri a rictu 0·7.

♀ supra mari similis : subtus alba, plumis cervicis et laterum macula discali viridi notatis, rectricibus utrinque tribus albis, fascia subterminali obliqua nigra notatis. (Descr. maris et feminæ ex Chiriqui, Panama. Mus. nostr.)

Hab. COSTA RICA, Dota [3] [9] (*Carmiol* [6]); PANAMA, near David (*Warszewiez* [1] [2]), Volcan de Chiriqui [5], Calovevora [5] (*Arcé*).

This species was discovered by Warszewiez near David in Chiriqui, and was described by Gould in 1850 [1]. The types (a male and a female) are in the National collection. With them a number of other specimens from the same district and from Costa Rica agree in every particular.

A Costa Rica example sent by Carmiol from Dota was described by Mr. Lawrence as *E. niveicauda* in 1865 [9], but its identity with *E. chionura* was soon recognized [3].

2. **Elvira cupreiceps.**

Eupherusa cupreiceps, Lawr. Ann. Lyc. N. Y. viii. p. 348 [1]; ix. p. 127 [2].

Elvira cupreiceps, Muls. Hist. Nat. Ois.-Mouches, i. p. 268 [3]; Gould, Mon. Troch. Suppl. t. 53 (Aug. 1880) [4]; Zeledon, An. Mus. Nac. Costa Rica, 1887, p. 122 [5]; Salv. Cat. Birds Brit. Mus. xvi. p. 75 [6].

E. chionuræ similis, sed rostro breviore et magis arcuato, pileo et rectricibus duabus mediis saturate cupreis illius plumis nigro limbatis, rectricibus omnibus (præter duas medias) plus minusve albis fusco terminatis : rostri maxilla nigra, mandibulæ dimidio basali albido. Long. tota 3·3, alæ 2·0, caudæ 1·15, rostri 0·7.

♀ feminæ *E. chionuræ* similis, pileo et cauda supra cupreis et forma rostris differt.

Hab. COSTA RICA (*Carmiol, Endres*), Barranca (*Carmiol* [1], *Zeledon, in U.S. Nat. Mus.*), Tucurriqui (*Arcé* [6]), Naranjo de Cartago (*Zeledon* [5]).

E. cupreiceps was described by Mr. Lawrence in 1866 from male specimens sent to the United States National Museum by Carmiol from Barranca in Costa Rica[1]. A female from Tucurriqui had for some time been in our collection; but we did not venture to describe it from such insufficient material. The resemblance of this species to *E. chionura* is obvious; but at the same time its distinctive characters can readily be recognized in its more curved bill and coppery head.

Its range seems confined to Costa Rica, where it inhabits the mountain-forests at about an elevation of 3000 feet above sea-level.

d'''. *Rostrum robustum, maxillæ tomia haud incurva.*

e[4]. *Culmen ad basin plumatum, tegulæ nasales partim expositæ : sexus dissimiles ; plaga auricularis nitida nulla.*

c[5]. *Tectrices subcaudales magnæ, laxæ ; rectrices laterales purpureo haud tinctæ.*

HYPUROPTILA.

Agyrtria, δ. Chalybura, Reich. Aufz. d. Col. p. 10 (1854).
Hypuroptila, Gould, Mon. Troch. ii. t. 89 (May 1854).

In this and the following genera of this section the bill is stouter than in the genera immediately preceding, but the ends of the tomia of the maxilla are not curved inwards to any great extent. In *Hypuroptila* and in *Lampornis* the culmen is feathered at the base, but the nasal covers are partially exposed, and the sexes are dissimilar.

In *Hypuroptila* the under tail-coverts are large and full, and the rectrices are bronze or greenish-bronze—both characters by which it may at once be distinguished from *Lampornis.*

The range of this genus extends from Nicaragua to Colombia and Venezuela. Of the five species all but one occur within our limits ; *H. isauræ* and *H. melanorrhoa* are restricted to Panama and Costa Rica and Nicaragua respectively.

α. *Mandibula omnino et pedes nigricantes ; subcaudales elongatæ, laxæ.*

1. Hypuroptila buffoni.

Trochilus buffoni, Less. Hist. Nat. Troch. p. 331, t. 55 [1].
Hypuroptila buffoni, Gould, Mon. Troch. ii. t. 89 (May 1854) [2]; Salv. Cat. Birds Brit. Mus. xvi. p. 87 [3].
Chalybura buffoni, Lawr. Ann. Lyc. N. Y. vii. p. 319 [4]; Scl. & Salv. P. Z. S. 1864, p. 365 [5].

Supra nitenti-gramineo-viridis, capite summo et uropygio cupreo-tinctis : subtus nitenti-smaragdino-viridis, tectricibus subcaudalibus pure albis ; cauda chalybeo-cyanea, rectricibus mediis saturate cupreo-viridibus : rostro nigro. Long. tota 4·8, alæ 2·75, caudæ rectr. med. 1·5, rectr. lat. 1·85, rostri 1·2.

♀ subtus cinerea, hypochondriis viridi lavatis, rectricibus lateralibus albido terminatis. (Descr. maris et feminæ ex Lion Hill, Panama. Mus. nostr.)

Hab. PANAMA, Lion Hill (*M'Leannan*[4][5]), Obispo Station (*O. S.*), Paraiso (*Hughes*[3]), Chepo (*Arcé*[3]).—COLOMBIA[3]; VENEZUELA[3].

Lesson's type of this species was supposed to have come from Brazil[1], but it is now known that the range of *H. buffoni* is limited to the north-western portion of South America, where it is a common bird, and that it only enters our fauna as far as the line of the Panama Railway, where M'Leannan[4][5] and others procured many specimens, and where Salvin observed it in May 1873 near Obispo Station.

H. buffoni has a near ally in *H. cæruleiventris*, from which it differs in having the under surface pure green instead of being deeply tinged with blue.

The latter bird is found further inland in Colombia, and is sent in large numbers in the trade collections of Bogota.

H. buffoni seems to be strictly confined to the hotter parts of the countries it inhabits.

β. *Mandibula (bitriens basalis) et pedes carnei; subcaudales minores.*

2. Hypuroptila urochrysea.

Hypuroptila urochrysea, Gould, P. Z. S. 1861, p. 198[1]; Mon. Troch. ii. t. 90 (July 1861)[2]; Salv. Cat. Birds Brit. Mus. xvi. p. 89[3].
Chalybura buffoni, Scl. & Salv. P. Z. S. 1879, p. 529 (nec Less.)[4].

Supra saturate gramineo-viridis, uropygio et tectricibus supracaudalibus cupreo tinctis; cauda cupreo-aurea: subtus smaragdino-viridis, abdomine sordide griseo viridi lavato: maxilla nigra, mandibula carnea apice nigra. Long. tota 5·0, alæ 2·75, caudæ rectr. med. 1·6, rectr. lat. 1·8, rostri a rictu 1·15. (Descr. exempl. typ. ex Panama. Mus. Brit.)
♀ adhuc ignota.

Hab. PANAMA (*Warszewiez*[1]).—N. COLOMBIA.

Warszewiez was the discoverer of this species[1]. The single male specimen obtained by him passed into Gould's hands, and was described in 1861. This type is said to have been shot at Panama, but no other collector has met with it in that district. As Salmon found it in the State of Antioquia, both near Medellin and Remedios, and as Warszewiez also visited that portion of Colombia, it is just possible that the locality Panama may be founded on a mistaken record of locality, and that Antioquia is the only district in which this rare species is found. Salmon's birds were wrongly entered as *Chalybura buffoni* in the list of his collection[4].

H. urochrysea is closely allied to *H. isauræ*, but may be distinguished by the purer green colour of the throat.

3. Hypuroptila isauræ.

Hypuroptila isauræ, Gould, P. Z. S. 1861, p. 199[1]; Salv. Cat. Birds Brit. Mus. xvi. p. 89[2].
Chalybura isauræ, Gould, Intr. Troch. p. 72[3]; Salv. P. Z. S. 1867, p. 152[4].

H. urochryseæ similis, sed dorso vix cæruleo lavato, uropygio magis cupreo tincto; subtus gutture et]pectore cærulescentibus. Long. tota 4·7, alæ 2·8, caudæ rectr. med. 1·6, rectr. lat. 1·8, rostri a rictu 1·1.

35*

♀ subtus omnino sordide grisea, rectricibus duabus utrinque externis griseo terminatis, fascia subterminali obscura. (Descr. maris et feminæ ex Santa Fé, Panama. Mus. nostr.)

Hab. Costa Rica, Talamanca (*Zeledon, in U.S. Nat. Mus.*); Panama, Boca del Toro (fide *Verreaux* [1]), Santa Fé [4], Santiago de Veraguas (*Arcé*).

The single, somewhat immature, male specimen described by Gould under this name was sent him by MM. Verreaux of Paris, who received it from Boca del Toro, on the Atlantic coast of the State of Panama, near the frontier of Costa Rica [1]. This type remained unique for many years, until our collector E. Arcé rediscovered the bird at Santa Fé and other places in Central Panama, and sent us specimens of both sexes [4].

The range of the species would thus appear to be very limited, and confined to the western parts of the State of Panama, and Talamanca, the border State of Eastern Costa Rica. A little to the southward *H. urochrysea* takes its place, and to the northward in the rest of Costa Rica and Nicaragua we find *H. melanorrhoa*. It is closely allied to the first-mentioned bird, but may be distinguished by the bluish shade which overspreads the green of the under surface.

4. **Hypuroptila melanorrhoa.** (*Chalybura melanorrhoa*, Tab. LV. figg. 2 ♂, 3 ♀.)

Chalybura melanorrhoa, Salv. P. Z. S. 1864, p. 584 [1]; Ibis, 1872, p. 319 [2]; Lawr. Ann. Lyc. N. Y. ix. p. 122 [3]; Nutting, Pr. U. S. Nat. Mus. vi. p. 406 [4]; Zeledon, An. Mus. Nac. Costa Rica, 1887, p. 121 [5].

Hypuroptila melanorrhoa, Gould, Mon. Troch., Suppl. t. 10 (July 1881) [6]; Salv. Cat. Birds Brit. Mus. xvi. p. 90 [7].

Chalybura carnioli, Lawr. Pr. Ac. Phil. 1865, p. 39 [8].

Similis præcedentibus, sed uropygio et cauda læte purpureo-cupreis: subtus colore viridi saturate cæruleo haud tincto, tectricibus subcaudalibus purpureo-nigris haud albis facile distinguenda. Long. tota 4·5, alæ 2·8, caudæ rectr. med. 1·6, rectr. lat. 1·8, rostri a rictu 1·1. (Descr. maris exempl. typ. ex Tucurriqui, Costa Rica. Mus. nostr.)

♀ a femina *H. isauræ* tectricibus subcaudalibus griseis haud albis differt.

Hab. Nicaragua, Chontales (*Belt* [2]), Los Sabalos (*Nutting* [4]); Costa Rica (*Endres*), Angostura [8], Pacuare (*Carmiol* [3]), Tucurriqui (*Arcé* [1]), Jimenez (*Zeledon* [5]), Talamanca (*Zeledon, in U.S. Nat. Mus.*).

A series of specimens of this species from Eastern Costa Rica sent us by our collector E. Arcé were the first that reached us. These were described in the 'Proceedings of the Zoological Society' in 1864 under the name the species now bears [1]. The following year Mr. Lawrence described the same bird, also from Costa Rica specimens, as *Chalybura carnioli* [8]. Other specimens have since been obtained in Costa Rica, where the bird is now well known. It also occurs in Nicaragua, as Belt secured several examples of both sexes at Chontales [2], and where Mr. Nutting also found it at Los Sabalos [4].

Though clearly allied to both *H. isauræ* and *H. urochrysea*, this species may at once be distinguished by the rich purple-bronze colour of the upper tail-coverts and tail; the tint of the green of the under surface is dark but without blue shade, and the under tail-coverts are purple-black instead of white.

We have no evidence of the existence of any member of this genus in Chiriqui, at least not on the Pacific side of the mountain-range. Nor is the genus represented in Western Costa Rica.

d[5]. *Tectrices subcaudales normales; rectrices laterales purpureo tinctæ.*

LAMPORNIS.

Lampornis, Swainson, Zool. Journ. iii. p. 358; Salv. Cat. Birds Brit. Mus. xvi. p. 91.

The purple colour of the greater part of the lateral rectrices in nearly all the species of *Lampornis,* the shorter rounder tail, and normal under tail-coverts serve to distinguish this genus from *Hypuroptila,* which otherwise has structural points in common with it.

The genus contains ten species, of which four occur within our limits, one of them being the very widely ranging *L. violicauda,* which enters the State of Panama as far as the Line of Railway. The most extensively distributed is *L. prevosti,* which spreads from the middle of the State of Vera Cruz to Costa Rica, a modified form, *L. hendersoni,* occupying the island of Old Providence. The fourth species, *L. veraguensis,* has a very restricted range in the western part of the State of Panama.

1. Lampornis violicauda.

Le Colibri à queue violette de Cayenne, Buff. Pl. Enl. 671. f. 2 [1].
Trochilus violicauda, Bodd. Tabl. Pl. Enl. p. 41 [2].
Lampornis violicauda, Elliot, Ibis, 1872, p. 351 [3]; Salv. Cat. Birds Brit. Mus. xvi. p. 93 [4].
Lampornis mango, Lawr. Ann. Lyc. N. Y. vii. p. 319 [5]; Scl. & Salv. P. Z. S. 1864, p. 365 [6].

Supra nitenti-aureo-viridis, capite summo obscuriore: subtus gutture et abdomine medio nigris, cervicis lateribus micanti-viridibus, hoc colore cyaneo gradatim transeunte ad guttur nigrum; hypochondriis viridibus, subcaudalibus nigris saturate viridescenti-cyaneo lavatis; caudæ rectricibus mediis saturate viridibus, lateralibus læte purpureis chalybeo-cyaneo marginatis: rostro nigro, pedibus nigricantibus. Long. tota 4·5, alæ 2·6, caudæ 1·4, rostri a rictu 1·1.

♀ subtus alba, fascia longitudinali nigra a mento usque ad crissum extendente, subcaudalibus viridibus albo marginatis, rectricibus lateralibus chalybeo-cyaneo-purpureis, plaga mediana purpureo-rubida, apicibus albis.

Hab. PANAMA, Lion Hill (*M'Leannan* [4] [5] [6]), Paraiso (*Hughes* [4]). — SOUTH AMERICA, generally from Colombia to South Brazil [4].

This well-known and widely-ranging species is only found within our limits at the extreme south-eastern portion, *i. e.* between the line of the Panama Railway and the mainland of South America. In the south it ranges over nearly the whole of Tropical South America, keeping its specific characters with remarkable precision. Only in the birds of Western Ecuador has any separation been attempted of late years, and these were described by Gould as *L. iridescens,* but the differences are hardly appreciable.

The great diversity between the sexes of this bird led to their being described as distinct species by the old authors. All of these titles are now collected under *Lampornis violicauda*, though the application of this name is questioned. For a long time Linnæus's *Trochilus mango* was considered its proper appellation, but Mr. Elliot showed that this name belonged to the very distinct Jamaican *Lampornis*, and we have followed him in this opinion.

Lampornis violicauda is not uncommon on the line of the Panama Railway both at Lion Hill and Paraiso Stations. We have received examples from both places; and M'Leannan, who collected principally at Lion Hill, also sent specimens to Mr. Lawrence.

2. **Lampornis prevosti.**

Trochilus prevosti, Less. Hist. Nat. Col. p. 87, t. 24 [1].

Lampornis prevosti, Gould, Mon. Troch. ii. t. 75 (May 1858)[2]; Scl. P. Z. S. 1857, p. 287[3]; 1859, pp. 367[4], 385[5]; Scl. & Salv. Ibis, 1859, p. 127[6]; 1870, p. 837[7]; Salv. Ibis, 1860, p. 272[8]; 1864, p. 380[9]; 1889, p. 365[10]; Cat. Strickl. Coll. p. 362[11]; Cat. Birds Brit. Mus. xvi. p. 98[12]; Lawr. Bull. U. S. Nat. Mus. no. 4. p. 32[13]; Sumichrast, La Nat. v. p. 250[14]; Boucard, Ann. Soc. Linn. Lyon, xx. p. 275[15]; P. Z. S. 1883, p. 451[16]; Stone, Pr. Ac. Phil. 1890, p. 207[17].

Lampornis thalassinus, Ridgw. Pr. Biol. Soc. Wash. iii. p. 23[18].

Lampornis prevosti thalassinus, Ridgw. Pr. U. S. Nat. Mus. viii. p. 573[19].

Lampornis mango, de Oca, La Nat. iii. p. 62[20]; Sanchez, An. Mus. Nac. Mex. i. p. 96[21].

Supra nitenti-aureo-viridis: subtus abdomine medio viridi-cyaneo tincto, hypochondriis aureis, gutture medio nigro lateribus suis micanti-viridibus, subcaudalibus purpureo-nigris; caudæ rectricibus mediis saturate viridibus, lateralibus rufo-purpureis, chalybeo-cyaneo marginatis: rostro nigro. Long. tota 4·5, alæ 2·6, caudæ 1·45, rostri a rictu 1·2.

♀ subtus alba, fascia mediana nigra a mento ad crissum apud pectus plumis viridibus intermixta, cervicis lateribus et hypochondriis aureo-viridibus, subcaudalibus viridi-fuscis albo terminatis; caudæ rectricibus lateralibus apicibus albis, fascia lata subterminali chalybeo-cyanea. (Descr. maris et feminæ ex Santa Ana, Peten. Mus. nostr.)

Hab. MEXICO (*Sallé*[3]), Altamira, Tampico and Tantina in Tamaulipas (*W. B. Richardson*[12]), Misantla (*de Oca, F. D. G.*), Jalapa (*de Oca*), Choapam (*Boucard*[5]), Cordova (*Boucard*[15], *Sumichrast*[14]), Uvero (*Sumichrast*[14]), Northern Yucatan (*G. F. Gaumer*[16]), Meco I., Mugeres I. (*G. F. G.*[10]), Cozumel I. (*Benedict, G. F. G.*[10]), road from Ticul to Uxmal, Labna (*Stone*), Santa Efigenia (*Sumichrast*[13]); BRITISH HONDURAS, Belize (*Blancaneaux*[12]); GUATEMALA (*Skinner*[6]), Santa Ana near Peten, Escuintla, Hacienda de la Concepcion (*O. S.*[12]); HONDURAS, Bonacca I. (*G. F. Gaumer*[10]), San Pedro (*G. M. Whitely*[7]); COSTA RICA, Bebedero de Nicoya (*Arcé*[12]).—VENEZUELA[12].

Lesson's figure of this bird was taken from a female or young male specimen of a *Lampornis* from an unknown locality. In his 'Index Général des genre Trochilus,' p. xii, he gave its locality with doubt as Surinam. Bonaparte, who included this bird in his 'Conspectus Avium,' assigned it to the island of Tobago, and Gould was the first person to attach Lesson's name to the Mexican *Lampornis*, and in this course he has been followed by all recent writers.

With a general resemblance to *L. violicauda* this species may readily be distinguished by the middle of the abdomen being green and not black, and this character is shared by the following closely allied species.

The range of *L. prevosti* is very extensive, and includes the whole of the Mexican State of Vera Cruz, and even spreads a little further north to Tampico and Altamira in the State of Tamaulipas. It thence passes through Yucatan, British Honduras, Guatemala, and as far south as Western Costa Rica. In Guatemala it is by no means common, and we do not recollect to have seen any skins of it in the great collections made near Coban. It occurs, however, in the province of Peten and near Escuintla on the side of mountains bordering the Pacific Ocean. In both places we found this bird feeding from the flowers of a species of *Erythrina*, commonly planted to form hedges. Boucard says [15] that it frequents the gardens of Cordova and Jalapa, and builds in the coffee-trees; and according to de Oca [20] it is common and resident in the State of Vera Cruz, but in no other part of Mexico.

It is common on most of the islands lying off the coast of Yucatan, British Honduras, and the Republic of Honduras. The Cozumel bird was separated by Mr. Ridgway as *L. thalassinus* [18], but we cannot trace any difference between our series from that island and others from the mainland.

The presence of *L. prevosti* in Venezuela seems to be assured. Not only did Mr. Spence procure a specimen in that country [12], but we believe Count Berlepsch has also obtained skins from there which are certainly referable to this species.

3. Lampornis hendersoni.

Lampornis hendersoni, Cory, Auk, iv. p. 177 [1]; Salv. Cat. Birds Brit. Mus. xvi. p. 99 [2].

L. prevosti similis, sed rostro breviore forsan distinguendus. Long. tota 4·4, alæ 2·65, caudæ 1·4, rostri a rictu 0·9.

♀ a femina *L. prevosti* rostro brevi differt. (Descr. maris et feminæ ex Ins. Old Providence. Mus. nostr.)

Hab. PANAMA, Old Providence I. in the Caribbean Sea (*R. Henderson* [1] [2]).

This bird is very closely allied to *L. prevosti*, and the only difference that can be relied on with any certainty is the dimensions of the bill, that of the island bird being very short. Mr. Cory, in his description, speaks of the back being green instead of bronzy, the black patch on the throat longer and narrower, and the top of the head faintly tinged with ash colour. These are variable characters, and may be partly due to the age of the plumage and the way the skin is made up.

The birds which were described by Mr. Cory were all obtained by Mr. R. Henderson on the little island of Old Providence, which lies at some distance from the east coast of Central America in the Caribbean Sea. Three of these specimens were most kindly sent us by Mr. Cory.

4. Lampornis veraguensis.

Lampornis veraguensis, Gould, Mon. Troch. ii. t. 76 (May 1858) [1]; Scl. P. Z. S. 1856, p. 140 [2];
    Lawr. Ann. Lyc. N. Y. viii. p. 178 [3]; Salv. P. Z. S. 1867, p. 153 [4]; 1870, p. 207 [5]; Cat.
    Birds Brit. Mus. xvi. p. 99 [6].

L. prevosti similis, sed gula tota micanti-viridi, colore nigro omnino absente facile distinguendus. (Descr.
    maris exempl. typ. ex Chiriqui. Mus. Brit.)

Hab. PANAMA, Volcan de Chiriqui (*Warszewiez* [1]), David (*Bridges* [1] [2], *Hicks* [3] [4]), Cor-
    dillera del Chucu, Calobre (*Arcé* [5]), Agua Dulce (*Herrera, in U.S. Nat. Mus.*).

Gould's description of this species was taken from specimens sent to him by Warszewiez from Chiriqui, and the bird has since been found in the same district by several
more recent travellers. Arcé also met with it at Calobre, halfway between Chiriqui
and Panama.

The range of the species is very restricted, and probably does not extend beyond the
western half of the State of Panama. In Costa Rica the allied form, *L. prevosti*, is
found, and at Panama *L. violicauda*.

As a species *L. veraguensis* is easily distinguished, for the whole throat is glittering
green, the middle as well as the sides; in all the allied forms the middle of the
throat is black.

f [4]. *Culmen ad basin plumatum, tegulæ nasales quoque plumatæ (margine inferiore*
excepto); plaga auricularis nitida, violacea: sexus similes.

PETASOPHORA.

Petasophora, Gray, List Gen. Birds, p. 13 (1840); Salv. Cat. Birds Brit. Mus. xvi. p. 105.

In this genus the feathering of the forehead is carried further along the bill than in
Lampornis, so that the nasal covers are almost hidden. *Petasophora* has also a peculiarity in the conspicuous elongated glittering blue auricular tufts, which are to be
found in every one of the species. The character of the coloration of the throat is also
peculiar, each feather showing a dark disc with a glittering margin in certain lights.
The tomia of the maxilla are rather strongly serrate, so much so that a Brazilian species
bears the name *P. serrirostris* from this feature.

Seven species are included in *Petasophora*, one of which, however, is of doubtful
value.

All the species inhabit mountain-ranges, most of them living at a considerable
elevation. *P. delphinæ*, though also a bird of the mountains, likewise visits the lower
grounds.

Of the three species found within our limits, *P. thalassina* inhabits Southern Mexico
and Guatemala, *P. cyanotis* Costa Rica and the State of Panama, and the Andes of
South America as far south as Bolivia. *P. delphinæ* is a widely-ranging bird of the
northern portion of the southern continent, and reaches the eastern forests of
Guatemala.

Ptilosis plerumque nitidi-viridis.

1. Petasophora thalassina.

Trochilus thalassinus, Sw. Phil. Mag. new ser. i. p. 441[1].

Petasophora thalassina, Gould, P. Z. S. 1847, p. 8[2]; Mon. Troch. iv. t. 227 (May 1853)[3]; Scl.
    P. Z. S. 1858, p. 297[4]; 1859, pp. 367[5], 386[6]; 1864, p. 177[7]; Scl. & Salv. Ibis, 1859,
    p. 127[8]; Salv. Ibis, 1859, p. 468[9]; 1860, pp. 195[10], 260[11], 263[12]; Cat. Birds Brit. Mus.
    xvi. p. 109[13]; Lawr. Pr. Bost. Soc. N. H. xiv. p. 284[14]; Mem. Bost. Soc. N. H. ii. p. 292[15];
    de Oca, La Nat. iii. p. 64[16]; Sumichrast, La Nat. v. p. 250[17]; Ferrari-Perez, Pr. U. S. Nat.
    Mus. ix. p. 157[18]; Herrera, La Nat. (2) i. p. 322[19].

Ramphodon anais, Less. Hist. Nat. Troch. p. 146, t. 56[20].

Ornismya anais, Less. Hist. Nat. Ois.-Mouches, Suppl. p. 104, t. 3[21].

Trochilus anaïs, Sw. Birds Braz. & Mex. t. 75[22].

Supra nitenti-gramineo-viridis; subtus gutture micanti-viridi, plumis singulis disco obscuriore; abdomine
    medio saturate violaceo-cyaneo, hypochondriis et tectricibus subcaudalibus viridibus, his cervino lim-
    batis; mento, genis et plaga auriculari elongata, nitide violaceis; rectricibus mediis dorso fere concolor-
    ibus, reliquis cyanescentioribus, omnibus fascia subterminali nigricanti-chalybea: rostro nigro. Long.
    tota 4·5, alæ 2·7, caudæ 1·7, rostri a rictu 1·0.

♀ mari similis, sed coloribus omnibus paginæ inferioris minus nitidis. (Descr. maris et feminæ ex Dueñas,
    Guatemala. Mus. nostr.)

Hab. MEXICO[2] (*Benvelet*[20], *White*[7]), Guanajuato (*Sanchez*), Temiscaltepec (*Bullock*[1])
    Real del Monte, Ajusco (*W. B. Richardson*[13]), Hacienda Eslava, Chimalpa and
    Tetelco in the Valley of Mexico, Montaña de Orizaba, Coatepec[16], Cordova (*Sanchez,
    F. Ferrari-Perez*[13]), Jalapa (*de Oca*[5][16], *M. Trujillo*[13]), Orizaba (*Sumichrast*[17]),
    Puebla (*Ferrari-Perez*[18]), Totontepec (*A. Boucard*[6], *M. Trujillo*), Oaxaca[4]
    (*Fenochio*[13]): GUATEMALA (*Skinner*[8]), Quezaltenango (*O. S.*[13]), San Martin,
    Chuipache, Toliman (*W. B. Richardson*[13]), Dueñas[11], Volcan de Fuego[11], Montaña
    de Chilasco, Coban (*O. S. & F. D. G.*).

This species was first described by Swainson in 1827, from specimens obtained by
Bullock at Temiscaltepec in Central Mexico[1], and it is now known to be a not uncommon bird in the Valley of Mexico[16], chiefly in the months of June and July[16], and on the
eastern edge of the plateau in the State of Vera Cruz. It appears to be absent from
the sierras of Western * and North-western Mexico, and though we have not traced
it northward of Real del Monte in the State of Hidalgo, Señor J. Sanchez gives Guanajuato as one of its localities. In Guatemala it is a common characteristic bird of the
highlands, where it keeps almost exclusively to the region of evergreen oaks, its range
in altitude extending from about 5000 to 9000 feet above the level of the sea. In the
oak forests it frequents the brushwood, and its presence may often be detected by
the rather monotonous song the male utters when resting on a dead twig of some bush.

Lesson, who gave a very fair figure of this species in his 'Histoire Naturelle des

---

* *Petasophora thalassina*, Lawr. Mem. Bost. Soc. N. H. ii. p. 292, ex Tres Marias Is. (*Xantus*), is based upon
a bird wrongly located.

Trochilidées,' under the name of *Ramphodon anais*, seems to have confused it with the South-American bird we now know as *P. iolata*. His first description of *R. anais* was based upon a Mexican specimen.

P. thalassina may readily be distinguished from *P. cyanotis* by its blue abdomen. In very adult birds the chin is slightly tinged with blue, but not nearly so much so as in *P. iolata*.

2. **Petasophora cyanotis.**

Trochilus cyanotus, Bourc. & Muls. Ann. Sc. Phys. et Nat. Lyon, vi. p. 41 [1].

Petasophora cyanotus, Gould, P. Z. S. 1847, p. 8 [2].

Petasophora cyanotis, Gould, Mon. Troch. iv. t. 228 (May 1853) [3]; Cab. J. f. Orn. 1863, p. 162 [4];
    Lawr. Ann. Lyc. N. Y. ix. p. 125 [5]; Frantz. J. f. Orn. 1869, p. 316 [6]; Salv. P. Z. S. 1870,
    p. 210 [7]; Cat. Birds Brit. Mus. xvi. p. 110 [8]; Boucard, P. Z. S. 1878, p. 69 [9]; Nutting, Pr.
    U. S. Nat. Mus. v. p. 500 [10]; Zeledon, An. Mus. Nac. Costa Rica, 1887, p. 121 [11].

Petasophora cabanidis, Heine, J. f. Orn. 1863, p. 182 [12].

Petasophora cabanisi, Lawr. Ann. Lyc. N. Y. ix. p. 126 [13].

P. thalassinæ similis, sed colore violaceo a mento et abdomine medio omnino absente.

Hab. COSTA RICA (*Carmiol, Endres*), Barranca [5], Dota [5], Grecia (*Carmiol*), Cartago
    (*Cooper* [5]), Orosi (*Kramer* [8]), Irazu (*Boucard* [9], *Rogers* [8]), La Palma (*Nutting* [10]),
    Faldas de Irazu (*Zeledon* [11]), Las Cruces de Candelaria (*Zeledon*); PANAMA,
    Volcan de Chiriqui, Chitra, Calovevora (*Arcé* [7]).—SOUTH AMERICA, Andes, from
    Colombia and Venezuela [1] to Bolivia [7].

Birds of this species from Costa Rica have been separated from the South-American form both by F. Heine and Mr. Lawrence under the names of *P. cabanidis* and *P. cabanisi*; but their comparisons are chiefly made with *P. thalassina*, which is certainly a distinct species. The differences observable between the Costa Rican and Andean birds are very slight, and consist in the former being rather darker on the abdomen and in the bright feathers of the throat spreading further over the breast. We doubt if even these slight characters are constant, but due in a great measure to the way the skins are made up.

P. cyanotis is a common bird in the highlands of Costa Rica and the State of Panama. A gap then occurs in its range, and it reappears in the Andes of Venezuela and Colombia, and thence passes southwards as far as Bolivia.

Ptilosis plerumque fusca.

3. **Petasophora delphinæ.**

Ornismya delphinæ, Less. Rev. Zool. 1839, p. 44 [1].

Petasophora delphinæ, Gould, P. Z. S. 1847, p. 9 [2]; Mon. Troch. iv. t. 229 (May 1853) [3]; Salv.
    Ibis, 1860, pp. 194 [4], 195 [5], 261 [6], 276 [7]; 1872, p. 320 [8]; P. Z. S. 1870, p. 210 [9]; Cat.
    Birds Brit. Mus. xvi. p. 111 [10]; Scl. & Salv. P. Z. S. 1870, p. 837 [11].

Fusco-brunnea, tectricibus supracaudalibus obscurioribus et cum uropygio ferrugineo terminatis: subtus fuscescens, gutture pallidiore, medialiter plumis nitide viridibus (ad pectus cyaneis) ornato ; plaga auriculari elongata, nitide violacea ; subcaudalibus ferrugineis ; cauda viridi-brunnea, fascia subterminali obscura utrinque ferrugineo limbata : rostro nigro. Long. tota 4·5, alæ 2·6, caudæ 1·5, rostri a rictu 0·8.

♀ mari similis, plaga gulari viridi et auricularibus elongatis violaceis minoribus distinguenda. (Descr. maris et feminæ ex Coban, Guatemala. Mus. nostr.)

Hab. GUATEMALA (*Skinner* [11]), Coban (*O. S.* [4] [5]); HONDURAS, San Pedro (*G. M. Whitely* [11]); NICARAGUA, Chontales (*Belt* [8]); COSTA RICA (*Carmiol* [11]); PANAMA, Calovevora (*Arcé* [9]).—COLOMBIA ; ECUADOR ; PERU ; VENEZUELA ; GUIANA [11].

Petasophora delphinæ is a well-known bird in all the countries forming the northern portion of the South-American continent from Guiana on the east to Colombia on the west, and it passes southwards as far as Peru. In Central America it also enjoys a wide range, occurring at intervals throughout our country as far north as Coban in Vera Paz.

When staying at the latter town in November 1859, Salvin obtained several specimens which were shot in the neighbourhood, mostly when feeding amongst the *Salviæ* which abound there and are in full flower towards the close of the year.

As M'Leannan did not meet with this species on the line of the Panama Railway, it is probable that it is not found in the hottest part of the lowlands, but keeps mostly to the forest-clad hills at some elevation above sea-level.

Sect. B. TROCHILI INTERMEDII.

Tomia maxillæ ad apicem indistincte serrata.

a. *Culmen ad basin plumatum ; tegulæ nasales partim expositæ ; rostrum subrectum.*

PANTERPE.

Panterpe, Cabanis & Heine, Mus. Hein. iii. p. 43; Salv. Cat. Birds Brit. Mus. xvi. p. 158.

This genus has no near allies, so far as we know at present. In the feathering of the base of the bill it resembles *Heliangelus* and *Heliotrypha*, and it agrees with those genera in the absence of white at the end of the lateral rectrices ; but the sexes are alike instead of being widely different, the tail more rounded, and the glittering colours differently arranged.

Panterpe is restricted in its range to Costa Rica and the adjoining portions of the State of Panama.

1. Panterpe insignis.

Panterpe insignis, Cab. & Heine, Mus. Hein. iii. p. 43[1]; Gould, Mon. Troch. v. t. 336 (May 1861)[2]; Cab. J. f. Orn. 1862, p. 164[3]; Lawr. Ann. Lyc. N. Y. viii. p. 45 (partim)[4]; ix. p. 124[5]; Frantz. J. f. Orn. 1869, p. 316[6]; Boucard, P. Z. S. 1878, p. 71[7]; Zeledon, An. Mus. Nac. Costa Rica, 1887, p. 122[8]; Salv. Cat. Birds Brit. Mus. xvi. p. 158[9].

Supra nitenti-cæruleo-viridis, tectricibus caudæ superioribus cærulescentioribus; nucha nigra; pileo nitide cyaneo: subtus nitide aurea, hypochondriis viridescentioribus, gutture medio nitide rubro; plaga pectorali cyanea, tectricibus subcaudalibus saturate viridibus; cauda saturate cyaneo-chalybea: rostro nigro, mandibulæ dimidio basali carnea. Long. tota 4·2, alæ 2·5, caudæ 1·5, rostri a rictu 0·9. (Descr. maris ex Volcan de Chiriqui. Mus. nostr.)

♀ mari similis.

Hab. Costa Rica, San José (*Hoffmann* [1] [3]), La Candelaria (*v. Frantzius* [5] [6]), Volcan de Cartago (*E. Arcé* [9], *J. Cooper* [5], *Boucard* [7]), Faldas de Irazu [8], La Palma (*Zeledon*); Panama, Volcan de Chiriqui (*Arcé* [9]).

This beautiful species was discovered by the late Dr. Hoffmann in Costa Rica, and was described by Cabanis and Heine in 1860 from the single specimen sent by him to the Berlin Museum [1]. This specimen also formed the subject of Gould's plate [2]. A few years afterwards our collector, Enrique Arcé, procured a series of specimens from Costa Rica, and subsequently others from the Volcan de Chiriqui, the sexes of each specimen from the latter locality being noted on the label. We thus learn that there is no tangible difference between the sexes of this species, the female being hardly less brilliant than the male. At one time it was supposed that the bird described by Gould as *Anthocephala castaneiventris* (a female *Oreopyra*) was the female of *Panterpe insignis* [5], but this view has, we believe, been now definitely abandoned.

The range of *P. insignis* seems to be very limited, and probably does not extend beyond the upland zone of forest which occupies the higher volcanoes of Costa Rica and Chiriqui. Zeledon gives its Costa Rica habitat as the slopes of the Volcan de Irazu, which is another name for that of Cartago. The same collector has sent a specimen to the United States National Museum from La Palma.

b. *Culmen ad basin plumatum; tegulæ nasales (pars distalis) distincte expositæ; rostrum leviter arcuatum.*

a'. *Guttur album aut nitide viride aut cæruleo-viride.*

a''. *Cauda uniformis, subquadrata; pileus viridis, dorso concolor.*

a'''. *Sexus fere similes.*

AGYRTRIA.

Thaumantias, Bp. Rev. Zool. 1854, p. 255 (nec Eschsch.).
Agyrtria, Reich. Aufz. d. Col. p. 10; Salv. Cat. Birds Brit. Mus. xvi. p. 178.

Of the twenty-two species included in this genus only two occur within our limits, one of them being the widely-ranging *A. candida*, which extends from Eastern Mexico to Nicaragua, the other being *A. luciæ*, the only known specimen of which came from Honduras. It is somewhat remarkable that in Costa Rica and the State of Panama both *Agyrtria* and *Cyanomyia* are unrepresented, though both occur on each side of that district.

Though many of the species of *Agyrtria* are well defined, others are not so, and the specific limits of the latter are not clearly understood.

The genus extends over nearly the whole of the tropical portion of South America, its northern limit being defined by that of *A. candida* in the middle of the Mexican State of Vera Cruz. Several species occur in Southern Brazil and Bolivia, but none seem to pass beyond the limits of the tropical forests.

As a genus *Agyrtria* is very closely allied to *Cyanomyia*, and it is questionable whether they should be kept apart; the tail of the latter is perhaps slightly more forked, but the difference is hardly material. In colour there is more diversity, as none of the members of *Agyrtria* have the crown glittering blue. *Cyanomyia*, on the whole, seems a natural group of species, and on that account had better be kept apart.

1. Agyrtria luciæ.

Thaumatias luciæ, Lawr. Pr. Ac. Phil. 1867, p. 233 [1]; Elliot, Ibis, 1878, p. 52 [2].
Agyrtria luciæ, Elliot, Syn. Troch. p. 208 [3]; Salv. Cat. Birds Brit. Mus. xvi. p. 188 [4].

"Upper plumage of a dull bronzy dark green, the crown duller; the upper tail-coverts of a lighter bronzy green, somewhat golden; the tail-feathers are dull bronzy green, all except the two central ones are broadly marked near their ends with dark purplish bronze, the tips being ashy grey; the throat and breast are glittering bluish green, middle of the abdomen white; the under tail-coverts are light olive margined with white; wings brownish purple; upper mandible black, the under yellow with the end black; feet black. Length (skin) $3\frac{3}{4}$ inches, wing $2\frac{1}{8}$, tail $1\frac{3}{8}$, bill $1\frac{3}{16}$." (*Lawrence, l. s. c.*)

Hab. HONDURAS [1].

We have never seen a specimen of this species, which Mr. Lawrence compares with *A. linnæi* (=*A. viridissima*, nob.), which it resembles in size and colour, differing in the tail being like that of *A. niveipectus*.

The type was the only specimen of the species in the collection in which Mr. Lawrence found it, but there were many examples of *A. candida*.

2. Agyrtria candida.

Trochilus candidus, Bourc. & Muls. Ann. Sc. Phys. et Nat. Lyon, ix. p. 326 [1].
Thaumatias candidus, Scl. P. Z. S. 1858, p. 358 [2]; 1859, p. 386 [3]; Scl. & Salv. Ibis, 1859, p. 130 [4]; 1860, p. 40 [5]; Salv. Ibis, 1859, p. 467 [6]; 1860, p. 270 [7]; 1872, p. 320 [8]; Cat. Birds Brit. Mus. xvi. p. 190 [9]; G. C. Taylor, Ibis, 1860, p. 116 [10]; Gould, Mon. Troch. v. p. 292 (May 1860) [11]; de Oca, La Nat. iii. p. 206 [12]; Boucard, Ann. Soc. Linn. Lyon, xx. p. 277 [13]; Lawr. Bull. U. S. Nat. Mus. no. 4. p. 33 [14]; Sumichrast, La Nat. v. p. 250 [15]; Sanchez, An. Mus. Nac. Mex. i. p. 96 [16].

Supra nitenti-cupreo-viridis, pileo et uropygio magis cupreo tinctis: subtus nivea, tectricibus subcaudalibus concoloribus, cervicis lateribus et hyochondriis nitide aureo-viridibus; cauda olivescenti-viridi, rectricibus lateralibus fascia subterminali cupreo-purpurea ornatis: rostri maxilla nigra, mandibula carnea apice nigra. Long. tota 3·6, alæ 2·0, caudæ 1·2, rostri a rictu 0·75.

♀ mari similis, sed rectricum lateralium apicibus pallidioribus. (Descr. maris et feminæ ex Coban, Guatemala. Mus. nostr.)

Hab. MEXICO (*de Oca* [12]), Misantla (*F. D. G.*[9]), Cordova [13], Playa Vicente (*Boucard* [3]), Sochiapa (*M. Trujillo* [9]), Guichicovi (*Sumichrast* [14] [15]), Chimalapa (*W. B. Richardson* [9]), Temax in Yucatan (*G. F. Gaumer* [9]); BRITISH HONDURAS, Corosal (*Roe* [9]), Belize, Cayo and Great Southern Pine-ridge (*Blancaneaux* [9]); GUATEMALA (*Skinner* [4]), Coban [1] [7], Choctum, Yzabal [7] (*O. S. & F. D. G.*); HONDURAS (*G. Taylor* [10]), Truxillo (*Townsend, in U. S. Nat. Mus.*), Santa Ana (*Wittkugel, in U. S. Nat. Mus.*); NICARAGUA, La Libertad and Santo Domingo in Chontales, Matagalpa (*W. B. Richardson*), Chontales (*Belt* [8]).

This distinct species of *Agyrtria* was discovered by Delattre in Mexico [1]. It is there a common species from the middle of the State of Vera Cruz southwards to the eastern side of the Isthmus of Tehuantepec, occurring also in Yucatan and thence through British Honduras to Eastern Guatemala and Nicaragua. It is very abundant in the neighbourhood of Coban at an elevation of about 4300 feet in the month of November, and we also met with it at Yzabal in September at nearly the sea-level. At the latter place it frequented the flowers of the underwood under the forest trees. At Coban the flowering *Salviæ* were the chief attraction.

A. candida is the only species of *Agyrtria* which has the crown of nearly the same colour as the back and the whole of the under surface, including the under tail-coverts, pure white. The sexes are much alike, but the female may be distinguished by the tips of the lateral rectrices being paler than in the male.

b'''. *Sexus dissimiles.*

ARINIA.

Arinia, Muls. "Ann. Soc. Linn. Lyon, 1877, Oct. 12"; Salv. Cat. Birds Brit. Mus. xvi. p. 193.

This genus was based by Mulsant upon a bird discovered by M. Boucard at Punta Arenas in Costa Rica. It is apparently closely allied to *Agyrtria*, but a difference in the coloration of the sexes separates the two forms.

Arinia is restricted in its range to a limited district of Costa Rica, in which country neither *Agyrtria* nor *Cyanomyia* occur.

1. **Arinia boucardi.**

Arinia boucardi, Muls. Ann. Soc. Linn. Lyon, 1877, Oct. [1]; Elliot, Syn. Troch. p. 209 [2]; Sharpe, in Gould's Mon. Troch., Suppl. (April 1885) [3]; Salv. Cat. Birds Brit. Mus. xvi. p. 193 [4].
Arena boucardi, Muls. Hist. Nat. Ois.-Mouches, iv. p. 194, t. 121 [5].
Sapphironia boucardi, Boucard, P. Z. S. 1878, p. 71 [6].

"*Male.* Upper surface and flanks bronzy green, darkest on the head. Throat and breast shining bluish green.

Abdomen and under tail-coverts pure white. Median pair of rectrices dark bronze-green; next bronze-green with black tip, remaining lateral feathers bronze-green at base, rest black, the bronze-green decreasing in extent as it goes towards the external feather. All the lateral feathers edged with white at their tips. Maxilla black; mandible flesh-colour, tip black. Feet black. Total length $3\frac{1}{4}$ inches, wing 2, tail $1\frac{9}{16}$, culmen $1\frac{1}{16}$.

"*Female.* Differs in having the middle of the throat, breast, and underparts pure white. Median rectrices bronzy green; lateral feathers green at base, then black, and tipped with grey. Rest like the male." (*Elliot, l. s. c.*[2])

Hab. COSTA RICA, Punta Arenas (*Boucard* [1 6]).

This bird is only known from the types obtained by M. Boucard in 1876 at Punta Arenas, the chief port on the Pacific coast of Costa Rica.

b″. *Cauda uniformis, subfurcata; pileus micans aut cyaneus aut purpureo-cyaneus, obscure viridis aut obscure cyaneus.*

CYANOMYIA.

Cyanomyia, Bonaparte, Rev. Zool. 1854, p. 254; Salv. Cat. Birds Brit. Mus. xvi. p. 194.
Uranomitra, Cab. & Heine, Mus. Hein. iii. p. 41 (ex Reich.).

Cyanomyia contains eight or nine species, all but two of which are strictly confined to the northern section of our region—the two exceptions belonging to the Andes of Colombia and Peru. Of the northern species four or five are strictly confined to Mexico, one (*C. guatemalensis*) ranges from British Honduras to Nicaragua, and one is said to belong to Honduras alone.

In *Cyanomyia* the tail is slightly forked and uniform in colour, without any white at the base of the lateral feathers. The crown in nearly all the species is glittering blue, inclining to violet in some of them; in others the fore part of the crown is very dark dull green or dark dull indigo-blue.

The genus naturally divides into two groups: in one the whole of the maxilla, except the tip, is flesh-colour and the flanks are white; all of the birds possessing these characters are from Western or Central Mexico. The other group belongs to Eastern Mexico, and Central America as far south as Nicaragua, and in it the maxilla is black and the flanks shining green. The two Andean birds belong to this latter group.

α. *Maxilla (apex exceptus) carnea; hypochondriæ fere pure albæ.*

α′. *Pileus cyaneus aut purpureo-cyaneus micans.*

1. **Cyanomyia verticalis.**

Trochilus quadricolor, Vieill. Enc. Méth. p. 573 [1]??
Agyrtria β. Uranomitra quadricolor, Reich. Aufz. d. Col. p. 10 [2].
Cyanomyia quadricolor, Gould, Mon. Troch. v. t. 284 (May 1855) [3]; Scl. P. Z. S. 1859, p. 386 [4];
    Dugès, La Nat. i. p. 141 [5]; Villada, La Nat. ii. p. 362 [6]; de Oca, La Nat. iii. p. 209 [7];
    Lawr. Mem. Bost. Soc. N. H. ii. p. 292 [8]; Boucard, Ann. Soc. Linn. Lyon, xx. p. 276 [9];
    Herrera, La Nat. (2) i. p. 322 [10]; Sanchez, An. Mus. Nac. Mex. i. p. 96 [11].

Trochilus verticalis, Licht. Preis-Verz. Mex. Vög. p. 1 (*cf.* J. f. Orn. 1863, p. 55) [12].

Cyanomyia verticalis, Salv. Cat. Birds Brit. Mus. xvi. p. 194 [13].

Uranomitra ellioti, Berl. Pr. U. S. Nat. Mus. xi. p. 562 [14].

Supra brunnescenti-olivacea viridi vix tincta, cervice postica viridescentiore; capite summo et cervicis lateribus nitenti-cæruleis, his pallidioribus: subtus (tectricibus subcaudalibus inclusis) nivea, lateribus infra alas fuscis; cauda olivaceo-viridi, rectricibus lateralibus angustissime albo terminatis: rostro carneo, apice nigro. Long. tota 4·0, alæ 2·2, caudæ 1·25, rostri a rictu 1·05.

♀ mari similis; colore cæruleo capitis minus nitido. (Descr. maris et feminæ ex Bolaños, Mexico. Mus. nostr.)

Hab. MEXICO (*Deppe* [13], *Floresi* [3]), Mazatlan (*Grayson* [8], *A. Forrer* [13]), Bolaños, Sierra de Bolaños, Calvillo, Lake Chapala, San Blas, Zapotlan (*W. B. Richardson* [13]), Guadalajara (*Grayson* [8]), Volcan de Orizaba (*Sallé* and *Boucard* [9]), Choapam (*Boucard* [4]), Guanajuato (*Dugès* [5]), Jalisco (*Sanchez* [11]), valley of Mexico (*Villada* [6], *de Oca* [7], *Herrera* [10]).

This species has usually passed as *C. quadricolor* (Vieill.), but, as Count Berlepsch has shown [14], it cannot be that bird, the description of which, founded upon a specimen said to have come from Trinidad [1], better suits *Cyanomyia franciæ* of Colombia than the present species.

Count Berlepsch proposed to call this bird *Uranomitra ellioti* [14], but Lichtenstein's title, *Trochilus verticalis*, a synonym, according to Cabanis and Heine, of *C. quadricolor*, may be used for it, based as it is upon Deppe's specimens collected in Mexico.

The range of *C. verticalis* is chiefly confined to the sierras of North-western Mexico, from Mazatlan southwards through the States of Jalisco and Aguas Calientes *. The most southern place whence we have received specimens is Zapotlan, which is on the south side of the Rio Lerma and Lake Chapala. Floresi's specimens, of which Gould had a number in his collection, were probably all obtained at or near Bolaños.

M. Boucard tells us that he and M. Sallé found this species at a great elevation on the peak of Orizaba during an excursion to that mountain [9]. No specimens were obtained on Popocatepetl by Elwes and Godman in 1888, nor did Mr. Richardson find it on the upper parts of Ixtaccihuatl; but Herrera and other writers on Mexican birds say that it occurs in the Valley of Mexico, and M. Boucard says he found it breeding at Choapam in the month of March [4].

2. Cyanomyia violiceps.

Cyanomyia violiceps, Gould, Ann. & Mag. N. H. 1859, iv. p. 97 [1]; Mon. Troch. v. t. 285 (Sept. 1860) [2]; Scl. P. Z. S. 1859, p. 386 [3]; de Oca, La Nat. iii. p. 208 [4]; Lawr. Bull. U. S. Nat. Mus. no. 4, p. 32 [5]; Sumichrast, La Nat. v. p. 250 [6]; Boucard, Ann. Soc. Linn. Lyon, xx. p. 276 [7]; Sanchez, An. Mus. Nac. Mex. i. p. 96 [8]; Salv. Cat. Birds Brit. Mus. xvi. p. 196 [9].

Uranomitra violiceps, Cab. & Heine, Mus. Hein. iii. p. 41 [10].

* When in London last summer (1891) Mr. W. Brewster showed us a specimen of a *Cyanomyia* allied to this species from Sonora. It has not yet, so far as we know, been described.

C. verticali similis, sed colore cæruleo ; capitis summi plerumque magis violaceo, cervicis lateribus magis viridibus et cauda nitide rufescenti-cuprea distinguenda. (Descr. exempl. typ. ex Oaxaca, Mexico. Mus. Brit.)

Hab. MEXICO, Cuernavaca [7], Puebla [7], Atlixco, Oaxaca [1] (*Boucard* [3]), Putla (*Rébouch*), Sierra Madre del Sur, Chilpancingo, Venta de Zopilote (*Mrs. H. H. Smith*), Santa Efigenia and Tapana (*Sumichrast* [5] [6]).

M. Boucard discovered this species when collecting in the State of Oaxaca, and his specimens, sent to M. Sallé, were described by Gould [1] and subsequently figured in his Monograph [2].

It is, according to M. Boucard, found in Oaxaca at all seasons of the year. It builds its nest from March to May, and may be seen in the gardens of the town of Oaxaca, taking its food from the flowers of Cacti.

C. violiceps is closely allied to *C. verticalis*, but may usually be distinguished by the deeper violet-blue of the crown. More certain characters are the greener tints of the sides of the neck and the colour of the tail. The latter is of a bronzy-reddish hue, whereas in *C. verticalis* it is olive-green.

β'. *Pileus obscurus.*

3. Cyanomyia viridifrons.

Cyanomyia viridifrons, Elliot, Ann. & Mag. N. H. 1871, viii. p. 267 [1]; Ibis, 1876, p. 314 [2]; de Oca, La Nat. iii. p. 304 [3]; Boucard, Ann. Soc. Linn. Lyon, xx. p. 277 [4]; Salv. Cat. Birds Brit. Mus. xvi. p. 196 [5].

Uranomitra viridifrons, Elliot, Syn. Troch. p. 197 [6]; Sharpe, in Gould's Mon. Troch., Suppl. t. 49 (April 1885) [7]; Berl. Pr. U. S. Nat. Mus. xi. p. 562 [8].

Supra nitenti-aureo-viridis, tectricibus supracaudalibus et cauda cupreo tinctis ; capite summo ad frontem saturatiore obscure nigricanti-viridi, cervicis lateribus nitenti-viridi lavatis : subtus (tectricibus subcaudalibus inclusis) nivea, lateribus infra alas viridibus : rostro carneo, apice nigro. Long. tota 3·7, alæ 2·1, caudæ 1·2, rostri a rictu 1·0. (Descr. maris exempl. typ. ex Putla, W. Mexico. Mus. Brit.)

Hab. MEXICO, Putla (*Rébouch* [1] [4]), Oaxaca (*Fenochio* [5]), Tehuantepec (*W. B. Richardson* [5]; *Sumichrast, in U. S. Nat. Mus.*), Tonala in Chiapas (*W. B. R.*).

This species was discovered by M. Eugène Rébouch near Putla in the Mexican State of Oaxaca, and described by Mr. Elliot in 1871 [1].

One of the original specimens passed into Gould's collection, and is now before us. An immature specimen from Oaxaca sent us by Señor Fenochio appears to belong to the same species, and two others—one from Tehuantepec, the other from Tonala in Chiapas—agree very closely with the typical bird. But the specimens from the State of Guerrero obtained by Mrs. Herbert Smith, which we have hitherto considered to belong to this species, differ in having the forehead and crown dark indigo-blue instead of green, and it seems necessary to separate them.

The southern extension of *C. viridifrons* has not yet been determined. We trace it to Tonala, but when at Retalhuleu in 1862 Salvin saw in the collection of Dr. Bernoulli a skin of a *Cyanomyia* which, from a note made at the time, was most probably of this species.

4. Cyanomyia guerrerensis, sp. n.

C. viridifronti similis, sed capite summo et fronte saturate obscure cyaneis nec viridibus, dorso postico paulo grisescentiore, forsan distinguenda.

Hab. MEXICO, Rincon, Acaguizotla and Tierra Colorada in Guerrero (*Mrs. H. H. Smith*).

Five specimens of this *Cyanomyia* in Mrs. Smith's collection, made in the Sierra Madre del Sur in the State of Guerrero, all agree in having the forehead and crown dark indigo-blue, instead of dark green as in the type of *C. viridifrons*; the back, too, seems a little greyer, and the tail perhaps deeper bronze.

As this bird appears to have a distinct range from *C. viridifrons*, we now describe it, but the characters are undoubtedly slight and we do so with some diffidence.

The position of both these birds is to some extent made more doubtful from the fact of *C. violiceps* being found in the districts occupied by each of them. The green colour of the flanks under the wings in both *C. viridifrons* and the present bird contrasted with the dusky flanks of both *C. verticalis* and *C. violiceps*, as well as the total absence of glittering feathers on the crown in all stages of the two first-mentioned birds, is fair evidence of their distinctness.

We may further remark that one of the Guerrero birds is quite young in first complete plumage, the feathers of the head are in moult, and the new ones are of the dark indigo-blue of the other more adult specimens.

β. Maxilla nigra; hypochondriæ viride lavatæ.

5. Cyanomyia microrhyncha.

Cyanomyia microrhyncha, Elliot, Ibis, 1876, p. 316[1]; Muls. Hist. Nat. Ois.-Mouches, iv. p. 172, t. 119[2]; Salv. Cat. Birds Brit. Mus. xvi. p. 197[3].

Uranomitra microrhyncha, Elliot, Syn. Troch. p. 197[4]; Sharpe, in Gould's Mon. Troch. Suppl. (April 1885)[5].

"Top of head and occiput dark metallic blue. Hind neck and mantle shining metallic green; rest of upper parts bronzy red. Throat, upper part of breast, and centre of abdomen white, with a few metallic green feathers scattered among the white ones. Flanks and under tail-coverts bronzy red, metallic. Wings dark brown, slightly shaded with purple. Tail brilliant metallic bronze. Total length 3¼ inches, wing 2¼, tail 1⅛, bill along culmen ½." (*Elliot, l. s. c.*[1])

Hab. HONDURAS (*fide Elliot*[1]).

We have not met with any bird agreeing with the above description. Mr. Elliot, when describing the species, stated that the type was said to come from Honduras.

As it evidently belongs to the same section of the genus as *C. cyanocephala* this locality may be correct.   It must be noted, however, that *C. guatemalensis* has been found in Honduras and also in Nicaragua, so that this area seems occupied by an allied form.

6. Cyanomyia cyanocephala.

Ornismya cyanocephalus, Less. Hist. Nat. Ois.-Mouches, p. xlv [1]; Suppl. p. 134, t. 18 [2].

Cyanomyia cyanocephala, Gould, Mon. Troch. v. t. 286 (May 1856) [3]; Scl. P. Z. S. 1859, p. 367 [4]; de Oca, La Nat. iii. p. 159 [5]; Lawr. Bull. U. S. Nat. Mus. no. 4, p. 32 [6]; Elliot, Ibis, 1876, p. 314 [7]; Sanchez, An. Mus. Nac. Mex. i. p. 96 [8]; Sumichrast, La Nat. v. p. 250 [9]; Salv. Cat. Birds Brit. Mus. xvi. p. 197 [10].

Uranomitra cyanocephala, Ferrari-Perez, Pr. U. S. Nat. Mus. ix. p. 158 [11].

Agyrtria β. Uranomitra faustina, Reich. Troch. Enum. p. 7, t. 760. ff. 4756–7 [12].

Uranomitra lessoni, Cab. & Heine, Mus. Hein. iii. p. 41 [13].

Supra nitenti-cupreo-viridis, pileo nitide cæruleo, cervicis lateribus nitide viridibus cæruleo certa luce lavatis: subtus nivea, hypochondriis nitenti-viridibus, abdomine medio albo; cauda et tectricibus subcaudalibus olivaceis his albo stricte limbatis: maxilla nigra, mandibula carnea apice nigra.   Long. tota 4·0, alæ 2·3, caudæ 1·35, rostri a rictu 0·9.

♀ mari similis, colore cæruleo pilei minus nitido.   (Descr. maris et feminæ ex Cordova, Mexico. Mus. Brit.)

Hab. MEXICO, Jalapa [13] (*de Oca* [4][5], *F. D. G.* [10], *Ferrari-Perez* [11], *M. Trujillo* [10]), Coatepec (*de Oca* [5], *F. Ferrari-Perez, M. Trujillo* [10]), Mirador (*Sartorius, in U. S. Nat. Mus.*), Huatusco (*F. Ferrari-Perez*), Orizaba (*Sumichrast* [9], *F. D. G., de Oca* [5]), Cordova (*Sallé, de Oca* [5]), Oaxaca (*Sallé*), Guichicovi (*Sumichrast* [6][9]), Chimalapa (*W. B. Richardson* [10]), Gineta Mountains (*Sumichrast, in U. S. Nat. Mus.*).

Though stated by Lesson to be a bird of Brazil [1] his description and figure sufficiently indicate that it was this Mexican species that he was dealing with.   Other names have been suggested for it by Reichenbach [12], and by Cabanis and Heine [13], but we see no reason for not adhering to Lesson's title, which has been much used.

The bird is very common, according to de Oca [5], in the neighbourhood of Jalapa, Coatepec, Orizaba, and Cordova, where it remains throughout the year frequenting the gardens of those towns.   It builds its nest in April and May, constructing it of " tule " (*Cyperus*), and covering it on the outside with bits of lichen.   The hen bird makes the nest in three or four days, the male helping.

Several other travellers have observed this species in this part of the State of Vera Cruz, but it is not confined to so limited an area, for a specimen in the Gould collection of M. Sallé's preparation is marked Oaxaca; and we have received several examples from the Isthmus of Tehuantepec sent us by Mr. Richardson, and where others were obtained by Sumichrast.   The former were all shot in March and April.

7. Cyanomyia guatemalensis.

Cyanomyia cyanocephala, Scl. & Salv. Ibis, 1859, p. 127 (nec Less.) [1]; Salv. Ibis, 1860, pp. 39 [2], 195 [3], 261 [4]; G. C. Taylor, Ibis, 1860, p. 114 [5].

Cyanomyia guatemalensis, Gould, Intr. Troch. p. 148 [6]; Salv. Ibis, 1866, p. 204 [7]; Cat. Birds

Brit. Mus. xvi. p. 198[9]; Lawr. Pr. Bost. Soc. N. H. xiv. p. 284[9]; Mem. Bost. Soc. N. H. ii. p. 292[10].

Uranomitra guatemalensis, Berl. Pr. U. S. Nat. Mus. xi. p. 562[11].

C. cyanocephalæ persimilis, cauda cupreo- nec olivaceo-viridi tincta forsan distinguenda.

Hab. BRITISH HONDURAS, Southern Pine-ridge of the Western District (*Blancaneaux*[8]); GUATEMALA, Pine-ridge of Poctun, Coban, Mountains of Chilasco and San Gerónimo in Vera Paz, Dueñas[1] (*O. S. & F. D. G.*[9]), Panajachel (*W. B. Richardson*[9]); HONDURAS, Siquatepec (*G. C. Taylor*[5]); NICARAGUA, Matagalpa (*W. B. R.*[9]).

The difference between this bird and the Mexican *C. cyanocephala*, though slight, seems to be fairly definite when adults with plumage of about the same age are compared. It is then seen that the tail of the southern form is more decidedly tinged with a bronzy hue, that of the northern bird being nearly pure olive. Females and young birds are not always easy to distinguish.

The range of *C. guatemalensis* extends beyond the limits of Guatemala in both directions, being found in the pine-clad districts of the western parts of British Honduras at an elevation of 1500 to 2000 feet above sea-level, and near Matagalpa in Nicaragua, also in a pine-region, at an elevation of about 4000 feet. The specimens obtained by Mr. Richardson in the last-named locality were shot between June and October.

In the highlands of Guatemala it is a common bird, especially about the village of Dueñas, where it chiefly feeds from the flowers of a Euphorbiaceous tree which grows there to a height of twenty or thirty feet, and forms one of the chief trees of the scrubby forest. Nests were found in successive years near the house of the Hacienda at Dueñas, placed in the outer branches of a large cypress tree. In cutting one of these nests down it was thrown quite on one side, but the eggs did not fall out owing to a projecting rim inside the nest keeping them from being upset. This rim would preserve the eggs from danger during great oscillations caused by high wind.

Some birds of this species were very tame, one would even take cotton-wool from a table inside the house, doubtless for nest-building; the same bird would daily search the cut flowers in the rooms. On one occasion it was caught but showed little fear, and whilst in the hand sucked at sugar dipped in water, and on being liberated flew to a tree close by. The wind produced by the rapid action of the wings of these little birds is considerable, for the surface of the piece of wool over which the intruder hovered was violently agitated by the disturbance of the air.

b'. *Guttur nunquam omnino album; color nitido-cyaneus nullus; supra plumis micantibus nunquam ornatæ.*

AMAZILIA.

Les Amazilis, Lesson, Ind. gén. Troch. p. xxvii.

Amazilia, Reich. Av. Syst. t. 39; Salv. Cat. Birds Brit. Mus. xvi. p. 203.

In many respects *Amazilia* resembles *Cyanomyia* and *Agyrtria*, the main points of structure being similar, the culmen being feathered to the base, but so as to leave the nasal covers distinctly exposed on their anterior portion. In *Amazilia* the throat is never wholly white, and none of its members have any glittering blue colours, or any glittering colours on the top of the head.

We are more or less acquainted with twenty-nine species of *Amazilia*, but there are some others which we have not met with; the former are spread over the Andes as far south as Peru, and over the northern portion of South America, none, so far as we know, occurring in the valley of the Amazons nor in Brazil. In Central America and Mexico we recognize thirteen species, two of which range as far north as the mouth of the Rio Grande. On the western side of Mexico, Mazatlan is the most northern point reached. Only one species also occurs in South America. Generally speaking, all species of *Amazilia* are birds of comparatively low-lying lands, but they ascend the mountains at certain seasons to an elevation of at least 4000 feet.

α. *Corpus subtus omnino cinnamomeum.*

1. Amazilia cinnamomea.

Ornismya cinnamomea, Less. Rev. Zool. 1842, p. 175 [1].

Pyrrhophæna cinnamomea, Gould, Intr. Troch. p. 156 [2]; Salv. Ibis, 1866, p. 204 [3]; Lawr. Ann. Lyc. N. Y. ix. p. 204 [4]; Mem. Bost. Soc. N. H. ii. p. 292 [5]; Bull. U. S. Nat. Mus. no. 4, p. 32 [6]; Sanchez, An. Mus. Nac. Mex. i. p. 96 [7]; Sumichrast, La Nat. v. p. 250 [8].

Amazilia cinnamomea, Salv. Ibis, 1864, p. 380 [9]; 1870, p. 115 [10]; Cat. Birds Brit. Mus. xvi. p. 207 [11]; Boucard, P. Z. S. 1878, p. 71 [12]; 1883, p. 451 [13]; Ridgw. Pr. U. S. Nat. Mus. iv. p. 26 [14]; Nutting, Pr. U. S. Nat. Mus. vi. p. 386 [15].

Ornismya rutila, Delattre, Echo du Monde Sav. 1843, p. 1069 [16].

Trochilus corallirostris, Bourc. & Muls. Ann. Sc. Phys. et Nat. Lyon, ix. p. 328 [17].

Amazilia corallirostris, Gould, Mon. Troch. v. t. 307 (May 1857) [18]; Scl. P. Z. S. 1858, p. 358 [19]; 1859, p. 386 [20]; Scl. & Salv. Ibis, 1859, p. 130 [21]; Taylor, Ibis, 1860, p. 115 [22]; Salv. Ibis, 1860, p. 268 [23].

Supra nitenti-cupreo-viridis, pileo obscuriore, loris et corpore toto subtus cinnamomeis, hoc ad mentum pallidiore; cauda castanea, apice et marginibus externis obscure cupreis: rostro carneo (ave viva sanguineo), apice nigro. Long. tota 4·2, alæ 2·25, caudæ 1·3, rostri a rictu 0·9. (Descr. maris ex Retalhuleu, Guatemala. Mus. nostr.)

♀ mari similis, sed subtus pallidior.

Hab. MEXICO, Mazatlan [5] and Presidio de Mazatlan (*Grayson, Forrer* [11]), San Blas (*W. B. Richardson* [11]), Tecolapa, Culata (*W. Lloyd* [11]), Plains of Colima (*W. B. R.* [11]), Acapulco (*A. Lesson* [1]), Tierra Colorada, Rio Papagaio, Acaguizotla, La Venta, Dos Arroyos, Alto de Camaron, Venta de Pelegrino (*Mrs. H. H. Smith* [11]), State of Oaxaca (*Boucard* [20]), Santa Efigenia, Tapana (*Sumichrast* [6] [8]), Chimalapa (*W. B. R.* [11]), Potrero (*Sumichrast* [8]), Merida in Yucatan (*Schott* [4], F. D. G., G. F. Gaumer* [11]), Holbox I. (*G. F. G.* [11]); BRITISH HONDURAS, Orange Walk (*G. F.*

G. [11]), Belize (*Blancaneaux* [11]), Cays off the coast (*O. S.* [9]); GUATEMALA, San Gerónimo [23], Escuintla [17], Santana Mixtan (*O. S. & F. D. G.*), Retalhuleu (*O. S. & F. D. G., W. B. Richardson*); SALVADOR [14], Acajutla (*Capt. J. M. Dow, in U. S. Nat. Mus.*), La Libertad (*W. B. R.* [11]); HONDURAS, Tigre I. [19], Comayagua (*G. C. Taylor* [22]); NICARAGUA, Chinandega, El Volcan Chinandega, Momotombo (*W. B. R.* [11]), Sucuyá (*Nutting* [15]); COSTA RICA [10] [11], San Mateo, Punta Arenas (*Boucard* [12]).

This species was first described by R. P. Lesson from skins obtained by his brother, A. Lesson, at Acapulco in the Mexican State of Guerrero [1]. We have many examples from this district sent us by Mrs. Herbert H. Smith, and the species has been traced northwards along the coast of Mexico through the State of Colima to San Blas and Mazatlan. Southwards it occurs uninterruptedly as far as Costa Rica, and we have many specimens before us from Tehuantepec, the Pacific coast-region of Guatemala, Salvador, and Nicaragua. On the east side of the continent Sumichrast records it from Potrero in the State of Vera Cruz, but we have never seen specimens from that State. It occurs in Northern Yucatan and some of the islands off the coast, and in the northern part of British Honduras. In the interior of Guatemala the only place we ever met with it was San Gerónimo, where it was fairly common at an altitude of about 3000 feet above sea-level. In Honduras, G. C. Taylor says it was a common species at intervals as he travelled across the country from the Pacific to the Atlantic Oceans, especially near Comayagua at an altitude of 1900 feet, where many birds were feeding from the flowers of a cactus growing in open ground. In Guatemala we noticed that the blossoms of the orange-trees were usually frequented by this bird.

As a species *A. cinnamomea* is very distinct from all other *Amaziliæ* except *A. graysoni*, which is a considerably larger bird.

Its real affinity is probably with *A. yucatanensis* and its allies, as it agrees with them in having a flesh-coloured maxilla and dark wings without any chestnut at the base. It also has points in common with *A. pristina* and the other Andean species of that section of the genus.

2. Amazilia graysoni.

Amazilia (Pyrrhophæna) graysoni, Lawr. Ann. Lyc. N. Y. viii. p. 404 [1].

Pyrrhophæna graysoni, Grayson, Pr. Bost. Soc. N. H. xiv. p. 183 [2]; Lawr. Mem. Bost. Soc. N. H. ii. p. 292 [3].

Amazilia graysoni, Gould, Ibis, 1867, p. 247 [4]; Sharpe, in Gould's Mon. Troch., Suppl. (March 1887) [5]; Salv. Cat. Birds Brit. Mus. xvi. p. 209 [6].

A. cinnamomeæ similis et omnino ejusdem coloris, sed multo major. Long. tota 4·7, alæ 2·6, caudæ 1·7, rostri a rictu 1·1. (Descr. maris ex Tres Marias Is., Mexico Occ. Mus. nostr.)

Hab. MEXICO, Tres Marias Islands (*Grayson* [1] [2] [3], *Forrer*).

The late Col. A. J. Grayson discovered this species during his visits to the Tres

Marias Islands between 1865 and 1867; and Mr. Alphonse Forrer also found it when at the same islands in March 1881. Two skins, a male and a female, from the last-named collector are now before us, and confirm the characters set forth by Mr. Lawrence when describing Grayson's birds.

Grayson says that birds of this species are very abundant on the islands, where they seem to be constantly at war with one another. Sometimes combats between them become of a desperate nature. One day, while watching a number of them in active motion around some tobacco-flowers, of which they are very fond, he saw two fine males after darting at each other for some time at length come to a deadly struggle high above his head; they finally clinched each other, each having one of the mandibles of the other in his mouth, at the same time scratching with their claws and using their wings with the greatest force. Whilst in this situation they wheeled round and round and fell to the ground. He then caught both under his hat, but even then, when held apart, they showed a desire to continue the struggle.

Grayson also says that he frequently saw birds of this species dart from their perch upon diminutive flies after the manner of a real Flycatcher, and their gizzards when examined were always full of minute insects.

β. *Guttur et pectus viridi micantes.*

α'. *Alæ ad basin cinnamomeæ.*

α''. *Cauda aut purpureo-castanea aut chalybea.*

3. **Amazilia beryllina.**

Trochilus beryllinus, Licht. Preis-Verz. Mex. Vög. p. 1 (*cf.* J. f. Orn. 1863, p. 55) [1].

Amazilia beryllina, Gould, Mon. Troch. v. t. 312 (July 1861) [2]; Scl. P. Z. S. 1864, p. 177 [3];
 Dugès, La Nat. i. p. 141 [4]; Villada, La Nat. ii. p. 364 [5]; de Oca, La Nat. iii. p. 23 [6];
 Sanchez, An. Mus. Nac. Mex. i. p. 96 [7]; Herrera, La Nat. (2) i. p. 322 [8]; Salv. Cat. Birds
 Brit. Mus. xvi. p. 209 [9].

Ornismya arsinoe, Less. Suppl. Ois.-Mouches, p. 154, t. 28 [10].

Amazilia arsinoe, Scl. P. Z. S. 1859, pp. 297 [11], 366 [12].

Trochilus mariæ, Bourc. Ann. Sc. Phys. et Nat. Lyon, ix. p. 319 [13].

Amazilia mariæ, Ferrari-Perez, Pr. U. S. Nat. Mus. ix. p. 158 [14].

Supra nitenti-aureo-viridis, dorso postico magis cupreo, tectricibus supracaudalibus purpurascentibus: subtus micanti-gramineo-viridis, abdomine imo et tectricibus subcaudalibus castaneis, his purpureo tinctis; alis purpureo-nigris ad basin castaneis, subalaribus omnino castaneis; cauda nitenti-purpureo-cupreo-castanea: maxilla nigra, mandibula carnea apice nigra. Long. tota 4·0, alæ 2·1, caudæ 1·3, rostri a rictu 0·85.

♀ mari similis, sed coloribus minus nitidis abdomine grisescentiore. (Descr. maris et feminæ ex Jalapa, Mexico. Mus. nostr.)

Hab. MEXICO [10] (*Deppe* [1]), Choix in Sinaloa (*W. Lloyd* [9]), San Blas and Tepic (*W. B.
 Richardson* [9]), Guanajuato (*Dugès* [4], *Sanchez* [7]), Huayimo, Sierra de Tepic, Bolaños,
 Zapotlan (*W. B. R.* [9]), Tonila, San Marcos, Beltran, all in Jalisco (*W. Lloyd* [9]),

Patzcuaro (*Dugès* [4]), Volcan de Colima (*W. B. R.* [9]), Chilpancingo, Xautipa, Amula, Omilteme in Guerrero (*Mrs. H. H. Smith* [9]), Valley of Mexico (*White* [3], *Villada* [5], *de Oca* [6], *Sanchez* [7], *Herrera* [8]), Tetelco in the Valley of Mexico (*F. Ferrari-Perez* [9]), Cofre de Perote (*M. Trujillo* [9]), Jalapa (*de Oca* [6] [11] [12], *Sanchez* [7], *F. Ferrari-Perez* [14], *Trujillo* [9]), Coatepec (*F. Ferrari-Perez* [9], *Trujillo* [9]), Orizaba (*Botteri* [2], *de Oca* [6], *Sanchez* [7]), Cordova (*Sallé* [2], *de Oca* [6], *Sanchez* [7]), Omealca (*F. Ferrari-Perez*), Villa Alta, Totontepec (*M. Trujillo* [9]), Oaxaca (*Fenochio* [9]), Chimalapa, Tehuantepec (*W. B. Richardson* [9]).

Deppé's specimens, briefly described by Lichtenstein, were the first of this species that reached Europe [1]. The same bird was soon afterwards renamed *Ornismya arsinoe* by Lesson [10], and figured in the Supplement to his Histoire Naturelle Oiseaux-Mouches. Bourcier's name *Trochilus mariæ* [13] also, we feel sure, belongs here, though this name has been applied to the next species.

Amazilia beryllina is one of the commonest of the Mexican Humming-Birds, and is distributed over a large area of that country, from the northern confines of the State of Sinaloa in the north to the Isthmus of Tehuantepec, and over the plateau of Mexico to the State of Vera Cruz in the east. De Oca says that this bird is found in the Cantons of Jalapa, Cordova, and Orizaba, and other parts of the State of Vera Cruz [6]. It frequents the gardens of the houses of Jalapa during the whole year, but is more common in the months of May, June, and July, which are the nesting-season.

There is considerable variation in the colour of the tail in this species, and in some specimens the upper tail-coverts and the tail are deep violet-purple, but we are unable to fix these variations to any definite localities. As a rule the darker specimens are from the more northern parts of Western Mexico, but this is not always the case.

The range in altitude of this bird extends from the sea-level at San Blas to the plateau of Mexico.

4. **Amazilia devillii.**

Trochilus devillii, Bourc. Rev. Zool. 1848, p. 272 [1].

Amazilia devillii, Gould, Mon. Troch. v. t. 313 (May 1860) [2]; Salv. Cat. Strickl. Coll. p. 369 [3]; Cat. Birds Brit. Mus. xvi. p. 211 [4]; Boucard, P. Z. S. 1883, p. 451 [5].

Pyrrhophæna devillii, Salv. Ibis, 1866, p. 204 [6]; Lawr. Bull. U. S. Nat. Mus. no. 4, p. 33 [7]; Sumichrast, La Nat. v. p. 250 [8].

Amazilia arsinoe, Salv. Ibis, 1860, p. 195 [9].

Amazilia dumerilii, Salv. Ibis, 1860, pp. 263 [10], 270 [11].

Amazilia mariæ, Elliot, Syn. Troch. p. 222 (nec Bourc.) [12].

A. beryllinæ similis, sed alis ad basin minus castaneis, colore viridi subtus usque ad crissum extenso. ♀ minus nitida. (Descr. maris et feminæ ex Dueñas, Guatemala. Mus. nostr.)

Hab. Mexico, Yucatan (*Gaumer* [5]), ? Gineta Mountains in Chiapas (*Sumichrast* [7] [8]); Guatemala [1], Choctum, Yzabal [9], Dueñas [11], Volcan de Fuego, La Trinidad (*O. S. & F. D. G.*); Salvador, Volcan de San Miguel, La Libertad (*W. B. Richardson*).

Bourcier's description of this bird was based upon a specimen from Guatemala, where the species is abundant from the sea-level at Yzabal to an altitude of 5000 feet on the slopes of the Volcan de Fuego. On the plains of Dueñas, which stretch from the village to the foot of the volcano, *A. devillii* used to be a very common bird, especially in the months of July, August, and September, at the time the tree-convolvulus (*Ipomœa murucoides*) was in flower. During foggy afternoons at this rainy season, when clouds drifted with the southerly wind between the volcanoes of Agua and Fuego, these and other Humming-Birds were to be seen in greatest number feeding from the flowers and fighting with one another. In October it was met with at a lower elevation (3000 feet) on the Volcan de Fuego, but its migratory movements are doubtless influenced by the plants in flower at different places at different times.

Until lately we were not aware of *A. devillii* being found beyond the limits of Guatemala, but Mr. Richardson has sent us a good series of specimens from Salvador shot in February, March, and April at La Libertad on the Pacific coast and on the Volcan de San Miguel.

Mr. Lawrence and Sumichrast, confirmed by Mr. Ridgway, include this species in the birds of the Gineta Mountains of Chiapas. Mr. Richardson's specimens from Chimalapa certainly belong to the Mexican form *A. beryllina*, and have the extended chestnut bases to the primaries and secondaries of that bird. It would thus appear that these two species occur in very close proximity.

5. Amazilia cyanura.

Amazilia cyanura, Gould, Mon. Troch. v. t. 315 (Sept. 1859) [1]; Salv. Ibis, 1863, p. 239 [2]; Cat. Birds Brit. Mus. xvi. p. 212 [4]; Berl. Pr. U. S. Nat. Mus. xi. p. 562 [4].

Pyrrhophæna cyanura, Salv. Ibis, 1866, p. 195 [5].

Supra nitenti-viridis, ad dorsum posticum rufescenti-purpurea, tectricibus supracaudalibus et cauda saturate chalybeis : subtus gramineo-viridis micans, tectricibus subcaudalibus chalybeis ; alis ad basin castaneis : maxilla nigra, mandibula carnea apice nigra. Long. tota 3·6, alæ 2·1, caudæ 1·3, rostri a rictu 0·85. (Descr. maris ex Retalhuleu, Guatemala. Mus. nostr.)

Hab. GUATEMALA, Retalhuleu (*O. S.*[5], *W. B. Richardson* [3]), Mazatenango (*O. S.* [3]) ; NICARAGUA, Realejo (*Sir E. Belcher* [1]; *Capt. J. M. Dow, in U. S. Nat. Mus.*), El Volcan Chinandega, Matagalpa (*W. B. Richardson*), Chontales (*Belt* [3]).

The original specimens of this species were obtained at Realejo, Nicaragua, by Sir Edward Belcher, and presented by him to the Zoological Society, whence they passed into Gould's hands and finally to the British Museum.

Belt also found it in Nicaragua [3], and recently Mr. Richardson secured for us a good series of examples on the volcano near Chinandega, including a female which resembles the male in the characteristic colouring of the tail, but has less bright tints on the body ; the under tail-coverts, too, are dusky, with paler edges.

The range of *A. cyanura* extends to the Pacific coast-region of Guatemala, where

Salvin found it near Retalhuleu and Mazatenango in September 1862.   Mr. Richardson also met with it in the same district in April 1891.   Thus in all probability the range of the species extends uninterruptedly from Guatemala, close to the Mexican frontier, to Nicaragua.

β″. Cauda nitente olivacea aut cuprea.

6. Amazilia ocai.

Amazilia ocai, Gould, Ann. & Mag. N. H. 1859, iv. p. 96[1]; Mon. Troch. v. t. 289 (July 1861)[2]; Scl. P. Z. S. 1859, p. 367[3]; de Oca, La Nat. iii. p. 16, t. —[4]; Salv. Cat. Birds Brit. Mus. xvi. p. 213[5].
Hemistilbon ocai, Gould, Intr. Troch. p. 150[6].
Thaumatias lerdi, de Oca, La Nat. iii. p. 24?[7].

Supra nitenti-aureo-viridis, pileo cæruleo-viridi, dorso postico et tectricibus supracaudalibus viridi-cupreis, gutture et pectore gramineo-viridibus micantibus, plumis singulis albis macula discali viridi ornatis; maculis gutturalibus minoribus, abdomine medio griseo, hypochondriis aureo-viridi lavatis; tectricibus subcaudalibus pallide viridi-cupreis late albido marginatis; alis ad basin castaneis; cauda cupreo-olivaceo-viridi, rectricum lateralium rhachidibus et pogoniis externis ad basin castaneis: rostro nigro, mandibula ad basin carnea. Long. tota 4·0, alæ 2·3, caudæ 1·35, rostri a rictu 0·85. (Descr. maris exempl. typ. ex Jalapa, Mexico. Mus. Brit.)

Hab. MEXICO, Jalapa (*de Oca* [1 2 3]), Paso del Macho? (*de Oca* [7]).

The type specimen obtained by de Oca at Jalapa and described by Gould in 1859, and subsequently figured in his Monograph, is the only one we have seen; nor have we any other information regarding the species unless the bird described by de Oca as *Thaumatias lerdi* belongs to it, as seems to me to be not improbable.

The latter name was placed by Mr. Elliot as a synonym of *Agyrtria norrisi*, which was considered by Gould to be a second member of his genus *Hemistilbon*, *A. ocai* being the type.

Gould also gave the habitat of *A. norrisi* as Bolaños, but on what grounds he did so is not apparent.   Bourcier, the author of the name, gave its locality as Guayaquil, and we believe the bird to be the same as *Amazilia dumerilii*.

"*Agyrtria norrisi*" therefore must be erased from the list of Mexican Humming-Birds.

7. Amazilia sumichrasti.

Amazilia sumichrasti, Salv. Ann. & Mag. N. H. 1891, vii. p. 376[1]; Cat. Birds Brit. Mus. xvi. p. 213, t. 7. f. 2[2].

Supra nitenti-gramineo-viridis, pileo obscuriore dorso postico magis aurescente: subtus gramineo-viridis micans, colore albo ad basin plumarum vix obvio, abdomine et hypochondriis viridibus; tectricibus subcaudalibus pallide rufescentibus; cauda læte nitenti-cuprea; primariis internis et secundariis ad basin castaneis: maxilla nigra, mandibula carnea apice nigra. Long. tota 3·8, alæ 2·1, caudæ 1·2, rostri a rictu 0·9. (Descr. maris exempl. typ. ex Tehuantepec. Mus. nostr.)

Hab. MEXICO, Santa Efigenia, Tehuantepec (*F. Sumichrast* [1] [2]).

The only specimen we have seen of this distinct species was sent by the late Prof. F. Sumichrast to M. Boucard and ceded to us by him. The specimen is a male, and was shot in December 1877. It is named after its discoverer, who long resided at various places in South Mexico and studied the vertebrate fauna of that country with great industry and success.

A. sumichrasti has some resemblance to *A. ocai*, but the points of difference are many and obvious. Chief amongst them is the colour of the under tail-coverts and tail, and the denser green colour of the throat, on which the white bases of the feathers are hardly visible.

β'. *Alæ ad basin purpureo-nigræ.*

γ". *Abdomen posticum cinnamomeum; lora viridia.*

8. Amazilia yucatanensis.

Trochilus yucatanensis, Cabot, Pr. Bost. Soc. N. H. ii. p. 74 (1845)[1].
Amazilia yucatanensis, Gould, Mon. Troch. v. t. 308 (Sept. 1861)[2]; de Oca, La Nat. iii. p. 303, t. —[3]; Ridgw. Pr. U. S. Nat. Mus. iv. p. 25[4]; Boucard, P. Z. S. 1883, p. 451[5]; Salv. Cat. Birds Brit. Mus. xvi. p. 214[6].
Pyrrhophæna cerviniventris, Salv. Ibis, 1866, p. 195 (nec Gould)[7].

Supra nitenti-cupreo-viridis, pileo obscuriore; gutture et pectore viridibus micantibus, abdomine hypochondriis et tectricibus subcaudalibus castaneis; cauda castanea cupreo limbata et terminata; alis ad basin purpureo-nigris: rostro carneo, apice nigro. Long. tota 4·0, alæ 2·2, caudæ 1·5, rostri a rictu 0·95.
♀ mari similis, sed subtus pallidior, rectricibus duabus mediis ad basin cupreis. (Descr. maris et feminæ ex Santana, Peten. Mus. nostr.)

Hab. MEXICO, Yucatan (*Cabot* [1] [2]), Merida in Yucatan (*F. D. G.*[6], *G. F. Gaumer*[5]); GUATEMALA, Santa Ana in Peten (*O. S.*[7]).

Dr. Samuel Cabot, who accompanied Stephens in his well-known travels in Yucatan, was the discoverer and describer of this species. His type also formed the subject of the plate in Gould's Monograph of the Trochilidæ, the upper figure of which, supposed to represent a female of this species, was drawn from a specimen of *A. cinnamomea*, as Gould more than half suspected at the time.

Many years elapsed after the first discovery of this species before anything more was heard of it, and it was not until Salvin shot three specimens at the little village of Santa Ana, on the road from Vera Paz to Peten, in April 1862, that it was again noticed. Since that time a few more examples have reached us from Northern Yucatan, amongst them two males which were shot by Godman when at Merida in February 1888.

The Santa Ana birds were feeding from the flowers of an *Erythrina* in company with *Amazilia riefferi* and *Lampornis prevosti*.

38*

9. **Amazilia cerviniventris.**

Amazilia cerviniventris, Gould, P. Z. S. 1856, p. 150 [1]; Mon. Troch. v. t. 309 (May 1857) [2]; Scl.
  P. Z. S. 1856, p. 287 [3]; 1857, p. 17 [4]; de Oca, La Nat. iii. p. 209 [5]; Merrill, Bull. Nutt.
  Orn. Club, ii. p. 26 [6]; Coues & Sennett, Bull. U. S. Geogr. Surv. iv. p. 35 [7]; Ridgw. Pr.
  U. S. Nat. Mus. iv. p. 25 [8]; Salv. Cat. Birds Brit. Mus. xvi. p. 214 [9].

Amazilia yucatanensis, Elliot, Syn. Troch. p. 219 (partim) [10].

A. yucatanensi affinis, abdomine et tectricibus subcaudalibus pallidioribus, hypochondriis et abdomine antico
  viridi lavatis, margine pectoris postico viridi male definito.
♀ mari similis.   (Descr. maris et feminæ exempl. typ. ex Cordova, Mexico.   Mus. Brit.)

Hab. TEXAS [6] [7].—MEXICO, Presas de Aldama, Altamira, Tampico, Tantina in Tamau-
  lipas (*W. B. Richardson* [9]), Valles in San Luis Potosi (*W. B. R.* [9]), Misantla,
  Colipa (*F. D. G.* [9]), Vega del Casadero, Tomatla (*M. Trujillo* [9]), Jalapa
  (*de Oca* [5]), Cordova (*Sallé* [1] [3], *de Oca* [5]), Tlacotalpam, San Andres Tuxtla (*Sallé* [4]),
  Vera Cruz and Laguna near Vera Cruz (*W. B. Richardson* [9]), Sochiapa
  (*M. Trujillo* [9]).

Gould described this species from some of M. Sallé's specimens obtained near
Cordova, where the bird is now known to be common, and it has been traced southwards to Sochiapa near Playa Vicente and northwards throughout the States of Vera
Cruz and Tamaulipas across the Rio Grande into Texas.   It does not appear to be
found inland much beyond the eastern slope of the mountains of these States, Valles
in the State of San Luis Potosi being the furthest point from the coast.   Its presence
on the northern side of the Rio Grande was first announced by Dr. Merrill in 1877 [6],
and it is now known to be a common bird near Brownsville, whence Mr. Armstrong
has sent us many specimens.

The distinctness of *A. cerviniventris* from *A. yucatanensis* was questioned by
Mr. Elliot [10], but its status was re-established by Mr. Ridgway [8], and there can be no
doubt, we think, that the two birds are quite distinct.

δ″. *Abdomen posticum cinereum; lora rufi.*

10. **Amazilia riefferi.**

Trochilus riefferi, Bourc. Ann. Sc. Phys. et Nat. Lyon, vi. p. 45 [1].

Amazilia riefferi, Scl. & Salv. Ibis, 1859, p. 130 [2]; P. Z. S. 1864, p. 365 [3]; Gould, Mon. Troch. v.
  t. 311 (May 1860) [4]; Salv. Ibis, 1860, pp. 195 [5], 270 [6]; 1872, p. 320 [7]; P. Z. S. 1867,
  p. 156 [8]; 1870, p. 210 [9]; Cat. Strickl. Coll. p. 369 [10]; Cat. Birds Brit. Mus. xvi. p. 216 [11];
  Lawr. Ann. Lyc. N. Y. vii. p. 292 [12]; Berl. J. f. Orn. 1884, p. 311 [13].

Pyrrhophæna riefferi, Lawr. Ann. Lyc. N. Y. viii. p. 183 [14]; ix. p. 127 [15]; Bull. U.S. Nat. Mus.
  no. 4, p. 33 [16]; Frantz. J. f. O. 1869, p. 317 [17]; Gould, P. Z. S. 1870, p. 803 [18];
  Merrill, Bull. Nutt. Orn. Club, i. p. 88 [19]; Boucard, P. Z. S. 1878, p. 71 [20]; Sumichrast,
  La Nat. v. p. 250 [21]; Berl. J. f. Orn. 1887, p. 331 [22].

Trochilus dubusi, Bourc. Ann. Sc. Phys. et Nat. Lyon, (2) iv. p. 141 [23].

Amazilia dubusi, Scl. P. Z. S. 1859, p. 386 [24].

Pyrrhophæna dubusi, Cab. & Heine, Mus. Hein. iii. p. 36 [25]; Cab. J. f. Orn. 1862, p. 163 [26].

Trochilus fuscicaudatus, Fraser, P. Z. S. 1840, p. 17 [27]?

Amazilia fuscicaudata, Ridgw. Pr. U. S. Nat. Mus. i. p. 147 [28]; x. p. 591 [29]; Elliot, Syn. Troch. p. 220 [30]; Nutting, Pr. U. S. Nat. Mus. v. p. 398 [31]; vi. p. 406 [32]; Zeledon, An. Mus. Nac. Costa Rica, 1887, p. 122 [33].

Supra nitenti-cupreo-viridis, pileo obscuriore, tectricibus supracaudalibus castaneis: subtus viridis micans, abdomine antico et hypochondriis nitenti-viridibus, abdomine imo fusco, loris et tectricibus subcaudalibus castaneis; cauda castanea, cupreo limbata et terminata: rostro carneo, apice nigro. Long. tota 4·0, alæ 2·3, caudæ 1·35, rostri a rictu 0·93.

♀ maris similis, maxilla obscuriore. (Descr. maris et feminæ ex Choctum, Guatemala. Mus. nostr.)

Hab. TEXAS [18] [28].—MEXICO, Tampico (*W. B. Richardson* [11]), Cordova (*Sallé; Sumichrast, in U. S. Nat. Mus.*), Choapam (*Boucard* [24]), Playa Vicente (*Boucard* [24], *Trujillo*), Sochiapa (*M. Trujillo* [11]), Teapa (*Mrs. H. H. Smith* [11]), Guichicovi (*Sumichrast* [21]); BRITISH HONDURAS, Orange Walk (*G. F. Gaumer* [11]), Corosal (*Roe* [11]), Belize, Cayo (*Blancaneaux* [11]); GUATEMALA, Santa Ana in Peten (*O. S.*), Choctum, Coban [5], Lanquin, Yzabal [6] (*O. S. & F. D. G.* [11]); HONDURAS (*Bourcier* [23]), Segovia River (*Townsend* [29]); NICARAGUA, Matagalpa and La Libertad (*W. B. Richardson*), Chontales (*Belt* [7]), Los Sabalos (*Nutting* [32]), Greytown (*Holland* [14]), San Juan Bautista (*Rovirosa, in U. S. Nat. Mus.*); COSTA RICA, Orosi (*Kramer*), Irazu (*Rogers* [11], *Boucard* [20]), Tucurriqui (*Arcé* [11]), El Naranjo [33], San José [33], Talamanca (*Zeledon, in U. S. Nat. Mus.*), La Palma (*Nutting* [31]); PANAMA, David (*Warszewiez, Bridges* [8]), Chiriqui, Chitra, Boquete de Chitra, Cordillera del Chucu [9], Calovevora [9] (*Arcé*), Lion Hill (*M·Leannan* [3] [12]), Paraiso (*Hughes* [11]), Veragua [25].—COLOMBIA [1] [13]; ECUADOR [18].

Considering that Chachapoyas in Peru, where this bird is not known to occur, was stated by Fraser to be the origin of his type of *T. fuscicaudatus* [27], and seeing that there are points in the description of that bird that do not apply to the species usually known as *A. riefferi,* we continue to employ the latter name for the present species, though a different course is taken by Mr. Elliot and other American writers.

Bourcier's type of his *Trochilus riefferi* came from Fusagasugá iu Colombia [1], and the bird is very well known from that country, skins of it being frequently sent in numbers in the trade collections of Bogota. It is also abundant in Ecuador, where most collectors have met with it, and where Fraser noticed some birds of this species feeding from the bark of a large tree in the forest at Babahoyo, and others searching the eaves of houses in Esmeraldas. At Panama and thence northwards on the eastern side of Central America and Mexico to the mouth of the Rio Grande this species seems to enjoy an uninterrupted range from the sea-level to a height of 4300 feet at Coban in Vera Paz. At the latter place several specimens were procured in the months of November and January, but the species was not common. At Lanquin, in March, Salvin obtained two half-grown birds, showing that the nesting-season there must be quite early in the year.

A characteristic feature of this species is the chestnut lores, which are present at all ages and in both sexes, and are even shown in the young birds just referred to.

ε". *Abdomen posticum album.*

11. Amazilia edwardi.

Trochilus edward, Delattre & Bourc. Rev. Zool. 1846, p. 308 [1].

Erythronota edwardi, Gould, Mon. Troch. v. t. 318 (May 1858) [2]; Lawr. Ann. Lyc. N. Y. vii. p. 292 [3]; ix. p. 127 [4].

Saucerottia edwardi, Scl. & Salv. P. Z. S. 1864, p. 365 [5].

Amazilia edwardi, Elliot, Syn. Troch. p. 221 [6]; Salv. Cat. Birds Brit. Mus. xvi. p. 221 [7].

Supra nitenti-rufescenti-cuprea, cervice postica et pileo viridescentioribus, gutture et pectore gramineo-viridibus micantibus; abdomine niveo, tectricibus subcaudalibus rufescenti-fuscis albido limbatis; cauda nitenti-rufescenti-cuprea: maxilla nigra, mandibula carnea apice nigra. Long. tota 3·5, alæ 2·0, caudæ 1·2, rostri a rictu 0·9.

♀ mari similis. (Descr. maris et feminæ ex Panama. Mus. nostr.)

Hab. PANAMA (*Delattre* [1]), Lion Hill (*M'Leannan* [3] [5]), Paraiso (*Hughes* [7]), Line of Railway (*Arcé* [7]), Obispo (*O. S.*).

This species was discovered by Delattre at Panama, and described by Bourcier in 1846 [1]. Its range must be very restricted, as we have no record of its occurrence anywhere in the State of Panama except along the line of Railway which crosses from the Atlantic to the Pacific side of the Isthmus. Here, however, it is not uncommon, and has been observed at several points between Paraiso and Lion Hill Stations. During a short stay at Obispo Station in April 1873, Salvin saw several birds of this species frequenting the orange-trees near the station house.

12. Amazilia niveiventris.

Trochilus (—— ?) *niveoventer,* Gould, P. Z. S. 1850, p. 164 [1].

Erythronota niveiventris, Gould, Mon. Troch. v. t. 319 (May 1858) [2]; Salv. P. Z. S. 1867, p. 155 [3]; 1870, p. 210 [4].

Saucerottia niveiventris, Scl. & Salv. P. Z. S. 1864, p. 365 [5].

Amazilia niveiventris, Elliot, Syn. Troch. p. 222 [6]; Salv. Cat. Birds Brit. Mus. xvi. p. 221 [7].

A. edwardi similis, sed cauda purpureo-chalybea nec rufescenti-cuprea facile distinguenda. (Descr. maris ex Lion Hill, Panama. Mus. nostr.)

Hab. COSTA RICA (*fide Gould* [7]), Talamanca (*Zeledon, in U. S. Nat. Mus.*); PANAMA, near David (*Warszewiez* [3], *Bridges* [2]), Volcan de Chiriqui [4], Chitra [4], Cordillera del Chucu [4], Calovevora [4], Santiago de Veraguas [3], Calobre (*Arcé*), Lion Hill (*M'Leannan* [5]), Line of Railway (*Arcé*).

This is a more northern form of *A. edwardi,* ranging from the line of the Panama Railway to the confines of Costa Rica, and into the province of Talamanca in that country. It is nowhere abundant, though Arcé has sent us specimens from several places in the western part of the State of Panama, including the Volcan de Chiriqui, where Warszewiez's type was obtained.

Gould, in his original description, states that this specimen was shot at "David in the warm country of Veragua"; but in his monograph he says at an elevation between 5000 and 10,000 feet above sea-level. We doubt if it is found so high, as this bird as well as its near allies are all denizens of the hot low-lying forests such as cover the greater part of the Isthmus of Panama.

M'Leannan's collection contained only a single specimen of *A. niveiventris* which he procured near Lion Hill. The prevalent species of that district is *A. edwardi*.

ζ‴. *Abdomen totum micante viride.*

13. Amazilia sophiæ.

Trochilus sophiæ, Bourc. & Muls. Ann. Sc. Phys. et Nat. ix. p. 318 [1].

Erythronota sophiæ, Gould, Mon. Troch. v. t. 322 (July 1861) [2].

Saucerottia sophiæ, Gould, Intr. Troch. p. 162 [3]; Scl. Cat. Am. Birds, p. 315 [4]; Lawr. Ann. Lyc. N. Y. ix. p. 127 [5]; Boucard, P. Z. S. 1878, p. 71 [6].

Amazilia sophiæ, Elliot, Syn. Troch. p. 224 [7]; Zeledon, An. Mus. Nac. Costa Rica, 1887, p. 122 [8]; Salv. Cat. Birds Brit. Mus. xvi. p. 224 [9].

Hemithylaca hoffmanni, Cab. & Heine, Mus. Hein. iii. p. 38 [10]; Cab. J. f. Orn. 1862, p. 163 [11].

Supra nitenti-viridis, uropygio rufescenti-cupreo, tectricibus supracaudalibus et cauda chalybeis: subtus gramineo-viridis micans, tectricibus subcaudalibus chalybeis fusco limbatis, alis ad basin purpureo-nigris: maxilla nigra, mandibula carnea apice nigra. Long. tota 4·0, alæ 2·2, caudæ 1·2, rostri a rictu 0·85. (Descr. maris ex Tucurriqui, Costa Rica. Mus. nostr.)

♀ mari similis.

Hab. NICARAGUA (*Hepburn, in U. S. Nat. Mus.*); COSTA RICA, San José (*Hoffmann* [11]), Bebedero de Nicoya, Tucurriqui (*Arcé* [9]), San José (*Carmiol* [5], *Zeledon* [8], *Boucard* [6]), Dota (*Carmiol* [5]), Las Cruces de Candelaria (*Zeledon, in U. S. Nat. Mus.*), Cartago (*Boucard* [6]).

Bourcier's description of this species was based upon a bird said to have come from Bogota [1], but it best suits this Costa Rican species. Not only did Gould apply the name to the Costa Rica bird, but Mr. Elliot, who claimed to have the type before him, did the same, so that little doubt attaches to the question.

A. sophiæ in general appearance is exceedingly like *A. cyanura*, but the lower back is not quite so coppery, and the wings are dark to the base instead of being chestnut.

Except for a specimen in the United States National Museum from Nicaragua, the range of this species seems strictly confined to Costa Rica, where it occurs on both sides of the mountain range.

It has no near relative in the State of Panama, but in Northern Colombia and in the Cauca Valley two very closely allied forms are found in *A. warszewiezi* and *A. saucerottii*, which only differ in the colour of the lower back and tail.

c. *Culmen ad basin nudum; tegulæ nasales fere omnino expositæ.*

c′. *Rostrum elongatum, rectum; cauda brevis, rotundata, rectricibus lateralibus albo terminatis.*

FLORICOLA.

Floricola, Elliot, Syn. Troch. p. 82.
Heliomaster, auctt. nec Bonaparte.

The species here included in *Floricola* were usually placed under *Heliomaster* till Mr. Elliot showed that that name properly belongs to *H. furcifer*, and proposed a new generic name for them. In general appearance *Floricola* resembles *Heliomaster* and *Lepidolarynx*, and these three genera have always, we believe, been placed in juxtaposition. *Floricola*, however, has several points of difference from the other two forms which keeps it somewhat widely apart from them. Instead of the culmen being feathered at the base to such an extent that the nasal covers are completely hidden, the latter are fully exposed, and this character brings *Floricola* into the neighbourhood of a group of genera all of which have the culmen bare nearly to the base. It stands apart from all these genera by virtue of its long bill and short tail.

Four species are included in the genus, belonging to two sections, which may readily be distinguished by the colour of the crown. Of these the widely ranging *F. longirostris* in a slightly modified form extends as far as Central Vera Cruz. The other two species belonging to the plain-headed section are peculiar, the one to Mexico, the other to Central America.

α. *Pileus cæruleo-viridis micans.*

1. **Floricola longirostris.**

Oiseau-Mouche à long Bec, Aud. Ois. Dor. i. p. 128, t. 59 [1].
Trochilus longirostris, Vieill. N. Dict. d'Hist. N. vii. p. 366 [2].
Heliomaster longirostris, Gould, Mon. Troch. iv. t. 259 (May 1853) [3]; Scl. P. Z. S. 1856, p. 140 [4]; Salv. Ibis, 1860, pp. 195 [5], 263 [6], 276 [7]; 1869, p. 316 [8]; P. Z. S. 1867, p. 155 [9]; 1870, p. 210 [10]; Lawr. Ann. Lyc. N. Y. ix. p. 126 [11].
Floricola longirostris, Elliot, Syn. Troch. p. 83 [12]; Salv. Cat. Birds Brit. Mus. xvi. p. 229 [13].
Heliomaster sclateri, Cab. & Heine, Mus. Hein. iii. p. 54 [14]; Gould, Intr. Troch. p. 139 [15]; Lawr. Ann. Lyc. N. Y. viii. p. 4 [16]; ix. p. 126 [17].
Heliomaster pallidiceps, Gould, Intr. Troch. p. 139 [18]; Scl. Cat. Am. Birds, p. 310 [19]; Salv. Ibis, 1866, p. 205 [20]; 1869, p. 316 [21]; 1872, p. 320 [22]; Cat. Strickl. Coll. p. 367 [23]; Cat. Birds Brit. Mus. xvi. p. 229 [24]; Lawr. Ann. Lyc. N. Y. ix. p. 126 [25]; Bull. U. S. Nat. Mus. no. 4, p. 32 [26]; de Oca, La Nat. iii. p. 27 [27]; Sumichrast, La Nat. v. p. 250 [28]; Sanchez, An. Mus. Nac. Mex. i. p. 96 [29].
Heliomaster stewartæ, Lawr. Ann. Lyc. N. Y. vii. p. 291 [30]; Scl. & Salv. P. Z. S. 1864, p. 365 [31].

Supra nitenti-aureo-viridis, nucha et tectricibus supracaudalibus cupreo tinctis, dorso postico plaga irregulari alba notato, capite summo micanti-cæruleo-viridi ; stria rictali, plaga costali utrinque, et abdomine medio albis ; mento nigro ; plaga gulari micanti-rosaceo-rubra, pectore et abdominis lateribus griseis, hypochondriis nitide viridi lavatis, tectricibus subcaudalibus griseis ad basin fascia subterminali viridescente, apicibus albis ; caudæ rectricibus mediis cupreo-viridibus, reliquis ad basin viridescentibus ad apicem chalybeis, apicibus ipsis albis : rostro nigro. Long. tota 4·6, alæ 2·3, caudæ 1·25, rostri a rictu 1·45. (Descr. maris ex Jalapa, Mexico. Mus. nostr.)

♀ capite summo inornato dorso concolore, stria rictali latiore ; gula nigra, plumis singulis albo marginatis nonnunquam plumis rosaceis intermixtis.

Hab. Mexico, Jalapa (*de Oca*[27], *Sanchez*[29]), Oaxaca (*Boucard*), Sierra de San Domingo, Tehuantepec (*W. B. Richardson*), Santa Efigenia, Tapana and Tonila (*Sumichrast*[26][28]); Guatemala, Santa Ana in Peten, Las Salinas, Dueñas[7], Retalhuleu (*O. S. & F. D. G.*), Naranjo (*Goss, in U. S. Nat. Mus.*); Salvador, Volcan de San Miguel, La Libertad (*W. B. Richardson*); Nicaragua, Chontales (*Belt*[22]); Costa Rica, Bebedero de Nicoya, Tucurriqui (*Arcé*), San José and Angostura (*Carmiol*[11][17]); Panama, David (*Bridges*[4]), Chiriqui, Cordillera del Chucu[10], Laguna del Castillo[10], Chitra[10], Cordillera de Tolé[9], Calovevora[10], Calobre, Santa Fé[9] (*Arcé*), Lion Hill (*M'Leannan*[30][31]), Paraiso (*Hughes*[13]), Line of Railway, Chepo (*Arcé*). — South America, from Colombia to Trinidad[12] and Guiana, Amazons Valley and Ecuador.

Males of this species from Guiana and Venezuela have rather bluer heads than those from Mexico, Panama birds being nearly intermediate. The northern bird was separated by Gould under the name of *Heliomaster pallidiceps*[18], but with the series now before us we do not see our way to admitting any specific difference.

Floricola longirostris is not a common bird in Mexico, and does not seem to be found northward of Jalapa in the State of Vera Cruz. It is absent from Western Mexico, but occurs on the Isthmus of Tehuantepec, and thence southwards on both sides of the Cordillera of Guatemala, reaching an altitude of nearly 5000 feet in the mountains near Dueñas. Here it is rather a rare bird, though every now and then we secured a specimen when feeding from the flowers of *Ipomœa murucoides*. In the State of Panama this species seems to be very abundant, as our collector Arcé obtained us many specimens, finding it in nearly every place he visited. It is equally common in the parts of South America in which it is found.

Other attempts to divide the Central-American birds besides that of Gould have been made; Mr. Lawrence referred the Panama form to that of Colombia, which he called *Heliomaster stewartæ*, and Cabanis and Heine described the Venezuela bird as *H. sclateri*. In our opinion both birds belong to *F. longirostris*. The trifling paler shade of the crown, being variable in itself, is insufficient for definition, and other characters, such as the width of the bill, are equally untrustworthy.

β. *Pileus viridis dorso fere concolor.*

2. Floricola constanti.

Ornismya constantii, Delattre, Echo du Monde Savant, 1843, p. 1069 [1].

Heliomaster constanti, Gould, Mon. Troch. iv. t. 260 (May 1853) [2]; Scl. & Salv. Ibis, 1859,
p. 129 [3]; Salv. Ibis, 1860, p. 263 [4]; Cat. Strickl. Coll. p. 367 [5]; Cab. & Heine, Mus. Hein.
iii. p. 54 [6]; Lawr. Ann. Lyc. N. Y. ix. p. 126 [7]; Bull. U. S. Nat. Mus. no. 4, p. 32 [8];
Frantz. J. f. Orn. 1869, p. 317 [9]; Sumichrast, La Nat. v. p. 250 [10].

Floricola constanti, Elliot, Syn. Troch. p. 84 [11]; Zeledon, An. Mus. Nac. Costa Rica, 1887, p. 121 [12];
Salv. Cat. Birds Brit. Mus. xvi. p. 231 [13].

Supra (pileo incluso) nitenti-cupreo-viridis, plaga irregulari dorsali alba, stria rictali utrinque alba, mento
nigro, gutture micanti-rubido, plumis singulis stricte cinereo marginatis; abdomine medio albo, lateribus
et pectore cinereis, hypochondriis viridi lavatis, plaga costali alba, tectricibus subcaudalibus fuscis albo
marginatis; caudæ rectricibus mediis dorso concoloribus nigro terminatis, reliquis ad basin griseis, fascia
lata subterminali nigra, apicibus albis: rostro nigro. Long. tota 5·0, alæ 2·7, caudæ 1·45, rostri a rictu
1·5. (Descr. maris ex Guatemala. Mus. Brit.)

♀ mari similis, plaga gulari rubida aut parva aut omnino absente.

Hab. MEXICO, Gineta Mountains in Chiapas (*Sumichrast* [8] [10]); GUATEMALA [6] (*Delattre* [1],
Skinner [2] [3]), San Gerónimo (*O. S. & F. D. G.* [4]); SALVADOR, San Salvador (*Hardi-
man, in U. S. Nat. Mus.*), Volcan de San Miguel, La Libertad (*W. B. Richardson* [13]);
NICARAGUA, Matagalpa, Momotombo (*W. B. R.* [13]); COSTA RICA (*v. Frantzius* [7],
Carmiol [7]), Bebedero de Nicoya, Tempate (*Arcé* [13]), San José (*Zeledon* [12]).

Sumichrast states that this species is found in the Gineta Mountains in Chiapas [10] to
the southward of the Isthmus of Tehuantepec. This is the most northern record we
have of this species. In Guatemala it must be a very local bird, for we only
once met with it when a specimen was brought to us when staying at San Gerónimo,
3000 feet above sea-level. Yet Gould speaks of it as common in that country, whence
he had received many specimens. In the Republic of Salvador, Mr. Richardson
secured a good series of skins between February and April 1891, both on the sea-coast
at La Libertad, and on the slopes of the Volcan de San Miguel, a little distance in the
interior. It also occurs at Momotombo on the western side of the Lake of Managua,
and on the shores of the Gulf of Nicoya in Costa Rica. This seems to be the extreme
limit of its southern range, for in the State of Panama we find no trace of it.

3. Floricola leocadiæ.

Trochilus leocadiæ, Bourc. Ann. Sc. Phys. et Nat. Lyon, (2) iv. p. 141 [1].

Heliomaster leocadiæ, Gould, Intr. Troch. p. 140 [2]; Scl. Cat. Am. Birds, p. 310 [3]; Lawr. Mem.
Bost. Soc. N. H. ii. p. 292 [4]; Bull. U. S. Nat. Mus. no. 4, p. 32 [5]; Sumichrast, La Nat. v.
p. 250 [6].

Floricola leocadiæ, Elliot, Syn. Troch. p. 84 [7]; Salv. Cat. Birds Brit. Mus. xvi. p. 232 [8].

Heliomaster pinicola, Gould, Mon. Troch. iv. t. 261 (May 1853) [9]; de Oca, La Nat. iii. p. 299 [10];
Sanchez, An. Mus. Nac. Mex. i. p. 96 [11].

F. constanti similis, sed plaga gulari micanti-rubida multo minore et cauda supra plerumque obscuriore differt. (Descr. maris ex Alto de Camaron, Guerrero, Mexico. Mus. nostr.)

Hab. MEXICO, Pine-region of N. Mexico (*Sanchez* [11]), Sierra de Alamos in Sonora (*W. Lloyd* [8]), Mazatlan (*Grayson* [4]), Presidio de Mazatlan (*A. Forrer* [8]), San Blas, Bolaños (*W. B. Richardson* [8]), Valley of Mexico? (*le Strange* [8]), Acapulco (*Capt. J. M. Dow, in U. S. Nat. Mus.*), Dos Arroyos, Rio Papagaio, Alto de Camaron, and Venta de Pelegrino (*Mrs. H. H. Smith* [8]), Tehuantepec (*Sumichrast* [5 6]), Chimalapa (*W. B. Richardson* [8]).

Floricola leocadiæ is a northern form of *F. constanti*, and is entirely restricted to Mexico, where it is found almost exclusively on the western side from Sonora in the north to the Isthmus of Tehuantepec.

Gould, who described the species as *Heliomaster pinicola* [9], says that it inhabits the lofty pine-ridges of Northern Mexico; but this statement is hardly correct, for we have abundant evidence that its chief abode is at a low level, and even reaches the sea-coas at Mazatlan, San Blas, Acapulco, and Tehuantepec.

Our specimen from Alamos is quite young in its first plumage, and was shot on the 23rd May, 1888. One from San Blas is not fully grown, and was shot on 2nd May, 1889. A still younger bird from Bolaños was shot on 17th February, 1889. These specimens indicate that the breeding-season extends over several months.

d'. *Rostrum multo brevius sensim decurvatum; cauda longior, rotundata aut subfurcata.*

c''. *Cauda furcata, rectricibus lateralibus longissimis, angustis.*

CYANOPHAIA.

Cyanophaia, Reichenbach, Aufz. d. Col. p. 10; Salv. Cat. Birds Brit. Mus. xvi. p. 233.

Compared with *Floricola*, which has a similarly denuded culmen and nasal covers, this and the following genera have a much shorter, more curved, bill and longer tail in proportion to their size.

Cyanophaia has a distinctly forked tail, the lateral pair of rectrices being the longest.

The genus itself contains three species, all of which are found in Colombia, but not further south. Only one of these spreads over the State of Panama, and perhaps to Costa Rica.

1. Cyanophaia cæruleigularis.

Trochilus (——?) *cæruleigularis*, Gould, P. Z. S. 1850, p. 163 [1].
Sapphironia cæruleigularis, Scl. P. Z. S. 1856, p. 140 [2]; Gould, Mon. Troch. v. t. 346 (May 1860) [3];

39*

Scl. & Salv. P. Z. S. 1864, p. 365 [4]; Salv. P. Z. S. 1867, p. 156 [5]; 1870, p. 211 [6]; 1883, p. 425 [7]; Lawr. Ann. Lyc. N. Y. ix. p. 128 [8]; Wyatt, Ibis, 1871, p. 378 [9].

Cyanophaia cœruleigularis, Elliot, Syn. Troch. p. 238 [10]; Salv. Cat. Birds Brit. Mus. xvi. p. 233 [11].

Supra nitide gramineo-viridis; capite summo obscuriore, gutture et pectore micanti-violaceo-cyaneis, lateribus suis viridescentibus; abdomine et tectricibus subalaribus nitenti-viridibus, his albido marginatis; cauda chalybea, rectricibus mediis cupreo-viridibus: maxilla nigra, mandibula carnea apice nigra. Long. tota 4·0, alæ 1·9, caudæ rectr. med. 1·0, rectr. lat. 1·35, rostri a rictu 0·85. (Descr. maris ex Calobre, Panama. Mus. nostr.)

♀ supra niteuti-viridis, pileo obscuriore: subtus alba, cervicis lateribus cæruleo-viridibus, pectore et hypochondriis viridi lavatis; tectricibus subcaudalibus albis, medialiter pallide fuscis; cauda chalybea, rectricibus mediis dorso concoloribus, lateralibus albo terminatis. (Descr. feminæ ex Cordillera del Chucu, Panama. Mus. nostr.)

Hab. Costa Rica [8] (*Gould* [3]); Panama, near David (*Warszewiez* [1] [3], *Bridges* [2]), Laguna del Castillo [6], Castillo [6], Cordillera del Chucu [6], Calobre [6], Santa Fé [5] (*Arcé*), Lion Hill (*M'Leannan* [4]), Paraiso (*Hughes* [11]), Colon (*A. H. Markham* [7]).—Northern Colombia [9].

Gould's type of this species was obtained near David by Warszewiez [1], and Bridges found it near the same place [2] [3], but we have not received any specimens from quite so far to the westward. Arcé, however, sent us many specimens from Santa Fé and other places in the vicinity, and the bird is not uncommon on the line of the Panama Railway. Its presence in Costa Rica rests upon a statement of Gould's, and a specimen so marked is in his collection, but he gave no further authority for its presence in that country. No recent collectors, that we are aware of, have observed it there.

According to Bridges [2], *C. cœruleigularis* flies in the streets of David, and feeds from the flowers of *Tamarindus indicus* and also from orange-blossoms.

d″. *Cauda irregulariter rotundata, rectricibus lateralibus quam proximis brevioribus.*

c‴. *Minor; rostrum breve, guttur viride, abdomen cyaneo-micans.*

DAMOPHILA.

Cœligena, β. Damophila, Reichenbach, Aufz. d. Col. p. 7.
Damophila, Salv. Cat. Birds Brit. Mus. xvi. p. 235.

In *Damophila* the tail is rounded, the four middle rectrices being nearly equal, the outer pair much shorter. Glittering colours overspread the whole of the under surface of the body.

Two species are contained in the genus, one of which belongs to Colombia and Western Ecuador; the other is probably peculiar to the State of Panama.

1. Damophila panamensis.

Juliamyia typica, Lawr. Ann. Lyc. N. Y. vii. p. 292 (nec Bp.)[1]; ix. p. 128[2].
Damophila juliæ, Scl. & Salv. P. Z. S. 1864, p. 365[3]; Salv. P. Z. S. 1870, p. 211 (nec Bourc.)[4].
Damophila panamensis, Berl. J. f. Orn. 1884, p. 312[5]; Pr. U. S. Nat. Mus. xi. p. 563[6]; Salv. Cat.
   Birds Brit. Mus. xvi. p. 237[7].

Supra saturate nitenti-viridis, dorso postico et tectricibus subcaudalibus cupreo tinctis, gutture micanti-
   gramineo-viridi; abdomine micanti-violaceo-cyaneo; tectricibus subcaudalibus et cauda chalybeis: maxilla
   nigra, mandibula carnea apice nigra.   Long. tota 3·2, alæ 1·65, caudæ rectr. med. 1·2, rectr. lat. 0·8,
   rostri a rictu 0·65.
♀ supra nitenti-viridis: subtus griseo-alba; tectricibus subcaudalibus fuscis; cauda chalybea, tectricibus, mediis
   viridi tinctis, lateralibus griseo terminatis.   (Descr. maris et feminæ ex Paraiso, Panama.   Mus. nostr.)

Hab.   Costa Rica? (*Carmiol*[2]); Panama, Calovevora (*Arcé*[4]), Lion Hill (*M'Leannan*[1][3]),
   Paraiso (*Hughes*[7]), Line of Railway, Chepo (*Arcé*[7]).

All the specimens we have seen of this species are from the line of the Panama
Railway or from Chepo on the Rio Bayano, a little to the southward.   In the rest of
Colombia and in Western Ecuador *D. juliæ* is the prevalent form.   This closely allied
bird has the head of the same glittering green as the throat and not dull like the back,
as is the case in *D. panamensis*.   This feature was first noticed by Count Berlepsch,
and led him to separate the two forms[5].

   The presence of *D. panamensis* or any species of the genus in Costa Rica is somewhat
doubtful.   Mr. Lawrence includes *D. typica* in his list of Costa Rica[2] birds on the
authority of Julian Carmiol, but gives no precise habitat.   Its extension so far north
has not been confirmed, so far as we know, by other authorities.

2. Damophila juliæ.

Ornismyia julie, Bourc. Rev. Zool. 1842, p. 373[1]; Ann. Sc. Phys. et Nat. Lyon, v. p. 345, t. 21[?].
Juliamyia juliæ, Cass. Pr. Ac. Phil. 1860, p. 194[3].
Damophila juliæ, Cab. & Heine, Mus. Hein. iii. p. 40[4]; Salv. Cat. Birds Brit. Mus. xvi. p. 236[5].
Juliamyia typica, Bp. Rev. Zool. 1854, p. 255[6]; Gould, Mon. Troch. v. t. 337 (Sept. 1859)[7];
   Berl. Pr. U. S. Nat. Mus. xi. p. 563[8].

D. panamensi similis, sed capite summo micanti-viridi, gula nec dorso concolore facile distinguenda.

Hab. Panama, Turbo (*Schott*[3]).—Colombia[1][4]; Ecuador.

This older and better-known form of *Damophila* occurs at the extreme southern limit
of our region, where Mr. Schott obtained a bird at Turbo on the Isthmus of Darien.
Count Berlepsch, who examined this specimen, states that it agrees with the bright-
headed southern form and not with the comparatively dull-headed bird of Panama[8].

   D. juliæ was described by Bourcier from a specimen from Tunja in Colombia, and it
is now well known as a bird of that country, specimens being frequently included in the
trade collections of the Bogota bird-hunters.   It is also fairly common through Western
Ecuador, probably to the southern limits of the forest district.

d'''. *Major; rostrum longius; pectus tantum cyaneo-micans.*

POLYERATA.

Polyerata, Heine, J. f. Orn. 1863, p. 194; Salv. Cat. Birds Brit. Mus. xvi. p. 237.
Damophila, Gould, Mon. Troch. v. t. 341 ; Elliot, Syn. Troch. p. 233 (nec Reich., partim).

This genus was generally merged with *Damophila* until Herr Heine separated it. The form of the tail distinguishes it, the rectrices being all of nearly equal length, the outer pair being equal to the middle pair and only very slightly shorter than the rest. The glittering colour of the under surface is confined to the breast.

Two species constitute the genus, one of which spreads from Costa Rica (missing a considerable portion of the State of Panama) to Colombia and Western Ecuador. The other is restricted to the neighbourhood of Chiriqui.

1. Polyerata amabilis.

Trochilus (——?) amabilis, Gould, P. Z. S. 1851, p. 115 [1].
Damophila amabilis, Gould, Mon. Troch. v. t. 341 (Sept. 1859) [2]; Lawr. Ann. Lyc. N. Y. vii. p. 292 [3]; ix. p. 128 [4]; Scl. & Salv. P. Z. S. 1864, p. 365 [5]; 1879, p. 530 [6]; Boucard, P. Z. S. 1878, p. 71 [7]; Zeledon, An. Mus. Nac. Costa Rica, 1887, p. 122 [8].
Polyerata amabilis, Heine, J. f. Orn. 1863, p. 194 [9]; Berl. J. f. Orn. 1884, p. 312 [10]; 1887, p. 333 [11]; Salv. Cat. Birds Brit. Mus. xvi. p. 237 [12].

Supra nitenti-gramineo-viridis, tectricibus supracaudalibus purpureo-cupreis; pileo et capitis lateribus micanti-viridibus, gula media nigra, pectore micanti-cyaneo; abdomine medio griseo, hypochondriis viridibus; tectricibus subcaudalibus obscure fuscis pallide griseo limbatis; cauda rectricibus mediis rufescente cupreis, reliquis chalybeis: maxilla nigra, mandibula carnea apice nigra. Long. tota 3·6, alæ 2·1, caudæ 1·15, rostri a rictu 0·8.

♀ supra nitenti-gramineo-viridis, pileo vix obscuriore, tectricibus supracaudalibus et rectricibus intermediis sicut in mare: subtus griseo-alba, gutturis plumis macula discali viridi, rectricibus lateralibus griseo terminatis. (Descr. maris et feminæ ex Chepo, Panama. Mus. nostr.)

Hab. COSTA RICA (*Endres*), Pozo Azul de Pirris (*Zeledon* [8]), Pacuare (*Carmiol* [4]), San Carlos (*Boucard* [7]); PANAMA, Lion Hill (*M'Leannan* [3][5]), Paraiso Station (*Hughes* [12]), Line of Railway, Chepo (*Arcé* [12]), Turbo (*Schott*).—COLOMBIA [16]; ECUADOR.

Gould's description of this species was based upon a trade skin from Bogota [1]. The bird is now known as not unfrequently represented in the collections of the bird-hunters of Bogota, and as occurring southwards in Western Ecuador and northwards to the Quindiu mountains and the State of Antioquia [6] to the line of the Panama Railway. Here we seem to lose it in the rest of the State of Panama, but it reappears in Costa Rica, where several collectors have found it. Its place in Western Panama seems to be occupied by *P. decora*, a closely allied form.

2. Polyerata decora.

Damophila amabilis, Salv. P. Z. S. 1870, p. 211 [1].

Polyerata decora, Salv. Ann. & Mag. N. H. 1891, vii. p. 377 [2]; Cat. Birds Brit. Mus. xvi. p. 238 [3].

P. amabili affinis, sed rostro longiore; plumis micantibus capitis supra nucham magis extensis; tectricibus supracaudalibus et rectricibus intermediis saturate nitenti-viridibus purpureo vix tinctis. Long. rostri a rictu 1·1.

♀ quoque rostro longiore, uropygio et cauda magis viridescentibus differt. (Descr. maris et feminæ exempl. typ. ex Chiriqui, Panama. Mus. nostr.)

Hab. PANAMA, Volcan de Chiriqui, Bugaba (*Arcé* [1]).

After considerable hesitation, Salvin described this species in the 'Catalogue of Birds in the British Museum' [3], having previously noted some of the differences which distinguish it from *P. amabilis* [1].

This form seems to be strictly confined to the district of Chiriqui, and is probably found there only on the Pacific side of the mountains.

e″. *Cauda regulariter rotundata, rectricibus latis aut aureo-cupreis micantibus, aut chalybeis aut castaneis.*

e‴. *Cauda læte aureo-cuprea; stria elongata postoculari nulla.*

CHRYSURONIA.

Chrysuronia, Bonaparte, Consp. Av. i. p. 75; Salv. Cat. Birds Brit. Mus. xvi. p. 248.

In *Chrysuronia* the tail is rounded, the feathers being broad, and in this respect it resembles the next genus, *Basilinna*; but in all the members of *Chrysuronia* the tail is of bright glittering colour; moreover, there is no long postocular white stripe, which is a very marked feature in *Basilinna*.

The number of species in *Chrysuronia* is five, which are distributed over nearly the whole of Tropical America as far south as the Argentine Republic; no species, however, occurs in Eastern Brazil. In Central America one species, *C. eliciæ*, is found, which is peculiar to that country.

1. Chrysuronia eliciæ.

Trochilus eliciæ, Bourc. & Muls. Ann. Sc. Phys. et Nat. Lyon, ix. p. 314 [1].

Chrysuronia eliciæ, Gould, Mon. Troch. v. t. 328 (Sept. 1858) [2]; Scl. & Salv. Ibis, 1859, p. 130 [3]; Salv. P. Z. S. 1870, p. 211 [4]; Ibis, 1872, p. 320 [5]; Cat. Birds Brit. Mus. xvi. p. 251 [6].

Chrysurisca eliciæ, Cab. & Heine, Mus. Hein. iii. p. 42 [7].

Supra saturate nitenti-gramineo-viridis, pileo obscuriore, tectricibus supracaudalibus læte cupreis; gutture et pectore micanti-cyaneis, hypochondriis nitide viridibus, abdomine medio cervino, tectricibus subcaudalibus cupreis cervino limbatis; cauda micanti-aureo-cuprea: rostro carneo, apice nigro. Long. tota 3·5, alæ 1·9, caudæ 1·1, rostri 0·7.

♀ mari similis, sed gutturis plumis maculis discalibus cyaneis tantum notatis. (Descr. maris et feminæ ex La Libertad, Salvador. Mus. nostr.)

Hab. GUATEMALA (*Skinner* [2] [3]), Coban, Choctum, Masagua, Retalhuleu (*O. S. & F. D. G.*);

SALVADOR, La Libertad (*W. B. Richardson*); HONDURAS (*mus. Heine*[7]), Segovia R. (*Townsend, in U. S. Nat. Mus.*), Santa Ana (*Wittkugel, in U. S. Nat. Mus.*); NICARAGUA, Sucuya (*Nutting*), Chontales (*Belt*[5]), La Libertad and Santo Domingo in Chontales (*W. B. Richardson*); COSTA RICA (*Endres*); PANAMA, Volcan de Chiriqui, Bugaba[4], David, Chitra[4] (*Arcé*).

Chrysuronia eliciæ was described by MM. Bourcier and Mulsant from a specimen the origin of which was not known. The species now appears to belong to Central America exclusively, with a wide range embracing the whole of Guatemala and the country southwards to Chiriqui. We have specimens before us from various points of this wide district. In Guatemala it is by no means common; and though Gould was supplied with specimens by Skinner[2], we only met with the bird on rare occasions in the forest country on both sides of the main mountain-chain. Some of these were obtained at Coban and the country to the northward; the others were from the Pacific side of the country, where they occurred at an elevation of less than 1000 feet above sea-level. Mr. Richardson also found it on the sea-coast of Salvador at La Libertad, and it has been recorded from Nicaragua and Costa Rica on a few occasions. At Chiriqui it is more common, but has not been found on the line of the Panama Railway.

f'''. *Cauda chalybea aut castanea, stria postocularis elongata alba.*

BASILINNA.

Basilinna, Boie, Isis, 1831, p. 546; Salv. Cat. Birds Brit. Mus. xvi. p. 252.
Heliopædica, Gould, Mon. Troch. ii. t. 64 (May 1858).

Basilinna has a rounded tail like that of *Chrysuronia*, but it is not brightly coloured as in all the members of that genus. The nasal covers are fully exposed, owing to the denudation of the base of the culmen. A distinguishing feature of *Basilinna*, compared with its allied genera, is a long narrow postocular white stripe. A similar stripe is found in *Delattria* and some allied forms, which, however, are not so nearly related to the present genus as was at one time supposed.

Two distinct species belong to *Basilinna*—one of which is found over nearly the whole of the uplands of Mexico, Guatemala, and Nicaragua; the other is peculiar to Lower California.

1. Basilinna leucotis.

Trochilus leucotis, Vieill. N. Dict. d'Hist. N. xxiii. p. 428[1].
Basilinna leucotis, Reich. Aufz. d. Col. p. 13[2]; Cab. & Heine, Mus. Hein. iii. p. 45[3]; Elliot, Syn. Troch. p. 227[4]; Salv. Cat. Strickl. Coll. p. 360[5]; Cat. Birds Brit. Mus. xvi. p. 252[6].
Trochilus lucidus, Shaw, Gen. Zool. viii. p. 327[7].
Sapphironia lucida, Scl. P. Z. S. 1858, p. 297[8]; 1859, p. 386[9].

Trochilus melanotus, Sw. Phil. Mag. new scr. i. p. 441[10].

Trochilus cuculiger, Licht. Preis-Verz. Mex. Vög. p. 1 (*cf.* J. f. Orn. 1863, p. 55)[11].

Ornismyia arsennii, Less. His. Nat. Ois.-Mouches, pp. xxvii, xlvi[12]; Suppl. p. 152, t. 27[13].

Heliopædica melanotis, Gould, Mon. Troch. ii. t. 64 (May 1858)[14]; Sanchez, An. Mus. Nac. Mex. i. p. 96[15]; Scl. & Salv. Ibis, 1859, p. 130[16]; Salv. Ibis, 1860, pp. 195[17], 263[18], 271[19]; Scl. P. Z. S. 1864, p. 176[20]; A. Dugès, La Nat. i. p. 141[21]; Villada, La Nat. ii. p. 365[22]; de Oca, La Nat. iii. p. 28[23]; Boucard, Ann. Soc. Linn. Lyon, (2) xxii. p. 14[24]; Herrera, La Nat. (2) i. p. 322[25].

Supra nitenti-gramineo-viridis, ad nucham et ad pileum posticum nigricantior, ad uropygium magis aurescens; facie et mento micanti-cyaneis, stria postoculari elongata alba; pectore micanti-viridi, abdomine et tectricibus subcaudalibus nitenti-viridibus his griseo-albido limbatis, caudæ rectricibus mediis nitenti-aureo-viridibus, lateralibus chalybeis viridi terminatis: rostro carneo, apice nigro. Long. tota 3·5, alæ 2·0, caudæ 1·2, rostri a rictu 0·65.

♀ supra nitenti-aureo-viridis, capite summo et nucha obscure fuscis rufo marginatis, stria postoculari alba, infra eam et infra oculum plaga nigra: subtus fusco-alba, gutturis plumis macula discali micanti-viridi, hypochondriis quoque maculatis; tectricibus subcaudalibus albidis, macula discali fusca; rectricibus lateralibus griseo-albo terminatis: rostro fere nigro. (Descr. maris et feminæ ex Sierra Nevada de Colima. Mus. nostr.)

Hab. MEXICO, Tutuaca in Sonora (*W. Lloyd*[6]), Mazatlan (*Grayson, in U. S. Nat. Mus.*), Ciudad in Durango (*A. Forrer*[6]), Sierra de Victoria Tamaulipas, Sierra de San Luis Potosi, Sierra de Valparaiso, Sierra de Nayarit, Sierra de Bolaños, Tepic, Volcan de Colima, Sierra Nevada de Colima (*W. B. Richardson*[6]), Guanajuato (*Dugès*[21], *Sanchez*[15]), Real del Monte, Temiscaltepec (*Bullock*[10]), Amecameca, Pinal in Puebla (*F. D. G.*[6]), Rio Frio Ixtaccihuatl, Tenango del Valle (*W. B. R.*[6]), Valley of Mexico (*Sanchez*[15], *Villada*[22], *de Oca*[23], *Herrera*[25], *White*[20]), Ixtapalapa, Hacienda Eslava, Chimalpa, Tetelco, San Antonio Coapa, and Las Cruces in the Valley of Mexico, Las Vigas, Montañas de Orizaba (*F. Ferrari-Perez*[6]), Tlascala (*F. D. G.*[6]), Cofre de Perote (*M. Trujillo*[6]), Jalapa (*de Oca*[23], *Sanchez*[15]), Mirador (*Sartorius, in U. S. Nat. Mus.*), Cordova (*Sallé*), Amula, Omilteme in Guerrero (*Mrs. H. H. Smith*[6]), Villa Alta, Totontepec, Tonaguia in Oaxaca (*M. Trujillo*[6]), Oaxaca (*Fenochio*[6]); GUATEMALA (*Skinner*[16]), Quezaltenango, Totonicapam (*O. S. & F. D. G.*), Santa Maria, Chuipaché (*W. B. Richardson*[6]), Volcan de Fuego[19], V. de Agua, Chilasco, Santa Rosa above Salama, San Gerónimo[19], Santa Barbara, Coban[17][19] (*O. S. & F. D. G.*[6]); NICARAGUA, Matagalpa (*W. B. Richardson*).

This is one of the commonest and most characteristic of the Humming-Birds of the highlands of Mexico and Guatemala, its range extending from the States of Sonora and Tamaulipas to the uplands of Nicaragua, birds from these widely-separated districts presenting no appreciable difference. Its range in altitude is considerable. It does not occur much below 4000 feet above sea-level, and thence reaches as high as 7000 or 8000 feet. On the slopes of the Volcan de Fuego we used to find it not uncommonly in open glades in the oak-forests, where it took its food from any plants that happened to be in flower. Of the breeding-habits of this species we have no account, but a three-parts grown bird from Sierra de Victoria was shot by Mr. Richardson in April, so that the nesting-time in that district would commence in March or the end of February.

But the nesting-season probably extends over a considerable period, for de Oca says he once found a nest in December, though the usual nesting-time in the valley of Mexico, where the bird is more common than at Jalapa, is in July and August. According to Villada it feeds from the flowers of *Cacti* and *Agave*, and also from those of *Bouvardia* and *Salvia*[22].

Mr. Richardson's specimens were all shot at Matagalpa between June and October.

In Lower California an allied species occurs in *B. xantusi*, distinguished by its cinnamon abdomen and chestnut tail. This bird has not yet been detected on the eastern side of the Gulf of California.

Sect. C. TROCHILI LÆVIROSTRES.

Tomia (et maxillæ et mandibulæ) usque ad apicem lævia, haud serrata.

a. *Plerumque majores: cauda plerumque normalis, furcata, rotundata aut cuneata, rectricibus plerumque latis; gula vix unquam micanti-rubra; caput vix unquam cristatum, plumæ cervicales laterales elongatæ nullæ neque plumæ superciliares elongatæ; dorsum fere uniforme, fascia transversa conspicua nulla.*

a'. *Plerumque majores: cauda variabilis, cuneata, rotundata aut furcata (interdum profunde).*

a''. *Rostrum valde curvatum (usque ad circuli trientem); cauda rectricum apicibus acutis; tegulæ nasales nudæ, ptilosis simplex haud coloribus micantibus ornata; remigum externorum rhachides normales.*

EUTOXERES.

Eutoxeres, Reichenbach, Syst. Av. t. xl.; Salv. Cat. Birds Brit. Mus. xvi. p. 261.

Of this genus, remarkable for the very singular shape of the bill, only one species occurs within our limits, ranging from the western part of the State of Panama to Costa Rica. This bird has two close allies—one in Colombia and the other in Western Ecuador. Another species (*E. condaminii*) is very distinct, and is only found on the eastern slopes of the Andes of Ecuador and Peru. *Eutoxeres* is closely allied to *Phaethornis*, but may at once be distinguished by the bill, which is abruptly curved to a third of a circle.

1. **Eutoxeres salvini.**

Eutoxeres aquila, Gould, Mon. Troch. i. t. 3 (Nov. 1851) (nec Bourc.)[1]; Salv. P. Z. S. 1867, p. 152[2];
　　Lawr. Ann. Lyc. N. Y. ix. p. 120[3].
Trochilus aquila, Lawr. Ann. Lyc. N. Y. vi. p. 139[4].
Eutoxeres salvini, Gould, Ann. & Mag. N. H. 1868, i. p. 456[5]; Salv. P. Z. S. 1870, p. 204[6]; Cat.
　　Birds Brit. Mus. xvi. p. 262[7].

Supra saturate nitenti-viridis, pileo obscuriore, uropygio cæruleo tincto hoc fulvo limbato : subtus nigrescens, gutturis plumis medialiter pallide cervinis, abdominis albis ; cauda viridi-brunnea, apice alba : rostro nigro, mandibula ad basin flava. Long. tota 5·3, alæ 3·0, caudæ 2·3, rostri a rictu 1·2.

♀ mari similis. (Descr. maris et feminæ ex Calovevora, Panama. Mus. nostr.)

Hab. COSTA RICA, Turrialba (*Arcé*[7]), Rovalo (*Warszewiez*[1]) ; PANAMA, Belen (*Merritt*[4]), Chitra, Calovevora[6], Calobre (*Arcé*).

This remarkable bird is found in many parts of Western Panama, and thence northwards to the lowlands of Costa Rica lying on the Atlantic slope of the Cordillera.   It is apparently absent from the line of the Panama Railway, but two closely allied forms occur in South America—one in Colombia, the other in Ecuador.

The presence of this species in the State of Panama was first detected by Dr. Merritt, who observed it in the district of Belen, where he obtained several specimens, which he sent to Mr. Lawrence accompanied with the following note :—" It was as near as I can recollect during the month of September, 1852, that I saw for the first time and obtained a specimen of this (to me) curious and novel bird.   I was at that time stationed in the mountainous district of Belen, province of Veraguas, New Granada.

" My attention at that particular time was directed towards the collection of specimens of the Humming-Bird family.   One day while out hunting a short distance from the camp for these *chefs-d'œuvre* of nature in the feathered race, I was startled by the swift approach of a small object through the close thicket, which darted like a rifle-bullet past me, with a loud hum and buzzing of wings.   Indeed, it was this great noise that accompanied its flight, which being so much greater than I had ever heard before from any of these winged meteors of the southern forests, that especially attracted my attention as something uncommon.

" The bird continued its flight but a short distance beyond the spot where I stood, when it suddenly stopped in its rapid course directly in front of a flower.   There for a moment poising itself in this position, it darted upon the flower in a peculiar manner ; in fact, the movements which now followed of this little creature were exceedingly curious to me.   Instead of inserting its beak into the calyx by advancing in a direct line towards the flower, as customary with this class of birds according to my limited observations, this one performed a curvilinear movement, at first stooping forward while it introduced its beak into the calyx, and then, when apparently the point of the beak had reached the desired locality in the flower, its body suddenly dropped downwards, so that it seemed as though it was suspended from the flower by the beak.   That this was not actually the case, the continued rapid movement of its wings demonstrated beyond a doubt.   In this position it remained the ordinary length of time, and then by performing these movements in the reverse order and direction, it freed itself from the flower, and afterwards proceeded to the adjoining one, when the same operation was repeated as already described."

Dr. Merritt proceeds to describe the flower as that of a " species of palm, the blossoms

40*

of which are attached alternately on either side to a pendent stalk. Each flower resembles an inverted Roman helmet, and is attached as it were by the point of the crest to the stalk. It is a fleshy mass of a deep crimson colour, and the cavity of the calyx extends in a tortuous manner downwards towards the attachment of the flower to the stalk."

b″. *Rostrum elongatum plus minusve arcuatum ; tegulæ nasales partim expositæ : cauda rotundata aut cuneata, rectricibus mediis elongatis ; remigum rhachides normales.*

a‴. *Cauda rotundata.*

THRENETES.

Threnetes, Gould, Mon. Troch. i. t. 13 (Oct. 1852); Salv. Cat. Birds Brit. Mus. xvi. p. 263.

Threnetes contains five fairly well-defined species which are distributed over the northern portion of South America, from the valley of the Amazons to the north coast. One species is peculiar to our country, ranging from Panama to Guatemala, having a near ally in Western Ecuador.

In general form *Threnetes* resembles *Glaucis*, so much so that it has been merged in that genus by some writers. Besides some peculiarities in the coloration, it shows no serrations like those of *Glaucis* on the cutting-edges of the bill, which in all respects resembles that of *Phaethornis*. The tail is much more rounded and formed of wider feathers, the central rectrices not being produced far beyond the rest.

1. **Threnetes ruckeri.**

Trochilus ruckeri, Bourc. P. Z. S. 1847, p. 46 [1].

Glaucis ruckeri, Gould, Mon. Troch. i. t. 11 (Nov. 1851) [2]; Lawr. Ann. Lyc. N. Y. vii. p. 319 [3]; ix. p. 121 [4]; Scl. & Salv. P. Z. S. 1864, p. 364 [5]; Salv. P. Z. S. 1870, p. 204 [6]; Zeledon, An. Mus. Nac. Costa Rica, 1887, p. 121 [7].

Threnetes ruckeri, Reich. Aufz. d. Col. p. 15 [8]; Salv. Ibis, 1873, p. 428 [9]; Cat. Birds Brit. Mus. xvi. p. 265 [10]; Salv. & Elliot, Ibis, 1873, p. 278 (partim) [11].

Supra nitenti-aureo-viridis, pileo obscuriore, macula postoculari et stria maxillari cervinis, loris, tectricibus auricularibus et gula antica nigris, pectore cinnamomeo, corpore subtus reliquo fusco-griseo, tectricibus subcaudalibus aureo-viridibus fulvo limbatis, rectricibus mediis dorso concoloribus, reliquis ad basin albis, dimidio distali nigro, apicibus albis : maxilla nigra, mandibula carnea apice nigra. Long. tota 4·5, alæ 2·3, caudæ 1·3, rostri a rictu 1·35. (Descr. maris ex Panama. Mus. nostr.)
♀ mari similis.

Hab. GUATEMALA [9]; COSTA RICA (*Endres* [4], *Zeledon, in U. S. Nat. Mus.*), Angostura (*Carmiol, Zeledon* [7]), Jimenez [7] (*Zeledon, in U. S. Nat. Mus.*); PANAMA, Veraguas (*Warszewiez* [2]), Mina de Chorcha [6], Bibalaz (*Arcé*), Lion Hill (*M'Leannan* [3] [5]), Line of Railway (*Arcé* [10]), Paraiso (*Hughes* [10]).

Bourcier's description of this species was based upon a specimen from an unknown locality. A few years after it was published Warszewiez sent two specimens from

Veraguas to Gould, who figured them in his 'Monograph of the Trochilidæ.' The bird is now known to be not uncommon in some parts of the State of Panama and also in Costa Rica. An allied species of *Threnetes* from Ecuador was described by Gould as *T. fraseri*; this has been united to *T. ruckeri* by some writers, but seems to be distinct. It has a smaller cinnamon patch on the breast, is greyer on the under surface, and has darker median rectrices.

b'''. *Cauda cuneata.*

a⁴. *Majores: cauda rectricibus mediis productis.*

PHAETHORNIS.

Phæthornis, Swainson, Zool. Journ. iii. p. 357.
Phaethornis, auct., Salv. Cat. Birds Brit. Mus. xvi. p. 267.

This genus, consisting of about seventeen species, is spread over the lowland forests of the greater portion of Tropical America, none of the species ascending the mountains to any considerable height. Of the three main sections into which the genus is divisible, two only are represented within our limits, each by a single species. *P. emiliæ*, which is closely allied to *P. guyi*, reaches Costa Rica, and *P. longirostris* occurs throughout Central America and in Eastern Mexico as far as the middle of the State of Vera Cruz. The section of *Phaethornis* represented by the latter bird is remarkable for the form of the tail, which is cuneate, the central rectrices being elongated, and the rest gradually reduced in length towards the outside, and all of them conspicuously tipped with white or buff. The bill is long and curved, and no glittering marks enter into the coloration of the plumage.

1. Phaethornis emiliæ.

Trochilus emiliæ, Bourc. & Muls. Ann. Sc. Phys. et Nat. Lyon, ix. p. 317[1].
Phaethornis emiliæ, Gould, Intr. Troch. p. 44[2]; Salv. P. Z. S. 1867, p. 152[3]; 1870, p. 205[4]; Cat. Birds Brit. Mus. xvi. p. 268[5]; Lawr. Ann. Lyc. N. Y. ix. p. 121[6]; Salv. & Elliot, Ibis, 1873, p. 12[7]; Boucard, P. Z. S. 1878, p. 67[8]; Tacz. Orn. Pér. i. p. 268[9].
Phaethornis yaruqui, Cassin, Pr. Ac. Phil. 1860, p. 194[10].

Supra saturate nitenti-cæruleo-viridis, pileo nigricanti, tectricibus supracaudalibus cærulescentioribus albo stricte terminatis, fascia subterminali nigra; tectricibus auricularibus nigris: subtus obscure griseus, cervicis lateribus et pectore viridi lavatis, gula media stria indistincta fulva notota; cauda purpureo-nigra ad basin chalybea, rectricibus mediis elongatis ad apicem cum rhachide albis: rostro nigro, mandibula flavida apice nigra. Long. tota 5·7, alæ 2·4, caudæ rectr. med. 2·2, rectr. lat. 1·0, rostri a rictu 1·7.

♀ mari similis: subtus pallidior, gula nigra stria mediana distincta fulva, superciliis fulvis, caudæ rectricibus lateralibus albo terminatis, rectricibus mediis elongatis (long. 2·9). (Descr. maris et feminæ ex Tucurriqui, Costa Rica. Mus. nostr.)

Hab. Costa Rica (*Endres*), San José, Peorsnada (*Zeledon, in U. S. Nat. Mus.*), Angostura, Barranca (*Carmiol*[6]), Tucurriqui, Turrialba (*Arcé*[15]), Irazu (*Rogers*[5]), Tres Rios, Naranjo (*Boucard*[8]); Panama, Boquete de Chitra[4], Laguna del Castillo,

Cordillera del Chucu [4], Calovevora [4], Santa Fé [3] (*Arcé*), Truando Falls (*Wood* [10]).
—COLOMBIA [1]; PERU [9].

A very closely allied species to *P. guyi* of Venezuela, and perhaps not always to be
distinguished from that bird. Adult males, however, have the bases of the rectrices
and the upper tail-coverts distinctly tinged with blue, these feathers being green in
the allied form.

P. emiliæ was described by Bourcier and Mulsant from a specimen from Bogota,
whence we have received many examples, probably shot in the lowlands or deeper
valleys of the Andes. In the State of Panama near Santa Fé and elsewhere in that
neighbourhood and in Costa Rica on the Atlantic side of the mountain-range this
Phaethornis appears to be a common bird, but it has not been detected on the line of the
Panama Railway, though specimens formed part of the collection made during Lieut.
Michler's exploring expedition to Darien. These were named *P. yaruqui* by Cassin,
the bird of Ecuador, but they doubtless belong here.

2. Phaethornis longirostris.

Ornismya longirostris, Less. & Delattre, Echo du Monde Savant, 1843, p. 1070 [1].
Phaethornis longirostris, Gould, Intr. Troch. p. 42 [2]; Scl. P. Z. S. 1857, p. 227 [3]; Cab. &
    Heine, Mus. Hein. iii. p. 9 [4]; Lawr. Ann. Lyc. N. Y. vii. p. 319 [5]; ix. p. 121 [6]; Scl. &
    Salv. P. Z. S. 1864, p. 364 [7]; 1879, p. 528 [8]; Salv. Ibis, 1866, p. 204 [9]; 1872, p. 319 [10];
    P. Z. S. 1870, p. 205 [11]; Cat. Birds Brit. Mus. xvi. p. 272 [12]; Boucard, P. Z. S. 1878, p. 67 [13];
    Berl. Pr. A. S. Nat. Mus. ix. p. 560 [14]; Zeledon, An. Mus. Nac. Costa Rica, 1887, p. 121 [15].
Trochilus cephalus, Bourc. & Muls. Rev. Zool. 1848, p. 269 [16].
Phaethornis cephalus, Gould, Mon. Troch. i. t. 19 (Sept. 1858) [17]; Scl. & Salv. Ibis, 1859, p. 126 [18];
    de Oca, La Nat. iii. p. 206 [19].
Phaethornis moorii, Scl. P. Z. S. 1860, p. 296 (nec Lawr.) [20].
Phaethornis cassini, Lawr. Ann. Lyc. N. Y. viii. p. 347 [21].

Supra æneo-viridis, pileo obscuriore, plumis nuchæ uropygii et tectricum supracaudalium cervino marginatis, stria
    utrinque superciliari aliisque malaribus et una in gulæ medio pallide cervinis, genis nigricantibus : subtus
    griseo-cervinus, gula obscuriore : cauda nigra ad basin æneo-viridi, rectricibus lateralibus albo terminatis,
    rectricibus duabus mediis parte prolongata alba : rostro nigro, mandibula flavida apice nigra. Long.
    tota 6·4, alæ 2·5, rectr. med. 2·75, rectr. lat. 1·0, rostri a rictu 1·7. (Descr. exempl. ex Choctum,
    Guatemala. Mus. nostr.)
♀ mari similis.

Hab. MEXICO, near Cordova (*Sallé, de Oca* [19]), San Andres Tuxtla (*Boucard* [3]), Chimalapa,
    Tehuantepec (*W. B. Richardson*); BRITISH HONDURAS, San Felipe (*F. Blancaneaux*);
    GUATEMALA (*Skinner* [2 19]), Yzabal, Choctum, track to Peten (*O. S. & F. D. G.*);
    HONDURAS, Santa Ana (*Wittkugel, in U. S. Nat. Mus.*); NICARAGUA, Rio San Juan
    (*Sallé* [16]), Chontales (*Belt*); COSTA RICA, La Balza (*J. Carmiol* [6]), Jimenez [15],
    San José (*Zeledon*), Naranjo (*Boucard* [14]); PANAMA, Bugaba (*Arcé* [11]), Lion Hill
    (*M'Leannan* [5]), Obispo (*Salvin*), Chepo (*Arcé*), Turbo (*Schott* [21]).—N. COLOMBIA;
    W. ECUADOR.

According to de Oca this is a very rare species in Mexico, a statement confirmed by recent observation, for we are not aware of any specimens having been obtained in the State of Vera Cruz since M. Boucard sent the birds from San Andres Tuxtla to M. Sallé, as recorded by Mr. Sclater in 1857. It occurs, however, on the eastern side of the Isthmus of Tehuantepec, as Mr. Richardson secured specimens there at Chimalapa in March and April 1890 at an altitude of 4000 feet above sea-level. In British Honduras and thence southwards in Eastern Guatemala *P. longirostris* becomes more common. We found it fairly abundant in the heavily forested country of Northern Vera Paz in February 1862 at an altitude of about 1200 feet, and also near the sea-level at Yzabal. It also occurs in Eastern Nicaragua and in Costa Rica. It is rare in many parts of the State of Panama, but not uncommon on the line of Railway, and passes beyond our limits into Northern Colombia and Western Ecuador.

P. longirostris was discovered by Delattre, and described in 1843. Shortly afterwards M. Sallé, during his visit to Nicaragua, procured the specimens which were named *Trochilus cephalus* by Boucier and Mulsant. The same bird received yet another name when Mr. Lawrence described the birds obtained during Lieut. Michler's expedition to Darien as *Phaethornis cassini*, the types of which were examined by Count Berlepsch and pronounced to be inseparable from *P. longirostris*. A near ally to this species in South America is the widely ranging *P. superciliosus* (Linn.), which under somewhat varying forms extends over the whole of the Amazons Valley and Guiana. From this bird it differs in the greater width of the edges of the feathers of the lower back and the greater whiteness of the tips of the outer rectrices.

b⁴. *Minores: cauda regulariter cuneata.*

PYGMORNIS.

Pygmornis, Bonaparte, Rev. Zool. 1854, p. 250; Salv. Cat. Birds Brit. Mus. xvi. p. 280.

This small form of *Phaethornis* contains eight species, which occupy nearly the same area of South and Central America as their larger allies. Only one species is at all common within our limits, a second, which is abundant in Colombia, just reaches our southern frontier at Darien.

Many writers on Trochilidæ do not separate *Pygmornis* from *Phaethornis*; but on the whole we think it best to keep the two forms apart. *Pygmornis*, besides its small size, has a rather differently constructed tail, the central feathers not being distinctly prominent beyond the rest, but form the apex of a regular wedge. In the adult male the tail is shorter than in the female.

1. Pygmornis adolphi.

Phaethornis adolphi, Bourc. MS. apud Gould, Mon. Troch. i. t. 35 (Sept. 1857) [1]; Scl. P. Z. S. 1856, p. 287 (descr. nulla) [2]; 1859, pp. 367 [3], 385 [4]; Scl. & Salv. Ibis, 1859, p. 126 [5]; 1860,

p. 38 [6]; P. Z. S. 1864, p. 365 [7]; Salv. Ibis, 1860, pp. 195 [8], 260 [9]; 1872, p. 319 [10]; P. Z. S. 1867, p. 152 [11]; Lawr. Ann. Lyc. N. Y. vii. p. 291 [12]; ix. p. 121 [13]; Ridgw. Pr. U. S. Nat. Mus. x. p. 591 [14].

Pygmornis adolphi, Cab. & Heine, Mus. Hein. iii. p. 7 [15]; Salv. & Elliot, Ibis, 1873, p. 271 [16]; Boucard, P. Z. S. 1878, p. 67 [17]; Salv. Cat. Birds Brit. Mus. xvi. p. 282 [18].

Supra cupreo-viridis, capite summo obscuriore, tectricibus supracaudalibus elongatis rufescentibus, stria post-oculari cervina, tectricibus auricularibus nigricantibus : subtus rufescens, gutture obscuriore ; cauda æneo-viridi, rectricibus omnibus rufo terminatis duabus mediis ad apicem pallidioribus : rostro nigro, mandibula flava apice nigra, pedibus flavis. Long. tota 3·8, alæ 1·5, caudæ rectr. med. 1·35, rectr. lat. 0·7, rostri a rictu 1·0.

♀ mari similis, sed gutture pallidiore, cauda longiore rectricibus duabus mediis magis productis (long. 1·45) distinguenda. (Descr. maris et feminæ ex Cordova, Mexico. Mus. Brit.)

Hab. MEXICO, Cordova (*Sallé* [1] [2]), Jalapa (*de Oca* [3]), Playa Vicente (*Boucard* [4], *M. Trujillo*), Teotalcingo (*Boucard* [4]), Teapa (*Mrs. H. H. Smith*); GUATEMALA (*Skinner*), forests of Northern Vera Paz, Kamkal near Coban, Coban [8] [9], Lanquin, Yzabal [5] [6] (*O. S. & F. D. G.*); HONDURAS, Segovia River (*Townsend* [14]); NICARAGUA, Chontales (*Belt* [10]); COSTA RICA (*Endres* [13], Angostura (*Carmiol* [13], *Zeledon*), Talamanca (*Zeledon*), San Carlos (*Boucard* [17]); PANAMA, Santiago de Veraguas (*Arcé* [11]), Lion Hill (*M'Leannan* [7] [12]), Paraiso (*Hughes* [18]), Obispo (*Salvin*).

This species of *Pygmornis* was discovered by M. Sallé during his residence at Cordova in Mexico, the first description of it being published with a figure by Gould in his 'Monograph of the Trochilidæ.' It is not a common bird by any means in Mexico, though specimens have been obtained in several places in the States of Vera Cruz and Tabasco. In the dense forests of Eastern Guatemala, *P. adolphi* is usually to be seen up to an elevation of over 4000 feet above sea-level. At Coban we found it in the month of November, feeding from the blossoms of the numerous *Salviæ* which abound there. Though not common its presence could readily be detected by the peculiar sound produced by the wings. At Yzabal it was more numerous in the forest bordering the town, but always in the dense undergrowth beneath the forest trees. It was by no means shy, taking little notice of an observer, and searching the flowers within a few feet of him. Like most Humming-Birds it rests frequently, selecting a small dead twig for its perch, where it trims its feathers with its long bill, which it cleans by rubbing on the perch on which it stands.

Keeping to the eastern side of the main mountain-chain of Central America, *P. adolphi* is found in the Province of Chontales in Nicaragua and in Eastern Costa Rica. In the State of Panama it occurs on both sides of the mountains, the southern limit of its range terminating near the line of the Panama Railway, for in Darien the allied *P. striigularis* takes its place.

2. Pygmornis striigularis.

Phaethornis striigularis, Gould, Mon. Troch. i. t. 37 (Oct. 1854) [1]; Berl. Pr. U. S. Nat. Mus. xi. p. 560 [2].

Pygmornis striigularis, Cab. & Heine, Mus. Hein. iii. p. 7 [3]; Salv. & Elliot, Ibis, 1873, p. 273 [4]; Salv. Cat. Birds Brit. Mus. xvi. p. 281 [5].

Phaethornis, sp. ?, Cassin, Pr. Ac. Phil. 1860, p. 194 [6].

Phaethornis adolphi, Ridgw. Pr. U. S. Nat. Mus. iii. p. 309 (nec Bourc.) [7].

P. adolphi similis, sed corpore subtus grisescentiore, gulæ plumis medialiter fuscis quasi striatis. (Descr. exempl. typ. ex Colombia. Mus. Brit.)

Hab. PANAMA, Turbo (*Lieut. Michler* [2] [6] [7]).—COLOMBIA [1] [5]; ECUADOR [5]; UPPER AMAZONS VALLEY [5].

According to Count Berlepsch, the single female specimen obtained at Turbo during Lieut. Michler's expedition to Darien belongs to this species. It was left undetermined by Cassin, and referred to *P. adolphi* by Mr. Ridgway, before being submitted to Count Berlepsch, whose determination we now follow.

The species was described by Gould from trade skins from Bogota, and is now well known as an inhabitant of Colombia, Ecuador, and the Valley of the Upper Amazons; in the latter district E. Bartlett found it at Chyavetas at the foot of the Andes of Peru.

c". *Rostrum brevius, modice curvatum; tegulæ nasales partim expositæ; remigum trium externorum rhachides tumidæ, pogonio externo ad partem tumidam obsoleto.*

c'''. *Cauda cuneata.*

SPHENOPROCTUS.

Sphenoproctus, Cabanis & Heine, Mus. Hein. iii. p. 11; Salv. Cat. Birds Brit. Mus. xvi. p. 286.

In this and the next genus the males all have remarkably thickened shafts to the outermost three primaries of the wing, these feathers in the female being normal. Whether *Sphenoproctus* is really distinct as a genus from *Campylopterus* is open to question, and many writers unite them. *Sphenoproctus*, as its name implies, has a peculiar wedge-shaped tail, and as the coloration of the species is also peculiar, the two forms may be kept separate.

Sphenoproctus contains two doubtfully distinct species, one of which belongs to Mexico, the other to Guatemala.

1. Sphenoproctus pampa.

Ornismya pampa, Less. Hist. Nat. Ois.-Mouches, Suppl. p. 127, t. 15 [1].

Campylopterus pampa, Gould, Mon. Troch. ii. t. 43 (Sept. 1855) (partim) [2]; Scl. & Salv. Ibis, 1859, p. 127 [3]; Salv. Ibis, 1860, p. 260 [4].

Sphenoproctus pampa, Gould, Intr. Troch. p. 51 [5]; Boucard, P. Z. S. 1883, p. 450 [6]; Salv. Cat. Birds Brit. Mus. xvi. p. 286 [7].

Supra nitenti-viridis, capite summo micanti saturate cyaneo: subtus griseus medialiter pallidior, tectricibus auricularibus, cervicis lateribus, hypochondriis et tectricibus subcaudalibus obscurioribus; cauda purpureonigra, rectricibus mediis omnino reliquis ad basin nitenti-cæruleo-viridibus, rectricibus externis utrinque in pogonio externo medialiter pallidis: rostro nigro. Long. tota 5·5, alæ 2·7, caudæ rectr. med. 2·15, rectr. lat. 1·7, rostri a rictu 1·2.

♀ mari similis; caudæ rectricibus utrinque externis in pogonio externo ad apicem et apicibus omnino griseis, abdomine concoloribus. (Descr. maris et feminæ ex Choctum, Guatemala. Mus. nostr.)

Hab. Mexico, Izalam and Tizimin in Northern Yucatan (*G. F. Gaumer*[6]); Guatemala (*Skinner*[3]), Coban[4], Choctum[7], Chisec[7] (*O. S. & F. D. G.*).

Lesson's description and figure of this species were based upon a male specimen supposed to have come from Paraguay, and until a difference was recognized between the Mexican and Guatemalan birds the name was applied in common to both. Gould, however, in his 'Introduction to the Trochilidæ,' pointed out the slight distinction separating the two birds, and applied Lesson's title to the Guatemalan form, using Lichtenstein's name *S. curvipennis* for the Mexican. In this course he has been followed by subsequent writers; but it is rather doubtful if he was right in so doing; for if the colour of the central tail-feathers goes for anything, Lesson's figure represents the Mexican rather than the Guatemalan bird. The point is of slight importance, and we adhere to the assignment of these names as adopted by Gould.

S. pampa is limited in its range to the great forests of Northern Vera Paz, where it is not uncommon at an elevation of about 1500 feet above sea-level. On one occasion a specimen was obtained near Coban in November 1859[4], but it was an exceptional circumstance to find it at so high an elevation as 4300 feet.

2. Sphenoproctus curvipennis.

Trochilus curvipennis, Licht. Preis-Verz. Mex. Vög. p. 1 (*cf.* J. f. Orn. 1863, p. 56)[1].

Sphenoproctus curvipennis, Gould, Intr. Troch. p. 51[2]; Ferrari-Perez, Pr. U. S. Nat. Mus. ix. p. 156[3]; Salv. Cat. Birds Brit. Mus. xvi. p. 287[4].

Campylopterus pampa, Scl. P. Z. S. 1856, p. 287[5]; 1859, pp. 367[6], 385[7]; de Oca, Pr. Ac. Phil. 1860, p. 552[8]; La Nat. iii. p. 30[9]; Sanchez, An. Mus. Nac. Mex. i. p. 96[10].

S. pampæ similis, sed rostro paulo longiore, capite summo pallidiore cæruleo et cauda paulo viridescentiore distinguenda. (Descr. maris et feminæ ex Jalapa, Mexico. Mus. nostr.)

Hab. Mexico (*Deppe*[1]), Misantla, Colipa (*F. D. G.*[4]), Cuesta de Misantla (*M. Trujillo*[4]), Coatepec (*de Oca*[9], *M. Trujillo*[4]), Jalapa (*de Oca*[6], *F. Ferrari-Perez*[3], *F. D. G.*[4], *C. F. Höge*[4], *M. Trujillo*[4]), Mirador (*Sartorius, in U. S. Nat. Mus.*), Atoyac (*Mrs. H. H. Smith*[4]), Orizaba (*Sanchez*[10]), Cordova (*Sallé*[5]), Teotalcingo (*Boucard*[7]).

The first specimens of this bird to receive a name were sent from Mexico by Deppe and briefly described by Lichtenstein in his Price-list of the Duplicates of that collector's spoils. The species is now known to be common on the slopes of the mountains of Vera Cruz from Jalapa to Teotalcingo. De Oca says that it is found in the dense bush near Coatepec in winter, and also occurs in similar places near Cordova and Orizaba. Boucard, who met with it at Teotalcingo, records that it breeds there in the month of March, and a nest and eggs obtained by him were sent to M. Sallé. Deppe's specimens were probably secured near Misantla, where Godman found the bird not uncommon in the month of March. It occurs in the neighbourhood of this district during the greater part of the year, as we have records of it also in May, June, and October.

d'''. *Cauda rotundata.*

CAMPYLOPTERUS.

Campylopterus, Swainson, Zool. Journ. iii. p. 358; Salv. Cat. Birds Brit. Mus. xvi. p. 288.
Platystylopterus, Reich. Aufz. d. Col. p. 11.

Nine species are contained in this genus, which has a wide range in Tropical America from Bolivia and the Valley of the Amazons to Southern Mexico. Of these only two occur within our region, both of them being peculiar to it—one of them (*C. hemileucurus*) ranging from Southern Mexico to the State of Panama, keeping, however, to the forests of the more mountainous parts; the other (*C. rufus*) is only found in the Guatemalan highlands and the districts adjoining to the southwards.

The peculiar swollen shafts to the outer three primaries of the wing of the male, together with the rounded tail, are characters which distinguish *Campylopterus* from all its allies.

1. Campylopterus hemileucurus.

Trochilus hemileucurus, Licht. Preis-Verz. Mex. Vög. p. 1 (*cf.* J. f. Orn. 1863, p. 55)[1].
Campylopterus hemileucurus, Cab. & Heine, Mus. Hein. iii. p. 13[2]; Cab. J. f. Orn. 1862, p. 162[3];
    Scl. P. Z. S. 1864, p. 176[4]; Salv. Ibis, 1866, p. 204[5]; P. Z. S. 1870, p. 205[6]; Cat. Birds Brit.
    Mus. xvi. p. 291[7]; Lawr. Ann. Lyc. N. Y. ix. p. 121[8]; Bull. U. S. Nat. Mus. no. 4, p. 32[9];
    v. Frantz. J. f. Orn. 1869, p. 315[10]; Boucard, P. Z. S. 1878, p. 68[11]; Sumichrast, La Nat.
    v. p. 250[12]; Nutting, Pr. U. S. Nat. Mus. v. p. 501[13]; Ferrari-Perez, Pr. U. S. Nat. Mus.
    ix. p. 157[14]; Berl. J. f. Orn. 1887, p. 316[15]; Zeledon, An. Mus. Nac. Costa Rica, 1887,
    p. 121[16].
Ornismya delattrii, Less. Rev. Zool. 1839, p. 14[17].
Campylopterus delattrii, Gould, Mon. Troch. ii. t. 45 (Sept. 1855[18]); Scl. P. Z. S. 1856, p. 287[19];
    1859, pp. 367[20], 385[21]; Scl. & Salv. Ibis, 1859, p. 127[22]; Salv. Ibis, 1860, pp. 195[23], 260[24];
    de Oca, La Nat. iii. p. 20, t. —[25].

Læte saturate violaceo-cyaneus micans, capite summo obscure viridi-cyaneo, fere nigro, tectricibus alarum et supracaudalibus saturate viridibus; cauda chalybeo-nigra, rectricibus mediis viridi lavatis, rectricibus tribus utrinque lateralibus late albo terminatis: rostro nigro. Long. tota circa 6·0, alæ 3·3, caudæ 2·3, rostri a rictu 1·3.

♀ supra nitenti-viridis, capite summo nigricanti-cupreo tincto: subtus grisea, cervicis lateribus, hypochondriis et tectricibus subcaudalibus viridibus, gula micanti-violacea; caudæ rectricibus mediis dorso fere concoloribus, tribus utrinque lateralibus albo late terminatis: rostro nigro. (Descr. maris et feminæ ex Coban, Guatemala. Mus. nostr.)

Hab. MEXICO (*Deppe*[1]), Jalapa (*Delattre*[17], *de Oca*[20][25], *F. Ferrari-Perez*[14], *M. Tru-*

41*

jillo [7]), Huatusco (*F. Ferrari-Perez*), Cordova (*Sallé* [19]), Orizaba (*Sumichrast* [12]), Playa Vicente (*M. Trujillo*), Teotalcingo (*Boucard* [21]), Omilteme in Guerrero (*Mrs. H. H. Smith* [7]), Chimalapa and Sierra de San Domingo, Tehuantepec (*W. B. Richardson* [7]), Gineta Mts. (*Sumichrast* [9] [12]); GUATEMALA (*Skinner* [22]), Coban [24] (*O. S. & F. D. G.*), Kamkal, Choctum, Totonicapam, Volcan de Fuego, Volcan de Agua (*O. S. & F. D. G.* [6]), Retalhuleu (*W. B. Richardson* [7]); HONDURAS, Santa Ana (*Wittkugel, in U. S. Nat. Mus.*); NICARAGUA, San Rafael del Norte (*W. B. Richardson*); COSTA RICA, (*Carmiol*); San José (*Von Frantzius* [3]), La Palma de San José [16], Tucurriqui (*Zeledon*), Tres Rios, Rancho Redondo (*Boucard* [11]); PANAMA, Cordillera del Chucu [6], Chitra [6], Boquete de Chitra, Calovevora [6] (*Arcé*).

This very distinct species of *Campylopterus*, the largest Humming-Bird of our region, was discovered by Deppe in Mexico, and very briefly described by Lichtenstein in 1830, in his list of that collector's duplicate specimens, under the name it now bears. A few years later, in 1839, the same species received another name (*O. delattrii*) from MM. Delattre and Lesson, based upon specimens obtained by the former traveller at Jalapa in Mexico. The bird is now known to be not uncommon on the eastern slopes of the mountains of the State of Vera Cruz, and thence southwards through Central America to the State of Panama, occurring also in the Sierra Madre del Sur in Western Mexico, and in the mountains of Guatemala stretching towards the Pacific Ocean.

According to Delattre, *C. hemileucurus* is only found at Jalapa during two months of the year; and this statement is confirmed by de Oca, who says it is common there during October and November, flying from nine o'clock in the morning until noon. We have, however, several specimens from Mateo Trujillo which were shot at Jalapa in July, and at Playa Vicente in February, and it also occurs on the Isthmus of Tehuantepec in the latter month. Other dates of capture, both in Mexico and Guatemala, tend to show that this bird probably does not migrate in any wide sense of the term, but moves from place to place as certain flowers come into bloom.

At Coban, in Guatemala, *C. hemileucurus* is common during the month of November, feeding from the flowers of the various species of *Salviæ* which there abound. It also occurs in the heavily-forested region which lies to the northward, and in the forests of the volcanoes of Guatemala, and as low as 1000 feet on that side of the Cordillera which extends to the Pacific Ocean. Its range in altitude is thus great, as it reaches to at least 8000 feet above sea-level.

2. **Campylopterus rufus.**

Campylopterus rufus, Less. Rev. Zool. 1840, p. 73 [1]; Gould, Mon. Troch. ii. t. 50 (May 1852) [2]; Scl. & Salv. Ibis, 1859, p. 127 [3]; Salv. Ibis, 1860, pp. 38 [4], 195 [5], 263 [6], 264 [7]; Cat. Strickl. Coll. p. 360 [8]; Cat. Birds Brit. Mus. xvi. p. 294 [9].

Platystylopterus rufus, Reich. Aufz. d. Col. p. 11 [10].

Supra nitenti-aureo-viridis, capite summo obscuriore: subtus cinnamomeus, abdomine medio pallidiore, tectricibus auricularibus brunnescentioribus ; caudæ rectricibus mediis dorso fere concoloribus, reliquis ad basin cinnamomeis, subtus fascia subterminali nigra in rectrice extima usque ad rhachidem tantum extendente, pogonio externo igitur omnino cinnamomeo: rostro nigricante, pedibus carneis. Long. tota circa 5·3, alæ 2·8, caudæ 2·0, rostri a rictu 1·2.

♀ mari omnino similis, remigum trium externorum rhachidibus haud tumidis. (Descr. maris et feminæ ex Volcan de Fuego, Guatemala. Mus. nostr.)

Hab. GUATEMALA (*Constancia*[8], *Skinner*[3]), Dueñas[3][4], Volcan de Fuego[3], Plains near Pacicia and Patzum (*O. S. & F. D. G.*); SALVADOR, Volcan de San Miguel (*W. B. Richardson*[9]).

Lesson described this species in 1840 from a specimen without locality. The species was subsequently traced to Guatemala, where Constancia met with it and sent examples to Strickland, and where Skinner also found it and supplied Gould with a series of skins. In Guatemala *C. rufus* is decidedly a local bird, and the only district in which we met with it is situated between 5000 and 6000 feet above sea-level, and extends from the neighbourhood of the Lake of Atitlan to Dueñas and the great volcanoes in the vicinity. It probably ranges further southwards along the highlands, as we have a specimen from the Volcan de San Miguel in Salvador which was shot by Mr. Richardson in March 1891.

At some seasons *C. rufus* is very common near Dueñas. A nest found in August was in a cypress tree in a coffee-plantation, and was attached to a branch about five feet from the ground. It had two eggs when found, but the nest and eggs were destroyed the following day. The old bird sat very close, allowing one to approach within a foot of the nest. On the slopes of the Volcan de Fuego, near the edge of the Llano of Dueñas, this bird was also very common, especially near the road which leads to the hacienda of Calderas. On the higher ground near Pacicia *C. rufus* was observed feeding from the flowers of the large species of *Yucca* which grow on the open plain ; the flowers of the banana (*Musa*) are also eagerly sought by this bird. The habits of this species in thus frequenting more open country and second-growth woods are in strong contrast with those of *C. hemileucurus*, which is a denizen of the denser forest.

d″. Rostrum subrectum; tegulæ nasales magis expositæ; remigum rhachides plerumque normales.

PHÆOCHROA.

Phæochroa, Gould, Intr. Troch. p. 54; Salv. Cat. Birds Brit. Mus. xvi. p. 299.

Phæochroa was separated by Gould from the South-American *Aphantochroa* and from *Campylopterus,* from both of which it has slight points of difference. It most resembles the former in the sombre colour of both its species; but the lateral rectrices are tipped with white and the outer primaries are slightly thickened. The latter character, however, is not well defined, and is carried to nothing like the extent seen in *Campylopterus*.

Two species constitute the genus, one of them belonging to Eastern Guatemala and thence southward to Nicaragua, the other to Costa Rica, Panama, and probably the north-western corner of South America.

1. **Phæochroa cuvieri.**

Trochilus cuvieri, Delattre & Bourc. Rev. Zool. 1846, p. 310 [1].

Campylopterus cuvieri, Gould, Mon. Troch. ii. t. 52 (Sept. 1856) [2]; Scl. P. Z. S. 1856, p. 140 [3]; Lawr. Ann. Lyc. N. Y. vii. p. 319 [4]; Zeledon, An. Mus. Nac. Costa Rica, 1887, p. 121 [5].

Phæochroa cuvieri, Gould, Intr. Troch. p. 55 [6]; Scl. & Salv. P. Z. S. 1864, p. 365 [7]; Salv. P. Z. S. 1867, p. 153 [8]; 1870, p. 205 [9]; Cat. Birds Brit. Mus. xvi. p. 299 [10]; Lawr. Ann. Lyc. N. Y. ix. p. 121 [11].

Supra nitenti-viridis: subtus obscurior, plumis omnibus griseo marginatis, abdomine griseo, subcaudalibus viridi-griseis albido marginatis; caudæ rectricibus mediis viridibus, lateralibus albo terminatis et fascia subterminali nigra notatis: rostro nigro, mandibulæ bitriente basali carnea. Long. tota circa 4·6, alæ 2·7, caudæ 1·7, rostri a rictu 1.

♀ mari similis. (Descr. maris et feminæ ex Lion Hill, Panama. Mus. nostr.)

Hab. Costa Rica, Punta Arenas (*O. S.* [10]), Mirabayes, Bebedero de Nicoya (*Arcé* [10]), Pozo Azul de Pirris (*Zeledon* [4][5]); Panama (*Delattre* [1]), David (*Bridges* [3]), Bugaba [9] (*Arcé*), Lion Hill (*O. S., M'Leannan* [4][7]), Paraiso (*Hughes* [10]).—Colombia? Venezuela?

This species was discovered by Delattre and described by him and Bourcier in 1846 from specimens said to have been shot on the Isthmus of Panama and at Teleman. If the latter place is the village of that name on the banks of the Polochic river in Guatemala, both *P. cuvieri* and *P. roberti* were included in Delattre's collection. The description undoubtedly refers to the Panama bird, as the colour of the base of the mandible is given as white, that of *P. roberti* being wholly black.

The range of this species, as given by Gould, extends to Colombia and Venezuela, but we have never seen specimens from any place south of the line of the Panama Railway. Northwards and westwards of this line it spreads over the rest of the State of Panama to Western Costa Rica, where it is not uncommon on the shores of the Gulf of Nicoya. In Nicaragua, and thence northwards to British Honduras, its place is taken by *P. roberti*.

2. **Phæochroa roberti.**

Aphantochroa roberti, Salv. P. Z. S. 1861, p. 203 [1]; Heine, J. f. Orn. 1863, p. 178 [2].

Campylopterus roberti, Gould, Mon. Troch. ii. t. 53 (Sept. 1861) [3].

Phæochroa roberti, Gould, Intr. Troch. p. 55 [4]; Nutting, Pr. U. S. Nat. Mus. vi. p. 406 [5]; Salv. Cat. Birds Brit. Mus. xvi. p. 300 [6].

Trochilus cuvieri? (partim), Delattre & Bourc. Rev. Zool. 1846, p. 310 [7].

P. cuvieri similis, sed fascia caudæ subterminali chalybeo-nigra multo latiore, mandibula omnino nigra quoque differt. (Descr. maris exempl. typ. ex Choctum, Guatemala. Mus. nostr.)

Hab. BRITISH HONDURAS, San Felipe, western district, Cayo and Belize river (*F. Blancaneaux* [6]); GUATEMALA, Choctum (*R. Owen* [13], *O. S. & F. D. G.* [6]), Cautoöloc (*O. S. & F. D. G.*), Teleman? (*Delattre* [7]); HONDURAS, Santa Ana (*Wittkugel, in U. S. Nat. Mus.*); NICARAGUA, Los Sabalos (*Nutting* [5]).

Mr. Robert Owen, who was formerly interested in the estate of San Gerónimo in Vera Paz, and where he resided for some time, procured us the first specimen of this species from Choctum. It was described by Salvin in 1861, and figured by Gould the same year. In 1862, during a visit to the low-lying forest-region of Northern Vera Paz in the month of February, we obtained several specimens and saw others frequenting openings in the forest, such as the banks of a stream or a clearing. Mr. Blancaneaux also met with it at various places on the upper portion of the Belize river. Southwards of Guatemala we have no personal knowledge of its existence, but Mr. Ridgway informs us that two specimens are in the United States National Museum obtained at Santa Ana by Herr Wittkugel, and Mr. Nutting includes it in his list of birds from Los Sabalos in Nicaragua. In Costa Rica, at least on the western side, its place is taken by *P. cuvieri*.

e". *Rostrum variabile sed nunquam valde arcuatum; tegulæ nasales et spatio inter mandibulæ ramos magis plumatæ; remigum rhachides normales; ptilosis hic illic coloribus micantibus ornata.*

e"'. *Rostrum elongatum, rectum; cauda uniformis sensim furcata; macula postoculari alba.*

EUGENES.

Eugenes, Gould, Mon. Troch. ii. t. 59 (Sept. 1856); Salv. Cat. Birds Brit. Mus. xvi. p. 302.

Two closely allied beautiful species constitute this genus, which is a peculiarly Central-American one, spread over the highlands from Sonora and beyond the frontier of Southern Arizona in the north to Costa Rica in the south.

E. fulgens, which has by far the more extended range, keeps strictly to the high grounds of Mexico, Guatemala, Honduras, and Nicaragua, *E. spectabilis* taking its place in Costa Rica.

The long bill, the brilliant colours of the head and throat, the slightly forked uniform tail, are characteristic features of *Eugenes*, distinguishing it from *Sternoclyta* and *Urochroa*, its nearest allies.

1. Eugenes fulgens.

Trochilus fulgens, Sw. Phil. Mag. new ser. i. p. 441 [1].

Eugenes fulgens, Gould, Mon. Troch. ii. t. 59 [2]; Moore, P.Z. S. 1859, p. 53 [3]; Scl. &   b
    1859, p. 128 [4]; Salv. Ibis, 1860, pp. 261 [5], 263 [6]; Cat. Birds Brit. Mus. xvi. p. 302 [7]; Scl.
    P. Z. S. 1864, p. 176 [8]; Boucard, Ann. Soc. Linn. Lyon, xx. p. 273 [9]; Dugès, La Nat. i.
    p. 141 [10]; Henshaw, in Wheeler's Geogr. & Geol. Surv., Zool. v. p. 379 [11]; Villada, La Nat.
    ii. p. 349, t. i. fig. 5 [12]; de Oca, La Nat. iii. p. 164 [13]; Sumichrast, La Nat. v. p. 250 [14];
    Ferrari-Perez, Pr. U. S. Nat. Mus. ix. p. 157 [15]; Herrera, La Nat. (2) i. p. 322 [16].

Cœligena fulgens, Scl. P. Z. S. 1856, p. 287 [17]; 1858, p. 297 [18]; 1859, pp. 367 [19], 386 [20].

Ornismya rivolii, Less. Hist. Nat. Ois.-Mouches, pp. xxvi, 48, t. 4 [21].

Ornismya clemenciæ ♀, Less. Suppl. Ois.-Mouches, p. 115, t. 8 [22].

Trochilus melanogaster, Licht. in Mus. Ber., fide Cab. & Heine, Mus. Hein. iii. p. 20 [23].

Eugenes viridiceps, Boucard, Ann. Soc. Linn. Lyon, (2) xxv. p. 55 (1878) [24].

Supra saturate cupreo-viridis, nitidus, cervice postica et dorso antico nigris a fronte adspectis; capite summo
    læte micanti-violaceo: subtus gula micanti-viridi, pectore et abdomine medio nigris a fronte, viridibus a
    tergo adspectis, abdomine imo griseo, tectricibus subcaudalibus pallide viridibus griseo late marginatis;
    cauda cupreo-viridi: rostro nigro.   Long. tota circa 5·5, alæ 3·0, caudæ rectr. lat. 1·85, rectr. med. 1·5,
    rostri a rictu 1·4.

♀ supra saturate gramineo-viridis, nitida; capite summo fuscescente: subtus grisea, gula plumis medialiter
    fuscis, hypochondriis viridi lavatis; caudæ rectricibus lateralibus griseo-albo terminatis et fascia lata
    subterminali chalybeo-nigra ornatis. (Descr. maris et feminæ ex Volcan de Fuego, Guatemala.   Mus.
    nostr.)

Hab. NORTH AMERICA, Arizona [11].—MEXICO, Sierra de San Luis Potosi, Sierra de Val-
    paraiso, Sierra de Nayarit, Sierra de Bolaños (*W. B. Richardson* [7]), Guanajuato
    (*Dugès* [10]), Temiscaltepec (*Bullock* [1]), Valley of Mexico (*White* [8], *Herrera* [16]), Chi-
    malpa, Hacienda Eslava in the Valley of Mexico (*F. Ferrari-Perez* [7]), Ajusco Valley of
    Mexico (*W. B. Richardson* [7]), Rio Frio, Ixtaccihuatl (*W. B. R.* [7]), Puebla (*F. Ferrari-*
    Perez [15]), La Parada (*Boucard* [9]), Alpine region of Orizaba (*Sumichrast* [14]), Las Vigas
    (*Ferrari-Perez*), Jalapa (*de Oca* [13] [19], *Ferrari-Perez* [15], *M. Trujillo* [7]), Coatepec (*de*
    Oca [13]), Mirador (*Sartorius, in U. S. Nat. Mus.*), Cordova (*Sallé* [17]), Totontepec
    (*Boucard* [20]), Sierra Nevada de Colima (*W. B. Richardson*), Omilteme and Xucu-
    manatlan in Guerrero (*Mrs. H. H. Smith* [7]), Tonaguia (*M. Trujillo* [7]), Oaxaca
    (*Fenochio* [7]); GUATEMALA (*Skinner* [4]), El Rincon in San Marcos, Santa Maria, San
    Martin, Chuipaché in Quezaltenango (*W. B. Richardson* [7]), Volcan de Fuego [5],
    Dueñas [5], Mountains of Chilasco, Tactic [5], Coban [5] (*O. S. & F. D. G.* [7]); NICARAGUA,
    San Rafael del Norte (*W. B. Richardson*).

This well-known species of the Mexican highlands crosses the northern political
boundary of Mexico and enters Southern Arizona.   Thence it spreads southwards over
the sierras of North-western Mexico and over the tableland, including the valley and
the higher parts of the States of Vera Cruz, Colima, Guerrero, and Oaxaca.   In Guatemala it is only found in the mountainous portions at an elevation of from 4000 to 8000
feet.   Near Dueñas, where the ravines of the Volcan de Fuego open out into the plain,

this species is found in great abundance at certain seasons, feeding from the flowers of the tree-convolvulus (*Ipomœa murucoides*), and flying on cloudy misty afternoons, the males fighting incessantly with one another and with every other species of Humming-Bird frequenting the same place. The females do not join in the same company, and therefore are, or appear to be, much rarer than the males.

The southern limit of this species is Southern Nicaragua, whence we have recently received two specimens from Mr. Richardson, who shot them at San Rafael del Norte in March and April 1892.

In Mexico, in the neighbourhood of Jalapa and Coatepec, de Oca says [13] that this species is found in spring and summer, but is more common in autumn, feeding from the flowers of *Centaurea benedicta*. He also says that it is found in the Valley of Mexico, a statement confirmed by many other observers, but that he never found its nest. Villada tells us [12] that *E. fulgens* is one of the first Humming-Birds to arrive in spring, appearing in March when the species of *Cereus* are in flower, and frequenting other *Cacti* as well as *Agave*. Later in the year it seeks *Lobelia laxiflora* and *Erythrina corallodendron*. In the month of June, when these plants have finished flowering, it retires to the neighbouring hills where *Bouvadia* abounds; in August and September it returns to the plains when *Salvia patens* and *S. fulgens* bloom, and at the commencement of autumn it retires to the south-eastward not to return till the following spring. M. Boucard says [9] that it is very common in Mexico in June and July and equally abundant at La Parada, where he resided for a long time. He obtained many specimens when they were feeding from the flowers of *Carduaceœ* which grew in his garden.

The species was first discovered by Bullock in Mexico, and his specimens were described by Swainson in 1827 [1]. A few years afterwards Lesson redescribed and figured the bird as *O. rivolii* [21]. Lichtenstein's uncharacterized name *Trochilus melanogaster* [23] was probably based on birds sent to the Berlin Museum by Deppe. Lesson figured and described a female of this species as a female of *Cœligena clemenciœ* [22].

M. Boucard has very kindly lent us his type of *Eugenes viridiceps* which he described in 1878 from a single specimen found in a collection of bird-skins made near Coban in Vera Paz [24].

The specimen is a very curious one, and may be, we think, an immature male. The upper surface resembles that of *Eugenes fulgens*, except that the crown is partially covered with glittering olive-green feathers, which in a young *E. fulgens* would be rich violet-blue. The under surface is sordid grey, darker on the flanks, which are also washed with golden green. The feathers of the throat are shaped like those of the male *E. fulgens*, that is to say, they are squamose with rounded ends; but the glittering colour is entirely gone, except in the case of a few on the left side, and these are glittering green. The tail is peculiar, and differs from that of the female *Eugenes fulgens* in having wider white tips to the lateral rectrices, the bases of which are pale green, a male character. The bill is rather longer than the average in *E. fulgens*. As the glittering feathers of the crown are not quite uniform in colour, some being bluer than others, and as the bright colour has disappeared from the feathers of the throat, we are on the whole inclined to think that this bird is a specimen of *Eugenes fulgens* in an abnormal state of plumage, due probably to disease.   This view is further strengthened by the fact that it came from a country where birds have for many years been collected in tens of thousands, and no other has, so far as we know, been found like it.   At the same time, in placing it under *Eugenes fulgens*, we must state that we shall welcome further evidence, in the form of additional specimens in more perfect plumage, which will prove *Eugenes viridiceps* to be a valid species.

2. Eugenes spectabilis.

Heliomaster spectabilis, Lawr. Ann. Lyc. N. Y. viii. p. 472 [1]; Salv. Ibis, 1868, p. 251 [2].

Eugenes spectabilis, Salv. Ibis, 1869, p. 316 [3]; Cat. Birds Brit. Mus. xvi. p. 304 [4]; Lawr. Ann. Lyc. N. Y. ix. p. 121 [5]; x. p. 140 [6]; v. Frantz. J. f. Orn. 1869, p. 315 [7]; Boucard, P. Z. S. 1878, p. 68 [8]; Sharpe, in Gould's Mon. Troch., Suppl. t. 13 (April 1885) [9]; Zeledon, An. Mus. Nac. Costa Rica, 1887, p. 121 [10].

E. fulgenti similis, sed pectore nitenti-viridi nec nigro; rectricibus lateralibus ad apicem obscurioribus; cauda minus profunde furcata distinguendus. (Descr. maris ex Irazu, Costa Rica. Mus. nostr.)

Hab. COSTA RICA (*A. C. Garcia* [1], *Endres* [4]), Rancho Redondo (*Carmiol* [5], *Zeledon*), Volcan de Irazu (*Arcé* [3], *Boucard* [8], *Rogers* [4], *Zeledon* [10]).

Mr. Lawrence's original description of this species was based upon a female which he assigned to the genus *Heliomaster* [1]; but Gould on seeing the type considered it a *Eugenes*, in which opinion he was undoubtedly right [2].   Salvin for some time hesitated to admit the distinctness of *E. spectabilis* from *E. fulgens*, being guided by an immature male sent by Arcé from the Volcan de Irazu.   Now that adult males have been received, there can be no doubt that the two birds, though closely allied, are really separated by fairly definite characters.

E. spectabilis, like *E. fulgens*, doubtless frequents mountainous districts of considerable elevation, being found, according to M. Boucard, at an altitude ranging between 6000 and 8000 feet above sea-level on the Volcan de Irazu, where it resorts to a parasitic plant resembling a mistletoe which bears a red flower [8].   Its range seems to be very limited and confined to the mountains of Costa Rica.

f'''. *Rostrum breve; stria postocularis alba.*

c⁴. *Rostrum modice curvatum; cauda rectricibus lateralibus albo terminatis.*

CŒLIGENA.

Cæligena, Lesson, Ind. gén. Troch. p. xviii; Salv. Cat. Birds Brit. Mus. xvi. p. 304.

The single species belonging to this genus, though closely allied to *Delattria*, which has as often as not been placed in it, is nevertheless a somewhat peculiar bird.   The bill is slightly more curved than in the genera which follow, and none of them have the wide terminal white spots to the outer rectrices. The range of the only species is given below, and includes the highlands of Mexico from Arizona to Oaxaca.

1. Cœligena clemenciæ.

Ornismya clemenciæ, Less. Hist. Nat. Ois.-Mouches, pp. xlv, 216, t. 80 [1].

Delattria clemenciæ, Gould, Mon. Troch. ii. t. 60 (May 1855) [2]; Scl. P. Z. S. 1858, p. 297 [3]; 1859, p. 367 [4]; de Oca, La Nat. iii. p. 100 [5].

Cœligena clemenciæ, Cab. & Heine, Mus. Hein. iii. p. 15 [6]; Boucard, Ann. Soc. Linn. Lyon, xx. p. 274 [7]; Dugès, La Nat. i. p. 141 [8]; Villada, La Nat. ii. p. 350 [9]; Sumichrast, La Nat. v. p. 250 [10]; Brewster, Auk, ii. p. 85 [11]; Herrera, La Nat. (2) i. p. 322 [12]; Salv. Cat. Birds Brit. Mus. xvi. p. 304 [13].

Supra nitenti-cupreo-viridis, dorso viridescentiore, uropygio saturatiore cupreo in purpurascentem transeunte, alis et cauda ejusdem coloris; capite summo obscuro, stria postoculari elongata alba; tectricibus auricularibus obscuris: subtus grisea, gutture micanti-cæruleo, hypochoudriis viridi lavatis, tectricibus subcaudalibus albo marginatis; caudæ rectricibus lateralibus duabus utrinque late albo terminatis: rostro nigro. Long. tota circa 5·3, alæ 3·1, caudæ 2·0, rostri a rictu 1·5.

♀ mari similis, sed corpore toto subtus griseo, gula haud cærulea. (Descr. maris et feminæ ex Amecameca, Mexico. Mus. nostr.)

Hab. NORTH AMERICA, Arizona [11].—MEXICO [1] [6], Ciudad in Durango (*A. Forrer* [13]), Guanajuato (*Dugès* [8]), Sierra de Valparaiso, Sierra de San Luis Potosi (*W. B. Richardson* [13]), Las Vigas (*F. Ferrari-Perez* [13]), Jalapa [4], Coatepec (*de Oca* [5]), Cordova (*Sallé, de Oca* [5]), Mirador (*Sartorius, in U. S. Nat. Mus.*), Orizaba (*Sumichrast* [10]), Valley of Mexico (*de Oca* [5], *Herrera* [12]), Tetelco, Ixtapalapa, Hacienda Eslava in the Valley of Mexico (*F. Ferrari-Perez*), Ajusco (*W. B. Richardson* [13]), Amecameca (*F. D. G.* [13]), Rio Frio Ixtaccihuatl (*W. B. Richardson* [13]), Tehuacan (*Boucard* [7]), Omilteme in Guerrero (*Mrs. H. H. Smith* [13]), Oaxaca (*Boucard* [3] [7], *Fenochio* [13]), La Parada (*Boucard* [7]).

Lesson described and figured this species from a male specimen in the Rivoli collection from Mexico. The same author's subsequent description and figure of the female belong not to this species but to *Eugenes fulgens*.

C. clemenciæ is now known to occur over a considerable area in the mountains of Southern Mexico, and as far north as the Sierra of San Luis Potosi and the Sierra Madre of Durango, and even beyond the Mexican frontier in Arizona, where Mr. F. Stephens obtained an adult male at Camp Lowell in May 1884 [11]. De Oca says [5] it is found in the neighbourhood of Jalapa, Coatepec, and Cordova in the State of Vera Cruz, but more rarely in the Valley of Mexico, where it stays from spring till the end of autumn. At Oaxaca, according to M. Boucard [7], it arrives in September, but leaves again early in November. He adds that it is a bird of the mountains, and, like *Eugenes fulgens*, capable of resisting a considerable amount of cold.

This species has no very near ally; the colour of the throat is peculiar, and so also are the white tips to the lateral rectrices. The elongated white postocular stripe it has in common with the members of *Delattria* and *Oreopyra*.

42*

d[4]. *Rostrum fere rectum ; cauda fere uniformis.*

a[5]. *Cauda rotundata ; gula nunquam micanti-rosaceo-rubra.*

a[6]. *Pileus micans.*

OREOPYRA.

Oreopyra, Gould, P. Z. S. 1860, p. 312 ; Salv. Cat. Birds Brit. Mus. xvi. p. 305.

The four species included in this genus all belong to the highlands of Costa Rica and the western mountains of the State of Panama adjoining.   In these countries they nearly take the place of *Delattria,* most of the species of which are found further north.

From *Delattria, Oreopyra* differs in having the sexes widely distinct in coloration, and in having the top of the head of the males glittering in contrast to, instead of in uniformity with, the back.   The tail in both genera is nearly uniform, the females only exhibiting pale tips to the outer rectrices.

1. Oreopyra leucaspis.

Trochilus (——?) *castaneoventris,* Gould, P. Z. S. 1850, p. 163 [1].

Adelomyia? castaneiventris, Gould, Mon. Troch. iii. t. 203 (Sept. 1855) [2].

Oreopyra leucaspis, Gould, P. Z. S. 1860, p. 312 [3]; Mon. Troch. iv. t. 264 (May 1861) [4]; Salv.
    P. Z. S. 1867, p. 153 [5]; 1870, p. 205 [6]; Cat. Birds Brit. Mus. xvi. p. 306 [7]; Lawr. Ann. Lyc.
    N. Y. ix. p. 125 [8].

Oreopyra castaneiventris, Salv. P. Z. S. 1867, p. 153 [9]; Ibis, 1869, p. 316 [10].

Supra saturate gramineo-viridis, nitens, dorso medio cupreo tincto, capite summo micanti-cæruleo-viridi ; loris
    et tectricibus auricularibus nigricanti-viridibus, stria postoculari elongata et gula niveis, hujus lateribus et
    pectore nitide viridibus, abdomine medio cinereo, lateribus et tectricibus subcaudalibus viridi lavatis his
    quoque albo limbatis ; cauda chalybeo-nigra : rostro nigro.   Long. tota circa 4·0, alæ 2·5, caudæ 1·4, rostri
    a rictu 0·95.

♀ supra viridis, nitens ; capite summo nitentiore : subtus cinnamomea ; cauda viridi, tectricibus externis griseo-
    albo terminatis et fascia subterminali nigra notatis.   (Descr. maris et feminæ ex Chiriqui, Panama.
    Mus. nostr.)

Hab. PANAMA, Cordillera de Chiriqui (*Warszewiez* [1] [3]), Volcan de Chiriqui (*Arcé* [6]).

Warszewiez was the discoverer of this species during his visit to the Cordillera of Chiriqui, where he obtained five specimens—a male and four females.   The latter were described by Gould in 1850 as *Trochilus* (?) *castaneoventris* [1], and subsequently figured in his 'Monograph of the Trochilidæ' as *Adelomyia? castaneiventris* [2].   The male was not characterized until 1860, when Gould placed it in a separate genus as *Oreopyra leucaspis* [3].   The real relationship between these birds was not suspected until we received a large series of skins from our collector Arcé, and the point was discussed by Salvin in 1870 [6].   In point of priority *A. castaneiventris* is several years older than *O. leucaspis*; but as the former name was founded on female specimens, and as all the birds of this sex are exceedingly alike in the species of *Oreopyra*, the latter name based upon the male had better be used.

Though *O. leucaspis* has a very restricted range, confined to the Volcano of Chiriqui and the higher hills in its vicinity, it appears to be a very common bird in its own home. Arcé sent us a large series of skins including fully adult birds and young in all stages of advancing maturity. It appears from the latter that the young males are not like the females in their first plumage, but resemble the older birds, the white throat and glittering head being assumed gradually. In some birds purple feathers appear at the edge of the white throat and even in the middle of it, and thus show the close relationship *O. leucaspis* bears to *O. calolæma*, in which the whole throat is reddish purple.

2. Oreopyra cinereicauda.

Oreopyra cinereicauda, Lawr. Ann. Lyc. N. Y. viii. p. 485[1]; ix. p. 125[2]; Boucard, P. Z. S. 1878, p. 68[3]; Muls. Hist. Nat. Ois.-Mouches, iv. p. 163, t. 116[4]; Sharpe in Gould's Mon. Troch., -Suppl. t. 7 (April 1885)[5]; Salv. Cat. Birds Brit. Mus. xvi. p. 307[6].

O. leucaspi similis, sed rostro forsan longiore, capite summo cæruleo tincto et cauda grisea ad apicem obscuriore nec chalybeo-nigro distinguenda. (Descr. maris ex Costa Rica. Mus. nostr.)

Hab. COSTA RICA (*Garcia*[1][2], *Carmiol*[6]), Navarro (*Boucard*[3]).

This species was described by Mr. Lawrence from a specimen sent him from Costa Rica by Mr. A. C. Garcia[1], but the exact place where it was procured was not recorded. All the specimens we have received are in the same condition, and the only precise recorded locality where the species occurs is Navarro, where M. Boucard obtained a single specimen in May[3]. Judging from what we find in *O. leucaspis*, *O. cinereicauda* is probably restricted to the forests of some of the higher mountains of Costa Rica in the vicinity of San José, the capital.

As a species *O. cinereicauda* is quite distinct from *O. leucaspis*, though the two birds resemble each other in many respects. The females are probably not separable with certainty, and that sex of *O. calolæma* is almost exactly similar. The bird we believe to be a female of *O. cinereicauda* has a longer bill than the others, and we place it under this name on that account.

3. Oreopyra calolæma. (Tab. LIV. figg. 1, ♂; 2, ♀.)

Oreopyra calolæma, Salv. P. Z. S. 1864, p. 584[1]; 1867, p. 153[2]; 1870, pp. 205[3], 206[4]; Cat. Birds Brit. Mus. xvi. p. 307[5]; Salvad. Atti R. Acc. Tor. iv. p. 183[6]; Lawr. Ann. Lyc. N. Y. ix. p. 125[7]; v. Frantz. J. f. Orn. 1869, p. 316[8]; Boucard, P. Z. S. 1878, p. 69[9]; Nutting, Pr. U. S. Nat. Mus. v. p. 500[10]; Sharpe, in Gould's Mon. Troch., Suppl. t. 6 (April 1885)[11].

Oreopyra venusta, Lawr. Ann. Lyc. N. Y. viii. p. 484[12].

Anthocephala castaneiventris, Lawr. Ann. Lyc. N. Y. ix. p. 124[13]; v. Frantz. J. f. Orn. 1869, p. 316[14].

Supra saturate gramineo-viridis, nitens, uropygio obscuriore; capite summo cæruleo-viridi micante, stria post-oculari alba, loris et tectricibus auricularibus viridi-nigris; gula nitenti-rufo-purpurea, lateribus suis et pectore micanti-viridibus, abdomine medio cinereo, hypochondriis viridi lavatis, tectricibus subcaudalibus fuscis viridi tinctis et albo marginatis; cauda chalybeo-nigra: rostro nigro.   Long. tota circa 4·0, alæ 2·5, caudæ 1·45, rostri a rictu 1·0.

♀ supra mari similis, sed dilutior; capite summo dorso concolore: subtus cinnamomea; cauda ad basin viridi, rectricibus lateralibus albido terminatis, fascia lata subterminali chalybeo-nigra.   (Descr. maris et feminæ ex V. de Cartago, Costa Rica.   Mus. nostr.)

Hab. Costa Rica, Volcan de Cartago (*Arcé* [1]), Rancho Redondo [7] [8] [14], San José, Dota (*v. Frantzius, Carmiol, Boucard* [9]), La Palma (*Nutting* [10]), Peorsnada, Las Cruces de Candelaria [7] [8] (*v. Frantzius, Zeledon*), Naranjo (*Boucard* [9]); Panama, Volcan de Chiriqui [3], Cordillera de Tolé [2], Cordillera del Chucu [3], Calovevora [3], Calobre [5] (*Arcé*).

Eastern Costa Rica and thence southwards to the higher mountains of Western Panama are the homes of this species, which was discovered by Arcé on the slopes of the Volcan de Cartago [1].   The same collector subsequently obtained us a good series of specimens from various points in the mountains of Western Panama.   According to M. Boucard this species is only met with in the forest [9].

4. Oreopyra pectoralis.

Oreopyra pectoralis, Salv. Ann. & Mag. N. H. 1891, vii. p. 377 [1]; Cat. Birds Brit. Mus. xvi. pp. 308, 664 [2].

O. calolæmæ similis, sed pectore (a fronte adspecto) nigro nec micanti-viridi distinguenda.   (Descr. exempl. typ. ex Costa Rica.   Mus. nostr.)

Hab. Costa Rica (*Endres* [1] [2]).

A single male in our collection and others in that of Gould, all apparently prepared by Endres, are all that we have seen of this species, which differs from the ordinary form in having a black instead of a glittering green breast.   Though the types are marked as coming from Costa Rica, we have as yet no clue to which district the species belongs.

The female of this bird is probably undistinguishable from that sex of *O. calolæma*. The female specimens we associate with the males of *O. pectoralis* are made up by the same collector in a precisely similar way.

b[6]. *Pileus dorsum concolor.*

DELATTRIA.

Delattria, Bonaparte, Consp. Av. i. p. 70; Salv. Cat. Birds Brit. Mus. xvi. p. 308.

This genus, which was first separated by Bonaparte, has frequently been united to *Cœligena*, with which it has several characters in common, but the bill is straighter and the lateral rectrices are of nearly uniform colour, and without the conspicuous white tips which distinguish *Cœligena clemenciæ*.   *Delattria* has also a close affinity to *Oreopyra*, but the style of coloration is different and none of the species have the glittering crown possessed by all the members of the latter genus.

With the exception of the somewhat abnormal Costa Rican *D. hemileuca*, all the species of *Delattria* belong to the northern section of our region. Two occur in Mexico, one of which is also found in Guatemala, the latter country possesses a peculiar species, and the fourth occurs in the highlands of Nicaragua and probably of Honduras.

1. **Delattria henrici.**

Ornismya henrica, Less. & Delattre, Rev. Zool. 1839, p. 17[1].

Delattria henrici, Gould, Mon. Troch. ii. t. 62 (Oct. 1854)[2]; Scl. P. Z. S. 1858, p. 297[3]; 1859, pp. 367[4], 386[5]; Scl. & Salv. Ibis, 1859, p. 129[6]; Salv. Ibis, 1860, p. 196[7]; 1862, p. 96[8]; Cat. Birds Brit. Mus. xvi. p. 308[9]; Villada, La Nat. ii. p. 351[10]; Herrera, La Nat. (2) i. p. 322[11].

Cœligena henrici, Cab. & Heine, Mus. Hein. iii. p. 15[12]; Boucard, Ann. Soc. Linn. Lyon, xx. p. 275[13]; Ferrari-Perez, Pr. U. S. Nat. Mus. ix. p. 157[14].

Supra saturate cupreo-viridis, uropygio brunnescente, tectricibus supracaudalibus longioribus sicut rectricibus purpureo-nigris; capite summo fusco nigricante, plumis singulis viridi limbatis; stria postoculari elongata alba, stria rictali fulva: subtus gula rosaceo-rubra, corpore reliquo griseo-brunneo, hypochondriis viridi lavatis, tectricibus subcaudalibus abdomine concoloribus albido marginatis, rectricibus lateralibus ad apicem pallidis: rostro nigro. Long. tota circa 4·5, alæ 2·6, caudæ 1·6, rostri a rictu 1·0.

♀ supra mari similis, subtus pallidior, pectore rufescente, gula rosacea nulla, rectricibus lateralibus griseo-albido terminatis. (Descr. maris et feminæ ex Calderas, Volcan de Fuego, Guatemala. Mus. nostr.)

Hab. MEXICO, Valley of Mexico (*Le Strange* [9], *Herrera* [11]), Hacienda Eslava (*F. Ferrari-Perez* [9]), Jalapa (*de Oca* [4], *F. Ferrari-Perez* [14]), Coatepec (*Delattre* [1], *M. Trujillo* [9]), Cordova (*F. Ferrari-Perez* [14], *Boucard* [13]), Mountains of Orizaba (*F. Ferrari-Perez* [9]), Playa Vicente (*Boucard* [13]), Sierra Nevada de Colima (*W. B. Richardson* [9]), Totontepec (*Boucard* [3][5]); GUATEMALA (*Skinner* [6]), El Rincon in San Marcos, Cuipaché, San Martin, and Quezaltenango (*W. B. R.* [9]), Totonicapam [9], Volcan de Fuego and Calderas on V. de Fuego [8] (*O. S. & F. D. G.*).

Delattria henrici was one of Delattre's discoveries during his journey to Mexico, and was described by himself and Lesson in 1839, and named after Henri Delattre, the brother of the traveller [1]. The species appears to be fairly common in the forests of the slopes of the mountains of Vera Cruz, thence it passes inland to the Valley of Mexico, where, however, it is a comparatively rare bird, and across the country to the Sierra Nevada de Colima, where Mr. Richardson secured a male specimen in December 1889. This bird is not old, and is paler grey beneath than birds from Eastern Mexico; but a specimen from Cuipaché, in Quezaltenango, is similar, so that there can be little doubt that the Colima bird is really the same as that of the Valley of Mexico. Totontepec is the most southern place in Mexico where *D. henrici* is found [5], but it occurs in many parts of the main mountain-range of Guatemala in the upland forests as high as 10,000 feet above sea-level. Guatemalan specimens, of which we have a large series, are exactly like those of Eastern Mexico.

On the ridge above Calderas (8000 feet) this bird was abundant in September, the flowers of an arborescent *Fuchsia* being the chief attraction.

2. **Delattria margarethæ.**   (Tab. LIV. A. figg. 1, ♂ ; 2, ♀ .)

Delattria margarethæ, Salv. & Godm. Ibis, 1889, p. 239[1] ; Salv. Cat. Birds Brit. Mus. xvi. p. 310[2].

D. henrici similis, sed gula violacea nec rosaceo-rubra facile distinguenda.

♀ feminæ *D. henrici* omnino similis.   (Descr. maris et feminæ exempl. typ. ex Omilteme, Guerrero, Mexico. Mus. nostr.)

Hab. MEXICO, Omilteme in the Sierra Madre del Sur, Guerrero, Mexico (*Mrs. H. H. Smith* [1] [2]).

The males of a series of specimens obtained by Mrs. Herbert Smith at Omilteme, in the high mountain-range called the Sierra Madre del Sur, all agree in having the throat violet instead of rosy red as in the well-known *D. henrici.*   For this reason we separated this form under the name it now bears, calling the species after its energetic discoverer.

Omilteme is a small hamlet situated at an elevation of about 8000 feet above the sea, where Mr. and Mrs. Smith spent the months of July and August 1888.

3. **Delattria viridipallens.**

Trochilus viridipallens, Bourc. & Muls. Ann. Sc. Phys. et Nat. Lyon, ix. p. 321[1].

Delattria viridipallens, Gould, Mon. Troch. ii. t. 63 (May 1855)[2] ; Scl. & Salv. Ibis, 1859, p. 129[3] ; Salv. Ibis, 1859, p. 468[4] ; 1860, pp. 40[5], 195[6], 263[7] ; Cat. Birds Brit. Mus. xvi. pp. 310[8], 664[9].

Supra cupreo-viridis, pileo viridescentiore, uropygio magis cupreo, tectricibus supracaudalibus longioribus sicut rectricibus mediis purpureo-nigris, rectricibus lateralibus grisescentioribus ; stria postoculari elongata alba, tectricibus auricularibus viridi-nigris : subtus alba, plumis gulæ singulis macula discali micanti-viridi, hypochondriis viridi lavatis, tectricibus subcaudalibus fuscis albido marginatis : rostro nigro. Long. tota circa 4·4, alæ 2·7, caudæ 1·65, rostri a rictu 0·9.

♀ mari similis, maculis gulæ viridibus absentibus, rectricibus lateralibus albido terminatis.   (Descr. maris et feminæ ex Volcan de Fuego, Guatemala.   Mus. nostr.)

Hab. GUATEMALA (*Skinner* [3]), Coban [1] [8] (*Delattre*), Chilasco [8], Volcan de Fuego [8] (*O. S. & F. D. G.*), Pie de la Cuesta in San Marcos, Santa Maria near Quezaltenango, Toliman (*W. B. Richardson* [8] [9]).

This pretty species, distinguished by the delicate green colour of the throat, was described from specimens obtained at Coban in Vera Paz, where numerous specimens were subsequently secured by Skinner's collectors and by ourselves.

Most of our examples were, however, shot in the upland forests of the Volcan de Fuego, where the bird is common up to an elevation of about 7000 to 8000 feet.   It frequents the same woods as *Petasophora thalassina,* never leaving the oak-forests, and is not found with *Eugenes fulgens* and other species in the more open plains.   It probably occurs in all suitable places over the highlands of Guatemala, as we also met with it in the higher mountains of Vera Paz, and Mr. Richardson has sent us a series of specimens from the Altos of Guatemala, close to the frontier of the Mexican State of Chiapas.   In Northern Nicaragua its place is taken by the next species.

4. Delattria sybillæ. (Tab. LIV. A. figg. 3, ♂ ; 4, ♀.)

Delattria sybillæ, Salv. & Godm. Ibis, 1892, p. 327 [1]; Salv. Cat. Birds Brit. Mus. xvi. p. 664 [2].

D. viridipallenti proxime affinis, sed pectore et hypochondriis viridibus gula concoloribus, dorso imo vix cupreo tincto, rectricibus lateralibus griseis facile distinguenda : rostro nigro. Long. tota circa 4·5, alæ 2·6, caudæ rectr. med. 1·3, rectr. lat. 1·7, rostri a rictu 0·95. (Descr. maris exempl. typ. ex Matagalpa, Nicaragua. Mus. nostr.)

♀ supra mari similis, subtus alba, gula leviter cervino tincta, cervicis lateribus et hypochondriis viridi punctatis, rectricibus lateralibus griseo-albis fascia angusta indistincta subapicali fusca notatis. (Descr. feminæ ex San Rafael del Norte, Nicaragua. Mus. nostr.)

Hab. NICARAGUA, Matagalpa [1] [2], San Rafael del Norte (*W. B. Richardson*).

Of this distinct species Mr. Richardson sent us in the first instance six adult males from Matagalpa, which place he visited in August 1891. During a second expedition to the same district in April and May of the following year he obtained examples of the young male and females at San Rafael del Norte, a place a short distance to the north-westward of Matagalpa, and nearer the Honduras frontier.

Though clearly allied to *D. viridipallens*, this species has several points of distinction. In the former bird the throat alone has green discal spots, whilst in *D. sybillæ* the green colour overspreads the whole under surface, leaving only the middle of the abdomen white. The tail, too, has the outer rectrices greyish white, the shafts alone being dark.

5. Delattria hemileuca. (Tab. LIV. figg. 3, ♂ ; 4, ♀.)

Oreopyra hemileuca, Salv. P. Z. S. 1864, p. 584 [1]; Lawr. Ann. Lyc. N. Y. ix. p. 125 [2]; v. Frantz. J. f. Orn. 1869, p. 316 [3]; Muls. Hist. Nat. Ois.-Mouches, iv. p. 167, t. 118 [4]; Boucard, P. Z. S. 1878, p. 69 [5].

Cœligena hemileuca, Elliot, Syn. Troch. p. 31 [6]; Sharpe, in Gould's Mon. Troch., Suppl. t. 5 (April 1885) [7]; Zeledon, An. Mus. Nac. Costa Rica, 1887, p. 121 [8].

Delattria hemileuca, Salv. Cat. Birds Brit. Mus. xvi. p. 311 [9].

Supra nitenti-viridis, capite summo et genis vix lætioribus, rectricibus mediis cupreo tinctis ; stria postoculari elongata alba : subtus alba, gula media læte micanti-violacea, lateribus micanti-viridibus, hypochondriis viridi lavatis, tectricibus subcaudalibus albis medialiter pallide fuscis ; rectricibus lateralibus griseo-viridibus, fascia subterminali obscura, apicibus pallidioribus : rostro nigro. Long. tota 4·0, alæ 2·4, caudæ 1·5, rostri a rictu 0·9.

♀ supra mari similis, capite summo dorso fere concolore : subtus gulæ plumis medialiter viridibus, plaga violacea nulla, caudæ rectricum apicibus latiore pallidis. (Descr. maris et feminæ exempl. typ. ex Turrialba, Costa Rica. Mus. nostr.)

Hab. COSTA RICA (*Endres, Zeledon, Alfaro in U. S. Nat. Mus.*), Turrialba, Tucurriqui (*Arcé* [1]), Candelaria and Rancho Redondo (*v. Frantzius* [3]), Naranjo de Cartago (*Boucard* [5], *Zeledon* [8]).

Little is known of this well-marked species, the first specimens of which were sent us by our collector Enrique Arcé, by whom they were obtained on the slopes of Turrialba and near Tucurriqui, on the eastern side of the mountains of Costa Rica.

b[5]. *Cauda furcata ; gula micanti-rosaceo-rubra.*

LAMPROLÆMA.

Lamprolæma, Gould, Mon. Troch. ii. t. 61 (May 1856) ; Salv. Cat. Birds Brit. Mus. xvi. p. 314.

The coloration of *Lamprolæma rhami,* the only member of its genus, is quite peculiar; this and the tail being forked render its separation necessary, though in many other points of structure it comes near *Cœligena* and *Delattria.* The bill, however, is decidedly shorter than in any member of those genera.

The range of *Lamprolæma* is strictly confined to the higher mountains of Southern Mexico and Guatemala.

1. **Lamprolæma rhami.**

Ornismya rhami, Less. Rev. Zool. 1838, p. 315[1] ; Less. & Delattre, Rev. Zool. 1839, p. 13[2].

Lamprolæma rhami, Gould, Mon. Troch. ii. t. 61 (May 1856)[3] ; Scl. & Salv. Ibis, 1859, p. 129[4] ; Salv. Ibis, 1859, p. 468[5] ; 1860, p. 196[6] ; Cat. Birds Brit. Mus. xvi. p. 314[7] ; Cab. & Heine, Mus. Hein. iii. p. 30[8] ; Scl. P. Z. S. 1864, p. 176[9] ; de Oca, La Nat. iii. p. 25[10] ; Sumichrast, La Nat. v. p. 250[11] ; Boucard, Ann. Soc. Linn. Lyon, xx. p. 275[12].

Delattria rhami, Scl. P. Z. S. 1858, p. 297[13] ; 1859, p. 367[14].

Supra nitenti-gramineo-viridis, antice lætior postice obscurior ; alis castaneis, tectricibus majoribus et secundariis anguste primariis quoque late nigricante terminatis ; cauda saturate rubro-purpurea : subtus gula nigra, medialiter rosaceo-rubra micante ; pectore micanti-violaceo, abdomine fusco-nigricante, hypochondriis viridi lavatis, tectricibus subcaudalibus purpureo-nigris : rostro nigro. Long. tota circa 5·0, alæ 3·2, caudæ 2·0, rostri a rictu 0·8.

♀ supra mari similis, alis quoque eodem modo castaneo notatis : subtus griseo-brunnea, gula interdum plumis rosaceis irregulariter ornata, pectore et hypochondriis viridi lavatis. (Descr. maris et feminæ ex Calderas, Volcan de Fuego, Guatemala. Mus. nostr.)

Hab. MEXICO (*Delattre*[1][2]), Cofre de Perote (*M. Trujillo*[7]), Jalapa[7][12][14], Coatepec[7][10] (*de Oca, Boucard, Trujillo*), Cordova (*Sallé, de Oca*[10]), Orizaba (*de Oca*[10], *F. Ferrari-Perez*), Alpine region of Orizaba (*Sumichrast*[11]), Omilteme in Guerrero (*Mrs. H. H. Smith*[7]), Tonaguia and Totontepec (*M. Trujillo*[7]), La Parada (*Boucard*[12]), Oaxaca (*Boucard*[13], *Fenochio*[7]); GUATEMALA[8] (*Skinner*[4]), El Rincon in San Marcos, Santa Maria, and San Martin near Quezaltenango (*W. B. Richardson*[7]), Calderas on Volcan de Fuego[5][6][7], Volcan de Agua, Chilasco[7] (*O. S. & F. D. G.*), Cahabon? (*fide Gould*[7]).

This beautiful and very distinct species was discovered by Delattre in Mexico, and it is now known to have a wide range in the southern portion of that country, being found in the upland forests on both sides of the main mountain-range. Its name is included in Mr. White's list of the birds of the Valley of Mexico[9], but its presence there is not confirmed by subsequent writers. According to de Oca it is common on the slopes of the Cofre de Perote near Coatepec, and in the neighbourhood of Cordova and Orizaba, but he never found its nest. The same writer says that it appears in these districts in the months of June and July, and is supposed to migrate to Guatemala to breed. This, however, is not the case, as Trujillo obtained specimens on the Cofre de Perote in November, and at Tonaguia and Totontepec in February.

M. Boucard, who observed this species at La Parada and elsewhere, says that it feeds from the flowers of Bromeliaceæ.

In Guatemala *L. rhami* is a bird of the upland forests lying at an elevation of from 6000 to 10,000 feet above the sea-level. We found it to be tolerably abundant in September on the slopes of the Volcan de Fuego and the ridges adjoining, where the vegetation is dense, and in other similar places in the higher mountains of Guatemala. It flies amongst the undergrowth, and feeds from such trees and shrubs that happen to be in flower.

f″. Rostrum variabile, rectum aut modice curvatum ; tegulæ nasales omnino plumatæ ; remigum rhachides normales.

g‴. Rostrum robustum, rectum.

HELIODOXA.

Heliodoxa, Gould, P. Z. S. 1849, p. 95 ; Salv. Cat. Birds Brit. Mus. xvi. p. 317.

Heliodoxa is the only representative of a small group of genera distinguished by their straight strong bills, some of which, as in *Docimaster*, are extraordinarily lengthened. The nasal covers are completely feathered, the tail forked, and the tail-feathers normal in the present genus. The under surface, especially the throat, is glittering green.

This genus has a wide range in the Andes from Bolivia to Colombia and Venezuela, and occurs also in the highlands of Guiana. One species of Colombia also appears in the mountainous parts of Panama and Costa Rica, and is the only one found within our limits.

1. Heliodoxa jacula.

Heliodoxa jacula, Gould, P. Z. S. 1849, p. 96[1]; Mon. Troch. ii. t. 94 (Sept. 1858)[2]; Cab. & Heine, Mus. Hein. iii. p. 22[3]; Salv. P. Z. S. 1867, p. 154[4]; 1870, p. 207[5]; Ibis, 1869, p. 316[6]; Cat. Birds Brit. Mus. xvi. p. 319[7]; Lawr. Ann. Lyc. N. Y. ix. p. 122[8]; Boucard, P. Z. S. 1878, p. 69[9]; Zeledon, An. Mus. Nac. Costa Rica, 1887, p. 121[10].

Heliodoxa henryi, Lawr. Ann. Lyc. N. Y. viii. p. 402[11].

Supra saturate gramineo-viridis, capite summo fronte et corpore toto subtus micanti-viridibus, abdomine obscuriore; plaga gulari micanti-violacea, tectricibus subcaudalibus brunneis medialiter viridi lavatis; cauda chalybeo-cyanea, rectricibus mediis cupreo tinctis: rostro nigro. Long. tota circa 4·7, alæ 2·8, caudæ rectr. med. 1·35, rectr. lat. 2·0, rostri a rictu 1·1.

♀ supra mari similis, capite summo dorso concolore: subtus alba, plumis singulis macula discali micanti-viridi ornatis, rectricibus lateralibus albo terminatis. (Descr. maris et feminæ ex Cordillera de Tolé, Panama. Mus. nostr.)

Hab. COSTA RICA, Angostura, Juiz (*Carmiol* [8,11]), Birris de Cartago (*Zeledon* [10]), Tucur-

43*

riqui (*Arcé*[7]), Naranjo and Volcan de Irazu (*Boucard*[9]), Talamanca (*Zeledon, in U. S. Nat. Mus.*); PANAMA, Boquete de Chitra[5], Cordillera de Tolé[4], Castillo[6], Calovevora[5], Santiago de Veraguas[4], Calobre (*Arcé*).—COLOMBIA[1].

Gould's description of this species was based upon specimens from Colombia, where this bird is not common, but is occasionally represented in the trade collections sent from Bogota. It is apparently absent from the low-lying lands of the Isthmus of Panama, but occurs in the more mountainous parts of that State and thence northwards into Costa Rica, where its range terminates. In Ecuador its place is taken by *H. jamesoni*, an allied but distinct species.

Hardly any difference can be traced between Colombian and more northern specimens, but the former have, as a rule, rather more bronze colour on the central rectrices; but this of itself is a variable feature, being absent altogether in some specimens and just visible in others, so that it is not available as a differential character.

H. henryi was described by Mr. Lawrence from a young male specimen from Juiz in Costa Rica[11], in which the bright spot on the throat and the bright crown had not been developed. The receipt of fully adult birds from Costa Rica has proved that *H. henryi* is a synonym of *H. jacula*.

h'''. *Rostrum debile, decurvum.*

FLORISUGA.

Florisuga, Bonaparte, Consp. Av. i. p. 73; Salv. Cat. Birds Brit. Mus. xvi. p. 328.

Florisuga stands as a rather isolated genus in the Trochilidæ, having no near allies. It comes, perhaps, next to *Lafresnaya*. As in *Heliodoxa*, the nasal covers are feathered, but the bill is much more slender and decidedly curved; the tail is barely forked. This latter character, its normal instead of lengthened under tail-coverts, and the rounded ends to the rectrices separate it from *Lafresnaya*.

The range of the genus extends over a large portion of Tropical South America, one species occupying the lowlands from Southern Mexico to the Amazons Valley, a second species being found in South-eastern Brazil.

1. **Florisuga mellivora.**

Trochilus mellivorus, Linn. Syst. Nat. i. p. 193[1].

Florisuga mellivora, Bonaparte, Consp. Av. i. p. 73[2]; Gould, Mon. Troch. ii. t. 113 (Nov. 1851)[3]; Moore, P. Z. S. 1859, p. 53[4]; Scl. & Salv. Ibis, 1859, p. 128[5]; P. Z. S. 1864, p. 365[6]; 1870, p. 837[7]; Salv. P. Z. S. 1867, p. 155[8]; Ibis, 1872, p. 319[9]; Cat. Birds Brit. Mus. xvi. p. 329[10]; Lawr. Ann. Lyc. N. Y. vii. p. 292[11]; ix. p. 122[12]; Pr. Bost. Soc. N. H. xiv. p. 284[13]; Mem. Bost. Soc. N. H. ii. p. 291[14]; Sumichrast, La Nat v. p. 250[15]; Berl. Pr. U. S. Nat. Mus. xi. p. 561[16].

Florisuga sallei, Boucard, The Humming Bird, i. p. 18[17].

Supra saturate nitenti-gramineo-viridis, cervice postica ad basin alba, capite toto et cervice usque ad pectus saturate nitenti-cyaneis, cervice postica viridi tincta, abdomine albo, hypochondriis viridibus; caudæ rectricibus mediis cæruleo-viridibus, lateralibus albis, apicibus omnibus et marginibus externis anguste (rectrice extima excepta) purpureo-nigris: rostro nigro. Long. tota circa 4·0, alæ 2·6, caudæ 1·4, rostri a rictu 0·9.

♀ supra omnino viridis, plaga cervicali alba nulla: subtus albida, plumis plaga magna discali saturate viridi notatis, abdomine medio fere albo, tectricibus subcaudalibus nigricantibus albo marginatis; caudæ rectricibus lateralibus ad basin viridescentibus, fascia subterminali chalybea, apicibus albis. (Descr. maris et feminæ ex Choctum, Guatemala. Mus. nostr.)

Hab. MEXICO, Orizaba (*Sumichrast* [15]); BRITISH HONDURAS, Belize (*Leyland* [4]), Western district (*F. Blancaneaux* [10]); GUATEMALA (*Skinner* [5]), Choctum [10], near Peten (*O. S. & F. D. G.*); HONDURAS, San Pedro (*G. M. Whitely* [7]); NICARAGUA, Chontales (*Belt* [9]), Rio San Juan (*Rovirosa, in U. S. Nat. Mus.*); COSTA RICA (*Endres* [10] [12]), Bebedero de Nicoya (*Arcé*); PANAMA, Volcan de Chiriqui [10], Cordillera de Tolé [8], Santiago de Veraguas [8] (*Arcé*), Lion Hill (*M'Leannan* [6] [11]), Paraiso (*Hughes* [10]).—SOUTH AMERICA from Colombia to Guiana, Trinidad, Tobago, the Amazons Valley, and Ecuador.

Florisuga mellivora is a very common species of the lowlands of the northern portion of South America, from the Valley of the Amazons to the Caribbean Sea, occurring also in the islands of Trinidad and Tobago. Within our limits it is equally abundant in the State of Panama, and thence northwards through Costa Rica to Eastern Nicaragua, and keeping to the eastern side of the Cordillera to Guatemala and the State of Vera Cruz. In Mexico, however, it must be a rare bird, as we have no skins of it from that country, and its presence there rests upon Sumichrast's statement that it occurs near Orizaba [15]. M. Boucard's description of *F. sallæi* was taken from a specimen shot by himself in Southern Mexico [17]. This last-mentioned bird appears to be a stained specimen, either through damp or exposure, of the ordinary form. At one time *F. mellivora* was stated to be found in the Tres Marias Islands on the authority of Xantus [13] [14]; but Count Berlepsch [16] has shown that this and other Humming-Birds stated to have come from the same islands were included in the list of their birds by some oversight. Their presence there was not confirmed by Grayson or by Mr. Forrer.

So far as our own observations go, *F. mellivora* is a forest-loving bird, and in Guatemala its vertical range probably does not exceed 2000 feet.

b'. *Minores: cauda rotundata; rostrum debile; tegulæ nasales celatæ; caput haud cristatum.*

g". *Rostrum parvum, breve; caput dorsum concolor.*

ABEILLIA.

Abeillia, Bonaparte, Consp. Av. i. p. 79; Salv. Cat. Birds Brit. Mus. xvi. p. 358.

This genus and the next belong to a section of Humming-Birds which are of small size, with small feeble bills, the tomia of both maxilla and mandible being decidedly rolled inwards towards the tip ; the nostrils are concealed by feathers, which, however, do not extend so far along the culmen as in some of the other genera. The tail is rounded and the rectrices normal ; the head is uncrested.

Abeillia differs from *Klais* in having a smaller, shorter bill, and in the crown being green like the back. The sole species of the genus extends from Southern Mexico and the highlands of Guatemala to those of Nicaragua.

1. Abeillia typica.

Ornismya abeillei, Delattre & Less. Rev. Zool. 1839, p. 16 [1].

Abeillia typica, Bp. Consp. Av. i. p. 79 [2] ; Salv. Cat. Birds Brit. Mus. xvi. pp. 358, 666 [3] ; Salv. & Godm. Ibis, 1892, p. 327 [4].

Myiabeillia typica, Bp. Rev. Zool. 1854, p. 253 [5] ; Gould, Mon. Troch. iii. t. 211 (Oct. 1854) [6] ; Scl. & Salv. Ibis, 1859, p. 128 [7] ; Salv. Ibis, 1860, pp. 195 [8], 262 [9], 263 [10] ; de Oca, La Nat. iii. p. 205 [11].

Baucis abeillei, Cab. & Heine, Mus. Hein. iii. p. 72 [12] ; Boucard, Ann. Soc. Linn. Lyon, xxii. p. 23 [13].

Supra nitenti-gramineo-viridis, plaga postoculari magna alba, tectricibus auricularibus nigris ; mento et gula antica micanti-viridibus, infra nigro marginatis ; corpore reliquo subtus fusco, cervicis lateribus, hypochondriis et tectricibus subcaudalibus medialiter viridibus ; caudæ rectricibus mediis cupreo-viridibus, lateralibus chalybeo-cyaneis ad basin viridescentibus, apicibus griseis : rostro nigro.   Long. tota circa 3·2, alæ 1·85, caudæ 1·15, rostri a rictu 0·6.

♀ mari similis, sed corpore toto subtus fusco-griseo, hypochondriis viridi lavatis.   (Descr. maris et feminæ ex Coban, Guatemala.   Mus. nostr.)

Hab. MEXICO, Jalapa (*Delattre* [1], *de Oca* [11]), Cordova (*Boucard* [13]) ; GUATEMALA [12], Coban (*Skinner* [7], *O. S. & F. D. G.* [8] [9]), Volcan de Fuego (*O. S. & F. D. G.* [9] [10]), Pie de la Cuesta in San Marcos, Toliman in Sololá (*W. B. Richardson* [3]) ; NICARAGUA, Matagalpa (*W. B. R.* [3] [4]).

This distinct species was discovered by Delattre at Jalapa in Mexico [1], where, however, he says that it is very rare in the forests, seeking its food from the wild flowers of that district.   De Oca confirms this statement of its occurrence near Jalapa [11], but in none of the large Mexican collections we have recently examined have we found an example, nor does its name occur in the original list of de Oca's collections (P. Z. S. 1859, p. 367). In the British Museum are three skins of this species which were supposed to have reached Gould from Floresi, and we believe they once formed part of his collection. From the mode of preparation of these skins we now think that they were made up by Delattre, and therefore perhaps typical specimens.   On the other hand, if they were from Delattre, they may have been shot in Coban and not in Mexico at all.

In Guatemala *A. typica* is a characteristic species of the upland forests, being abundant at certain seasons in the ravines of the volcanoes amongst the second-growth woods.   Near Coban it was found in all the mountain hollows, feeding from the *Salviæ* in flower in November.

The most southern locality reached by *A. typica* is Matagalpa in Nicaragua, whence Mr. Richardson has recently sent us two specimens which, though females, seem undoubtedly referable to this species [3] [4].

h″. *Rostrum longius ; pileus cyaneus, micans ; gula concolor.*

KLAIS.

Klais, Gould, Mon. Troch. iv. t. 110 (Sept. 1857) ; Salv. Cat. Birds Brit. Mus. xvi. p. 359.

Though closely allied to *Abeillia*, this genus may be distinguished by its longer bill and in having the crown glittering blue like the throat. Its sole species has a wide range in South America from the valley of the Upper Amazons northwards. It enters our fauna at Panama, and spreads thence as far north as Nicaragua.

1. **Klais guimeti.**

Trochilus guimeti, Bourc. & Muls. Ann. Sc. Phys. et Nat. vi. p. 38, t. 2 [1].

Klais guimeti, Gould, Mon. Troch. iv. t. 110 (Sept. 1857) [2] ; Boucard, P. Z. S. 1878, p. 69 [3] ; Zeledon, An. Mus. Nac. Costa Rica, 1887, p. 122 [4] ; Salv. Cat. Birds Brit. Mus. xvi. pp. 359, 666 [5].

Clais guimeti, Salv. P. Z. S. 1867, p. 155 [6].

Mellisuga merrittii, Lawr. Ann. Lyc. N. Y. vii. p. 110 [7] ; Gould, Ibis, 1860, p. 309 [8].

Clais merritti, Salv. P. Z. S. 1870, p. 209 [9] ; Ibis, 1872, p. 319 [10].

Supra nitenti-gramineo-viridis ad nucham saturatior ad uropygium cæruleo lavata ; capite summo late micanti-violaceo ; plaga postoculari magna alba : subtus fusco-grisea, gula violacea, cervicis et pectoris lateribus et hypochondriis cæruleo lavatis ; caudæ rectricibus mediis cæruleo-viridibus, lateribus ad basin viridibus ad apicem chalybeo-nigris : rostro nigro. Long. tota circa 3·4, alæ 2·0, caudæ 1·2, rostri a rictu 0·6.

♀ supra mari similis, capite summo micanti-cyaneo : subtus omnino grisea ; hypochondriis viridi lavatis ; caudæ rectricibus lateralibus griseo terminatis. (Descr. maris et feminæ ex Chepo, Panama. Mus. nostr.)

Hab. NICARAGUA, Chontales (*Belt* [10]), La Libertad in Chontales (*W. B. Richardson*) [5] ; COSTA RICA (*Endres* [5]), Navarro (*Boucard* [3], *Cooper, in U. S. Nat. Mus., Zeledon* [4]) ; PANAMA, Volcan de Chiriqui [9], Bugaba [9], Laguna del Castillo [9], Castillo [9], Chitra [9], Calovevora [9], Santiago de Veraguas [6], Santa Fé [6] (*Arcé*), El Mineral (*Dr. J. K. Merritt*), Chepo (*Arcé* [5]).—COLOMBIA ; VENEZUELA ; ECUADOR ; UPPER AMAZONS [5].

This little species was described by Bourcier and Mulsant in 1843 [1], but the locality whence the type came was not recorded. We now know that it is not an uncommon bird in the north-western portion of the South-American continent, being found in the valley of the Upper Amazons as well as in Ecuador and Venezuela. It is also frequently represented in trade collections from Bogota.

Though not included in M'Leannan's collections from the Line of the Panama Railway, we have little doubt that it occurs throughout the low-lying lands of the State of Panama and spreads thence northwards through Eastern Costa Rica to Eastern Nicaragua. From the latter country we have specimens from Belt's collection and others recently sent us by Mr. Richardson.

Dr. Merritt, who found this species in the district of Veragua called El Mineral, says that it is very pugnacious, seeking its food from the flowers of the guava. The specimens sent by this collector to Mr. Lawrence were described as *Mellisuga merrittii*[7]; they were, from the characters given, evidently females. Males have since reached us, and though Gould at one time considered this Central-American form to be distinguishable from the true *K. guimeti*, in which opinion he was followed by Salvin, we are now convinced that no such distinction exists.

b. *Minores: cauda plerumque abnormalis vix unquam regulariter rotundata aut furcata sed valde variabilis, rectrice utrinque extima sæpe attenuata; gula plerumque rubra, micans, interdum violacea; caput cristatum aut simplex, cervix nonnunquam plumis elongatis ornata; dorsum uniforme, aut fascia transversa albida ornatum.*

c'. *Cauda variabilis, sed haud cuneata aut spatulata; gula plerumque micanti-rubra, interdum violacea; fascia dorsalis nulla.*

i". *Cauda elongata, furcata haud transfasciata; rostrum longum et arcuatum; gula micanti-rubra, violaceo tincta.*

DORICHA.

Calliphlox, β. Doricha, Reich. Aufz. d. Col. p. 12.
Doricha, Gould, Intr. Troch. p. 94; Salv. Cat. Birds Brit. Mus. xvi. p. 380.

Though this and the following genera are very varied as to their structural details, they all seem to be more nearly allied to one another than to the other members of the family.

Doricha is distinguished by the long tail of all its species, the outer feathers having no transverse bands as in *Tilmatura*. The throat is usually of a ruby-red colour, with shades of violet and sometimes, as in *D. enicura*, of an amethystine-purple. The tail, though long, varies considerably in this respect, and diagnostic specific characters are to be found in the way in which the outer rectrices are edged with rufous.

The range of *Doricha* is peculiar, inasmuch as all the species except two are peculiar to Southern Mexico and Central America. The exceptions are closely-allied species restricted to certain groups of the Bahama Islands, no species being found in the larger intervening Antilles.

Of the three species found in our country, *D. elizæ* is peculiar to Southern Mexico, including Northern Yucatan, *D. enicura* to Guatemala, and *D. bryantæ* to Costa Rica and the adjoining portion of the State of Panama.

1. Doricha enicura.

Trochilus enicurus, Vieill. N. Dict. d'Hist. N. xxiii. p. 429 [1]; Temm. Pl. Col. 66. f. 3 [2].

Thaumastura enicura, Gould, Mon. Troch. iii. t. 157 (Oct. 1852) [3]; Scl. & Salv. Ibis, 1859, p. 129 [4]; Salv. Ibis, 1860, pp. 196 [5], 264 [6].

Doricha enicura, Gould, Intr. Troch. p. 95 [7]; Salv. Cat. Birds Brit. Mus. xvi. pp. 381, 667 [8].

Doricha henicura, Salv. Cat. Strickl. Coll. p. 365 [9].

Ornismya heteropygia, Less. Hist. Nat. Ois.-Mouches, pp. xxi, 72, t. 15 [10]; Suppl. p. 97 [11].

Trochilus swainsoni, Less. Hist. Nat. Troch. p. 167, t. 66 [12].

Supra nitenti-aureo-viridis; capite summo obscuriore, capitis lateralibus et mento nigris vix viridi tinctis, gula micanti-amethystina; pectore cervino-albo; abdomine medio albicante; hypochondriis et tectricibus sub-caudalibus aureo-viridibus; rectricibus sex intermediis dorso concoloribus, duabus utrinque externis pur-pureo-nigris ea extima proxima in pogonio interno rufo limbata: rostro nigro. Long. tota circa 4·7, alæ 1·3, caudæ rectr. med. 0·37, rectr. lat. 2·4, rostri a rictu 0·8.

♀ supra mari similis, capite summo obscuriore, dorso medio cupreo tincto: subtus pallide rufescens, loris et area infra oculos nigricantibus; rectricibus quatuor mediis dorso concoloribus, reliquis ad basin rufes-centibus, apicibus albis et fascia subterminali lata nigra notatis. Long. caud. rectr. med. 0·6, rectr. lat. 1·0. (Descr. maris et feminæ ex Dueñas, Guatemala. Mus. nostr.)

Hab. GUATEMALA (*Constancia* [9], *Skinner* [3]), Dueñas [4] [6], Coban [5] (*O. S. & F. D. G.*), Atitlan and Panajachel (*W. B. Richardson* [8]).

The male of this species was described by Vieillot under the name of *Trochilus enicurus* [1], and subsequently figured by Temminck with the same title [2]. Lesson also described and figured the same bird, his drawing being a reproduction of that of Temminck, and proposed that the name should be changed to *O. heteropygia* [10]. The same author subsequently described and figured the female as *Trochilus swainsoni* [12]. None of these writers give any trustworthy account of the origin of their specimens.

Doricha enicura is now known to be a common bird in the highlands of Guatemala, beyond the limits of which country we have no certain evidence of its occurrence. It is true that de Oca says that it is found in Yucatan, but in default of any direct evidence on this point we believe that he mistook *D. elizæ* for the present bird *.

The name is also included, with doubt, in Mr. Henshaw's paper accompanying Wheeler's Report †, but the specimen now proves to be a female of *Calothorax lucifer* ‡.

This species is one of the most familiar of the whole family of Humming-Birds at Dueñas and its vicinity, and during our visits there we had constant opportunities of watching its habits. In 1858 a large portion of the hacienda was under cactus-cultivation for rearing cochineal, and during the month of May the flowers of the cactus were much sought by Humming-Birds, especially this species, both males and females flying together. During the winter months the females were much more frequently seen than the males, which no doubt associated apart in more secluded places. In August 1859 three nests were found: one of them was placed on the cup-shaped top of a fruit of the cactus and fastened most dexterously to the clusters of

---

* La Nat. iii. p. 203.   † Wheeler's Expl. west of the 100th Merid. v. Zool. p. 381.

‡ Ridgway, Rep. U. S. Nat. Mus. for 1890, p. 360 (1892).

prickles of the fruit, the whole structure being thus held firmly in its place; this nest was very shallow, not being subject to oscillation by wind. Another nest was in a coffee-tree. The third was placed on the upper shoots of a dahlia which grew in the garden of the house. The hen bird seemed to have the entire duty of rearing the young, as no male ever approached the nest. When the hen was sitting she would allow an observer to go quite close and even to hold the branch still from being swayed by the wind without evincing any alarm. But it was only when a hot sun was shining that she would allow so close an inspection; on dull and rainy days four or five yards was the nearest approach permitted. After being disturbed she would soon return, bringing a small piece of lichen in her bill, which, after settling in her nest, she would attach to the outside. When sitting, the whole cavity of the nest was filled with her puffed-out feathers, the wings, except their tips, being entirely concealed by the feathers of the back. When the young were first hatched they looked little black shapeless things with long necks and hardly any bill; they soon, however, grew and entirely filled the nest. The old bird was never observed to sit after the young were hatched; she seemed to leave them alike in sun and rain. When feeding them she would stand on the edge of the nest with her body nearly upright. One of the young ones first flew on 15th October. It was standing on the edge of the nest and, being alarmed, attempted to fly, but fell amongst the flowers below; on being replaced in the nest it essayed again to fly, nothing daunted by its first failure—the second time with better success, for it flew over a wall close by and settled on a tree on the other side. The same day the old bird was seen feeding it, and it was observed to fly again with increased vigour to an orange-tree, where it tried at first to rest on one of the fruit, but failing, found a more fitting perch on the edge of a leaf. It was not seen again. The other young one flew two days later.

The down of the seeds of the willow and bulrush are favourite materials for the lining of the nest of *D. enicura*, whilst lichen is freely used outside.

Willow trees grow plentifully near Dueñas, especially on the borders of the lake. About the latter males were sometimes noticed to congregate in some numbers; but the special attraction to these trees was not apparent.

2. Doricha elizæ.

Trochilus eliza, Less. & Delattre, Rev. Zool. 1839, p. 20 [1].

Thaumastura elizæ, Gould, Mon. Troch. iii. t. 155 (May 1857) [2]; de Oca, Pr. Ac. Phil. 1860, p. 552 [3]; La Nat. iii. p. 17, t. — [4].

Doricha elizæ, Gould, Intr. Troch. p. 94 [5]; Boucard, Ann. Soc. Linn. Lyon, xxii. p. 22 [6]; P. Z. S. 1883, p. 451 [7]; Ferrari-Perez, Pr. U. S. Nat. Mus. ix. p. 157 [8]; Salv. Ibis, 1889, p. 365 [9]; Cat. Birds Brit. Mus. xvi. p. 382 [10].

Supra nitenti-aureo-viridis; capite summo obscuriore: subtus gula micanti-rosaceo-rubra, plaga infra oculos fusca, pectore albo, abdomine medio et tectricibus subcaudalibus albidis, hypochondriis aureo-viridi lavatis; caudæ rectricibus quatuor mediis dorso concoloribus, reliquis (tribus utrinque) purpureo-nigris, omnibus, extimis exceptis, in pogonio interno cinnamomeo marginatis: rostro nigro. Long. tota circa 3·9, alæ 1·45, caudæ rectr. med. 0·4, rectr. lat. 1·5, rostri a rictu 0·9.

♀ supra mari similis, sed dilutior: subtus alba cervina vix tincta, hypochondriis leviter viridi lavatis; caudæ rectricibus utrinque tribus ad basin cervinis albo terminatis et fascia lata subterminali nigra notatis. (Descr. maris et feminæ ex Jalapa, Mexico. Mus. Brit.)

Hab. MEXICO, Jalapa (*Delattre* [1], *de Oca*, *Ferrari-Perez* [8]), Barranca de Jico near Jalapa (*de Oca* [3][4]), Mirador (*Sartorius, in U. S. Nat. Mus.*), Cordova, Llano de Camerones near Vera Cruz (*Sallé*), Progreso (*Gaumer* [7]), Sisal (*Schott* [10]), Merida in Yucatan (*Schott, in U. S. Nat. Mus.*), Northern Yucatan, Holbox Island (*G. F. Gaumer* [9][10]).

This species was discovered by Delattre between Vera Cruz and Jalapa, where he says it is very rare, living in societies, flying early and resting during the day from 9 o'clock in the morning to 4 o'clock in the afternoon [1].

Delattre obtained specimens of both sexes, as well as young birds and the nest and eggs.

De Oca gives a similar account of its habits [3][4]. He says that it is one of the rarest of Mexican Humming-Birds. It is very shy, flying very early in the morning and never seen between 8 o'clock in the morning and 5 o'clock in the afternoon, when it flies again till dusk, frequenting the same flowers day after day, those of the tobacco being favourites. De Oca also found it at the Barranca de Jico, about thirty miles from Jalapa, and here he discovered its nest, which he describes as very small, round, and flat at the bottom, being neither so deep nor so thick on the lower part as in those of the generality of Humming-Birds. The nest is covered on the outside with moss and lined on the inside with Tule, or cotton from the seeds of *Cyperus*.

Other collectors have met with this species in this part of the State of Vera Cruz, but always in sparing numbers. On the north coast of Yucatan and on some of the adjoining islands *D. elizæ* appears to be more common, and we have seen specimens from there from several collectors.

The female is very like that sex of *D. enicura*, but is much whiter on the under surface.

3. Doricha bryantæ.

Doricha bryantæ, Lawr. Ann. Lyc. N. Y. viii. p. 483 [1]; ix. p. 123 [2]; Frantz. J. f. Orn. 1869, p. 316 [3]; Salv. P. Z. S. 1870, p. 209 [4]; Cat. Birds Brit. Mus. xvi. p. 384 [5]; Boucard, P. Z. S. 1878, p. 70 [6]; Gould, Mon. Troch. Suppl. t. 33 (Jan. 1881) [7]; Zeledon, An. Mus. Nac. Costa Rica, 1887, p. 122 [8].

Supra saturate nitenti-aureo-viridis: subtus gula micanti-rubra, pectore albicante, abdomine medio albido, hypochondriis antice viridi lavatis, postice cinnamomeis; tectricibus subcaudalibus rufescentibus viridi lavatis; caudæ rectricibus mediis olivescenti-nigricantibus, proximis externe ejusdem coloris interne purpureo-nigris, reliquis purpureo-nigris, omnibus pogonio interno cinnamomeo limbatis: rostro nigro. Long. tota circa 3·7, alæ 1·6, caudæ rectr. med. 0·45, rectr. lat. 1·4, rostri a rictu 0·7.

♀ supra mari similis, subtus pallide rufescens; gula, hypochondriis, et tectricibus subcaudalibus saturatioribus, pectore et abdomine medio pallidioribus; rectricibus lateralibus ad basin et apicibus rufescentibus, fascia subterminali lata nigra notatis. (Descr. maris et feminæ ex Castillo, Panama. Mus. nostr.)

Hab. Costa Rica (*Endres, Carmiol*[1]), Dota (*Carmiol*[2]), San José, Volcan de Irazu (*Boucard*[6]), Las Cruces de Candelaria[2], Naranjo de Cartago[8] (*Zeledon*); Panama, Volcan de Chiriqui, Cordillera del Chucu, Castillo, Laguna del Castillo (*Arcé*[4]).

Doricha bryantæ was described by Mr. Lawrence from specimens sent by Julian Carmiol from Costa Rica to the United States National Museum. The precise localities where these specimens were procured was not stated in the first instance; but in his List of Costa-Rica birds Mr. Lawrence gives Dota and Las Cruces de Candelaria as places where this bird is found. In parts of the State of Panama it appears to be a very common bird, as our collector Arcé sent us a large series of specimens, mostly obtained at Castillo.

Mr. Lawrence compared *D. bryantæ* with *D. evelynæ* of the Bahama Islands, and no doubt the two birds have some characters, such as the colour of the apices of the lateral rectrices of the females, in common. But *D. bryantæ* is the only species of the genus which has all the outer rectrices edged on the inner webs with rufous—a small but significant character.

j″. Cauda elongata, furcata, rectricibus lateralibus transfasciatis.

TILMATURA.

Tryphæna, Gould, Mon. Troch. iii. t. 158 (nec Ochsenheimer).
Tilmatura, Reichenbach, Aufz. d. Col. p. 8; Salv. Cat. Birds Brit. Mus. xvi. p. 385.

The single species constituting this genus is a very peculiar bird as regards the coloration of the outer rectrices of the tail; these are conspicuously tipped and banded with white in a way not found in any other Humming-Bird. The outermost rectrices are peculiarly shaped, being reduced in width towards the end and then slightly expanded to form an incipient spatula. In other structural characters *Tilmatura* seems to come next to *Doricha*.

The range of the genus extends over Southern Mexico and Guatemala to Northern Nicaragua.

1. **Tilmatura duponti.**

Ornismya dupontii, Less. Suppl. Ois.-Mouches, p. 100, t. 1[1]; de Oca, La Nat. iii. p. 103[2].
Tryphæna duponti, Gould, Mon. Troch. iii. t. 158 (June 1849)[3]; Scl. & Salv. Ibis, 1859, p. 129[4]; Salv. Ibis, 1860, p. 266[5]; Villada, La Nat. ii. p. 360[6]; Herrera, La Nat. (2) i. p. 322[7].
Tilmatura duponti, Cab. & Heine, Mus. Hein. iii. p. 59[8]; Ferrari-Perez, Pr. U. S. Nat. Mus. ix. p. 157[9]; Salv. Cat. Birds Brit. Mus. xvi. pp. 385, 667[10]; Salv. & Godm. Ibis, 1892, p. 327[11].
Ornismya cœlestis, Less. Traité d'Orn. p. 276[12].
Ornismya zémès, Less. Rev. Zool. 1838, p. 315[13].
Tilmatura lepida, Reich. Aufz. d. Col. p. 8[14]; Troch. Enum. t. 711. ff. 4610–4[15].

Supra nitenti-gramineo-viridis : subtus gula nigra, plumis singulis saturate violaceo marginatis ; pectore albo, abdomine dorso concolore, tectricibus subcaudalibus viridibus albo limbatis ; caudæ rectricibus quatuor mediis viridibus, duabus proximis purpureo-nigris, extrorsum viridi marginatis et albo terminatis, pogonio externo quoque macula alba notato ; rectricibus utrinque duabus externis purpureo-nigris ad basin, deinde fascia rufa, deinde fascia alba, altera obscura et apicibus albis ; duabus externis prope apicem constrictis : rostro nigro.   Long. tota 3·8, alæ 1·4, caudæ rectr. med. 0·35, rectr. lat. 1·9, rostri a rictu 0·6.

♀ supra mari similis, aureo magis tincta, loris et corpore toto subtus cinnamomeis, infra oculos, hypochondriis et tectricibus subalaribus saturatioribus ; caudæ rectricibus mediis viridibus, lateralibus purpureo-nigris, apicibus rufo (in rectrice utrinque extima fere albo) terminatis.   Long. caudæ rectr. med. 0·55, rectr. lat. 0·85.   (Descr. maris et feminæ ex Amula, Guerrero, Mexico.   Mus. nostr.)

Hab. Mexico [1] [12], Jalapa (*de Oca* [2], *F. Ferrari-Perez* [9], *M. Trujillo* [10]), Los Cerillos, Cuesta de Misantla (*M. Trujillo* [10]), Coatepec (*de Oca* [2]), Valley of Mexico (*de Oca* [2], *Villada* [6], *F. Ferrari-Perez* [9], *Herrera* [7]), Volcan de Colima (*W. B. Richardson* [10]), Amula, Chilpancingo in Guerrero (*Mrs. H. H. Smith* [10]) ; Guatemala (*Skinner* [3]), Coban, San Gerónimo (*O. S. & F. D. G.* [5]), Volcan de Santa Maria near Quezaltenango (*W. B. Richardson* [10]) ; Nicaragua, Matagalpa (*W. B. R.* [11]).

Lesson, who first described this species under the name of *Ornismya duponti*, was also the author of two of its synonyms, *O. zémès* and *O. cœlestis*, and referred in each case to the plate accompanying his first description.

According to de Oca [2] *T. duponti* is found during the summer in the vicinity of Jalapa and Coatepec, and it also occurs, though rarely, in the Valley of Mexico.   We have no specimens from the latter locality, but from Jalapa and its neighbourhood we have several shot in the months of May and June by Mateo Trujillo.   Mr. Richardson secured specimens in January on the Volcan de Colima, and Mrs. Herbert Smith an interesting series of nicely prepared specimens on the Sierra Madre del Sur in August.

The species has long been known as an inhabitant of Guatemala, but we only met with an occasional specimen during our stay in that country, and only in the department of Vera Paz.   Mr. Richardson, however, seems to have found it in numbers near Santa Maria, in the department of Quezaltenango, whence he sent us many specimens, all of them shot in the months of August and September.

The same collector also met with it in the mountains near Matagalpa in Northern Nicaragua [10] [11].

This singular bird has no near ally, the peculiar shape and coloration of the tail rendering it quite unlike any other member of the family.

k". *Cauda brevior sed plus minusve irregulariter constructa, rectricibus mediis haud abnormaliter brevibus.*

i'''. *Rostrum elongatum, decurvum ; plumæ gulares laterales elongatæ.*

CALOTHORAX.

Calothorax, Gray, List Gen. B. p. 13 (1840) ; Salv. Cat. Birds Brit. Mus. xvi. p. 390.

In this and the following genera the tail is not deeply forked as in *Doricha*, but is more or less irregularly formed, some of the rectrices being peculiar either for their attenuated width or for their comparative length. The central rectrices are, however, not abnormally short, as is the case in *Chætocercus* and other allied South-American forms.

Calothorax differs from *Selasphorus* and its allies in having a longer more arched bill.

Two allied species are included in *Calothorax*—one of them ranging over North-western Central Mexico to Puebla and Orizaba ; the other occurring in the State of Oaxaca.

1. Calothorax lucifer.

Cynanthus lucifer, Sw. Phil. Mag. new ser. i. p. 442[1].

Calothorax lucifer, Gray, Gen. Birds, i. p. 110[2] ; Cab. & Heine, Mus. Hein. iii. p. 55[3] ; Scl. P. Z. S. 1856, p. 288[4] ; 1864, p. 177[5] ; Salv. Cat. Strickl. Coll. p. 364[6] ; Cat. Birds Brit. Mus. xvi. p. 390[7] ; Sumichrast, La Nat. v. p. 250[8].

Trochilus lucifer, Finsch, Abh. nat. Ver. zu Bremen, 1870, p. 324[9] ; Herrera, La Nat. (2) i. p. 322[10].

Ornismya cyanopogon, Less. Hist. Nat. Ois.-Mouches, pp. xvi, xlvi, 50, t. 5[11] ; Suppl. pp. 117, 119, tt. 9, 10[12].

Trochilus cyanopogon, Sw. Birds Brazil & Mex. t. 77[13].

Calothorax cyanopogon, Gould, Mon. Troch. iii. t. 143 (Sept. 1857)[14] ; Villada, La Nat. ii. p. 357[15] ; de Oca, La Nat. iii. p. 104[16] ; Boucard, Ann. Soc. Linn. Lyon, xxii. p. 21[17].

Trochilus simplex, Less. Hist. Nat. Col. p. 86, t. 23[18].

Trochilus corruscus, Licht. Preis-Verz. Mex. Vög. p. 1 (*cf.* J. f. Orn. 1863, p. 55)[19].

Supra nitenti-aureo-viridis, capite summo obscuriore, uropygio magis aurescente : subtus gula micanti-lilaceo-rubra, pectore, abdomine medio et tectricibus subcaudalibus albis, hypochondriis pallide fulvis viridi lavatis ; caudæ rectricibus quatuor mediis dorso concoloribus, reliquis purpureo-nigris, lateribus albo terminatis, extima angusta acuta : rostro nigro. Long. tota circa 3·5, alæ 1·5, caudæ rectr. med. 0·6, rectr. longissimi 1·2, rostri a rictu 1·0.

♀ supra maris similis, subtus pallide rufescens, abdomine medio albicantiore, plaga infra oculos fusca ; rectricibus lateralibus ad basin fulvis, apicibus albis fascia lata subterminali nigra. (Descr. maris et feminæ ex Ajusco, Valley of Mexico. Mus. nostr.)

Hab. MEXICO[3][6] (*T. Mann*[6]), Sierra Madre of Sinaloa (*Grayson*, fide *Finsch*[9]), Sierra de San Luis Potosi, Bolaños and Lake Chapala in Jalisco, Ajusco in the Valley of Mexico (*W. B. Richardson*[7]), Temiscaltepec (*Bullock*[1]), Valley of Mexico

(*White* [5], *de Oca* [16], *Sumichrast* [8], *Herrera* [10]), San Antonio Coapa, Hacienda Eslava, Tetelco and Ixtapalapa in the Valley of Mexico (*F. Ferrari-Perez* [7]), Tupataro in Guanajuato (*Dugès, in U. S. Nat. Mus.*), Puebla, San Andres Chalchicomula (*Boucard* [17]), Orizaba (*Sumichrast* [8]), Cordova (*Sallé* [4]).

The Mexican highlands seem to be the chief resort of this species, its range extending from the Sierras of the north-west to the Valley of Mexico and the country immediately adjoining. It is also recorded in the first list of M. Sallé's collections made when he resided chiefly at Cordova. The birds then obtained were probably from the neighbouring mountains.

De Oca says [16] that *C. lucifer*, is peculiar to the valley of Mexico, where it lives from the commencement of spring to the end of autumn. He adds that it is never seen near Jalapa. We have seen specimens from the Valley of Mexico shot in January, so that this bird is probably in that neighbourhood throughout the year, shifting its ground according to the florescence of the vegetation.

M. Boucard [17], who observed this species at Puebla and elsewhere, says that it feeds chiefly from the flowers of a *Convolvulus* which grows in the upland cold country. Like so many of its family it is a very quarrelsome bird.

2. Calothorax pulcher.

Calothorax pulchra, Gould, Ann. & Mag. Nat. Hist. 1859, iv. p. 97 [1]; Mon. Troch. iii. t. 144 (May 1860) [2]; Scl. P. Z. S. 1859, p. 386 [3]; de Oca, La Nat. iii. p. 105 [4]; Boucard, Ann. Soc. Linn. Lyon, xxii. p. 22 [5]; Salv. Cat. Birds Brit. Mus. xvi. p. 391 [6].

C. pulchri similis quoad colores corporis gulæ plnmis lateralibus minus elongatis, rostro breviore et minus robusto, caudæ quoque rectrice utrinque extima normali ad apicem vix angustiore et nullo modo acuta, distinguenda.

♀ minor et rostro breviore.

Hab. MEXICO, Venta de Zopilote in Guerrero (*Mrs. H. H. Smith* [6]), Putla (*Rébouch* [5]), Oaxaca (*Boucard* [1 2 3], *Fenochio* [6]), Tehuantepec (*W. B. Richardson* [6]).

The discovery of this species is due to M. Boucard, who first found it at Oaxaca, as he tells us, on 28th June, 1857 [5]. He forwarded his specimens to M. Sallé, who sent them on to Gould, who described [1] and figured [2] them. According to M. Boucard this bird feeds from the flowers of a cactus which is used to form the hedges surrounding the properties of the Indians of Oaxaca.

Female specimens sent us by Mrs. Herbert Smith from Guerrero we believe belong to this species, and according to M. Boucard it is found at Putla, whence examples were forwarded to him by M. Rébouch [5]. The southern limit of its range extends to Tehuantepec, whence Mr. Richardson sent us two males in abraded plumage, which were shot in February [6].

j'''. Rostrum brevius, rectius; cauda rectricibus mediis abrupte acutis.

e⁴. Aut remex alæ extimus aut caudæ rectrices laterales ad apicem filiformes.

SELASPHORUS.

Selasphorus, Swainson, Faun. Bor.-Am. ii. p. 496; Salv. Cat. Birds Brit. Mus. xvi. p. 391.

This genus is closely allied to *Trochilus,* both having the bill in all their species shorter and straighter than in *Calothorax.* In *Selasphorus* either the outermost primary is reduced to a filiform end as in *S. platycercus,* or the outer rectrices are so reduced, as in the other members of the genus. The throat of the males of all the species is glittering red. In one section of the genus the lateral gular feathers are elongated, in the others they are not so.

Selasphorus contains eight species, all of which, except the Californian *S. alleni,* occur within our limits. Of these, *S. rufus, S. platycercus,* and the little-known *S. floresii* pass beyond our northern frontier—the first named wintering only in Mexico. The other four species are all peculiar to the mountains of the southern section of our country.

1. Selasphorus floresii.

Selasphorus floresii, Gould, Mon. Troch. iii. t. 139 (Sept. 1861)[1]; de Oca, La Nat. iii. p. 101, t. —[2]; Salv. Cat. Birds Brit. Mus. xvi. p. 392[3].

Trochilus floresii, Bryant, Forest & Stream, xxvi. p. 426[4]; Chapman, Auk, 1888, p. 396[5].

Trochilus rubromitratus, Ridgw. Auk, 1891, p. 114[6].

"Capite summo et gula micanti-rubris violaceo tinctis præcipue in pileo et gulæ apicibus; pectore et abdomine medio griseo-albis; corpore supra et tectricibus supracaudalibus cupreo-viridibus, hypochondriis ejusdem coloris sed pallidioribus, caudæ rectricibus duabus mediis viridibus purpureo tinctis, rectricibus lateralibus in pogonio externo purpureis, in pogonio interno rufescenti-cervinis; alis purpureo-brunneis: rostro nigro." (*Ex Gould.*)

Hab. CALIFORNIA [4][5].—MEXICO, Bolaños (*Floresi* [1]).

Very little is known of this bird, which for many years remained in obscurity, the only specimen seen having been described by Gould in 1861, in his well-known 'Monograph of the Trochilidæ'[1]. This specimen was obtained, it was said, at Bolaños, in the State of Jalisco, by Floresi, and sent to Loddiges, in whose collection it, we believe, still remains. In 1886 another specimen was secured in California, and recorded by Mr. Bryant[4] and subsequently by Mr. Chapman[5]. Partly with a view to the rediscovery of this species, Mr. Richardson made two visits to Bolaños, and though he secured good collections of birds on both occasions, no trace of *Selasphorus floresii* appeared. As the greatest uncertainty prevails regarding the localities of Floresi's specimens, none of them being marked in any way, it is very possible that *S. floresii* may not be a Mexican bird at all, but belongs exclusively to California.

2. Selasphorus rufus.

Trochilus rufus, Gm. Syst. Nat. i. p. 497 [1].
Trochilus (Selasphorus) rufus, Sw. Faun. Bor.-Am. ii. p. 324 [2].
Selasphorus rufus, Gould, Mon. Troch. iii. t. 137 (May 1852) [3]; Scl. P. Z. S. 1864, p. 177 [4];
Baird, Brewer, & Ridgw. N. Am. B. ii. p. 459 (partim) [5]; de Oca, La Nat. iii. p. 99 [6]; Sumi-
chrast, La Nat. v. p. 250 [7]; Herrera, La Nat. (2) i. p. 322 [8]; Salv. Cat. Birds Brit. Mus.
xvi. p. 392 [9].
Selasforus rufus, Dugès, La Nat. i. p. 141 [10]; Villada, La Nat. ii. p. 355 [11].
Selasphorus henshawi, Elliot, Bull. Nutt. Orn. Club, ii. p. 102 [12]; Syn. Troch. p. 111 [13].

Supra (cervice postica et tectricibus supracaudalibus inclusis) cinnamomeo-rufus, capite summo obscure aureo-
viridis, plumis singulis ciunamomeo limbatis: subtus gula micanti-rubra, pectore et abdomine medio
albis, hypochondriis et tectricibus subcaudalibus cinnamomeis; cauda saturate cinnamomea nigro terminata, rectricibus medianis proximis ad apicem profunde excavatis in pogonio interno, minus profunde in
pogonio externo: rostro nigro. Long. tota circa 3·5, alæ 1·6, caudæ 1·1, rostri a rictu 0·75.

♀ supra nitenti-gramineo-viridis, capite summo obscuriore: subtus alba, gula maculis discalibus fuscis notata,
et plumis micanti-rubris irregulariter ornata, hypochondriis et tectricibus subcaudalibus cinnamomeo
lavatis; cauda ad basin cinnamomea, rectricibus mediis nitenti-viridibus saturatioribus et cærulescentioribus ad apicem, lateralibus late albo terminatis et fascia subterminali nigra notatis. (Descr. maris et
feminæ ex Zacatecas, Mexico. Mus. nostr.)

Hab. NORTH AMERICA, western portion from British Colombia to Arizona.—MEXICO,
Guanajuato (*Dugès* [10]), Zacatecas and Xeres in Zacatecas, Plains of San Luis
Potosi, Sierra de Valparaiso, Ajusco in the Valley of Mexico (*W. B. Richardson* [9]),
Valley of Mexico (*White* [4], *Villada* [11], *de Oca* [6], *Sumichrast* [7], *Herrera* [8]), Tetelco,
Valley of Mexico (*F. Ferrari-Perez* [9]), Patzcuaro (*F. D. G.* [9]), Volcan de Colima
(*W. B. Richardson* [9]), La Parada, Oaxaca (*Boucard*), Mirador (*Sartorius, in U. S.
Nat. Mus.*).

Selasphorus rufus is a winter visitor to the highlands of Mexico, where it arrives in
August and remains until the following spring. The remainder of the year it spends
in the Western States of North America, reaching British Columbia in its northern
migration. Its breeds during the summer months, and it is only in males from the
north that the full beauty of its plumage is seen. All specimens of that sex from
Mexico are in more or less faded and worn plumage.

According to de Oca [6] it is abundant in the Valley of Mexico in autumn, at which
time Villada says it breeds [11]; but this statement, we think, requires confirmation. The
highlands of the State of Oaxaca are the extreme southern limit of the autumn
migration of this species. It is quite unknown in the highlands of Guatemala.

3. Selasphorus scintilla.

Trochilus (Selasphorus) scintilla, Gould, P. Z. S. 1850, p. 162 [1].
Selasphorus scintilla, Gould, Mon. Troch. iii. t. 138 (May 1852) [2]; Cab. J. f. Orn. 1862, p. 165 [3];
Salv. P. Z. S. 1867, p. 155 [4]; 1870, p. 209 [5]; Cat. Birds Brit. Mus. xvi. p. 395 [6]; Lawr.
Ann. Lyc. N. Y. ix. p. 123 [7]; v. Frantz. J. f. Orn. 1869, p. 315 [8]; Boucard, P. Z. S.
1878, p. 70 [9].

Supra (tectricibus supracaudalibus inclusis) nitenti-aureo-viridis ; capite summo paulo obscuriore, loris et regione circum oculos cinnamomeis : subtus gula micanti-rubra, pectore albo, hypochondriis et tectricibus subcaudalibus cinnamomeis illis viridi lavatis, abdomine medio pallide cinnamomeo ; caudæ rectricibus mediis cinnamomeis medialiter stria longitudinali purpureo-nigra, lateralibus purpureo-nigris, pogonio interno fere ad rhachidem cinnamomeo : rostro nigro, mandibulæ basi carnea. Long. tota circa 2·7, alæ 1·3, caudæ 1·0, rostri a rictu 0·55.

♀ subtus alba, gula cervina maculis discalibus fuscis notata, cauda cinnamomea fascia lata subterminali nigra. (Descr. maris et feminæ ex Volcan de Chiriqui, Panama. Mus. nostr.)

Hab. Costa Rica, Barranca, Cervantes (*Carmiol*[7]), Rancho Redondo, Las Cruces de Candelaria[7], San José (*Zeledon, in U. S. Nat. Mus.*), Irazu (*Rogers*[6]), Tabacales (*v. Frantzius*[8]), Tucurriqui (*Arcé*[6]), Cartago and Volcan de Irazu (*Boucard*[9]) ; Panama, Chiriqui (*Warszewiez*[1]), Volcan de Chiriqui (*Arcé*[5]).

This beautiful little species was discovered by Warszewiez during his visit to the Volcan de Chiriqui, and his specimens were described by Gould in 1850, and figured in his 'Monograph of the Trochilidæ' two years afterwards[2]. It was next discovered in Costa Rica by Von Frantzius[7][8] and other collectors, and subsequently Arcé sent us a good series of examples from Chiriqui[5].

In some respects *S. scintilla* is like *S. alleni* of California on a small scale, but it may readily be distinguished by the flesh-coloured base to the mandible.

M. Boucard, who observed this species in Costa Rica[9], says that it flies as high as 10,000 feet on the Volcan de Irazu, and feeds from the flowers of small low-growing plants, making little noise with the vibration of its wings. He thought that by its silent low flight it escaped the notice of other Humming-Birds frequenting the same places.

4. Selasphorus torridus. (Tab. LVI. figg. 2, ♂ ; 3, ♀.)

Selasphorus torridus, Salv. P. Z. S. 1870, p. 208[1] ; Cat. Birds Brit. Mus. xvi. p. 395[2] ; Ridgw. Pr. U. S. Nat. Mus. vii. p. 14[3] ; Zeledon, An. Mus. Nac. Costa Rica, 1887, p. 122[4].
Selasphorus flammea, Nutting (nec Salv.), Pr. U. S. Nat. Mus. v. p. 497[5].

Supra nitenti-gramineo-viridis, loris cinnamomeis : subtus gula micanti-lilacino-rubra plumbescente tincta, plumis ad basin cervinis, pectore, abdomine medio et tectricibus subcaudalibus albis, hypochondriis viridi lavatis ; caudæ rectricibus mediis saturate nitenti-viridibus ad basin cinnamomeo limbatis, lateralibus purpureo-nigris, macula cinnamomea in pogonio interno ad apicem : rostro nigro, mandibula ad basin carnea. Long. tota circa 2·7, alæ 1·6, caudæ 1·1, rostri a rictu 0·65.

♀ capite summo obscuriore : subtus alba, gulæ plumis singulis macula discali fusca, hypochondriis et tectricibus subcaudalibus cervino lavatis, caudæ rectricibus lateralibus ad basin cinnamomeis, apicibus albicantibus et fascia subterminali nigra notatis. (Descr. maris et feminæ exempl. typ. ex Volcan de Chiriqui. Mus. nostr.)

Hab. Costa Rica (*Van Patten*[3]), Volcan de Cartago (*Nutting*[5], *Zeledon*[4]) ; Panama, Volcan de Chiriqui (*Arcé*[1][2]).

The colour of the throat of this species is very peculiar, being of a lilac tint overcast with a leaden hue. It has all the appearance of being faded, but from the number of specimens we have seen this can hardly be so. Its nearest ally is no doubt *S. scintilla*, from which it differs not only in the colour of the thorax, but also in that of the tail, the inner web of the outer rectrices being wholly purple-black instead of nearly wholly rufous.

All the specimens of this species that we have seen were sent us by our collector Arcé from the Volcan de Chiriqui. It has also been found by several collectors on the Volcan de Irazu in Costa Rica [3] [4] [5].

5. Selasphorus platycercus.

Trochilus platycercus, Sw. Phil. Mag. new ser. i. p. 441 [1].

Selasphorus platycercus, Gould, Mon. Troch. iii. t. 140 (May 1852) [2]; Scl. & Salv. Ibis, 1859, p. 129 [3]; Salv. Ibis, 1860, p. 196 [4]; Cat. Strickl. Coll. p. 364 [5]; Cat. Birds Brit. Mus. xvi. p. 396 [6]; Scl. P. Z. S. 1864, p. 177 [7]; Baird, Brew., and Ridgw. N. Am. Birds, ii. p. 462 [8]; de Oca, La Nat. iii. p. 204, t. — [9]; Sumichrast, La Nat. v. p. 250 [10]; Boucard, Ann. Soc. Linn. Lyon, xxii. p. 19 [11]; Herrera, La Nat. (2) i. p. 322 [12].

Selasforus platycercus, Dugès, La Nat. i. p. 141 [13]; Villada, La Nat. ii. p. 352 [14].

Ornismya tricolor, Less. Suppl. Ois.-Mouches, p. 125, t. 14 [15].

Trochilus montanus, Less. Ind. gén. Troch. p. xxxiv [16]; Sw. Birds Brazil & Mex. t. 74 [17].

Supra nitenti-olivaceo-viridis : subtus gula micanti-rosaceo-rubra, pectore albo, abdomine medio et tectricibus subcaudalibus albidis, hypochondriis viridi lavatis ; caudæ rectricibus mediis dorso fere concoloribus, reliquis purpureo-nigris, sublateralibus ad basin cinnamomeo limbatis : rostro nigro. Long. tota circa 3·3, alæ 1·95, caudæ 1·3, rostri a rictu 0·8.

♀ supra magis aurescens : subtus pallide cervina, gula et pectore albicantioribus, hypochondriis et tectricibus subcaudalibus magis cinnamomeis, gula maculis discalibus fuscis notata ; caudæ rectricibus lateralibus ad basin cinnamomeis, medialiter nigricantibus, apicibus albis. (Descr. maris et feminæ ex Ajusco, Valley of Mexico. Mus. nostr.)

Hab. NORTH AMERICA, Utah, New Mexico, Colorado, and Arizona.—MEXICO (*Bullock* [1], *Mann* [5]), Micoba in Sonora (*W. Lloyd* [6]), Sierra de Valparaiso, Sierra de Calvillo, Sierra de Bolaños, Volcan and Sierra Nevada de Colima, Real del Monte, Tenango del Valle, Ajusco (*W. B. Richardson* [6]), Hacienda Eslava in the Valley of Mexico (*F. Ferrari-Perez* [6]), Patzcuaro (*Dugès* [13]), Rio Frio Ixtaccihuatl (*W. B. R.* [6]), Pinal Puebla (*F. D. G.* [6]), Puebla (*Boucard* [11]), Tonaguia (*M. Trujillo* [6]), Valley of Mexico (*de Oca* [9], *White* [7], *Sumichrast* [10], *Herrera* [12]), Mirador (*Sartorius, in U. S. Nat. Mus.*), Alpine region of Orizaba (*Sumichrast* [10]); GUATEMALA (*Skinner* [3]), Quezaltenango (*O. S. & F. D. G.* [4], *W. B. Richardson* [6]), Chuipache and San Martin in Quezaltenango, Rincon in San Marcos (*W. B. R.* [6]), Mountains above Totonicapam, Paramos (*O. S.* [4]).

This species was first described by Swainson in his paper on Bullock's Mexican collection [1], and subsequently figured by the same author in his 'Birds of Brazil and Mexico' [17], when he suppressed his original name in favour of Lesson's *Trochilus montanus*, which had been bestowed on a bird supposed to have come from Brazil [16]. From Mexico it has been traced northwards across the frontier as far as Utah, and it appears to be found, at least in the summer months, in all the South-western States of America from May to August.

In Mexico it seems to be essentially a bird of the highlands, being common in the Valley of Mexico.   According to de Oca [9], it feeds from the flowers of *Centaurea mexicana* during the months of May and June.   It then, according to that observer, ascends the mountains to the southward, remaining there two months, during which time it breeds.   M. Boucard says [11] it is very common in the environs of Mexico from June to August, and passes on to the State of Oaxaca from September to November.   Its presence in the State of Vera Cruz is probably confined to the mountains at the edge of the plateau ; and though specimens are recorded from Jalapa and Mirador, there can be little doubt that they came from the lofty mountains in the neighbourhood of those places.

In Guatemala we believe *Selasphorus platycercus* to be restricted to the Altos of San Marcos and Quezaltenango, and thence southwards to the edges of the plain of Chimaltenango which lies at an elevation of 6000 feet above the sea.   On one occasion, in February, many of these birds were noticed in the mountains above the town of Totonicapam as high as 10,000 feet above sea-level.

The peculiar formation of the outermost primary in the male of this bird is characteristic of the species.   The inner web is much reduced in width so that the feather has a filiform point.   It is this structure that no doubt produces the shrill sound when the bird is in flight.   This was very noticeable in birds that frequented the gardens of the town of Quezaltenango, especially when alarmed they flew rapidly away.

6. **Selasphorus ardens.**   (Tab. LVI. fig. I.)

Selasphorus ardens, Salv. P. Z. S. 1870, p. 209 [1]; Cat. Birds Brit. Mus. xvi. p. 398 [2]; Sharpe, in
    Gould's Mon. Troch., Suppl. t. 31 (Jan. 1883) [3]; Ridgw. Pr. U. S. Nat. Mus. vii. p. 14 [4].

S. platycerco similis, sed minor, supra saturatior, loris et tectricibus auricularibus rufis his nigro intermixtis ;
    caudæ rectricibus mediis purpureo nigris ad basin cinnamomeo limbatis, rectricibus lateralibus purpureo-
    nigris, in pogonio interno ad basin cinnamomeis et macula subterminali ejusdem coloris notatis : rostro
    nigro.   Long. tota circa 2·8, alæ 1·55, caudæ 1·15, rostri a rictu 0·65.

♀ *juv.* gula maculis fuscis aut rosaceo-rubris notata ; caudæ rectricibus lateralibus ad basin cinnamomeis
    medialiter viridibus, apicibus pallide cervinis fascia subterminali obscura, rectricibus mediis nitenti-
    viridibus ad basin cinnamomeis, apicibus obscuris.   (Descr. exempl. typ. ex Castillo, Panama.   Mus.
    nostr.)

Hab. COSTA RICA (*Van Patten* [4]), Volcan de Poas (*Alfaro, in U. S. Nat. Mus.*), Las Cruces
    de Candelaria (*Zeledon, in U. S. Nat. Mus.*); PANAMA, Calovevora, Castillo (*Arcé* [1]).

Selasphorus ardens was discovered by our collector Arcé, who sent us two specimens —one from Castillo, the other, a young male, from Calovevora in the State of Panama [1]. Other specimens have been since obtained in Costa Rica by several collectors, and identified as belonging to the species by Mr. Ridgway [4].

Like *S. placycercus*, *S. ardens* belongs to the section of the genus in which the lateral gular feathers are not elongated.   It differs from that bird in having the outermost primary normal, and from *S. flammula* in the colour of the central rectrices.

7. Selasphorus flammula.

Selasphorus flammula, Salv. P. Z. S. 1864, p. 586 [1] ; Cat. Birds Brit. Mus. xvi. p. 398 [2] ; Lawr. Ann.
Lyc. N. Y. ix. p. 123 [3] ; v. Frantz. J. f. Orn. 1869, p. 315 [4] ; Boucard, P. Z. S. 1878, p. 70 [5] ;
Sharpe, in Gould's Mon. Troch., Suppl. t. 31 (Jan. 1883) [6].

S. ardenti similis, sed gula magis rosacea ; caudæ rectricibus mediis nitenti-viridibus cinnamomeo limbatis,
rectricibus lateralibus purpureo-nigris, apicibus albis in pogonio interno ad basin stricte cinnamomeo
limbatis : rostro nigro, mandibulæ basi carnea. (Descr. maris exempl. typ. ex Volcan de Cartago, Costa
Rica. Mus. nostr.)

Hab. COSTA RICA, Volcan de Cartago (*Arcé* [1], *Boucard* [5], *Zeledon, in U. S. Nat. Mus.*) [,]
Rancho Redondo (*Zeledon, in U. S. Nat. Mus.*), Candelaria Mts. (*v. Frantzius* [4]).

A single male specimen sent us by Arcé from the Volcan de Cartago in Costa Rica
formed the type of this species [1]. It is in rather faded plumage, but, when freshly
moulted, males show a throat as brilliant as that of *Selasphorus platycercus*. Other
collectors have since obtained specimens of this species, which appears to be restricted
in its range to the higher mountains of Central Costa Rica.

M. Boucard says [5] that it feeds from the flowers of mistletoe growing on small alpine
trees near the summit of tbe Volcan de Cartago at an elevation of 10,000 feet and
upwards above sea-level.

f⁴. *Nec remex extimus nec rectrices laterales ad apicem filiformes.*

TROCHILUS.

Trochilus, Linnæus, Syst. Nat. i. p. 189 ; Salv. Cat. Birds Brit. Mus. xvi. p. 398.

Neither the primaries nor the outer rectrices are filiform in the members of this
genus, and in this respect it differs from *Selasphorus*, to which it is otherwise closely
allied. Thus restricted, *Trochilus* contains two well-known species, and a third is
included in it which we have not seen.

Trochilus colubris, the best-known member of the genus, performs an extended annual
migration from the British Provinces of North America to the Isthmus of Panama.
T. alexandri is a more western bird, and its migrations are not so wide, and in winter
do not pass the tablelands of Mexico.

1. Trochilus colubris.

Trochilus colubris, Linn. Syst. Nat. i. p. 191 [1] ; Gould, Mon. Troch. iii. t. 131 (May 1858) [2] ; Scl.
& Salv. Ibis, 1859, p. 129 [3] ; Scl. P. Z. S. 1859, pp. 367 [4], 386 [5] ; 1864, p. 176 [6] ; Salv. Ibis,
1860, pp. 195 [7], 263 [8], 266 [9] ; P. Z. S. 1870, p. 208 [10] ; 1889, p. 365 [11] ; Cat. Strickl. Coll.
p. 364 [12] ; Cat. Birds Brit. Mus. xvi. pp. 399, 667 [13] ; Lawr. Ann. Lyc. N. Y. ix. p. 123 [14] ; Bull.
U. S. Mus. no. 4, p. 32 [15] ; v. Frantz. J. f. Orn. 1869, p. 315 [16] ; Villada, La Nat. ii. p. 352 [17] ;
Baird, Brewer & Ridgw. N. Am. Birds, ii. p. 448 [18] ; de Oca, La Nat. iii. p. 22 [19] ; Boucard,

P. Z. S. 1878, p. 70[20]; 1883, p. 451[21]; Sumichrast, La Nat. v. p. 250[22]; Nutting, Pr. U. S. Nat. Mus. vi. p. 394[23]; Ridgw. Pr. U. S. Nat. Mus. viii. p. 573[24]; Ferrari-Perez, Pr. U. S. Nat. Mus. ix. p. 157[25]; Herrera, La Nat. (2) i. p. 322[26].

Supra nitenti-gramineo-viridis; capite summo obscuro, uropygio magis nitido: subtus abdomine medio sordide albo, pectore albo, hypochondriis viridi lavatis, gula micanti-rubra, mento et regione infra oculos nigris; caudæ rectricibus mediis dorso concoloribus, reliquiis chalybeo-nigris: rostro nigro. Long. tota 3·5, alæ 1·5, caudæ rectr. longissimis 1·1, rectr. med. 0·65.

♀ supra mari similis: subtus alba, caudæ rectricibus lateralibus ad basin griseis, apicibus albis et fascia sub-terminali nigra notatis. (Descr. maris et feminæ ex Ajusco, Valley of Mexico. Mus. nostr.)

Hab. EASTERN NORTH AMERICA from Canada southwards.—MEXICO, Sierra de Victoria, Escandon, Tamesi, Tampico (*W. B. Richardson*[13]), Misantla (*F. D. G.*[13]), Coatepec[19], Jalapa[4] (*de Oca, Ferrari-Perez*[25]), Mirador (*Sartorius, in U. S. Nat. Mus.*), Orizaba (*Botteri, Sumichrast*[22]), Playa Vicente (*M. Trujillo*[13]), Ajusco in the Valley of Mexico (*W. B. Richardson*[13]), Valley of Mexico (*White*[6], *de Oca*[19], *Sumichrast*[22], *Herrera*[26]), Puebla (*W. B. R.*[13]), Amecameca (*F. D. G.*[13]), Volcan de Colima (*W. B. R.*[13]), Chilpancingo, Venta de Zopilote, Amula, Acaguizotla (*Mrs. H. H. Smith*[13]), Tonaguia (*M. Trujillo*[13]), La Parada, Tuxtla, Oaxaca[5] (*Boucard*), Santa Efigenia (*Sumichrast*[15][22]), Chimalapa and Tehuantepec (*W. B. Richardson*[13]), Northern Yucatan (*Gaumer*[21]), Merida in Yucatan (*Schott*), Progreso, Holbox I.[11], Cozumel I.[11] (*Gaumer*); GUATEMALA (*Constancia*[12]), Santa Ana in Peten, Coban[7][9], San Gerónimo[9], Dueñas[7][9], Acatenango (*O. S.*[3] & *F. D. G.*), Rincon in San Marcos, Panajachel (*W. B. Richardson*[13]); NICARAGUA, Omotepe I. (*Nutting*[23]); COSTA RICA[10][16], Bebedero de Nicoya (*Arcé*[13]), Las Cruces de Candelaria (*v. Frantzius*[16], *Zeledon*[14]), San José (*Boucard*[20]); PANAMA, Volcan de Chiriqui (*Arcé*[10]).

This well-known bird is very common in Mexico and Central America during the winter months, all or nearly all the specimens migrating to North America in the spring, and remaining there to breed. In September and October de Oca says[19] *T. colubris* is very common at Jalapa and Coatepec as well as in the Valley of Mexico, where it may also be seen in November. M. Boucard also speaks of its abundance in Mexico, but he says that a few individuals remain to breed. This statement is confirmed to some extent by specimens obtained by Mr. Richardson in the State of Tamaulipas in the successive months of March, April, and May, at which time it also occurs on the north side of the mouth of the Rio Grande in Texas. Villada[17] also says a few individuals remain to breed in the Valley of Mexico, and he describes the nest in some detail.

In its southern migration it spreads to Nicaragua, Costa Rica, and Chiriqui, but in much diminished numbers, and it does not seem to pass beyond the last-mentioned district.

During its stay in the south, *T. colubris* is found at all altitudes from the sea-level at Tampico and in Yucatan to as high as 8000 feet in the Valley of Mexico.

2. **Trochilus alexandri.**

Trochilus alexandri, Bourc. & Muls. Ann. Sc. Phys. et Nat. Lyon, ix. p. 330 [1]; Gould, Mon. Troch. iii. t. 132 (Sept. 1851) [2]; Scl. P. Z. S. 1864, p. 177 [3]; Villada, La Nat. ii. p. 351 [4]; de Oca, La Nat. iii. p. 102 [5]; Herrera, La Nat. (2) i. p. 322 [6]; Salv. Cat. Birds Brit. Mus. xvi. p. 402 [7].

T. colubri similis, sed gula antica cum mento nigra, gula postica micanti-violacea facile distinguenda.
♀ feminæ *T. colubris* persimilis, sed rostro longiore forsan distinguenda.

Hab. NORTH AMERICA, from California and Utah southwards to Arizona.—MEXICO, Montemorelos, Sierra Madre, and Monterey in Nuevo Leon (*F. B. Armstrong* [7]), San Diego in Chihuahua (*Robinette, in U.S. Nat. Mus.*), Nuri in Sonora (*W. Lloyd* [7]), Xeres in Zacatecas, Plains of Colima (*W. B. Richardson* [7]), Valley of Mexico (*White* [3], *de Oca* [5], *Boucard, Herrera* [6]), Venta de Zopilote in Guerrero (*Mrs. H. H. Smith* [7]).

Trochilus alexandri is a close relative of *T. colubris* and appears to take its place in the Western States of America in the breeding-season, but the two mingle in the same localities in the winter months, which are spent in Mexico.

It probably breeds in the more northern parts of Mexico, as we have specimens of both sexes shot in the State of Nuevo Leon in May and at Nuri in Sonora in April. According to Villada [4] and de Oca [5], it visits the Valley of Mexico at the beginning of autumn, but is rare there—a statement confirmed by M. Boucard, who says that during his sojourn in Mexico he never met with this species except in the environs of the city *.

* The following species of *Calypte* have usually been attributed to Mexico, but we have not succeeded in obtaining any well-authenticated specimens of either of them from that country. Both are well-known Californian species :—

Calypte annæ.

Ornismya anna, Less. Hist. Nat. Ois.-Mouches, p. 205, t. 74.
Calypte annæ, Salv. Cat. Birds Brit. Mus. xvi. p. 403.

According to Gould and others this species is found in Mexico, but his specimens obtained from Floresi may well have come from California. M. Boucard (Ann. Soc. Linn. Lyon, xxii. p. 20) says that it is very rare in Mexico, but gives no authority for its occurrence there, and he does not seem to have met with it himself. Herrera mentions it as found in the Valley of Mexico, but gives no particulars ('La Naturaleza,' (2) i. p. 322). It certainly occurs near our northern frontier at Camp Grant, Arizona.

Calypte costæ.

Ornismya costæ, Bourc. Rev. Zool. 1839, p. 294.
Calypte costæ, Salv. Cat. Birds Brit. Mus. xvi. p. 404.

This species has likewise been attributed by Gould to Mexico, apparently on the authority of Floresi's specimens, all of which probably came from California. M. Boucard, however, states (Ann. Soc. Linn. Lyon, xxii. p. 20) that it is very rare in Mexico, but, as in the case of *C. annæ*, gives no authentic instance of its occurrence. Mr. Belding, also, gives its name in the list of birds he observed at Guaymas (Pr. U. S. Nat. Mus. vi. p. 343).

l″. *Cauda fere normalis, rotundata aut furcata.*

k‴. *Cauda rotundata, albo terminata; plumæ gulares laterales elongatæ.*

ATTHIS.

Trochilus, δ. Atthis, Reichenbach, Aufz. d. Col. p. 12.
Atthis, Gould, Intr. Troch. p. 89; Salv. Cat. Birds Brit. Mus. xvi. p. 411.

In *Atthis* the tail, though short, is nearly normal and rounded, the lateral rectrices being of full width and tipped with white. The lateral gular feathers are elongated and wholly glittering rosy red with a slight purple tinge.

Two closely-allied species inhabit Southern Mexico and Guatemala. They resemble each other in colour, but may be distinguished by the shape of the outermost primary, which in the northern form (*A. heloisæ*) is attenuated towards the extremity.

1. **Atthis heloisæ.**

Ornismya heloisa, Less. & Delattre, Rev. Zool. 1839, p. 15 [1].
Selasphorus heloisæ, Gould, Mon. Troch. iii. t. 141 (Oct. 1854) [2]; Scl. P. Z. S. 1859, p. 386 [3]; 1864, p. 177 [4]; de Oca, La Nat. iii. p. 19, t. — [5].
Tryphæna heloisæ, Scl. P. Z. S. 1858, p. 297 [6]; 1859, p. 367 [7].
Atthis heloisæ, Gould, Intr. Troch. p. 89 [8]; Dugès, La Nat. i. p. 141 [9]; Villada, La Nat. ii. p. 357 [10]; Ridgw. Pr. U. S. Nat. Mus. i. p. 10 [11]; Salv. Cat. Birds Brit. Mus. xvi. p. 411 [12].
Trochilus heloisa, Herrera, La Nat. (2) i. p. 322 [13].

Supra nitenti-aureo-viridis : subtus gula micanti-rosaceo-rubra purpureo leviter lavata, pectore, abdomine medio et tectricibus subcaudalibus albis, hypochondriis pallide cinnamomeis maculis discalibus aureo-viridibus notatis ; caudæ rectricibus mediis dorso concoloribus, lateralibus ad basin cinnamomeis, apicibus albis fascia subterminali lata nigra : rostro nigro. Long. tota circa 2·9, alæ 1·4, caudæ 0·9, rostri a rictu 0·55.

♀ capite summo obscuriore, gula tota alba maculis discalibus aureo-viridibus notata. (Descr. maris et feminæ ex Cuesta de Misantla (Jalapa), Mexico. Mus. nostr.)

Hab. MEXICO, Guanajuato (*Dugès* [9]), Sierra de San Luis Potosi (*W. B. Richardson* [12]), Cofre de Perote (*M. Trujillo* [12]), Jalapa (*Delattre* [1], *de Oca* [5][7], *C. F. Höge* [12], *M. Trujillo* [12]), Cuesta de Misantla (*M. Trujillo* [13]), Cordova, Orizaba, San Andres Tuxtla (*Boucard*), Valley of Mexico (*White* [4], *Villada* [10], *de Oca* [5], *Herrera* [13]), Patzcuaro (*Dugès* [9]), Tepic (*W. B. Richardson* [12]), Totontepec (*Boucard* [3]), Oaxaca (*Boucard* [6], *Fenochio* [12]).

Delattre discovered this species during his sojourn at Jalapa [1], where it has since been found by nearly every collector who has visited that district.

Most of our specimens came from this neighbourhood, but the species ranges far beyond the limits of the State of Vera Cruz, for we have received specimens from the Sierra de San Luis Potosi in Central Mexico, from Tepic near the west coast, and also from the State of Oaxaca.

Villada says [10] that it is only found in the Valley of Mexico in the months of June and July, seeking its food chiefly from the flowers of *Lythrum vulnerarium.*

At one time *A. heloisæ* was supposed to have occurred in Southern Texas, but this statement, we believe, has now been found to have been based upon a wrong identification.

2. Atthis ellioti.

Selasphorus heloisæ, Scl. & Salv. Ibis, 1859, p. 129[1]; Salv. Ibis, 1859, p. 468[2]; 1860, pp. 195[3], 271[4]; 1862, p. 96 (nec Less. & Del.)[5].

Atthis ellioti, Ridgw. Pr. U. S. Nat. Mus. i. p. 9[6]; Elliot, Syn. Troch. p. 114[7]; Salv. Cat. Birds Brit. Mus. xvi. pp. 412, 667[8].

A. heloisæ similis, sed rectrice extima integra haud ad apicem attenuata distinguenda.

Hab. GUATEMALA (*Skinner*[1]), El Rincon in San Marcos, Chuipaché and Volcan de Santa Maria in Quezaltenango, Atitlan (*W. B. Richardson*[8]), Volcan de Fuego[3][5], Chilasco and Coban (*O. S. & F. D. G.*[8]).

This species was long considered to be the same as *A. heloisæ*, and passed as such until Mr. Ridgway discovered a curious difference in the shape of the outermost primary, whereby the male of the Mexican and Guatemalan birds can always be distinguished[6]. This feather in the Mexican form is attenuated towards the end by the reduction in width of the inner web—in a similar way, but not to the same extent, as in *Selasphorus platycercus*. The Guatemalan form has this feather of the normal width throughout.

A. ellioti occurs in many parts of the uplands of Guatemala, but is much more common in the outskirts of the forests of the Altos and of the great volcanoes than in Vera Paz. We found it in some numbers on the ridge above Calderas, which forms a spur to the Volcan de Fuego. Here it sought a large thistle which grew in some profusion on the hill-side. It was also observed on the upper part of the Volcano near to where the two chief peaks unite. At certain seasons it has a cheerful song.

1‴. *Cauda subfurcata; plumæ gulares laterales elongatæ, albæ, macula terminali rubra notatæ.*

STELLULA.

Stellula, Gould, Intr. Troch. p. 90; Salv. Cat. Birds Brit. Mus. xvi. p. 413.

Stellula is closely allied to *Atthis*, but has a slightly forked tail, the outer rectrices being without white tips. The coloration of the throat is somewhat peculiar, inasmuch as the glittering red terminal spots of the feathers are so reduced in size as to show the white of the rest of the feathers amongst them.

Stellula calliope is the only member of the genus, its range extending from Oregon southwards to the tablelands of Mexico.

1. **Stellula calliope.**

Trochilus (Calothorax) calliope, Gould, P. Z. S. 1847, p. 11 [1].

Calothorax calliope, Gould, Mon. Troch. iii. t. 142 (Sept. 1857) [2]; de Oca, La Nat. iii. p. 27 [3].

Stellula calliope, Gould, Intr. Troch. p. 90 [4]; Elliot, B. N. Am. i. t. 23 [5]; Villada, La Nat. ii. p. 359 [6]; Salv. Cat. Birds Brit. Mus. xvi. p. 413 [7].

Trochilus calliope, Herrera, La Nat. (2) i. p. 322 [8].

Supra nitenti-aureo-viridis, capite summo obscuriore: subtus alba, gulæ plumis lateralibus valde elongatis, macula ovali rosaceo-rubra terminatis, colore ad basin albo (præcipue in mento) obvio, hypochondriis pallide cinnamomeis et viridi lavatis; caudæ rectricibus mediis dorso concoloribus, lateralibus nigricantibus haud albo terminatis sed ad basin stricte cinnamomeo limbatis: rostro nigro. Long. tota circa 2·9, alæ 1·5, caudæ 0·9, rostri a rictu 0·65. (Descr. maris ex Ajusco, Valley of Mexico. Mus. nostr.)

♀ subtus alba, gula maculis discalibus aureo-viridibus notatis, hypochondriis et tectricibus subcaudalibus cinnamomeo lavatis; caudæ rectricibus lateralibus ad basin griseis, albo terminatis et fascia lata subterminali nigra notatis.

Hab. NORTH AMERICA, Western States from Oregon southwards to Arizona.—MEXICO [1], Valley of Mexico (*de Oca* [3], *Herrera* [8]), Tetelco in the Valley of Mexico (*F. Ferrari-Perez*), Ajusco in the Valley of Mexico, Calvillo in Aguas Calientes (*W. B. Richardson* [7]), Amula in Guerrero (*Mrs. H. H. Smith* [7]), Cerros de Guadalupe Pedregal (*Villada* [6]).

Stellula calliope is by no means a common bird in Mexico, where it appears to be strictly confined to the highlands, from the mountains of Guerrero and the Valley of Mexico northwards.

Within the United States it would appear to be much more numerous, at least during the summer months, when no doubt it breeds.

The colour of the throat readily distinguishes this species, no other showing the white bases of the feathers of the throat amongst the glittering rosy spots at their ends. The female much resembles that sex of *Atthis heloisæ,* but may be recognized by its longer bill and by the bases of the lateral rectrices being greyish rather than cinnamon.

d′. *Cauda rotundata aut furcata haud cuneata; dorsum posticum fascia transversa albida notatum; cervix interdum plumis lateralibus elongatis ornatis.*

m″. *Cauda rotundata vix furcata; plumæ cervicales laterales elongatæ.*

LOPHORNIS.

Lophornis, Lesson, Hist. Nat. Ois.-Mouches, p. xxxvii; Salv. Cat. Birds Brit. Mus. xvi. p. 419.
Telamon, Muls. & Verr. Class. Troch. p. 75.
Paphosia, Muls. & Verr. Class. Troch. p. 75.
Dialia, Muls. Ann. Soc. Linn. Lyon, xxii. p. 223.

Lophornis is one of the most remarkable genera of Humming-Birds, on account of the development of the feathers of the head and neck and their diversity of shape and colour. These peculiarities have suggested the division of the genus into no less than six genera; but as there are only eleven species in *Lophornis* as a whole, and as the characters for its subdivision are all drawn from one set of modifications, it is perhaps as well to treat the subdivisions as sections of one genus. The most distinct from *Lophornis* is *Polemistria*, which contains three species, none of which occur in Central America.

All the species of *Lophornis* are very small birds, the males distinguished by the development of their lateral cervical plumes. In some of the species the head is conspicuously crested. All the species have rounded or slightly forked tails, and the rectrices are all of normal width. The lower back is crossed by a transverse white or whitish band.

Three of the eleven species occur within our limits. *L. helenæ*, the type of Mulsant and Verreaux's genus *Paphosia*, ranges from Southern Mexico to Costa Rica. *L. adorabilis*, the type of Mulsant's *Dialia*, occurs in Chiriqui and also in Costa Rica; and *L. delattrii*, the type of Mulsant and Verreaux's *Telamon*, is found in the State of Panama and also in more southern parts of Colombia. In South America the genus ranges over the greater part of the forest-region as far as South-eastern Brazil.

1. Lophornis delattrii.

Ornismya (Lophornis) delattrii, Less. Rev. Zool. 1839, p. 19[1].

Lophornis delattrii, Gould, Mon. Troch. iii. t. 121 (Sept. 1861)[2]; Lawr. Ann. Lyc. N. Y. vii. p. 465[3]; Scl. & Salv. P. Z. S. 1864, p. 365[4]; Salv. P. Z. S. 1870, p. 207[5]; Cat. Birds Brit. Mus. xvi. p. 423[6]; Tacz. Orn. Pér. i. p. 299[7].

Supra nitenti-aureo-viridis, uropygio et tectricibus supracaudalibus saturate purpureo-cupreis, fascia transversa dorsali cervino-albida; capite summo cinnamomeo, plumis valde elongatis angustis, acutis, punctis minutis nigris terminatis, loris et gutture toto micanti-viridibus illius plumis lateralibus ad basin cinnamomeis; pectore plumis paucis albis notato; corpore reliquo subtus viridi, subcaudalibus cinnamomeis; cauda cinnamomea, rectricibus mediis ad apicem viridibus, reliquis pogonio externo viride nigricante limbatis : rostro carneo, apice nigro. Long. tota circa 2·7, alæ 1·5, caudæ 0·9, rostri a rictu 0·5.

♀ supra aureo-viridis, fronte cinnamomea plumis elongatis nullis : subtus gula cervina fusco maculata, gutture imo fascia lata nigra notato et infra eam plaga albida; abdomine viridi, hypochondriis posticis et tectricibus subcaudalibus cinnamomeis; cauda cinnamomea fascia subterminali nigra, rectricibus mediis medialiter viridibus. (Descr. maris et feminæ ex Panama. Mus. nostr.)

Hab. PANAMA, Castillo, Laguna del Castillo (*Arcé*[5]), Lion Hill (*M'Leannan*[3][4]), Line of Railway and Chepo (*Arcé*[6]).—COLOMBIA[2][6]; PERU[7].

This beautiful species was discovered by Delattre, and described by him in conjunction with Lesson[1], but the exact locality where it was found was not stated. We now know it as a not uncommon bird in the trade collections from Bogota. It is also far from rare in the State of Panama as far westwards as Castillo, whence Arcé has sent us many specimens[5]. Beyond this point, however, it does not seem to occur, as we have no trace of it at Chiriqui, the country of *L. adorabilis*, nor from Costa Rica, where *L. helenœ* is found.

L. delattrii has two near allies in *L. regulus* and *L. stictolophus*, but it differs from both in its narrow crest-feathers, hardly any of which have a trace of a dark terminal spot.

2. **Lophornis helenæ.**

Ornismya helenæ, Delattre, Echo du Monde Sav. 1843, p. 1068[1]; Rev. Zool. 1843, p. 133[2].

Lophornis helenæ, Gould, Mon. Troch. iii. t. 123 (Sept. 1855)[3]; Scl. & Salv. Ibis, 1859, p. 130[4]; Salv. Ibis, 1860, pp. 194[5], 196[6], 267[7]; Cat. Birds Brit. Mus. xvi. p. 425[8]; de Oca, La Nat. iii. p. 300, t. —[9]; Boucard, Ann. Soc. Linn. Lyon, xxii. p. 15[10].

Paphosia helenæ, Boucard, P. Z. S. 1878, p. 70[11].

Supra nitenti-aureo-viridis, uropygio et tectricibus supracaudalibus rufo-purpurascentibus, fascia dorsali transversa cervino-albida; capite summo saturate viridi, plumis utrinque valde elongatis, longissimis angustis, plerumque nigris ad apicem filiformibus auricularibus nigris: subtus gula micanti-aureo-viridi, margine suo distali rotundato et undique nigro marginato, plumis lateralibus elongatis nigro et cinnamomeo intermixtis, pectore aureo-viridi, abdomine albo, plumis singulis macula magna aurea rotunda notatis; tectricibus subcaudalibus cinnamomeis medialiter aureo-viridi vix tinctis: cauda cinnamomea, rectricibus mediis viridibus ad apicem saturatioribus, reliquis viridi extrorsum limbatis: rostro carneo, apice nigro. Long. tota circa 3·0, alæ 1·6, caudæ 1·0, rostri a rictu 0·6.

♀ supra nitenti-aureo-viridis; capite summo fere unicolore, plumis elongatis nullis; gutture albo, plumis singulis macula discali aureo-nigricante notatis; cauda cinnamomea, fascia subterminali nigra, rectricibus mediis quoque medialiter viridibus. (Descr. maris et feminæ ex Coban, Guatemala. Mus. nostr.)

Hab. MEXICO, environs of Cordova, Santecomapam, Catemaco (*Boucard* [10]), Chiapas (*de Oca* [9]); GUATEMALA, "Petinck" (? Peten) (*Delattre* [1][2]), Coban (*Skinner* [4], *O. S. & F. D. G.* [7]); HONDURAS, San Pedro Sula (*Wittkugel, in U. S. Nat. Mus.*); COSTA RICA, Turrialba (*Arcé* [1], *Boucard* [11]), Tucurriqui (*Arcé* [8]), San Carlos (*Boucard* [11]), El Naranjo (*Zeledon, in U. S. Nat. Mus.*).

The range of *Lophornis helenæ* extends much further north than that of any other species of the genus, and even reaches the middle of the State of Vera Cruz, where so many purely neotropical birds find the northern limit of their distribution.

It was not in Mexico, as it has been sometimes stated, that Delattre discovered this bird, but in Vera Paz, the only Department of Guatemala where it is found. In the month of November it is not uncommon near Coban, feeding from the flowers of the *Salviæ*, the favourite resort of so many species of Humming-Birds. The flight of *L. helenæ* is very rapid, and hardly to be followed by the eye as it darts from flower to flower. Its cry is peculiarly shrill and unlike that of any other Humming-Bird, so that its presence in any place may at once be detected by a skilled ear. The females are either very much rarer than the males, or, which is probably the case, less in evidence. During a month spent at Coban only one female was secured to seventeen males.

M. Boucard observed this species during his residence in Mexico at several places near the town of Cordova. The same traveller subsequently met with it in Costa Rica.

3. Lophornis adorabilis. (Tab. LVII. fig. 1, ♂; 2, ♀.)

Lophornis adorabilis, Salv. P. Z. S. 1870, p. 207 [1]; Cat. Birds Brit. Mus. xvi. p. 425 [2]; Gould, Mon. Troch., Suppl. t. 35 (Aug. 1880) [3]; Zeledon, An. Mus. Nac. Costa Rica, 1887, p. 122 [4]; Ridgway, Pr. U. S. Nat. Mus. xi. p. 542 [5].

Dialia adorabilis, Muls. Hist. Nat. Ois.-Mouches, iii. p. 208, t. 91. fig. 1 [6].

Supra aureo-viridis, fascia dorsali transversa albida, uropygio et tectricibus supracaudalibus purpureis; capite summo medio pure albo, plumis lateralibus elongatis acutis antice divergentibus postice confluentibus, fronte, loris et capitis lateribus micanti-cupreis, plumis ad basin albis: subtus gula micanti-viridi, plumis ad basin albis, plumis lateralibus valde elongatis et acutis postice retractis, plaga magna pectorali alba, abdomine et tectricibus subcaudalibus cinnamomeis; cauda cinnamomea, rectricibus mediis apicibus et omnium marginibus viridi nigricantibus: rostro carneo, apice nigro. Long. tota circa 2·8, alæ 1·5, caudæ 1·0, rostri a rictu 0·5. (Descr. maris exempl. typ. ex Volcan de Chiriqui. Mus. nostr.)

♀ capite summo nigricante, fronte cupreo lavata, genis nigricantibus: subtus gutture toto cum pectore albis, hujus plumis omnibus macula discali aurea notatis; cauda fascia subterminali nigra, rectricibus mediis quoque medialiter viridibus. (Descr. feminæ ex Bugaba, Panama. Mus. nostr.)

Hab. COSTA RICA, San José (*Zeledon* [4] [5]); PANAMA, Volcan de Chiriqui [1], Bugaba [2], Bibalaz [2] (*Arcé*).

Our collector Enrique Arcé, who worked so diligently in the western portion of the State of Panama, discovered this remarkable species. The first specimen sent was a female which he shot near Bugaba, but it was only when the male arrived that it was described by Salvin, and subsequently figured by Gould and Mulsant in their respective works. The further extension of the range of the species is proved by a specimen having been obtained near San José, as recorded by Mr. Ridgway [5] and Mr. Zeledon [4].

Lophornis adorabilis has no near allies, so much so that Mulsant proposed a new generic name, *Dialia*, for it. This we think hardly necessary, and prefer to let this species and also *L. helenæ* stand in *Lophornis* in sections by themselves.

n″. *Cauda elongata profunde furcata, rectricibus lateralibus angustissimis acutis, mediis brevissimis; plumæ cervicales haud elongatæ.*

PRYMNACANTHA.

Gouldia, Bonaparte, Consp. Av. i. p. 86 (nec Adams).
Prymnacantha, Cabanis & Heine, Mus. Hein. iii. p. 64; Salv. Cat. Birds Brit. Mus. xvi. p. 428.

The absence of any peculiar development of the lateral cervical feathers and the deeply-forked tail consisting of very narrow pointed rectrices, the median pair being very short, the outermost very long, and the general green colour of all the species distinguish *Prymnacantha* from *Lophornis*, which it resembles in the small size of its component species, and in the common character of a transverse white dorsal band. It differs from *Discura* in the absence of the large spatules which terminate the outer rectrices of that genus.

Four species are contained in *Prymnacantha*, all of which belong to South America, one only, *P. conversi*, extending northwards to the State of Panama and to Costa Rica.

1. Prymnacantha conversi.

Trochilus conversi, Bourc. & Muls. Ann. Sc. Phys. et Nat. Lyon, ix. p. 313[1].

Gouldia conversi, Gould, Mon. Troch. iii. p. 129 (May 1854)[2]; Lawr. Ann. Lyc. N. Y. vii. p. 319[3];
    ix. p. 123[4]; Salv. P. Z. S. 1867, p. 154[5]; 1870, p. 208[6].

Prymnacantha conversi, Cab. & Heine, Mus. Hein. iii. p. 65[7]; Salv. Cat. Birds Brit. Mus. xv.
    p. 430[8].

Supra nitenti-gramineo-viridis, fascia transversa dorsali alba, tectricibus supracaudalibus purpureis: subtus
    gutture toto nitenti-viridis, plaga pectorali cyanea, abdomine viridi plumis ad basin nigris, tectricibus
    subcaudalibus viridibus; cauda chalybea, rhachidibus supra pallide fuscis, subtus albis: rostro nigro.
    Long. tota circa 3·5, alæ 1·6, caudæ rectr. med. 0·35, rectr. lat. 2·4, rostri a rictu 0·55.

♀ mari similis: subtus gula nigra utrinque albo marginata, pectore et hypochondriis viridibus plumis ad basin
    nigris, abdomine medio nigro utrinque macula magna albo notato; cauda chalybea, rectricibus lateralibus
    rhachidibus subtus albis, pogonio externo et apicibus quoque albis. Long. caudæ rectr. med. 0·5, rectr.
    lat. 0·95. (Descr. maris et feminæ ex Tucurriqui, Costa Rica. Mus. nostr.)

Hab. Costa Rica, Tucurriqui (*Arcé* [4] [5]), Angostura (*Carmiol* [8]), Naranjo de Cartago
    (*Zeledon, in U. S. Nat. Mus.*); Panama, Calovevora [6], Santa Fé [5], Cordillera del
    Chucu (*Arcé*), Lion Hill (*M'Leannan* [3]).—Colombia [1] [2] [7]; Ecuador [8].

The original specimen of *P. conversi* described by Bourcier came from Colombia, and
was sent thence by M. Convers, who lived for some time at Bogota [1]. The presence of
the species within our limits was first noticed by M'Leannan, who obtained a single
male specimen in the dense forest near the Line of the Panama Railway, and sent it
to Mr. Lawrence [3]. It was subsequently found in Costa Rica by Arcé, and also at
several places within the limits of the State of Panama. Its southern range reaches
Ecuador, where specimens have been obtained by several collectors. Stolzmann's
examples from that country were described by Von Berlepsch and Taczanowski as
Gouldia conversi æquatorialis, but they hardly differ from the typical Colombian form.
The head and throat are perhaps a little brighter, and in this respect the Central-
American birds agree with those of Western Ecuador.

Suborder CYPSELI.

Fam. CYPSELIDÆ.

This suborder is spread over the whole of the temperate and tropical portions of the
globe, and comprises about 78 species, the American Continents claiming about one-
third of these.

Recent authors divide the Cypselidæ into two sections, based upon the number of
phalanges in the third and fourth digits of the adult bird. The first of these sections
forms the subfamily Cypselinæ, in which the second, third, and fourth digits have each
three phalanges. In the second section the toes are of normal structure, the third toe

having four and the fourth toe five phalanges. This section is again divided into Chæturinæ and Malcopteryginæ, the latter being restricted to the Indo-Malayan region and New Guinea.

We have therefore here only to do with the Cypselinæ and Chæturinæ, which are differentiated by the structure of their toes.

This curious feature has long been known, but its development has only recently been examined by Herr L. Zehntner ('Zoologischer Anzeiger,' No. 319 (1889), and 'Ibis,' 1890, p. 196) in embryos of *Cypselus melba*. The result shows pretty conclusively that in the intermediate stages of development the embryo of that species possesses the normal number of phalanges, but that as growth advances one phalange in the third toe and two in the fourth are lost by absorption into adjoining joints.

The exceedingly rapid flight, often at a great height in the air, of the Cypselidæ generally, is a reason for their being seldom represented in collections of bird-skins, few native collectors being able to shoot them. It is only by resorting to their nesting- or roosting-places that any number of specimens can be obtained.

Subfam. *CYPSELINÆ*.

To this subfamily belong the genera of Cypselidæ which have an abnormal number of phalanges to the middle and outer toes, the middle toe having only three phalanges instead of four and the outer also three instead of five. The true Swifts of the Old World all belong here, and two South-American species are comprised in the same genus *Cypselus*. It includes *Aëronautes* and *Panyptila*, both peculiar to America, and also one of the Palm-Swifts of the genus *Tachornis* and its ally *Claudia*.

Of the twenty-four or twenty-five known species of Cypselinæ only seven or eight occur in the New World, and of these only one, *Aëronautes melanoleucus*, a bird of our country, is found north of Mexico. *Panyptila* is represented within our limits by all its species. *Cypselus* itself (in the New World) is confined to the Andes of South America, neither *Tachornis* nor *Claudia* occurring at all. With *Tachornis*, a genus represented in some of the larger Antilles by *T. phœnicobia*, Mr. Hartert associates the Palm-Swifts of the East, and assigns a new generic name (*Claudia*) to *Cypselus squamatus* of South America.

AËRONAUTES.

Aëronautes, Hartert, Cat. Birds Brit. Mus. xvi. p. 459 (1892).
Panyptila (partim), Baird et auctt.

This genus is very closely allied to *Cypselus* on the one hand and *Panyptila* on the other, so much so that the single species it contains has been placed sometimes in one genus and sometimes in the other. Its position is best recognized under a distinct name and placed between the two above-mentioned genera. From *Cypselus*, *Aëronautes* may be distinguished by the toes as well as the tarsi being feathered and in having the outermost tail-feather on either side shorter than the next. *Aëronautes* agrees with *Panyptila* in having feathered toes, but the tail is much less deeply forked, the feathers wider, less acute at their ends, and the outermost pair shorter than the next. The outermost primary is shorter than the second and equal to the third, and is thus shorter as well as blunter than the same feather of *Panyptila*. In nidification *Aëronautes* agrees with *Cypselus* rather than with *Panyptila*.

The range of *Aëronautes* as given in detail below extends from Wyoming Territory southwards through California to Arizona and Western Texas and to Mexico and Guatemala.

1. **Aëronautes melanoleucus.**

"*Acanthylis saxatilis*," Woodh. Expl. Zuñi and Colorado Rivers, p. 64 (1853) [1]; Coues, Ibis, 1865, p. 536 [2].

Panyptila saxatilis, Coues, Birds N. W. p. 265 [3]; Hensh. in Wheeler's Surv., Zool. v. p. 370 [4].

Cypselus melanoleucus, Baird, Pr. Ac. Phil. 1854, p. 118 [5].

Panyptila melanoleuca, Baird, Birds N. Am. p. 141, t. 18. f. 1 [6]; Scl. & Salv. Ibis, 1859, p. 125 [7]; Scl. P. Z. S. 1865, p. 607 [8]; Sumichrast, Mem. Bost. Soc. N. H. i. p. 562 [9]; Baird, Brew., & Ridgw. N.-Am. Birds, ii. p. 424 [10].

Micropus melanoleucus, Shufeldt, Ibis, 1887, p. 151, t. 5 [11].

Aëronautes melanoleucus, Hartert, Cat. Birds Brit. Mus. xvi. p. 459 [12].

Niger, fronte, cervice postica, et capitis lateribus magis fuliginosis; gutture toto, abdomine medio, plaga utrinque hypochondriali, campterio alari, et secundariis ad apicem albis, plumis ad gutturis latera et pectoris fusco marginatis: rectrice extima in pogonio externo stricte albo marginato, reliquis (duabus mediis exceptis) in pogonio interno plaga elongata alba ad basin notatis: rostro nigro, digitis cum unguibus suis flavidis. Long. tota circa 6·0, alæ 5·9, caudæ rectr. med. 1·8, rectr. lat. 2·3.

♀ mari similis. (Descr. maris ex Dueñas, Guatemala. Mus. nostr.)

Hab. NORTH AMERICA, Wyoming, California, Utah, New Mexico, Colorado, and Arizona [3][4].—MEXICO (*Mus. Brit.* [12]), Mountains of Orizaba? (*Sumichrast* [9]); GUATEMALA, Gorge of Rio Guacalate near Dueñas (*O. S. & F. D. G.* [7]).

Dr. Woodhouse no doubt saw birds of this species at Inscription Rock in 1851, when he accompanied Sitgreaves's Expedition to the Zuñi and Colorado Rivers [1]. As he did not obtain specimens, his name for the species, "*Acanthylis saxatilis*," rests upon a somewhat questionable basis. Dr. Coues [2][3], and after him Mr. Henshaw [4] and others, have, however, used the name *Panyptila saxatilis* in preference to that of *Cypselus melanoleucus* given to it in 1854 by Baird from a specimen obtained by Kennerly and Möllhausen in the San Francisco Mountains [5]. Recent American writers have now reverted to *melanoleucus*, which was for many years the only specific name employed.

Regarding the birds of Inscription Rock, there can, as we have already said, be hardly a doubt, for both Dr. Coues [2] and Mr. Henshaw [4] have seen them there, with full knowledge of the birds they were observing. We conclude, therefore, that the names *saxatilis* and *melanoleucus* refer to one and the same species.

The accounts of the habits of this Swift agree in most points, and are in full accord concerning the features of the localities in which alone it is to be found: these are gorges of the mountains with rocky precipitous sides, in the fissures and clefts of which the birds reside. Both Dr. Coues and Mr. Henshaw speak of the abundance of this species in Utah, Colorado, New Mexico, and Arizona, and as congregating in suitable places where the fissured cliffs afforded them suitable roosting- and breeding-places.

The presence of *A. melanoleucus* in Mexico rests upon the rather doubtful evidence of two skins in the British Museum [12], said to have come from that country, and the statement by Sumichrast [9] that he believed he recognized it flying about the mountains of Orizaba. There can, however, be little doubt that it is to be found in suitable places in Mexico, as in the countries further to the northward.

In Guatemala we only met with it in one locality, a gorge of the Rio Guacalate between the villages of Dueñas and Ciudad Vieja, at an elevation of about 5000 feet above sea-level [7], a fissured precipice of igneous rock on one side of the valley harbouring a good many individuals. During the daytime some of the birds of this colony might usually be seen soaring high in the air over the valley, others would be hidden in the crevices of the rock, keeping up a continuous chatter. Every now and then one or two would descend from the flock in the air and enter a crevice with the utmost rapidity; again others would dart out and join their companions in their flight.

Owing to the inaccessibility and narrowness of the fissures frequented by birds of this species their nests and eggs have not yet, so far as we know, been obtained. Dr. Coues states [2] that they breed on the face of high perpendicular cliffs, gluing their nests to the sides; and, again [3], that they were observed evidently nesting in the rocks, but he could not say whether they built against the open rocks or in the crevices, though they certainly did so upon the face of the cliffs. This account is not clear, and it is not fully supported by Mr. Henshaw, who says [4] that on several occasions he found colonies breeding in the faces of the cliffs; the inaccessibility of the crevices they had chosen for their retreats proved an insurmountable obstacle to any attempt to spy out their domestic arrangements.

Our own observations in Guatemala, which apply to cliffs of apparently much less elevation than those visited by Dr. Coues and Mr. Henshaw, lead us to conclude that the nests are placed inside the crevices and not against the face of the rock. We visited the Guacalate colony in several months of the year (in February, July, and November), and we never saw any trace of a nest outside a fissure. Debris from inside one of the most frequented crevices consisted of feathers and pieces of dry grass, the latter probably brought for nest-building.

Authentic information concerning the migration of this species, if any, is also very deficient. The presence of birds in countries north of Mexico has been recorded between the months of February and September, and in December at San Bernardino in Southern California; and Dr. Cooper believed[3] that they winter in the cañons of the Colorado river; but this appeared improbable to Dr. Coues, who was inclined to look upon the Guatemala individuals as birds in their winter-quarters. So far as our own experience goes we are satisfied that the Guacalate colony is resident throughout the year, whatever the movements of the northern birds may be.

PANYPTILA.

Panyptila, Cabanis in Wiegm. Arch. für Naturgesch. 1847, xiii. p. 345; Hartert, Cat. Birds Brit. Mus. xvi. p. 461.

Prof. Cabanis separated this genus from *Cypselus* in 1847 in his well-known paper on the Classification of Birds, and made *P. cayennensis* the type.

Panyptila can be readily distinguished from *Cypselus* by the feathering of the toes from the end of the tarso-metatarsus to the base of the claws. Its nidification also is very different from that of *Cypselus*, as it constructs a large pendent nest of silky seeds which it glues to the under surface of an overhanging rock, *Cypselus* resorting to crevices and caves in rocks or roofs of buildings. From *Aëronautes*, *Panyptila* differs in its more deeply forked tail, the outer rectrices being considerably the longest and very pointed; the first primary, too, is as long as, instead of shorter than, the second and also sharply pointed.

Only two species are contained in the genus, of which *P. cayennensis* has a wide range over Tropical America and just enters our fauna in the State of Panama. The other, *P. sancti-hieronymi*, so far as we know at present, is confined to Guatemala.

1. **Panyptila cayennensis.**

Le Martinet à collier blanc, D'Aub. Pl. Enl. p. 725. fig. 2 [1].

Hirundo cayennensis, Gm. Syst. Nat. i. p. 1024 [2].

Panyptila cayennensis, Cab. in Wiegm. Arch. f. Naturg. 1847, xiii. p. 345 [3]; Layard, Ibis, 1873, p. 389 [4]; Salv. Ibis, 1885, p. 436 [5]; W. L. Scl. Ibis, 1887, p. 318 [6].

Panyptila cayanensis, Scl. P. Z. S. 1865, p. 606 [7]; Scl. & Salv. P. Z. S. 1879, p. 531 [8]; Hartert, Cat. Birds Brit. Mus. xvi. p. 461 [9].

Velutino-nigra, macula supra lorali, torque cervicali, gutture toto, macula utrinque hypochondriali et rectricibus externis in pogonio externo ad basin pure albis; secundariis ad apicem et primariis internis in pogonio interno (stricte) albo marginatis; alarum margine externo et campterio fusco variegatis: rostro nigro, unguibus fuscis. Long. tota circa 5·6, alæ 5·0, caudæ rectr. med. 1·1, rectr. lat. 2·2. (Descr. maris ex Samiria, E. Peru. Mus. nostr.)

Hab. PANAMA, Rio Chagres (*Merritt*).—SOUTH AMERICA generally from Colombia [8] and Venezuela [9] to Guiana [1][5][6], the Amazons Valley [4], and South-east Brazil [9].

Though well known for more than a century, this species is still somewhat rarely represented in collections, due most probably to the difficulty of securing specimens of a bird possessing such power ot rapid flight. By degrees it has been traced over a large portion of Tropical America, and examples have been obtained from widely distant places. Discovered in Guiana [1], where also Whitely met with it [5], it occurs at Para [4], where a specimen was secured by Mr. Layard, into whose dining-room it dashed during his residence in that city. It has been recorded from South Brazil, though Natterer did not meet with it. We recently found a beautiful specimen in one of Hauxwell's collections made at Samiria on the Upper Amazons. It occurs also in Venezuela and Ecuador, and in the Colombian State of Antioquia [8], the last-named locality bringing it close to our borders.

We have no specimen from our country, but Salvin was shown by Mr. Lawrence in 1874 a specimen with its nest which was found near the Chagres river by Dr. T. K. Merritt, the discoverer of *Microchera albocoronata*. Writing in 1884, Mr. Lawrence says that the bird was captured in its nest, the latter being a remarkable structure, composed of some kind of silk-weed, and, being probably waterproof, was used by the bird as a domicile in the rainy season. Its shape was like a sleeve, three or four inches in diameter and nine or ten inches long. This nest was therefore somewhat similar to that of *P. sancti-hieronymi*, but a good deal smaller, and had probably been attached to a rock in a similar way.

2. Panyptila sancti-hieronymi.

Panyptila sancti-hieronymi, Salv. P. Z. S. 1863, p. 190, t. 23 [1]; Ibis, 1866, p. 195 [2]; 1874, p. 188 [3]; Hartert, Cat. Birds Brit. Mus. xvi. p. 462 [4].

P. cayennensi persimilis, sed multo major, primariis internis latiore albo-marginatis. Long. tota circa 7·8, alæ 7·5, caudæ rectr. med. 1·35, rectr. lat. 3·4. (Descr. exempl. typ. ex San Gerónimo, Guatemala. Mus. nostr.)

Hab. GUATEMALA, San Gerónimo [1], Volcan de Fuego (*O. S. & F. D. G.*, *H. Hague*), vicinity of Antigua (*V. Constancia*).

The first intimation we had of the existence of this fine species was when Mr. Carter, the manager of the estate of San Gerónimo in Vera Paz, brought us two specimens confined in one of the lamps of his gig! They had been caught by an Indian under a rock near the village of Matanzas, and were nearly dead, but one of them had sufficient energy to show the great grasping powers of its strong feet. Soon after this the nest was brought us from the hills above San Gerónimo. It was taken from a rock near some Indian ruins called Pueblo Viejo, situated at the extremity of a spur of the mountain chain. Some years later we visited this spot and found a half-finished nest, but no birds were flying about [3].

Though birds of this species were afterwards observed in other parts of Guatemala we were never able to secure a specimen. On several occasions birds were seen sweeping over the second-growth woods of the Volcan de Fuego, and attempts were made to shoot some, but in vain, their flight being far too rapid for our skill. From this cause *P. sancti-hieronymi* is a very rare bird in collections. There are specimens,

47*

Mr. Ridgway informs us, in the United States National Museum which were sent there by Mr. Henry Hague, who succeeded Mr. Carter as manager of the San Gerónimo estate. Don Vicente Constancia, too, had a specimen in his collection, which passed at his death into the Museum of the Sociedad Economica de Guatemala. This last-named bird was obtained near Antigua, Guatemala, and probably belonged to the colony which flew round the Volcan de Fuego.

The nest of this species is a remarkable structure, made entirely of the downy seeds of some plant; these are glued together, doubtless by the saliva of the bird, so as to form a long bag-like structure with the opening below. The nest itself is near the top of the inverted bag, and the bird on entering the mouth must climb to the top by its feet. The eggs are not known.

Panyptila sancti-hieronymi is a large form of *P. cayennensis*, and resembles it in nearly every particular of the distribution of its black and white colour. The difference in size is nearly half as large again, the wing measuring 7·5 inches as against 5·6.

Subfam. *CHÆTURINÆ.*

In this subfamily Mr. Hartert includes the genera *Chætura*, its near ally *Cypseloides*, and the builders of the edible nests, *Collocalia*. The latter genus is purely Eastern, and does not concern us here.

All the members of *Chætura* as distinguished from *Cypseloides* have stiff tail-feathers, the shafts of which are produced beyond the webs and form sharp points, which no doubt enable the birds to support themselves against rocks, buildings, and trees, as a Woodpecker or Creeper does against a tree.

CHÆTURA.

Chætura, Stephens in Shaw's Gen. Zool. xiii. pt. 2, p. 76 (1826); Hartert, Cat. Birds Brit. Mus.
    xvi. p. 470.
Hemiprocne, Nitzsch, Pter. p. 123.

This genus contains the spine-tailed Swifts found throughout the greater part of the tropical portion of the world, and includes, according to Mr. Hartert, the large *C. caudacuta* and its allies, by some separated into a distinct genus *Hirundinapus,* as well as the larger forms of South and Central America to which the name *Hemiprocne* has been applied. Both these groups appear to be natural sections, but their definition is not easy and hardly necessary. *Chætura,* then, in its wide sense, contains about thirty-six species, of which just half belong to the New World. The rest are found in various parts of the Old World as far east as New Guinea and Australia, Tropical Africa and Madagascar possessing species of their own.

Of the eighteen American species, eight occur within our region, two of them being winter visitants from the north. *C. semicollaris* is peculiar to Mexico, and *C. gaumeri* has not been noticed beyond the limits of Central America. The remaining four all extend beyond our southern border, and are found on the continent of South America.

a. *Majores: torques cervicalis albus aut integer aut interruptus.*

1. Chætura zonaris.

Hirundo zonaris, Shaw in Mill. Cim. Phys. p. 100, t. 55 (1796)[1].

Hemiprocne zonaris, Cab. & Heine, Mus. Hein. iii. p. 83[2]; Scl. & Salv. Ibis, 1859, p. 125[3]; Salv.
Ibis, 1860, p. 37[4]; Boucard, P. Z. S. 1878, p. 67[5]; Sumichrast, La Nat. v. p. 250[6];
Zeledon, An. Mus. Nac. Costa Rica, 1887, p. 120[7]; Scl. & Huds. Arg. Orn. ii. p. 11[8].

Chætura zonaris, Scl. P. Z. S. 1865, p. 609[9]; Sumichrast, Mem. Bost. Soc. N. H. i. p. 562[10]; Salv.
P. Z. S. 1870, p. 204[11]; Hartert, Cat. Birds Brit. Mus. xvi. p. 476[12].

Cypselus collaris, Temm. Pl. Col. 195[13].

Fuliginoso-nigra, alis metallice olivaceo vix tinctis, torque cervicali albo, margine alari albo stricte fasciato:
rostro et pedibus nigris. Long. tota circa 8·0, alæ 8·2, caudæ 2·4, tarsi 0·85. (Descr. feminæ ex
Dueñas, Guatemala. Mus. nostr.)

♂ feminæ similis.

Av. juv. quoque feminæ similis, sed torque pectorali indistincto, plumis albo marginatis.

Hab. MEXICO, Tierra Caliente of both coasts, Uvero, Cordova, State of Vera Cruz
(*Sumichrast*[6][10]), Mirador (*Sumichrast*[6], *Sartorius, in U. S. Nat. Mus.*), Villa Alta
(*M. Trujillo*[12]), Santa Efigenia, Cacoprieto (*Sumichrast*[6]); GUATEMALA (*Skinner*[3]),
Retalhuleu, Patzicia, Calderas (8300 feet), Dueñas[4], San José de Guatemala (*O. S.
& F. D. G.*); COSTA RICA (*Van Patten, in U. S. Nat. Mus.*), Volcan de Irazu
(*Boucard*[5]), La Palma de San José (*Zeledon*[7]); PANAMA, Chitra, Calovevora
(*Arcé*[11]).—SOUTH AMERICA generally[12] from Colombia to South Brazil and
Argentina[8]; GREATER ANTILLES; GRENADA[12].

Chætura zonaris has a very wide range in South America, extending over nearly the
whole of the tropical portion of that continent from the Sierra de Mendoza in the
Argentine Republic to Colombia, and thence northwards through Central America to
Southern Mexico. It is also found in all the larger Antilles and in the island of
Grenada, where Mr. Wells obtained specimens. The bird of British Guiana was
separated by Cabanis as *Hemiprocne albicincta,* and a bird from Bogota by Mr. Lawrence
as *H. minor.* These seem only to differ from the ordinary form in being rather smaller.
Still the Guiana birds at any rate are localized, and the fact of their small size is
noteworthy.

In other respects but little difference is to be found in specimens from localities
widely separated. Central-American birds are, on an average, perhaps rather smaller
than southern examples, but the difference is not material. Mr. Hartert notices that
the Antillean birds have the forehead brownish grey, but none of the specimens he
examined are in freshly moulted plumage, and the difference, if any, seems to us to
be trivial.

In Mexico the recorded range of this species does not extend beyond the middle of
the State of Vera Cruz[6]. Sumichrast obtained specimens, which are now in the United
States National Museum, on the Rio Seco near Cordova, and Sartorius others at the
Hacienda of Mirador near Huatusco. Our collector Mateo Trujillo also found this

Swift at Villa Alta in Oaxaca, but no specimens, so far as we know, were included in MM. Sallé's and Boucard's collections.

Nor have we any tidings of it from any of the more northern or western parts of the Republic of Mexico.

In Guatemala we believe it to be pretty generally distributed, and we observed it at different places from the sea-level at San José de Guatemala to as high as the mountain ridge above Calderas on the Volcan de Fuego, an altitude of 8300 feet.

In the rainy season flocks of this Swift were frequently to be seen flying high over the plain of Dueñas, occasionally descending to within gun-shot, when a few specimens could be secured. A roosting-place of a flock of these birds was in the rocks over which the Guacalate formed a cascade near the village of Ciudad Vieja. On one occasion a number of these birds which had been observed flying over the valley suddenly descended and disappeared behind the fall.

2. Chætura semicollaris.

Acanthylis semicollaris, De Sauss. Rev. Zool. 1859, p. 118[1].

Chætura semicollaris, Scl. P. Z. S. 1865, p. 609[2]; Scl. & Salv. Ex. Orn. p. 103, t. 52[3]; Sumichrast, Mem. Bost. Soc. N. H. i. p. 562[4]; Herrera, Apuntes de Ornit. p. 15[5]; Hartert, Cat. Birds Brit. Mus. xvi. p. 479[6].

Hemiprocne semicollaris, Sumichrast, La Nat. v. p. 250[7].

Fuliginoso-nigra, capite toto et gutture vix pallidioribus, fascia transversa angusta nuchali alba. Long. tota circa 9·5, alæ 9·2, caudæ 2·9. (Descr. exempl. typ. ex Mexico. Mus. Brit.)

Hab. MEXICO [1], San Joaquin near the capital (*Sumichrast* [7]).

Several specimens of this large Swift were killed near Mexico city by Sumichrast when he was in company with M. H. de Saussure in 1856 [7]. These birds were described by the latter naturalist in 1859 [1], and one of the typical specimens passed into Mr. Sclater's possession and was figured in 'Exotic Ornithology' [3]. This last-named bird, which is now in the British Museum, is the only one we have seen.

Of the species very little is known; Sumichrast does not seem to have met with it again, and Herrera speaks of it as probably a bird of accidental occurrence [5]. Neither Sallé nor Boucard notice it; nor have we any tidings of it in the large collections of Richardson, Lloyd, and others recently formed in various parts of Mexico.

C. semicollaris is most nearly allied to *C. zonaris*, but may readily be distinguished from that species by its large size and by the white collar being restricted to the back of the neck, and not forming a complete ring round it, as is the case in the allied form.

b. *Minores: torques cervicalis nullus.*

3. Chætura pelagica.

Hirundo pelagica, Linn. Syst. Nat. i. p. 192 (1758)[1].

Chætura pelagica, Baird, Brew., & Ridgw. N. Am. Birds, ii. p. 432[2]; Coues, Birds N. W. p. 267[3]; Salv. Ibis, 1889, p. 367[4]; Hartert, Cat. Birds Brit. Mus. xvi. p. 480[5].

Hirundo pelasgia, Linn. Syst. Nat. i. p. 345[6]; Wils. Am. Orn. v. p. 48, t. 39[7].

Chætura pelasgia, Baird, Birds N. Am. p. 144 (1858)[8]; Scl. P. Z. S. 1865, p. 610[9].

Saturate murino-brunnea, alis saturatioribus, dorso postico et cauda dilutioribus, vitta superciliari indistincta: subtus gutture toto sordide albicante ad pectus murino transeunte: rostro et pedibus nigris. Long. tota circa 5·0, alæ 5·1, caudæ 1·6. (Descr. maris ex Ins. Cozumel, Yucatan. Mus. nostr.) ♀ mari similis.

Hab. NORTH AMERICA from Labrador and lat. 50° W. southwards[2].—MEXICO, Jalapa (*Boucard*[5]), Cozumel I. (*G. F. Gaumer*[4]); GUATEMALA[5]?

This Swift is a well-known summer visitant to the eastern portion of the United States, where it breeds, making its nest in the chimneys of buildings or in hollow trees in the forest. The nest is described as constructed of sticks firmly stuck together with the saliva of the bird, and attached to the brickwork of a chimney or to a tree by the same material. Brewer[2] gives an account of the way in which the bird collects the twigs during its flight, and the passage is quoted at length by Dr. Coues[3]. The former author states that the number of eggs laid in each nest is four; the latter gives the number as from four to six.

Dr. Coues[3] was unable to find any statement giving the winter-quarters of *C. pelagica*, and we are very much in the same position, though we have ascertained a few spots outside the limits of the United States where this bird has been noticed in the winter months. It occurs at Jalapa, where M. Boucard met with it, and Mr. Gaumer obtained several examples during his stay on the Island of Cozumel[4]. It also occurs in South-eastern Texas, but probably only on passage. In Florida, too, it has been noticed in spring, but whence the individuals arrive is unknown, as we have no record of the appearance of the bird in any of the West-Indian Islands or on the mainland of South America. Practically, therefore, we know next to nothing of the winter-quarters of the great mass of birds which must pass and repass in spring and autumn to their summer nesting-quarters in the United States, as the few birds noticed in Eastern Mexico can only belong to the fringe of the main body of migrants. The occurrence of this species in Guatemala rests upon a skin in the British Museum which was formerly in Lord Tweeddale's collection[5]. Its locality is not otherwise authenticated.

4. Chætura vauxi.

Cypselus vauxi, Towns. Journ. Ac. Phil. viii. p. 148 (1839)[1].

Chætura vauxi, Baird, Birds N. Am. p. 145, t. 18 (1858)[2]; Salv. Ibis, 1861, p. 147[3]; Scl. P. Z. S. 1865, p. 611[4]; Baird, Brew., & Ridgw. N. Am. Birds, ii. p. 435[5]; Sumichrast, Mem. Bost. Soc. N. H. i. p. 562[6]; La Nat. v. p. 250[7]; Lawr. Bull. U. S. Nat. Mus. no. 4, p. 32[8]; Ferrari-Perez, Pr. U. S. Nat. Mus. ix. p. 158[9]; Hartert, Cat. Birds Brit. Mus. xvi. p. 481[10].

Chætura ——?, Scl. & Salv. Ibis, 1860, p. 37[11].

Chætura similis, Lawr.[12]

C. pelagicæ affinis, sed minor dorso postico et tectricibus caudæ superioribus pallidioribus: subtus omnino pallidior, abdomine quam guttur paulo obscuriore. Long. tota circa 4·0, alæ 4·5, caudæ 1·55. (Descr. maris ex Mexico. Mus. nostr.)

Hab. NORTH AMERICA, Western States from British Columbia southwards [5].—MEXICO (*de Saussure*), Sierra de Mexico (*Rébouch*), Rio Seco near Cordova, Valley of Mexico [7] (*Sumichrast*), Puebla (*Mus. Brit.*[10]), Laguna del Rosario in Tlaxcala (*F. Ferrari-Perez*[9]), Guichicovi [7], Tehuantepec (*Sumichrast, in U. S. Nat. Mus.*[8]); GUATEMALA, Raxche [3], Coban [11], Dueñas, Alotenango and Tierra Caliente generally (*O. S. & F. D. G.*); HONDURAS (*Dyson, in Mus. Brit.*[11]); NICARAGUA, Rio Escondido (*C. W. Richmond, in U. S. Nat. Mus.*); COSTA RICA (*Van Patten, in U. S. Nat. Mus.*).

This species is a near ally of *C. pelagica*, but may be distinguished by its smaller size, the wing being on an average nearly an inch shorter ; the tarsi and toes, however, are relatively longer ; in colour it is generally paler.

C. vauxi was discovered by Townsend in the Columbia river, where he found it common, breeding in the hollow trunks of trees, in the same manner as *C. pelagica*, and laying four white eggs [1]. The bird is now known to be widely spread in Western North America from Puget's Sound to California. It occurs also in Mexico and Guatemala, and thence southwards to Costa Rica. In Guatemala we used to see it not unfrequently in the winter months flying over the open ground between the volcanoes of Agua and Fuego, and occasionally a flock would fly low enough to enable us to secure a few specimens. We also observed it in various parts of the department of Vera Paz. Though there can hardly be a doubt that these southern birds are simply individuals of *C. vauxi* in their winter-quarters, some attempts have been made to separate them as distinct. Thus Mr. Lawrence at one time referred a Dueñas specimen to his *C. gaumeri*, and associated with it an example from Tehuantepec, and these birds he seems afterwards to have discriminated under the name of *C. similis* *. When due allowance is made for small individual differences in size, and for the wear and tear of the plumage, we do not think it possible to define these southern birds as distinct from the true *C. vauxi*.

5. Chætura gaumeri.

Chætura vauxi, Lawr. (nec Townsend) Ann. Lyc. N. Y. ix. p. 204 [1].

Chætura gaumeri, Lawr. Ann. N. Y. Ac. Sc. ii. p. 245 [2]; Boucard, P. Z. S. 1883, p. 451 [3]; Ridgw. Pr. U. S. Nat. Mus. vi. p. 415 [4]; Salv. Ibis, 1889, p. 367 [5]; Stone, Pr. Ac. Phil. 1890, p. 206 [6]; Hartert, Cat. Birds Brit. Mus. xvi. p. 482 [7].

Chætura yucatanica, Lawr. Ann. N. Y. Ac. Sc. iii. p. 156 [8].

hætura peregrinator, Lawr. Ann. N. Y. Ac. Sc. iii. p. 273 [9].

C. vauxi similis, sed plerumque minor supra saturatior, abdomine et tectricibus subcaudalibus quoque obscu-rioribus. Long. tota circa 4·0, alæ 4·2, caudæ 1·4. (Descr. maris ex Cozumel I., Yucatan. Mus. nostr.)

---

* Probably the same bird is referred to by Mr. Ridgway as *C. affinis* (Pr. U. S. Nat. Mus. ix. p. 158). We have not been able to find any description of it or of *C. similis*.

Hab. MEXICO, N. Yucatan (*G. F. Gaumer* [2][3]), Merida (*Schott, in U. S. Nat. Mus.* [1]), Silam [8], Temax [9], Cozumel I. [5] (*G. F. Gaumer*), Tunkas and Ticul (*W. Stone* [6]); NICARAGUA, Rio Escondido (*C. W. Richmond*); COSTA RICA (*Van Patten* [4]); PANAMA, Chiriqui (*Arcé* [5]).

Chætura gaumeri seems to be a small resident form of *C. vauxi*, chiefly restricted to Eastern Central America from the promontory of Northern Yucatan and the islands adjoining to Nicaragua and Costa Rica. In the former country it frequents the large ' senotes' or caves formed like wells in the limestone formation of that peculiar district, and where Dr. Gaumer says the species is abundant. Mr. Richmond found *C. gaumeri* to be common on the Rio Escondido towards the end of May, when he supposed it to be breeding *.

Dr. Gaumer sent us a number of specimens of this bird captured during his visit to Cozumel Island. From these we learn that there is a certain amount of individual variation in size, and much in the extent to which the projecting ends of the shafts of the rectrices are worn. It thus becomes evident that neither *C. yucatanica* nor *C. peregrinator*, both described by Mr. Lawrence from Yucatan birds, can be recognized as distinct. This view was fully confirmed when we had an opportunity of seeing the types, which were submitted to Mr. Hartert when compiling his Catalogue of Cypselidæ in the British Museum [7].

6. Chætura fumosa.

Chætura fumosa, Salv. P. Z. S. 1870, p. 204 [1]; Wyatt, Ibis, 1871, p. 375 [2]; Hartert, Cat. Birds Brit. Mus. xvi. p. 483 [3].

Chætura spinicauda, Layard (nec Temm.), Ibis, 1873, p. 389 [4].

Chætura cinereiventris guianensis, Ridgw. Pr. U. S. Nat. Mus. xvi. p. 43 (partim) [5]; Richmond, Pr. U. S. Nat. Mus. xvi. p. 516 [6].

Nigra vix purpureo nitens; uropygio et tectricibus supracaudalibus proximis cineriis, rhachidibus nigris: subtus gutture sordide cinereo-albo, pectore et abdomine toto nigricantibus. Long. tota circa 4·6, alæ 4·4, caudæ 1·5. (Descr. exempl. typ. ex Bugaba, Panama. Mus. nostr.)

Hab. NICARAGUA, Rio Escondido (*C. W. Richmond* [6]); COSTA RICA, Rio Frio (*C. W. R.* [6]); PANAMA, Bugaba [1], Volcan de Chiriqui (*Arcé*).—COLOMBIA [2]; AMAZONS VALLEY, Santarem [3], Para [4].

Chætura spinicauda of Guiana and Trinidad is the most nearly allied species to *C. fumosa*, but the latter bird has a wider gray band across the rump, this colour extending to the proximal upper tail-coverts, the shafts of these feathers alone being dark; the lower surface, too, of the body is darker and more uniform, the chin and throat being of a dingy ashy white.

* Pr. U. S. Nat. Mus. xvi. p. 516. Mr. Richmond's birds have been already mentioned, *anteà* p. 376, as *C. vauxi*, the name sent us by Mr. Ridgway, who first examined them. In the paper cited Mr. Richmond puts this right.

Skins of this Swift sent us by our collector Arcé from Chiriqui were the first that reached us and were described by Salvin in 1870 [1]. Soon afterwards Mr. C. W. Wyatt shot a specimen in a clearing in the forest near Naranjo in Colombia at an elevation of 2500 feet above the sea [2]. Mr. Wickham obtained a specimen at Santarem on the Amazons river, and Mr. Layard others at Para, where he says the bird is common throughout the year [4].

We have recently acquired a specimen of the Swift found in Nicaragua and Costa Rica by Mr. C. W. Richmond and referred by Mr. Ridgway [5] and by him [6] to Mr. Hartert's *C. cinereiventris guianensis*. This we have compared with our types of *C. fumosa*, and can find no tangible differences; in fact the only point that we notice is that the longest upper tail-coverts are slightly darker in *C. fumosa*, and in Mr. Richmond's specimen grayer, but the latter are somewhat abraided and the difference at most but very slight. As the Costa Rica and Nicaragua bird occurs on the outskirts of the northern range of *C. fumosa*, we have no hesitation in placing it under that name.

Mr. Richmond shot two specimens on the Rio Frio from a large company of Swifts, and collected others on the estate of the International Plantation Company on the Rio Escondido, where it appeared to be common, associating with *C. gaumeri* [6].

c. *Minor: mas torque cervicali ferrugineo.*

7. Chætura brunneitorques.

Chætura brunneitorques, Lafr. Rev. Zool. 1844, p. 81 [1]; Salv. & Godm. Ibis, 1882, p. 83 [2]; Zeledon, An. Mus. Nac. Costa Rica, 1887, p. 120 [3]; Cherrie, Auk, 1892, p. 324 [4].

Cypseloides brunneitorques, Hartert, Cat. Birds Brit. Mus. xvi. p. 493 [5].

Chætura rutila, Scl. & Salv. (nec Vieill.), Ibis, 1860, p. 37, t. 3 [6]; P. Z. S. 1869, p. 363 [7]; Sumichrast, Mem. Bost. Soc. N. H. i. p. 562 [8]; La Nat. v. p. 250 [9].

Fuliginoso-nigra, gula et abdomine vix dilutioribus, torque cervicali undique rufo, antice latiore, et plumarum omnium rhachidibus nigris : rostro et pedibus nigris. Long. tota circa 5·0, alæ 5·0, caudæ 1·2, tarsi 0·45. ♀ mari similis, sed torque cervicali rufo nullo. (Descr. maris et feminæ ex Dueñas, Guatemala. Mus. nostr.)

Hab. MEXICO (*le Strange* [7]), Tuxpango near Orizaba (*Sumichrast* [8][9]), Orizaba (*Sumichrast, in U. S. Nat. Mus.*), San Miguel Molino (*F. Ferrari-Perez*); GUATEMALA, Plains near Dueñas (*O. S. & F. D. G.* [6]); COSTA RICA (*Van Patten, in U. S. Nat. Mus.*), San José (*Zeledon* [3], *Cherrie* [4]); PANAMA, Chiriqui, Calovevora (*Arcé*).— COLOMBIA [1]; ECUADOR [2][7].

This species was described in 1844 by Lafresnaye from specimens from Colombia [1], from which country there are several examples in the British Museum. These agree with a series from various parts of Central America and Southern Mexico, including the birds obtained by us on various occasions at Dueñas and its neighbourhood.

In the last-named locality *C. brunneitorques* is not unfrequently to be seen in flocks flying over the open country, especially in the wet season from July to October. On cloudy rainy afternoons the birds would fly near the ground and within gun-shot, at other times they would circle round like ordinary Swifts high in the air.

The fact of there being a marked difference in the plumage between the sexes of this species is a peculiarity in the family only shared by *C. rutila* of Guiana and Trinidad. Dissected specimens proved that the male has the red collar, and that the female is without it.

The southern extension of the range of *C. brunneitorques* reaches Ecuador, whence we have seen several specimens [2]. Its northern limit includes Southern Mexico, where Mr. le Strange found it and where Sumichrast says that it is resident and breeds in the State of Vera Cruz near Tuxpango and Orizaba [8], Señor Ferrari-Perez also found it at San Miguel Molino in the State of Puebla.

The only species at all nearly related to *C. brunneitorques* is *C. rutila* (Vieill.) of Guiana and Trinidad, and with which it was for some time confounded[2]. *C. rutila* has, however, the chin as well as the cervical collar of a clearer paler rusty red, the dark crown being more restricted posteriorly, and other slight differences.

Mr. Hartert, in his Catalogue of the Cypselidæ in the British Museum, removed *C. brunneitorques* and *C. rutila* from *Chætura*, and placed them in *Cypseloides*. As the shafts of the rectrices are distinctly spinous, though perhaps hardly so much so as in typical *Chæiura* (in *Cypseloides* the points are not at all prominent), the two species in question are best placed in *Chætura*.

CYPSELOIDES.

Cypseloides, Streubel, Isis, 1848, p. 366 ; Hartert, Cat. Birds Brit. Mus. xvi. p. 492.

The shafts of the rectrices in this genus are not produced beyond the webs of the feathers, and therefore the tail is not provided with the spiny points which form such a conspicuous feature in *Chætura*. *Cypseloides* thus to outward appearance much more resembles the true Swifts, but it has the normal number of phalanges to the third and fourth toes, so that it really falls into this section of the family.

Mr. Hartert includes five species in the genus, but we think that *C. rutila* and *C. brunneitorques* belong more properly to *Chætura*. To the three remaining species *C. cherriei* must be added, making four in all, of which two occur within our limits. The other two are confined to South America.

1. Cypseloides niger.

Hirundo apos dominicensis, Briss. Orn. ii. p. 514, t. 46. f. 3 [1].

Hirundo niger, Gm. Syst. Nat. i. p. 1025 [2].

Cypselus niger, Gosse, Birds Jam. p. 63 [3] ; Ill. Birds Jam. t. 10 [4].

Cypseloides niger, Scl. P. Z. S. 1865, p. 615 [5] ; Zeledon, An. Mus. Nac. Costa Rica, 1887, p. 120 [6] ; Cory, Birds W. Ind. p. 140 [7] ; Hartert, Cat. Birds Brit. Mus. xvi. p. 494 [8] ; Cherrie, Auk, 1892, p. 324 [9].

Nephæcetes niger, Sumichrast, Mem. Bost. Soc. N. H. i. p. 562 [10] ; Baird, Brew., & Ridgw. N. Am. Birds, ii. p. 429 [11].

Cypselus borealis, Kennerly, Pr. Ac. Phil. 1857, p. 202 [12].

Cypseloides borealis, Scl. P. Z. S. 1865, p. 615 [13] ; Hartert, Cat. Birds Brit. Mus. xvi. p. 495 [14].

Fuliginoso-niger, dorso, alis et cauda saturatioribus et certa luce nitidis, loris et superciliis indistincte canescentibus: rostro et pedibus nigris. Long. tota circa 6·3, alæ 6·5, caudæ rectr. med. 2·1, rectr. lat. 2·35 tarsi 0·5. (Descr. maris ex San Miguel Molino, Puebla, Mexico. Mus. nostr.)

♀ mari similis.

Hab. NORTH AMERICA, from British Columbia southwards [10].—MEXICO, Sierra Madre de Tepic (*W. B. Richardson* [14]), San Miguel Molino in Puebla (*F. Ferrari-Perez* [14]), State of Vera Cruz (*Sumichrast* [9]); COSTA RICA, San José (*Zeledon* [6], *Cherrie* [9]).—WEST INDIES generally [7]; BRITISH GUIANA [13].

Opinions vary concerning this Swift, whether the bird of Western North America and Mexico should be considered distinct from that of the West Indian Islands. The question appears to rest simply on the relative size of the two birds, the former being slightly larger than the latter. Mr. Sclater kept the two birds separate in his Monograph published in 1865 [13], and Mr. Hartert also admits the continental bird to subspecific rank [14]. American ornithologists differ on the subject, but Mr. Ridgway in his Manual places both forms under *C. niger*. In our opinion the difference is of too slight importance to justify separation, though the continental birds appear to be undoubtedly a little larger than the average of those from the West Indies.

Little is known of this bird in Mexico. Sumichrast states that it is found in the State of Vera Cruz and breeds there [10]. The latter fact is confirmed by the specimen from Puebla, which is scarcely adult and was shot on the 5th July; and also by Mr. Richardson's examples, all of which are immature and were shot in June [14]. It is probable that the "Black Swift" about the size of *C. brunneitorques*, which Mr. Richmond (Pr. U. S. Nat. Mus. xvi. p. 516) saw in numbers on the Rio Frio in Costa Rica, belonged to this species. It has been recorded from that country by Mr. Zeledon [6] and confirmed by Mr. Cherrie [9], and the latter naturalist says that on the label of Mr. Zeledon's specimen in the National Museum is a note to the effect that the bird was breeding when shot.

2. Cypseloides cherriei.

Cypseloides cherriei, Ridgw. Pr. U. S. Nat. Mus. xvi. p. 44 [1].

"Similar in size and general form to *C. brunneitorques* (Lafr.), but tail quite truncated, with feathers less rigid and only very minutely mucronate. Colour, uniform sooty black (much darker than in *C. brunneitorques*), the under surface somewhat paler, especially anteriorly, where becoming light grayish on the chin. A large, sharply defined spot of silky white on each side of the forehead, immediately over the lores, and a short streak of the same colour immediately behind the eye; lores velvety black, in very sharp contrast with the white spot above them. Length (skin) 5 inches, wing 6, tail 1·87, tarsus 0·50." (*Ridgway, l. c.*)

Hab. COSTA RICA, Volcan de Irazu (*G. K. Cherrie* [1]).

"This apparently new species needs no comparison with any other, the peculiar white markings of the head being sufficient to at once distinguish it." (*Ridgway.*)

We have seen no bird at all answering to the above description of Mr. Ridgway. The species appears to be remarkably distinct, and we shall be glad to hear more about it.

Note.—*Panyptila cayennensis* (*anteà*, p. 370, Jan. 1893) was included in this work on the evidence of a specimen obtained with its nest on the banks of the Chagres River by Dr. Merritt. Since then we have seen Mr. Richmond's very interesting account of the bird and its breeding-habits published in the 'Auk' for 1893 (p. 84). Mr. Richmond was staying at the estate of the Imperial Plantation Company, on the Rio Escondido, about fifty miles from Blewfields, Nicaragua, and the substance of his note we now transcribe:—

" On Aug. 23, 1892, after an early morning trip in the woods, I had nearly reached the edge of the plantation when my attention was drawn to a mixed company of birds feeding on berries in an immense tree. The tree belonged to a species common in these forests, a giant among its surroundings, the trunk at least five feet in diameter, and the first limb over seventy feet from the ground . . . . Wounding a Yellowtail (*Ostinops montezumæ*), I was endeavouring to keep sight of it, when a small bird dashed past and disappeared on the trunk of the tree about seventy feet from the ground. Looking in that direction I noticed a nest, eight or nine inches in length, hanging from the trunk, and so nearly resembling it in colour that ordinarily it would have been passed unnoticed. The trunk was perfectly straight for a distance of seventy feet, at which point there was a division, the portion with the nest leaning very slightly, and the nest was attached to the smooth grayish bark on the underside of the trunk, hanging vertically and at the same time almost against the bark, rendering it a very inconspicuous object. The nest when first observed was still quivering from the movements made by the bird, proving it to be made of some soft, yielding material. The nest almost exactly matched the bark in colour; the entrance, at the bottom, was very large, nearly the diameter of the nest, which appeared to be about three inches at the lower end with a slight bulging near the top. On shooting into the nest there was a struggle inside which shook it considerably, and presently the bird dropped to the ground. It was a *Panyptila cayennensis*, and on dissection proved to be a male, with the sexual organs only slightly developed.

" Visiting the spot the next day with a pair of field-glasses, I tried to identify the material composing the nest, but beyond its having the appearance of being stuccoed with some substance resembling the bark in colour, I could determine nothing. The bark was quite smooth, and the nest appeared to be glued on, although this was not positively ascertained to be the case.

" This Swift is quite abundant here, as is also the small gray-rumped *Chætura*. They usually fly very high, though apparently not faster than the Chimney Swift of Eastern North America. On cloudy afternoons, particularly after rain-storms, they often fly so low that specimens may be easily obtained."

We have recently acquired several of Mr. Richmond's specimens and find them rather smaller than some of the South-American series in the British Museum. As they vary *inter se* in this respect, and as the smallest is not larger than a specimen from British Guiana, we do not consider this difference of size of any importance.

Suborder CAPRIMULGI.

Fam. CAPRIMULGIDÆ.

The Goatsuckers, under which name these birds are commonly known, like the Swifts, are found nearly throughout the tropical and temperate portions of the globe. None occur in the colder regions of either the northern or southern hemispheres, and they appear to be absent from the islands of the Pacific Ocean eastward of the Solomon Islands.

The members of the family Caprimulgidæ are, as a rule, easily recognized by characters both of structure and plumage; the allied forms Podargidæ and Steatornithidæ, which were once included under the same family, being removed, the remainder constitute a uniform group, divisible, like the Swifts, into two subfamilies by the structure of the foot.

Mr. Hartert, in his Catalogue of the Caprimulgidæ, recognizes nineteen genera; of these *Caprimulgus* is common to both the Old and New Worlds. Of the remaining eighteen genera, thirteen occur in America only, all but two of which are Neotropical. In Mexico and Central America seven genera are represented: one of these is the widely spread *Caprimulgus*; *Phalœnoptilus*, a North-American genus, occurs in Northern Mexico; *Otophanes* is peculiar to Northern and Western Mexico; *Nyctidromus*, *Stenopsis*, and *Nyctibius* are all southern forms; and *Chordeiles* extends its range both into North and South America.

Subfam. *CAPRIMULGINÆ.*

In this subfamily, which includes all but one of the genera of American Caprimulgidæ, the outer toe has only four instead of five phalanges, the claw of the middle toe is pectinated, and there are no powder-down patches on the body.

a. *Rictus setis fortibus armatus.*

CAPRIMULGUS.

Caprimulgus, Linnæus, Syst. Nat. i. p. 346 (1766); Hartert, Cat. Birds Brit. Mus. xvi. p. 521.
Antrostomus, Nuttall, Man. Orn. ed. 2, p. 729 (1840); Sclater, P. Z. S. 1866, p. 136.

The Common Goatsucker, *Caprimulgus europæus*, the oldest and best known of the whole family, is the type of the genus *Caprimulgus* as defined by Linnæus, the name being derived from older writers.

In 1840, Nuttall separated the American from the Old World birds under the name of *Antrostomus*, and this separation has been almost universally adopted by subsequent writers. Mr. Hartert, however, failing to find characters whereby to separate *Antrostomus* from *Caprimulgus*, united them in his Catalogue under the latter name; in so doing, he followed up the hint thrown out by Mr. Sclater in his "Notes on American Caprimulgidæ."

The tarsus in *Caprimulgus*, as in the three following genera, is more or less feathered in front, and is shorter than the middle toe including its claw; the tail is rounded; the head unadorned with ear-like tufts, but with distinct longitudinal markings.

Of the forty-three species constituting the genus only seven occur within our limits. Two of these, *C. carolinensis* and *C. vociferus*, pass some way into North America; one, *C. macromystax*, occurs on the frontier and throughout Mexico and Guatemala; one, *C. saturatus*, is restricted to Costa Rica and Panama; one, *C. yucatanicus*, to Yucatan; and one, *C. salvini*, to Mexico; the seventh is *C. rufus*, a southern species occurring as far north as Panama.

The patterns of the plumage of all the Caprimulgidæ are very intricate, so much so that specific differences of coloration, though apparent to the eye, are not easily described in words. To render the Mexican and Central-American species more readily distinguished the following key may serve:—

A. Alæ, primariis in ambobus pogoniis maculatis.
    a. Rectrices tres externæ macula magna, supra alba, infra isabellina.
        a′. Setæ rictales filamentis lateralibus instructæ . . . . . . 1. *carolinensis.*
        b′. Setæ rictales simplices . . . . 2. *rufus.*
    b. Rectrices tres externæ macula magna, supra et subtus alba.
        c′. Maculæ caudales magnæ.
            a″. Rectrices externæ rotundatæ, maculæ albæ extrorsum decrescentes.
               a‴. Maculæ caudales majores, caput summum in medio longitudinaliter striatum . . . . . 3. *vociferus.*
               b‴. Maculæ caudales minores, caput summum undique maculatum . . . . 4. *macromystax.*
            b″. Rectrices externæ majus acutæ, maculæ albæ extrorsum increscentes . . . . 5. *salvini.*
        d′. Maculæ caudales minutæ, angustæ . . . . 6. *yucatanicus.*
B. Alæ, primariis in pogonio interno unicoloribus, in pogonio externo tantum maculatis . . . . 7. *saturatus.*

1. Caprimulgus carolinensis.

Caprimulgus carolinensis, Gm. Syst. Nat. i. p. 1028 [1] ; Wils. Am. Orn. v. p. 95, t. 54. f. 20 [2]; Hartert, Cat. Birds Brit. Mus. xvi. p. 565 [3].

Antrostomus carolinensis, Salv. Ibis, 1866, p. 195 [4] ; P. Z. S. 1870, p. 203 [5]; Lawr. Ann. Lyc. N. Y. ix. p. 120 [6]; v. Frantzius, J. f. Orn. 1869, p. 314 [7]; Baird, Brew., & Ridgw. N. Am.

Birds, ii. p. 410[8]; Scl. & Salv. P. Z. S. 1879, p. 531[9]; Nutting, Pr. U. S. Nat. Mus. vi. p. 375[10]; Ridgway, Man. N. Am. Birds, p. 298[11].

Supra saturate nigricans, fulvo minute irroratus; capite summo et dorso striis elongatis nigris ornatis, scapularibus quoque nigro striatis et maculis fulvis notatis, torque cervicali plumis medialiter pallide cervinis composita; alis nigricantibus, maculis irregularibus rufis in pogonio externo subrotundatis, in pogonio interno transversim elongatis, nigro interruptis: subtus quoque fulvo irroratus et fasciatus, gula regulariter nigro transfasciata, torque cervicali isabellino plumis singulis nigro terminatis, pectore sparsim nigro sagittato, hypochondriis isabellino guttatis, tectricibus subcaudalibus fulvis nigro transfasciatis; cauda supra nigro et fulvo irrorata, rectricibus duabus mediis nigro indistincte sed regulariter transfasciatis, rectricibus utrinque tribus externis in pogonio interno (rhachide inclusa) plaga magna, fere ad apicem extensa, supra nivea, infra fulva notatis. Setis rictalibus filamentis lateralibus instructis. Long. tota circa 12·0, alæ 8·5, caudæ 5·5, tarsi 0·8, dig. med. cum ungue 1·1. (Descr. maris ex Costa Rica. Mus. nostr.)

♀ mari similis, maculis magnis caudalibus absentibus.

Hab. North America, Atlantic and Gulf States [11].—Mexico, Nuevo Leon (*F. B. Armstrong* [3]), Sierra de Santo Domingo in Tehuantepec (*W. B. Richardson* [3]).—Guatemala, Dueñas (*O. S. & F. D. G.* [4]); Nicaragua, San Juan del Sur (*Nutting* [10]); Costa Rica (*Endres* [3]), Guadelupe (*v. Frantzius* [7]), Las Cruces de Candelaria (*Zeledon* [6][7]); Panama, Volcan de Chiriqui (*Arcé* [5]). — Colombia [9]; Antilles [3].

This Goatsucker is the oldest known of its kind in North America. Though not fully recognized as distinct from *Caprimulgus europæus* by Linnæus it figures in Catesby's work, and now passes under Gmelin's title of *Caprimulgus carolinensis* *.

The South Atlantic and Gulf States and the Lower Mississippi Valley are the summer residence of this species, its northern extension reaching, according to Mr. Ridgway [11], to North Carolina and Southern Illinois. Its migration southward commences in August [8], and in the winter months it has been traced to several of the West Indian Islands, to Mexico and Central America, and as far south as Northern Colombia. The return journey northwards begins in March [8]. The eggs are laid on the bare ground amongst leaves in the darker thickets of the woods. As usual in this family, two is the full complement of eggs; their shape is oval, the ground-colour white, and they are more or less spotted with blotches of various sizes of dark purplish-brown, mixed with grayish-lavender, with occasional marks of raw-umber brown [8].

In Mexico and Central America *C. carolinensis* is apparently by no means common, as but few specimens have reached us. This is probably due to its nocturnal habits and the silence maintained during the winter season.

---

* We have no doubt Catesby (Car. i. t. 8) intended to give an accurate figure of his Carolina Goatsucker, but it may be remarked that he represents the wing with large white spots as in *Chordeiles virginianus*, a feature not possessed by any North-American species of *Caprimulgus*! Moreover, Latham, Brisson, and Gmelin all refer to these white spots; but Pennant (Arct. Zool. i. p. 133. no. 336), though referring to Catesby, gives an accurate description of the bird we now call *C. carolinensis*, omitting all mention of the white wing-spots.

2. Caprimulgus rufus.

Engoulevent roux de Cayenne, Montb. Hist. Nat. Ois. vi. p. 581 [1].
Crapaud volant, ou Tette-chèvre, de Cayenne, D'Aub. Pl. Enl. 735 [2].
Caprimulgus rufus, Bodd. Tabl. Enl. p. 46 [3]; Hartert, Cat. Birds Brit. Mus. xvi. p. 566 [4].
Antrostomus rufus, Cassin, Pr. Ac. Phil. 1851, p. 183 [5]; Cory, Birds W. Ind. p. 136 [6].
Antrostomus carolinensis, Salv. P. Z. S. 1870, p. 203 (partim) [7].

C. carolinensi similis sed minor, supra et subtus nigricantior, maculis magnis caudalibus paulo brevioribus, iis in rectrice secunda et tertia pogonio externo extendentibus; setis rictalibus simplicibus, fiamentis lateralibus haud instructis. Long. tota circa 10·5, alæ 7·1, caudæ 4·7, tarsi 6·5, dig. med. cum ungue 0·9. (Descr. maris ex Volcan de Chiriqui. Mus. nostr.)

Hab. PANAMA, Volcan de Chiriqui (*Arcé* [7]).—SOUTH AMERICA generally from Colombia to South Brazil [4]; SANTA LUCIA, W.I. [6]

Though this Goatsucker has a close general resemblance to *C. carolinensis*, so much so that our only Central-American specimen was at first referred to that species [7], the two birds are in fact very distinct. The present species may at once be distinguished from its ally by the structure of the long strong rictal bristles; the shafts of these are bare and not furnished with the fine lateral filaments found in *C. carolinensis*, and in it alone of the American Caprimulgidæ. *C. rufus* therefore, in this respect, resembles the rest of the family.

The range of this Goatsucker is very extensive and includes a large portion of tropical South America. Its southern range includes the Brazilian province of Rio Janeiro and its northern the West-Indian Island of Santa Lucia and Chiriqui within our limits: from the latter country a single male specimen was sent us by our collector E. Arcé in 1870 [4][7]; it was accompanied with a male of *C. carolinensis*.

3. Caprimulgus vociferus.

Caprimulgus vociferus, Wils. Am. Orn. v. p. 71, t. 41 [1]; Hartert, Cat. Birds Brit. Mus. xvi. p. 568 [2].
Antrostomus vociferus, Scl. P. Z. S. 1859, p. 367 [3]; Scl. & Salv. Ibis, 1860, p. 275 [4]; Baird, Brew., & Ridgw. Man. N. Am. Birds, ii. p. 413 [5]; Lawr. Bull. U. S. Nat. Mus. no. 4, p. 31 [6]; Sumichrast, La Nat. v. p. 249 [7]; Salv. Cat. Strickl. Coll. p. 379 [8]; Ferrari-Perez, Pr. U. S. Nat. Mus. ix. p. 158 [9]; Herrera, La Nat. (2) i. pp. 179 [10], 322 [11]; Ridgw. Man. N. Am. Birds, ii. p. 299 [12]; Cory, Auk, 1889, p. 276 [13].

Supra nigricans, fulvo minute irroratus; capite summo griseo et nigro dense irrorato, stria lata mediana nigra; alis et scapularibus magis rufescentibus, his maculis quibusdam nigris, aliis fulvis notatis, primariis nigricantibus, maculis in pogoniis ambobus rufis, regulariter fasciatis: subtus niger fulvo irroratus; gula nigra fulvo tenuiter fasciata, torque cervicali alba, pectore griseo irrorato, lateralibus isabellino indistincte guttatis; cauda nigricante, supra undique sed indistincte griseo irrorata, rectricibus tribus externis albo late terminata, maculis his extrorsum decrescentibus. Long. tota circa 9·0, alæ 7·1, caudæ 5·0, tarsi 0·72, dig. med. cum ungue 0·85. (Descr. maris ex Sonteh, Guatemala. Mus. nostr.)
♀ mari similis, maculis caudalibus parvis et isabellinis nec albis.

Hab. NORTH AMERICA, Eastern States from Nova Scotia and Manitoba southwards; Texas [5][12].—MEXICO, Rio Fuerte in Sinaloa (*W. Lloyd* [2]), Sierra de Tepic (*W. B.*

Richardson [2]), Valley of Mexico (*Herrera* [10]), Jalapa (*de Oca* [3]), Tlacotepec and Jaguey in Puebla [9], San Miguel Molino (*F. Ferrari-Perez*), Tehuantepec city (*Sumichrast* [6] [7]); GUATEMALA (*Constancia* [8]), Coban [4], Sonteh [2], San Gerónimo [4] (*O. S. & F. D. G.*); SALVADOR, La Libertad (*W. B. Richardson* [4]).—PUERTO RICO [13].

The Whip-poor-will, the name by which this bird is familiarly known in North America, is common during the summer months throughout the Eastern States and as far north as Montreal and Manitoba. In its northern migration it first shows itself in the Southern States early in March, but in more northern localities its appearance is delayed till the end of April and even the early part of May [5]. After the breeding-season, on the approach of autumn, it leaves for the south again in September. The winter months are passed in Mexico and Guatemala: the port of La Libertad in Salvador, on the shores of the Pacific, is the most southern point to which we have as yet traced it; here Mr. Richardson secured an example in February. Though chiefly found in Eastern Mexico it is not confined to that region, as Mr. Ridgway states, for we have specimens from Sinaloa and Tepic, on the western side of the Mexican Cordillera.

In Guatemala it is not by any means abundant, or at least not much in evidence. Our only specimens from that locality were obtained in Vera Paz on the eastern side of the country.

According to Brewer [5] the Whip-poor-will makes no nest, but lays its eggs in the thickest and most shady portions of the woods amongst fallen leaves in a hollow excavated for that purpose or on the leaves themselves. The eggs, two in number, are oval, of a creamy-white colour, irregularly spotted and marbled with lines and patches of purplish-lavender mingled with reddish-brown, the latter much more distinct.

4. Caprimulgus macromystax.

Caprimulgus macromystax, Wagl. Isis, 1831, p. 533 [1]; Hartert, Ibis, 1892, p. 286 [2]; Cat. Birds Brit. Mus. xvi. p. 570 [3].

Antrostomus macromystax, Scl. P. Z. S. 1858, p. 296 [4]; Salv. Cat. Strickl. Coll. p. 379 [5].

Antrostomus vociferus arizonæ, Brewster, Bull. Nutt. Orn. Club, vi. p. 69 [6]; Scott, Auk, 1886, p. 429 [7]; Ridgw. Man. N. Am. Birds, p. 299 [8].

Antrostomus ——?, Owen, Ibis, 1861, p. 64 [9].

C. vocifero similis, sed major, maculis caudalibus minoribus, tectricibus auricularibus fulvescentioribus, maculis verticis nigris magis dispersis; setis rictalibus plerumque longioribus. (Descr. maris ex Ixtaccihuatl, Mexico. Mus. nostr.)

Hab. NORTH AMERICA, Southern Arizona [6].—MEXICO (*Wagler* [1], *Galeotti* [4]), Sierra de Valparaiso, Sierra de Bolaños, Ajusco, Tenango del Valle, Rio Frio Ixtaccihuatl (*W. B. Richardson* [5]), Hacienda de San Marcos, Zapotlan (*W. Lloyd* [5]), Volcan de Colima (*W. B. Richardson* [5]), Amula in Guerrero (*Mrs. H. H. Smith*), La Parada (*Boucard* [3]); GUATEMALA, Coban, Volcan de Fuego (*O. S. & F. D. G.*), Santa Barbara in Vera Paz (*R. Owen* [9]).

C. macromystax is apparently a resident species in the Mexican tablelands, the western districts of that country, and in Guatemala. It also passes the northern frontier into Arizona.

Concerning its name there was long a certain amount of doubt, Wagler's description not being sufficiently explicit to distinguish between *C. macromystax* and *C. vociferus*. This question has been finally settled by Mr. Hartert [2], who has examined the type lent to him by its custodian at Munich and compared it with the series in the British Museum. The result shows that the bird named *C. macromystax* by Sclater and others was rightly so called, and that Mr. Brewster's *Antrostomus vociferus arizonæ* must be referred to the same species, the *C. macromystax* of American authors being a very different species.

On 20th April, 1860, Mr. R. Owen found, in the Santa Barbara Mountains in Vera Paz, two eggs of this species, and secured the female parent [9]. These eggs, though of the shape and texture usual in the Caprimulgidæ, are pure spotless white; they were deposited on the ground at the foot of a large pine-tree, but there was no nest. That these eggs belonged to the bird secured cannot be reasonably doubted; but their colour is quite unusual and perhaps abnormal, though it must be remembered *Phalænoptilus nuttalli* lays white eggs, and those of *Stenopsis ruficervix* are of the same colour.

In quoting a letter from Salvin, dated 10th March, 1872, Brewer, in his history of the last species, gives a correct account of the present bird, so far as its southern range is concerned; its extension northwards into Arizona was ascertained subsequently.

5. **Caprimulgus salvini.** (Tab. LVIII. b.)

Antrostomus macromystax, Baird, Brew., & Ridgw. (nec Wagler), N. Am. Birds, ii. p. 409 [1]; Boucard, P. Z. S. 1883, p. 451 [2].

Caprimulgus salvini, Hartert, Ibis, 1892, p. 287 [3]; Cat. Birds Brit. Mus. xvi. p. 568 [4].

Supra nigricans, fulvo et griseo minute irroratus, maculis magnis nigris in capite summo undique dispersis, cervice postica torque angusto rufescente, scapularibus et tectricibus alarum striis hastiformibus conspicue notatis : subtus gula nigricante fasciis tenuibus rufis, plumis gulæ lateralibus albo variegatis, torque cervicali alba, infra eam in pectore maculis albis ; abdomine nigro rufo fasciato et maculis albis conspicue guttato, tectricibus subcaudalibus fulvis nigro sparsim fasciatis ; alis nigris, maculis parvis rufis in pogoniis ambobus ; cauda nigra, fasciis crebris indistinctis maculosis grisescentibus supra notata, rectricibus tribus externis macula magna alba terminata extrorsum increscente. Long. tota circa 11·0, alæ 7·7, caudæ 5·0, tarsi 0·68, dig. med. cum ungue 0·9. (Descr. maris exempl. typ. ex Merida, Yucatan. Mus. nostr.)

♀ mari similis, maculis caudalibus minoribus et isabellinis.

Hab. Mexico, Nuevo Leon (*F. B. Armstrong* [3]), Merida in Yucatan (*G. F. Gaumer* [3]).

This bird is the *Antrostomus macromystax* of Baird, Brewer, and Ridgway [1] and subsequent American writers, but not *C. macromystax* of Wagler. This point has been amply proved by Mr. Hartert, who found it necessary to give the bird a new name.

We have seen but few specimens of this Goatsucker, but a male obtained by

Dr. Gaumer on 7th January, 1879, near Merida in Yucatan has long been in our possession.　Mr. Armstrong obtained us another in the North Mexican State of Nuevo Leon. It would thus appear to approach the limits of the United States, but at present there is no evidence of its crossing the frontier.　Of its habits nothing has yet been recorded, but it is probably resident in the countries in which it is found.

6. **Caprimulgus yucatanicus.**　(Tab. LVIII. A.)

Caprimulgus yucatanicus, Hartert, Cat. Birds Brit. Mus. xvi. p. 575 [1].

Supra capite summo vinaceo-rufo, plumis singulis medialiter nigricantibus, corpore reliquo rufo et nigro minute irrorato; scapularibus maculis conspicuis hastiformibus nigris, tectricibus alarum majoribus similiter ornatis, minoribus quoque albo guttulatis: subtus fascia lata gulari candida, pectore vinaceo-rufo minute nigro irrorato, plumis singulis rhachidibus nigris; abdomine nigro et fulvo vermiculato, maculis albidis quoque notato; alis nigricantibus, pogoniis ambobus rufo regulariter maculatis; cauda (imperfecta, rectricibus quatuor mediis absentibus) rectricibus tribus utrinque lateralibus albo anguste terminatis.　Long. tota circa 8·5, alæ 4·3, caudæ 3·8, tarsi 0·63, dig. med. cum ungue 0·75.　(Descr. exempl. typ. ex Tizimin, Yucatan.　Mus. nostr.)

Hab. MEXICO, Tizimin in Yucatan (*G. F. Gaumer* [1]).

A single specimen shot on 10th June, 1879, by Dr. Gaumer, is the only example we have seen of this singular species.　It is marked as a female, and so recorded by Mr. Hartert, but the pure white band across the throat and the white tips to the outer tail-feathers, so frequently characteristic of the male in Caprimulgidæ, makes us doubt if the sex has been correctly recorded.

C. yucatanicus is the smallest of this section of Central-American Caprimulgidæ.　It has no near allies, though some of its markings, especially the size and shape of the terminal white spots to the tail, call to mind *C. ocellatus* of South America.　These spots are similarly shaped in *Otophanes macleodi*.　The comparative length of the outermost primary in both these species appears to be similar, but, unfortunately, our specimens (one of each) are not in sufficiently good condition to make a satisfactory comparison.　At a future time, with better materials, it would be well to examine further into the relationship subsisting between these two forms.

7. **Caprimulgus saturatus.**　(Tab. LVIII.)

Antrostomus saturatus, Salv. P. Z. S. 1870, p. 203 [1]; Ridgw. Pr. U. S. Nat. Mus. xvi. p. 609 [2]?
Caprimulgus saturatus, Hartert, Cat. Birds Brit. Mus. xvi. p. 572 [3].
Antrostomus rufomaculatus, Ridgw. Pr. U. S. Nat. Mus. xiv. p. 466 [4].

Nigricans, rufo-maculatus, alis nigris in pogonio externo tantum maculatis, plaga alari alba nulla: subtus niger rufescente transfasciatus, vitta gulari alba nulla, ventre medio albo maculato; cauda nigra rufo transfasciata, rectricibus tribus utrinque externis albo late terminatis; setis rictalibus longissimis.　Long. tota circa 8·5, alæ 6·1, caudæ 4·8, tarsi 0·65, dig. med. cum ungue 0·85.　(Descr. maris exempl. typ. ex Volcan de Chiriqui.　Mus. nostr.)

Hab. COSTA RICA, Volcan de Irazu (*Alfaro* [4]); PANAMA, Volcan de Chiriqui (*Arcé* [1]).

A single male specimen sent us by our collector Arcé in 1870, in one of his collections made in the Volcan de Chiriqui, is the only one we have received. This was described in the second paper on Arcé's Veraguan collections [1]. More than twenty years afterwards, Mr. Ridgway having received a specimen from Señor Anastasio Alfaro, of the Costa Rica National Museum, redescribed the species under the name of *Antrostomus rufomaculatus* [4]. He subsequently sent us the type for examination, when its identity with *A. saturatus* was at once evident and the fact recorded by Mr. Hartert.

C. saturatus has no near allies that we are acquainted with. In having the inner web of the primaries uniform, the outer web being spotted, it agrees with *C. sericeocaudatus* and a few extra-American species. In its general aspect it is not unlike *C. nigrescens*, a species with large white spots on the primaries; but the relationship is not at all close.

There is much to learn concerning this interesting species, the female even being unknown.

PHALÆNOPTILUS.

Phalænoptilus, Ridgway, Pr. U. S. Nat. Mus. iii. p. 5 (1880); Hartert, Cat. Birds Brit. Mus. xvi. p. 579.

Mr. Ridgway separated this genus from *Caprimulgus* on account of its "short even tail (much shorter than the wing), and lengthened perfectly naked tarsus (longer than the middle toe), the first quill shorter than the fourth, and the plumage with a peculiar velvety moth-like surface."

Regarding the relative length of the tarsus and middle toe, if the claw of the latter is omitted Mr. Ridgway's statement is correct, but the toe and claw together are considerably longer than the tarsus as stated by Mr. Hartert. Nor can the tarsus be said to be entirely naked in front (Ridgway), for the proximal end is certainly slightly feathered though the rest of the joint is bare. Regarding the relative lengths of the first and fourth primaries, the first is, as Mr. Ridgway says, usually the shorter of the two, but in some of the specimens before me they are nearly equal.

We would therefore define *Phalænoptilus* as having a short even tail, much shorter than the wing; tarsi stout, feathered in front only at the extreme proximal end, and longer relatively to the middle toe and claw than in *Caprimulgus*. Plumage exceedingly soft.

The range of the genus is that of its single species as given below.

1. Phalænoptilus nuttalli.

Caprimulgus nuttalli, Aud. Birds Am. vii. p. 250, t. 495 [1].
Antrostomus nuttalli, Baird, Brew., & Ridgw. N. Am. Birds, ii. p. 417 [2]; Coues, Birds N. W. p. 261 [3].
Phalænoptilus nuttalli, Ridgw. Pr. U. S. Nat. Mus. iii. p. 5 [4]; Hartert, Cat. Birds Brit. Mus. xvi. p. 579 [5].

Supra griseus, nigro. minute irroratus; capite summo plumis singulis fascia nigra medialiter transfasciatis; scapularibus maculis hastiformibus nigris distincte notatis: subtus gula grisea nigro indistincte transfasciata, gutture plaga magna transversa nivea infra nigro limbata, pectoris plumis albis nigro fasciatis; abdomine albicante regulariter nigro fasciato, tectricibus subcaudalibus isabellino-albis; alis nigricantibus pallide fulvo transfasciatis; cauda supra griseo et nigro minute irrorata fasciis indistinctis notata, rectricibus tribus lateralibus albo extrorsum increscente terminatis. Long. tota circa 7·5, alæ 5·4, caudæ 3·3, tarsi 0·65, dig. med. cum ungue 0·8. (Descr. exempl. ex Guanajuato, Mexico. Mus. nostr.) ♀ mari similis, sed maculis caudalibus minoribus.

Hab. NORTH AMERICA, Western States from Oregon and Washington territory south-wards; Arizona and Texas [2][4].—MEXICO, Guanajuato (*mus. nostr.* [2]).

Though this species is apparently common on our north-western frontier and is doubtless found in Sonora and Sinaloa, we have only the evidence of a single specimen to prove its existence in Mexico. This is an adult male which came into our possession many years ago from Verreaux, who may have received it from his correspondent, Señor E. Dugès, as the label bears the locality Guanajuato on it. None of our collectors in Northern and Western Mexico met with this species, and we have found no other record of its occurrence within our limits.

P. nuttalli has been separated into two or, perhaps, three races, dependent upon size and a slight difference of shade of colour; but Mr. Hartert considers that the points of distinction are not satisfactory. If, however, on further evidence they prove sufficient, the Mexican bird should bear the name of the typical form *P. nuttalli*, being inter-mediate in colour between Mr. Brewster's *P. nuttalli nitidus* and Mr. Ridgway's *P. nuttalli californicus*. The dimensions, however, of our only Mexican skin, which is not in good condition, are rather small. A full account of the history and habits of this bird are given by Brewer [2] and by Dr. Coues [3], from which it would appear that it is common in all the frontier States from Arizona to Texas. Mr. Ridgway found an egg from which the male bird flew at the foot of the East Humboldt Mountains. This egg was unspotted dead-white, and was laid on the bare ground beneath a sage-bush. In colour, therefore, the eggs of this species resemble those of *Caprimulgus macro-mystax*, taken by Mr. R. Owen in Vera Paz, to which we have already alluded.

OTOPHANES.

Otophanes, Brewster, Auk, v. p. 89 (1888); Hartert, Cat. Birds Brit. Mus. xvi. p. 581.

Mr. Brewster has given an excellent description of this genus, the substance of which is as follows:—Bill long, narrow, slender, with tubular nostrils opening forward and outward, not upward; the gape with long, stiff, naked bristles curving downwards and inwards, meeting and overlapping under the chin; tarsus naked, about equal to the middle toe; tail long (only ·80 inch shorter than the wing) and slightly rounded (graduation about ·25 inch); wing comparatively short and rounded, the second and third quills equal and longest, the fourth slightly shorter, the first and fifth decidedly shorter than the fourth and equal. Plumage peculiarly soft and velvety; eyes bordered in front by semicirclets of radiating feathers, the tips directed upwards and outwards, forming distinct superciliary ruffs or shields which extend from the gape along the sides of the crown to the occiput, where they terminate in tufts of elongated feathers, erectile in life and precisely similar in form and position to the ear-tufts of a Scops-Owl. The superciliary shields, as well as the feathers along the maxillary line and many of the auriculars, are tipped with a fringe of delicate, black, hair-like bristles of varying length, the longest extending about 0·3 inch beyond the ends of the feathers. These bristles are the elongated shafts of feathers and a few barbs without their barbules.

The tarsi are not quite naked as Mr. Brewster states, as the extreme proximal end in front has small feathers, much as in *Phalœnoptilus*.

The only known species is *O. macleodi*, the range of which is given below.

1. Otophanes macleodi.

Otophanes macleodi, Brewster, Auk, v. p. 89 [1]; viii. p. 320, t. 1 [2]; Hartert, Cat. Birds Brit. Mus. xvi. p. 581 [3].

Rufo-brunneus, fulvo minute irroratus; verticis lateribus, genis et gula grisescentioribus; cervice postica fulvo et brunneo transfasciata; scapularibus maculis magnis saturate brunneis griseo limbatis, tectricibus alarum maculis albis brunneo marginatis ornatis: subtus fascia gutturali transversa alba, abdomine maculis quibusdam albis notata; alis nigricantibus fulvo transfasciatis; cauda nigricante indistincte fasciata, rectricibus externis albo anguste terminatis. Long. tota circa 8·5, alæ 5·1, caudæ 4·1, tarsi 0·63, dig. med. cum. ungue 0·85. (Descr. maris ex Hacienda de San Marcos, Zapotlan, Mexico. Mus. nostr.)

♀ mari similis, sed (ut videtur) omnino rufescentior.

Hab. MEXICO, Sierra Madre of Chihuahua (*McLeod* [1]), Hacienda de San Marcos near Zapotlan in Jalisco (*W. Lloyd* [3]).

The first specimen of this curious bird was obtained by Mr. R. R. Macleod in December 1884, and passing into Mr. Brewster's collection was described by him in 1888. Mr. McLeod omitted to record the exact locality where the specimen was obtained, as the bird was brought to him alive by a Mexican boy when staying in the State of Chihuahua. Mr. Brewster considers that El Carmen was most likely the place where the bird was captured, or perhaps Durasno. It was kept in a cage for two weeks, during which time it refused food, which had to be forced upon it. It moved the ear-tufts precisely as an Owl does, erecting them when approached or startled by any sudden noise, allowing them to drop back on the crown when it thought itself alone and safe. Mr. Brewster's specimen is a female, and was carefully figured by Mr. Ridgway in the volume of the 'Auk' for 1891.

The only specimen we have received from Mexico was shot by Mr. William Lloyd when staying at the hacienda of San Marcos near Zapotlan in the State of Jalisco, and therefore a long way from Mr. McLeod's locality. Our specimen is a male and is in much greyer plumage than the female type, as represented in the figure, but there can be no doubt that the two birds belong to the same species.

Mr. Lloyd shot our bird on 11th May, 1889, at an elevation of 8000 feet above the sea in the mountains of Jalisco. We may therefore infer that this species is a mountain-bird and has a range extending from the Sierra Madre of Chihuahua to that of Jalisco.

In the width and shape of the white patches on the outer rectrices *Otophanes* resembles *Caprimulgus yucatanicus* and *C. ocellatus*, a fact which may prove of significance when we know more about these birds.

STENOPSIS.

Stenopsis, Cassin, Pr. Ac. Phil. 1851, p. 179; Hartert, Cat. Birds Brit. Mus. xvi. p. 582.

Stenopsis is closely allied to *Caprimulgus*, but has a squarer even emarginate tail, a character which is more evident in the type *S. cayennensis* than in the other species of the genus. The bill is more elongated in comparison with its breadth, the nostrils more exposed, the first primary is nearly equal to the second, the tarsi are feathered along the front for about one third of their proximal ends; the sexes differ in colour, especially as regards the pattern of the outer rectrices and the outer primaries.

The genus contains five species, which are spread over the greater part of South America, even as far south as Northern Patagonia. Only one species, *S. cayennensis*, enters our fauna as far as Costa Rica; but *S. ruficervix* is found in the Colombian State of Antioquia, just beyond our southern boundary.

1. **Stenopsis cayennensis.**

Engoulevant varié de Cayenne, Montb. Hist. Nat. Ois. ii. p. 577 [1].

Crapaud-volant de Cayenne, D'Aub. Pl. Enl. 760 [2].

Caprimulgus cayennensis, Gm. Syst. Nat. i. p. 1031 [3].

Stenopsis cayennensis, Cass. Pr. Ac. Phil. 1851, p. 179 [4]; Scl. P. Z. S. 1866, p. 140 [5]; Salv. P. Z. S. 1870, p. 204 [6]; Hartert, Cat. Birds Brit. Mus. xvi. p. 583 [7].

Stenopsis albicauda, Lawr. Ann. Lyc. N. Y. xi. p. 89 [8].

Supra brunneo-grisea, nigro irrorata et vermiculata; capite summo plumis singulis medialiter nigris, cervice postica cervina; scapularibus maculis nigris et pallide cervinis ornatis, tectricibus alarum minoribus albo, mediis et majoribus cervino maculatis: subtus gula albida nigricante transfasciata, fascia transversa gutturali alba, pectore et abdomine antico cervinis nigro transfasciatis, ventre imo albicante, tectricibus subcaudalibus pallide cervinis; alis nigricantibus, primariis quatuor externis macula alba obliqua et altera ad basin in pogonio interno cervina, secundariis fasciis duabus medianis et apicibus albis; cauda rectricibus duabus mediis griseis nigro vermiculatis et stricte fasciatis, reliquis macula magna alba fere ad apicem extendente, in pogonio interno ad basin nigro trifasciatis.

♀ mari similis, primariis cervino nec albo maculatis, rectricibus externis nigricantibus cervino regulariter transfasciatis. (Descr. maris et feminæ ex Chitra, Panama. Mus. nostr.)

Hab. COSTA RICA, Talamanca (*J. Cooper* [8]); PANAMA, Calovevora (*Arcé* [6]). — SOUTH AMERICA, northern portion from Colombia to Guiana, Trinidad and Tobago [7].

This well-known species of the northern parts of South America is the only one of the genus *Stenopsis* that enters our fauna. Here it occurs sparingly in the State of Panama and in Eastern Costa Rica. From the former country we have only received a pair, which formed part of one of our collector Arcé's consignments[6]. Subsequently a male was obtained in the district of Talamanca in Costa Rica by Mr. J. Cooper, the naturalist attached to Prof. Gabb's expedition. This bird was described in 1875 by Mr. Lawrence as *Stenopsis albicauda*[8] and distinguished from *S. cayennensis* by its longer tail with narrower feathers, the absence of the transverse median black bar on the tail-feathers, and the darker rufous colour of the abdomen and under tail-coverts. These prove to be all variable characters and are not confirmed by our Panama specimens.

In South America *S. cayennensis* has been found over a wide area and has been recorded from Guiana, the islands of Tobago and Trinidad, from Forte do Rio Branco on a tributary of the Rio Negro, and thence along the northern districts of the continent to Colombia. In the latter country it is occasionally met with by the bird-hunters of Bogota, and was found by Salmon in the State of Antioquia.

We are not acquainted with any account of its breeding-habits or of its eggs.

NYCTIDROMUS.

Nyctidromus, Gould, Icon. Av. ii. t. 2 (1838); Hartert, Cat. Birds Brit. Mus. xvi. p. 587.

The only species of this genus differs in several characters from the typical members of *Caprimulgus* and the preceding genera. The habits are more terrestrial, and, perhaps in consequence, the tarsus is bare and longer in proportion to the toes; the tail is long and peculiarly marked, the conspicuous white marks of the male being on the second and third feathers from the outside and not on the outer feather.

The range of the genus is that of its only species and is given below.

1. Nyctidromus albicollis.

Tette-chèvre roux de la Guyane, D'Aub. Pl. Enl. 733 (♀)[1].

Caprimulgus albicollis, Gm. Syst. Nat. i. p. 1030[2]; Licht. Preis-Verz. Mex., Vög. p. 3 (*cf.* J. f. Orn. 1863, p. 58)[3].

Nyctidromus albicollis, Burm. Syst. Ueb. ii. p. 389[4]; Scl. P. Z. S. 1866, p. 144[5]; Lawr. Ann. Lyc. N. Y. ix. pp. 120[6], 204[7]; Mem. Bost. Soc. N. H. ii. p. 291[9]; Bull. U. S. Nat. Mus. no. 4, p. 31[9]; Cab. J. f. Orn. 1862, p. 166[10]; v. Frantz. J. f. Orn. 1869, p. 314[11]; Scl. & Salv. P. Z. S. 1870, p. 837[12]; Merrill, Bull. Nutt. Orn. Club, i. p. 88[13]; Boucard, P. Z. S. 1878, p. 67[14]; 1883, p. 451[15]; Nutting, Pr. U. S. Nat. Mus. v. p. 398[16]; vi. pp. 375[17], 386[18], 394[19]; Ferrari-Perez, Pr. U. S. Nat. Mus. ix. p. 158[20]; Ridgw. Pr. U. S. Nat. Mus. x. p. 592[21]; Zeledon, An. Mus. Nac. Costa Rica, 1887, p. 120[22]; Herrera, La Nat. (2) i. pp. 179, 322[23]; Salv. Ibis, 1889, p. 368[24]; Stone, Pr. Ac. Phil. 1890, p. 206[25]; Hartert, Cat. Birds Brit. Mus. xvi. p. 587[26].

Nyctidromus americanus, Scl. (nec Linn.), P. Z. S. 1856, p. 285[27]; 1859, p. 367[28]; Scl. & Salv. Ibis, 1859, p. 125[29]; Lawr. Ann. Lyc. N. Y. vii. p. 290[30].

Caprimulgus guianensis, Gm. Syst. Nat. i. p. 1030 [31].

Nyctidromus guianensis, Cassin, Pr. Ac. Phil. 1860, p. 133 [32]; Lawr. Ann. Lyc. N. Y. vii. p. 290 [33];
    Scl. P. Z. S. 1864, p. 176 [34]; Scl. & Salv. P. Z. S. 1864, p. 364 [35]; Salv. P. Z. S. 1870,
    p. 204 [36].

Nyctidromus albicollis merrilli, Sennett, Auk, 1888, p. 44 [37].

Nyctidromus merrilli, Hartert, Cat. Birds Brit. Mus. xvi. p. 591 [38].

Supra brunneus griseo et rufo minute irroratus, plumis verticis medialiter nigris striam medianam formantibus, plumis verticis lateralibus et dorsi stria angusta nigra notatis ; scapularibus fascia lata subterminali nigra cervino limbata, tectricibus alarum cervino vermiculatis et macula subrotunda terminali ornatis: subtus cervinus, mento et gulæ lateribus nigro fasciatis, gutture plaga magna mediana nivea supra eam plaga nigra; pectore crebre, abdomine sparsim fasciis nigris notatis ; alis nigris, primariis quinque externis fascia obliqua nivea notatis, primariis internis et secundariis fulvo fasciatis ; cauda nigra, rectricibus mediis griseo irroratis fasciis indistinctis exhibentibus, rectricibus secunda et tertia ab externo in pogonio interno plaga magna nivea ornatis. Long. tota circa 10·5, alæ 6·5, caudæ 6, tarsi 1·0, dig. med. cum ungue 1·1. Descr. maris ex Chimalapa, Tehuantepec. Mus. nostr.)

♀ mari similis, sed caudæ rectrice subexterno in pogonio interno ad apicem tantum albo.

Hab. NORTH AMERICA, S.E. Texas [13] [37] [38].—MEXICO, Tampico (*W. B. Richardson* [26]), Valley of Mexico (*Herrera* [23]), Misantla (*F. D. G.* [26]), Jalapa (*de Oca* [28], *Ferrari-Perez*), Coatepec, Huatusco, Rio Rancho Nuevo, Santa Ana (*F. Ferrari-Perez*), Orizaba (*Botteri*), Cordova (*Sallé* [27]), Playa Vicente (*M. Trujillo*), Tres Marias Is. (*Grayson* [8]), Presidio de Mazatlan (*Forrer*), Mazatlan, Plains of Colima (*Xantus* [8]), Tepic, San Blas, Colima, Santiago (*W. B. Richardson*), Mazatiopam in Puebla (*F. Ferrari-Perez* [20]), Chihuitan, Santa Efigenia (*Sumichrast* [9]), Tehuantepec, Tonala, Salina Cruz, Chimalapa (*W. B. Richardson*), Acapulco, Teapa (*Mrs. H. H. Smith*), Northern Yucatan [15], Peto, Buctzotz, Temax (*G. F. Gaumer*), Tunkas, Shkolak and Ticul (*W. Stone* [25]), Merida (*Schott* [7]), Mugeres and Cozumel Islands (*G. F. Gaumer* [24]); BRITISH HONDURAS (*Dyson*), Orange Walk (*G. F. Gaumer*), Belize (*Blancaneaux*); GUATEMALA [29], Pine-ridge of Poctum, Chisec, Choctum, Coban, Cahabon, Teleman, San Gerónimo, Dueñas, Retalhuleu (*O. S. & F. D. G.*); HONDURAS, San Pedro (*G. M. Whitely* [12]), Segovia River (*Townsend* [21]); SALVADOR, La Libertad, Volcan de San Miguel (*W. B. Richardson*); NICARAGUA, Chinandega, Momotombo (*W. B. R.*), Sucuyá [18], Omotepe [19], San Juan del Sur [17] (*Nutting*); COSTA RICA, San José, Angostura (*J. Carmiol* [6], *Cherrie*), Irazu (*Boucard* [14], *Rogers*), La Palma (*Nutting* [16]), Orosi, Turrialba, Moravia, Pacuar, Chirripo (*v. Frantzius* [11]), Las Trojas, Pozo Azul de Pirris, Alajuela, Naranjo de Cartago (*Zeledon* [22]); PANAMA, Chiriqui, Bugaba, Mina de Chorcha, Chitra, Calovevora (*Arcé* [36]), Line of Railway (*McLeannan* [30] [33] [35]), Turbo (*Wood* [32]).—SOUTH AMERICA generally, from Colombia and Guiana [31] to South Brazil [26].

The extent of individual variation shown in this species is considerable, and it exists to a very great extent without reference to locality, sex, or age. The general cast of the upper plumage is sometimes grey, sometimes rich rufous, and there is every intermediate gradation of tone between these colours. There is also great difference in size. The bird from the Lower Rio Grande Valley has been recently separated by Mr. Sennett as *Nyctidromus albicollis merrilli*[37], and this course was endorsed by Mr. Hartert[38]. But on re-examining the large series of specimens in the British Museum we do not think such a distinction can be maintained. Rio Grande birds are, perhaps, rather greyer on the upper plumage, especially on the head, and they are rather large; but they can be matched almost exactly by birds from many other places. Moreover, the range of this species is no doubt quite continuous, and the Rio Grande birds only represent it at its extreme northern boundary.

Nyctidromus albicollis is by far the commonest species of Goatsucker in Mexico and Central America. Its distribution is nearly universal in the low-lying districts up to an elevation of about 5000 feet in the mountains. It affects the more open thinly wooded districts rather than the dense forests, though it occurs in open glades. After nightfall its presence is made known to the traveller by its habit of flitting in front of the horseman and settling from time to time in the middle of the track. Its familiar note, which resembles the words " Who are you?" may be heard throughout the night.

This bird makes no nest, but lays its two eggs on the bare ground. These are of a pinkish-buff colour with darker spots. Salvin found an egg on bare ground about the middle of May near Obispo Station on the Panama Railway, close to the edge of the forest; and Mr. Merrill also took a nest near Hidalgo in Southern Texas on 15th May; but Mr. Sennett met with one in the same district as early as 20th April.

b. *Rictus glaber, setis elongatis nullis.*

CHORDEILES.

Chordeiles, Swainson, Fauna Bor.-Am. ii. p. 496 (1831); Hartert, Cat. Birds Brit. Mus. xvi. p. 609.

Chordeiles is the only Central-American genus of Caprimulgidæ which is destitute of the strong, long, rictal bristles so characteristic of the foregoing genera. Three other genera, *Nyctiprogne*, *Podager*, and *Lurocalis*, all of them belonging to South America, have the same character; and two Old World forms, *Lyncornis* and *Eurystopodus*, are also destitute of rictal bristles. Amongst other characters distinguishing *Chordeiles* from Central-American forms is the forked tail.

Of the four definite species recognized by Mr. Hartert, divisible into nine imperfectly segregated forms, two only occur within our limits. One of these is the well-known *C. virginianus* and its modification *C. henryi*, and the other, *C. texensis*, a northern form of the South-American *C. acutipennis*. Both, after the usual habit of their kind, are probably more or less migratory.

1. Chordeiles virginianus.

Le Tette-chèvre de Virginie, Briss. Orn. ii. p. 477[1].

Caprimulgus virginianus, Gm. Syst. Nat. i. p. 1028[2].

Chordeiles virginianus, Sw. Faun. Bor.-Am. ii. p. 496[3]; Scl. & Salv. Ibis, 1860, p. 275[4]; P. Z. S. 1864, p. 364[5]; Scl. P. Z. S. 1866, p. 133[6]; Hartert, Cat. Birds Brit. Mus. xvi. p. 610[7].

Caprimulgus popetue, Vieill. Ois. Am. Sept. i. p. 56, t. 24[8].

Chordeiles popetue, Salv. P. Z. S. 1870, p. 203[9]; Baird, Brew., & Ridgw. N. Am. Birds, ii. p. 401[10].

Chordeiles henryi, Cassin, Ill. Birds Cal. & Texas, p. 239[11]; Scl. P. Z. S. 1866, p. 133[12]; Hartert, Cat. Birds Brit. Mus. xvi. p. 612[13].

Chordeiles popetue, var. *henryi*, Baird, Brew., & Ridgw. N. Am. Birds, ii. p. 404[14].

Chordeiles sennetti, Coues, Auk, 1888, p. 37[15].

Supra nigricans plus minusve albo et fulvo maculatus, humeris nigris, tectricibus alarum reliquis albo guttulatis, primariis nigris pennis quinque externis plaga magna ad medium alba, secundariis albo indistincte fasciatis: subtus gulæ lateribus nigris fulvo maculatis, gutture plaga magna transversa alba usque ad mentum extendente, pectore nigricante fulvo guttato, abdomine nigro et albido regulariter transfasciato; tectricibus subcaudalibus albis nigro sparsim transfasciatis; cauda nigricante indistincte griseo fasciata, rectricibus omnibus (duabus mediis exceptis) fascia subterminali alba. Long. tota circa 9·5, alæ 8·0, caudæ rectr. med. 3·85, rectr. lat. 4·5, tarsi 0·65, dig. med. cum ungue 0·8. (Descr. maris ex San Agustin, Nuevo Leon, Mexico. Mus. nostr.)

♀ mari similis, sed subtus rufescentior, fascia cauda subterminali alba nulla.

Juv. supra niger rufo dense variegatus: subtus (cauda inclusa) undique nigro et rufo regulariter transfasciatus.

Hab. NORTH AMERICA[2], generally in summer from Hudson's Bay southwards, Texas.— MEXICO, San Agustin, Vaqueria in Nuevo Leon (*F. B. Armstrong*), Xeres in Zacatecas (*W. B. Richardson*[13]), Atotonilco (*F. Ferrari-Perez*); BRITISH HONDURAS, Southern Pine-ridge (*F. Blancaneaux*[13]); GUATEMALA, Coban (*O. S. & F. D. G.*[4]), La Grande (*F. Oates*); PANAMA, Calovevora (*Arcé*[9]), Lion Hill (*M'Leannan*[5]).—SOUTH AMERICA, Colombia, Amazons Valley; BAHAMA IS.; GREATER ANTILLES.

Though some specimens from our north-eastern frontier are paler than the more typical form, and whiter on the abdomen and under tail-coverts, we are quite unable to separate them from the darker birds, which are no doubt typical *Chordeiles virginianus*, the paler ones being *C. henryi*. So far as we can see, and we have examined a large series of skins, any attempt to arrange the series in more than one group must leave a considerable number undetermined as equally referable to one form or the other. A still larger series cannot fail to render any separation more difficult. We should have preferred to keep *C. henryi* separate, and used the name for the pale bird of our northern frontier, but with these birds we find others of the darker type and all associating together towards the end of May in their breeding-season.

Dr. Coues[15] has separated *C. virginianus* into four subspecies, making two of the so-called light-coloured western form. Mr. Hartert, in his recent Catalogue of the Caprimulgidæ, kept *C. virginianus* and *C. henryi* as subspecies, and made a section of the former to include specimens supposed to blend the two together. This is certainly not satisfactory, and we think any attempt to recognize the variations of this species by names will not in the end simplify matters.

It is somewhat surprising that we know so little of *C. virginianus* in its southern winter-quarters; our records of it beyond Mexico are few and far between, though they extend over a vast extent of the southern continent, even as far as Patagonia!

C. virginianus lays its eggs in open situations on the ground and on rocks, and even on the flat roofs of houses. The eggs, two in number, are of the oval shape usual in this family; the ground is of various shades of stone-colour, with slaty and yellowish-brown markings diffused over the whole surface.

2. **Chordeiles texensis.**

Chordeiles texensis, Lawr. Ann. Lyc. N. Y. vi. p. 167[1]; ix. pp. 120[2], 204[3]; Mem. Bost. Soc. N. H. ii. p. 291[4]; Bull. U. S. Nat. Mus. no. 4, p. 31[5]; Scl. P. Z. S. 1866, p. 134[6]; Sumichrast, La Nat. v. p. 249[7]; Boucard, P. Z. S. 1883, p. 451[8]; Ridgw. Pr. U. S. Nat. Mus. x. p. 581[9]; Salv. Ibis, 1889, p. 368[10]; Cherrie, Auk, 1892, p. 324[11]; Hartert, Cat. Birds Brit. Mus. xvi. p. 616[12].

Chordeiles acutipennis, var. *texensis*, Baird, Brew., and Ridgw. B. N. Am. ii. p. 406[13].

Chordeiles brasilianus, Cab. J. f. Orn. 1862, p. 165[14]; v. Frantz. J. f. Orn. 1869, p. 314[15].

Supra niger undique cervino et griseo albido variegatus, capite summo colore nigro magis obvio, superciliis indistinctis albidis, tectricibus alarum maculis rotundis albidis ornatis; cauda nigro fasciata, area inter fascias griseo variegato: subtus gulæ lateribus nigro et cervino variegatis, gula macula triangulari magna alba, pectore summo nigricante fulvo intermixto, imo griseo irrorato, abdomine et tectricibus subalaribus cervinis nigro regulariter transfasciatis; alis primariis quatuor externis macula magna mediana alba, primariis internis et tectricibus majoribus fulvo transversim maculatis; cauda infra nigra, in pogonio interno cervino late fasciata, fascia subterminali alba et pogonio externo albo maculato. Long. tota circa 9·0, alæ 7·2, caudæ rectr. med. 3·9, rectr. lat. 4·5, tarsi 0·55, dig. med. cum ungue 0·72. (Descr. maris ex Dueñas, Guatemala. Mus. nostr.)

♀ mari similis, macula gulari cervino, maculis remigum quoque cervinis, et macula caudali subterminali nulla distinguenda.

Hab. NORTH AMERICA, Southern frontier States[13].—MEXICO, San Antonio, San Pedro, San Agustin, Monte Morelos in Nuevo Leon (*F. B. Armstrong*), Altamira and Xicotencal in Tamaulipas (*W. B. Richardson*[12]), Mexicalcingo[12], Coapa[12], Culhuacan, Chimalpa in the valley of Mexico (*F. Ferrari-Perez*), Atotonilco, San Baltazar in Puebla[12] (*F. F.-P.*), Sierra de Alamos[12] (*W. Lloyd*), Mazatlan (*Grayson*[4], *Forrer*[12]), San Blas (*Grayson*[4]), Santana near Guadalajara (*W. Lloyd*[12]), Plains of Colima (*W. B. Richardson*[12]), Juchatengo (*M. Trujillo*[12]), San Mateo, Sta. Efigenia (*Sumichrast*[5][7]), Tonala (*W. B. Richardson*[12]), N. Yucatan[8], Cozumel I.[10] (*G. F. Gaumer*), Merida (*Schott*[3]); GUATEMALA, Dueñas, San Gerónimo[12], Coban (*O. S. & F. D. G.*); HONDURAS, Ruatan I. (*G. F. Gaumer*[10]), Trujillo (*Townsend*[9]); NICARAGUA, Realejo (*O. S.*[12]); COSTA RICA, Rio Tirribi (*Zeledon*[2]), San José (*Cherrie*[11]); PANAMA, Veraguas (*Arcé*).

Chordeiles texensis is a northern form of the South-American *C. acutipennis*, from which it differs chiefly, if not only, in its larger size[6].   Its northern range hardly passes the limits of our fauna into the frontier States of North America, its southern extending to Panama, but not into the continent of South America.

C. texensis may readily be distinguished from *C. virginianus* by its smaller size, more fawn-colour of the abdomen, the greater distance of the white wing-spots from the shoulder, their limitation to four, or at most five, quills, and the rufous markings on the inner primaries.

In Central America *C. texensis* is a much more common species than *C. virginianus*, and its presence has been recorded from many places ranging from the sea-coast at Realejo to as high as 7000 feet in the mountains of Mexico and Guatemala.

Grayson says[4] that this species is common in Western Mexico, especially in the neighbourhood of Mazatlan and San Blas. He describes the eggs as deposited on withered leaves, without any nest, in some retired spot in the woods. They are of a cream-colour, sometimes two in number, but usually only one. This description does not agree with that given by Brewer. who, on the authority of Dr. Berlandier, says the eggs are like those of *C. virginianus*, and resemble a piece of polished marble of a dark grey colour by the combination of small irregular confluent black, umber, and purplish-grey spots and blotches. Mr. Ridgway describes them as smaller and usually paler than those of *C. virginianus henryi*. Mr. Armstrong's Nuevo Leon skins were all obtained in the latter half of May, when no doubt the birds were breeding.

Subfam. *NYCTIBIINÆ*.

The singular birds forming this subfamily differ from the Caprimulginæ in having the normal number of phalanges to the toes; the claw of the middle toe is not pectinated; the tarsi are exceedingly short and stout; the bill peculiarly constructed, the gape very wide, and the body with powder-down patches.

Nearly all the species are birds of large size, some of them rivalling members of the Australian *Podargi*, to which they bear some superficial resemblance.

NYCTIBIUS.

Nyctibius, Vieillot, N. Dict. d'Hist. N. xvi. p. 6 (1817); Hartert, Cat. Birds Brit. Mus. xvi.
    p. 623.

Six species constitute this genus, which is a purely Neotropical one, and spread from the northern confines of the region in Mexico to Southern Brazil. One, *N. jamaicensis*, the type of *Nyctibius*, occurs throughout our region, and one of the southern forms, *N. grandis*, has been met with in the State of Panama.

1. Nyctibius jamaicensis.

Wood-Owle, Sloane, Nat. Hist. Jamaica, ii. p. 295 (1725)[1].

Cyprimulgus jamaicensis, Gm. Syst. Nat. i. p. 1029[2].

Nyctibius jamaicensis, Gosse, Birds Jamaica, p. 41[3]; Ill. t. 6[4]; Salv. Ibis, 1866, p. 194[5]; 1889, p. 368[6]; P. Z. S. 1870, p. 203[7]; Lawr. Bull. U. S. Nat. Mus. no. 4, p. 32[8]*; Ridgw. Pr. U. S. Nat. Mus. iv. p. 336[9]; Herrera, La Nat. (2) i. p. 322[10]; Hartert, Cat. Birds Brit. Mus. xvi. p. 625[11].

Caprimulgus cornutus, Vieill. N. Dict. d'Hist. N. p. 245[12].

Nyctibius cornutus, Cab. J. f. Orn. 1869, p. 314 (note)[13].

Nyctibius pectoralis, Gould, Icon. Av. ii. t. 8[14].

Supra griseus, albo irroratus; plumis omnibus rhachidibus nigris, capite summo et humeris nigris; tectricibus alarum minoribus rufescente tinctis: subtus griseus, albo irroratus; rhachidibus omnibus anguste nigris, pectore maculis distinctis nigris ornato; alis nigricantibus, fasciis maculosis indistinctis notatis, subalaribus nigris albo guttatis; cauda nigra, profuse griseo marmorata, fasciis vix distinctis notata. Long. tota circa 16·0, alæ 12·0, caudæ 8·1, tarsi 0·5, dig. med. cum ungue 1·3. (Descr. maris ex Presidio de Mazatlan, Mexico. Mus. nostr.)

Hab. MEXICO, Presidio de Mazatlan (*Forrer*[11]), Valley of Mexico (*Herrera*[10]), Jalapa (*Höge*), Mirador (*U. S. Nat. Mus.*), La Antigua in Vera Cruz (*M. Trujillo*), Teapa in Tabasco (*Mrs. H. H. Smith*), Santa Efigenia, Tehuantepec (*Sumichrast*[8]); GUATEMALA (*Mus. Berol.*[13]), near the city (*Constancia*[5]), Vera Paz (*J. Rodriguez*), Tactic (*Sarg*); HONDURAS, Ruatan I. (*G. F. Gaumer*[6]); COSTA RICA, Sarchi (*U. S. Nat. Mus.*[9]); PANAMA, Volcan de Chiriqui (*Arcé*[7]), Lion Hill (*M'Leannan*).—SOUTH AMERICA, from Colombia to Guiana, Brazil, and Paraguay[12]; JAMAICA[1][2].

There is much difference both in colour and size between individuals of this species, some specimens being greyer, others more rufescent. Mr. Hartert is disposed to divide it into a large northern and a small southern race, the latter being Gould's *N. pectoralis*[14]; but as gradations are clearly indicated, and the range probably uninterrupted, such a division seems hardly necessary or possible.

This *Nyctibius* has been long known, having been mentioned by Sloane, in his 'Natural History of Jamaica,' as a "Wood-Owle"[1], and, being thus associated with the Island of Jamaica, received from Gmelin the name of *Caprimulgus jamaicensis*[2]. Though not found in any other island of the Antilles, it is by no means confined to Jamaica, but enjoys a very wide range over Tropical America, at least as far south as Bahia in Brazil[11]. Northwards it occurs sparingly over the whole of Central America and Mexico, as far as Mazatlan on the west and the State of Vera Cruz on the east. Herrera says[10] that in the Valley of Mexico it is migratory, and when residing in that district it frequents the large pine-trees, where it is with difficulty detected. In Guatemala we never met with it ourselves, but there is a specimen from that country in the Berlin Museum[13]: the late Don Vicente Constancia, of Antigua Guatemala, had two specimens, one of which passed into our possession[5]; another, which was in the

* According to v. Frantzius (J. f. Orn. 1869, p. 314) the bird called by Lawrence with doubt *Nyctibius jamaicensis* from S. José de Costa Rica (Ann. Lyc. N. Y. ix. p. 120) was a young *Pharomacrus mocinno*.

collection of the Sociedad Economica de Guatemala in 1874, we were informed, was obtained from a native in the city of Guatemala; and, lastly, in the same year Don Juan Rodriguez had one which was sent him from Vera Paz. In all the other Central-American States *Nyctibius jamaicensis* occurs as far south as the Line of the Panama Railway, where M'Leannan obtained a specimen and sent it to Mr. Lawrence.

Gosse[3] gives an excellent account of the habits of this species; he says that in Jamaica "it is not unfrequently seen in the evening, taking its station soon after sunset on some dead tree or fence-post, or floating by on noiseless wing, like an Owl, which the common people suppose it to be...... Now and then it is seen by day; but it is half concealed in the bushy foliage of some thick tree, which it can with difficulty be induced to quit...... As it sits in the fading twilight it ever and anon utters a loud and hoarse *ho-hoo*, and sometimes the same syllables are heard, in a much lower tone, as if proceeding from the depth of the throat." The food of specimens examined by Gosse consisted of large Coleoptera, such as *Megasoma titanus*, a species of black *Phanæus*, and other Lamellicorns. Individuals kept alive for a short time would always sit across the finger or stick, never lengthwise as is the habit of so many Caprimulgidæ. The iris in life is brilliant yellow, and the inside of the mouth violet passing into flesh-colour.

2. Nyctibius grandis.

Le grand Tette-chèvre tacheté du Brésil, Briss. Orn. ii. p. 485[1].
Grand Crapaud-volant de Cayenne, Daub. Pl. Enl. 325[2].
Caprimulgus grandis, Gm. Syst. Nat. i. p. 1029[3].
Nyctibius grandis, Vieill. N. Dict. d'Hist. N. xvi. p. 7[4]; Lawr. Ann. Lyc. N. Y. vii. p. 290[5];
        Hartert, Cat. Birds Brit. Mus. xvi. p. 628[6].

Supra griseus, albo vermiculatus, interscapulio, humeris et tectricibus alarum fulvo tinctis: subtus albus
    nigricante griseo vermiculatus, gutture fulvo tincto; alis nigricantibus indistincte fasciatis, subalaribus
    nigris albido et fulvo guttulatis; cauda nigricante, fasciis vermiculosis griseis notatis. Long. tota
    circa 20·0, alæ 14·3, caudæ 9·5, tarsi 0·55, dig. med. cum ungue 1·3. (Descr. exempl. ex Sarayacu,
    Ecuador. Mus. nostr.)

Hab. PANAMA, Lion Hill (*M'Leannan*[5]).—SOUTH AMERICA, from Colombia to the
        Amazons Valley[6] and Guiana[1,2,3].

Nyctibius grandis is one of the largest species of the genus, equalling, if not exceeding, in size the Brazilian *N. æthereus*, from which it differs in being much lighter in tint, the ground-colour of the plumage being nearly white, on which the darker markings are overspread.

The range of this *Nyctibius* extends over the northern portions of South America from Guiana to Colombia, and its presence has also been recorded from several places in the Valley of the Amazons. Its presence in our country is proved by a single specimen obtained by M'Leannan at his station on the Panama Railway. This was sent to Mr. Lawrence, and is correctly named in his first list of M'Leannan's birds[5].

Order PICI.

Fam. PICIDÆ.

This family of birds is usually, and properly, divided into three subfamilies, of which by far the largest is the stiff-tailed scansorial species commonly known as Woodpeckers, or Picinæ. The other two subfamilies have soft rounded tails, not stiffened or used for scansorial purposes. Only one of these two subfamilies—the Picumninæ—is represented in America, the other, the Iynginæ or Wrynecks, being exclusively an Old-World group.

The family, as a whole, is distributed over a large portion of the world, with the exception of Madagascar, New Guinea and the adjoining islands, Australia, and the whole of the islands of the Pacific Ocean.

Mr. Hargitt, in his recent catalogue of the Picidæ in the British Museum, includes 385 species and subspecies in the whole family. Of these considerably more than half, viz. 227, are found in America. Only two of the genera admitted by Mr. Hargitt occur in both Old and New Worlds, viz. *Dendrocopus* and *Picoides*. The proportion of genera found in America is not so large as that of the species, the numbers being— America 21, Old World 39.

In Mexico and Central America we are able to enumerate in the following pages about 43 species, which is a large number for the area investigated.

Subfam. *PICINÆ.*

Cauda rigida, scansoria.

a. *Cervix haud contracta, plumis normalibus vestita; caput haud amplificatum.*

a'. *Digitus pedis medius quam digitus externus (reversus) longior, aut æqualis.*

a". *Tarsus quam digitus pedis externus (reversus) cum ungue longior; maxilla supra nares fere lavis.*

COLAPTES.

Colaptes, Swainson, Zool. Journ. iii. p. 353 (1827); Hargitt, Cat. Birds Brit. Mus. xviii. p. 10 (1890).

Mr. Hargitt includes thirteen species in the genus *Colaptes,* but from these *C. ayresi* must be deducted, being, by many ornithologists, considered to be a hybrid between *C. auratus* and *C. mexicanus.* Of the remaining twelve species, only three occur within our limits, all of them belonging to one section of the genus, and that of northern domicile. Of these three species, one (*C. mexicanus*) has a wide range in western North America and throughout the Mexican highlands, *C. chrysoides* is restricted to the countries bordering the Gulf of California, and *C. mexicanoides* to the uplands of Guatemala, Honduras, and Central Nicaragua. No member of the genus is found in Costa Rica, nor do we meet with it again till the Andes of Peru, Bolivia, and Chili are reached. *Colaptes* is unrepresented in the Valley of the Amazons, nor are any members of it found in Guiana or Venezuela. Two species occur in Eastern and Southern Brazil, and one of them as far south as Patagonia. All these southern birds differ rather materially from those of the north.

In *Colaptes* the bill is curved, and has no distinct ridge running parallel to the culmen; the wing is pointed; the tarsus is longer than the outer toe (reversed); the shafts of the wing-primaries are brightly coloured, so also are the inner webs of the same feathers beneath, and the tail-feathers beneath for at least two-thirds of their length from the base.

1. Colaptes mexicanus.

Colaptes mexicanus, Sw. Phil. Mag. new ser. i. p. 440 (1827)[1]; Scl. P. Z. S. 1856, p. 307[2]; 1858, p. 305[3]; 1859, p. 367[4]; Dugès, La Nat. i. p. 139[5]; Baird, Brew., and Ridgw. N. Am. Birds, ii. p. 578[6]; Sumichrast, La Nat. v. p. 240[7]; Salv. Cat. Strickl. Coll. p. 400[8]; Ferrari-Perez, Pr. U.S. Nat. Mus. ix. p. 160[9]; Hargitt, Cat. Birds Brit. Mus. xviii. pp. 17[10], 568[11].

Picus cafer, Gm. Syst. Nat. i. p. 431[12] *.

Colaptes cafer, Coues, Check-list N. Am. Birds, p. 218[13]; Herrera, La Nat. (2) i. pp. 179[14], 322[15]; Stone, Pr. Ac. Phil. 1890, p. 214[16]; Allen, Bull. Am. Mus. N. H. iv. p. 21 et seq.[17]

Picus rubricatus, Wagl. Isis, 1829, p. 516[18].

Colaptes rubricatus, Bp. P. Z. S. 1837, p. 109[19].

Supra vinaceo-fuscus, pileo immaculato paulo rufescentiore, dorso et tectricibus alarum plumis omnibus nigro bifasciatis, dorso imo albo, tectricibus supracaudalibus longioribus albis nigro transfasciatis; capite, cervicis lateribus et gutture griseis, stria malari coccinea, fascia magna pectorali lunata nigra, abdomine albicante, plumis omnibus macula magna discali nigra, hypochondriis imis et tectricibus subalaribus nigro fasciatis; alis nigricantibus, extrorsum vinaceo-fusco maculatis, rhachidibus rubidis: subtus plerumque rubidis, subalaribus rosaceis nigro maculatis; cauda bitriente basali rubida, apice nigra; rectrice subexterna in pogonio externo nigro et rosaceo variegato; rostro et pedibus plumbeis. Long. tota circa 10·5, alæ 6·2, caudæ rectr. med. 4·0, rectr. subexterna 3·6, rectr. lat. 1·4, rostri a rictu 1·65, tarsi 1·15, dig. med. absque ungue 0·9, dig. ext. 0·7. (Descr. maris ex Mexico Vall. Mus. nostr.)

♀ mari similis, stria malari coccinea nulla, sed cinnamomeo interdum irregulariter vix notata.

Hab. Western North America, from the eastern base of the Rocky Mountains to the Pacific, north to British Columbia[6].—MEXICO (*T. Mann*[8]), Hermosillo in Sonora

---

* We have no doubt Gmelin's name applies to *C. mexicanus*, and is much older than it; but we are not prepared to call an American bird by the specific name of *cafer*—one suggested in complete ignorance of the true origin of the species.

(*Ferrari-Perez*), Chupadero, San José, Concepcion, Chihuahua city, Temosachic, all in Chihuahua (*W. Lloyd*), Ciudad in Durango (*A. Forrer*), Sierra de Bolaños, Sierra de Xeres, Sierra de San Luis Potosi, Sierra de Calvillo, Aguas Calientes, Sierra de Nayarit, Sierra Madre de Tepic (*W. B. Richardson*), Zapotlan (*W. Lloyd*), Guanajuato (*Dugès* [5]), Tetelco, Chimalpa, Ixtapalapa, Huipulco, in the Valley of Mexico (*Ferrari-Perez*), Valley of Mexico (*Herrera* [14] [15]), Temiscaltepec, Real del Monte (*Bullock* [1]), S. Miguel Molino, Texmelucan [9], Totimehuacan [9], in Puebla (*Ferrari-Perez*), Ixtaccihuatl, Popocatepetl (*Baker* [16]), Volcan de Colima (*W. Lloyd*), Omilteme in the Sierra Madre del Sur, Guerrero (*Mrs. H. H. Smith*), Las Vigas (*Ferrari-Perez*), Suapam (*Sallé* [2]), Jalapa (*de Oca* [4]), Orizaba (*Baker* [16]), Monte Alto (*Sumichrast* [7]), Cofre de Perote (*Sumichrast* [7], *M. Trujillo*), La Parada (*Boucard* [3]), Totontepec, Tonaguia, Villa Alta (*M. Trujillo*) *.

Colaptes mexicanus was described by Swainson from specimens obtained by Bullock at Temiscaltepec and Real del Monte in the tablelands of Central Mexico [1], and it has since proved to be a common species all over this region wherever a suitable country exists. Its northern extension reaches far beyond the limits of Mexico, and spreading from the base of the Rocky Mountains to the shores of the Pacific stretches to Sitka in the far north-west. The birds from this distant region, according to Mr. Ridgway, present some slight differences, and are his *C. cafer saturatior*. Within the limits of Mexico some variations also exist, but these cannot well be traced to definite localities; the differences seem all due to some slight shades of colour and of dimensions. Birds from our northern frontier States are generally paler and greyer above, whilst those from Oaxaca are darker and redder, especially on the head, the birds from the tablelands being intermediate.

A point of considerable interest is associated with this species as regards its relations with *Colaptes auratus* along their common boundary. It was long ago shown by Baird that a strip of country between the ranges of the two birds is occupied by a mixed form, which he called *C. hybridus*, believing it to be the result of the interbreeding of the two definite species. This interpretation of the facts has been adopted by several writers as the most probable explanation of them. Mr. Hargitt, in his 'Catalogue,' accepted this view, and from his treatment of the subject Mr. Allen was induced to examine a very large number of specimens, with the result that he came practically to the same conclusion. But the question cannot be considered settled, for the difficulty in accepting the hybridization-theory suggested by Dr. Coues † still remains unexplained.

Though *C. auratus* approaches our boundary in Texas, we are not aware that it

* Mr. Allen's map gives Tehuantepec as within the breeding-range of *C. mexicanus*, but without authority. We have not traced the bird beyond the uplands of Oaxaca.

† Birds N.-W. p. 293.

occurs anywhere within Mexican territory. Only one of our Chihuahua specimens shows the red nape of *C. auratus*, otherwise it exactly resembles its fellows, and we are not inclined to think that hybridization has had anything to do with its peculiarity.

Full details of the habits of this species are given by Brewer, who describes the nest as made usually in oak- or pine-trees, the eggs, as is universally the case in this family, being pure white.

2. Colaptes mexicanoides.

Colaptes mexicanoides, Lafr. Rev. Zool. 1844, p. 42 [1]; Scl. & Salv. Ibis, 1859, p. 137 [2]; Salv. Cat. Strickl. Coll. p. 400 [3]; Allen, Bull. Am. Mus. N. H. iv. p. 21 [4]; Salv. & Godm. Ibis, 1892, p. 327 [5].

Colaptes rubricatus, Gray (nec Wagl.), Gen. Birds, ii. p. 446, t. 111 [6].

Picus submexicanus, Sundev. Consp. Av. Pic. p. 72 [7].

Colaptes submexicanus, Hargitt, Cat. Birds Brit. Mus. xviii. p. 21 [8].

C. mexicano similis, sed supra capite summo et cervice postica læte castaneis, dorso fasciis nigris latioribus notatis, dorso imo nigro guttato. Long. tota circa 11·0, alæ 5·8, caudæ 3·9, rostri a rictu 1·55.

♀ stria malari castanea bene definita facile distinguenda.

Hab. GUATEMALA [7], Coban (*Delattre, Constancia* [3]), Tactic (*O. S. & F. D. G.*), El Rincon in San Marcos, Ciupaché, San Martin, Plain of Quezaltenango (*W. B. Richardson*), Quezaltenango and ridges above Totonicapam, Barranco de los Chocoyos [2], Calderas and Pajal Grande on Volcan de Fuego (*O. S. & F. D. G.*); NICARAGUA, Matagalpa (*W. B. Richardson* [5]).

This species entirely takes the place of *C. mexicanus* in Guatemala, and thence southwards to Northern Nicaragua. It inhabits similar upland districts to those frequented by the Mexican bird, seldom or never descending below an elevation of 5000 feet above sea-level, and occurring as high as 8000 or 9000 feet. Its favourite woods are the evergreen-oaks and pines which occur at intervals all over the highland districts. The occurrence of this bird in Nicaragua has only recently been made known to us by Mr. Richardson, who sent us a series of specimens from the neighbourhood of Matagalpa, a district which forms the southern boundary of the highland fauna of the mountains of Guatemala, Honduras, and Nicaragua, and is also the southern limit of true pines in Central America [5].

It has been suggested that *C. mexicanoides* is not a definite species, but probably blends with *C. mexicanus* [4]. A study of the mountain masses of the countries occupied by the two birds, and the fact that both are upland species, at once show that it is very unlikely that any such transitional forms exist; for the range of the genus is completely interrupted at the Isthmus of Tehuantepec, which contains no suitable mountain area to support such intermediate birds. Moreover, we are not aware that migration of either species takes place between Mexico and Guatemala, nor do we believe that any such movement occurs. Still the fact remains that the Oaxaca form of *C. mexicanus* departs from the more typical form of the Valley of Mexico in the direction of *C. mexicanoides.* On the other hand, the latter bird is very uniform in its coloration, and practically no difference exists between specimens from Quezaltenango and Matagalpa.

3. Colaptes chrysoides.

Geopicus (Colaptes) chrysoides, Malh. Rev. Zool. 1852, p. 553[1]; Mon. Pic. ii. p. 261, t. 109[2].

Colaptes chrysoides, Reich. Scans. Picinæ, p. 413[3]; Baird, Brew., & Ridgw. N. Am. Birds, ii. p. 583[4]; Belding, Pr. U. S. Nat. Mus. vi. p. 344[5]; Hargitt, Cat. Birds Brit. Mus. xviii. p. 16[6]; Allen, Bull. Am. Mus. N. H. iv. p. 21[7].

Supra vinaceo-cinnamomeo-fuscus, capite summo et cervice postica immaculatis, illo rufescentiore, dorso et scapularibus nigro transfasciatis, plumis singulis fascia subterminali altera discali nigra, dorso imo albo, tectricibus supracaudalibus albis nigro transfasciatis; capitis lateribus et gutture toto griseis vix cinnamomeo tinctis, stria malari utrinque coccinea; pectore plaga magna lunata nigra, abdomine toto et tectricibus subcaudalibus albidis, plumis singulis macula magna discali nigra, margine ultra eam cervino tincto; alis nigris, rhachidibus flavis, remigibus internis in pogonio externo albido indistincte notatis, remigibus subtus ad basin flavidis, subalaribus albidis nigro variegatis; cauda nigra bitriente basali flava, rectrice utrinque subexterna in pogonio externo ad apicem flavo notato; rostro et pedibus plumbeis. Long. tota circa 10·0, alæ 5·6, caudæ rectr. med. 3·7, rectr. subext. 3·0, rectr. lat. 1·3, rostri a rictu 1·65, tarsi 1·1, dig. med. absque ungue 0·9, dig. ext. 0·8. (Descr. maris ex La Paz, Cal. inf. Mus. nostr.)

♀ mari similis, sed stria malari coccinea nulla.

Hab. NORTH AMERICA, S. California, Arizona, Lower California[2][4].—MEXICO, State of Sonora, Guaymas (*Belding*[5]), Hermosillo (*Ferrari-Perez*), La Cobrisa, Cedros, Ysleta in Sonora (*W. Lloyd*).

In having the base of the tail and the shafts of the primaries and their inner webs yellow instead of red, *C. chrysoides* resembles the eastern *C. auratus.* On the other hand, the absence of a red nuchal patch and the presence of a red instead of a black malar stripe in the male are characters possessed in common with *C. mexicanus.*

The range of *C. chrysoides* is much more limited than that of *C. mexicanus,* and is restricted to a narrow area, including Lower and Southern California, and the western side of the mountains of Mexico stretching towards the Gulf of California. The Mexican State of Sonora thus comes within its limits, but it hardly passes beyond into any of the adjoining States.

Though its range, to some extent, overlaps that of *C. mexicanus,* we believe no intermingling of the two birds takes place, as is the case with *C. mexicanus* and *C. auratus.*

Xantus noted birds of this species breeding at Cape San Lucas, the nest being formed in the stems of *Cereus giganteus,* the giant cactus of the district[4].

b″. *Tarsus quam digitus pedis externus (reversus) cum ungue aut brevior,*
    aut æqualis; maxilla supra nares rugosa.

CHLORONERPES.

Chloronerpes, Swainson, Classif. Birds, ii. p. 307 (1837); Hargitt, Cat. Birds Brit. Mus. xviii. p. 69.

This is a purely Neotropical genus containing, according to Mr. Hargitt, seventeen species, which are spread over the greater part of the region from its most northern boundary in Mexico to Paraguay and Argentina. Six species are found within our limits, all of them peculiar, except *C. yucatanensis,* which ranges into the north-western parts of the southern continent. Of the other species, three are restricted to Mexico and two to Costa Rica and Panama.

The bill is curved, with a distinct ridge on each side of the culmen; the tarsus is less than the outer reversed toe and its claw; the wing moderately long; the tail rather short, the short outer rectrix reaching nearly to the tips of the longest coverts.

α. *Majores, remigibus intus ad basin pallide flavidis.*

1. Chloronerpes æruginosus.

? *Picus poliocephalus,* Licht. Preis-Verz. mex. Vög. p. 1 (1830) (*cf.* J. f. Orn. 1863, p. 55) [1].
Chloronerpes rubiginosus, Gray (nec Sw.), Gen. Birds, ii. p. 443, t. 110 (1846) [2].
Chloronerpes æruginosus, Licht. Mus. Ber. [3]; Gray, Gen. Birds, App. p. 22 [4]; Scl. P. Z. S. 1859, p. 388 [5]; 1864, p. 177 [6]; Sumichrast, La Nat. v. p. 240 (partim) [7]; Hargitt, Cat. Birds Brit. Mus. xviii. p. 81 [8].
Chloronerpes yucatanensis, Scl. P. Z. S. 1856, p. 307 [9]; 1859, p. 367 [10].

Supra olivaceus, alis extrorsum oleagineis, uropygio fasciis indistinctis flavidis notato, capite summo plumbeo, nucha cum regione parotica, supra oculos evanescente et stria malari coccineis, loris et oculorum ambitu sordide albis, auricularibus paulo obscurioribus: subtus obscure olivaceus, plumis gulæ utrinque albis, vitta mediana olivacea, corpore toto reliquo fasciis sagittiformibus flavis ornato; alis subtus interne pallide flavis; cauda supra olivacea, rectricum apicibus nigris: subtus pallide olivacea, rectricum rhachidibus flavis; rostro et pedibus nigricanti-plumbeis. Long. tota circa 8·5, alæ 5·3, caudæ 3·1, rostri a rictu 1·25, tarsi 0·95, dig. med. absque ungue 0·8, dig. ext. 0·7. (Descr. maris et Ciudad Victoria, Tamaulipas. Mus. nostr.)
♀ mari similis, sed stria malari coccinea nulla.

Hab. MEXICO (*Deppe & Schiede* [3]), Sierra above Ciudad Victoria, Tamaulipas, Tampico (*Richardson*), Cordova (*Sallé* [9]), Jalapa (*Deppe in Mus. Ber.,* de Oca [10], *F. D. G., Ferrari-Perez*), Coatepec, Huatusco, Zentla (*Ferrari-Perez*), Orizaba (*Sumichrast* [7], *Ferrari-Perez*), Atoyac (*Mrs. H. H. Smith*), Teotalcingo (*Boucard* [5]).

The Eastern Cordillera of Tamaulipas, and thence southwards through the whole of the central and northern portion of the State of Vera Cruz on the flanks of the mountains sloping towards the Atlantic Ocean and onwards to the State of Oaxaca, is the home of this Woodpecker, where it ranges from the sea-level to as high as 5000 feet in the mountains. It appears to be strictly confined to this region, for immediately to the southwards, in Southern Vera Cruz, in the State of Tabasco, and in

Yucatan, the next species entirely takes it place; and though the two birds are evidently closely allied, they can nearly always be distinguished with certainty. A male from Atoyac, however, has the red over the eye carried forward in a very narrow line to the base of the bill; the bars of the breast are, however, those of *C. æruginosus*. In Western Mexico two other birds, *C. auricularis* and *C. godmani*, take its place—one in the Sierra Madre del Sur, and the other in the Sierras of the State of Jalisco.

C. æruginosus may always be recognized by the red band on the side of the head becoming evanescent over the eye, and by the hastate character of the transverse light bands on the abdomen.

Some time elapsed before Lichtenstein's name for this species became established. In the first place, it is very probably the *Picus poliocephalus* of Lichtenstein's list of Deppe and Schiede's duplicates[1], a name unaccompanied by any description. It is certainly the *Chloronerpes æruginosus* of Lichtenstein's 'Nomenclator,' as testified by the specimens now in the Berlin Museum. This name was indirectly established by Gray, who first figured the bird in the 'Genera of Birds' as Swainson's *C. rubiginosus*, but in the Appendix applied to it the name the bird now bears. Mr. Sclater for some time called it *C. yucatanensis*[9][10], but eventually recognized its correct name[5].

C. æruginosus is doubtless a resident species where it occurs. We have records of its presence at various places nearly throughout the year.

2. Chloronerpes yucatanensis.

Picus yucatanensis, Cabot, Journ. Bost. Soc. N. H. 1845, p. 92[1].

Chloronerpes yucatanensis, Moore, P. Z. S. 1859, p. 60[2]; Scl. & Salv. Ibis, 1859, p. 136[3]; 1860, p. 44[4]; Lawr. Ann. Lyc. N. Y. ix. p. 131[5]; v. Frantz. J. f. Orn. 1869, p. 364[6]; Salv. Cat. Strickl. Coll. p. 396[7]: Boucard, P. Z. S. 1883, p. 452[8]; Zeledon, An. Mus. Nac. Costa Rica, 1887, p. 124[9]; Hargitt, Cat. Birds Brit. Mus. xviii. p. 84[10].

Chloronerpes uropygialis, Cab. J. f. Orn. 1862, p. 321[11].

Chloronerpes canipileus, Salv. (nec. d'Orb.), P. Z. S. 1870, p. 212[12].

Chloronerpes æruginosus, Lawr. Bull. U. S. Nat. Mus. no. 4, p. 35[13]; Sumichrast, La Nat. v. p. 240 (partim)[14].

C. æruginoso similis, sed stria coccinea supra oculos usque ad frontem producta, fasciis corporis subtus multo rectioribus nullo modo sagittiformibus. Long. tota circa 8·0, alæ 4·7, caudæ 2·55, rostri a rictu 1·15, tarsi 0·9, dig. med. 0·7, dig. ext. 0·65. (Descr. maris ex Peto, Yucatan. Mus. nostr.)

♀ mari similis, plaga coccinea ad nucham restricta supra oculos ad frontem haud producta, stria malari coccinea nulla.

Hab. MEXICO, Playa Vicente (*M. Trujillo*), Teapa in Tabasco (*Mrs. H. H. Smith*), Chimalapa (*W. B. Richardson*), Tapana, Guichicovi, Gineta Mts. (*Sumichrast*[13][14]), Yucatan (*Cabot*[1]), Tizimin[8], Izamal[8], Peto (*G. F. Gaumer*); BRITISH HONDURAS (*Leyland*[3]), Orange Walk (*Gaumer*); GUATEMALA (*Constancia*[7]), Chisec, Coban[4], Tactic, San Gerónimo, Dueñas[3], Barranco Hondo, Savana Grande, Volcan de Agua (*O. S. & F. D. G.*), Toliman, Retalhuleu (*W. B. Richardson*); SALVADOR, La Libertad, Volcan de San Miguel (*W. B. Richardson*); NICARAGUA, Leon, Chinandega,

Volcan de Chinandega, Matagalpa, San Rafael del Norte (*W. B. Richardson*); Costa Rica, Candelaria Mts. (*Hoffmann*[11]), Barranca (*v. Frantzius*[6], *Carmiol*[5]), Turrialba (*v. Frantzius*[6], *J. Cooper*[5]), Tres Rios (*v. Frantzius*[6]), Naranjo de Cartago, Rio Sucio, Sarchi de Alajuela (*Zeledon*[9]); Panama, Volcan de Chiriqui[12], Cordillera del Chucu[12], Bibalaz, Calobre (*Arcé*).—Colombia[10]; W. Ecuador[10].

Dr. Cabot, who accompanied Stephens on his memorable expedition to Central America, was the first person to describe this Woodpecker[1], and having found it in Yucatan, named it *Picus yucatanensis*. We have several specimens from that country, and we trace its range thence southwards throughout Central America. It also occurs in the Mexican State of Vera Cruz as far north as Playa Vicente and in the State of Tabasco, a district which belongs rather to Guatemala than to the portion of Mexico which lies immediately to the north-westward. A specimen from Tehuantepec, sent us by Mr. Richardson, suggests that all Sumichrast's birds from that neighbourhood belong to this species. In Guatemala *C. yucatanensis* is common in all the mountain-districts up to an elevation of about 5000 feet.

C. yucatanensis can be distinguished from *C. æruginosus* by the bands of the under surface being much straighter, and by the red superciliary streak extending forwards to the nostril and sometimes even passing across the forehead.

3. **Chloronerpes auricularis.** (Tab. LIX. A. fig. 3, ♂.)

Chloronerpes auricularis, Salv. & Godm. Ibis, 1889, p. 381[1]; Hargitt, Cat. Birds Brit. Mus. xviii. p. 83[2].

Oleagineo-olivaceus, dorso fere unicolore, alis extus saturatioribus, uropygio pallide viridi-flavo stricte fasciato; capite summo toto cinereo; genis et tectricibus auricularibus albidis cinereo tenuiter fasciatis: subtus oleagineis, fasciis pallide viridi-albicantibus hastiformibus vittatus, gula cinerea albo punctata, stria malari utrinque coccinea; alis subtus interne pallide flavis; cauda oleaginea, rectricibus duabus mediis, rhachidibus et apicibus nigris, rectricibus externis obsolete transfasciatis, subtus olivaceis, rhachidibus flavis; rostro et pedibus nigricanti-plumbeis. Long. tota circa 8·0, alæ 4·6, caudæ 2·65, rostri a rictu 1·2, tarsi 0·75, dig. med. absque ungue 0·8, dig. ext. 0·6. (Descr. maris exempl. typ. ex Xautipa, Mexico. Mus. nostr.) ♀ adhuc ignota.

Hab. Mexico, Xautipa in Guerrero (*Mrs. H. H. Smith*).

A single male specimen was obtained by Mrs. Herbert H. Smith during the expedition made with her husband to the Sierra Madre del Sur, in the Mexican State of Guerrero, in 1888. This specimen was shot in July near the village of Xautipa. No more examples have reached us, so that we have not seen a female. That sex, judging from what we know to be the case in the closely allied *C. godmani*, no doubt only differs from the male in wanting the red malar stripe on either side of the throat.

C. auricularis, though resembling in many respects its commoner relatives *C. æruginosus* and *C. yucatanensis*, differs from both in the entire absence of any red on the head, with the exception of the malar stripes. The nape is grey like the crown. The ear-coverts, too, are somewhat conspicuously banded with grey.

4. **Chloronerpes godmani.** (Tab. LIX. A. figg. 1, ♂; 2, ♀.)

Chloronerpes godmani, Hargitt, Cat. Birds Brit. Mus. xviii. p. 83[1].

C. auriculari persimilis, regione oculari sordide albido, tectricibus auricularibus indistincte fasciatis, pileo toto pallidiore cinereo, dorso viridescentiore oleagineo vix tincto: subtus gula albicantiore, fasciis corporis pallidis angustioribus forsan dignoscendus.

♀ mari similis, sed stria malari coccinea nulla.

Hab. MEXICO, Hacienda de San Marcos, Jalisco (*W. Lloyd* [1]), Hacienda de Santa Gertrudis, Jalisco (*Dr. A. C. Buller*), Mineral de San Sebastian near Mascota, Jalisco (*Dr. A. C. Buller, in Mus. Rothschild*).

We have some doubts whether this species is really distinct from *C. auricularis,* which it resembles in almost every particular, though slight modifications of tone in the coloration of the plumage can be noticed. The female, upon which Mr. Hargitt based his description, certainly has the area round the eye, the lores, and ear-coverts uniform whity-brown, without grey bands across the latter, but in the male these are to some extent visible. In both sexes the head is paler grey, and the back, too, is of a paler shade than in the allied bird.

Our first specimen, a female, was sent us by Mr. William Lloyd, who shot it on 12th May, 1889, near the Hacienda of San Marcos in the State of Jalisco, at an altitude of 5200 feet above sea-level. We have since obtained a male shot by Dr. A. C. Buller on 20th July, 1892, near the Hacienda of Santa Gertrudis in the same State. Mr. Rothschild also has two specimens, a male and female, from the same collector, which were shot at Mineral de San Sebastian, near Mascota, also in the State of Jalisco, on the 5th May, 1892, and 3rd February, 1893, respectively.

β. *Minores, remigibus intus ad basin cinnamomeis nigro maculatis.*

5. **Chloronerpes callopterus.** (Tab. LIX. fig. 1.)

Chloronerpes callopterus, Lawr. Ann. Lyc. N. Y. vii. p. 476[1]; Salv. Ibis, 1874, p. 317[2]; Hargitt, Cat. Birds Brit. Mus. xviii. p. 80[3].

Supra oleagineo-olivaceus, capite summo et capitis lateribus brunnescentioribus, nucha coccinea, stria ab ore infra oculos flava: subtus oleagineus, gula flavo striata, gutture et pectore flavo guttatis, abdomine flavo et oleagineo regulariter transfasciatis; alis cinnamomeis, apicibus nigris et nigro in ambobus pogoniis maculatis, secundariis extrorsum fere omnino oleagineis; cauda oleaginea, rectricibus mediis apicibus et rhachidibus nigris; rostro et pedibus nigricante plumbeis. Long. tota circa 7·0, alæ 4·3, caudæ 2·3, rostri a rictu 1·0, tarsi 0·7, dig. med. absque ungue 0·6, dig. ext. 0·55. (Descr. feminæ ex Veraguas, Panama. Mus. nostr.)

♂ adhuc ignotus.

Hab. PANAMA, Veraguas (*Arcé* [2]), Lion Hill (*M'Leannan* [1]).

We are not aware of the existence of more than two specimens of this species in collections, both of them females. Mr. Lawrence received the first from M'Leannan from the Line of the Panama Railway and described it as a male in 1862[1]. The second specimen was sent us by Arcé in one of his last collections made in Veraguas subsequently to the publication of the second list of his birds in 1870[2]. These two specimens were compared together by Salvin in 1875, and found to be quite alike. The Veraguas bird is now figured. The male of *C. callopterus* will doubtless have a large amount of red on the head as well as a red malar stripe, and that sex will be distinguished from the male of *C. simplex* by a yellow stripe passing from the corner of the mouth under the eye.

The range of this species will doubtless prove to be very restricted, and probably hardly passes the limits of the State of Panama.

6. **Chloronerpes simplex.** (Tab. LIX. fig. 2.)

Chloronerpes simplex, Salv. P. Z. S. 1870, p. 212[1]; Ibis, 1874, p. 317[2]; Hargitt, Cat. Birds Brit. Mus. xviii. p. 81[3].

Oleagineo-virescens, gula, pectore et regione auriculari paulo obscurioribus; capite toto, nucha et stria lata malari coccineis, pectore maculis discalibus ochraceis guttato, abdomine pallide ochraceo-flavido, transfasciato; alis intus castaneis, remigibus omnibus apicibus nigricantibus et nigro transfasciatis; cauda fusco-nigricante extrorsum dorso concolori; rostro et pedibus plumbeis. Long. tota circa 7·0, alæ 4·5, caudæ 2·55, rostri a rictu 1·0, tarsi 0·7, dig. med. absque ungue 0·6, dig. ext. 0·55. (Descr. maris ex Chontales, Nicaragua. Mus. nostr.)

♀ mari similis, sed capite toto (nucha excepta) dorso fere concolore paulo obscuriore.

Hab. NICARAGUA, La Libertad in Chontales (*W. B. Richardson*); COSTA RICA, Talamanca (*Gabb*[2]); PANAMA, Bugaba[1], Chiriqui[3] (*Arcé*).

A female specimen sent by Arcé from Bugaba, in the district of Chiriqui, was described by Salvin in 1870[1], and a male recognized as of the same species, obtained by Prof. Gabb's expedition to Talamanca, was also described by him in 1874[2]. Arcé subsequently sent a second female specimen from Chiriqui *. Since then we have received two males and a female from Mr. Richardson, who obtained them at La Libertad, in the district of Chontales, Nicaragua, in January and February 1892, the female agreeing closely with the type.

C. simplex resembles *C. callopterus* in many respects, but may readily be distinguished by the absence of the yellow stripe of the latter, which runs from the corner of the mouth below the eye, and by the throat being of a uniform colour, unbroken by yellow marks.

Our figure is taken from the type from Bugaba.

MELANERPES.

Melanerpes, Swainson, Class. Birds, ii. p. 310 (1837); Ridgw. Man. N. Am. Birds, p. 290; Hargitt, Cat. Birds Brit. Mus. xviii. p. 139.

Centurus, Swainson, Class. Birds, ii. p. 310 (1837); Ridgw. Pr. U. S. Nat. Mus. iv. p. 93.

Tripsurus, Swainson, Class. Birds, ii. p. 311 (1837).

We use the name *Melanerpes* in the wide sense adopted by Mr. Ridgway and

---

* Mr. Hargitt[3] states that this is the type—an obvious mistake.

Mr. Hargitt; so that it includes all the species usually placed in *Centurus*. The two groups are chiefly, if not only, separated by colour-characters, and these, again, are connected by such species as *Melanerpes pucherani*.

As in *Chloronerpes*, *Melanerpes* has a short tarsus, which is less than the middle toe and claw and less than the outer toe (reversed) and its claw; but the wing is considerably longer, and the style of coloration very different.

The Mexican and Central-American species may be divided into three groups as follows:—

    α. Back uniform black, glossed bluish or green. =*Melanerpes* (type *M. erythrocephalus*).

    β. Back black, with a broad median stripe of pale drab.

    γ. Back black, distinctly barred with white. =*Centurus* (type *M. carolinus*).

The first of these groups is represented by *M. formicivorus*; the second by *M. chrysauchen*; the third by *M. pucherani*, *M. wagleri*, *M. rubriventris*, *M. aurifrons* (and its allies), *M. uropygialis*, *M. elegans*, and *M. hypopolius*—in all twelve species, the whole genus containing about thirty-three species, more or less distinct. Of these only four are found in North America, of which *M. carolinus* reaches Canada. Each of the larger Antilles, and several of the smaller islands, as well as some of the Bahamas, have species of their own. The rest belong exclusively to South America, and mostly appertain to group *β*; South Brazil and Western Argentina being the furthest points reached.

The chief memoirs on *Melanerpes* are Mr. Hargitt's 'Catalogue of Picidæ in the British Museum,' which treats of the genus as a whole; Dr. Cabanis's notes on *Centurus* in the 'Journal für Ornithologie' for 1862; and Mr. Ridgway's review of the genus *Centurus* in the 'Proceedings of the United States National Museum' for 1881. On the whole, we have followed Mr. Hargitt's arrangement, which was based almost entirely upon the series of skins gathered by us for the present work.

One point as regards the inter-relationship of some of the species of *Melanerpes* calls for special notice, and that is the intergradation or blending which seems certainly to take place along the boundary-lines of the ranges of some of them. This fact induced Mr. Ridgway to use trinomials largely in their nomenclature. We have thought it best to adhere to the old plan of binomials wherever a form proved to be definite over a certain area, and also where the modifications seem to indicate only a general tendency towards a not thoroughly established character. We have not attempted to differentiate by name the intermediates between otherwise fairly precise forms.

Mr. Ridgway's plan has this difficulty, which is well illustrated by his treatment of *M. aurifrons* and its allies. Thus we have *M. aurifrons*, *M. a. santacruzi*, *M. a. dubius*, *M. a. hoffmanni*, and subsequently *M. santacruzi pauper*. Now the connection between *M. aurifrons* and *M. dubius*, on the one hand, and *M. hoffmanni*, on the other, is certainly not direct, but through *M. santacruzi*. Therefore, to be thorough in this matter of names, we ought to read *M. aurifrons santacruzi dubius*, *M. a. s. hoffmanni*, and

M. a. s. pauper. And even further as regards Mr. Ridgway's *M. leei*, which was at one time called *M. dubius leei*; for *M. dubius*, through the connection of *M. santacruzi*, is *M. aurifrons santacruzi dubius*, and hence *M. leei* becomes *Melanerpes aurifrons santacruzi dubius leei*! By making *M. santacruzi* the central form, one of these names may be eliminated at the cost of strict priority, but *M. leei* would still be left with four names.

Mr. Ridgway, when compiling his 'Manual of North-American Birds,' seems to have seen all this difficulty, for he calls the whole of the members of this section of the genus by simple binomials. But what, then, has become of the intergradation, the existence of which he so strongly insisted upon in his first paper, and which is probably much more evident to us now than it was to him at the time?

α. Dorsum nigrum, cærulescenti-chalybeo lavatum.

1. Melanerpes formicivorus.

Picus formicivorus, Sw. Phil. Mag. new ser. i. p. 439 (1827)[1]; Wagl. Isis, 1829, p. 515[2].

Melanerpes formicivorus, Bp. P. Z. S. 1837, p. 109[3]; Scl. P. Z. S. 1856, pp. 143[4], 307[5]; 1858, p. 305[6]; 1859, p. 367[7]; Moore, P. Z. S. 1859, p. 60[8]; Scl. & Salv. Ibis, 1859, p. 137[9]; Cab. J. f. Orn. 1862, p. 322[10]; Dugès, La Nat. i. p. 139[11]; Lawr. Ann. Lyc. N. Y. ix. p. 131[12]; Mem. Bost. Soc. N. H. ii. p. 294[13]; Bull. U. S. Nat. Mus. no. 4, p. 35[14]; v. Frantz. J. f. Orn. 1869, p. 364[15]; Sumichrast, Mem. Bost. Soc. N. H. i. p. 562[16]; La Nat. v. p. 240[17]; Salv. P. Z. S. 1870, p. 213[18]; Cat. Strickl. Coll. p. 397[19]; Boucard, P. Z. S. 1878, p. 49[20]; Ridgw. Pr. U. S. Nat. Mus. v. p. 497[21]; x. p. 591[22]; Ferrari-Perez, Pr. U. S. Nat. Mus. ix. p. 159[23]; Zeledon, An. Mus. Nac. Costa Rica, 1887, p. 124[24]; Hargitt, Cat. Birds Brit. Mus. xviii. pp. 149, 569[25].

Picus melanopogon, Temm. Pl. Col. 451 (1828)[26]; Wagl. Isis, 1829, p. 515[27].

Picus melanopogon, Licht. Preis-Verz. mex. Vög. p. 1 (*cf.* J. f. Orn. 1863, p. 55)[28].

Melanerpes melanopogon, Hargitt, Cat. Birds Brit. Mus. xviii. p. 151[29].

Melanerpes formicivorus, var. *formicivorus*, Baird, Brew., & Ridgw. N. Am. Birds, ii. p. 566[30].

Melanerpes formicivorus bairdi, Coues, Check-l. N. Am. Birds, p. 79[31].

Supra chalybeo-niger, uropygio et tectricibus supracaudalibus niveis his strictissime nigro limbatis; capite summo et nucha coccineis, fronte postica et torque gutturali (linea ante oculos conjunctis) albis, hac flavo suffuso, fronte antica et gula antica nigris; pectore nigro chalybeo squamato, parte postica et hypochondriis utrinque albo limbatis, illius plumis in pectore medio macula alba in pogonio interno tantum notatis ciliis omnibus nigris, ventre medio albo; alis et cauda nigris, illis speculo alari albo, remigibus omnibus ad basin in pogonio interno albis, subalaribus nigro et albo variegatis; rostro et pedibus nigris. Long. tota 8·5, alæ 6·0, caudæ 3·35, rostri a rictu 1·3, tarsi 0·9, dig. med. absque ungue 0·7, dig. ext. 0·65.

♀ mari similis, capite summo chalybeo-nigro dorso concolore; pectore antico plumis quibusdam coccineis ornato. (Descr. maris et feminæ ex Real del Monte, Mexico. Mus. nostr.)

Hab. NORTH AMERICA, Western States from British Columbia southwards to Arizona and Western Texas[30].—MEXICO (*Temminck*[26], *Wagler, Mus. Ber.*[27]), Santa Rosa, Yecæra in Sonora (*W. Lloyd*), Pinos Altos in Chihuahua (*Buchan-Hepburn*), Refugio, San José, Tomochic, Jesus Maria, all in Chihuahua (*W. Lloyd*), Ciudad in Durango (*Forrer*), Guanajuato (*Dugès*[11]), Sierra de Valparaiso, Sierra de Bolaños, Sierra de Jerez, Sierra de San Luis Potosi, Sierra de Tepic, Sierra above Ciudad Victoria in

Tamaulipas, Real del Monte (*W. B. Richardson*), Temiscaltepec (*Bullock* [1]), Chimalpa, Mexicalcingo in the Valley of Mexico (*F. Ferrari-Perez*), Rio Frio Ixtaccihuatl (*W. B. Richardson*), Cordova (*Sallé* [5]), Las Vigas, Coatepec, Misantla, Huatusco, S. Lorenzo near Cordova, San Bartolo, Zentla, Chachapa [23], La Resurreccion, S. Miguel Molino (*F. Ferrari-Perez*), Potrero (*Sumichrast* [17]), Jalapa (*de Oca* [7], *F. D. G.*, *F. Ferrari- Perez* [23]), Zapotlan (*W. Lloyd*), Sierra Nevada de Colima (*W. B. Richardson*), Tonila (*Xantus* [13]), Omilteme, Xautipa, Sierra Madre del Sur (*Mrs. H. H. Smith*), La Parada (*Boucard* [6]), Sola, Juchatengo (*M. Trujillo*), Oaxaca (*Fenochio, Sumichrast* [17]), Guichicovi, Gineta Mts. [17] (*Sumichrast* [14]), Chimalapa (*W. B. Richardson*); BRITISH HONDURAS, Pine-ridge of Belize, Chilomo (*Leyland* [8]), Cayo, Southern Pine-ridge (*Blancaneaux*), Punta Placentia (*O. S.*); GUATEMALA (*Constancia* [19]), Chilasco, Rabinal, Ridge above Totonicapam, Calderas [9], Volcan de Fuego [9], Volcan de Agua, Alotepeque (*O. S. & F. D. G.*), Toliman (*W. B. Richardson*); HONDURAS, Segovia River (*Townsend* [22]); NICARAGUA, Matagalpa, San Rafael del Norte (*W. B. Richardson*); COSTA RICA, Volcan de Irazu (*v. Frantzius, Hoffmann* [10], *Arcé, Nutting* [21], *Boucard* [20]), Cartago, Monte Redondo, Zarcero de Alajuela, La Palma de S. José (*Zeledon* [24]), Naranjo (*Boucard* [20]), S. José (*v. Frantzius* [12][15]), Barranca (*Carmiol* [12], *Zeledon*), Dota Mts. (*v. Frantzius* [15], *Zeledon* [12]), Birris (*Zeledon* [12]), Grecia, Potrero, Cervantes (*v. Frantzius* [15]); PANAMA, David (*Bridges* [4]), Volcan de Chiriqui (*Arcé* [18]).

A close examination of a very large series of specimens of this species from all parts of Mexico convinces us that it is not possible to recognize with any certainty the two races of *Melanerpes formicivorus* that have, of recent years, been called *M. formicivorus* and *M. f. bairdi* by American writers or *M. melanopogon* by Mr. Hargitt. The character chiefly relied on is the extent to which the white markings of the feathers of the pectoral band are carried forward towards the anterior margin of this band. In northern birds these markings are only shown towards the lower edge, leaving the band itself wide and of a nearly uninterrupted black colour; the white marks become more extensive and more prominent in specimens from more southern regions, but nowhere, at least in Mexico, is one type prevalent to the entire exclusion of the other. Mr. Hargitt endeavoured to sort the British Museum specimens into the two forms; but the result is not satisfactory, for in several instances both forms are assigned to the same district. Thus the type from Temiscaltepec is called *M. formicivorus*, but other specimens from the Valley of Mexico are named *M. melanopogon*; the birds of the Sierra Madre del Sur are placed under the former title, but those from Oaxaca appear under both.

We do not think it advisable to attempt any division, but include all under one name, the species being on the whole very constant in its characters, but variable to a slight extent as regards the width of the dark band across the chest.

M. formicivorus is one of the most abundant of the Woodpeckers of our region, and is found wherever pines or oaks, or both, are the chief trees of a district. As these trees are found at short intervals over the whole of the Mexican and Central-American highlands, *M. formicivorus* occurs in profusion. But it is not in the highlands alone that it is found, for as oaks grow near the shores of the Gulf of Mexico near Misantla and pines within sight of the sea on the coast of British Honduras, there, too, *Melanerpes formicivorus* is present. It thus has a range in altitude extending from the sea-level to a height of at least 8000 or 9000 feet in the mountains.

The first specimens sent to Europe were obtained by Bullock at Temiscaltepec [1], on the borders of the Valley of Mexico. These were named by Swainson in 1827 as *Picus formicivorus*. The following year Temminck described and figured a female bird as *Picus melanopogon* [26]. Both names belong to the bird of the highlands of Central Mexico, whence we have lately received many specimens. The northern bird was separated by Dr. Coues as *M. f. bairdi*, and a name has been suggested for the bird of Costa Rica, but apparently without description. All these names we now place under Swainson's title.

A curious habit of this species has been described by Sumichrast [16], viz. the storing of acorns in the hollow trunks of the maguey and in the clefts behind the peeling bark of dry trees. He also says these birds pick round holes in the bark of oak trees, and into each one insert an acorn and fix it there firmly. On one occasion, Salvin observed a number of birds evidently engaged in this operation. This was on the high mountain-ridge which lies between the Guatemalan town of Rabinal and the Valley of the Motagua. The trees whose bark was perforated in this case were pines, and a portion of the bark was split off and brought home and may be now seen in the British Museum. The habit has also been noticed by Leyland [8] and by Dr. Berendt [30] in the neighbourhood of Belize, and extended details on the subject are given by Brewer [30].

This curious labour may be undertaken by this Woodpecker for the purpose of extracting larvæ infesting the acorns; but, as Sumichrast says, it is not easy to understand why the birds should take so much trouble to get these small larvæ in a country where insect-life exists in profusion.

A close ally of *M. formicivorus*, in its wide sense, is *M. flavigula* of Colombia, in which the male is coloured on the head like the female of the northern bird, and the female has no red on the head at all. Another closely allied form, and perhaps not really different, occurs in Lower California.

β. *Dorsum nigrum, stria lata longitudinali mediana alba aut pallide isabellina.*

2. **Melanerpes chrysauchen.** (Tab. LX.)

Melanerpes chrysauchen, Salv. P. Z. S. 1870, p. 213 [1]; Hargitt, Cat. Birds Brit. Mus. xviii. p. 160 [2].

Supra niger, dorso medio et uropygio albis, illo nigro maculato, fronte et nucha flavis, pileo medio coccineo; alis nigris, intus albo notatis; cauda nigra: subtus sordide albidus flavo lavatus, ventre medio coccineo, hypochondriis imis et tectricibus subcaudalibus nigro transfasciatis; rostro et pedibus plumbeis. Long. tot. circa 7·0, alæ 4·5, caudæ 2·3, rostri a rictu 1·2, tarsi 0·73, dig. med. absque ungue 0·65, dig. ext. 0·6.

♀ mari similis, sed pileo medio vitta arcuata nigra transfasciato, colore coccineo nullo. (Descr. maris et feminæ exempl. typ. ex Bugaba, Panama. Mus. nostr.)

Hab. PANAMA, Bugaba (*Arcé* [1]).

This pretty species is only known to us from the few specimens obtained by our collector Arcé in the district of Chiriqui, State of Panama. Its nearest ally appears to be the Brazilian *M. flavifrons*, from which it may readily be distinguished by the wider black band behind the eye and by the lores being entirely yellow instead of black. Moreover, in the present bird the throat is a dingy, not a clear, yellow, and the red is confined to the lower belly instead of being spread over the whole of the middle of the abdomen.

γ. *Dorsum nigrum, albo regulariter transfasciatum.*

α'. *Abdomen totum nigro transfasciatum.*

3. **Melanerpes pucherani.**

Zebrapicus pucherani, Malh. Rev. Zool. 1849, p. 542 [1]; Mon. Pic. ii. p. 227, t. 103. figg. 1–3 [2].

Centurus pucherani, Bp. Consp. Av. i. p. 120 [3]; Scl. P. Z. S. 1857, p. 229 [4]; Moore, P. Z. S. 1859, p. 60 [5]; Scl. & Salv. Ibis, 1859, p. 136 [6]; 1860, p. 43 [7]; P. Z. S. 1864, p. 367 [8]; 1867, p. 280 [9]; 1870, p. 837 [10]; Lawr. Ann. Lyc. N. Y. vii. p. 299 [11]; viii. p. 184 [12]; Salv. Ibis, 1872, p. 320 [13]; Boucard, P. Z. S. 1878, p. 49 [14]; Sumichrast, La Nat. v. p. 240 [15]; Ridgw. Pr. U. S. Nat. Mus. x. pp. 583 [16], 591 [17].

Tripsurus pucherani, Salvad. Atti R. Acc. Sc. Tor. 1868, p. 183 [18].

Melanerpes pucherani, Nutting, Pr. U. S. Nat. Mus. vi. p. 406 [19]; Zeledon, An. Mus. Nac. Costa Rica, 1887, p. 124 [20]; Hargitt, Cat. Birds Brit. Mus. xviii. p. 164 [21].

Zebrapicus gerinii, Malh. Mon. Pic. ii. p. 231 [22].

Centurus gerinii, Lawr. Ann. Lyc. N. Y. ix. p. 131 [23]; v. Frantz. J. f. Orn. 1869, p. 364 [24].

Supra niger, dorso medio albo transfasciato, uropygio et tectricibus supracaudalibus albis; alis nigris, sparsim albo maculatis; pileo toto et nucha coccineis, fronte albida aurantio tincta; capitis lateribus albis, macula postoculari alba: subtus fuscus, gula albicante, pectore immaculato, abdomine toto nigro transfasciato, ventre medio coccineo; cauda nigra, rectricibus mediis unicoloribus (interdum in pogonio interno albo ad basin fasciatis), rectricibus subexternis obsolete fasciatis; rostro nigricante, pedibus plumbeis. Long. tota circa 7·5, alæ 4·5, caudæ 2·4, rostri a rictu 1·2, tarsi 0·8, dig. med. absque ungue 0·7, dig. ext. 0·65.

♀ mari similis, sed pileo medio albido postice nigro marginato; nucha tantum coccineo. (Descr. maris et feminæ ex La Libertad, Chontales, Nicaragua. Mus. nostr.)

Hab. MEXICO, Orizaba [4] (*Mus. Brit.*), Santecomapam (*Sallé* [4]), Uvero (*Sumichrast* [15]); BRITISH HONDURAS (*Blancaneaux*); GUATEMALA, Coban [7], Choctum, Chisec, Yzabal [7] (*O. S. & F. D G.*); HONDURAS, Omoa (*Leyland* [5]), San Pedro (*G. M. Whitely* [10]), Truxillo [16], R. Segovia [17] (*Townsend*); NICARAGUA, Blewfields (*Wickham* [9]), Los Sabalos (*Nutting* [19]), Chontales (*Belt* [13]), La Libertad, Rama (*W. B. Richardson*), Rio Escondido (*Richmond*), Greytown (*Holland* [12], *Richmond*); COSTA RICA (*Durando* [18], *v. Frantzius* [24]), Rio Frio (*Richmond*), San José (*Carmiol* [23]), San Carlos, Naranjo (*Boucard* [14]), Turrialba (*Arcé*), Cartago, Jimenez, Rancho Redondo, Talamanca (*Zeledon* [20]); PANAMA, Lion Hill (*M'Leannan* [8] [11]).—COLOMBIA [2] [21]; W. ECUADOR [21]; TOBAGO [1].

Melanerpes pucherani, though belonging to the section of the genus with the back barred with black and white, is aberrant, inasmuch as the whole of the abdomen, from the breast downwards, is barred; the lesser wing-coverts and the primaries externally are spotless black; and there are other points of difference.

The species has a very wide range over the whole of our region from the Mexican State of Vera Cruz southwards, and passes into Colombia and Western Ecuador. So far as we know, it does not occur in Western Mexico or the part of Guatemala bordering the Pacific Ocean, but keeps strictly to the denser forests of the low-lying lands of the eastern side of the main mountain-range, not ascending the hills to any great elevation.

According to Fraser, who obtained specimens in Western Ecuador, the irides are hazel.

β'. *Corpus subtus unicolor, ventre imo et tectricibus subcaudalibus tantum fasciatis.*

α". *Capitis latus, circum oculos haud nigro notatus.*

α'''. *Uropygium et tectrices supracaudales plerumque pure albi* *.

4. **Melanerpes wagleri.**

Picus tricolor, Wagl. (nec Gm.), Isis, 1829, p. 512[1].

Centurus tricolor, Cab. J. f. Orn. 1862, p. 327[2]; Scl. & Salv. P. Z. S. 1864, p. 367[3]; Salv. P. Z. S. 1867, p. 157[4]; 1870, p. 213[5].

Melanerpes tricolor, Hargitt, Cat. Birds Brit. Mus. xviii. p. 174[6].

Centurus subelegans, Bp. Consp. Av. i. p. 119 (nec P. Z. S. 1837, p. 109)[7]; Scl. P. Z. S. 1856, p. 143[8].

Centurus rubriventris, Lawr. (nec Sw.), Ann. Lyc. N. Y. vii. p. 299[9].

Supra niger, frequenter albo transfasciatus, pileo toto et nucha coccineis, fronte albida ad nares flavo tincta, tectricibus supracaudalibus albis; capitis lateribus et corpore subtus sordide albis, abdomine medio coccineo, hypochondriis imis et tectricibus subcaudalibus nigro transfasciatis; alis nigris, albo guttatis et fasciatis, remigibus externis ad basin tantum in pogonio externo fasciatis; cauda nigra, rectricibus subexternis ad apicem et mediis fere omnino albo distincte transfasciatis; rostro et pedibus plumbeis. Long. tota circa 7·0, alæ 4·2, caudæ 2·1, rostri a rictu 1·2, tarsi 0·78, dig. med. absque ungue 0·67, dig. ext. 0·6. ♀ mari similis, sed pileo toto sordide albido, nucha tantum coccinea. (Descr. maris et feminæ ex Lion Hill, Panama. Mus. nostr.)

Hab. PANAMA, David (*Bridges*[8]), Cordillera de Tolé[4], Castillo[5], Chitra[5], Calovevora[5], Santa Fé[4] (*Arcé*), Lion Hill (*M'Leannan*[3][9]), Paraiso Station (*Hughes*).—COLOMBIA[2]; VENEZUELA[2].

Wagler's name for this species cannot be retained. It was based upon a bird supposed to be the *Picus tricolor* of Gmelin, a name applied to the Mexican "Quauhchochopitli" of Hernandez[1], which, though probably a *Melanerpes*, cannot now be recognized, but was certainly not the present bird. It is, no doubt, the *Centurus subelegans* of Bonaparte's 'Conspectus;' but, unfortunately, this name was first

---

* In some island-specimens of *M. dubius* these parts are irregularly banded.

applied to *Melanerpes aurifrons* and is a synonym of it. We cannot consider Wagler's description an amended one of that of Gmelin, for though the former author gives Mexico as the habitat of his *M. tricolor*, his type, as Dr Cabanis tells us, really came from Cartagena[2]. The proper solution of the difficulty is to give the present bird a fresh name, and we apply to it that of the author who first described it fully [*].

The range of *Melanerpes wagleri* is very restricted, and appears to be confined to parts of Venezuela and Colombia, including the State of Panama. A closely-allied species is *M. terricolor* (Berl.), a larger bird with the upper tail-coverts barred.

M. rubriventris is also allied, but may be distinguished by its smaller size, more closely barred back, and by the yellow colour which surrounds the mouth.

5. Melanerpes rubriventris.

Centurus rubriventris, Sw. An. in Menag. p. 354[1]; Lawr. Ann. Lyc. N. Y. ix. p. 206[2]; Ann. N. Y. Ac. Sc. ii. p. 247[3]; Boucard, P. Z. S. 1883, p. 452[4]; Salv. Ibis, 1885, p. 192[5]; 1889, p. 369[6]; 1890, p. 88[7].

Zebrapicus rubriventris, Malh. Mon. Pic. ii. p. 248, t. 107. fig. 1[8].

Melanerpes rubriventris, Hargitt, Cat. Birds Brit. Mus. xviii. p. 176[9].

Centurus rubriventris pygmæus, Ridgw. Pr. U. S. Nat. Mus. viii. p. 576[10].

Melanerpes pygmæus, Ridgw. Man. N. Am. Birds, p. 293[11].

Supra niger, dorso toto et alis extus crebre albo transfasciatis; pileo summo et nucha rubris, uropygio et tectricibus supracaudalibus albis; capitis lateribus, stria transversa inter oculos et corpore subtus sordide albis, facie tota cum mento aureis, abdomine medio rubro, subcaudalibus nigro fasciatis, remigibus extus nigris ad basin in pogonio externo albo maculatis, secundariis extrorsum maculatis; cauda nigra, rectricibus mediis ad basin albo variegatis, rectricibus duabus subexternis in pogonio externo extrorsum albido maculatis; rostro et pedibus plumbeis. Long. tota 7·0, alæ 4·2, caudæ 2·5, rostri a rictu 1·1, tarsi 0·72, dig. med. absque ungue 0·6, dig. ext. 0·6.

♀ mari similis, sed capite summo cinereo, nucha tantum rubra. (Descr. maris et feminæ ex Peto, Yucatan. Mus. nostr.)

Hab. MEXICO, Merida in Yucatan (*Schott*[2][3], *Gaumer*[4]), Peto in Yucatan (*Gaumer*), Cozumel I. (*Devis*[5], *Benedict*[10], *Gaumer*[6][7]); HONDURAS, Bonacca I. (*Gaumer*[6][7]).

This little species, though characterized by Swainson in 1837, and figured by Malherbe in 1862, was scarcely known until Mr. Lawrence described a male specimen in 1869 obtained by Schott near Merida in Yucatan[2]. During the last ten years many specimens have been sent us by Dr. Gaumer, both from the mainland of Northern Yucatan, the islands off the east coast, and from Bonacca Island in the Bay of Honduras. The Cozumel bird was separated by Mr. Ridgway from the mainland *M. rubriventris* first as *Centurus rubriventris pygmæus* and subsequently as *Melanerpes pygmæus*. The average size of the island birds is rather small, the colour rather dark, and the central rectrices whiter at the base, but it is not difficult to match island and mainland birds both as to size and colour.

* This name need not be confused with *Dyctiopicus wagleri*, Bp., a synonym of *Dendrocopus cancellatus* (Wagl.), or *Picus wagleri*, Hartl., a synonym of *Dendrocopus macii* (Vieill.).

In size and general appearance *M. rubriventris* resembles *M. wagleri*, and the two birds at one time were confused together. The bright orange of the whole of the feathers surrounding the base of the bill and the narrowness of the white bars of the upper surface readily distinguish *M. rubriventris* from its more southern ally. The Bonacca Island bird, however, is somewhat intermediate between the two, both in size and colour; but as the adult has the yellow colouring round the base of the bill, we assign it to *M. rubriventris*.

6. Melanerpes aurifrons.

Picus aurifrons, Wagl. Isis, 1829, p. 512 [1]; Licht. Preis-Verz. mex. Vög. p. 1 (*cf.* J. f. Orn. 1863, p. 55) [2].

Centurus aurifrons, Cab. J. f. Orn. 1862, p. 323 [3]; Dugès, La Nat. i. p. 139 [4]; Baird, Brew., & Ridgw. N. Am. Birds, ii. p. 557 [5]; Ridgw. Pr. U. S. Nat. Mus. iv. p. 104 [6].

Melanerpes aurifrons, Hargitt, Cat. Birds Brit. Mus. xviii. p. 177 [7].

Centurus subelegans, Bp. P. Z. S. 1837, p. 109 (nec Consp. Av. i. p. 118) [8].

Picus ornatus, Less. Rev. Zool. 1839, p. 102 [9].

Supra niger, dorso et alis albo transfasciatis, uropygio et tectricibus supracaudalibus albis; capite summo griseo, plaga magna occipitali rubra, nucha et fronte aureis hac pallidiore, capite antico lateribus et corpore subtus albicantibus; ventre medio flavo; tectricibus subalaribus et tibiis nigro transfasciatis, remigibus nigris, fascia lata irregulari alba, rhachidibus nigris; cauda nigra, rectrice subexterni ad apicem et in pogonio externo albo fasciato; rostro nigro; pedibus plumbeis. Long. tota circa 9·0, alæ 5·5, caudæ 3·4, rostri a rictu 1·7, tarsi 0·93, dig. med. absque ungue 0·8, dig. ext. 0·73. (Descr. maris ex Julines, Chihuahua, Mexico. Mus. nostr.)

♀ mari similis, sed plaga rubra capitis summi nulla.

Hab. N. AMERICA, Texas [5].—MEXICO [9], Julines in Chihuahua (*W. Lloyd*), Nuevo Laredo, Ceralvo, Hacienda de las Escobas, San Agustin in Nuevo Leon (*F. B. Armstrong*), Ismiquilpam (*Deppe, in Mus. Berol.* [3]), Sierra above Ciudad Victoria and Soto la Marina in Tamaulipas, Aguas Calientes and Calvillo in Aguas Calientes (*W. B. Richardson*), Silao (*mus. nostr.*), Valley of Mexico (*mus. nostr.*), Morelia (*F. D. G.*), Guanajuato (*Dugès* [4]), Santana near Guadalajara (*W. Lloyd*).

Wagler's description of this Woodpecker was based on Mexican specimens in the Berlin Museum, which were probably those obtained by Deppe at Ismiquilpam. In North Mexico we now know the bird is by no means rare. Its southward extension reaches to Morelia in the State of Michoacan, and we have a specimen said to have come from the Valley of Mexico, but this is perhaps open to question. On the eastern side it occurs throughout the States of Tamaulipas and Nuevo Leon; but we have no record of its occurrence in Vera Cruz, its place being taken by a closely allied form. In South Texas it appears to be very common, and has been noticed by all collectors who have written on the birds of that State. Mr. Sennett found it at Lomita, where it was breeding, making its nest-hole in the large hard-wood trees. It also bores into the telegraph-poles in search of larvæ. The eggs are of the usual white colour and vary in number from four to six in a nest.

The widely separated white bars of the upper plumage, the pure white upper tail-coverts of the adult, and the wholly black exposed portion of the central rectrices distinguish this species. The colour of the nape varies from golden yellow to orange and even red; the occipital spot is generally isolated, but sometimes almost confluent with the nuchal band.

7. Melanerpes hoffmanni.

Centurus hoffmanni, Cab. J. f. Orn. 1862, p. 322 [1]; Lawr. Ann. Lyc. N. Y. ix. p. 131 [2]; v. Frantzius, J. f. Orn. 1869, p. 364 [3]; Boucard, P. Z. S. 1878, p. 49 [4]; Zeledon, An. Mus. Nac. Costa Rica, 1887, p. 124 [5]; Cherrie, Auk, 1892, p. 327 [6].

Melanerpes hoffmanni, Hargitt, Cat. Birds Brit. Mus. xviii. p. 181 [7].

Centurus aurifrons hoffmanni, Ridgw. Pr. U. S. Nat. Mus. iv. p. 110 [8]; v. p. 501 [9]; Nutting, Pr. U. S. Nat. Mus. v. p. 399 [10]; vi. pp. 375 [11], 387 [12], 394 [13].

M. aurifronti similis, sed multo minor, rostro breviore et magis arcuato; corpore subtus fuscescentiore, remigibus externis ad basin albo vix transfasciatis, caudæ remigibus mediis in pogonio interno regulariter. albo fasciatis. Long. tota circa 7·5, alæ 4·5, caudæ 2·2, rostri a rictu 1·3, tarsi 0·83, dig. med. absque ungue 0·8, dig. ext. 0·7.

♀ mari similis, pileo toto sordide cinereo, colore coccineo nullo. (Descr. maris et feminæ ex Punta Arenas. Costa Rica. Mus. nostr.)

Hab. NICARAGUA, Leon (*W. B. Richardson*), San Juan del Sur [11], Sucuya [12], Omotepe [13] (*Nutting*); COSTA RICA (*Hoffmann, Ellendorf* [1]), Punta Arenas (*O. S*), La Palma (*Nutting* [10]), San José (*v. Frantzius* [3], *M. J. Calleja, Carmiol* [2], *Boucard* [4], *Zeledon* [5], *Nutting* [9], *Cherrie* [6]), Cartago (*Boucard* [4], *Zeledon* [5]), Grecia (*Carmiol* [2], *v. Frantzius* [3]), Alajuela (*Zeledon* [5]).

Dr. Cabanis described this species from specimens sent to the Berlin Museum from Costa Rica by Dr. Hoffmann, to whom it was dedicated [1]. With the description Dr. Cabanis added a useful summary of the whole of the members of the genus, in which some valuable notes on their synonymy are to be found.

The relationship of this species to *M. aurifrons* is obvious, but the characters separating the two forms seem fairly constant and their respective ranges quite distinct, the intermediate country of Guatemala, Honduras, and Salvador being occupied by *M. santacruzi,* a bird which, again, differs in several points.

M. hoffmanni is a common species in Costa Rica. It occurs at Punta Arenas, where Salvin secured some specimens and where M. Boucard also met with it [4]; and it is also found in the neighbourhood of San José, and to an altitude, according to Mr. Cherrie, of 6500 feet [6]. The last-named naturalist found two nests near San José of this Woodpecker, one of which was 25 feet from the ground in an old rotton snag, and contained two fresh eggs: the other was only about three feet from the ground, in an old stump, and contained three fresh eggs; the entrance-hole to this nest was two inches in diameter, and there was no lining. The eggs were glossy white, measuring about 1·03 × 0·7 inch.

53*

In Nicaragua *M. hoffmanni* appears to be equally common, as Mr. Nutting observed it in numbers at most of the localities he explored, and speaks of it as the most abundant of the Woodpeckers of the district. Mr. Richardson also found it in Nicaragua and sent us several specimens.

8. **Melanerpes santacruzi.**

? *Picus albifrons*, Sw. Phil. Mag. new ser. i. p. 439 (1827)[1]; Wagl. Isis, 1829, p. 514[2].

Centurus albifrons, Cab. J. f. Orn. 1862, p. 324[3]; Scl. & Salv. P. Z. S. 1869, p. 364[4]; Salv. Cat. Strickl. Coll. p. 399[5].

Centurus santacruzi, Bp. P. Z. S. 1837, p. 116[6]; Scl. P. Z. S. 1856, p. 307[7]; 1858, p. 359[8]; 1859, p. 367[9]; Moore, P. Z. S. 1859, p. 60[10]; Scl. & Salv. Ibis, 1859, p. 136[11]; P. Z. S. 1870, p. 837[12]; R. Owen, Ibis, 1861, p. 67[13].

Melanerpes santacruzi, Hargitt, Cat. Birds Brit. Mus. xviii. p. 179[14].

Picus grateloupensis, Less. Rev. Zool. 1839, p. 41[15].

Centurus polygrammus, Cab. J. f. Orn. 1862, p. 326[16].

Centurus aurifrons, Lawr. (nec Wagl.) Bull. U. S. Nat. Mus. no. 4, p. 35[17]; Sumichrast, La Nat. v. p. 240[18].

Centurus aurifrons santacruzi, Ridgw. Pr. U. S. Nat. Mus. iv. p. 106[19].

Centurus santacruzi pauper, Ridgw. Pr. U. S. Nat. Mus. x. p. 582[20].

Supra niger, dorso toto et alis stricte albo transfasciatis, pileo et nucha coccineis, fronte albida, plumis ad nares aurantiis, uropygio et tectricibus supracaudalibus albis: subtus fuscus, olivaceo vix tinctus, gula albida, hypochondriis imis et tectricibus subcaudalibus nigro transfasciatis, abdomine medio aurantio, remigibus externis nigris, in pogonio interno ad basin tantum albo maculatis; cauda nigra, rectricibus duabus mediis ad basin in pogonio interno albo variegatis, interdum fasciis indistinctis albis notatis, subalaribus nigris albo transfasciatis; rostro et pedibus plumbeis. Long. tota circa 8·5, alæ 5·2, caudæ 2·85, rostri a rictu 1·5, tarsi 0·85, dig. med. absque ungue 0·7, dig. ext. 0·65. (Descr. maris ex Panajachel, Guatemala. Mus. nostr.)

♀ mari similis, sed pileo toto sordide albido ad nucham fusco, nucha tantum coccinea.

Hab. MEXICO [15], Tampico (*W. B. Richardson*), Las Vigas, Jalapa (*de Oca* [9]), Coatepec (*Ferrari-Perez*), Misantla (*F. D. G.*), Cuesta de Misantla, Vega del Casadero (*M. Trujillo*), Atoyac (*Mrs. H. H. Smith*), Cordova (*Sallé* [7]), Jomotla (*M. Trujillo*), Santana, Plan del Rio, Huatusco, Cuichapa (?), Zentla, Rio Rancho Nuevo, Hacienda Tortugas (*Ferrari-Perez*), Vera Cruz (*W. B. Richardson*), Orizaba (*Sumichrast* [18]), Sochiapa, Playa Vicente (*M. Trujillo*), Juchitan, Sta. Efigenia, Chihuitan (*Sumichrast* [17] [18]), Chimalapa, Sierra de S. Domingo, Tehuantepec (*W. B. Richardson*); GUATEMALA (*Velasquez* [6], *Constancia* [5]), Santa Maria de Quezaltenango (*W. B. Richardson*), Salama (*Skinner* [11]), San Gerónimo (*R. Owen* [13]), Retalhuleu, Escuintla, El Baoul, Dueñas [11] (*O. S. & F. D. G.*), Toliman, Panajachel (*W. B. Richardson*); HONDURAS, Julian, San Pedro (*G. M. Whitely* [12]), Truxillo (*Townsend* [20]), Omoa (*Leyland* [10]), Comayagua (*G. C. Taylor*); SALVADOR, Volcan de S. Miguel, La Libertad (*W. B. Richardson*).

It has frequently been considered that Swainson's name *Picus albifrons*[1] is the correct title for this bird ; but this decision has been questioned by Mr. Ridgway and by Mr. Hargitt, who agree that it is more probably a synonym of the Jamaican *Melanerpes superciliaris*, the locality Mexico having been wrongly assigned to the type. As this type is not now forthcoming, it is not possible to settle the question, but nevertheless we accept Mr. Ridgway's view.

The next title available is Bonaparte's *Centurus santacruzi*[6], which was given to a Guatemala bird obtained by Col. Velasquez in that country, and named after a " Scientific Professor in Mexico."

Taking the Guatemalan form as typical, we find that the red of the crown joins that of the nape, where there is hardly any trace of the golden yellow along its lower margin ; the transverse white bands of the back are narrow, the central rectrices have ill-defined white marks on the inner web towards the base with a tendency to develop into cross-bands, the under surface is dusky with an olive tinge, and the nasal feathers and central abdomen orange-yellow.

In the State of Vera Cruz most specimens resemble the type form ; but examples from Playa Vicente and Sochiapa, and some, but not all, from Cuichapa, have the nasal feathers and the abdomen red, and thus resemble *M. dubius*, except that the red is not so pure. As birds from Teapa appear to be typical *M. dubius*, Playa Vicente and places near are on the boundary between the ranges of *M. santacruzi* and *M. dubius*, and they there apparently blend together. So, again, at Tampico there seems to be a transition towards *M. aurifrons*, as birds from that district have rather wider white bands on the back, the lower part of the nape is more tinged with orange-yellow, and the central rectrices have hardly any white at the base of their inner webs. Tehuantepec birds are most divergent in having much more orange-yellow on the nape, but in other respects resemble the typical Guatemalan form. In Honduras a form occurs which, besides its small size, has very narrow white bands on the back and is generally of a dark colour. This form, which appears to be variable where it is found, Mr. Ridgway has separated as *Centurus santacruzi pauper*. With it Mr. Ridgway is inclined to associate a bird from Salvador, but which he says links *M. santacruzi* with *M. s. pauper*. Our Salvador specimens are all females, and are only to be distinguished, if at all, from *M. santacruzi* by the distinct white bars on the inner webs of the central rectrices, a character showing a divergence towards *M. hoffmanni*.

In Guatemala *M. santacruzi* is a common bird in the thinner woods of the hot and temperate regions from near the sea-level to a height of at least 7000 feet in the mountains.

Mr. R. Owen found on 2nd June, 1860, a pair of this species which had a nest in one of the high trees scattered over the plain of San Gerónimo in Vera Paz (alt. 3000 feet), and secured one of the parents and four eggs, which were quite fresh, though stained with spots of foreign matter.

9. **Melanerpes dubius.**

Picus carolinensis, Cabot (nec Linn.), in Steph. Trav. in Yucatan, ii. p. 475 [1].

Picus dubius, Cabot, Pr. Bost. Soc. N. H. i. p. 164 [2]; Bost. Journ. N. H. v. p. 91 [3].

Centurus dubius, Boucard, P. Z. S. 1883, p. 452 [4]; Salv. Ibis, 1885, p. 192 [5]; 1889, p. 369 [6]; Stone, Pr. Ac. Phil. 1890, p. 206 [7].

Melanerpes dubius, Hargitt, Cat. Birds Brit. Mus. xviii. p. 172 [8].

Centurus aurifrons dubius, Ridgw. Pr. U. S. Nat. Mus. iv. p. 108 [9].

Centurus albifrons, Lawr. Ann. Lyc. N. Y. ix. p. 205 [10].

Centurus leei, Ridgw. Pr. Biol. Soc. Wash. iii. p. 22 [11].

Centurus dubius leei, Ridgw. Pr. U. S. Nat. Mus. viii. p. 575 [12].

M. santacruzi similis, fronte antica ad nares et abdomine medio coccineis pileo concoloribus, nucha pure coccinea; capitis lateribus et corpore subtus pallidioribus, rectricibus duabus mediis omnino nigris. Long. tota 9·0, alæ 5·2, caudæ 3·3, rostri a rictu 1·6, tarsi 0·85, dig. med. absque ungue 0·8, dig. ext. 0·75.

♀ mari similis, sed pileo toto canescente ad nucham saturatiore. (Descr. maris et feminæ ex Izamal, Yucatan. Mus. nostr.)

Obs. Specimina ex Insula Cozumel sæpe differunt uropygio et tectricibus supracaudalibus nigro fasciatis, unde *M. leei,* Ridgway.

Hab. MEXICO, Teapa in Tabasco (*Mrs. H. H. Smith*), Merida in Yucatan (*Schott* [10]), Buctzotz, Temax, Izamal and Peto in N. Yucatan (*Gaumer* [4]), Tunkas, Shkolak, Tekanto, Labna (*Stone* [7]), Tabi (*F. D. G.*), Cozumel I. (*Benedict* [11] [12], *Gaumer* [6]), Meco I. (*Gaumer* [6]); BRITISH HONDURAS, Cayo, San Felipe, Rio Mopan, Belize (*Blancaneaux*).

Dr. S. Cabot, who accompanied Stephens in his travels in Yucatan, first noticed this species [1]. According to Dr. Gaumer it is found in all parts of Yucatan, where it is said to do much damage to young cocoa-nuts by piercing them. It usually frequents the cities and haciendas, but is not uncommon in the larger forests [4].

Dr. Gaumer procured us many specimens during his visit to the island of Cozumel. These vary a good deal in the amount to which the rump and upper tail-coverts are barred with black, upon which character Mr. Ridgway separated his *Centurus leei.* The island-specimens show every gradation, from the pure white form like that of the mainland to a distinctly-banded form which seems restricted to Cozumel. It is, perhaps, significant that this tendency is in the direction of the Jamaican bird *M. superciliaris.*

The southern range of *M. dubius* reaches the western district of British Honduras, and its western limits pass the State of Tabasco, where Mrs. H. H. Smith obtained several specimens at Teapa, all of which are of the typical form of Northern Yucatan. In the southern parts of the State of Vera Cruz *M. dubius* seems to pass into *M. santacruzi,* as we find intermediate birds at Playa Vicente and its neighbourhood. Whether the same state of things prevails to the south-westward of Tabasco we are unable to say, as a large tract of country still remains unexplored in that direction.

10. **Melanerpes canescens.**

Centurus dubius, Ridgw. Pr. U. S. Nat. Mus. x. p. 579[1].
Centurus canescens, Salv. Ibis, 1889, p. 370[2].
Melanerpes canescens, Hargitt, Cat. Birds Brit. Mus. xviii. p. 174[3].

C. dubio affinis, sed fasciis albis corporis superioris et alarum paulo latioribus, remigibus externis ad basin distincte albo fasciatis; genis et corpore subtus plerumque albicantioribus, fascia frontali albida multo latiore, narium plumis vix coccineo tinctis. Long. tota circa 9·7, alæ 5·1, caudæ 3·15, rostri a rictu 1·6, tarsi 0·8, dig. med. absque ungue 0·78, dig. ext. 0·78.
♀ mari similis, pileo summo cano. (Descr. maris et feminæ exempl. typ. ex Ins. Ruatan. Mus. nostr.)

Hab. HONDURAS, Ruatan I. (*Townsend*[1], *Gaumer*[2]).

Dr. Gaumer obtained many specimens of this Woodpecker when visiting the island of Ruatan in the Bay of Honduras. It is no doubt very closely allied to *M. dubius*, being an island-form of that bird distinguished by the very pale colour of the sides of the head and under surface. There is very little red on the feathers covering the nostrils, so that the transverse band across the forehead is wide; the primaries, too, show externally much more of the white spots near the base.

On the mainland of Honduras, opposite the island of Ruatan, the small dark form of *M. santacruzi* called by Mr. Ridgway *M. s. pauper* occurs, no doubt replacing *M. dubius*; but where these two forms meet in British Honduras has not yet been traced.

β'''. Uropygium et tectrices supracaudales nigro regulariter fasciati.

11. **Melanerpes uropygialis.**

Centurus uropygialis, Baird, Pr. Ac. Phil. 1854, p. 120[1]; Cab. J. f. Orn. 1862, p. 330[2]; Baird, Brew., & Ridgw. N. Am. Birds, ii. p. 558[3]; Lawr. Mem. Bost. Soc. N. H. ii. p. 294[4]; Ridgw. Pr. U. S. Nat. Mus. iv. p. 112[5]; Belding, Pr. U. S. Nat. Mus. vi. p. 344[6].
Melanerpes uropygialis, Hargitt, Cat. Birds Brit. Mus. xviii. pp. 182, 569[7].

Supra niger, dorso toto, uropygio et alis albo regulariter transfasciatis; capite toto, cervice et corpore subtus pallide brunneo-fuscescentibus, fronte et plumis narium albicantioribus, pileo medio coccineo, hypochondriis imis et tectricibus subcaudalibus nigro distincte transfasciatis, abdomine medio vix flavo tincto; remigibus externis ad basin distincte albo fasciatis; cauda nigra, rectricibus subexterniis albo fasciatis, duabus mediis quoque fasciatis in pogonio interno, in pogonio externo stria elongata juxta rhachidem notatis; rostro et pedibus plumbeis. Long. tota circa 8·5, alæ 5·0, caudæ 2·8, rostri a rictu 1·4, tarsi 0·9, dig. med. absque ungue 0·78, dig. ext. 0·75.
♀ mari similis, pileo medio haud coccineo. (Descr. maris et feminæ ex Nuri, Sonora. Mus. nostr.)

Hab. N. AMERICA, New Mexico[1], Southern and Lower California, S. Arizona[3,5].—MEXICO, Moctezuma, Hermosillo in Sonora (*Ferrari-Perez*), Guaymas (*Belding*[6]), Ysleta, Rio Mayo, Nuri, Cedros (*W. Lloyd*), Mazatlan (*Grayson*[4], *Forrer*), Presidio de Mazatlan (*Forrer*), San Blas (*W. B. Richardson*), Hacienda de San Ramon, Rancho de San Pablo in the Sierra de Alica, Hacienda de Ambas Aguas, Ixtlan, all in the Terr. de Tepic (*Dr. A. C. Buller, in Mus. Rothschild*), Tepic, Guadalajara (*Grayson*[4]), Santana near Guadalajara (*W. Lloyd*), Barranca de Portillo near Guadalajara (*Dr. A. C. Buller, in Mus. Rothschild*), Sierra de Bolaños, Calvillo (*W. B. Richardson*).

M. uropygialis is a very distinct species with no near allies. The upper tail-coverts are distinctly banded; there is no nuchal red patch in either sex or colouring on the nasal feathers.

Its range is restricted to the countries lying on our north-western frontier and Western Mexico, as far south as the sierras of the States of Jalisco and Aguas Calientes. Grayson says that it is found at all seasons of the year in some localities in Western Mexico, but is not abundant. It makes its nest by boring into decayed trees, sometimes selecting the stems of palms. In Arizona, according to Dr. Hermann, the giant cactus trees, which reach a height of forty feet, are often riddled with holes made by birds of this species. The pith of the plant is extracted until a chamber of suitable size is formed; the wounded surface hardens and forms a smooth dry coating to the cavity, and thus a convenient place for incubation is constructed.

According to Dr. Cooper the food of this Woodpecker largely consists of the berries of mistletoe, but no doubt insects are also eaten in numbers.

β″. *Capitis latus circum oculos nigro notatus.*

12. Melanerpes elegans.

Picus elegans, Sw. Phil. Mag. new ser. i. p. 439 [1]; Wagl. Isis, 1829, p. 514 [2]; Finsch, Abh. nat. Ver. Bremen, 1870, p. 356 [3].

Centurus elegans, Cab. J. f. Orn. 1862, p. 327 [4]; Scl. P. Z. S. 1864, p. 177 [5]; Lawr. Mem. Bost. Soc. N. H. ii. p. 294 [6]; Ridgw. Pr. U. S. Nat. Mus. iv. p. 114 [7]; Salv. Cat. Strickl. Coll. p. 399 [8]; P. Z. S. 1883, p. 425 [9]; Ferrari-Perez, Pr. U. S. Nat. Mus. ix. p. 160 [10]; Stone, Pr. Ac. Phil. 1890, p. 218 [11].

Melanerpes elegans, Hargitt, Cat. Birds Brit. Mus. xviii. p. 184 [12].

Supra niger, dorso toto, alis, uropygio, tectricibus supracaudalibus, rectricibus mediis et duabus subexternis regulariter albo transfasciatis, pileo toto coccineo, nucha læte flavo-aurantia, fronte albida, plumis supra nares et area infra oculos quoque flavo lavatis, oculorum ambitu nigerrimo: subtus fuscus, gula et abdomine imo pallidieribus, hoc cum hypochondriis imis et subcaudalibus nigro transfasciatis, ventre medio flavo; remigibus externis nigris albo ad basin distincte notatis, apicibus quoque albis, subalaribus albis nigro variegatis; rostro et pedibus plumbeis. Long. tota circa 8·7, alæ 5·1, caudæ 3·1, rostri a rictu 1·3, tarsi 0·9, dig. med. absque ungue 0·8, dig. ext. 0·7. (Descr. maris ex Dos Arroyos, Guerrero, Mexico. Mus. nostr.)

♀ mari similis, sed pileo toto sordide albo nec coccineo.

Hab. Mexico, Coast region (*Bullock* [1]), Sonora (*Grayson* [6]), Mazatlan (*Grayson* [6], *Forrer*), Santiago, San Blas, Tepic (*W. B. Richardson*), Tuxpan in the Terr. de Tepic (*Dr. A. C. Buller, in Mus. Rothschild*), Beltran, Hacienda de San Marcos (*W. Lloyd*), Plains of Colima (*Xantus*), La Playa V. de Jorullo (*Baker* [11]), Acapulco (*Mus. Berol.* [4], *A. H. Markham* [9], *Mrs. H. H. Smith*), Dos Arroyos (*Mrs. H. H. Smith*), Guadalajara (*Grayson* [6]), Matamoros Izucar [10], Epatlan (*Ferrari-Perez*).

This pretty Woodpecker was first described by Swainson in 1827, from a specimen sent by Bullock from the " maritime land" of Mexico. It was no doubt from the western slope of the central highlands, as all subsequent records show that it is strictly confined to Western Mexico from the State of Sinaloa to those of Guerrero and Puebla.

Grayson, who observed *M. elegans* at Mazatlan as well as at Guadalajara, Tepic, and in Sonora, has some interesting notes concerning it. He says it is one of the commonest species inhabiting the region of Mazatlan, and is noted for boring its nest in the giant cactus (*Cereus giganteus*), in which, with wonderful perseverance and labour amid innumerable sharp spines of this singular plant, it picks out a hole slanting downwards sufficiently ample for its nest. The entrance is just sufficiently large, but the hole gradually widens as it descends to the depth of six or eight inches, where the eggs are deposited on the bare wood. Both male and female work at the nest till finished. The nest once made is used for some years, if not too much distorted by the growth of the plant. This Woodpecker, however, does not confine itself to the cactus for making its nest: the smooth trunk of the palm is also a favourite; sometimes as many as two or three nests may be seen in the stem of one palm.

The eggs are generally three in number and of a transparent white.

13. Melanerpes hypopolius.

Picus hypopolius, Wagl. Isis, 1829, p. 514[1].

Centurus hypopolius, Cab. J. f. Orn. 1862, p. 329[2]; Lawr. Bull. U. S. Nat. Mus. no. 4, p. 35[3]; Sumichrast, La Nat. v. p. 240[4]; Ridgw. Pr. U. S. Nat. Mus. iv. p. 113[5]; Ferrari-Perez, Bull. U. S. Nat. Mus. ix. p. 160[6].

Melanerpes hypopolius, Hargitt, Cat. Birds Brit. Mus. xviii. p. 186[7].

Supra niger, dorso toto et alis albo transfasciatis, uropygio albo nigro striato; capite, collo et corpore subtus fuscis, fronte pallidiore, pileo medio coccineo, oculorum ambitu nigro, ciliis albis, area infra oculos coccineo lavata; abdomine medio albo, imo et tectricibus subcaudalibus albidis nigro transfasciatis; cauda nigra, rectricibus mediis in pogonio interno ad basin albo fasciatis, rectricibus subexternis quoque fasciatis, remigibus quatuor externis in pogonio externo omnino nigris, reliquis ad basin albo fasciatis, subalaribus albis nigro variegatis; rostro et pedibus plumbeis. Long. tota circa 8·0, alæ 5·0, caudæ 3·3, rostri a rictu 2·25, tarsi 0·8, dig. med. absque ungue 0·65, dig. ext. 0·6. (Descr. maris ex Epatlan, Mexico. Mus. nostr.)

♀ mari similis, sed pileo summo omnino fusco.

Hab. Mexico (*Wagler*[1], *le Strange*), Tehuacan (*Mus. Berol.*[2], *Sumichrast*[4]), Tecuapan (*Mus. Berol.*[2]), Huehuetlan[6], Izucar de Matamoros[6], San Miguel Molino, Chietla, San Bartolo, Epatlan (*Ferrari-Perez*), Chapulco (*Sumichrast*[3] [4]), Sierra Madre del Sur (*Mrs. H. H. Smith*).

Melanerpes hypopolius was described by Wagler in 1829, from Mexican specimens in the Berlin Museum[1], which Dr. Cabanis since informs us were from Tehuacan and Tecuapan in the State of Puebla[2]. Our subsequent records of this bird show that it is nearly restricted in its range to this State, though it is also found in that of Guerrero, where Mrs. Herbert Smith secured a specimen in the Sierra Madre del Sur.

This Woodpecker is a well-marked one, having no near allies. The middle of the abdomen is nearly white, without any tint of yellow or red, as in the other members of this section of the genus. It has black round the eyes as in *M. elegans,* but there is no yellow or orange on any portion of the head. The bill, too, is much more slender than that of *M. elegans.*

We have no account as yet of its habits.

Species dubiæ.

MELANERPES XANTHOLARYNX, Reich. Scans. Picinæ, p. 384, t. dcxliii. figg. 4293–4; Hargitt, Cat. Birds Brit. Mus. xviii. p. 155.

A species allied to *M. formicivorus,* said to be from Mexico, but only known from Reichenbach's figures. These differ from the above-mentioned species in showing a white face, the side of the neck being also white without any black patch behind the eye, the malar region alone being black. The underparts are striated with black, but there is no black band on the breast.

PICUS AUROCAPILLUS, Vig. P. Z. S. 1832, p. 4.

A bird described by Vigors from a specimen in Cuming's collection, but without locality, but presumably from Chili, though stated by Lesson (Compl. Buff. ix. p. 315) to be from Mexico.

The species has not since been recognized, nor is the name mentioned by Mr. Hargitt. Vigors's description is as follows:—

"PICUS AUROCAPILLUS. Pic. supra ater, albo fasciatus maculatusque; striga lata supra oculos ad humeros extendente, alteraque suboculari interrupta, gulaque albis; pectore abdomineque sordide albescentibus, strigis parcis fuscis notatis; capite atro, fronte aureo strigatim notato, vertice aureo.
"Longitudo 6½ unc."

b'. *Digitus pedis medius quam digitus externus (reversus) brevior.*

c". *Cauda quam remex secundus haud brevior.*

SPHYROPICUS.

Sphyrapicus, Baird, Birds N. Am. p. 101 (1858).
Sphyropicus, Baird, Brew., & Ridgw. N. Am. Birds, ii. p. 535; Hargitt, Cat. Birds Brit. Mus. xviii. p. 187.

The structure of the tongue in the members of this genus departs from the usual arrangement of that organ in the Woodpeckers, inasmuch as it is scarcely extensible. Dr. Coues, who carefully examined the tongues of several species of *Sphyropicus,* states that the hyoid bones are much shorter than in other Woodpeckers, and that the apo-hyal and cerato-hyal portions of the hyoid do not reach back much beyond the tympano-maxillary articulation, instead of, as in *Picus,* round over the occiput to the top of the cranium, or even curving into an osseous groove round the orbit. The basi-hyoids supporting the tongue are shorter and differently-shaped. The tongue itself is short and flattened, with a superior longitudinal median groove and a corresponding inferior edge; the tip is broad and flattened, obtusely rounded, and with numerous long soft bristly hairs (Pr. Ac. Phil. 1866, p. 52).

The peculiar food of the birds of this genus probably accounts for the modifications of the tongue. The chief portion of their nutriment is derived from the cambium-layer of trees, the soft substance lying beneath the bark. To get at this the bark is stripped off in patches, to the serious injury and generally the destruction of the tree. Besides this food the sap issuing from the injured trees is largely partaken of as well as insects attracted to the sap. Insects also are frequently caught in the air.

The range of *Sphyropicus* is chiefly confined to North America, all the species being found there. *S. varius* is migratory and visits Mexico, Central America, and some of the West-Indian Islands in winter. *S. nuchalis* and *S. thyroideus* occur in Western and North-western Mexico.

1. Sphyropicus varius.

The Yellow Belly'd Woodpecker, Catesby, Nat. Hist. Carol. i. p. 21, t. 21[1]; F. Bolles, Auk, 1891, p. 256[2].

Picus varius, Linn. Syst. Nat. i. p. 176[3]; Sw. Phil. Mag. new ser. i. p. 439[4]; Licht. Preis-Verz. mex. Vög. p. 1 (*cf.* J. f. Orn. 1863, p. 55)[5]; Gosse, Birds Jam. p. 270[6]; Scl. P.Z.S. 1856, p. 308[7]; 1859, pp. 367[8], 388[9]; Taylor, Ibis, 1860, p. 119[10]; Sumichrast, La Nat. v. p. 240[11].

Sphyrapicus varius, Baird, Birds N. Am. p. 103[12]; Lawr. Mem. Bost. Soc. N. H. ii. p. 294[13]; Bull. U. S. Nat. Mus. no. 4, p. 35[14]; Gundl. Orn. Cub. p. 115[15]; Ferrari-Perez, Pr. U. S. Nat. Mus. ix. p. 159[16]; Herrera, La Nat. (2) i. pp. 179[17].

Sphyropicus varius, Scl. & Salv. Ibis, 1859, p. 136[18]; Lawr. Ann. Lyc. N. Y. ix. p. 205[19]; Baird, Brew., & Ridgw. N. Am. Birds, ii. p. 539[20]; Salv. Cat. Strickl. Coll. p. 389[21]; Hargitt, Cat. Birds Brit. Mus. xviii. p. 188[22].

Supra niger, dorso toto sordide albo variegato, pileo medio coccineo undique nigro circumcincto, stria post-oculari utrinque apud nucham conjuncta sordide alba; uropygio medio albo; alis nigris, tectricibus mediis et majoribus late albo terminatis; remigibus omnibus in pogoniis ambobus ad margines albo guttatis: subtus flavido-albus, pectore et stria utrinque malari nigris, gutture medio coccineo, stria quoque a nares usque ad ventrem albida, regione parotica nigricante albo variegata; hypochondriis fuscescentibus, nigro fasciatis; cauda nigra, rectricibus duabus mediis in pogonio interno albis, nigro fasciatis; rostro et pedibus nigricanti-plumbeis. Long. tota circa 7·5, alæ 4·9, caudæ 3·0, rostri a rictu 1·0, tarsi 0·75, dig. med. absque ungue 0·56, dig. ext. 0·6. (Descr. maris ad. ex Coapa, Mexico. Mus. nostr.)

♀ mari similis, sed gutture medio albicante.

♂ juv. pectore variegato.

♀ interdum pileo toto nigerrimo (an av. juv.?).

Hab. NORTH AMERICA, Eastern and Southern States, Texas[21].—MEXICO (*Deppe & Schiede*[5]), Sierra above Ciudad Victoria (*W. B. Richardson*), Real del Monte (*Bullock*[4], *W. B. Richardson*), Temiscaltepec (*Bullock*[4]), Cofre de Perote,

Coatepec (*M. Trujillo*), Jalapa (*de Oca* [8], *F. D. G.*, *Ferrari-Perez*), Hacienda de los Atlixcos (*F. D. G.*), Cordova (*Sallé* [7]), Orizaba (*Sumichrast* [11]), Valley of Mexico (*Sumichrast* [11], *Herrera* [17]), Coapa, Ixtapalapa, Mexicalcingo, Hacienda Eslava, Culhuacan, Coajimalpa, Chimalpa, and Tetelco in the Valley of Mexico, Huexotitla in Puebla [16] (*Ferrari-Perez*), Tenango del Valle (*W. B. Richardson*), Plains of Colima (*Xantus* [13]), Colima, Volcan de Colima, Zapotlan (*W. B. Richardson*), La Parada, Llano Verde (*Boucard* [9]), Villa Alta, Totontepec, Tonaguia (*M. Trujillo*), Sta. Efigenia, Gineta Mts. (*Sumichrast* [14]), Merida in Yucatan (*Schott* [19]) ; GUATE-MALA (*Skinner* [18], *Constancia* [21]), Coban, San Gerónimo, Dueñas, Volcan de Agua, upper pine-region of Volcan de Fuego 10,000 to 11,000 feet (*O. S. & F. D. G.*), Toliman (*W. B. Richardson*); HONDURAS, Siquatepeque (*G. C. Taylor* [10]); NICA-RAGUA, San Rafael del Norte (*W. B. Richardson*); COSTA RICA (*Mus. Brit.*).

Except along our northern frontier *Sphyropicus varius* is probably only a winter visitor to Mexico and Central America. All our records of it refer to that time of year, nearly all the dates ranging from November to March and the beginning of April. Mr. Richardson found it as late as May in the sierras of Tamaulipas ; but possibly the specimens he obtained would have bred in the district.

In the United States the " Yellow-bellied Woodpecker " or " Sap-Sucker," under which names *S. varius* is known, is a common bird, arriving in April and May and remaining to breed. It is well known in the New England States and has even been recorded from Greenland.

Its winter resorts include Central America as far south as Honduras and Northern Nicaragua—that is, as far as the southern extension of the upland pines. It also occurs in many of the West India Islands. Mr. Cory mentions several of the Bahamas, Gosse and others the island of Jamaica, and Dr. Gundlach Cuba, where it arrives every autumn on passage.

The range in altitude of this species in its winter-quarters is very considerable, for it occurs in Northern Yucatan near the sea-level and in the upland pine-region of the higher volcanoes of Guatemala at least 10,500 feet above the sea. It is, however, most commonly met with in the highlands between 4000 and 8000 feet.

In 1891, Mr. Frank Boller published an interesting account of the feeding-habits of this species in a paper entitled " Yellow-bellied Woodpeckers and their uninvited Guests " [2]. From his observations he concludes that this species is in the habit for successive years of drilling holes in several kinds of trees for the purpose of taking from them the " elaborated sap " and sometimes the cambium-layer of the bark ; that the birds consume the sap in large quantities for its own sake and not for the insects which it occasionally contains ; that the sap attracts many insects of various kinds, a few of which form a considerable part of the food of this bird, but whose capture does not occupy nearly so much time as sap-drinking ; that different families of these

Woodpeckers occupy different "orchards," each family consisting of a male, female, and several young; that the "orchards" consist of several trees a few rods apart, and that these trees are regularly and constantly visited from sunrise to long after sunset, not only by the Woodpeckers themselves but by numerous Humming-Birds, which feed from the same holes on the sap and insects contained therein. The trees attacked generally die after the second or third year of use.

The excavation for the nest is usually made in large decaying trees at a considerable height from the ground. The white eggs, four to six in number, are laid on chips at the bottom of the hole.

2. Sphyropicus nuchalis.

Sphyrapicus nuchalis, Baird, Birds N. Am. p. 103, t. 35. figg. 1, 2 [1].
Sphyropicus nuchalis, Hargitt, Cat. Birds Brit. Mus. xviii. p. 192 [2].
Sphyropicus varius, var. *nuchalis,* Baird, Brew., & Ridgw. N. Am. Birds, ii. p. 542 [3].

S. vario similis, sed fascia transversa nuchali coccinea nec albida, gutture quoque colore coccineo latiore usque ad fasciam albidam longitudinalem cervicalem extendente.
♀ gula quoque plerumque coccinea.

Hab. NORTH AMERICA, Rocky Mountain region [1], Arizona [2].— MEXICO, Temosachic, Guerrero, Casa Colorada, Refugio, all in Chihuahua (*W. Lloyd*), Sierra de Bolaños (*W. B. Richardson*); GUATEMALA, Panajachel (*W. B. Richardson*).

This is a western form of *S. varius,* closely allied but distinguishable by the slight characters referred to above. We have received several adult birds from the Mexican States of Chihuahua and Jalisco. Also a single male from Guatemala, which was shot by Mr. Richardson at Panajachel, on the borders of the lake of Atitlan, at an elevation of 5000 feet above the sea. This bird has the scarlet nape-band clearly shown, and also the lateral extension of the scarlet throat; it is the only one we have seen from so far south. We have no female specimen from Mexico answering to the description of the adult bird—that is, with half the throat-patch red.

It would appear that the seasonal movements of this Woodpecker are not at all comparable with those of *S. varius.* Dr. Coues found it an abundant and permanent resident in Arizona, living amongst the cotton-wood trees and willows. Mr. Ridgway says it is one of the most characteristic birds of the Wasatch and Uintah mountains, its favourite resort during summer being the aspen-groves in the mountains at an altitude of about 7000 feet. It nested in the aspen trees in preference to pines. In winter it sought the cotton-woods and willows of the river valleys.

In Mexico it is also probably resident, but our evidence is not complete on this point.

Of the presence of *S. ruber* in our country we have as yet no trace. This is the bird found in the Pacific coast-region of North America, and the extreme form so far as development of the red colour is concerned, of which *S. nuchalis* is the intermediate between it and *S. varius*.

3. Sphyropicus thyroideus.

Picus thyroideus, Cassin, Pr. Ac. Phil. 1851, p. 349 [1].

Sphyrapicus thyroideus, Baird, Birds N. Am. p. 106 [2].

Sphyropicus thyroideus, Baird, Brew., & Ridgw. N. Am. Birds, ii. p. 547 [3]; Hargitt, Cat. Birds Brit. Mus. xviii. p. 196 [4].

Picus williamsoni, Newberry, Pac. R. R. Rep. vi. p. 89, t. 24. fig. 1 [5].

Sphyropicus williamsoni, Baird, Brew., & Ridgw. N. Am. Birds, ii. p. 545 [6].

Supra niger, dorsi plumis striis celatis albis notatis, uropygio pure albo; vitta postoculari elongata utrinque apud nucham tamen vix conjuncta, altera a naribus infra oculos albis; gutture et pectore nigris, illo plaga elongata media a mento coccinea; abdomine flavicante, hypochondriis et tectricibus subalaribus nigris albo variegatis; alis nigris, tectricibus mediis et majoribus plerumque albis, remigibus extrorsum nigris, mediis in pogonio externo sparsim albo maculatis, omnibus in pogonio interno maculis albis (apicibus exceptis) in margine notatis; cauda omnino nigra; rostro et pedibus nigricantibus. Long. tota circa 8·8, alæ 5·5, caudæ 3·5, rostri a rictu 1·15, tarsi 0·75, dig. med. absque ungue 0·56, dig. ext. 0·6. (Descr. maris ex Refugio, Chihuahua, Mexico. Mus. nostr.)

♀ fere omnino diversa. Supra (pileo fusco-brunneo et uropygio albo exceptis) nigra undique fusco-albido transversim fasciata, alis quoque similiter fasciatis, gula media et regione parotica pileo concoloribus, gulæ lateribus nigro striatis, pectore plaga mediana rotunda nigra ornato; pectoris lateribus, hypochondriis et tectricibus subcaudalibus sicut dorsum fasciatis, abdomine medio flavicante; cauda nigra, rectricibus duabus mediis in pogoniis ambobus albo fasciatis, fasciis haud concurrentibus; rostro et pedibus nigricantibus. (Descr. feminæ ex Sierra de Bolaños, Mexico. Mus. nostr.)

Av. juv. plagam pectoralem nigram caret.

Hab. NORTH AMERICA, Rocky Mountains to the Pacific coast [3].—MEXICO, Pinos Altos (*Buchan-Hepburn*), Jesus Maria, Casa Colorada, and Refugio in Chihuahua (*W. Lloyd*), Sierra de Bolaños (*W. B. Richardson*), Tinguindi near Guadalajara (*Dr. A. C. Buller, in Mus. Rothschild*).

The female of this remarkable species was described by Cassin as long ago as 1851, and the male six years later by Dr. Newberry as a distinct species under the name of *Picus williamsoni*. The relationship of the two birds was not suspected for many years, and even in 1874 they were kept distinct by the authors of the 'History of North-American Birds.'

It is now well known that the bird called *P. williamsoni* is the male and *P. thyroideus* the female of one and the same species. The great sexual difference of plumage in this species does not occur in any other Woodpecker.

S. thyroideus, however, is a true *Sphyropicus*, having, according to Dr. Coues, the tongue constructed as in the other members of the genus; its habits and food being also similar.

Until recently the range of this Woodpecker was supposed to be confined to the Rocky Mountain region, and thence to the Pacific coast of North America, where it is said to keep chiefly to the pine-belt, of which it is one of the characteristic birds.

Its range into Mexico was first made known to us on the receipt of a male specimen from Mr. Buchan-Hepburn, who shot it near Pinos Altos in Chihuahua. We have since received several examples from Mr. Lloyd from the same State, and others from Mr. Richardson from as far south as Bolaños in the sierras of Jalisco. Dr. Buller also met with it near Guadalajara and sent specimens to Mr. Rothschild, which we have seen.

DENDROCOPUS.

Dendrocopus, Koch, Baier. Zool. i. p. 72 (1816) (nec Vieill. 1816=*Dendrocolaptes*, Herm.);
   Hargitt, Cat. Birds Brit. Mus. xviii. p. 201.
Dryobates, Boie, Isis, 1829, p. 977, et auctt. Amer.

This genus has a wide range over nearly the whole of North America, Northern Europe, and Asia to Japan, and southwards in the New World to Costa Rica and Chiriqui, and in the Old to North Africa, Northern India, and Burmah, as well as Malacca and Java. In South America there is also an isolated colony of species inhabiting Chili, Argentina, and the extreme south of Brazil. No species is found in the Ethiopian region. In America by far the larger number of species belong to the north, beyond the limits of our region; but we find within our boundary two closely allied forms in *Dendrocopus harrisi* and *D. jardinii*, as well as such well-defined species as *D. stricklandi*, *D. arizonæ*, and *D. scalaris*—a small proportion of only five representatives of the whole forty-five species and subspecies recognized by Mr. Hargitt in his recent Catalogue of the Picidæ.

With many of the features of *Sphyropicus*, *Dendrocopus* can be distinguished by the development of the stiff curved bristly feathers which completely hide the nostrils and also the angle between the rami of the mandible; the groove and the ridge above it which runs above the nostril parallel to the culmen are very strongly developed.

In using Koch's generic name *Dendrocopus* for these Woodpeckers, we follow Swainson (1837) and Mr. Hargitt. The same name was applied to a totally different group of birds by Vieillot, also in 1816. Which title has actual priority is not easy to say. Anyhow Vieillot's name can never be used, as it is simply a synonym of *Dendrocolaptes*; so *Dendrocopus*, Koch, may be allowed to stand.

   α. Alæ externe et plumæ scapulares uniformes; nucha maris coccinea.

1. Dendrocopus harrisi.

Picus harrisii, Aud. Orn. Biogr. v. p. 191 [1].
Picus villosus, var. *harrisi*, Baird, Brew., & Ridgw. N. Am. Birds, ii. p. 507 [2].
Dendrocopus harrisi, Hargitt, Cat. Birds Brit. Mus. xviii. p. 234 [3].

Supra nitenti-niger, dorso medio plaga elongata alba notata, nucha coccinea; plumis nasalibus, superciliis et stria elongata infra oculos albis: subtus albus, plumis pectoris laterum medialiter nigris, hypochondriis sparsim nigro striatis; remigibus externis in pogonio externo et alis subtus omnino albo maculatis; caudæ rectricibus duabus subexternis fere omnino albis, in pogonio interno nigro irregulater albo notatis; rostro nigro; pedibus plumbeis. Long. tota circa 8·0, alæ 5·0, caudæ 3·9, rostri a rictu 1·4, tarsi 0·8, dig. med. absque ungue 0·54, dig. ext. 0·54.

♀ mari similis, plaga nuchali coccinea absente. (Descr. maris et feminæ ex Rio de Urique, Chihuahua, Mexico. Mus. nostr.)

Hab. NORTH AMERICA, Rocky Mountains to the Pacific Coast from Alaska southwards [2]. —MEXICO, Casa Colorada, Pinos Altos, Temosachic, Rio de Iglesias, Rio de Emeritano, Refugio and Rio de Urique in Chihuahua (*W. Lloyd*), Ciudad in Durango (*Forrer*), Sierra de Nayarit, Sierra de Valparaiso, Sierra de Bolaños, Sierra de San Luis Potosi (*W. B. Richardson*).

In North America this Woodpecker is considered a race of *Dendrocopus villosus* (Linn.), a very variable form divided into six subspecies by Mr. Ridgway, and an equal number by Mr. Hargitt, but of rather different relative value. Thus *D. villosus*, besides the typical bird, has a large northern and a small southern form, called respectively by Mr. Ridgway *D. villosus*, *D. v. leucomelas*, and *D. v. auduboni*, the other three forms being subsp. α. *D. maynardi*, Hargitt, = *D. v. maynardi*, Ridgw., subsp. β. *D. harrisi*, Hargitt, = *D. v. harrisi*, Ridgw., and subsp. γ. *D. jardinii*, Hargitt, = *D. v. jardinii*, Ridgw. We have here only to do with the two latter birds, which we may call *Dendrocopus harrisi* and *D. jardinii*, nothing resembling the true *D. villosus* occurring within our limits.

D. harrisi is restricted to the Northern and Western States of Mexico, as far south as the sierras of Jalisco; birds from this district can be distinguished without much difficulty by the lighter purer white of their light markings, which show but a slight tinge of the smoky tint which pervades *D. jardinii*.

Specimens from the more southern districts of Jalisco and Colima are slightly darker than more northern birds, and thus there is an area within which *D. harrisi* passes into *D. jardinii*. In Eastern and Southern Mexico all the birds are undoubtedly *D. jardinii*.

2. **Dendrocopus jardinii.**

Picus jardinii, Malh. Rev. Zool. 1845, p. 374 [1]; Scl. P. Z. S. 1856, p. 308 [2]; 1857, p. 214 [3]; 1859, pp. 367 [4], 388 [5]; 1864, p. 177 [6]; Scl. & Salv. Ibis, 1859, p. 136 [7]; Taylor, Ibis, 1860, p. 119 [8]; Lawr. Ann. Lyc. N. Y. ix. p. 130 [9]; v. Frantzius, J. f. Orn. 1869, p. 364 [10]; Salv. P. Z. S. 1870, p. 212 [11]; Cat. Strickl. Coll. p. 387 [12].

Dyctiopicus jardinii, Boucard, P. Z. S. 1878, p. 49 [13].

Dryobates jardinii, Zeledon, An. Mus. Nac. Costa Rica, 1887, p. 123 [14]; Cherrie, Auk, 1892, p. 327 [15].

Dendrocopus jardinii, Hargitt, Cat. Birds Brit. Mus. xviii. p. 237 [16].

Dryobates villosus jardinii, Ferrari-Perez, Pr. U. S. Nat. Mus. ix. p. 159 [17].

Picus harrisi, Cab. J. f. Orn. 1862, p. 175 [18]; Sumichrast, La Nat. v. p. 240 [19].

D. harrisi affinis, sed forsan minor, coloribus albicantibus totius corporis plus minusve fuliginoso lavatis.

Hab. MEXICO [1] (*T. Mann* [13]), valley of Mexico (*le Strange*), Tenango del Valle (*W. B. Richardson*), Mexicalcingo, Chimalpa, San Pedro and Tetelco in the valley of Mexico, Teziutlan [17], San Miguel Molino (*Ferrari-Perez*), Alpine region of Orizaba (*Sumichrast* [18]), Popocatepetl 10,000 to 12,000 feet (*F. D. G.*), El Jacale (*Sallé* [2]),

Jalapa (*de Oca* [4]), Cofre de Perote (*M. Trujillo*), Sierra Madre de Colima (*W. B. Richardson*), Oaxaca (*Boucard* [5]), Tonaguia (*M. Trujillo*), Sierra Madre del Sur, Omilteme, Amula (*Mrs. H. H. Smith*); GUATEMALA, El Rincon in San Marcos, Santa Maria near Quezaltenango, Cuipache, Toliman (*W. B. Richardson*), Chilasco, San Gerónimo, Dueñas, Volcan de Fuego (*O. S. & F. D. G.*); HONDURAS, Siquatepeque (*G. C. Taylor* [8]); NICARAGUA, Matagalpa, San Rafael del Norte (*W. B. Richardson*); COSTA RICA, Desengaño (*Hoffmann* [18]), Candelaria Mts. (*v. Frantzius* [10]), San José (*Carmiol, Cherrie* [16]), Volcan de Irazu (*Arcé, Rogers, Boucard* [13], *Zeledon* [14]), Navarro (*Boucard* [13]), Cervantes (*Carmiol* [9]), Birris (*Zeledon* [9] [14]); PANAMA, Volcan de Chiriqui (*Arcé* [11]).

This dark form of *D. harrisi* occurs in the valley of Mexico and the surrounding hills, even ascending to a height of 10,000 to 12,000 feet above the sea on the slopes of Popocatepetl. It is also found on the Cofre de Perote and the Alpine region generally of the State of Vera Cruz, on the Sierra Madre del Sur, and the highlands of the State of Oaxaca. Southward of Mexico it spreads over the mountains of Guatemala, Honduras, and Costa Rica, the Volcano of Chiriqui being its most southern domicile.

It appears to be everywhere a highland bird, doubtless keeping to the upland pine- and oak-forests wherever they are found.

There is a considerable amount of difference between individuals as regards the sooty colour of the under plumage. The darkest we have are from the Volcan de Santa Maria and its neighbourhood, in the Guatemalan department of Quezaltenango, but a specimen from Tonaguia, Oaxaca, is nearly as dark.

The iris in life is reddish hazel, the tarsi and toes greenish slate.

3. **Dendrocopus stricklandi.**

Picus stricklandi, Malh. Rev. Zool. 1845, p. 373 [1]; Scl. P. Z. S. 1859, p. 367 [2]; Salv. Cat. Strickl. Coll. p. 387 [3].

Threnopipo stricklandi, Cab. & Heine, Mus. Hein. iv. Heft 2, p. 71 [4].

Dendrocopus stricklandi, Hargitt, Cat. Birds Brit. Mus. xviii. p. 243 [5].

Dryobates stricklandi, Stone, Pr. Ac. Phil. 1890, p. 214 [6].

Picus cancellatus, Scl. (nec Wagl.) P. Z. S. 1856, p. 308 [7].

Fuliginoso-niger, nucha coccinea, dorso medio toto albo late transfasciato, stria postoculari, altera infra oculos ad nucham extendente albis: subtus albidus undique nigricante striatus, striis pectoris latioribus; remigibus externis in pogonio externo et alis subtus fere omnino albo maculatis; caudæ rectricibus externis albis, nigro distincte bifasciatis; rostro nigro; pedibus nigricanti-plumbeis. Long. tota circa 7·4, alæ 4·7, caudæ 3·9, rostri a rictu 1·0, tarsi 0·75, dig. med. absque ungue 0·5, dig. ext. 0·56.

♀ mari similis, plaga nuchali coccinea absente. (Descr. maris et feminæ ex Rio Frio Ixtaccihuatl, Mexico. Mus. nostr.)

Hab. MEXICO [1] (*T. Mann* [3]), Tetelco in the Valley of Mexico, Las Vigas, San Miguel Molino (*Ferrari-Perez*), San Andres, Suapam (*Sallé* [7]), Jalapa [5] (*de Oca* [2]), Cofre de Perote (*M. Trujillo*), base of the Volcan de Orizaba (*Baker* [6]), Rio Frio Ixtaccihuatl (*W. B. Richardson*).

Dendrocopus stricklandi has always been a rare bird in collections, probably due to the high elevation at which it is found over a limited area of Mexico. Sallé and his immediate successors secured a few specimens, which were recorded by Mr. Sclater[2][7]. More recently Don F. Ferrari-Perez found it on the hills surrounding the Valley of Mexico and at Las Vigas; Mr. W. B. Richardson on the slopes of Ixtaccihuatl; Trujillo on the Cofre de Perote; and Mr. Baker at the foot of the peak of Orizaba, at an altitude of 8700 feet[6].

The only species *D. stricklandi* at all resembles is *D. arizonæ*, which, indeed, passed under the former name until Mr. Hargitt showed that the two birds belonged to quite distinct species.

The dark portion of the plumage of both birds is of a similar shade of brown, but *D. stricklandi* not only has the breast streaked instead of spotted as in *D. arizonæ*, but the back is transversely banded with broad white bars.

4. Dendrocopus arizonæ.

Picus stricklandi, Gray (nec Malh.), List Picid. Brit. Mus. p. 37[1]; Hensh. U. S. Geogr. Surv. W. of 100th Merid. p. 389[2].

Dryobates stricklandi, A. O. U. List N. Am. Birds, p. 213[3].

Picus arizonæ, Hargitt, Ibis, 1886, p. 115[4].

Dendrocopus arizonæ, Hargitt, Cat. Birds Brit. Mus. xviii. p. 228[5].

Dryobates arizonæ fraterculus, Ridgw. Man. N. Am. Birds, p. 286[6].

Supra brunneus, uropygio paulo saturatiore, nucha coccinea, stria postoculari, altera infra oculos ad cervicis latera extendente albis: subtus albus, gutture fere immaculato, plumis reliquis macula brunnea discali notatis; hypochondriis imis brunneo transfasciatis; remigibus in pogonio externo et alis subtus fere omnino albo maculatis; caudæ rectricibus externis albis, regulariter fusco fasciatis; rostro et pedibus nigricantibus. Long. tota circa 7·5, alæ 4·6, caudæ 3·8, rostri a rictu 2·2, tarsi 0·8, dig. med. absque ungue 0·5, dig. ext. 0·55.

♀ mari similis, plaga nuchali coccinea absente. (Descr. maris et feminæ ex Temosachic, Chihuahua, Mexico. Mus. nostr.)

Hab. North America, Arizona[2][3].—Mexico, near Oposura in Sonora (*Cahoon*), Yecæra (*W. Lloyd*), Chihuahua (*Buchan-Hepburn, W. Lloyd*), Rio Verde, Temosachic, Tomochic, and Rio de Urique in Chihuahua (*W. Lloyd*), La Laguna in the Sierra de Alica (*Dr. A. C. Buller, in Mus. Rothschild*), Tepic, Sierra de Nayarit, Sierra de Valparaiso, Sierra de Bolaños (*W. B. Richardson*), Hacienda de San Marcos (*W. Lloyd*), Volcan de Colima (*W. B. Richardson*), Sierra Nevada de Colima (*Xantus*[6]).

This Woodpecker is found in the North-western and Western Sierras of Mexico, passing the political frontier into Arizona, where it has of recent years been found by many collectors.

Its southern range extends to the Sierra Nevada de Colima, where Xantus found it, and in the same district Mr. Lloyd procured us several specimens near the Hacienda de

San Marcos in May 1889. Some of these examples are rather smaller than those from more northern localities, and upon such a small specimen (a female) Mr. Ridgway founded his *D. arizonæ fraterculus*. The difference, however, is by no means constant, and some southern birds quite equal their northern relatives in size; so that failing more positive characters no separation should be made.

Though known for some time as a bird of Arizona, it passed under the name of *D. stricklandi*, until Mr. Hargitt, having occasion to refer to the question, detected the differences, and described the bird under the name it now bears.

β. *Alæ externe et plumæ scapulares distincte albo notatæ ; pileus fere totus maris coccineo ornatus.*

5. **Dendrocopus scalaris.**

Picus scalaris, Wagl. Isis, 1829, p. 511[1]; Scl. P. Z. S. 1856, p. 307[2]; 1859, p. 367[3]; Dugès, La Nat. i. p. 139[4]; Lawr. Ann. Lyc. N. Y. ix. p. 205[5]; Mem. Bost. Soc. N. H. ii. p. 294[6]; Bull. U. S. Nat. Mus. no. 4, p. 34[7]; Grayson, Pr. Bost. Soc. N. H. xiv. p. 273[8]; Baird, Brew., & Ridgw. N. Am. Birds, ii. p. 515[9]; Sumichrast, La Nat. v. p. 240[10]; Belding, Pr. U. S. Nat. Mus. vi. p. 344[11]; Boucard, P. Z. S. 1883, p. 452[12]; Salv. Ibis, 1885, p. 191[13]

Dryobates scalaris, Ridgw. Pr. U. S. Nat. Mus. viii. p. 575[14]; Ferrari-Perez, Pr. U. S. Nat. Mus. ix. p. 159[15]; Herrera, La Nat. (2) i. pp. 179[16], 322[17]; Salv. Ibis, 1889, p. 368[18]

Dendrocopus scalaris, Hargitt, Cat. Birds Brit. Mus. xviii. p. 246[19].

Dictyopipo scalaris, Cab. & Heine, Mus. Hein. iv. Heft 2, p. 74[20].

Picus parvus, Cabot, Bost. Journ. N. H. v. p. 92[21].

Dryobates scalaris parvus, Ridgw. Man. N. Am. Birds, p. 284[22]; Stone, Pr. Ac. Phil. 1890, p. 206[23].

Picus bairdi, Malh. Mon. Pic. i. p. 118, t. 27. figg. 7, 8[24]; Scl. Cat. Am. Birds, p. 333[25].

Picus scalaris, var., Malh. Mon. Pic. t. 27. fig. 6[26].

Picus orizabæ, Cassin, Pr. Ac. Phil. 1863, p. 196[27].

Picus lucasianus, Finsch, Abh. nat. Ver. z. Bremen, 1870, p. 354[28].

Dryobates scalaris sinaloensis, Ridgw. Man. N. Am. Birds, p. 285[29].

Picus scalaris, var. *graysoni*, Lawr. Mem. Bost. Soc. N. H. ii. p. 294[30].

Dryobates scalaris graysoni, Ridgw. Man. N. Am. Birds, p. 285[31].

Dendrocopus graysoni, Hargitt, Cat. Birds Brit. Mus. xviii. p. 250[32].

Supra niger, distincte et regulariter albo transfasciatus, tectricibus supracaudalibus nigricantibus, pilei plumis ad basin nigris medialiter albis et coccineo terminatis, fronte tantum albo guttata, nucha pure coccinea; capitis lateribus nigricantibus, stria superciliari (cervicis lateribus albidis conjuncta) et stria infra oculos albidis: subtus albidus, corporis lateribus sparsim nigricante guttatis; alis nigricantibus albo fasciatis, tectricibus quoque albo guttatis; cauda nigra, rectricibus externis distincte albo transfasciatis; rostro et pedibus nigricanti-plumbeis. Long. tota circa 6·0, alæ 3·9, caudæ 3·0, rostri a rictu 0·85, tarsi 0·6, dig. med. absque ungue 0·45, dig. ext. 0·5. (Descr. maris ex Chietla, Puebla, Mexico. Mus. nostr.)

♀ mari similis, capite summo omnino nigricante.

Hab. NORTH AMERICA, States of the southern frontier, from Arizona to Texas[9].— MEXICO (*Wagler*[1]), Hermosillo, Moctezuma (*Ferrari-Perez*), Guaymas (*Belding*[11]), Cedros, Guadalupe in Sonora, Indines in Chihuahua (*W. Lloyd*), Presidio de

Mazatlan (*Forrer*), Mazatlan (*Grayson* [28] [29] [30]), Tres Marias Is. (*Grayson* [8] [28] [30], *Forrer*), Nuevo Laredo, Topo Chico, Hacienda de las Escobas, Nuevo Leon (*F. B. Armstrong*), Sierra above Ciudad Victoria, Soto La Marina, Aldama, Tampico, Plains of San Luis Potosi, Aguas Calientes, Sierra de Nayarit, Bolaños, Calvillo (*W. B. Richardson*), Mineral de San Sebastian near Mascota, Jalisco (*Dr. A. C. Buller, in Mus. Rothschild*), Guanajuato (*Dugès* [4]), Santana, Zapotlan, Beltran, Zacoalco (*W. Lloyd*), Volcan de Colima (*W. B. Richardson*), Valley of Mexico (*Sumichrast* [7] [10], *Herrera* [16]), Tetelco, Chimalpa (*Ferrari-Perez*), Jalapa [20] (*de Oca* [3] [27], *F. D. G., Höge*), Coatepec, Huatusco, Plan del Rio, Cordova (*Ferrari-Perez*), Orizaba (*Sumichrast* [10], *Botteri* [25]), Puente Colorado (*Sumichrast* [10]), Chietla [15], San Miguel Molino (*Ferrari-Perez*), Pinal near Puebla (*F. D. G.*), Amula (*Mrs. H. H. Smith*), Oaxaca (*Fenochio*), Sola, Juchatengo (*M. Trujillo*), Merida in Yucatan (*Schott* [5], *Gaumer* [12]), Pocul in Yucatan (*Cabot* [1]), Tunkas, Tekanto (*Stone & Baker* [23]), Tizimin, Chable (*Gaumer* [12]), Cozumel I. (*Devis* [18]).

This little Woodpecker was described by Wagler from Mexican specimens, the precise origin of which was not stated. In all probability they came from the highlands of Central Mexico.

It is now known to be generally distributed over nearly the whole of the tablelands of Mexico, and in various forms to the Rio Grande Valley, the western coast of Mexico, the Tres Marias Islands, and to Northern Yucatan. The birds from all these localities have had names bestowed upon them, but from the large series of specimens before us we find it hardly possible to differentiate between them. We thus go rather further than Mr. Hargitt in this conclusion, for he kept the Tres Marias Islands' bird as a subspecies, whereas we are unable to distinguish it from the bird of the opposite mainland, which again seems to merge into the generalized type.

The bird of the north, which crosses the Rio Grande into Texas and Arizona, has been called *Picus bairdi*; it is usually a large bird, and has the white dorsal bands rather wide. It seems to pass gradually into the bird of Central Mexico. The bird of Sinaloa has been called *Dryobates scalaris sinaloensis* on account of the deficient barring of the outer web of the outer rectrix, in which it agrees with the larger form found in Lower California, *D. lucasianus*; this character is decidedly variable, and we are not disposed to lay much stress upon it. The Tres Marias Islands' bird was separated as *D. scalaris graysoni* chiefly on the absence of spots on the primary coverts, but in this respect our specimens agree with those from Mazatlan and with others from the Valley of Mexico. The bird of Northern Yucatan was described by Dr. Cabot as *Picus parvus*, and is the *Dryobates scalaris parvus* of Mr. Ridgway. Birds from this district are small, but can be matched with others from Jalapa and its neighbourhood.

In the Tres Marias Islands, Grayson says [8], " this Woodpecker is more abundant than on the main coast, where it is also a common species. I have met with it along the tierra caliente bordering the Pacific coast from Sonora to Tehuantepec. It seems to thrive better in the Marias than elsewhere, for there it is very numerous and may be seen, or its gentle tappings heard, in the quiet woods at all hours of the day, busy drilling into the dried branches and logs in search of borers or white ants, upon which it becomes very fat. I found a nest (in the month of April) of a pair of these little Woodpeckers upon the island near the sea-shore, bored into the green flower-stem of a large maguey plant. The entrance of the nest was beautifully rounded, and about twelve feet from the ground. This small, slender, smooth stem, not more than four inches in diameter, with its soft spongy wood, afforded a convenient material to work out the nest, as well as a sure protection against the raccoon or other intruders, the long spear-shaped leaves, armed with spines at the root, preventing the possibility of a near approach to it from the ground without some labour of cutting them away. Both birds evinced a great deal of uneasiness at my presence. As I had no instrument, however, to cut away the dagger-shaped leaves of the maguey, I left the birds with their well-fortified domicile."

Dr. Gaumer [12] says that this Woodpecker occurs in all parts of Yucatan, though it is not at all common, and is met with both in the towns and ranchos. The iris in life is reddish brown. In the island of Cozumel Mr. Devis says [13] it is rarer than the other Woodpeckers, but found with them in the uncleared woods.

d″. *Cauda quam remex secundus brevior.*

DENDROBATES.

Dendrobates, Swainson, Faun. Bor.-Am., Birds, p. 301 (1831) ; Hargitt, Cat. Birds Brit. Mus. xviii. p. 337.

Mr. Hargitt recognizes twenty-five species belonging to this genus, which is a purely Neotropical one. Only four of these occur within our limits, and of these three are exceedingly closely allied to one another and to *D. fumigatus* of the Southern Continent; the fourth, *D. ceciliæ,* only just enters our fauna in the State of Panama.

The culmen is a sharp ridge, the bill on either side being scooped into a smooth channel, which is bounded along the lower edge by the ridge above the nostrils; the groove beneath this is well defined and deep. The tarsus is usually slightly longer than the outer toe (reversed), which again is longer than the middle toe.

α. *Subtus feré unicolor ; dorsum posticum et tectrices supracaudales concolores.*

1. **Dendrobates oleagineus.**

Picus oleagineus, Licht. Preis-Verz. mex. Vög. p. 1 (*cf.* J. f. Orn. 1863, p. 55) [1].

Chloronerpes (Phaionerpes) oleagineus, Reich. Scansores, p. 356, t. dclxxv. figg. 4467–8 [2].

Chloronerpes oleagineus, Scl. P. Z. S. 1856, p. 307 [3]; 1859, pp. 367 [4], 388 [5]; Sumichrast, La Nat. v. p. 240 [6]; Ferrari-Perez, Pr. U. S. Nat. Mus. ix. p. 159 [7].

Phæonerpes oleagineus, Cab. & Heine, Mus. Hein. iv. Heft 2, p. 140 [8].

Dendrobates oleaginus, Hargitt, Cat. Birds Brit. Mus. xviii. p. 344 [9].

Supra oleagineo-brunneus, pileo toto summo fuliginoso-nigricante, plumis omnibus coccineo terminatis, tectricibus supracaudalibus brunneo-nigricantibus, loris et capitis lateribus sordide albidis, tectricibus auricularibus saturate oleagineis : subtus fere ut supra, gula tota obscure griseo-nigricante ; alis extus unicoloribus, intus in pogonio interno maculis albis notatis ; cauda brunneo-nigricante immaculata ; rostro et pedibus plumbeo-nigricantibus.   Long. tota circa 6·5, alæ 4·0, caudæ 2·15, rostri a rictu 1·0, tarsi 0·7, dig. med. absque ungue 0·5, dig. ext. 0·62.

♀ mari similis, sed pileo summo coccineo haud ornato.   (Descr. maris et feminæ ex Coatepec, Vera Cruz, Mexico.   Mus. nostr.)

Hab. MEXICO, Papantla (*Deppe* [2]), Mineral de San Sebastian near Mascota, Jalisco (*Dr. A. C. Buller, in Mus. Rothschild*), Jalapa (*de Oca* [4], *Ferrari-Perez* [7], *F. D. G.*), Coatepec (*Ferrari-Perez, M. Trujillo*), Cordova (*Sallé* [3]), Uvero, Potrero (*Sumichrast* [6]), Orizaba (*Sumichrast* [6], *Botteri*), Playa Vicente (*Boucard* [5]).

This little Woodpecker seems fairly abundant in the temperate and lower regions of Mexico on both sides of the Cordillera, but perhaps more so in the State of Vera Cruz than elsewhere.

The bird first came under the notice of Deppe during his travels in Mexico, and specimens were included in the list of his duplicates by Lichtenstein under the name of *Picus oleagineus*, but no description was given [1].   The title, however, became current through the writings of Reichenbach, Sclater, and others, the female being characterized by the latter from specimens obtained by Sallé [3].   Deppe's specimens, according to Reichenbach, came from Papantla in Vera Cruz.   In size *D. oleagineus* exceeds both the more southern Central-American races of the same group, and in this respect fully equals the South-American *D. fumigatus*.   The latter is a darker bird, with the sides of the head dark, and is thus slightly differentiated.

2. **Dendrobates caboti.**

Chloronerpes oleagineus, Scl. & Salv. (nec Licht.) Ibis, 1860, p. 400 [1]; Lawr. Ann. Lyc. N. Y. ix. p. 131 [2]; v. Frantz. J. f. Orn. 1869, p. 364 [3]; Boucard, P. Z. S. 1883, p. 452 [4]; Zeledon, An. Mus. Nac. Costa Rica, 1887, p. 124 [5].

Mesopicus caboti, Malh. Mon. Pic. ii. p. 53, t. 57. figg. 1, 2 [8].

Chloronerpes caboti, Scl. Cat. Am. Birds, p. 337 [7]; Salv. Ibis, 1866, p. 206 [8]; P. Z. S. 1867, p. 157 [9]; 1870, p. 212 [10].

Dendrobates caboti, Hargitt, Cat. Birds Brit. Mus. xviii. p. 344 [11].

D. oleagineo valde affinis, sed minor, capitis lateribus plerumque obscurioribus vix distinctus.

Hab. MEXICO, Teapa in Tabasco (*Mrs. H. H. Smith*), Tizimin in Yucatan (*Gaumer* [11] *), BRITISH HONDURAS (*F. Blancaneaux*), Orange Walk (*G. F. Gaumer*);

* Mr. Hargitt places this specimen with *D. oleagineus*; but the specimen in question is a young male with a few red spots on the crown; the sides of the head are rather light, but the dimensions are those of the southern form.

GUATEMALA, Choctum [1], Saonchil, Savana Grande, Retalhuleu (*O. S. & F. D. G.*), Pie de la Cuesta in San Marcos (*W. B. Richardson*); COSTA RICA (*Endres*), Barranca (*Carmiol* [2]), Turialba (*Carmiol* [2], *Zeledon* [5]); PANAMA, Cordillera de Tolé [9], Cordillera del Chucu [10], Bugaba (*Arcé*).

There is little to distinguish *D. caboti* with certainty from *D. oleagineus*, except its smaller size, a character of slight value. The sides of the head in fully adult males are nearly uniformly dark, but in younger birds and in most females light lores and cheeks are usual, and therefore in this respect they resemble *D. oleagineus*.

D. caboti was described by Malherbe from specimens supposed to have come from Colombia, and named after Dr. Cabot, the companion of Stephens during his travels in Yucatan. Dr. Cabot, however, does not seem to have met with the species in Yucatan, as no specimen was in his collection when Salvin examined it in 1874.

Its distribution now has been traced over the lowlands of Guatemala on both sides of the main mountain-chain, and thence southwards to Costa Rica and the forests of the Cordillera of Tolé; but no Woodpecker of this group has been found on the Isthmus of Panama. In South America, from Colombia to Bolivia, *D. fumigatus* is the prevalent form.

3. Dendrobates sanguinolentus.

Chloronerpes sanguinolentus, Scl. P. Z. S. 1859, p. 60, t. 151 [1]; Scl. & Salv. Ibis, 1859, p. 136 [2].
Dendrobates sanguinolentus, Hargitt, Cat. Birds Brit. Mus. xviii. p. 346 [3].

D. caboti similis, sed dorso toto medio coccineo suffuso, statura quoque paulo minor. Long. tota circa 6·0, alæ 3·15, caudæ 1·75. (Descr. maris ex S. Domingo, Nicaragua. Mus. nostr.)

Hab. HONDURAS, Omoa (*Leyland* [1][2]); NICARAGUA, Santo Domingo in Chontales (*W. B. Richardson*), Rio Escondido (*Richmond*).

Mr. Sclater described this Woodpecker from a specimen obtained by Leyland at Omoa, in Honduras. This specimen is in the Derby Museum at Liverpool, and until recently has remained the only one known. About two years ago, Mr. Richardson secured several examples of a Woodpecker of this group at Santo Domingo, in the Province of Chontales, in Nicaragua. One of these is a male with the back richly suffused with dark red, and belongs doubtless to *D. sanguinolentus*; the others are not so coloured, nor are two specimens from the Rio Escondido nearer the coast, which formed part of Mr. Richmond's collection. They all, however, agree closely in dimensions, and undoubtedly belong to the same species. We have never seen the red colouring of the back on any specimen of *D. caboti*, and are thus driven to the conclusion that this peculiarity is characteristic of old males of *D. sanguinolentus* only and that younger males and females are not so adorned.

Mr. Hargitt considers *D. reichenbachi*, Cab. & Heine, to belong probably to this species [3]. If this is correct, its range extends to Venezuela.

β. *Subtus transfasciatus; dorsum posticum et tectrices supracaudales coccineæ.*

4. Dendrobates ceciliæ.

Mesopicos cecilii, Malh. Rev. Zool. 1849, p. 538 [1].

Chloronerpes cecilii, Scl. P. Z. S. 1856, p. 143 [2].

Chloronerpes ceciliæ, Salv. P. Z. S. 1867, p. 157 [3]; 1870, p. 213 [4].

Dendrobates ceciliæ, Hargitt, Cat. Birds Brit. Mus. xviii. p. 366 [5].

Supra læte oleagineo-brunnescens, dorso postico, tectricibus supracaudalibus et pileo toto coccineis, nucha flavo-aurantiaca; alis extus immaculatis dorso fere concoloribus: subtus fusco-brunneus, albido stricte trans-fasciatus; alis intus fuscis, albo distincte maculatis; cauda fusca, indistincte transfasciata; rostro et pedi-bus saturate plumbeis. Long. tota circa 6·0, alæ 3·45, caudæ 2·2, rostri a rictu 1·05, tarsi 0·6, dig. med. absque ungue 0·5, dig. ext. 0·6. (Descr. maris ex Mina de Chorcha, Panama. Mus. nostr.)

♀ mari similis, sed pileo toto fusco nec coccineo.

Hab. PANAMA, David (*Bridges* [2] [3]), Mina de Chorcha [4], Bibalaz (*Arcé*).—COLOMBIA [1]; W. ECUADOR [5].

This Woodpecker belongs to a small section of the genus *Dendrobates* in which the lower back and upper tail-coverts are bright red in both sexes. It thus differs conspicuously from *D. oleagineus* and its allies; moreover it is banded below, a character shared by many South-American members of the genus, and the nape is yellow. Only one other species in South America is at all nearly allied to *D. ceciliæ*, and that is *D. kirki* of the islands of Tobago and Trinidad. The latter species may always be distinguished by the wing-coverts being spotted with yellow.

D. ceciliæ was described by Malherbe from Colombian specimens, and it is not unfrequently represented in the trade collections of skins made by the bird-hunters of Bogota. Salmon found it in the Province of Antioquia, and Bridges obtained specimens in Chiriqui, as recorded by Mr. Sclater. The only Panama specimens we have seen are from the latter district, whence Arcé sent us two males. Bridges [2] says this Woodpecker is found on the trees in the outskirts of the town of David, but he only observed one pair.

b. *Cervix contracta, plumis parvis vestita; caput magnum.*

c'. *Nares apertæ haud plumis obtectæ.*

CELEUS.

Celeus, Boie, Isis, 1831, p. 542; Hargitt, Cat. Birds Brit. Mus. xviii. p. 420.

Mr. Hargitt includes fourteen species in *Celeus*, keeping two small genera, *Cerchnei-picus*, with three species, and *Crocomorphus*, with two species, distinct. The species of both of these genera have usually been included in *Celeus*. The former, according to Mr. Hargitt, differs in having an elongated and not a rounded nostril, and the latter is without a distinct ridge on the side of the bill running from above the nostril parallel to the culmen.

The species of *Celeus* are strictly Neotropical birds and inhabitants of the hot forests wherever they are found. One species, *C. castaneus*, is restricted to our region, and ranges from the State of Vera Cruz to Costa Rica. Another, *C. loricatus*, occurs in Eastern Costa Rica and in the State of Panama, and thence southwards to Peru. A third species, referred to below, may also occur in the State of Panama.

The bill of *Celeus* has the culmen slightly arched; the nostrils are exposed, the postnasal feathers being erect but not curved forward as in many Woodpeckers; above the nostrils is a ridge running parallel to the culmen and disappearing halfway along the side of the maxilla. The feathers of the occiput are long, those of the neck short. Rich chestnut with cross markings of black are the chief colours of the plumage; and a well-defined red rictal stripe marks the male in most of the species. In *C. loricatus* these stripes unite under the chin. The outer toe (reversed) without its claw is shorter than the middle toe.

1. Celeus castaneus.

Picus castaneus, Wagl. Isis, 1829, p. 515 [1].

Celeus castaneus, Scl. P. Z. S. 1858, p. 359 [2]; 1859, p. 388 [3]; Moore, P. Z. S. 1859, p. 60 [4]; Scl. & Salv. Ibis, 1859, p. 137 [5]; P. Z. S. 1870, p. 837 [6]; Taylor, Ibis, 1860, p. 119 [7]; Lawr. Ann. Lyc. N. Y. viii. p. 184 [8]; ix. p. 130 [9]; v. Frantz. J. f. Orn. 1869, p. 364 [10]; Salv. Ibis, 1872, p. 320 [11]; Sumichrast, La Nat. v. p. 240 [12]; Boucard, P. Z. S. 1883, p. 452 [13]; Zeledon, An. Mus. Nac. Costa Rica, 1887, p. 123 [14]; Hargitt, Cat. Birds Brit. Mus. xviii. p. 433 [15].

Picus badioides, Less. Cent. Zool. p. 56, t. 14 [16].

Celeus badioides, Scl. P. Z. S. 1857, p. 229 [17].

Castaneo-rufus, corpore toto (dorso postico excepto) lunulis nigris ornato; pileo toto et crista occipitali elongata, ochracco-rufescentibus; capitis lateribus et mento ejusdem coloris, stria utrinque rictali et regione parotica coccineis; remigibus fuscis, intus ad basin castaneis; secundariis castaneis, internis medialiter maculis sagittiformibus nigris sparsim notatis, subalaribus flavis; cauda nigra, dimidio basali saturate castaneo; rostro eburneo-albo; pedibus fuscis. Long. tota circa 9·0, alæ 5·1, caudæ 3·3, rostri a rictu 1·2, tarsi 0·8, dig. med. absque ungue 0·8, dig. ext. 0·6.

♀ mari similis, stria rictali coccinea utrinque nulla. (Descr. maris et feminæ ex Choctum, Guatemala. Mus. nostr.)

Hab. MEXICO [16], Cuesalpa [17], Santecomapam [17], Playa Vicente [3] (*Boucard*), Orizaba (*Botteri* [15]), Omealca, Uvero (*Sumichrast* [12]), Atoyac (*Mrs. H. H. Smith*), Tizimin in Yucatan (*Gaumer* [13] [15]), Chimalapa, Tehuantepec (*W. B. Richardson*); BRITISH HONDURAS, Orange Walk (*Gaumer*); GUATEMALA, Teleman, Choctum (*O. S. & F. D. G.*); HONDURAS (*Dyson* [15]), Omoa (*Leyland* [4]), Julian, San Pedro (*G. M. Whitely* [6]), Potrerillos (*G. C. Taylor* [2] [7]); NICARAGUA, Chontales (*Belt* [11]), La Libertad (*W. B. Richardson*), Greytown (*Holland* [8]); COSTA RICA (*v. Frantzius* [10]), Turrialba (*Cooper* [9], *Zeledon* [14]), Pacuare (*Zeledon* [14]), Angostura (*Carmiol* [9]).

This *Celeus* has long been known as an inhabitant of Mexico and Central America, having been described by Wagler in 1829, and since observed, though in sparing numbers, by most of the collectors who have worked in the country now examined. It is only, however, in the hottest and densest forests of the districts bordering the Atlantic Ocean that *C. castaneus* is found occurring in such places, from the Mexican State of Vera Cruz to Nicaragua and Costa Rica. We have no record of its occurrence in any of the forests of the districts on the Pacific side of the mountain-range, though many such exist apparently suitable to its habits.

In Guatemala it is strictly confined to the vast forest-tracts of Vera Paz which stretch from Coban to the Mexican frontier, and to the lower portion of the Valley of the Polochic river beyond the village of Teleman.

Celeus castaneus has no very near allies—*C. grammicus* of Guiana and the Amazons Valley being, perhaps, its nearest relative, a species differing in many points.

In Yucatan Dr. Gaumer says[13] this Woodpecker is very rare, and during a whole year he only saw two specimens. He noticed that the bird had a strong and peculiar odour, which he supposed to be derived from its food, which consists exclusively of a small Hymenopterous insect known as the "*Uss.*" He adds that *C. castaneus* is solitary in its habits, living in the deepest part of the forest. The specimens obtained were very tame; they jumped nimbly about the trees, constantly catching the small insects which seem to be attracted to them by their odour.

2. Celeus loricatus.

Meiglyptes loricatus, Reich. Scansores, Picinæ, p. 405, t. 681. figg. 4495-96[1].

Celeus loricatus, Scl. & Salv. P. Z. S. 1879, p. 533[2]; Zeledon, An. Mus. Nac. Costa Rica, 1887, p. 124[3]; Hargitt, Cat. Birds Brit. Mus. xviii. p. 432[4].

Celeus mentalis, Cassin, Pr. Ac. Phil. 1860, p. 137[5]; Journ. Ac. Phil. v. p. 461, t. 52. figg. 2, 3[6] Scl. & Salv. P. Z. S. 1864, p. 367[7].

Celeus fraseri, Malh. Mon. Pic. ii. p. 16, t. 43 bis, fig. 5[8].

Celeus squamatus, Lawr. Ibis, 1863, p. 184[9]; Ann. Lyc. N. Y. viii. p. 11[10].

Supra rufescenti-castaneus, interscapulio fere unicolore, dorso toto et tectricibus supracaudalibus pallidioribus nigro fasciatis, occipite rufescenti-castaneo, frontis plumis medialiter nigris; alis rufescenti-castaneis, secundariis et tectricibus omnibus lineis angustis nigris sparsim transfasciatis, remigibus nigricantibus castaneo guttatis : subtus ochraceo-albidus, plumis omnibus fascia distincta subterminali nigra, pectore castaneo lavato, mento et stria utrinque rictali coccineis, subalaribus castaneis; cauda nigra, pallide castaneo regulariter transfasciata; rostro corneo; pedibus plumbeis. Long. tota circa 8·0, alæ 4·8, caudæ 2·8, rostri a rictu 1·0, tarsi 0·7, dig. med. absque ungue 0·75, dig. ext. 0·6. (Descr. maris ex Veraguas, Panama. Mus. nostr.)

♀ mari similis, mento et striis rictalibus castaneis, colore coccineo nullo.

Hab. Costa Rica, Talamanca, Jimenez (*Zeledon*[3]); Panama, Veraguas (*Arcé*), Lion Hill (*M'Leannan*[7][9]), Turbo (*W. S. & C. J. Wood*[5]).—Colombia[2]; W. Ecuador[8]; N. Peru[1].

Specimens of this distinct species have been obtained from various places scattered over a wide area of North-western South America, but in very small numbers; nevertheless the names bestowed upon the bird are, unfortunately, many. Messrs. Wood, who accompanied Lieut. Michler's expedition to Darien, first obtained specimens in our region at Turbo, and these were described and figured by Cassin as *Celeus mentalis* [5]. Then Mr. Lawrence described a female specimen from Panama as *Celeus squamatus* [9], considering it distinct from *Celeus fraseri* of Western Ecuador. Subsequent investigations have settled that all these names are synonyms of *Meiglyptes loricatus* of Reichenbach. based on a bird said to have been obtained in Peru by Warszewiez [1].

M'Leannan sent us two females from Panama, and subsequently Arcé obtained a male from Veraguas. This marks the extreme limit of the range of the species so far as our own information goes; but Mr. Zeledon records it from the Costa-Rican province of Talamanca, where it must closely approach the domain of *C. castaneus*, which occurs at Angostura on the same side of the mountain-range.

We have no record of its habits, but Salmon, who met with the bird in the Colombian State of Antioquia, states that the iris in life is dark [2].

3. Celeus immaculatus.

Celeus immaculatus, Berl. Ibis, 1880, p. 113 [1].

"Allied to *C. elegans*, from which it seems only to differ in having the inner webs of the wing-feathers plain yellow, without the black bands or spots to be seen in that species." (*Berlepsch, l. s. c.*)

Hab. PANAMA, Agua Dulce (*fide Berlepsch*).

We know nothing of this species, nor was Mr. Hargitt acquainted with it when he wrote his 'Catalogue of Picidæ.' It was described from a female specimen by Count Berlepsch, and supposed to have been sent from Panama from the style of preparation of the skin.

C. elegans belongs to the section of the genus in which the under surface of the body is nearly or quite uniform. Its habitat is the northern countries of South America from Guiana to Trinidad and Venezuela.

d'. *Nares plumis obtectæ.*

Digitus pedis externus (reversus) quam digitus medius longior.

CAMPOPHILUS.

Campephilus, Gray, List Gen. Birds, 1840, p. 54.
Campophilus, Cabanis & Heine, Mus. Hein. iv. Heft 2, p. 100; Hargitt, Cat. Birds Brit. Mus. xviii. p. 460.
Cniparchus, Cab. & Heine, Mus. Hein. iv. Heft 2, p. 98.
Scapaneus, Cab. & Heine, Mus. Hein. iv. Heft 2, p. 90.

Excluding *Ipocrantor magellanicus*, which has frequently been considered a *Campophilus*, Hargitt* includes fourteen species in this genus, which is almost

* It is with great regret that we notice the recent death of Edward Hargitt, whose careful and concentrated work on the Woodpeckers and their allies has done so much to elucidate their classification. As will be seen

exclusively a Neotropical one, the exceptions being *C. principalis* of the Southern States of North America, to which may perhaps be added its near allies *C. bairdi* and *C. imperialis*, though both are found beyond the boundaries of the United States.

Of the narrow-necked large-headed Woodpeckers, *Campophilus* has the nostrils hidden by antrorse bristly feathers, similar plumes extending forwards on the chin over the interramal angle. The outer (reversed) toe is considerably longer than the middle toe; the tail is long, the central feathers peculiarly formed, so that the stiffened webs when closely pressed to the stem or branch of a tree assist largely in supporting the bird, the points of the feathers not apparently being used for this purpose and therefore soft and but slightly worn; the shafts of these feathers are hollowed out beneath. The head carries a distinct crest, very pronounced in *C. imperialis*, and the bill is very strong, being wide at its base as compared with its height.

Of the fourteen known species of the genus four only occur within our limits. The most northern of these is the giant of the whole family, *C. imperialis*, restricted in its range to the pine-clad heights of the Sierra Madre of North-western Mexico. *C. guatemalensis* is by far the most widely distributed of our species, and extends from Mazatlan and Tampico to Costa Rica. The other two species are both of southern connection and do not enter our fauna beyond the limits of the State of Panama. The southern species spread over nearly the whole of the southern continent as far as Paraguay and the Argentine Republic.

α. *Ingens, corpore subtus omnino nigro.*

1. Campophilus imperialis.

Picus imperialis, Gould, P. Z. S. 1832, p. 140 [1].

Campophilus imperialis, Cab. & Heine, Mus. Hein. iv. Heft 2, p. 101 [2]; Hargitt, Cat. Birds Brit. Mus. xviii. p. 465 [3].

Campephilus imperialis, Ridgw. Auk, 1887, p. 161 [4].

Purpureo-niger, interscapulio utrinque albo marginato, stria lata post oculos utrinque ad nucham conjunctis, plumis valde elongatis coccineis cum plumis elongatis occipitalibus nigris crista magna formantibus; remigibus quinque externis nigris, sexto ad apicem albo, reliquis cum secundariis omnibus externe albis; rostro eburneo; pedibus nigricanti-plumbeis, unguibus corneis. Long. tota circa 22·0, alæ 12·5, caudæ 8·0, tarsus 1·8, dig. med. absque ungue 1·45, dig. ext. 1·65.

♀ mari similis, crista haud coccinea, sed plumis valde elongatis et recurvatis nigris composita. (Descr. maris et feminæ ex Ciudad in Durango, Mexico. Mus. nostr.)

Hab. MEXICO (*Floresi* [3]), Sierra Madre de Sonora (*Benson* [4]), Ciudad in Durango (*Forrer*), Sierra de Valparaiso (*W. B. Richardson*), Sierra de Juanacatlan, Mascota, Jalisco (*Dr. A. C. Buller, in mus. Rothschild*).

---

in these pages, his Catalogue of the Picidæ in the British Museum has been of the greatest service to us in our present undertaking.

This magnificent Woodpecker, by far the largest of the whole family, was first made known to science by the late John Gould [1], who having obtained five or six skins of it, exhibited some of them at a meeting of the Zoological Society held 14th August, 1832, the descriptions of male and female appearing in the 'Proceedings' of the Society for that year. Gould gave no details of the source whence he obtained his specimens, merely stating that they came from "that little-explored district of California which borders the territory of Mexico."

Probably on the strength of this statement *Campophilus imperialis* was long included in the North-American fauna, but its name is omitted in recent works.

Two of Gould's skins passed some years ago into our possession, and from the manner of their preparation we believe them to have been made by the Mining Engineer Floresi, who formed a considerable collection of Humming-Birds, and also preserved skins of a few other species, all of which passed into Gould's possession. Amongst the latter were specimens of *Amphispiza quinquestriata* and *Euptilotis neoxenus*, birds exclusively restricted in their range to the country inhabited by *Campophilus imperialis*. Moreover, Floresi is known to have visited this region.

Besides Gould's specimens others were obtained many years ago, for an adult male was in the Heine Collection when the Catalogue was compiled in 1863, the origin of which is given as Mexico [2].

From an account given to him in 1858 of a large Woodpecker frequenting the upland forests of the Volcan de Fuego, in Guatemala, Salvin was inclined to think the bird might be *C. imperialis* ('Ibis,' 1859, p. 136); but this suggestion was subsequently abandoned ('Ibis,' 1866, p. 204). Guatemala, nevertheless, appears, with the addition of South Mexico, in the 'History of North-American Birds' (ii. p. 496), as the countries in which *C. imperialis* is found.

All doubt as to its habitat is now set at rest, for it has been traced definitely to the Sierras of North-western Mexico, which stretch from Arizona to Jalisco, in a lofty chain of pine-clad mountains running more or less parallel to the shores of the Pacific Ocean, and attaining in places an altitude of at least 10,000 feet.

Forrer secured several specimens in the State of Durango, near the village of Ciudad, in the sierra of that district *. Mr. Richardson, when in the Sierra de Valparaiso, in the State of Jalisco, saw a specimen and shot at it, but, much to his disgust, failed to secure the bird. More recently in the same State, Dr. A. C. Buller obtained several specimens in the Sierra de Juanacatlan, near Mascota. These are now in the collection of the Hon. W. Rothschild, and Mr. Hartert, writing to us respecting them, says that a young male killed 18th May resembles the female but has large white tips to the primaries; another young male is similar, but a number of the crest-feathers are partly red, the tips being black.

* This place is often given in the 'Catalogue of Birds' as Ciudad Durango, suggesting the "City of Durango," a very different place in a comparatively open country.

The most northern record of this species is reported by Mr. Ridgway, who says [4] that Lieut. H. C. Benson, of the U.S. Army, when scouting in the Apaché country, found *C. imperialis* to be common in the Sierra Madre, in Sonora, fifty miles south of the frontier-line in the pine-forests. A head only was brought home, sufficient, however, to render the determination of the species certain.

Whether *C. imperialis* crosses the frontier into United States Territory or not has yet to be determined. The probability of its doing so depends upon the continuity of the great pine-forests which clothe the sierras of these districts. The political boundary is quite arbitrary so far as any physical features of the country are concerned.

β. *Dorsum posticum nigrum ; abdomen regulariter fasciatum.*

2. **Campophilus guatemalensis.**

Picus guatemalensis, Hartl. Rev. Zool. 1844, p. 214 [1].

Campephilus guatemalensis, Gray, Gen. Birds, ii. p. 436 [2]; Scl. P. Z. S. 1864, p. 177 [3]; Salv. P. Z. S. 1867, p. 157 [4]; Lawr. Ann. Lyc. N. Y. ix. p. 130 [5]; Mem. Bost. Soc. N. H. ii. p. 293 [6]; Bull. U. S. Nat. Mus. no. 4, p. 34 [7]; v. Frantz. J. f. Orn. 1869, p. 363 [8]; Sumichrast, La Nat. v. p. 240 [9]; Nutting, Pr. U. S. Nat. Mus. v. p. 398 [10]; vi. pp. 387 [11], 406 [12]; Boucard, P. Z. S. 1883, p. 452 [13]; Ferrari-Perez, Pr. U. S. Nat. Mus. ix. p. 158 [14]; Ridgw. Pr. U. S. Nat. Mus. x. pp. 582 [15], 591 [16]; Zeledon, An. Mus. Nac. Costa Rica, 1887, p. 123 [17]; Stone, Pr. Ac. Phil. 1890, p. 206 [18]; Cherrie, Auk, 1892, p. 327 [19].

Campophilus guatemalensis, Hargitt, Cat. Birds Brit. Mus. xviii. p. 473 [20].

Dryocopus guatemalensis, Scl. P. Z. S. 1857, p. 229 [21]; 1858, p. 359 [22]; 1859, pp. 367 [23], 388 [24]; Scl. & Salv. Ibis, 1859, p. 135 [25].

Phlæoceastes guatemalensis, Cab. J. f. Orn. 1862, p. 175 [26].

Scapaneus guatemalensis, Cab. & Heine, Mus. Hein. iv. Heft 2, p. 92 [27]; Salvad. Atti R. Acc. Tor. 1868, p. 183 [28].

Picus lessoni, Less. Echo du Monde Savant, 1845, p. 920 [29].

Dryotomus odoardus, Bp Notes Ornith. p. 85 (1854) [30].

Campephilus regius, Reich. Scans. Picinæ, p. 393, t. 649. figg. 4331-2 [31].

Dryocopus erythrops, Scl. (nec Valenc.), P. Z. S. 1856, p. 306 [32].

Supra niger, vittis (una cervicis lateribus utrinque) in dorso convergentibus flavido-albis ; capite toto undique cum gula antica coccineis ; subtus abdomine toto nigro et flavido-albido regulariter fasciato, pectore et gutture nigris, subcaudalibus nigris flavido-fusco indistincte fasciatis ; alis nigris, subalaribus et remigibus omnibus ad basin sulphureo-flavis ; rostro albicanti-corneo ; pedibus plumbeis. Long. tota circa 14·0, alæ 7·1, caudæ 4·3, rostri a rictu 2·2, tarsi 1·4, dig. med. absque ungue 1·0, dig. ext. 1·13. (Descr. maris ex San Marcos, Guatemala. Mus. nostr.)

♀ mari similis, capite toto summo medialiter et gutture usque ad mentum nigris, loris et mento ipso cum capitis lateribus coccineis.

Hab. MEXICO, Mazatlan (*Grayson* [6], *Forrer*), Presidio de Mazatlan (*Forrer*), Tepic (*W. B. Richardson*), Santiago, Tonila, Culata, Jacolapa in Colima (*W. Lloyd*), Rio de la Armeria (*Xantus* [6]), Dos Arroyos in Guerrero (*Mrs. H. H. Smith*),

Tampico, Tamesi (*W. B. Bichardson*), Papantla (*Deppe* [31]), Misantla, Colipa (*F. D. G.*), Jalapa (*de Oca* [23]), Santana near Jalapa [14], Paso de la Milpa [14], San Juan Martin (*Ferrari-Perez*), Laguna Verde (*M. Trujillo*), Orizaba, Uvero (*Sumichrast* [9]), Cordova (*Sallé* [32]), Santecomapam [21], Llano Verde [24], Playa Vicente [24] (*Boucard*), Tehuantepec (*W. B. Richardson*), Tehuantepec city [7], Santa Efigenia [9], Chihuitan [7] (*Sumichrast*), Teapa (*Mrs. H. H. Smith*), N. Yucatan [13], Buctzotz, Izamal (*Gaumer*), Tunkas, Labna (*Stone & Baker* [18]); BRITISH HONDURAS, Orange Walk (*Gaumer*), Cayo, Belize (*Blancaneaux*); GUATEMALA [1], Rabinal, San Gerónimo, Volcan de Fuego, Savana Grande, Medio Monte, Retalhuleu (*O. S. & F. D. G.*); SALVADOR, Volcan de San Miguel (*W. B. Richardson*); HONDURAS (*Dyson*), Omoa (*G. C. Taylor* [22]), Truxillo [15], Segovia river [16] (*Townsend*); NICARAGUA, Matagalpa, Momotombo (*W. B. Richardson*), Sucuya [11], Los Sabalos [12] (*Nutting*), Woods near Virgin Bay (*Bridges*), Rio Escondido (*Richmond*); COSTA RICA (*v. Frantzius, Hoffmann* [27], *Durando* [28]), Bebedero (*Arcé*), Lepanto (*Ellendorf* [27]), Rio Frio (*Richmond*), Dota Mts., Candelaria Mts. [8], Grecia [5], Angostura [5] (*v. Frantzius, Carmiol*), La Palma (*Nutting* [10]), San José (*v. Frantzius* [5], *Cherrie* [19]), Jimenez, Las Trojas, Cartago (*Zeledon* [17]); PANAMA, Santiago de Veraguas (*Arcé* [4]).

Campophilus guatemalensis is a very distinct species, easily recognized by the side of the head in both sexes being scarlet with no white marks whatever, the ear-coverts alone being slightly tinged with brown.   The entire head as well as the upper throat are scarlet in the male, but in the female the centre of the crown and crest, and the throat, except the antrorse feathers on the chin, are black.   The nearest ally of *C. guatemalensis* is *C. melanoleucus*, a species of wide distribution in South America, which has white markings about the head.

The range of this species extends over nearly the whole of the lowlands of our region, from Mazatlan on the west and Tampico on the east to the State of Panama, being everywhere a bird of the heavily wooded country, and ranging in altitude from the sea-level to a height of 3000 to 6000 feet in the mountains.   At Mazatlan, Grayson says it is common in the larger forests and a constant resident.   Dr. Gaumer notes its abundance in all parts of Yucatan, not only in the large forests but about the dead trees in clearings, and he once counted as many as fourteen on one tree, all working hard at the decaying wood.   Mr. Stone also observed it in the woods of Tunkas and Labna.

In Guatemala *C. guatemalensis* is not uncommon in the forests of the Volcan de Fuego up to a height of about 6000 feet, and is found at all elevations below this throughout the country bordering the Pacific Ocean.   It also occurs in the interior near San Gerónimo and Rabinal.   We noticed nothing peculiar in its habits, which were those of Woodpeckers generally.

In Costa Rica Mr. Cherrie says [19] that it occurs accidentally at San José, but is common on both the Atlantic and Pacific slopes of the mountains down to the coast-line. At La Palma Mr. Nutting did not notice its presence until 27th April, when it suddenly became quite common, and so continued as long as he remained in the district. He adds that one of the commonest sounds in the forest was its quick, loud tap. It usually taps but twice in rapid succession, hunts in pairs, and seems to prefer the thick forests to the more open woods.

Sumichrast noted that the iris of this species is light yellow, the bill horny-white, and the feet ashy.

3. Campophilus malherbii.

Campephilus malherbii, Gray, Gen. Birds, ii. p. 436, t. 108 [1]; Scl. & Salv. P. Z. S. 1864, p. 366 [2]; Salv. P. Z. S. 1867, p. 157 [3]; 1870, p. 212 [4].

Campophilus malherbii, Hargitt, Cat. Birds Brit. Mus. xviii. p. 472 [5].

Dryocopus malherbii, Cassin, Pr. Ac. Phil. 1860, p. 137 [6]; Lawr. Ann. Lyc. N. Y. vii. p. 299 [7].

Supra niger, vittis (una cervicis lateribus utrinque) in dorso convergentibus albis; capite summo et capitis lateribus coccineis, loris et macula ad maudibulæ basin albis, illis supra linea angusta nigra marginatis, auricularibus infra albis supra nigris; abdomine toto subtus nigro et pallide ferrugineo regulariter transfasciato; alis nigris, subalaribus et remigibus omnibus ad basin pallidissime flavido-albis; rostro et pedibus plumbeis. Long. tota circa 13·0, alæ 7·3, caudæ 4·5, rostri a rictu 2·0, tarsi 1·45, dig. med. absque ungue 0·93, dig. ext. 1·1. (Descr. maris ex Lion Hill, Panama. Mus. nostr.)

♀ mari similis, capite summo medialiter omnino nigro, vitta cervicali alba usque ad mandibulæ basin extensa.

Hab. PANAMA, Chiriqui (*Kellett & Wood*[5]), Santa Fé[3], Cordillera de Tolé[4], Calovevora[4], Santiago de Veraguas (*Arcé*), Lion Hill (*M'Leannan*[2 7]), Turbo (*C. J. Wood*[6]) — COLOMBIA.

This Woodpecker has a very limited range, being restricted to an area in Colombia reaching in the south to the neighbourhood of Bogota and spreading thence northwards so as to include the State of Panama. Skins of it are not unfrequently found in the trade collections of Bogota. Salmon met with it at several places in the Cauca Valley, and Mr. Simons at Atanques in the Sierra of Santa Marta at an elevation of 4000 feet. Mr. Wood, who accompanied Lieut. Michler's expedition to Darien, says that it is occasionally seen in the forest at Turbo, but is very shy and difficult to approach.

In the State of Panama M'Leannan met with it on the Line of the Panama Railway, and Arcé at several places in Veraguas. But the latter collector sent us no specimens from Chiriqui, though it is said to be found there, as a specimen in the British Museum obtained by Capt. Kellett and Capt. Wood is marked as coming from that district.

C. malherbii can readily be distinguished from *C. guatemalensis* by the white marks at the base of the bill in both sexes. Its nearest ally is *C. melanoleucus*, from which it differs in having a darker bill, the intervals between the dark bars of the under surface more rufescent, and in the male by the red of the crown and cheeks being connected in front of the orbit, and other characters.

Mr. Simons states that the iris of *C. malherbii* is white.

γ. *Dorsum posticum coccineum, abdomen plerumque concolor.*

4. Campophilus splendens.

Campephilus hæmatogaster, Salv. (nec Tsch.), P. Z. S. 1867, p. 157[1]; 1870, p. 212[2]; Scl. & Salv. P. Z. S. 1879, p. 532[3].

Campophilus spendens, Hargitt, Ibis, 1889, p. 58[4]; Cat. Birds Brit. Mus. xviii. p. 480[5].

Supra niger, dorso imo, pileo toto, cervice et corpore subtus (mento excepto) coccineis, stria frontali per oculos utrinque ducta nigra, supra eam post oculos et infra eam a naribus ochraceo-alba, pectoris lateribus nigris, hypochondriis fusco et nigro fasciatis; subalaribus et maculis magnis in pogoniis internis remigum ochraceis; rostro et pedibus plumbeo-nigricantibus. Long. tota 15·5, alæ 7·3, caudæ 3·9, rostri a rictu 2·2, tarsi 1·55, dig. med. absque ungue 0·85, dig. ext. 1·2.

♀ mari similis, sed gula antica nigra, stria ochracea infra oculos cervicis lateres occupante. (Descr. maris et feminæ ex Antioquia, Colombia. Mus. Brit.)

Hab. PANAMA, Santiago de Veraguas[1], Calovevora[2] (*Arcé*[5]).—COLOMBIA, State of Antioquia[3].

This species is closely allied to *C. hæmatogaster*, Tsch., and was not separated from that bird till 1889, when Hargitt detected the differences, and gave it a distinct name. In the male *C. splendens* the red colour spreads much further up the throat than in *C. hæmatogaster*, leaving little more than the chin pure black; the spots, too, of the primaries are more stained with ochre in the former bird, and this character is shared by the female. Hargitt states that the bases of the feathers of the hind neck in *C. splendens* are black, whereas they are white in *C. hæmatogaster*. In the contracted skin of Bogota make this character cannot be examined, but in other specimens, so far as we can see, little difference is observable; if anything, the short feathers in both birds at the back of the neck are indistinctly barred towards their bases.

The only adult male of this bird that we have seen was obtained by Salmon in the Colombian State of Antioquia. Three skins sent us by Arcé are all females, and are narrowly and irregularly barred towards the base of each feather of the under surface, the tips alone being red. Whether this extensive barring of these feathers is characteristic of *C. splendens* or not, we are unable at present to say. In the skins of *C. hæmatogaster* before us not nearly so much is seen, and the barred feathers are so irregularly placed that it seems probable that they would disappear in the fully adult bird.

Salmon noted the iris of *C. splendens* to be yellow[3].

Digitus pedis externus (reversus) quam digitus medius brevior.

CEOPHLŒUS.

Ceophlœus, Cabanis, J. f. Orn. 1862, p. 176; Cab. & Heine, Mus. Hein. iv. Heft 2, p. 85 (1863); Hargitt, Cat. Birds Brit. Mus. xviii. p. 506.

Ceophlœus, according to Hargitt, contains five species, which we would reduce to four—*C. fuscipennis* being, in our opinion, indistinguishable from *C. lineatus*. These are distributed over the greater part of the Neotropical region, from Mexico to South Brazil. One common South-American species, *C. lineatus*, occurs within our limits,

another closely allied, *C. scapularis*, is restricted to Mexico and Central America.   The
genus is thus purely Neotropical, and its range northwards follows the woods on each
side of the Mexican highlands to the States of Nuevo Leon and Tamaulipas on the
east, and to Sonora on the west.

With a general resemblance to the species of *Campophilus*, which are barred on the
under surface, *Ceophlœus* is not quite so stoutly built, and has a more feeble bill; the
proportion of the toes, too, is different, and forms a good distinguishing character, for
in *Campophilus* the outer toe (reversed) is longer than the middle toe, whereas in
Ceophlœus the reverse is the case, and the middle toe is the longer of the two.

1. Ceophlœus scapularis.

Picus scapularis, Vig. Zool. Journ. iv. p. 354[1]; Zool. Voy. 'Blossom,' p. 23[2].

Dryocopus scapularis, Scl. P. Z. S. 1856, p. 306[3]; 1858, p. 359[4]; 1859, p. 367[5]; Moore, P. Z. S.
1859, p. 60[6]; Scl. & Salv. Ibis, 1859, p. 135[7]; P. Z. S. 1870, p. 837[8]; Lawr. Ann. Lyc.
N. Y. ix. p. 205[9]; Mem. Bost. Soc. N. H. ii. p. 293[10]; Bull. U. S. Nat. Mus. no. 4, p. 34[11];
v. Frantz. J. f. Orn. 1869, p. 364[12]; Sumichrast, La Nat. v. p. 240[13]; Salv. Cat. Strickl.
Coll. p. 385[14].

Ceophlœus scapularis, Cab. J. f. Orn. 1862, p. 176[15]; Ferrari-Perez, Pr. U. S. Nat. Mus. ix. p. 159[16];
Ridgw. Pr. U. S. Nat. Mus. x. p. 582[17]; Zeledon, An. Mus. Nac. Costa Rica, 1887, p. 123[18];
Hargitt, Cat. Birds Brit. Mus. xviii. p. 510[19].

Hylotomus scapularis, Nutting, Pr. U. S. Nat. Mus. vi. p. 387[20].

Picus similis, Less. Descr. Mamm. et Ois. p. 204[21].

Campephilus leucorhamphus, Reich. Scans. Picinæ, p. 393, t. 648. figg. 4327–8[22].

Dryotomus delattrii, Bp. Compt. Rend. xxxviii. p. 656[23].

Supra niger, scapularibus extus albis, pileo toto plumis ad nucham elongatis cristam formantibus et stria
malari coccineis; capitis lateribus, oculorum ambitu incluso, saturate plumbeis, linea angusta utrinque a
naribus usque ad pectoris latera albida, parte antica aurantio tincta: subtus gula alba nigro guttata,
cervice et pectore nigris, abdomine toto albido nigro regulariter transfasciato; alis et cauda nigricantibus,
hujus remigibus ad basin et tectricibus subalaribus fulvo-flavicantibus; rostro eburneo; pedibus plumbeis.
Long. tota circa 12·0, alæ 7·0, caudæ 4·65, rostri a rictu 1·75, tarsi 1·1, dig. med. absque ungue 0·9, dig.
ext. 0·7.   (Descr. maris ex La Libertad, Salvador.   Mus. nostr.)
♀ mari similis, pileo antico et regione malari nigricantibus.

Hab. MEXICO, Hacienda de la Cruz and Villa Grande in Nuevo Leon (*F. B. Armstrong*),
Sierra above Ciudad Victoria, Aldama, Tampico, Valles (*W. B. Richardson*),
Jalapa (*de Oca*[5], *Ferrari-Perez*[16]), R. Juan Martin, Hacienda Tortugas, Omealca,
San Lorenzo, Alvarado, Plan del Rio, Zentla (*Ferrari-Perez*), Cordova (*Sallé*[3],
Sumichrast[13]), Mirador, Uvero (*Sumichrast*[13]), Atoyac (*Mrs. H. H. Smith*), Vega
del Casadero, Playa Vicente (*M. Trujillo*), Sierra de Alamos (*W. Lloyd*), Mazatlan
(*Grayson*[10], *Xantus*[10], *Forrer*), San Blas (*Collie*[1], *W. B. Richardson*), Plains of
Colima, R. Tupila (*Xantus*[10]), Putla (*Rébouch*), Acapulco (*Mrs. H. H. Smith*),
Chihuitan[11], Santa Efigenia[11], Cacoprieto[13], Tonala (*Sumichrast*), Tehuantepec
(*W. B. Richardson*), Merida in Yucatan (*Schott*[9]), Izamal, Buctzotz (*Gaumer*);
BRITISH HONDURAS, Belize (*Blancaneaux*); GUATEMALA, Vera Paz (*Skinner*[7]), San

Gerónimo, Dueñas, Savana Grande, Retalhuleu (*O. S. & F. D. G.*); SALVADOR, La Libertad (*W. B. Richardson*); HONDURAS, Omoa (*Leyland* [6]), Truxillo (*Townsend* [17]), San Pedro (*G. M. Whitely* [8]), Tigre I. (*G. C. Taylor* [4]); NICARAGUA, Leon, Momotombo (*W. B. Richardson*), Sucuya (*Nutting* [20]), Rio Escondido (*Richmond*); ? COSTA RICA (*Carmiol* [19]), Aguacate Mts. (*Hoffmann* [15]), Candelaria (*Zeledon* [18]).

This is one of the commonest of the larger Woodpeckers of our region, its range being very similar to that of *Campophilus guatemalensis*, the southern limit of the two species reaching Costa Rica, but not extending beyond into the State of Panama, where its place is taken by *C. lineatus*. In Mexico its northern range is more extensive, as it has been traced in the west to the Sierra de Alamos in Sonora by Mr. W. Lloyd, and in the east to the Hacienda de la Cruz and Villa Grande in Nuevo Leon by Mr. Armstrong and to the Sierra above Ciudad Victoria in Tamaulipas by Mr. Richardson. From these points it is found uninterruptedly throughout Central America on both sides of the main Cordillera, perhaps as far as Costa Rica. Its range in altitude is rather less than that of *C. guatemalensis*, as we have no record of it at higher elevations in Guatemala than the woods near Dueñas—that is, about 5000 feet above sea-level.

The iris in life is white.

2. Ceophlœus lineatus.

Picus lineatus, Linn. Syst. Nat. i. p. 174 [1].
Dryocopus lineatus, Scl. & Salv. P. Z. S. 1879, p. 532 [2].
Ceophlœus lineatus, Hargitt, Cat. Birds Brit. Mus. xviii. p. 508 [3].
Dryocopus scapularis, Lawr. (nec Vigors), Ann. Lyc. N. Y. vii. p. 333 [4].
Dryocopus fuscipennis, Scl. & Salv. P. Z. S. 1864, p. 366 [5].

C. scapulari similis, sed major, rostro corneo nec eburneo, subalaribus albicantioribus facile distinguendus.

Hab. PANAMA, Chiriqui (*Kellett & Wood* [3]), Santa Fé (*Arcé*), Lion Hill (*M'Leannan* [4][5]), Chepo (*Arcé*).—SOUTH AMERICA, from Colombia to Brazil [3].

This common South-American Woodpecker, whose range extends over nearly the whole of the northern part of the continent, and even reaches the south-western and eastern provinces of Brazil, entirely replaces *C. scapularis* in the State of Panama. We have several records of it from that State, a specimen obtained by Capt. Kellett and Capt. Wood in Chiriqui being the most westerly occurrence. Arcé sent us examples from Santa Fé and also from Chepo, and M'Leannan found it on the Line of the Panama Railway. The birds sent us by the latter collector were referred by Sclater and Salvin to *C. fuscipennis* of Western Ecuador, with an expressed doubt as to the distinctness of that bird from *C. lineatus*, and in the 'Nomenclator Avium Neotropicalium' they were considered identical. Hargitt, however, in his 'Catalogue,' resuscitates *C. fuscipennis* as a distinct species, but places the Panama birds with *C. lineatus*. On re-examining the question, and in view of the worn and faded condition of the types of *C. fuscipennis*, we do not hesitate to adhere to the opinion expressed in the

'Nomenclator,' and subsequently confirmed in the paper on Salmon's collection from Antioquia.

With regard to the extension of the range of this species to Costa Rica, as given by Hargitt, it would seem that he was induced, by Dr. Cabanis's note (J. f. Orn. 1862, p. 176) on three specimens sent to Berlin by Dr. von Frantzius and Hoffmann, to place all the Costa-Rica references to *C. scapularis* under *C. lineatus*. These are described as rather larger than Mexican examples, with a darker horn-coloured bill, and with the light parts under the wing of a purer white, without a yellowish tint. All these characters certainly point to *C. lineatus*, though Dr. Cabanis, looking upon his specimens as somewhat intermediate, called them *C. scapularis*, in which he has been followed by other writers on Costa-Rica birds. In the following year Cabanis and Heine described the same specimens as *C. mesorhynchus* (Mus. Hein. iv. Heft 2, p. 86, note), and further suggested that probably the same form occurred throughout Central America. This we now know to be not the case, as the bird found in Central America north of Costa Rica is certainly the same as that of Mexico.

Unfortunately a series of specimens from Costa Rica is not accessible to us, for the only example we have seen from that country is a female, and this appears to be a true *C. scapularis*, to which species Hargitt has already referred it.

In answer to enquiries, Mr. Ridgway writes that the only adult specimen in the U. S. National Museum appears to be intermediate between *C. scapularis* and *C. lineatus*. It therefore seems probable that in Costa Rica the two forms intergrade.

Subfam. *PICUMNINÆ*.

Cauda laxa haud scansoria, rectricibus rotundatis haud acutis.

Of the four genera contained in this subfamily, only one, *Picumnus*, is represented in Central America. Of the others, *Nesoctites* (a modification of *Picumnus*) is found in the island of Hispaniola. The remaining genera are both Old-World forms, viz.: *Verreauxia* of West Africa, and *Sasia* of the Indo-Malayan sub-region. *Picumnus* is also an Old-World genus, according to Hargitt, who includes *Vivia* within its limits.

PICUMNUS.

Picumnus, Temminck, Pl. Col. livr. 62 (1825); Hargitt, Cat. Birds Brit. Mus. xviii. p. 521.

Including the Old-World genus *Vivia* with two species, Hargitt admits thirty-three species of *Picumnus*, which we would reduce to thirty-two, as we do not consider *P. granadensis* separable from *P. olivaceus*. All the thirty American species are found in South America, the only one occurring within our limits being the bird just named.

1. Picumnus olivaceus.

Picumnus olivaceus, Lafr. Rev. Zool. 1845, pp. 7[1], 111[2]; Salv. P. Z. S. 1870, p. 212[3]; Scl. & Salv. P. Z. S. 1870, pp. 837[4], 839[5]; Hargitt, Cat. Birds Brit. Mus. xviii. p. 548[6].

Picumnus granadensis, Lafr. Rev. Zool. 1847, p. 78[7]; Lawr. Ann. Lyc. N. Y. vii. p. 333[8]; Hargitt, Cat. Birds Brit. Mus. xviii. p. 549[9].

Picumnus flavotinctus, Ridgw. Pr. U. S. Nat. Mus. xi. p. 543[10].

Supra saturate olivaceus, secundariis extus pallidiore flavo-olivaceo limbatis, capite summo nigro, nuchæ plumis albo pilei antici aurantio terminatis : subtus sordide olivaceus, gula pallidiore, plumis singulis stricte nigro limbatis, abdomine sordide flavido olivaceo flammulato; alis nigricanti-brunneis, remigibus ad basin et subalaribus albidis; cauda nigra, longitudinaliter flavido-albido tristriata; rostro et pedibus plumbeis. Long. tota circa 3·5, alæ 2·1, caudæ 1·1, tarsi 0·47, dig. med. absque ungue 0·4, dig. ext. 0·4.

♀ mari similis, pileo toto albo punctato. (Descr. maris et feminæ ex Bugaba, Panama. Mus. nostr.)

Hab. HONDURAS, Julian and San Pedro (*G. M. Whitely*[4][5]); COSTA RICA, Pozo Azul (*Zeledon*[10]); PANAMA, Mina de Chorcha, Bugaba (*Arcé*[3]), Lion Hill (*McLeannan*[8]), Obispo (*O. S.*).—COLOMBIA, Bogota[1], Cali[7]; ECUADOR[9].

In his Catalogue Hargitt admitted the birds described by Lafresnaye in 1845 as *Picumnus olivaceus*[1] and in 1847 as *P. granadensis*[7] as subspecies, basing their difference upon the colour of the spots on the anterior part of the crown—these in *P. olivaceus* being described as "orange-scarlet" and in *P. granadensis* as "golden-yellow." As the distribution of the two supposed forms, he gives Honduras and the neighbourhood of Bogota for the former, and the intermediate country of Panama, the northern portion of Colombia, and Western Ecuador for the latter. The assignment of the specimens to these disconnected areas is evidently extremely unlikely to be correct. On examining the specimens there is no doubt in the most marked individuals a perceptible difference of colour in the spots of the crown; moreover, on an average, in the Bogota specimens these spots seem the reddest and in the Panama birds the yellowest; but the differences are so blended by intermediate forms that we consider the evidence in favour of their being more than one species very insufficient, and more likely than not the difference is due to the age of the feathers themselves or to the age of the birds.

In 1874 Salvin examined the type of Lafresnaye's *P. granadensis* at Boston, and he then believed it to be only a young example of *P. olivaceus*, and this has been our opinion since.

In 1888 Mr. Ridgway described a Costa Rica *Picumnus* as *P. flavotinctus*, and with it he placed the Panama form, suggesting, however, that the bird might be a geographical race of *P. olivaceus*. No comparison is made with *P. granadensis*, the bird most nearly allied if distinct at all.

P. olivaceus is the only species of *Picumnus* which has the upper plumage olive, the chest plain olive, and the abdomen striped and not barred. Its range extends from North-eastern Honduras to the United States of Colombia, and thence southwards to Western Ecuador. Skins of it are by no means uncommon in the trade collections made in the neighbourhood of Bogota.

When staying at Obispo Station on the Panama Railway in 1873, Salvin had opportunities of watching birds of this species. They perch on trees like an ordinary insessorial bird, and never climb after the manner of Woodpeckers.

Order COCCYGES.

Suborder COCCYGES ANISODACTYLÆ.

Fam. MOMOTIDÆ.

Sclater, P. Z. S. 1857, p. 248; Murie, Ibis, 1872, p. 383; Sharpe, Cat. Birds Brit. Mus. xvii. p. 313 (1892).

The Momotidæ form a very homogeneous family of birds peculiar to the Neotropical Region. The nearest ally is no doubt the Iodidæ of the Greater Antilles, and a more remote relationship to the Alcedinidæ is hardly questioned. The chief connected memoirs on the family are three:—one by Mr. Sclater, published in 1857, in which four genera and seventeen species were admitted; one by Dr. Murie in 1872, in which the osteological characters of several species were examined, the genera admitted being also four, but not with the same limits as Mr. Sclater's. The third memoir is by Mr. Sharpe, who, in the 'Catalogue of Birds in the British Museum,' recognized seven genera and eighteen species. Unfortunately the key to the genera is, to a great extent, vitiated owing to a wrong estimate of the number of rectrices in several cases, and to the value placed on certain characters leading to an unnatural arrangement.

In revising the family we think that six genera are as many as can be recognized, *Urospatha* merging with *Baryphthengus*, and we are in some doubt if *Aspatha* should be separated from *Hylomanes*.

Five of these six genera have ten rectrices, *Momotus* alone having twelve. In *Baryphthengus* the antrorse loral feathers are longer than in any of the other genera and reach beyond the nostrils; in *Hylomanes* they are shortest, *Aspatha* hardly differing. Other characters are concisely included in the following key:—

A. Bill compressed, stout, serration of the tomia large.
    a. Rectrices 12 . . . . Momotus.
    b. Rectrices 10 . . . . Baryphthengus.
B. Bill wide, serration small; rectrices 10.
    c. Culmen rounded . . . . Eumomota.
    d. Culmen flattened, serration of tomia minute . . . . Prionornis *.
C. Bill moderate, tarsi relatively to the wing long; rectrices 10.
    e. Tail longer than the wing, serration of tomia moderate . . . . . Aspatha.
    f. Tail and wing subequal, serration of tomia small . . . . Hylomanes.

In the above key it will be seen that no use is made of the presence or absence of spatules at the end of the two central rectrices. These spatules are now known to be produced by the birds themselves, the feathers in a natural state being at the most narrowed at the place where the webs are subsequently stripped off. In 1873 (P. Z. S.

---

* A name suggested by Mr. Sclater in place of his *Prionirhynchus*, which is preoccupied [Crustacea: Jacquinot and Lucas, Voy. au Pôle Sud, Zool. iii. Crust. p. 8 (1853)].

p. 429) Salvin gave an account of this curious practice on the part of Motmots, with the evidence then forthcoming on the subject. Since then Mr. Cherrie has, as quoted below, watched young of *Momotus lessoni* in confinement performing the operation; so that there can be no further doubt on the subject. Instances in which the process is neglected or imperfectly executed often occur in individuals of the same species, so that the use of the character in a generic sense cannot be entertained.

Southern Mexico and Central America is the metropolis of the Momotidæ; all the genera are found within these limits, and three of them, *Eumomota*, *Aspatha*, and *Hylomanes*, do not occur elsewhere.

Dr. Gaumer, who during his long residence in Northern Yucatan had constant opportunity of studying the habits of the Motmots of that region, has published some interesting notes on them (Trans. Kansas Ac. Sc. viii. p. 63). After giving various native accounts of the way the birds acquire the spatules to the tail, which we need not repeat here, he goes on to say: " The Momotidæ all live beneath the surface of the earth; some in the deserted dens of the Armadillo and other burrowing quadrupeds; some live in caves, some in the crevices of the rocks and cliffs, while others take up their abode near the homes of men, living in their wells and 'senotes.' Their food consists of small frogs, worms, and other things which their subterranean abodes furnish them, with a few insects which they catch on the wing. They are seldom seen in bad weather, early in the morning, in the heat of the day, and never at night. This exclusion from light, and exposure to perpetual moisture, gives them a loose, pale flesh and almost colourless blood, and soft muscles, thus rendering them very lazy and stupid, though they sometimes retreat very quickly when the hunter tries to get a shot at them. The nests are made in some secluded corner of their underground homes. They consist of sticks and mud, or grass and mud, and are seldom large enough for the bare shafts of the tail-feathers to rest upon the rim; nor would this account for the mutilation of the feathers even were the conditions of the nest favourable, for the web of the feather is arranged laterally upon the shaft, and a vertical motion would be required to wear it away, whereas the movement of the tail is from side to side. Some of the Momotidæ are very tame, and seem to have no fear of man, but rather to prefer his company, making their nests in his wells and his cellars. . . . ." Dr. Gaumer's further remarks relate chiefly to *Eumomota superciliaris*, and will be found under the account of that species.

MOMOTUS.

Momotus, Brisson, Orn. iv. p. 465 (1760); Sharpe, Cat. Birds Brit. Mus. xvii. p. 318.
Prionites, Illiger, Prodr. p. 224 (1811).

Momotus is the most widely distributed genus of the family and contains the largest number of species. Its range extends from North-eastern Mexico and the southern side of the lower Rio Grande Valley to Eastern and Southern Brazil. The species of the genus readily divide into two groups—one containing those with the crown blue or black with a blue cincture, the other those with a chestnut head. The number of species admitted by Mr. Sharpe is eleven; Mr. Sclater recognizing ten in 1857. Of these five occur within our limits, viz. three of the first section and both the species of the second, which is peculiar to Western Mexico and Guatemala.

The bill of *Momotus* is stout and compressed, the culmen curved and transversely rounded without any definite ridge, the serrations of the tomia are large and extend along the middle portion of both maxilla and mandible; the antrorse loral feathers when directed forwards reach as far as the nostrils without covering them; the nostrils themselves are nearly round, and are at the extremity of the nasal fossa, with a membrane behind. The tarsi as compared with the wing are rather long: the tail consists of twelve feathers, the outer pair reaching a little beyond the ends of the under tail-coverts; the middle pair are usually trimmed by the bird so as to leave a spatule at the end.

α. *Pileus aut cæruleus aut niger cæruleo circumcinctus.*

1. Momotus lessoni.

Momotus lessoni, Less. Rev. Zool. 1842, p. 174[1]; Des Murs, Icon. Orn. t. 62[2]; Scl. P. Z. S. 1856, pp. 139[3], 285[4]; 1857, p. 253[5]; 1859, p. 387[6]; Moore, P. Z. S. 1859, p. 54[7]; Scl. & Salv. Ibis, 1859, p. 131[8]; P. Z. S. 1870, p. 837[9]; Salv. Ibis, 1860, p. 100[10]; 1872, p. 321[11]; P. Z. S. 1867, p. 150[12]; 1870, p. 201[13]; Cat. Strickl. Coll. p. 413[14]; Lawr. Ann. Lyc. N. Y. viii. p. 178[15]; ix. pp. 117[16], 204[17]; Bull. U. S. Nat. Mus. no. 4, p. 29[18]; v. Frantz. J. f. Orn. 1869, p. 311[19]; Boucard, P. Z. S. 1878, p. 48[20]; 1883, p. 453[21]; Sumichrast, La Nat. v. p. 239[22]; Nutting, Pr. U. S. Nat. Mus. v. p. 399[23]; vi. p. 387[24]; Ridgw. Pr. U. S. Nat. Mus. v. p. 501[25]; x. pp. 582[26], 591[27]; Zeledon, An. Mus. Nac. Costa Rica, 1887, p. 119[28]; Cherrie, Auk, 1892, p. 322[29]; Richmond, Pr. U. S. Nat. Mus. xvi. p. 510[30].
Momotus psalurus, Bp. Compt. Rend. xxxviii. p. 659 (1854)[31].
Prionites psalurus, Cab. J. f. Orn. 1861, p. 255[32].
Prionites momotus, Bp. P. Z. S. 1837, p. 114[33].

Supra olivaceo-viridis, capite summo nigro argenteo-cæruleo circumcincto, ad nucham cyaneo-purpureo tincto nigro distincte marginato; capitis lateribus nigris, cæruleo anguste limbatis: subtus paulo rufescentior, gula viridi tincta, plaga pectorali nigra cæruleo limbata; alis extus cærulescentioribus; cauda quoque cærulescente, rectricibus duabus mediis nigro terminatis. Long. tota circa 15·5, alæ 5·2, caudæ rectr. med. 8·5, rectr. latr. 3·0, rostri a rictu 1·7, tarsi 1·1. (Descr. feminæ ex Izamal, Yucatan. Mus. nostr.)
♂ feminæ similis.

Hab. MEXICO, Xacaltepec (*Deppe, in Mus. Berol.*), Orizaba, Cordova (*Sallé*[4], *Sumichrast*[22]), Huatusco, Cuichapa (*Ferrari-Perez*), Vera Cruz (*W. B. Richardson*), Playa Vicente (*Boucard*[6], *M. Trujillo*), Teotalcingo (*Boucard*[6]), Atoyac, Teapa (*Mrs. H. H. Smith*), Chimalapa (*Sumichrast*[18], *W. B. Richardson*), Guichicovi (*Sumichrast*[18][22]), Temax[21], Buctzotz and Peto in N. Yucatan (*G. F. Gaumer*), Merida (*Schott*[17]); BRITISH HONDURAS, Cayo and San Felipe in the western district (*F. Blancaneaux*); GUATEMALA (*Velasquez* [32], *Skinner* [8], *Constancia* [8] [14]), Pie de la Cuesta in San Marcos (*W. B. Richardson*), Retalhuleu (*O. S. & F. D. G.*, *W. B. Richardson*), Toliman (*W. B. R.*), Savana Grande, Alotenango, Dueñas, San Gerónimo, Coban, Lanquin, Choctum, Chisec (*O. S. & F. D. G.*); SALVADOR, San Miguel (*W. B. Richardson*); HONDURAS, San Pedro (*G. M. Whitely* [9]), Truxillo [27], Segovia River [26] (*Townsend*); NICARAGUA, Realejo (*A. Lesson* [1]), Chinandega (*W. B. Richardson*), Sucuya (*Nutting* [24]), Chontales (*Belt* [11]); COSTA RICA (*Hoffmann, v. Frantzius*), San José (*v. Frantzius* [19], *Carmiol* [16], *Boucard* [21], *Nutting* [23], *Cherrie* [29]), San Carlos, Dota Mts., Grecia (*Carmiol* [16]), Alajuela, Santa Ana, Las Trojas, Cartago, Naranjo de Cartago (*Zeledon* [28]), La Palma (*Nutting* [23]); PANAMA, David (*Bridges* [3], *Hicks* [15]), Cordillera de Tolé [12], Chitrá [13], Mina de Chorcha [13], Bugaba [13], Volcan de Chiriqui [13] (*Arcé*).

Momotus lessoni is the commonest species of the family in Mexico and Central America, having a wide range, extending from the middle of the State of Vera Cruz to the Pacific Ocean at Tehuantepec, to Northern Yucatan, and thence southwards to Costa Rica and the district of Chiriqui, where it appears to stop, and its place taken on the Line of the Panama Railway by the closely allied *M. subrufescens*. In the north, too, it is supplanted from the middle of Vera Cruz to the States of Tamaulipas and Nuevo Leon by *M. cœruleiceps*, but in this case there is a district on the confines of the ranges of the two birds in which intermediate forms are far from uncommon. In altitude *M. lessoni* also has a considerable range, for it occurs from near the sea-level to a height of between 3000 and 4000 feet in the mountains. Its haunts are in the forests, where it keeps to the undergrowth and the lower branches of the higher trees. The nest is made, like that of a Kingfisher, in a bank. Its shape and position is well described by Mr. Cherrie [29], who, quoting Mr. Zeledon, says that the bird is common and resident near San José, in Costa Rica. "The nests are built in the ground, some bank, like the side of a stream, being selected. The entrance tunnel extends back horizontally sometimes for a distance of six feet. At about half its length there is a sharp bend upwards for some six inches, then the course is again horizontal as far as the chamber occupied by the nest. The nest space is twelve or fourteen inches in diameter, being round, and about six inches high, with level floor and ceiling. A few rather coarse dry twigs are strewn over the floor. The eggs I am not acquainted with." Mr. Zeledon also informed Mr. Cherrie that "if one of these nests be opened at about the time the young are ready to leave the nest, it is found to be one of the dirtiest, foul-smelling places that can well be imagined. The young birds occupy the centre of the nest, while all about them, and especially at the sides of the opening, are piles of the excrement mixed with the pellets, composed of the hard chitinous parts of the beetles and other insects composing the chief food of the 'Bobos' that are ejected from the mouth. This mass is reeking with maggots."

Mr. Cherrie gives the following interesting notes on this species:—" On the 8th May, 1889, I bought five young birds, the pin-feathers not yet concealed, and the eye light sepia-brown. By the 25th of the same month they were fully feathered, the iris had changed to a decided chestnut shade, and the tail of one of the birds measured 3·55 inches. On the 28th the birds commenced imitating the notes of the adults; their eyes had become bright chestnut. With the first utterances of the notes of the adults the peculiar jerky motions of the tail commenced. It was most amusing to watch the four birds sitting in a row together, almost motionless, only giving the tail first a jerk to this side, then to that, now up and now down, to see it held for the space of a couple of minutes almost at right angles to the body, and then go with a whisk to the other side, the birds all the time uttering their peculiar cooing notes. On May 30th I measured the tail of one of the birds and found it to be 4·25 inches, an increase of ·7 inch in five days. I fed the birds on raw meat, and about this time they began to fight vigorously for their shares. If two happened to get hold of the same piece, neither was willing to let go, and each would close its eyes and hang on for dear life, both squealing as hard as they could. On 3rd June the serration of the bill began to show. On the 16th the tails were apparently full-grown, and the birds began to tear at the webs at the points of the middle pair of feathers. By the 1st July the tail-feathers were fully trimmed." He adds, " on one occasion I found the stomach of a bird I had shot filled with snails of a species having a delicate easily crushed shell. The birds I had in confinement greedily ate earthworms, and one day when I had placed a small live Warbler in the cage I returned in about half an hour's time and found the feet and tail of my Warbler protruding from the mouth of one of the Bobos!"

The specimens described by R. P. Lesson in 1842 were obtained by his brother Adolphe Lesson at Realejo, on the Pacific coast of Nicaragua [1].

2. Momotus cæruleiceps.

Prionites cæruleiceps, Gould, P. Z. S. 1836, p. 18 [1]; Cab. & Heine, Mus. Hein. ii. p. 113 [2].

Momotus cæruleiceps, Scl. P. Z. S. 1857, pp. 201 [3], 253 [4]; 1859, p. 367 [5]; 1864, p. 176 [6]; Baird, U. S. Bound. Surv., Birds, p. 7, t. 8 [7]; Ferrari-Perez, Pr. U. S. Nat. Mus. ix. p. 160 [8]; Sharpe, Cat. Birds Brit. Mus. xvii. p. 327 [9].

Momotus cæruleocephalus, Jard. & Selby, Ill. Orn. iv. t. 42 [10].

Momotus subhutu, Less. Descr. Mamm. et Ois. p. 265 (1847) [11].

M. lessoni affinis, sed capite summo omnino cæruleo distinguendus.

Hab. MEXICO (*Lesson* [11]), Tamaulipas (*Gould* [1]), Boquillo in Nuevo Leon (*Couch* [7]), Villa Grande, Hacienda de la Cruz, Rio Camarcho in Nuevo Leon (*F. B. Armstrong*), Sierra Madre above Ciudad Victoria, Xicotencal, Tampico, Valles (*W. B. Richardson*), Misantla, Colipa (*F. D. G.*), Cuesta de Misantla (*M. Trujillo*), Jalapa (*Sallé* [3], *de Oca* [5], *Ferrari-Perez* [8]), Santa Ana, Plan del Rio, Hacienda Tortugas, Rio San Juan Martin, Cuichapa (*Ferrari-Perez*).

Gould described this Motmot in 1836 from a specimen said to have come from Tamaulipas [1]; it was figured shortly afterwards by Jardine and Selby, from a specimen of unknown origin, under the name of *M. cœruleocephalus* [10], and it received yet another appellation from Lesson in 1847 [11]. Its range is restricted to the eastern portion of Mexico which extends from about the middle of the State of Vera Cruz northwards to Tamaulipas and Nuevo Leon. From the last-named States we have many specimens, sent us by Mr. Richardson and Mr. Armstroug. In the neighbourhood of Jalapa it is found with its head uniformly blue, but a little to the southward of this district, on the road from Vera Cruz to Cordova and beyond it at Playa Vicente, birds show a slight admixture of black in the centre of the crown, and are thus intermediate between *M. cœruleiceps* and *M. lessoni*, the prevalent species throughout the more southern portion of Mexico and the whole of Central America.

We have no special account of the habits of this species, which doubtless are like those of its close ally *M. lessoni*.

3. Momotus subrufescens.

Momotus subrufescens, Scl. Rev. Zool. 1853, p. 489 [1]; P. Z. S. 1857, p. 252 [2]; Lawr. Ann. Lyc.
  N. Y. vii. p. 318 [3]; Sharpe, Cat. Birds Brit. Mus. xvii. p. 321, t. 10. fig. 1 [4].
Momotus lessoni, Lawr. Ann. Lyc. N. Y. vii. p. 290 [5]; Scl. & Salv. P. Z. S. 1864, p. 362 [6].

M. lessoni quoque affinis, abdomine plerumque rufescentiore, corona capitis argenteo-cærulea ad nucham rufescente nec nigro limbata.

Hab. PANAMA, Lion Hill (*M'Leannan*), Chepo (*Arcé*).—COLOMBIA [1] [2]; VENEZUELA and
  Matto Grosso in BRAZIL [4].

Mr. Sclater separated this species from *M. swainsoni* (sive *bahamensis*), the bird of Trinidad and Tobago, basing his description on specimens from Santa Marta in Northern Colombia [1]. With this birds from the Line of the Panama Railway agree.

M. subrufescens can be readily distinguished from *M. lessoni* by the absence of the black margin to the back of the blue coronet, the feathers there being slightly edged with chestnut. The body, too, beneath, is more rufescent. The range of this bird in the State of Panama is very restricted, and does not seem to pass beyond the Line of the Railway, where, however, it is far from uncommon. In the more western portion of the State, where Arcé collected so industriously, *M. lessoni* alone is found *.

The range of *M. subrufescens* in South America is restricted to the northern coast-region of Colombia and Venezuela; but Mr. Sharpe suggests a separation between the birds from these countries, and further remarks that Mr. Herbert Smith's specimens from Matto Grosso are intermediate.

* Mr. Sharpe * places one of Arcé's specimens from Mina de Chorcha, a place not far from Chiriqui, under this species, but it is undoubtedly an example of the true *M. lessoni*.

β. Pileus castaneus.

4. Momotus mexicanus.

Momotus mexicanus, Swains. Phil. Mag. new ser. i. p. 442 (1827) [1]; Zool. Ill. ser. 2, ii. t. 81 [2]; Scl. P. Z. S. 1857, p. 253 [3]; 1859, p. 387 [4]; 1860, p. 252 [5]; Lawr. Mem. Bost. Soc. N. H. ii. p. 289 [6]; Bull. U. S. Nat. Mus. no. 4, p. 29 [7]; Sumichrast, La Nat. v. p. 239 [8]; Salv. Cat. Strickl. Coll. p. 413 [9]; P. Z. S. 1883, p. 426 [10]; Ferrari-Perez, Pr. U. S. Nat. Mus. ix. p. 160 [11]; Sharpe, Cat. Birds Brit. Mus. xvii. p. 328 [12].

Crybelus mexicanus, Cab. & Heine, Mus. Hein. ii. p. 112 [13].

Prionites mexicanus, Wagl. Isis, 1831, p. 528 [14].

Momotus martii, Jard. & Selby, Ill. Orn. i. t. 23 [15].

Supra olivaceo-virescens, capite summo toto castaneo, cervice postica quoque castanea ad dorsi colorem insensim transeunte; loris et regione suboculari cum tectricibus elongatis auricularibus nigris, his supra et subtus intense violaceis, macula in regione malari quoque violacea: subtus virescentior, gula cæruleo lavata, abdomine imo albicante, macula pectorali nigra; alis extus et cauda cærulescentibus, hujus rectricibus duabus mediis nigro terminatis, remigibus intus ad basin et subalaribus pallide cinnamomeis; rostro nigro; pedibus corylinis. Long. tota 14·0, alæ 4·9, caudæ rectr. med. 7·5, rectr. lat. 1·95, rostri a rictu 1·75, tarsi 1·05. (Descr. maris ex Tonala, Chiapas. Mus. nostr.)

♀ mari similis.

Hab. MEXICO (*Wagler* [14], *Galeotti* [9]), Mazatlan [6] (*Grayson, Xantus, Bischoff*), Presidio de Mazatlan (*Forrer*), Santiago and San Blas in the Territory of Tepic, Bolaños (*W. B. Richardson*), Plains of Colima (*Xantus* [6], *W. B. Richardson*), Colima, Beltran and Tonila in Jalisco (*W. Lloyd*), Temiscaltepec (*Bullock* [1]), Cuernavaca (*le Strange*), Chietla (*Ferrari-Perez* [11]), Amula, Rincon, and Chilpancingo in Guerrero (*Mrs. H. H. Smith*), Acapulco (*A. H. Markham* [10]), Rio Grande (*Boucard* [4]), Lucapa (*Mus. Liverp.* [3]), Golan (*Delattre* [3]), Quicatlan (*Deppe* [3]), Sola in Oaxaca (*M. Trujillo*), Chihuitan [7], Santa Efigenia [7][8], Barrio [7], Los Cues [7], Tonala [8], Tapanatepec [8] (*Sumichrast*), Tehuantepec [8] (*Sumichrast, W. B. Richardson*).

Momotus mexicanus is restricted in its range to Western Mexico, where it is found from Mazatlan to Tehuantepec, and is apparently by no means a rare species in that region. Grayson says [6] that it frequents the darkest woods of the Tierra Caliente, breeding in the ground like the Kingfishers, and laying three or four clear white eggs. He adds that it is a constant resident in the neighbourhood of Mazatlan and quite common at Tehuantepec. It subsists chiefly on insects.

Besides frequenting the lowlands bordering the Pacific Ocean, this species is found some distance in the interior, and has been recorded from Temiscaltepec, where Swainson's original specimen came from [1], and also from Cuernavaca and Chietla [11], places on the slope of the Cordillera at some elevation above sea-level.

Though found by all collectors who have visited Western Mexico, hardly any notice has been taken of the habits of this species. Sumichrast states that the iris is red, the bill black, the base of the mandible whitish horn-colour, and the feet dull cinereous [7].

The bird figured by Jardine and Selby under the name of *Momotus martii* was one of Bullock's Mexican specimens and bought at the sale of his collection. It has, of course, nothing to do with *M. martii*, Spix.

5. Momotus castaneiceps.

Momotus castaneiceps, Gould, P. Z. S. 1854, p. 154 [1]; Scl. P. Z. S. 1857, p. 254 [2]; Salv. Ibis, 1861, p. 354 [3]; Sharpe, Cat. Birds Brit. Mus. xvii. p. 329 [4].

M. mexicano similis, capite summo intense castaneo, tectricibus auricularibus elongatis fere omnino nigris, plaga malari violacea nulla, macula pectorali nigra majore facile distinguendus. Long. tota circa 14·5, alæ 5·2, caudæ rectr. med. 7·5, rectr. lat. 1·5, rostri a rictu 1·6, tarsi 1·1.

Hab. GUATEMALA (*Gould* [1], *Mus. Liverpool* [2], *Mus. Philad. Ac.* [2], *Mus. Bremen* [2]), Valley of the Rio Motagua from Guastatoya and La Magdalena to Gualan (*O. S. & F. D. G.* [3]).

The late John Gould described this species in 1854 from a specimen sent him from Guatemala [1], and in 1857 Mr. Sclater stated [2] that he had seen specimens in the Bremen Museum also from Guatemala, and others in the Museum of the Academy of Philadelphia and that of Lord Derby at Liverpool. He also gives Coban in Guatemala, on the authority of Delattre, as the precise locality where this bird is found. The latter statement we think is very doubtfully correct, as we have never met with a single specimen of it in any of the large collections of bird-skins from Coban and its neighbourhood which we have examined.

The only part of Guatemala that we know of where *Momotus castaneiceps* occurs is the valley of the Motagua river, between the narrow gorge near Guastatoya and La Magdalena, and the denser forest which commences above Gualan. This includes the whole of the plain of Zacapa, which is comparatively open country, large cacti and mimosa trees being the characteristic plants. Here *M. castaneiceps* is by no means an uncommon bird, and individuals may frequently be seen along the roadside, their habits being precisely like those of *M. lessoni* and other well-known members of the family.

Though closely allied to *M. mexicanus*, this species is readily distinguished by the deeper colour of the chestnut head, and the nearly total absence of the violet-blue marks on either side of the black band which runs from the lores to the ear-coverts. The black feathers which form the pectoral patch are also larger.

BARYPHTHENGUS.

Baryphthengus, Cabanis & Heine, Mus. Hein. ii. p. 114 (1859).

Urospatha, Salvadori, Atti R. Acc. Sc. Tor. iv. p. 179 (1868); Sharpe, Cat. Birds Brit. Mus. xvii. p. 314.

The type of this genus is the *Tutu* of Azara, *Baryphonus ruficapillus* of Vieillot.

With this bird we place *Urospatha martii*, as has been already done by Count Berlepsch. *Urospatha*, so far as we can see, differs only in having spatules to the ends of the central rectrices, an ornament produced by the bird itself, and, as our specimens show, often absent.

The number of rectrices is ten, the bill stout and compressed, and the serrations to both the maxilla and mandible very large, even coarser than in *Momotus*. The antrorse loral feathers are long, the radii being distinct; these feathers reach beyond the nostril when stretched forwards, lying below and not covering the opening. The nostrils themselves are at the extremity of the nasal fossa, are slightly oval, and bordered behind by membrane. The tarsi are rather strong and have about the same relative proportion to the wing as is found in *Eumomota*, and are thus comparatively shorter than in *Momotus*, but the difference is small.

Of the two species of *Baryphthengus*, *B. martii* occurs in the whole of the Upper Amazonian region, in Colombia, and in Central America as far north as Nicaragua, while *B. ruficapillus* is found in Eastern and South-eastern Brazil and Paraguay.

1. **Baryphthengus martii.**

Prionites martii, Spix, Av. Bras. ii. p. 64, t. 60[1].

Momotus martii, Gray, Gen. Birds, i. p. 68[2]; Cassin, Pr. Ac. Phil. 1860, p. 136[3]; Lawr. Ann. Lyc. N. Y. vii. p. 290[4]; ix. p. 117[5]; Salv. P. Z. S. 1867, p. 151[6]; 1870, p. 201[7]; Ibis, 1872, p. 320[8]; v. Frantz. J. f. Orn. 1869, p. 311[9].

Urospatha martii, Salvad. Atti R. Acc. Sc. Tor. iv. p. 179[10]; Boucard, P. Z. S. 1878, p. 49[11]; Tacz. Orn. Pér. iii. p. 111[12]; Zeledon, An. Mus. Nac. Costa Rica, 1887, p. 119[13]; Sharpe, Cat. Birds Brit. Mus. xvii. p. 314[14].

Momotus semirufus, Scl. Rev. Zool. 1853, p. 489[15]; P. Z. S. 1857, p. 254[16]; Schl. Mus. Pays-Bas, *Momotus*, p. 5[17]; Scl. & Salv. P. Z. S. 1864, p. 363[18].

Supra viridis, capite, cervice et corpore subtus usque ad medium ventris læte castaneis, gutture paulo dilutiore; loris, capitis lateribus cum tectricibus auricularibus et plaga pectorali nigerrimis; hypochondriis et ventre imo, tibiis et tectricibus subcaudalibus viridibus cæruleo tinctis; remigibus nigris, extrorsum saturate cyaneis, in pogoniis internis apud rhachidem nigram viridibus, alula spuria cyaneo marginata; cauda subtus nigra, supra viridi cærulea, rhachidibus nigris; rostro nigro; pedibus saturate corylinis. Long. tota 22·0, alæ 6·3, caudæ rectr. med. 13·5, rectr. lat. 2·8, rostri a rictu 2·4, tarsi 1·3. (Descr. maris ex Panama. Mus. nostr.)

♀ mari similis.

Hab. NICARAGUA, Chontales (*Belt*[8]), La Libertad (*W. B. Richardson*); COSTA RICA (*Durando*[10]), San Carlos (*v. Frantzius*[9], *Boucard*[11]), Pacuare (*v. Frantzius*[9], *Carmiol*[5]), Angostura (*Carmiol*[14]), Naranjo de Cartago, Jimenez (*Zeledon*[12]); PANAMA, Santa Fé[6], Santiago[6], Calobre[7] (*Arcé*), Lion Hill (*M'Leannan*[4][18]), R. Nercua (*C. J. Wood*[3]).—SOUTH AMERICA, from Colombia[15] and Upper Amazons[1], to Peru[12] and Bolivia[14]; Para[1].

Baryphthengus martii was discovered by Spix during his travels in Brazil, and named after his companion and coadjutor in their great work on the fauna and flora of that vast region. The specimens obtained were from the woods of Para, at the mouth of the Amazons Valley, a district in which it has not since been met with; but several recent travellers have found it in the Upper Amazons, so that the range of the species probably embraces the whole of the forest country at the base and lower slopes of the Eastern Andes from Bolivia to Colombia. Crossing the Cordillera of the latter country it occurs in the valley of the Cauca river, where Salmon found it near Remedios and Neche; in Western Ecuador, at Chimbo, where Stolzmann and Siemiradzki secured specimens; and near Santa Marta, examples from which locality were described by Mr. Sclater as *Momotus semirufus* [15]. In Central America it has been traced from Darien and the Isthmus of Panama throughout that State; it occurs also in Costa Rica and in Nicaragua, where Belt met with it at Chontales, and where Mr. Richardson has since found it. Regarding *Momotus semirufus* of Sclater, it may be observed that the name was originally given under the impression that *Prionites martii* of Spix was the same as *Momotus platyrhynchus* of Leadbeater. When this error was discovered, *M. semirufus* was still maintained as distinct from *P. martii* by Schlegel and others, on the ground of slight distinctions of colour between the two birds. The series now collected in the British Museum proves, we think, that there is no real difference between the northern and western birds and those from the eastern side of the Andes. All, therefore, should pass under Spix's name.

Very little is on record concerning the habits of this species. M. Boucard, who found small flocks of it in the forests of San Carlos, in Costa Rica, says it is a very noisy bird, its cry resembling that of *Momotus lessoni* but louder [11]. Salmon noted the iris as dark, and he found the remains of beetles in the stomachs of those he dissected.

The central rectrices of certain specimens of this species are often not nibbled so as to leave the spatule at the end; in others the operation is imperfectly performed. In Spix's type the feathers are entire. The presence of the spatule tail, therefore, is not valid as a generic character.

EUMOMOTA.

Eumomota, Sclater, P. Z. S. 1857, p. 257; Sharpe, Cat. Birds Brit. Mus. xvii. p. 317.
Spathophorus, Cabanis & Heine, Mus. Hein. ii. p. 112 (1859).

This genus was separated from *Momotus* by Mr. Sclater in 1857, and a comparison made between it and *Prionornis*, the other genus of wide-billed Momotidæ. It differs from *Prionornis* in having the culmen of the bill rounded transversely and the sides of the maxilla on either side of the culmen are not hollowed out; the serrations of the tomia of both maxilla and mandible are much smaller than in *Momotus*, and extend nearly to the tip; the antrorse loral feathers are much as in *Momotus*, and do not reach beyond the nostril, which is also like that of *Momotus*. The characteristic markings of the plumage are not quite like those of any other of the Momotidæ;

the conspicuous black stripe, bordered with blue, of the middle of the throat perhaps represents the black pectoral spot of many other species; the conspicuous superciliary stripe is a modification of the blue cincture of *Momotus lessoni* and its allies. The tail differs from that of all other species in having the two central feathers very much longer than the rest, and ending in a very large spatule, between which and the ends of the next pair of feathers the shaft is denuded.

The range of *Eumomota* is restricted to Central America—in the north occurring in Yucatan and Tehuantepec, and in the south not passing beyond the limits of Costa Rica.

1. Eumomota superciliaris.

Prionites superciliaris, Sandbach, Rep. Brit. Assoc. 1837, p. 99 [1].

Prionites (Crypticus) superciliaris, Jard. & Selby, Ill. Orn. iv. t. 18 [2].

Eumomota superciliaris, Scl. P. Z. S. 1857, p. 257 [3]; Scl. & Salv. Ibis, 1859, p. 132 [4]; P. Z. S. 1870, p. 837 [5]; Owen, Ibis, 1861, p. 64 [6]; Lawr. Ann. Lyc. N. Y. ix. p. 204 [7]; Bull. U. S. Nat. Mus. no. 4, p. 30 [8]; v. Frantz. J. f. Orn. 1869, p. 311 [9]; Scl. Ibis, 1873, p. 373 [10]; Boucard, P. Z. S. 1878, p. 49 [11]; 1883, p. 453 [12]; Sumichrast, La Nat. v. p. 239 [13]; Nutting, Pr. U. S. Nat. Mus. v. p. 399 [14]; vi. p. 387 [15]; Salv. Cat. Strickl. Coll. p. 413 [16]; Ibis, 1889, p. 371 [17]; 1890, p. 88 [18]; Gaumer, Trans. Kansas Ac. Sc. viii. p. 65 (1883) [19]; Stone, Pr. Ac. Phil. 1890, p. 206 [20]; Sharpe, Cat. Birds Brit. Mus. xvii. p. 317 [21].

Spathophorus superciliaris, Cab. & Heine, Mus. Hein. ii. p. 112 [22]; Cab. J. f. Orn. 1861, p. 255 [23].

Crypticus superciliosus, Swains. An. in Men. p. 358 [24]; Less. Descr. Mamm. et Ois. p. 267 [21].

Crypticus apiaster, Less. Rev. Zool. 1842, p. 174 [26].

Momotus yucatanensis, Cabot, Pr. Bost. Soc. N. H. 1843, p. 156 [27].

Viridis, dorso medio cinnamomeo lavato, superciliis latis argenteo-cæruleis, loris et lineis supra et infra oculos cum tectricibus auricularibus elongatis nigris, macula post oculari cinnamomea, plumis nigris infra oculos et ad mandibulæ basin cæruleo terminatis, gutture medio nigro utrinque plumis elongatis cæruleis marginato, abdomine cinnamomeo; alis extus cæruleis nigro terminatis, tectricibus majoribus nigris; cauda cærulea, rectricibus omnibus rhachidibus nigris et nigro terminatis; rostro nigro; pedibus corylinis. Long. tota circa 15·0, alæ 4·6, caudæ rectr. med. 9·3, rectr. lat. 2·6, rostri a rictu 0·9, tarsi 0·85. (Descr. maris ex San Gerónimo, Guatemala. Mus. nostr.)

♀ mari similis.

Hab. Mexico, Bay of Campeche (*Mus. Brit.* [1][2][21]), N. Yucatan (*G. F. Gaumer* [12]), Merida (*Schott* [7]), Temax [19], Buctzotz, Peto, Meco I. [17] (*G. F. Gaumer*), Tekanto, Tunkas, Ticul (*Stone & Baker* [20]), Tapana [8][13], Cacoprieto [8][13], Santa Efigenia [13] in Tehuantepec (*Sumichrast*); Guatemala [16], Zacapa and Motagua Valley, San Gerónimo [6] (*O. S. & F. D. G.* [21], *R. Owen*), Retalhuleu (*W. B. Richardson* [21]), San José de Guatemala [21] to Escuintla and Palin, Medio Monte (*O. S. & F. D. G.*); Salvador, La Libertad, San Miguel (*W. B. Richardson*); Honduras, San Pedro (*G. M. Whitely* [5]); Nicaragua, Chontales (*Belt* [10]), Sucuyá (*Nutting* [15]), Chinandega (*W. B. Richardson* [20]); Costa Rica (*Ellendorf* [22]), Bebedero in Nicoya (*Arcé* [21]), La Palma (*Nutting* [14]), Barranca (*Boucard* [11]).

This species, the most beautiful of its family, was first made known to science at the

Meeting of the British Association held at Liverpool in 1837, by Mr. Sandbach, the Curator of the Museum of that town, to whom, so we are informed by Jardine and Selby, upwards of twenty specimens were brought by a vessel sailing from Campeche. One of these was acquired by Sir William Jardine and figured by Jardine and Selby in the following year. The bird described by Swainson as *Crypticus superciliosus* was doubtless from the same source. The same Motmot was soon afterwards found in Yucatan by Cabot, who gave it the name of *Momotus yucatanensis*, and it has been noticed by all subsequent travellers in that country. The only other portion of Mexican territory in which it occurs is the Isthmus of Tehuantepec, where Sumichrast obtained specimens. From Tehuantepec it occurs all along the Pacific coast-region of Central America as far as Costa Rica, and is very abundant in some places in the hotter parts of the country. Thus, in March 1874, it was a very common bird all along the road between Escuintla in Guatemala and the port of San José. Further inland we met with it as high as the village of Palin, which is on the slope of the cordillera between Escuintla and Amatitlan. In the interior of Guatemala it occurs in the plains of Salamá and Zacapa, a region of large cacti and mimosa trees. It is not a forest bird, but keeps to the second-growth woods and more open districts, and thus probably has increased considerably in numbers with the destruction of the older forests of the coast-region bordering the Pacific Ocean.

On the eastern side of Central America we have, besides the records of it in Yucatan already mentioned, only notices of its occurrence at San Pedro in Honduras and in Chontales, where Belt met with it. It is also said to occur near Comayagua. In Costa Rica its range seems confined to the country bordering the Gulf of Nicoya and the Pacific Ocean. Beyond Costa Rica it has not been traced, so that *Eumomota superciliaris* is one of the marked and characteristic species of Central America.

It has been suggested that there are two forms of this species, a western and an eastern race—the former redder, the latter bluer. Variation to some extent certainly exists, but this appears to be individual and not localized in any way.

In habits *Eumomota superciliaris* is sluggish, fearless, and silent during the greater part of the year; but from the following interesting note on its breeding-habits from the pen of Mr. Robert Owen it would appear that it is both noisy and active during the breeding-season. He writes from San Gerónimo, Vera Paz, 21st May, 1860:—
"This appears to be the height of the breeding-season with the 'Torovoces' (='Bull-voice,' a local name for this species). They are in full song, if their croaking note may be so termed, and are as noisy and busy now as they are mute and torpid during the rest of the year. I do not know of any sound that will convey a better idea of the note than that produced by the laboured respiration occurring after each time the air is exhausted in the lungs by the spasms of the hooping-cough.

"The nest of the 'Torovoz' is subterranean, and is usually found in the banks of rivers, or of watercourses which empty into them. The excavation is horizontal, and at a distance from the surface, varying with the depth of the barranco or bank in which it is situated. The size of the orifice is sufficient to allow the bare arm to be introduced, the shape being round and regular for three or at most for eight feet, where the shaft terminates in a circular chamber about eight inches in diameter and five inches high. In this chamber the eggs, usually four in number, are deposited on the bare soil. The banks of the river which winds through the plain of San Gerónimo are full of excavations made by this bird—that is to say, in such places where the soil is light and the bank chops down perpendicularly. It is a simple matter to hit upon those that are inhabited, as the entrance to the abandoned ones will be found perfectly smooth, whereas the mouth of those which contain eggs or young is ploughed up in two parallel furrows made by the old bird when passing in and out. The 'Torovoz' is exceedingly tame, and, when startled from its nest, will, perched upon a bough a few yards distant, watch the demolition of its habitation with a degree of attention and fancied security more easily imagined than described."

The eggs are glossy white, and measure 1.0×0.8 inch.

Dr. Gaumer was also much interested in *Eumomota superciliaris*, and of it he writes [19] :—" During my residence of nearly four months in the city of Temax, near the north coast of Yucatan, about twenty of these birds lived in a well from which I used to draw water every day. The well was almost forty feet deep, had been cut through a porous shell-limestone, and its walls contained many cavities, into which a man could crawl many feet, but was obliged to back out. Within these cavities the Motmots lived, and oftentimes very poisonous little reptiles called 'cauchæ' by the natives. Risking the poisonous serpents, I have frequently gone many yards into these caverns to investigate the home of the Motmots and their work therein, and I have always come out feeling well repaid for all the danger, having invariably seen something new and interesting. At one time I have found only the nest, with four or six roundish, white eggs, with the shell so thin and transparent that the yolk was plainly visible; at another I have found the young birds in almost every stage of development—those with the tail-feathers just starting growth being always the most interesting. The feathers all seem to grow alike to a certain point, except the middle ones, which are always a little broader towards the end, then all cease to grow except the two middle ones, which soon pass the others by about an inch and a half. Up to this point the webs of these two feathers are just the same throughout, except the subterminal portion, which is much narrower. Thus far no mutilation has taken place, but as soon as these feathers exceed the others a little more the webs begin to disappear, and the outer web of each feather is taken off first. This, however, is not always the case, as the inner webs sometimes go first. In a very few cases have I ever seen a web trimmed further up than just to the ends of the other tail-feathers; and just as these pass the shorter ones, so are they trimmed until their growth ceases.

"I have never seen the bird arrange its feathers, and especially not its tail, when above ground, though I have seen them work for a long time with the bill arranging the tail, while they were in the well—catching hold of it and drawing it round, first on one side, then upon the other, always using the point and not the whole of the bill.

" On examining the bill, it is found to be dentated at the middle portion and smooth at the tip and base. The smooth portion at the tip of the upper mandible fits very closely with the lower one, something after the fashion of scissors, and the bill therefore is well adapted to the work of feather-trimming.

" On closer inspection of the shaft, we find that traces of a web still remain, showing that it did not come so by a natural growth; so that after a careful examination of the structure of the bill, and considering the unevenness of the shaft where the webs are missing, as well as the time of disappearance of the latter, we must conclude that what nature does not do by narrowing the feather, the bird by its natural instinct of beauty and symmetry does by its bill."

Dr. Gaumer further states [11] that he has seen as many as a hundred birds issue from a single well or " senote."

PRIONORNIS.

Crypticus, Swainson, Classif. Birds, ii. p. 338 (1837) (nec Latreille).
Prionirhynchus, Sclater, P. Z. S. 1857, p. 256 (nec Jacquin and Lucas, 1854); Sharpe, Cat. Birds Brit. Mus. xvii. p. 315.

In some respects this genus is the most definite of the Momotidæ; its wide, flattened, curved bill with its distinct ridge along the culmen, which is even hollowed out for the greater part of its length, is not like the bill of the members of any of the other genera. On each side of the culmen the bill is concave instead of convex, as in all the others, and the serrations of the maxilla and mandible are exceedingly fine and numerous. The tarsi are considerably shorter in proportion to the wings than in the rest of the family, and the feet relatively smaller. The antrorse loral feathers are short, not reaching nearly to the line of the round nostrils. The tail consists of ten feathers, which are graduated much as in *Momotus*.

Two species of *Prionornis* are known, both of them occurring within our limits; of these, *P. platyrhynchus* has a wide range in the Valley of the Upper Amazons, is found in the State of Panama, and as far north as Nicaragua. The other species, *P. carinatus*, is restricted to Eastern Central America, from British Honduras to Nicaragua, and has also been recorded from Costa Rica.

Mr. Sclater's name *Prionirhynchus* being unfortunately preoccupied in Crustacea, he suggests *Prionornis* as a substitute for it.

1. Prionornis platyrhynchus.

Momotus platyrhynchus, Leadbeater, Trans. Linn. Soc. xvi. p. 92[1]; Jard. & Selb. Ill. Orn. iii. t. 106[2].
Crypticus platyrhynchus, Swains. Classif. Birds, ii. p. 338[3]; Cassin, Pr. Ac. Phil. 1860, p. 136[4]; Lawr. Ann. Lyc. N. Y. vii. p. 290[5].

59*

Prionirhynchus platyrhynchus, Scl. P. Z. S. 1857, p. 256[6]; Scl. & Salv. P. Z. S. 1864, p. 362[7]; 1867, p. 279[8]; Salv. P. Z. S. 1867, p. 151[9]; Ibis, 1872, p. 321[10]; Lawr. Ann. Lyc. N. Y. ix. p. 117[11]; v. Frantz. J. f. Orn. 1869, p. 311[12]; Zeledon, An. Mus. Nac. Costa Rica, 1887, p. 119[13]; Sharpe, Cat. Birds Brit. Mus. xvii. p. 315[14].

Crypticus martii, Bp. (nec Spix) P. Z. S. 1837, p. 119[15]; Consp. Av. i. p. 165[16].

Supra viridis, capite, cervice et pectore læte castaneis, loris et regione suboculari et auricularibus nigris, plaga permagna pectorali quoque nigra, mento et abdomine viridibus; alis nigris, extrorsum viridi limbatis; cauda subtus nigra, supra viridi, rhachidibus et rectricibus duabus mediis ad apicem nigris; rostro nigro; pedibus saturate corylinis. Long. tota circa 12·0, alæ 4·3, caudæ rectr. med. 6·8, rectr. lat. 2·0, rostri a rictu 1·75, tarsi 0·7. (Descr. maris ex Panama. Mus. nostr.)

♀ mari similis.

Hab. NICARAGUA, Chontales (*Belt*[10]), Blewfields (*Wickham*[8]); COSTA RICA (*v. Frantzius*[12]), Atirro (*Carmiol*[11]), Barranca, Angostura (*Carmiol*[11], *Zeledon*[13]), Jimenez (*Zeledon*[13]); PANAMA, Santa Fé (*Arcé*[9]), Lion Hill (*M'Leannan*[5][7]), Chepo (*Arcé*[14]), R. Nercua (*C. J. Wood*[4]).—SOUTH AMERICA, from Colombia[16] to Ecuador and Upper Amazons Valley[14].

The similarity of the colour of the plumage of this bird to that of *Baryphthengus martii* has led to their being mistaken for the same species. But besides the smaller size of the present bird, a glance at the formation of the bill of the two birds at once reveals their complete distinctness.

Prionornis platyrhynchus was described by Leadbeater in 1833, and shortly afterwards figured in Jardine and Selby's 'Illustrations of Ornithology'; but for many years little was known about it until specimens were obtained on the Isthmus of Darien by Lieut. Michler's party, and shortly afterwards others were secured by M'Leannan on the Line of the Panama Railway. We now know of its occurrence throughout the State of Panama, in Costa Rica, and in the eastern provinces of Nicaragua. It occurs also in the valley of the Cauca river in Colombia and in Eastern Ecuador and Peru. Its range therefore almost exactly corresponds with that of *Baryphthengus martii*, but it has not yet been found in Western Ecuador or in Bolivia.

Of its habits we can find nothing recorded.

2. **Prionornis carinatus.**

Prionites carinatus, DuBus, Bull. Ac. Brux. xiv. pt. 2, p. 108[1]; Rev. Zool. 1848, p. 249[2].

Crypticus carinatus, Bp. Consp. Av. i. p. 165[3].

Prionirhynchus carinatus, Scl. P. Z. S. 1857, p. 257, t. 128[4]; 1858, p. 357[5]; Scl. & Salv. Ibis, 1859, p. 132[6]; Taylor, Ibis, 1860, p. 117[7]; Salv. Ibis, 1872, p. 321[8]; Boucard, P. Z. S. 1878, p. 49[9]; Ridgw. Pr. U. S. Nat. Mus. x. p. 591[10]; Sharpe, Cat. Birds Brit. Mus. xvii. p. 316[11].

Supra omnino viridis, fronte tantum castaneo tincta, superciliis læte cæruleis; loris, regione suboculari et tectricibus auricularibus nigris, plaga permagna pectorali quoque nigra: subtus viridis pallidior, mento tantum cæruleo; subalaribus obscure castaneis; cauda cæruleo-viridi, rectricibus mediis nigro terminatis; rostro nigro; pedibus obscure corylinis. Long. tota circa 12·0, alæ 4·5, caudæ rectr. med. 6·8, rectr. lat. 2·05, rostri a rictu 1·85, tarsi 0·7. (Descr. exempl. ex Belize, Brit. Honduras. Mus. nostr.)

Hab. BRITISH HONDURAS, Belize (*Blancaneaux* [11]); GUATEMALA [1] [2] [4] (*O. S. & F. D. G.*), Chixoy Valley near Santa Ana? (*O. S.*); HONDURAS, Lake Yojoa (*G. C. Taylor* [5] [6] [7]), Segovia river (*Townsend* [10]); NICARAGUA, Chontales (*Belt* [8]); COSTA RICA, San Carlos (*Boucard* [9]).

Specimens of this well-marked species have come before us at rare intervals and very few in number, though the bird is spread over a wide area in Central America.

It was first described by Vicomte DuBus from a specimen from Guatemala in the Brussels Museum. A figure of this bird accompanies Mr. Sclater's memoir on Momotidæ in the 'Proceedings of the Zoological Society.' We have seen a few other specimens from Guatemala, but we are not certain of the exact origin of any of these. *P. carinatus* never came directly under our notice, though Salvin believes he saw a bird of this species when riding in March 1874 near the banks of the Rio Chixoy, not far from Santa Ana and the remarkable gorge called La Campana.

A specimen was found in one of the collections sent us by Mr. F. Blancaneaux from the neighbourhood of Belize. The late Capt. G. C. Taylor secured one near Lake Yojoa in Honduras, which he shot in dense forest between Taulevi and the lake, when sitting on a low branch of brushwood beneath some lofty mahogany trees [7].

Mr. Townsend secured two specimens on the Segovia river in June. Belt met with it at Chontales in Nicaragua; and M. Boucard includes the species in his list of Costa Rica birds, a specimen having been obtained by him at San Carlos in February, and he remarked that the bird was to be seen in the forest in pairs. This last record is the only one we have from Costa Rica, but there seems no reason to doubt the identification; as both *P. platyrhynchus* and *P. carinatus* occur together in Nicaragua, they may also be found in the same locality in Costa Rica.

ASPATHA.

Aspatha, Sharpe, Cat. Birds Brit. Mus. xvii. pp. 313, 331 (1892).

In several points this genus agrees with *Hylomanes* rather than with any of the other genera of Momotidæ. The bill has a rounded culmen with no concave depression on either side, but it is not nearly so compressed as in *Momotus*, and the serrations of the maxilla and mandible are much more feeble; the antrorse loral feathers are short, and these feathers, as well as the region round the eye, are buff, though the ear-coverts are black, and there is a black pectoral spot. The tarsi are long in comparison with the wings, and the tail of ten (*not twelve*) feathers is graduated, the points of the central pair are never trimmed into spatules. *Aspatha* is thus intermediate between *Hylomanes* and *Momotus*, and for this reason Strickland united all the genera of the family under *Momotus*. Mr. Sclater, on the other hand, placed *A. gularis* with *Hylomanes*. On the whole we think it best to retain Mr. Sharpe's genus *Aspatha*, but the characters are not very pronounced, and in associating *Aspatha* with *Baryphthengus* in the same section of his key, as Mr. Sharpe has done, he has, we consider, suggested a very unnatural arrangement.

Aspatha only contains one species, *A. gularis*, a bird of the upland forests of certain districts of Guatemala.

1. Aspatha gularis.

Prionites gularis, Lafr. Rev. Zool. 1840, p. 130 [1].

Momotus gularis, Strickl. Contr. Orn. 1849, p. 33, t. 5 [2].

Hylomanes gularis, Scl. P. Z. S. 1857, p. 256 [3]; Scl. & Salv. Ibis, 1859, p. 131 [4]; Salv. Cat. Strickl. Coll. p. 414 [5].

Aspatha gularis, Sharpe, Cat. Birds Brit. Mus. xvii. p. 331 [6].

Viridis, supra fere unicolor, loris et regione oculari pallide cinnamomeis, tectricibus auricularibus elongatis et plaga pectorali nigris; gutture et abdomine cæruleis, pectore et hypochondriis olivaceo tinctis; alis et cauda dorso fere concoloribus, hac ad apicem cæruleo tincta, rhachidibus nigris; rostri maxilla cornea, mandibula et pedibus flavidis. Long. tota circa 11·0, alæ 4·0, caudæ rectr. med. 5·3, rectr. lat. 1·75, rostri a rictu 1·3, tarsi 1·0.

♀ mari similis.

Hab. GUATEMALA [1] [2] [3] (*Constancia* [5], *Skinner* [4]), Santa Maria near Quezaltenango (*W. B. Richardson*), Volcan de Fuego, Dueñas, Barranco Hondo near Alotenango (*O. S. & F. D. G.*), Cunen (*F. Sarg*).

Aspatha gularis is not known to occur outside the boundaries of the Republic of Guatemala, and it is hardly known beyond a limited district in that country, viz. the oak-region of the main cordillera situated between 4000 and 7000 feet above the sea-level. It has also been reported from Cunen in the department of Huehuetenango in an elevated district, a spur of the Cordillera, where Quezals and other peculiarly upland species are found.

When staying at Dueñas in 1873–74 we saw many birds of this species in the oak-forests of the Volcan de Fuego, where they frequented the undergrowth and had all the sluggish, quiet habits of the other members of the family. A good many specimens were brought to us by Indian hunters, apparently uninjured, but we were not able to keep them alive for more than a few days. Some of them would often remain motionless in the hand for several minutes, and even allow themselves to be laid down on a table without stirring, and then they would come suddenly as it were to life. Their food would be held in the bill for some time without any movement and then suddenly swallowed. All their motions were done in this spasmodic way, but without the slightest fear or uneasiness or wish to escape.

The breeding-habits of this species never came under our observation.

As skins of *A. gularis* do not occur in the collections of the native hunters of Coban, the species is not common in collections. Strickland's specimen was sent·him by Constancia, who resided in the city of Antigua Guatemala, not far from the Volcan de Fuego and the oak-forests frequented by this bird.

HYLOMANES.

Hylomanes, Lichtenstein, Abh. Ak. Wissensch. Berl. 1838, p. 449; Sharpe, Cat. Birds Brit. Mus. xvii. p. 332.

Hylomanes was defined by Lichtenstein to contain the singular bird known as *H. momotula*, the smallest of the Momotidæ, and on that account suggestive of a closer relationship with the diminutive Todidæ of the Greater Antilles than shown by any of the larger members of the family.

With a bill similar to that of *Aspatha*, the antrorse loral feathers are still shorter and their points less distinctly visible. The ear-coverts as usual are black, but there is no black pectoral spot. The tarsi are long, bearing the same proportion to the wing as those of *Aspatha*. The tail has ten feathers, the middle pair hardly exceeding the next pair in length. The tail is thus comparatively short.

The genus has only one species, a bird of the hot lowland forests of South Mexico and Guatemala.

1. **Hylomanes momotula.**

Hylomanes momotula, Licht. Abh. Ak. Wissensch. Berl. 1838, p. 449, t. 4[1]; Scl. P. Z. S. 1857, pp. 201[2], 256[3]; 1859, p. 387[4]; Moore, P. Z. S. 1859, p. 54[5]; Scl. & Salv. Ibis, 1860, p. 400[6]; Sumichrast, La Nat. v. p. 239[7]; Sharpe, Cat. Birds Brit. Mus. xvii. p. 332[8].

Momotus momotula, Gray & Mitch. Gen. Birds, i. p. 68, t. 24[9].

Supra viridis, capite summo et nucha castaneis, illo fuscescentiore, stria superciliari cærulea, loris albicantibus, stria postoculari (tectricibus auricularibus inclusis) nigra, infra albido marginata : subtus olivaceus, gula media et abdomine medio albicantibus, abdomine antico cæruleo lavato ; alis et cauda fuscescenti-viridibus ; rostro corneo, mandibulæ basi et pedibus flavidis. Long. tota circa 6·5, alæ 2·8, caudæ rectr. med. 2·6, rectr. lat. 1·1, rostri a rictu 1·2, tarsi 0·7. (Descr. maris ex Choctum, Guatemala. Mus. nostr.)

♀ mari similis.

Hab. MEXICO, Valle Real (*Mus. Berol.*[3]), Jalapa (*Sallé*[2]), Uvero (*Sumichrast*[7]), Playa Vicente (*Boucard*[4], *M. Trujillo*); BRITISH HONDURAS, Cayo in the western district (*Blancaneaux*); GUATEMALA, Choctum[6], Cubilguitz, Khamkal, Volcan de Agua above San Diego, La Trinidad on the slope of the Volcan de Fuego, Savana Grande (*O. S. & F. D. G.*).

Hylomanes momotula is a bird of the lowland forests of South-eastern Mexico and of Guatemala, occurring also in British Honduras. It has not been recorded from Western Mexico or Tehuantepec, but is found in the forests of Guatemala, on both sides of the main mountain chain, from the sea-level to a height of about 3000 feet. Its habits resemble those of the rest of the family, of which it is the smallest member, and the least conspicuous from the dense nature of the forests in which it lives. Of its nesting-habits nothing has as yet been recorded.

Fam. ALCEDINIDÆ.

The members of this family are spread over the tropical and temperate regions of the globe, by far the majority of the species occurring in the Austro-Malayan and Papuan subregions—India, Africa, and Australia being fairly represented. America, both north and south, with its vast river-systems, which one would have thought would have maintained an immense variety of Kingfishers, is only tenanted by a single genus, shared with the Ethiopian and Indian regions, and about ten or eleven species and subspecies.

Mr. Sharpe, who has paid great attention to this family, and has published not only an illustrated Monograph of it, but also the portion of the 'Catalogue of Birds in the British Museum' containing an account of the Alcedinidæ, divides the family into two subfamilies—the Alcedininæ and Daceloninæ. Twenty genera are included in these groups, and these again contain about 200 species and "subspecies." Only one of the genera, *Ceryle* (belonging to the Alcedininæ), is found in America, one species having a wide range throughout the northern continent, the rest being South-American birds spreading into Central America and Mexico, and in some cases beyond these limits into the frontier States of North America.

CERYLE.

Ceryle, Boie, Isis, 1828, p. 316; Sharpe, Cat. Birds Brit. Mus. xvii. p. 107.
Streptoceryle, Bp. Consp. Vol. Anis. p. 10 (1854).

With the exception of *Ceryle alcyon*, which is a North-American species, all the American members of *Ceryle* belong to the southern continent, and range northwards through Central America and Mexico. In the Old World we find *Ceryle rudis* and its close ally *C. varia* in the countries bordering the Eastern Mediterranean and thence eastwards to India; *C. lugubris* in India, China, and Japan; and the fine large *C. maxima* and its ally *C. sharpii* over the greater part of the African continent.

The comparatively long tail of the species of *Ceryle* distinguishes them from all Kingfishers except *Pelargopsis*, which are again distinguished by their very robust bills.

α. Corpus supra lœte schistaceum haud nitidum.

1. Ceryle alcyon.

The Kingfisher, Catesby, Nat. Hist. Carol. i. p. 69, t. 69 (1731) [1].
The American Kingfisher, Edwards, Nat. Hist. Birds, iii. p. 115, t. 115 (1750) [2].
Alcedo alcyon, Linn. Syst. Nat. i. p. 180 (1766) [3].
Ceryle alcyon, Moore, P. Z. S. 1859, p. 53 [4]; Scl. & Salv. Ibis, 1859, p. 131 [5]; Scl. P. Z. S. 1859, p. 367 [6]; 1860, p. 252 [7]; Lawr. Ann. Lyc. N. Y. vii. p. 318 [8]; ix. p. 118 [9]; Mem. Bost. Soc.

N. H. ii. p. 289[10]; Bull. U. S. Nat. Mus. no. 4, p. 30[11]; Sharpe, Mon. Alced. p. 79, t. 23[12]; Cat. Birds Brit. Mus. xvii. p. 125[13]; v. Frantzius, J. f. Orn. 1869, p. 311[14]; Dugès, La Nat. i. p. 139[15]; Grayson, Pr. Bost. Soc. N. H. xiv. p. 284[16]; Salv. Ibis, 1872, p. 321[17]; 1889, p. 371[18]; 1890, p. 88[19]; Cat. Strickl. Coll. p. 416[20]; Baird, Brew., & Ridgw. N. Am. Birds, ii. p. 392[21]; Gundl. Orn. Cub. p. 111[22]; Sumichrast, La Nat. v. p. 239[23]; Nutting, Pr. U. S. Nat. Mus. vi. pp. 375[24], 394[25]; Ferrari-Perez, Pr. U. S. Nat. Mus. ix. p. 160[26]; Herrera, La Nat. (2) i. pp. 178, 321[27]; Stone, Pr. Ac. Phil. 1890, p. 206[28]; Richmond, Pr. U. S. Nat. Mus. xvi. p. 511[29].

Streptoceryle alcyon, Cab. J. f. Orn. 1862, p. 162[30].

Supra schistacea, capite cristata, plumis elongatis singulis medialiter nigris; capitis lateribus schistaceis, macula infra oculos altera supra lora albis: subtus alba, torque pectorali schistacea, cervicis lateribus postice fere conjunctis albis, hypochondriis schistaceis; alis extus schistaceis, tectricibus et secundariis albo stricte terminatis, remigibus nigris in pogonio externo albo maculatis, in pogonio interno, bitriente basali, fere omnino albo, axillaribus albis; cauda nigra, extrorsum schistacea, rectricibus omnibus (duobus mediis exceptis) frequenter albo transfasciatis, fasciis singulis ad rhachidem interruptis; rostro nigro; pedibus fuscis. Long. tota 12·0, alæ 6·0, caudæ 3·4, rostri a rictu 2·75, tarsi 0·4. (Descr. maris ex Tampico, Mexico. Mus. nostr.)

♀ mari similis, hypochondriis (supra abdomen anticum vix conjunctis) et axillaribus castaneis.

Hab. North America generally[21].—Mexico (*T. Mann*[20]), Rio de Ermitaño (*W. Lloyd*), Mazatlan (*Grayson*[10][16], *Forrer*), Tres Marias Is. (*Grayson*[6][10][16]), Zapotlan in Jalisco (*W. B. Richardson*), Guanajuato (*Dugès*[15]), Valley of Mexico (*Herrera*[27]), Tampico (*W. B. Richardson*), Vega del Casadero (*M. Trujillo*), Epatlan[26], Puebla[26], Chapulco (*Ferrari-Perez*), Orizaba (*Sallé*[7], *Ferrari-Perez*), Jalapa (*de Oca*[6]), Santa Efigenia (*Sumichrast*[11]), Progreso in N. Yucatan (*Devis, Stone & Baker*[28]), Shkolak (*Stone & Baker*[28]), Cozumel I. (*G. F. Gaumer*[18]); British Honduras, Belize (*O. S.*[5]); Guatemala, Rio Dulce (*O. S.*[5]), San Gerónimo, Dueñas, San José, Huamuchal, Santana Mixtan (*O. S. & F. D. G.*); Honduras, Omoa (*Leyland*[4]), Ruatan I. (*G. F. Gaumer*[18]); Nicaragua, Chontales (*Janson*[17]), San Juan del Sur[24], Omotepe[25] (*Nutting*), Escondido R. (*Richmond*[29]); Costa Rica (*J. Cooper*), Rio Frio (*Richmond*[29]), Navarro[14], Cartago (*v. Frantzius, Carmiol*[9]), Agua Caliente, Orosi (*v. Frantzius*[14]); Panama (*M'Leannan*[8]). — Colombia, Santa Marta[13]; Antilles[13].

The Belted Kingfisher is the only member of the Alcedinidæ that enjoys a wide range over the North-American continent, where it is found from the Arctic Ocean southwards and from the Atlantic to the Pacific. So far as the rigour of the winter season permits, it is resident in the United States. Its range southwards extends on the mainland nearly everywhere in Mexico and Central America, as far as the Isthmus of Panama, and even beyond our limits to Northern Colombia.

Grayson says it is common at all seasons at Mazatlan[16]; but on the Tres Marias Islands he only met with solitary individuals, sitting on rocks on the sea-shore. In Guatemala we saw *Ceryle alcyon* on nearly every river and lake from the sea-level to a height of about 5000 feet in the mountains, but, so far as we could ascertain, it was only observed in the winter season. These southern birds, therefore, are probably those that visit the far north in the breeding-season.

We never met with a nest in Central America; but in the States, according to Brewer [21], the nest is made in an excavation in the bank of a pool or stream, but not necessarily in the immediate vicinity of water. The hole or tunnel excavated by the bird varies from 4 to 15 feet in length, and is enlarged at the end, where six or sometimes seven glossy white eggs are laid.

In its delicate grey back this species agrees with *C. torquata* and differs from the other Central-American Kingfishers; but in the coloration of the sexes the difference between the two species is marked. The male of *C. alcyon* is devoid of chestnut colour on the under surface, whereas in *C. torquata* this colour is more pronounced in the male than in the opposite sex.

2. Ceryle torquata.

Alcedo torquata, Linn. Syst. Nat. i. p. 180 (1766) [1]; Licht. Preis-Verz. mex. Vög. p. 1 (*cf.* J. f. Orn. 1863, p. 55) [2].

Ceryle torquata, Bp. P. Z. S. 1837, p. 108 [3]; Scl. P. Z. S. 1857, p. 202 [4]; Moore, Ibis, 1859, p. 53 [5]; Scl. & Salv. Ibis, 1859, p. 131 [6]; P Z. S. 1864, p. 363 [7]; 1867, p. 280 [8]; 1870, p. 837 [9]; Cassin, Pr. Ac. Phil. 1860, p. 133 [10]; Lawr. Ann. Lyc. N. Y. vii. p. 290 [11]; Mem. Bost. Soc. N. H. ii. p. 289 [12]; Bull. U. S. Nat. Mus. no. 4, p. 30 [13]; v. Frantzius, J. f. Orn. 1869, p. 311 [14]; Sharpe, Mon. Alced. p. 73, t. 22 [15]; Cat. Birds Brit. Mus. xvii. p. 121 [16]; Sumichrast, La Nat. v. p. 239 [17]; Nutting, Pr. U. S. Nat. Mus. v. p. 399 [18]; vi. pp. 375 [19], 387 [20], 394 [21]; Ferrari-Perez, Pr. U. S. Nat. Mus. ix. p. 160 [22]; Ridgw. Pr. U. S. Nat. Mus. x. p. 591 [23]; Zeledon, An. Mus. Nac. Costa Rica, 1887, p. 119 [24]; Richmond, Pr. U. S. Nat. Mus. xvi. p. 510 [25].

Streptoceryle torquata, Cab. J. f. Orn. 1862, p. 161 [26].

Supra schistacea, plumis singulis rhachidibus nigris, capite cristata; capitis lateribus, alis extus et pectoris lateribus dorso concoloribus; macula infra oculos, altera supra lora, gula et torque cervicali albis; abdomine toto læte castaneo, hypochondriis et axillaribus concoloribus, subalaribus albis, remigibus in pogonio interno maculis albis ad marginem concurrentibus albis, tectricibus subcaudalibus albis schistaceo variegatis (interdum pure albis); cauda nigra, extrorsum schistacea, pogoniis ambobus regulariter albo maculatis; rostro nigro ad basin rufescente; pedibus flavescenti-fuscis. Long. tota circa 16·0, alæ 7·5, caudæ 4·5, rostri a rictu 4·0, tarsi 0·6. (Descr. maris ex Lion Hill, Panama. Mus. nostr.)

♀ mari similis, torque pectorali schistacea, subalaribus et tectricibus subcaudalibus omnino castaneis, abdomine concoloribus.

Hab. MEXICO, Rio Grande, Nuevo Leon (*F. B. Armstrong*), Tampico (*W. B. Richardson*), Real del Monte (*Mus. Brit.*), Jalapa (*Sallé* [4]), Paso de la Milpa [22], Vega de Alatorre [22], Santa Ana, Rio Rancho Nuevo (*Ferrari-Perez*), Mazatlan (*Grayson* [12]), Presidio de Mazatlan (*Forrer*), San Blas (*W. B. Richardson*), Tonala, Chihuitan [13], Santa Efigenia [13] (*Sumichrast*), Teapa (*Mrs. H. H. Smith*); BRITISH HONDURAS, Belize river (*O. S.*), Cayo in the western district (*Blancaneaux*); GUATEMALA, Rio Dulce (*O. S.* [6]), Lanquin, Choctum, Huamuchal, San José de Guatemala (*O. S. & F. D. G.*), Peten (*Leyland* [5]); HONDURAS, Omoa (*Leyland* [5]), San Pedro (*G. M. Whitely* [9]),

Segovia river (*Townsend* [23]) ; NICARAGUA, Momotombo (*W. B. Richardson*), San Juan del Sur [19], Sucuyá [20], Omotepe [21] (*Nutting*), Escondido R. (*Richmond* [25]) ; COSTA RICA, Agua Caliente, Orosi, Navarro (*v. Frantzius* [14]), La Palma (*Nutting* [18]), Gulf of Nicoya (*Sir E. Belcher* [16]), Peje (*Carmiol*), Liberia, Jimenez (*Zeledon* [24]) ; PANAMA, Lion Hill (*M'Leannan* [7] [11]), Chepo (*Arcé*).—SOUTH AMERICA generally, except Patagonia and the west coast of Chili and Peru.

Ceryle torquata is much the largest of the Central-American Kingfishers, and in the southern continent is only equalled by forms that are barely separable from it. Though allied to *C. alcyon*, it has a wholly different range, being in fact a South-American species, extending northwards through Central America to both Western and Eastern Mexico even to the Rio Grande, where a specimen was shot a few years ago near Laredo, its capture being recorded by Mr. Stone.

In South America its range is nearly universal, and only in Southern Patagonia and the west coast of the continent between the Andes and the Pacific is its place taken by the closely-allied *C. stellata*. In altitude *C. torquata* does not reach nearly so high as *C. alcyon*, as it keeps to the stiller waters of the rivers as they approach the sea and the lakes and swamps near the coast. Grayson says that he only saw it near the sea in the vicinity of Mazatlan, but not in the river itself [12]. It preferred stagnant pools and lagoons densely shaded with overhanging trees. Our experience was somewhat different, for during canoe journeys down the Belize river and on the Rio Dulce birds of this species were seldom out of sight, flying ahead of the boat and alighting from time to time to start again as she approached, till at last, being driven beyond their usual haunts, they would dash past in the opposite direction.

So far as we know, *C. torquata* makes no migratory movements, but remains sedentary throughout its range the whole year.

β. Corpus supra nitente viride.

3. Ceryle amazona.

Amazonian Kingfisher, Lath. Gen. Syn., Suppl. i. p. 116 [1].

Alcedo amazona, Lath. Ind. Orn. i. p. 257 [2].

Ceryle amazona, Scl. P. Z. S. 1857, p. 202 [3] ; Moore, P. Z. S. 1859, p. 53 [4] ; Scl. & Salv. Ibis, 1859, p. 131 [5] ; P. Z. S. 1864, p. 363 [6] ; 1867, p. 279 [7] ; Cassin, Pr. Ac. Phil. 1860, p. 133 [8] ; Salv. Ibis, 1860, p. 195 [9] ; P. Z. S. 1867, p. 152 [10] ; 1870, p. 201 [11] ; Cat. Strickl. Coll. p. 416 [12] ; Lawr. Ann. Lyc. N. Y. vii. p. 290 [13] ; Mem. Bost. Soc. N. H. ii. p. 295 [14] ; Bull. U. S. Nat. Mus. no. 4, p. 30 [15] ; v. Frantz. J. f. Orn. 1869, p. 311 [16] ; Sharpe, Mon. Alced. p. 83, t. 24 [17] ; Cat. Birds Brit. Mus. xvii. p. 129 [18] ; Finsch, Abh. nat. Ver. z. Bremen, 1870, p. 328 [19] ; Sumichrast, La Nat. v. p. 239 [20] ; Boucard, P. Z. S. 1883, p. 453 [21] ; Nutting, Pr. U. S. Nat. Mus. vi. p. 394 [22] ; Ferrari-Perez, Pr. U. S. Nat. Mus. ix. p. 161 [23] ; Zeledon, An. Mus. Nac. Costa Rica, 1887, p. 119 [24] ; Richmond, Pr. U. S. Nat. Mus. xvi. p. 511 [25].

Chloroceryle amazonia, Cab. J. f. Orn. 1862, p. 161 [26].

Supra nitide viridis, stria malari, pectoris lateribus concoloribus, hypochondriis quoque viridi striatis ; macula infra oculos, gula, torque cervicali integra, abdomine et tectricibus subcaudalibus albis, pectore medialiter et abdomine antico plaga magna castanea ornatis ; alis nigris, subalaribus albis ; cauda viridi-nigricante, rectricum lateralium marginibus albo maculatis, rectricibus externis in pogonio externo ad basin quoque maculatis ; rostro et pedibus nigris. Long. tota circa 11·0, alæ 5·5, caudæ 3·15, rostri a rictu 3·0, tarsi 0·5.

♀ mari similis, subtus medialiter omnino albus, plaga pectorali castanea nulla.

Hab. MEXICO, Mazatlan (*Grayson* [14]), Presidio de Mazatlan (*Forrer*), San Blas (*W. B. Richardson*), Tupila river (*Xantus* [14]), Jalapa (*Sallé* [3], *Ferrari-Perez* [23]), Santa Ana, Misantla, Plan del Rio (*Ferrari-Perez*), La Antigua, Vega del Casadero (*M. Trujillo*), Teapa (*Mrs. H. H. Smith*), Chihuitan [15], Santa Efigenia [15], Tehuantepec [20] (*Sumichrast*), N. Yucatan (*G. F. Gaumer* [21]) ; BRITISH HONDURAS, Cayo in the western district (*Blancaneaux*) ; GUATEMALA (*Skinner* [5], *Constancia* [12]), Vera Paz, San Gerónimo, San José de Guatemala, Huamuchal (*O. S. & F. D. G.*) ; HONDURAS, Omoa (*Leyland* [4]) ; NICARAGUA, Omotepe (*Nutting* [22]), Escondido R. (*Richmond* [25]), Blewfields (*Wickham* [7]) ; COSTA RICA [26], Agua Caliente, Orosi, Navarro (*v. Frantzius* [16]), Pacuare (*Zeledon* [24]) ; PANAMA, Chitra [11], Calovevora [11], Santiago de Veraguas [10] (*Arcé*), Lion Hill (*McLeannan* [6] [13]), Nercua (*Wood* [8]).—SOUTH AMERICA generally, from Colombia and Guiana to Argentina [18].

The Amazonian Kingfisher of Latham has been known for more than a century, and is one of the commonest of the Kingfishers of South America. It has a similar range to *C. torquata*, but not quite so extended in Eastern Mexico, its limits northward probably not passing the State of Vera Cruz. In altitude it is found from the sea-level to a height of 3000 or 4000 feet in the rivers and lakes of the mountainous parts of the country it inhabits.

Like the other South-American species of Alcedinidæ, *C. amazona* seems to be resident throughout the year wherever it is found.

4. **Ceryle septentrionalis.**

Alcedo americana, Swains. Phil. Mag. new ser. i. p. 366 (nec Gmelin) [1].

Ceryle americana, Scl. P. Z. S. 1856, pp. 139 [2], 286 [3] ; 1858, p. 358 [4] ; 1859, p. 367 [5] ; Moore, P. Z. S. 1859, p. 53 [6] ; Scl. & Salv. Ibis, 1859, p. 131 [7] ; Lawr. Ann. Lyc. N. Y. vii. p. 290 [8] ; Dugès, La Nat. i. p. 139 [9].

Ceryle cabanisi, Salv. P. Z. S. 1867, p. 152 [10] ; 1870, p. 201 [11] ; Ibis, 1872, p. 321 [12] ; Scl. & Salv. P. Z. S. 1867, p. 280 [13] ; 1870, p. 837 [14] ; Lawr. Ann. Lyc. N. Y. ix. p. 118 [15] ; Sharpe, Mon. Alced. p. 87 (partim) [16] ; v. Frantzius, J. f. Orn. 1869, p. 311 [17] ; Boucard, P. Z. S. 1878, p. 48 [18] ; 1883, p. 453 [19] ; Sumichrast, La Nat. v. p. 239 [20] ; Ferrari-Perez, Pr. U. S. Nat. Mus. ix. p. 161 [21] ; Ridgw. Pr. U. S. Nat. Mus. x. pp. 582 [22], 591 [23] ; Zeledon, An. Mus. Nac. Costa Rica, 1887, p. 119 [24] ; Herrera, La Nat. (2) i. p. 321 [25] ; Cherrie, Auk, 1892, p. 322 [26].

Ceryle americana, var. *cabanisi,* Baird, Brew., and Ridgw. N. Am. Birds, ii. p. 396 [27] ; Lawr. Mem. Bost. Soc. N. H. ii. p. 290 [28] ; Bull. U. S. Nat. Mus. no. 4, p. 30 [29].

Ceryle americana cabanisi, Nutting, Pr. U. S. Nat. Mus. v. p. 399 [30]; vi. pp. 375 [31], 387 [32], 394 [33];
407 [34]; Ridgw. Pr. U. S. Nat. Mus. v. p. 501 [35].

Chloroceryle cabanisi, Cab. J. f. Orn. 1862, p. 256 [36]; Scl. P. Z. S. 1864, p. 176 [37].

Ceryle septentrionalis, Sharpe, Cat. Birds Brit. Mus. xvii. p. 134 [38].

Ceryle americana septentrionalis, Richmond, Pr. U. S. Nat. Mus. xvi. p. 511 [39].

Supra nitide virescens, capite toto et cauda saturatioribus, alis albo guttatis; macula infra oculos, gutture,
torque cervicali integra et ventre albis, vitta malari angusta viridi, torque pectorali lata castanea, hypochondriis et tectricibus subcaudalibus maculis magnis nigricanti-viridibus notatis; alis intus in pogonio
interno albo maculatis; cauda ad basin alba, rectricibus externis fere ad apicem albis in pogonio interno
albo variegatis; rostro et pedibus nigricantibus. Long. tota circa 7·5, alæ 3·4, caudæ 2·2, rostri a rictu 2·0,
tarsi 0·4.

♀ mari similis, pectore et abdomine nigricanti-viridi bitorquatis, colore castaneo nullo. (Descr. maris et
feminæ ex San Gerónimo, Guatemala. Mus. nostr.)

Hab. NORTH AMERICA, South-western States, Texas to Arizona; Lower California [27].—
MEXICO (*Bullock* [1]), Hermosillo in Sonora (*Ferrari-Perez*), Isleta (*W. Lloyd*),
Mazatlan (*Grayson* [28]), Presidio de Mazatlan (*Forrer*), San Blas (*W. B. Richard-
son*), Tepic (*Grayson* [28]), Colotlan, Aguas Calientes (*W. B. Richardson*), Guanajuato,
Guadalajara (*Dugès* [9]), Plains of Colima, R. Tupila (*Xantus* [28]), Rio Salado in
Nuevo Leon (*F. B. Armstrong*), Sierra Madre above Ciudad Victoria, Aldama,
Tampico, Valles (*W. B. Richardson*), Misantla, Vega del Casadero (*M. Trujillo*),
Jalapa (*de Oca* [5], *Ferrari-Perez* [21]), Coatepec, Santa Ana, Rio Rancho Nuevo,
Hacienda Tortugas (*Ferrari-Perez*), Orizaba (*Botteri, Sumichrast* [20], *Ferrari-Perez,
F. D. G.*), Cordova (*Sallé* [3], *Sumichrast* [20]), Atoyac (*Mrs. H. H. Smith*), Playa
Vicente (*M. Trujillo*), Valley of Mexico (*White* [36], *Herrera* [25]), Morelia (*F. D. G.*),
Chietla, Izucar de Matamoros (*Ferrari-Perez* [21]), Sola, Juchatengo, Oaxaca city
(*M. Trujillo*), Chihuitan [29], Santa Efigenia [20][29], Tepanatepec [20] (*Sumichrast*),
Chimalapa, Sierra de Santo Domingo, Tehuantepec (*W. B. Richardson*), Teapa
(*Mrs. H. H. Smith*), N. Yucatan (*G. F. Gaumer* [19]); BRITISH HONDURAS, Cayo in
the western district, Old River (*Leyland* [6]); GUATEMALA, Rio Dulce (*O. S.*), Toliman
(*W. B. Richardson*), Dueñas [7], Rio Guacalate [7], San Gerónimo, Huamuchal (*O. S.
& F. D. G.*); SALVADOR (*Mus. Brit.*), La Libertad (*W. B. Richardson*); HONDURAS,
San Pedro (*G. M. Whitely* [14]), Truxillo [22], Segovia R. [23] (*Townsend*), Lake Yojoa
(*Taylor* [4]); NICARAGUA, Momotombo, Matagalpa (*W. B. Richardson*), Chontales
(*Belt* [12]), Escondido R. (*Richmond* [39]), Blewfields (*Wickham* [13]), San Juan del Sur [31],
Omotepe [33], Sucuyá [32], Los Sabalos [34] (*Nutting*); COSTA RICA (*Hoffmann* [35],
Ellendorf [35], *v. Frantzius, Boucard*), San José (*v. Frantzius* [17], *Carmiol* [15], *Zeledon* [24],
Nutting [35], *Cherrie* [26]), Jimenez, Naranjo de Cartago (*Zeledon* [24]), Valza, San Carlos
(*Carmiol* [15]), Cartago (*v. Frantzius* [17], *Cooper* [15]), La Palma (*Nutting* [30]); PANAMA,
David (*Bridges* [2][10]) Calovevora, Calobre (*Arcé* [11]), Lion Hill (*M'Leannan* [8]), Paraiso
Station (*Hughes*), Chepo (*Arcé*).

This northern form of *Ceryle americana* is closely allied to that species, the differences consisting in its stouter bill and rather stronger build. It has usually been considered to be the same as the bird of Peru described by Tschudi as *Alcedo cabanisi*; but Mr. Sharpe has recently shown that the true *Ceryle cabanisi* has much more conspicuous and wider white bars on the quills, the bill being only slightly stouter than that of *C. americana*.

The range of this species is nearly universal throughout Central America and Mexico, and even passes the Rio Grande into the frontier States of Arizona and Texas; it is everywhere common, frequenting the mountain-streams as high as 5000 feet as well as the larger rivers of the lowlands. Its habits are like those of its congeners of the same region, and, like them, it is resident wherever it is found.

5. Ceryle inda.

The Spotted Kingfisher, Edwards, Glean. Nat. Hist. iii. p. 262, t. 335 [1].

Alcedo inda, Linn. Syst. Nat. i. p. 179 (1766) [2].

Ceryle inda, Cassin, Pr. Ac. Phil. 1860, p. 133 [3]; Lawr. Ann. Lyc. N. Y. vii. p. 290 [4]; viii. p. 184 [5]; Scl. & Salv. P. Z. S. 1864, p. 363 [6]; Sharpe, Mon. Alced. p. 91, t. 27 [7]; Cat. Birds Brit. Mus. xvii. p. 137 [8]; Richmond, Pr. U. S. Nat. Mus. xvi. p. 512 [9].

Supra nitente viridis, alis et cauda albo maculatis; macula infra oculos, altera supra lora fulvis; gutture toto et torque cervicali fulvescenti-albidis; corpore toto subtus reliquo rufescenti-castaneo, subalaribus concoloribus.

Hab. NICARAGUA, Greytown (*Holland* [5], *Richmond* [9]), Escondido R. (*Richmond* [9]); PANAMA, Veraguas (*Arcé*), Lion Hill (*M'Leannan* [4] [6]), Turbo (*C. J. Wood* [3]).— SOUTH AMERICA, Ecuador, Peru, Amazonia, Guiana, and Eastern Brazil [8].

Though one of the long-known species of the Kingfishers of America, having been figured as long ago as 1764 by George Edwards, *Ceryle inda* is certainly the rarest of the species of our region, if not of Tropical America generally. Its range, too, is more limited, as we have not been able to trace it beyond Eastern Nicaragua near Greytown and the Escondido or Blewfields river of the Mosquito Territory. Though doubtless found in Costa Rica, we have not yet met with an authentic record of its occurrence. In the State of Panama it has been noticed several times, and in South America its range traced over the whole of that portion lying eastwards of the Andes and as far south as Bahia on the coast of Brazil.

6. Ceryle superciliosa.

Little Green and Orange-coloured Kingfisher, Edwards, Glean. Nat. Hist. i. p. 73, t. 245 [1].

Alcedo superciliosa, Linn. Syst. Nat. i. p. 179 (1766) [2].

Ceryle superciliosa, Scl. P. Z. S. 1857, p. 227 [3]; 1859, p. 387 [4]; Moore, P. Z. S. 1859, p. 53 [5]; Scl. & Salv. Ibis, 1859, p. 131 [6]; P. Z. S. 1864, p. 363 [7]; 1870, p. 837 [8]; Cassin, Pr. Ac. Phil. 1860, p. 134 [9]; Lawr. Ann. Lyc. N. Y. vii. p. 290 [10]; ix. p. 204 [11]; Bull. U. S. Nat. Mus. no. 4, p. 30 [12]; Sharpe, Mon. Alced. p. 93, t. 28 [13]; Cat. Birds Brit. Mus. xvii. p. 138 [14]; v. Frantz. J. f. Orn. 1869, p. 311 [15]; Sumichrast, La Nat. v. p. 239 [16]; Nutting,

Pr. U. S. Nat. Mus. v. p. 400 [17] ; Boucard, P. Z. S. 1883, p. 453 [18]; Salv. Ibis, 1889, p. 371 [19] ; 1890, p. 88 [20].

Chloroceryle superciliosa, Cab. J. f. Orn. 1862, p. 256 [21] ; Scl. P. Z. S. 1864, p. 176 [22].

Ceryle superciliosa stictoptera, Ridgw. Pr. Biol. Soc. Wash. ii. p. 95 [23]; Richmond, Pr. U. S. Nat. Mus. xvi. p. 511 [24].

Ceryle stictoptera, Sharpe, Cat. Birds Brit. Mus. xvii. p. 139 [25].

Supra nitide viridis, pileo vix obscuriore, alis extus albo triseriatim maculatis, macula supra lora castanea : subtus gutture toto pallide castaneo, pectore et hypochondriis saturate castaneis, abdomine medio et tectricibus subcaudalibus albis; cauda viridi-nigricante, rectricibus præter duas medias ad basin albis et in pogonio interno albo maculatis ; rostro nigro, mandibula infra ad basin carnea ; pedibus nigris. Long. tota circa 5·6, alæ 2·25, caudæ 1·6, rostri a rictu 1·5, tarsi 0·35. (Descr. maris ex Choctum, Guatemala. Mus. nostr.)

♀ mari similis, fascia transversa pectorali saturate viridi, plumis singulis albo limbatis.

Hab. MEXICO (*White* [22]), San Andres Tuxtla [3], Playa Vicente [4] (*Boucard*), Uvero [16], Omealca [16], Santa Efigenia [12] (*Sumichrast*), Chimalapa (*W. B. Richardson*), Sisal in Yucatan (*Schott* [11] [23]), Rio Lagartos, Cozumel I. [19] (*G. F. Gaumer*); GUATEMALA, Peten (*Leyland* [5]), Choctum (*O. S. & F. D. G.*), Mouth of Rio Samala (*O. S.* [6]); HONDURAS, San Pedro (*G. M. Whitely* [8]) ; NICARAGUA, Escondido R. (*Richmond* [24]); COSTA RICA (*Ellendorf* [21], *v. Frantzius* [15] [21]), Rio Frio (*Richmond* [24]), La Palma (*Nutting* [17]) ; PANAMA, Lion Hill (*M'Leannan* [7] [10]), Turbo (*C. J. Wood* [9]).—SOUTH AMERICA generally, to Guiana, Amazonia, and Brazil.

Mr. Ridgway separated the Yucatan bird from the South-American *Ceryle superciliosa* under the name of *C. superciliosa stictoptera,* stating that the wings are spotted with white, those of the southern birds being nearly or quite plain. All our specimens from Central America agree with this definition ; but only four out of twenty-one birds from South America have unspotted wings, the other seventeen have the wings all more or less spotted, and are thus not distinguishable from the northern birds. As the character thus breaks down dividing these birds we are unable to discriminate more than one species, to which the old name *Ceryle superciliosa* is applicable. There appears to be no break whatever in the range of the species, as it is found, though sparingly, in every river and stream of the lowlands of Tropical America. In Mexico it has been found in several places in the southern portion of the State of Vera Cruz and also on the Isthmus of Tehuantepec. In Guatemala we found it close to the shore of the Pacific at the mouth of the Rio Samala, and also at Choctum, one of the favourite hunting-resorts of the bird-collectors of Coban, in the interior of Vera Paz, at an elevation of about 1200 feet above the sea. It has also been met with in all the other Central-American States and in the State of Panama, both on the Line of Railway as well as on the Isthmus of Darien.

In habits this species has no peculiarities that we know of to distinguish it from the other species of *Ceryle* inhabiting the same districts.

Suborder COCCYGES HETERODACTYLÆ.

Fam. TROGONIDÆ.

Trogonidæ, Gould, Mon. Trog. ed. 2 (1858–1875) ; Ogilvie-Grant, Cat. Birds, Brit. Mus. xvii.
pp. 429 et seq. (1892).

This remarkable family is well represented in Central America and Mexico ; for of
the known species, numbering in all about fifty, sixteen occur within our limits, and
of these not more than four pass beyond our region into the northern parts of South
America.   But the forty-nine or fifty known species of Trogonidæ spread far beyond
the limits of America, for three occur in tropical Africa and eighteen in the eastern
parts of tropical Asia and the great islands of Java, Sumatra, and Borneo.   We thus
have thirty-one or thirty-two species belonging to the New World, at least half of them
Central American.

The American genera are distinguished from those of the Old World.   They are :—
Pharomacrus with four species, one Central American ; *Euptilotis* with one exclusively
Mexican species ; *Tmetotrogon* and *Prionotelus* with one Hispaniolan and one Cuban
species respectively ; and, lastly, *Trogon* with twenty-four species, of which fourteen
occur within our limits.   Africa has *Hapaloderma* with three species to itself, and South-
eastern Asia and its islands *Harpactes* with eleven species and *Harpalarpactes* with two
species.   An interesting and suggestive fact concerning the former distribution of the
Trogonidæ is the discovery of fossil remains of a species ascribed to *Trogon* in the miocene
beds of Allier in France, described by Prof. A. Milne-Edwards as *Trogon gallicus* (Ois.
Foss. de la France, ii. p. 395).   These remains show that the family had a much wider
distribution in these early times, and was spread over a much less broken area.   Since
then species have disappeared from large districts and the remainder left in the
isolated countries in which we now find them.

Trogons are inhabitants of more or less heavily forested districts, but are by no means
restricted to the lowlying hotter country—*Pharomacrus, Euptilotis,* and several species
of *Trogon* frequenting mountain-ranges to a height of at least 8000 or 9000 feet.

The members of the family Trogonidæ, being remarkably brilliant in the colours of
their plumage, early attracted the attention of Gould, and a monograph of it, finished
in 1838, formed the second of his great monographic works.   A second edition, but
really a distinct volume, was commenced in 1858, and completed in 1875.   Since then
we have in vol. xvii. of the Catalogue of Birds of the British Museum a complete
account of the Trogons in that institution from the pen of Mr. Ogilvie-Grant.   As this
volume contains lists of nearly the whole of the specimens collected by us for this work,
it has been of great use to us in preparing our account of the family which follows.

PHAROMACRUS.

Pharomacrus, De la Llave, Registro Trimestre, i. p. 48 (1831); Gould, Mon. Trog. ed. 2, Intr. p. xvii (1875); Grant, Cat. Birds Brit. Mus. xvii. p. 430.
Calurus, Swains. Class. Birds, ii. p. 337.

Pharomacrus may readily be distinguished from *Trogon* by the development of the wing- and tail-coverts and by the feathers of the crown being more or less drawn together from either side so as to form a crest. These characters are all of them most distinctly shown in the Central-American representative of the genus, *P. mocinno*, in which two of the upper tail-coverts are often four times as long as the tail itself, and the wing-coverts curve over the primaries.

Mr. Grant unites Gould's *Pharomacrus fulgidus* to *P. antisiensis* of d'Orbigny, and recognizes four species of *Pharomacrus*, of which *P. mocinno* alone is found in our region—the other three being of South-American domicile, ranging along the Andes from Venezuela and Colombia to Bolivia. No species of the genus has as yet been found in the upland forests of Guiana or in Eastern Brazil.

1. **Pharomacrus mocinno.**

Trogon pavoninus, Temm. Pl. Col. 372 (nec Spix) [1].
Pharomacrus mocinno, De la Llave, Regis. Trim. i. p. 48 (1831) [2]; Scl. P. Z. S. 1856, p. 139 [3]; Cab. & Heine, Mus. Hein. iv. Heft 1, p. 211 [4]; Salv. P. Z. S. 1867, p. 151 [5]; 1870, p. 202 [6]; Salvad. Atti R. Acc. Sc. Tor. 1868, p. 183 [7]; v. Frantz. J. f. Orn. 1869, p. 313 [8]; Gould, Mon. Trog. ed. 2, t. 1 [9]; Grant, Cat. Birds Brit. Mus. xvii. p. 431 [10].
Trogon resplendens, Gould, P. Z. S. 1835, p. 29 [11].
Trogon (Calurus) resplendens, Gould, Mon. Trog. t. 21 [12]; Delattre, Echo du Monde Savant, 1843 [13], et Rev. Zool. 1843, p. 163 [14].
Trogon paradiseus, Bp. P. Z. S. 1837, p. 101 [15].
Pharomacrus paradiseus, Scl. & Salv. Ibis, 1859, p. 132 [16]; Moore, P. Z. S. 1859, p. 52 [17]; Taylor, Ibis, 1860, p. 118 [18]; Salv. P. Z. S. 1860, p. 374 [19]; Ibis, 1861, p. 138 [20]; R. Owen, Ibis, 1861, p. 66 [21]; Cab. J. f. Orn. 1862, p. 175 [22].
Pharomacrus costaricensis, Cab. J. f. Orn. 1869, p. 313 [23]; Zeledon, An. Mus. Nac. Costa Rica, 1887, p. 120 [24].
Pharomacrus mocinno, var. *costaricensis*, Boucard, P. Z. S. 1878, p. 48 [25]; in Rowley's Orn. Misc. iii. p. 21 [26].
Pharomacrus mocinno costaricensis, Ridgw. Pr. U.S. Nat. Mus. v. pp. 497 [27], 501 [28].
Nyctibius jamaicensis?, Lawr. Ann. Lyc. N. Y. ix. p. 120 [29].

Nitide gramineo-viridis, abdomine toto et tectricibus subcaudalibus coccineis his dilutioribus, illo ad pectus saturate coccineo-brunnescente; alis et cauda nigris, hujus rectricibus tribus utrinque plerumque albis, rhachidibus nigris; tectricibus alarum mediis valde elongatis falciformibus dorso concoloribus, tectricibus supracaudalibus elongatis, quatuor caudam superantibus, quarum duabus longissimis; rostro flavo, pedibus carneis. Long. tota ad caudæ apicem circa 16·5, alæ 8·2, caudæ 8, tectricibus supracaudalibus longissimis 34·0, rostri a rictu 1·0, tarsi 0·85.

♀ nitide viridis, capite fusco cupreo lavato, pectore et cervice antico griseis viridi lavatis, abdomine griseo, ad crissum et tectricibus subcaudalibus coccineis; alis nigricantibus, remigibus extus cervino limbatis; cauda nigricante griseo-albido transversim regulariter fasciata, tectricibus supracaudalibus elongatis sed caudam haud superantibus.

♂ *juv.* ♀ similis, capite virescentiore, secundariis nonnunquam cervino guttatis, caudæ rectricibus tribus utrinque externis acutis et albo distincte terminatis. (Descr. maris, maris juv. et feminæ ex Volcan de Fuego, Guatemala. Mus. nostr.)

Hab. GUATEMALA [17], forests of the higher mountains, San Martin in Quezaltenango, Pie de la Cuesta in San Marcos (*W. B. Richardson*), Cerro Zunil, Volcan de Fuego 7000 feet [16], Volcan de Agua (*O. S. & F. D. G.*), Chiacaman in the Chiantla range (*fide O. S.*), vicinity of Coban [16], and the higher forests of Vera Paz, Raxché [20], Chilasco, &c. (*Delattre, O. S. & F. D. G.*), Santa Cruz Mts. (*R. Owen* [21]); HONDURAS, mountains south and east of Comayagua (*Taylor* [18]); NICARAGUA, San Rafael del Norte (*W. B. Richardson*); COSTA RICA [22] (*Durando* [7]), Turrialba, Cervantes (*v. Frantzius* [8]), Volcan de Irazu (*v. Frantzius* [8], *Boucard* [25], *Zeledon* [24] [29], *Nutting* [27]), San José (*Nutting* [28]), Navarro, Candelaria Mts. (*Boucard* [25]), El Zarcero de Alajuela, La Palma de San José (*Zeledon* [24]); PANAMA, Boquete (*Bridges* [3] [5]), Volcan de Chiriqui, Calovevora, Calobre (*Arcé* [6]).

The earlier history of this remarkable bird is best given in some extracts from the 'Ornithology' of Francis Willughby, who describes it in an "Appendix (p. 385) to the History of Birds, containing Such Birds as we suspect for fabulous, or such as are too briefly and unaccurately described to give us a full and sufficient knowledge of them, taken out of Franc. Hernandez especially." After describing the Quetzaltototl he goes on to say:—"The feathers of this Bird are highly esteemed among the Indians, and preferred even before Gold itself; the longer ones for crests, and other ornaments both of the head and whole body, both for War and Peace: But the rest for setting in feather-works, and composing the figures of Saints and other things; which they are so skilful in doing, as not to fall short of the most artificial pictures drawn in colours. For this purpose they also make use of, and mingle and weave in together with these the feathers of the humming bird. These Birds live in the Province of Tecolotlan beyond Quauhtemallam towards Honduras, where great care is taken that no man kill them: Only it is lawful to pluck off their feathers, and so let them go naked; yet not for all men indifferently, but only for the Lords and Proprietors of them; for they descend to the Heirs as rich possessions. Fr. Hernandez, in some pretermitted annotations adds concerning the manner of the taking these birds some things worth the knowing. The Fowlers (saith he) betake themselves to the Mountains, and there hiding themselves in small Cottages, scatter up and down boil'd Indian Wheat, and prick down in the ground many rods besmeared with Birdlime, wherewith the Birds intangled become their prey. They fly in flocks among trees, on which they are wont to sit, making no unpleasant noise with their whistling and singing in consort. They have by the instinct of nature such knowledge of their riches, that once sticking to the Birdlime, they remain still and quiet, not strugling at all, that they may not mar or injure their feathers. The beauty whereof they are so in love with, that they chuse rather to be taken and killed, than by endeavouring to get their liberty do anything that may deface or prejudice them. They are said to pick holes in trees, and therein to build and breed up their Young. They feed upon Worms, and certain wild Pinnæ, of that sort which the Mexicans are wont to call Matzatli. They love the open air, nor hath it been yet found, that ever they would be kept tame, or brought up in houses. They make a noise not much unlike Parrots: But they have a chearful and pleasant whistle, and they sing thrice a day, to wit, in the Morning, about Noon, and about Sun-set."

Hernandez wrote in 1651 and Willughby in 1678, and no trace of the doubtful Quetzaltototl so fully described by the former author came to light until the year 1825, when Temminck figured a magnificent Trogon in his 'Planches Coloriées des Oiseaux' from a specimen lent him by Leadbeater [1]. This bird was supposed to be the same as Spix's *Trogon pavoninus*, and it was not until 1831 that De la Llave gave it the distinctive but barbarous name of *Pharomacrus mocinno* [2]. It is true Bonaparte in 1837 [15] claimed that he had named the bird *Trogon paradiseus* in 1826, but a reference to any description or name at that date has not been forthcoming to this day. In 1835 Gould, unaware of De la Llave's previous paper, called the bird *Trogon resplendens* [11], and figured it in the first edition of his Monograph of the Family [12].

The haunts of the Quezal having been traced to the mountain-forests of Vera Paz, one of the Departments of Guatemala (the Quahtemallam of Hernandez), the French traveller Delattre visited the district and gave an account of his experiences in the 'Echo du Monde Savant' [13] in an article which was subsequently reprinted in the 'Revue Zoologique' for 1843 [14]. From that time a regular trade in Quezal skins was established, without the restrictions of the early days, and large numbers were yearly exported, Coban, the capital of Alta Vera Paz, being the central collecting ground. In 1860 Salvin stayed some weeks in this district and made a special expedition with skilled hunters to forests inhabited by Quezals, and the following account of the habits of this bird and the method of hunting them is taken from the paper he published on the subject [20].

The scene of these notes was in the high range of hills which form the northern boundary of the valley of the Cahabon river and the watershed between it and the upper or southern tributaries to the Rio de la Pasion; the summit and northern slopes of this range were at that time clothed with dense forest, and the altitude being 4000 feet above the sea and upwards the climate was cool but very damp.

The Quezal never leaves the forests of this description, and on entering the part referred to from the village of Lanquin in the valley birds of this species were at once met with. The experienced hunter when at work imitates the various calls of the bird and entices it within shot. One of these calls consists principally of a low double note "*whe-oo*," "*whe-ou*," which the bird repeats, whistling it softly at first, and then gradually swelling it into a loud but not unmelodious cry. This is often succeeded by a long note, which after swelling dies away as it began. Both these notes can be easily imitated by the mouth. The bird's other cries are harsh and discordant: they are best produced by doubling a pliant leaf over the first fingers, which must be kept about two inches apart; the two edges of the leaf being then placed in the mouth and the breath drawn in, the required sound is produced. When searching for Quezals the hunter whistles as he walks along, here and there sitting down and repeating the other notes. As soon as he hears a bird answering at a distance he stops, and imitates the bird's cries until it has approached near enough to enable him either to shoot it from where he stands or to creep up to within shot. The female generally flies up first and perches on a tree near the hunter, who takes no notice of her, but continues calling till the male, who usually quickly follows the female, appears. Should the male not show himself, the hunter will sometimes shoot the female. It is thus that so large a proportion of males are shot. The flight of the Quezal is rapid and straight; the long tail-feathers, which never seem in his way, stream after him. It sits almost motionless on its perch, the body remaining in the same position, the head only moving slowly from side to side. The tail does not hang perpendicularly, the angle between the true tail and the vertical being perhaps as much as 15 or 20 degrees; it is occasionally jerked open and closed again, and now and then slightly raised, causing the long coverts to vibrate gracefully. The food consists principally of fruit, which is plucked on the wing, but an occasional caterpillar is also eaten.

The nest of the Quezal is made in the hollow of a tree, and the following note by Mr. Robert Owen, who was then living at the hacienda of San Gerónimo in Vera Paz, gives a good account of its first discovery [21]:—

"Mountains of Santa Cruz, 11th June, 1860.—In an expedition to the mountains of Santa Cruz one of our hunters told me that he knew of a Quezal's nest about a league from Chilasco, a place in the same range, and offered to shoot for me the female and bring me the eggs if I would send my servant to help him. This I accordingly did, and my man returned with the hen and two eggs. They stated that they found the nest in a hollow of a decayed forest-tree, about 26 feet from the ground. There was but one orifice, not more than sufficiently large to allow the bird to enter, and the whole interior cavity was barely large enough to admit of the bird turning round. Inside there were no signs of a nest, beyond a layer of small particles of decayed wood upon which the eggs were deposited. The mountaineers all say that the bird avails itself of the deserted hole of a Woodpecker for its nesting-place, probably founding the supposition on the evident inaptness of the birds for boring into trees."

These eggs are of a bluish-green tint without spots or markings, and measure axis 1·4 in., diam. 1·15 in.

The above account of the nesting-habits of the Quezal and the colour and number of its eggs corresponds exactly with that given by Salmon of the allied *P. auriceps* which he found breeding in the valley of the Cauca in Colombia. The story put in circulation by Bonaparte [15] that the Quezal builds a nest in the shape of a bag or barrel open at both ends, by which means injury to its long tail-feathers is avoided, is finally discredited.

The range of the Quezal extends beyond the limits of Vera Paz, for it occurs where ancient upland forest remains in all the higher parts of Guatemala, such as the mountains beyond the Rio Negro above Chiacaman and Cunen, in the forests of Quezaltenango, and in the great volcanoes of Agua and Fuego, in the belt of mixed forest which encircles those mountains between 7000 and 10,000 feet above the sea. In these mountains we obtained several specimens when staying at the hospitable hacienda of Dueñas. Southward of Guatemala the late Capt. G. C. Taylor gave good evidence of Quezals being found in the higher mountains south and east of Comayagua in Honduras [18], and quite recently Mr. W. B. Richardson has sent us several examples from the neighbourhood of San Rafael del Norte in Nicaragua. Southward of this point there is a distinct gap in the range of the Quezal, the mountain-chain sinking below the height suitable for its economy; but when the hills and volcanos rise again in Costa Rica and Chiriqui, the Quezal reappears in a slightly smaller form, which was named *P. costaricensis* by Cabanis [23], or *P. mocinno* var. *costaricensis* [25] or *P. m. costaricensis* [27], according to the taste of some authors. The difference is slight and only of dimensions, and in our opinion the southern bird is not worthy of being separated by name. Of the Costa Rica bird M. Boucard [26] has given some interesting details in the third volume of Rowley's 'Ornithological Miscellany.'

EUPTILOTIS.

Euptilotis, Gould, Mon. Trog. ed. 2, t. 6 (1858); Grant, Cat. Birds Brit. Mus. xvii. p. 436.

Leptuas, Cab. & Heine, Mus. Hein. iv. Heft 1, p. 206 (1863).

Euptilotis is a peculiar monotypic genus of restricted range. It differs from true *Trogon* in several points of more or less significance. The central rectrices instead of differing in the sexes are coloured alike in both male and female. The ear-coverts are produced and end in long hair-like filaments, a character not found in any other member of the family. The bill is slate-colour, rather flatter and less stout than in *Trogon*, the oval nostrils are more exposed, and the maxilla has a single subterminal notch; and in this respect *Euptilotis* resembles *Pharomacrus* rather than *Trogon*, which has several notches along the end of the tomia.

The genus was founded by Gould in 1858, and in 1863 Cabanis and Heine, apparently overlooking Gould's title, renamed it *Leptuas*.

1. Euptilotis neoxenus.

Trogon neoxenus, Gould, Mon. Trog. t. 25 (1838) [1].

Euptilotis neoxenus, Gould, Mon. Trog. ed. 2, t. 6 (1858) [2]; Grant, Cat. Birds Brit. Mus. xvii. p. 437 [3]; Allen, Bull. Am. Mus. N. H. v. p. 34 [4].

Leptuas neoxenus, Cab. & Heine, Mus. Hein. iv. Heft 1, p. 206 [5].

Supra saturate gramineo-viridis, nitens, capite summo plumbescenti-nigro, cupreo-viridi vix tincto: subtus
　　gutture toto plumbeo-nigro nitenti viridi lavato, corpore toto reliquo rosaceo-coccineo; alis plumbeo-nigris,
　　remigibus ad basin in pogonio externo albidis; cauda chalybeo-nigra, rectricibus tribus utrinque externis
　　late albo terminatis; rostro plumbeo, pedibus corylino-carneis.　Long. tota circa 13·0, alæ 7·9, caudæ 8·0,
　　rostri a rictu 1·5, tarsi 0·7.

♀ supra mari similis, capite summo plumbeo: subtus a mento usque ad medium ventris plumbeo ad medium
　　pectus brunneo tincta, ventre reliquo et tectricibus subcaudalibus coccineis, cauda sicut in mare.　(Descr.
　　maris et feminæ ex Sierra de Valparaiso, Mexico.　Mus. nostr.)

Hab. Mexico (*J. Taylor* [1], *Floresi apud Gould* [1][2]), El Pinita in Chihuahua (*F. Robinette* [4]),
Sierra de Valparaiso, Sierra Madre de Nayarit (*W. B. Richardson* [3]).

In the first edition of his ' Monograph of the Trogonidæ,' Gould tells us that the
first intimation he had of the existence of this interesting species was the presentation
by Mr. John Taylor to the Zoological Society of an immature specimen about the year
1836, which he described and figured under the name of *Trogon neoxenus.*　In the
second edition of the same work he states that he subsequently received an adult male
and female from the late Mr. Floresi, but was unable to say for certain from what part of
Mexico they were brought, but thought they came from the neighbourhood of Real del
Monte, a supposition since proved to be erroneous.　Besides the specimens mentioned by
Gould, two others were acquired for the Berlin Museum, as recorded by Cabanis [5], both
from Mexico, but without more precise locality.　It is only quite recently that the true
domicile of *Euptilotis neoxenus* was ascertained by our collector, Mr. W. B. Richardson,
who obtained five specimens for us in the Sierra de Valparaiso and the Sierra Madre de
Nayarit districts, towards the southern end of the great mountain-range which runs
more or less parallel to the Pacific Ocean, through the States of Jalisco and Durango
to the north-western frontier of the Republic.　Since then this Trogon has been found
much further north in the same range at El Pinita, in the State of Chihuahua,
by Mr. F. Robinette, who was attached to the Lumholtz Archæological Expedition
of 1890–91 [4].　It is thus extremely probable that Floresi's examples were secured in
the mountains near Bolaños, where he certainly resided for some time, and where some
of his collections were made.　This place is close to where Mr. Richardson secured his
birds.　The species is doubtless restricted in its range to suitable forests on the great
mountain-range already referred to, and forms one of its most characteristic birds, the
great Woodpecker, *Campophilus imperialis,* being another.

No particulars of the habits of this fine bird have reached us.

TROGON.

Trogon, Linnæus, Syst. Nat. i. p. 167 (1766); Grant, Cat. Birds Brit. Mus. xvii. p. 440.
Pothinus, Cab. & Heine, Mus. Hein. iv. Heft 1, p. 180 (1863).
Aganus, Cab. & Heine, op. cit. p. 184.
Troctes, Cab. & Heine, op. cit. p. 201.

The genus *Trogon* is essentially Neotropical, its species ranging from the northern confines of the region to the limits of the Brazilian fauna, being absent in Argentina, Chili, and the extreme south. Of the twenty-four species admitted in Mr. Grant's Catalogue * no less than fourteen are found within our limits. Of these seven occur in Mexico, some of them nearly reaching the northern frontier, and one even passing it into Arizona; six occur in Guatemala and five in Honduras. The more southern forms then begin to appear, for in Nicaragua we find seven species, and eight in Costa Rica and Panama.

The only species with wide southern range is *T. atricollis*, which penetrates as far north as the Segovia river, dividing Honduras from Nicaragua. In the south this species is subject to local variations which are discussed at length below. Other species passing into the southern continent are *T. chionurus* and *T. caligatus* as far as Western Ecuador, both of them with close southern allies, and *T. macrurus*, a species restricted to Panama and Colombia. The other ten species are restricted to our fauna: of these, *T. bairdi* and *T. clathratus* belong to Costa Rica and Panama; *T. chrysomelas* to Eastern Nicaragua; *T. mexicanus* to Southern Mexico and Guatemala; *T. ambiguus* and *T. citreolus* to Mexico; *T. melanocephalus* to Mexico and Costa Rica and the intervening country; *T. massena* to Mexico and Panama and all between; *T. elegans* to the country between Guatemala and Costa Rica, and *T. puella* to that lying between Southern Mexico and Panama.

The genus *Trogon*, of which *T. viridis* has been considered the type, has been much subdivided by various authors; but the characters are trivial, with the exception, perhaps, of *Troctes* of Cabanis and Heine, represented by *Trogon massena*. This is a stouter form without white ends to the lateral rectrices, but these characters are hardly of sufficient importance to render any division of *Trogon* desirable.

As in *Euptilotis* the upper tail-coverts are comparatively short and do not extend nearly to the end of the rectrices, nor are the wing-coverts lengthened as in *Pharomacrus*. The central pair of rectrices are differently coloured in the sexes, those of the male being of some shade of glittering green, those of the female brown or slate-colour.

The colouring of the lateral rectrices and of the females furnishes natural characters for the subdivision of the genus.

A. *Rectrices utrinque tres laterales plus minusve albo terminatæ.*

a. *Femina supra brunnea aut rufo-brunnea.*

1. **Trogon mexicanus.**

Trogon mexicanus, Swains. Phil. Mag. new ser. i. p. 440 (1827) [1]; Zool. Ill. ser. 2, tt. 82, 107 [2]; Wagl. Isis, 1831, p. 523 [3]; Gould, Mon. Trog. tt. 1, 2 [4]; ed. 2. t. 7 [5]; Scl. P. Z. S. 1859,

---

* Of these we unite *T. aurantiiventris* with *T. puella* and add Mr. Richmond's *T. chrysomelas*, a species unknown to us.

pp. 367[6], 387[7]; Scl. & Salv. Ibis, 1859, p. 132[8]; 1860, p. 41[9]: Cab. & Heine, Mus. Hein. iv. Heft 1, p. 167[10]; Sumichrast, La Nat. v. p. 239[11]; Salv. Cat. Strickl. Coll. p. 425[12]; Ferrari-Perez, Pr. U. S. Nat. Mus. ix. p. 161[13]; Herrera, La Nat. (2) i. pp. 178[14], 321[15]; Grant, Cat. Birds Brit. Mus. xvii. p. 444[16].

Togon glocitans, Licht. Preis-Verz. Mex. Vög. p. 1 (*cf.* J. f. Orn. 1863, p. 55)[17].

Trogon morgani, Swains. apud Gould, Mon. Trog. t. 1 (text)[18].

Supra nitide gramineo-viridis, dorso vix cupreo tincto; loris, capitis lateribus et gula nigris, gutture dorso concolore, torque pectorali nivea, abdomine et tectricibus subcaudalibus coccineis; alis nigris, secundariis extrorsum et tectricibus mediis et minoribus nigris minutissime griseo irroratis; cauda nigra, rectricibus macula terminali magna quadrata alba, rectricibus duabus mediis dorso fere concoloribus nigro late terminatis; rostro flavo, pedibus corylinis, oculorum ambitu ave vivo coccineo. Long. tota circa 11·0, alæ 5·8, caudæ 6·7, rostri a rictu 0·85, tarsi 0·6.

♀ supra rufo-brunnea, capitis lateribus et gula nigricantioribus, macula postoculari alba, gutture dorso concolore, torque pectorali albida, ventre antico brunneo, ventre imo et tectricibus subcaudalibus coccineis; alis nigricantibus, tectricibus minutissime fulvo irroratis, remigibus extrorsum albo limbatis; cauda nigra, rectricibus tribus utrinque externis in pogonio externo regulariter albo vittatis et albo terminatis, rectricibus duabus mediis brunneis nigro terminatis. (Descr. maris et feminæ ex Sierra Nevada de Colima, Mexico. Mus. nostr.)

Juv. tectricibus alarum macula subterminali magna fulva ornatis.

Hab. MEXICO[17] (*Wagler*[3], *T. Mann*[12]), Temiscaltepec (*Bullock*[1]), Real del Monte (*J. Taylor*[4]), Valley of Mexico (*Herrera*[14][15]), Alpine region of Orizaba, Monte Alto, Popocatepetl (*Sumichrast*[11]), Rio Frio Ixtaccihuatl (*W. B. Richardson*), Chimalpa, Coapa, Cerro de San Mateo[13] (*Ferrari-Perez*), Jalapa (*de Oca*[6], *Ferrari-Perez*[13]), Cofre de Perote, Coatepec (*M. Trujillo*), Tenango de Valle, Sierra de Nayarit, Sierra de Bolaños (*W. B. Richardson*), Sierra Nevada de Colima (*W. B. Richardson, W. Lloyd*), Omilteme in Guerrero (*Mrs. H. H. Smith*), Real Arriba (*Deppe*), La Parada (*Rébouch*), Cinco Señores (*Boucard*[7]), Villa Alta, Oaxaca (*M. Trujillo*); GUATEMALA (*Constancia*[12]), Santa Cruz Mts., San Gerónimo, Chuacus, Volcan de Fuego[9] (*O. S. & F. D. G.*), Santa Maria, San Martin and Cuipaché in Quezaltenango (*W. B. Richardson*).

Trogon mexicanus is a well-known and characteristic species of the forests of the highlands of Mexico and Guatemala, beyond which latter country it has not been traced. It was first discovered in Mexico by Bullock at Temiscaltepec, on the borders of the plateau, and it has since been found in suitable places in all the surrounding country—the Sierras of Jalisco and the Sierra Nevada of Colima, as well as the volcanos of Orizaba, Popocatepetl, and Cofre de Perote. In Guatemala we found it in many parts of the upland districts from an elevation of about 3000 feet to as high as 7000 or 8000 feet or more above sea-level. The forests of evergreen oaks are its chief resort, but it is also found in the thinner forest which clothes the hills of the interior at a lower elevation. On one occasion, when riding along the road from the city of Guatemala to Vera Paz, near the village of Chuacus, we observed a male bird of this species fly from a hole in a small tree growing near the road-side. This hole was about 15 or 20 feet from the ground, and contained three slightly-pointed eggs of a very pale greenish colour. There was no nest, the eggs lying on the floor of the hole.

Like other members of the family, *Trogon mexicanus* does not fly much, but rests almost motionless on the lower branches of the higher trees in an upright position. Its flight is quick but not sustained, as it moves from one perch to another.

The bare eyelid surrounding the eye in both sexes is red, of a tint corresponding with that of the breast in each case, that of the male being the brighter of the two.

2. **Trogon elegans.**

Trogon elegans, Gould, P. Z. S. 1834, p. 26 [1]; Mon. Trog. t. 3 [2]; ed. 2, t. 9 [3]; Scl. P. Z. S. 1858, p. 357 [4]; Taylor, Ibis, 1860, p. 117 [5]; Salv. Ibis, 1866, p. 194 [6]; 1872, p. 322 [7]; Cab. & Heine, Mus. Hein. iv. Heft 1, p. 170 [8]; Cherrie, Pr. U. S. Nat. Mus. xvi. p. 536 [9]; Grant, Cat. Birds Brit. Mus. xvii. p. 449 [10].

Supra læte nitide viridis, fronte, capitis lateribus et gula nigris: subtus gutture et pectore dorso concoloribus, fascia pectorali nivea, corpore toto reliquo et tectricibus subcaudalibus coccineis; alis nigris, remigibus extus albo limbatis, secundariis, tectricibus mediis et minoribus nigris minutissime griseo-albido vermiculatis; cauda supra cupreo-viridi, rectricibus sex mediis nigro terminatis, rectricibus tribus utrinque externis nigris late albo terminatis et regulariter albo stricte transversim fasciatis; rostro flavo, oculorum ambitu coccineo, pedibus corylinis. Long. tota circa 11·0, alæ 5·0, caudæ 6·7, rostri a rictu 0·85, tarsi 0·65.

♀ supra fusco-brunnea, pileo saturatiore; loris, capitis lateribus et gula nigricantibus, macula malari, altera auriculari et oculorum ambitu albis: subtus gutture dorso concolori, fascia pectorale albida, hypochondriis imis et tectricibus subalaribus rosaceo-coccineis, abdomine medio albo; alis nigris, remigibus albo limbatis, secundariis et tectricibus mediis et minoribus pallide fuscis vix nigro irroratis; cauda supra castanea nigro terminata, rectricibus tribus utrinque externis nigris albo late transfasciatis et albo terminatis. (Descr. maris et feminæ ex La Libertad, Salvador. Mus. nostr.)

Hab. GUATEMALA (*fide Gould* [1], *mus. Heineanum* [8]); SALVADOR, La Libertad, Volcan de San Miguel (*W. B. Richardson*); HONDURAS, Plain of Comayagua (*Taylor* [4][5]); NICARAGUA, Chinandega, Volcan de Chinandega, Leon (*W. B. Richardson*), Virgin Bay, Lake of Nicaragua (*Bridges* [7]), Chontales (*Belt* [7]); COSTA RICA, San Lucas I., Gulf of Nicoya (*Alfaro & Cherrie* [9]).

The specimens from which Gould took his original description of this species in 1834 were stated to have been brought from Guatemala [1]; and a male in the Heine collection is supposed to have come from the same country, a young female in the same collection being attributed to Mexico [8]. We have no further evidence that this Trogon occurs in either country, and, judging from the number of skins we have lately received from Salvador and Nicaragua, we are inclined to doubt its occurrence in Guatemala, and to disbelieve in its existence in any part of Mexico. If it is found in the former country it is probably restricted to the southern portion of the lowlands bordering the Pacific Ocean, which form an extension of the lowlands of Salvador, where we have abundant evidence of its occurrence. From this point along the coast of the Pacific through Nicaragua, *T. elegans* seems to be abundant, as Mr. Richardson has sent us many specimens from various places visited by him in this region. It also occurs as far in the interior of Honduras as Comayagua, and in the woods on the shore of the great lake of Nicaragua. The most southern point recorded for the occurrence of this species is the island of San Lucas in the Gulf of Nicoya, where Don A. Alfaro and Mr. Cherrie met with it [9].

T. elegans most resembles *T. ambiguus*, but may readily be distinguished in the adult dress by the more distinct banding of the outer tail-feathers and the coarser freckling of the wing-coverts. *T. ambiguus*, as will be seen below, has a much more northern range, and the two birds are not found together so far as we know.

3. Trogon ambiguus.

Trogon ambiguus, Gould, P. Z. S. 1835, p. 30 [1]; Mon. Trog. t. 4 [2]; ed. 2, t. 8 [3]; Scl. P. Z. S. 1859, p. 387 [4]; Finsch, Abh. naturw. Ver. zu Bremen, 1870, p. 326 [5]; Grayson, Pr. Bost. Soc. N. H. xiv. p. 272 [6]; Lawr. Mem. Bost. Soc. N. H. ii. p. 290 [7]; Sumichr. La Nat. v. p. 239 [8]; Ferrari-Perez, Pr. U. S. Nat. Mus. ix. p. 161 [9]; Ridgw. Pr. U. S. Nat. Mus. x. p. 147 [10]; Grant, Cat. Birds Brit. Mus. xvii. p. 451 [11].

Trogon mexicanus, Baird, U. S. Bound. Surv. Birds, p. 5, t. 2 (nec Swains.) [12].

? *Trogon puella*, Dugès, La Nat. i. p. 139 [13].

T. eleganti similis, sed capite summo fere toto nigro, caudæ rectricibus tribus utrinque externis in dimidio distali albis minute nigro punctatis (nec nigro fasciatis), plaga terminali quadrata tantum pure alba dignoscendus. ♀ rectricibus caudæ externis quoque punctatis nec striatis distinguenda. (Descr. maris et feminæ ex Santiago Territorio de Tepic, Mexico. Mus. nostr.)

Juv. Supra brunneus, secundariis alarum tectricibus mediis et minoribus maculis rotundis conspicuis subapicalibus cervinis ornatis, gutture brunneo, abdomine albido, fusco indistincte fasciato.

Hab. NORTH AMERICA, Arizona [10].—MEXICO [1], Ysleta, Sierra de Alamos (*W. Lloyd*), Mazatlan (*Grayson* [5] [7]), Presidio de Mazatlan (*Forrer*), Tres Marias Is. (*Grayson* [5] [6] [7], *Forrer*), Tepic, Santiago, San Blas, Sierra Madre de Jalisco, Sierra de Valparaiso, Sierra de Nayarit, Bolaños, Zapotlan (*W. B. Richardson*), Beltran (*W. Lloyd*), Volcan de Colima (*W. B. R.*), Boquillo in Nuevo Leon (*Couch* [12]), Rio Camacho, Villa Grande, Hacienda de la Cruz in Nuevo Leon (*F. B. Armstrong*), Tamaulipas, Sierra Madre above Ciudad Victoria, Soto La Marina, Tantina, Tampico, Sierra de San Luis Potosi (*W. B. Richardson*), Alpine region of Orizaba (*Sumichrast* [8]), Coajimalpa in the Valley of Mexico, Chietla [9] and Chachapa in Puebla (*Ferrari-Perez*), Amula and Omilteme in Guerrero (*Mrs. H. H. Smith*), Talea (*Boucard* [4]), Xacautepec (*Deppe*), Oaxaca (*Fenochio*), Juchatengo (*M. Trujillo*).

Gould described this species in 1835 [1], defining its differences from *T. elegans* as consisting of the outer rectrices being obscurely and finely dotted, instead of being marked with strong well-defined bars. In his 'Monograph of the Trogonidæ' he further drew attention to the finer freckling of the wing-coverts and the deeper bronze colour of the upper surface, particularly of the central rectrices. Many specimens have reached us, and these characteristic features of *T. ambiguus* have been abundantly confirmed.

The range of this species seems quite distinct from that of *T. elegans*, and is much more northerly, extending on both sides of the Mexican highlands to the State of

Sonora on the west, and even beyond the limits of Mexico to Arizona [10], and also to Nuevo Leon and Tamaulipas on the east. It is also found in the Valley of Mexico and in the Alpine region of Orizaba, but apparently not in the lowlands of the State of Vera Cruz.

The range in altitude is unusually great for a member of the family of the Trogonidæ, for, as just stated, it occurs in the highlands near Mexico and Orizaba, and in many places in the mountain-ranges of the States of Jalisco, Guerrero, and Oaxaca. It also is found at Mazatlan, the Tres Marias Islands, and San Blas, and near Tampico and other places in the vicinity in the State of Tamaulipas, all near the sea-level.

The range of *T. elegans* is much further south, and, as already stated under the account of that species, is chiefly restricted to Nicaragua and Salvador.

Of the habits of this species little is on record, and they doubtless differ little or not at all from those of other members of the genus. Grayson, who observed it at Mazatlan [7] and the Tres Marias Islands [6], says that it is to be met with only in the dark forests of the tierra caliente, where it breeds in the hollows of trees like Parrots, incubating in June and July. Mr. Ridgway, in 1887, reported that a young bird of this species had been obtained in the Huachuca Mountains in Arizona on Aug. 24, 1885, by Lieut. H. C. Benson, U.S.A., and gave a full description of this specimen [10]. The species had previously been recorded from near the frontier by Baird [12] in his account of the birds collected by the Boundary Survey, and there called *T. mexicanus*.

The name *T. puella* appears in Dugès's list of the birds of Guanajuato and Guadalajara [13]. This should probably be *T. ambiguus*, as the district is far outside the recognized range of *T. puella*.

4. Trogon puella.

Trogon puella, Gould, P. Z. S. 1845, p. 18 [1]; Mon. Trog. ed. 2. t. 11 [2]; Scl. P. Z. S. 1856, p. 286 [3]; 1859, pp. 367 [4], 387 [5]; 1864, p. 176 [6]; Scl. & Salv. Ibis, 1859, p. 132 [7]; Cab. J. f. Orn. 1862, p. 173 [8]; Lawr. Ann. Lyc. N. Y. ix. p. 118 [9]; Bull. U. S. Nat. Mus. no. 4. p. 31 [10]; Salvad. Atti R. Acc. Sc. Tor. 1868, p. 181 [11]; v. Frantz. J. f. Orn. 1869, p. 312 [12]; Salv. P. Z. S. 1870, p. 202 [13]; Boucard, P. Z. S. 1878, p. 48 [14]; 1883, p. 454 [15]; Sumichrast, La Nat. v. p. 239 [16]; Zeledon, An. Mus. Nac. Costa Rica, 1887, p. 120 [17]; Grant, Cat. Birds Brit. Mus. xvii. p. 452 [18].

Trogon xalapensis, Du Bus, Esq. Orn. t. 2 [19].

Trogon aurantiiventris, Gould, P. Z. S. 1856, p. 107 [20]; Mon. Trog. ed. 2, t. 12 [21]; Scl. P. Z. S. 1856, pp. 139 [22], 286 [23]; Salv. Ibis, 1866, p. 194 [24]; P. Z. S. 1867, p. 151 [25]; 1870, p. 202 [26]; Lawr. Ann. Lyc. N. Y. ix. p. 118 [27]; v. Frantz. J. f. Orn. 1869, p. 312 [28]; Zeledon, An. Mus. Nac. Costa Rica, 1887, p. 120 [29]; Grant, Cat. Birds Brit. Mus. xvii. p. 454 [30].

Pothinus aurantiiventer, Cab. & Heine, Mus. Hein. iv. Heft 1, p. 182 [31].

Trogon luciani, Less. apud Bonaparte [32]; Bp. Compt. Rend. xlii. p. 955 (1856) [33].

Trogon sallæi, Bp. Compt. Rend. xlii. p. 955 [34].

Pothinus sallæi, Cab. & Heine, Mus. Hein. iv. Heft 1, p. 183 [35].

Supra læte nitide aureo-viridis, loris, capitis lateribus et mento nigris: subtus gutture et pectore dorso concoloribus, hoc late albo marginato; corpore toto reliquo et tectricibus subcaudalibus coccineis; alis nigris, remigibus albo limbatis, tectricibus alarum minute albo vermiculatis; cauda nigra, rectricibus utrinque tribus parte exposita anguste sed distincte albo transfasciatis, duabus mediis extrorsum fere dorso concoloribus nigro terminatis, reliquis in pogonio externo quoque dorso concoloribus; oculorum ambitu ave vivo coccineo; rostro flavo, pedibus corylinis. Long. tota 10·5, alæ 5·0, caudæ rectr. med. 5·6, rectr. lat. 3·5, tarsus 0·55.

♀ supra omnino brunnea, gutture et pectore concoloribus, mento et capitis lateribus nigricantibus, torque pectorali alba, abdomine rosaceo; alis fusco-nigricantibus extrorsum albido limbatis, tectricibus dorso concoloribus minutissime nigro irroratis; cauda fusco-nigricante, rectricibus duabus mediis extrorsum castaneis nigro terminatis, rectricibus tribus externis in pogonio externo et ad apicem albidis nigro variegatis, apicibus albis, fascia subterminali nigra. (Descr. maris et feminæ ex Dueñas, Guatemala. Mus. nostr.)

♂ juv. cauda plus minusve feminæ caudi similis.

Var. abdomine plus minusve aurantio nec coccineo unde *Trogon aurantiiventris*, Gould.

Hab. MEXICO (*White*[6]), Jalapa (*de Oca*[4]), Cofre de Perote, Coatepec, Vega del Casadero (*M. Trujillo*), Misantla (*F. D. G.*), Cordova (*Sallé*[3 23]), Uvero (*Sumichrast*[16]), Atoyac (*Mrs. H. H. Smith*), Playa Vicente (*Boucard*[5]), Guichicovi (*Sumichrast*[10]), Chimalapa (*Sumichrast*[10 16], *W. B. Richardson*), Izamal, Tizimin in Yucatan (*G. F. Gaumer*[15]); BRITISH HONDURAS, Western District (*F. Blancaneaux*); GUATEMALA, Pie de la Cuesta, Santa Maria near Quezaltenango, Retalhuleu, Toliman (*W. B. Richardson*), Pacific coast region[7], Medio Monte, Alotenango, Dueñas, Volcan de Fuego (*O. S. & F. D. G.*), Escuintla (*Gould*[1]), Chiriquyu near Coban, Yaxcamnal, Choctum[24], Teleman (*O. S. & F. D. G.*); NICARAGUA, Matagalpa, San Rafael de Norte (*W. B. Richardson*); COSTA RICA[8 28] (*Durando*[11]), Turrialba[9 17], Angostura (*Carmiol*), S. José[9], Dota Mts.[12] (*v. Frantzius*), Candelaria Mts. (*v. Frantzius*[12], *Boucard*[14]), Barranca (*Carmiol*[27], *Zeledon*[29]), Navarro (*Boucard*[14]), Naranjo de Cartago (*Zeledon*[17]); PANAMA, David, Boquete (*Bridges*[20 21]), Volcan de Chiriqui[13], Calovevora[26], Castillo[26], Sta Fé[25], Cordillera de Tolé[25] (*Arcé*).

This Trogon was described by Gould in 1845, from a specimen said to have been sent from Escuintla in "South America"[1], the well-known town of that name in the lowlands of Guatemala bordering the Pacific Ocean no doubt being the place referred to. It was again described in the same year by Vicomte Du Bus as *Trogon xalapensis*, and figured in his 'Esquisses Ornithologiques'[19]. The range of the species is now known to be very extensive, reaching in the north to about the middle of the Mexican State of Vera Cruz, where it is found in some abundance from the neighbourhood of Jalapa southwards. It occurs on the Isthmus of Tehuantepec[10], but probably only on the eastern side, for we have no record of its being traced to any part of Western Mexico. It is found in Northern Yucatan[15], in British Honduras, and is a common bird throughout the heavily forested district of Central Guatemala up to Coban and the valley of the Polochic river. In Western Guatemala it is also abundant throughout the region bordering the Pacific Ocean, and in the mountains inland up to an elevation of about 5000 feet above the level of the sea. Absent, apparently, from Honduras and Nicaragua, it reappears in Costa Rica, where it has been found by most collectors, and also in many places in the district of Chiriqui in the State of Panama, and as far in this direction as Santa Fé, which seems to be its extreme southern limit, as we have no tidings of it on the isthmus itself or any place on the mainland of South America.

The habits of this species resemble those of *T. mexicanus*. Of its nest and eggs nothing is on record.

Regarding the orange-breasted bird usually known as *Trogon aurantiiventris*, which was described by Gould in 1856[20] from a specimen obtained by T. Bridges in Chiriqui, and has since been traced to Guatemala[24] and Cordova[23] in Mexico, we have little doubt that it is only an aberrant form of *T. puella*. Though not nearly so common, the range of the two birds is practically the same; moreover, in the series from the more southern parts of its range, the orange colour of the abdomen varies from a lighter to a darker redder tint.

Mr. Ogilvie-Grant, when writing the Catalogue of Trogonidæ in the British Museum, expressed his great doubt as to the distinctness of the two birds[30]. We now go a little further and unite them.

5. Trogon atricollis.

Trogon curucui, var. γ, Gm. Syst. Nat. i. p. 403[1].

Trogon atricollis, Vieill. N. Dict. d'Hist. N. viii. p. 318[2]; Gould, Mon. Trog. t. 8[3]; ed. 2, t. 14[4]; Cassin, Pr. Ac. Phil. 1860, p. 136[5]; Scl. & Salv. P. Z. S. 1864, p. 364[6]; Salv. P. Z. S. 1867, p. 151[7]; 1870, p. 202[8]; Ibis, 1872, p. 321[9]; Ridgw. Pr. U. S. Nat. Mus. x. p. 591[10]; Zeledon, An. Mus. Nac. Costa Rica, 1887, p. 120[11]; Grant, Cat. Birds Brit. Mus. xvii. p. 455[12].

Trogon tenellus, Cab. J. f. Orn. 1862, p. 173[13]; Lawr. Ann. Lyc. N. Y. viii. pp. 3[14], 184[15]; ix. p. 119[16]; v. Frantz. J. f. Orn. 1869, p. 312[17].

Trogon atricollis tenellus, Richm. Pr. U. S. Nat. Mus. xvi. p. 513[18].

Trogon aurantiiventris, Lawr. Ann. Lyc. N. Y. vii. p. 290 (nec Gould)[19].

Supra nitente viridis, tectricibus supracaudalibus vix cyaneo tinctis; loris, capitis lateribus et mento nigris, gula et pectore dorso concoloribus, abdomine citrino, tectricibus subcaudalibus concoloribus, torque pectorali vix obvia albida; alis nigris albo limbatis, tectricibus alarum albo minute irroratis; caudæ rectricibus duabus mediis uropygio concoloribus nigro terminatis, rectricibus tribus externis nigris extrorsum albo regulariter transfasciatis et albo late terminatis, reliquis in pogonio externo duabus mediis concoloribus; oculorum ambitu cæruleo; rostro viridescente, pedibus plumbeis. Long. tota 9·5, alæ 4·3, caudæ rectr. med. 5·5, rectr. lat. 3·0, tarsi 0·55.

♀ supra brunnea, gutture toto et pectore concoloribus, abdomine et tectricibus subcaudalibus pallide citrinis, torque pectorali alba; alis nigricantibus, extrorsum albo limbatis, tectricibus alarum brunneis minute nigro irroratis; caudæ rectricibus duabus mediis castaneis nigro terminatis, rectricibus tribus externis sicut in mare fasciatis. (Descr. maris et feminæ ex La Libertad, Nicaragua. Mus. nostr.)

Hab. HONDURAS, Segovia R. (*Townsend*[10]); NICARAGUA, Chontales (*Belt*[9]), La Libertad and S. Domingo in Chontales (*W. B. Richardson*), Escondido R. (*Richmond*[18]), Greytown (*Holland*[15]); COSTA RICA (*v. Frantzius*[13][17]), Pacuare, Angostura (*Carmiol*[16], *Zeledon*[11]), Barranca, Guaitil (*Carmiol*[16]), Las Trojas (*Zeledon*[11]);

PANAMA, Volcan de Chiriqui [8], Bugaba [8], Cordillera de Tolé [7], Chitra [8], Calovevora [8], Santiago de Veraguas [7], Santa Fé [7] (*Arcé*), Lion Hill (*McLeannan* [6] [14] [19]), Chepo (*Arcé*), Truando R. (*C. J. Wood* [5]).—SOUTH AMERICA generally in forest country, from Colombia to Guiana and Brazil [12].

This Trogon, in one or other of its forms, has been long known. The Brazilian bird was figured by Edwards in 1758 as the "Yellow-bellied Green Cuckoo," a species mentioned in the earlier work of Marcgrave. Upon the female of the Guiana form the name of "Couroucou à queue rousse de Cayenne" was bestowed by Buffon, and figured by D'Aubenton in the 'Planches Coloriées des Oiseaux,' and this subsequently became the *Trogon rufus* of Gmelin. The male, also from Guiana, was described by Vieillot in 1817 as *Trogon atricollis*. Other titles were subsequently bestowed upon it, amongst these *Trogon chrysochloros* by v. Pelzeln on the Brazilian bird, and *Trogon tenellus* by Cabanis on that of Costa Rica. It is with the latter that we have now to deal.

A revision of the large series of skins of *T. atricollis* in the British Museum, supplemented with additions to the list in Mr. Grant's catalogue, mostly from Nicaragua, show that the notes on the variation of the species supplied by Salvin to Gould for the second edition of the 'Trogonidæ' are fully confirmed. They are briefly as follows:—

Central America (*Nicaragua to Panama*).—The male has the central rectrices of a rather bluer shade of green; the bars on the outer tail-feathers are wider and fewer, and the abdomen is clear yellow with hardly any shade of orange.

Colombia (*Cauca Valley*).—The central rectrices are not tinged with blue, but have a slight bronze tint; the barring of the tail agrees with that of the Central-American bird, and there is a slight tinge of orange on the breast.

Eastern Ecuador (*Sarayacu*).—The central rectrices are of a deeper bronze tint than any of the series, the bands of the outer rectrices being wide as in more northern examples; the abdomen is still deeper orange.

Guiana.—Central rectrices slightly bronze as in the Cauca Valley birds, the bands of the outer rectrices being rather narrower, the abdomen slightly orange.

Brazil.—Tail rather long, central rectrices slightly tinged with bronze, outer rectrices more narrowly and more numerously barred, the abdomen slightly orange.

These characters, always very slight, are not absolutely restricted to the birds of these districts, but indicate rather their general features. It will be thus seen that if any separation is to be made the number of divisions can hardly be confined to two. We think ourselves that this is one of those cases where a single name will be found sufficient, the variation being acknowledged.

The range of *Trogon atricollis* in Central America reaches as far as Eastern Nicaragua, where it was noticed by Belt, who, writing of it and *T. caligatus*, says ('Naturalist in Nacaragua,' p. 122), "Both species take short, quick, jerky flights, and are often met with along with flocks of other birds—Flycatchers, Tanagers, Creepers, Woodpeckers, &c., that hunt together, traversing the forests in troops of hundreds belonging to more than a score of different species. . . . . The Flycatchers and Trogons sit on branches and fly after the larger insects, the Flycatchers taking them on the wing, the Trogons from the leaves upon which they have settled. In the breeding-season the Trogons are continually calling out to each other, and are easily discovered. The Spainards call them 'Viudas.'"

Mr. Richmond says [18] that Trogons are almost invariably found in pairs (probably during the breeding-season), rarely in small flocks. He adds that the iris of this species is very dark brown, the feet plumbeous, the orbital ring blue, and the bill chromium-yellow.

In Costa Rica this species appears to be equally common, and also in the State of Panama, both in Chiriqui and along the Line of Railway.

In South America it is represented in nearly every collection of any extent formed in lowlying forests of the hotter parts of the continent.

b. *Femina supra schistacea aut schistaceo-nigra.*

6. Trogon chionurus.

Trogon melanopterus, Cassin, Pr. Ac. Phil. 1860, p. 136 (nec Swainson) [1].

Trogon viridis, Lawr. Ann. Lyc. N. Y. vii. p. 290 (nec Linn.) [2]; Scl. & Salv. P. Z. S. 1864, p. 364 [3].

Trogon chionurus, Scl. & Salv. P. Z. S. 1870, p. 843 [4]; 1879, p. 535 [5]; Grant, Cat. Birds Brit. Mus. xvii. p. 460 [6].

Trogon eximius, Lawr. Ann. Lyc. N. Y. x. p. 11 [7].

Supra dorso medio et scapularibus nitide cyaneo-viridescentibus, cervice postica et uropygio læte nitide purpureis, capite summo nigro purpureo lavato; loris, capitis lateribus et gula nigris, pectore nigro purpureo lavato, abdomine et tectricibus subcaudalibus citrino-aurantiis, hypochondriis saturate schistaceis; alis nigris, tectricibus concoloribus; caudæ rectricibus duabus mediis viridescenti-cyaneis, nigro terminatis, rectricibus tribus utrinque lateralibus ad basin nigris parte exposita omnino alba, rectricibus reliquis in pogonio externo duabus mediis concoloribus; rostro flavido ad basin plumbeo, pedibus fuscis. Long. tota 11·0, alæ 6·0, caudæ rectr. med. 6·3, rectr. lat. 4·3, tarsus 0·5.

♀ schistacea, abdomine et tectricibus subcaudalibus aurantiis, secundariis internis et tectricibus alarum omnibus albo stricte transversim lineolatis, remigibus extus albido maculatis; caudæ rectricibus utrinque tribus in pogonio externo ad basin et ad apices omnino albo transfasciatis, apicibus ipsis late albis. (Descr. maris et feminæ exempl. typ. ex Panama. Mus. nostr.)

Hab. PANAMA [7], Veraguas (*Arcé*), Lion Hill (*M'Leannan* [2] [3] [4]), Truando R. (*C. J. Wood* [1]). —COLOMBIA [5]; W. ECUADOR [6].

Little has transpired concerning this fine Trogon beyond the account of it given by Salvin in the second edition of Gould's 'Monograph of the Trogonidæ,' which we transcribe below. The range is now found to be a little more extended, as Arcé sent us an adult male from Veraguas, and we have adults of both male and female from the

Colombian State of Antioquia, and an adult male from the Balzar Mountains, north of the Gulf of Guayaquil, in Western Ecuador. Salmon, who met with *Trogon chionurus* in Antioquia, also found its nest, which he says is made in holes of palm-trees, in which two white eggs are laid [5].

The notes in the 'Monograph of the Trogonidæ' are as follows:—" This beautiful Trogon may readily be distinguished from the well-known *T. viridis* by the much greater development of white in the tail-feathers. The first outer pair are all pure white, except a narrow basal patch concealed by the tail-coverts. Of the second pair considerably more than the apical half is white; in the third pair the white apices measure two inches in length. When the tail is closed the under surface appears perfectly white. Comparing the amount of white in the tail with that shown in *T. viridis*, the distinctness of the two birds is apparent. Notwithstanding this difference, the species remained several years undescribed both in Mr. Lawrence's cabinet and in our own; but in 1870 Mr. Sclater and I had occasion to examine the question, when it became manifest that this fine species required a name. About the same time Mr. Lawrence also bestowed the name *T. eximius* upon it."

The first specimens of this species were forwarded to Lawrence from the Panama Railway Line by the late James M'Leannan, who afterwards supplied our collection with specimens of both sexes. The bird does not seem to extend its range into Central America much beyond the Line of Railway. Mr. Wyatt, when travelling in the valley of the Magdalena river in Colombia, shot a female of this species in the forest near Paturia, and heard the male calling further in.

The bird found by the hunters of Bogota is the true *T. viridis*, which occurs over a wide range of country lying to the east of the Andes, as far as Guiana and Eastern Brazil. It is therefore most probable that Colombian birds of this form are all obtained on the slope of the mountains drained by the upper waters of the Rio Meta, a district much frequented by the Bogota bird-hunters.

7. **Trogon bairdi.**

Trogon bairdi, Lawr. Ann. Lyc. N. Y. ix. p. 119 [1]; Salv. Ibis, 1869, p. 316 [2]; P. Z. S. 1870, p. 202 [3];
v. Frantz. J. f. Orn. 1869, p. 313 [4]; Gould, Mon. Trog. ed. 2, t. 23 [5]; Zeledon, An. Mus. Nac. Costa Rica, 1887, p. 120 [6]; Grant, Cat. Birds Brit. Mus. xvii. p. 461 [7].
Trogon clathratus, Lawr. Ann. Lyc. N. Y. ix. p. 119 (nec Salv.) [8].

T. chionuri similis, abdomine et tectricibus subcaudalibus coccineis nec aurantiis facile distinguendus, femina caudæ rectricibus tribus utrinque lateralibus ad apices fasciatis nec late albo terminatis. (Descr. maris et feminæ ex Bugaba, Panama. Mus. nostr.)

Hab. Costa Rica, San Mateo (*Cooper* [1] [8], *v. Frantzius* [4]), Pozo Azul de Pirris, Las Trojas (*Zeledon* [6]); Panama, Bugaba [3], Bibalaz (*Arcé*), Veraguas (*Merritt*).

This fine species is closely allied to *T. chionurus*, but may readily be distinguished by its scarlet breast. It range, too, is distinct, being confined to Costa Rica and the district of Chiriqui; whereas *T. chionurus* is a more southern bird, whose northern limits do not reach much beyond the Line of the Panama Railway.

T. bairdi was described by Lawrence from specimens obtained by J. Cooper at San Mateo in Costa Rica [1], and others have been secured in the same country by J. Zeledon [6]. All our examples were sent in by Arcé from Bugaba [3] and other places in the vicinity, the bird being evidently not uncommon in the district of Chiriqui.

The specimen described by Lawrence as a female of *T. clathratus*, an identification to which Mr. Grant disagreed, proves after re-examination by Mr. Ridgway to belong to *T. bairdi*.

Long prior to the description of this species by Lawrence, specimens were secured by Dr. Merritt in Veraguas, and were in his collection when Salvin examined it in 1874.

Nothing concerning its habits is on record.

8. Trogon citreolus.

Trogon citreolus, Gould, P. Z. S. 1835, p. 30 [1]; Mon. Trog. t. 13 [2]; ed. 2, t. 26 [3]; Scl. & Salv. Ibis, 1859, p. 132 [4]; Finsch, Abh. naturw. Ver. zu Bremen, 1870, p. 326 [5]; Lawr. Mem. Bost. Soc. N. H. ii. p. 290 [6]; Bull. U. S. Nat. Mus. no. 4, p. 31 [7]; Sumichrast, La Nat. v. p. 239 [8]; Ferrari-Perez, Pr. U. S. Nat. Mus. ix. p. 162 [9]; Grant, Cat. Birds Brit. Mus. xvii. p. 461 [10].

Aganus citreolus, Cab. & Heine, Mus. Hein. iv. Heft 1, p. 197 [11].

Trogon capistratum, Less. Rev. Zool. 1842, p. 136 (apud Cab. & Heine) [12].

Trogon lucidus, Licht. in Mus. Berol. [13]

Supra nitide chalybeo-viridis, dorso antico et uropygio purpureo tinctis, capite summo schistaceo-nigro cyaneo-viridi lavato; loris, capitis lateribus, gutture et pectore schistaceo-nigris hoc cyaneo-viridi lavato, torque pectorali late alba, abdomine et tectricibus subcaudalibus citrino-aurantiis; alis schistaceo-nigris, remigibus albo limbatis; caudæ rectricibus duabus mediis nitide viridibus nigro terminatis, rectricibus tribus lateralibus late albo terminatis, rectricibus reliquis in pogonio externo mediis concoloribus; rostro corneo. Long. tota 10·7, alæ 5·3, caudæ rectr. med. 6·0, rectr. lat. 4·0.

♀ corpore supra omnino, gutture et pectore schistaceis, torque pectorali alba, abdomine citrino; caudæ rectricibus tribus lateralibus ad apicem albis, pogonio externo quoque albo maculatis. (Descr. maris et feminæ ex Mazatlan, Mexico. Mus. nostr.)

Hab. MÉXICO, Mazatlan (*Grayson* [5] [6], *Xantus, Forrer*), Presidio de Mazatlan (*Forrer*), Santiago and San Blas in the Territory of Tepic (*W. B. Richardson*), Colima, Culata near Manzanillo (*W. Lloyd*), Acapulco, Rincon in Guerrero (*Mrs. H. H. Smith*), Tequistlan (*Deppe* [11]), Ianhuitlan (?) (*Ferrari-Perez* [9]), Tehuantepec (*Deppe* [11], *Grayson* [6], *Sumichrast, Richardson*), Chihuitan, Sta. Efigenia, Tapanatepec, Cacoprieto, Tapana, Ventosa (*Sumichrast* [7]).

This species, which was described by Gould in 1835 from specimens from an unknown locality [1], was at one time supposed to be an inhabitant of Yucatan [4]; but this is now known to be erroneous, the bird being restricted to Western Mexico from Mazatlan to the Isthmus of Tehuantepec.

The first examples obtained were doubtless those sent by Deppe to the Berlin

Museum from Tequistlan and Tehuantepec, where they were labelled *Trogon lucidus* by Lichtenstein, but never characterized, and for many years nothing more was heard of this peculiar Trogon.

When the ornithology of Western Mexico was so carefully investigated by Grayson, *T. citreolus* again appeared before us as, in the words of its rediscoverer, "well distributed throughout the forests of the tierra caliente of this region." He adds that he found it also at Tehuantepec, and that it is a native and does not migrate. Since then we have received a plentiful supply of specimens from our collectors in Western Mexico—Forrer, Richardson, Lloyd, and Mrs. Herbert Smith, who found it at various points in the States of Sonora, Jalisco, Colima, Guerrero, Oaxaca, and on the Isthmus of Tehuantepec.

Whether it is found further to the south we are as yet unable to say, but it very likely occurs in the Department of Soconusco, if not in the Costa Grande of Guatemala.

The type from Gould's collection and the specimen from Mazatlan have a distinct bluish-green tint over the crown and the lower part and sides of the breast, which is not present in any of the examples from Tehuantepec or from the coast northwards till we come to Santiago, which lies on the north of the river of that name and not far from Mazatlan. A male from this place has a slight tint over the feathers of the crown. If it is found expedient to recognize two forms of *T. citreolus*, the original name should be retained for the Mazatlan bird, and the southern form might be called *T. capistratus*, Less., if, as may have been the case, the locality Realejo was wrongly given for Acapulco. Should *T. capistratus* prove to belong to *T. melanocephalus*, Lichtenstein's uncharacterized title *Trogon lucidus*, given to Deppe's Tehuantepec birds, may be employed.

9. Trogon melanocephalus.

Trogon melanocephalus, Gould, Mon. Trog. t. 12 [1]; ed. 2, t. 27 [2]; Scl. P. Z. S. 1857, p. 227 [3]; 1858, p. 357 [4]; 1859, pp. 367 [5], 387 [6]; Moore, P. Z. S. 1859, p. 53 [7]; Scl. & Salv. Ibis, 1859, p. 132 [8]; P. Z. S. 1870, p. 837 [9]; Taylor, Ibis, 1860, p. 117 [10]; Lawr. Ann. Lyc. N. Y. viii. p. 184 [11]; Salv. Ibis, 1870, p. 115 [12]; 1872, p. 322 [13]; 1889, p. 371 [14]; 1890, p. 88 [15]; Sumichrast, La Nat. x. p. 239 [16]; Nutting, Pr. U. S. Nat. Mus. v. p. 400 [17]; vi. pp. 376 [18], 387 [19], 395 [20]; Boucard, P. Z. S. 1883, p. 454 [21]; Ridgw. Pr. U. S. Nat. Mus. x. p. 581 [22]; Herrera, La Nat. (2) i. p. 321 [23]; Grant, Cat. Birds Brit. Mus. xvii. p. 462 [24]; Richmond, Pr. U. S. Nat. Mus. xvi. p. 515 [25].

Aganus melanocephalus, Cab. & Heine, Mus. Hein. iv. Heft 1, p. 197 [26].

Supra nitide cyaneo-viridis, uropygio nitide purpureo; capite toto, gula, pectore et alis nigris, harum remigibus ad basin albo limbatis, abdomine toto et tectricibus subcaudalibus citrino-aurantiis; caudæ rectricibus duabus mediis dorso concoloribus nigro terminatis, rectricibus tribus lateralibus nigris macula subquadrata alba terminatis, rectricibus reliquis nigris in pogonio externo mediis concoloribus. Long. tota 10·5, caudæ rectr. med. 5·8, rectr. lat. 4·0.

♀ supra schistaceo-nigra, rectricibus mediis nigro terminatis, gula et pectore dorso concoloribus, abdomine et tectricibus subcaudalibus citrino-aurantiis; caudæ rectricibus tribus utrinque albo late terminatis. (Descr. maris et feminæ ex Teapa, Tabasco, Mexico. Mus. nostr.)

♂ *juv.* caudæ rectricibus tribus lateralibus albo terminatis et in pogonio externo albo maculatis.

Hab. MEXICO [26], Tamaulipas (*Gould* [1]), Tampico (*W. B. Richardson*), Misantla, Laguna Verde (*M. Trujillo*), Jalapa (*de Oca* [5]), Vera Cruz (*W. B. R.*), Playa Vicente (*Boucard* [6], *M. Trujillo*), Uvero (*Sumichrast* [16]), Valle Real, Alvarado (*Deppe*), Cateman (*Boucard* [3]), Teapa (*Mrs. H. H. Smith*), Yak-Jonat [21], Chem-zonat [21], Buctzotz, Izamal, Peto, Meco [14] (*G. F. Gaumer*), Merida (*Schott*); BRITISH HONDURAS, Corosal (*Roe*), Orange Walk (*G. F. Gaumer*), Belize, San Antonio, Cayo, San Felipe (*Blancaneaux*); GUATEMALA [8], Choctum (*O. S. & F. D. G.*); SALVADOR, Volcan de San Miguel (*W. B. Richardson*), La Union (*O. S.*); HONDURAS [8], Omoa (*Leyland* [7]), Truxillo (*Townsend* [22]), Medina, San Pedro (*G. M. Whitely* [9]), Tigre I. [4] and Taulevi (*Taylor* [10]); NICARAGUA, Escondido R. (*Richmond* [25]), Greytown (*Holland* [11]), Chontales (*Belt* [13]), La Libertad in Chontales, Leon (*W. B. Richardson*), San Juan del Sur [18], Sucuya [19], Omotepe [20] (*Nutting*), Virgin Bay (*Bridges*), Volcan de Chinandega (*W. B. Richardson*); COSTA RICA (*Carmiol* [12]), La Palma (*Nutting* [17]).

Gould's original specimen, on which he based his description and drew the plate in the first edition of his Monograph, was stated to have come from the Mexican State of Tamaulipas [1]. Mr. Richardson sent us an adult male from Tampico, on the boundary of the States of Tamaulipas and Vera Cruz, and we have many examples both from him and other collectors from thence southwards, all through the lowlands of Vera Cruz and Tabasco. *Trogon melanocephalus* also occurs in Yucatan and British Honduras, but in Eastern Guatemala it appears to be quite rare, as very few specimens have come under our notice from that country. It appears to be common on both sides of the mountain-range of Honduras, and also in Nicaragua. In Costa Rica, according to Mr. Nutting, it is common at La Palma, where it is to be seen in flocks of a dozen or more in the dry open woods away from water. It has a sort of chattering note, low and soft. A report of a gun does not startle them, and an entire flock can be secured from the same tree. Mr. Richmond gives [25] a similar account of the bird in the parts of Nicaragua he visited, where it is abundant, wandering into the plantations and sometimes found as many as six or eight together.

The only occasion on which Salvin met with *T. melanocephalus* was when coasting from Guatemala to Panama. An opportunity of going ashore occurring when the steamer was calling at La Union, he found several birds of this species in the woods close to the shore of the Bay of Fonseca. In habits they resembled other Trogons. *Trogon melanocephalus* and *T. citreolus* are closely allied, but the former may readily be distinguished by the smaller squarer terminal white spots to the three lateral tail-feathers on either side, the absence of the white pectoral band, and the deeper orange of the abdomen.

Mr. Nutting noted that the skin round the eye in the fresh bird is sky-blue.

63*

10. **Trogon caligatus.**

Trogon caligatus, Gould, Mon. Trog. t. 7 [1]; ed. 2, t. 16 [2]; Scl. P. Z. S. 1856, p. 286 [3]; 1859,
  pp. 367 [4], 387 [5]; 1864, p. 176 [6]; Moore, P. Z. S. 1859, p. 53 [7]; Scl. & Salv. Ibis, 1859,
  p. 132 [8]; P. Z. S. 1864, p. 364 [9]; Lawr. Ann. Lyc. N. Y. vii. p. 290 [10]; ix. p. 118 [11]; Salv.
  P. Z. S. 1867, p. 151 [12]; 1870, p. 202 [13]; Ibis, 1869, p. 316 [14]; 1872, p. 322 [15]; Sumichrast,
  La Nat. v. p. 239 [16]; Boucard, P. Z. S. 1883, p. 454 [17]; Nutting, Pr. U. S. Nat. Mus. v.
  p. 400 [18]; Zeledon, An. Mus. Nac. Costa Rica, 1887, p. 120 [19]; Stone, Pr. Ac. Phil. 1890,
  p. 206 [20]; Grant, Cat. Birds Brit. Mus. xvii. p. 465 [21]; Richmond, Pr. U. S. Nat. Mus. xvi.
  p. 513 [22].

Trogon concinnus, Lawr. Ann. Lyc. N. Y. vii. p. 463 [23]; ix. p. 119 [24]; v. Frantzius, J. f. Orn. 1869,
  p. 312 [25].

Aganus braccatus, Cab. & Heine, Mus. Hein. iv. Heft 1, p. 184 [26].

Trogon braccatus, Lawr. Bull. U. S. Nat. Mus. no. 4, p. 31 [27]; Sumichrast, La Nat. v. p. 239 [28].

Trogon lepidus, Cab. & Heine, Mus. Hein. iv. Heft 1, p. 187 [29].

Supra nitide cupreo-viridis, certa luce cyaneo tinctus, nucha et pectore nitide purpureo; capite toto et gula
  nigris, torque pectorali alba, abdomine et tectricibus subcaudalibus aurantiis; alis nigris, remigibus albo
  limbatis, tectricibus minutissime albo irroratis; caudæ rectricibus duabus mediis dorso concoloribus nigro
  terminatis, tectricibus tribus externis apicibus albis et albo, parte exposita, transfasciatis, rectricibus
  reliquis in pogonio externo mediis concoloribus; oculorum ambitu citrino. Long. tota 9·0, alæ 5·0, caudæ
  rectr. med. 5·0, rectr. lat. 3·0.

♀ supra schistacea, gula et pectore concoloribus, caudæ apicibus nigris, alarum tectricibus stricte sed regulariter
  albo transfasciatis; caudæ rectricibus tribus externis albo terminatis, pogoniis externis tantum albo transfasciatis. (Descr. maris et feminæ ex La Libertad, Salvador. Mus. nostr.)

Hab. MEXICO (*White* [6]), Tampico (*W. B. Richardson*), Colipa (*F. D. Godman*),
  Misantla, Los Cerrillos (*M. Trujillo*), Jalapa (*de Oca* [4]), Cordova (*Sallé* [3]), Uvero,
  Omealca (*Sumichrast* [16]), Atoyac (*Mrs. H. H. Smith*), Playa Vicente (*Boucard* [5]),
  Valle Real (*Déppe*), Cacoprieto [16], Guichicovi [18] [27] (*Sumichrast*), Chimalapa, Tehu-
  antepec (*W. B. Richardson*), Teapa in Tabasco (*Mrs. H. H. Smith*), N. Yucatan [17],
  Peto, Izamal (*G. F. Gaumer*), Tunkas (*Stone & Baker* [20]); GUATEMALA [8], Choctum,
  Yaxcamnal, Chisec, Teleman, Dueñas, Volcan de Fuego, Alotenango (*O. S. &
  F. D. G.*), Retalhuleu, Toliman (*W. B. Richardson*); SALVADOR, Volcan de San
  Miguel (*W. B. R.*); HONDURAS, Omoa (*Leyland* [7]); NICARAGUA, Matagalpa, San
  Rafael del Norte, El Volcan Chinandega, San Carlos, Leon, La Libertad in
  Chontales (*W. B. Richardson*), Chontales (*Belt* [15]), Escondido R. (*Richmond* [22]);
  COSTA RICA, La Palma (*Nutting* [18]), San Mateo, Turrialba (*Cooper* [11]), Birris de
  Cartago [11] [19], San Juan [11] [24] [25], Alajuela [19], Las Trojas [19], Naranjo de Cartago [19],
  Cartago [19], Jimenez [19] (*Zeledon*), Guaitil [25], San José [11] [19] (*v. Frantzius*), Angostura
  (*Carmiol*); PANAMA, Calovevora [13], Castillo [13], Santiago de Veraguas, Santa Fé [12]
  (*Arcé*), Lion Hill (*M'Leannan* [9] [10] [23]), San Pablo (*O. S.*), Paraiso (*Hughes*).—
  COLOMBIA; W. ECUADOR [29].

There has been a good deal of confusion respecting this bird, owing to an error in
the colouring of the original plate in the first edition of Gould's 'Monograph of the
Trogonidæ,' in which the head is represented as blue instead of black. This is explained
by Gould in the second edition of his work with the original specimen before him.

We now know that *T. caligatus* throughout its range has a black head, its allies on the southern continent having the head distinctly washed with blue. The Mexican bird received the name of *Aganus braccatus* from Cabanis and Heine, who also described the bird of Western Ecuador as *Aganus lepidus*. The large series of specimens before us prove that no real distinctions exist. There remains the name *Trogon concinnus* of Lawrence bestowed upon a Panama bird, which, on further examination, turns out to be only a young male example of *T. caligatus*.

The range of this Trogon extends from Tampico throughout the hotter parts of Vera Cruz. It then divides, and crossing to the west side at the Isthmus of Tehuantepec passes along the Costa Grande of Guatemala through the whole west-coast region of Central America to Panama, and beyond to the end of the western forest-region of Ecuador. The eastern portion covers the whole of Yucatan and probably British Honduras, Eastern Guatemala, and the Republic of Honduras, and meets the western section in Nicaragua.

In Guatemala, *T. caligatus* as a rule keeps to the forests of the lowlands, but is not uncommon in the oak-woods of the Volcan de Fuego, near the village of Alotenango, and reaches an elevation of at least 4500 feet above sea-level. In Costa Rica, Mr. Nutting says [18], it is not so common as *T. melanocephalus* at La Palma, though frequently seen in the neighbourhood. It is the only Trogon he ever heard that gives utterance to a clear distinct whistle.

The bare skin round the eye of this bird in life is lemon-yellow.

11. **Trogon chrysomelas.**

Trogon chrysomelas, Richmond, Pr. U. S. Nat. Mus. xvi. p. 513 [1].

" *Sp. char.* Exactly like *T. atricollis tenellus*, except that the metallic green of the male is wholly replaced by opaque black, without the slightest trace of metallic gloss.

" *Adult male* (type, no. 127338, Escondido River, Nicaragua, Sept. 23, 1892 : *Chas. W. Richmond*). Entire head, neck, and chest uniform ' dead ' black ; back, scapulars, and rump dull, dusky greyish-brown, tinged or mixed with blackish ; upper tail-coverts and middle tail-feathers brownish black, the latter abruptly tipped with deep black (about 0·4 in. wide). Wing-coverts and outer surface of closed secondaries very finely vermiculated with black and white ; rest of the wing black, the primaries edged with white, this occupying the whole outer web at the base. Three outer tail-feathers mostly white (the outermost wholly white for the exposed portion), broadly tipped (for about 0·45 in. on the first to 0·7 in. on the third feather) with white, the remaining portion sharply and regularly barred on both webs with black, the black bars averaging very nearly as wide as the white interspaces. Underparts, posterior to the chest, wholly rich cadmium-yellow, becoming a little paler next the black of the chest. Bill greenish horn-colour, with tomia and culmen yellowish ; feet horn-colour. Length (skin) 9·25 in., wing 4·3, tail 5·4, the outermost feather 2·35 shorter, culmen 0·75.

" *Adult female* (type, no. 128377, Escondido River, Nicaragua, Jan. 17, 1893 : *Chas. W. Richmond*). Upper parts, including upper tail-coverts, sides of neck, malar region and auriculars, slate-black, almost pure black on the pileum ; middle pair of tail-feathers slate-black with a terminal bar of 0·2 in. Wings black, primaries, second to sixth, with outer webs edged with white ; secondaries and wing-coverts narrowly barred with white, bars 0·1 in. apart. A white spot before and one behind the eye ; throat and breast between mouse- and smoke-grey, a narrow band of white posteriorly and bordering the yellow of the lower breast. Lower breast, abdomen, and under tail-coverts deep cadmium-yellow ; sides olive-grey ; feathers of tarsus black, whitish at the base. Second pair of rectrices black, somewhat lighter on the outer web ; third pair black ; three outer pairs tipped with white, broad on the outer web, but narrowing down to a mere edging on the inner web at the tips of the feathers; the outer feather barred for its exposed length, but the basal half of this barring more in the nature of spots, which do not touch the shaft, and become smaller towards the base; the second feather is similar, but has less barring, the third still less. Exposed culmen 0·66 in., width of bill at base 0·69, wing 4·7, longest tail-feather 5·1, shortest 3·28, tarsus 0·58. Orbital ring clove-brown; iris dark brown.

" The female just described resembles that of *T. caligatus* almost exactly, but the barring on the wing-coverts and secondaries is very different, and there is a slight difference on the upper parts, a perceptible gloss being present on these parts in the bird just described."—*C. W. Richmond, l. s. c.*

Hab. NICARAGUA, Escondido R. (*C. W. Richmond*).

The above is Mr. Richmond's description of this *Trogon*, of which we know nothing ourselves. In reply to enquiries, Mr. Ridgway writes that it agrees closely with *T. caligatus* in the colour of the underparts, the pattern of the lateral rectrices, and fine vermiculation of the wing-coverts; but there is not a trace of metallic colouring on the chest or upper parts—the former being uniform black like the head, the back, scapulars, and rump similar but greyer, and the middle rectrices dark brownish-slate with the usual terminal black bar. If not a distinct species it must be a very abnormal *T. caligatus.*

B. *Rectrices utrinque tres laterales haud albo terminatæ.*

c. *Rectrices laterales unicolores.*

12. **Trogon macrurus.**

Trogon macroura, Gould, Mon. Trog. t. 17[1]; Lawr. Ann. Lyc. N. Y. vii. p. 290[2].
Trogon macrourus, Cassin, Pr. Ac. Phil. 1860, p. 135 note[3].
Trogon macrurus, Scl. & Salv. P. Z. S. 1864, p. 364[4]; 1879, p. 535[5]; Gould, Mon. Trog. ed. 2, t. 30[6]; Grant, Cat. Birds Brit. Mus. xvii. p. 474[7].

Supra nitide cupreo-viridis, uropygio vix cyanescentiore; loris, capitis lateribus et mento nigris, pectore dorso concolore, torque pectorali alba, abdomine et tectricibus subcaudalibus coccineis; alis nigricantibus, remigibus albido limbatis, secundariis internis et tectricibus albo minute irroratis; caudæ rectricibus duabus mediis cyanescenti-viridibus, rectricibus tribus externis omnino nigris, rectricibus reliquis in pogonio externo dorso concoloribus; rostro flavido. Long. tota 12·0, alæ 6·6, caudæ rectr. med. 7·0, rectr. lat. 4·8.
♀ schistacea, abdomine imo et tectricibus subcaudalibus coccineis, remigibus albo limbatis; maxilla cornea, basi et mandibula flavida. (Descr. maris et feminæ ex Lion Hill, Panama. Mus. nostr.)

Hab. PANAMA, Lion Hill (*M'Leannan*[2][4]), Paraiso (*Hughes*[7]), Truando R. and Delta of the Atrato (*W. S. & C. J. Wood*[3]).—COLOMBIA[5].

The only Central-American species at all closely allied to this is *Trogon massena,* from which it may readily be distinguished by the distinct white pectoral band which divides the green of the throat from the scarlet of the abdomen. From *T. melanurus* of South America it is not so easily distinguished, the two birds being very much alike. *T. macrurus,* however, besides having a distinct range, seems to be a larger bird with a decidedly longer tail, whence its name.

Of the species itself we know next to nothing. It was described and figured by Gould in the first edition of his Monograph[1], and included by Lawrence in his list of M'Leannan's collections made on the Panama Railway Line[2], and the same collector supplied us with specimens. Cassin states that amongst a number of skins of young birds of *Trogon massena* brought from the Truando river and the delta of the Atrato is one specimen that may belong to *T. macrurus*[3]. Salmon, who found it in the Cauca Valley of Colombia, states that it feeds on fruit[5].

13. **Trogon massena.**

Trogon massena, Gould, Mon. Trog. t. 16[1]; Scl. P. Z. S. 1858, p. 96[2]; 1859, p. 387[3]; Moore, P. Z. S. 1859, p. 53[4]; Scl. & Salv. Ibis, 1859, p. 132[5]; P. Z. S. 1864, p. 364[6]; Cassin, Pr. Ac. Phil. 1860, p. 135[7]; Salv. Ibis, 1861, p. 146[8]; 1872, p. 321[9]; P. Z. S. 1867, p. 151[10]; 1870, p. 202[11]; Lawr. Ann. Lyc. N. Y. vii. p. 290[12]; viii. p. 184[13]; ix. p. 119[14]; Cab. J. f. Orn. 1862, p. 174[15]; v. Frantz. J. f. Orn. 1869, p. 313[16]; Boucard, P. Z. S. 1878, p. 48[17]; Sumichrast, La Nat. v. p. 239[18]; Nutting, Pr. U. S. Nat. Mus. v. p. 400[19]; vi. p. 407[20]; Ridgw. Pr. U. S. Nat. Mus. x. p. 591[21]; Zeledon, An. Mus. Nac. Costa Rica, 1887, p. 120[22]; Grant, Cat. Birds Brit. Mus. xvii. p. 474[23]; Richmond, Pr. U. S. Nat. Mus. xvi. p. 514[24].

Troctes massena, Cab. & Heine, Mus. Hein. iv. Heft 1, p. 204[25]; Gould, Mon. Trog. ed. 2, t. 31[26].

Troctes hoffmanni, Cab. & Heine, Mus. Hein. iv. Heft 1, p. 204[27].

Supra nitide viridis, loris, capitis lateribus et mento nigris, pectore toto dorso concoloro, abdomine et tectricibus subcaudalibus coccineis; alis nigricantibus, secundariis internis et tectricibus minute albo irroratis; caudæ rectricibus duabus mediis nitide viridibus æneo tinctis, rectricibus tribus externis nigris, pogonio externo indistincte albido irrorato, rectricibus reliquis in pogonio externo mediis concoloribus; rostro flavido. Long. tota 13·0, alæ 7·0, caudæ rectr. med. 7·2, rectr. lat. 5·0.

♀ schistacea, alis et cauda saturatioribus, abdomine imo et tectricibus subcaudalibus coccineis. (Descr. maris et feminæ ex Choctum et Chisec, Guatemala. Mus. nostr.)

♂ *juv.* caudæ rectricibus tribus lateralibus albo anguste terminatis et pogoniis suis externis albo variegatis.

Hab. MEXICO (*Verreaux*[2]), Playa Vicente (*Boucard*[3]), Uvero (*Sumichrast*[18]), Chimalapa (*W. B. Richardson*), Teapa (*Mrs. H. H. Smith*); BRITISH HONDURAS. Western District, San Felipe, Cayo (*Blancaneaux*); GUATEMALA, Chisec, Choctum, Raxché[8], Teleman (*O. S. & F. D. G.*); HONDURAS[8], Omoa, San Pedro (*Leyland*[4]), Segovia R. (*Townsend*[21]); NICARAGUA, Greytown (*Holland*[13]), Chontales (*Belt*[9]), Los Sabalos (*Nutting*[20]), San Carlos, Rana (*W. B. Richardson*), Virgin Bay (*Bridges*); COSTA RICA[15][16], Rio Frio (*Richmond*[24]), La Palma (*Nutting*[19]), Angostura[14], Valza (*Carmiol*), Tucurriqui[14], Pozo Azul de Pirris[22], Jimenez[22], Naranjo de Cartago[22] (*Zeledon*), San Carlos (*Boucard*[17]); PANAMA, Bugaba[11], Volcan de Chiriqui[11], Cordillera de Tolé[10], Santiago de Veraguas[10] (*Arcé*), Lion Hill (*M'Leannan*[6][12]), Truando R. and Delta of the Atrato (*W. S. & C. J. Wood*[7]).

Gould described this species in the first edition of his 'Monograph of the Trogonidæ' from specimens said to have been received from Guatemala[1], and according to Mr. Grant now in the collection of the British Museum. In his second edition Gould adopted Cabanis and Heine's genus *Troctes* for this bird, a course which has not been followed.

To the account furnished by Salvin of *T. massena* for Gould we have little to add, and the following notes give the substance of what is there stated.

This Trogon, though abundant in many parts of the vast forests which clothe the warmer portions of the eastern side of the great Central-American Isthmus from Mexico to Panama, does not appear to occur in similar tracts on the western or Pacific side of those countries north of Costa Rica, nor is it to be found in the more broken and thinner forests of the central portion of the Isthmus. Though it occurs in Mexico, it does not seem to be at all common in that country; M. Boucard found it at Playa Vicente and Sumichrast at Uvero, near Cordova, Richardson on the eastern side of the Isthmus of Tehuantepec, and Mrs. Herbert Smith at Teapa. It is absent from Northern Yucatan, but abundant in British Honduras and the forests of Vera Paz, where we had frequent opportunities of observing it. It is essentially a bird of the deep forest, never emerging into sunlight or the brushwood of an old clearing. It usually flies amongst the lower branches of the forest trees, but still a good way from the ground. Its habits are quick and spasmodic while in motion, and the very reverse when perched and at rest. A bird is observed to fly past overhead; it alights on a bough, and in a moment assumes an attitude that would lead one to suppose it had not moved for an hour. When thus perched the glittering green of the upper plumage and breast is inconspicuous, but the brilliant red of the underparts is an object of mark against the dark foliage of the trees. Its cries are various, but harsh and discordant, none of them being so soft as the call-notes of the Quezal. Its food consists principally of ripe fruits, which are plucked whilst the bird is on the wing. Occasionally a caterpillar is added to its repast. Mr. Richmond, writing on birds observed by him on the Escondido river in Nicaragua, also says that this bird feeds largely on berries and fruit. The birds, while picking at the fruit, sometimes hang from the end of the branch, back downwards, with wings fluttering, at such times presenting a very striking appearance. Mr. Nutting, in his notes on the birds of La Palma, Costa Rica, says that he has never seen this species associating in flocks as others do, but that it is a rather silent bird, preferring the deep recesses of the tropical forests, its note being a kind of clucking noise hard to describe *. In the Museum Heineanum, Cabanis and Heine refer to Costa Rica specimens as smaller than those from Mexico, and suggest that the southern bird should be called *Troctes hoffmanni*. Southern examples are certainly smaller, but we are not prepared to admit of their being specifically distinct on the score of a trifling difference in size.

d. *Rectrices laterales albo stricte transfasciatæ.*

14. Trogon clathratus.

Trogon clathratus, Salv. P. Z. S. 1866, p. 75[1]; 1867, p. 151[2]; 1870, p. 202[3]; Ibis, 1869, p. 316[4]; 1874, p. 329[5]; v. Frantz. J. f. Orn. 1869, p. 313[6]; Gould, Mon. Trog. ed. 2, t. 28[7]; Grant, Cat. Birds Brit. Mus. xvii. p. 476[8].

Supra nitide viridis cyaneo tinctus, capite summo et uropygio vix saturatioribus; loris, capitis lateribus et mento nigris, pectore toto dorso concolore, abdomine et tectricibus subcaudalibus saturate coccineis; alis nigricantibus, remigibus albo limbatis, tectricibus minutissime albo irroratis; caudæ rectricibus duabus mediis uropygio concoloribus nigro terminatis, rectricibus tribus utrinque externis stricte sed regulariter

---

* In his notes on the birds of Los Sabalos, Nicaragua, Mr. Nutting gives a different account of this Trogon, speaking of its gregarious habits and of the bare orbital space being sky-blue—perhaps inadvertently referring to another species (Pr. U. S. Nat. Mus. vi. p. 407).

albo transfasciatis; rostro flavido. Long. tota 12·0, alæ 6·2, caudæ rectr. med. 6·2, rectr. lat. 4·6. (Descr. maris exempl. typ. ex Santa Fé, Panama. Mus. nostr.)

♀ schistacea, abdomine antico brunneo, imo et tectricibus subcaudalibus coccineis, caudæ rectricibus tribus externis indistincte albo stricte transfasciatis. (Descr. feminæ ex Cordillera de Tolé, Panama. Mus. nostr.)

Hab. COSTA RICA [6], Angostura (*Carmiol* [8]); PANAMA, Santiago de Veraguas [1] [2], Cordillera de Tolé [2], Calovevora [3], Santa Fé [1] [2] (*Arcé*), Veraguas (*Merritt* [5]).

The first specimens of this fine species that came under our notice were sent us by Enrique Arcé from Santa Fé in the State of Panama, and the same collector subsequently secured for us a good series of examples, including specimens of both sexes. These were all obtained in the same district. But long before Arcé visited this little worked region, Dr. Merritt, the discoverer of *Microchera albocoronata*, obtained a specimen of this Trogon, which Salvin saw in his collection in 1874 [5]. *Trogon clathratus* also occurs in Costa Rica, whence we have examples. It is also mentioned in Lawrence's Catalogue, where a description is given of a female bird supposed to be of this species; but this Mr. Grant decided was an error [8], and it now proves to be a female of *T. bairdi*.

Though bearing some resemblance to *Trogon massena*, this species is really very distinct not only on account of the fine rather widely separate white bars on the tail, but also on account of its inferior size. The bill has five distinct notches on the edges of both the maxilla and mandible, but they are neither so deep nor so large as in *Trogon massena*.

Of the habits of this species nothing has been recorded.

Suborder COCCYGES ZYGODACTYLÆ.

Fam. GALBULIDÆ.

Galbulidæ, Cabanis; Scl. Mon. Jacamars and Puff-birds, p. xix; Cat. Birds Brit. Mus. xix. pp. 161–177.

The Galbulidæ constitute a small family of birds of well-defined characters and of purely Neotropical domicile. The nearest allies are the Bucconidæ of the same region, but more numerous in species. These two families are usually associated together by systematists, as they have many points of structure in common, the most obvious being the formation of the feet. They may at once be distinguished by the narrow, slender, pointed bill of the members of the Galbulidæ and the more slender build of most of them, the Bucconidæ being rather heavily-built birds with strong bills, the maxilla ending in a distinct hook. The habits of the two are, as will be seen below, for the most part, rather widely distinct.

Of the six recognized genera of Galbulidæ only two, viz. *Galbula* and *Jacamerops*, are represented in our region, each by a single species, the total number of species in the family being twenty-one.

GALBULA.

Galbula, Brisson, Orn. iv. p. 85 (1760); Scl. Mon. Jacamars and Puff-birds, p. xxi; Cat. Birds Brit. Mus. xix. p. 163.

Of the ten recognized species of this genus only one occurs within our limits, where it is widely distributed. The remaining nine are distributed over the rest of Tropical America, the Amazons Valley being the metropolis of the genus—only one species, *G. rufo-viridis*, reaching the forests of South-eastern Brazil.

The bill of *Galbula* is long, straight, compressed, and sharp-pointed; the nostrils rounded and exposed, with a few long overhanging bristles; the outer rectrix on either side of the tail is small, the tail itself long and cuneate, the middle pair of rectrices slightly exceeding the next pair. The plumage generally is glittering green.

1. **Galbula melanogenia.**

Galbula melanogenia, Scl. Contr. Orn. 1852, p. 61, t. 90[1]; P. Z. S. 1856, p. 139[2]; 1858, p. 357[3]; 1859, p. 387[4]; Mon. Jacamars and Puff-birds, p. 19, t. 5[5]; Cat. Birds Brit. Mus. xix. p. 166[6]; Moore, P. Z. S. 1859, p. 53[7]; Scl. & Salv. Ibis, 1859, p. 131[8]; 1860, p. 40[9]; P. Z. S. 1870, p. 837[10]; Taylor, Ibis, 1860, p. 116[11]; Salv. P. Z. S. 1867, p. 151[12]; 1870, p. 201[13]; Ibis, 1872, p. 321[14]; Lawr. Ann. Lyc. N. Y. ix. p. 118[15]; v. Frantz. J. f. Orn. 1869, p. 311[16]; Boucard, P. Z. S. 1878, p. 47[17]; Nutting, Pr. U. S. Nat. Mus. v. p. 401[18]; vi. p. 407[19]; v. Berl. & Tacz. P. Z. S. 1883, p. 572[20]; Ridgw. Pr. U. S. Nat. Mus. x. p. 591[21]; Zeled. Ann. Mus. Nac. Costa Rica, 1887, p. 119[22]; Richmond, Pr. U. S. Nat. Mus. xvi. p. 512[23].

Galbula ruficauda, Cassin, Pr. Ac. Phil. 1860, p. 134[24].

Supra nitente aureo-viridis, loris et regione oculari nigris, capitis lateribus reliquis dorso concoloribus: subtus mento nigro, gula pure albo, pectore dorso concolore, abdomine læte castaneo; alarum remigibus et tectricibus suis majoribus nigricantibus, secundariis internis et tectricibus reliquis viridibus; caudæ rectricibus quatuor mediis dorso concoloribus, rectricibus tribus utrinque externis castaneis; rostro nigro, pedibus rubidis. Long. tota 9·8, alæ 3·3, caudæ rectr. med. 4·3, rectr. lat. 2·75, rostri a rictu 2·95, tarsi 0·5.

♀ mari similis, sed gula pallide castanea nec alba, abdomine dilutiore. (Descr. maris et feminæ ex Teleman, Guatemala. Mus. nostr.)

Hab. MEXICO, Playa Vicente (*Boucard*[4]); BRITISH HONDURAS, Belize (*Blancaneaux*); GUATEMALA (*Delattre*[1][5][6]), Coban[9], Chisec, Choctum, Teleman[5], Yzabal[5] (*O. S. & F. D. G.*); HONDURAS, Omoa (*G. C. Taylor*[3], *Leyland*[7]), San Pedro (*G. M. Whitely*[10]), Segovia R. (*Townsend*[21]); NICARAGUA, Chontales (*Belt*[14]), Los Sabalos (*Nutting*[19]), Rana (*W. B. Richardson*), Escondido R. (*Richmond*[23]); COSTA RICA, Bebedero, Nicoya (*Arcé, C. F. Underwood*), La Palma (*Nutting*[18]),

Jimenez, Las Trojas, San Mateo, Pozo Azul de Pirris (*Zeledon* [22]), San Carlos (*v. Frantzius* [16], *Carmiol* [15], *Boucard* [17]), Turrialba (*v. Frantzius* [16], *J. Cooper* [15]), Pacuare (*v. Frantzius* [16], *Carmiol* [15], *Zeledon* [22]), Angostura (*Carmiol*); PANAMA, David (*Bridges* [2]), Volcan de Chiriqui, Bugaba, Mina de Chorcha (*Arcé* [13]), R. Nercua (*C. J. Wood* [24]).—W. ECUADOR [6] [20].

We have little to add to the account given of this bird by Mr. Sclater in his latest Monograph of the Galbulidæ. The greater part of the information concerning it was supplied by Salvin, and the substance of these notes we now reproduce, with the additional information since acquired. Mr. Sclater tells us [5] that his original specimens, described in 1852, were most probably part of the ornithological spoils of the French collector Delattre; thus they very likely came from Vera Paz, where Delattre collected for some time, and was one of the earliest explorers of the district.

The species is not uncommon in the heavily-forested country lying to the north of Coban, the chief town of Alta Vera Paz, and skins of it are usually included in the collections of the bird-hunters of that place. We visited its haunts in 1862, but were not fortunate enough to see living birds, though our Indian hunters not unfrequently brought us specimens. Northward of Vera Paz it has been traced to the neighbourhood of Belize, whence Blancaneaux sent us examples, and it has even been noticed as far north as Playa Vicente on the eastern foot of the Mexican cordillera, on the borders of the States of Oaxaca and Vera Cruz. Tracing its range southwards we find it in the Valley of the Polochic and on the borders of the Lake of Yzabal, where Salvin met with it on more than one occasion. In Honduras it has been observed by several travellers. Leyland, who met with it on the road from Omoa to Comayagua, says it is quite solitary in its habits, frequenting the deep ravines overhung with trees [7]. It has a quick darting flight, utters no cry, and feeds on insects. Taylor [3], Whitely [10], and Townsend [21] also found it in Honduras. In Nicaragua it was noticed by Belt in Chontales [14], and by Mr. Richmond on the Escondido river [23], where, however, he says, it is rather rare. This traveller describes its cry as piercing, resembling the syllables " Keé-u," with the first syllable very shrill and strongly accented. It jerks its tail, he says, after the fashion of a Kingfisher; Mr. Richardson has also sent us specimens from this part of Nicaragua. From this district northwards the range of *G. melanogenia* is restricted to the forests of the eastern or Atlantic side of the great Central-American isthmus, but southwards of Nicaragua its range divides—part continuing along the Atlantic side of the Cordillera and part crossing to the Pacific side, as we have specimens sent us by Arcé from Bebedero on the shores of the Gulf of Nicoya, and there are other records of its occurrence in the same district. The most southern point of its range in Central America is Chiriqui, where it was found by Bridges as early as 1856 [2], and subsequently at several places by Arcé [13]. Curiously enough, it appears to be wholly absent

64*

from the portion of Panama crossed by the inter-oceanic railway, where its place seems to be entirely taken by *Jacamerops aurea*; but it reappears on the Isthmus of Darien, where the naturalists of Lieut. Michler's expedition obtained a specimen*, and in Western Ecuador, whence we received specimens in a collection of skins made by Mr. Illingworth in the Balzar Mountains, and where Stolzmann and Siemiradzki found it at Chimbo, as recorded by Count Berlepsch and Taczanowski [20].

The flight of *Galbula melanogenia* is quick and rather spasmodic, and not long sustained, for on being disturbed it quickly alights again and remains almost motionless on its perch, like a Trogon or Motmot. Of its nesting-habits nothing is on record, but they doubtless resemble those of its near ally, *G. ruficauda*, described by Kirk, who says that it builds in marl banks in the island of Tobago, like the Motmot, without any nest beyond digging a hole an inch and a half in diameter. The distance of the eggs from the entrance is about 18 inches; they are three in number, pure white, and nearly circular in shape.

JACAMEROPS.

Jacamerops, Lesson, Traité d'Orn. p. 234 (1831); Scl. Mon. Jacamars and Puff-birds, p. xxiv; Cat. Birds Brit. Mus. xix. p. 176.

A monotypic genus, its only species being of wide distribution in the northern part of Tropical America and entering our limits in the State of Panama, where it is tolerably common on the Line of Railway. It has also been recorded from Costa Rica.

Instead of a nearly straight bill, as in *Galbula*, *Jacamerops* has a gradually incurved bill, which is widened at the base; the outer rectrix on either side is of medium size, not quite half the length of the central pair. The tarsi are feathered instead of bare for the distal portion.

In his Catalogue Mr. Sclater divides the Galbulidæ into two subfamilies, making *Jacamerops* the sole representative of his Jacameropinæ. We do not adopt this division, as it appears to us that *Jacamerops aurea* is but a modified *Galbula* with similar style of plumage, its generic distinction resting on the modification of the bill. Other Galbulidæ, such as *Galbalcyrhynchus leucotis*, seem much more widely separated.

1. **Jacamerops aurea.**

Alcedo aurea, P. L. S. Müller, Natursyst. Suppl. p. 94 (1776) [1].

Great Jacamar, Lath. Gen. Syn. i. p. 605 [2].

Alcedo grandis, Gm. Syst. Nat. i. p. 458 (1788) [3].

Jacamerops grandis, Less. Traité d'Orn. p. 234 [4]; Cassin, Pr. Ac. Phil. 1860, p. 134 [5]; Lawr. Ann.

---

* At our request Mr. Ridgway has kindly examined this specimen, which Cassin with doubt called *Galbula ruficauda*, and he pronounces it to belong to *G. melanogenia*.

Lyc. N. H. vii. p. 291[6]; Scl. & Salv. P. Z. S. 1864, p. 363[7]; Zeledon, An. Mus. Nac. Costa Rica, 1887, p. 119[8]; Scl. Mon. Jacamars and Puff-birds, p. 57, t. 18[9]; Cat. Birds Brit. Mus. xix. p. 176[10].

Supra nitide aureo-viridis, interscapulio cupreo nitens; pileo antico, capitis lateribus et gula antica paulo cyanescentioribus, gutture plaga conspicua mediana alba, corpore reliquo subtus castaneo; alarum remigibus nigris, secundariis internis et tectricibus dorso concoloribus; cauda chalybeo-nigra, supra extrorsum dorso paulo cyanescentiore; rostro nigro, pedibus fuscis. Long. tota 10·7, alæ 4·3, caudæ rectr. med. 5·6, rectr. lat. 2·5, rostri a rictu 2·1, tarsi 0·5.

♀ mari similis, plaga gutturali alba nulla et corpore subtus dilutiore castaneo. (Descr. maris ex Chepo, feminæ ex Lion Hill, Panama. Mus. nostr.)

Hab. Costa Rica, Jimenez (*Zeledon*[8]); Panama, Veraguas (*Arcé*), Lion Hill (*M‘Leannan*[6][7]), Chepo (*Arcé*), Truando R. (*C. J. Wood*[5]).—South America, from Colombia to Peru, Amazons Valley, and Guiana[6][10].

Jacamerops aurea has long been known, having been described by Vosmaer in 1768 as a "long-tailed Kingfisher with two fingers turned forwards and two behind," from a specimen in the Prince of Orange's collection from the Dutch plantation of Berbice. This, in 1776, became the *Alcedo aurea* of P. L. S. Müller[1], which, as Mr. Sclater fully admits, is undoubtedly its oldest title. He, however, follows custom in using Gmelin's name of *Alcedo grandis* given in 1788[3]. We should prefer to do the same, but the law of priority gives no escape on the plea of uncertainty. Moreover, the name *Jacamerops aurea* is certainly preferable on other grounds, were they of any weight.

The range of *Jacamerops aurea* extends over nearly the whole of the northern part of Tropical America from Guiana and the Amazons Valley to the base of the Andes, to Colombia and the State of Panama. Schomburgk, and subsequently Whitely, found it generally distributed in British Guiana; and the former traveller says that it is usually met with as solitary individuals or in pairs, preferring trees on the banks of streams to more open places in the forest. They here watch for passing insects, which they catch on the wing and return to their position. They often remain almost motionless for hours without stirring a feather. According to Schomburgk they are said to breed in holes in banks like *Galbula viridis*; but Mr. E. Bartlett, who observed the bird at Chamicurros and Santa Cruz in Eastern Peru, was informed that stumps of old trees were also employed for this purpose.

In Colombia *J. aurea* seems to be generally distributed in suitable forests. It occasionally comes within the grasp of the bird-hunters of Bogota, but whether they meet with it on the eastern or western side of the Cordillera of Bogota has not yet been made sure. It certainly occurs in the Cauca Valley, as Salmon secured specimens during his residence in that district. Approaching our fauna, it occurs on the Truando river, where the naturalists of Lieut. Michler's Darien Expedition found it, and record that it sits in a tree and darts after insects like a Flycatcher[5]. From the Isthmus of Panama, Arcé sent us a specimen from Chepo, and M‘Leannan many from his station on the Panama Railway. This district we supposed at one time to be the extreme limit of its range in this direction; but we have a skin from our collector Arcé from a point westward of the railway, and in his most recent list Mr. Zeledon records its presence at Jimenez in Costa Rica [8].

Fam. BUCCONIDÆ.

Bucconidæ, Sclater, Mon. Jacamars and Puff-birds, pp. xxvii et seq. (1882); Cat. Birds Brit. Mus. xix. pp. 178–208.

The Bucconidæ, like the Galbulidæ, is a family of purely Neotropical birds with nearly the same geographical range over Continental America, both being absent from the Antillean subregion. The Bucconidæ is divided into seven genera, four of which are represented in our region; these are: *Bucco* with five species, *Malacoptila* with two, *Nonnula* with one, and *Monasa* with two. Of the total number of forty-three species we find ten in Central America, only two of which, viz. *Malacoptila inornata* and *Monasa grandior*, are not found outside our limits, but both of them have very close external allies.

Compared with the Galbulidæ, the Bucconidæ have a much stouter bill, which is wider at the base, and the culmen evenly curved for the greater part of its length and depressed (in *Bucco* to a distinct hook) at the end; the rictal bristles are strong and curved, the nostrils are deeply sunk and overhung by strong, curved, bristle-like feathers. The wings are short and rounded, the tail usually short, but elongated in *Monasa*. The character of the plumage differs completely from that of the typical Galbulidæ, being destitute of any metallic tints, and the birds generally are of much stouter build.

The structure of various members of the family was fully examined by Forbes, and his notes are given in the introduction to Sclater's Monograph.

A. *Rostrum robustum, apice hamato.*

BUCCO.

Bucco, Brisson, Orn. iv. p. 92 (1760); Scl. Mon. Jacamars and Puff-birds, p. xxxv; Cat. Birds Brit. Mus. xix. p. 179.
Tamatia, Lesson, Traité d'Orn. p. 166.
Notharchus, Cab. & Heine, Mus. Hein. iv. Heft 1, p. 149.

Mr. Sclater admits twenty species of *Bucco*, which he divides into two subgenera, *Bucco* and *Nyctalus*, on the shape of the bill, which is dilated at the base in the species arranged under the former name, the sides nearly straight and more compressed, in the latter the sides being slightly concave. These differences are more distinct in the large species of the *B. dysoni* section when compared with *B. radiatus* and its allies, but other forms are somewhat intermediate. The bill has a distinct hook at the end of the maxilla, which is preceded by a depression in the tomia; and opposite this is a corresponding depression in the maxilla. In many species the end of the mandible is cleft, and the point of the maxilla fits into the fork when the bill is closed. This is very clearly seen in *B. ruficollis*, but is present to a slight extent in the other species.

The species of *Bucco* range over the greater part of the Neotropical region, and extending northwards as far as the Isthmus of Tehuantepec spread over the whole of the lowlands of Central and South America as far as Southern Brazil and Bolivia, the metropolis of the genus being probably Guiana and the Amazons Valley.

Five species occur within our limits, of which *B. dysoni* only has a wide range; the other four are found in the State of Panama, none of them passing much beyond the Line of the Panama Railway, and one, *B. ruficollis*, only reaching the Isthmus of Darien. None of the species are peculiar to our region.

1. **Bucco dysoni.**

Bucco dysoni, G. R. Gray in Mus. Brit.[1]; Scl. P. Z. S. 1855, p. 193[2]; Mon. Jacamars and Puff-
birds, p. 67, t. 21[3]; Cat. Birds Brit. Mus. xix. p. 182[4]; Scl. & Salv. Ibis, 1860, p. 40[5];
P. Z. S. 1864, p. 363[6]; Lawr. Ann. Lyc. N. Y. vii. p. 318[7]; Bull. U. S. Nat. Mus. no. 4,
p. 30[8]; Salv. P. Z. S. 1870, p. 201[9]; Ibis, 1872, p. 322[10]; Cat. Strickl. Coll. p. 429[11];
Sumichrast, La Nat. v. p. 239[12]; Nutting, Pr. U. S. Nat. Mus. v. p. 401[13]; Zeledon, An.
Mus. Nac. Costa Rica, 1887, p. 120[14]; Richmond, Pr. U. S. Nat. Mus. xvi. p. 513[15].

Notharchus dysoni, Cab. & Heine, Mus. Hein. iv. Heft 1, p. 149[16].

Tamatia gigas, Bp. Consp. Vol. Zyg. p. 13[17].

Bucco leucocrissus, Scl. P. Z. S. 1860, p. 284[18].

Bucco napensis, Scl. Cat. Am. Birds, p. 269[19].

Supra niger, dorso, uropygio necnon alis et tectricibus suis stricte albo fimbriatis, interscapulio et capite summo
immaculatis; fronte, superciliis, gutture toto, tectricibus auricularibus, torque cervicali et abdomine albis,
loris cum stria postoculari et torque subpectorali nigris, hypochondriis albis nigro transfasciatis; cauda
nigricante; rostro nigro, pedibus plumbeis. Long. tota 10·0, alæ 4·6, caudæ 3·45, rostri a rictu 1·9,
tarsi 0·85. (Descr. maris ex Escuintla, Guatemala. Mus. nostr.)

♀ mari omnino similis.

Hab. MEXICO, Santa Efigenia[8][12] and Tapanatepec[12] in Tehuantepec (*Sumichrast*);
BRITISH HONDURAS, Cayo (*Blancaneaux*); GUATEMALA (*mus. Strickland*[11]), Forests
of Northern Vera Paz, above Escuintla, alt. 3000 feet (*O. S. & F. D. G.*);
HONDURAS (*Dyson*[1][2][5]); NICARAGUA, Chontales (*Belt*[10]), Escondido R. (*Richmond*[15]),
La Libertad in Chontales, Chinandega, and El Volcan Chinandega (*W. B. Rich-
ardson*); COSTA RICA, La Palma (*Nutting*[13]), Pacuare, Pozo Azul de Pirris
(*Zeledon*[14]); PANAMA, Bugaba, Mina de Chorcha (*Arcé*[9]), Lion Hill (*M'Lean-
nan*[6][7]), Chepo (*Arcé*).—SOUTH AMERICA, Colombia[4], Ecuador[4][18][19], Upper
Amazons Valley[4].

Bucco dysoni is one of a small group of black and white species of the genus *Bucco* which extend over most of tropical America, from Southern Brazil to the confines of Mexico, and has the most northern range of them all. It is the only species of the larger members of this section found within our limits. In South America the allied forms are:—*B. macrorhynchus* of Guiana and the Lower Amazons Valley, in which the white of the forehead is very restricted and does not reach to a line drawn between the eyes; *B. hyperrhynchus* of the Amazons Valley generally, in which the white of the forehead is wide and reaches quite to the middle of the crown, the bill in this species being very large; and *B. swainsoni* of South Brazil, more readily distinguished by the rufescent tinge of the abdomen. *B. dysoni* is somewhat intermediate between *B. macrorhynchus* and *B. hyperrhynchus*, having a rather wide frontal white band which is produced over each eye as a superciliary stripe. The name *B. dysoni* was based upon a specimen in the British Museum obtained by Dyson in Honduras, to which the late G. R. Gray had attached the discoverer's name[1], subsequently adopted by Mr. Sclater[2]. Bonaparte's uncharacterized title, *Tamatia gigas*[17], most probably refers to the same bird, as do also Mr Sclater's *B. napensis*[19] and *B. leucocrissus*[18]—the former based upon a bird from the Napo Valley in Eastern Ecuador, the latter from Fraser's specimens obtained in the same country but on the western side of the Andes. Mr. Sclater now merges all these names under *B. dysoni*[3][4], and we think rightly so, though we notice that the Napo birds before us and others from Sarayacu in the same district have very dark flanks, the light cross-bands being not nearly so distinct as in the northern bird.

The northern limit of the range of *B. dysoni* is the Isthmus of Tehuantepec, where Sumichrast noticed it[8][12], and it also occurs in the western parts of British Honduras. In Guatemala it is found in the vast forests of northern Vera Paz, where we observed it on more than one occasion, but perched on such lofty trees that we did not succeed in securing a specimen. On the Pacific side of the mountains, however, near Escuintla, Godman shot a pair from a high tree at an elevation of about 3000 feet above the sea. In Nicaragua, Belt met with it at Chontales[10], and Mr. Richmond on the Rio Escondido[15], where he says the specimen he shot was in forest catching insects very like a *Tyrannus*, but after making a capture flew leisurely to a fresh perch. Mr. Richardson has also sent us several examples from Nicaragua. From Costa Rica it has been recorded from several places[9], and throughout the State of Panama it would appear to be not uncommon[6][7].

Of the nesting-habits of this species nothing is recorded. In life it is rather an apathetic bird, and from its perch on withered branches of the loftiest forest trees it takes little notice of the hunter far below, and even when shot at merely turns its head to look down for a moment to see what the disturbance was about. Only after several ineffectual shots would it shift its position.

2. Bucco pectoralis.

Bucco pectoralis, Gray, Gen. Birds, i. p. 74, t. 26 [1]; Scl. P. Z. S. 1855, p. 196 [2]; Mon. Jacamars and
Puff-birds, p. 75, t. 24 [3]; Cat. Birds Brit. Mus. xix. p. 184 [4]; Lawr. Ann. Lyc. N. Y. vii.
p. 464 [5]; Scl. & Salv. P. Z. S. 1864, p. 363 [6]; 1879, p. 536 [7]; Wyatt, Ibis, 1871, p. 374 [8].

Supra chalybeo-niger, nitens, dorso medio, uropygio et tectricibus alarum stricte albo fimbriatis; capite toto
summo (fronte inclusa), capitis lateribus et pectore lato pure chalybeo-nigris; tectricibus auricularibus,
torque cervicali postica, gutture toto et abdomine albis, hypochondriis albis nigro transfasciatis; cauda
nigricante; rostro nigro, pedibus nigricantibus. Long. tota 7·7, alæ 4·0, caudæ 3·2, rostri a rictu 1·6,
tarsi 0·7. (Descr. maris ex Lion Hill, Panama. Mus. nostr.)
♀ mari similis.

Hab. PANAMA, Lion Hill (*M'Leannan* [5] [6]), Chepo (*Arcé*).—COLOMBIA [7] [8].

This *Bucco* was for many years known only from the plate in Gray and Mitchell's
'Genera of Birds,' taken from a specimen in the British Museum from an unknown
locality and acquired in 1843 [1]. It was not until M'Leannan began to explore the
Isthmus of Panama along the Railway Line that fresh information concerning the bird
came to light through specimens sent to Lawrence and to us. Arcé obtained us a
single example during a short visit to Chepo on the Rio Bayano, south of Panama, but
he never came across it during his subsequent journeys between Panama and Chiriqui.
From the mainland of Colombia we have two records of the species, for Mr. C. W.
Wyatt met with it in the dense forest situated between Naranjo and the Magdalena
river [8], and Salmon found it at Nichi in the Cauca Valley [7]. It will thus be seen that
the range of *Bucco pectoralis* is very restricted.

As a species this *Bucco* is quite distinct from *B. dysoni* and its allies; this is readily
seen not only by its smaller size, but by the white throat being surrounded by black on
the sides of the neck, the wholly black forehead, and the conspicuous white ear-coverts,
which are connected by a white band round the back of the neck. According to
Mr. Wyatt the iris is brown [8].

3. Bucco subtectus.

Bucco subtectus, Scl. P. Z. S. 1860, p. 296 [1]; Mon. Jacamars and Puff-birds, p. 83, t. 27 [2]; Cat.
Birds Brit. Mus. xix. p. 186 [3]; Scl. & Salv. P. Z. S. 1864, p. 363 [4]; 1879, p. 536 [5].
Bucco tectus, Lawr. Ann. Lyc. N. Y. vii. p. 318 [6].

Supra niger, fronte et pileo antico albo punctatis, plaga scapulari utrinque alba: subtus albus, torque pectorali
et stria infra oculos nigris, hypochondriis albis nigro variegatis; cauda nigra, rectricibus utrinque quatuor
externis albo medialiter fasciatis et macula in pogonio interno albo terminatis; rostro nigro, pedibus
nigricantibus. Long. tota 5·8, alæ 2·7, caudæ 2·3, rostri a rictu 1·1, tarsi 0·5. (Descr. maris ex Lion
Hill, Panama. Mus. nostr.)
♀ mari similis.

Hab. PANAMA, Veraguas (*Arcé*), Lion Hill (*M'Leannan* [4] [6]).—COLOMBIA [5]; W. ECUADOR [1].

This is a western form of the old Guianan *Bucco tectus* of Boddaert, the "Barbu à
poitrine noir de Cayenne" of the 'Planches Enluminées,' no. 688, fig. 2, from which it
may be distinguished by its much narrower black band across the chest.

It was first described by Mr. Sclater from a specimen sent from Esmeraldas in Western Ecuador by Fraser [1], and, like so many of the birds of that district, was subsequently traced to Panama, where M'Leannan obtained specimens for Lawrence and ourselves [4][6]. Then Arcé found it a little further along the Isthmus, and Salmon at Nichi in the Cauca Valley of Colombia [5].

None of these collectors have given us any account of the habits of the bird, and on this point we are in ignorance. Of the closely allied *B. tectus*, Mr. Layard shot several specimens near Para from some low trees in an abandoned clearing. Their stomachs contained fragments of insects. Of the same bird Natterer says that it lives solitary, perched on high dried trees.

4. Bucco ruficollis.

Capito ruficollis, Wagl. Isis, 1829, p. 658 [1].

Bucco ruficollis, Gray, Gen. Birds, i. p. 74 [2]; Scl. P. Z. S. 1855, p. 196 [3]; Mon. Jacamars and Puff-birds, p. 89, t. 29 [4]; Cat. Birds Brit. Mus. xix. p. 187 [5]; Cassin, Pr. Ac. Phil. 1860, p. 134 [6]; Wyatt, Ibis, 1871, p. 374 [7].

Supra fuscus, cervino guttatus, fronte rufescente; loris et tectricibus auricularibus, nucha et cervice postica albis: subtus cervino albidus, torque pectorali nigro, gutture medio rufo, hypochondriis nigro guttatis; alis fusco-nigris, remigibus (duobus externis exceptis) macula cervina mediana in pogonio externo notatis, secundariis cervino extrorsum limbatis; cauda fusco-nigricante; rostro nigro, pedibus plumbeis. Long. tota 8·4, alæ 3·4, caudæ 3·2, rostri a rictu 1·55, tarsi 0·75. (Descr. exempl. ex Valle Dupar, Colombia. Mus. nostr.)

Hab. PANAMA, Truando R. (*C. J. Wood* [6]).—COLOMBIA [4][5].

Passing over Wagler's erroneous statement that this species occurs in Mexico [1], we admit this *Bucco* into the present work on Cassin's record of the capture of a single specimen on the Truando river by Mr. C. J. Wood, one of the naturalists of Lieut. Michler's Darien Expedition [6]. It was only once seen, at the first camp on the Truando after leaving the Atrato. The occurrence of this species at this place is easily explained, seeing that its regular haunts are at no great distance, for it is known to be found near Santa Marta and a short way up the Magdalena Valley at Canuto, where Mr. Wyatt met with it [7]. He records that the iris is straw-yellow, and that the crops of those he shot were found to be full of beetles.

Bucco ruficollis is the only species of the genus dealt with here which has the curious cleft tip to the maxilla, referred to in our account of the genus, prominently shown.

5. Bucco fulvidus, sp. n.

Bucco radiatus, Scl. Mon. Jacamars and Puff-birds, p. 109 (partim), t. 36 (figura proxima) [1]; Cat. Birds Brit. Mus. xix. p. 192 (partim) [2]; Scl. & Salv. P. Z. S. 1879, p. 536 [3]; v. Berl. & Tacz. P. Z. S. 1883, p. 572 [4].

Supra castaneus, nigro transversim radiatus, pileo postico et interscapulio plerumque nigris, torque cervicali fulva; loris albidis, capitis lateribus et abdomine antico fulvis nigro transfasciatis, gula albida, abdomine imo et tectricibus subcaudalibus pure fulvis; alis castaneis nigro transfasciatis, remigum apicibus nigri-

cantibus; cauda castanea, nigro regulariter fasciata; rostro plumbescente, mandibula infra pallida; pedibus corylinis. Long. tota 8·5, alæ 3·65, caudæ 3·3, rostri a rictu 1·65, tarsi 0·75. (Descr. exempl. ex Veraguas, Panama. Mus. nostr.)
Sexus similis.

Hab. PANAMA, Veraguas (*Arcé* [2]), Lion Hill (*M'Leannan, in mus. G. N. Lawrence*).— COLOMBIA [2]; ECUADOR [3].

Skins of this *Bucco* from the State of Panama agree accurately with others from Antioquia, as represented on the larger figure of Mr. Sclater's plate, in being of a distinct fulvous tint over the whole of the under surface and the cervical collar, whereas in the types of *B. radiatus* and some other skins of Bogota make the under plumage is nearly pure white. The ranges of these two forms cannot be yet traced with accuracy. As might be expected the fulvous race is found in Western Ecuador [3], but it also occurs on the eastern side of the Andes of that country at Sarayacu, and both races occur in collections made by the bird-hunters of Bogota. The latter fact may probably be explained by the supposition that the white-breasted form is obtained on the eastern side of the cordillera drained by the Rio Meta, while the fulvous form comes from the valleys of the Rio Magdalena. The bird-hunters work in both directions, and their spoils are mixed in the capital by the merchants who export the skins. No *Bucco* is found near Bogota itself. Mr. Sclater duly noted these differences in his Monograph [1], but was inclined to think the pale colour of the typical birds was due to bleaching from damp. We do not agree to this suggestion, but fully believe each form has its own exclusive range, and therefore deserving of recognition by name.

Though noticed by several collectors, Salmon in Antioquia [3], Buckley, Illingworth, and Stolzmann [4] in Ecuador, we have only the brief note concerning it from the latter traveller to the effect that the irides of specimens obtained at Chimbo were ochre of the same colour as the abdomen [3].

The evidence of the occurrence of this *Bucco* in the State of Panama rests on specimens sent by Arcé in his later collections made at some place west of the Line of Railway. Its name does not appear in the lists prepared by Salvin up to 1870. M'Leannan did not meet with it on the Railway itself at the time Lawrence was compiling the lists of his collections, but he subsequently sent him a pair, which Salvin saw in Lawrence's possession in 1874.

B. *Rostrum debilius, apice minime hamato.*

MALACOPTILA.

Malacoptila, Gray, List Gen. Birds, p. 13 (1841); Scl. Monogr. Jacamars and Puff-birds, p. xxxvi; Cat. Birds Brit. Mus. xix. p. 193.

The number of supposed species of *Malacoptila* was reduced to seven by Mr. Sclater in his 'Monograph of the Bucconidæ,' and this number was maintained in his Catalogue of these birds in the British Museum. These seven species are spread over nearly the same area as the members of *Bucco*, and extend from Eastern Guatemala to South-eastern Brazil. They are inhabitants of the hot forests of the lowlands wherever they are found.

The bill in *Malacoptila* is much more slender than in *Bucco*, the culmen gradually curved for most of its length, but rather more abruptly towards the tip; there is no hook nor any notch at the end of the tomia in either maxilla or mandible. The nostrils are open but deeply sunken and overhung by long curved bristle-like feathers; the rictal bristles are strong and long; the feathers from the rictus are long and pendent, and often conspicuous from their white colour. The wings are short and rounded, the tail moderate and rounded, the feet feeble. In several species, notably those of Central America, there is a marked difference of colour between the sexes, the males being of a ferruginous tint, the females greyer. Moreover there seems to be a considerable amount of local and individual variation. Of the two species found within our limits, *M. inornata* marks the northern extension of the genus, and spreads from Guatemala to Nicaragua on the eastern side of those countries; *M. panamensis* takes its place in Costa Rica, and is found thence as far south as Venezuela, Ecuador, and Peru.

1. **Malacoptila panamensis.**

Malacoptila panamensis, Lafr. Rev. Zool. 1847, p. 79 [1]; Scl. P. Z. S. 1855, p. 196 [2]; Mon. Jacamars and Puff-birds, p. 119, t. 40 [3]; Cat. Birds Brit. Mus. xix. p. 196 [4]; Cassin, Pr. Ac. Phil. 1860, p. 134 [5]; Lawr. Ann. Lyc. N. Y. vii. p. 290 [6]; Scl. & Salv. P. Z. S. 1864, p. 363 [7]; 1879, p. 536 [8]; Salv. P. Z. S. 1870, p. 201 [9]; Boucard, P. Z. S. 1878, p. 47 [10]; Zeledon, An. Mus. Nac. Costa Rica, 1887, p. 119 [11].

Malacoptila costaricensis, Cab. J. f. Orn. 1862, p. 172 [12]; Cab. & Heine, Mus. Hein. iv. Heft 1, p. 135 [13]; Lawr. Ann. Lyc. N. Y. ix. p. 118 [14]; v. Frantz. J. f. Orn. 1869, p. 312 [15].

Malacoptila inornata, Lawr. Ann. Lyc. N. Y. viii. p. 4 [16]; ix. p. 118 [17]; Scl. & Salv. P. Z. S. 1864, p. 363 [18]; v. Frantz. J. f. Orn. 1869, p. 311 [19].

Malacoptila veræpacis, Lawr. Ann. Lyc. N. Y. ix. p. 118 [20]; v. Frantz. J. f. Orn. 1869, p. 311 [21].

Supra ferruginea, interscapulio et tectricibus alarum fulvo punctatis, capitis lateribus indistincte fulvo striatis : subtus plumis mystacalibus albidis, gutture toto ferrugineo, pectore imo et hypochondriis fulvis nigricante striolatis, abdomine medio albicante, tectricibus subcaudalibus pallide fulvis; alis nigricanti-fuscis, intus læte cinnamomeis; cauda et uropygio rufo-ferrugineis; rostro corneo, mandibula infra albida; pedibus corylinis. Long. tota 7·0, alæ 3·4, caudæ 3·2, rostri a rictu 1·4, tarsi 0·7.

♀ supra omnino grisescentior, distincte punctata, fronte et loris albo variegatis, capitis lateribus distincte cervino striolatis, gutture medio cervino, pectore imo et hypochondriis distincte nigro striatis, abdomine medio albido. (Descr. maris et feminæ ex Liou Hill, Panama. Mus. nostr.)

Hab. Costa Rica (*v. Frantzius* [12] [19] [21]), San Mateo (*v. Frantzius* [15], *J. Cooper* [14]), Guaitil, Angostura (*v. Frantzius* [15], *Carmiol* [17] [20], *Zeledon* [11]), Pacuare (*v. Frantzius* [15], *Carmiol* [20]), Las Trojas, Pozo Azul de Pirris, Jimenez (*Zeledon* [11]), Dota Mts. [17], Peje (*Carmiol*), San Carlos (*Boucard* [10]); Panama (*Delattre* [1]), Volcan de Chiriqui,

Bugaba, Mina de Chorcha (*Arcé*[9]), Lion Hill (*M'Leannan*[6][7][16]), Truando R. (*C. J. Wood*[5]).—COLOMBIA[3][4][8]; VENEZUELA[3][4]; ECUADOR[3][4]; PERU[3][4].

This species was described by Lafresnaye in 1847, from skins obtained at Panama by Delattre[1]: and from this district we have seen many specimens of both sexes, the description of the type being evidently taken from a male. Many names have subsequently been proposed for nearly every local form, and not unfrequently the sexes have been described as distinct species—the difference of the coloration of the plumage not having been recognized before 1864, when M'Leannan's dissected specimens from Panama showed the relationship between the two forms[18].

The gradual accumulation of a large series of specimens has demonstrated that the close subdivision made cannot be maintained in view of the amount of variation which evidently exists both locally and individually. Mr. Sclater has fully discussed this question, both in his Monograph and in the Catalogue of Birds, and unites the Costa Rican *M. costaricensis*, Cab.[12], the Colombian and Venezuelan *M. mystacalis*, Lafr., the Ecuadorian *M. æquatorialis*, together with the birds called *M. aspersa*, Scl., *M. poliopsis*, Scl., and *M. blacica*, Cab., all under Lafresnaye's title *M. panamensis*.

The range of *M. panamensis* extends from Costa Rica throughout the Isthmus of Panama, and thence spreads southwards to Colombia, Western Ecuador, and Peru, and eastwards to Venezuela. Beyond these countries other definite species take its place. Northwards of Costa Rica the *Malacoptila* of Nicaragua has been called *M. panamensis*; but specimens recently received from Mr. Richardson, as well as others from Mr. Richmond, show that if *M. inornata* is to be kept distinct they belong to it rather than to the more southern bird.

Of the habits of *M. panamensis* little has been recorded. Like the other members of the genus it is a forest bird, keeping to the lower branches of the trees and the bushes of the undergrowth. Mr. Wood says[5] that it is a very quiet inactive bird, starting out occasionally from its perch to capture an insect and then returning.

2. **Malacoptila inornata.**

Monasa inornata, DuBus, Bull. Ac. Brux. xiv. pt. 2, p. 107 (1847)[1].

Malacoptila inornata, Scl. Ann. & Mag. N. H. 1854, xiii. p. 478[2]; Mon. Jacamars and Puff-birds, p. 125, t. 41[3]; Cat. Birds Brit. Mus. xvi. p. 197[4]; Scl. & Salv. Ibis, 1860, p. 40[5]; Cab. & Heine, Mus. Hein. iv. Heft 1, p. 137[6]; Salv. P. Z. S. 1870, p. 201[7].

Malacoptila veræpacis, Scl. & Salv. Ibis, 1860, p. 40[8]; Lawr. Ann. Lyc. N. Y. viii. p. 184[9].

Malacoptila panamensis, Richmond, Pr. U. S. Nat. Mus. xvi. p. 512[10].

? *Malacoptila fuliginosa*, Ridgw. Pr. U. S. Nat. Mus. xvi. p. 512[11].

M. panamensi persimilis et vix certe distincta, abdomine toto ferrugineo nec pectore imo neque hypochondriis fusco striolatis; corpore subtus fere unicolore, abdomine paullo pallidiore.

♀ a femina *M. panamensis* vix differt. (Descr. maris, *M. veræpacis* typ. et feminæ ex Vera Paz, Guatemala. Mus. nostr.)

Hab. BRITISH HONDURAS (*Blancaneaux*); GUATEMALA, Coban (*V. Constancia* [8]), Choctum, Chisec (*O. S. & F. D. G.*); NICARAGUA, San Carlos, Santo Domingo, Rana (*W. B. Richardson*), Escondido R. (*Richmond* [10]), Greytown (*Holland* [9]).

M. inornata was described in 1847 by Vicomte DuBus [1] from a Guatemalan specimen, the characters given indicating that the specimen in question must have been a female bird. The male was subsequently named *M. veræpacis* by Sclater and Salvin in 1860 [8], the differences between the sexes in some species of this genus not having then been appreciated.

In 1870 Salvin [7] had occasion to compare this northern bird with the more southern *M. panamensis,* and gave the result as follows :—" In the northern bird, for which the term *inornata* is the older and must be adopted, the male is distinguished by the rufous colouring extending nearly uniformly over the whole surface below, being slightly paler on the lower belly, and bearing very slight traces of dark markings on the margins of the feathers. In the southern form, for which the name *panamensis* must be retained, the breast alone is clear ferruginous, and is succeeded below by strongly mottled plumage, formed by the black lateral margins of each feather; the lower belly is pale fulvous, nearly white. . . . . The females of the two forms are so exactly alike that it is not possible to distinguish them."

Until quite recently *M. inornata* was only known to live in the vast forest-region of northern Vera Paz, whence we have received many specimens from the collectors who frequent that district from Coban, but where we were not fortunate enough actually to see it ourselves. Within the last year or two we have received specimens from Eastern Nicaragua and the Mosquito coast, both from Mr. Richardson and Mr. Richmond; and though the latter naturalist has referred his examples to *M. panamensis,* we have no hesitation in stating that they are very much nearer to *M. inornata* and cannot really be distinguished from it. Mr. Richmond, in his paper on the collections he made on the Escondido river, speaks of some very dark examples, which Mr. Ridgway describes, suggesting the name *M. fuliginosa* for them [11]. In view of the variability of these birds and our extreme reluctance to admit the likelihood of two closely-allied forms coexisting in the same district, we prefer to leave the question of the status of these birds in abeyance for the present, awaiting further information respecting this form.

M. inornata, like the other members of the genus, seems restricted to the hotter lowland forests of the countries in which it lives, and probably does not pass beyond an altitude of 2000 feet in the mountains. It is wholly absent from the lowlands of Guatemala and the countries south of it bordering the Pacific Ocean.

NONNULA.

Nonnula, Sclater, P. Z. S. 1853, p. 124; Mon. Jacamars and Puff-birds, p. xxxviii; Cat. Birds
   Brit. Mus. xix. p. 199.

Nonnula is a small weak form of *Malacoptila*, containing, according to Mr. Sclater,
five species, which are spread from the Isthmus of Panama to South-eastern Brazil.
Only one of these occurs just within our border in the State of Panama.

The bill of *Nonnula* is flatter than that of *Malacoptila*, especially at the base, though
the curve of the culmen is similar and the tomia without notch; the bristle-like
feathers curving forwards over the nostrils and under the chin are very long and strong,
the rictal bristles themselves being also very strong. There are no pendent elongated
feathers from the rictus, as in *Malacoptila*. The wings are short and rounded, the tail
moderate and rounded, the rectrices narrow. The feet are feeble. In coloration the
plumage resembles that of *Malacoptila*, but the tints are uniform without any darker
marks, and the size of all the species much less.

1. **Nonnula frontalis.**

Malacoptila frontalis, Scl. Ann. & Mag. N. H. 1854, xiii. p. 479[1]; Synops. Bucc. p. 20[2]; P. Z. S.
   1855, pp. 136[3]; Lawr. Ann. Lyc. N. Y. vii. p. 318[4].
Nonnula frontalis, Scl. P. Z. S. 1855, p. 196[5]; Mon. Jacamars and Puff-birds, p. 139[6]; Cat. Birds
   Brit. Mus. xix. p. 201[7].

Supra fusca, pileo rufescente tincto, loris et capitis lateribus cinereis: subtus ferruginea, gutture et pectore
   saturatioribus, abdomine medio et tectricibus subcaudalibus albicantibus; alis et cauda saturate fuscis,
   hujus rectricibus externis (dimidio distali) indistincte pallide fusco terminatis; rostro corneo, mandibula
   infra pallida; pedibus corylinis. Long. tota 5·5, alæ 2·2, caudæ 2·15, rostri a rictu 0·95, tarsi 0·5.
   (Descr. maris ex Lion Hill, Panama. Mus. nostr.)
♀ mari similis.

Hab. PANAMA, Lion Hill (*M'Leannan* [4]).—COLOMBIA [1] [6] [7].

Nonnula frontalis is a northern form of *N. ruficapilla*, of the interior of Brazil and
Peru, from which it differs but slightly. Mr. Sclater described it in 1854 [1] from
specimens found in a collection of trade skins sent from Bogota, which were probably
obtained in the upper part of the valley of the Magdalena river. Mr. Sclater
subsequently (P. Z. S. 1860, p. 60) referred a specimen contained in a collection from
the valley of the Napo in Ecuador, with doubt, to this species; but as nothing
further is said in his Monograph of the family concerning this bird beyond the reference
to the paper, we suppose the southern extension must be considered unconfirmed.

The only other records of this bird are from Panama, where M'Leannan met with it,
as noted by Lawrence [4].

The differences separating it from *N. ruficapilla* are thus given by Mr. Sclater [6]:—
"The cap, instead of being bright chestnut, well defined, is of a brownish colour.
There is no cinereous on the sides of the head and nape, cutting off the cap from the

back, but the brownish cap passes gradually into the less bright brown of the upper surface."

We find nothing on record respecting the habits of this bird. *N. ruficapilla* is stated by Natterer to live solitary in the forest, sitting on branches near the ground.

MONASA *.

Monasa, Vieillot, Anal. p. 27 (1816).
Lypornix, Wagler, Syst. Av. fol. 10, p. 15 (1827).
Monastes, Nitzsch, Pter. p. 135 (1840).
Monacha, Sclater, Monogr. Jacamars and Puff-birds, p. xl (1882) ; Cat. Birds Brit. Mus. xix. p. 202.

This genus is very distinct, not only on account of the dark colour of its members, all of which are either black or dark grey, slightly relieved in some cases by white on the forehead or chin. Other structural characters distinguish it from the rest of the genera of Bucconidæ.

The bill is much as in *Malacoptila,* but, relatively to the size of the body, smaller, the culmen evenly curved, and the maxilla without notch. The feathers curving over the nostrils and those of the chin are not nearly so long nor so bristle-like as in *Malacoptila* and *Nonnula.* The tail is long and the rectrices wide.

Of the seven known species, two occur within our limits; of these, *M. grandior* is restricted to Nicaragua and Costa Rica, but has a close ally in *M. peruana* of the southern continent. The other, *M. pallescens,* is found on the Isthmus of Darien and other parts of Colombia. The remaining five species are distributed over Tropical South America, from Colombia and Guiana to South-eastern Brazil.

The species of *Monasa* are strictly forest birds.

1. **Monasa grandior.**

Monasa grandior, Scl. & Salv. P. Z. S. 1868, p. 327 [1]; Salv. Ibis, 1869, p. 315 [2]; 1872, p. 322 [3];
　　　Zeledon, An. Mus. Nac. Costa Rica, 1887, p. 120 [4].
Monacha grandior, Scl. Mon. Jacamars and Puff-birds, p. 155, t. 52 [5]; Cat. Birds Brit. Mus. xix.
　　　p. 205 [6].
Monasa peruana, Lawr. Ann. Lyc. N. Y. ix. p. 118 [7]; v. Frantz. J. f. Orn. 1869, p. 312 [8].

Saturate schistacea, capite, gutture, remigibus et cauda nigris; fronte, mento et gula antica albis; tectricibus
　　　alarum dorso concoloribus, tectricibus subcaudalibus nigricantibus; rostro ruberrimo, pedibus nigri-
　　　cantibus.　　Long. tota 12·0, alæ 5·6, caudæ 5·0, rostri a rictu 1·8, tarsi 0·8.　(Descr. exempl. ex
　　　Chontales, Nicaragua.　Mus. nostr.)
♀ mari similis.

Hab. NICARAGUA, Mosquito Coast (*Bell* [1]), Chontales (*Belt* [3]), La Libertad in Chontales

---

* Mr. Sclater altered Vieillot's name *Monasa* into *Monacha,* the former being probably intended either for *Monacha* or *Monastes,* Nitzsch's suggestion. But we already have *Monarcha* in Aves, written *Monacha* by Swainson, so that on the whole it seems best to let *Monasa* stand. If a change must be made, Wagler's title *Lypornix* has priority, and after it Nitzsch's *Monastes.*

(*W. B. Richardson*); Costa Rica, Angostura (*Carmiol* [1]), Pacuare, San Carlos (*v. Frantzius* [8], *J. Cooper* [7]), San José (*v. Frantzius, J. Cooper* [7]), Rio Sucio, Jimenez (*Zeledon* [4]).

This species is very closely allied to two South-American birds, which are again barely separable. Of these, *M. morpheus* of Brazil and the Lower Amazons is perhaps the nearest, and has about the same amount of white on the forehead and chin. *M. morpheus* is, however, a rather smaller bird, and not quite so darkly coloured on the head and neck. The other, *M. peruana* of the Upper Amazons and Ecuador, is also a smaller bird and the white on the forehead and chin is rather more restricted.

M. grandior being apparently completely isolated in its range from both these allied forms by the intervention of the distinct *M. pallescens*, it may be safely treated as a distinct species.

The first intimation of the existence of a *Monasa* in Central America was from a drawing of one being included amongst others of birds found in the Mosquito Territory made by a Mr. Bell and submitted to Mr. Sclater [1]. But the first skin that came before us was one sent by Carmiol from Costa Rica, and this was duly described in 1868 [1]. About the same time Lawrence examined several Costa Rica skins, but noting their large size called them *Monasa peruana* in his first list of Costa Rica birds [7].

We have now seen several Nicaraguan skins, both from Belt and Mr. Richardson, as well as others from Costa Rica; but no account of the habits of the bird has reached us.

2. **Monasa pallescens.**

Monasa pallescens, Cassin, Pr. Ac. Phil. 1860, p. 134 [1]; 1864, p. 287, t. 4 [2]; Wyatt, Ibis, 1871, p. 374 [3]; Scl. & Salv. P. Z. S. 1879, p. 536 [4].

Monacha pallescens, Scl. Mon. Jacamars and Puff-birds, p. 157, t. 53 [5]; Cat. Birds Brit. Mus. xix. p. 206 [6].

M. grandiori similis, sed mento et gula antica omnino nigra, fronte tantum alba distinguenda. Long. tota 11·0, alæ 5·1, caudæ 5·1, rostri a rictu 1·7, tarsi 0·8. (Descr. maris ex Remedios, Colombia. Mus. nostr.)

Hab. Panama, Truando R. (*C. J. Wood & W. S. Wood* [1] [2]).—Colombia [3] [4].

Monasa pallescens is the only species of the genus which has a white forehead and black throat and chin, and is thus easily recognized. Its name would imply that it is much paler in colour than its allies, and is so figured on the plate of one of the types [2]. But the specimens before us from several places in Northern Colombia do not show much difference in coloration, and are quite as dark as the usual tint of *M. grandior*.

The first specimens secured of this species formed part of the collection made on the Isthmus of Darien by Mr. C. J. Wood and Mr. W. S. Wood, Jun., who accompanied Lieut. Michler in his survey of that region, and were named by Cassin in 1860 [1]. Birds of this species were only once seen in the cordillera on the river Truando in January

1858. A party of eight or ten individuals was observed sitting very quietly in a tree at some distance from the ground, and being quite regardless of the gun, or the presence of man, several were obtained. The specimens labelled as females proved to be slightly larger than those marked as males. We have no representatives of *M. pallescens* from this region; but a little further south Mr. Wyatt once met with it in the forest near Paturia in the Magdalena Valley [3], and Salmon secured several examples in the Cauca Valley [4], and he noted the contents of the stomach as "lizards &c.," a variation from the usual insect diet of all the members of the family.

Fam. CUCULIDÆ.

The family of Cuculidæ is one of nearly world-wide distribution, being absent only in the extreme northern and southern portions of the world. In the temperate regions the species are few and migratory, whilst in the tropics they abound, and here we find most of the genera.

In Captain Shelley's recently compiled 'Catalogue of the Cuculidæ,' the family is divided into six subfamilies containing in all forty-two genera and about 172 species. Of these the Cuculinæ, with seventeen genera, is represented in America by *Coccyzus* alone with about eleven species. The Centropodinæ is a purely Old-World subfamily. The Phœnicophainæ containing sixteen genera has, as purely American representatives, *Saurothera* with five species, *Hyetornis* with one, and *Piaya* with four species. The Neomorphinæ is more strictly American, and is only represented in the Old World by the Bornean and Sumatran *Carpococcyx*; *Neomorphus*, *Geococcyx*, and *Morococcyx* being purely American, and contain five, two, and one species respectively. The Diplopterinæ, with *Diplopterus* (one species) and *Dromococcyx* (two species), is found in America alone, as is the Crotophaginæ with two genera, *Crotophaga* (three species) and *Guira* (one species).

America, then, owns exclusively two subfamilies—Diplopterinæ and Crotophaginæ; it shares the Cuculinæ, Phœnicophainæ, and Neomorphinæ with the Old World, but has no representative of the Centropodinæ.

Only eleven of the total of forty-two of the genera of Cuculidæ are found in America, and only thirty-six of about 172 species.

Comparing the representatives of the family in the Nearctic and Neotropical regions, we find *Coccyzus* in North America, with three species (two of which are migrants), some of which pass their breeding-season in the North-American continent. One of the species of *Geococcyx* is found along the southern border of the region, and two species of *Crotophaga* just pass beyond the limits of the Neotropical region.

In Mexico and Central America eight of the eleven genera are found, and fifteen of the thirty-six species. These are widely distributed over the area, the greater number of species occurring in the southern portion bordering the southern continent.

Geococcyx almost exclusively, and *Morococcyx* entirely, are peculiarly Central-American and Mexican genera, a larger numerical proportion as compared with the southern continent than usual in other families of birds.

The position of the Cuculidæ is one of marked isolation, and its position in the Systema Avium has been much discussed. Huxley placed it in his Coccygomorphæ, associating it with the Bucconidæ, Capitonidæ, Rhamphastidæ, &c., and this is the place we here assign to it.

Subfam. *CUCULINÆ.*

This subfamily contains genera the species of which are arboreal in habits, with long pointed wings and somewhat powerful flight. The tarsi are short, the tail moderately long and rounded and consisting of ten rectrices. Seventeen genera are included in it, of which *Coccyzus* alone is American.

COCCYZUS.

Coccyzus, Vieillot, Anal. p. 28 (1816); Shelley, Cat. Birds Brit. Mus. xix. p. 302.

Of this genus there are seven recognized species, one of them (*C. minor*) being subdivided into three subspecies, two of them belonging to certain West-Indian Islands and of rather doubtful value. The species found in Central America are *C. americanus*, the type of the genus, *C. erythrophthalmus*, and *C. minor*; the two former being amongst the recognized summer visitants to North America, and the latter a bird found round the shores of the Caribbean Sea and many of the West-Indian Islands.

The other members of the genus are all of South-American domicile, with the exception of *C. ferrugineus*, which seems restricted to Cocos Island, an isolated islet in the Pacific outside the Bay of Panama.

Coccyzus belongs to the Cuculinæ, and in general shape is not unlike *Cuculus canorus*, being an arboreal genus with short tarsi and rather long pointed wings, the third and fourth quills of which are the longest and form the point of the wing; the tail is long and much graduated, the outermost feathers being rather more than half the length of the central ones, and in several species all but the middle pair are conspicuously tipped with white; both maxilla and mandible of the bill are curved and drawn gradually to a point, with an even tomia without notch; the nostrils are open oval apertures at the base of the nasal fossa, with the upper margin membranous; the eyelashes are not simple bristles, as in most of the American Cuculidæ, the shafts having distinct barbs.

1. Coccyzus minor.

Cuculus minor, Gm. Syst. Nat. i. p. 411[1].

Coccyzus minor, Gray, Gen. Birds, ii. p. 457[2]; Scl. & Salv. P. Z. S. 1870, p. 837[3]; Baird, Brew., & Ridgw. N. Am. Birds, ii. p. 482[4]; Gundl. Orn. Cub. p. 121[5]; Boucard, P. Z. S. 1878;

p. 47 [6]; Sumichrast, La Nat. v. p. 239 [7]; Ridgw. Pr. U. S. Nat. Mus. x. p. 577 [8]; xvi. p. 518 [9]; Salv. Ibis, 1889, p. 372 [10]; 1890, p. 88 [11]; Cherrie, Pr. U. S. Nat. Mus. xiv. p. 536 [12]; Auk, 1892, p. 326 [13]; Shelley, Cat. Birds Brit. Mus. xix. p. 304, t. 12. f. 2 [14]; Cory, Birds W. Indies, p. 102 [15]; Richmond, Pr. U. S. Nat. Mus. xvi. p. 518 [16].

Coccyzus seniculus, Vieill. Enc. Méth. iii. p. 1346 [17]; Nutting, Pr. U. S. Nat. Mus. v. p. 401 [18]; vi. pp. 376 [19], 388 [20].

Supra fusco-griseus, æneo vix micans, capite summo grisescentiore ad frontem pure plumbeo, loris vix obscurioribus, stria lata utrinque infra oculos (tectricibus auricularibus includente) nigra; subtus fulvidus, gula antica albescente; alis et caudæ rectricibus mediis dorso concoloribus, his ad apicem nigricantibus, rectricibus reliquis nigris, macula alba terminali notatis, subalaribus et remigibus intus fulvidis; rostro nigricante, mandibula infra ad basin flavida; pedibus plumbeis. Long. tota circa 12·0, alæ 5·3, caudæ rectr. med. 6·5, rectr. lat. 4·3, rostri a rictu 1·2, tarsi 1·1. (Descr. exempl. ex Cozumel I., Yucatan. Mus. nostr.) Sexus similes.

Hab. North America, Louisiana, Florida, Key West [4].—Mexico, Tampico (*W. B. Richardson*), Dos Arroyos (*Mrs. H. H. Smith*), Tapana, Cacoprieto (*Sumichrast* [7]), Temax, Izamal, Buctzotz, Cozumel I. [10] (*G. F. Gaumer*); Salvador, La Libertad (*W. B. Richardson*); Honduras, Ruatan I. (*G. F. Gaumer* [10]), Puerto Cabello (*G. M. Whitely* [3]); Nicaragua, Chinandega (*W. B. Richardson*), San Juan del Sur [19], Sucuya [20] (*Nutting*), Greytown (*Richmond* [16]); Costa Rica, Punta Arenas (*Boucard* [6]), La Palma (*Nutting* [18]), San José (*Cherrie* [12] [13]); Panama, Chiriqui (*Capt. Kellett & Lieut. Wood*).—South America, from Colombia and Venezuela to Guiana [1] and the Lower Amazons [14]; Antilles generally [15], Swan Island [8].

This Cuckoo may be easily recognized by the fulvous colouring of its under surface, by the dark patch over the ears, by the orange base of the mandible, and by the distinct white ends to the lateral rectrices. Both *C. americanus* and *C. erythrophthalmus* have the under surface white, and the latter a wholly black bill and indistinct marks at the end of the lateral rectrices. *C. melanocoryphus* of South America has a fulvous under surface, but the bill is wholly black.

The range of *C. minor* may be generally defined as extending over nearly the whole of the West-Indian Islands and the countries surrounding the western and southern shores of the Caribbean Sea. It has also been found sparingly in Florida and Louisiana. In Central America, though widely dispersed from Tampico to Panama, and even to the shores of the Pacific, it is nowhere common, and we have traced its range by degrees from a few specimens that have come before us from time to time in the various collections we have examined. Whether it is a resident or a migrant within our area we are unable to say, but probably, from what we know of its congeners, some periodic change of its residence takes place at times. The name " Mangrove Cuckoo," by which it is known in the United States, implies that it is a bird of the mangrove swamps of the sea-shore, and it would seem that such places are its chief resort, but from Dr. Gaumer's records, as well as those of other collectors, it occurs in inland localities as well. Mr. Cherrie states that besides frequenting both coasts of

Costa Rica, it is found as high as 6000 feet in the mountains. He remarks that birds from the Atlantic coast seem to be decidedly the darkest, those from the Pacific coast considerably paler, while specimens from the interior are palest [13].

We never met with it in Guatemala, but it has been recorded from all the other Central-American States, as well as from Eastern and Western Mexico.

Its breeding-habits, as described by Brewer [4], resemble those of *C. americanus*. Its nest is a very slight flat structure of twigs, and the eggs, usually three in number, are oval and of a glaucous-green colour.

Two other forms of *C. minor* have been recognized in the bird of the Bahamas, which is the *C. maynardi* of Ridgway, and the Dominica bird, which Capt. Shelley has called *C. dominicæ*. The differential characters of the three forms are given on plate xii. of the 'Catalogue of Birds' [14].

2. Coccyzus americanus.

Cuculus americanus, Linn. Syst. Nat. i. p. 170 [1].

Coccyzus americanus, Bp. Journ. Ac. Phil. iii. pt. 2, p. 267 [2]; Scl. P. Z. S. 1860, p. 252 [3]; 1864, p. 177 [4]; Scl. & Salv. Ibis, 1860, p. 43 [5]; P. Z. S. 1864, p. 366 [6]; Cab. J. f. Orn. 1862, p. 167 [7]; v. Frantz. J. f. Orn. 1869, p. 361 [8]; Baird, Brew., & Ridgw. N. Am. Birds, ii. p. 477 [9]; Lawr. Mem. Bost. Soc. N. H. ii. p. 293 [10]; Gundl. Orn. Cub. p. 120 [11]; Ferrari-Perez, Pr. U. S. Nat. Mus. ix. p. 162 [12]; Ridgw. Pr. U. S. Nat. Mus. x. p. 577 [13]; Zeledon, An. Mus. Nac. Costa Rica, 1887, p. 123 [14]; Salv. Ibis, 1889, p. 372 [15]; Shelley, Cat. Birds Brit. Mus. xix. p. 308 [16]; Cherrie, Auk, 1892, p. 327 [17]; Cory, Birds West Indies, p. 102 [18].

Supra fusco-griseus, æneo vix micans, capite summo et caudæ rectricibus mediis unicoloribus, his ad apicem nigricantibus, rectricibus reliquis nigris, macula terminali alba notatis ; alis dorso concoloribus, remigibus intus ferrugineis interdum medialiter omnino hujus coloris, subalaribus albis cervino vix tinctis: subtus albus, pectore vix griseo lavato ; rostro nigro, maxillæ margine inferiore et maxilla præter apicem flavidis ; pedibus plumbeis. Long. tota circa 12·0, alæ 5·8, caudæ rectr. med. 6·0, rectr. lat. 3·7, rostri a rictu 1·2, tarsi 0·1. (Descr. exempl. ex Cozumel I., Yucatan : April. Mus. nostr.)

Sexus similes.

Hab. NORTH AMERICA, temperate regions from New Brunswick, Canada, and British Colombia southwards [9].—MEXICO, Moctezuma (*Ferrari-Perez*), Mazatlan (*Grayson*), Calvillo (*W. B. Richardson*), Nuevo Leon (*F. B. Armstrong*), Xicotencal, Tampico (*W. B. Richardson*), Mexico city (*White* [4]), Las Vigas, Plan del Rio, Paso Nuevo (*Ferrari-Perez* [12]), Jalapa (*de Oca, Ferrari-Perez*), Vera Cruz (*Sallé* [3]), La Antigua (*M. Trujillo*), Cozumel I. (*G. F. Gaumer* [15]); GUATEMALA (*Constancia*), Coban [5], Dueñas (*O. S. & F. D. G.*); HONDURAS, Ruatan I. (*G. F. Gaumer* [15]); NICARAGUA, Volcan de Chinandega (*W. B. Richardson*); COSTA RICA (*v. Frantzius* [7][8]), San Juan, Cartago (*Zeledon* [14]), San José (*Cherrie* [17]); PANAMA, Lion Hill (*M·Leannan* [6]). —SOUTH AMERICA generally, from Colombia to Buenos Ayres [16]; ANTILLES [18], Swan Island [13].

The Yellow-billed Cuckoo is found sparingly throughout Mexico and Central America from the coast to an altitude of at least 5000 or 6000 feet in the mountains.

According to Grayson, it is a summer visitant to the neighbourhood of Mazatlan, arriving in June and leaving again in September. During its sojourn it usually frequents the mangrove-swamps and breeds there [10]. In other parts of the country we have records of its occurrence extending from April to October, but none indicating that the bird remains during the autumn and winter months; the latest date recorded being October 20, when Mr. Cherrie found it at San José, Costa Rica [15]. This confirms Grayson's statement, and shows that during the winter *C. americanus* passes to the South-American continent, where it spreads as far as Argentina, and that Central America and Mexico, at least on the coast, are included in its breeding-area. Northward of our region it is, of course, a well-known bird, being found during the summer from Canada to Florida and Texas, and from the Atlantic to the Pacific coasts [9]. The western birds from Oregon to New Mexico and Colorado are noted for their larger size and stouter bill, and have been described by Mr. Ridgway as *C. americanus occidentalis*. A specimen before us from Sonora is no doubt one of this large race, but we have not been able to identify with certainty any other examples as belonging to it; and as the dimensions of the two forms, as given by Mr. Ridgway, completely overlap, we do not attempt any separation.

In the West-Indian Islands *C. americanus* is not uncommon, and there are records of its breeding in many of the islands [18]. In Cuba, Gundlach says he met with it on few occasions in the western districts, where he found its nest [11]. Sir E. Newton also met with it in the island of Santa Cruz, and describes a nest he examined at the end of June 1858. This nest was a very slight platform of sticks laid across one another with a few finer twigs and a little grass as a lining, but so slightly put together that on attempting to take it from the tree it fell to pieces. The eggs are three or four in number, oval, and of a pale green colour.

A few individuals of this Cuckoo have strayed to Europe.

3. Coccyzus erythrophthalmus.

Cuculus erythrophthalmus, Wils. Am. Orn. iv. p. 16, t. 28. f. 2 [1].

Coccyzus erythrophthalmus, Bp. Journ. Ac. Phil. iii. p. 307, t. 2 [2]; Scl. P. Z. S. 1857, p. 214 [3];
    1860, p. 252 [4]; Scl. & Salv. Ibis, 1860, p. 276 [5]; Lawr. Ann. Lyc. N. Y. vii. p. 477 [6]; ix.
    p. 128 [7]; v. Frantzius, J. f. Orn. 1869, p. 361 [8]; Baird, Brew., & Ridgw. N. Am. Birds,
    ii. p. 484 [9]; Gundl. Orn. Cub. p. 120 [10]; Sumichrast, La Nat. v. p. 239 [11]; Zeledon, An.
    Mus. Nac. Costa Rica, 1887, p. 123 [12]; Herrera, La Nat. (2) i. pp. 178 [13], 321 [14]; Salv. Ibis,
    1889, p. 373 [15]; Shelley, Cat. Birds Brit. Mus. xix. p. 311 [16]; Cherrie, Auk, 1892, p. 327 [17].

C. americano similis, sed minor, supra brunnescentior; caudæ rectricibus angustioribus, lateribus fere unicoloribus stricte albo terminatis et fascia angusta subterminali nigricante notatis, remigibus intus et subalaribus pallide cervinis; rostro fere omnino nigro. Long. tota circa 10·5, alæ 5·4, caudæ rectr. med. 5·5, rectr. lat. 3·5, rostri a rictu 1·1, tarsi 0·8. (Descr. exempl. ex Acapulco, Mexico: September. Mus. nostr.)

Sexus similes.

Hab. NORTH AMERICA, Eastern States, north to Labrador, Manitoba, and Assiniboia, west to the Rocky Mountains [9].—MEXICO, Vera Cruz (*Sallé*), Orizaba [4] (*Botteri* [3], *Sumichrast* [11]), Valley of Mexico (*Herrera* [13] [14]), Acapulco, Dos Arroyos (*Mrs. H. H. Smith*), Cozumel I. (*G. F. Gaumer* [15]); GUATEMALA, Dueñas (*O. S. & F. D. G.* [5]); COSTA RICA (*v. Frantzius* [8]), Barranca (*Carmiol* [7], *Zeledon* [12]), San José (*Cherrie* [17]); PANAMA, Lion Hill (*M'Leannan* [6]).—SOUTH AMERICA, from Colombia to Eastern Peru [16]; CUBA [10] and TRINIDAD [16].

The distribution of the Black-billed Cuckoo is very similar to that of the Yellow-billed Cuckoo, but it does not occur westwards of the Rocky Mountains, where the large-billed form of the latter bird is found. Its breeding-range extends as far north as Labrador, Manitoba, and Eastern Assiniboia, but it does not, as in the case of *C. americanus*, breed outside the southern limits of the United States. The only island of the West Indies where it has been observed is Cuba, where Dr. Gundlach says it is very rare, and noted by him in the months of April and May, probably during the northward spring migration [10]. In Mexico we have records of its occurrence from May till November, and some birds probably remain the whole winter. In Costa Rica Mr. Cherrie says it occurs on both coasts, but is very rare; he secured a specimen on October 1st at San José [17]. In South America *C. erythrophthalmus* does not have nearly so extensive a range as *C. americanus*, but it has been recorded from Colombia (Bogota), from Northern and Eastern Peru, and from the island of Trinidad, and, like *C. americanus*, a few individuals have strayed to Europe.

In its nesting-habits this species resembles *C. americanus*, the eggs being similar, but rather smaller.

Subfam. PHŒNICOPHAINÆ.

Of the sixteen genera which Captain Shelley places in this subfamily only three, viz. *Saurothera*, *Hyetornis*, and *Piaya*, occur in America; and of these the two former belong exclusively to the larger West-Indian Islands and the Bahamas. *Piaya* is purely Neotropical, and has a wide range in that region, as stated below.

The members of this subfamily are arboreal in their habits. The tarsi are short; the wings short and much rounded; the tail long and composed of ten soft curved feathers—the flight of the American species being feeble and of short duration.

PIAYA.

Piaya, Lesson, Traité d'Orn. p. 139 (1831); Shelley, Cat. Birds Brit. Mus. xix. p. 373.
Pyrrhococcyx, Cabanis in Schomb. Reise n. Guiana, iii. p. 713.
Coccyzusa, Cabanis & Heine, Mus. Hein. iv. Heft 1, p. 89.

A purely Neotropical genus, with close allies in the Antilles. The number of species belonging to *Piaya* is very variously estimated, owing to the views entertained as to the desirability of dividing up the common widely distributed *P. cayana*. In Central

America we find two fairly distinct forms of this bird occupying for the most part distinct districts, and we treat them as different species, so that, with *P. minuta*, which occurs at the extreme southern end of our fauna, and *P. melanogaster* of South America, we recognize four forms in all, which is one more than is admitted by Capt. Shelley. The northern range of the genus extends to the Mexican State of Tamaulipas on one side to that of Sinaloa on the other, and thence spreads southwards, and to a height of about 5000 feet in the mountainous districts.

The bill of *Piaya* is much like that of *Coccyzus* in its general shape and curvature, but is shorter and stouter; the nostrils are oval openings at the lower edge of the nasal fossa; the wings are short and rounded, the sixth quill being the longest, the third falling far short of the extremity; the primaries themselves do not project much beyond the secondaries, and the whole wing when closed fits compactly to the body; the tail is very long, and composed of wide, curved, soft feathers; all but the middle pair are distinctly tipped with white, and the lateral pair are little more than half the middle pair; the eyelashes are simple strong bristles, without barbs as in *Coccyzus*.

1. **Piaya cayana.**

Cuculus cayanus, Linn. Syst. Nat. i. p. 170[1]; Licht. Preis-Verz. Mex. Vög. p. 1 (*cf. J. f. Orn.* 1863, p. 55)[2]; Wagl. Isis, 1831, p. 524[3].

Piaya cayana, Less. Traité d'Orn. p. 140[4]; Lawr. Bull. U. S. Nat. Mus. no. 4, p. 33[5]; Sumichrast, La Nat. v. p. 239[6]; Salv. Cat. Strickl. Coll. p. 441[7]; Ibis, 1889, p. 372[8]; Boucard, P. Z. S. 1883, p. 454[9]; Ferrari-Perez, Pr. U. S. Nat. Mus. ix. p. 162[10]; Ridgw. Pr. U. S. Nat. Mus. x. pp. 582[11], 591[12]; Stone, Pr. Ac. Phil. 1890, p. 206[13]; Shelley, Cat. Birds Brit. Mus. xix. p. 373 (partim)[14].

Piaya mexicana, Scl. P. Z. S. 1856, p. 308[15]; 1858, p. 359[16]; Moore, P. Z. S. 1859, p. 60[17]; Scl. & Salv. Ibis, 1859, p. 133[18].

Piaya melheri, Bp. Consp. Av. i. p. 110[19]; Scl. P. Z. S. 1864, p. 177[20]; Lawr. Ann. Lyc. N. Y. ix. pp. 128[21], 205[22]; Salv. Ibis, 1866, p. 204[23]; P. Z. S. 1867, p. 156[24]; 1870, p. 211[25]; Ibis, 1872, p. 323[26]; Scl. & Salv. P. Z. S. 1867, p. 280[27]; 1870, p. 837[29]; v. Frantz. J. f. Orn. 1869, p. 361[29]; Boucard, P. Z. S. 1878, p. 48[30]; Sumichrast, La Nat. v. p. 239[31].

Pyrrhococcyx melheri, Cab. J. f. Orn. 1862, p. 167[32].

Piaya cayana melheri, Nutting, Pr. U. S. Nat. Mus. v. p. 401[33]; vi. pp. 376[34], 388[35]; Ridgw. Pr. U. S. Nat. Mus. v. p. 498[36]; Zeledon, An. Mus. Nac. Costa Rica, 1887, p. 123[37]; Cherrie, Auk, 1892, p. 326[39]; Richmond, Pr. U. S. Nat. Mus. xvi. p. 517[38].

Piaya thermophila, Scl. P. Z. S. 1859, p. 368[40]; Scl. & Salv. Ibis, 1860, p. 43[41].

Piaya nigricrissa, Scl. P. Z. S. 1860, p. 285[42]; Lawr. Ann. Lyc. N. Y. vii. p. 300[49]; viii. p. 175[44]; Scl. & Salv. P. Z. S. 1864, p. 366[45].

Piaya ridibunda, Lawr. Bull. U. S. Nat. Mus. no. 4, p. 33[46]; Sumichrast, La Nat. v. p. 239[47].

Supra castaneus, capite summo fuscescentiore ad frontem pallidiore: subtus gutture toto pallide rufescente; abdomine griseo, ventre imo, tectricibus subcaudalibus et tibiis griseo-nigricantibus; alis et cauda dorso concoloribus paulo saturatioribus, remigum apicibus fusco-nigricantibus, subalaribus pallide griseis; caudæ rectricibus mediis ad apicem nigris, apicibus ipsis albis, rectricibus reliquis supra rufescentibus ad apicem nigris et albo terminatis, subtus omnino nigris, apicibus tantum albis; rostro flavescenti-viridi ad basin saturatiore viridi; pedibus plumbeis. Long. tota circa 18·0, alæ 5·6, caudæ rectr. med. 10·5, rectr. lat. 5·5, rostri a rictu 1·3, tarsi 1·4. (Descr. maris ex San Lorenzo, Canton de Cordova, Mexico. Mus. nostr.) ♀ mari similis.

Hab. MEXICO (*Deppe*[2], *Wagler*[3], *White*[20]), Tamaulipas, Tampico, Valles (*W. B. Richard-son*), Misantla (*F. D. G.*), Jalapa (*de Oca*[40], *Ferrari-Perez*[11], *F. D. G.*), Cofre de Perote (*M. Trujillo*), Coatepec (*Ferrari-Perez*), Cordova (*Sallé*[15], *Sumichrast*[31]), San Lorenzo near Cordova (*Ferrari-Perez*), Orizaba (*F. D. G.*, *Ferrari-Perez*), Atoyac, Teapa (*Mrs. H. H. Smith*), Tonala, Chihuitan, Barrio (*Sumichrast*[5][6]), N. Yucatan[9], Peto, Izalam, Temax (*G. F. Gaumer*), Merida (*Schott*[22]), Meco, Holbox I., Mugeres I. (*G. F. Gaumer*[8][9]), Ticul (*Stone & Baker*[13]); BRITISH HONDURAS, Western District (*Blancaneaux*); GUATEMALA (*Constancia*[7][18]), Peten (*Leyland*[17]), Coban[41], Yzabal[41], Chisec, Cahabon, San Gerónimo, Dueñas, Retalhuleu (*O. S. & F. D. G.*); SALVADOR, La Libertad (*W. B. Richardson*); HONDURAS, Omoa (*Leyland*[17]), Truxillo[11], Segovia R.[12] (*Townsend*), San Pedro (*G. M. Whitely*[28]), Comayagua (*G. C. Taylor*[16]); NICARAGUA, Chontales (*Belt*[26]), Leon, Chinandega (*W. B. Richardson*), San Juan del Sur[34], Sucuya[35] (*Nutting*), Escondido R. (*Richmond*), Blewfields (*Wickham*[27]); COSTA RICA (*Hoffmann, v. Frantzius*[32]), S. José (*v. Frantzius*[29], *Carmiol*[21], *Boucard*[30], *Zeledon*[37], *Cherrie*[38]), Angostura (*v. Frantzius*[29], *Carmiol*[21]), V. de Irazu[36], La Palma[33] (*Nutting*), Alajuela, Liberia, Cartago, Jimenez (*Zeledon*[37]); PANAMA, David (*Bridges*[24], *Hicks*[44]), Castillo, Calovevora (*Arcé*[25]), Lion Hill (*M'Leannan*[43][45]).— SOUTH AMERICA generally, from Colombia to Guiana, Brazil, and Argentina[14].

Much difference of opinion exists respecting this *Piaya*, as to whether it is divisible into several local races, for which many names have been proposed, or whether all should be merged under one title. In the 'Nomenclator Avium Neotropicalium' the latter course was adopted, which has been followed by Capt. Shelley in the 'Catalogue of Birds in the British Museum.' On the other hand, Mr. Allen (Bull. Am. Mus. Nat. Hist. v. p. 136) has recently revived the treatment of the authors of the 'Museum Heineanum' (iv. Heft 1, pp. 82 *et seq.*), and makes six races of *P. cayana*, to each of which he assigns a subspecific name, his remarks being inspired by the examination of a series of specimens collected by Mr. Herbert Smith in the Brazilian province of Matto Grosso. That differences occur in specimens from various points of the wide area over which this bird extends is obvious, and they are to a certain extent localized. But in most cases they are not very pronounced, and we feel sure that the greater the amount of material examined and our knowledge of the distribution extended, it will prove, as has been already anticipated, that it will be hardly possible to define all the races of the southern continent that have been proposed. It remains, therefore, for us to examine the relationship of the two forms found within our limits, which we call *P. cayana* and *P. mexicana*. The typical forms of these two birds are distinct enough, and may be recognized at once—*P. cayana* being of a darker colour above, darker beneath, and with the under surface of the tail black; *P. mexicana*, on the other hand, is light rufous above and has a rufous tail beneath, the white terminal spots being banded inwardly by a black subterminal bar.

The ranges of the two birds are also distinct, *P. cayana* being found in Eastern Mexico and thence southwards to the Isthmus of Panama, whence it spreads in various forms over nearly the whole of South America as far as South Brazil and Paraguay. *P. mexicana*, on the other hand, is restricted to Western Mexico, and is not found elsewhere within our region. The only difficulty that arises is that on the Isthmus of Tehuantepec we find intermediate birds which have a rusty tint over the under surface of the tail-feathers, and thus we have a case similar to what we find in *Melanerpes santacruzi* (*antea*, p. 421) and also in *Psilorhinus morio* and *P. mexicanus*, where forms mingle along their respective boundaries. In the present case, as in the others referred to, we think it best to treat each form as distinct, recording the fact that a certain amount of mixture takes place where the two come in contact.

P. cayana is a common species throughout our region from the Mexican State of Tamaulipas southwards. It keeps to the eastern side of the mountains, as far south as the Isthmus of Tehuantepec, where it also crosses to the Pacific coast, and is the only form throughout the rest of Central America. In altitude it ranges from the sea-level to a height of at least 6000 feet in the mountains of the interior. Though strictly arboreal in its habits, *P. cayana* is not restricted to any particular kind of forest, but frequents the trees on the margins of clearings, sometimes resting close to the ground, at others amongst the upper branches. It is also found in the woody margins of streams. It is a bird that usually sits quietly on a bough; but both Mr. Richmond[39] and Mr. Cherrie[38] mention a habit it has of running along the boughs of trees, and thus resembles a squirrel, so much so that in Costa Rica it is called " Pajaro Ardilla," or Squirrel-bird. It also, from its tameness, is called " Bobo," or Foolish bird.

Mr. Nutting says it is silent and solitary, but when disturbed utters a loud harsh note at regular intervals and flits its tail with angry jerks. The same observer says that the cry of this Cuckoo is frequently heard around San Juan del Sur. In Yucatan Dr. Gaumer says[10] it is a common bird, and he is the only observer that speaks of its habit of frequenting the neighbourhood of hive-bees and feeding freely on them, taking them when resorting to flowers in search of honey.

Mr. Cherrie[38] describes the nest from the notes of Señor Alfaro, who found one amongst some scraggy trees on the banks of the Rio de Poas in Costa Rica. The female bird, which he shot, was sitting on the nest, but flew to a short distance on being disturbed. The nest was placed about nine feet from the ground in the branches of a small tree, and was well hidden by the broad leaves of a climbing plant. It was constructed of decayed leaves, and could not be preserved. The two eggs were opaque white without markings, elliptical-oval in shape, and measured 35 × 24 and 33 × 24 millim.

2. **Piaya mexicana.**

Cuculus mexicanus, Sw. Phil. Mag. new ser. i. p. 440 [1].

Piaya mexicana, Scl. P. Z. S. 1859, p. 388 [2].

Pyrrhococcyx mexicanus, Finsch, Abhandl. naturw. Ver. zu Bremen, 1870, p. 356 [3].

Piaya melheri, Dugès, La Nat. i. p. 138 [4].

Piaya ridibundus, Lawr. Mem. Bost. Soc. N. H. ii. p. 293 [5]; Bull. U. S. Nat. Mus. no. 4, p. 33 (?) [6];
  Sumichrast, La Nat. v. p. 239 (?) [7].

Piaya cayenensis, Salv. P. Z. S. 1883, p. 426 [8].

Piaya cayana, Ferrari-Perez, Pr. U. S. Nat. Mus. ix. p. 162 [9]; Shelley, Cat. Birds Brit. Mus. xix.
  p. 373 (partim) [10].

P. cayanæ similis, sed supra omnino pallidior et rufescentior : subtus quoque pallidior, ventre imo, tectricibus subcaudalibus et tibiis griseis, quam abdomen reliquum paulo saturatioribus ; caudæ rectricibus lateralibus subtus et supra rufescentibus, apicibus albis et fascia subterminali conspicua nigra notatis. Long. tota 18·0, alæ 0·2, caudæ rectr. med. 12·6, rectr. lat. 6·0, rostri a rictu 1·25, tarsi 1·4. (Descr. feminæ ex Chietla, Puebla, Mexico. Mus. nostr.)

♂ feminæ similis.

Hab. Mexico, Mazatlan (*Grayson* [3] [5], *Xantus* [5], *Bischoff* [5]), San Blas (*W. B. Richardson*), Hacienda de San Marcos (*W. Lloyd*), Zapotlan (*W. B. Richardson*), Guanajuato, Guadalajara (*Dugès*), Bolaños, Colima (*W. B. Richardson*), Tupila R., Plains of Colima (*Xantus* [5]), Temiscaltepec (*Bullock* [1]). Acapulco (*A. H. Markham* [8], *Mrs. H. H. Smith*), Xautipa in Guerrero (*Mrs. H. H. Smith*), Chietla in the Canton de Cordova (*Ferrari-Perez* [9]), Juchatengo (*M. Trujillo*), Juquila (*Boucard* [2]), Oaxaca (*Fenochio*), Tehuantepec? (*Sumichrast* [6] [7]).

This is a Western Mexican form of the eastern and southern *P. cayana*, and is found as far north as the neighbourhood of Mazatlan, and thence southwards through the States of Jalisco, Guerrero, and Oaxaca. On the Isthmus of Tehuantepec, as already stated, it blends with *P. cayana*, and beyond this district no trace of it is found in Central America, but in the far south the peculiar feature of the rufous tail reappears. In size it slightly exceeds its close ally, and this, too, is characteristic of the southern form.

Swainson's type was obtained by Bullock at Temiscaltepec [1], on the western edge of the Mexican tableland ; and it has been found since that time by all collectors who have worked in the western parts of the republic, from the edge of the highlands to the sea-coast.

Its habits, of which nothing is on record, doubtless resemble those of *P. cayana*.

3. **Piaya minuta.**

Cuculus cyanus, var. β, Linn. Syst. Nat. i. p. 170 [1].

Cuculus minutus, Vieill. N. Dict. d'Hist. N. viii. p. 277 [2].

Piaya minuta, Gray, Gen. Birds, ii. p. 457 [3]; Scl. & Salv. P. Z. S. 1866, p. 195 [4]; 1879, p. 537 [5];
  Layard, Ibis, 1873, p. 393 [6]; Shelley, Cat. Birds Brit. Mus. xix. p. 378 [7].

? *Cuculus rutilus,* Illig. Abh. Ak. Wissensch. Berl. 1812, p. 224 [8].

Piaya rutila, Lawr. Ann. Lyc. N. Y. vii. p. 300 [9].

Coccyzusa gracilis, Heine, J. f. Orn. 1863, p. 356[10].

Piaya gracilis, Scl. & Salv. P. Z. S. 1864, p. 366[11].

Supra castanea, capite summo ad frontem rufescentiore, uropygio et cauda saturatioribus : subtus gutture toto rufescente, abdomine griseo, ventre imo, tectricibus subalaribus et tibiis griseo-nigricantibus ; caudæ rectricibus omnibus ad apicem fusco-nigricantibus et albo terminatis, rectricibus lateralibus subtus fere omnino nigris usque ad maculam albam terminalem vix castaneo tinctis, sed supra castaneis usque ad fasciam subterminalem nigram ; rostro flavido, maxillæ basi fusca ; pedibus plumbeis. Long. tota circa 10·0, alæ 3·9, caudæ rectr. med. 6·0, rectr. lat. 3·0, rostri a rictu 0·85, tarsi 1·1. (Descr. maris ex Lion Hill, Panama. Mus. nostr.)

Hab. PANAMA, Lion Hill (*M'Leannan*[9][11]). — SOUTH AMERICA, from Colombia and Ecuador[10] to Guiana, Amazons Valley, and Brazil[7].

This Cuckoo is a miniature form of *P. cayana,* the tints and distribution of the colours of its plumage being very similar. It has a wide range over the northern parts of the South-American continent from Guiana and the mouth of the Amazons to Western Ecuador. It just enters our fauna, being not uncommon on the Isthmus of Panama, where M'Leannan met with it and sent specimens to Lawrence and to ourselves. The bird of Western Ecuador was separated by Heine as *Coccyzusa gracilis*[10], but there appears to be no difference of any importance between it and birds from further east.

Of the habits of *P. minuta* little is recorded. Mr. Layard[6] shot one about ten miles from Para in a garden. It crept through the bushes and trees just like a *Colius* (a bird with which he was familiar in South Africa), always, on his approach, flying out on the opposite side of the bush. Its stomach contained spiders and caterpillars. The iris in life is red.

Subfam. *NEOMORPHINÆ.*

Of the four genera contained in this subfamily, *Carpococcyx* of Borneo and Sumatra has a general resemblance to *Neomorphus,* but differs in some important particulars. *Geococcyx* is a very isolated form peculiar to Mexico and the northern frontier States and to the northern section of Central America ; *Morococcyx* is another isolated form. All these birds are of terrestrial habits, though they rest on low trees and scrub-wood. The wings are short, the primaries hardly exceeding the secondaries in length, and the whole wing when closed fitting close to the body ; the tail is long, rounded, and consists of ten wide feathers ; the tarsi are long, and the distal ends of the tibiæ clothed with short feathers.

NEOMORPHUS.

Neomorphus, Gloger, in Froriep's Notiz. xvi. p. 278 (1827) ; Lawr. Ibis, 1873, pp. 287 et seq.;
    Shelley, Cat. Birds Brit. Mus. xix. p. 415.

Cultrides, Pucheran, Rev. Zool. 1845, p. 51.

Of this remarkable genus of Cuckoos five species are now known, but all of them are rare birds, though found over a large area, including the greater part of Tropical America. *N. geoffroyi*, the oldest known, belongs to South-eastern Brazil; *N. rufipennis* to Guiana; *N. pucherani* to the Amazons Valley; *N. radiolosus* to Eastern Ecuador; whilst *N. salvini*, the species which belongs to our country, occurs from Nicaragua to Ecuador.

All the species of *Neomorphus* are of large size and of rich tints of bronze and purple on the upper surface; the head carries a long, full nuchal crest; the wings are very short, the sixth quill being the longest and hardly exceeding the secondaries in length; the tail consists of long, wide, slightly curved feathers, the outermost pair are rather more than half the length of the middle pair; the legs are long, and the tarsi bare, the tibiæ covered with small closely set feathers, and not full like those of *Coccyzus* and *Piaya*; the bill is compressed, and the culmen drawn into a sharp curved edge; the nostrils are horizontal slits along the lower edge of the nasal fossa; the eyelashes are long bristles, with some long hair-like barbs from near the base.

The only genus at all like *Neomorphus* is the Bornean and Sumatran *Carpococcyx*, to which it has a general resemblance; but the latter genus has a wider culmen at the base, the area over the nostrils less feathered, and the nostrils themselves more open.

1. **Neomorphus salvini.**

Neomorphus salvini, Scl. P. Z. S. 1866, p. 60, t. 5 [1]; Salv. P. Z. S. 1867, p. 156 [2]; Ibis, 1872, p. 323 [3]; Lawr. Ibis, 1873, p. 291 [4]; Shelley, Cat. Birds Brit. Mus. xix. p. 417 [5].

Supra æneo-viridis, lilacino-purpureo micans; capite summo rufescente, fronte dilutiore, crista nuchali elongata violaceo-viridi: subtus griseo-fuscus, pectoris plumis pallide marginatis, torque pectorali nigra, ventre imo et tectricibus subcaudalibus rufo-brunneis, tibiis rufescentibus; alis et cauda æneo-virescentibus, hac supra rufa certa luce lavata; rostro corneo, culmine et tomiis pallidis; pedibus plumbeis. Long. tota circa 20·0, alæ 6·6, caudæ rectr. med. 10·0, rectr. lat. 6·2, rostri a rictu 2·2, tarsi 2·8. (Descr. feminæ, exempl. typ. ex Veraguas, Panama. Mus. nostr.)

Hab. NICARAGUA, Chontales (*Belt* [3]); PANAMA (*Mus. Brit.*), Santiago de Veraguas [1], Cordillera de Tolé (*Arcé* [2]).—COLOMBIA [1]; ECUADOR [5].

Mr. Sclater's description and figure of this distinct species were taken from a female specimen sent us in the second collection of birds made by Enrique Arcé after he left Panama and commenced his fruitful researches in the rich country lying to the westward of the interoceanic railway, and extending to Chiriqui and the frontier of Costa Rica. This collection was formed near Santiago de Veraguas, and reached us in January 1866. A second specimen, a male, was subsequently sent us from the Cordillera de Tolé, and reached us in September 1866; this passed into Mr. Sclater's possession, and thence with the rest of his collection to the British Museum *.

In 1872 Salvin found a specimen in Belt's collection formed in Nicaragua, another

* We give these particulars, as Capt. Shelley credits Mr. Sclater's collection with the type of the species, which is an error.

from Panama was in Seebohm's collection.　These four birds are all that we know with certainty as coming from Central America; but in the Rivoli collection, now the property of the Academy of Natural Sciences of Philadelphia, is, as Lawrence has pointed out, a bird of this species said to have come from Mexico, but without further particulars.　Though doubtless found in Costa Rica, it has as yet escaped the notice of the careful collectors who have worked in that country during the last thirty years. The extension of the range of *N. salvini* into South America is shown by a bird of Colombian origin in the British Museum, and by a specimen procured by Buckley on the Rio Cotopaza in Eastern Ecuador.

The species most nearly allied to *N. salvini* is *N. geoffroyi* of South Brazil, from which it may be distinguished by the lilac tint of the back, upper tail-coverts, and wings, and by other slight characters.

Of the habits of *N. salvini* nothing has been recorded.　It is evidently a rare bird, as is each of the other members of the genus.

GEOCOCCYX.

Geococcyx, Wagler, Isis, 1831, p. 524; Shelley, Cat. Birds Brit. Mus. xix. p. 419.

A genus containing two closely allied but distinct species, remarkable amongst the Cuckoos of America for their form, colour, and habits.　They belong to the group of Ground-Cuckoos, as they pass their time mostly on the ground and run with great swiftness.　Their food consists of insects, and they build in low bushes and rear their own broods.

The range of *Geococcyx* extends from Nicaragua northwards, and passes beyond our northern limit into the frontier States of North America.

Both species are of large size with long tails, and the plumage of the upper surface distinctly striated with light markings upon a dark purple-black ground.　The bill is long, the culmen nearly straight towards the base, but curving downwards rather abruptly towards the tip; the nostrils are oval and placed at the lower edge of the nasal fossa, which is feathered over nearly the whole of its surface; surrounding the orbit is a brightly coloured space, which ends posteriorly in a scarlet patch; the eyelashes are strong, simple, flattened bristles; the tarsi are long, the toes short, and the tibiæ clothed with short feathers; the tail long and cuneate, the lateral feathers reaching to about two-thirds of the whole length.

1. **Geococcyx californianus.**

? *Phasianus mexicanus*, Gm. Syst. Nat. i. p. 741[1].

Geococcyx mexicanus, Strickl. Ann. & Mag. N. H. 1842, viii. p. 544[2]; Cassin, Birds Cal. & Tex. p. 213, t. 36[3]; Scl. P. Z. S. 1857, p. 205[4]; 1864, p. 177[5]; Dugès, La Nat. i. p. 139[6]; Lawr. Mem. Bost. Soc. N. H. ii. p. 293[7]; Sumichrast, La Nat. v. p. 239[8]; Salv. Cat. Strickl. Coll. p. 442[9]; Shelley, Cat. Birds Brit. Mus. xix. p. 419[10].

Saurothera californiana, Less. Compl. Buff., Ois. vi. p. 420 (1829)[11].

Geococcyx californianus, Baird, Brew., & Ridgw. N. Am. Birds, ii. p. 472[12]; Sennett, Bull. U. S.
    Geol. Surv. v. p. 413[13]; Belding, Pr. U. S. Nat. Mus. vi. p. 344[14]; Shufeldt, Ibis, 1885,
    p. 286, t. 7[15]; P. Z. S. 1886, p. 466, tt. 42, 45[16]; Herrera, La Nat. (2) i. pp. 178, 321[17].

Cuculus viaticus, Licht. Preis-Verz. Mex. Vög. p. 1 (*cf.* J. f. Orn. 1863, p. 55)[18].

Geococcyx variegata, Wagl. Isis, 1831, p. 524[19].

Supra æneo-viridescens, plumis omnibus (præter apices) cervino limbatis, crista nuchali saturate purpurea:
    subtus sordide albus, gutturis et pectoris plumis medialiter stria rachali nigra utrinque fulvo limbata, gula
    immaculata, tectricibus subcaudalibus abdomine concoloribus; alis purpureo-nigris, remigibus maculis
    duabus elongatis in pogonio externo albis, una mediana, altera apicali; cauda æneo-viridi, rectricibus
    quatuor utrinque lateralibus albo terminatis; rostro corneo; pedibus plumbeis; iride (ave vivo) rubro
    bicincta, oculorum ambitu nudo cæruleo medialiter cretaceo-albo, postice plaga coccinea ornato. Long.
    tota circa 21·0, alæ 7·3, caudæ rectr. med. 11·5, rectr. lat. 8·0, rostri a rictu 2·55, tarsi 2·5. (Descr.
    feminæ ex San Salvador, Puebla, Mexico. Mus. nostr.)

♂ feminæ similis.

Hab. NORTH AMERICA, Southern frontier States[12], Texas[13]. — MEXICO (*Deppé*[18],
    Wagler[19], *T. Mann*[9], *White*[5], *Sumichrast*[8]), Guaymas (*Belding*[14]), Mazatlan
    (*Grayson*[7], *Xantus*[7]), Guanajuato (*Dugès*[6]), Zapotlan (*W. Lloyd, W. B. Richard-
    son*), Nuevo Leon (*F. B. Armstrong*), Sierra Madre above Ciudad Victoria,
    Xicotencal, Soto La Marina, Tamesi near Tampico, Tenango del Valle (*W. B.
    Richardson*), San Salvador in Puebla (*Ferrari-Perez*), Valley of Mexico (*Herrera*[17]),
    Velasco (*le Strange*), Jalapa (*Sallé*[4]).

This species has frequently been called by Gmelin's name, *Phasianus mexicanus*,
which was applied to the Hoitlallotl of Hernandez. This may be correct; but as the
name *mexicanus* has also been applied to the smaller *G. affinis*, and the description
is so vague that it is impossible to decide to which bird it should belong, we think
it best to take Lesson's title *californianus* for it, as is the practice with American
ornithologists.

The range of this species is extended over the whole of Northern Mexico as far as
the States of Jalisco and Sonora and the southern extremity of Tamaulipas. It is also
found in the Valley of Mexico, in small numbers, according to Herrera, in winter near
Tlalpam[17]. The only record we have of it south of this district is a specimen sent us
by Don F. Ferrari-Perez from San Salvador in the State of Puebla. In altitude the
range of this species is great, and extends from the sea-level at Mazatlan and Tampico
to the Valley of Mexico. Beyond the northern frontier of Mexico it occurs in all the
border States from Texas to California, and is a well-known bird in those countries.

The habits of *Geococcyx californianus* have been fully described by several writers,
and a summary of their observations is so well given by Brewer in the 'History of North-
American Birds'[12], that we need only add Grayson's notes[7] concerning the bird, and
those of Mr. Sennett[13] which relate to its breeding. Grayson writes:—" This remarkable
bird, which the Mexicans call 'Churea del Camino' (Road-runner)—so called from the
habit it sometimes has of running along a path or road,—seldom fails to attract the

attention of the traveller by its solitary and peculiar habits, and often, too, in the mountainous regions and desert countries, where no other living creature is to be seen. Although met with in such localities, it is, however, not entirely confined to them, as it is an equal inhabitant of some portions of the thinly wooded parts of the *tierra caliente* of the west, where the trees are scrubby and the country open, as the barren and rocky great central plains of Mexico. It seems to prefer a hilly country but scantily supplied with vegetation, where the numerous species of cacti form impenetrable thorny thickets. Here the Road-runner wanders in solitude, subsisting on grasshoppers, mice, lizards, &c.

"It is most usually met with upon the ground, and as soon as it discovers the presence of danger, or the intruder, instantly runs off with remarkable fleetness to the nearest thicket or hill, where it generally escapes from its pursuers, either by concealment or a short flight from one hill to another. If a tree with low branches be convenient it will spring into that, and soon reaching the top will fly off to the distance of a hundred yards or more; it appears to rise from the level ground with much difficulty. It is very quick in its motions, active and vigilant; indeed its fleetness enables it to elude its pursuers, although one may be mounted on a good horse or a dog may be in the train; but this only for a short distance, as it would soon be run down by the horse or dog, were not some convenient thicket or hill near, from which to take its flight from the latter or conceal itself among the branches of the former."

Mr. Sennett, during one of his visits to Lomita, about sixty miles up the Rio Grande river of Texas, found a score of nests of this Cuckoo, some containing as many as eight or nine eggs. The nests were found in all sorts of places at heights varying from four to eight feet from the ground, and in various trees, a large prickly-pear cactus or a thick clump of thorny bushes being often chosen. The nests vary in size according to the position, sometimes being bulky, sometimes very fragile, but composed always of sticks with a lining of grasses, and having a depression about equal to the diameter of the egg. The eggs are laid with much irregularity, but mostly in April, though fresh eggs were obtained as late as the end of May. Their colour is opaque-white.

2. Geococcyx affinis.

Geococcyx affinis, Hartl. Rev. Zool. 1844, p. 215 [1]; Scl. P. Z. S. 1858, p. 305 [2]; 1859, pp. 368 [3], 387 [4]; Scl. & Salv. Ibis, 1859, p. 134 [5]; R. Owen, Ibis, 1861, p. 67 [6]; Sumichrast, La Nat. v. p. 239 [7]; Salv. Cat. Strickl. Coll. p. 442 [8]; Boucard, P. Z. S. 1883, p. 454 [9]; Ferrari-Perez, Pr. U. S. Nat. Mus. ix. p. 162 [10]; Stone, Pr. Ac. Phil. 1890, p. 205 [11]; Shelley, Cat. Birds Brit. Mus. xix. p. 421 [12].

? *Geococcyx mexicanus*, Lawr. Ann. Lyc. N. Y. ix. p. 205 [13]; Bull. U. S. Nat. Mus. no. 4, p. 34 [14].

G. californiano similis, sed minor, supra æneo-brunneus vix viridi tinctus, striis pallidis similibus sed angustioribus: subtus cervinus medialiter immaculatus, pectoris lateribus tantum nigro striatis; tectricibus subcaudalibus saturate brunneis; iride (ave vivo) brunnea, annulo aurantiaco, oculorum ambitu cretaceocæruleo macula conspicua coccinea postice ornato. Long. tota circa 18·5, alæ 6·0, caudæ rectr. med. 11·0, rectr. lat. 6·6, rostri a rictu 2·0, tarsi 2·0. (Descr. exempl. ex San Gerónimo, Guatemala. Mus. nostr.)

Hab. MEXICO, Sierra de Alamos (*W. Lloyd*), Presidio de Mazatlan (*Forrer*), Hacienda de San Marcos, Zapotlan (*W. Lloyd*), Volcan de Colima (*W. B. Richardson*), Jalapa (*de Oca* [3], *F. D. G.*), Zentla, Huehuetlan [10] (*Ferrari-Perez*), Durasnal (*Boucard* [2]), Morelia (*le Strange*), Juquila (*Boucard* [4]), Soledad, Potrero, Juchitan, Cacoprieto (*Sumichrast* [7] [14]), Sierra de S. Domingo, Tehuantepec (*W. B. Richardson*), Peto, Temax, Izalam, Progreso, Rio Lagartos [9] (*G. F. Gaumer*), Tekanto (*Stone & Baker* [11]); GUATEMALA [1] generally [5] [8], Vera Paz, hills above Quiché, Gorge of La Campana Rio Chixoy, Dueñas (*O. S. & F. D. G.*), San Gerónimo (*R. Owen* [6]), Toliman (*W. B. Richardson*); NICARAGUA, San Rafael del Norte, Matagalpa (*W. B. Richardson*).

This species, which Dr. Hartlaub separated from *Geococcyx californianus* in 1844, has a very similar general appearance to that bird, but is smaller, without stripes on the middle of the breast, and has the under tail-coverts dark brown. Its range extends much further south, but in Western Mexico both species occur together over a considerable area, reaching from the State of Sonora to that of Puebla. In Yucatan, and thence southwards through Guatemala and as far as Northern Nicaragua, *G. affinis* is found alone.

Dr. Gaumer says [9] it is a rather rare bird in Northern Yucatan, except at Rio Lagartos, and may be generally seen perched upon the stone fences or upon some elevated object, but rarely in trees. When startled it jumps quickly to the ground and runs away, hiding itself in the thick undergrowth. Mr. Stone [11] only met with it in the scrubby woods about Tekanto, where a few individuals were seen running rapidly through the bush, and when thus running they look very like the Iguanas which abound in the district. We also noticed the likeness they have to the large lizards, and in Guatemala they are in some places called "Iguana" and "Siguamonte" or "Guarda camino." When riding along a road where these birds are found one may be seen occasionally to cross the track rapidly, first peering out of the underwood before making a rush, and now and then stopping to make a final survey just before diving in again. The bird is not shy but inquisitive, and will often remain quite still by the side of the path and watch a passer-by without alarm.

Mr. Robert Owen [6] procured us a bird and four eggs from near San Gerónimo, in Guatemala, on 3rd April, 1860. The nest was placed in the fork of a tree about twelve feet from the ground, and was a loose unfinished-looking structure consisting of a few dried twigs and lined with stalks of grass. The eggs are pure white with a smooth surface, and measure 1·45 × 1·05 inch.

The large space round the eye in life is of a chalky bluish-white colour, and has at its further end a large crescent-shaped patch of vermilion. The legs are of a slate-colour.

MOROCOCCYX.

Morococcyx, Sclater, Cat. Am. Birds, p. 322 (1862); Shelley, Cat. Birds Brit. Mus. xix. p. 422.

A monotypic genus peculiar to Central America with no near allies. It belongs to the section of Ground-Cuckoos, but is a much smaller bird than either species of *Geococcyx*, which are, perhaps, its next of kin.

Its range in Mexico seems confined to the Western States from Sinaloa to Tehuantepec; in Guatemala it is chiefly found in the valley of the Motagua river, and it also occurs in Nicaragua and Costa Rica.

The general tint of the plumage is nearly uniform above with bronze tints, and pale chestnut beneath, and with dull whitish spots on the outer rectrices; the bill is short, the culmen regularly arched; the nostrils are oval and at the lower edge of the nasal fossa; the space round the eye is bare, and coloured blue in life, the eyelashes simple, strong bristles; the tarsi are moderately long, and the toes longer in proportion than in *Geococcyx*; the primaries short, hardly exceeding the secondaries, the wings thus being much rounded; the outer rectrices are about two-thirds the length of the middle pair, the tail being rounded.

1. Morococcyx erythropygus.

Coccyzus erythropyga, Less. Rev. Zool. 1842, p. 210 [1].

Piaya erythropygia, Des Murs, Icon. Orn. t. 66 [2]; Scl. & Salv. Ibis, 1859, p. 133 [3]; G. C. Taylor, Ibis, 1860, p. 118 [4].

Morococcyx erythropygia, Scl. Cat. Am. Birds, p. 322 [5]; Lawr. Ann. Lyc. N. Y. ix. p. 128 [6]; Mem. Bost. Soc. N. H. ii. p. 293 [7]; Bull. U. S. Nat. Mus. no. 4, p. 34 [8]; v. Frant. J. f. Orn. 1869, p. 361 [9]; Scl. & Salv. P. Z. S. 1870, p. 551 [10]; Boucard, P. Z. S. 1878, p. 48 [11]; Sumichrast, La Nat. v. p. 239 [12]; Nutting, Pr. U. S. Nat. Mus. vi. p. 388 [13]; Zeledon, An. Mus. Nac. Costa Rica, 1887, p. 123 [14].

Morococcyx erythropygus, Shelley, Cat. Birds Brit. Mus. xix. p. 422 [15].

Supra murinus æneo vix nitens, capite summo cervino striato, dorso postico saturate brunneo, lineis paucis cervinis transfasciato, stria superciliari cervina, oculorum ambitu nudo plumulis nigris undique marginato: subtus saturate fulvus, gula pallidiore, tectricibus subcaudalibus rufo-brunneis; caudæ rectricibus utrinque tribus cervino terminatis et fascia indistincta subterminali nigricante notatis; rostro flavido, maxilla supra nigricante; pedibus pallide corylinis. Long. tota 10·7, alæ 3·9, caudæ rectr. med. 5·2, rectr. lat. 3·6, rostri a rictu 1·2, tarsi 1·5. (Descr. maris ex La Libertad, Salvador. Mus. nostr.)

♀ mari similis.

Hab. MEXICO, Mazatlan (*Grayson* [7]), San Blas, Plains of Colima (*W. B. Richardson*), Acapulco, Dos Arroyos (*Mrs. H. H. Smith*), San Juan del Rio (*Rébouch* [10]), Chihuitan [8], Tehuantepec city [8], Santa Efigenia [12], Tonala [12], Juchitan [12] (*Sumichrast*), Sierra de Santo Domingo, Chimalapa (*W. B. Richardson*); GUATEMALA, Laguna [3], Valley of the Rio Motagua (*O. S. & F. D. G.*), Volcan de Fuego (*Sarg, in Mus. Bremen*); SALVADOR, Chinandega (*W. B. Richardson*), Sucuyá (*Nutting* [13]); COSTA RICA (*Carmiol*), Pacuare (*v. Frantzius* [9], *Zeledon* [6]), Liberia (*Zeledon* [14]), Atenas (*Boucard* [11]).

This peculiar Cuckoo was first described by Lesson in 1842 [1] from a specimen obtained by Adolphe Lesson at "San Carlos," Central America, and was afterwards figured by Des Murs in his 'Iconographie Ornithologique' [2]. In Mexico it seems to be restricted in its range to the western side of the mountains, and is found from Mazatlan to Tehuantepec, and is by no means rare. In Guatemala we only observed it in the valley of the Motagua river; but it probably also occurs on the Pacific side of the mountains, as there is a specimen in the Bremen Museum said to have been obtained on the slopes of the Volcan de Fuego by Mr. Sarg. Southwards of Guatemala it is found through Salvador, Nicaragua, and Costa Rica, which is the extreme limit of its range in this direction, as we have no record of its occurrence in Chiriqui or any part of the State of Panama.

In habits this bird somewhat resembles *Geococcyx affinis*, but is not nearly so conspicuous. It lives in the brushwood, and may be seen walking on the ground, now running rapidly, now standing still with its head erect. It climbs, too, about the branches of the low underwood. It is very tame, and is difficult to shoot without damaging the specimen, as both Taylor and ourselves found. Its note is short and rich, and uttered at intervals, so that the natives both in Guatemala [3] and Nicaragua [13] call it "El reloj," or Clock-bird, saying that its song marks the hours. Mr. Nutting, who says it is abundant at Sucuyá [13], also remarks that its nest is placed in grass, but he is silent as to the colour and texture of the eggs.

The bare skin round the eye in life is cobalt-blue.

Subfam. *DIPLOPTERINÆ*.

The two genera which constitute this subfamily are very different in their general appearance and in the shape of the bill, but they have a common character in the great length and fullness of the upper tail-coverts, the longest of which nearly reach to the end of the rectrices. In habits the members of both genera are semiterrestrial, that is to say, they live on or near the ground. They fly readily, but for short distances. The subfamily is purely neotropical, and has no near allies in the Old World.

DIPLOPTERUS.

Diplopterus, Boie, Isis, 1826, p. 977; Shelley, Cat. Birds Brit. Mus. xix. p. 423.

The single species of this genus is a peculiar bird of wide range in South and Central America. In having long upper tail-coverts it resembles *Dromococcyx*, but has little else in common with that genus. The bill is short and compressed, the culmen arched, the nostrils elongated, opening along the lower edge of the nasal fossa; the eyelashes are strong curved bristles, the posterior ones having barbs on one side near the base. The wings are more pointed than in the preceding genera, the secondaries being short; the feathers of the bastard wing are large and full, and are spread in life, and being black show conspicuously; the tail is composed of rather narrow feathers, the outer ones being about half as long as the central pair; the upper tail-coverts are long and narrow, and reach to within an inch of the tip of the tail. The general colour of the plumage is tawny with dark centres to the feathers; the head has a tolerably conspicuous crest.

, The range of the only species is fully given below.

1. Diplopterus nævius.

Cuculus nævius, Linn. Syst. Nat. i. p. 170[1].

Diplopterus nævius, Boie, Isis, 1826, p. 977[2]; Lawr. Ann. Lyc. N. Y. viii. p. 178[3]; ix. p. 128[4]; Bull. U. S. Nat. Mus. no. 4, p. 33[5]; Scl. & Salv. P. Z. S. 1864, p. 366[6]; Salv. P. Z. S. 1867, p. 156[7]; 1870, p. 211[8]; v. Frantz. J. f. Orn. 1869, p. 361[9]; Nutting, Pr. U. S. Nat. Mus. vi. pp. 376[10], 387[11]; Zeledon, An. Mus. Nac. Costa Rica, 1887, p. 123[12]; Cherrie, Auk, 1892, p. 326[13]; Shelley, Cat. Birds Brit. Mus. xix. p. 423[14]; Chapman, Bull. Am. Mus. Nat. Hist. vi. p. 64[15].

Diplopterus excellens, Scl. P. Z. S. 1857, p. 229[16]; Moore, P. Z. S. 1859, p. 60[17]; Scl. & Salv. Ibis, 1859, p. 133[18]; Lawr. Ann. Lyc. N. Y. vii. p. 300[19].

Supra saturate fulvus, plumis omnibus medialiter striis latis nigricantibus notatis, capite summo pallide castaneo nigro striato, uropygio et tectricibus supracaudalibus elongatis pallide fulvis, rhachidibus nigris, superciliis albidis, stria angusta mystacali et auricularibus nigris: subtus albus, gutture toto ad pectus et tectricibus subcaudalibus cervinis; alis fuscis, extrorsum fulvo limbatis; cauda fusco-nigricante late fulvo marginata; rostro flavido, maxillæ basi corneo; pedibus plumbeis. Long. tota circa 11·5, alæ 4·8, caudæ rectr. med. 6·8, rectr. lat. 3·8, rostri a rictu 0·95, tarsi 1·3. (Descr. maris ex Chinandega, Nicaragua. Mus. nostr.)

♀ mari similis.

Juv. plumis omnibus supra et tectricibus alarum macula conspicua fulva terminatis.

Hab. MEXICO, San Andres Tuxtla (*Boucard*[16]), Playa Vicente (*M. Trujillo*), Teapa in Tabasco (*Mrs. H. H. Smith*), Sta. Efigenia (*Sumichrast*[5]); GUATEMALA, Retalhuleu, Dueñas, Savana Grande (*O. S. & F. D. G.*); SALVADOR, Volcan de San Miguel (*W. B. Richardson*); HONDURAS, San Pedro (*Leyland*[17][18]); NICARAGUA, Chinandega, Matagalpa (*W. B. Richardson*), San Juan del Sur[10], Sucuyá[11] (*Nutting*); COSTA RICA, San José (*Cherrie*[13]), San Mateo (*v. Frantzius*[9], *Cooper*[4], *Zeledon*[12]), Guaitil (*v. Frantzius*[9], *Carmiol*[4]), Pozo Azul de Perris (*Zeledon*[12]), Barranca (*Arcé*); PANAMA, David (*Bridges*[7], *Hicks*[3]), Calovevora, Mina de Chorcha, Chitra (*Arcé*[8]), Lion Hill (*M'Leannan*[6][19]).—SOUTH AMERICA generally, from Colombia to Guiana[1] and Trinidad[15] and to South Brazil[14].

Diplopterus nævius is found sparingly but regularly distributed over a very wide area, extending from the middle of the State of Vera Cruz throughout Central America, and thence southwards over nearly the whole of the continent of South America as far as the southern provinces of Brazil. Its range in altitude is considerable, for, though chiefly a bird of the low hot districts, we found it as high as the neighbourhood of Dueñas—that is, nearly 5000 feet above sea-level.

In 1857[16] Mr. Sclater separated a bird sent from San Andres Tuxtla by M. Boucard as *Diplopterus excellens*, on the ground of its being larger than the southern form, more rufescent on the back, the upper tail-coverts cinnamon-rufous with a median black stripe, purer white beneath, the breast slightly rufescent and without greyish tint, its bill longer and higher, the tarsus longer, &c. These characters, so far as the plumage is concerned, point to a not very old bird in freshly-moulted feather, and do not seem of much weight when a large series of specimens is examined, such as now exists in the British Museum. The difference of size, too, is unimportant, so that it is not now deemed necessary to separate the Mexican bird.

The resort of this Cuckoo is scrubby woods, where it lives mostly on or near the ground. One we shot near Dueñas was in such a place, and rose rapidly from the ground, and flew swiftly away on being disturbed. Mr. Nutting shot one out of a hedge in an open field near San Juan del Sur in Nicaragua [10]. Mr. Cherrie says it is rare near San José, Costa Rica, where it is a straggler, but common at low elevations down to the shores of the Pacific [13].

Mr. Chapman [15] found *D. nœvius* to be common in the island of Trinidad, but a rather shy bird, living in and near thickets. He says it passes much of its time on the ground, but frequently ascends to the topmost branches of the smaller trees to call. Its calls are also uttered on the ground. They are given more or less throughout the day, and are among the most pleasing and characteristic bird-notes to be heard at the place where he stayed. They are of two kinds—one being heard quite as frequently as the other. Both are in a minor key, the first consisting of two notes, the second half a tone lower than the first. The second call is translated by the negroes as *chloë, chloë, chloë-dead, chloë-dead*. On one occasion, whilst watching one of these birds walking over some recently burnt ground, Mr. Chapman was surprised at a most singular action on its part. The bird walked rapidly for a few yards, then stopping raised and lowered its crest, and turned the black feathers of the bastard wing forwards until they pointed towards the breast. This was repeated several times.

We are not aware of anything being on record respecting the nesting-habits or the eggs of this species.

DROMOCOCCYX.

Dromococcyx, Wied, Beitr. Naturg. Bras. iv. p. 351 (1832); Shelley, Cat. Birds Brit. Mus. xix. p. 425.

With the upper tail-coverts long and largely developed as in *Diplopterus*, this genus differs in having a much straighter, flatter, and more slender bill, the nostrils being long narrow slits at the lower edge of the nasal fossa; the tail-feathers are much wider and the tail itself larger, and the upper coverts very fully developed and reaching to the tips of the longest rectrices. The tarsi are moderately long, and the tibiæ clothed with short feathers.

The general colour of the upper plumage is dark brown, relieved on the wings with fulvous spots; the under plumage is white, with spots on the breast.

Two closely allied species constitute the genus, of which *D. phasianellus* has a wide range and occurs throughout Central America; the other, *D. pavoninus*, is found in Guiana and some of the adjoining districts.

1. Dromococcyx phasianellus.

Macropus phasianellus, Spix, Av. Bras. i. p. 53, t. 42 (1824) [1].

Dromococcyx phasianellus, Wied, Beitr. iv. p. 353 [2]; Cab. J. f. Orn. 1862, p. 171 [3]; Salv. Ibis, 1868, p. 486 [4]; v. Frantz. J. f. Orn. 1869, p. 361 [5]; Sumichrast, La Nat. v. p. 239 [6]; Boucard, P. Z. S. p. 455 [7]; Zeledon, An Mus. Nac. Costa Rica, 1887, p. 123 [8]; Shelley, Cat. Birds Brit. Mus. xix. p. 426 [9].

Dromococcyx mexicana, Bp. Compt. Rend. xlii. p. 957 [10].

Dromococcyx mexicanus, Scl. P. Z. S. 1856, p. 308 [11]; 1859, p. 368 [12]; Scl. & Salv. Ibis, 1859, p. 133 [13]; Lawr. Ann. Lyc. N. Y. vii. p. 300 [14].

Dromococcyx rufigularis, Lawr. Pr. Ac. Phil. 1867, p. 233 [15].

Supra saturate fuscus, interscapulii plumis stricte rufo marginatis, tectricibus supracaudalibus elongatis macula parva albida termiuatis, capitis et cervicis lateribus pileo concoloribus, stria postoculari ad cervicem utrinque producta et corpore subtus albis, gutture et pectore nigro guttatis; alis fuscis, tectricibus omnibus fulvo limbatis; cauda fusca, infra griseo tincta, rectricibus omnibus (mediis exceptis) albo terminatis et fascia subterminali nigra notatis; rostro corneo, mandibula pallida; pedibus corylinis. Long. tota circa 15·0, alæ 6·6, caudæ rectr. med. 8·5, rectr. lat. 4·7, rostri a rectu 1·17, tarsi 1·4. (Descr. maris ex Coban, Guatemala. Mus. nostr.)

♀ mari similis.

Juv. gutture toto et stria postoculari læte fulvis.

Hab. MEXICO, Cordova (*Sallé* [11]), Jalapa (*de Oca* [12]), Potrero, Santa Efigenia, Cacoprieto (*Sumichrast* [6]), N. Yucatan [7], Buctzotz, Izamal (*G. F. Gaumer*); GUATEMALA (*Van Patten* [15]), Coban, Cahabon [13], Choctum, Mirandilla (*O. S. & F. D. G.*); SALVADOR, Volcan de San Miguel (*W. B. Richardson*); COSTA RICA (*v. Frantzius* [3] [5]), Santa Maria de Dota (*Zeledon* [8]); PANAMA, Lion Hill (*McLeannan* [14]), Paraiso (*A. Hughes*).—SOUTH AMERICA, from Colombia to South Brazil [9].

Though as widely distributed as *Diplopterus nævius*, this Cuckoo is much less known owing doubtless to its greater rarity, our own experience respecting it being confined to the capture of a few specimens by our hunters at rare intervals. We have no notes on its habits. Like *D. nævius* it appears to be a bird of the lowlands, but is found as high as 4000 feet in the mountains of Vera Cruz, and also in Vera Paz in Guatemala.

Though the Mexican bird was separated by Bonaparte from that of South America under the name of *Dromococcyx mexicana* [10], no differential characters were given, and it now appears that practically none exist between them. In 1867 Lawrence described a bird sent from Guatemala by Van Patten, "from a high mountian region," as *Dromococcyx rufigularis* [15]. We have similar birds from Paraiso Station on the Panama Railway Line, which we have no hesitation in pronouncing to be young examples of *D. phasianellus*, and thus place Lawrence's name as a synonym of this bird, a position long ago assigned it by Salvin.

Subfam. *CROTOPHAGINÆ*.

The Crotophaginæ form a most distinct subfamily of Cuckoos, and differ from all others in its members having only eight rectrices in the tail. Two genera are known— the widely spread *Crotophaga* with three species, and *Guira*, which is confined to Brazil and Paraguay. The eggs of the members of both genera are peculiarly covered with a cretaceous coating, evenly overspread in the case of *Crotophaga*, but in mottled lines in *Guira*, between which the blue ground-colour is shown.

CROTOPHAGA.

Crotophaga, Linnæus, Syst. Nat. i. 154 (1766); Shelley, Cat. Birds Brit. Mus. xix. p. 427.

Crotophaga differs widely from most of the other genera of Cuckoos. Its members have only eight rectrices, a feature shared by the South-American *Guira*, from which *Crotophaga* differs in the colour of the plumage and in the shape of the bill.

The latter is much compressed with a high arched culmen, the sides of the maxilla are either smooth or furrowed, the lores and orbital region nearly naked, with a few scattered bristle-like feathers; the tarsi are moderately long, about equalling the middle toe; the wings are moderately long, the primaries considerably exceeding the secondaries; the tail is long and rounded, the feathers straight and moderately stiff; the plumage is black with steel-blue or greenish lustre, and with the feathers of the anterior portion of the body and head edged so as to give a scale-like appearance.

The nesting-habits of *Crotophaga* are peculiar in that several birds seem to use a common nest in which to lay their eggs. The food consists largely of ticks, which the birds pick from the skins of cattle, in whose society they are usually found.

Three species of the genus are known: one, *C. ani,* is common all through the West-Indian Islands, in Florida, and many parts of South America, and also occurs in some widely separated districts in Central America. *C. sulcirostris* is the best known and commonest species in Mexico and Central America, and is found everywhere from the Rio Grande Valley southwards; in South America it occurs in countries bordering the Pacific Ocean as far south as Peru. *C. major*, the third species, is a common South-American bird found along our southern border.

1. **Crotophaga major.**

Crotophaga major, Gm. Syst. Nat. i. p. 363[1]; Cass. Pr. Ac. Phil. 1860, p. 138[2]; Scl. & Salv. P. Z. S. 1879, p. 536[3]; Shelley, Cat. Birds Brit. Mus. xix. p. 428[4].

Nitenti-chalybeo-nigra, capitis, cervicis, dorsi, scapularium, tectricum alarum et pectoris plumis æneo-viridi inconspicue marginatis; cauda purpurascenti; rostro et pedibus nigris, rostri culmine acuto medialiter abrupte elevato, lateribus glabris. Long. tota 19·0, alæ 7·5, caudæ rectr. med. 10·0, rectr. lat. 7·7, rostri a rictu 1·8, tarsi 1·7. (Descr. maris ex Nichi, Colombia. Mus. nostr.)

♀ mari similis.

Hab. PANAMA, R. Atrato (*Wood*[2]).—SOUTH AMERICA generally, from Colombia[3] to Peru, Guiana, Brazil, and La Plata[4].

The name of this *Crotophaga* is included in Cassin's list of birds collected by Lieut. Michler's party during their exploration of the Isthmus of Darien, but we have no other evidence of its occurrence elsewhere within our boundaries. It has been recorded from other parts of Colombia by Salmon and others, and its range spreads thence over the valley of the Amazons and to Guiana and southwards throughout Brazil to the valley of the La Plata.

In general colour *Crotophaga major* is a much brighter bird than either of its sombre congeners, being of a shiny steel-blue with greenish edgings to the feathers. It is, too, a much larger bird.

In habits it resembles *C. ani* and *C. sulcirostris*, which are described more at length below.

The iris, according to Prince Wied, is light green, with a narrow yellow ring round the pupil.

2. Crotophaga ani.

Crotophaga ani, Linn. Syst. Nat. i. p. 154[1]; Lawr. Ann. Lyc. N. Y. vii. p. 301[2]; Scl. & Salv. P. Z. S. 1864, p. 366[3]; Salv. P. Z. S. 1870, p. 211[4]; Ibis, 1889, p. 372[5]; 1890, p. 88[6]; Ridgw. Pr. U. S. Nat. Mus. viii. p. 577[7]; Cory, Birds W. Indies, p. 102[8]; Shelley, Cat. Birds Brit. Mus. xix. p. 429[9].

Nigra, plumis omnibus corporis anticis, cervicis et capitis æneo-nigro limbatis; rostri culmine acuto elevato regulariter arcuato, lateribus glabris; rostro et pedibus nigris. Long. tota circa 13·0, alæ 5·7, caudæ rectr. med. 7·0, rectr. lat. 6·0, rostri a rictu 1·16, tarsi 1·5. (Descr. maris ex Lion Hill, Panama. Mus. nostr.) ♀ mari similis.

Hab. NORTH AMERICA, Florida &c.—MEXICO, Holbox I., Cozumel I. (*G. F. Gaumer*[5][6]); HONDURAS, Ruatan I. (*G. F. Gaumer*[5]); PANAMA, Mina de Chorcha (*Arcé*[4]), Lion Hill (*M'Leannan*[2][3]), Obispo (*O. S.*).—SOUTH AMERICA, from Colombia to Brazil[9]; ANTILLES generally[8].

Though the range of *Crotophaga ani* is general in the Antilles and over a large portion of the South-American continent, it is quite partial in Central America and confined to the islands of Holbox and Cozumel off the coast of Yucatan and Ruatan in the Bay of Honduras. It is also found on the Isthmus of Panama as far westward as the district of Chiriqui. All through the rest of Mexico and Central America *C. sulcirostris* takes its place. It occurs sparingly in Southern Florida, and has been recorded from various places in the South-eastern States of America.

The familiar habits of this bird have been frequently described, and the notes of Gosse, Newton, and others give a good account of them. Several birds live together in small flocks in open savanas and pastures, and are usually to be seen amongst herds of cattle, from which they pick the ticks which infest them. Their flight is a laboured performance and much upset by even a slight breeze. Their cries are harsh and incessant. All authorities testify to the habit of several birds laying in a common nest, which is usually placed against the trunk of a tree a few feet from the ground; it is composed of a collection of sticks and twigs and partly filled with dead leaves, amongst which the eggs are placed. These vary in number, and in one nest Mr. Newton found at one time as many as fourteen. The eggs are oval, of a greenish-blue colour, and overspread when fresh with a soft cretaceous coating, which shows plainly every scratch of the claws of the birds.

3. Crotophaga sulcirostris.

Crotophaga sulcirostris, Sw. Phil. Mag. new ser. i. p. 440[1]; Scl. P. Z. S. 1856, p. 309[2]; 1858, p. 359[3]; 1859, pp. 368[4], 388[5]; Moore, P. Z. S. 1859, p. 59[6]; Scl. & Salv. Ibis, 1859, p. 135[7]; P. Z. S. 1867, p. 280[8]; 1870, p. 837[9]; Cab. J. f. Orn. 1862, p. 171[10]; Lawr. Ann. Lyc. N. Y. viii. p. 11[11]; ix. pp. 128[12], 205[13]; Mem. Bost. Soc. N. H. ii. p. 292[14]; Bull. U. S. Nat. Mus. no. 4, p. 33[15]; v. Frantz. J. f. Orn. 1869, p. 361[16]; Salv. P. Z. S. 1870, p. 211[17]; Cat. Strickl. Coll. p. 443[18]; Ibis, 1889, p. 372[19]; 1890, p. 88[20]; Boucard, P. Z. S. 1878, p. 47[21]; 1883, p. 454[22]; Sumichrast, La Nat. v. p. 239[23]; Nutting, Pr. U. S. Nat. Mus. v. p. 401[24]; vi. pp. 376[25], 387[26], 395[27]; Ridgw. Pr. U. S. Nat. Mus. v. p. 498[28]; x. pp. 582[29], 591[30]; Ferrari-Perez, Pr. U. S. Nat. Mus. ix. p. 162[31]; Zeledon, An. Mus. Nac. Costa Rica, 1887, p. 122[32]; Shelley, Cat. Birds Brit. Mus. xix. p. 432[33]; Stone, Pr. Ac. Phil. 1890, p. 205[34]; Cherrie, Auk, 1892, p. 325[35]; Richmond, Pr. U. S. Nat. Mus. xvi. p. 517[36].

Crotophaga ani, Licht. Preis-Verz. Mex. Vög. p. 1 (nec Linn.) (*cf.* J. f. Orn. 1863, p. 55[37]).

C. ani similis, sed rostri lateribus rugis tribus aut quatuor elevatis culmini plus minusve parallelis instructis, mandibulæ lateribus quoque rugosis; rostro et pedibus nigris. Long. tota circa 12·0, alæ 5·3, caudæ rectr. med. 6·7, rectr. lat. 5·2, rostri a rictu 0·92, tarsi 1·32. (Descr. exempl. ex Izamal, Yucatan. Mus. nostr.)

Hab. NORTH AMERICA, Texas and Lower California.—MEXICO (*Deppe*[37]), Mazatlan (*Grayson*[14], *Xantus*[14], *Bischoff*[14]), Presidio de Mazatlan (*Forrer*), San Blas (*W. B. Richardson*), Tepic (*Grayson*[14]), Bolaños (*W. B. Richardson*), Santana, Santiago, Manzanilla (*W. Lloyd*), Plains of Colima (*Xantus*[14]), Putla (*Rébouch*), Temiscaltepec (*Bullock*[1]), Nuevo Leon (*F. B. Armstrong*), Sierra Madre above Ciudad Victoria, Xicotencal, Tampico (*W. B. Richardson*), Jalapa (*de Oca*[4], *F. D. G.*), Izucar de Matamoros, Plan del Rio[31], Epatlan (*F. Ferrari-Perez*), Cordova (*Sallé*[2]), Oaxaca (*Boucard*[5]), Juchitan (*Sumichrast*[15]), Tehuantepec (*W. B. Richardson*), Teapa (*Mrs. H. H. Smith*), N. Yucatan[22], Peto, Buctzotz, Izamal, Holbox I.[19], Mugeres I.[19], Meco[19] (*G. F. Gaumer*), Merida (*Schott*[13]), Progreso (*Stone & Baker*[34]); BRITISH HONDURAS, Orange Walk (*G. F. Gaumer*); GUATEMALA[18] generally, Dueñas[7] (*O. S. & F. D. G.*); SALVADOR, La Libertad (*W. B. Richardson*); HONDURAS, Omoa (*Leyland*[6]), Truxillo[29], Segovia R.[30] (*Townsend*), San Pedro (*G. M. Whitely*[9]), Comayagua (*G. C. Taylor*[3]); NICARAGUA, Chinandega (*W. B. Richardson*), San Juan del Sur[25], Sucuya[26], Omotepe[27]

(*Nutting*), Blewfields (*Wickham* [8]), Escondido R. (*Richmond* [36]); COSTA RICA (*Hoffmann* [10], v. *Frantzius* [16]), San José (*Carmiol* [12], *Boucard* [21], *Zeledon* [32], *Cherrie* [35]), La Palma [24], V. de Irazu [28] (*Nutting*), Alajuela, Cartago (*Zeledon* [32]); PANAMA, Calovevora, Castillo (*Arcé* [17]), Lion Hill (*M'Leannan* [11]).—COLOMBIA [33]; W. ECUADOR [33]; PERU [33].

One of the most familiar birds in Central America is *Crotophaga sulcirostris*, occurring everywhere in open pastures and savanas and associating in small flocks with cattle, from which they pick the ticks adhering to their skins. It occurs beyond the Rio Grande, in Texas, where Mr. Sennett first noticed it at Lomita, and whence Mr. Armstrong has sent us a series of specimens from Brownsville. Lower California is also included in its range. In South America it is found exclusively on the western side of the continent as far south as Peru.

Writing concerning it in Western Mexico, Grayson says:—"This is a common resident species in this locality, and throughout the western *tierra caliente*. Eight or ten birds associate together in small flocks, and are fond of picking the ticks off the cattle. The nest is usually built in a thorny tree or bush, at a moderate height, and composed of thorns and dry twigs exteriorly, and lined with fibrous roots ; the eggs are usually five, the outside of the shell is rough and white, the inside is green." This note gives no indication that Grayson was aware of the fact of several birds laying in a common nest. This is made clear by Señor Alfaro's observations, as given by Mr. Cherrie [35]:—"The 'Zopilotillo' is very abundant in the fields near Tambor (a little town about twenty miles north-west of San José), where, along the hedgerows and in the scrubby timber, as well as on the skins of cattle, they find those insects which constitute their food—the ticks, or garrapatas, which adhere to the head and neck and legs of the cattle. In this locality I have collected three nests in the month of May, the first with nine eggs, the second with eleven, the third with thirteen. The nests that I have collected agree with the observations made by Zeledon. The structure is voluminous, composed chiefly of coarse dead twigs, but presents one peculiarity not observed in any other bird, viz. the nest being lined with fresh green leaves. My specimens were all placed in low trees, and none were at a greater height than three metres. One had been built above an old nest of one of the larger Tyrannidæ. On the 20th May I noticed a Zopilotillo with a dry stick in its bill, which was immediately carried to a hedgerow and deposited with three others. After assuring myself that the bird was building its nest there I retired, with the intention of returning at a more opportune moment. And when, one week later, I returned to the same spot, what was my surprise to see not only the nest completed and containing six eggs, but in the thorns and leaves about it were scattered seven more eggs ; so that if the collection was not the produce of several Zopilotillos, a single bird would have deposited at least two eggs daily. In finding some of the eggs scattered in the leaves one of the architect's peculiarities was shown. A hole had been left in the centre of the nest and only recently filled with leaves, whose fresh green colour testified that they had been cut and placed there later than the others forming the carpeting of the bottom of this common incubator. The eggs were all fresh, the six occupying the nest having the rough white calcareous surface perfectly clean and without the slightest variation in colour: not so the eggs found about the outside of the nest. Those found in contact with the leaves had taken on a dirty yellowish tinge. Those held suspended among the leaves and thorns showed various spots and lines of the lustrous blue colour forming the base for the chalky external coat." In form the eggs vary in shape from an oval to an elliptical oval, and differ greatly in size.

Fam. CAPITONIDÆ.

The family Capitonidæ contains, so far as we know at present, about 118 species, which are divided into nineteen genera. Of these all but seventeen species of two genera belong to the Old World, and are distributed over the tropical portions of Africa and Asia as far as China, the Philippine Islands, and in the south-east to Borneo and Java. The family is unrepresented in Celebes and the whole of the New Guinea region, Australia, and the islands of the Pacific Ocean. Nor is it found in any portion of the Palæarctic region, nor in America north of Costa Rica.

The Neotropical members of the family, seventeen in all, belong to the genera *Capito* (15) and *Tetragonops* (2). *Capito* is distributed over the northern portion of the continent of South America from the valley of the Amazons to the north coast and along the Isthmus as far as Costa Rica, but no further. Eastern Peru and Ecuador seem to be the metropolis of the family, as nine species of *Capito* and one *Tetragonops* occur on the eastern slopes of the Andes and the upper waters of the Amazons.

In Central America we find two species of *Capito* and one *Tetragonops*, but none occur beyond the mountains of Costa Rica.

As to the position of the Capitonidæ in the "Systema Avium," it is now generally agreed that the Rhamphastidæ is the nearest allied family, the Indicatoridæ not far removed. Garrod and Forbes always placed these families close to the Picidæ and away from the Cuculidæ, considering that the great similarity of the body anatomy overruled the differences plainly observable in the structure of the head.

The two chief recent authorities on the Capitonidæ are the Messrs. Marshall, who completed an illustrated Monograph of it in 1871, and Capt. Shelley, who wrote the catalogue of these birds in the British Museum (1891).

The arrangement of the genera *Capito* and *Tetragonops* differs in these two works: in the former *Tetragonops* is placed with the other dentate forms with the African *Pogonorhynchus* in the Pogonorhynchinæ, whilst *Capito* finds a place with the smooth-billed

69*

forms, such as *Trachyphonus*, in the Capitoninæ. In the latter *Tetragonops* is assigned a place to itself, *Pogonorhynchus* being at the opposite end of the arrangement.

Capito is associated with *Megalæma*, *Trachyphonus*, &c., but has a separate section to itself.

When the anatomy of these genera has been more fully worked out we should look for characters to connect *Capito* with *Tetragonops*, so as to remove these American forms from the Old World members of the family *.

CAPITO.

Capito, Vieillot, Anal. p. 27 (1816); Marshall, Mon. Capit. pp. xxxi, xxxvi; Shelley, Cat. Birds Brit. Mus. xix. pp. 15, 107.

Two of the fifteen species of *Capito* recognized by Capt. Shelley are found within the limits of our region—one, the very peculiar *C. maculicoronatus* of Panama and the adjoining State of Antioquia; the other, *C. salvini* of Panama and Costa Rica, a close ally of the more widely ranging southern form *C. bourcieri*.

The tomia of the maxilla in *Capito* is even and without tooth or notch near the extremity, the point of the mandible fits into that of the maxilla in the ordinary way. A few strong black bristles extend far over the nostrils, others spread forwards from the chin. The wings are short, close-fitting, and rounded; the tail short and much rounded. In coloration the sexes differ greatly—so much so, that the males and females of several of the species have been treated as distinct species until their true relationship was recognized.

1. **Capito maculicoronatus.**

Capito maculicoronatus, Lawr. Ann. Lyc. N. Y. vii. p. 300[1]; Scl. Ibis, 1862, p. 1, t. 1[2]; Scl. & Salv. P. Z. S. 1864, p. 366[3]; 1879, p. 537[4]; Salv. P. Z. S. 1867, p. 157[5]; Marshall, Mon. Capit. p. 153, t. 61[6]; Shelley, Cat. Birds Brit. Mus. xix. p. 109[7].

Nitente niger, pileo medio plaga maculosa ornato, plumis singulis albicantibus saturate fusco limbatis: subtus albus, cervicis lateribus et pectore aurantio suffusis, hypochondriis nigro guttatis et plaga elongata læte aurantiaca notatis; rostro corneo; pedibus nigricantibus. Long. tota 6·3, alæ 3·1, caudæ 2·0, rostri a rictu 1·1, tarsi 0·9.

♀ mari similis, gutture et pectore toto nigris. (Descr. maris et feminæ ex Lion Hill, Panama. Mus. nostr.)

Hab. PANAMA, Santiago de Veraguas (*Arcé*[5]), Lion Hill (*M‘Leannan*[1 2 3]).—COLOMBIA[4].

This remarkable species, which has no near allies, was discovered by M‘Leannan on the Isthmus of Panama, and was described by Lawrence in 1861 in his first paper on the birds of that region[1]. Subsequently specimens of both sexes carefully dissected were obtained by M‘Leannan and Galbraith[2], and by them our collections have been supplied. Arcé, too, met with this Barbet near Santiago de Veraguas[5], but beyond

---

* Since the above paragraph was in type Mr. Beddard has published a note on this subject [P. Z. S. 1896, p. 557], in which he says that a possible means of differentiating the Old World from the New World Barbets lies in the pterylosis of the spinal tract.

this point in this direction it has not been traced. It also occurs in the State of Antioquia, where Salmon met with it both at Neche and Remedios[4]. The only notes we have on its habits were supplied to Lawrence by Galbraith, who states that it is not often met with on the Isthmus of Panama, that it is found on high trees, and that the iris in life is brown[2]. The species was figured by Mr. Sclater[2] and by Messrs. Marshall[6], but the latter give no additional information respecting it. Captain Shelley[7] places *C. maculicoronatus* in the same section as *C. auratus* and its allies; but it has little in common with them, being a very isolated form.

2. **Capito salvini.**

Capito bourcieri, Lawr. Ann. Lyc. N. Y. ix. p. 130 (nec Lafr.)[1]; v. Frantz. J. f. Orn. 1869, p. 363[2]; Salv. P. Z. S. 1870, p. 212[3]; Marshall, Mon. Capit. p. 165 (partim)[4]; Boucard, P. Z. S. 1878, p. 47[5]; Zeledon, An. Mus. Nac. Costa Rica, 1887, p. 123[6].

Capito hartlaubi, Lawr. Ann. Lyc. N. Y. ix. p. 130 (nec Lafr.)[7]; v. Frantz. J. f. Orn. 1869, p. 363[8].

Capito salvini, Shelley, Cat. Birds Brit. Mus. xix. p. 119[9].

Supra viridis, capite toto et gutture coccineis, loris et mento nigris, macula cervicis utrinque glauco-albida: subtus abdomine toto olivaceo-flavo ad pectus coccineo lavato, hypochondriis distincte olivaceo flammulatis; rostro flavido; pedibus nigricantibus. Long. tota circa 5·8, alæ 2·7, caudæ 1·8, rostri a rictu 0·85, tarsi 0·8.

♀ capite summo et cervicis lateribus viridibus aureo lavatis, fronte nigra, superciliis et genis glauco-cæruleis, gutture viridi-flavo, pectore aurantio a mari differt. (Descr. maris et feminæ ex Costa Rica. Mus. nostr.)

Hab. Costa Rica (*v. Frantzius*[2][8]), Barranca (*Carmiol*[1][7]), Turrialba (*Cooper*[2]), Orosi, Navarro (*Boucard*[5]), Naranjo de Cartago, Birris de Cartago, Jimenez (*Zeledon*[6]); Panama, Volcan de Chiriqui (*Arcé*[3]).

This *Capito* is very nearly allied to, if really distinct from, *C. bourcieri* of the more southern parts of Colombia and Ecuador. The only distinction is to be found in the female, which has no bluish-grey colour bordering the black band of the forehead on the inside. This difference occurs in all the Central-American specimens we have examined, but was not noticed until Captain Shelley wrote his catalogue of the birds of this family[9].

We have no notes concerning this bird, but Salmon says of the allied *C. bourcieri* that its food is fruit.

The range of *C. salvini* seems restricted to Costa Rica and the western portion of the State of Panama. Most of the collectors who have worked in the former country have met with it, and Arcé sent us specimens from Chiriqui[3]. On the Isthmus of Panama itself it appears to be absent, and in the State of Antioquia the closely allied *C. bourcieri* takes its place. Concerning the latter bird, as observed by him at Nanegal and Pallatanga in Ecuador, Fraser says that he found in one bird that the gizzard contained green fruit and minute seeds, and that the bare skin round the eye was yellowish; and again that in another the iris in life was red, the bill greenish-yellow, the legs and feet green, and that the gizzard contained fruit and remains of insects. A solitary bird, living in high trees and rather stupid[4].

TETRAGONOPS.

Tetragonops, Jardine, Edinb. Phil. Journ. new ser. i. p. 404; Marshall, Mon. Capit. pp. xxii, xxiv; Shelley, Cat. Birds Brit. Mus. xix. pp. 15, 120.

Of this singular form two species are known—one, inhabiting Ecuador, a bright-coloured bird of robust build with many of the colours characteristic of the Rhamphastidæ. This is the type of the genus, *T. rhamphastinus*, discovered in Ecuador by Prof. Jameson, and described by Jardine in 1855. The other, *T. frantzii*, is peculiar to Costa Rica and the adjoining parts of Panama, and is fully described below.

The bill is shorter and stouter than that of *Capito*, deeply grooved at the base, the nostrils being sunk between ridges; the culmen is sharp at the base instead of rounded. The tomia of the maxilla has a distinct tooth near the end, and the point of the maxilla, when the bill is shut, rests between the forked end of the mandible.

The sexes are nearly alike in colour, but the male has a long shiny black nuchal tuft, wanting in the female bird.

1. Tetragonops frantzii.

Tetragonops frantzii, Scl. Ibis, 1864, p. 371, t. 10[1]; v. Frantzius, Ibis, 1865, p. 551[2]; J. f. Orn. 1869, p. 363[3]; Lawr. Ann. Lyc. N. Y. ix. p. 130[4]; Marshall, Mon. Capit. p. 3, t. 2[5]; Boucard, P. Z. S. 1878, p. 47[6]; Zeledon, An. Mus. Nac. Costa Rica, 1887, p. 123[7]; Shelley, Cat. Birds Brit. Mus. xix. p. 121[8].

Supra olivaceus, fronte et pileo aureo suffusis, crista nuchali plumis elongatis nitenti-nigris composita, loris nigris : subtus gutture et pectore toto fulvescentibus, torque pectorali (medialiter interrupto) cinerea, ventre et tectricibus subcaudalibus olivaceis in medio flavido suffusis; rostro plumbeo; pedibus nigricantibus. Long. tota circa 7·0, alæ 3·5, caudæ 2·4, rostri a rictu 8·5, tarsi 1·0.

♀ mari similis, sed crista nuchali nigra nulla. (Descr. maris et feminæ ex Costa Rica. Mus. nostr.)

Hab. COSTA RICA, Birris[2][4], Rancho Redondo[7] (*Zeledon*), La Palma (*v. Frantzius*[3], *Zeledon*[4][7]), Irazu (*Rogers*), Navarro (*Cooper*[4], *Boucard*[6]), Quebrada Honda (*v. Frantzius*[3]), Cervantes de Cartago (*v. Frantzius*[2], *Carmiol*[4], *Zeledon*[7]), San José (*v. Frantzius*[4]); PANAMA, Veraguas (*Arcé*[8]).

This remarkable species was discovered in Costa Rica by Dr. von Frantzius, and the type, sent to the late Prof. Baird, was submitted to Mr. Sclater, who described and figured it in 'The Ibis' for 1864[1]. The same collector subsequently obtained another specimen near Birris[2]. Since then many examples have been secured from various places in the mountainous parts of Costa Rica, where, according to von Frantzius, it occurs as high as 5000 or 6000 feet above sea-level[3], and according to whom it lives socially in flocks, and utters a cry like that of a chicken, whence its local name "Gallineta." M. Boucard[6] found birds of this species in the forest at Navarro near streams.

On seeing the original type we were inclined to believe that it was a female of a much brighter-coloured male[1]; but this proves not to be the case, for the female is a duller bird, inasmuch as it lacks the shining black long nuchal crest shown in the original figure of the type and in all dissected male birds.

This difference in the sexes is also shown in *Tetragonops rhamphastinus*, but is not noticed by Captain Shelley in his catalogue; and though mentioned in Marshall's monograph in the case of *T. frantzii* is not alluded to in the case of the allied form.

All the specimens of this bird we have seen came from Costa Rica, except one, and this was sent by Arcé from Veraguas after the second paper on his birds was published in 1870.

Fam. RHAMPHASTIDÆ.

The Family Rhamphastidæ is restricted to the Neotropical region, and is found almost universally over the heavily forested districts from Southern Mexico to the confines of Argentina, some forms being restricted to the upland woods of the higher mountains, others to the vast forests of the lowlands.

Of the five genera into which the family is divided, four occur within our limits, *Andigena* alone being absent. *Rhamphastos* is represented by three species out of a total of fourteen, *Pteroglossus* by three out of eighteen, *Selenidera* by one out of seven, and *Aulacorhamphus* by three out of fourteen. We thus have ten species out of a total of fifty-nine known forms, and our region is fairly stocked with members of this singular family; but far larger numbers are found in South America, the metropolis of the Rhamphastidæ being the upper waters of the great Amazons basin and the eastern slopes of the Andes from Colombia to Bolivia.

The enormous size of the bill in the Rhamphastidæ at once renders these birds easily recognizable. This organ is of curious structure, very light, but strongly built within by a bony network. The tongue is also very peculiar, being long, narrow, and thin, and deeply lacerated towards the end. The tail-feathers, as in the Capitonidæ, are ten in number, the oil-gland is tufted, and there are no cæca. The Rhamphastidæ further differ from the Capitonidæ in the form of the vomer, which, instead of being bifurcated at its distal end, is truncated and has a rounded extremity.

In the general structure of the body the Toucans closely resemble the Capitos and Woodpeckers—so much so, that, apart from the cranial characters, slight grounds of separation exist, a point strongly insisted upon by Garrod and Forbes.

The Rhamphastidæ attracted Gould's attention early in his career, and he produced two large illustrated monographs of the family. A small edition, also illustrated, was brought out by J. H. C. F. and J. W. Sturm in 1841, and the 'Catalogue of Birds in the British Museum,' vol. xix., contains a complete synopsis of the family by Mr. P. L. Sclater. The latter book contains lists of all the specimens gathered by us for this work, and has been of great use to us in our account of the species here treated of.

RHAMPHASTOS.

Rhamphastos, Linnæus, Syst. Nat. i. p. 150 (1766) ; Sclater, Cat. Birds Brit. Mus. xix. p. 124.

The genus *Rhamphastos* contains fourteen species, so far as is at present known, which are distributed over the whole of the low-lying heavily forested districts of the Neotropical region, from Southern Mexico to the confines of Argentina. Three species occur within our limits, viz. *R. carinatus* and its close ally *R. brevicarinatus*—the former with a more northerly range, extending from Honduras through Eastern Guatemala to the middle of the Mexican State of Vera Cruz; the latter ranges from Eastern Nicaragua through Costa Rica and Panama, and just enters Northern Colombia. The third species is *R. tocard,* which is found from Eastern Nicaragua to Colombia and Ecuador.

Rhamphastos is the most distinct of the genera of Rhamphastidæ : the bill is larger, the proximal edge of the maxilla runs nearly evenly across the forehead ; the nostrils are completely hidden on the inside of the margin of the covering of the bill—in all the other genera they are more or less exposed.

1. **Rhamphastos carinatus.**

Rhamphastos piscivorus, Linn. Syst. Nat. i. p. 151[1]?

Rhamphastos carinatus, Sw. Zool. Ill. i. t. 45[2]; Wagl. Syst. Av. fol. 1, p. 3[3] ; Gould, P. Z. S. 1834, p. 73[4]; Mon. Rhamph. t. 7, ed. 2, t. 2[5]; Bp. P. Z. S. 1837, p. 108[6]; Scl. P. Z. S. 1856, p. 308[7]; 1859, pp. 368[8], 388[9]; Cat. Birds Brit. Mus. xix. p. 125[10]; Moore, P. Z. S. 1859, p. 59[11]; Scl. & Salv. Ibis, 1859, p. 135[12] ; P. Z. S. 1870, p. 837[13]; Sumichrast, La Nat. v. p. 238[14]; Boucard, P. Z. S. 1883, p. 455[15]; Ferrari-Perez, Pr. U. S. Nat. Mus. ix. p. 163[16]; Salv. Ibis, 1889, p. 373[17]; 1890, p. 88[18].

Rhamphastos pœcilorhynchus, Licht. Preis-Verz. Mex. Vög. p. 1 (*cf.* J. f. Orn. 1863, p. 54)[19].

Niger, cervice postica saturate rufo tincta ; tectricibus supracaudalibus albis : subtus gutture toto luteo postice coccineo anguste limbato, tectricibus subcaudalibus coccineis ; rostro (ave sicco) nigro, apice rubido, maxilla ad medium, tomia et culmine flavida ; pedibus plumbeis. Long. tota circa 18·0, alæ 8·0, caudæ 6·5, rostri a rictu 5·0, tarsi 1·8. (Descr. feminæ ex Choctum, Guatemala. Mus. nostr.)

♂ feminæ similis, forsan paulo major.

Hab. MEXICO[4] (*Deppe*[19], *le Strange*), Misantla, Colipa, Hacienda de los Atlixcos (*F. D. G.*), Jalapa (*de Oca*[8]), Rio Juan Martin, Rio Rancho Nuevo, Santana[16], Hacienda Tortugas, Vega del Casadero, San Lorenzo near Cordova, Alvarado (*Ferrari-Perez*), Cordova (*Sallé*[7], *Sumichrast*[14]), Cosamaloapam, Uvero (*Sumichrast*[14]), Atoyac (*Mrs. H. H. Smith*), Vera Cruz (*W. B. Richardson*), Playa Vicente (*Boucard*[9]), Teapa (*Mrs. H. H. Smith*), Northern Yucatan (*G. F. Gaumer*[15]), Meco I. (*G. F. Gaumer*[17][18]) ; BRITISH HONDURAS, Orange Walk (*G. F. Gaumer*), Belize (*Blancaneaux*) ; GUATEMALA, Choctum, sources of Rio de la Pasion, Lanquin, Izabal (*O. S. & F. D. G.*), Rio Dulce (*O. S.*[12]) ; HONDURAS (*Dyson*[10], *Leyland*[11]), San Pedro (*G. M. Whitely*[13]).

It is quite possible that Linnæus's name *Rhamphastos piscivorus*[1] was applied to this bird, but there are points in the description, such as the white throat, that make it doubtful what Linnæus's bird really was. We quite accept the general verdict that Swainson's title *R. carinatus* [2] may continue to be applied to this Toucan, though the description is not satisfactory.

The range of this species extends far further north than that of any of its congeners, as it is found from the middle of the State of Vera Cruz throughout Eastern Guatemala to Honduras. It seems to be wholly absent from Western Mexico and the whole of the low-lying land of Guatemala, between the mountains and the Pacific Ocean. Where it occurs on the eastern side of the Cordillera, it is by no means uncommon, as we have records of it from many places in Vera Cruz, and thence southwards into Yucatan, British Honduras, and Guatemala. It is a bird that never leaves the vicinity of the great forests, and its presence may be known by its harsh cries. It does not leave the hotter districts, and its range in the mountains probably does not much exceed 2500 feet.

The colours of the bill in life are very vivid, but these almost wholly disappear in the dried skin. The maxilla in life is for the most part yellowish-green, the tip being blood-red, and there is a large elongated orange patch along the proximal half of the side; the mandible is blood-red at the tip, then follows a sky-blue band, succeeded by yellowish-green to the base; a black ridge surrounds the base of the bill. The bare space round the eye is greenish-yellow, becoming green under the eye itself. The iris is greenish-yellow. These notes on the colours of these parts were taken from a specimen freshly killed on the Rio Dulce, Guatemala, in December 1857 [12].

2. Rhamphastos brevicarinatus.

Rhamphastos brevicarinatus, Gould, Mon. Rhamph. ed. 2, t. 3 [1]; Salv. Ibis, 1869, p. 317 [2]; Scl. Cat. Birds Brit. Mus. xix. p. 126 [3]; Richmond, Pr. U. S. Nat. Mus. xvi. p. 518 [4].

Rhamphastos approximans, Cab. J. f. Orn. 1862, p. 333 [5]; v. Frantz. J. f. Orn. 1869, p. 362 [6]; Lawr. Ann. Lyc. N. Y. ix. p. 128 [7].

Rhamphastos carinatus, Cassin, Pr. Ac. Phil. 1860, p. 136 [8]; Lawr. Ann. Lyc. N. Y. vii. p. 299 [9]; Scl. & Salv. P. Z. S. 1864, p. 366 [10]; Salv. P. Z. S. 1867, p. 156 [11]; 1870, p. 211 [12]; Nutting, Pr. U. S. Nat. Mus. vi. p. 407 [13]; Zeledon, An. Mus. Nac. Costa Rica, 1887, p. 123 [14]; Underwood, Ibis, 1896, p. 445 [15].

Rhamphastos piscivorus, Lawr. Ann. Lyc. N. Y. viii. p. 184 [16]; Scl. & Salv. P. Z. S. 1867, p. 280 [17].

R. carinato persimilis et forsan vix distinguendus; gutture luteo, postice late coccineo limbato, et statura forsan minore diversus.

Hab. NICARAGUA, Matagalpa (*W. B. Richardson*), Escondido river (*Richmond* [3]), Blewfields (*Wickham* [16]), Los Sabalos (*Nutting* [13]), La Libertad, San Emilio (*W. B. Richardson*), Greytown (*Holland* [16]); COSTA RICA [5], San José (*v. Frantzius* [7]), Grecia, Angostura, Dota Mts. (*v. Frantzius* [6], *Carmiol* [7]), Candelaria Mts., Aguacate, Machuca, Orosi, Tucurriqui (*v. Frantzius* [6]), Cartago, Naranjo de Cartago (*Zeledon* [13]), Turrialba (*Arcé, Zeledon* [14]), Miravalles (*Underwood* [15]); PANAMA, Chitra [12], Santa Fé [11] (*Arcé*), Lion Hill (*M'Leannan* [9] [10]).—N. COLOMBIA [4].

This is a race closely allied to *R. carinatus*—so much so, that, since it was separated by Gould [1], doubts have always existed whether it can really be distinguished. It appears to be a smaller bird, with a shorter and comparatively deeper bill, characters of little value ; but a more definite point is the width of the scarlet band which borders the yellow throat. This in *R. brevicarinatus* is wide and distinct, but scarcely shown in *R. carinatus*.

The range of the latter bird extends from Eastern Nicaragua through Costa Rica and Panama. It just enters the northern part of Colombia, where Mr. Simons obtained a specimen at Manaure, near Santa Marta.

In habits, *R. brevicarinatus* resembles *R. carinatus*, and appears to be equally common in the countries where it is found. Both Mr. Nutting [11] and Mr. Richmond [3] found it at Nicaragua, and we have many records of it in Costa Rica and Panama.

R. approximans, Cab., was kept separate from *R. brevicarinatus* by Cassin in his review of the Rhamphastidæ (Pr. Ac. Phil. 1867, p. 103), but their distinctness cannot, we think, now be maintained.

3. Rhamphastos tocard.

Le Tocard, Levaill. Hist. Nat. Ois. de Parad. ii. p. 25, t. 9 [1].

Rhamphastos tocard, Vieill. N. Dict. Hist. N. xxxiv. p. 281 [2]; Wagl. Syst. Av. fol. 1, p. 3 [3];
   Gould, Mon. Rhamph. ed. 2, t. 4 [4]; Cassin, Pr. Ac. Phil. 1860, p. 136 [5]; Lawr. Ann. Lyc.
   N. Y. vii. p. 299 [6]; ix. p. 128 [7]; Cab. J. f. Orn. 1862, p. 324 [8]; Scl. & Salv. P. Z. S. 1864,
   p. 366 [9]; v. Frantz. J. f. Orn. 1869, p. 362 [10]; Salv. P. Z. S. 1870, p. 211 [11]; Ibis, 1872,
   p. 323 [12]; Boucard, P. Z. S. 1878, p. 46 [13]; Nutting, Pr. U. S. Nat. Mus. vi. p. 407 [14];
   Ridgw. Pr. U. S. Nat. Mus. x. p. 591 [15]; Zeledon, An. Mus. Nac. Costa Rica, 1887, p. 123 [16];
   Richmond, Pr. U. S. Nat. Mus. xvi. p. 518 [17]; Scl. Cat. Birds Brit. Mus. xix. p. 127 [18].

Niger, supra rufo lavatus, alis et cauda pure nigris paulo nitidis ; tectricibus supracaudalibus albis ; gutture
   toto luteo, postice albo deinde coccineo limbato ; tectricibus subcaudalibus coccineis ; rostri maxilla culmine
   aurantiaco, basi rubida, inter hos colores nigra ; mandibula nigricante ad basin rubida ; oculorum ambitu
   nudo luteo ; pedibus plumbeis. Long. tota circa 24·0, alæ 9·3, caudæ 6·5, rostri a rictu 6·5, tarsi 2·0.
   (Descr. maris ex Chiriqui. Mus. nostr.)
♀ mari similis.

Hab. NICARAGUA, Segovia river (*Townsend* [15]), Escondido river (*Richmond* [17]), Chontales
   (*Belt* [12]), Los Sabalos (*Nutting* [14]); COSTA RICA [8], San Carlos (*v. Frantzius* [10], *Carmiol* [7],
   Boucard [13]), Turrialba (*v. Frantzius* [10], *Carmiol* [7]), Tucurriqui (*v. Frantzius* [10]),
   Angostura (*Carmiol* [7]), Naranjo de Cartago, Jimenez, Las Trojas, Pozo Azul de
   Pirris (*Zeledon* [16]); PANAMA, Bugaba, Volcan de Chiriqui (*Arcé* [11]), Lion Hill
   (*M‘Leannan* [6][9]), Rio Nercua (*Wood* [5]).—COLOMBIA ; ECUADOR ; PERU.

Rhamphastos tocard is one of the largest species of Toucans, and has been known since Levaillant's time, the figure in his great work ' Oiseaux de Paradis' being now generally accepted as a representation of this bird. Upon this figure Vieillot based his name.

This species is not at all uncommon in the lowlands of the north-western countries of South America, from Peru northwards through Ecuador and Colombia. It thence passes into the Isthmus of Central America, and is found as far north as the eastern parts of Nicaragua up to the Segovia river, where Mr. Townsend met with it.

Mr. Nutting says [14] that *R. tocard* is common at Los Sabalos, in Nicaragua, nesting in trunks of trees. Its note is a loud clear whistle, followed by two or more softer and lower ones. Mr. Richmond [17] also found it to be common on the Escondido river, where, however, it is seldom seen during the summer months, but from October or November on through the winter birds are seen daily, sometimes in large flocks, and often come out into the plantations. He describes their note as a curious croaking noise made when several birds are assembled in some solitary tree or retired place. When disturbed they fly silently away.

The colouring of the bill and naked space round the eye in Gould's plate [4] was taken from a specimen and notes supplied him by Bourcier, formerly French Consul at Quito. Mr. Nutting describes the former as having the maxilla above a line drawn from the base of the culmen to the lower edge, to a point on the tomia one-fifth of its length from the tip, as "corn-yellow," the remaining parts black; mandible very dark maroon; iris green; feet bronze-blue. The colour of the bill alters entirely in the dried skin, but the base of the maxilla in some specimens distinctly shows the remains of a maroon colour like that of the mandible.

PTEROGLOSSUS.

Pteroglossus, Illiger, Prodr. p. 202 (1811); Scl. Cat. Birds Brit. Mus. xix. p. 137.

Of the eighteen recognized species of *Pteroglossus* only three occur within our limits, all belonging to the same section in which the breast is banded, the sexes alike, and there is a large black pectoral spot. *P. erythropygius* is the only other species of this section, a southern form from which *P. sanguineus* hardly differs.

P. torquatus has the base of the culmen very flat between the nostrils, and the posterior margin of the sheath of the maxilla instead of being nearly straight across as in *Rhamphastos* is undulating, a deep notch running forwards on each side so as to include the open nostril. *Pteroglossus* is the least homogeneous of the Toucans, as in some of the species there is a sexual difference of plumage, and *P. beauharnasi* with its curiously curled crown-feathers is a very remarkable bird. All belong to the hot low-lying regions, and the metropolis of the genus is probably the valley of the Upper Amazons.

1. Pteroglossus torquatus.

Rhamphastos torquatus, Gm. Syst. Nat. i. p. 354 [1].

Pteroglossus torquatus, Wagl. Isis, 1829, p. 508 [2]; Gould, Mon. Rhamph. ed. 2, t. 20 [3]; Scl. P. Z. S. 1857, p. 205 [4]; 1858, p. 359 [5]; 1859, p. 388 [6]; Cat. Birds Brit. Mus. xix. p. 141 [7]; Moore, P. Z. S. 1859, p. 59 [8]; Scl. & Salv. Ibis, 1859, p. 135 [9]; P. Z. S. 1864, p. 366 [10]; 1870,

p. 837 [11]; Lawr. Ann. Lyc. N. Y. vii. p. 299 [12]; ix. p. 129 [13]; Bull. U. S. Nat. Mus. no. 4, p. 34 [14]; Cab. J. f. Orn. 1862, p. 331 [15]; v. Frantz. J. f. Orn. 1869, p. 362 [16]; Salv. Ibis, 1872, p. 323 [17]; Boucard, P. Z. S. 1878, p. 46 [18]; 1883, p. 455 [19]; Sumichrast, La Nat. v. p. 238 [20]; Nutting, Pr. U. S. Nat. Mus. v. p. 401 [21]; vi. pp. 388 [22], 407 [23]; Ferrari-Perez, Pr. U. S. Nat. Mus. ix. p. 163 [24]; Ridgw. Pr. U. S. Nat. Mus. x. p. 591 [25]; Zeledon, An. Mus. Nac. Costa Rica, 1887, p. 123 [26]; Richmond, Pr. U. S. Nat. Mus. xvi. p. 518 [27]; Underwood, Ibis, 1896, p. 445 [28].

Pteroglossus regalis, Licht. in Mus. Berol. apud Wagl. Isis, 1829, p. 508 [29]; Gould, P. Z. S. 1834, p. 75 [30].

Pteroglossus erythropygius, Lawr. Ann. Lyc. N. Y. viii. p. 179 [31]; Salv. P. Z. S. 1867, p. 157 [32].

Supra saturate nigricanti-olivaceus, capite toto undique nigro, torque nuchali angusta castanea; uropygio et tectricibus supracaudalibus coccineis : subtus gutture toto, plaga pectorali et fascia abdominali nigris, corpore reliquo flavo-coccineo irregulariter tincto; tibiis castaneis; rostri culminis apice et mandibula tota nigris, maxilla reliqua albicante ad basin rufescente; oculorum ambitu coccineo, infra oculos nigricante; iride flava; pedibus viridibus. Long. tota circa 18·0, alæ 6·0, caudæ 7·0, rostri a rictu 4·3, tarsi 1·4. (Descr. exempl. ex Choctum, Guatemala. Mus. nostr.)

♀ mari similis.

Hab. MEXICO, Tustepec, Xacatepec (*Wagler* [29]), Jalapa (*Ferrari-Perez* [24]), San Andres Tuxtla (*Sallé* [4]), Uvero, Cosamaloapam, Omealca (*Sumichrast* [20]), San Lorenzo near Cordova, Alvarado (*Ferrari-Perez*), Playa Vicente (*Boucard* [6], *M. Trujillo*), Sochiapa (*M. Trujillo*), Teapa in Tabasco (*Mrs. H. H. Smith*), N. Yucatan [19], Izalam (*G. F. Gaumer*), Santa Efigenia [14], Tapanatepec, Tonala (*Sumichrast* [20]); BRITISH HONDURAS, Orange Walk, Cayo, Belize (*Blancaneaux*); GUATEMALA, Savana Grande, Retalhuleu, Patio Bolas, Choctum, Rio Dulce [9] (*O. S. & F. D. G.*); HONDURAS (*Leyland* [8]), Omoa (*G. C. Taylor* [5]), San Pedro (*G. M. Whitely* [11]), Segovia river (*Townsend* [25]); NICARAGUA, Matagalpa, La Libertad, Volcan de Chinandega, Leon, Momotombo, San Emilio (*W. B. Richardson*), Chontales (*Belt* [17]), Escondido river (*Richmond* [27]), Sucuya [22], Los Sabalos [23] (*Nutting*); COSTA RICA, Bebedero (*Arcé*), Angostura, Turrialba (*v. Frantzius* [16], *Carmiol* [13]), San Miguel [15], Sarapiqui [16] (*v. Frantzius*), San Carlos (*Boucard* [18]), Naranjo de Cartago, Jimenez, Liberia (*Zeledon* [26]), La Palma (*Nutting* [21]), Miravalles (*Underwood* [28]); PANAMA, David (*Hicks* [30] [31]), Lion Hill (*M'Leannan* [10] [12]).—N. COLOMBIA [7]; VENEZUELA [7].

This is perhaps the commonest species of Toucan in Central America; for though not more numerous than *Rhamphastos carinatus* in places where both species occur, it has a wider range, extending to the Isthmus of Tehuantepec and the coast region of Guatemala bordering the Pacific Ocean. It is also found in other parts of Western Central America where neither *R. carinatus* nor *R. brevicarinatus* occur. It is usually found in companies of five or more birds, which are not easily frightened, but when disturbed call excitedly and rattle their bills on the bough on which they are perched [27]. As to the range of *P. torquatus* beyond our southern boundary, Gould doubted Sturm's statement that specimens had been received in Bogota collections. Certain is it, however, that both Salmon and Simons found it in Northern Colombia, the former in the Cauca valley, the latter near Santa Marta. It also reaches Venezuelan territory, as Goering met with it near Puerto Cabello.

A specimen shot by Mr. Nutting had a large beetle in its mouth [23].

2. Pteroglossus frantzii.

Pteroglossus frantzii, Cab. Sitz. Ber. Ges. naturf. Freunde z. Berlin, 1861 [1]; J. f. Orn. 1862, p. 333 [2]; Lawr. Ann. Lyc. N. Y. ix. p. 129 [3]; v. Frantz. J. f. Orn. 1869, p. 362 [4]; Salv. P. Z. S. 1870, p. 211 [5]; Ibis, 1874, p. 329 [6]; Boucard, P. Z. S. 1878, p. 47 [7]; Zeledon, An. Mus. Nac. Costa Rica, 1887, p. 123 [8]; Scl. Cat. Birds Brit. Mus. xix. p. 142 [9].

Supra saturate olivaceus, capite toto undique nigro, torque nuchali saturate castanea, uropygio et tectricibus supracaudalibus coccineis: subtus gutture toto et plaga pectorali nigris, fascia lata abdominali coccinea; corpore subtus reliquo flavo-coccineo irregulariter tincto; tibiis castaneis; rostri maxilla (culmine nigro excepto) fere omnino flavida ad basin rufescente; mandibula nigra; oculorum ambitu forsan coccineo et pedibus viridibus ut in *Pt. torquato*. Long. tota circa 18·0, alæ 6·0, caudæ 6·0, rostri a rictu 4·7, tarsi 1·7. (Descr. maris ex Volcan de Chiriqui. Mus. nostr.)
♀ mari similis.

Hab. COSTA RICA [1], Aguacate Mts. [2], San Mateo [4] (*v. Frantzius*), San José, Angostura (*Carmiol* [3]), San Carlos (*Boucard* [7]), Pozo Azul de Pirris, Las Trojas, Monte Redondo (*Zeledon* [8]); PANAMA, Bugaba, Volcan de Chiriqui (*Arcé* [5]), Veraguas (*Merritt* [6]).

This species has not been found outside the limits of Costa Rica and the adjoining parts of the State of Panama, where, however, it appears to be common in the latter country to the exclusion apparently of its near ally *P. torquatus*. It differs from that species in the colour of the maxilla, which is wholly yellow towards the end. Across the abdomen is a broad scarlet band instead of a much narrower black one as in the allied form.

Long before the discovery of this species in Costa Rica, Dr. Merritt had obtained specimens in Veraguas, which remained undescribed in his collection and unnoticed until Salvin saw them in 1874 [6].

3. Pteroglossus sanguineus.

Pteroglossus sanguineus, Gould, Mon. Rhamph. ed. 2, sub t. 21 [1]; Cassin, Pr. Ac. Phil. 1867, p. 109 [2]; Scl. Cat. Birds Brit. Mus. xix. p. 143 [3].
Pteroglossus erythropygius, Cassin, Pr. Ac. Phil. 1860, p. 136 [4].

Supra saturate nigricanti-olivaceus, capite toto intense nigro, torque cervicali nulla, uropygio et tectricibus supracaudalibus coccineis: subtus gutture, plaga pectorali et fascia abdominali nigris, corpore subtus reliquo flavo coccineo tincto; tibiis castaneis; rostro albicanti-flavido, culmine stria laterali (interrupta) et mandibula plerumque nigris. Long. tot. circa 18·0, alæ 5·6, caudæ 6·5, rostri a rictu 4·2, tarsi 1·4. (Descr. exemp. typ. in Mus. Brit. ex patria ignota.)

Hab. PANAMA, R. Truando (*Wood* [3] [4]).

This form was only doubtfully separated by Gould from his *P. erythropygius*, but accepted by Cassin and Mr. Sclater as distinct, the former writer fixing its habitat to the Isthmus of Darien by referring six specimens obtained during Lieut. Michler's exploring expedition to it rather than to *P. erythropygius*, to which he had previously considered them to belong.   From the latter bird *P. sanguineus* differs in having the culmen and mandible black.   Some sexual difference, according to Cassin, is found in the colour of the bill [1].   The true *P. erythropygius*, of which the type was obtained by Dr. Hind during the voyage of H.M.S. 'Sulphur,' was said to have been shot in the Nicaraguan port of Realejo.   As several specimens have since been sent from Western Ecuador by more than one collector, we have no doubt an error was made in giving this species a Central-American habitat which has never been confirmed.   There is a strong lateral ridge on the side of the maxilla in both these species.

SELENIDERA.

Selenidera, Gould, Icones Av. pl. 7, text (1837) ; Scl. Cat. Birds Brit. Mus. xix. p. 148.

Though the members of this genus form a very compact group, the characters by which to separate *Selenidera* from *Pteroglossus* are not very trenchant.   The culmen is not quite so flat between the nostrils, but the bill otherwise is much the same as in that genus.   There is a marked difference in the sexes, the males having a conspicuous long tuft of yellow feathers beneath the bare space surrounding the eye, wholly absent in the females.   Of the seven recognized species of *Selenidera* only one is found within our limits; the other six are distributed over the South-American continent, one belonging to South-eastern Brazil, the rest to the Amazons Valley and Guiana.   The range of the single Central-American species, *C. spectabilis*, is given below.

1. **Selenidera spectabilis.**

Selenidera spectabilis, Cassin, Pr. Ac. Phil. 1857, p. 214 [1]; 1860, p. 136 [2]; Journ. Ac. Phil. ser. 2, iv. p. 1, t. 1 [3]; Lawr. Ann. Lyc. N. Y. vii. p. 474 [4]; ix. p. 129 [5]; Salv. P. Z. S. 1857, p. 157 [6]; 1870, p. 211 [7]; Ibis, 1872, p. 323 [8] ; v. Frantz. J. f. Orn. 1869, p. 362 [9]; Boucard, P. Z. S. 1878, p. 47 [10]; Zeledon, An. Mus. Nac. Costa Rica, 1887, p. 123 [11]; Scl. Cat. Birds Brit. Mus. xix. p. 153 [12].

Supra olivaceus, capite summo et cervice postica nigris ; cauda griseo-nigricante : subtus omnino niger, plaga elongata infra oculos lutea, hypochondriis aurantiacis, subalaribus isabellinis ; tibiis castaneis ; tectricibus subcaudalibus coccineis ; maxilla supra a naribus usque ad apicem olivacea, lateribus et mandibula fusco-grisescentibus ad basin obscure olivascentibus, basi ipsa nigra; pedibus plumbeis.   Long. tota circa 16·0, alæ 5·4, caudæ 5·0, rostri a rictu 4·0, tarsi 1·4.   (Descr. maris ex Chontales, Nicaragua.   Mus. nostr.)

♀ capite toto summo et cervice postica saturate castaneis, plaga infra oculos lutea nulla.

Hab. NICARAGUA, Chontales (*Belt* [8]), La Libertad, Santo Domingo (*W. B. Richardson*) ; COSTA RICA [5], Tucurriqui (*Arcé, v. Frantzius* [9]), Naranjo (*Boucard* [10]), Rio Sucio (*Zeledon* [11]) ; PANAMA, Cordillera de Tolé [6], Santiago [6], Sante Fé [6], Calovevora [7] (*Arcé*), Cocuyos de Veragua (*R. W. Mitchell* [1]), Lion Hill (*M'Leannan* [4]), R. Truando (*Wood* [2]).

The first specimen of this fine species was sent to Cassin by Mr. Mitchell from Cocuyos de Veragua [1], and soon afterwards a pair came into the same writer's hands from the Darien Exploring Expedition under Lieut. Michler [2]. The latter were procured at the falls of the Rio Truando. Since then the species has been gradually traced northwards through the Isthmus of Panama to Costa Rica and Eastern Nicaragua, where Belt found it during his stay at Chontales, a specimen being included in his collection of bird-skins. Mr. Richardson has also recently sent us specimens from the same district.

Little is on record concerning this species; M. Boucard says he found it at Naranjo in Costa Rica in small flocks, living chiefly on fruit [10].

AULACORHAMPHUS.

Aulacorhamphus, Gould, P. Z. S. 1834, p. 147; Scl. Cat. Birds Brit. Mus. xix. p. 153.

Aulacorhamphus, again, is a genus of very similar structure to *Pteroglossus* and its allies, but the common character of the green plumage of all the species makes the group a very homogeneous one. The bill is smaller in proportion than in the other genera of Rhamphastidæ, and the base of the culmen rather more elevated; otherwise there is not much structural difference. *Aulacorhamphus* also has the peculiarity of being an upland genus, all the species belonging to the thick forests which cover many tropical mountains up to a height of 9000 or 10,000 feet.

Three of the fourteen known species are found in Mexico and Central America. One of them is peculiar to South-western Mexico, one to the eastern mountain-ranges of the same country, and thence southwards to Northern Nicaragua, and the third to the mountains of Costa Rica and the State of Panama. The southern species are found at various stations throughout the Andes from Colombia to Bolivia and in the higher mountains of Venezuela and Guiana.

1. Aulacorhamphus prasinus.

Pteroglossus prasinus, Licht. in Mus. Berol. [1]; Gould, P. Z. S. 1834, p. 78 [2]; Mon. Rhamph. t. 29 [3].
Aulacorhamphus prasinus, Bp. Consp. Av. i. p. 96 [4]; Gould, Mon. Rhamph. ed. 2, t. 47 [5]; Scl. P. Z. S. 1856, p. 308 [6]; 1859, p. 368 [7]; 1864, p. 177 [8]; Cat. Birds Brit. Mus. xix. p. 156 [9]; Scl. & Salv. Ibis, 1859, p. 135 [10]; P. Z. S. 1870, p. 837 [11]; Sumichrast, La Nat. v. p. 239 [12]; Ferrari-Perez, Pr. U. S. Nat. Mus. ix. p. 163 [13]; Salv. & Godm. Ibis, 1892, p. 327 [14].
Pteroglossus pavoninus, Wagl. Isis, 1829, p. 507 [15].

Supra viridis, capite vix obscuriore, uropygio lætiore: subtus dilutior, pectore vix cærulescentiore, gula alba, tectricibus subalaribus castaneis; cauda supra viride ad apicem cærulescente, subtus nigra, rectricibus omnibus castaneo terminatis; rostro viridescenti-luteo, culmine basi et macula infra nares confluente sanguineo-nigris, tomia quoque hujus coloris; mandibula nigra; oculorum ambitu castaneo; pedibus plumbeis. Long. tota circa 14·0, alæ 5·0, caudæ 4·5, rostri a rictu 3·5, tarsi 1·3. (Descr. maris ex Orizaba, Mexico. Mus. nostr.)

♀ mari similis, sed minor, rostro minore.

Hab. MEXICO (*White*[9]), Valle Real (*Wagler*[15]), Jalapa (*de Oca*[7], *Ferrari-Perez*[13]), Cordova (*Sallé*[6]), Orizaba, Mirador (*Sumichrast*[12]), Cofre de Perote (*M. Trujillo*), Coatepec, Huatusco, Hacienda Tortugas, Zeutla, Rio Juan Martin, Orizaba (*Ferrari-Perez*), Tonaguia (*M. Trujillo*); BRITISH HONDURAS, Western District (*Blancaneaux*); GUATEMALA, Coban, Chilasco, Raxché, Cerro Zunil, Las Nubes, Totonicapam, Volcan de Fuego, Calderas[10] (*O. S. & F. D. G.*); SALVADOR, Volcan de San Miguel (*W. B. Richardson*); HONDURAS, San Pedro (*G. M. Whitely*[11]); NICARAGUA, Matagalpa (*W. B. Richardson*[14]).

Though Wagler's description of the colouring of the base of the maxilla of his *Pteroglossus pavoninus* makes it almost certain that that name and Lichtenstein's *P. prasinus* were applied to the same species, if not to the same specimen, we do not think it at all desirable to supercede the specific name *prasinus* for the older title *pavoninus*. The latter has been frequently used for the allied *Aulacorhamphus wagleri*; and, moreover, if Sturm's statement, as quoted by Gould, is correct, that the inappropriate name "*pavoninus*" was suggested by extraneous feathers inserted in the skin, additional justification for rejecting the title is afforded.

We adhere, therefore, to the practice which has prevailed till now of calling this Toucan *Aulacorhamphus prasinus*.

This species is common in all the upland forests of Eastern Mexico from the slopes of the Cofre de Perote southwards. It also occurs in the western district of British Honduras, where the mountains attain an elevation of upwards of 2000 feet. In Guatemala it is common in Alta Vera Paz and in the forest belt of the Volcan de Fuego. In the latter locality its loud call was familiar to us during our rambles in those attractive regions. Southwards of Guatemala it is doubtless found in suitable districts till we come to the mountains of Matagalpa in Northern Nicaragua, and here probably it stops, as in Costa Rica its place is taken by *A. cœruleogularis*.

There is little to be said respecting the habits of this species; birds are rather solitary and silent when observed, and keep in the upper branches of the higher trees. We have no notes on its nesting peculiarities.

2. Aulacorhamphus wagleri.

Pteroglossus pavoninus, Gould, P. Z. S. 1835, p. 158[1]; Mon. Rhamp. t. 30[2] (Wagl. in Mus. Munich; nec Isis, 1829, p. 507).

Aulacorhamphus pavoninus, Bp. Consp. Av. i. p. 95[3]; Salv. & Godm. Ibis, 1889, p. 240[4].

Pteroglossus wagleri, Sturm, Mon. Rhamph. ii. t. 7[5].

Aulacorhamphus wagleri, Gould, Mon. Rhamph. ed. 2, t. 48[6]; Scl. P. Z. S. 1859, p. 388[7]; Cat. Birds Brit. Mus. xix. p. 157[8]; Cassin, Pr. Ac. Phil. 1867, p. 120[9].

A. prasino similis, mandibula basi omnino nigra, margine tumido multo latiore, fronte lutescente, cervicis lateribus et gutture cæruleo lavato distinguendus. Long. tota circa 11·0, alæ 5·2, caudæ 4·8, rostri a rictu 4·0, tarsi 1·2. (Descr. feminæ ex Amula, Mexico. Mus. nostr.)

Hab. MEXICO, Sacatepec (*Boucard* [6]), Amula in Guerrero (*Mrs. H. H. Smith* [3]).

A green Toucan in the Museum at Munich was supposed by Wagler to belong to the same species he had previously named *Pteroglossus pavoninus* in Berlin. Their distinctness was discovered by Sturm, and the Munich bird named *P. wagleri*. Some confusion has arisen concerning the application of these names, but we are now convinced that Wagler's name *P. pavoninus* belongs to *Aulacorhamphus prasinus* and not to the present bird, though we thought otherwise in 1889 [4].

Of *A. wagleri* very little is known. Besides the original specimen, which no doubt came from Mexico, only two others have been recorded; one of these was obtained by M. Boucard at Sacatepec [6], and is now in the British Museum. The other formed part of a large collection made for us by Mrs. H. H. Smith, when she, in company with her husband, explored the mountain-range traversing the Mexican State of Guerrero called the Sierra Madre del Sur; it is a female and was shot near a place called Amula, in the higher part of the range.

A. wagleri is more distinct from *A. prasinus* than appears at first sight, for besides the difference of the colouring of the base of the bill, the dark edging of the tomia runs nearly parallel to the edge instead of arching over it. The forehead is tinged with yellowish at the base of the feathers, and the sides of the neck and the throat washed with blue. The swollen margin to the base of the maxilla, too, is much wider and more prominent.

3. Aulacorhamphus cæruleigularis.

Aulacorhamphus cæruleigularis, Gould, P. Z. S. 1853, p. 45 [1]; Mon. Rhamph. ed. 2, t. 51 [2]; Cassin, Pr. Ac. Phil. 1867, p. 121 [3]; Salv. P. Z. S. 1867, p. 157 [4]; 1870, p. 211 [5]; Lawr. Ann. Lyc. N. Y. ix. p. 129 [6]; v. Frantz. J. f. Orn. 1869, p. 362 [7]; Boucard, P. Z. S. 1878, p. 47 [8]; Zeledon, An. Mus. Nac. Costa Rica, 1887, p. 123 [9]; Scl. Cat. Birds Brit. Mus. xix. p. 159 [10].

Aulacorhynchus cæruleogularis, Cab. J. f. Orn. 1862, p. 330 [11].

Supra viridis, capite summo et cervice postica fusco vix lavatis: subtus pallidior, gutture toto læte cæruleo, tectricibus subcaudalibus castaneis; cauda supra viridi ad apicem cærulescente, subtus nigricante, rectricibus omnibus castaneo terminatis; rostro flavido, culmine basi et tomia margine sanguineo-nigricantibus, basi tumida flavicante, mandibula (basi albida excepta) nigra; pedibus plumbeis. Long. tota circa 12·0, alæ 4·5, caudæ 4·0, rostri a rictu 4·0, tarsi 1·3. (Descr. maris ex Santa Fé, Panama. Mus. nostr.)

♀ mari similis, sed minor, rostro minore.

Hab. COSTA RICA [7], Volcan de Barba (*Hoffmann* [11]), Birris, La Palma, San José (*v. Frantzius* [3]), Barranca, Dota Mts., Turrialba (*Carmiol* [6]), Naranjo (*Boucard* [8]), Naranjo de Cartago, Cartago, Volcan de Irazu, Monte Redondo, Navarro de Cartago (*Zeledon* [9]); PANAMA, Volcan de Chiriqui, Calovevora [5], Santa Fé [4] (*Arcé*), Veraguas (*Seemann* [1] [2]).

The first specimen of this species was obtained by the late Berthold Seemann in

Veragua during his expedition in H.M.S. 'Herald,' and was described by Gould in 1853 [1], and subsequently figured in the second edition of his 'Monograph of the Rhamphastidæ' [2].

The bird has since been found in some numbers in the same district by our collector Arcé, and in many places in Costa Rica.

We have few notes of its habits, but according to v. Frantzius it inhabits similar districts as its ally *A. prasinus*,—*i. e.*, the upland forests of the higher mountain-ranges of the countries in which it is found. It is wholly absent from the Line of the Panama Railway, and other species take its place further south.

Order PSITTACI.

In treating of the Mexican and Central-American species of Parrots we have followed closely Count Salvadori's Catalogue of Psittaci in the collection of the British Museum, published in 1891. The order is there divided into six families, which are distributed over the greater part of the tropical regions of the World. New Guinea and the islands adjoining, and Australia, are especially rich in species and genera, whilst Africa is comparatively poor. In America we find many species, but few genera ; and so distinct are the Parrots of the New World that though all belong to the family Psittacidæ, which is nearly world-wide, America monopolizes the whole of the subfamily Conurinæ and all the Pioninæ with the exception of the African genus *Pæocephalus*.

Count Salvadori recognizes 450 species of Psittaci, belonging to seventy-nine genera ; of these 180 species of twenty-four genera belong to America. Thus, while the species of America amount to 40 per cent. of the total known, the genera only reach a little over 30 per cent. The absence of variety in the American Parrots is still further shown by all of them belonging to a single one of the six families, viz. the Psittacidæ, and these to only two of the six subfamilies into which Count Salvadori subdivides the Psittacidæ.

In Mexico and Central America we find thirty-four species belonging to ten genera. The species are therefore only about 19 per cent. of the number found in America, while the genera reach nearly 42 per cent.

Apart from *Conurus carolinensis*, an outlying species found in the southern States of North America, no Parrot passes beyond the northern frontier of Mexico, though several approach near to it. This fact is of importance, as the northern limit of the range of the Psittaci in Mexico is a valuable element in tracing the boundary between the Neotropical and Nearctic regions.

As an order the Parrots form a very compact and isolated group with no outlying members leading to other orders. The Striges and Accipitres are considered by some to be the most nearly allied birds, but the affinity cannot be close nor are these two orders at all nearly related to one another.

Fam. PSITTACIDÆ.

The Psittacidæ, which, as we have already said, is the only one of the six families which here concerns us, belongs to Count Salvadori's second division of the order, in which the maxilla has towards the end of the palate two series of ridges more or less transverse or oblique, producing a file-like surface, the tongue is simple without fringe, the sternum complete with a well-defined keel, the orbital ring is mostly incomplete, but, if complete, without a process bridging the temporal fossa.

Subfam. *CONURINÆ*.

Conurinæ, Salvadori, Cat. Birds Brit. Mus. xx. p. 145.

Tail soft as contrasted with the spiny tail of the Nasiterninæ. Furcula present (except in *Psittacula*); the left carotid superficial; orbital ring complete; tail usually long and always cuneate.

ARA.

Ara, Cuvier, Leç. d'Anat. Comp. t. ii. (1799); Salvadori, Cat. Birds Brit. Mus. xx. p. 150.
Sittace, Wagler, Mon. Psitt. p. 499 (1830).

After assigning the three great Blue Macaws to the genus *Anodorhynchus*, and *Sittace spixi*, Wagl., to *Cyanopsittacus*, Count Salvadori leaves fifteen species of these large Parrots in the genus *Ara*, its range extending over most of the tropical portion of the Neotropical region, with the exception of nearly all the West-Indian islands, Cuba alone possessing *A. tricolor*, a species now nearly, if not quite, extinct. Six species are found in Central America and Mexico, three of which only just enter the fauna, as far as the Line of the Panama Railway. Of the remaining three, *A. macao* is the only species extending over nearly the whole country as far as Southern Mexico, both forms of the great Green Macaws having a more restricted range: one, *A. militaris*, being found chiefly in Western Mexico; the other, *A. ambigua*, in Nicaragua, Costa Rica, and Panama, and thence southwards into Western Ecuador.

The genus *Ara* contains birds of very different sizes, ranging from *A. ambigua*, one of the largest of the American Parrots, to *A. hahni*, a bird less than some members of *Conurus*.

In *Ara*, as in all the following genera, the tail is long and cuneate, but the " orbital

71*

ring," or ring of bone surrounding the eye, is complete, and the furcula is present. The lores are naked, as are also, for the most part, the cheeks, except in such cases as the latter are traversed by narrow lines of small feathers, as in *A. chloroptera*. These latter characters distinguish *Ara* from the other genera of this subfamily, and from *Conurus* and *Rhynchopsittacus*, to which it is most nearly allied.

1. Ara ararauna.

The Blue and Yellow Maccaw, Edw. Birds, iv. p. 159, t. 159 [1].

Psittacus ararauua, Linn. Syst. Nat. i. p. 139 [2].

Ara ararauna, G. R. Gray; Cassin, Pr. Ac. Phil. 1860, p. 137 [3]; Salv. Ibis, 1871, p. 90 [4]; Salvad. Cat. Birds Brit. Mus. xx. p. 152 [5].

Supra cærulea, certa luce viridescens, fronte et pileo antico olivaceis; genis nudis, lineis plumosis nigricantibus notatis; gula nuda, plumis nigris postice marginata; tectricibus auricularibus, cervicis lateribus, corpore subtus et tectricibus subalaribus aurantio-flavis; rostro et pedibus nigris; iride (ave viva) viridigrisea. Long. tota circa 31·0, alæ 15·0, caudæ rectr. med. 20·0, rectr. lat. 12·0, rostri culminis 1·9, tarsi 1·1. (Descr. maris ex Chepo, Panama. Mus. nostr.)

Hab. PANAMA, Chepo (*Arcé* [4]).—SOUTH AMERICA, Colombia [3], Amazons Valley, Bolivia, and Guiana [5].

Our knowledge of the existence of this Macaw is of very early date, going back as far as the works of Aldovrandus (1646) and Marcgrave (1648), and in the following century it was figured by George Edwards [1] and described by Linnæus [2].

It is a very well-known South-American species as a tenant of menageries from early times.

The range of *Ara ararauna* extends over a large part of tropical South America, and it is found from Colombia in the extreme north-west to Guiana and the whole of the valley of the Amazons to the base of the Andes of Ecuador, Peru, and Bolivia. In Paraguay its place is taken by an allied form, *A. caninde*, which has a similar coloration, but the throat is bluish-green instead of black, and the lines of small feathers which cross the naked space of the lores and cheeks are dark green.

Ara ararauna only just enters our limits. It was found at the mouth of the Atrato, in the Gulf of Uraba, by the naturalists who accompanied Lieut. Michler in his exploring expedition to the Isthmus of Darien [3]; and our collector Arcé sent us a single specimen from Chepo, a place on the Isthmus of Panama, about 40 miles south of the city. Dr. Finsch quotes Leyland as an authority for its occurrence in Honduras; but its name does not appear in the published lists of Leyland's birds, nor has any subsequent collector, and there have been many, found it in this region. We therefore conclude that the southern extremity of the Isthmus of Panama is the limit of the northern range of this Macaw.

2. Ara macao.

The Red and Blue Maccaw, Edw. Birds, iv. p. 158, t. 158 [1].

Psittacus macao, Linn. Syst. Nat. i. p. 139 [2].

Ara macao, G. R. Gray; Taylor, Ibis, 1860, p. 119 [3]; Cassin, Pr. Ac. Phil. 1860, p. 137 [4]; Lawr.
Ann. Lyc. N. Y. vii. p. 474 [5]; Bull. U. S. Nat. Mus. no. 4, p. 35 [6]; Salv. Ibis, 1871,
p. 89 [7]; Boucard, P. Z. S. 1878, p. 46 [8]; Sumichrast, La Nat. v. p. 238 [9]; Nutting, Pr.
U. S. Nat. Mus. v. p. 402 [10]; vi. pp. 376 [11], 388 [12], 395 [13], 407 [14]; Zeledon, An. Mus. Nac.
Costa Rica, 1887, p. 124 [15]; Salvad. Cat. Birds Brit. Mus. xx. p. 154 [16]; Richmond, Pr.
U. S. Nat. Mus. xvi. p. 519 [17]; Underwood, Ibis, 1896, p. 445 [18].

Sittace macao, Finsch, Papag. i. p. 398 [19]; Lawr. Ann. Lyc. N. Y. ix. p. 131 [20]; v. Frantz. J. f.
Orn. 1869, p. 364 [21].

Psittacus aracanga, Gm. Syst. Nat. i. p. 313 [22]; Licht. Preis-Verz. Mex. Vög. p. 1 (*cf.* J. f. Orn.
1863, p. 54) [23].

Ara aracanga, G. R. Gray; Moore, P. Z. S. 1859, p. 59 [24]; Scl. & Salv. Ibis, 1859, p. 137 [25];
P. Z. S. 1864, p. 367 [26]; Lawr. Ann. Lyc. N. Y. viii. p. 11 [27].

Coccinea, dorso postico et tectricibus supracaudalibus pallide cæruleis; tectricibus alarum majoribus et mediis
et scapularibus flavis saturate viridi terminatis, remigibus cyaneis, subtus tectricibus majoribus fusco-
coccineis; rectricibus quatuor mediis coccineis, rhachidibus nigris, tertia utrinque ad basin coccinea
cæruleo terminata, reliquis fere omnino cæruleis, subtus omnibus (quatuor mediis exceptis) fusco-coccineis;
rostri maxilla albida ad basin et ad apicem nigra, mandibula nigra; capitis lateribus nudis, carneis; iride
(ave viva) flavido-alba. Long. tota circa 36·0, alæ 16·0, caudæ rectr. med. 23·5, rectr. lat. 8·0, rostri
culminis 3·1, tarsi 1·1. (Descr. exempl. ex Aguna, Guatemala. Mus. nostr.)

Hab. MEXICO (*Deppe* [23]), Tampico [9], Tuxpam [9], Uvero [9], Tehuantepec [6][9], Santa Efigenia [6][9],
Cacoprieto [9], Tonala [6][9] (*Sumichrast*), Chimalapa (*W. B. Richardson*); GUATEMALA,
Aguna [25], Savana Grande, San Agustin, Huamuchal, Plain of Salama [7], Choctum,
Pine-ridge of Poctun [7] (*O. S. & F. D. G.*); SALVADOR, La Union (*O. S.*); HONDURAS,
Omoa (*Leyland* [24]), Comayagua, Tigre I. (*G. C. Taylor* [3]); NICARAGUA, Matagalpa,
San Rafael del Norte (*W. B. Richardson*), San Juan del Sur (*O. S., Nutting* [11]),
Sucuyá [12], Omotepe I. [13], Los Sabalos [14] (*Nutting*), R. Escondido (*Richmond* [17]);
COSTA RICA (*v. Frantzius* [21]), Miravalles (*Underwood* [18]), Las Anonas [20], Tres Rios,
Jimenez, Rio Sucio, Las Trojas (*Zeledon* [15]), Peje (*Carmiol*), La Palma (*Nutting* [10]),
San Carlos (*Boucard* [8]); PANAMA, Lion Hill (*M'Leannan* [5][26][27]).—SOUTH AMERICA,
from Guiana and the Amazons Valley to Bolivia [16].

The Red and Blue Macaw (*Psittacus macao*, Linn., *P. aracanga*, Gm.) is far the
commonest and most widely-spread species of *Ara* in Central America, and is found
from Tampico in Eastern Mexico, over the whole of Central America, and thence
southwards over a large part of tropical South America, where it extends from the
north coast to the valley of the Amazons, and to the base of the Andes of Ecuador,
Peru, and Bolivia. It seems to be absent from all parts of Western Mexico north of
the Isthmus of Tehuantepec. In Guatemala it is abundant on both sides of the
cordillera, and may at times be seen flying over the valleys of the interior as high as
3000 feet above the sea. Its harsh discordant cries and showy plumage make it a bird

much in evidence wherever it occurs.   It frequents forest-clearings and open pine-clad savanas like those of Poctun in the district of Peten, and flies in pairs or a number of pairs together.   In Honduras and Nicaragua *Ara macao* seems to be very abundant, as testified by G. C. Taylor[3], Leyland[24], Nutting[12], and Richmond[17]; the last-named collector found two eggs in a tree which he cut down in February.   In Costa Rica it appears to be equally common, and we have specimens from the Line of the Panama Railway, where it occurs with *Ara chloroptera*.

3. Ara chloroptera.

Ara chloropterus, G. R. Gray, List Psitt. Brit. Mus. p. 26 (1859)[1].

Ara chloroptera, Scl. & Salv. P. Z. S. 1864, p. 367[2]; Salv. Ibis, 1871, p. 90[3]; Salvad. Cat. Birds Brit. Mus. xx. p. 156[4].

Saturate coccinea, dorso postico et tectricibus supracaudalibus pallide cæruleis ; tectricibus alarum minoribus coccineis, mediis olivaceis, majoribus cæruleis, interscapulio olivaceo ; remigibus supra cyaneis, subtus et tectricibus omnibus fusco-coccineis ; rectricibus mediis medialiter fusco-coccineis ad apicem et ad basin cæruleis, duabus proximis similibus sed magis cæruleis, reliquis plerumque cæruleis, omnibus subtus fusco-coccineis ; tectricibus subcaudalibus cæruleis ; rostri maxilla albida ad basin nigra, mandibula nigra, capitis lateribus nudis, carneis, undique plumulis coccineis ornatis ; pedibus nigris.   Long. tota circa 34·0, alæ 15·5, caudæ rectr. med. 20·0, rectr. lat. 7·0, rostri culminis 3·7, tarsi 1·2.   (Descr. maris ex Panama. Mus. nostr.)

Hab. PANAMA, Lion Hill (*M'Leannan*[2][3]).—SOUTH AMERICA, Colombia, Ecuador, Bolivia, Amazons Valley, and Guiana[4].

This *Ara* closely resembles *A. macao* in general coloration, but on examination may readily be distinguished by the median wing-coverts being green instead of chrome-yellow, the darker tint of the red colour, and by the naked cheeks being traversed by narrow lines of scarlet feathers.

It was not until 1859 that this Macaw was definitely separated from *Ara macao* by G. R. Gray[1], who gave it the name it now bears.   It had previously been called by names strictly applicable to the allied form, as shown in Count Salvadori's recently published Catalogue[4].

Its range, though apparently equally wide as that of *A. macao* on the South-American continent, is much more restricted in our country and it has as yet only been found on the Isthmus of Panama along the Line of the Railway.   It is true that it has been reported from Guatemala, but we should like further evidence before admitting its existence so far north.

4. Ara militaris.

The Great Green Macaw, Edw. Glean. vii. p. 224, t. 313[1].

Psittacus militaris, Linn. Syst. Nat. i. p. 139[2]; Licht. Preis-Verz. Mex. Vög. p. 1 (*cf.* J. f. Orn. 1863, p. 54)[3]; Wagl. Isis, 1831, p. 525[4].

Macrocercus militaris, Vieill. N. Dict. d'Hist. N. ii. p. 261[5]; Sw. Phil. Mag. new ser. i. p. 439[6]; Bp. P. Z. S. 1837, p. 109[7]; Dugès, La Nat. i. p. 138[8].

Ara militaris, G. R. Gray; Salv. Ibis, 1871, p. 88 (partim)[9]; Lawr. Bull. U. S. Nat. Mus. no. 4, p. 35[10]; Sumichrast, La Nat. v. p. 338[11]; Salvad. Cat. Birds Brit. Mus. xx. p. 158[12]; Jouy, Pr. U. S. Nat. Mus. xvi. p. 786[13].

Sittace militaris, Finsch, Abh. naturw. Ver. Bremen, 1870, p. 352[14]; Lawr. Mem. Bost. Soc. N. H. ii. p. 295[15].

Olivaceo-viridis, dorso postico et tectricibus supracaudalibus cæruleis, pileo et nucha viridibus, fronte et loris coccineis, tectricibus alarum majoribus et remigibus cæruleis; cauda medialiter saturate coccinea, basi et apice cærula, rectricibus lateralibus plerumque cæruleis, omnibus subtus olivaceis; rostro corneo; capitis lateribus nudis, carneis, plumulis ante oculos rubris, infra oculos nigris notatis. Long. tota circa 27·0, alæ 15·0, caudæ rectr. med. 15·0, rectr. lat. 7·5, rostri culminis 2·8, tarsi 1·0. (Descr. maris ex San Blas, W. Mexico. Mus. nostr.)

Hab. MEXICO [6] (*Deppe* [3], *le Strange* [9]), Mazatlan (*Grayson* [14] [15]), Presidio de Mazatlan (*Forrer*), Quiriego in Sonora (*Lloyd*), San Blas (*W. B. Richardson*), Guanajuato (*Dugès* [8]), Culata in Colima (*Lloyd*), Acapulco (*Grayson* [15]), Huamelula near Zapotlan (*Sumichrast* [11]), Rio de la Armeria (*Xantus* [15]), Barranca de Beltran, Agosta (*Jouy* [13]), Temiscaltepec (*Bullock* [6]), Sierra Madre de Tamaulipas (*W. B. Richardson*).—COLOMBIA; PERU; BOLIVIA.

This is the smaller of the two Green Macaws found in our region, and its range is chiefly restricted to Western Mexico from the State of Guerrero to that of Sinaloa. It is also found on the eastern side of the cordillera, as Mr. Richardson sent us a specimen from the Sierras of the State of Tamaulipas. It is said to occur in the mountains to the north of Tehuantepec [9] and also in Guatemala, but we have no specimens to confirm either statement, and the correctness of the latter we hesitate to accept.

Grayson's account [15] of this species is very complete, and the following notes give the substance of his remarks. *Ara militaris* inhabits the belt of land called the tierra caliente of Western Mexico lying between the sea-coast and the base of the cordillera, and in this district it moves from one locality to another as food upon which it subsists comes into season. It is sometimes found as high as 3000 or 4000 feet above the sea in the mountains, attracted there from the lowlands by suitable food. It may be seen at all seasons near the sea-coast from Mazatlan to Acapulco, but is especially numerous about the Rio Mazatlan, the great forest of that district affording it subsistence in abundance.

"Guacamayo" is the native name for all the Macaws both in Mexico and Guatemala, and the "Guacamayo" of Western Mexico is said to descend to the ground only during the month of May in search of a certain hard nut which is then shed from the trees which bear them. This nut is the fruit of a tree called "Ava" by the Mexicans, a species of "Nux vomica," the milky sap of which as well as the fruit being a deadly poison to most animals, but not to the *Ara*. This tree grows to a large size on the banks of rivers or over rich alluvial valleys. The pod which contains the fruit is spherical and about twelve inches in circumference, divided into sixteen sections, in each of which is a button-shaped seed. The shell of these is exceedingly hard, but the powerful bill of the Macaw splits it with apparent ease. From the time this nut ripens in December until the spring it forms the principal food of the Macaw, but it also feeds on a small cocoa-nut or nuts of the "Royal Palm," which are also very hard. The weight of the "Ava"-pod when green exceeds a pound, yet the Macaws, after gnawing off the tough stem, handle it in their strong claws with ease, and even fly with it in their jaws for a short distance. Acacia-beans of various kinds and other wild fruits form food for this Macaw, and cornfields are sometimes visited by it.

This *Ara* is gregarious, except during the breeding-season, but continues in pairs throughout the year. When shifting their feeding-ground they fly at a great height, but always in pairs, and utter harsh discordant cries. They congregate to roost from many miles, selecting the highest branches of the tallest trees in some chosen spot, which they frequent for many months together.

They breed in holes of trees, usually selecting a wild fig-tree, one of the largest of the forest. The eggs are laid on the bare wood, are two in number, rather less than those of the common hen, and pure white. The breeding-season commences in April, both male and female incubating the eggs in turn.

The late P. L. Jouy [13] found this *Ara* in the Barranca de Beltran in Southern Jalisco in some numbers, and also in the pine-forests of Agosto. He was informed that it also occurs in the Barranca de Ibarra near Guadalajara. It is a bird that joins the noisy evening flights of Parrots, flying very high and uttering piercing cries. He noted the iris as yellow, and the naked skin round the eye as carmine.

5. Ara ambigua.

Psittacus ambiguus, Bechst. Kurze Ueb. iv. p. 65 [1].
Ara ambigua, Salvad. Cat. Birds Brit. Mus. xx. p. 160 [2].
Ara militaris, Cassin, Pr. Ac. Phil. 1860, p. 137 [3]; Lawr. Ann. Lyc. N. Y. vii. p. 299 [4]; Salv. P. Z. S.
    1870, p. 213 [5]; Boucard, P. Z. S. 1878, p. 46 [6]; Nutting, Pr. U. S. Mus. vi. p. 407 [7]; Zeledon,
    An. Mus. Nac. Costa Rica, 1887, p. 124 [8]; Richmond, Pr. U. S. Nat. Mus. xvi. p. 519 [9].
Sittace militaris, Lawr. Ann. Lyc. N. Y. ix. p. 131 [10]; v. Frantz. J. f. Orn. 1869, p. 364 [11].

A. *militari* similis, sed omnino major, rostro majore, colore corporis olivaceo pallidiore et flavescentiore, uropygio
    pallidiore cæruleo. Long. tot. circa 33·0, alæ 16·0, caudæ rectr. med. 18·5, rectr. lat. 8·0, rostri
    culminis 3·3, tarsi 1·1. (Descr. maris ex Calovevora, Panama. Mus. nostr.)

Hab. NICARAGUA, R. Escondido (*Richmond* [9]), Los Sabalos (*Nutting* [7]), San Emilio (*W.
    B. Richardson*); COSTA RICA (*v. Frantzius* [10], *Zeledon* [7]), Barba (*Carmiol* [10]), San
    Carlos, Zarcero (*Boucard* [5]), Talamanca (*Gabb, U. S. Nat. Mus.*); PANAMA, Calovevora
    (*Arcé* [5]), Lion Hill (*M'Leannan* [4]), R. Nercua (*Wood* [3]).—WESTERN ECUADOR [2].

This is a large form of *A. militaris*, exceeding that bird considerably in size, and differing from it in some slight modifications of colour.

With the specimens now before us we are able to state that its range extends to Nicaragua, whence we have several specimens, and it thence spreads southwards over

Costa Rica and the State of Panama to Western Ecuador. In Colombia a small form again appears which may or may not be the same as that of Mexico. The only southern specimen accessible to us is even smaller than any of our series from the latter country, so that we do not feel in a position to decide this question. Mr. Ridgway also writes to say that a trade-skin from Bogota in the United States National Museum is also very small, and he, in fact, was the first person to draw our attention to the point. Should this southern bird be found to be sufficiently distinct for separation it will be somewhat difficult to say whether the Mexican or the southern bird should bear the name *Ara militaris*, but it will be advisable to continue its use for the northern form.

We have no special account of the habits of this species, which Mr. Richmond[7] says resemble those of *Ara macao*. He adds that the naked skin on the head is pale carmine-purple, the iris dark yellow, but varying in different individuals. A specimen from the Rio Nercua, obtained during Lieut. Michler's expedition to Darien, and now in the United States National Museum, was obtained in the cordillera in which that river takes its rise[3].

6. **Ara severa.**

Brasilian Green Macaw, Edw. Glean. v. p. 41, t. 229[1].
Psittacus severus, Linn. Syst. Nat. i. p. 140[2].
Ara severa, G. R. Gray; Cassin, Pr. Ac. Phil. 1860, p. 137[3]; Lawr. Ann. Lyc. N. Y. vii. p. 474[4];
    Salv. Ibis, 1871, p. 91[5]; Salvad. Cat. Birds Brit. Mus. xx. p. 161[6].

Viridis, capite summo cæruleo lavato, fronte, capitis lateribus et mento marginibus castaneo-fuscis, lineis plumosis genarum nigris; tectricibus alarum majoribus et remigibus glauco-cæruleis nigro marginatis, secundariis extrorsum medialiter rubidis et cæruleo terminatis, reliquis plerumque extrorsum cæruleis, omnibus subtus rubro lavatis: alis subtus quoque rubidis, margine carpali et tectricibus minoribus coccineis, majoribus viridescentibus; genis nudis, albido-carneis; iride (ave viva) flava. Long. tota circa 18·0, alæ 9·3, caudæ rectr. med. 9·0, rectr. lat. 4·5, rostri culminis 1·8, tarsi 0·8. (Descr. exempl. ex Colombia. Mus. nostr.)

Hab. PANAMA, Lion Hill (*M'Leannan*[4]), mouth of the R. Nercua (*Wood*[3]).—COLOMBIA; ECUADOR; PERU; BOLIVIA; AMAZONS VALLEY and GUIANA[6].

Of the presence of this *Ara* within our region we have only two records—a specimen having been sent by M'Leannan to Lawrence[4] in one of his earlier collections from the Isthmus of Panama, another was obtained during Lieut. Michler's expedition to the Isthmus of Darien[3]. No Central-American example has reached our hands. On the continent of South America *A. severa* has a wide range over the eastern slopes of the Andes from Colombia to Bolivia, and is found throughout the Amazons Valley and in Guiana, though we have seen no specimens from the latter country[6].

RHYNCHOPSITTACUS.

Rhynchopsitta, Bonaparte, Rev. et Mag. Zool. 1854, p. 149.
Rhynchopsittacus, Salvadori, Cat. Birds Brit. Mus. xx. p. 168.

This genus contains the single species *R. pachyrhynchus,* which resembles some of the Macaws in size, but differs from them in having the lores feathered as in *Conurus.* From the latter genus it can be distinguished by its much more compressed bill, the mandible being flattened and grooved in front, the culmen of the maxilla rounded, and the nostrils completely hidden. The known range of the genus is restricted to Central and Northern Mexico, but it probably crosses the border into South-western Texas and Southern New Mexico; the details of its distribution are given below.

1. **Rhynchopsittacus pachyrhynchus.**

Macrocercus pachyrhynchus, Sw. Phil. Mag. new ser. i. p. 439 [1].
Sittace pachyrhyncha, Wagl. Mon. Psitt. p. 667, t. 25 [2].
Ara pachyrhyncha, Scl. P. Z. S. 1859, p. 368 [3].
Rhynchopsitta pachyrhyncha, Bp., Souancé, Icon. Perr. t. 5 [4]; Scl. P. Z. S. 1857, p. 230 [5]; Sumichrast, Mem. Bost. Soc. N. H. i. p. 562 [6]; La Nat. v. p. 232 [7]; Salv. Ibis, 1871, p. 91 [8]; Cat. Strickl. Coll. p. 464 [9]; Allen, Bull. Am. Mus. N. H. v. p. 34 [10]; Ridgw. Man. N. Am. Birds, ed. 2, p. 269 [11].
Rhynchopsittacus pachyrhynchus, Salvad. Cat. Birds Brit. Mus. xx. p. 169 [12].
Psittacus strenuus, Licht. Preis-Verz. Mex. Vög. p. 1 (*cf.* J. f. Orn. 1863, p. 54) [13].
Psittacus pascha, Wagl. Isis, 1831, p. 525 [14].

Viridis, genis et tectricibus auricularibus lætioribus; fronte, pilei dimidio antico, superciliis, humeris et tibiis cocciueis, macula ante oculos nigricante; tectricibus alarum majoribus subtus luteis, alis et cauda viridibus, subtus fusco-nigricantibus; rostro et pedibus nigricantibus. Long. tota circa 15·0, alæ 10·5, caudæ rectr. med. 0·7, rectr. lat. 4·8, rostri culminis 1·8, tarsi 0·75. (Descr. maris ex Ciudad in Durango. Mus. nostr.)

Hab. NORTH AMERICA, Southern New Mexico, S.W. Texas [11] ?—MEXICO [9][13][14] (*T. Mann* [9]), Tablelands (*Bullock* [1]), Pachico in Chihuahua (*Robinette* [10]), Ciudad in Durango (*Forrer*), Cofre de Perote, Moyoapam, Popocatepetl (*Sumichrast* [6][7]), Jalapa (*de Oca* [3]).

This very distinct species of Parrot was discovered by Bullock on the tablelands of Mexico, and described by Swainson in 1827 as *Macrocercus pachyrhynchus* [1]. Specimens were shortly afterwards sent to Berlin by Deppe, and called *Psittacus strenuus* by Lichtenstein [13], and then *P. pascha* by Wagler [14], the latter name being a substitute for that of Swainson.

Its range seems restricted to the highlands of Mexico; and Sumichrast names Popocatepetl, Mozoapam on the volcano of Orizaba, and the Cofre de Perote as upland localities where it is to be met with [6]. De Oca's collection from Jalapa [3] contained specimens which probably came from the Cofre de Perote. None of the collectors recently employed by us in Mexico met with this bird; but Mr. Forrer secured specimens on the Sierra Madre between Mazatlan and Durango, and Mr. Robinette obtained three examples near Pachico in Chihuahua when he was with the Lumholtz Archæological Expedition of 1890–91[10].

These records of localities are all we have concerning this Parrot; no account of its habits have reached us.

R. pachyrhynchus has been placed amongst the North-American birds on the strength of a specimen said to have been shot on the Rio Grande, Texas. But in the second edition (1895) of the 'Check-list of North-American Birds' (p. 330) it is relegated to the hypothetical list. It has since been again brought forward by Mr. Ridgway as a North-American bird in the second edition (1896) of his 'Manual' (p. 269)[11], Dr. R. W. Shufeldt having reported its presence in Southern New Mexico.

Being an inhabitant of upland pine-forests, it may well occur in such districts across the frontier of Northern Mexico.

CONURUS.

Conurus, Kuhl, Consp. Psitt. p. 4 (1820); Salvad. Cat. Birds Brit. Mus. xx. p. 170.

A characteristic genus of South-American Parrots, numerous in species and individuals. Count Salvadori admits twenty-eight species, to which *C. rubritorquis* must be added, making a total of twenty-nine, which are spread over a wide area, extending from Socorro I. and Southern Mexico to Bolivia and Paraguay.

In our region seven species only are found, and, though having no very marked characters, none of them occur beyond our limits in South America.

As a genus, *Conurus* may be distinguished from *Rhynchopsittacus* by the bill not being compressed, but the sides of the maxilla are rather swollen, the mandible broad and rounded, not flattened in front nor grooved, the culmen of the maxilla being both. The fourth primary is attenuated at the end, and the nostrils fully exposed, but surrounded by small scattered feathers. According to Garrod the ambiens muscle is always present.

1. Conurus finschi.

Conurus finschi, Salv. Ibis, 1871, p. 91, t. 4[1]; Zeledon, An. Mus. Nac. Costa Rica, 1887, p. 124[2]; Salvad. Cat. Birds Brit. Mus. xx. p. 184[3]; Cherrie, Auk, 1892, p. 327[4]; Richmond, Pr. U. S. Nat. Mus. xvi. p. 519[5].

Viridis, fronte et pileo antico coccineis, margine carpali et tectricibus alarum subtus minoribus proximis coccineis, reliquis interioribus luteo-viridibus, tectricibus majoribus subtus oleagineis, extimis paucis pure luteis; remigibus et rectricibus subtus oleagineis; rostro flavido; pedibus carneis. Long. tota circa 11·5, alæ 6·3, caudæ rectr. med. 5·5, rectr. lat. 2·7, rostri culminis 1·2, tarsi 0·6. (Descr. exempl. typ. ex Bugaba, Chiriqui. Mus. nostr.)

Hab. NICARAGUA, R. Escondido (*Richmond*[5]), Rama (*W. B. Richardson*); COSTA RICA, Naranjo de Cartago (*Zeledon*[2]), San José (*Zeledon*[2], *Cherrie*[4]); PANAMA, Bugaba (*Arcé*[1]).

Conurus finschi is the most northern member of a small section of the genus found in the western countries of South America from Bolivia to Colombia, and distinguished by their having a more or less wide scarlet band across the forehead and anterior portion of the crown. The lores being only partially instead of wholly red associates this Parrot with *C. wagleri*, from which it is again to be distinguished by the scarlet lesser wing-coverts of the under surface of the wing.

It was first discovered by Arcé, who sent us three specimens from Bugaba, in the district of Chiriqui [1], and has now been traced to Costa Rica, and even to Eastern Nicaragua, where Mr. Richmond [5] found it to be common on the Rio Escondido, where it was usually to be seen feeding in the large trees standing in the plantations, but at times in small trees bordering the forest. Here he once saw a flock of about twenty-five scattered in low trees that were laden with berries. These birds were tame and allowed him to approach them very closely. Mr. Richardson also met with *C. finschi* in the same district. In Costa Rica Mr. Cherrie says this species is a rare straggler about San José [4].

2. Conurus holochlorus.

Conurus holochlorus, Scl. Ann. & Mag. N. H. 1859, iv. p. 224 [1]; P. Z. S. 1859, p. 368 [2]; 1864, p. 177 [3]; Scl. & Salv. Ibis, 1860, p. 44 [4]; Salv. Ibis, 1871, p. 92 [5]; Cat. Strickl. Coll. p. 465 [6]; Sumichrast, La Nat. v. p. 238 [7]; Nutting, Pr. U. S. Nat. Mus. vi. p. 395 [8]; Salvad. Cat. Birds Brit. Mus. xx. p. 189 [9].

Psittacus guianensis, Licht. Preis-Verz. Mex. Vög. p. 1 (*cf.* J. f. Orn. 1863, p. 54) [10].

Viridis, fere unicolor, subtus paulo pallidior, tectricibus alarum majoribus et margine alari vix cæruleo tinctis: alis et cauda subtus olivescentibus, tectricibus subalaribus majoribus ejusdem coloris, reliquis viridibus; oculorum ambitu carneo; rostro flavido; pedibus carneis. Long. tota circa 12·0, alæ 6·7, caudæ rectr. med. 5·7, rectr. lat. 3·3, rostri culminis 1·15, tarsi 0·65. (Descr. exempl. ex Jalapa, Mexico. Mus. nostr.)

Hab. Mexico (*Deppe*) [10], Rio Camacho in Nuevo Leon (*F. B. Armstrong*), Sierra Madre and Xicotencal in Tamaulipas, Valles in San Luis Potosi (*W. B. Richardson*), Misantla, Santana, Rio Juan Martin, Hacienda Tortugas (*F. Ferrari-Perez*), Jalapa (*de Oca* [2], *C. F. Höge*), Omealca (*Sumichrast* [7]); Guatemala (*Constancia* [6]), El Rincon in San Marcos and Santa Maria de Quezaltenango (*W. B. Richardson*), Dueñas, San Gerónimo (*O. S. & F. D. G.* [4]); Salvador, Volcan de San Miguel (*W. B. Richardson*); Nicaragua, Omotepe (*Nutting* [8], *W. B. Richardson*).

In Count Salvadori's key to the species of *Conurus* this species is placed in a section in which the plumage has normally no red patches of feathers. Now that we know more of *C. rubritorquis* with its red throat, and which is evidently a near ally of *C. holochlorus*, this definition must be modified to include *C. rubritorquis*. If the words "except the throat" were added to the definition the key may still stand. The

only species, besides that mentioned, at all closely allied to the present bird is
C. brevipes.

C. leucophthalmus (Müll.), commonly called *C. pavua* (Bodd.) or *P. guianensis* (Gm.),
has a general resemblance, but may at once be distinguished by its yellow greater
under wing-coverts.

Deppe seems to have been the first collector to send specimens of *C. holochlorus* to
Europe; but his specimens were ascribed to *C. guianensis* [11], and it was not until 1859
that Mr. Sclater separated it under the name it now bears [1].

This Parrot is common in Eastern Mexico from the States of Nuevo Leon and
Tamaulipas southwards through Vera Cruz, but we have no record of it in Western
Mexico, nor even on the Isthmus of Tehuantepec. In Guatemala it is abundant all
over the central plateau and the mountain-slopes towards the Pacific, ranging from an
altitude of 6000 or 7000 feet down to less than 1000 feet above the sea-level. At the
ripening of the crops of maize or Indian corn large flocks assemble and do great
damage by eating the grain before it is gathered. It is said to breed in the ravines
intersecting the mountains between Chimaltenango and Panajachel, and one of them
is called El Barranco de Los Chocoyos from the number of these birds frequenting it—
" Chocoyo " being its familiar name. Southward of Guatemala we trace it to Salvador
and Nicaragua, where, on the island of Omotepe, Mr. Nutting says [8] that the number
of these Parrots to be seen around the lagoons is something almost incredible, and the
air seems fairly to tremble with their cries. He could recall no other species of bird
swarming in such numbers. In Costa Rica we have no tidings of it, its place being
taken by *C. finschi.*

3. Conurus rubritorquis.

Conurus rubritorquis, Scl. P. Z. S. 1886, p. 538, t. 56 [1]; Salv. & Godm. Ibis, 1892, p. 328 [2]; Salvad.
     Ibis, 1893, p. 122 [3].

C. holochloro similis, sed minor, rostro minore; gutture toto plumis coccineis notato. Long. tota circa 11·0,
     alæ 5·7, caudæ rectr. med. 4·8, rectr. lat. 2·5, rostri culminis 1·1, tarsi 0·65. (Descr. exempl. typ. ex
     patria ignota. Mus. Brit.)

Hab. SALVADOR, Volcan de San Miguel (*W. B. Richardson*); NICARAGUA, Matagalpa
     (*W. B. Richardson* [2]).

This *Conurus* was described by Mr. Sclater from a specimen living in the Gardens
of the Zoological Society. It had been obtained from a Liverpool dealer, but from
what part of America was unknown. Mr. Sclater says nothing as to its affinity to the
known species, merely comparing it in size with *C. euops* of Cuba. Count Salvadori
examined the type in 1891 when compiling his catalogue of Psittacidæ, and came to
the conclusion that it was an abnormal individual of *C. holochlorus*, in which an unusual
number of red feathers had been developed on the throat. The following year we

received from our collector Mr. Richardson a number of specimens from Matagalpa, all of which had the red throat, and the fact was noted in 'The Ibis' for that year; Count Salvadori, having examined these birds, then admitted the distinctness of *C. rubritorquis* from *C. holochlorus.*

Besides the Matagalpa specimens, Mr. Richardson has also sent us examples from the Volcan de San Miguel in Salvador, so that the range of this Parrot seems restricted to the highlands of Northern Nicaragua and the adjoining parts of Honduras and Salvador. *C. holochlorus* also occurs on the Volcan de San Miguel and as far south as the island of Omotepe in the Lake of Nicaragua. In Eastern Nicaragua the only *Conurus* of this group is *C. finschi.*

The type was probably brought from the interior of Nicaragua, and shipped for Liverpool at the port of Greytown.

4. Conurus brevipes.

Conurus holochlorus, var. *brevipes,* Baird, Ann. Lyc. N. Y. x. p. 54 [1]; Grayson, Pr. Bost. Soc. N. H. xiv. p. 298 [2]; Lawr. Mem. Bost. Soc. N. H. ii. p. 295 [3].

Conurus brevipes, Salvad. Cat. Birds Brit. Mus. xx. p. 191 [4].

C. holochloro similis, sed pedibus debilioribus, digito externo breviore, colore omnino subtus saturatiore viridi. Long. tota circa 12·5, alæ 6·6, caudæ rectr. med. 6·0, rectr. lat. 3·7, rostri culminis 1·3, tarsi 0·7. (Descr. exempl. ex Socorro I. Smiths. Inst. no. 55,913. Mus. nostr.)

Hab. MEXICO, Socorro I. (*Grayson* [2] [3]).

This bird is very closely allied to *C. holochlorus,* so much so that it has usually been treated as a " variety " of that species. But its isolated island home and the constancy of the slight characters which distinguish it make its recognition as a species desirable. We therefore follow Count Salvadori in so treating it.

The late Col. Grayson discovered this Parrot when he visited the island of Socorro in May 1867, and his is the only account of it as yet published. His notes concerning it are as follows:—" This Parrakeet is quite abundant, and evidently belongs to this locality (Socorro I.), which it never leaves; they are to be met with in flocks or in pairs. In the mornings they left the cove in which we were encamped for the higher regions of the interior to feed, returning again in the evening to roost. This cove, in which the trees are larger and the shade more dense than in other parts of the island, seems to be their favourite resort. I saw them at times walking about on the ground beneath these trees, apparently picking up clay or gravel; they were remarkably tame, exhibiting no fear in our presence. Three cages were soon filled with them, which were caught by hand, and their constant whistling for their mates brought many of them into camp, perching upon the cages and elsewhere; they feed upon a hard nut which they find in the mountain-gorges, but on account of the inaccessible localities where this fruit grew I was unable to discover it. The powerful jaws of this Parrakeet would indicate the fruit to be very hard."

In his further account of this bird, published in Lawrence's 'Birds of North-western Mexico,' Grayson speaks of its great tameness and his reluctance to kill specimens for his collection[3].

The habits of *C. brevipes* thus differ greatly from those of *C. holochlorus*.

5. Conurus aztec.

Conurus astec, Souancé, Rev. et Mag. Zool. 1857, p. 97 [1]; Scl. P. Z. S. 1859, p. 388 [2]; Moore, P. Z. S. 1859, p. 59 [3]; Scl. & Salv. Ibis, 1859, p. 137 [4]; P. Z. S. 1867, p. 280 [5]; 1870, p. 837 [6]; Taylor, Ibis, 1860, p. 120 [7]; Boucard, P. Z. S. 1878, p. 46 [8]; Sumichrast, La Nat. v. p. 238 [9]; Ferrari-Perez, Pr. U. S. Nat. Mus. ix. p. 163 [10]; Salv. & Godm. Ibis, 1889, p. 373 [11]; 1890, p. 88 [12].

Conurus aztec, Souancé, Icon. Perr. t. 12. f. 2 [13]; Lawr. Ann. Lyc. N. Y. viii. p. 185 [14]; ix. p. 207 [15]; Bull. U. S. Nat. Mus. no. 4, p. 35 [16]; Salv. Ibis, 1871, p. 93 [17]; Boucard, P. Z. S. 1883, p. 455 [18]; Nutting, Pr. U. S. Nat. Mus. vi. p. 407 [19]; Salv. & Godm. Ibis, 1889, p. 291 [20]; Stone & Baker, Pr. Ac. Phil. 1890, p. 205 [21]; Salvad. Cat. Birds Brit. Mus. xx. p. 192 [22]; Richmond, Pr. U. S. Nat. Mus. xvi. p. 519 [23].

Psittacus pertinax, juv., Licht. Preis-Verz. Mex. Vög. p. 1 (*cf.* J. f. Orn. 1863, p. 54) [24].

Supra viridis, fronte anguste fusca, cera inter et circum nares plumulis aurantiacis semivestita; capitis lateribus et genis dorso concoloribus: subtus fusco-viridis, abdomine flavescentiore, plumarum rhachidibus omnibus nigricantibus; alis cærulescentibus, extrorsum viridibus et nigricante terminatis, subtus fuscis, tectricibus majoribus concoloribus, reliquis viridibus; rostro corneo, apice pallido; pedibus nigricantibus. Long. tota circa 9·5, alæ 5·2, caudæ rectr. med. 4·6, rectr. lat. 2·4, rostri culminis 0·8, tarsi 0·5. (Descr. exempl. ex Yucatan. Mus. nostr.)

Hab. MEXICO [1] (*Deppe* [24]), Tampico (*W. B. Richardson*), Vera Cruz (*Boucard*), Misantla (*F. D. G., Ferrari-Perez, M. Trujillo*), Vega del Casadero, La Antigua, Sochiapa, Playa Vicente (*Boucard* [2], *M. Trujillo*), Jalapa, San Lorenzo near Cordova, Plan del Rio [10] (*Ferrari-Perez*), Omealca, Cosamaloapam (*Sumichrast* [9]), Atoyac, Teapa (*Mrs. H. H. Smith*), N. Yucatan, Citilpech, Tekanto, Ticul, Labna (*Stone & Baker* [21]), Merida (*Schott* [15]), Izamal [18], Holbox I. [11] (*G. F. Gaumer*), Guichicovi (*Sumichrast* [9] [16]); BRITISH HONDURAS, Belize river (*Leyland* [3] [4]), Orange Walk, Belize (*G. F. Gaumer*); GUATEMALA, Peten, Cahabon (*O. S. & F. D. G.* [17]); HONDURAS, Omoa (*Leyland* [3]), San Pedro (*G. M. Whitely* [6]), Comayagua (*G. C. Taylor* [7]); NICARAGUA, La Libertad (*W. B. Richardson*), Los Sabalos (*Nutting* [19]), Blewfields (*Wickham* [5]), R. Escondido (*Richmond* [23]), Greytown (*Holland* [14]); COSTA RICA (*Carmiol*), San Carlos (*Boucard* [8]).

The wings of the species of the section of *Conurus* to which *C. aztec* belongs are partly blue, the primary-coverts and the quills being more or less tinted with blue. In having no wide orange-red band across the forehead it can be distinguished at once from *C. canicularis*, and in the absence of yellow about the eye from *C. ocularis*. The most nearly allied species is *C. nanus* of Jamaica, but may be recognized by the throat and breast being olive tinged with brown instead of dusky brown, and in the small orange feathers between the nostrils being always present instead of sometimes absent.

The range of *C. aztec* extends over the whole of the hotter parts of the State of Vera Cruz from Tampico southwards, and thence to the State of Tabasco and Yucatan, and some of the islands off the north-east coast. It is found also in British Honduras and in Eastern Guatemala, where we met with it near Peten and also near Cahabon. It is, however, by no means so common in Guatemala as in Eastern Mexico. Passing south it occurs in Honduras at San Pedro and Comayagua, being not uncommon, according to Taylor, at the latter place[7]. In Eastern Nicaragua it is abundant, occurring, according to Mr. Richmond[23], on the Rio Escondido in large flocks, and in this district nearly every collector has found it. Mr. Nutting secured three specimens at Los Sabalos[19], and noted that the iris was yellow, and the cere and orbital region white.

The only authority we have for its occurrence in Costa Rica is a specimen sent us from that country by Carmiol, but without precise locality; but M. Boucard shot a specimen out of a large flock that was feeding on fruits and seeds in the forest at San Carlos in February[8].

6. Conurus ocularis.

Conurus pertinax ?, Lawr. Ann. Lyc. N. Y. vii. p. 333[1].
Conurus chrysogenys, Lawr. Ann. Lyc. N. Y. viii. p. 11[2].
Conurus ocularis, Scl. & Salv. P. Z. S. 1864, p. 367[3]; Salv. P. Z. S. 1870, p. 214[4]; Ibis, 1871, p. 93[5]; Salvad. Cat. Birds Brit. Mus. xx. p. 197[6].

Viridis, pileo antico vix cæruleo tincto, fronte stricte fusca, area oculorum aurantiaca, parte infra oculos latiore; capitis lateribus, genis, gutture et pectore toto viridi-fuscis, abdomine viridi vix aurantiaco tincto : alis subtus sicut in *C. aztec*; rostro corneo, apice pallido; pedibus fuscis. Long. tota circa 9·0, alæ 5·5, caudæ rectr. med. 4·4, rectr. lat. 2·6, rostri culminis 0·8, tarsi 0·55. (Descr. maris exempl. typ. ex Panama. Mus. nostr.)

Hab. PANAMA, Calobre (*Arcé*[4]), Lion Hill (*M'Leannan*[1][2][3]).

Conurus ocularis is very closely allied to *C. æruginosus* of Venezuela and Guiana, but has the green colour of the crown scarcely tinged with blue, and the orange ring round the eye wider below than above, and the abdomen nearly destitute of the orange patch in the middle. These differences are very slight, but seem possessed by the birds of Panama alone, and thus we were led to separate them by a distinct name in 1864, and this course has been endorsed by Count Salvadori.

Our first specimens were sent us by M'Leannan from his station on the Panama Railway[3], others subsequently reached us from other parts of the State of Panama[4]; but the bird does not appear to extend far to the westward, and is apparently absent in Chiriqui and in Costa Rica.

7. Conurus canicularis.

The red-and-blue-headed Parrakeet, Edw. Birds, iv. p. 176, t. 176 [1].

Psittacus canicularis, Linn. Syst. Nat. i. p. 142 [2].

Conurus canicularis, Finsch, Papag. i. p. 503 [3]; Salv. Ibis, 1871, p. 88, note [4]; Salvad. Cat. Birds Brit. Mus. xx. p. 201 [5].

Psittacus petzi, Leibl. in Mus. Würz. fide Wagl. Mon. Psitt. p. 650 [6].

Conurus petzi, Gray, Souancé, Icon. Perr. t. 9 [7]; Scl. P. Z. S. 1857, p. 230 [8]; Taylor, Ibis, 1860, p. 120 [9]; Scl. & Salv. Ibis, 1860, p. 401 [10]; Lawr. Ann. Lyc. N. Y. ix. p. 131 [11]; Mem. Bost. Soc. N. H. ii. p. 296 [12]; Bull. U. S. Nat. Mus. no. 4, p. 36 [13]; Frantz. J. f. Orn. 1869, p. 365 [14]; Salv. Ibis, 1871, p. 92 [15]; P. Z. S. 1883, p. 426 [16]; Sumichrast, La Nat. v. p. 238 [17]; Zeledon, An. Mus. Nac. Costa Rica, 1887, p. 124 [18]; Cherrie, Auk, 1892, p. 327 [19]; Jouy, Pr. U. S. Nat. Mus. xvi. p. 786 [20].

Eupsittaca petzii, Cab. J. f. O. 1862, p. 335 [21].

Psittacus (Aratinga) eburneirostris, Less. Rev. Zool. 1842, p. 135 [22].

Viridis, fronte late rubro-aurantiaca, pileo postico et loris cæruleis: subtus a mento usque ad pectus imum olivaceus, abdomine pallide viridi; alis cæruleis, extrorsum viridibus et nigro terminatis, subtus griseo-fuscis, tectricibus majoribus concoloribus, reliquis viridibus; mandibulæ basi plumbea, dimidio distali albido. Long. tota circa 9·5, alæ 5·5, caudæ rectr. med. 4·5, rectr. lat. 2·8, rostri culminis 0·85, tarsi 0·5. (Descr. maris ex Mazatlan, Mexico. Mus. nostr.)

Hab. MEXICO, Mazatlan (*Grayson* [12], *Bischoff* [12], *Forrer*), Santiago and San Blas in Tepic (*W. B. Richardson*), Plains of Colima (*Xantus* [12], *W. B. Richardson*), Rio de Coahuyana, Manzanilla Bay (*Xantus* [12]), Manzanilla, Beltran, Hacienda de San Marcos (*W. Lloyd*), Barranca de Beltran (*Jouy* [20]), Acapulco [8] (*A. H. Markham* [16], *Mrs. H. H. Smith*), Tierra Colorada, Dos Arroyos (*Mrs. H. H. Smith*), Putla (*Rébouch*), Cacoprieto, Juchitan [13], Chihuitan [13], Santa Efigenia [13], Tapanatepec (*Sumichrast* [17]), Tonala (*Sumichrast* [13] [17], *W. B. Richardson*); GUATEMALA, Retalhuleu (*W. B. Richardson*), Rio Motagua (*O. S. & F. D. G.* [10] [15]); SALVADOR, La Libertad (*W. B. Richardson*); HONDURAS, Pacific slope (*Taylor* [9]); NICARAGUA (*Mus. Brit.*); COSTA RICA (*v. Frantzius* [14]), San José (*Carmiol* [11], *Zeledon* [18], *Cherrie* [19]), Sarchi (*Carmiol* [11]), Alajuela, Liberia (*Zeledon* [18]), San Juan (*v. Frantzius* [14]).

Conurus petzi is the name by which this Parrot is more commonly known, but Count Salvadori has shown that it must be referred to Edwards's Red-and-Blue-headed Parrakeet, upon which Linnæus's *Psittacus canicularis* was mainly founded [5].

It has only one near ally, and that is *C. aureus,* a common bird over a wide area in South America. Both have a wide orange patch on the forehead, extending over nearly the anterior half of the crown. *C. canicularis* has the inner webs of the quills blackish instead of olive, the forehead redder and more restricted, and no yellow surrounding the eyes. But this last character is sometimes absent in specimens, probably young, of *C. aureus.*

Conurus canicularis is a very common species in Western Mexico, where it is resident according to Grayson [12], and Jouy [20] found it in small flocks in the Barranca de Beltran in Southern Jalisco in March. It is everywhere abundant on the Isthmus of Tehuantepec, living in woods, on plains, and in the neighbourhood of inhabited places. Passing southwards into Guatemala it occurs in the coast-lands bordering the Pacific at Retalhuleu; but the only place we ever saw it on the eastern side of the cordillera was the neighbourhood of some hot springs on the roadside between the Rio Motagua and Chuacus in Vera Paz. Here we never failed when passing to see a small flock of these birds in the trees about the springs, where they kept company with a flock of *Chrysotis albifrons*. In Salvador, *C. canicularis* has been found at La Libertad on the coast, and still keeping to the Pacific side of the mountains in Honduras, where Taylor says it is abundant [9]. There is a specimen in the British Museum said to have come from Nicaragua, but we have no skins from the collectors who have recently worked in that country. It is recorded from Costa Rica, and this is the extremity of its range in that direction [11] [14].

PYRRHURA.

Pyrrhura, Bonaparte, Naumannia, 1856, p. 383; Salvadori, Cat. Birds Brit. Mus. xx. p. 211.

Pyrrhura is a purely Neotropical genus, containing nineteen species, only one of which is found within our limits, the rest being distributed over nearly the whole of South America as far south as the northern provinces of Argentina. The single Central-American species, *P. hoffmanni*, is only found in Costa Rica and the adjoining part of the State of Panama.

As a genus, *Pyrrhura* has a general resemblance to *Conurus*, so far as its shape is concerned, but differs much in coloration and in several points of structure. The naked cere has no small isolated feathers surrounding the nostril as in many *Conuri*; the fourth primary is not attenuated at the end; the tail beneath is red or brownish red. and in many species on the upperside also. The ambiens muscle, according to Garrod, is absent, being present in *Conurus*, and on this fact he laid much stress when constructing his classification of Parrots.

1. **Pyrrhura hoffmanni.**

Conurus hoffmanni, Cab. Sitz.-Ber. der Ges. naturf. Freunde zu Berlin, 13 Nov. 1861 [1]; Lawr. Ann. Lyc. N. Y. ix. p. 131 [2]; Scl. & Salv. Ex. Orn. p. 161, t. 81 [3]; Frantz. J. f. Orn. 1869, p. 365 [4]; Salv. P. Z. S. 1870, p. 214 [5]; Ibis, 1871, p. 93 [6]; Boucard, P. Z. S. 1878, p. 46 [7]; Zeledon, An. Mus. Nac. Costa Rica, 1887, p. 124 [8].

Pyrrhura hoffmanni, Cab. J. f. Orn. 1862, p. 335 [9]; Salvad. Cat. Birds Brit. Mus. xx. p. 230 [10].

Viridis, pilei plumis flavido terminatis, regione oculari coccinea, mento calvo plumulis sparsis aurantiacis (postice rubidis) notato; primariis externis ad basin cærulescentibus, alula spuria, tectricibus majoribus et primariis internis ad basin flavis; primariis externis subtus et tectricibus majoribus griseo-fuscis, olivaceo tinctis, remigibus reliquis ad basin flavis, tectricibus minoribus viridibus; cauda supra rufo-olivacea, ad basin viridescentiore, rhachidibus basi albis, subtus brunneo-rufa; rostro eburneo-albo; pedibus fuscis. Long. tota circa 9·0, alæ 5·2, caudæ rectr. med. 4·3, rectr. lat. 2·2, rostri culminis 0·8, tarsi 0·5. (Descr. maris ex Angostura, Costa Rica. Mus. nostr.)

Hab. Costa Rica [8], Aguas Calientes (*Hoffmann* [1] [9], *Boucard* [7]), Candelaria Mts. (*v. Frantzius* [4], *Boucard* [9]), Navarro (*Cooper* [12]), Dota Mts., Angostura, Frailes (*Carmiol* [2]); Panama, Volcan de Chiriqui, Veraguas (*Arcé* [5]).

Pyrrhura hoffmanni belongs to a small section of the genus which, having no brown patch of feathers on the lower back, has no distinct bars on the underside but red ear-coverts; the tail above is olive, but beneath reddish brown, and the base of the quills yellow. These characters taken together distinguish it from *P. hæmatotis* and *P. rhodocephala*, which are, perhaps, its nearest allies.

This Parrot was discovered by Dr. Hoffmann, and was described by Dr. Cabanis in 1861 [1], when the collections sent by the former to Berlin first revealed the richness of the ornithological fauna of Costa Rica. The specimens were obtained at Aguas Calientes, near Cartago, where M. Boucard also found the species, as well as at the foot of the Candelaria Mountains [7]. He says that the conspicuous colour of the wings, alluding no doubt to the yellow bases of the primaries, renders a flock of these birds a beautiful object when flying.

In the State of Panama *P. hoffmanni* is not uncommon on the Volcan de Chiriqui, and it is found further to the eastward, but is not known to occur on the Isthmus or any point south of it.

BOLBORHYNCHUS.

Bolborhynchus, Bonaparte, Compt. Rend. xliv. p. 596 (1857); Salvadori, Cat. Birds Brit. Mus. xx. p. 233.

In *Bolborhynchus* and in the two following wedge-shaped tailed Parrots the orbital ring, according to Count Salvadori, is incomplete, the opposite being the case in the genera just discussed. *Bolborhynchus* itself may be distinguished from *Brotogerys* by its more swollen bill, the maxilla being more rounded; the cere is tumid, with a few short inconspicuous isolated bristles, the nostrils being fully exposed. The tail is of moderate length, bluntly cuneate, each rectrix acute. The tomia of the maxilla undulating but scarcely toothed. There is a tufted oil-gland and complete furcula (Salvadori); but no difference in the plumage of the sexes.

Seven species are known of the genus. These are distributed over nearly the whole of Tropical America from Southern Mexico to Argentina. Only one species, and that a well-marked one, occurs within our limits. This is probably peculiar to the mountainous parts, but it is said to occur also in Venezuela.

1. Bolborhynchus lineolatus.

Psittacula lineola, Cassin, Pr. Ac. Phil. vi. p. 372 [1]; Journ. Ac. Phil. iii. p. 154, t. 14. f. 1 [2].
Conurus lineola, Scl. P. Z. S. 1864, p. 177 [3].
Myiopsitta lineola, Zeledon, An. Mus. Nac. Costa Rica, 1887, p. 124 [4].
Psittacula lineolata, Scl. P. Z. S. 1856, p. 306 [5].

73*

Conurus lineolatus, Scl. & Salv. Ibis, 1859, p. 137[6]; 1862, p. 96[7]; Salv. Ibis, 1869, p. 319[8].

Bolborhynchus lineolatus, Finsch, Papag. ii. p. 130[9]; Salv. Ibis, 1871, p. 94[10]; Salvad. Cat. Birds Brit. Mus. xx. p. 239[11].

Myiopsitta catharina, Bp. Compt. Rend. xliv. p. 538[12].

Supra viridis, fronte et loris paulo cærulescentioribus, dorso toto, cervicis lateribus, hypochondriis et tectricibus alarum plumis omnibus nigro terminatis: subtus medialiter viridis immaculatus, tectricibus subcaudalibus nigro punctatis, remigibus nigris extrorsum viridi limbatis, subalaribus prasinis; rostro et pedibus flavis. Long. tota circa 6·5, alæ 4·1, caudæ 2·3, rostri culminis 0·6, tarsi 0·45. (Descr. exempl. ex Volcan de Fuego, Guatemala.   Mus. nostr.)

Hab. Mexico[12] (*White*[3]), Cordova (*Sallé*[5]), Coatepec (*Ferrari-Perez*), Cozumel I. (*Cabot*[6])?; Guatemala, Volcan de Fuego (*O. S. & F. D. G.*[7][10]), Chiquimula (*Mus. Soc. Econ. de Guatemala*); Costa Rica, Angostura (*Carmiol*[8]), Naranjo de Cartago (*Zeledon*[4]); Panama, Volcan de Chiriqui (*Arcé*).—Venezuela[12]?

This pretty little Parrot differs from all other members of the genus *Bolborhynchus* in having the back and flanks conspicuously banded with black.   It was first described by Cassin from Mexican specimens in 1853, in the 'Proceedings of the Academy of Philadelphia'[1], and figured two years afterwards in the 'Journal' of the same Society[2]. Its range in Mexico seems restricted to the mountains of Vera Cruz, where Sallé obtained a specimen near Cordova[5], and Señor Ferrari-Perez others in August and September at Coatepec, near Jalapa.   The origin of a specimen in Mr. White's collection[3] cannot be given with certainty, as it may have been taken to Mexico from a distance.   It has been stated that Dr. Cabot had a specimen in his collection from the island of Cozumel[6], but no trace of it existed when Salvin examined this collection in 1874.

In Guatemala, *B. lineolatus* is by no means common, and but few specimens occurred in the native-made collections of Vera Paz.   We once came across a small flock in November 1861, in a tree overhanging the road which winds up the mountain-side above the rancheria of Calderas on the northern slope of the Volcan de Fuego, and secured several specimens before the rest took fright and flew away.   In 1873 there was a mounted bird of this species in the museum of the Sociedad Economica de Guatemala, labelled as having been obtained at Chiquimula, a town to the eastward of the city, in a valley draining into that of the Motagua river.

In Costa Rica this Parrot has been reported from several places, and in the adjoining part of the State of Panama it seems to be not uncommon on the slopes of the Volcan de Chiriqui.

PSITTACULA.

Psittacula, Illiger, Prodr. p. 200 (1811); Salvadori, Cat. Birds Brit. Mus. xx. p. 240.

This genus contains the smallest Parrots of the American continent.   As in *Bolborhynchus,* the bill is rather swollen, the cere bare with a few isolated bristles, the nostrils being fully exposed; the tomia of the maxilla has a very distinct tooth; the tail is short and but slightly cuneate, the rectrices pointed ; there is a tufted oil-gland, but no furcula (Salvadori).

The ten or twelve species composing the genus are distributed over nearly the whole of continental Tropical America from Western Mexico to Brazil and Bolivia. Only one species is found within our region, and this is peculiar to the Tres Marias Islands off the coast of Western Mexico, and the mainland opposite from Sonora to Manzanilla. The next species in point of distance is found in Colombia, leaving a wide hiatus in the range of the genus unoccupied by any species of *Psittacula*.

1. Psittacula cyanopygia.

Psittacula cyanopygia, Souancé, Rev. et Mag. Zool. 1856, p. 157[1]; Icon. Perr. t. 42 (1857)[2]; Finsch, Abh. nat. Ver. Bremen, 1870, p. 353[3]; Grayson, Pr. Bost. Soc. N. H. xiv. p. 271[4]; Ridgw. Pr. U. S. Nat. Mus. x. p. 540[5]; Salvad. Cat. Birds Brit. Mus. xx. p. 249[6].

Psittacula cyanopyga, Salv. Ibis, 1871, p. 100[7]; Lawr. Mem. Bost. Soc. N. H. ii. p. 297[8]; Salv. & Godm. Ibis, 1889, p. 242[9].

Psittacula insularis, Ridgw. Pr. U. S. Nat. Mus. x. p. 541[10].

Psittacula cyanopyga pallida, Brewster, Auk, vi. p. 85[11].

Pallide viridis, fronte, capitis lateribus et corpore subtus dilutioribus ; dorso postico, uropygio, tectricibus subalaribus et axillaribus pallide cœruleis; tectricibus remigum, secundariis et remigibus internis ad basin saturatiore cœruleis, margine alarum viridi : alis subtus fuscis viridi-cœruleo lavatis, tectricibus supra-caudalibus et cauda viridibus ; rostro pallide corneo, ad basin fusco ; pedibus fusco-carnescentibus. Long. tota circa 5·0, alæ 3 4, caudæ 1·6, rostri culminis 0·6.

♀ mari similis, sed omnino viridis, colore cœruleo omnino absente. (Descr. maris et feminæ ex Mazatlan, Mexico. Mus. nostr.)

Hab. MEXICO, Alamos (*Frazar*[11]), Sierra de Alamos (*Lloyd*), Mazatlan (*Grayson*[3][4][8], *Bischoff*[5]), Presidio de Mazatlan (*Forrer*), Tres Marias Is. (*Grayson*[4][10], *Forrer*), Manzanilla Bay (*Xantus*[8]), Jalisco (*U. S. Nat. Mus.*).

The types of this species, from the Massena collection, are in the British Museum[6]. They are marked as from Bolivia, but no doubt wrongly. They are quite as dark as the birds from the Tres Marias Islands which Mr. Ridgway separated as *P insularis*[10]. Mr. Brewster subsequently described a pale form from Sonora as *P. cyanopygia pallida*[11]. Col. Grayson noticed that the island bird differed somewhat from that of the mainland. Lawrence placed them together in 1874[8], but Mr. Ridgway separated them in 1889[10]. Count Salvadori again, in 1891, united all three forms under the oldest title[6], and we follow him in so doing. The island birds are a little darker, but the difference is very slight. Two Sonora specimens from the same place as Mr. Brewster's types of *P. c. pallida* are in rather abraded plumage, but are so close to the typical birds that we see no grounds for separating them. It may be remarked that the materials for a satisfactory comparison of the supposed races of this Parrot do not exist in any one museum, so that there may be more difference between them than appears from the ten specimens before us. The only fully adult male specimen we have seen is the type of that sex.

The range of *P. cyanopygia* is restricted to the Tres Marias Islands and Western Mexico, where it is found from the Sierra de Alamos in Sonora to Manzanilla Bay [8] in the State of Colima. About Mazatlan and in the islands Grayson says [3] it is very abundant and resident, forming flocks of considerable size. In the islands, birds were very tame, but too delicate to undergo confinement for any length of time. Their notes are rather feeble, and they never learnt to imitate words.

BROTOGERYS.

Brotogeris, Vigors, Zool. Journ. ii. p. 400 (1825).
Brotogerys, Agass. Nomencl. Zool. Ind. Univ. p. 54; Salvadori, Cat. Birds Brit. Mus. xx. p. 253.

Brotogerys differs in several respects from the previous genera. The bill is rather compressed; the tomia of the maxilla undulating, but not toothed; the cere large and tumid, completely naked, with the nostrils fully exposed. There is no tufted oil-gland.

Of the eleven known species of the genus only one is found in our region, extending from the Isthmus of Tehuantepec through the western lowlands of Central America into Colombia. The other species are spread through continental Tropical America as far south as Brazil and Bolivia.

1. Brotogerys jugularis.

Petite Perruche à gorge jaune d'Amérique, Daub. Pl. Enl. 190. f. 1 [1].
Psittacus jugularis, Müller, Syst. Nat. Suppl. p. 80 [2]; Cassin, Pr. Ac. Phil. 1864, p. 240 [3].
Brotogerys jugularis, Salvad. Cat. Birds Brit. Mus. xx. p. 259 [4].
Psittacus tovi, Gm. Syst. Nat. i. p. 351 [5].
Psittovius tovi, Scl. & Salv. Ibis, 1860, p. 44 [6]; Taylor, Ibis, 1860, p. 121 [7]; Lawr. Ann. Lyc. N. Y. vii. p. 299 [8].
Brotogerys tovi, Finsch, Papag. ii. p. 99 [9]; Lawr. Ann. Lyc. N. Y. ix. p. 131 [10]; Bull. U. S. Nat. Mus. no. 4, p. 36 [11]; Frantz. J. f. Orn. 1869, p. 364 [12]; Salv. P. Z. S. 1870, p. 214 [13]; Ibis, 1871, p. 93 [14]; Cat. Strickl. Coll. p. 470 [15]; Wyatt, Ibis, 1871, p. 381 [16]; Boucard, P. Z. S. 1878, p. 46 [17]; Sumichrast, La Nat. v. p. 238 [18]; Nutting, Pr. U. S. Nat. Mus. v. p. 402 [19]; vi. pp. 377 [20], 395 [21]; Zeledon, An. Mus. Nac. Costa Rica, 1887, p. 124 [22]; Richmond, Pr. U. S. Nat. Mus. xvi. p. 519 [23]; Underwood, Ibis, 1896, p. 445 [24].
Psittovius subcæruleus, Lawr. Ann. Lyc. N. Y. vii. p. 475 [25].
Brotogerys subcæruleus, Finsch, Papag. ii. p. 97, t. 2 [26].

Viridis, interscapulio olcagineo tincto, tectricibus alarum minoribus oleagineo-brunneis, tectricibus remigum ad apicem cæruleis: subtus pallidior et flavescentior, mento aurantiaco-rubro, abdomine cæruleo sensim lavato, tectricibus subalaribus minoribus luteis, majoribus et remigibus subtus saturate viridibus; rostro et pedibus carneis. Long. tota circa 6·5, alæ 4·2, caudæ 2·65, rostri culminis 0·8, tarsi 0·45. (Descr. maris ex Mina de Chorcha, Panama. Mus. nostr.)
♀ mari similis.

Hab. MEXICO, Santa Efigenia, Tonala, Tapana [11], Cacoprieto (*Sumichrast* [18]); GUATEMALA [6], La Concepcion, Chiapam (*O. S. & F. D. G.* [14]), Retalhuleu (*W. B. Richardson*); SALVADOR, La Libertad (*W. B. Richardson*); HONDURAS, Tigre Island

(*Taylor* [7]) ; NICARAGUA, Omotepe I.[21], San Juan del Sur [20] (*Nutting*), San Carlos (*Richmond* [23]), Chinandega, San Emilio (*W. B. Richardson*) ; COSTA RICA, Nicoya (*v. Frantzius* [12]), Puntarenas, San Mateo (*Zeledon* [22]), La Palma (*Nutting* [18]), Bebedero (*Arcé* [14], *Underwood* [24]), Miravalles (*Underwood* [24]), San Carlos (*Boucard* [17]) ; PANAMA, Volcan de Chiriqui [13], Mina de Chorcha, Bugaba [13], Calovevora (*Arcé*), Lion Hill (*M'Leannan* [8] [25]), Paraiso Station (*Hughes*).— COLOMBIA [16].

Brotogerys jugularis belongs to the short-tailed section of the genus, and its distinguishing features, taken as a whole together, are the absence of a yellow patch on the sinciput, its rather long bill, its green cheeks, and orange chin. The primary-coverts are blue, not yellow, the upper wing-coverts are tinged with brown, and the under wing-coverts yellow.

Its range seems to be exclusively restricted to the western tropical parts of Central America from the Isthmus of Tehuantepec, where it is common, through the coast-region of Guatemala, Salvador, Honduras, Nicaragua (abundant at San Juan del Sur and on the island of Omotepe), and Costa Rica, bordering the Pacific Ocean. Passing along the Isthmus of Panama it occurs in Northern Colombia in the Cauca Valley, and is found in the trade collections sent from Bogota, the skins being probably obtained from the valley of the Magdalena.

Of the habits of this species there seems little to record. We found it in the lowlands of the Pacific coast, associating in flocks, and having the usual habits of the smaller members of the family.

Lawrence's *Psittovius subcœruleus* [25] was based upon a bluish individual of this species shot by M'Leannan from a flock of the ordinary form. Though recognized as a distinct species by Dr. Finsch, and figured in his work [26], there can be no doubt the type is only an abnormally-coloured specimen of *B. jugularis*. No similar specimens have been since seen [14].

CHRYSOTIS.

Psittacus (*Amazona*), Lesson, Traité d'Orn. p. 189 (1831).
Chrysotis, Swainson, Classif. Birds, ii. p. 300 (1837) ; Salvadori, Cat. Birds Brit. Mus. xx. p. 268.
Amazona, Lesson, Descr. Mamm. et Ois. p. 194 (1847) ; Ridgway, Man. N. Am. Birds, p. 587.

The genus *Chrysotis* is the largest of the order in South America, containing, according to Count Salvadori, forty-two species. Many of these species are numerous in individuals, so that this group of Parrots is a marked feature in the bird-fauna of the hotter parts of Central and South America, and is represented by several very striking forms in some of the West-Indian Islands. The northern limit of the range of *Chrysotis* reaches to that of the Neotropical region in Northern Mexico, and in the south it extends to South Brazil, Argentina, Paraguay, and Bolivia.

Twelve species are found in our region, of which no less than eight occur in Mexico, no other of the divisions of the country possessing more than four.

The species of *Chrysotis* found within our limits may readily be divided into two groups by the presence or absence of a scarlet speculum on the wing. Ten species have this speculum, but it is wanting in the two small species, *C. albifrons* and *C. albilora*.

We continue to use the name *Chrysotis* for these Parrots, and in doing so we have the high authority of Count Salvadori. Mr. Ridgway, in employing *Amazona* of Lesson in a generic sense, gives it a value not originally intended by its author, and not used by him as a full genus title until ten years after *Chrysotis* had been introduced.

As is the case in *Pionus*, *Chrysotis* has no tufted oil-gland, which is present in *Pionopsittacus*, the only other genus of Pioninæ found in our region. Its members may be distinguished from those of *Pionus* by their longer, wider tails and by the under tail-coverts being always green.

a. *Species majores, speculo alari coccineo ornati.*

1. Chrysotis guatemalæ.

Psittacus, sp. n. ex Guatemala, Hartl. Verz. Brem. Samml. p. 87 [1].

Chrysotis, sp. ?, Moore, P. Z. S. 1859, p. 59 [2]; Scl. & Salv. Ibis, 1859, p. 138 [3].

Chrysotis guatemalæ, Hartl. Mus. Brem.; Scl. & Salv. Ibis, 1860, p. 44 [4]; P. Z. S. 1870, p. 837 [5]; Scl. P. Z. S. 1860, p. 253 [6]; Finsch, Papag. ii. p. 562, t. 4 [7]; Salv. Ibis, 1871, p. 98 (partim) [8]; Lawr. Ibis, 1871, p. 250 [9]; Salvad. Cat. Birds Brit. Mus. xx. p. 279 [10].

Chrysotis farinosa, Sumichrast, La Nat. v. p. 238 [11].

Viridis, pileo toto cæruleo, plumis singulis partis posticæ et cervicis nigro terminatis, genis et corpore subtus viridibus vix flavescente tinctis; speculo alari coccineo, remige primo nigro, reliquis in pogonio externo ad basin saturate viridibus, secundariis cyaneo terminatis: alis subtus saturate viridibus, remigibus extus nigris; cauda viridi, fascia lata terminali pallide viridi-flava; rostro corneo; pedibus plumbeis. Long. tota circa 15·0, alæ 9·5, caudæ 5·5, rostri culminis 1·8, tarsi 1·1. (Descr. exempl. ex R. de la Pasion, Guatemala. Mus. nostr.)

♀ mari similis.

Hab. MEXICO [1] [9], Orizaba (*Sallé* [6]), Potrero near Cordova, Chimalapa (*Sumichrast* [11]); GUATEMALA (*Mus. Bremen* [1]), R. de la Pasion, Choctum (*O. S. & F. D. G.*); HONDURAS, Omoa (*Leyland* [2] [3] [4]), San Pedro (*G. M. Whitely* [4]).

A supposed young bird in Mr. Sclater's collection obtained by Leyland at Omoa [2], but which Count Salvadori considers adult, was the first indication we had of the existence of this species [2]. On a second example being seen by Mr. Sclater in the Bremen Museum with Dr. Hartlaub's name *C. guatemalæ* attached to it [1], the bird was described under that title in 1860 [3].

The species belongs to a section of large green Parrots of which *C. farinosa* is the oldest known form; from this it differs in having the metacarpal edge of the wing green instead of red. The next species (*C. virenticeps*) is its nearest ally, and the two were long considered the same. They differ in the colour of the head, that of *C. guatemalæ* being tinted blue, that of *C. virenticeps* (as its name implies) green.

C. guatemalæ does not seem to be a common bird in Mexico, and we have only seen a few specimens from the State of Vera Cruz. Sumichrast, however, states that it occurs near Chimalapa, which we suppose to be the village of that name on the Isthmus of Tehuantepec [10]. In Guatemala we found it to be very local, but common in the lowland forests of Vera Paz, and, when staying at Choctum, where it is called by the natives "Cho-cho," we secured several specimens from flocks which frequented the edge of the small patch of open savanna at that place. These flocks commence flying from tree to tree soon after daybreak, and in the evening they are again restless and noisy. As usual with all Parrots, a flock consists of a number of birds which keep in pairs both when at rest and when flying about.

Southward of Guatemala the only certain localities for the occurrence of this species are Omoa, where Leyland obtained the type, and San Pedro, whence Whitely sent specimens [4]. Mr. Nutting's record of it in Nicaragua is wrong, so Mr. Ridgway tells us, and refers to a young specimen of *C. auropalliatus*.

2. Chrysotis virenticeps.

Chrysotis pulverulenta, Lawr. Ann. Lyc. N. Y. ix. p. 131 (nec Gm.) [1].
Chrysotis guatemalæ, Frantz. J. f. Orn. 1869, p. 365 [2]; Lawr. Ann. Lyc. N. Y. ix. p. 145 [3]; Salv.
    P. Z. S. 1870, p. 214 [4]; Ibis, 1870, 113 [5]; 1871, p. 98 (partim) [6].
Amazona guatemalæ, Zeledon, An. Mus. Nac. Costa Rica, 1887, p. 124 [7].
Chrysotis farinosa, Lawr. Ibis, 1871, p. 249 (partim) [8]; Boucard, P. Z. S. 1878, p. 46 [9].
Chrysotis virenticeps, Salvad. Cat. Birds Brit. Mus. xx. p. 280 [10].

C. guatemalæ similis, sed pileo toto viride nec cæruleo lavato differt. (Descr. maris exempl. typ. ex Bugaba, Panama. Mus. nostr.)

Hab. Costa Rica, Cervantes (*v. Frantzius* [2], *Carmiol* [1][3][4]), Angostura (*Carmiol*), San Carlos (*Boucard* [8]), San Mateo (*Zeledon* [6]); Panama, Bugaba, Volcan de Chiriqui (*Arcé* [4]).

C. virenticeps is the Costa Rica and Chiriqui form of *C. guatemalæ*, and was separated from that bird by Count Salvadori in his Catalogue of the order [10]. The difference is slight, but apparently constant, and consists in the colour of the head being green instead of distinctly blue.

It has been noticed by most of the Costa Rica collectors, and M. Boucard found it to be common at San Carlos in February [9].

3. Chrysotis inornata.

Psittacus pulverulentus, Lawr. Ann. Lyc. N. Y. viii. p. 11 [1].
Chrysotis farinosa, Lawr. Ibis, 1871, p. 250 [2]; Scl. & Salv. P. Z. S. 1879, p. 538 [3].
Chrysotis inornata, Salvad. Cat. Birds Brit. Mus. xx. p. 281 [4].

Viridis, pileo postico vix cæruleo lavato, plumis omnibus cervicis posticæ nigro marginatis, genis et corpore subtus pallidiore viridibus margine alarum et speculo alari coccineis, remigibus nigris ad basin viridibus, medialiter cyaneo-nigricantibus, secundariis cyaneo-nigro terminatis, remigibus subtus nigris, pogonio interno dimidio basali oleagineo-viridi late marginatis; cauda viridi, triente basali luteo-viridi; rostro flavido; pedibus fuscis. Long. tota circa 17·0, alæ 9·8, caudæ 5·3, rostri culminis 1·9, tarsi 1·0. (Descr. exempl. ex Veragua, Panama. Mus. nostr.)

Hab. PANAMA, Veraguas (*Arcé*), Lion Hill (*M'Leannan* [1]).—SOUTH AMERICA, from Colombia [3] to Peru and the Amazons Valley [4].

Count Salvadori [4] separated this *Chrysotis* from its near ally *C. farinosa*, from its wanting the yellow spot in the centre of the crown, the slightly brighter tint of its green colour, and its rather larger size, especially of the bill.

It is the largest of the species of *Chrysotis* found within our limits, but occurs only in the eastern part of the State of Panama, though it has a rather wide range in South America.

4. Chrysotis panamensis.

Chrysotis ochrocephala, Salv. Ibis, 1871, p. 99 [1].
Chrysotis panamensis, Cab. J. f. Orn. 1874, p. 349 [2]; Salvad. Cat. Birds Brit. Mus. xx. p. 291 [3].

Viridis, uropygio lætiore, pileo antico, fronte et tibiis parte distali luteis: subtus pallidior, campterio et speculo alari coccineis, remigibus cyaneo-nigris ad basin viridibus; cauda viridi, luteo-viridi terminata, rectricibus omnibus (duabus mediis exceptis) in pogonio interno ad basin coccineis; rostro flavicante, maxilla ad apicem cornea; pedibus carneis. Long. tota circa 12·0, alæ 7·6, caudæ 4·0, rostri culminis 1·5, tarsi 1·0. (Descr. exempl. ex Chitra, Panama. Mus. nostr.)

Hab. PANAMA [2], Chitra (*Arcé* [1]).—COLOMBIA [3].

This *Chrysotis* is very closely allied to the common *C. ochrocephala* of South America, but differs in several small points which Count Salvadori gives as follows [3]:—" Very much like *C. ochrocephala*, but smaller, and with the yellow of the head confined to the sinciput and extended to the frontal edge, where there is no glaucous-green colour; the hairy feathers round the nostrils are partially golden; the vertex is tinged with glaucous green, and the thighs are yellow; bill yellowish, with the tip lead-colour."

Though not included in M'Leannan's collections made along the Line of the Panama Railway, *C. panamensis* appears to be far from uncommon in parts of Veragua, judging from the number of skins sent from there. It also occurs in trade collections sent from Bogota.

Living tame birds may be seen in some numbers for sale both at Colon and Panama, and several specimens have reached the Gardens of the Zoological Society from time to time.

5. Chrysotis auropalliata.

Psittacus (Amazona) auropalliatus, Less. Rev. Zool. 1842, p. 135 [1].
Chrysotis auropalliata, Scl. & Salv. Ibis, 1859, p. 138 [2]; Taylor, Ibis, 1860, p. 121 [3]; Salv. Ibis, 1871, p. 99 [4]; Cat. Strickl. Coll. p. 467 [5]; Lawr. Bull. U. S. Nat. Mus. no. 4, p. 36 [6]; Sumichrast, La Nat. v. p. 238 [7]; Nutting, Pr. U. S. Nat. Mus. v. p. 402 [8]; vi. p. 377 [9]; Salv. & Godm. Ibis, 1889, p. 373 [10]; 1890, p. 88 [11]; Salvad. Cat. Birds Brit. Mus. xx. p. 291 [12]; Underwood, Ibis, 1896, p. 445 [13].

Amazona auropalliata, Zeledon, An. Mus. Nac. Costa Rica, 1887, p. 124 [11].

Psittacus flavinuchus, Gould, Voy. 'Sulphur,' p. 45, t. 27 [15].

Chrysotis guatemalæ, Nutting, Pr. U. S. Nat. Mus. vi. p. 395 (fide Ridgway) [16].

Viridis, uropygio lætiore, capite summo pallidior, viridi-cæruleo leviter lavato; cervice postica late lutea, plumulis circum nares nigris, speculo alari coccineo, remigibus cyaneo-nigrescentibus ad basin viridibus; cauda viridi, viridi-luteo terminata, rectricibus lateralibus in pogonio interno ad basin coccineis; rostro corneo, maxillæ lateribus pallidis; pedibus fuscis. Long. tota circa 14·0, alæ 8·8, caudæ 4·8, rostri culminis 1·8, tarsi 0·9. (Descr. maris ex Huamuchal, Guatemala. Mus. nostr.)

Hab. MEXICO, Santa Efigenia [6], Tapanatepec, Cacoprieto, Tonala (*Sumichrast* [7]), Tapachula; GUATEMALA [2] (*Constancia* [5]), Huamuchal, Retalhuleu, La Grande, San José (*O. S. & F. D. G.*); SALVADOR (*Mus. Brit.*); HONDURAS, Ruatan I. (*G. F. Gaumer* [10]), Tigre I. (*Taylor* [3]); NICARAGUA, Realejo (*Lesson* [1], *O. S.*), Chinandega, Momotombo (*W. B. Richardson*), San Juan del Sur [9], Omotepe [16] (*Nutting*); COSTA RICA, Bagaces, Miravalles (*Underwood* [13]), Liberia (*Zeledon* [14]), La Palma (*Nutting* [8]).

The yellow nape of this Parrot at once distinguishes it from all its allies as it is a prominent feature in all adult birds. With the exception of the island of Ruatan in the Bay of Honduras, *C. auropalliata* is exclusively found on the western side of the mountains of Central America from Tehuantepec to Costa Rica, and wherever it occurs it is abundant in the woods, and is also to be seen in captivity in many of the houses of the natives, as it is readily tamed and a fluent talker.

Its presence in Ruatan, so far from its usual haunts, is singular, and may possibly be due to the multiplication of birds escaped from domestication, which had some time or other been brought from the west coast.

6. Chrysotis levaillanti.

Perroquet à tête jaune, Levaill. Perr. t. 86 [1].

Psittacus ochrocephalus, Licht. Preis-Verz. Mex. Vög. p. 1 (*cf.* J. f. Orn. 1863, p. 54) (nec Gm.) [2].

Psittacus xanthops, Wagl. Mon. Psitt. p. 583 (partim) (nec Spix) [3].

Chrysotis xanthops, Souancé, Rev. et Mag. Zool. 1856, p. 153 [4]; Taylor, Ibis, 1860, p. 317 [5].

Chrysotis ochroptera, Scl. P. Z. S. 1859, p. 389 [6].

Chrysotis levaillanti, G. R. Gray, List Psitt. Brit. Mus. p. 79 (1859) (nec *Amazona levaillanti*, Lesson) [7]; Salv. Ibis, 1866, p. 195 [8]; 1871, p. 100 [9]; Grayson, Pr. Bost. Soc. N. H. xiv. p. 271 [10]; Lawr. Ibis, 1871, p. 250 [11]; Mem. Bost. Soc. N. H. ii. p. 296 [12]; Bull. U. S. Nat. Mus. no. 4, p. 36 [13]; Sumichrast, La Nat. v. p. 238 [14]; Ferrari-Perez, Pr. U. S. Nat. Mus. ix. p. 163 [15]; Salv. & Godm. Ibis, 1889, p. 241 [16]; Salvad. Cat. Birds Brit. Mus. xx. p. 293 [17].

Amazona oratrix, Ridgw. Man. N. Am. Birds, p. 587 [18].

Viridis, subtus pallidior, tectricibus supracaudalibus flavescentibus, cervicis plumis undique nigro limbatis, capite toto, margine alarum et tibiis luteis; campterio alari, humeris anticis et speculo alari coccineis; alis cyaneo-nigris ad basin viridibus, secundariis cyaneo-nigro terminatis: alis subtus oleagineo-viridibus, remigibus nigro terminatis; cauda viridi apice lutescente, rectricibus lateralibus in pogonio interno ad basin coccineis; rostro flavo; pedibus carneis. Long. tota circa 14·0, alæ 9·0, caudæ 5·0, rostri culminis 1·55, tarsi 0·75. (Descr. maris ex Aldama, Tamaulipas, Mexico. Mus. nostr.)

♀ mari similis.

74*

Hab. Mexico (*Deppe* [2]), Tres Marias Is. (*Grayson* [10] [12], *Forrer*), Rio Tupila, R. de Coahuyana (*Xantus* [12]), Villa Grande in Nuevo Leon (*F. B. Armstrong*), Sierra Madre above Ciudad Victoria, Aldama (*W. B. Richardson*), Tierra Caliente of Vera Cruz (*Sumichrast* [14]), Rio Grande, Playa Vicente (*Boucard* [6]), Santana [15], Rio Rancho Nuevo, Alvarado (*Ferrari-Perez*), Barrio, Petapa (*Sumichrast* [13]); British Honduras, Belize (*O. S.*); Honduras, Ruatan I. (*G. F. Gaumer* [16]), Yojoa (*G. C. Taylor* [5]).

The amount of yellow on the head and neck of different specimens of this Parrot varies greatly, probably due to the age of each individual bird. A specimen from the Tres Marias Islands has the entire head and neck yellow, and yellow feathers mixed with red ones on the bend of the wing. Some specimens from Aldama in Tamaulipas have yellow feathers irregularly scattered over the breast and abdomen.

The range of *Chrysotis levaillanti* in Mexico is wide and extends along both the Atlantic and Pacific coasts—on the lowlands bordering the former well into the frontier States of Nuevo Leon and Tamaulipas, and on the latter to the Tres Marias Islands, where the late Col. Grayson found it in considerable numbers when he first visited the islands in 1865. But it was much less common in 1867, the woodcutters who frequented the islands having in the meantime captured and transported for sale at Mazatlan and elsewhere on the mainland large numbers of birds, which realized prices varying from one to five dollars each [10].

When first visited, the birds of the Marias were exceedingly tame, and they could be easily caught by passing a string with running-noose attached to a slender pole over their heads as they were feeding or sitting on the trees. They, however, soon became shy and even difficult of approach.

The nests of this Parrot seen by Grayson were all in the hollows of large trees, and he was only able to reach one in a tree known as "Palo prieto." The two eggs lay upon the bare rotten wood in a slight depression. They were pure white, a good deal larger than those of a tame pigeon and of an elliptical form.

Xantus records [12] this species from the Rio Tupila and the Rio de Coahuyana on the mainland, but possibly these birds may have been brought from the Marias Islands.

On the east coast Mr. Armstrong obtained specimens for us near Villa Grande in Nuevo Leon, and Mr. Richardson a good series from various parts of Southern Tamaulipas, the bird being apparently especially common near Aldama, a little to the northward of Tampico; thence it is found southwards throughout the hotter parts of the State of Vera Cruz.

Count Salvadori continues to use Gray's name, *Chrysotis levaillanti*, for this species, though the specific title was previously applied to an African *Pœocephalus* by Lesson, and placed with his American species of *Amazona*. For this reason Mr. Ridgway renamed our bird *Amazona oratrix* [18].

7. Chrysotis finschi.

Chrysotis viridigenalis, Scl. P. Z. S. 1857, p. 230 (nec Cassin) [1].

Chrysotis finschi, Scl. P. Z. S. 1864, p. 298 [2]; 1874, p. 206, t. 34 [3]; Salv. Ibis, 1871, p. 97 [4];
 Lawr. Ibis, 1871, p. 250 [5]; Mem. Bost. Soc. N. H. ii. p. 296 [6]; Bull. U. S. Nat. Mus.
 no. 4, p. 37 [7]; Sumichrast, La Nat. v. p. 238 [8]; Salv. & Godm. Ibis, 1889, p. 242 [9];
 Salvad. Cat. Birds Brit. Mus. xx. p. 298 [10].

Amazona finschi, Jouy, Pr. U. S. Nat. Mus. xvi. p. 786 [11].

Viridis, subtus pallidior, cervicis posticæ plumis (late), dorsi (stricte) et corporis totius subtus nigro terminatis,
 plumulis circum oculos nigris, pileo et nucha cæruleis, hujus plumis stricte nigro terminatis, loris et fronte
 saturate coccineis, genis et regione auriculari læte viridibus immaculatis; speculo alari coccineo; alis
 cyaneo-nigris, ad basin viridibus, subtus oleagineo-viridibus, remigibus nigro terminatis, tectricibus pallide
 viridibus; cauda viridi, tectricibus lateralibus ad apicem lutescentibus; rostro flavicante; pedibus carneis.
 Long. tota circa 13·0, alæ 8·0, caudæ 4·8, rostri culminis 1·6, tarsi 0·75. (Descr. maris ex Mazatlan,
 Mexico. Mus. nostr.)

♀ mari similis.

Hab. MEXICO [1] [2], Choix, Culebra in Sinaloa (*W. Lloyd*), Mazatlan (*Grayson* [6], *Forrer*),
 Presidio de Mazatlan (*Forrer*), San Blas in Tepic (*W. B. Richardson*), Rio de la
 Ameria (*Xantus* [6]), Beltran in Jalisco (*W. Lloyd, Jouy* [11]), Putla (*Rébouch* [3]),
 Ventosa, Zanatepec, Tehuantepec [7] (*Sumichrast* [8]).

This distinct *Chrysotis* is characteristic of Western Mexico, and according to
Grayson [6] inhabits the tierra caliente between the mountains and the Pacific from
Southern Sonora to Tehuantepec, being especially abundant near Mazatlan. He goes
on to say that the forests in some localities, particularly when certain fruits are in
season, appear at times to be alive with them, but only in the morning and evening
when they are seeking their favourite food; they then fly hither and thither through
the woods, perching and climbing amongst the branches of the trees which bear the
fruit, keeping up at the same time an incessant din, which, with the loud and harsh
screams of the large green Macaws, produces a very discordant and disagreeable forest
music. They often visit the cornfields or milpas in great numbers about the time the
green corn or maize commences to mature, committing great depredations, and even
destroying small milpas unless watched.

Young birds if taken from the nest when unfledged may be taught to pronounce
some words very distinctly and to whistle tunes. The season of incubation begins in
the latter part of March or early in April, at which time birds quietly divide off into
pairs and seek a hollow in some large tree, where they deposit their eggs on the bare
rotten wood, which is smoothed a little by the birds, both parents taking equal parts
in the task of incubation. The eggs, two in number, are clear white, and the young
are fed by the old birds some time after they can fly. The pair from the same nest
generally remain together through life*. By an extraordinary provision of nature, it

---

* This is hardly likely to be the case; but it is much more probable that birds once paired remain together
for life, and it is these pairs that make up the constituents of a flock.

is seldom if ever that the young of a nest are of the same sex, but always male and female.

Grayson also says that it is usually supposed that Parrots do not drink; but this is a mistake, as they have their watering-places, such as brooks overhung with trees, whither they resort about ten or eleven o'clock in the forenoon to drink, and sometimes to bathe also.

The late Mr. Jouy [11] found *Chrysotis finschi* to be the most abundant species of the family in Southern Jalisco, being common in the Barranca de Beltran in March. During the day these birds are scattered in small flocks all over the country, feeding on various wild fruits, but towards evening they assemble in flocks of thirty or more and delight in taking long flights up and down the barranca screaming in noisy chorus all the time. Suddenly they swerve in their course and alight in a large tree, and for a few moments all is silent, when, apparently without cause, they fly forth and seek another tree and repeat the performance, which they keep up until darkness sends them to their final roosting-place. Ordinarily stupid and easily approached they seem to be unusually suspicious at nightfall, and occasionally fly quite high, when their rapid and powerful flight much resembles that of a wild duck.

Jouy describes the colours of the soft parts as follows:—Inner ring of iris brown-ochre, central portion chrome, outer edge orange; bill pale yellow, brightest on the sides of the mandible. Naked skin round the eye dusky lead-colour; toes lead-colour, nails dusky."

8. Chrysotis viridigena.

Chrysotis viridigenalis, Cassin, Pr. Ac. Phil. vi. p. 371 [1]; Journ. Ac. Phil. iii. p. 153, t. 13 [2]; Salv. & Godm. Ibis, 1889, p. 241 [3].

Chrysotis viridigena, Salvad. Cat. Birds Brit. Mus. xx. p. 297 [4].

Chrysotis coccineifrons, Souancé, Rev. et Mag. Zool. 1856, p. 154 [5]; Lawr. Ibis, 1871, p. 251 [6].

C. finschi similis, sed capite toto summo cum fronte et loris læte coccineis, colore cæruleo areæ postocularis restricto, plumis cervicis posticæ late nigro terminatis, sed corpore subtus et dorso fere unicoloribus. Long. tota circa 13·0, alæ 8·3, caudæ 4·4, rostri culminis 1·4, tarsi 0·8. (Descr. maris ex Colipa, Mexico. Mus. nostr.)

Hab. MEXICO, Monte Morelos, Rio Comacho in Tamaulipas (*F. B. Armstrong* [3]), Sierra Madre above Ciudad Victoria, Tampico, Tantina, Tamesi (*W. B. Richardson* [3]), Colipa in Vera Cruz (*F. D. G.* [3]).

Though this Parrot was described as long ago as 1853 by Cassin [1], and living specimens have from time to time been brought to the Zoological Gardens of Europe, it is only quite recently that its native home has been ascertained.

In March 1888 Godman obtained two specimens during a short excursion from Jalapa to Colipa in the lowlands of Vera Cruz, and soon afterwards our collectors Richardson and Armstrong secured us many examples from the district lying to the north of Misantla, as far north as the Rio Comacho and Monte Morelos in the State of Nuevo Leon, and from various places all through the State of Tamaulipas. It thus appears to be abundant to within a short distance of the Rio Grande.

Its nearest ally is *C. finschi* of Western Mexico, but it may readily be distinguished by the entirely red crown of the adult birds, the wide black margins to the feathers of the hind neck, and other points mentioned above.

9. Chrysotis autumnalis.

The Lesser Green Parrot, Edw. Birds, iv. p. 164, t. 164 [1].

Psittacus autumnalis, Linn. Syst. Nat. i. p. 147 [2]; Licht. Preis-Verz. Mex. Vög. p. 1 (*cf. J. f. Orn.* 1863, p. 54) [3].

Chrysotis autumnalis, Scl. P. Z. S. 1857, p. 205 [4]; 1859, p. 389 [5]; Moore, P. Z. S. 1859, p. 59 [6]; Scl. & Salv. Ibis, 1860, p. 401 [7]; P. Z. S. 1870, p. 837 [8]; Salv. Ibis, 1871, p. 98 [9]; Lawr. Ibis, 1871, p. 250 [10]; Bull. U. S. Nat. Mus. no. 4, p. 36 [11]; Sumichrast, La Nat. v. p. 238 [12]; Ferrari-Perez, Pr. U. S. Nat. Mus. ix. p. 163 [13]; Salv. & Godm. Ibis, 1889, pp. 241 [14], 373 [15]; 1890, p. 88 [16]; Salvad. Cat. Birds Brit. Mus. xx. p. 302 [17].

Viridis, fronte late, loris et speculo alari coccineis, pilei et cervicis posticæ plumis ad basin viridibus, nigro terminatis, illis fascia lilacina subterminali notatis, his plerumque tantum nigro terminatis : subtus pallidior, genis viridibus, plaga magna suborbitali lutea ; alis nigris cyaneo lavatis, remigibus extus viridibus, secundariis cyaneo-nigro terminatis ; cauda viridi, luteo-viridi terminata, rectricibus lateralibus in pogonio interno ad basin luteis vix coccineo notatis ; rostro pallide corneo ; pedibus plumbeis. Long. tota circa 14·0, alæ 8·3, caudæ 4·5, rostri culminis 1·3, tarsi 0·9. (Descr. maris ex Colipa, Mexico. Mus. nostr.)

♀ mari similis.

Hab. MEXICO (*Deppe* [3]), Tamaulipas, Tampico, Tamesi, Tantina (*W. B. Richardson*), Tierra Caliente of Vera Cruz (*Sumichrast* [12]), Jalapa (*de Oca, Höge*), Colipa (*F. D. G.*), Potrero (*Sumichrast* [12]), Plan del Rio, San José Acateno (*Ferrari-Perez* [13]), Vega del Casadero (*M. Trujillo*), Playa Vicente (*Boucard* [5], *M. Trujillo*), Barrio (*Sumichrast* [10]) ; BRITISH HONDURAS, Belize (*Blancaneaux*) ; GUATEMALA, Choctum, Las Salinas (*O. S. & F. D. G.* [9]) ; HONDURAS, Ruatan I. (*G. F. Gaumer* [15] [16]), Omoa (*Leyland* [6]), San Pedro (*G. M. Whitely* [8]).

Mexican and Guatemalan specimens of this Parrot are readily distinguished from those of the more southern form from Nicaragua to Panama by the presence in the adult bird of a large patch of yellow feathers beneath the eye. The feathers of the back of the neck are, for the most part, destitute of the lilac subterminal band, the red of the forehead is wide, and the outer tail-feathers seldom have any red on the inner web near the base. In the typical *C. salvini* from Panama the cheeks are wholly green, and the feathers of the nape and back of the neck, besides their black edge, have a lilac subterminal band ; the red of the forehead is narrow, and there is a large red patch on the inner web of the outer rectrices.

These distinguishing characters are not constant in birds from Nicaragua and Costa Rica, many of which are certainly intermediate. Thus, a small suborbital yellow patch, not always symmetrical, is not unfrequently seen. The subterminal lilac band of the nape-feathers is not quite so pronounced as in more southern examples. On the whole, it seems better to assign these intermediate specimens to *C. salvini* rather than to *C. autumnalis*.

Young birds of *C. autumnalis* show no yellow suborbital patch, and old birds often have this patch of a nearly pure scarlet; and scarlet feathers are often freely mixed with the green ones surrounding the bare chin. The latter features are not observable in the southern form.

Mr. Ridgway, in writing to us on the birds of these forms in the United States National Museum, describes the same intermediate characters between *C. autumnalis* and *C. salvini*. Count Salvadori, when describing the latter bird, seems to have had the true *C. diademata* more in view, as for a long time *C. salvini* was considered to belong to that species. But *C. diademata* (apparently a rare bird) differs distinctly in the colouring of the lores, which are of a " deep purple-red."

C. autumnalis is a common species in the lowlands of the forest-region of Vera Paz, where it may be seen in numerous flocks in the same districts as *C. guatemalæ*. Domesticated birds of this Parrot are commonly seen about the houses of Vera Paz, as its tameness and readiness in learning words render it a great favourite.

10. Chrysotis salvini.

Chrysotis viridigenalis, Scl. P. Z. S. 1864, p. 298 (nec Cassin) [1]; Scl. & Salv. P. Z. S. 1864, p. 368 [2]; Lawr. Ann. Lyc. N. Y. ix. p. 131 [3]; Frantz. J. f. Orn. 1869, p. 365 [4].

Chrysotis autumnalis, Frantz. J. f. Orn. 1869, p. 365 [5].

Chrysotis diademata, Salv. P. Z. S. 1870, p. 214 [6]; Ibis, 1870, p. 113 [7]; 1871, pp. 97 [8], 251 [9]; Lawr. Ibis, 1871, p. 250 [10]; Scl. & Salv. P. Z. S. 1879, p. 538 [11]; Nutting, Pr. U. S. Nat. Mus. vi. p. 407 [12].

Amazona diademata, Zeledon, An. Mus. Nac. Costa Rica, 1887, p. 124 [13].

Chrysotis salvini, Salvad. Cat. Birds Brit. Mus. xx. p. 300, t. 7. f. 3 [14].

Amazona salvini, Richmond, Pr. U. S. Nat. Mus. xvi. p. 519 [15].

C. autumnali similis, sed genis plerumque omnino viridibus, fronte angustiore coccinea, plumis cervicis posticæ omnibus lilacino subterminatis, rectricibus lateralibus in pogonio interno ad basin plaga coccinea notatis. (Descr. exempl. typ. ex Panama. Mus. nostr.)

Hab. NICARAGUA, Matagalpa, San Emilio (*W. B. Richardson*), Greytown, R. Escondido (*Richmond* [15]), Los Sabalos (*Nutting* [12]); COSTA RICA, San José [3] (*v. Frantzius* [5], Carmiol), Peje (*Carmiol*), Talamanca (*Gabb, U. S. Nat. Mus.*), Jimenez (*Zeledon* [13]); PANAMA, Calovevora, Bugaba (*Arcé* [6]), Lion Hill (*M'Leannan* [2]).—COLOMBIA [11]; RIO NEGRO VALLEY.

As already stated under *C. autumnalis*, we restrict the title of *C. salvini* to the bird found in Nicaragua, Costa Rica, and Panama, though specimens from the first-named country nearly all have intermediate characters, and some of those from Costa Rica.

We have many specimens of this bird from Nicaragua, sent us by Mr. Richardson from Matagalpa and San Emilio at the southern end of the lake. Mr. Richmond says it is common on the Escondido and at Greytown, and that the iris is orange.

b. *Species minores, speculo alari nullo.*

11. Chrysotis albifrons.

White-crowned Parrot, Lath. Gen. Syn. i. p. 280[1].

Psittacus albifrons, Sparrm. Mus. Carls. iii. t. 52[2].

Chrysotis albifrons, Bp. Souancé, Icon. Perr. t. 30[3]; Scl. P. Z. S. 1858, p. 359[4]; Scl. & Salv. Ibis, 1859, p. 138[5]; Taylor, Ibis, 1860, p. 121[6]; Lawr. Ann. Lyc. N. Y. ix. p. 131[7]; Ibis, 1871, p. 251[8]; Mem. Bost. Soc. N. H. ii. p. 296[9]; Bull. U. S. Nat. Mus. no. 4, p. 37[10]; Frantz. J. f. Orn. 1869, p. 366[11]; Finsch, Abh. nat. Ver. Bremen, 1870, p. 252[12]; Salv. Ibis, 1871, p. 96[13]; 1885, p. 192[14]; Boucard, P. Z. S. 1883, p. 455[15]; Sumichrast, La Nat. v. p. 238[16]; Nutting, Pr. U. S. Nat. Mus. vi. pp. 376[17], 388[18]; Salv. & Godm. Ibis, 1889, p. 242[19]; Stone & Baker, Pr. Ac. Phil. 1890, p. 205[20]; Salvad. Cat. Birds Brit. Mus. xx. p. 312[21].

Amazona albifrons, Zeledon, An. Mus. Nac. Costa Rica, 1887, p. 124[22].

Chrysotis apophænica, Reichw. Orn. Centralb. 1880, p. 16[23].

Viridis, interscapulii et cervicis posticæ plumis nigro marginatis, pilei dimidio antico albo, dimidio postico cæruleo; loris, oculorum ambitu, margine alarum, alula spuria et tectricibus majoribus coccineis; remigibus cyaneo-nigris, ad basin viridibus, secundariis cyaneis extrorsum viridi limbatis; cauda viridi, ad apicem pallidiore, rectricibus lateralibus ad basin coccineis; rostro flavescenti-corneo; pedibus carneis. Long. tota circa 10·5, alæ 7·0, caudæ 3·5, rostri culminis 1·3, tarsi 0·6. (Descr. maris ex Tehuantepec, Mexico. Mus. nostr.)

♂ et ♀ *juv.* colorem coccineum alarum omnino carent.

Hab. MEXICO, Quiriego, Sierre de Alamos in Sonora (*W. Lloyd*), Mazatlan (*Grayson*[9][12], *Bischoff*[9]), Presidio de Mazatlan (*Forrer*), Acapulco (*Mrs. H. H. Smith*), Tehuantepec, Tonala (*Sumichrast*[10][16], *W. B. Richardson*), Juchitan[10], Chihuitan[10], Santa Efigenia, Cacoprieto (*Sumichrast*[16]), N. Yucatan[15], Merida, Buctzotz, Izamal (*G. F. Gaumer*), Tunkas, Citilpech (*Stone & Baker*[20]); GUATEMALA, Retalhuleu, Rio Chiguate, Agua Caliente near Chuacus, Peten (*O. S. & F. D. G.*[13]), Volcan de Fuego, 8000 ft. (*O. S.*[13]); HONDURAS, Yojoa, San Pedro (*Taylor*[6]); NICARAGUA, La Libertad, Matagalpa (*W. B. Richardson*), San Juan del Sur[17], Sucuya[18] (*Nutting*); COSTA RICA, Nicoya, San Mateo (*v. Frantzius*[11]), Liberia[22] (*Zeledon*), Desmonte (*v. Frantzius*[7]), Nicoya (*Zeledon*[7]).

Specimens of this Parrot vary a good deal as to the relative amount of the white and blue colouring of the top of the head, the white in some specimens encroaching on the blue, and in others the opposite is the case. Most specimens, but not all, have a narrow frontal edge of red feathers.

The range of *C. albifrons* is somewhat remarkable. In Mexico it is a bird of the west coast from Sonora to Tehuantepec. It is absent from the Eastern States, but in Yucatan it is abundant. In Guatemala, again, it appears as a western bird, with the exception of the flock or flocks which frequent the hot springs situated on the road to Vera Paz between the Rio Motagua and the village of Chuacus. Our skins from Nicaragua are from the central region and Chontales on the eastern side. In Costa Rica it appears to be a western bird.

In Western Mexico, Grayson says, it is found in the warmer regions, and is found in the same localities as *C. finschi*, though each species keeps in distinct flocks. It is a bird easily domesticated when young, and readily learns to pronounce words; it is therefore a great favourite with the natives.

12. Chrysotis xantholora.

Chrysotis xantholora, G. R. Gray, List Psitt. Brit. Mus. p. 83 (1859) [1]; Salv. Ibis, 1861, p. 354 [2]; 1871, p. 97 [3]; 1874, p. 327 [4]; 1885, pp. 186 [5], 192 [6]; Lawr. Ibis, 1871, p. 251 [7]; Scl. P. Z. S. 1875, p. 157, t. 26 [8]; Boucard, P. Z. S. 1883, p. 455 [9]; Ridgw. Pr. U. S. Nat. Mus. viii. p. 577 [10]; Salv. & Godm. Ibis, 1889, p. 373 [11]; 1890, p. 88 [12]; Salvad. Cat. Birds Brit. Mus. xx. p. 313 [13].

Viridis, plumis corporis omnibus nigro distincte marginatis, tectricibus supracaudalibus luteo-viridibus, pileo toto summo albo, postice cæruleo limbato, loris luteis, oculorum ambitu reliquo coccineo, regione auriculari nigro; alis nigris, remigibus in pogonio externo ad basin viridibus ad apicem cyaneis, secundariis cyaneis, tectricibus majoribus et humeris coccineis; cauda viridi, ad apicem lutescente, rectricibus externis ad apicem coccineis; rostro flavo; pedibus carneis. Long. tota circa 10·0, alæ 6·9, caudæ 3·5, rostri culminis 1·25, tarsi 0·6. (Descr. exempl. ex Cozumel I., Mexico. Mus. nostr.)

♀ pileo summo cærulea, parte antica solum alba, tectrice majore tertia tantum coccinea, reliquis viridibus, humeris viridibus et colore coccineo circum oculos vix obvio a mare differt.

Hab. MEXICO, N. Yucatan (*Cabot* [4]), Merida, Izamal, Cozumel I. (*G. F. Gaumer* [11] [12]); BRITISH HONDURAS (*Dyson* [1]), Orange Walk (*G. F. Gaumer*).

Though this species has a general resemblance to *C. albifrons*, it has many points of difference. The lores are yellow instead of scarlet, the ear-coverts black, the bastard-wing green, the shoulders scarlet, and the black margins to the feathers of the body more distinct.

Though Kuhl seems to have seen a specimen of this bird as early as 1820, and Dr. S. Cabot obtained one during his visit to Yucatan with Stephens in 1841–2 (which Salvin saw in his collection in Boston in 1874), it was not until 1859 that G. R. Gray named it from a specimen obtained by Dyson in Honduras. When the ornithology of Yucatan became better known, chiefly through the exertions of Dr. Gaumer, *C. xantholora* was found to be not uncommon in the northern part of that country, where it occurs with *C. albifrons*, but in much smaller numbers [9]. On the island of Cozumel it is very abundant, judging from the series of skins Dr. Gaumer sent us from there after his visit in 1887–8. The same collector afterwards secured a specimen at Orange Walk in British Honduras. In Guatemala and the rest of Central America *C. xantholora* seems quite unknown.

PIONUS.

Pionus, Wagler, Mon. Psitt. p. 497 (1832); Salvadori, Cat. Birds Brit. Mus. xx. p. 321.
Pionias, Finsch, Papag. ii. p. 366.

The short, nearly even tail, and the invariably red under tail-coverts in all the species of *Pionus* distinguish them from *Chrysotis*. In general size, too, they are smaller, except in the cases of *C. albifrons* and *C. xantholora*, and the colours of the plumage less uniformly green.

Ten species of *Pionus* are recognized by Count Salvadori, of which two occur within our limits, viz. *P. senilis*, which is not found elsewhere, and *P. menstruus*, which has a wide range in South America and is found throughout the State of Panama, but not beyond.

1. Pionus menstruus.

Blue-headed Parrot, Edw. Glean. Nat. Hist. vii. p. 226, t. 314 [1].

Psittacus menstruus, Linn. Syst. Nat. i. p. 148 [2].

Pionus menstruus, Wagl. Mon. Psitt. p. 602 [3]; Scl. & Salv. P. Z. S. 1864, p. 368 [4]; 1879, p. 538 [5]; Salv. P. Z. S. 1867, p. 158 [6]; 1870, p. 214 [7]; Ibis, 1871, p. 95 [8]; Scl. in Rowley's Orn. Misc. iii. p. 6 [9]; Salvad. Cat. Birds Brit. Mus. xx. p. 322 [10].

Pionius menstruus, Lawr. Ann. Lyc. N. Y. vii. p. 299 [11].

Viridis, alis extus oleagineo tinctis, capite toto, cervice et corpore subtus usque ad pectus imum cæruleis, regione auriculari nigra, pectoris plumis medialiter plus minusve rosaceo tinctis, subcaudalibus et rectricibus lateralibus ad basin coccineis, illis viridi limbatis; remigibus viridibus, rhachidibus et pogonio interno juxta iis nigris; rostro nigro, maxillæ lateribus ad basin rubris; pedibus fuscis. Long. tota circa 10·0, alæ 6·9, caudæ 3·3, rostri culminis 1·2, tarsi 0·6. (Descr. maris ex Santa Fé, Panama. Mus. nostr.)
♀ mari similis.
Juv. capite et pectore viridescentioribus.

Hab. PANAMA, Bugaba [7], Mina de Chorcha [7], Veraguas [6], Santa Fé [6], Calobre [7] (*Arcé*), Lion Hill (*M'Leannan* [4] [11]), Chepo (*Arcé* [8]).—SOUTH AMERICA, from Colombia to Guiana, the Amazons Valley, Peru, and Bolivia [10].

A long-known Parrot of South America, over which continent it has a very wide range. In Central America it is found throughout the State of Panama, and we have specimens from many points extending from Chiriqui and the frontier of Costa Rica to beyond the Line of the Panama Railway. Mr. Zeledon includes it in his list of Costa Rica birds, but does not refer to any specimens in the Museum at San José, and as yet we have not seen any from that country, where *P. senilis* is not uncommon.

P. menstruus may readily be distinguished from *P. senilis* by its blue head and the colour of the primaries and their coverts, which are green, and not blue as in the allied form.

2. Pionus senilis.

Psittacus senilis, Spix, Av. Bras. i. p. 42, t. 31. f. 1 [1].

Pionus senilis, Wagl., Scl. P. Z. S. 1856, p. 306 [2]; in Rowley's Orn. Misc. iii. p. 6 [3]; Scl. & Salv. Ibis, 1859, p. 138 [4]; P. Z. S. 1870, p. 837 [5]; Cab. J. f. Orn. 1862, p. 335 [6]; Frantz. J. f. Orn. 1869, p. 366 [7]; Salv. Ibis, 1871, p. 95 [8]; Boucard, P. Z. S. 1878, p. 46 [9]; Sumichrast, La Nat. v. p. 238 [10]; Zeledon, An. Mus. Nac. Costa Rica, 1887, p. 124 [11]; Salvad. Cat. Birds Brit. Mus. xx. p. 331 [12]; Richmond, Pr. U. S. Nat. Mus. xxi. p. 331 [13].

Pionius senilis, Lawr. Ann. Lyc. N. Y. viii. p. 184 [14]; ix. p. 131 [15].

Psittacus leucorhynchus, Sw. Phil. Mag. new ser. i. p. 438 [16].

Olivaceo-viridis, tectricibus alarum minoribus oleagineis, pallide fusco terminatis ; pileo summo et loris niveis, plumis omnibus cervicis, capitis laterum et pectoris late cæruleo limbatis, gutture medio albo ; alis saturate cyaneis viridi terminatis, tectricibus majoribus ejusdem coloris, secundariis cyaneis viridi marginatis ; cauda viridi, rectricibus lateralibus ad basin et tectricibus subcaudalibus coccineis ; rostro albicante corneo ; pedibus carneis. Long. tota circa 9·0, alæ 6·9, caudæ 3·2, rostri culminis 1·3, tarsi 0·6. (Descr. maris ex Cuesta de Misantla, Vera Cruz, Mexico. Mus. nostr.)

♀ mari similis, coloribus omnibus pallidioribus, pileo antico tantum albo.

Hab. MEXICO (*Bullock* [16]), Cuesta de Misantla (*F. D. G.*), Mirador (*Sartorius, Sumichrast* [10]), Cordova (*Sallé* [2]), Potrero, Orizaba (*Sumichrast* [10]), Villa Alta (*Boucard*) ; BRITISH HONDURAS, Orange Walk (*G. F. Gaumer*), Belize (*Blancaneaux*) ; GUATEMALA (*Skinner* [4]), Chisec, Choctum, Coban, Lanquin (*O. S. & F. D. G.* [8]) ; HONDURAS, San Pedro (*G. M. Whitely* [5]) ; NICARAGUA, Escondido R. (*Richmond* [13]), La Libertad, Rama, San Emilio (*W. B. Richardson*), Greytown (*Holland* [14]) ; COSTA RICA, Angostura (*Carmiol*), San José (*v. Frantzius* [15], *M. L. Calleja* [14]), Alajuela, Zarcero de Alajuela, Los Trojas, Barranca, Jimenez, Monte Redondo (*Zeledon* [11]), San Carlos (*Boucard* [9]), Orosi, Tucurriqui (*v. Frantzius* [7]).

Though described by Spix in his great work on the birds of Brazil, this *Pionus* does not belong to that country, but is a purely Mexican and Central-American species, ranging from the State of Vera Cruz through British Honduras, Guatemala, and Nicaragua to Costa Rica, but, so far as we know, keeping strictly to the country lying to the eastward of the central mountain-range. We found it to be abundant in Vera Paz as high as the town of Coban, and low down in the valley to the eastward at Lanquin. Mr. Richmond speaks of it as abundant on the Escondido in Nicaragua, and he noted that the iris in life is orange [13].

The white head of the adult bird of this species renders it easily distinguished from the blue-headed *P. menstruus,* the only other *Pionus* found within our limits.

PIONOPSITTACUS.

Pionopsitta, Bonaparte, Rev. et Mag. Zool. 1854, p. 152.
Pionopsittacus, Salvadori, Cat. Birds Brit. Mus. xx. p. 338.

This genus has much the appearance of *Pionus,* but its members generally are smaller, more brightly coloured birds ; but the essential difference is the presence of a tufted oil-gland which *Pionopsittacus* possesses in common with a number of other South-American genera of Pioninæ not represented in Central America. Its nearest ally is *Caica,* from which it differs, according to Count Salvadori, in the outline of the wing, the second and third primaries being the longest, and the first equal to the fourth, instead of the second, third, and fourth being the longest, and the first equal to the fifth.

Count Salvadori admits nine species of *Pionopsittacus,* of which two belong to our region, viz.: *P. hæmatotis,* of rather wide range from Southern Mexico to Western Panama, and the very closely-allied *P. coccineicollaris,* which is only known from the Line of the Panama Railway.

1. **Pionopsittacus hæmatotis.**

Pionus hæmatotis, Scl. & Salv. P. Z. S. 1860, p. 300 [1]; Ibis, 1860, p. 401, t. 13 [2]; Salv. Ibis, 1861,
    p. 147 [3]; Frantz. J. f. Orn. 1869, p. 366 [4].
Pionius hæmatotis, Lawr. Ann. Lyc. N. Y. ix. p. 131 [5].
Caica hæmatotis, Scl. P. Z. S. 1862, p. 20 [6]; Salv. P. Z. S. 1867, p. 158 [7]; Ibis, 1871, p. 96 [8]; 1874,
    p. 329 [9]; Scl. & Salv. P. Z. S. 1870, p. 837 [10]; Zeledon, An. Mus. Nac. Costa Rica, 1887,
    p. 124 [11].
Pionopsittacus hæmatotis, Salvad. Cat. Birds Brit. Mus. xx. p. 343 [12].
Pionopsitta hæmatotis, Richmond, Pr. U. S. Nat. Mus. xvi. p. 520 [13].

Viridis, torque cervicali et pectore oleagineo tinctis, pileo et nucha fuscis, plumis singulis rufo-brunneo marginatis,
    margine frontali et loris albis; capitis lateribus et gula nigricanti-fuscis; tectricibus auricularibus
    sanguineis; hypochondriis, axillaribus et tectricibus subalaribus juxta humeros coccineis; margine alarum
    et alula spuria saturate cyancis, remigibus nigris cervino stricte limbatis; secundariis et tectricibus mediis
    extrorsum viridibus introrsum cyaneis; cauda viridi, apice cyanea, rectricibus lateralibus ad basin coccineis;
    rostro flavido; pedibus carneis. Long. tota circa 8·5, alæ 6·0, caudæ 2·4, rostri culminis 1·0, tarsi 0·6.
    (Descr. exempl. typ. ex Raxché, Vera Paz, Guatemala. Mus. nostr.)
♀ mari similis, sed omnino pallidior.

Hab. MEXICO, San Lorenzo near Cordova (*Ferrari-Perez*), Playa Vicente (*Boucard* [6]);
    BRITISH HONDURAS, Orange Walk (*G. F. Gaumer*); GUATEMALA, Raxché [1], Choctum,
    Yaxcamnal, Sources of R. Sarstoon near Chimuchuch (*O. S. & F. D. G.* [8]);
    HONDURAS, San Pedro (*G. M. Whitely* [10]); COSTA RICA, Rio Frio (*Richmond* [13]),
    Angostura (*Carmiol* [4]), Pacuare (*Carmiol* [5], *Zeledon* [11], *v. Frantzius* [4]), Naranjo de
    Cartago (*Zeledon* [11]); PANAMA, Santa Fé (*Arcé* [6]), Veraguas (*Merritt* [9]).

This species belongs to the section of the genus in which the inner webs of the
outer tail-feathers are red and not yellow, the axillaries are bright scarlet, and the ear-
coverts red. The only other Parrot having these characters is *P. coccineicollaris*, which
differs as stated under the account of that bird.

Originally discovered in the forests of the mountains of Vera Paz, and subsequently
traced to the lower districts of the same department, it is now known to occur in
Southern Mexico, where Boucard met with it near Playa Vicente [6], and more recently
Don F. Ferrari-Perez near Cordova, but where it is apparently very rare. A single
specimen was also procured by Dr. Gaumer at Orange Walk in British Honduras. It
occurs also near San Pedro in the Republic of Honduras [10], and in greater abundance in
Costa Rica. In the last-named country Mr. Richmond observed a flock of a dozen in a
fruit-tree on the Rio Frio [13]. The birds were quite quiet, making no noise even after
being shot at several times.

Our own experience of *P. hæmatotis* was very similar, and specimens were very
difficult to secure, and remaining so still in the lofty trees of the forest they were hard
to discover in the foliage and could seldom be shot at so great a height.

2. Pionopsittacus coccineicollaris.

Pionus hæmatotis, ? var., Lawr. Ann. Lyc. N. Y. vii. p. 299 (nec Scl. & Salv.)[1].
Caica hæmatotis, Scl. & Salv. P. Z. S. 1864, p. 368[2]; Salv. Ibis, 1871, p. 96 (partim)[3].
Pionius coccineicollaris, Lawr. Ann. Lyc. N. Y. vii. p. 475[4].
Pionopsittacus coccineicollaris, Salvad. Cat. Birds Brit. Mus. xx. p. 344[5].

P. *hæmatoti* similis, sed pectore summo plumis rosaceo-rubris notato, pilei plumis haud rufo-brunneo marginatis
    vix distinguendus. (Descr. maris ex Lion Hill, Panama. Mus. nostr.)

Hab. PANAMA, Lion Hill (*M'Leannan* [1] [2] [4]), Paraiso Station (*Hughes*).

We have long been reluctant to admit the distinctness of this bird from *P. hæmatotis*, so closely are they allied; but we do so now rather out of deference to Count Salvadori's opinion. The most obvious distinction is the presence of rose-red feathers across the throat, but these are not always to be seen; a more certain difference, but one that is not easily detected, is the edging of the feathers of the crown, which is olive-brown rather than red-brown. There is white about the chin, which may or may not be constant.

P. coccineicollaris is only found, so far as we know as yet, on the Isthmus of Panama, where it is crossed by the railway. A little further to the westward, at Santa Fé, the true *P. hæmatotis* is found.

END OF VOL. II.